THE NEW COMPLETE INVESTOR

THE NEW COMPLETE INVESTOR

GEOFFREY A. HIRT

STANLEY B. BLOCK

BUSINESS ONE IRWIN
Homewood, Illinois 60430

Acquisitions editor: Amy Hollands
Project editor: Lynne Basler
Production manager: Ann Cassady
Artist: Publication Services
Compositor: J. M. Post Graphics, Corp.
Typeface: 10/12 Bembo
Printer: R. R. Donnelley & Sons Company

Library of Congress Cataloging-in-Publication Data

Hirt, Geoffrey A.
   The new complete investor/Geoffrey A. Hirt, Stanley B. Block.
      p.   cm.
   Rev. ed. of: The complete investor. c1987.
   Includes bibliographical references and index.
   ISBN 1-55623-367-1
   1. Investments.   2. Investments—United States.   3. Investment
analysis.   I. Block, Stanley B.   II. Hirt, Geoffrey A. Complete
investor.   III. Title.
   HG4521.H579   1990b
   332.6—dc20   90–3370

TO OUR PARENTS

PREFACE

A visit to any well-stocked bookstore will convince the reader of the breadth and depth of the investment field. Books about stocks, bonds, options, futures, real estate, mutual funds, and the many other topics that this interesting discipline comprises line the shelves. Some of these books are intended for the novice, others are addressed to the advanced investor.

In *The New Complete Investor* we have attempted to provide the reader with a thorough coverage of all important investment subjects, beginning with the basics, and building to a conceptual level that is both challenging and useful. Every effort has been made to make the discussion clear, and to avoid esoteric subjects or models having little or no application in the real world. All information has been updated in addition to the inclusion of new investment vehicles developed and popularized since the first edition.

We believe that the book will provide a sound foundation of understanding for those beginning their studies of investing, and that advanced readers will be challenged to expand the boundaries of their knowledge. We think *The New Complete Investor* explains concepts and demonstrates analytical techniques that can be applied by those wishing to tackle investing for the first time as well as by those serious investors looking for some depth of analysis.

We are grateful to the following individuals for their thoughtful reviews and suggestions for this edition: Joe B. Copeland (University of North Alabama), Marcia M. Cornett (Southern Methodist University), Adam Gehr (DePaul University), David Heskel (Bloomsburg University), James Khule (California State University-Sacramento), Carl Luft (DePaul University), Roger R. Palmer (College of St. Thomas), Linda L. Richardson (University of Southern Maine), Joseph F. Singer (University of Missouri-Kansas City), Allan. J. Twark (Kent State University), and Howard E. Van Auken (Iowa State University).

For their prior reviews and helpful comments, we are grateful to Keith E. Boles (University of Colorado, Colorado Springs), Jerry D. Boswell (College of Financial Planning), Paul Grier (SUNY-Binghamton), John D. Markese (DePaul University), John W. Peavy III (Southern Methodist University), Tom S. Sale (Louisiana Tech University), Ira Smolowitz (Siena College), Frank N. Tiernan (Drake University), Bismarck Williams (Roosevelt University), Sheri Kole (Copeland Companies), Art Schwartz (University of South Florida), Jane H. Finley (University of South Alabama), Don Taylor (University of Wisconsin, Platteville), Carol J. Billingham (Central Michigan University), and Gerald A. Blum (University of Nevada, Reno).

Geoffrey A. Hirt
Stanley B. Block

CONTENTS

4
SOURCES OF INVESTMENT INFORMATION 87

ANALYSIS AND VALUATION OF EQUITY SECURITIES 136

5
ECONOMIC AND INDUSTRY ANALYSIS 139

6
VALUATION OF THE INDIVIDUAL FIRM 180

11
DURATION AND REINVESTMENT CONCEPTS   320

12
CONVERTIBLE SECURITIES AND WARRANTS   338

13
PUT AND CALL OPTIONS   358

Part Four

BROADENING THE INVESTMENT PERSPECTIVE   402

14
INVESTMENTS IN SPECIAL SITUATIONS   405

THE NEW COMPLETE INVESTOR

Part One

INTRODUCTION TO INVESTMENTS

■ OUTLINE

■ INTRODUCTION

In Part One of the text, we establish the groundwork essential to the development of investment strategy and the management of financial resources.

The place to begin is with the setting of investment objectives. Not only is this the first step in any well-managed investment program, but it is often the most important ingredient. Among the factors the investor considers are willingness to take risks, desire for current income, need for liquidity, tax considerations, and retirement and estate planning. The reader also considers the concepts of risk and return and examines historical rates of return on different types of investments. Career opportunities in the areas of investments and security analysis are also described in an appendix to Chapter 1.

A discussion of security markets follows in Chapter 2. An important distinction is made between primary markets (for new issues) and secondary markets (for existing issues). We discuss the major organized exchanges, such as the New York Stock Exchange, the American Stock Exchange, the Chicago Board Options Exchange, as well as the over-the-counter market. We also take a look at future developments in the securities industry relating to computerized security trading and to the internationalization of financial markets.

In Chapter 3, the actual steps necessary to participate in the market are considered, with a description of the types of accounts that can be opened, the forms of orders that can be executed, and the commission costs involved. Tax considerations are also covered, with an emphasis on the proper timing of investment decisions to minimize taxes. The influence of the Tax Reform Act of 1986 on investments is also discussed.

As part of the goal of establishing the groundwork for investment management in Part One, sources of investment information are covered in Chapter 4. The reader is presented with an overview of aggregate economic data sources generated by the government and industry/company data developed by investment advisory services, such as Value Line and Standard & Poor's. The uses of periodical indexes, journals, and particularly, computer data bases are also highlighted.

1

THE INVESTMENT SETTING

F rom early 1982 to October 19, 1987, the issues of the New York Stock Exchange increased by 250 percent in value. On the Tokyo Stock Exchange, the advance over the same five and a half years was even greater, with a gain in excess of 400 percent. One Japanese stock alone, Nippon Telephone and Telegraph Company, carried a larger value than the entire West German stock market. This was one of the great bull markets of the post–World War II period.

Then came the great panic on Monday, October 19, 1987. In one day, the Dow Jones Industrial Average, the most-watched stock market indicator in the world, declined 22.6 percent. By contrast, the largest single day decline in the fabled stock market crash of 1929 was slightly over 12 percent. On Black Monday of 1987, IBM declined $31^1/_4$ points; Eastman Kodak, 26 points; Westinghouse Electric, $20^1/_2$ points; and DuPont $18^1/_2$ points. Over $500 billion in stock values was erased in one day on U.S. stock markets and over $1 trillion worldwide.

Of course, common stocks are not the only volatile investment. In the last two decades, silver has gone from $5 an ounce to $50 and back again to the $6–8 range. Gold has moved from $35 an ounce to $875 and retreated to half that value. The same can be said of investments in oil, real estate, and a number of other items. By the publication date of this book, other examples will have taken place both on the upside and downside as fortunes are increased or diminished.

How does one develop an investment strategy in such an environment? Suggestions come from all directions. The investor is told how to benefit from the coming monetary disaster as well as how to grow rich in a new era of prosperity. The intent of this text is to help the investor sort out the various investments that are available and to develop analytical skills that suggest what securities and assets might be most appropriate for a given **portfolio.**

We shall define an **investment** as the commitment of current funds in anticipation of receiving a larger future flow of funds. The investor hopes to be compensated for forgoing immediate consumption, for inflation, and for taking a risk.

The process of investing may be both exciting and challenging. The first-time investor who pours over the financial statements of a firm and then makes a dollar commitment to purchase a few shares of stock often has a feeling of euphoria as he or she charges out in the morning to secure the daily newspaper and read the market quotes. Even the professional analyst may take pleasure in leaving his Wall Street office to evaluate an emerging high-technology firm in Austin or Palo Alto. Likewise, the buyer of a rare painting, late 18th-century U.S. coin, or invaluable baseball card may find a sense of excitement in attempting to outsmart the market. Even the purchaser of a bond or money market instrument must do proper analysis to assure that anticipated objectives are being met. Let us examine the different types of investments.

TABLE 1–1   OVERVIEW OF INVESTMENT ALTERNATIVES

A. Financial assets
    1. Equity claims—direct
        Common stock
        Warrants
        Options
    2. Equity claims—indirect
        Investment company shares
    3. Creditor claims
        Savings accounts
        Money market funds
        Commercial paper
        Treasury bills
        Bonds (straight and convertible to common stock)
    4. Preferred stock (straight and convertible to common stock)
    5. Commodity futures
B. Real assets
    1. Real estate—office buildings, apartments, shopping centers, personal residences
    2. Precious metals—gold, silver
    3. Precious gems—diamonds, rubies, sapphires
    4. Collectibles
        Art
        Antiques
        Stamps
        Coins
        Rare books
    5. Other
        Cattle
        Oil
        Common metals

FORMS OF INVESTMENT

In the text, we break down investment alternatives between financial and real assets. A **financial asset** represents a financial claim on an asset that is usually documented by some form of legal representation. An example would be a share of stock or a bond. A **real asset** represents an actual tangible asset that may be seen, felt, held, or collected. An example would be real estate or gold.

In Table 1–1, we list the various forms of financial and real assets.

As indicated in Part A of Table 1–1, financial assets may be broken down into five categories. *Direct equity claims* represent ownership interests and include common stock as well as other instruments that can be used to purchase common stock, such as warrants and options. Warrants and options allow the holder to buy a stipulated number of shares in the future at a given price. Warrants usually convert to one share and are long-term in nature, whereas options are generally based on 100 share units and are short-term in nature.

Indirect equity can be acquired through placing funds in investment companies (such as a mutual fund). The investment company pools the resources of many investors and reinvests them in common stock (or other investments). The individual enjoys the advantages of diversification and professional management (though not necessarily higher returns).

Financial assets may also take the form of *creditor claims* as represented by debt instruments offered by financial institutions, industrial corporations, or the government. The rate of return is often initially fixed, though the effective yield may vary with changing market conditions. Other forms of financial assets are *preferred stock,* which is a hybrid form of security combining some of the elements of equity ownership and creditor claims, and *commodity futures,* which represent a contract to buy or sell a commodity in the future at a given price. Commodities may include wheat, corn, copper, or even such financial instruments as Treasury bonds or foreign exchange.

As shown in Part B of Table 1–1, there are also numerous categories of real assets. The most widely recognized investment in this category is *real estate,* either commercial property or one's own residence. For greater risk, *precious metals* or *precious gems* can be considered, and for those seeking psychic pleasure as well as monetary gain, *collectibles* are an investment outlet. Finally, the *other (all-inclusive)* category includes cattle, oil, and other items that stretch as far as the imagination will go.

Throughout the text, each form of financial and real asset is considered. What assets the investor ultimately selects will depend on his or her investment objectives as well as the economic outlook for the future. For example, the investor who believes that inflation will be relatively strong in the future may have a preference for real assets that have a replacement value reflecting increasing prices. In a more moderate inflationary environment, stocks and bonds may be preferred.

THE SETTING OF INVESTMENT OBJECTIVES

The setting of investment objectives may be as important as the selection of the investment. In actuality, they tend to go together. A number of key areas should be considered.

Risk and Safety of Principal

The first factor the investor must consider is the amount of risk he or she is prepared to assume. In a relatively efficient and informed capital market environment, risk tends to be closely correlated with return. Most of the literature of finance would suggest that those who consistently demonstrate high returns of perhaps 20 percent or more are greater-than-normal risk takers. While some clever investors are able to prosper on their wits alone, most high returns may be perceived as compensation for risk.

And there is not only the risk of losing invested capital directly (a dry hole perhaps) but also the danger of a loss in purchasing power. At 8 percent inflation (compounded annually), a stock that is held for four years without a gain in value would represent a 36 percent loss in purchasing power.

The investor who wishes to assume low risks will probably confine a large portion of his or her portfolio to short-term debt instruments in which the party responsible for payment is the government or a major bank or corporation. Some conservative investors may choose to invest in a money market fund in which the funds of numerous investors are pooled together and reinvested in high-yielding, short-term instruments. More aggressive investors may look toward longer-term debt instruments and common stock. Real assets, such as gold, silver, or valued art, might also be included in an aggressive portfolio.

It is not only the inherent risk in an asset that must be considered but also the extent to which that risk is being diversified away in a portfolio. Though an investment in gold might be considered risky, such might not be fully the case if it is combined into a portfolio of common stocks. Gold thrives on bad news, while common stocks generally do well in a positive economic environment. An oil embargo or foreign war may drive down the value of stocks while gold is advancing, and vice versa.

The age and economic circumstances of an investor are important variables in determining an appropriate level of risk. Young, upwardly mobile people are generally in a better position to absorb risk than are elderly couples on a fixed income. Nevertheless, each of us, regardless of our plight in life, has different risk-taking desires. A surgeon earning $200,000 a year may be more averse to accepting a $2 per share loss on a stock than an aging taxicab driver.

One cruel lesson of the last decade is that those who thought they were buying conservative investments often found quite the opposite to be true. For example, a 7 percent U.S. government bond maturing in 2008 was trading at 75 percent of its stated value in the late 1980s.

Current Income versus Capital Appreciation

A second consideration in the setting of investment objectives is a decision on the desire for current income versus capital appreciation. Though this decision is closely tied to an evaluation of risk, it is a separate matter.

In purchasing stocks, the investor with a need for current income may opt for high-yielding, mature firms in such industries as public utilities, machine tools, or apparel. Those searching for price gains may look toward smaller, emerging firms in high technology, energy, or electronics. The latter firms may pay no cash dividend at all, but the investor hopes for an increase in value to provide the desired return.

Liquidity Considerations

Liquidity is measured by the ability of the investor to convert an investment into cash within a relatively short period of time with a minimum capital loss on the transaction. Most financial assets provide a high degree of liquidity. Stocks and bonds can generally be sold within a matter of minutes at a price reasonably close to the last traded value. Such may not be the case for real estate. Almost everyone has seen a house or piece of commercial real estate sit on the market for weeks or months.

Liquidity can also be measured indirectly by the transaction costs or commissions involved in the transfer of ownership. Financial assets generally trade on a relatively low commission basis (perhaps 1 or 2 percent), whereas many real assets have transaction costs that run from 5 percent to 25 percent or more.

In many cases, the lack of immediate liquidity can be justified if there are unusual opportunities for gain. An investment in real estate or precious gems may provide sufficient return to more than compensate for the added transaction costs. Of course, a bad investment will be all the more difficult to unload.

The investor must carefully assess his or her own situation to determine the need for liquidity. If you are investing funds to be used for the next house payment or the coming semester's tuition, then immediate liquidity will be essential, and financial assets will be preferred. If funds can be tied up for long periods of time, bargain-buying opportunities of an unusual nature can also be evaluated.

Short-Term versus Long-Term Orientation

In setting investment objectives you must decide whether you will assume a short-term or long-term orientation in managing the funds and evaluating performance. You do not always have a choice. Those who manage funds for others may be put under tremendous pressure to show a given level of performance in the short run. The appliers of pressure may be a concerned relative or a large pension fund that has placed funds with a bank trust department. Even though you are convinced your latest stock purchase will double in the next three years, the fact that it is currently down by 15 percent may provide some discomfort to those around you.

Market strategies may also be short-term or long-term in scope. Those who attempt to engage in short-term market tactics are termed *traders*. They may buy a stock at 15 and hope to liquidate if it goes to 20. To help reach decisions, short-term traders often make use of technical analysis, which is based on evaluating market indicator series and charting. Those who take a longer-term perspective try to identify fundamentally sound companies for a buy-and-hold approach. A long-term investor does not necessarily anticipate being able to buy right at the bottom or sell at the exact peak.

Tax Factors

Investors in high tax brackets will have different investment objectives than those in lower brackets or tax-exempt charities, foundations, or similar organizations. An investor in a high tax bracket may prefer municipal bonds (interest is not taxable), real estate (with its depreciation and interest write-off), or investments that provide tax credits or limited tax shelters, such as those in oil and gas or railroad cars.

In recent times, many investment advisers have cautioned investors not to be blinded by the beneficial tax aspects of an investment but to look at the economic factors as well. Furthermore, the Tax Reform Act of 1986 has greatly diminished the ability to use tax shams and tax shelters to protect income from taxation. One of the best tax-planning features is the individual retirement account (IRA), which is discussed in this chapter and later chapters.

Ease of Management

Another item of consideration in setting up an investment program is ease of management. The investor must determine the amount of time and effort that can be devoted to an investment portfolio and act accordingly. In the stock market, this may determine whether you want to be a daily trader or to assume a longer-term perspective. In real estate, it may mean the difference between personally owning and managing a handful of rental houses or going in with 10 other investors to form a limited partnership in which a general partner takes full management responsibility and the limited partners merely put up the capital.

Of course, there is a minimum amount of time that must be committed to any investment program. Even when investment advisers or general partners are in charge, their activities must be monitored and evaluated.

Retirement and Estate Planning Considerations

Even the relatively young must begin to consider the effect of their investment decisions on their retirement and the estates they will pass along to their "potential families" someday. Those who wish to remain single will still be called upon to advise others as to the appropriateness of a given investment strategy for their family needs.

Most good retirement questions should not be asked at "retirement" but 40 or 45 years before because that's the time period with the greatest impact. One of the first questions a person is often asked after taking a job upon graduation is whether he or she wishes to set up an individual retirement account (IRA). An IRA allows a taxpayer to deduct $2,000 from taxable income and invest the funds at a bank, savings and loan, brokerage house, mutual fund, or other financial institution. The funds are normally placed in interest-bearing instruments, such as a certificate of deposit, or perhaps in other securities, such as common stock. Not only can the $2,000 be deducted from earned income to reduce current taxes, but the income earned on the funds is allowed to grow tax-free until withdrawn at retirement. As an example, if a person places $2,000 a year in an IRA for 45 consecutive years and the funds earn 10 percent over that time period, $1,437,810 will have been accumulated. Similar retirement and estate-planning issues will be mentioned later.

PROFILE ANALYSIS

The editors of *Consumer Guide* have developed an interesting survey to see what types of investments are appropriate for investors, based on their age and economic circumstances. The questionnaire is presented in Appendix 1–A. After you have read this chapter, you may want to try it. You can apply the questions to your own or your family's economic conditions.

BROKER'S NEW CRY: ASSET ALLOCATION

Eager to drum up new business, Wall Street is touting an investment technique to small investors that it has been pushing to institutional clients for years—asset allocation.

That's a fancy way of saying split up your money among stocks, bonds, cash equivalents and other investments. Just how that split works depends on things like your age, investment objectives, and willingness to take risk.

Asset allocation can be done many ways, all building on the idea of diversification to spread risk. Some plans call for a never-changing portfolio makeup, such as the widely publicized "fixed mix" of equal investments in U.S. stocks, U.S bonds, foreign stocks, real estate, and cash equivalents.

A look at Prudential-Bache's plan shows how big brokerage firms are tailoring allocation programs in a bid to capture the largest number of investors. Prudential-Bache's computer can spin out any one of 300 basic investment portfolios based on the investor's answers to its questionnaire.

Investors find that they often need to do fairly regular buying and selling to stay in line with their recommended asset mix. This is, in part, because the formulas themselves change along with an investor's age, family obligations, and general economic conditions.

Source: James A. White, *The Wall Street Journal,* October 6, 1988, p. C1. Reprinted by permission of *The Wall Street Journal* © Dow Jones & Co., Inc., 1988. All rights reserved.

SELLING ASSET ALLOCATION
(Portfolios Currently Recommended under Prudential-Bache's Strategy)

Characteristic	25-Year Old		45-Year Old		65-Year Old	
Risk Level*	Moderate		Aggressive		Very Conservative	
Portfolio size	$160,000		$600,000		$1.2 million	
Excess cash flow	Low		High		Low	
Desired investments						
Income	60%		10%		100%	
Growth	40%		90%		0%	
Investments Recommended						
Cash and equivalents	$64,000	(40%)	$30,000	(5%)	$120,000	(10%)
Fixed income	$40,000	(25%)	$60,000	(10%)	$780,000	(65%)
Moderate growth	$32,000	(20%)	$270,000	(45%)	$240,000	(20%)
Aggressive growth	$8,000	(5%)	$90,000	(15%)	0	—
Direct ownership	$8,000	(5%)	$120,000	(20%)	0	—
Tangible assets	$8,000	(5%)	$30,000	(5%)	$60,000	(5%)

*Data provided by investor.

MEASURES OF RISK AND RETURN

Now that you have some basic familiarity with the different forms of investments and the setting of investment goals, we are ready to look at concepts of measuring the return from an investment and the associated risk. The return you receive from any investment (stocks, bonds, real estate) has two primary components: capital gains (or increase in value) and current income. The rate of return from an investment can be measured as:

$$\text{Rate of return} = \frac{(\text{Ending value} - \text{Beginning value}) + \text{Income}}{\text{Beginning value}} \qquad (1-1)$$

Thus, if a share of stock goes from \$20 to \$22 during 1989 and also pays a dollar in dividends during the year, the total return is 15 percent. Using Formula (1–1):

$$\frac{(\$22 - \$20) + \$1}{\$20} = \frac{\$2 + \$1}{\$20} = \frac{\$3}{\$20} = 15\%$$

Where the formula is being specifically applied to stocks, it is written as:

$$\text{Rate of return} = \frac{(P_1 - P_0) + D_1}{P_0} \qquad (1-2)$$

Where:

P_1 = Price at the end of the period
P_0 = Price at the beginning of the period
D_1 = Dividend income

Risk

The risk for an investment is related to the uncertainty associated with the outcomes from an investment. For example, an investment that has an absolutely certain return of 10 percent is said to be riskless. Another investment that has a likely or expected return of 12 percent but also has the possibility of minus 10 percent in hard economic times and plus 30 percent under optimum circumstances is said to be risky. An example of three investments with progressively greater risk is presented in Figure 1–1. Based on our definition of risk, investment C is clearly the riskiest because of the large uncertain (wide dispersion) of possible outcomes.

In the study of investments, you will soon observe that the desired or required rate of return for a given investment is generally related to the risk associated with that investment. Because most investors do not like risk, they will require a higher rate of return for a more risky investment. That is not to say the investors are unwilling to take risks—they simply wish to be compensated for taking the risk. For this reason, an investment in common stocks (which inevitably carries some amount of risk) may require an anticipated return 5 or 6 percent higher than a certificate of deposit in a commercial bank. This 5 or 6 percent represents a risk premium. You never know for sure whether you will get the returns you anticipate, but at least your initial requirements will be higher to justify the risk you are taking.

FIGURE 1–1   EXAMPLES OF RISK

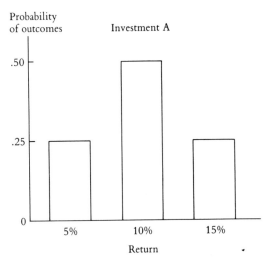

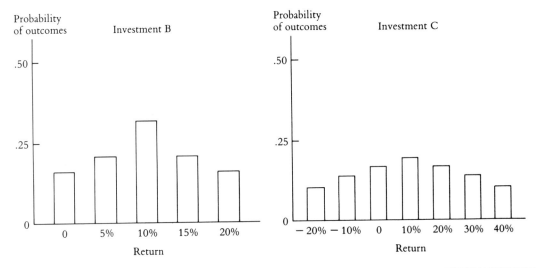

ACTUAL CONSIDERATION OF REQUIRED RETURNS

Let's consider how return requirements are determined in the financial markets. Although the following discussion starts out on a theoretical "what if" basis, you will eventually see empirical evidence that different types of investments do provide different types of returns.

Basically, three components make up the required return from an investment:

1. The real rate of return.
2. The anticipated inflation factor.
3. The risk premium.

Real Rate of Return

The **real rate of return** is the return that investors require for allowing others to use their money for a given time period. This is the return that investors demand for passing up immediate consumption and allowing others to use their savings until the funds are returned. Because the term *real* is employed, this means it is a value determined before inflation is included in the calculation. The real rate of return is also determined before considering any specific risk for the investment.

Historically, the real rate of return in the U.S. economy has been of the magnitude of 2 to 3 percent. More recently, it has been somewhat higher (4 to 6 percent). It is possible that the greater volatility in the financial markets (in terms of interest rates and stock prices) has led to this higher real-rate-of-return requirement. Over the long term, perhaps 3 percent may still be the most reasonable estimate of the real rate of return.

Anticipated Inflation Factor

The anticipated factor must be added to the real rate of return. For example, if there is a 3 percent real-rate-of-return requirement and the **anticipated rate of inflation** is 4 percent, we combine the two to arrive at an approximate 7 percent required return factor. Combining the real rate of return and inflationary considerations gives us the required return on an investment before explicitly considering risk. For this reason, it is called the risk-free required rate of return or, simply, **risk-free rate (R_F).**

We can define the risk-free rate as:

$$\text{Risk-free rate} = (1 + \text{Real rate})(1 + \text{Expected rate of inflation}) - 1$$

$$(1\text{--}3)$$

Plugging in numerical values, we would show:

$$= (1.03)(1.04) - 1 = 1.0712 - 1 = .0712, \text{ or } 7.12\%$$

The answer is approximately 7 percent. You can simply add the real rate of return (3 percent) to the anticipated inflation rate (4 percent) to get a 7 percent answer or go through the more theoretically correct process of Formula 1–3 to arrive at 7.12 percent. Either approach is frequently used.

The risk-free rate (R_F) of approximately 7 percent applies to any investment

FIGURE 1–2   THE COMPONENTS OF REQUIRED RATE OF RETURN

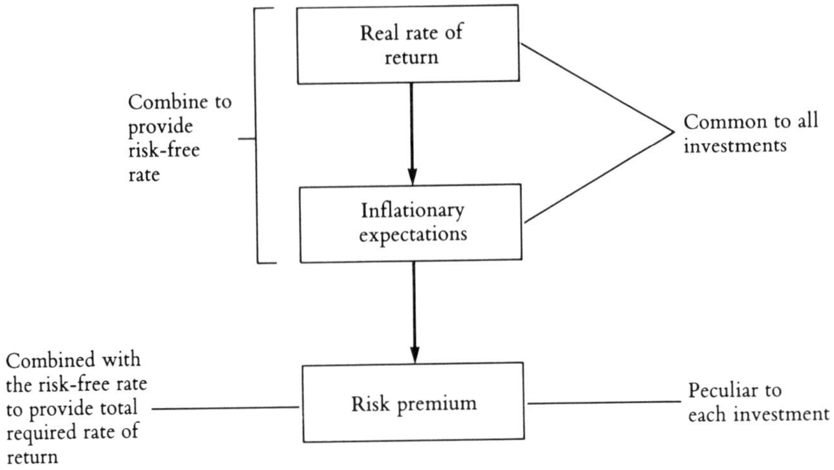

as the minimum required rate of return to provide a 3 percent *real return* after inflation. Of course, if the investor actually receives a lower return, his real rate of return may be quite low or negative. For example, if the investor receives a 3 percent return in a 4 percent inflationary environment, there is a negative real return of 1 percent. The investor will have 1 percent less purchasing power than before he started. He would have been better off to spend the money *now* rather than save at a 3 percent rate in a 4 percent inflationary economy. In effect, he is *paying* the borrower to use his money. Of course, real rates of return and inflationary expectations change from time to time, so the risk-free required rate (R_F) also changes.

We now have examined the two components that make up the minimum risk-free rate of return that apply to investments (stock, bonds, real estate, etc.). We now consider the third component, the risk premium. The relationship is depicted in Figure 1–2.

Risk Premium

The **risk premium** will be different for each investment. For example, for a federally insured certificate of deposit at a bank or for a U.S. government Treasury bill, the risk premium approaches zero. All the return to the investor will be at the risk-free rate of return (the real rate of return plus inflationary expectations). For common stock, the investor's required return may carry a 5 or 6 percent risk premium in addition to the risk-free rate of return. If the risk-free rate were 7 percent, the investor might have an overall required return of 12 to 13 percent on common stock.

+ Real rate	3%
+ Anticipated inflation	4%
= Risk-free rate	7%
+ Risk premium	5% to 6%
= Required rate of return	12% to 13%

Corporate bonds fall somewhere between short-term government obligations (virtually no risk) and common stock in terms of risk. Thus, the risk premium may be 2 to 4 percent. Like the real rate of return and the inflation rate, the risk premium is not a constant but may change from time to time. If investors are very fearful about the economic outlook, the risk premium may be 8 to 10 percent for a high-risk investment.

The normal relationship between selected investments and their rates of return is depicted in Figure 1–3.

FIGURE 1–3   RISK-RETURN CHARACTERISTICS

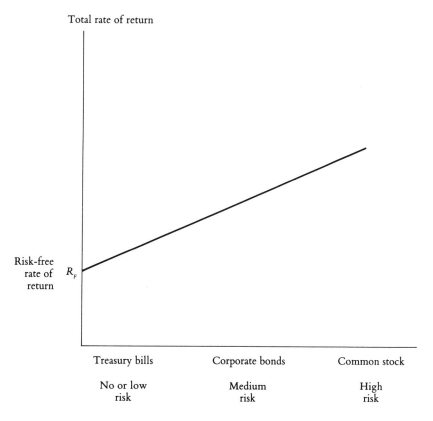

Source: The CFA Candidate Program (Charlottesville, Va.: The Institute of Chartered Financial Analysts, 1988–89), pp. 11–15.

A number of empirical studies tend to support the risk-return relationships shown in Figure 1–3 over a long period of time. Perhaps the most widely cited is the Ibbotson and Sinquefield study presented in Table 1–2, which covers data from 1926 to 1987. Note the high-to-low return scale is in line with expectations based on risk. Of particular interest is the first column, labeled geometric mean. Nonstatisticians will be pleased to know that this is simply the compound annual rate of return. The arithmetic mean in Column 2 is an average of yearly rates of return and has less meaning. We will study the concept of standard deviation (Column 3) later in the text.

TABLE 1–2	ANNUAL RETURNS OF FINANCIAL ASSETS (1926–1987)		
Series	(1) Geometric Mean	(2) Arithmetic Mean	(3) Standard Deviation
Common stocks	9.7%	12.0%	20.9%
Small stocks	11.9	17.7	35.6
Long-term corporate bonds	4.9	5.2	8.4
Long-term government bonds	4.2	4.6	8.4
U.S. Treasury bills	3.4	3.5	3.2
Inflation	3.0	3.1	4.8

Source: *Stocks, Bonds, Bills and Inflation, 1987 Yearbook* (Chicago: R.G. Ibbotson and Associates, Inc., 1987).

Because the study covered over half a century (including a decade of depression), the rates of return may be somewhat lower than those currently available in the economy. This is particularly true for the bonds and Treasury bills shown in the table.

In Table 1–3, you see a study by Salomon Brothers, an investment banking firm, that covers 14 different investment categories and the CPI (consumer price index).

The study is different from Table 1–2 in that it covers real assets as well as financial assets. The information runs through June 1, 1988.

For the 20-year and 10-year periods, real assets tend to dominate the return rankings. This is primarily due to the high rate of inflation that was present during the 1970s and early 1980s. Real assets, because of increasing replacement value and scarcity, tend to perform best during periods of high inflation. However, in the 5-year column, you will observe that many real assets, such as U.S. stamps, gold, and oil performed poorly as inflationary expectations diminished in the 1983–88 time frame. Stocks, which were poor performers over the 20-year period, showed a strong performance during the 5-year time frame. The one-year rankings are almost meaningless because of short-term influences.

Because most of the material in the Salomon Brothers study was gathered during one of the most-inflationary time periods in U.S. history (aided by major oil price increases), you should not overly generalize from the results. Over longer periods of time, common stock tends to perform at approximately

TABLE 1–3   COMPOUNDED ANNUAL RATES OF RETURN

	20 Years	Rank	10 Years	Rank	5 Years	Rank	1 Year	Rank
Coins	15.1	1	13.4	1	10.1	4	14.0	3
U.S. Stamps	12.9	2	10.5	3	0.2	12	1.4	13
Gold	12.8	3	9.6	7	2.2	11	3.1	10
Chinese Ceramics[a]	12.0	4	9.2	8	5.5	8	10.5	5
Oil[b]	9.9	5	3.7	12	−10.7	14	19.5	2
Diamonds[c]	9.9	6	9.6	6	7.5	7	24.9	1
Old Masters[a]	8.8	7	8.0	9	12.0	3	13.4	4
Treasury Bills	8.5	8	10.1	5	7.6	6	6.0	8
Bonds	8.1	9	10.3	4	13.4	2	6.2	7
Housing	7.7	10	6.2	10	5.0	9	2.0	12
Stocks	6.8	11	13.3	2	13.6	1	−4.9	14
CPI	**6.3**	**12**	**6.1**	**11**	**3.3**	**10**	**3.1**	**9**
Silver	5.9	13	2.8	14	−11.6	15	−7.4	15
U.S. Farmland	5.9	14	0.6	15	−6.5	13	3.1	11
Foreign Exchange	4.7	15	3.2	13	9.5	5	8.6	6

[a]Source: Sotheby's 1988 index level for Chinese Ceramics does not reflect sales held May 17–19 in Hong Kong.
[b]Oil index figures have been revised to reflect refiners' acquisition cost of crude oil. Source: U.S. Department of Energy.
[c]Source: The Diamond Registry.
Note: All returns are for the period ended June 1, 1988, based on latest available data.
CPI: Consumer Price Index.
Source: Salomon Brothers Inc., June 6, 1988.

the same level as such real assets as real estate, coins, stamps, and so forth,[1] with each tending to show a different type of performance in a differing economic environment. More will be said about the impact of inflation and disinflation on investments in later parts of the text.

Determining the Risk Premium

We have attempted to demonstrate the importance of risk in determining the required rate of return for an investment. As previously discussed, it is the third key component that is added to the risk-free rate (composed of the real rate of return and the inflation premium) to determine the total required rate of return. How does one *actually* go about determining the risk that is to be rewarded from a given instrument?

Systematic and Unsystematic Risk

You will recall that earlier we defined risk as related to the uncertainty of outcomes for a given investment. But it is not just the risk for an individual security that must be considered. Financial theory also requires that we consider

---

[1]Examples of longer-term studies on comparative returns between real and financial assets are: Roger G. Ibbotson and Carol F. Fall, "The United States Wealth Portfolio," *The Journal of Portfolio Management,* Fall 1982, pp. 82–92; Roger G. Ibbotson and Lawrence B. Siegel, "The World Market Wealth Portfolio," *The Journal of Portfolio Management,* Winter 1983, pp. 5–17; and Alexander A. Robichek, Richard A. Cohn, and John J. Pringle, "Returns on Alternative Media and Implications for Portfolio Construction," *Journal of Business,* July 1972, pp. 427–43. (While Ibbotson and Siegel showed superior returns for metals between 1960 and 1980, metals have greatly underperformed other assets in the 1980s.)

the relationship between two or more investments to determine the combined risk level. Part of the risk of one investment may be **diversified** away with a second investment. For example, an investment in an oil company may be somewhat risky in nature because oil prices may drop, but if you have a second investment in a petrochemical company that will benefit from lower oil prices, then you have diversified away part of the risk. Similarly, investments in foreign stocks often move in the opposite direction of investments in U.S. stocks. If you combine stocks from two or more countries, part of the risk is diversified away. Because diversification can *eliminate* part of the risk in an investment, not all risk is thought to be compensated for by proportionally higher returns.

Financial theory can be used to break down risk that is systematic and unsystematic in nature. We'll talk about the latter item first. **Unsystematic risk** is risk that can be diversified away in a well-constructed portfolio and thus is not assumed to be rewarded with higher returns in the financial markets. It represents the type of risk described in the preceding paragraph. **Systematic risk,** on the other hand, is inherent in the investment and cannot be diversified away and is assumed to be rewarded in the marketplace. The relationship is indicated below.

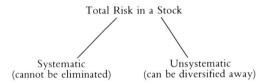

Total Risk in a Stock

Systematic
(cannot be eliminated)

Unsystematic
(can be diversified away)

Systematic risk is measured by the related movement of a stock to the market. Even in a totally diversified portfolio, each stock will be vulnerable to changes in the *overall* market even if individual characteristics of the stocks have been largely diversified away. Based on systematic risk, if the market goes up or down by 10 percent, our stock may go up or down by 10 percent. The joint movement between a security and the market in general is defined as the **beta** coefficient. If a stock has equal volatility to the market (if the market changes by 10 percent, the stock changes by 10 percent) the beta coefficient is 1. If the stock is 50 percent more volatile than the market, the beta coefficient is 1.5 and so on. Systematic risk, as measured by the beta coefficient, is assumed to be compensated for by higher potential returns. That is, stocks that have high systematic risk or betas are assumed to provide higher returns to compensate for the additional risk. This same type of risk analysis can be applied to other types of investments as well.

In a later chapter, we will give a more thorough mathematical definition of how you separate out systematic and unsystematic risk. It is enough for now that you understand that the differences exist and that the two forms of risk are not equally compensated. In the prior discussion of unsystematic risk, we mentioned the importance of diversifying away nonmarket–related risks.

We discussed oil versus petrochemicals as presenting potential for diversifying oil price risks. Also foreign stocks versus U.S. stocks were given as an example. Undoubtedly, you can think of others. The auto part replacement market may move in the opposite direction of new auto sales; the same can be said for the market for defense systems and public works projects. In order to establish an efficiently diversified portfolio, the investor must consider how projects correlate with each other. Generally, highly correlated projects provide little diversification benefits, while projects that have low correlations or are negatively correlated provide maximum diversification benefits.

Summary of Return Considerations

Based on our analysis to this point, we can say that each investment requires a total return that comprises a real rate of return, compensation for inflationary expectations, and a risk premium. The risk premium should be related to systematic risk (as opposed to unsystematic risk). In Chapter 6, "Valuation of the Individual Firm," you will become familiar with K_e, which is the total return on common stock. You should keep in mind that K_e represents a risk-free rate plus a risk premium and that this risk premium is directly related to systematic risk. By glancing back to Table 1–2, you can observe that over the very long term, the difference between a risk-free asset (such as a Treasury bill) and common stock is often of the magnitude of 6 percent. This is the risk premium.

Also, in Chapter 6, you will see how the required rate of return influences the valuation of an investment. You should also be aware that just because an investor has a required return expectation does not mean that the expectation will be met. For example, an investor may purchase a bond with an expected return of 10 percent. But if the inflation expectations go up, the new required return on such a bond may now be 13 percent. The only way for the old bond to offer the going market rate, based on its low 10 percent interest payments, will be for the bond to go down in value. This lower value will offer the *new* bondholders the return they desire but will mean *old* bondholders are suffering market value losses in the meantime. They started out hoping to receive 10 percent, but now their annual rate of return will be less because of the drop in the bond value.[2] The same thing can happen to common stock investors.

WHAT YOU WILL LEARN

The first part of the book covers the general framework for investing. You will look at an overview of the security markets (New York Stock Exchange, Chicago Board Options Exchange, and so on). Then you will examine the basics for participating in the market, such as opening an account, executing an order, investing individually or through a mutual fund, and so forth. Also

---

[2]Of course, if inflation expectations go down, the required return would be less and the bond price would go up. Now investors would receive a return higher than the 10 percent they initially expected.

in the first section of the book, you will become familiar with sources of important investment information so that you can begin to make your university or public library a valuable asset.

You will then go through the classic process of analyzing and valuing a security. You will start with examining the economy, then move to the industry level, and finally move to the actual company. The authors go through the process of actually putting a value on a stock. There is also heavy emphasis on financial analysis. One chapter provides an in-depth analysis of The Coca-Cola Company to demonstrate the procedures that should be utilized in identifying the strengths and weaknesses of a company. For enthusiasts of charting and other forms of technical analysis, we examine the advantages and disadvantages of such approaches.

You will then move from stocks to bonds. Your level of interest should not diminish because bonds also offer an opportunity for income and, surprisingly, for large gains or losses. Because an emphasis of the book is to give the student a wide investment horizon from which to choose, we then consider a variety of other investment alternatives. These include convertible securities and warrants, put and call options, commodities and financial futures, stock index futures and options, and real assets such as real estate and precious metals. We realize some of these terms may have little meaning to you now, but they soon will.

In the latter part of the book, we also consider the concepts of portfolio theory and how to put together the most desirable package of investments in terms of risk and return. We also consider the consequences of investing in a reasonably efficient stock market environment, one in which information is acted upon very quickly. Can superior return be achieved in such a setting?

Many students taking an investments course are not sure of their ultimate career goals. We hope this course can be equally valuable to a future banker, CPA, insurance executive, marketing manager, or anyone else. However, for those specifically considering a career in investments, the authors present a brief summary of career opportunities in the second appendix at the back of this chapter, Appendix 1–B.

APPENDIX 1-A: INVESTOR PROFILE

PROFILE ANALYSIS: WHAT SHOULD YOU INVEST IN NOW?

Directions: Circle the answer that most nearly applies to you or your family. Write that number in the space at right. Then add up the numbers and divide by 9 to get a median score.

AGE—My age is closest to:

(9) 30   (7) 40   (5) 50   (3) 60   (1) 70   _____

INCOME—My present annual income from all sources is nearest to (in thousands):

(2) 10   (4) 20   (5) 30   (6) 40   (8) 50   _____

ANNUAL EXPENSES—In relation to income, my annual expenses approximate:

(1) 100%   (3) 90%   (5) 80%   (7) 70%   (9) 50%   _____

NUMBER OF DEPENDENTS—I presently have these dependents:

(9) 0   (8) 1   (6) 2–3   (4) 4–5   (1) 6 or more   _____

ESTIMATED VALUE OF ASSETS—My house, insurance, savings, and investments total (in thousands):

(1) 50   (3) 100   (5) 250   (7) 350   (9) 500 or more   _____

LIABILITIES—My bills, mortgages, installment payments, and debts in relation to assets approximate (in thousands):

(9) 30%   (7) 50%   (5) 75%   (3) 90%   (1) 100%   _____

SAVINGS—I have cash on hand in savings or other liquid assets to equal this amount of expenses:

(1) 1 month   (3) 2 months   (5) 3 months   (7) 4 months   (9) 6 months or more   _____

LIFE INSURANCE—My life insurance coverage equals (in thousands):

(9) 250   (7) 150   (5) 100   (3) 50   (1) 25 or less   _____

HEALTH INSURANCE—My health insurance coverage includes:

(9) Basic, major medical, catastrophic   (5) Major medical plus basic   (1) Basic   _____

Add up your scores and divide by 9 to get the average. Then consider the investment strategies that follow.

The investment strategy rating numbers below correlate with the average score you got from the profile analysis. The investment strategy ratings indicate investment categories ranging from (1) ultraconservative to (9) highly speculative. By matching the profile score with the nearest investment strategy numbers, you get some feel for investments that may be appropriate for you. You would probably choose from two or three categories.

1. Insured savings accounts.
2. High-grade government securities.
3. High-quality corporate and municipal bonds, preferred stocks, investment trusts, and annuity income.
4. Lower-rated corporate and municipal bonds, preferred stocks, investment trusts, convertible bonds and preferred stocks, and variable insurance.
5. Higher-rated common stocks and investment trusts and investment annuities.
6. Lower-rated common stocks and investment trusts.
7. Speculative bonds, stocks, and investment trusts.
8. Gold and silver-related investments and foreign investment trusts.
9. Rare and exotic investments: stamps, rare coins, art, antiques, gems and jewelry, rare books, autographs, prints, and lithographs.

Source: The Editors of *Consumer Guide,* with Peter A. Dickinson, *How to Make Money during Inflation Recession* (New York: Harper & Row, 1980).

APPENDIX 1–B: CAREER OPPORTUNITIES IN INVESTMENTS

Career opportunities in the field of investments include positions as a stockbroker, security analyst or portfolio manager, investment banker, or financial planner.

Stockbroker

A stockbroker generally works with the public in advising and executing orders for individual or institutional accounts. Although he or she may have a salary base to cushion against bad times, most of the compensation is in the form of commissions. Successful brokers do quite well financially.

Most brokerage houses look for people who have effective selling skills as well as an interest in finance. In hiring, some (though not all) brokerage houses require prior business experience and a mature appearance. A listing of the 30 largest brokerage houses is presented in Table 1B–1. Further information on these firms (as well as others not included on the list) can be found in the *Securities Industry Yearbook* published by the Securities Industry Association, 10 Broad Street, New York, N.Y. 10005.

Security Analyst or Portfolio Manager

Security analysts study various industries and companies and provide research reports to their clientele. A security analyst might work for a brokerage house, a bank trust department, or any other type of institutional investor. Security analysts often specialize in certain industries, such as banking or the airlines. They are expected to have an in-depth knowledge of overall financial analysis as well as the variables that influence their industry.

The role of the financial analyst has been upgraded over the years through the establishment of a certifying program in which you can become a Chartered Financial Analyst (CFA). There are approximately 10,000 CFAs in the United States and Canada. Achieving this designation calls for a three-year minimum appropriate-experience requirement and extensive testing over a three-year period. Each of the annual exams is six hours long and costs approximately $225 (the fee changes somewhat from year to year). There is also an initial, one-time registration fee (currently, $175). You can actually begin taking the

TABLE 1B–1   30 LARGEST U.S. BROKERAGE HOUSES

1987 Rank	Name of Firm	Total Capital ($ Millions)
1	Salomon Brothers	$3,209.2
2	Shearson Lehman Brothers	3,122.0
3	Merrill Lynch, Pierce, Fenner & Smith	2,864.8
4	Goldman, Sachs & Co.	1,951.0
5	Drexel Burnham Lambert	1,870.5
6	First Boston	1,363.8
7	Prudential-Bache Securities	1,288.7
8	Dean Witter Reynolds	1,213.6
9	Bear, Stearns & Co.	1,057.2
10	E.F. Hutton & Co.	986.4
11	Morgan Stanley & Co.	901.2
12	Donaldson, Lufkin & Jenrette	766.1
13	Paine Webber	635.1
14	Kidder, Peabody & Co.	595.5
15	Stephens	418.8
16	Smith Barney, Harris Upham & Co.	407.9
17	Shelby Cullom Davis & Co.	366.6
18	Allen & Co.	359.5
19	Thomson McKinnon Securities	298.0
20	L.F. Rothschild, Unterberg, Towbin	289.3
21	Van Kampen Merritt	236.5
22	Spear, Leeds & Kellogg	234.0
23	A.G. Edwards & Sons	231.0
24	Oppenheimer & Co.	211.0
25	Dillon, Read & Co.	190.9
26	John Nuveen & Co.	185.6
27	UBS Securities	170.3
28	Allen & Co. Inc.	150.8
29	Neuberger & Berman	144.1
30	Nomura Securities International	128.0

Source: "Ranking America's Biggest Brokers." *Institutional Investor,* April 1987, pp. 197–98.

exams while still in school (you can complete your experience requirement later).

Each exam covers the topics shown in Table 1B–2, but the degree of difficulty increases as you progress from Exam I through Exam III. The bars show how much of the information is to be covered in Exams I, II, and III. An undergraduate degree in business with a major in finance or accounting or an economics degree is quite beneficial to the exam process (though other degrees are also acceptable). Of course, educational background must be supplemented with additional study prescribed by the Institute of Chartered Financial Analysts.

The address for more information is: The Institute of Chartered Financial Analysts, P.O. Box 3668, Charlottesville, Virginia 22903 (phone 804 977-6600).

While many security analysts are not CFAs, those who carry this designation tend to enjoy higher salary and prestige. The number of openings for security

TABLE 1B–2   AREAS OF STUDY FOR CFA EXAMS

**Ethical and Professional Standards
Securities Law and Regulations**

Candidate level

I   II   III

Applicable laws and regulations
Nature and applicability of fiduciary standards
Pertinent laws and regulations
Organization and purpose of governing regulatory bodies

Professional code and standards
Code of Ethics
Standards of Professional Conduct
By-Laws, Article VII, Sections 4, 5, and 6
Rules of Procedure

Ethical standards and professional obligations
Public
Customers and clients
Corporate management
Employers
Associates
Other analysts
Insider information
Supervisory responsibilities
Research reports and investment recommendations
Compensation
Conflicts of interest
Fiduciary duties
Professional misconduct

Identification of issues and administration of ethical conduct
Takeovers and the institutional investor
General business ethical values and obligations
Intrafirm relationships
Competency and proper care
Social responsibility
Soft dollars
Nonvoting shares

(continued in next column)

Financial Accounting

I   II   III

Role and function of basic accounting statements
Income statement
Statement of financial position
Statement of changes in financial position

Interpretation of accounting statements
Revenue recognition
Inventory costing
Depreciation methods
Investments in marketable securities
Off-balance sheet financing
Troubled debt restructuring
Leases
Postemployment benefits
Income taxes
Prior period adjustments
Earnings per share
Foreign currency translation
Intercorporate investments
Business combinations

Not Assigned

Special topics
Goals of financial statement analysis
Implications of efficient market hypothesis
The setting of accounting standards
Analysis of liquidity
Cash flow analysis
Adjustments to financial statements

Quantitative Analysis

I   II   III

Introduction to quantitative methods
Mathematics of valuation
Statistics and data analysis

(continued in next column)

TABLE 1B–2   *(continued)*

Candidate level

I. II. III

Uncertainty and valuation
Rate of return
Time weighted and dollar weighted rate
of return

Equity analysis
Equity valuation
Factor analysis

Fixed income analysis
Fixed income valuation
Determinants of bond yields
Factors that affect bond markets

Real estate analysis
Property valuation issues
Portfolio analysis

Derivative security analysis
Boundaries and basic properties of option
values
Arbitrage and option valuation
Option pricing models
Empirical analysis of options
Option pricing theory applied to other
assets
Asset Allocation
Expected return and risk
Estimation issues
The optimal portfolio
Dynamic asset allocation

Performance measurement
Universe comparisons
Risk adjustment
Benchmark error
Ambiguity between skill and chance
Performance attribution
Normal portfolio
Nonparametric performance
measurement
Incentive fees
Gaming performance measurement

Economics

I   II   III

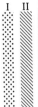

Focus on macroeconomics
Concept and measurement of GNP
Business fluctuations and economic
forecasting
Inflationary process
Aggregate supply and demand
Macro schools of thought
Forecasting tools and success

**Focus on microeconomics and
analysis**
Consumer behavior and business decision
making
Costs and supply of goods
Product life cycle
Business structure and regulation

International economics
Comparative advantage
International payments and exchange

**Focus on analysis, policy, and
investment application**
Applications to portfolio management
Economic factors of return
Structural change
Current issues

**Techniques of Analysis — Fixed
Income Securities**

I   II   III

Types and characteristics
Taxable, non-taxable
Type of issuer

(continued in next column)   *(continued in next column)*

TABLE 1B–2   *(continued)*

Candidate level

I   II   III

Maturities
Indenture provisions
Convertible, non-convertible

Mathematical properties
Interest on interest
Determinants of prices and yields
Duration

Credit evaluation
Ratings and rating services
Earning power
Asset protection
Terms and covenants

Interest rates
Term structure
Forecasting

Bond trading
Analysis
Techniques

Risk management
Futures
Options

New features
Contingent options and early
redemptions
International bond investing

Techniques of Analysis — Equity Securities

I   II   III

Investment context
Equity instruments (common stocks,
convertible and participating issues,
rights, warrants, options and futures)
Development and application of equity
instruments

(continued in next column)

I   II   III

Characteristics of equity markets:
indices, economic relationship,
comparative risk and return
International instruments,
developments, and markets

**Economic framework
industry analysis and evaluation**
Identification of company's business(es)
External factors: political, regulatory,
social
Demand analysis: end uses, growth (real
and nominal), cyclicality
Supply analysis: degree of concentration,
ease of entry, capacity
Profitability: demand/supply balance,
pricing and cost
International aspects

Company analysis and evaluation
Position within industry
Sales analysis: growth (real and nominal),
cyclicality
Earnings analysis: earnings by business
segment, consolidated results,
components of return on equity
Flow of funds analysis
Balance sheet analysis
Dividends: payout policy and divided
growth
Management appraisal
International equity analysis

Risk analysis
Qualitative factors: external (political,
social, environmental); company
business (economic sensitivity, size,
growth, financial leverage); stock
market (price volatility, share
characteristics, market sub-groups)
Quantitative factors: capital asset
pricing model (beta, nonsystematic),
factor analysis (identification, exposure)

Valuation
Earnings multiples
Dividend discount and other valuation
models

(continued in next column)

TABLE 1B–2   *(concluded)*

Candidate level

Technical analysis
Stock market perceptions

Derivative securities
Characteristics of options, futures, warrants
Markets for derivative securities
Valuation models
Application of derivative securities

Equity analysis and the efficient markets
Weak, semistrong and strong forms of efficient market hypothesis
Implications relative to fundamental and technical analysis
Market anomalies

Organization of the equity analysis process
General investment philosophy
Techniques of information collection and processing
Analysts' interaction with other investment professionals
Communication of information inside and outside organizations

Equity analysis performance measurement
Criteria
Techniques
Evaluation process

Objective of Analysis — Portfolio Management

I   II   III

Principle of financial asset management
Definition of portfolio management, basic concepts–return, risk, diversification, portfolio efficiency

I   II   III

Evolution of portfolio management–traditional and recent developments

Investor objectives, constraints and policies
Liquidity requirement
Return requirement
Risk tolerance
Time horizon
Tax considerations
Regulatory and legal considerations
Unique needs, circumstances and preferences
Determination of portfolio policies

Expectational factors
Social, political and economic
Capital markets
Individual financial assets

Integration of portfolio policies and expectional factors
Portfolio construction–asset allocation, active/passive strategies
Monitoring portfolio and responding to change–objectives, constraints and policies, expectational factors
Execution–timing, commission costs, price effects

Portfolio performance appraisal
Performance criteria–absolute performance, relative to portfolio objectives and risk level, relative to other portfolios with similar objectives.
Measurement of performance–valuation of assets, accounting for income, rates of return and volatility
Evaluation of results–relationship to performance criteria, sources of results.

(continued in next column)

analysts has shrunk in recent times because of the tight research budgets of many brokerage houses. This came about in the mid 1970s when commission charges went from fixed to freely competitive and fewer dollars were allocated to research.

In spite of this situation, really top analysts are still in strong demand and six-figure salaries for top analysts are common. A magazine entitled *The Institutional Investor* actually picks an all-American team of security analysts, the best in energy, banking, and so on. As we will see later in the text, some academic researchers question the legitimacy of such designations.

Portfolio managers have the responsibility for managing large pools of funds, and they are generally employed by insurance companies, mutual funds, bank trust departments, pension funds, and other institutional investors. They often rely on the help of security analysts and brokers in designing their portfolios. They not only must decide which stocks to buy or sell, but they also must determine the risk level with the optimum trade-off between the common-stock and fixed-income components of a portfolio. Portfolio managers often rise through the ranks of stockbrokers and security analysts.

Investment Banker

Investment bankers are primarily involved in the distribution of securities from the issuing corporation to the public. Investment bankers also advise corporate clients on their financial strategy and may help to arrange mergers and acquisitions.

The investment banker is one of the most prestigious participants in the securities industry. Although the hiring of investment bankers was once closely confined to Ivy League graduates with the right family ties, such is no longer the case. Nevertheless, an MBA and top credentials are usually the first prerequisites.

Financial Planner

A new field of financial planning is emerging to help solve the investment and tax problems of the individual investor. Financial planners may include specially trained representatives of the insurance industry, accountants who have expertise in this area, and Certified Financial Planners (actually an individual may fall into more than one of these categories).

Certified Financial Planners (CFPs) are so designated by the College for Financial Planning in Denver. The CFP program includes the following parts.

CFP I   Introduction to financial planning.
CFP II   Risk management.
CFP III Investments.

TABLE 1B–3   AREAS OF STUDY FOR THE CFP (CERTIFIED FINANCIAL PLANNER) PROGRAM

PROGRAM OVERVIEW

CFP 1—Introduction to Financial Planning

The purpose of CFP I is threefold. First, it presents the six-stage financial planning process and an introduction to regulations affecting financial planners. Emphasis is placed on constructing financial statements and analyzing the client's current financial situation. Second, CFP I presents three critical areas applicable to financial planning: communication skills, the economic environment, and time value of money concepts. Third, it provides an introduction and overview of the content of CFP Program Parts II through VI.

CFP II—Risk Management

In CFP II, the candidate first studies principles of risk management and insurance to identify a client's risk exposures and select the appropriate risk management techniques. Because transferring risk through the use of insurance is the principal method of handling risk, the candidate is introduced to the basic insurance contract and practical insurance checklists. The study guide deals with property and liability insurance, including homeowners, personal auto, and umbrella policies. The candidate then analyzes life insurance, using a 13-step life insurance selection process that utilizes a 10-step needs determination approach. Finally, medical and disability insurance, social insurance, and compulsory compensation are covered.

CFP III—Investments

CFP III addresses the wide variety of investment vehicles that can be included in the client's personal investment portfolio. In this unit, the candidate learns the importance of the economic and business environment and studies the fundamentals of investing, including tools and mechanics of investing, security markets, tax considerations, sources of investment information, types of investment risk, and the analysis of corporate financial statements. In addition, the characteristics and valuation techniques of several investment vehicles are examined. The case analysis section introduces the portfolio construction and management process for the individual and also incorporates time value of money calculations. In the case section, the candidate is required to recommend asset categories and investment vehicles based on the client's needs, resources, and financial goals.

CFP IV—Tax Planning and Management

The first 11 assignments in CFP IV focus on the fundamentals of individual income taxation, tax implications of various forms of business, planning for the acquisition and disposition of property, tax-advantaged investments, and tax planning for the family. More technical topics are discussed in the following three assignments: employee compensation issues and planning, special tax computations, and tax traps. Concepts are integrated in the final assignment, which prepares the candidate to evaluate client cases and make recommendations concerning tax planning techniques.

CFP V—Retirement Planning and Employee Benefits

The materials in CFP V begin with a discussion of personal tax-deferred retirement programs available to many working adults and include a framework for use in calculating annual savings needed to reach retirement income goals. Next, the candidate focuses on the key features of qualified retirement plan design, with emphasis on the advantages and disadvantages of specific types of qualified plans for the owners of small- to medium-sized businesses, including a flow chart of the retirement plan development and maintenance process with funding considerations. Government-sponsored plans, including Social Security, Medicare, and federal and civil service and military programs, also are presented. In addition, CFP V examines life, health, and disability insurance; nonqualified deferred compensation; and other commonly provided employee benefits. The case study requires the candidate to select an appropriate qualified retirement plan for a small business owner and to analyze the tax implications of employee benefits.

CFP VI—Estate Planning

The final part of the CFP Program introduces the candidate to the process applied to the development of an estate plan. The fundamentals of federal estate and gift taxation are emphasized, as well as specific exclusion and valuation techniques that reduce the size of the gross estate. CFP VI highlights the characteristics of wills, intestacy, and the probate process. The use of trusts, property ownership forms, and will substitutes also is introduced. Specific assignments address life insurance, lifetime gifting, and coordination of the unified credit with the marital deduction as a part of estate planning, as well as charitable, intrafamily, and business transfers, and postmortem planning techniques that play an important part in estate planning. CFP VI concludes with a comprehensive case analysis that requires the candidate to select appropriate estate planning techniques based on a client's constraints and objectives.

Source: *College of Financial Planning Catalog* (Denver, Colo.: The College for Financial Planning, 1988) pp. 9 and 11.

CFP IV   Tax planning and management.
CFP V   Retirement planning and employee benefits.
CFP VI   Estate planning.

The parts of the CFP program are further described in Table 1B–3. Each part is concluded with a comprehensive written exam. The program normally takes 24 months to complete and the program participant may study on his or her own or attend formal classes. Appropriate experience requirements are also needed for final certification. Information on the CFP program can be obtained by contacting the College for Financial Planning, 9725 East Hampden Avenue, Denver, Colorado 80231-4993 (phone 303 755-7101).

2

SECURITY MARKETS— PRESENT AND FUTURE

THE MARKET ENVIRONMENT

Changes in the securities markets that began a decade ago have greatly accelerated. Deregulation of financial institutions created new competitors for retail brokerage houses and allowed banks and savings and loans to offer discount brokerage services and money market deposit accounts. Mergers continue to increase the consolidation of financial resources into well-capitalized financial-service-oriented companies such as Merrill Lynch, Sears, Prudential-Bache, and Shearson Lehman Hutton. Insurance companies have entered the financial services arena with offerings of mutual funds to take advantage of retirement planning and the increased emphasis on individual retirement accounts (IRAs). One result of these market changes is that investors probably have more alternative investments (securities) currently available to them than at any other time in history. They are able to buy traditional stocks and bonds, short-term money market instruments, real estate investments, and international securities as well as other more-risky alternatives.

The markets for stocks, bonds, options, and futures have become much more international in scope in the last few years. The increased listing of foreign securities on international stock exchanges has led to around-the-world trading from one time zone to another and virtual 24-hour trading in stocks of large international corporations. The fall of the dollar against the yen and the dramatic rise in the Japanese stock market has made the Japanese stock market the largest in the world followed by the New York Stock Exchange and London markets. These three markets, as well as the smaller international markets, have created an international market that currently trades securities 24 hours a day. The trading starts in Japan, is passed to London, then to New York, and back to Japan. The three markets encompass enough time zones to make continuous trading almost a reality. International markets are covered separately in Chapter 18.

The Chicago Mercantile Exchange (MERC), the Chicago Board Options Exchange, and the Chicago Board of Trade are at the center of options and futures trading with the MERC very much in the forefront of the international markets. The market for stock options and financial futures has become more integrated with the stock and bond markets through stock index options and futures contracts on stock indexes and bonds. The futures market led by the Chicago Mercantile Exchange is now operating 24 hours a day using a computerized trading system.

Even the traditional markets for common stocks have changed as the over-the-counter market through its NASDAQ automated quotation system has successfully increased its share of equity trades at the expense of the New York and American Stock Exchanges. Computer and communications technology are affecting the way securities are traded not only in the international market systems but are also affecting the way individuals and institutional investors trade. Much of the blame for the Crash of '87 on October 19, 1987, was focused on new trading methods made possible by computerized trading. The Dow Jones Industrial Average declined 508 points, or 22.6 percent on that day, creating a record drop far in excess of the largest daily decline of October 1929 (slightly over 12 percent).

The impact of these changes as well as a complete discussion of securities available for investment will be presented in various chapters throughout the book. In this chapter, we examine how the market system operates, with an eye towards efficiency, liquidity, and allocation of capital. We then look at the role of the secondary or resale markets for stocks, bonds, and other securities. Finally, we examine some key protective legislation for the investor.

MARKET FUNCTIONS

Many times people will call their stockbroker and ask, "How's the market?" What they are referring to is usually the market for common stocks as measured by the Dow Jones Industrial Average, the New York Stock Exchange Index, or some other measure of common stock performance. The stock market is not the only market. There are markets for each different kind of investment that can be made.

A **market** is simply a way of exchanging assets, usually cash, for something of value. It could be a used car, a government bond, gold, or diamonds. There doesn't have to be a central place where this transaction is consummated. As long as there can be communication between buyers and sellers, the exchange can occur. The offering party does not have to own what he sells, but can be an agent acting for the owner in the transaction. For example, in the sale of real estate, the owner usually employs a real estate broker/agent who advertises and sells the property for a percentage commission. Not all markets have the same procedures, but certain trading characteristics are desirable for most markets.

Market Efficiency and Liquidity

In general, markets are efficient when prices respond quickly to new information, when each successive trade is made at a price close to the preceding price, and when the market can absorb large amounts of securities or assets without changing the price significantly. The more efficient the market, the faster prices react to new information, the closer in price is each successive trade, and the greater the amount of securities that can be sold without changing the price.

In order for markets to be efficient in this context, they must be liquid. Liquidity is a measure of the speed with which an asset can be converted into cash at its fair market value. Liquid markets exist when continuous trading occurs, and as the number of participants in the market becomes larger, price continuity increases along with liquidity. Transaction costs also affect liquidity. The lower the cost of buying and selling, the more likely it is that people will be able to enter the market.

Competition and Allocation of Capital

An investor must realize that all markets compete for funds: stocks against bonds, mutual funds against real estate, government securities against corporate securities, and so on. The competitive comparisons are almost endless.

Because markets set prices on assets, investors are able to compare the prices against their perceived risk and expected return and thereby choose assets that enable them to achieve their desired risk-return trade-offs. If the markets are efficient, prices adjust rapidly to new information, and this adjustment changes the expected rate of return and allows the investor to alter his or her investment strategy. Without efficient and liquid markets, the investor would be unable to do this. This allocation of capital takes place on both secondary and primary markets.

Secondary Markets

Secondary markets are markets for existing assets that are currently traded between investors. It is these markets that create the prices and allow for liquidity. If secondary markets did not exist, investors would have no place to sell their assets. Without liquidity, many people would not invest at all. Would you like to own $10,000 of Eastman Kodak common stock but be unable to convert it into cash if needed? If there were no secondary markets, investors would expect a higher return to compensate for the increased risk of illiquidity and the inability to adjust their portfolios to new information.

Primary Markets

Primary markets are distinguished by the flow of funds between the market participants. Instead of trading between investors as in the secondary markets, participants in the primary market buy their assets directly from the source of the asset. A common example would be a new issue of corporate bonds sold by AT&T. You would buy the bonds through a brokerage firm acting as an agent for AT&T. Your dollars would flow to AT&T rather than to another investor. The same would be true of buying a piece of art directly from the artist rather than from an art gallery. Primary markets allow corporations, government units, and others to raise needed funds for expansion of their capital base. Once the assets or securities are sold in the primary market, they begin trading in the secondary market. Price competition in the secondary markets between different risk-return classes enables the primary markets to price new issues at fair prices to reflect existing risk-return relationships. So far, our discussion of markets has been quite general but applicable to most free markets. In the following section, we will deal with the organization and structure of specific markets.

ORGANIZATION OF THE PRIMARY MARKETS— THE INVESTMENT BANKER

The most active participant in the primary market is the investment banker. Since corporations, states, and local governments do not sell new securities daily, monthly, or even annually, they rely on the expertise of the investment banker when selling securities.

TABLE 2–1   CORPORATE ISSUES BY METHOD OF DISTRIBUTION AND BY TYPE OF SE-
CURITY: 1981–1987 (Primary Issues Registered under the Security Act of 1933 in Millions)

	Underwritten				*Best Efforts*			
Year	Total	Debt	Preferred	Common	Total	Debt	Preferred	Common
1987	$84,726	$45,871	$6,332	$32,523	$10,053	$2,031	$162	$ 7,860
1986	85,509	45,755	9,319	30,435	10,914	431	11	10,472
1985	54,377	32,288	4,959	17,130	9,833	504	5	9,324
1984	31,168	21,745	3,258	6,165	8,473	224	9	8,240
1983	40,826	16,049	4,918	19,859	8,454	152	16	8,286
1982	36,674	21,570	4,558	10,546	9,935	1,305	10	8,620
1981	46,678	32,499	1,678	12,451	10,139	1,206	4	8,929

	Direct by Issuer			
Year	Total	Debt	Preferred	Common
1987	$4,552	$ 320	$278	$3,954
1986	4,647	1,753	8	2,886
1985	2,683	308	49	2,326
1984	2,940	520	167	2,253
1983	2,543	339	28	2,176
1982	4,138	2,589	6	1,542
1981	6,689	3,091	10	3,589

Source: U.S. Securities and Exchange Commission.

Underwriting Function

The **investment banker** acts as a middleman in the process of raising funds, and in most cases, he takes a risk by **underwriting** an issue of securities. Underwriting refers to the guarantee the investment banking firm gives the selling firm to purchase its securities at a fixed price, thereby eliminating the risk of not selling the whole issue of securities and having less cash than desired. The investment banker may also sell the issue on a **"best-efforts"** basis where the issuing firm assumes the risk and simply takes back any securities not sold after a fixed period of time.

We can see by inspecting Table 2–1 that on average the best-efforts offerings in recent years only equal 10–15 percent of the total securities sold through public distribution, and the overwhelming majority of these issues were common stock. The more risk the investment banker takes, the higher the selling fee to the corporation. Some stock issues are so risky that the investment banker may charge too much of a fee for underwriting risk and distribution so the firm chooses the best-efforts method as a cheaper alternative. With underwriting, once the security is sold, the investment banker will usually make a market in the security, which means active buying and selling to ensure a continuously liquid market and wider distribution. In the case of best efforts and for direct offerings by the issuer, which are even smaller than best efforts, the firm assumes the risk of not raising enough capital and has no guarantees that a continuous market will be made in the company's securities. Table 2–1 shows that most long-term capital-raising efforts by corporations are through investment bankers and not directly by corporations.

TABLE 2–2   GROSS PROCEEDS OF CORPORATE BONDS PUBLICLY OFFERED AND PRIVATELY PLACED (Dollars in Millions)

		Publicly Offered		Privately Placed	
	Total Issues	Amount	Percent of Total	Amount	Percent of Total
1987	$301,349	$209,279	69.45%	$92,070	30.55%
1986	312,697	231,936	74.17	80,761	25.83
1985	165,754	119,559	72.13	46,195	27.87
1984	109,683	73,357	66.88	36,326	33.12
1983	68,495	47,369	69.16	21,126	30.84
1982	54,066	44,278	81.90	9,788	18.10
1981	44,642	37,653	84.34	6,989	15.66
1980	53,206	41,587	78.16	11,619	21.84
1979	40,208	25,814	64.20	14,394	35.80
1978	36,872	19,815	53.74	17,057	46.26
1977	42,015	24,072	57.29	17,943	42.71
1976	42,380	26,453	62.42	15,927	37.58
1975	42,755	32,583	76.21	10,172	23.79
1970	30,315	25,384	83.73	4,931	16.27
1965	13,720	5,570	40.60	8,150	59.40
1960	8,081	4,806	59.47	3,275	40.53
1955	7,420	4,119	55.51	3,301	44.49
1950	4,920	2,360	47.97	2,560	52.03

Source: Selected issues of the *Federal Reserve Bulletin.*

Corporations may also choose to raise capital through private placements rather than through a public offering. With a private placement, the company may sell its own securities to a financial institution such as an insurance company, a pension fund, or a mutual fund, or it can engage an investment banker to find an institution willing to buy a large block of stock or bonds. Most private placements involve bonds (debt issues) instead of common stock. Table 2–2 demonstrates a huge increase in the volume of total bonds issued during the bull market that began in 1982. As the total volume rose, the basic percentages between publicly offered and privately placed bonds maintained their historical relationship with publicly offered bonds issued through underwriters being by far the most popular method of raising debt capital.

Distribution

In a public offering, the distribution process is extremely important, and on some large issues, an investment banker does not undertake this alone. Investment banking firms will share the risk and the burden of distribution by forming a group called a syndicate. The larger the offering in dollar terms, the more participants there generally are in the syndicate. For example, the tombstone advertisement in Figure 2–1 for Hawaiian Electric's issue of common stock shows two separate groups of investment bankers. One group will sell 1.5 million shares in the United States, and the second group will sell 1 million shares in foreign countries. This split of the offering is a new development initiated over the last several years and indicates the globalization of capital flows from country to country. Goldman, Sachs & Co. and Shearson

FIGURE 2–1   ADVERTISEMENT OF DISTRIBUTION

2,500,000 Shares

Hawaiian Electric Industries, Inc.

Common Stock
(without par value)

Price $30.875 Per Share

Upon request, a copy of the Prospectus describing these securities and the business of the Company may be obtained within any State from any Underwriter who may legally distributed it within such State. The securities are offered only by means of the Prospectus, and this announcement is neither an offer to sell nor a solicitation of any offer to buy.

1,500,000 Shares

This portion of the offering is being offered in the United States by the undersigned.

Goldman, Sachs & Co.   Shearson Lehman Hutton Inc.

Bear, Stearns & Co. Inc.   The First Boston Corporation   Daiwa Securities America Inc.   Drexel Burnham Lambert
Incorporated

Kiddler, Peabody & Co,   Merrill Lynch Capital Markets   Morgan Stanley & Co.   Paine Webber Incorporated
Incorporated   Incorporated

Prudential-Bache Captial Funding   Salomon Brothers Inc.   Smith Barney, Harris Upham & Co.
Incorporated

Dean Witter Capital Markets   William Blair & Company   Blunt Ellis & Loewl   A. G. Edwards & Sons, Inc.
Incorporated

McDonald & Company   Oppenheimer & Co., Inc.   Piper, Jaffray & Hopwood   Prescott, Ball & Turben, Inc.
Securities, Inc.   Incorporated

The Robinson-Humphrey Company, Inc.   Tucker, Anthony & R. L. Day, Inc.   Wheat, First Securities, Inc.

Robert W. Baird & Co.   Bateman Eichler, Hill Richards   Boettcher & Company, Inc.   The Chicago Corporation
Incorporated   Incorporated

Fahnestock & Co. Inc.   Howard, Well, Labouisse, Friedrichs   Johnson, Lane, Space, Smith & Co., Inc.
Incorporated

Johnston, Lemon & Co.   Ladenburg, Thalmann & Co. Inc.   Legg Mason Wood Walker
Incorporated   Incorporated

Nomura Securities International, Inc.   Stifel, Nicolaus & Company   Sutro & Co.   Crowell, Weedon & Co.
Incorporated   Incorporated

Morgan, Olmstead, Kennedy & Gardner   Seidler Amdec Securities Inc.
Incorporated

Van Kasper & Company   Wedbush Securities, Inc.

1,000,000 Shares

This portion of the offering is being offered outside the United States by the undersigned.

Goldman Sachs International Corp.

Daiwa Europe Limited

Shearson Lehman Hutton International

Banque Paribas Capital Markets Limited   County NatWest Limited

Daishin Securities Co. Ltd.   Deutsche Bank Capital Markets Limited

IBJ International Limited   Morgan Stanley International

The Nikko Securities Co., (Europe) Ltd.   Nomura International Limited

N. M. Rothschild & Sons Limited   Salomon Brothers International Limited

Sumitomo Finance International   SBCI Swiss Bank Corporation Investment banking

Union Bank of Switzerland (Securities) Limited   Yamaichi International (Europe) Limited

July 5, 1988

TABLE 2–3   1987 LEADING UNDERWRITERS FOR U.S. ISSUERS—DOMESTIC AND FOREIGN SALES OF U.S. ISSUES (Dollars in Billions)

	Total Amount	Common Stock	Mortgage-Backed	Asset-Backed	Junk Bonds	Other
Salomon Brothers	$40.8	$1.8	$17.3	$3.1	$1.2	$17.4
First Boston	37.6	2.2	12.1	5.1	4.0	14.2
Merrill Lynch	31.8	4.1	9.6	0.2	3.4	14.5
Morgan Stanley	31.8	2.2	7.1	—	4.4	18.1
Goldman Sachs	29.2	3.3	8.8	1.0	2.0	14.1
Drexel Burnham	21.2	2.4	4.1	0.5	11.6	2.6
Shearson Lehman	20.0	2.5	5.9	1.4	0.3	9.9
Kidder Peabody	10.0	1.4	4.4	0.2	0.5	3.5
Prudential-Bache	5.7	1.1	2.4	—	0.1	2.1
Bear Stearns	5.6	0.3	3.5	—	0.1	1.7
Top 10 total	$233.70	$21.30	$75.20	$11.50	$27.60	$98.10

Source: *The Wall Street Journal,* January 4, 1988, p. 25.

Lehman Hutton Inc. are the managing underwriters domestically and are listed first under the 1.5 million shares offering. For the 1 million shares to be issued in foreign countries, Daiwa Europe Limited is also a managing underwriter and joins the other two firms' international divisions. The firms are usually listed in the tombstone advertisement based on their clout in the investment banking community. The firms at the top of the advertisement usually have taken the biggest dollar position, and the firms at the bottom, a relatively small position. This is true in bond offerings as well as stock offerings. Each banker in the syndicate is responsible for selling the agreed-upon number of bonds or stock.

For most original offerings, the investment banker is extremely important as a link between the original issuer and the security markets. By taking much of the risk, the investment banker enables corporations and others to find needed capital and thus allows investors an opportunity to participate in the ownership of securities through purchase in the secondary markets. Notice that the common stock is priced at $30.875 per share. This is the price paid by the public. In the case of Hawaiian Electric, the investment banker took some risk that the stock market would not fall much during the offering period. Since the October 19, 1987 market crash, there is more uncertainty and risk in the new-issues market because of the high volatility of stock prices. If the price should fall below $30.875 while the shares are still being sold to the public, the investment bankers in the syndicate will not make their original estimated profit on the issue. The risk also exists that if the stock price drops too much below $30.875, the investment bankers could lose money on the offering.

Some significant changes are taking place in the investment banking industry. The number of firms in the syndicate is shrinking, but the size of the individual investment banking firms in the syndicate is increasing as investment bankers expand their capital base to compete in an international market for stocks and bonds. The financial strength of the investment bankers has increased to the point where they are able to assume more risk and thus larger dollar positions in new offerings. Also the rise of shelf registration under SEC Rule 415 (discussed in Chapter 9) increased the dominance of the large investment bankers. A shelf registration allows issuing firms to register their securities (mostly bonds and notes) with the Securities and Exchange Commission and then sell them at will as funds are needed. This allows investment bankers to buy portions of the shelf issue and immediately resell the securities to institutional clients without forming the normal syndicates or tying up capital for several weeks. Shelf registration is popular with new bond offerings but less so with stock offerings where the traditional syndicated offering tends to exist.

Table 2–3 shows the top 10 lead underwriters for 1987. The categories of securities indicate that each investment banking firm has its own leadership position in certain types of securities. Salomon Brothers leads in mortgage-backed securities, First Boston in asset-backed securities, Merrill Lynch in common stock, and Drexel Burnham in junk bonds.

ORGANIZATION OF THE SECONDARY MARKETS

Once the investment banker or the Federal Reserve (for U.S. government securities) has sold a new issue of securities, it begins trading in secondary markets that provide liquidity, efficiency, continuity, and competition. The **organized exchanges** fulfill this need in a central location where trading takes place between buyers and sellers. The **over-the-counter markets** also provide markets for exchange but not in a central location. We will first examine the organized exchanges and then the over-the-counter markets.

Organized Exchanges

Organized exchanges are either national or regional, but both classifications are organized in a similar fashion. Exchanges have a central trading location where securities are bought and sold in an auction market by brokers acting as agents for the buyer and seller. Stocks usually trade at various trading posts on the floor of the exchange. Brokers are registered members of the exchanges, and their number is fixed by each exchange. The national exchanges are the New York Stock Exchange (NYSE), located at the corner of Broad and Wall Street in New York City, and the American Stock Exchange (AMEX), located at the corner of Hanover and Wall Street, also in New York City. Both these exchanges are governed by a board of directors consisting of one half exchange members and one half public members.

The regional exchanges began their existence trading securities of local firms. As the firms grew, they became listed on the national exchanges, but they also continued to trade on the regionals. Many cities, such as Chicago, Cincinnati, Baltimore, Detroit, and Boston have regional exchanges. Today, most of the trading on these exchanges is done in nationally known companies. Trading in the same companies is common between the NYSE and such regionals as the Midwest Exchange in Chicago, the Pacific Coast Exchange in San Francisco and Los Angeles, and the smaller regionals. In fact, about 90

TABLE 2–4	DATA ON TRADING VOLUME—BREAKDOWN OF TRADING IN NYSE STOCKS		
By Market	Monday, October 19, 1987	Tuesday, October 20, 1987	1987 Daily Average
New York	604,330,000	608,120,000	188,937,980
Midwest	21,666,900	24,326,200	12,529,086
Pacific	12,743,900	12,897,600	6,617,917
NASD	4,341,330	4,516,920	4,156,177
Philadelphia	6,602,100	6,294,600	3,072,138
Boston	4,788,100	4,223,900	2,825,407
Cincinnati	1,399,500	1,367,100	928,094
Instinet	261,900	128,100	193,498
Composite	661,874,420	656,133,730	219,260,296

Source: *New York Stock Exchange Fact Book,* 1988, p. 6. *The Wall Street Journal,* October 21, 1987, page 57. Reprinted by permission of *The Wall Street Journal,* © Dow Jones & Company, Inc., 1987. All rights reserved.

percent of the companies traded on the Midwest and Pacific Coast Exchanges are also listed on the NYSE. This is referred to as dual trading.

October 20, 1987, the day following the Crash of '87, was the busiest day in the history of the New York Stock Exchange. On October 19, 1987, the day of the crash, 604 million shares traded, and on the next day, 608 million shares traded. Table 2–4 shows this information as well as data on New York Stock Exchange firms that trade on other markets also. The all-time composite trade volume for NYSE firms trading *on all markets* was 661.8 million shares on October 19 (the actual day of the crash).

Consolidated Tape

Although dual listing and trading has existed for some time, it was not until June 16, 1975, that a consolidated ticker tape was instituted. This allows brokers on the floor of one exchange to see prices of transactions on other exchanges in the dually listed stocks. Any time a transaction is made on a regional exchange or over-the-counter in a security listed on the NYSE, this transaction and any made on the floor of the NYSE are displayed on the composite tape. The composite price data keeps markets more efficient and prices more competitive between exchanges at all times.

The NYSE and AMEX are both national exchanges and for years did not allow dual listing of companies traded on their exchanges, but as of August 1976, securities were able to be dually listed between these exchanges. There doesn't seem to be any advantage to this since both are located in New York City, and traditionally, shares that trade on one exchange are not traded on the other.

Table 2–5 displays the number of trades (not number of shares) on all markets participating in the consolidated tape. We can see that trading volume has risen dramatically since 1977. However, the New York Stock Exchange

TABLE 2-5 NUMBER OF TRADES SHOWN ON THE CONSOLIDATED TAPE

Consolidated Tape Trades by Market, 1987

	NYSE	AMEX	PSE	MSE	PHLX	BSE	CSE	NASD	INST	Total
1987	22,634,989	0	2,863,513	2,749,171	1,074,834	712,071	81,236	630,559	6,412	30,752,785
1986	18,971,943	0	2,757,958	2,223,131	953,009	588,062	76,833	522,711	8,260	26,101,907
1985	14,648,648	0	1,876,326	1,609,287	752,781	428,112	62,307	334,837	19,163	19,731,461
1984	12,953,946	0	1,534,707	1,365,991	705,206	305,106	58,109	241,424	14,733	17,179,222
1983	15,050,791	43	1,661,907	1,138,868	751,002	241,520	94,171	248,820	7,250	19,374,372
1982	12,609,104	13	1,326,460	944,862	628,217	159,865	134,106	231,036	6,304	16,039,967
1981	11,701,098	673	910,634	644,176	547,219	129,593	123,911	136,519	3,329	14,197,152
1980	13,074,382	1,021	817,957	548,416	530,659	118,000	108,169	112,923	3,019	15,314,546
1979	10,442,237	244	665,073	402,196	333,805	78,087	63,689	71,858	4,123	12,061,312
1978	10,087,834	725	653,769	366,654	255,359	75,471	54,065	96,165	1,911	11,591,953
1977	8,264,036	1,982	548,507	328,653	150,234	74,263	155,804	178,020	2,062	9,703,561

Distribution of Consolidated Tape Trades, 1977–1987

	NYSE	AMEX	PSE	MSE	PHLX	BSE	CSE	NASD	INST	Total
1987	73.60%	0.00%	9.31%	8.94%	3.50%	2.32%	0.26%	2.05%	0.02%	100.00%
1986	72.68	0.00	10.57	8.52	3.65	2.25	0.29	2.00	0.03	100.00
1985	72.24	0.00	9.51	8.16	3.82	2.17	0.32	1.70	0.10	100.00
1984	75.40	0.00	8.93	7.95	4.10	1.78	0.34	1.41	0.09	100.00
1983	77.68	0.00	8.58	6.81	3.88	1.25	0.49	1.28	0.04	100.00
1982	78.61	0.00	8.27	5.89	3.92	1.00	0.84	1.44	0.04	100.00
1981	82.42	0.00	6.41	4.54	3.85	0.91	0.87	0.96	0.02	100.00
1980	85.37	0.00	5.34	3.58	3.47	0.77	0.71	0.74	0.02	100.00
1979	86.58	0.00	5.51	3.33	2.77	0.65	0.53	0.60	0.03	100.00
1978	87.02	0.01	5.64	3.16	2.20	0.65	0.47	0.83	0.02	100.00
1977	85.16	0.02	5.65	3.39	1.55	0.77	1.61	1.83	0.02	100.00

Participating markets: NYSE, New York; AMEX, American; PSE, Pacific; MSE, Midwest; PHLX, Philadelphia; BSE, Boston; CSE, Cincinnati; NASD, National Association of Securities Dealers; INST, Instinet.

Source: *New York Stock Exchange Fact Book, 1988,* p. 19.

is getting a smaller piece of the total number of trades in its own listed stock.[1] In general, it is seeing tough competition from other exchanges and the over-the-counter NASDAQ system, and it is faced with a possible loss of prestige and profits during the 1990s as competition becomes even more intense.

Listing Requirements for Firms

Securities can only be traded on an exchange if they have met the listing requirements of the exchange and have been approved by the board of governors of that exchange. All exchanges have minimum requirements that must be met before trading can take place in a company's common stock. Since the NYSE is the biggest exchange and generates the most dollar volume in large, well-known companies, it is not surprising that its listing requirements are the most restrictive.

Initial Listing.   Although each case is decided on its own merits, according to the *NYSE Fact Book,* the minimum requirements for a company to be listed on the New York Stock Exchange for the first time are as follows:

1. Demonstrated earning power under competitive conditions of: *either* $2.5 million before federal income taxes for the most recent year and $2 million pre-tax for each of the preceding two years *or* an aggregate for the last three fiscal years of $6.5 million *together with* a minimum in the most recent fiscal year of $4.5 million. (All three years must be profitable.)
2. Net tangible assets of $18 million, but greater emphasis is placed on the aggregate market value of the common stock.
3. Market value of publicly held shares, subject to adjustment depending on market conditions, within the following limits.

Maximum	$18,000,000
Minimum	9,000,000
Present (2/13/87)	18,000,000

4. A total of 1 million common shares publicly held.
5. *Either* 2,000 holders of 100 shares or more *or* 2,200 total stockholders *together with* average monthly trading volume (for the most recent six months) of 100,000 shares.

The other exchanges have requirements covering the same areas, but the amounts are smaller.

Corporations desiring to be listed on exchanges have made the decision that public availability of the stock on an exchange will benefit their shareholders

---

[1]The NYSE has a larger percentage of the share volume than the trade volume (Table 2–5) because its average trade involves more shares than other exchanges. Its percentage of share volume is approximately 85 percent.

by providing liquidity to owners or by allowing the company a more viable means for raising external capital for growth and expansion. The company must pay annual listing fees to the exchange and some fees based on the number of shares traded each year.

Delisting.   The New York Stock Exchange also has the authority to remove (delist) a security from trading when the security fails to meet certain criteria. There is much latitude in these decisions, but generally, a company's security may be considered for delisting if there are fewer than 1,200 round-lot (100 shares) owners, 600,000 shares or fewer in public hands, and a market value of the security of less than $5 million. A company that easily exceeded these standards on first being listed may fall below them during hard times.

Membership for Market Participants

We've talked about listing requirements for corporations on the exchange, but what about the investment houses or traders that service the listed firms or trade for their own account on the exchanges? These privileges are reserved for a select number of people. The NYSE has 1,366 members who own "seats," which may be leased (508 leased at end of 1987) or sold with the approval of the NYSE. Multiple seats are owned by many member firms such as Merrill Lynch, so the number of member organizations totaled 1,192. The NYSE also has memberships available that provide electronic access (96) and physical access (23) to this membership category. In recent years, the price of NYSE seats has ranged from a low of $35,000 in 1977 to a high of $1,150,000 in 1987. Prices fluctuate with market trends going up in bull markets and down in bear markets. The members owning these seats can be divided into five distinct categories, each with a specific job.

Commission Brokers.   **Commission brokers** represent commission houses, such as Merrill Lynch or Shearson Lehman Hutton, that execute orders on the floor of the exchange for customers of that firm. Many of the larger retail brokerage houses have more than one commission broker on the floor of the exchange. If you call your account executive (stockbroker) and place an order to buy 100 shares of Exxon, he or she will teletype your order to the NYSE where it will be transmitted to one of the firm's commission brokers who will go to the appropriate trading post and execute the order.

Floor Brokers.   You can imagine that a commission broker could get very busy running from post to post on a heavy volume day. In times like these, he will rely on some help from a **floor broker,** who is registered to trade on the exchange but is not an employee of a member firm. Instead, the floor broker owns his own seat and charges a small fee for his services (usually around $4 per 100 shares).

Registered Traders.   **Registered traders** own their own seats and are not associated with a member firm (such as Merrill Lynch). They are registered to trade for their own accounts and, of course, do so with the objective of earning a profit. Because they are members, they don't have to pay commissions on these trades; but in so trading, they help to generate a continuous market and liquidity for the market in general. There is always the possibility that these traders could manipulate the market if they acted in mass, and for that reason, the exchanges have rules governing their behavior and limiting the number of registered traders at one specific trading post.

Odd-Lot Dealers.   Odd lots (less than 100 shares) are not traded on the main floor of the exchange, so if a customer wants to buy or sell 20 shares of AT&T, the order will end up being processed by an **odd-lot dealer.** The dealer owns his own inventory of the particular security and buys and sells for his own account. If he accumulates 100 shares, he can sell them in the market, or if he needs 20 shares, he can buy 100 in the market and hold the other 80 shares in his inventory. A few very large brokerage firms, such as Merrill Lynch, have begun making their own odd-lot market in actively traded securities, and it is expected that this trend will become common practice at the other large commission houses. Odd-lot trading on other exchanges is usually handled by the specialist in the particular stock.

Specialists.   **Specialists** are a very important segment of the exchange and make up about one fourth of total membership. Each stock traded has a specialist assigned to it, and most specialists are responsible for more than one stock. The specialist has two basic duties with regard to the stocks he supervises. First, he must handle any special orders that commission brokers or floor brokers might give him. For example, a special order could limit the price someone is willing to pay for General Telephone (GTE) stock to $40 per share for 100 shares. If the commission broker reaches the General Telephone trading post and GTE is selling at $41 per share, the broker will leave the order with the specialist to execute if and when the stock of GTE falls to $40 or less. The specialist puts these special limit orders in his "book" with the date and time entered so he can execute orders at the same price by the earliest time of receipt. A portion of the broker's commission is then paid to the specialist.

The second major function of specialists is to maintain continuous, liquid, and orderly markets in their assigned stocks. This is not a difficult function in the actively traded securities, such as General Motors, Du Pont, and American Telephone, but it becomes more difficult in those stocks where there are no large, active markets. For example, suppose you placed an order to buy 100 shares of Ametek at the market price. If the commission broker reaches the Ametek trading post and no seller is present, he can't wait for one to appear since he has other orders to execute. Fortunately, he can buy the shares from the specialist who acts as a dealer—in this case buying for and selling from his own inventory. To ensure his ability to maintain continuous markets, the exchange requires a specialist to have $500,000 or enough capital to own 5,000 shares of his assigned stock, whichever is greater. At times, specialists are placed under tremendous pressure to make a market for securities. A classic

TABLE 2–6	MARKET QUALITY AND SPECIALISTS' STABILIZATION			
	(1) Price Continuity	(2) Quotation Spreads	(3) Market Depth	(4) Stabilization Rate
1987	89.0%	67.5%	87.2%	90.7%
1986	90.2	69.8	89.2	90.2
1985	92.3	70.6	89.8	89.2
1984	91.1	64.7	88.0	88.8
1983	88.7	60.7	86.2	90.0
1982	89.5	65.1	85.2	88.9
1981	87.2	60.4	81.6	90.2
1980	86.4	60.6	80.4	90.9
1979	90.6	71.1	84.9	90.0
1978	90.8	72.9	84.4	90.0
1977	92.5	75.9	86.0	90.8
1976	90.3	71.0	—	92.5
1975	88.1	59.9	—	91.4
1974	84.3	44.9	—	91.1

Source: *New York Stock Exchange Fact Book*, 1988.

case occurred when President Eisenhower had a heart attack in the 1950s and specialists stabilized the market by absorbing wave after wave of sell orders.

The New York Stock Exchange actually keeps statistics on specialist performance and their ability to maintain price continuity, quotation spreads, market depth, and price stabilization. These data are given in Table 2–6. Price continuity is measured by the size of the price variation in successive trades. Column 1 is the percentage of transactions with no change in price or a minimum change of $1/8$ of a dollar. Column 2 presents the percentage of the quotes where the bid and asked price was equal to or less than $1/4$ of a point. Market depth (Column 3) is displayed as a percentage of the time that 1,000 shares of volume failed to move the price of the stock more than $1/8$ of a point. Finally, the NYSE expects the specialist to stabilize the market by buying and selling from his own account against the prevailing trend. This is measured in Column 4 as the percentage of shares purchased below the last different price and the percentage of shares sold above the last different price. While these statistics are not 100 percent, it would be quite unreasonable for us to expect specialists to maintain that kind of a record in all types of markets. However, some critics of the specialist system on the NYSE think that these performance measures could be improved by having more than one specialist for each stock. Many market watchers feel that competing dealers on the over-the-counter market provide more price stability and fluid markets than the NYSE specialist system.

OTHER ORGANIZED EXCHANGES

The American Stock Exchange

The American Stock Exchange trades in smaller companies than the NYSE, and except for one dually listed company on the NYSE in 1983, the stocks traded on the AMEX are completely different from those on any other exchange. Because many of the small companies on the AMEX do not meet the liquidity needs of large institutional investors, the AMEX has been primarily a market for individual investors.

In an attempt to differentiate itself from the NYSE, the AMEX traded warrants in companies for many years before the NYSE allowed them. Even now, the AMEX has warrants listed for stocks trading on the NYSE. The AMEX also trades put and call options on approximately 200 stocks, with most of the underlying common stocks being listed on the NYSE. This market has been a stabilizing force for the AMEX.

The Chicago Board Options Exchange

Trading in call **options** started on the Chicago Board Options Exchange (CBOE) in April 1973 and proved very successful. The number of call options listed grew from 16 in 1973 to approximately 560 by 1988. A call option gives the owner the right to buy 100 shares of the underlying common stock at a set price for a certain period of time. The establishment of the CBOE standardized call options into three-month, six-month, and nine-month expiration periods on a rotating monthly series. Also other sequences have since been developed. The CBOE and the AMEX currently have many options that are dually listed, and the competition between them is fierce. The two exchanges also trade put options (options to sell). A number of smaller regional exchanges also provide for option trading, and the New York Stock Exchange began trading options in 1985.

A new wrinkle in the options game has been options on stock market indexes or industry groupings (called subindexes). The CBOE offers puts and calls on the Standard & Poor's 100 Index; the NYSE has options on the NYSE Index; the AMEX has options on the AMEX Market Value Index, and so on. More about these markets will be presented in Chapter 16.

Futures Markets

Futures markets have traditionally been associated with commodities but, more recently, also with financial instruments. Purchasers of commodity futures own the right to buy a certain amount of the commodity at a set price for a specified period of time. When the time runs out (expires), the futures contract will be delivered unless sold before expiration. One major futures markets is the Chicago Board of Trade, which trades corn, oats, soybeans, wheat, silver, plywood, and Treasury bond futures. There are also other important futures markets in Chicago, Kansas City, Minneapolis, New York, and other cities. These markets are very important as hedging markets and help set commodity prices. They are also known for their wide price swings and volatile speculative nature.

In recent years, trading volume has increased in foreign exchange futures such as the West German mark, Japanese yen, and British pound as well as in

Treasury bill and Treasury bond futures. One recent product having a direct effect in the stock market is the development of futures contracts on stock market indexes. The Chicago Merchantile Exchange, Chicago Board of Trade, New York Futures Exchanges (a division of the NYSE), and the Kansas City Board of Trade have all developed contracts in separate market indexes such as the Standard & Poor's 500 and the Value Line Index. Market indexes will be presented in the following chapter, and we will spend more time discussing futures markets in Chapters 15 and 16.

OVER-THE-COUNTER MARKETS

Unlike the organized exchanges, the over-the-counter markets (OTC) have no central location where securities are traded. Being traded over-the-counter implies that the trade takes place by telephone or electronic device and that dealers stand ready to buy or sell specific securities for their own accounts. These dealers will buy at a bid price and sell at an asked price that reflects the competitive market conditions. By contrast, brokers on the organized exchanges merely act as agents who process orders. The National Association of Securities Dealers (NASD), a self-policing organization of dealers, requires at least two market makers (dealers) for each security, but often there are 5 or 10 or even 20 for government securities. As previously mentioned, the multiple-dealer function in the over-the-counter market is an attractive feature for many companies in comparison to the single specialist arrangement on the NYSE and other organized exchanges.

OTC markets exist for stocks, corporate bonds, mutual funds, federal government securities, state and local bonds, commercial paper, negotiable certificates of deposits, and various other securities. Altogether these securities make the OTC the largest of all markets in the United States in dollar terms.

In the OTC market, the difference between the bid and asked price is the spread; it represents the profit the dealer earns by making a market. For example, if XYZ common stock is bid 10 and asked $10\frac{1}{2}$, this simply means the dealer will buy at least 100 shares at $10 per share or will sell 100 shares at $10.50 per share. If his prices are too low, more buyers than sellers will appear, and he will run out of inventory unless he raises prices to attract more sellers and balances the supply and demand. If his price is at equilibrium, he will match an equal number of shares bought and sold, and for his market-making activities, he will earn 50 cents per share traded. Although in the future, many OTC stocks will no longer be reported on the basis of bid and ask prices but simply at a closing price, the concept of dealer spreads will remain.

Actually, the over-the-counter stock market has several segments and the National Association of Securities Dealers divides the 6,000+ companies into the National Market System, the national list, and regional and local companies. Stocks in the National Market System receive the quickest and best reporting of their trading activity.

On the National Market System, stocks of companies such as Apple Computer, Coors Brewing, Intel, and MCI Communications can be found. These companies all have a diversified geographical shareholder base,[2] while the national list and regional or local companies are usually smaller or closely held by management or the founding family. The small local stocks may not appear in *The Wall Street Journal* but will be found on the financial pages of large city newspapers in Dallas, Cleveland, Chicago, Minneapolis, Los Angeles, and other major cities under the heading "Local Over-The-Counter Markets." Many are also listed on special pink sheets put out by investment houses. OTC markets have always been very popular for bank stocks and insurance stocks because these stocks do not generate enough trading volume or have enough stockholders to merit their listing on the organized exchanges. Another reason is that many only have local interest.

NASDAQ

NASDAQ stands for the National Association of Securities Dealers Automated Quotations System. This system is linked together by a computer network and provides up-to-the-minute quotations on approximately 5,000 of the OTC stocks traded on the NASDAQ system.

Table 2–7 presents the qualification standards for initial and continued listing on various OTC markets. The big difference between the OTC standards and the NYSE listing requirements is that the OTC requires fewer shareholders of record, smaller assets, and less net income. While these qualifications allow many small companies to be included in the trading system, they do not preclude many large companies such as Apple Computer or MCI from trading. In fact, the National Association of Securities Dealers estimates that over 600 companies on the National Market System would be eligible for listing on the New York Stock Exchange, and many more would be eligible for the American Stock Exchange.

The OTC market used to be thought of as only an equity market for low-priced common stocks, but that is all changing with the advent of the National Market System. Table 2–8 depicts the OTC market and the most active stocks in dollar volume on October 20, 1987, the day after the crash. On this day when the NYSE set a new trading high of 608 million shares, the OTC's volume was 284 million shares. Notice that some of the names of the most active stocks may be familiar to you. On October 20, 1987, the total number of issues traded was 4,864, which is more issues than traded on the NYSE and AMEX combined.

During the mid-1980s, many articles appeared comparing the New York Stock Exchange and the American Stock Exchange to the over-the-counter market and, in particular, to the inroads that the National Association of Securities Dealers had made in retaining companies on their automated quotation system. Traditionally, companies that would reach listing qualifications would jump to the AMEX and then eventually to the NYSE. This cannot be

---

[2]The standards for inclusion on the National Market System were reduced by the NASD in 1984 (with permission of the SEC). By 1988, 3700 OTC firms were listed on the National Market System.

TABLE 2-7   NASDAQ, NATIONAL LIST AND NASDAQ NMS QUALIFICATION STANDARDS

Standard	For Initial NASDAQ Inclusion (Domestic Common Stocks)*	For Continued NASDAQ Inclusion (Domestic Common Stocks)*	For Newspaper National List Inclusion — Alternative 1	For Newspaper National List Inclusion — Alternative 2	SEC Criteria for Mandatory NMS† Inclusion‡	SEC Criteria for Voluntary NMS† Inclusion‡
Registration under Section 12(g) of the Securities Exchange Act of 1934 or equivalent	Yes	Yes	Yes	Yes	Yes	Yes
Total assets	$2 million	$750,000	$2 million	$2 million	—	—
Tangible assets	—	—	—	—	$2 million	$2 million
Capital and surplus	$1 million	$375,000	$1 million	$8 million	$1 million	$1 million
Net income	—	—	$300,000 in latest or 2 of 3 last fiscal years	—	—	—
Operating history	—	—	—	4 years	—	—
Public float (shares)	100,000	100,000	350,000	800,000	500,000	250,000
Market value of float	—	—	$2 million	$8 million	$5 million	$3 million
Minimum bid	—	—	$3	—	$10 on 5 business days	$5 on 5 business days
Trading volume	—	—	—	—	Average 600,000 shares/month for 6 months	Average 100,000 shares/month for 6 months
Shareholders of record	300	300	300	300	300	300
Number of market makers	2	1	2	2	4 on 5 business days	4 on 5 business days

*Qualification standards for other types of securities are available upon request from the NASDAQ Operations Department in Washington, D.C.
†NMS—National Market System.
‡A number of their standards were further reduced in 1984 to expand participation in the National Market System.
Source: *NASDAQ Fact Book* (Washington, D.C.: National Association of Securities Dealers, Inc., annual issue).

TABLE 2–8	OVER-THE-COUNTER MARKETS—QUOTATIONS FROM THE NASDAQ SYSTEM

	Tuesday, October 20, 1987
Issues traded	4,864
Advances	214
Declines	3,571
Unchanged	1,079
New highs	5
New lows	2,101
Advance volume (000)	20,895
Decline volume (000)	208,376
Total volume (000)	284,117
Block trades*	4,310

NASDAQ Most Active	October 20, 1987
MCI Communications	5,255,200
Apple Computer	5,080,800
Genentech	3,322,600
Seagate Technology	3,221,000
Intel Corporation	2,664,600
Tele Com A	2,612,000
Liz Claiborne	2,368,700

*A block trade is a trade of 10,000 or more shares at one time.
Source: *The Wall Street Journal,* October 21, 1987, p. 57. Reprinted by permission of *The Wall Street Journal,* © Dow Jones & Company, Inc., 1987. All rights reserved.

assumed to happen any more. The AMEX seems to be suffering most of all in this battle, as the number of listings has fallen by about one third since 1974. The multiple-dealer system as well as the enhanced reporting capability can be listed as reasons for the increased competitive nature of the OTC markets.

Debt Securities Traded Over-the-Counter

Debt securities also trade over-the-counter. Actually, government securities of the U.S. Treasury provide the largest dollar volume of transactions on the OTC and account for billions of dollars in trades each week. These securities are traded by government securities dealers who are often associated with a division of a large financial institution, such as a New York, Chicago, or West Coast money market bank or a large brokerage house like Merrill Lynch. These dealers make markets in government securities, such as Treasury bills and Treasury bonds, or federal agency securities like Federal National Mortgage Association issues.

Municipal bonds of state and local governments are traded by specialized municipal bond dealers who, in most cases, work for large commercial banks. Commercial paper, representing unsecured, short-term corporate debt, is traded directly by *finance* companies, but a large portion of commercial paper sold by *industrial* companies is handled by OTC dealers specializing in this market.

Every security has its own set of dealers and its own distribution system. On markets where large dollar trades occur, the spread between the bid and ask price could be as little as $1/16$ or $1/32$ of \$1 per \$1,000 of securities.

The Third and Fourth Markets—Part of Over-the-Counter Trading

Prior to the mid-1970s, commissions on the NYSE were fixed. This meant that the same commission schedule applied to all transactions of a given size, and one broker could not undercut the other on the New York Stock Exchange. Several OTC dealers, most notably Weeden & Co., decided to make a market in about 200 of the most actively traded NYSE issues and to do this at a much smaller cost than the NYSE commission structure would allow. This trading in NYSE-listed securities in over-the-counter markets became known as the **third market.**

The third market diminished in importance for a while as the NYSE became more price competitive. However, in the 1980s, this market made somewhat of a comeback. One advantage of the OTC market is that more than one specialist trades a security and there is greater flexibility in trading. During July of 1984, ITT Corporation reported a significant dividend cut and lower earnings after the NYSE was closed, but Jefferies Corporation, an over-the-counter trading firm, traded 3 million shares by the time the NYSE opened the next morning. Another example occurred when the Justice Department announced the breakup of AT&T on a Friday. MCI, a competitor in communications, traded OTC, while AT&T traded on the NYSE. AT&T trading was halted until Monday because the specialist was unable to stabilize the market, whereas the 29 market makers in MCI stock in the OTC market transacted over \$75 million of securities before AT&T opened on Monday morning. At the time of this writing, much discussion is being held at the New York Stock Exchange about expanding trading hours, revising rules, and generally competing more effectively with the third market and the OTC.

The **fourth market** is that market in which institutions trade between themselves, bypassing the middleman broker altogether (replacing him with a computer). Much of the trading in this market is done through Instinet, Institutional Networks Inc. Instinet provides a low-cost automated stock trading system, with transactions available on over 3,500 securities, both listed and over-the-counter. The system allows banks, insurance companies, mutual and pension funds to enter an order over a computer terminal for up to 1,000 shares. The computer searches a nationwide trading network until it finds the trader with the best price, then the computer holds the order 30 seconds so that another trader may offer a better price. While Instinet is only a small trading system, Merrill Lynch bought 8 percent of the company and has plans to tie the trading system into the quote-terminal desktop computer that it is developing with IBM.

TABLE 2–9   INSTITUTIONAL ACTIVITY ON THE NEW YORK STOCK EXCHANGE

Year	Total Number of Large Block Transactions per Year	Average Number of Large Block Transactions per Day	Block Shares (Thousands)	Block Trades as a Percent of Reported NYSE Volume
1965	2,171	9	49,262	3.1%
1967	6,685	27	N.A.	6.7
1969	15,132	61	N.A.	14.1
1970	17,217	68	450,908	15.4
1971	26,941	106	692,536	17.8
1973	29,223	116	721,356	17.8
1975	34,420	136	778,540	16.6
1977	54,275	215	1,183,924	22.4
1979	97,509	385	2,164,726	26.5
1981	145,564	575	3,771,442	31.8
1982	254,707	1,007	6,742,481	41.0
1983	363,415	1,436	9,842,080	45.6
1984	433,427	1,713	11,492,091	49.8
1985	539,039	2,139	14,222,272	51.7
1986	665,587	2,631	17,811,335	49.9
1987	920,679	3,639	24,497,241	51.2

N.A. = Not available.
Source: *New York Stock Exchange Fact Book,* 1988, p. 75.

THE TRANSFORMATION AND FUTURE OF THE CAPITAL MARKETS

Financial institutions, such as banks, pension funds, insurance companies, and investment companies (mutual funds), have always invested and traded in securities. However, the growth of these institutions and their participation in the capital markets has increased dramatically in recent years. Part of the increased share activity can be found in the accelerated growth of pension plans during this period. Also, the rapid rise in stock prices during the post–World War II period attracted a lot of individual investors into mutual funds.

Table 2–9 on institutional activity shows that significant changes have taken place over the last two decades as institutional trading has accounted for a relatively larger percentage of total trading on the New York Stock Exchange. A block trade is a transaction of 10,000 shares or more and is almost always carried out by institutions rather than individuals. In 1965, block trades accounted for only 3.1 percent of the reported volume on the NYSE, but by 1987, block trades increased to over 51 percent. This increased institutional activity is also evident by an examination of the second column of Table 2–9 which shows that between 1965 and 1987 the average number of block trades per day increased from 9 to 3,639.

Proof of the decreased importance of small investors and the increased importance of the institutional trader also is seen in Table 2–10. The average size of a trade on the NYSE in 1965 was 224 shares (last column) while in 1987, it was almost 10 times as great, averaging 2,112 shares per trade. Another enlightening statistic is the percent turnover rate (average shares traded divided

TABLE 2–10   REPORTED VOLUME, TURNOVER RATE, REPORTED TRADES (Millions of Shares)

Year	Reported Share Volume	Average of Shares Listed	Percent Turnover	Reported Trades (Thousands)	Average Size of Trade
1965	1,556.3	9,643.6	16%	—	224
1967	2,530.0	11,280.5	22	9,822	257
1969	2,850.8	14,139.1	20	8,004	356
1970	2,937.4	15,573.6	19	7,566	388
1971	3,891.3	16,782.6	23	9,094	428
1973	4,053.2	20,062.6	20	9,025	449
1975	4,693.4	22,107.5	21	9,481	495
1977	5,273.8	25,296.5	21	8,222	641
1979	8,155.9	28,803.0	28	10,369	787
1981	11,853.7	36,003.5	33	11,696	1,013
1982	16,458.0	38,907.0	42	12,609	1,305
1983	21,589.6	42,316.9	51	15,051	1,434
1984	23,071.0	47,104.8	49	12,954	1,781
1985	27,510.7	50,759.4	54	14,649	1,878
1986	35,680.0	56,023.8	64	18,972	1,881
1987	47,801.3	65,711.4	73	22,635	2,112

Source: *New York Stock Exchange Fact Book*, 1988, p. 73.

by average shares outstanding). The 1987 figure of 73 percent indicates that of the 65 billion shares outstanding, 47 billion changed owners during the year. In 1965, the turnover rate was 16 percent. This stark contrast indicates that markets are much more oriented toward institutional trading than the traditional long-term buy and hold strategy practiced by individual investors. These statistics do not mean that individuals are getting out of the stock market entirely but that many are investing indirectly in stocks through mutual funds, IRAs, and private pension plans. The market crash of 1987 and the high volatility of stock price movements subsequent to that event have scared off many small investors. However, as markets eventually settle down and new regulations are put into place, the individual investor will continue to have a meaningful role in the market.

Competition in Financial Services

In 1975, the New York Stock Exchange and other security markets went from a fixed to a negotiated commission system. After negotiated commissions were in place, brokerage houses started charging individuals for research reports that previously had been distributed free of charge. This forced the individual to either buy research or simply take his or her account executive's advice. Under these conditions, the individual investor started looking for services on a competitive fee basis, and many ended up using brokers that only charged for making trades but gave no research advice. Because these brokers charged lower prices than the large retail brokerage firms, they became known as discount brokers. This segment of the market is growing rapidly as many banks and savings and loans are now indirectly offering discount brokerage service to their customers. For example, in an attempt to retain bank clients and their funds, many banks have simply lined up with the large discount brokers and are providing this investment service through trading desks located in their own buildings.

As previously mentioned, the rise of financial service companies has become commonplace. Starting in 1981, financial service firms purchased brokerage houses in order to diversify their consumer base. Prudential Insurance bought Bache Halsey Stuart Shields; Sears acquired Dean Witter; American Express bought Shearson and, later, Lehman Brothers and E.F. Hutton; and Equitable Life purchased Donaldson, Lufkin and Jenrette. Most of these firms were adding brokerage houses to other financially oriented companies. Sears, with its Allstate Insurance, Sears Savings Bank, and Dean Witter brokerage services, now has financial service centers in many of its retail stores and is trying to take advantage of its relationship with 25 million Sears credit-card holders.

American Express is a better example of a financial service company. Known worldwide for its card and travelers checks, it bought Fireman's Fund Insurance, a large casualty insurance company, in 1968. In 1981, it acquired Shearson, a large retail brokerage firm; in 1983, it bought IDS, a Minneapolis-based life insurance company and one of the biggest mutual fund management companies; and in 1984, it purchased Lehman Bros. Kuhn Loeb Inc., a prestigious investment banking house specializing in bonds. By 1986, American Express had sold about 35 percent of Shearson/Lehman[3] and 45 percent of Fireman's Fund to the public. These sales allowed American Express to get some of its invested capital back while still maintaining control of the companies. In 1987, American Express, through its stock brokerage subsidiaries, bought E.F. Hutton, making its total stock brokerage operation the second largest investment firm in the United States.[4] Size seems to be the name of the game as we head into the 1990s.

The National Market System

A national market system was mandated by Congress in the Securities Amendments Act of 1975. This is envisioned as a coordinated national system of security trading with no barriers between the various exchanges or the OTC market. There is sometimes confusion between the concept of a national market system and the **National Market System** listing segment of the OTC market. It is the former system that is the subject of the present discussion. The latter has already been discussed.

Despite some delay in the implementation of a national market system due to industry foot-dragging and political changes in Washington, it is still a goal for the future. The implementation of the system is strongly supported by the

---

[3]Shearson/Lehman represented the joint operation of two of its prior acquisitions in the securities industry.

[4]The name of the American Express subsidiary is Shearson Lehman Hutton, Inc.

SEC. No one knows exactly what form this national market might take, but several things will be required. Some are easily achieved, while others are not. The first is already in place—the composite tape that reflects trades on all exchanges for listed NYSE companies. There will also have to be competition between specialists and market makers. This is already occurring between the regional exchanges and the NYSE in dually listed securities. The prices seem to be more stable and the spreads between the bid and ask prices are closer for securities with competing market makers. A third occurrence is that the NYSE will most likely have to abolish Rule 390, which prohibits members of the NYSE from trading off the exchange in NYSE-listed securities. This has yet to take place.

Possibly the biggest dilemma in creating a national market system is fully developing a computerized system to execute limit orders. Currently, NYSE specialists execute most limit orders, which specify that a security must be bought or sold at a limited price or better. The national market system will need a computerized system to handle limit orders from all markets. Progress along these lines was being required by the SEC, and by the late-1980s, the NYSE had created several computer systems to aid in trading. The designated order turnaround system (Super DOT) allows members to transmit orders of up to 599 shares directly to the correct trading post on the floor of the exchange. After the transaction, the execution report is returned to the order origination point, and the NYSE states that 95 percent of the market orders are confirmed in two minutes. This electronic system transmits market and limit orders. In 1984, the AMEX announced that it had installed Autoper, an electronic order execution system that processes specialists' trades in a few seconds. This system uses a touch-screen that virtually eliminates clerical errors and allows market price trades of 300 shares or limit orders of up to 500 shares.

The national market system mandated by Congress could eventually take the form of NASDAQ, where several competing dealers make markets electronically. Clearly, the National Association of Securities Dealers hopes that the national market system will follow its trading practices rather than the auction markets of the exchanges. The exchanges have complained to the SEC that the NASD's use of the term *National Market System* for its largest OTC companies should not be allowed because it gives the appearance that the OTC is *the* national market. Certainly, the NYSE will not capitulate easily to an over-the-counter system of trading. The traditional exchange auction markets have been able to absorb block trades without difficulty and serve the needs of institutional customers and individuals. The NYSE does not want to give up its dominant market position, but it had better stop to look at who is catching up to it.

It is clear that any truly national market system will rely on computers more than ever, and the trend seems to show no sign of ceasing. Some systems in existence today even allow individual investors to use their personal computers to place stock market orders.

Of course, any national market system will also have to interface with international markets whose continuous around-the-clock, around-the-world trading was mentioned earlier in the chapter.

REGULATION OF THE SECURITY MARKETS

Organized securities markets are regulated by the **Securities and Exchange Commission (SEC)** and by the self-regulation of the exchanges. The OTC market is controlled by the National Association of Securities Dealers. Three major laws govern the sale and subsequent trading of securities. The **Securities Act of 1933** pertains to new issues of securities, while the **Securities Exchange Act of 1934** deals with trading in the securities markets. The **Securities Acts Amendments of 1975** are the latest legislation, and their main emphasis is on a national securities market. The primary purpose of these laws was to protect unwary investors from fraud and manipulation and to make the markets more competitive and efficient.

Securities Act of 1933

The Securities Act of 1933 was enacted after congressional investigations of the abuses present in the securities markets during the 1929 crash and again in 1931. The act's primary purpose was to provide full disclosure of all pertinent investment information whenever a corporation sold a new issue of securities. For this reason, it is sometimes referred to as the "truth in securities" act. The Securities Act has several important features:

1. All offerings except government bonds and bank stocks that are to be sold in more than one state must be registered with the SEC.[5]
2. The registration statement must be filed 20 days in advance of the date of sale and include detailed corporate information. If the SEC finds the information misleading, incomplete, or inaccurate, they will delay the offering until the registration statement is corrected. The SEC in no way certifies that the security is fairly priced but only that the information seems to be factual and accurate. Under certain circumstances, the previously mentioned shelf registration is being used to modify the 20-day waiting period concept.
3. All new issues of securities must be accompanied by a *prospectus,* a detailed summary of the registration statement. Included in the prospectus is usually a list of directors and officers; their salaries, stock options, and shareholdings; financial reports certified by a CPA; a list of the underwriters; the purpose and use for the funds to be provided from the sale of securities; and any other reasonable information that investors may need to know before they can wisely invest their money. A preliminary prospectus may be distributed to potential buyers before the offering date, but it will not contain the offering price or underwriting fees. It is called a **red herring** because stamped on the front in red letters are the words *Preliminary Prospectus.*

---

[5]Actually, the SEC did not come into existence until 1934. The Federal Trade Commission had many of these responsibilities prior to the formation of the SEC.

4. Officers of the company and other experts preparing the prospectus or registration statement can be sued for penalties and recovery of realized losses if any information presented was fraudulent or factually wrong or if relevant information was omitted.

Securities Exchange Act of 1934

This act created the Securities and Exchange Commission to enforce the securities laws. It was empowered to regulate the securities markets and those companies listed on the exchanges. Specifically, the major points of the 1934 Act are as follows:

1. Guidelines for insider trading were established. Insiders must hold securities for at least six months before they can sell them. This is to prevent them from taking quick advantage of information which could result in a short-term profit. All short-term profits were payable to the corporation. Insiders were generally thought to be officers, directors, major stockholders, employees, or relatives. In the last two decades, the SEC widened its interpretation to include anyone having information that was not public knowledge. This could include security analysts, loan officers, large institutional holders, and many others who had business dealings with the firm.

2. The Federal Reserve Board of Governors became responsible for setting margin requirements to determine how much credit one had available to buy securities.

3. Manipulation of securities by conspiracies between investors was prohibited.

4. The SEC was given control over the proxy procedures of corporations (a proxy is an absent stockholder vote).

5. In its regulation of companies traded on the markets, it required certain reports to be filed periodically. Corporations must file quarterly financial statements with the SEC, send annual reports to the stockholders, and file 10-K Reports with the SEC annually. The 10-K Report has more financial data than the annual report and can be very useful to an investor or loan officer. Most companies will now send 10-K Reports to stockholders on request.

6. The act required all securities exchanges to register with the SEC. In this capacity, the SEC supervises and regulates many pertinent organizational aspects of exchanges such as listing and trading mechanics.

The Securities Acts Amendments of 1975

The major focus of the Securities Acts amendments of 1975 was to direct the SEC to supervise the development of a national securities market. No exact structure was put forth, but the law did assume that any national market would make extensive use of computers and electronic communication devices. Additionally, the law prohibited fixed commissions on public transactions and also prohibited banks, insurance companies, and other financial institutions from buying stock exchange memberships to save commission costs for their own institutional transactions. This act is a worthwhile addition to the securities laws since it fosters greater competition and more efficient prices.

Other Legislation

In addition to these three major pieces of legislation, a number of other acts deal directly with investor protection. For example, the Investment Advisor Act of 1940 is set up to protect the public from unethical investment advisers. Any adviser with over 15 public clients (excluding tax accountants and lawyers) must register with the SEC and file semiannual reports. The Investment Company Act of 1940 provides similar oversight for mutual funds and investment companies dealing with small investors. The act was amended in 1970 and currently gives the NASD authority to supervise and limit commissions and investment advisory fees on certain types of mutual funds.

Another piece of legislation dealing directly with investor protection is the Securities Investor Protection Act of 1970. The **Securities Investor Protection Corporation (SIPC)** was established to oversee liquidation of brokerage firms and to insure investors' accounts to a maximum value of $500,000 in case of bankruptcy of a brokerage firm. It functions much the same as the Federal Deposit Insurance Corporation (for banks) and the Federal Savings and Loan Insurance Corporation. SIPC resulted from the problems encountered on Wall Street during the period from 1967 to 1970 when share volume surged to then all-time highs, and many firms were unable to process orders fast enough. A back-office paper crunch caused Wall Street to shorten the hours the exchanges were formally open for new business, but even this didn't help. Investors lost large sums, and for many months, they were unable to use or get possession of securities held in their names. Even though SIPC insures these accounts, it still does not cover market value losses suffered while waiting to get securities from a bankrupt brokerage firm.

Insider Trading

The Securities Exchange Act of 1934 established the initial restrictions on insider trading. However, over the years, these restrictions have often proved to be inadequate. As previously indicated, the definition of *insider* may go beyond officers, directors, and major stockholders to include anyone with special insider knowledge. Both the Congress and the Securities and Exchange Commission are attempting to grapple with the issue of making punitive measures severe enough to discourage the illegal use of nonpublic information for profits.[6] Current and future legislation is likely to include tougher civil

---

[6]Insiders, of course, may make proper long-term investments in a corporation.

penalties and stiffer criminal prosecution. Also the penalties for improper action will expand beyond simple recovery of profits to a penalty three or more times the profits involved.

The 1980s have seen a continuous rash of insider trading scandals involving major investment banking houses, traders, analysts, and investors. Ivan Boesky and Dennis Levine were the first of the well-known investors to end up in jail, and in June of 1988, Steven Wang, Jr., an analyst at Morgan Stanley, was charged by the SEC of insider trading activities evolving from confidential information passed on to a wealthy Taiwanese businessman, Fred Lee. These insider trading scandals have plagued Wall Street and tarnished its image as a place where investors can get a fair deal.

On balance, all the legislation we have discussed has tended to increase the confidence of the investing public. In an industry where public trust is so critical, some form of supervision, whether public or private, is necessary and generally accepted.

Program Trading and Market Price Limits

Program trading is identified by some market analysts as the primary culprit behind the 508-point market crash on October 19, 1987. Program trading simply means that computer-based trigger points are established in which large volume trades are initiated by institutional investors. For example, if the Dow Jones Industrial Average (or some other market measure) hits a certain point, a large sale or purchase may automatically take place. When many institutional investors are using program trading simultaneously, this process can have a major cumulative effect on the market. This was thought to be the case not only in the October 19th crash but for many other highly volatile days in the market.

Some have suggested that program trading be made illegal by a congressional act or, at a minimum, be voluntarily restricted in scope by the security exchanges and their member firms. The latter seems to be the more likely path now. Furthermore, it should be pointed out that not all market participants envision program trading to be necessarily bad. One can argue that program trading simply accelerates the inevitable and gets it over with more quickly. Instead of the market going down by 500 points over a period of six months because of a series of negative factors, it perhaps can happen in one day.[7] One thing is certain: the topic of program trading will get continued attention in the future.

Another topic that received much publicity after the market crash was the possibility of establishing price limits on daily market movements so that the market would not be allowed to go up or down by more than 50, 100, or perhaps 200 points in a given day. The prestigious Brady Commission that was appointed by the president to investigate the causes and cures for the crash

---

[7]Program trading is also used to arbitrage price differentials between the futures market and the cash market for securities. This is not only a potentially profitable transaction for market participants but may increase market efficiency by ensuring that price discrepancies are quickly eliminated.

actually made such a recommendation. This, once again, is a controversial issue. Some would argue that price limits (collars) on market movements might create confidence in the market by restricting the potential for large daily moves, while others would argue that closing down the market because of a large price move would only cause panic. (There might be a run on the stock market similar to the run on the banks in the 1930s.) Once again, the issue is public trust and confidence and how it can be maintained in the marketplace. Only the passage of time will help to answer these questions. For now, the exchanges have adopted a limited use of price movement limits.

3

PARTICIPATING IN THE MARKET

Many different kinds of investors participate in the market, from the individual to the professional, and each participant needs to know about the structure and mechanics of the market in which he or she might invest. In this chapter, we examine the use of indexes to gauge market performance, the rules and mechanics of opening and trading in an account, and basic tax considerations for the investor.

MEASURES OF PRICE PERFORMANCE— MARKET INDEXES

We first look at tracking market performance for stocks and bonds. Each market has several market indexes published by Moody's, Standard & Poor's, Dow Jones, and other financial services. These indexes allow investors to measure the performance of their portfolios against an index which approximates their portfolio composition; thus, different investors prefer different indexes. While a professional pension fund manager might use the Standard & Poor's 500 Stock Index, a mutual fund specializing in small, over-the-counter stocks might prefer the NASDAQ (National Association of Securities Dealers Automated Quotations) Index, and a small investor might use the Value Line Average as the best approximation of his or her portfolio.

INDEXES AND AVERAGES

Dow Jones Averages

Since there are many stock market indexes and averages, we will cover the most widely used ones. Dow Jones, the publisher of *The Wall Street Journal* and *Barron's,* publishes several market averages of which the **Dow Jones Industrial Average (DJIA)** is the most popular. This average consists of 30 large industrial companies and is considered a "blue chip" index (stocks of very high quality). Many people criticize the DJIA for being too selective and representing too few stocks.[1] Nevertheless, the Dow Industrials do follow the general trend of the market, and these 30 common stocks comprise over 25 percent of the market value of the 1,550 firms listed on the New York Stock Exchange. Dow Jones also publishes an index of 20 transportation stocks and 15 utility stocks. Figure 3–1 shows a listing of the stocks in the Dow Jones Industrial, Transportation, and Utility averages as well as the daily price movements for the averages over a six-month time period. In Table 3–1, you also see a listing of the daily movement of the three Dow Jones averages for April 22, 1988. In that table is also a Dow Jones 65 stock composite average that summarizes the performance of the Dow Jones industrial, transportation and utility issues. You will observe that many other market averages are presented in the table, which we shall later discuss.

---

[1]On October 3, 1988, Dow Jones & Company began quoting a comparison index to the Dow Jones Industrial Average called the Dow Jones Equity Index. It is composed of 693 stocks but is not widely followed.

FIGURE 3–1

20
Transportation

30
Industrials

15
Utilities

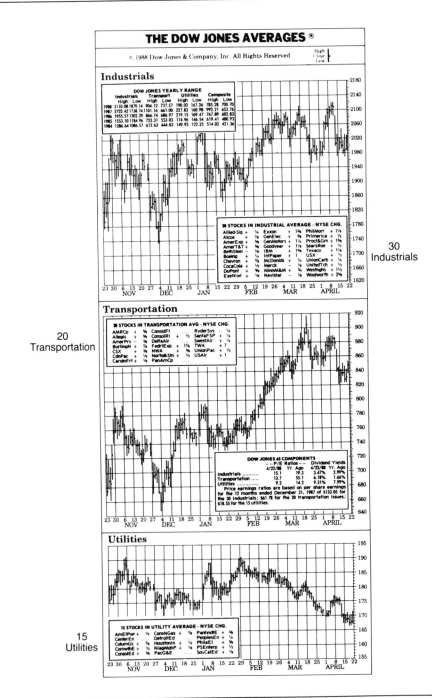

Source: *Barron's*, April 25, 1988, p. 44. *Reprinted by permission of Barron's,* © Dow Jones & Company, Inc., 1988.
All rights reserved.

TABLE 3–1   INDEXES AND AVERAGES FOUND IN *THE WALL STREET JOURNAL*

STOCK MARKET DATA BANK   Apr. 22, 1988

Major Indexes

HIGH	LOW	(12 MOS)	CLOSE	NET CH	% CH	12 MO CH	%	FROM 12/31	%
DOW JONES AVERAGES									
2722.42	1738.74	30 Industrials	2015.09	+ 27.69	+ 1.39	− 220.28	− 9.85	+ 76.26	+ 3.93
1101.16	661.00	20 Transportation	847.67	+ 17.17	+ 2.07	− 65.80	− 7.20	+ 98.81	+13.19
213.79	160.98	15 Utilities	x169.87	+ 2.20	+ 1.31	− 29.46	−14.78	− 5.21	− 2.98
992.21	653.76	65 Composite	x752.07	+ 11.59	+ 1.57	− 83.10	− 9.95	+ 37.80	+ 5.29
NEW YORK STOCK EXCHANGE									
187.99	125.91	Composite	147.03	+ 1.79	+ 1.23	− 12.34	− 7.74	+ 8.80	+ 6.37
231.05	149.43	Industrials	179.16	+ 2.26	+ 1.28	− 14.60	− 7.54	+ 12.12	+ 7.26
80.22	61.63	Utilities	68.66	+ 0.75	+ 1.10	− 2.10	− 2.97	+ 1.35	+ 2.01
168.20	104.76	Transportation	132.24	+ 2.06	+ 1.58	− 2.50	− 1.86	+ 13.67	+11.53
165.36	107.39	Finance	120.56	+ 1.21	+ 1.01	− 24.44	−16.86	+ 5.99	+ 5.23
STANDARD & POOR'S INDEXES									
336.77	223.92	500 Index	260.14	+ 3.72	+ 1.45	− 21.38	− 7.59	+ 13.06	+ 5.29
393.17	255.43	Industrials	302.92	+ 4.26	+ 1.43	− 23.92	− 7.32	+ 17.06	+ 5.97
274.20	167.59	Transportation	207.32	+ 2.68	+ 1.31	− 11.97	− 5.46	+ 17.15	+ 9.02
121.11	91.80	Utilities	103.02	+ 1.59	+ 1.57	− 3.46	− 3.25	+ 0.90	+ 0.88
32.56	20.39	Financials	22.21	+ 0.35	+ 1.60	− 5.15	−18.82	+ 0.58	+ 2.68
NASDAQ									
455.26	291.88	Composite	374.04	+ 0.84	+ 0.23	− 38.58	− 9.35	+ 43.57	+13.18
488.92	288.30	Industrials	384.22	+ 1.69	+ 0.44	− 55.14	−12.55	+ 45.28	+13.36
475.78	333.66	Insurance	396.46	+ 0.60	+ 0.15	− 17.48	− 4.22	+ 45.40	+12.93
510.24	365.63	Banks	444.41	− 0.65	− 0.15	− 35.82	− 7.46	+ 53.75	+13.76
195.37	124.98	Nat. Mkt. Comp.	161.61	+ 0.36	+ 0.22	− 14.58	− 8.28	+ 19.02	+13.34
187.94	110.21	Nat. Mkt. Indus.	148.55	+ 0.66	+ 0.45	− 18.77	−11.22	+ 17.44	+13.30
OTHERS									
365.01	231.90	AMEX	298.03	+ 1.32	+ 0.44	− 23.77	− 7.39	+ 37.68	+14.47
1926.2	1232.0	Fin. Times Indus.	1411.6	− 11.8	− 0.83	− 169.3	−10.71	+ 38.3	+ 2.79
27111.35	21036.80	Nikkei Stock Avg.	26837.12	+ 8.96	+ 0.03	+2830.72	+11.79	+5273.12	+24.45
289.02	181.09	Value-Line(geom)	227.64	+ 1.28	+ 0.57	− 27.98	−10.95	+ 26.02	+12.91
3299.44	2188.11	Wilshire 5000	2589.55	+ 26.54	+ 1.04	− 225.61	− 8.01	+ 172.42	+ 7.13

Source: *The Wall Street Journal,* April 25, 1988, p. 45. Reprinted by permission of *The Wall Street Journal,* © Dow Jones & Company, Inc. 1988. All rights reserved.

For now, let's return to the Dow Jones Industrial Average of 30 stocks. The Dow Jones Industrial Average used to be a simple average of 30 stocks, but when a company splits its stock price, the average has to be adjusted in some manner. For the Dow Jones Industrials, the divisor in the formula has been adjusted downward from the original 30 to slightly more than 1. Each time a company splits its shares of stock (or provides a stock dividend), the divisor is reduced to maintain the average at the same level prior to the stock split. If this were not done, the lower-priced stock after the split would reduce the average, giving the appearance that investors were worse off.

The Dow Jones Industrial Average is a **price-weighted average,** which means that each stock in the average is weighted by its price. To simplify the meaning of price-weighted: If you had three stocks in a price-weighted *index*

TABLE 3–2   BARRON'S GROUP STOCK AVERAGES

1988 High-a	Low-a			Apr. 7	Mar. 31	% chg.
1,113.79	943.61	Aircraft mfg		1,077.60	1,067.74	+ 0.92
286.04	222.47	Air transport		281.39	287.15	− 2.01
162.75	147.68	Automobiles	H	163.24	156.28	+ 4.46
463.15	389.92	Automobile equip	H	483.58	463.15	+ 4.41
341.42	297.37	Banks		318.46	317.79	+ 0.21
552.18	383.55	Bldg mat, equip	H	552.85	552.18	+ 0.12
777.63	653.08	Chemicals		755.23	734.20	+ 2.86
32.00	29.37	Closed-end invest		31.02	30.71	+ 1.01
5,404.19	4,928.41	Drugs		5,118.18	4,930.78	+ 3.80
1,454.93	1,300.80	Electrical equip		1,415.40	1,368.61	+ 3.42
584.37	430.26	Farm equipment		581.96	584.37	− 0.41
1,430.13	1,304.12	Foods and bev		1,391.84	1,351.86	+ 2.96
753.19	646.97	Gold mining		662.94	658.64	+ 0.65
1,188.65	884.70	Grocery chains		1,134.32	1,115.04	+ 1.73
662.97	492.89	Installment fin		659.24	650.46	+ 1.35
1,557.98	1,446.24	Insurance		1,465.92	1,474.27	− 0.57
2,265.25	1,981.35	Liquor		2,150.74	2,103.04	+ 2.27
239.50	176.95	Machine tools		235.61	221.05	+ 6.59
244.38	210.90	Machinery (heavy)	L	203.48	224.33	− 9.29
2,573.35	2,230.29	Motion pictures		2,387.70	2,407.86	− 0.84
504.23	394.96	Non-ferrous metal		449.19	434.23	+ 3.44
4,524.90	3,950.91	Office equip		4,010.15	3,950.91	+ 1.50
1,117.65	961.63	Oil	H	1,135.94	1,093.32	+ 3.90
1,258.50	961.78	Packing		1,214.21	1,209.46	+ 0.39
794.01	668.77	Paper		779.89	737.42	+ 5.76
268.68	219.58	Railroad equip		260.10	255.99	+ 1.60
2,199.83	1,378.27	Retail merch	H	2,222.99	2,176.08	+ 2.16
1,142.66	721.63	Rubber	H	1,166.08	1,142.66	+ 2.05
162.53	133.23	Steel and iron		154.78	148.40	+ 4.30
328.66	291.92	Television	H	331.21	319.86	+ 3.55
937.06	518.10	Textiles	H	976.00	931.07	+ 4.83
778.09	690.54	Tobacco		766.23	753.27	+ 1.72
2,090.19	1,879.14	Dow-Jones Indus		2,062.17	1,988.06	+ 3.73
904.12	737.57	Dow-Jones Transp		874.25	863.05	+ 1.30
190.02	171.29	Dow-Jones Utils		174.37	171.47	+ 1.69
782.23	700.70	Dow-Jones Comp		771.62	750.87	+ 2.76

a-1988 highs and lows through preceding week ended Thursday. In this table, daily closings for trading week ended last Friday used in the range for the Dow Jones Averages. H-New high L-New low.

that had values of 10, 40, and 100, you would add the prices and divide by three. In this case, you would get an average of 50 (150 divided by 3). A price-weighted index is similar to what you normally use in computing averages. Price-weighted *averages* tend to give a higher weighting bias to high-price stocks than to low-price stocks. For example, in the above analysis, if the $100 stock goes up by 10 percent, with all else the same, the average will go up over three points from 50 to 53.3. However, if the $10 stock goes up by 10 percent, with all else the same, the average will only go from 50 to 50.3. It is not necessary that you go back and do these computations, only that you understand the basic principle.

In mid-1988, Procter & Gamble was trading at 88, while Navistar (formerly International Harvester) was trading at 6. Clearly, an up or down 10 percent price movement in Procter & Gamble would have a greater impact on the

TABLE 3–3   DOW JONES INDUSTRY GROUPS

October 14, 1988, 4:30 p.m. Eastern Time

GROUPS LEADING (and strongest stocks in group)				GROUPS LAGGING (and weakest stocks in group)			
GROUP	CLOSE	CHG	% CHG	GROUP	CLOSE	CHG	% CHG
Health care	195.04	+ 5.45	+ 2.87	Heavy construction	173.74	– 1.81	– 1.03
Hospital Amer	48.25	+ 3.75	+ 8.43	Fluor Corp	20.75	– 0.38	– 1.78
Amer Med Intl	17.88	+ 0.25	+ 1.42	Foster Wheeler	14.50	– 0.25	– 1.69
Humana Inc	24.50	+ 0.13	+ 0.51	Dover Corp	30.50	– 0.38	– 1.21
Other non-ferrous	180.38	+ 4.68	+ 2.66	Retailers,broadline	360.86	– 3.53	– 0.97
Phelps Dodge	47.00	+ 1.88	+ 4.16	Sears Roebuck	41.00	– 1.38	– 3.24
Asarco Inc	26.88	+ 0.63	+ 2.38	Zayre Corp	25.63	– 0.38	– 1.44
Magma Copper	6.63	+ 0.13	+ 1.92	May Dept Store	36.25	– 0.50	– 1.36
Coal	178.33	+ 1.99	+ 1.13	Retailers,drug-based	266.16	– 2.21	– 0.82
Cyprus Minrl	35.25	+ 0.88	+ 2.55	Medco Contain	13.63	– 0.25	– 1.80
Pittston Co	14.50	+ 0.13	+ 0.87	Walgreen Co	33.75	– 0.50	– 1.46
Westmoreland	14.25	unch	unch	Mckesson Corp	33.50	– 0.25	– 0.74
Oilfield equip/svcs	88.30	+ 0.99	+ 1.13	Forest products	212.51	– 1.65	– 0.77
Schlumberger	33.50	+ 0.63	+ 1.90	Louisiana Pac	28.75	– 0.88	– 2.95
Halliburton Co	25.25	+ 0.13	+ 0.50	Potlatch Corp	30.38	– 0.38	– 1.22
Dresser Indus	28.38	+ 0.13	+ 0.44	Boise Cascade	43.00	– 0.50	– 1.15
Aluminum	270.22	+ 2.80	+ 1.05	Precious metals	249.17	– 1.85	– 0.74
Reynolds Mtls	53.25	+ 1.25	+ 2.40	Homestake Min	14.25	– 0.25	– 1.72
Alum Co Amer	55.25	+ 0.25	+ 0.45	A S A Ltd	38.75	– 0.63	– 1.59
Kaisertech Ltd	18.63	unch	unch	Battle Mt Gold	15.00	unch	unch

INDUSTRY GROUP PERFORMANCE (June 30, 1982=100)

GROUP	CLOSE	CHG	% CHG	GROUPS	CLOSE	CHG	% CHG
Basic Materials	285.95	– 0.75	– 0.26	Banks,regional	305.87	– 0.72	– 0.23
Aluminum	270.22	+ 2.80	+ 1.05	Banks-Central	348.74	+ 0.27	+ 0.08
Other non-ferrous	180.38	+ 4.68	+ 2.66	Banks-East	333.70	– 0.74	– 0.22
Chemicals	322.18	– 1.07	– 0.33	Banks-South	238.71	– 1.43	– 0.60
Forest products	212.51	– 1.65	– 0.77	Banks-West	325.74	– 0.53	– 0.16
Mining,diversified	210.92	– 0.53	– 0.25	Financial services	262.14	– 0.16	– 0.06
Paper products	356.63	– 1.33	– 0.37	Insurance,all	261.53	– 0.31	– 0.12
Precious metals	249.17	– 1.85	– 0.74	Ins-Full line	206.00	– 0.25	– 0.12
Steel	125.24	– 0.77	– 0.61	Ins-Life	316.35	+ 0.31	+ 0.10
Conglomerate	291.56	+ 0.70	+ 0.24	Property/Casualty	306.25	– 0.47	– 0.15
Consumer,Cyclical	324.77	+ 0.00	+ 0.00	Real estate	389.57	+ 1.61	+ 0.41
Advertising	279.70	+ 0.98	+ 0.35	Savings & loans	429.71	– 0.88	– 0.20
Airlines	259.77	– 0.11	– 0.04	Securities brokers	249.15	+ 1.86	+ 0.75
Auto manufacturers	333.74	+ 3.01	+ 0.91	Industrial	280.01	+ 0.29	+ 0.10
Auto parts & equip	286.75	– 0.74	– 0.26	Air freight	179.08	+ 1.60	+ 0.90
Casinos	376.42	– 0.24	– 0.06	Building materials	413.78	– 0.27	– 0.07
Home construction	325.42	– 1.02	– 0.31	Containers/pkging	488.46	– 0.34	– 0.07
Home furnishings	217.27	– 0.86	– 0.39	Elec comp/equip	274.06	+ 1.46	+ 0.54
Lodging	368.52	– 1.42	– 0.38	Factory equipment	261.17	– 1.55	– 0.59
Media	430.46	– 1.11	– 0.26	Heavy construction	173.74	– 1.81	– 1.03
Recreation products	218.31	+ 2.03	+ 0.94	Heavy machinery	166.02	– 1.07	– 0.64
Restaurants	325.00	+ 0.22	+ 0.07	Industrial services	319.59	+ 0.82	+ 0.26
Retailers,apparel	636.25	+ 4.78	+ 0.76	Industrial,divers	247.80	– 0.76	– 0.31
Retailers,broadline	360.86	– 3.53	– 0.97	Marine transport	423.77	+ 2.82	+ 0.67
Retailers,drug-based	266.16	– 2.21	– 0.82	Pollution control	593.43	+ 0.92	+ 0.16
Retailers,speciality	303.90	– 1.48	– 0.48	Railroads	252.22	+ 2.08	+ 0.83
Textiles and apparel	396.45	+ 0.72	+ 0.18	Transportation equip	239.20	– 1.45	– 0.60
Consumer,Non-Cycl	322.71	+ 0.86	+ 0.27	Trucking	247.63	– 0.89	– 0.36
Beverages	335.43	+ 1.22	+ 0.37	Technology	234.08	+ 0.73	+ 0.31
Consumer services	310.17	+ 2.05	+ 0.67	Aerospace/Defense	313.29	+ 1.39	+ 0.45
Cosmetics	272.57	+ 1.36	+ 0.50	Commu-w/AT&T	249.80	+ 2.49	+ 1.01
Food	442.13	+ 1.62	+ 0.37	Commu-wo/AT&T	161.09	– 0.89	– 0.55
Food retailers	442.79	+ 1.42	+ 0.32	Comptrs-w/IBM	218.86	+ 0.69	+ 0.32
Health care	195.04	+ 5.45	+ 2.87	Comptrs-wo/IBM	260.91	– 1.43	– 0.55
Household products	279.87	– 0.42	– 0.15	Diversified tech	201.57	– 0.60	– 0.30
Medical supplies	246.31	+ 1.91	+ 0.78	Industrial tech	247.29	+ 2.04	+ 0.83
Pharmaceuticals	309.28	+ 0.29	+ 0.09	Medical/Bio tech	212.66	+ 2.21	+ 1.05
Energy	202.04	+ 0.47	+ 0.23	Office equipment	246.00	+ 0.77	+ 0.31
Coal	178.33	+ 1.99	+ 1.13	Semiconductor	182.15	+ 0.17	+ 0.09
Oil drilling	64.27	+ 0.31	+ 0.48	Software	768.54	– 0.49	– 0.06
Oil-majors	243.52	+ 0.41	+ 0.17	Utilities	203.29	+ 0.46	+ 0.23
Oil-secondary	181.15	+ 0.10	+ 0.06	Telephone	252.91	+ 1.34	+ 0.53
Oilfield equip/svcs	88.30	+ 0.99	+ 1.13	Electric	173.05	+ 0.07	+ 0.04
Pipelines	150.77	+ 0.27	+ 0.18	Gas	166.58	– 1.23	– 0.73
Financial	259.31	– 0.19	– 0.07	Water	389.80	+ 0.81	+ 0.21
Banks,money center	179.56	+ 0.06	+ 0.03	DJ Equity Market	259.30	+ 0.34	+ 0.13

History compiled by Dow Jones and Shearson Lehman Hutton Inc.

Source: *The Wall Street Journal,* October 17, 1988, p. C6. Reprinted by permission of *The Wall Street Journal,* © Dow Jones & Company, Inc. 1988. All rights reserved.

Dow Jones Industrial Average than a 10 percent movement in Navistar. Thus, we see the bias toward high-priced stocks in the Dow Jones Industrial Average.

Barron's, a weekly Dow Jones publication, carries *Barron's* 50 Stock Average as well as an index of low-priced securities that meets the needs of many small investors. *Barron's* also publishes a weekly average, *Barron's* Group Stock Averages, covering 32 industry groups. These averages are especially useful to the analyst following the performance of a specific industry relative to the general market, and they are shown in Table 3–2. For example, observe that automobile and textile stocks were particularly strong in the week covered in the table.

For another view of industry performances, the analyst may also wish to observe the Dow Jones Industry Groups data found daily in *The Wall Street Journal.* Here we can also view the leading and lagging group for a given day as shown in Table 3–3.

Standard & Poor's Indexes

Standard & Poor's Corporation publishes several indexes, but two of the most important are the S&P 400 Industrials and the S&P 500 Stock Index. These indexes are followed by professional investors and others as measures of broad stock market activity. The S&P 400 consists of industrial common stocks and makes up over 50 percent of the market value of NYSE-listed companies. The S&P 500 Stock Index includes the 400 industrials, plus 20 transportation firms, 40 utilities, and 40 financial firms. The stocks in the S&P 500 Stock Index are equivalent to 75 percent of the total value of the 1,550 firms listed on the New York Stock Exchange.[2]

These are true indexes in that they are linked to some base value, in this case stock prices in the period from 1941 to 1943. The base period price in 1941 to 1943 was 10, so the S&P 500 Stock Index of 260.14 on April 22, 1988, previously shown in Table 3–1 indicates that the index has increased by 2,501.4 percent over this period.

These indexes are **value-weighted,** which means that each company is weighted in the index by its own total market value as a percentage of the total market value for all firms. For example, in a value-weighted index comprising the following three firms, the weighting would be:

Stock	Shares	Price	Total Market Value	Weighting
A	150	$10	$ 1,500	12.0%
B	200	20	4,000	32.0
C	500	14	7,000	56.0
			$12,500	100.0%

---

[2]Actually, there are also some large, over-the-counter firms in the S&P Indexes, though the indexes are predominantly made up of New York Stock Exchange firms.

In each case, the weighting is determined by dividing the total market value of the stock by the total market value for all firms. In the case of stock A, that would be $1,500 divided by $12,500, or 12 percent. The same procedure is followed for stocks B and C.

Even though stock C has only the second highest price, it makes up 56 percent of the average because of its high total market value based on 500 shares outstanding. This same basic effect carries through in the Standard & Poor's Indexes, with large companies such as IBM, AT&T, and Exxon having a greater impact on the index than do small companies. For example, IBM makes up approximately 3.9 percent of the 500-company index, while Quaser Corp. makes up .01 percent. Value-weighted indexes do not require special adjustments for stock splits because the increase in the number of shares automatically compensates for the decline in the stock value caused by the split.

The S&P 400 and S&P 500 indexes provide a good measure of the direction of the market for large firms. Often they are used as a proxy for market return when calculating the risk measures (betas) of individual stocks and portfolios.

Standard & Poor's also compiles value-weighted indexes for 90 different industries, and they are reported in the *Outlook,* a weekly Standard & Poor's publication.

Value Line Average

The Value Line Average represents 1,700 companies from the New York and American Stock Exchanges and the over-the-counter market. Some individual investors use the Value Line Average because it more closely corresponds to the variety of stocks small investors may have in their portfolios.

Unlike the previously discussed price-weighted average (the Dow Jones Industrial Average) and value-weighted indexes (S&P 400 and 500), the Value Line Average is **equal-weighted.** This means that each of the 1,700 stocks, regardless of market price or total market value, is weighted equally. It is as if there were $100 to be invested in each and every stock. In this case, IBM or Exxon is weighted no more heavily than Wendy's International or Mattel Inc. This equal-weighting characteristic also more closely conforms to the portfolio of individual investors.

Other Market Indexes

Indexes are also computed and published by the New York Stock Exchange, American Stock Exchange, and the National Association of Securities Dealers. Each index is intended to represent the performance of stocks traded in a particular exchange or market. As is seen in Table 3–1, the NYSE publishes a composite index as well as an industrial, utility, transportation, and financial index. Each index represents the stocks of a broad group or type of company. The American Exchange Market Value Index (AMEX) is composed of all stocks trading on the American Stock Exchange. This index is also shown in Table 3–1.

TABLE 3–4   WORLD STOCK MARKET AVERAGES

Stock Market Indexes

EXCHANGE	FRIDAY CLOSE	NET CHG	PCT CHG
Tokyo Nikkei Average-s	27058.37	+ 221.25	+ 1.21
Tokyo First Section-s	2166.99	+ 14.49	+ 1.49
London FT 30-share	1411.6	− 11.8	− 0.83
London 100-share	1771.6	− 20.3	− 1.13
London Gold Mines	205.7	− 2.9	− 1.39
Frankfurt FAZ	452.45	− 0.17	− 0.04
Zurich Credit Suisse	446.8	− 3.9	− 0.87
Paris CAC General	308.0	+ 6.5	+ 2.16
Milan Stock Index	1044	− 8	− 0.76
Amsterdam ANP-CBS General	245.6	− 1.2	− 0.49
Stockholm Affarsvarlden	794.7	− 0.3	− 0.04
Brussels Stock Index	4661.06	− 9.76	− 0.21
Sydney All Ordinaries	1436.1	− 1.7	− 0.12
Hong Kong Hang Seng	2591.35	+ 38.94	+ 1.51
Singapore Straits Times	955.77	+ 11.28	+ 1.19
Johannesburg J'burg Gold	1186	− 32	− 2.63
Toronto 300 Composite	3332.91	+ 3.31	+ 0.10
Europe, Australia, Far East	870.8	− 5.8	− 1.51

s-Saturday trading.

Source: *The Wall Street Journal*, April 25, 1986, p. 35. Reprinted by permission of *The Wall Street Journal*, © Dow Jones & Company, Inc. 1986. All rights reserved.

The National Association of Securities Dealers, which is the self-governing body of the over-the-counter markets, also constructs several indexes to represent the companies in their market. They publish the NASDAQ OTC composite, industrial, insurance, and banking indexes. The NASDAQ also publishes subindexes for stocks listed in the National Market System (See Table 3–1).

The indexes of the New York Stock Exchange, the American Stock Exchange, and NASDAQ are all *value-weighted* indexes.[3]

A relatively new index is the Wilshire 5000 Equity Index. It represents the *total dollar value* of 5,000 stocks, including all New York Stock Exchange and American Stock Exchange issues and the most active over-the-counter issues. By the very fact of including total dollar value, it is *value-weighted*. On April 22, 1988, the Wilshire Index had a value of $2,589.55 billion. The index tells you the total value of virtually all important equities daily.

The direction of the indexes are all closely related, but they do not necessarily move together all the time. If a pension fund manager is trying to "outperform the market," then the choice of index may be as crucial as to whether the fund manager maintains his or her accounts. The important thing for you, as well as for a professional, when measuring success or failure of performance, is to use an index that represents the risk characteristics of the portfolio being compared to the index. If you only want a general idea as to whether the market is going up or down over time, the choice of the average or index is not that critical since they all move fairly closely together.

---

[3]Until October 1973, the American Stock Exchange Index was price-weighted.

TABLE 3–5   BOND INDEXES

INDEX	FRI	FRI YIELD	THU	THU YIELD	YR AGO	12-MO HIGH	12-MO LOW
Shearson Lehman Hutton treas.	1256.54	9.05%	1254.01	9.07%	1130.33	1329.29	1152.47
DJ 10 Industrial	90.00	9.49	89.93	9.50	84.61	90.64	83.00
DJ 10 Utilities	90.08	9.91	90.25	9.88	79.95	91.88	79.51
Bond Buyer municipal	91-5	7.81	91	7.83	77-26	99	76-9
Merrill Lynch corporate	93.75	9.85	93.80	9.84	87.89	96.50	87.33

Source: *The Wall Street Journal,* October 17, 1988, p. C1. Reprinted by permission of *The Wall Street Journal,* © Dow Jones & Company, Inc., 1988. All rights reserved.

International Stock Averages.   On a daily basis, *The Wall Street Journal* provides information on stock market averages across the globe. In Table 3–4, you see 18 different market indicators for price changes in foreign markets. No doubt, the most-watched foreign equity market is Japan, with many sophisticated investors and analysts following the Tokyo Nikkei Average as closely as the Dow Jones Industrial Average.

Bond Market Indicators.   Performance in the bond market is not widely followed by an index or average but is usually gauged by interest-rate movements. Since rising interest rates mean falling bond prices and falling rates signal rising prices, investors can usually judge the bond market performance by yield-curve changes or interest-rate graphs. Dow Jones (DJ) does publish an index of 20 bonds (10 utility bonds and 10 industrial bonds), and additional bond indexes are published by Shearson Lehman Hutton, Merrill Lynch, and others. An example from *The Wall Street Journal* is shown in Table 3–5.

Mutual Fund Averages.   Lipper Analytical Services publishes the Lipper Mutual and Investment Performance Averages shown in Table 3–6. While mutual funds will be considered in depth in Chapter 19, for now it is interesting to observe the various categories that the funds are broken down into for purposes of computing measures of performance (capital appreciation, growth, etc.). Also, observe in the next few columns of Table 3–6 that the starting point of the measurement period is very important in relation to the presence or absence of pluses (or minuses) in performance.

BUYING AND SELLING IN THE MARKET

Once you are generally familiar with the market and perhaps decide to invest directly in common stocks or other assets, you will need to set up an account with a retail brokerage house. Some of the largest and better-known retail brokers are Merrill Lynch, Shearson Lehman Hutton, and Prudential-Bache, but there are many other good houses, both regional and national. When you set up your account, the account executive (often called stockbroker) will ask you to fill out a card listing your investment objectives, such as conservative,

TABLE 3–6   LIPPER MUTUAL FUND INVESTMENT PERFORMANCE AVERAGES

| Managed Indexes Total Reinvested Cumulative Performance | | | | | | | | | | |
No. of Current Funds	Type of Fund	12/03/87- 4/14/88		8/20/87- 4/14/88		4/16/87- 4/14/88		Year-to-Date 12/31/87- 4/14/88		Weekly 4/07/88- 4/14/88
154	Capital Appreciation	+	19.29%	−	16.85%	−	8.05%	+	8.16%	− 1.18%
245	Growth Funds	+	19.53%	−	17.33%	−	7.36%	+	8.19%	− 1.33%
62	Small Company Growth	+	29.28%	−	15.70%	−	10.07%	+	14.50%	− 0.79%
174	Growth and Income	+	15.55%	−	14.14%	−	4.09%	+	7.39%	− 1.23%
49	Equity Income	+	9.21%	−	10.98%	−	4.47%	+	5.22%	− 1.04%
684	Gen. Equity Funds Avg.	+	18.56%	−	15.81%	−	6.71%	+	8.32%	− 1.20%
8	Health Funds	+	21.75%	−	20.70%	−	13.53%	+	8.32%	− 1.61%
14	Natural Resources	+	22.82%	−	15.51%	−	4.26%	+	12.19%	− 0.36%
26	Science & Technol.	+	24.38%	−	19.97%	−	12.29%	+	8.46%	− 1.01%
10	Utility Funds	+	6.96%	−	5.66%	−	1.05%	+	5.53%	− 0.97%
43	Specialty Funds	+	18.21%	−	17.35%	−	10.26%	+	9.93%	− 0.91%
33	Global Funds	+	17.82%	−	11.51%	−	2.51%	+	9.03%	+ 0.82%
55	International Funds	+	20.63%	−	4.27%	+	4.05%	+	11.98%	+ 2.20%
25	Gold Oriented Funds	−	10.80%	−	26.10%	−	23.26%	−	8.74%	+ 0.00%
4	Option Growth Funds	+	6.56%	−	1.00%	+	10.37%	+	1.58%	− 0.67%
20	Option Income Funds	+	15.25%	−	12.59%	−	3.77%	+	6.88%	− 1.57%
922	All Equity Funds Avg.	+	17.81%	−	15.28%	−	6.62%	+	8.15%	− 0.86%
26	Conv. Sec Funds	+	13.60%	−	10.23%	−	5.54%	+	8.66%	+ 0.08%
39	Balanced Funds	+	11.46%	−	8.39%	−	1.11%	+	5.46%	− 0.84%
19	Income Funds	+	7.31%	−	1.30%	+	1.77%	+	5.37%	− 0.46%
25	World Income Funds	+	5.47%	+	13.09%	+	12.91%	+	1.35%	+ 0.68%
416	Fixed Income Funds	+	4.62%	+	4.27%	+	4.32%	+	3.54%	− 0.11%
1447	All Funds Average	+	13.46%	−	8.93%	−	3.08%	+	6.62%	− 0.60%
1447	All Funds-Median	+	13.20%	−	10.73%	−	2.51%	+	5.65%	− 0.58%
	No. of Funds in Universe		1406		1346		1284		1419	1428

preservation of capital, income oriented, growth plus income, or growth. The account executive will also ask for your social security number for tax reporting, the level of your income, net worth, employer, and other basic information. Basically, he or she needs to know your desire and ability to take risk in order to give good advice and proper management of your assets. Later in this section, we will also talk about discount brokers; that is, brokers who charge very low commissions but give a stripped-down form of service.

Cash or Margin Account

The account executive will need to know if you want a cash account or **margin account.** Either account allows you five business days to pay for any purchase. A cash account requires full payment, while a margin account allows the investor to borrow a percentage of the purchase price from the brokerage firm. The percentage of the total cost the investor must pay is called the margin and is set by the Federal Reserve Board. During the great crash in the 1920s, margin on stock was only 10 percent, but it was as high as 80 percent in 1968. It has been at 50 percent since January 1974. The margin percentage is used to control speculation. When the Board of Governors of the Federal Reserve

System thinks that the markets are being pushed too high by speculative fervor, they raise the margin requirement, which means that more cash must be put up. The Fed has been hesitant to take action in this area in recent times.

Margin accounts are used mostly by traders and speculators or by investors who think their long-run return will be greater than the cost of borrowing. Most brokerage houses require a $2,000 minimum in an account before loaning out money, although many brokerage houses have higher limits. Here is how a margin account works. Assume you purchased 100 shares of General Dynamics at $60 per share on margin and that margin is 50 percent.

Purchase: 100 shares at $60 per share	$6,000
Borrow: Cost (1 − margin percentage)	−3,000
Equity contributed—cash or securities	$3,000

You can borrow $3,000 or the total cost times (1 − margin percentage). The percentage cost of borrowing is generally 1 to 2 percent above the prime rate, depending on the size of the account. Rather than putting up $3,000 in cash, a customer could put $3,000 of other approved financial assets into the account to satisfy the margin. Not all stocks may be used for margin purchases. The Securities and Exchange Commission publishes a list of approved securities which may be borrowed against.

One reason people buy on margin is to leverage their returns. Assume that General Dynamics stock rises to $80 per share. The account would now have $8,000 in stock and an increase in equity from $3,000 to $5,000.

100 shares at $80	$8,000
Loan	−3,000
Equity	$5,000

This $2,000 increase in equity creates a 67 percent return on the initial $3,000 of equity. The 67 percent return was accomplished on the basis of only a 33 percent increase in the price of stock ($60 to $80). With the increased equity in the account, the customer could now purchase additional securities on margin.

Margin is a two-edged sword, however, and what works out to your advantage in up markets works to your disadvantage in down markets. If General Dynamics stock had gone to $40, your equity would decrease to $1,000.

100 shares at $40	$4,000
Borrowed	−3,000
Equity	$1,000

There are minimum requirements for equity in a margin account called *minimum maintenance standards* (usually 25 percent). Your equity would now be at minimum maintenance standards where the equity of $1,000 equals 25 percent of the current market value of $4,000. A fall below $1,000 would bring a margin call for more cash or equity. Many brokerage firms have maintenance requirements above 25 percent, and when margin calls are made, the equity often needs to be increased to 35 percent or more of the portfolio value. Normally, you must maintain a $2,000 minimum in your account, so you would have been called for more equity when the stock was at $50 even though the minimum maintenance requirement had not yet been reached.

One feature of a margin account is that margined securities may not be delivered to the customer. In this case, the General Dynamics stock would be kept registered in the street name of your retail brokerage house (e.g., Shearson Lehman Hutton), and your account would show a claim on 100 shares which are held as collateral for the loan. It is much like an automobile loan; you don't hold title to the car until you have made the last payment. In the use of margin, however, there is no due date on the loan. The use of margin increases risk and is not recommended for anyone who cannot afford large losses or who has no substantial experience in the market.

Long or Short?—That Is the Question

Once you have opened the account of your choice, you are ready to buy or sell. When investors establish a position in a security, they are said to be **long** if they purchase the security for their account. It is assumed that the reason they purchased the security was to profit on an increase in price over time and/or to receive dividend income. An investor who is long may take delivery of the securities (keep them in physical possession) if he or she has a cash account. An investor with a cash account may also choose to keep them on deposit in his/her brokerage account to facilitate bookkeeping, dividends, safekeeping, and ease of sale. A margin account user has no choice but to keep them with the broker in street name.

Sometimes investors anticipate that the price of a security may drop in value. If they are long in the stock, some may sell out their position. Those who have no position at all may wish to take a **short** position in order to profit from the expected decline. When you short a security, you are borrowing the security from the broker and selling it with the obligation to replace the security at a future time. How you can sell something you don't own is an obvious question. Your broker will simply loan you the security from the brokerage house inventory. If your brokerage house doesn't have an inventory of the particular stock you want to short, the firm will borrow the stock from another broker.

Once you go short, you begin hoping and praying that the price of the security will go down so that you can buy it back and replace the security that you sold at a lower price. In a perverse way, bad news starts to become good news. When you read the morning paper, you look for signs of unemployment, high inflation, and high interest rates in hopes of a stock market decline.

A short sale can only be made on a trade where the price of the stock advances (an uptick), or if there is no change in price, the prior trade must have been positive. These rules are intended to stop a snowballing decline in stock values caused by short sellers.

There is a margin requirement associated with short selling, and it is currently equal to 50 percent of the securities sold short. Thus, if you were to sell 100 shares of Monsanto Co. short at $70 per share, you would be required to put up $3,500 in margin (50 percent of $7,000). In a short sale, the margin is considered to be good-faith money and obviously is not a down payment toward purchase. The margin protects the brokerage house in case you start losing money on your account.

The way that you would lose money on a short sales position is if the stock that you sold short starts going up. Assume that Monsanto goes from $70 to $80. Since you initially sold 100 shares short at $70 per share, you have suffered a $1,000 paper loss. Your initial margin or equity position has been reduced from $3,500 to $2,500.

Initial margin (equity)	$3,500
Loss	−1,000
Current margin (equity)	$2,500

We previously specified that there is a minimum 25 percent margin maintenance requirement in buying stock. There is a similar type requirement in selling short. The equity position must equal at least 30 percent of the *current* value of the stock that has been sold short. In the present example, the equity position is equal to $2,500, and the current market value of Monsanto is $8,000 ($80 × 100). Your margin percentage is 31.25 percent ($2,500 ÷ $8,000) or slightly above the minimum requirement. However, if the stock goes up another point or two and your losses increase, you will be asked to put up more margin to increase your equity position.

Of course, if the value of Monsanto stock goes down from its initial base of $70, you would be making profits off the bad news. A 20-point drop in Monsanto would mean a $2,000 profit on your 100 shares. Most market observers agree that it requires a "special breed of cat" to be an effective short seller. You often need nerves of steel and a contrarian outlook that can not be easily shaken by good news.

Aside from risk takers, some investors sell short to establish beneficial tax positions. For example, if you had bought Digital Equipment at $60 and five months later it was $100, you would have a $40 per share profit on paper. If you want to preserve the profit but wait until next year to pay the tax, you can **sell short against the box.** This means you can short shares against those you already hold. Since you own the stock and also have a short position, you can neither gain nor lose by price movements in the stock. In the following tax year, you can deliver the shares you hold to cover your short position. At that point, you will incur the tax obligations associated with the transactions. The total net profit will still be $40.

One final point on selling short. In the last 10 or 15 years, some investors have chosen to use other ways to take a negative position in a security. These normally involve put and call options, which are discussed in Chapter 13.

Both selling short or option transactions can be effectively utilized for strategic purposes.

TYPES OF ORDERS

When an investor places an order to establish a position, he or she has many different kinds of orders from which to choose. When the order is placed with the account executive on a NYSE-listed stock, it is teletyped to the exchange where it is executed by the company's floor broker in an auction market. Each stock is traded at a specific trading post on the floor of the exchange, so the floor broker knows exactly where to go to find other brokers buying and selling the same company's shares.

Most orders placed will be straightforward market orders to buy or sell. The market order will be carried by the floor broker to the correct trading post and will usually trade close to the last price or within $1/4$ of a point. For example, if you want to sell 100 shares of AT&T at market, you would probably have no trouble finding a ready buyer, since AT&T may be trading a few million shares per day. On the other hand, if you wanted to sell 100 shares of Bemis, there might be as few as 1,000 shares traded in a day, and no other broker would be waiting at the Bemis post to make a transaction with the floor broker. If the broker finds no one else wishing to buy the shares he is selling, he will transact the sale with the specialist who is always at the post ready to buy and sell 100-share round lots. If the broker wants to sell, the specialist will either buy the shares for his own account at $1/8$ to $1/4$ less than the last trade or will buy out of his book in which special orders of others are kept.

The two basic special orders are the **limit order** and the **stop order.** A limit order limits the price at which you are willing to buy or sell and assures that you will pay no more than the limit price on a buy or receive no less than the limit price on a sell. Assume you are trying to buy a thinly traded stock that fluctuates in value and you are afraid that with a market order you might risk paying more than you want. So you would place a limit order to buy 100 shares of Bell Industries, as an example, at $16^1/_2$ or a better price. The order will go to the floor broker who goes to the post to check the price. The broker finds Bell Industries trading at its high for the day of $16^7/_8$, and so he leaves the limit order with the specialist who records it in his book. The entry will record the price, date, time, and brokerage firm. There may be other orders in front of yours at $16^1/_2$, but once these are cleared, and assuming the stock stays in this range, your order will be executed at $16^1/_2$ or less. Limit orders are used by investors to buy or sell thinly traded stocks or to buy securities at prices thought to be at the low end of a price range and to sell securities at the high end of the price range. Investors who calculate fundamental values have a basic idea of what they think a stock is worth and will often set a limit to take advantage of what they view to be discrepancies in values.

Many traders are certain that they want their order to be executed if a certain price is reached. A limit order does not guarantee execution if orders are ahead of you on the specialist's book. In cases where you want a guaranteed "fill" of the order, a stop order is placed. A stop order is a two-part mechanism. It is placed at a specific price like a limit order, but when the price is reached, the stop turns into a market order which will be executed at close to the stop price but not necessarily at the exact price specified. Often there will be a common price that many short-term traders will view with optimism for a certain trading strategy. When the stock hits the price, it may pop up on an abundance of buy orders or decline sharply on a large volume of sell orders, and your "fill" could be several dollars away from the top price. Assume that AXE Corporation stock has been trading between $25 and $40 per share over the last six months, reaching both these prices three times. A trader may follow several strategies. One strategy would be to buy at $25 and sell at $40 using a stop buy and a stop sell order. There may be some traders putting in a stop buy at $41 thinking that if the stock breaks through its peak trading range it will go on to new highs, and finally some may put in a stop sell at $23 to either eliminate a long position or establish a short position with the assumption that the stock has broken its support and will trend lower. When used to eliminate a long position, a stop order is often called a stop-loss order.

Limit orders and stop orders can be "day orders" that expire at the end of the day if not executed, or they can be GTC (good till cancelled) orders. GTC orders will remain on the specialist's books until taken off by the brokerage house or executed. If the order remains unfilled for several months, most brokerage houses will send reminders that the order is still pending so that the client does not get caught buying stock for which he is unable to pay. Orders have been known to stay on the specialist's books for years.

COST OF TRADING

Since May 1, 1975, commissions have been negotiated between the broker and customer, with larger orders getting smaller percentage charges. Before "May Day," commissions were fixed, and all brokers charged the same fee out of a published table for a given size order. Now there are individual variations, so check with several brokers. If commissions are of concern, you may want to do business with a "discount" broker who charges a discount of 30–75 percent from the old fixed-commission schedule.

Discount brokers sprung up as bare-bones operators providing only trans-actions and no research. They have found a niche with those investors who make up their own minds and do not need advice or personal service. The largest national discount broker is Charles Schwab & Co. To get a quote on the commission for a trade, you can call them from anywhere in the country with a toll-free number (listed in your phone book). Many banks in local communities may also have subsidiaries that offer discount brokerage services, so you may wish to check with your local financial institution.

Regular brokerage houses still offer more personal service and more variety of services and are often part of a financial corporation involved in underwriting and investment banking, managing mutual funds and pension funds, economic advising, government bond dealings, and more. Unfortunately, you pay extra

TABLE 3–7	EXAMPLE OF ROUND-LOT COMMISSIONS

	Commissions
Under $800	2.500% + $11
$801–$2,500	1.875 + 16
$2,500–$5,000	1.395 + 28
$5,000–$20,000	1.255 + 35
$20,000–$30,000	0.910 + 104
Over $30,000	0.560 + 209

when dealing with a full-service broker. Table 3–7 sets forth the fees for one national brokerage house.

Most full-service brokers still use a formula for computing commissions, but they also negotiate rates on large transactions and are willing to give actively trading customers discounts from the formula if their business over the year makes them a large trader in volume.

The fees in Table 3–7 are not necessarily an industry standard, and you may find variations of these fees from broker to broker. However, most firms will have a similar structure, charging a commission based on the dollar value of the transactions. Don't be embarrassed to ask your broker what the commission will be before you make any trades.

TAXES

In making many types of investments, an important consideration will be the tax consequences of your investment (taxes may turn out to be more significant than the brokerage commissions just discussed).

This section is only intended as a brief overview of tax consequences. For more detailed coverage, the student should consult a tax guide. Consultation with a CPA, CFP (Certified Financial Planner), or similar sources may also be advisable. Also, some instructors may consider this material as optional reading, so we have put it at the end of the chapter.

Before we specifically talk about the tax consequences of investment gains and losses, let's briefly look at the new tax rates under the Tax Reform Act of 1986. The rates are presented in Table 3–8.

Refer to Table 3–8 and assume you have appropriately computed your taxable income after all deductions as $23,800. Further assume you are single so that you fall into the first category of the table. How much is your tax obligation? The answer is shown below.

Amount		Rate	Tax
1st	$17,850	15%	$2,678
Next	5,950	28	1,666
	$23,800		$4,344

COMPUTER INVESTMENT SYSTEMS THRIVE AS PEOPLE SEEK CONTROL OVER PORTFOLIOS

Considering the reduced interest in the stock market among individual investors, computerized investing is doing surprisingly well. In fact, it is one of the few areas in the battered discount-brokerage business showing any life. Charles Schwab & Co., the nation's largest discount broker, now has 26,000 customers for its Equalizer computerized trading system, up from 15,000 a year ago.

Many people say they've become computerized because they believe it's the only way to compete with institutional investors. "On-line" systems, the basic service connecting investors to the brokerage firms, typically allow users to check current stock prices, place their orders, and check their portfolios through programs that automatically update the value of their holdings. Investors can also check current news, usually at extra cost.

"Off-line" software programs, for which the brokerage firms act as marketers, enable investors to do fundamental and technical analysis on stocks and bonds.

Many people, however, see computerized trading as a significant advance. The crash is one reason: While it drove many investors from the stock market, it impressed on many others the importance of being able to stay up-to-the-minute on the market and place orders quickly in a crisis. "If you can buy and sell with a personal computer, you can't be put on hold," says one brokerage-firm executive.

The total tax is $4,344. The rates of 15 percent and 28 percent are referred to as *marginal* tax rates. They are the rates that apply to income within a given tax bracket. The *average* tax paid is a slightly different concept. It is simply the amount of taxes paid divided by taxable income or 18.25 percent in this case.

$$\frac{\text{Taxes paid}}{\text{Taxable income}} = \frac{\$4,344}{\$23,800} = 18.25\%$$

Elimination of Capital Gains Tax Treatment

Perhaps no element in the Tax Reform Act of 1986 is more important (or controversial) than the elimination of the preferential tax treatment for long-term capital gains. Let us first review what was eliminated and then examine the consequences.

Prior to the passage of the 1986 act, gains on investments held for longer than six months received very special tax treatment when the security or asset was sold. Sixty percent of the gain was exempted from taxation so that only 40 percent was taxable. Assume an investor was in a 50 percent "pre–tax reform" marginal tax bracket. If the investor qualified an investment for long-

TABLE 3–8	TAX RATES UNDER THE TAX REFORM ACT OF 1986 (Based on Taxable Income)

Single:
$0–$17,850	15% of the amount
$17,850–$43,150	28% of the amount over $17,850
$43,150–$89,560★	33% of the amount over $43,150

Married (joint return):
$0–$29,750	15% of the amount
$29,750–$71,900	28% of the amount over $29,750
$71,900–$149,250★	33% of the amount over $71,900

Unmarried head of household:
$0–$23,900	15% of the amount
$23,900–$61,650	28% of the amount over $23,900
$61,650–$123,790★	33% of the amount over $61,650

★The third bracket in each case is extended by $10,920 per personal exemption. After that point, it reverts back to 28 percent. A personal exemption means that a person is entitled to a deduction of approximately $2,000 as a result of being appropriately claimed on a tax form.

term capital gains treatment, the gain would only be taxed at 40 percent of the normal 50 percent rate or 20 percent in total.

$$
\begin{array}{r}
50\%\ \text{Normal tax rate} \\
\times\ \underline{40\%\ \text{Long-term capital gains provision}} \\
20\%\ \text{Effective tax rate on long-term capital gains}
\end{array}
$$

With a $1,000 long-term capital gain, the tax obligation only would be $200.

The passage of the Tax Reform Act of 1986 changed all this. No longer are long-term capital gains treated any differently than short-term capital gains (investments held for six months or less) or any other income for that matter. That is, interest you receive on a certificate of deposit, cash dividends you receive on stock, or even the wages or salary you earn are now taxed precisely the same as long-term capital gains. In the example above, the $1,000 long-term capital gain would simply be taxed at your applicable marginal tax rate, whether it be 15, 28, or 33 percent.

Consequences of the Change to Capital Gains

First, this means there is no longer any incentive to hold an asset for at least six months to qualify for long-term capital gains. Second, and perhaps more important, it means that there is less incentive for investors to take risks in their investments in order to generate capital gains. Since interest or dividend income is taxed precisely the same as gains from appreciation in the value of a security, some investors are less willing to provide risk capital in hopes of generating a gain.

Many corporations have increased their dividend payments in an attempt to attract investors. Of course, tax considerations aside, double-digit annual gains to investors (perhaps 20 or 30 percent) must always come from capital appreciation, so there are still many investors trying to pick the big winners in spite of the lack of tax incentives.

Because the elimination of the preferential capital gains tax treatment is one of the most-controversial aspects of the Tax Reform Act of 1986, there is some chance that the provision may be once again restored in the 1990s. One scenario is that overall tax rates will be increased (perhaps to 40 percent or higher), and then a differential will be restored to long-term capital gains. Interestingly enough, the IRS still makes tax filers distinguish between short-term and long-term gains and losses even though the distinction is of no tax consequence. Perhaps the IRS is anticipating some changes in the future.

Deductions and Timing of Losses

Even though the investor no longer has to be concerned about the length of time a security is held for tax planning, other timing related considerations are still significant. The most important is that you can deduct up to $3,000 in security transaction losses in a given year against other forms of income. Thus, if you have a salary of $25,000 and you incur $3,000 in stock trading losses, your taxable income will only be $22,000 for that year. Prior to tax reform, long-term capital losses (losses on securities held over six months) could only be deducted at 40 percent of the dollar loss, so there was much incentive to take the loss (sell the stock) before the six-month period closed, but this is no longer the rule. Any loss, whether it is short-term or long-term in nature, can be used at full value in accumulating the $3,000 deduction.

Investors still have some incentive to take losses (that is, translate dollar losses on paper to actual losses by selling the security or securities) before year-end. Perhaps an investor has sold $5,000 worth of stock at a profit during the year. When December comes around, he or she may attempt to identify up to $8,000 of stocks to sell at a loss to cancel out the profit and create the maximum net loss of $3,000 for the year.

While investors should not let tax considerations override sound investment decisions (don't sell a potential long-term winner just for tax considerations), they have many ways to take losses and still maintain their basic position. For example, an investor might take a loss in one oil stock and buy another similar oil company at the same time (sell Exxon and buy Mobil, or vice versa). Furthermore, even a stock that has been sold for tax purposes can be repurchased after 30 days, and the loss is still deductible. Also, investors have many sophisticated ways to use options, convertibles, and other securities to maintain the potential for an upside move in a security that they just sold.

One final point in dealing with the timing of losses. Although the maximum net loss (losses minus gains) deduction is $3,000 per year, a person can carry over larger losses to subsequent years and take up to a maximum of $3,000 in each ensuing year. In Table 3–9, the loss carryover potential for an investor is examined.

We see the investor had net losses of $8,000 in 1989 of which $3,000 was written off against other income, leaving $5,000 to be carried forward. In 1990, another $3,000 was written off, so that $2,000 in losses was carried forward

TABLE 3–9	TAX LOSS CARRYOVER ANALYSIS		
		1989	
	$6,000 Gains	$14,000 Losses	$8,000 Net losses − 3,000 Tax write-off $5,000 Tax loss carryover
		1990	
	$7,000 Gains	$ 7,000 Losses	0 Net loss $3,000 Tax write-off (carried over from 1989) $2,000 Remaining tax loss carryover ($5,000 − $3,000)
		1991	
	$4,200 Gains	$6,000 Losses	$1,800 Net loss 1,200 Tax loss carryover $3,000 Tax write-off $ 800 Remaining tax loss carryover ($2,000 − $1,200)

to 1991. In 1991, the investor had net losses of $1,800 during the year so that only $1,200 of the remaining $2,000 was utilized to accumulate the maximum $3,000 deduction. This left $800 to be carried over in subsequent years. Although not explicitly shown in the table, if the investor had net gains of $800 in 1992, the loss carryforward of $800 would simply mean no taxes would be owed on the gains.

IRAs and Taxes

Another important tax consideration for the investor is the use of individual retirement accounts (IRAs) to reduce current tax burdens and accumulate long-term wealth. The process through which a person may deduct $2,000 a year from current income and invest it tax-free until a future withdrawal was touched upon in Chapter 1 and is covered in more detail in Appendix 3–A.

APPENDIX 3–A   MORE INFORMATION ON IRAS AND TAXES

An individual retirement account (IRA) allows a taxpayer to deduct $2,000 from taxable income and invest the funds at a bank, savings and loan, brokerage house, or other financial institution. Not only is the $2,000 allowed to be deducted from earned income to reduce current taxes, but the income is allowed to grow tax-free until withdrawn at retirement. For the young investor, the use of IRAs may be particularly appropriate as an investment vehicle. Instead of investing $2,000 directly in the market, an investor may wish to set up an IRA with a brokerage house so that he or she can deduct the $2,000 from earned income before it is invested. While an individual may qualify for a $2,000 deduction, a couple filing a joint return may qualify for a $2,250 deduction if there is only one working spouse and $4,000 if there are two working spouses. The money initially put into an IRA must be actually earned income and not gifts from others, inheritance funds, and so forth.

In Table 3A–1, we look at the potential accumulation in an IRA account based on annual contributions of $2,000 and various compound rates of growth on the funds. Note that the age at which contributions begin and the compounding rate are both significant. For example, a person who begins contributions at age 25 and earns a 10 percent return will accumulate $1,437,810 at age 70. If the same person had waited to age 45, the accumulation at age 70 (based on a 10 percent growth rate) would only be $196,694.

When you begin to withdraw funds from your IRA in later life, you do have to pay your normal tax rate on your annual withdrawals (but you have had the potential for tremendous tax-free accumulation up to that point). It should be pointed out that one can wait to begin withdrawing funds until

TABLE 3A–1   VALUE OF IRA FUND AT AGE 70 ($2,000 Annual Contribution)

Age Contributions Begin	Compound Annual Rate of Return			
	8 Percent	10 Percent	12 Percent	14 Percent
20	$1,147,540	$2,327,817	$4,800,036	$9,989,043
25	773,011	1,437,810	2,716,460	5,181,130
30	518,113	885,185	1,534,183	2,684,050
35	344,634	542,049	863,327	1,387,145
40	226,566	328,988	482,665	713,574
45	146,212	196,694	266,668	363,742
50	91,524	114,550	144,105	182,050
55	54,304	63,545	74,559	87,685
60	28,973	31,875	35,097	38,675

anywhere from age $59^1/_2$ up to age $70^1/_2$ (it's up to you to choose). At that time, you must withdraw a specified minimum amount each year based upon your life expectancy and the amount of funds in your IRA. One disadvantage of withdrawing funds before age $59^1/_2$ is that you pay a 10 percent penalty on the early withdrawal as well as the normal tax rate on the funds withdrawn (this depends on your marginal tax bracket).

Because IRAs can be such an advantageous way to make stock market investments or draw interest on savings instruments, the IRS restricts the use of IRAs of those who also participate in work-related retirement plans. In Table 3A–2, we see the phaseout of allowable annual contributions to an IRA for those who participate in such work-related plans. For example, an individual who makes $30,000 and is in a work-related plan can only contribute $1,100 annually to an IRA as a tax-deductible item. If an individual is not in a work-related retirement plan, he or she can take the full $2,000 taxable deduction regardless of income level. Even those individuals who do not qualify for the $2,000 deduction can still put the funds in an IRA and allow them to grow tax-free until retirement. The taxpayer does not get the initial $2,000 deduction from income, but the subsequent return on the funds grows tax-free until retirement.

In summary, IRAs are generally a desirable way to shelter income from taxation initially (if you qualify) and allow it to grow tax-free until retirement. IRAs, however, are not a desirable investment if you are likely to have a liquidity problem one or two years after you make the contribution and end up having to pay a 10 percent withdrawal penalty[1] as well as your normal taxes on the funds withdrawn. Also, keep in mind that even if you make a contribution to an IRA in one year, you are not required to make a similar contribution in subsequent years (though the accumulations in Table 3A–1 are based on regular annual contributions).

TABLE 3A–2	PHASEOUT OF ALLOWABLE IRA CONTRIBUTIONS FOR TAXPAYERS IN A WORK-RELATED PENSION PLAN			
	Individual		*Joint Filing*	
	Income Level	Maximum IRA Deduction	Income Level	Married, 1 Spouse Works	Married, 2 Spouses Work
	$25,000	$2,000	$40,000	$2,250	$4,000
	26,000	1,900	41,000	2,138	3,800
	27,000	1,700	42,000	1,913	3,400
	28,000	1,500	43,000	1,688	3,000
	29,000	1,300	44,000	1,463	2,600
	30,000	1,100	45,000	1,238	2,200
	31,000	900	46,000	1,013	1,800
	32,000	700	47,000	788	1,400
	33,000	500	48,000	563	1,000
	34,000	300	49,000	338	600
	35,000	100	50,000	113	200
	Over $35,000	0	Over $50,000	0	0

[1]Generally, the break-even point for using an IRA is about five years. That is, it takes about that long for the tax advantages to overcome the withdrawal penalty.

4

SOURCES OF INVESTMENT INFORMATION

W e are continually exposed to much information in this world of expanding and rapid communications. As the scope of investments has grown to include more than stocks and bonds, investment information has expanded to cover items such as gold and silver, diamonds, original art, antiques, stamps and coins, real estate, farm land, oil and gas, tax shelters, commodities, mutual funds, and other specialized assets. The problem investors are faced with is not only which investments to choose from the many available but also where to find relevant information on specific investments.

First, the investor needs a basic knowledge of the economic environment. After determining the economic climate, the investor will proceed to a more detailed analysis of industries and unique variables affecting a specific investment. It is often said that the sign of an educated person is whether he or she knows where to find information to make an intelligent decision. The rest of this chapter will attempt to provide a list and descriptions of the basic information sources for some of the more common forms of investments as well as sources for general economic data.

You may want to refer to this chapter as you go through the chapters that follow. This chapter is not intended to be a guide for analysis—only an overview of what information is available. You may have heard the old phrase "a picture is worth a thousand words." You will find that is certainly true of the tables and figures in this chapter. It is virtually impossible to discuss each and every variable found in them. To acquaint yourself more fully with information sources, we suggest you visit your college and local library and spend time browsing through their collections of economic and financial services. Appendix 4–A at the end of the chapter contains the addresses of a number of the sources mentioned in the chapter.

AGGREGATE ECONOMIC DATA

Economic data are necessary for analyzing the past and predicting future trends of the economy. The economic environment that exists today and the one expected in the future will bear heavily on the types of investments selected when creating or managing an investment portfolio. Information on inflation, wages, disposable income, economic growth rates, interest rates, money supply, demographic trends, and so on are important economic data that will influence investor decisions. This information is available in many publications from the government, commercial banks, and periodicals. What follows is a brief description of some of the major sources of economic data.

Federal Reserve Bulletin

The *Federal Reserve Bulletin* is published monthly by the Board of Governors of the Federal Reserve System, Washington, D.C. It contains an abundance of monetary data such as money supply figures, interest rates, bank reserves, and various statistics on commercial banks. Fiscal variables such as U.S. budget receipts and outlays and federal debt figures are also found in the *Bulletin*. This publication also contains data on international exchange rates and U.S. dealings with foreigners and overseas banks.

Since a complete description of the *Federal Reserve Bulletin* is outside the scope of this chapter, a partial listing of the table of contents should suffice to provide a better idea of what information it contains. Each heading may be divided into more detailed sections that provide information for the previous month, the current year on a monthly basis, and several years of historical annual data.

Domestic Financial Statistics
Federal Reserve Banks
Monetary and Credit Aggregates
Commercial Banks
Financial Markets
Federal Finance
Securities Markets and Corporate Finance
Real Estate
Consumer Installment Credit
Domestic Non-Financial Statistics
International Statistics
Securities Holdings and Transactions
Interest and Exchange Rates

The Federal Reserve Board also publishes a *Federal Reserve Quarterly Chart Book* and an annual *Historical Chart Book* depicting the data in the *Bulletin* in graphic form.

Federal Reserve Banks

The 12 Federal Reserve banks in the Federal Reserve System represent different geographical areas (districts) of the United States. Each bank publishes its own monthly letter or review which includes economic data about its region and sometimes commentary on national issues or monetary policy. The 12 banks by district are as follows: Boston (1), New York (2), Philadelphia (3), Cleveland (4), Richmond (5), Atlanta (6), Chicago (7), St. Louis (8), Minneapolis (9), Kansas City (10), Dallas (11), and San Francisco (12).

Federal Reserve Bank of St. Louis

One district bank, the Federal Reserve Bank of St. Louis, publishes some of the most-comprehensive economic statistics on a weekly and monthly basis. *U.S. Financial Data* is published weekly and includes data on the monetary base, bank reserves, money supply, a breakdown of time deposits and demand deposits, borrowing from the Federal Reserve banks, and business loans from the large commercial banks. The publication also includes yields and interest rates on a weekly basis on selected short-term and long-term securities. An example of these published interest rates appears in Figures 4–1 and 4–2.

Monetary Trends, published monthly, includes charts and tables of monthly data. The information is similar to that found in *U.S. Financial Data* but covers a longer time period. The tables provide compound annual rates of change, while the graphs include the raw data with trend changes over time. Additional data are available on the federal government debt and its composition by type of holder and on the receipts and expenditures of the government for both the National Income Account Budget and the High Employment Budget.

National Economic Trends is also published by the Federal Reserve Bank of St. Louis and presents monthly economic data on employment, unemployment rates, consumer and producer prices, industrial production, personal income, retail sales, productivity, compensation and labor costs, gross national product, the implicit price deflator for the GNP, personal consumption expenditures, gross private domestic investment, government purchases of goods and services, disposable personal income, corporate profit after taxes, and inventories. This information is presented in graphic form and in tables showing the compounded annual rate of change on a monthly basis. If raw data is needed, other economic publications are required.

Survey of Current Business

The *Survey of Current Business* is published monthly by the Bureau of Economic Analysis of the U.S. Department of Commerce. It contains monthly and quarterly raw data rather than compound annual growth rates as found in the St. Louis Federal Reserve's publications. The *Survey of Current Business* contains a monthly update and evaluation of the business situation, analyzing such data as GNP, business inventories, personal consumption, fixed investment, exports, labor market statistics, financial data, and much more. For example, if personal consumption expenditures are broken down into subcategories, one would find expenditures on durable goods such as motor vehicles and parts and furniture and equipment; nondurables such as food, energy, clothing, and shoes; and services.

The *Survey* can be extremely helpful for industry analysis as it breaks down data into basic industries. For example, data on inventory, new plant and equipment, production, and more can be found on such specific industries as coal, tobacco, chemicals, leather products, furniture, and paper. Even within industries such as lumber, production statistics can be found on hardwoods and softwoods right down to Douglas fir trees, southern pine, and western pine. The Commerce Department publishes a weekly update to the *Survey* called *Weekly Business Statistics.* This publication updates the major series found in the *Survey of Current Business* and includes 27 weekly series and charts of selected series. To provide a more comprehensive view of what is available in the *Survey of Current Business* and *Weekly Business Statistics,* a list of the major series updates follows on page 93.

FIGURE 4–1

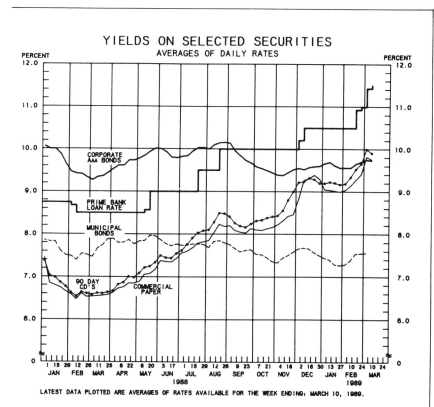

Source: Federal Reserve Bank of St. Louis, March 9, 1989.

FIGURE 4–2

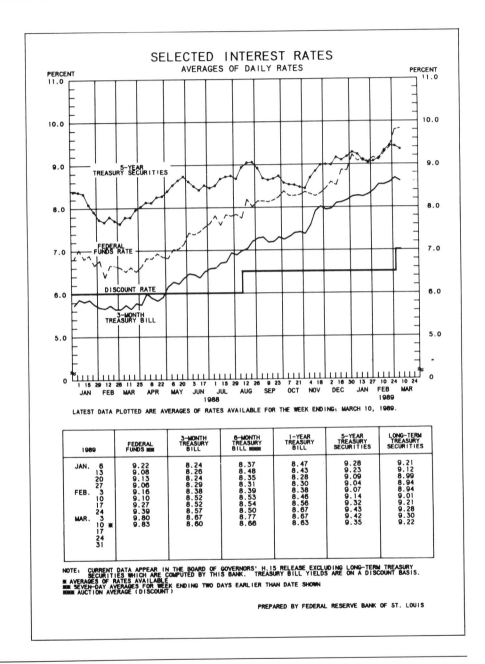

GNP	Housing Starts and Permits
National Income	Retail Trade
Personal Income	Labor Force, Employment and
Industrial Production	Earnings
Manufacturers' Shipments,	Banking
Inventories and Orders	Consumer Installment Credit
Consumer Price Index	Stock Prices
Producer Price Index	Value of Exports and Imports
Construction Put in Place	Motor Vehicles

Business Conditions Digest

The *Business Conditions Digest* is published monthly by the Bureau of Economic Analysis of the U.S. Department of Commerce. The information differs from the other publications previously discussed in that its primary emphasis is on cyclical indicators of economic activity. The National Bureau of Economic Research (NBER) analyzes and selects the time series data based on each series' ability to be identified as a leading, coincident, or lagging indicator over several decades of aggregate economic activity.

Over the years, the NBER has identified the approximate dates when aggregate economic activity reached its cyclical high or low point. Each time series is related to the business cycle. Leading indicators move prior to the business cycle, coincident indicators move with the business cycle, and lagging indicators follow directional changes in the business cycle. Figure 4–3 represents the composite index of 11 leading, 4 coincident, and 6 lagging indicators that have consistently performed well relative to the general swings in the economy. These 21 indicators were selected from several hundred found in the *Business Conditions Digest* and were time-tested by the NBER. This publication can be very helpful in understanding past economic behavior and in forecasting future economic activity with a higher degree of success.

Other Sources of Economic Data

So far, we have presented the basic sources of economic data. Much other data is available in other publications. What is available to each investor may vary from library to library, so here are some brief notes on other sources of data.

Many universities have bureaus of business research that provide statistical data on a statewide or regional basis. Major banks, such as Citicorp, Morgan Guaranty Trust, Harris Trust, and Bank of America, publish monthly or weekly letters or economic reviews, including raw data and analysis. Several other government sources are available, such as *Economic Indicators* prepared by the Council of Economic Advisors and the *Annual Economic Report of the President*. Additionally, many periodicals, such as *Business Week, Fortune,* and *Barron's,* contain raw data as well as economic commentary. Moody's and

FIGURE 4–3   CYCLICAL INDICATORS (Composite Indexes and Their Components)

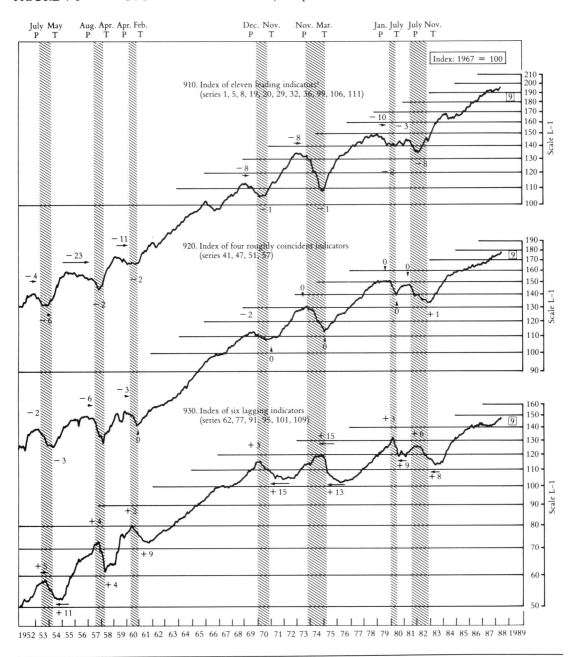

Note: Numbers entered on the chart indicate length of leads (−) and lags (+) in months from reference turning dates.
[1]Values of this index prior to January 1984 include a 12th component, series 12, which has been suspended from the current index.
Source: *Business Conditions Digest* (U.S. Department of Commerce Bureau of Economic Analysis, October 1988).

Standard & Poor's investment services (introduced on the following pages) both publish economic data along with much other market-related information.

INVESTMENT ADVISORY SERVICES

Investment information and advice is available from many sources—from large corporate financial services to individuals writing investment letters. A look through such financial magazines as *Barron's, Forbes,* and *Financial World* will turn up hundreds of investment services charging fees large and small for the information they sell. Most public libraries and universities subscribe from several of the major publishers, such as Moody's, Standard & Poor's, or Value Line.

Moody's

Moody's is owned by Dun & Bradstreet and publishes several data bases for bonds and stocks. *Moody's Manuals* are widely used and present historical financial data on the companies listed, on their officers, and on the companies' general corporate condition. The *Manuals* are divided into several categories (Banks and Finance, Industrial, Municipals and Government, OTC Industrial, Public Utility, and Transportation). Each manual has a biweekly news supplement that updates quarterly earnings, dividend announcements, mergers, and other news of interest. *Moody's Manuals* are comprehensive, with each category taking up one or two volumes and several thousand pages.

Moody's Bond Record, a monthly publication, contains data on corporates, convertibles, governments, municipals, and ratings on commercial paper and preferred stock. Corporate bond information includes the interest coupon, payment dates, call price, Moody's rating, and yield to maturity. The current price as well as the yearly and historical high-low prices are presented. The total amount of the bond issue outstanding is given with a designation for a sinking fund and the original issue date. Data on convertible bonds also include the conversion price, conversion value, and conversion period. Information on industrial revenue and municipal bonds is usually limited to the Moody's rating. *Moody's Bond Record* also contains historical yield graphs for various types of bonds over at least 30 years.

Moody's also publishes a weekly *Bond Survey* that reviews the week's activity in the bond market, rating changes, new issues, and bonds called for redemption. *Moody's Dividend Record* presents quarterly dividends and the date of declaration, date of record, date payable, and ex-dividend dates. This is an annual publication. *Moody's Handbook of Common Stock* is a quarterly reference guide that summarizes a company's 10-year historical financial data along with a discussion of corporate background, recent developments, and prospects. Approximately 1,000 companies are listed in the *Handbook. Moody's Stock*

Survey is a weekly publication that discusses the weekly investment climate and market performance. This publication also presents some selected stocks for purchase. Only a brief description has been given for each Moody's publication, but enough has been presented for you to know whether a particular one may be worth looking at further.

Standard & Poor's

A second major source of information is the Standard & Poor's Corporation, a subsidiary of McGraw-Hall. Standard & Poor's has very comprehensive coverage of financial data. The following items will not all be discussed, but they provide a good look at what Standard & Poor's makes available to the investor.

Analysts Handbook	*The Outlook*
Bond Guide	*Poor's Register of Corporations,*
Called Bond Record	*Directors and Executives*
Convertible Bond Reports	*Registered Bond Interest Record*
Corporation Records	*The Review of Securities Regulation*
Daily Stock Price Records	*Security Dealers Directory*
Dividend Record	*Stock Guide*
Fixed Income Investor	*Stock Reports (A.S.E., N.Y.S.E.,*
Industry Survey	*O-T-C and Regional Exchanges)*
International Stock Reports	*Stock Summary*
Investment Advisory Survey	*Standard & Poor's Statistical Service*
Municipal Bond Selector	*Transportation Service*
Opportunities in Convertible Bonds	*Trendline Charts*

Standard & Poor's Corporate Records are similar to *Moody's Manuals* except they are organized alphabetically rather than by trade categories. The *Corporate Records* are published monthly, and the six volumes are updated by daily supplements. Information found in the volumes includes historical company background, financial statements, news announcements, earnings updates, and other news of general interest. Companies found in the *Corporate Records* are listed, and their subsidiary companies are cross-listed.

Something that may be overlooked when examining the *Corporate Records* is the statistical section found in the T–Z volume. The statistical section includes a mutual fund summary, an address list of many no-load mutual funds, and foreign bond statistics. Special tables contained in the T–Z volume list new stock and bond offerings on a monthly basis. This volume also presents a classified index of industrial companies listed by standard industrial classification code numbers (SIC). For example, if you want to find out about cereal breakfast food companies, you would first find the corresponding SIC number for cereal breakfast foods which is listed in alphabetical order. The number,

FIGURE 4-4   SAMPLE PAGES, STANDARD & POOR'S STOCK GUIDE

212 TER-THR

Standard & Poor's Corporation

February, 1989

Index	Ticker Symbol	Name of Issue (Call Price of Pfd Stocks)	Market	Com. Rank. & Pfd. Rating	Par Val	Inst. Hold Cos	Inst. Hold Shs. (000)	Principal Business	Price Range 1971-87 High	Low	1988 High	Low	1989 High	Low	Feb. Sales in 100s	Last Sale Or Bid High	Low	Last	%Div Yield	P-E Ratio
1	TMEXF	Terra Mines Ltd .... OTC		NR	50¢	9	509	Int'l expl prod prec metals	8¼	1¼	⅞	1⅝	¼	1⅝	2612	12½	¼	⅛		d
2	TSO	Tesoro Petroleum .... NY,B,M,P,To		C	16¾¢	29	3794	Integrated oil company	32¼	6¾	13¾	8¼	12¾	11½	9144	12⅞	11¾	12½		d
3	Pr	$2.16 cm Cv Pfd(25)vtg .... NY,M		C		3	34	Trinidad, Indonesia, U.S.	55½	18¾	25	16¾	25	6¼	1908	25½	20¾	23	9.4	
4	TEVIY	Teva Pharm Indus ADR⁴⁴ .... OTC		NR		9	1099	Pharmac'ls;veterinary prod	12	1¾	7½	4¼	7¾	6¼	1256	17⅞	6¾	⅞	2.0	3.5
5	TXC	Texaco Canada⁴⁴ .... AS,Mo,To,Ph		B+	No			Large factor in Canadian oil	38	5⅝	37½	21¼	38⅛	32¼	19812	34¾	33⅝	34		12

Uniform Footnote Explanations—See Page 1. Other: ¹Ph:Cycle 2. ²Vc:Cycle 3. ³ASE:Cycle 1. ⁴Ph:Cycle 1. ⁵P:Cycle 1. ⁶CBOE:Cycle 1. ⁷To.

(Table continues — full data rows for Texaco Inc., Texas Air, Texas Amer'n Bancsh, Texas Amer'n Energy, Texas East'n Corp, Texas Indus, Texas Instruments, Texas Meridian Resources, Texas Pac Ld Tr, Texas Utilities, Texfi Indus, Textron Inc, Thai Fund, $1.40 cm Cv B Pfd, TGI Friday's, TGX Corp, Thackeray Corp, Therapeutic Technologies, Thermedics Inc, Thermo Cardiosystems, Thermo Electron, Thermo Environmental, Thermo Instrument Sys, Thermo Process Sys, Thermwood Corp, Thomas & Betts, Thomas Indus, Thomas Nelson, Thomaston Mills 'A', Thomson McKinnon, Thomson Newspaper A, Thor Energy Res, Thor Industries, Thortec Int'l, Thousand Trails, Three D Depts Cv Cl B, Class 'A')

FIGURE 4–4 *(concluded)*

Common and Preferred Stocks

TER-THR 213

Splits ◆ Index	Cash Divs. Ea. Yr. Since	Dividends: Latest Payment Period $	Date	Ex. Div.	Total $ So Far 1989	Ind. Rate	Paid 1988	Financial Position Mil-$ Cash& Equiv.	Curr. Assets	Curr. Liab.	Balance Sheet Date
1◆	....	5%Stk	1-28-85	1-8	....	Nil	....	3.92	5.73	0.61	j12-31-87
2	....	0.10	8-25-86	8-5	....	Nil	....	96.8	229	118	9-30-88
3	1976	a2.16	3-15-89	2-23	a[61]2.16	2.16	0.54	Cv into 1.7241 common,$14.50			
4	1984	0.036	12-30-88	12-6	....	0.14	0.165	40.8	112	49.6	12-31-87
5	1944	g†0.75	3-1-89	2-15	†g[67]7.25	e1.20	g1.20	1003	1677	591	j9-30-88
6	1903	Q0.75	3-10-89	2-1	0.75	3.00	2.25	2479	8470	6505	9-30-88
7	....	0.04	7-31-83	7-6	....	Nil	....	777	2153	2320	9-30-88
8	....	0.10	1-5-87	12-8	....	Nil	....	Book Value Neg			9-30-88
9◆	....	5%Stk	9-30-85	8-28	....	Nil	....	28.6	28.7	3.17	9-30-88
10◆	1950	Q0.25	3-1-89	2-14	0.25	1.00	1.00	239	950	891	9-30-88
11◆	1962	Q0.20	2-28-89	1-30	0.20	0.80	†s0.785	90.0	303	105	11-30-88
12◆	1962	Q0.18	1-23-89	12-22	0.18	0.72	0.72	607	2494	1202	9-30-88
13	....	0.32	3-5-86	1-27	....	Nil	....	0.70	4.86	6.49	9-30-88
14	1956	A0.40	3-13-89	2-28	0.40	0.40	0.40	3.37	...	...	9-30-88
15	1917	Q0.73	4-3-89	2-28	1.45	2.92	2.86	58.4	865	951	9-30-88
16◆	....	None Paid			....	Nil	....	5.89	51.7	19.3	10-28-88
17	1988	Q0.27½	3-1-89	2-9	0.27½	1.10	1.103	....	...	...	
18	1988	Q0.25	1-1-89	12-9	0.25	1.00	0.547	....	...	...	
19◆	1942	Q0.25	4-1-89	3-6	0.50	1.00	1.00	13.6	2297	1035	10-01-88
20	1968	Q0.52	4-1-89	3-6	1.04	2.08	2.08	Cv into 2.2 common			
21	1968	Q0.35	4-1-89	3-6	0.70	1.40	1.40	Cv into 1.8 common			
22	....	None Since Public			....	Nil	....	45.2	57.7	23.4	10-03-88
23	....	None Paid			....	Nil	....	2.96	42.0	28.3	9-30-88
24	....	0.30	6-5-74	5-6	....	Nil	....	0.38	42.2	18.9	9-30-88
25	1989	[69]0.29	1-16-89	12-23	[69]0.29	0.29	....	Net Asset Val $11.36			2-24-89
26	....	None Since Public			....	Nil	....	0.44	1.52	0.41	9-30-88
27◆	....	None Since Public			....	Nil	....	23.8	32.5	3.14	10-01-88
28	....	None Since Public			....	Nil	....	....	0.96	0.24	10-01-88
29◆	....	None Paid			....	Nil	....	122	313	110	10-01-88
30◆	....	None Since Public			....	Nil	....	7.08	24.8	6.15	10-01-88
31◆	....	None Since Public			....	Nil	....	49.7	101	30.6	10-01-88
32◆	....	None Since Public			....	Nil	....	3.60	20.7	10.7	12-31-88
33	....	None Paid			....	Nil	....	....	4.62	3.29	10-31-88
34◆	1934	Q0.46	4-3-89	2-28	0.92	1.84	1.76	50.5	262	116	9-30-88
35◆	1955	Q0.18	4-1-89	2-27	s0.351	0.72	s0 64	9.61	133	39.1	9-30-88
36◆	....	h[71]....	9-30-88	9-12	....	Nil h[71]	....	5.39	30.7	11.5	12-31-88
37	1939	Q0.10	1-1-89	12-15	0.10	0.40	0.20	0.78	51.2	14.2	12-31-88
38	1988	0.35	2-10-89	1-26	0.35	1.25	1.00	Equity per shr $0.79			9-30-88
39◆	1966	gQ0.18½	3-15-89	2-23	g0.18½	0.74	g0.71½	113	262	85.9	j12-31-87
40	....	None Since Public			....	Nil	....	1.57	4.55	2.50	10-31-88
41◆	1987	Q0.03	1-4-89	12-14	0.03	0.12	0.12	15.1	45.2	19.2	10-31-88
42◆	....	5%Stk	9-11-87	8-26	....	Nil	....	2.20	42.4	26.0	7-31-88
43◆	....	None Since Public			....	Nil	....	Equity per shr $1.57			3-31-88
44	1978	Q0.01½	2-17-89	1-30	0.15	0.06	0.06	3.75	16.1	5.95	10-29-88
45	1984	Q0.02½	2-17-89	1-30	0.02½	0.10	0.10	....	...	...	

Index	Capitalization Lg Trm Debt Mil-$	Shs. 000 Pfd.	Com.	Earnings $ Per Shr. Years End	1984	1985	1986	1987	1988	Last 12 Mos.	Interim Earnings Period	$ per Shr. 1987	1988	Index
1	....	...	19131	Dc	d1.10	d0.17	■d0.89	d0.18	....	jd0.19	9 Mo Sep	d0.06	d0.07	1
2	110	4197	14011	Sp	0.59	d7.01	d9.76	d0.80	d2.04	d1.33	3 Mo Dec	d0.65	0.06	2
3	....	1322	...	Sp	b1.56	bd3.87	bd3.73	b0.61	b0.28	....				3
4	15.3	...	[63]267609	Dc	0.41	0.47	[64]0.72	‡[66]0.53	....	....	9 Mo Sep	n/a	0.42	4
5	82.0	...	120768	Dc	3.41	2.74	2.34	2.65	P2.75	j2.75				5
6	7695	★833	244312	Dc	■1.03	5.11	3.01	■d18.15	P5.35	5.35				6
7	5053	25357	±41626	Dc	*1.24	*2.49	*0.65	d12.58	Pd18.88	d18.88				7
8	111	...	11110	Dc	▲4.06	2.40	d10.51	d7.05	Pd45.93	d45.93				8
9	12.1	...	7501	Dc	0.13	d4.24	d1.91	*0.91	....	2.43	9 Mo Sep	0.08	*△1.60	9
10	1734	[60]77	★55499	Dc	4.04	0.75	■0.02	1.80	P□3.13	3.13				10
11	273	6	8858	My	1.32	1.93	2.26	Nil	△0.44	1.19	6 Mo Nov	△0.10	0.85	11
12	627	5	80212	Dc	▲4.35	d1.59	□0.38	*2.96	P4.05	4.05				12
13	12.0	9275	15189	Dc	d2.13	d1.91	d3.70	d1.01	....	d0.93	9 Mo Sep	d0.33	△d0.25	13
14	....	...	3670	Dc	1.77	1.77	0.82	0.73	P0.70	0.70				14
15	5870	[60]1143	★168850	Dc	4.15	4.35	4.45	4.55	P4.00	4.00				15
16	15.1	2501	p7554	Oc	d2.77	*△0.08	△d0.06	*0.58	1.18	1.13	3 Mo Jan△	0.28	0.23	16
17	....	891	...	Oc	...	...	...	....	b3.53	....				17
18	....	1610	...	Oc	...	...	...	....	b3.53	....				18
19	1932	924	84909	Dc	1.55	△2.99	□2.97	□3.29	P□3.10	3.10				19
20	....	677	...	Dc	b3.76	b1.81	b2.23	b1.95	....	....				20
21	....	247	...	Dc	b3.76	b1.81	b2.23	b1.95	....	....				21
22	10.5	40323	11107	Dc	0.65	0.52	0.08	0.44	P0.70	0.70				22
23	97.5	300	26106	Dc	0.10	d0.05	0.03	0.21	....	0.10	9 Mo Sep	0.19	0.08	23
24	35.1	...	5107	Dc	*d0.17	*d0.20	*d0.22	△0.02	....	0.09	9 Mo Sep	△d0.10	d0.03	24
25	....	...	★8333	Dc	...	...	...	....	§10.24	....				25
26	0.03	...	5782	Sp	d1.42	d0.94	d0.56	d0.16	△Nil	d0.02	3 Mo Dec	0.02	Nil	26
27	6.78	...	16814	Dc	d0.05	d0.05	d0.04	*0.06	P*0.08	0.08				27
28	....	...	★4500	Dc	...	...	...	pd0.05	....	....	9 Mo Sep	n/a	p0.01	28
29	157	...	17261	Dc	0.45	0.67	0.83	1.00	P1.15	1.15				29
30	19.9	...	8770	Dc	...	0.19	0.16	△0.17	P△0.31	0.31				30
31	45.6	...	14678	Je	...	0.00	0.30	0.39	[70]0.52	0.59	6 Mo Dec	0.24	0.31	31
32	....	...	7357	Mr	...	0.09	0.12	0.08	....	0.22	9 Mo Dec	0.04	0.18	32
33	2.03	...	4862	Jl	d0.86	d0.38	*0.02	*0.04	0.08	0.09	3 Mo Oct	0.01	0.02	33
34	40.3	...	16964	Dc	2.51	2.15	2.44	2.88	P3.46	3.46				34
35	38.8	...	p10162	Dc	1.47	1.49	1.17	1.56	P△1.62	1.62				35
36	4.29	...	±5568	Mr	d0.45	d0.94	△0.03	0.38	....	0.45	9 Mo Dec	0.30	△0.37	36
37	14.9	...	±3136	Je	0.88	d0.05	d0.32	*3.43	3.32	1.24	27 Wk Dec	1.87	△d0.21	37
38	0.59	...	3630	Dc	...	...	...	....	P1.29	1.29				38
39	120	121	±148159	Dc	1.04	1.19	*□1.36	1.56	P1.72	1.72				39
40	0.25	...	6350	Ja	0.12	d0.07	d0.04	Nil	....	d0.09	9 Mo Oct	0.05	d0.04	40
41	....	...	5049	Jl	0.96	0.91	1.15	1.46	1.13	1.04	3 Mo Oct	0.34	0.25	41
42	52.5	...	6900	Oc	0.59	d1.71	0.93	△d3.72	Pd2.53	d2.53				42
43	77.4	...	24022	Je	1.78	0.17	d5.16	△[74]d4.34	E0.00	....	6 Mo Dec	n/a	*0.15	43
44	....	...	±2922	Jl	0.41	0.27	0.26	0.22	0.24	0.23	3 Mo Oct	0.13	0.12	44
45	....	...	±442	Jl	0.41	0.27	0.26	0.22	0.24	0.23	3 Mo Oct	0.13	0.12	45

◆**Stock Splits & Divs By Line Reference Index** [1]Adj for 5%,'85. [9]Adj to 5%,'85. [10]2-for-1,'84. [11]Adj to 4%,'88. [12]3-for-1,'87. [16]4-for-3,'87. [19]2-for-1,'87. [27]5-for-4,'85:4-for-3,'85:3-for-2,'86. [29]3-for-2,'85,'86. [30]3-for-2,'88. [31]3-for-2,'88. [32]6-for-5,'88:To split 6-for-5,ex Mar 17. [34]2-for-1,'84. [35]10%,'84,'86:Adj for 5%,'88. [36]Adj to 5%,'88(in Cl'B'). [39]3-for-1,'85. [41]3-for-2,'86. [42]Adj to 5%, Aug'87. [43]3-for-2,'84.

Source: *Standard & Poor's Stock Guide*, March 1989.

2043, then leads you to the cross-listing of companies. These are the companies one would find listed under *2043 Cereal Breakfast Foods:*

Carnation Co.	Kellogg Company
The Clorox Company	Liggett Group Inc.
General Mills, Inc.	Nestlé S.A.
Gerber Products Co.	The Quaker Oats Co.
Iroquois Brands, Ltd.	Ralston Purina Co.

All of these companies make up an industry classification and may be found in the *Corporate Records.* This industry listing can certainly be helpful when trying to put together a list of companies for an industry analysis.

Several other Standard & Poor's publications are quite useful and present concise, thumbnail sketches of companies, common stock variables, and corporate bonds. Figure 4–4 depicts two pages from the *Stock Guide.* This is a monthly publication that enables investors to take a preliminary look at the common and preferred stock of several thousand companies and over 400 mutual funds. The introduction to the *Stock Guide* presents name changes, new exchange listings, common stock rating changes, and a graph of Standard & Poor's Stock Price Indexes.

The *Bond Guide* has the same format as the *Stock Guide.* A monthly publication in booklet form, it presents data on corporate and convertible bonds. Figure 4–5 shows one page on corporate bonds with a long list of Texas–New Mexico Power bonds in the middle. The Standard & Poor's rating is presented along with the bond form (either a coupon or registered bond), call prices, sinking funds, yields, prices, and other information. Figure 4–6 shows one page of convertible bonds from the *Bond Guide.* Looking at the figure, we see convertible bonds having different coupons, interest payment dates, and maturities. Again, the Standard & Poor's rating is given. All the conversion data is presented with bond prices and common stock prices. Can you find how many shares of common stock an investor will receive for each $1,000 bond of Addington Resources?[1]

One of the more popular of Standard & Poor's publications is the *Corporate Reports.* These reports are often mailed out from brokerage houses to customers who want basic information on a company. In Figure 4–7, Texas Instruments provides a good example of what one would expect to find in such reports. This information can be compared to the entry in Figure 4–4, line 12, for Texas Instruments to see the difference in the depth of coverage between the *Corporate Reports* and the *Stock Guide.* The *Corporate Reports* are contained in three separate multiple-volume sets, the New York Stock Exchange Stocks, American Stock Exchange Stocks, and Over-the-Counter and Regional Stocks. Each company is updated quarterly with new earnings, dividends, and recent developments. About 1,020 NYSE stocks are selected and bound in an annual publication called the Standard & Poor's *Stock Market Encyclopedia,* which

---

[1]The answer is 35.71 shares.

FIGURE 4–5   PAGE FROM *STANDARD & POOR'S BOND GUIDE* (Corporate Bonds)

174 TEX-TEX

Standard & Poor's Corporation

The table lists Texas bond issues including Texas Gas Transmission (Cont.), Texas Industries, Texas Instruments, Texas International, Texas & New Orleans RR., Texas-New Mexico Pwr², Texas Oil & Gas, Texas & Pacific Ry., and Texas Power & Light, with columns for Title-Industry Code & Co. Finances, Interest Dates, S&P Debt Rating, Date of Last Rating Change, Prior Rating, Fixed Charge Coverage (1985, 1986, 1987), Year End, Eligible Bond Form, Redemption Provisions (Regular, Sinking Fund, Refund/Other Restriction), Balance Sheet Date, Million $ (Cash & Equiv., Curr. Assets, Curr. Liab.), L. Term Debt, Capitalization, Outst'g, Underwriting Firm Year, Total Debt % Capital, Price Range 1989 (High, Low), Mo. End Price Sale(s) or Bid, Curr. Yield, and Yield to Mat.

Uniform Footnote Explanations–See Page 1. Other: ¹ Incl disc. ² Subsid of TNP Enterprises. ³ Int incr fr 4 ½%,7/1/74. ⁴ Int incr fr 4 ¾%,8/1/74. ⁵ Int incr fr 5 ⅜%,11/1/74.

source: *Standard & Poor's Bond Guide*, February 1989.

FIGURE 4-6 PAGE FROM *STANDARD & POOR'S BOND GUIDE* (Convertible Bonds)

Convertible Bonds

Exchange	Issue, Rate, Interest Dates and Maturity	S&P Debt Rating	B.F.o.o.d.m	Outstg. Mil-$	Conv. Expires	Shares per $1,000 Bond	Price per Share	Div. Income per Bond	1988 Price Range High	1988 Price Range Low	Curr. Bid Sale(a) Ask(A)	Curr. Yield	Yield to Mat.	Stock Value of Bond	Conv. Parity	Stock Data Curr. Price	Stock Data P/E Ratio	Yr. End	1987	1988	Last 12 Mos
Addington Resources	8s Jl 2013	BB	R	40.0	2013	35.71	28.00	8.84	118	99½	118	6.78	6.52	81¼	33	30	12	Dc	p2.12		p2.40
Advest Group	9s Ms15 2010	NR	R	26.5	2010	73.89	13.57		85½	80½	85½	10.53	10.81	61%	11½	8½	18	Sp	1.34	0.32	0.47
Air Wis Services	7¾s Jd15 2010	BBB	R	40.0	2010	57.90	17.27		94	92	94	8.24	8.36	81	16%	14	22	Dc	0.71		1.47
Airborne Freight	7¾s Jd15 2011	BB	R	35.0	2011	36.17	27.65	21.70	100%	96	s96	7.81	7.88	86¼	26½	•22½	10	Dc	0.90		1.01
Alaska Air Gr	7¾s Jd15 2010	BB	R	30.6	2010	35.40	28.25	7.08	97%	94½	97½	7.96	7.92	80½	27%	•22½		Dc	0.85	E2.15	2.02
Alexander & Alex Sv	11s Ao15 2007	A-	R	67.6	2007	25.64	39.00	25.64	105	105	105	10.48	10.38	60½	40%	•23½	16	Dc	1.53		1.46
Alliant Computer Sys	7¾s Mn15 2012	NR	R	50.0	2012	25.16	39.75		44	41	42	17.26	17.74	8¾	16%	3½	d	Dc	0.34		0.88
Allis Inc	8s Ao 1995	NR	R	17.3	1995	53.33	18.75		110	108	110	7.27	6.03	102%	20%	19¾	96	Dc	0.20		0.20
Amer West Airlines	11¾s Jl 2009	NR	R	49.5	2009	95.24	10.50		97	84	97	11.86	11.90	72½	10%	8	d	Dc	d3.85	△Pd0.67	d0.67
Amer West Airlines	7¾s 1A 2010	NR	R	37.4	2010	74.07	13.50		72½	65	72½	10.69	11.14	56¾	9%	8	d	Dc	d3.85	△Pd0.67	d0.67
America West Airlines	7½s Ao 2011	NR	R	36.2	2011	71.43	14.00	36.63	70	62	70	10.71	11.19	54%	9¾	8	d	Dc	d3.85	△Pd0.67	d0.67
Amer Bkrs Ins Gr(''91)	9¾s JD 2004	B	R	35.0	2004	73.26	13.65	127.08	103	103	103	9.47	9.38	87½	14	12	7	Dc	d2.66		1.62
Amer Cap Bd Fd(''Ext)	11.35s Jl 1995	AAA	R	89.6	1995	52.08	19.20		105%	105½	105½	10.76	10.09	105%	20%	•20%	d	Je	d4.08	Pd5.53	d5.53
Amer Century Corp*	7s Ao 1990	NR	R	31.67	1990	76.33	13.09		38	22	s38	18.42	117.30	3%	4%	½		Je	d4.08	Pd5.53	d5.53
7Amer Century Tr*	6¼s Jd15 1991	NR	R	38.41	1991	56.95	17.56		No Sale		22		Flat	2%	3½	•½		Je	d4.08		d5.53
Amer Hoist & Der	5¾s Jd 1993	NR	R	6.21	1993	57.18	17.49		87	84	85	6.47	9.83	77%	14½	•13½	20	Nv	0.90	P0.66	0.66
9Amer Maize-Prod	7¾s Jd15 2001	BBB	R	25.0	2001	186.58	11.55		No Sale		87½	8.55	9.18	79	10%	•8½	6	Dc	±1.11		0.36
Amer Medical Int'l	9½s mN15 2001	BB+	R	92.6	2001	41.02	24.38	29.53	98	94½	s96	9.90	9.90	67%	23%	•16%	17	Au	□1.26	△□1.21	10.95
Amer Medical Int'l	8¼s Ao 2008	BB+	R	48.4	2008	45.00	40.00	18.00	74¼	70	s74	11.15	11.67	41%	23¾	•16%	17	Au	□1.26	△□1.21	10.95
8Amoco Canada Petroleum	7¾s smN8 2013	BBB	R	407	2013	39.52	105.00	36.18	100¼	95½	99	7.45	7.46	74	103%	•77%	d	Je	5.31	P8.01	8.01
Anacomp, Inc¹4	13⅜s Jl15 2002	NR	R	*23.2	2002	57.14	17.50		100%	95½	100%		Flat	37%	17½	•6%	9	Sp	0.47	*0.72	0.72
Anadarko Petroleum	5¾s Ao 2012	BBB+	R	100	2012	30.65	32.63	10.73	100%	95½	s95½	6.02	6.12	76%	31%	•25¼	33	Dc	0.18	P0.76	0.76
Andal¹4Corp¹6	6½s mS15 1997	BBB	R	2.02	1997	44.44	22.50		84		85	14.96	13.40	26%	12%	•5%	d	Au	d0.94	Pd0.16	40.73
Andersen Group	10½s sO15 2002	NR	R	9.95	2002	61.84	16.17		82	82	82	12.80	12.73	44%	13%	7%	7	Fb	4.89		42.73
17Antec Image Tech	5⅝s Ms15 2012	BBB+	R	75.0	2012	16.45	60.80	24.35	95	89	95	6.18	6.29	83%	57¼	•51	d	Dc	3.68	P6.57	6.57
18Anixter Bros	8¾s Jl 2003	NR	R	20.1	2003	Conv into $1020.04			102%	102	102	8.01	8.09	152	22	22	29	Dc	d0.09	E0.75	0.71
Anthony Indus	11¾s 29gd15 2000	NR	R	21.9	2000	120.48	8.30	53.01	148	137	s148	7.60	7.60	76%	12½	•12½	8	Dc	1.08		1.39
Apache Corp	8¼s Mn 2006	B	R	69.0	2006	89.89	11.13	25.17	96	91%	95	8.95	9.08	76%	8½	•8½	d	Dc	d3.55		3.29
Apache Corp	7¼s Ao 2012	B	R	82.7	2012	72.07	13.88	20.18	79½	75%	81	9.26	9.55	61¾	11½	•8½	d	Dc	d3.55		3.29
21Apache Cp²7/Key Cp²³	9s Jl15 2001	B	R	13.0	2001	Cv into Common²⁴			73	72	73	12.33	13.55			•1%	d	Dc	2.13		1.95
Apollo Computer	7¼s Fa 2011	NR	R	115	2011	55.56	18.00		68	64	64	11.33	11.90	43	11½	7¾		Dc	0.60	P△0.01	0.01
Arkansas Best²⁶	7s Ao 2011	NR	R	20.6	2011	Conv into $1002.31			100¼	98	100¼	11.33	13.85	17%	24%	•1%	d	Dc	d1.24		P△0.39
Arrow Electronics	9s 1A 2003	B-	R	30.0	2003	28.74	34.80		74	74	74	12.86	2.25	20¼	34%	•1%	d	Mr	d2.33		24.31
Ashland Oil	4¾s 1A15 1993	A-	R	1.43	1993	59.99	16.67	59.99	79½	75½	s211½	2.25	11.93	30%	11	•35	8	Sp	2.13	△3.29	1.28
AST Research	8¼s Jl15 2013	B	R	50.7	2013	64.52	15.50		72	71¼	71¼	11.93	12.22	50		7%	21	Je	1.13		0.36
Astrex Inc²⁸	9½s mS 2000	NR	R	0.95	2000	68.97	14.50		40	35	35	27.14	29.50	11½	5	•1%	d	Mr	d2.33		2.62
Astrex²⁸Inc¹B²⁸	9½s mS 2000	NR	R	11.6	2000	125.00	8.00		40	35	35	27.14	29.50	20¼	2%	•1%	d	Mr	d2.33		2.62
Atalanta/Scanoff Cap	7⅛s Jd15 2001	NR	R	18.2	2001	56.98	17.55	22.79	No Sale		77	9.25	10.49	30%	13½	•5%	6	Dc	0.87	PD0.78	0.78
Atari Corp²⁹	5¼s ²⁹Apr29 2002	B-	R	75.0	2002	30.65	32.63		No Sale		46	11.41	14.56	16	15	•5%	10	Dc	*0.76		0.54
Atlantic Amer'n	8s Mn15 1997	CCC+	R	30.0	1997	91.41	10.94		59½	59½	59½	13.45	17.41	28½	6½	3½	d	Dc	0.14		0.41
Atlantic Fin'l Fed'l	7½s Ao15 2011	NR	R	36.8	2011	50.00	20.00	14.00	56	52	53	14.62	15.17	19%	10½	3%	2	Sp	0.19	*1.57	1.57
Audiotronics Corp	10¼s ³¹Qdc31 2002	NR	R	5.37	2002	320.00	3.13		33½	33	33%	14.29	29.29	21%	1	•%	d	Je	0.25	d1.33	1.45
Autodie Corp	7s Mn 2011	NR	R	29.1	2011	28.88	34.63		65	65	65%	10.69	11.26	41%	22%	14%	16	Au	0.04	P△0.52	10.86
Automatic Data Proc	6½s Ms 2011	A+	R	150	2011	23.96	41.73	12.46	109¾	105¾	s107½	6.05	5.89	95%	44%	•40½	17	Je	1.76	2.20	2.33
Avalon Corp³²	7s Fa15 1992	NR	R	5.82	1992	40.00	25.00		87		87		Flat	24½	21¼	•6¼	d	Dc	△0.02		0.43

Uniform Footnote Explanations—See Page 224. Other: ¹ (HRO)On 12-1-91 at 110. ² Rating(BBB-)has been suspended. ³ Incl disc. ⁴ (HRO)On 1-1-90. ⁵ Int thru 12-31-89,adj aft as defined.
⁶ Was Amer Century Mtg Inv. ⁷ Now Amer Century Corp:was Amer Century Mtg Inv. ⁸ Int of 12-15-88 to be pd 2-17-89. ⁹ Into Amer Century Corp Com. ¹⁰ Data of American Fructose
¹¹ Exch'ble for American Fructose Cl'A'com. ¹² Subsid & data of Amoco Corp. ¹³ Into Amoco Corp com. ¹⁴ Int¹-1-15-84,pd 3-21-84:7-15-84,pd 8-15-84. ¹⁵ Was Nat'l Kinney.
¹⁷ Conv into & data of Int'l Paper. ¹⁸ Into Int'l Paper com. ¹⁹ Subsid & data of Itel Corp. ²⁰ Due Jan 31. ²¹ Data of Apache Corp. ²² Oblig jointly of Key Corp & Apache Petroleum L.P.
²⁴ Into Apache & data of Int'l Paper. ²⁵ Acquired by Kelso & Co.L.P. ²⁶ (HRO)On ea Sep 1,1990-2 at 100. ²⁷ Co may pay int in cash/com. ²⁸ Hldrs opt to redeem on chge of ctrl,as defined.
²⁹ Offered outside U.S. ³⁰ Int pd annually Apr 29. ³¹ Due 4-21-2002. ³² Was Tri-South(Mtg)Inv.

FIGURE 4–7   SAMPLE PAGES, *STANDARD & POOR'S CORPORATE REPORTS*

Texas Instruments

2208

NYSE Symbol TXN   Options on CBOE (Jan-Apr-Jul-Oct)   In S&P 500

Price	Range	P-E Ratio	Dividend	Yield	S&P Ranking	Beta
Oct. 11'88 40½	1988 60-37½	12	0.72	1.8%	B+	1.49

Summary

Texas Instruments is one of the world's largest producers of semiconductors. It also derives over half of its revenues from defense electronics, computers, terminals and calculators. A 40% interest is held in a seismic services company. Despite sharply lower royalty income, which totaled $191 million in 1987, earnings are projected to rise sharply in 1988 due largely to strong sales of semiconductors. Further progress is likely in 1989 as well.

Current Outlook

Earnings for 1989 should approximate $5.00 a share, up from the $4.25 estimated for 1988.

The $0.18 quarterly dividend is likely to be increased in 1988.

Sales for 1989 are likely to increase close to 10%. The gain should be led by defense electronics operations, which are experiencing an increase in orders and backlog despite the slowing of defense spending generally. Components are also expected to have higher sales, although the rate of growth will be far below the extremely strong increase projected for 1988 due to a slowing of the industry's expansion. Digital products should benefit from new product introductions. Margins are expected to continue to benefit from the higher volume, aggressive cost reductions and reduced losses at the digital products segment. Somewhat restraining will be a decline in royalty income.

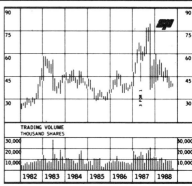

TRADING VOLUME
THOUSAND SHARES

Net Sales (Million $)

Quarter:	1988	1987	1986	1985
Mar.	1,467	1,272	1,145	1,288
Jun.	1,558	1,372	1,244	1,237
Sep.	---	1,416	1,249	1,191
Dec.	---	1,535	1,336	1,209
	---	5,595	4,974	4,924

Sales for the six months ended June 30, 1988 rose 14%, year to year, primarily because of major increases in semiconductors and defense electronics. Margins widened substantially, and operating income rose 125%. Following a 40% decline in other income, pretax income advanced 21%. After taxes at 28.8%, versus 24.0%, net income increased 13%, to $1.97 a share from $1.90 (restated).

Common Share Earnings ($)

Quarter:	1988	1987	1986	1985
Mar.	0.95	0.92	d0.18	0.12
Jun.	1.02	0.56	0.12	d0.05
Sep.	E1.00	0.63	0.14	d1.10
Dec.	E1.28	0.85	0.30	d0.55
	E4.25	2.96	0.38	d1.59

Important Developments

Jul. '88—TXN said that its higher margins in the first half principally resulted from improvement in the components segment. Profits in the defense electronics segment remained essentially unchanged despite a $14 million charge. Digital products operated at a loss.

Next earnings report expected in late October.

Per Share Data ($)

Yr. End Dec. 31[1]	1987	1986	1985	1984	1983	1982	1981	1980	1979	1978
Book Value	21.95	18.60	18.91	20.86	16.69	19.18	17.81	16.69	13.92	12.37
Earnings[1]	2.96	0.38	d1.59	4.35	d2.03	2.03	1.54	2.53	2.53	2.05
Dividends	0.70⅝	0.66¾	0.66¾	0.66¾	0.66¾	0.66¾	0.66¾	0.66¾	0.66¾	0.58¾
Payout Ratio	23%	180%	NM	16%	NM	33%	43%	22%	26%	29%
Prices—High	80¼	49½	43⅞	49⅞	58¾	50⅞	42⅛	50¼	33¾	30⅞
Low	36¼	34¼	28¾	37¼	33¾	23½	25	26¼	26	20½
P/E Ratio—	27-12	NM	NM	11-9	NM	25-12	27-16	16-9	13-10	15-10

Data as orig. reptd. Adj. for stk. div(s). of 200% Jun. 1987. 1. Bef. spec. item(s) of +0.63 in 1987, −0.14 in 1986. NM-Not Meaningful. d-Deficit. E-Estimated.

October 19, 1988

Standard & Poor's Corp.
25 Broadway, NY, NY 10004

FIGURE 4–7   (*concluded*)

2208   Texas Instruments Incorporated

Income Data (Million $)

Year Ended Dec. 31	Revs.	Oper. Inc.	% Oper. Inc. of Revs.	Cap. Exp.	Depr.	Int. Exp.	Net Bef. Taxes	Eff. Tax Rate	²Net Inc.	% Net Inc. of Revs.
1987	5,594	597	10.7%	¹463	380	33.4	415	38.1%	257	4.6%
1986	4,974	528	10.6%	447	426	38.2	99	59.6%	40	0.8%
1985	4,924	488	9.9%	515	516	55.0	d115	NM	d119	NM
1984	5,742	948	16.5%	722	423	48.9	487	35.0%	316	5.5%
1983	4,580	63	1.4%	479	351	36.0	d323	NM	d145	NM
1982	4,327	574	13.3%	342	339	33.1	213	32.4%	144	3.3%
1981	4,206	586	13.9%	350	333	41.3	175	38.0%	109	2.6%
1980	4,075	676	16.6%	548	257	44.3	379	44.0%	212	5.2%
1979	3,224	507	15.7%	435	187	19.5	309	44.0%	173	5.4%
1978	2,550	385	15.1%	311	131	8.4	257	45.5%	140	5.5%

Balance Sheet Data (Million $)

Dec. 31	Cash	Current Assets	Current Liab.	Ratio	Total Assets	Ret. on Assets	Long Term Debt	Common Equity	Total Cap.	% LT Debt of Cap.	Ret. on Equity
1987	663	2,563	1,247	2.1	4,256	6.7%	487	1,726	2,733	17.8%	14.8%
1986	214	1,781	1,113	1.6	3,337	1.2%	191	1,727	1,919	10.0%	1.8%
1985	159	1,531	1,129	1.4	3,076	NM	382	1,428	1,810	21.1%	NM
1984	274	1,858	1,412	1.3	3,423	10.2%	381	1,541	1,921	19.8%	22.8%
1983	185	1,452	1,231	1.2	2,713	NM	225	1,203	1,428	15.8%	NM
1982	420	1,527	959	1.6	2,631	5.8%	214	1,361	1,575	13.6%	11.0%
1981	150	1,197	765	1.6	2,311	4.6%	212	1,260	1,472	14.4%	8.9%
1980	140	1,299	971	1.3	2,414	9.7%	212	1,165	1,376	15.4%	19.9%
1979	117	1,083	882	1.2	1,908	10.1%	18	953	970	1.8%	19.2%
1978	115	915	637	1.4	1,518	10.1%	19	845	864	2.2%	17.7%

Data as orig. reptd. 1. Net of curr. yr. retirement and disposals. 2. Bef. spec. item(s) in 1986. NM-Not Meaningful. d-Deficit.

Business Summary

Texas Instruments produces a variety of electrical and electronics products for industrial, consumer and government markets. Contributions (profits in million $) by industry segment in 1987:

	Sales	Profits
Components	42%	$346
Defense electronics	35%	212
Digital products	16%	−28
Metallurgical materials	3%	10
Services	4%	−10

Foreign sales accounted for 40% of revenues and 35% of operating income in 1987. Sales to the U.S. Government were 25% of the total.

Components include semiconductor integrated circuits, semiconductor discrete devices, assembled modules, and electrical and electronic control devices.

Defense electronics products include radar infrared surveillance systems and missile guidance and control systems.

Digital products include minicomputers, electronic data terminals and peripherals, geophysical and scientific equipment, electronic calculators, learning aids and other products.

Metallurgical materials primarily involve clad metals which are used in variety of applications.

Services (40%-owned since February, 1988) are petroleum-exploration related.

Dividend Data

Dividends have been paid since 1962. A "poison pill" stock purchase right was adopted in 1988.

Amt. of Divd. $	Date Decl.	Ex-divd. Date	Stock of Record	Payment Date
0.18	Nov. 20	Dec. 24	Dec. 31	Jan. 25'88
0.18	Mar. 18	Mar. 23	Mar. 29	Apr. 25'88
0.18	Jun. 17	Jun. 24	Jun. 30	Jul. 25'88
0.18	Sep. 16	Sep. 21	Sep. 27	Oct. 24'88

Next dividend meeting: late Nov. '88.

Capitalization

Long Term Debt: $630,400,000.

Market Auction Pref. Stk.: 3,000 shs.

Conv. Money Market Cum. Pfd. Stk.: 2,208 shs. in 3 series.

Common Stock: 79,760,187 shs. ($1 par). Institutions hold approximately 74%. Shareholders of record: 32,914.

Office—13500 North Central Expressway, Dallas, Texas 75265. Tel—(214) 995-3773. Pres & Chrmn—J. R. Junkins. VP-Secy—R. J. Agnich. CFO & Treas—W. A. Aylesworth. Investor Contact—M. Poet. Dirs—B. M. Farber, G. W. Fronterhouse, D. C. Garrett, Jr., J. R. Junkins, E. R. Kane, D. M. Roderick, M. Shepherd, Jr., J. C. Toomay, J. M. Voss, W. P. Weber. Transfer Agents & Registrars—First RepublicBank Dallas; Morgan Shareholder Services Trust Co., NYC. Incorporated in Delaware in 1938. Empl—75,347.

Information has been obtained from sources believed to be reliable, but its accuracy and completeness are not guaranteed.   Paul H. Valentine, CFA

Source: *Standard & Poor's Corporate Reports,* October 19, 1988.

contains end-of-the-year *Corporate Reports*. To develop an appreciation for the other Standard & Poor's services, try perusing this material at your library.

Value Line

Value Line Investment Survey, a publication of Arnold Bernhard & Co., is one of the most widely used investment services by individuals, stockbrokers, and small bank trust departments. The *Value Line Investment Survey* follows 1,700 companies, and each common stock is covered in a one-page summary (see the one for Texas Instruments in Figure 4–8). Value Line is noted for its comprehensive coverage, which can be seen by comparing Figure 4–8 to Figures 4–4 and 4–7. Raw financial data is available as well as trendline growth rates, price history patterns in graphic form, quarterly sales, earnings and dividends, and a breakdown of sales and profit margins by line of business. Value Line contains 13 sections divided into several industries each. The first few pages beginning an industry classification are devoted to an overview of the industry, with the company summaries following. Each section is revised on a 13-week cycle.

Value Line has a unique evaluation system that is primarily dependent on historical relationships and regression analysis. From the valuation model, each company is rated 1 through 5, with 1 being the highest positive rating and 5 the lowest. Each company is rated on timeliness and safety. It should be noted that Value Line minimizes human judgment in making its evaluation.

Other Investment Services

Dun & Bradstreet publishes *Key Business Ratios* in bound form. This publication contains 14 significant ratios on 800 different lines of business listed by SIC (standard industrial classification) code. Examples of ratios included are current assets to current debt, net profits on net sales, and total debt to tangible net worth. This publication has replaced the old Dun & Bradstreet 11-page pamphlet on key business ratios for 125 lines of business. Another good source of ratios is Robert Morris Associates, which provides ratios on over 150 industry classifications.

Dun's Marketing Services division of Dun & Bradstreet also publishes the *Million Dollar Directory* and *Billion Dollar Directory*. Companies are listed in alphabetical order, by geographical location, and by product classification. The data provide names, addresses, phone numbers, and sales for each company. This could be helpful in identifying companies in the same industry or in writing to request such information as annual reports or product lists.

Another publication is the *Dow Jones-Irwin Business Almanac*. Almost everyone has looked through an almanac at some time and probably remembers being overwhelmed by all the facts and figures. This almanac is no exception. For our specific purposes, a section on finance and accounting covers key business ratios, financial statement ratios by industry, and corporate profits and margins. A section on the stock market covers over 100 pages and includes market averages, mutual funds, dividends, common stock prices and yields,

FIGURE 4–8   THE VALUE LINE INVESTMENT SURVEY

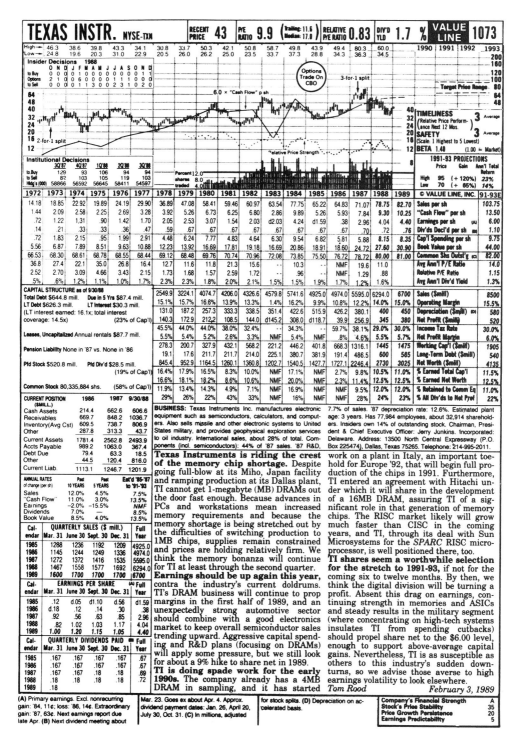

and much more. Information on commodities, banks, financial institutions, economic data, and a great deal more is contained in this 700-page business almanac.

Wiesenberger Services, Inc., publishes one of the best-known sources of information on mutual funds. The annual issue covers a 10-year statistical history (a sample page appears in Chapter 19). Another publication which is like an investment service is the annual issue of *The Individual Investor's Guide to No-Load Mutual Funds* published by the American Association of Individual Investors.

Retail stockbrokers have long provided information to their clients. Of course, the more you can afford to pay and the bigger your account, the more research you may receive. Most large brokers, such as Merrill Lynch; Shearson Lehman Hutton; Prudential-Bache; and Dean Witter Reynolds, will provide investors information free or perhaps for a fee. You name what you want, and they have it—industry-company analysis, bond market analysis, futures and commodities, options advice, tax shelters in oil and gas and real estate, and so on. The brokerage industry provides much more sophisticated coverage of investments outside of stocks and bonds than they have in the past. This is partly because investors themselves have become more sophisticated and partly because of the increasing numbers and complexity of alternative investments.

INDEXES, SEC FILINGS, PERIODICALS, AND JOURNALS

Indexes

One way to find relevant articles in periodicals and journals is to use indexes. Many will lead an analyst to useful information. The *Business Periodicals Index* references subjects in approximately 170 periodicals in the fields of accounting, advertising, banking, communications, economics, finance, insurance, investments, labor management, marketing, taxation, and other specific topics. The *Funk and Scott Index of Corporations and Industries* indexes articles from over 750 publications in two volumes. Each article covered includes a brief description of the article's contents. The articles are taken from business, financial, and trade magazines, major newspapers, bank newsletters, and investment advisory services. One very popular index is *The Wall Street Journal Index,* which identifies the date, page, and column of articles appearing in *The Wall Street Journal.* The index is presented in two parts—corporate news and general news. Many libraries have several years of *The Wall Street Journal* on microfiche or microfilm. Among the many other indexes are *Who's Who in Finance and Industry,* Dun & Bradstreet's *Reference Book of Corporate Management,* and Standard & Poor's *Register of Corporations, Directors and Executives.* These last three focus on people and can provide important qualitative information about management.

FIGURE 4–9 SECURITIES AND EXCHANGE COMMISSION FILINGS

REPORT CONTENTS	10-K	19-K 20-F	10-Q	8-K	10-C	6-K	Proxy Statement	Prospects	Registration Statements '34 Act F-10 8-A 8-B	'33 Act "S" Type	ARS	Listing Application	N-1R	N-1Q
Auditor														
Name	A	A	▨				▨	A	A		A	▨	A	
Opinion	A	A							A		A		A	
Changes				A		▨								
Compensation Plans														
Equity	▨		▨				F	F	A	F		▨	▨	
Monetary							F	A		F				
Company Information														
Nature of Business	A	A				F		A	A		A	▨		
History	F	A						A		A				
Organization and Change	F	F		A	▨	F	▨	A	F	A	▨			
Debt Structure	A					F	▨	A	A	A	A		A	
Depreciation & Other Schedules	A	A				F		A	A	A				
Dilution Factors	A	A	F			F		A	A	A	A			
Directors, Officers, Insiders														
Identification	F	A				F	A	A	A	A	F			
Background	▨	A				F	F	A	▨	A	▨			
Holdings	▨	A		▨			A	A	A	A				
Compensation	▨	A		▨			A	A	A	A				
Earnings Per Share	A	A	A			F		A		A	A		A	
Financial Information														
Annual Audited	A	A						A		A	A		A	
Interim Audited		A					▨		▨					
Interim Unaudited	▨		A	▨		F		F		F	F			
Foreign Operations	A						▨	A	A	A	▨	F		
Labor Contracts		▨	▨						F	F				
Legal Agreements	F	▨	▨						F	F				
Legal Counsel			▨					A		A		▨		
Loan Agreements	F		F	▨			▨		F	F			▨	
Plants and Properties	A	F	▨					F	A	F	▨			
Portfolio Operations														
Content (Listing of Securities)														A
Management												A		
Product-Line Breakout	A							A		A	▨			
Securities Structure	A	A			▨			A	A	A				
Subsidiaries	A	A				▨		A	A	A	▨			
Underwriting			▨					A	A	A				
Unregistered Securities	▨		▨				▨	F		F				
Block Movements	▨			F			▨		A			▨		

TENDER OFFER ACQUISITION REPORTS	13D	13G	14D-1	14D-9	13E-3	13E-4
Name of Issuer (Subject Company)	A	A	A	A	A	A
Filing Person (or Company)	A	A	A	A	A	A
Amount of Shares Owned	A	A				
Percent of Class Outstanding	A	A				
Financial Statements of Bidders			F		F	F
Purpose of Tender Offer			A	A	A	A
Source and Amount of Funds	A		A		A	
Identity and Background Information			A	A	A	
Persons Retained, Employed or to be Compensated			A	A	A	A
Exhibits	F		F	F	F	F

Legend   **A**-always included-included-if occurred or significant   **F**-frequently included

▨-special circumstances only

Source: *A Guide to SEC Corporate Filings* (Bethesda, Md.: Disclosure, Inc., April 1983), pp. 12–13.

Securities and Exchange Commission Filings

As discussed in Chapter 2, the Securities and Exchange Commission (SEC) was established by the Securities Exchange Act of 1934 and has the power to regulate trading on the exchanges and to require corporate disclosure of information relevant to the stockholders of publicly traded companies. The SEC even has the power to dictate accounting conventions.

Information available through the SEC consists primarily of corporate income statements, balance sheets, detailed support of accounting information, and internal data not always found in a company's annual report. There are specific reports that companies are required to file with the SEC. The annual 10-K report is perhaps the most widely known and can usually be obtained free of charge directly from the company rather than paying the SEC a copying charge. This report should be read in combination with the firm's annual report as it contains the same type of information but in greater detail. The 8-K report must be filed when the corporation undergoes some important event that stockholders would be interested in knowing about such as changes in control, bankruptcy, resignation of officers or directors, and other material events. 10-Q statements are filed quarterly no later than 45 days after the end of the quarter. This report includes quarterly financial statements, changes in stockholdings, legal proceedings, and other matters.

There are many other SEC reports. The most common are proxy statements that disclose information relevant to stockholders' votes; a prospectus which must be issued whenever a new offering of securities is made to the public; and a registration trading statement which is normally required for new issues by firms trading on an organized exchange or over-the-counter. Figure 4–9 presents a detailed listing of information available from SEC filings, including reports required for tender offers and acquisitions. This table is taken from Disclosure, Inc., a firm providing on-line computer access to SEC filings and other information sources to subscribers. These reports can be obtained from the Disclosure retrieval system with a one-business-day turnaround, or they can be ordered from the Securities and Exchange Commission with a seven-business-day turnaround. They can also be read at the SEC regional office, where the corporation is headquartered, or in the SEC's regional New York, Chicago, or Los Angeles offices.

Periodicals and Newspapers

After using the *Business Periodical Index,* an investor will most likely be referred to several of the most-popular business periodicals such as *Fortune, Business Week, Forbes, Dun's Business Month,* and *Financial World. Fortune* is published biweekly and is known for its coverage of industry problems and specific company analysis. *Fortune* has several regular features that make interesting reading. One, "Business Roundup," usually deals with a major business concern such as the federal budget, inflation, or productivity. Another feature,

"Personal Investing," is always a thought-provoking article presenting ideas and analysis for the average investor.

Forbes is also a biweekly publication featuring several company-management interviews. This management-oriented approach points out various management styles and provides a look into the qualitative factors of security analysis. Several regular columnists discuss investment topics from a diversified perspective. *Business Week* is somewhat more general in nature than *Forbes*. It includes a weekly economic update on such economic variables as interest rates, electricity consumption, and market prices while also featuring articles on industries and companies. Many other periodicals, such as *The Harvard Business Review* and *Money* magazine, are helpful to the financial manager or personal investor. Unfortunately, space limits describing very many.

Newspapers in most major cities (Chicago, Dallas, and Cleveland, to name a few) have good financial sections. *The New York Times* has an exceptional financial page. However, the most widely circulated financial daily is *The Wall Street Journal*, published by Dow Jones. It is read by millions of investors who want to keep up with the economy and business environment. Feature articles on labor, business, economics, personal investing, technology, and taxes appear regularly. Corporate announcements of all kinds are published. Figure 4–10, "Digest of Earnings Reports," is a daily feature that updates quarterly and annual earnings of firms.

New offerings of stocks and bonds are also advertised by investment bankers in the *Journal*. Prices of actively traded securities are presented by the market in which they trade. Common and preferred stock prices are organized by exchange and over-the-counter markets. Figure 4–11 is an example of common and preferred stock prices on the New York Stock Exchange.

Many other prices are printed in *The Wall Street Journal*. An investor will find prices of government Treasury bills, notes, and bonds, mutual funds, put and call prices from the option exchanges, government agency securities, foreign exchange prices, and commodities future prices. Figure 4–12 is an example of the commodity future prices from the *Journal*. The prices are listed by category and exchange. Because of the comprehensive price coverage on a daily basis and other features, it is hard to believe that an up-to-date intelligent investor would be able to function without *The Wall Street Journal*. Each fall *The Wall Street Journal* publishes an educational edition which explains how to read *The Wall Street Journal* and interpret some of the data presented.

Barron's National Business and Financial Weekly, also published by Dow Jones (every Monday), contains regular features on dividends, put and call options, international stock markets, commodities, a review of the stock market, and many pages of prices and financial statistics. *Barron's* takes a weekly perspective and summarizes the previous week's market behavior. It also has regular analyses of several companies in its section called "Investment News and Views." The common stock section of *Barron's* not only provides weekly high-low-close prices and volume, but also informs investors as to the latest earnings per share, dividends declared, and dividend record and payable dates. This can be seen in the middle portion of Figure 4–13.

One unique feature of *Barron's* is the "Market Laboratory" covering the last

FIGURE 4–10   *THE WALL STREET JOURNAL* "DIGEST OF EARNINGS REPORTS"

ABBREVIATIONS

A partial list of frequently used abbreviations: Net Inv Inc (net Investment Income); Loss dis op (Loss from discontinued operations); Inco cnt op (Income from continuing operations.)

COLLINS INDUSTRIES INC. (A)

Year Oct 31:	1988	a1987
Sales	$120,061,000	$96,003,000
Inco cnt op	625,000	1,229,000
Loss dis op	1,768,000	604,000
Loss	1,143,000	c625,000
Extrd cred		489,000
Net loss	1,143,000	c1,114,000
Shr earns:		
Inco cnt op ..	.18	.33
Loss	....	c.17
Net loss	....	c.30
Quarter:		
Sales	33,087,000	26,197,000
Loss cnt op	237,000	c300,000
Loss dis op	196,000	186,000
Loss	433,000	c114,000
Extrd cred		149,000
Net loss	433,000	c263,000
Shr earns:		
Loss cnt op .	....	c.08
Loss	....	c.03
Net loss	....	c.07

a-Restated to reflect discontinued operations. c-Income.

DATAMETRICS CORP. (A)

Year Oct 29:	1988	1987
Revenues	$29,460,762	$24,063,539
Income	1,482,181	809,728
aExtrd	576,000	...,000
N...	2,058,1..	

Net income	..	.1.
Shr earns (fully diluted):		
Income	.06	.05
Net income ..	.06	.10

a-Tax benefit from tax-loss carry-forwards.

DRESSER INDUSTRIES INC. (N)

Year Oct 31:	a1988	1987
Revenues ..	$3,941,700,000	$3,119,700,000
Inco cnt op ..	122,800,000	16,300,000
Inco dis op ..	22,700,000	26,700,000
Income	145,500,000	43,000,000
cExtrd cred	11,300,000	5,900,000
bNet income	156,800,000	48,900,000
Avg shares .	69,100,000	75,300,000
Shr earns:		
Inco cnt op	1.78	.22
Income	2.11	.57
Net income	2.27	.65
Quarter:		
Revenues ...	973,200,000	865,100,000
Inco cnt op	60,900,000	23,100,000
Inco dis op ..	....	b10,500,000
Income	60,900,000	33,600,000
Extrd item .	d14,600,000	c4,800,000
bNet income	46,300,000	38,400,000
Avg shares .	67,200,000	73,700,000
Shr earns:		
Inco cnt op ..	.89	.30
Income	.90	.44
Net income .	.69	.51

a-Includes the results of M.W. Kellogg Co., acquired in January 1988. b-Includes gains related to the settlement of pension liabilities of $13,600,000 in the year and $10,700,000 the quarter of 1988 and $88,900,000 and $25,600,000, respectively, in the like periods of 1987. Also, the 1987 year end includes a net gain of $6,600,000 from the sale of real estate. c-Credit; tax benefit from tax-loss carry-forwards. d-Charge; reversal of tax-loss carry-forwards.

EATON VANCE CORP. (O)

Year Oct 31:	1988	1987
Net income	$10,740,948	$11,550,297
Avg shares	3,915,295	4,275,902
Shr earns:		
Net income .	2.74	2.70
Qtuarter:		
Net income	1,797,783	2,643,572
Avg shares	3,668,945	4,263,826
Shr earns:		
Net income .	.49	.62

GOLDEN ENTERPRISES INC (O)

Quar Nov 30:	1988	1987
Revenues	$29,584,482	$30,152,801
Net income	1,109,424	1,413,302
Avg shares	12,801,800	13,053,334
Shr earns:		
Net income .	.09	.11
6 months:		
Revenues	61,313,962	61,206,297
Income	3,149,327	2,714,919
Acctg adj		a1,025,000
Net income ...	3,149,327	3,739,919
Avg shares	12,828,565	13,067,438
Shr earns:		
Income	.25	.21
Net income .	.25	.29

a-Credit; cumulative effect of an accounting change for income taxes.

HARDING ASSOCIATES INC. (O)

Quar Nov 30:	1988	1987
Revenues	$13,032,412	$9,199,562
Net income	824,320	500,102
Avg shares	2,903,740	2,918,130
Shr earns:		
Net income .	.28	.17
6 months:		
Revenues	24,985,841	18,722,82..
Income	...893,108	1,31...
Acctg ad...		

...nths:		.37
Revenues	262,800,000	223,100,000
Net income ...	14,520,000	13,294,000
Shr earns:		
Net income	1.38	1.25

ICO INC (O)

Year Sept 30:	1988	1987
Revenues	$40,178,000	$29,220,000
Loss	2,425,000	7,378,000
Extrd cred	a11,795,000	
Net income	9,370,000	d7,378,000
Shr earns:		
Net income .	1.22	....

a-From gain on debt restructure. d-Loss.

INTERNAT'L MULTIFOODS (N)

Quar Nov 30:	1988	1987
Sales	$508,451,000	$462,078,000
Net income	11,303,000	10,616,000
Shr earns:		
Net income .	.78	.73
9 months:		
Sales	1,394,618,000	1,245,556,000
Net income .	28,102,000	25,246,000
Shr earns:		
Net income	1.93	1.73

LA QUINTA MOTOR INNS INC. (N)

Quar Nov 30:	1988	1987
Revenues	$45,245,000	$42,063,000
Net income ...	528,000	d699,000
Shr earns:		
Net income .	.04	....
6 months:		
Revenues	99,737,000	92,590,000
Net income ...	5,421,000	3,586,000
Shr earns:		
Net income .	42	.26

d-Loss.

MACHINE TECHNOLOGY (O)

Quar Dec 4:	1988	1987
Sales	$5,979,087	$6,433,101
Income	92,426	27,505
aExtrd cred	48,000	14,000
Net income	140,426	41,505
Shr earns:		
Income	.02	.01
Net income .	.03	.01

a-Tax benefit from tax-loss carry-forwards.

MICROPRO INTERNATONAL (O)

Quar Nov 30:	1988	1987
Revenues	$9,656,000	$10,278,000
Net loss	2,607,000	c9,000

c-Income.

MOOG INC. (A)

^ Year Sep 30:	1988	1987
Sales	$296,889,000	$307,069,000
Loss cnt op	16,426,000	c9,211,000
aLoss dis op ..	197,000	c2,620,000
Loss	16,623,000	c11,831,000
Acctg adj	b2,740,000	....
Net loss	13,883,000	c11,831,000
Shr earns:		
Loss cnt op ..	....	c1.03
Loss	....	c1.33
Net loss	....	c1.33

a-Includes loss of $197,000 in 1988 and gain of $3,330,000 in 1987 from sale of discontinued operations. b-Credit; cumulative effect on prior periods of an accounting change. c-Income.

POSEIDON POOLS OF AMER (O)

Year Aug 31:	1988	1987
Sales	$30,826,897	$24,801,013
Income	354,820	1,074,941
Extrd cred		a49,500
Net income	354,820	1,124,441
Avg shares	2,394,100	1,255,700
Shr earns:		
...ncome .		.15

ST... ...LANNI...

Quar ...ov 30:	1988	1987
Revenues	$9,578,329	$13,227,153
Net loss	1,606,437	c1,351,124
Shr earns:		
Net loss	....	a.26

a-Income; adjusted for a four-for-three stock split paid in August 1988. c-Income.

TCA CABLE TV INC. (O)

Year Oct 31:	1988	1987
Revenues	$68,580,000	$60,397,000
Net income	9,573,000	5,070,000
Shr earns:		
Net income .	.79	.46
Quarter:		
Revenues	18,143,000	15,897,000
Net income	3,304,000	1,115,000
Shr earns:		
Net income .	.27	.09

VWR CORP. (O)

Quar Nov 30:	1988	1987
Sales	$155,892,000	$143,633,000
Net income	2,352,000	1,972,000
Shr earns:		
Net income .	.43	.36
9 months:		
Sales	467,770,000	419,247,000
Income	6,053,000	5,992,000
Acctg adi		a570,000
Net income	6,053,000	6,562,000
Shr earns:		
Income	1.10	1.07
Net income .	1.10	1.17

a-Credit; cumulative effect on prior periods of an accounting change.

(N) New York Stock Exchange (A) American Exchange (O) Over-the-Counter (Pa) Pacific (M) Midwest (P) Philadelphia (B) Boston (T) Toronto (Mo) Montreal (F) Foreign.

Source: *The Wall Street Journal*, December 23, 1988, p. C6. Reprinted by permission of *The Wall Street Journal*, © Dow Jones & Company, Inc., 1988. All rights reserved.

FIGURE 4–11 NEW YORK STOCK EXCHANGE COMPOSITE TRANSACTIONS (Common Stock Prices)

Quotations as of 4:30 p.m. Eastern Time
Thursday, December 22, 1988

52 Weeks Hi	Lo	Stock	Sym	Div	Yld %	PE	Vol 100s	Hi	Lo	Close	Net Chg
		—A—A—A—									
27⅞	16⅝	AAR	AIR	.44	1.8	17	69	24¾	24⅜	24¾	+ ¼
n 10⅛	8⅜	ACM OppFd	AOF	1.01	11.4	...	598	9	8⅜	8⅞	+ ⅛
12⅛	10⅜	ACM Gvt Fd	ACG	1.26a	12.0	...	1517	10⅝	10⅜	10½	...
n↓ 10⅛	9⅜	ACM MgdIncFd	AMF	.08e	.9	...	211	9¼	9	9¼	− ⅛
nx 12⅛	10¼	ACM SecFd	GSF	1.26	12.3	...	x1596	10⅜	10¼	10¼	− ⅛
n 10⅛	8½	ACM SpctmFd	SI	1.01a	11.5	...	1232	8¾	8½	8¾	
5⅜	2⅝	AMCA	AIL	12e	3.7	...	23	3⅜	3¼	3¼	+ ⅛
6⅛	3⅜	AM Int	AM		...	...	1112	4⅞	4⅝	4⅞	+ ¼
23¼	18⅛	AM Int pf		2.00	9.3	...	41	21⅝	21½	21½	...
55	32⅝	AMR	AMR		...	9	4229	52¼	51½	52	−1
24⅜	20⅝	ANR pf		2.12	9.0	...	1	23½	23½	23½	+ ⅛
9½	5⅜	ARX	ARX		...	10	353	6	5¾	5¾	− ¼
51¾	35¼	ASA	ASA	3.00a	7.9	...	472	38⅛	37⅝	37¾	− ⅛
20¼	12¾	AVX	AVX	18e	1.1	12	140	16⅞	16⅝	16⅞	+ ⅛
52⅜	42⅞	AbbotLab	ABT	1.20	2.6	15	3145	47¼	46½	46⅝	− ¾
21¾	15⅜	Abitibi g	ABY	1.00	...	...	64	15¾	15⅝	15¾	...
13⅞	7½	AcmeCleve	AMT	.40	4.6	...	433	8⅞	8¾	8¾	...
8⅞	5⅞	AcmeElec	ACE	.32b	5.1	27	14	6¼	6⅛	6¼	...
29½	15¾	Acuson	ACN		...	24	392	25¾	25½	25½	− ⅛
17	14½	AdamsExp	ADX	1.82e	12.3	...	121	14⅞	14¾	14¾	...
16⅞	7⅛	AdvMicro	AMD		...	16	4055	8⅝	8¼	8⅜	
43½	28¾	AdvMicro pf		3.00	10.1	...	30	30⅛	29½	29¾	− ⅛
8½	4⅞	AdobeRes	ADB		...	...	167	6¾	6⅝	6⅝	− ⅛
18½	16¼	AdobeRes pf		1.84	10.7	...	13	17¼	17¼	17¼	− ¼
21¾	19¼	AdobeRes pf		2.40	11.9	...	15	20½	20¼	20¼	− ⅜
9¾	5⅞	Advest	ADV	.12	1.7	23	252	7½	7¼	7¼	...
52½	39½	AetnaLife	AET	2.76	5.8	8	2641	47¾	46¾	47½	+ ¾
s 35¾	24	AffilPub	AFP	.22	.6	...	388	34⅜	34	34⅛	− ⅛
18⅝	13¾	Ahmanson	AHM	.88	5.7	9	890	15⅝	15⅜	15½	− ⅛
4⅝	1⅞	Aileen	AEE		...	...	1030	3⅝	3¼	3⅜	− ⅛
53⅜	36½	AirProduct	APD	1.20	3.0	10	1831	40¾	40⅜	40½	+ ¼
22¼	12¾	AirbornFrght	ABF	.60	2.8	21	536	21½	20½	21¼	...
16¾	9⅜	Airgas	ARG		...	16	6	14⅞	14⅞	14⅞	− ⅛
20	14½	Airlease	FLY	2.40	12.2	9	70	20	19⅝	19⅝	− ⅛
26⅝	22½	AlaPwr pf		2.10e	9.0	...	6	23⅜	23⅜	23⅜	− ⅛
9¾	8½	AlaPwr pf		.87	9.7	...	22	9⅛	8⅞	9	...
97	89	AlaPwr pf		9.00	9.7	...	z150	93	92	93	...
22½	13¼	AlaskaAir	ALK	.20	1.0	10	909	20⅝	20¼	20½	− ⅛
19¾	11	AlbanyInt	AIN	.25	1.6	11	864	16	15¾	15¾	− ¼
38¼	19⅜	AlbertoCl	ACV	.30	.8	18	77	36⅜	36⅛	36⅛	...
28¼	14¾	AlbertoCl A	ACVA	.30	1.1	13	11	26¼	26	26¼	+ ⅛
38¾	24	Albertsons	ABS	.56	1.5	16	536	38	37	37⅞	−1
s 33⅜	23½	Alcan	AL	1.20	3.7	7	4130	32¼	31⅞	32¼	+ ⅜
27⅞	20⅛	AlcoStd	ASN	.76	2.8	12	1496	27	26¾	26⅞	+ ⅛
28⅛	17⅜	Alex&Alex	AAL	1.00	4.2	16	632	24	23¾	24	+ ⅛
77	39½	Alexanders	ALX		...	94	14	68¼	67¾	67¾	− ¾
76⅛	67⅞	AlleghanyCp	Y		...	10	77	71	70½	71	+ ½
6⅞	1½	vjAllegInt	AG		...	...	907	1¾	1½	1⅝	+ ⅛
10⅜	2	vjAllegInt pr			...	...	26	3⅝	3⅜	3⅝	+ ¼
35⅞	7½	vjAllegInt pf			...	...	18	11¼	11	11	− ⅜
32¾	19	AllegL		1.00a	3.3	7	1174	30	29⅝		
41½	35⅞				8.3	10	1243	37¾			

52 Weeks Hi	Lo	Stock	Sym	Div	Yld %	PE	Vol 100s	Hi	Lo	Close	Net Chg
2⅜	⅛	vjBasix	BAS		...	...	473	9/32	15/64	¼	...
19¼	12⅞	BattleMtn	BMG	.10	.7	14	1096	14¼	14	14	...
48	31¾	BauschLomb	BOL	1.00	2.3	14	1351	42⅞	42¼	42¾	+ ⅜
26⅛	16¼	BaxterInt	BAX	.50	2.8	14	7309	17⅝	17⅜	17⅝	+ ⅛
49	37⅛	BaxterInt pf		3.67e	9.4	...	71	39	38½	39	+ ⅝
83	56¾	BaxterInt pf		3.50	6.0	...	747	58⅝	58	58¼	+ ¼
19¾	10¼	BayFnl	BAY	.05j	...	...	14	11¾	11⅝	11¾	...
26	19¾	BayStGas	BGC	1.68	6.6	10	143	25⅝	25⅛	25⅝	+ ⅜
15⅜	10	BearStearns	BSC	.50	4.0	8	895	12¾	12⅜	12⅜	− ¼
41⅞	23½	BearingsInc	BER	.80	2.3	13	31	35½	35¼	35½	...
n 19	17⅝	BeckmanInstr	BEC		...	...	76	17⅞	17¾	17¾	+ ⅛
62⅛	46½	BectonDksn	BDX	1.00	1.9	14	1034	51¾	51	51¾	...
40	20¼	BeldenHem	BHY	.52	1.7	12	7	30⅛	30	30⅛	+ ¼
74½	62¼	BellAtlantic	BEL	4.08	5.7	11	24497	72⅝	71¾	71¾	− ¾
16⅛	12⅛	BellIndus	BI	.28	1.9	15	47	15¼	15	15⅛	+ ⅛
43⅞	35⅛	BellSouth	BLS	2.36	5.9	12	2739	40½	40	40	− ½
32	22⅜	Belo AH	BLC	.44	1.9	28	88	23½	22⅞	22⅞	− ⅝
s 25½	16	Bemis	BMS	.44	1.9	16	84	22¾	22½	22⅝	...
53¾	34⅛	Beneficial	BNL	2.00	4.6	9	1126	44⅝	43½	43¾	− ¾
45	38½	Beneficial pf		4.30	10.6	...	10	40¾	40½	40½	− ¾
4⅝	3	Benguet B	BE	.19r	4.9	5	102	4	3¾	3⅞	− ⅛
4½	⅜	vjBerkey	BKY		...	...	95	7/16	7/16	7/16	...
5050	2755	BerkHathwy	BRK		...	181	z230	4800	4675	4700	−50
15⅝	6⅝	BestBuy	BBY		...	40	198	8⅞	8⅝	8⅞	+ ⅛
25½	15¼	BethSteel	BS		...	5	4041	22⅝	22	22½	+ ¼
55¼	40⅛	BethSteel pf		5.00	9.8	...	23	51⅛	50⅞	51	...
27½	20⅜	BethSteel pf		2.50	10.0	...	73	25	24⅞	25	+ ⅛
8	3¾	BeverlyEnt	BEV	.05j	...	...	3551	5⅜	5	5⅜	+ ⅛
20⅜	9¾	BeverlyInv	BIP	1.98e	17.2	8	328	11⅝	11⅛	11½	+ ¼
21⅜	7½	BiocraftLabs	BCL		...	14	229	8	7¾	7¾	− ⅛
s 25	12¾	BirmghamStl	BIR	.30	1.3	8	582	23⅜	22¾	23⅛	− ⅛
24¾	16½	BlackDeck	BDK	.40	1.8	14	1318	23	22⅝	22⅝	− ⅜
28¼	21⅝	BlackHills	BKH	1.40	5.7	10	69	24¾	24½	24¾	+ ¼
n 10⅛	9⅛	BlackstnIncTr	BKT	1.10	11.6	...	2082	9⅝	9¼	9½	+ ¼
n↓ 10⅛	9¾	BlackstnTgt	BTT	.08e	.8	...	1917	9⅞	9⅝	9⅝	− ⅛
34⅜	22¾	BlockHR	HRB	1.04	3.7	17	473	28¼	27⅝	28⅛	+ ⅛
n 22¾	14⅝	BlueArrow	BAW	.14e	.9	...	543	15⅝	15	15⅝	+ ¼
6½	5⅛	BlueChipFd	BLU	.19e	3.2	...	218	6	5⅞	5⅞	− ⅛
67⅝	36⅞	Boeing	BA	1.60	2.7	16	13100	59⅝	58⅝	59⅛	+ ⅝
50	36	BoiseCasc	BCC	1.40	3.5	7	920	39¾	39⅜	39½	− ⅛
↓ 19⅜	10⅜	BoltBerNew	BBN	.06	.6	12	2138	10⅝	9⅞	10½	...
n 11¾	6¾	BondIntGold	BIG		...	...	370	7	6¾	7	...
4⅛	1⅛	BondIntGold wt			...	...	182	1⅜	1¼	1⅜	+ ¼
20⅛	10⅞	BordChm pr		2.46e	13.8	...	1070	17⅞	17⅝	17⅞	+ ¼
n↑ 17⅛	17	BordChm	BCU		...	...	1077	17¼	17⅛	17¼	+ ⅛
61⅛	47⅛	BordenInc	BN	1.56	2.7	14	1282	58⅛	57¾	58	− ⅛
25¾	7¾	Bormans	BRF	.05j	...	...	196	25¼	25	25⅛	...
15¾	11⅜	BostCelts	BOS	1.60e	11.4	9	44	14	13¾	14	+ ⅛
19¼	12½	BostEdsn	BSE	1.82	11.2	10	784	16⅝	16¼	16¼	− ¼
92	82	BostEdsn pf		8.88	10.6	...	z1210	84¾	84	84	− ½
15⅞	13¾	BostEdsn pf		1.46	10.2	...	4	14⅜	14⅜	14⅜	...
36⅞	25¼	Bowater	BOW	1.12	4.2	7	1442	26¾	26⅛	26¾	+ ⅝
n 14¼	7⅜	BrazilFd	BZF		...	...	1235	8¼	7¾	8⅛	+ ⅜
36	24¼	BriggsStrat	BGG	1.60			227	27¼	26⅞	27⅛	+ ⅛
41½	38⅛	BristMyrs	BMY						45⅜	45½	− ¼
	43¾	BritAir							29¼	29¼	

52 Weeks Hi	Lo	Stock	Sym	Div	Yld %	PE	Vol 100s	Hi	Lo	Close	Net Chg
17⅞	13¼	CRI InsMtgII	CII	3.21e	23.1	8	32	13⅞	13¾	13⅞	+ ⅛
n 19	13⅞	CRI InsMtgIII	CTH	1.60	10.8	10	132	15	14½	14⅞	+ ¼
s 26½	10⅝	CRS Sirr	CRX	.24	.9	18	7	26	25¾	25¾	− ¼
32½	24⅜	CSX	CSX	1.24	3.9	58	1511	31¾	31⅝	31¾	+ ⅛
27⅜	17½	CTS	CTS	.50	2.3	9	152	22	22	22	...
14½	9½	C3 Inc	CEE		...	14	491	12⅞	12⅝	12⅞	− ⅛
41¾	29⅛	Cabot Cp	CBT	.92	2.5	16	237	36¾	36½	36¾	− ⅛
32⅜	18⅜	CaesarWld	CAW		...	11	1463	31⅞	30⅞	30⅞	− ⅞
8¼	6⅛	CalFedInco	CFI	1.00	15.4	...	410	6⅝	6⅜	6½	+ ⅛
29	20⅝	CalFed	CAL	1.40	6.4	4	634	22	21⅝	21¾	...
6⅜	4⅛	CalifREIT	CT	.40	7.0	...	23	5¾	5¾	5¾	− ⅛
24¼	14¼	CallahnMng	CMN	.20	1.4	...	151	14⅜	14¼	14¼	− ⅛
46⅛	24⅜	CalMat	CZM	.48	1.7	15	396	28¾	27⅞	28	− ½
6⅞	2⅜	Calton Inc	CN		...	5	462	3	2⅞	3	...
18½	10	Cammiron	CIW	.04	.3	...	776	15	14¾	14⅞	...
49¾	35⅞	Cammiron pf		3.50	8.4	...	98	41¾	41½	41½	+ ¼
1⅞	⅝	CampblRes g	CCH		...	...	687	11/16	⅝	11/16	+ 1/16
35¼	23⅞	CampblSoup	CPB	.92	2.9	17	527	32	31½	31⅞	− ⅛
20⅛	15⅜	CdnPac g	CP	.76	4.3	...	2663	17⅞	17¾	17⅞	+ ⅛
9⅛	4⅜	Canal Cap	COW		...	...	75	5⅜	5¼	5⅜	+ ⅜
10¾	8½	Canal Cap pf		1.30	15.1	...	13	8⅝	8⅝	8⅝	+ ⅛
5⅛	3	CannonGp	CAN		...	...	104	4⅜	4⅛	4⅛	− ⅛
369¾	297	CapCities	CCB	.20	.1	17	125	357	356	356	...
34	25⅝	CapHldg	CPH	1.00	3.1	11	346	33	32½	32½	− ⅛
s 15⅝	6¾	Careercom	PTA		...	14	1186	9¼	9⅛	9¼	+ ⅛
37⅝	26¼	Carlisle	CSL	1.16	3.6	11	84	32¾	32¼	32⅝	+ ¼
11	5⅞	CarolcoPic	CRC		...	8	241	7⅛	7	7⅛	+ ⅛
2	15/16	CarolcoPic wt			...	...	40	1⅛	1⅛	1⅛	+ ⅛
30⅝	18	CarolFrght	CAO	.54	2.3	27	803	24	23⅝	24	+ ¼
36⅞	31⅞	CarolPwr	CPL	2.84	7.8	16	544	36⅝	36⅜	36⅝	...
51¼	40	CarpTech	CRS	2.10	4.7	14	91	45⅛	44½	45	+ ½
6¼	3½	Carriage	CGE	.10	2.0	9	112	5⅜	5⅛	5⅛	− ⅛
16½	7¼	CarsonPirie	CRN	.10	.8	67	203	12⅛	12	12	...
12½	7¾	CarterHaw	CHH		...	9	440	7⅞	7¾	7⅞	...
43¼	30¼	CarterWal	CAR	.68	1.7	15	269	40⅜	40	40	− ¼
16¼	13½	CascadeNG	CGC	1.28	8.6	11	75	15	14⅝	14⅞	+ ⅛
29⅜	17	CastlCook	CKE		...	13	478	27⅜	26¾	26¾	− ½
68½	53⅞	Caterpillar	CAT	1.20	1.9	11	1230	63⅞	63¼	63⅜	− ½
10¼	7⅝	CedarFair	FUN	1.08	10.5	10	176	10¼	10	10¼	+ ⅛
52¼	34¼	Centel	CNT	1.84	3.7	14	712	50⅝	50⅛	50⅛	− ⅛
18	12¼	CentrEngy	CX	1.60	12.3	6	10519	13⅛	12¾	13	+ ⅛
29½	16½	Centex	CTX	.25	.9	14	870	26⅞	26⅝	26⅝	− ¼
34¾	28⅞	CentlSoWest	CSR	2.44	7.9	8	767	31¼	30⅞	31	− ⅛
21¾	16½	CentlHudGE	CNH	1.76	8.2	8	190	21¾	21½	21½	− ⅛
23½	19⅞	CentlIIIPS	CIP	1.76	8.1	9	290	22	21⅝	21¾	− ¼
33⅞	30	CentlLaElec	CNL	2.32	7.2	9	80	32¼	32	32¼	+ ¼
18⅝	14⅞	CentlMePwr	CTP	1.52	8.2	8	449	18½	18⅜	18½	...
26	21⅛	CentlVtPS	CV	1.98	8.3	8	76	23¾	23⅝	23¾	− ⅛
s 29½	12¾	CenturyTel	CTL	.60	2.1	24	375	29½	29¼	29¼	− ⅛
20⅜	14½	CenvillInv	CVI	2.00	12.5	7	1347	16	15¾	16	+ ⅛
38⅛	29½	ChampInt	CHA	1.00	3.2	7	2360	31½	30⅞	31⅜	+ ⅜
14⅞	10⅝	ChampSpk	CHM	.20	1.5	40	219	13⅞	13½	13¾	+ ¼
n 15⅝	10¼	ChaparlStl	CSM	.05e	.4	9	193	12⅜	11⅞	12⅜	+ ⅜
5¼	3½	Charter	CHR	.05e	1.3	2	175				+ ⅛
			CMB	2.16	7.6	3					
				5.25	10.7						

52 Weeks Hi	Lo	Stock	Sym	Div	Yld %	PE	Vol 100s	Hi	Lo	Close	Net Chg
s 10	6¼	ClayHomes	CMH		...	9	98	8	7⅞	8	+ ⅛
8¼	5½	ClemteGlob	CLM		...	...	64	7	6¾	6¾	− ⅛
28⅝	11¾	CleveCliff	CLF		...	6	344	27	26⅛	26¼	− ¼
76⅜	64¾	CleveElec pf		7.40	11.4	...	z150	65¼	65	65	− ¼
↓ 76	66	CleveElec pf		7.56	11.5	...	z3750	68¾	65½	65½	− 3½
33¾	26⅛	Clorox	CLX	1.04	3.3	13	300	31½	31¼	31¼	− ¼
16⅝	10¼	ClubMed	CMI	.20	1.5	18	91	13	12⅞	13	...
13⅝	6⅝	Coachmen	COA	.40	4.5	32	225	9	8¾	8⅞	− ⅛
22	13⅞	CoastS&L	CSA	.40	2.8	4	303	14¾	14½	14½	− ¼
35½	23⅜	Coastal	CGP	.40	1.1	16	1519	35¼	34½	35	+ ⅜
45¼	35	CocaCola	KO	1.20	2.7	16	3589	44⅝	44¼	44⅜	...
16¾	12⅝	CocaColaEnt	CCE	.05	.3	20	736	14¾	14⅜	14⅝	+ ⅛
4⅝	1	vjColeco	CLO		...	...	306	1¼	1⅛	1¼	+ ⅛
41½	31	Coleman	CLN	1.20	3.1	11	71	38¾	38⅛	38½	+ ¼
49½	37½	ColgatePalm	CL	1.48a	3.3	13	943	45½	45⅛	45¼	− ⅛
17⅜	10½	CollinsFds	CF	.16	1.0	14	246	16¾	16⅜	16½	− ¼
n 10	8¾	ColonHigh	CIF	.35e	3.9	...	334	9⅛	8¾	8⅞	...
9⅞	8⅛	ColonMuni	CMU	.79	8.1	...	527	9¾	9⅝	9¾	+ ⅛
44¾	26⅞	ColumGas	CG	2.00	5.8	17	335	34½	34⅛	34¼	...
12½	6¾	ColumbiaPic	KPE		...	...	1136	11⅛	10⅞	10⅞	− ¼
9⅝	6	ColumSL	CSV	.28	4.2	...	262	6⅞	6⅝	6⅝	− ⅛
9⅝	6⅛	ColumSL pf			...	...	41	7	6⅞	7	+ ⅛
29	27⅜	ColumSoPwr pf		3.45	12.3	...	9	28⅛	27¾	28⅛	+ ⅝
26½	24	ColumSoPwr pf		2.42	9.9	...	10	24½	24⅜	24½	+ ⅜
37½	25¾	CombustEngr	CSP	1.00	3.6	...	1097	28	27¼	27½	− ½
24⅞	17	Comdisco	CDO	.24	1.2	48	838	19⅞	19⅛	19⅝	− ⅛
31½	17½	CommercMtls	CMC	.44	1.7	9	92	26	25¼	25¾	+ ¾
13¾	6¾	CommodoreInt	CBU		...	8	739	12⅞	12⅜	12⅞	+ ⅜
↑ 32¾	22¾	ComwEd	CWE	3.00	9.1	9	46759	33⅜	31¼	33	+ ¾
↑ 32⅞	23¾	ComwEd pf		1.42	4.3	...	2	33⅜	33⅜	33⅜	+1
20¼	17⅜	ComwEd pr		1.90	9.9	...	24	19½	19¼	19¼	...
21¼	18⅜	ComwEd pr		2.00	9.9	...	5	20½	20¼	20¼	− ¼
92	87¼	ComwEd pfB		8.40	9.4	...	z100	89½	88½	89½	...
85½	75⅞	ComwEd pf		8.38	10.2	...	z2850	82⅜	82⅜	82⅜	+ ⅜
26	23¾	ComwEd pr		2.37	9.3	...	42	25½	24⅞	25½	+ ⅝
27¼	25¼	ComwEd pf		2.87	10.8	...	33	26¾	26⅝	26⅝	− ⅛
85	76	ComwEd pf		8.40	10.2	...	z750	82¾	82¼	82¾	− ¼
73½	65¼	ComwEd pr		7.24	10.2	...	z800	70¾	70	70¾	+ ¾
33	26½	ComwEngy	CES	2.80	9.0	10	50	31¼	31	31⅛	+ ¼
5⅝	1⅜	ComwMtg	CMA	1.10	38.3	...	814	2⅞	2½	2⅞	+ ⅛
30¾	25⅛	Comsat	CQ	1.32	5.0	9	254	26⅝	26⅛	26⅜	+ ¼
26⅛	19	CmuntyPsych	CMY	.36	1.5	16	1351	23¾	23¼	23¼	...
65¾	42	Compaq	CPQ		...	11	3277	60¾	60	60	− ⅞
12¼	6½	ComprehnCr	CMP	.40	4.9	10	361	8⅜	8	8⅛	− ⅛
32¾	23⅞	CptrAssoc	CA		...	21	4105	32⅜	31⅞	32	+ ⅛
17⅛	10	CptrFactry	CFA		...	10	1560	12⅛	11⅝	12	+ ⅜
55⅞	38	CptrSci	CSC		...	16	319	47⅞	47¼	47⅜	+ ⅛
17¼	9⅜	CptrTask	TSK	.05	.4	18	92	14⅜	14⅛	14¼	...
n 10⅛	8⅞	ComstockPtr	CPF	.49e	5.4	...	2357	9⅛	8⅞	9	+ ⅛
34	23¾	ConAgra	CAG	.77	2.7	13	3137	28⅞	28½	28¾	+ ⅛
22⅞	19⅞	ConnEngy	CNE	1.76	8.5	10	12	21	20¾	20¾	...
18¼	15¾	ConnNatGas	CTG	1.36	8.2	12	87	17	16½	16⅝	− ¼
14½	8⅝	Conseco	CNC	.20	1.7	3	34	12	11¾	11¾	− ⅜
24½	16⅛	Conseco					63	18¾	18¼	18⅜	− ⅛
47½	40⅞	Co						46⅜	46⅛	46⅜	+
54½									49¾	50	

Source: (Figures 4–11 and 4–12); *The Wall Street Journal,* December 23, 1988, pp. C3 and C12. Reprinted by permission of *The Wall Street Journal,* © Dow Jones & Company, Inc., 1988. All rights reserved.

FIGURE 4–12 COMMODITY FUTURES PRICES

Thursday, December 22, 1988

Open Interest Reflects Previous Trading Day.

GRAINS AND OILSEEDS

CORN (CBT) 5,000 bu.; cents per bu.

	Open	High	Low	Settle	Change	Lifetime High	Lifetime Low	Open Interest
Mar	284½	286½	283	283¼	– 1½	370	193½	132,311
May	291	291½	288½	289½	– ¼	369	207½	41,781
July	293½	294½	291½	292¼	– ¼	360	233	26,482
Sept	277¼	279	276	278½	+ 2½	317¾	245	5,558
Dec	270½	272¾	269	272¾	+ 1¾	295	234	21,074
Mr90	274½	278¼	274½	278¼	+ 2¼	278¼	257½	357

Est vol 35,000; vol Wed 40,047; open int 227,581, +2,537.

OATS (CBT) 5,000 bu.; cents per bu.

	Open	High	Low	Settle	Change	Lifetime High	Lifetime Low	Open Interest
Mar	232¾	232¾	229¼	232	– ½	367¾	161	5,442
May	234¼	234½	231	233	– 1	340	187	1,587
July	230½	231	226½	229¼	– 1	277	201½	1,744
Sept	228¾	229	226½	227¾	– 1¼	231½	200	430

Est vol 1,000; vol Wed 1,769; open int 9,203, –7.

SOYBEANS (CBT) 5,000 bu.; cents per bu.

	Open	High	Low	Settle	Change	Lifetime High	Lifetime Low	Open Interest
Jan	798	798½	791½	792¼	– 3¼	1034	553	24,011
Mar	812	814	806	806½	– 3½	1023	579	45,453
May	822½	824	817	818¼	– 2¼	1003	647	18,769
July	824	828	820	822	– ½	986	685	14,999
Aug	814	814	809	810	– 1	951	725	2,488
Sept	757	764	756	763	+ 6¼	835	701	3,266
Nov	721	725	716	724½	+ 6¾	793	663	12,378
Ja90	732	732	726½	734	+ 8½	748	684	727

Est vol 32,000; vol Wed 61,780; open int 122,170, +2,468.

SOYBEAN MEAL (CBT) 100 tons; $ per ton.

	Open	High	Low	Settle	Change	Lifetime High	Lifetime Low	Open Interest
Jan	256.50	257.00	255.00	255.10	– .60	313.00	177.00	14,867
Mar	258.00	259.00	256.50	256.60	– .60	308.00	193.50	35,140
May	257.00	257.30	255.00	255.20	....	304.00	200.50	9,522
July	253.50	253.50	251.00	252.10	+ .90	300.00	221.00	5,106
Aug	243.50	246.00	242.50	244.50	+ 3.50	298.00	217.50	1,474
Sept	229.00	232.00	228.00	231.50	...	290.00	214.00	1,755
Oct	217.00	217.00	214.50	216.00	– .20	237.00	203.00	1,658
Dec	214.00	214.30	211.50	212.70	+ 1.00	270.00	199.50	1,491

Est vol 14,000; vol Wed 23,520; open int 71,013, +569.

SOYBEAN OIL (CBT) 60,000 lbs.; cents per lb.

	Open	High	Low	Settle	Change	Lifetime High	Lifetime Low	Open Interest
Jan	23.46	23.77	23.42	23.53	– .03	33.95	20.75	11,965
Mar	24.12	24.29	23.93	24.06	– .06	33.60	21.25	34,094
May	24.65	24.80	24.45	24.61	– .01	33.00	22.45	12,350
July	25.18	25.30	24.95	25.07	+ .02	32.50	22.85	6,855
Aug	25.15	25.15	25.05	25.15	+ .03	32.05	23.15	2,262
Sept	25.35	25.42	25.05	25.15	– .02	28.70	23.30	1,575
Oct	25.38	25.38	25.10	25.25	....	26.95	23.30	2,067
Dec	25.40	25.40	25.10	25.30	....	28.05	22.80	2,613

Est vol 17,000; vol Wed 16,320; open int 73,813, +469.

WHEAT (CBT) 5,000 bu.; cents per bu.

	Open	High	Low	Settle	Change	Lifetime High	Lifetime Low	Open Interest
Mar	439	439½	436	438¾	....	442	323	34,744
May	429	429¾	426¼	427¾	– 1½	430	330	7,859
July	395	395	392	395	+ 1½	395½	327	20,096
Sept	398	399	397	398½	+ 1	399	350½	1,900
Dec	405	407¾	405	407¾	+ 1¼	407¾	378	632

Est vol 8,000; vol Wed 11,757; open int 65,374, +381.

WHEAT (KC) 5,000 bu.; cents per bu.

	Open	High	Low	Settle	Change	Lifetime High	Lifetime Low	Open Interest
Mar	429	430	427	429½	+ 1¾	434	322¾	25,522
May	422½	423½	420¼	422½	+ 1¼	423½	324	2,552
July	395½	396½	394½	395½	+ ½	396½	331	3,498
Sept	398	400	398	399	+ ½	400	353	423

Est vol 4,473; vol Wed 4,866; open int 32,007, +445.

WHEAT (MPLS) 5,000 bu.; cents per bu.

	Open	High	Low	Settle	Change	Lifetime High	Lifetime Low	Open Interest
Mar	411½	413	409	412¼	+ 1¾	472	347	4,666
May	412	414	410½	414	+ 2¼	428	399	916
July	402	407	402	407	+ 4	411	380	205
Sept	396	397½	396	396½	+ 1½	405	388	234

Est vol 1,388; vol Wed 1,388; open int 6,021, +131.

BARLEY (WPG) 20 metric tons; Can. $ per ton

	Open	High	Low	Settle	Change	Lifetime High	Lifetime Low	Open Interest
Dec	128.50	129.70	128.50	129.30	+ 1.40	135.70	78.90	218
Mr89	134.00	135.20	134.00	134.80	+ 1.00	142.00	105.00	14,957
May	138.70	139.00	138.70	138.70	+ .80	148.50	125.50	3,272
July	141.50	142.00	141.50	141.50	+ .50	147.00	132.60	2,837
Oct	133.80	133.90	133.80	133.90	+ .90	140.00	124.00	934

Est vol 1,455; vol Wed 2,225; open int 22,218, +526.

FLAXSEED (WPG) 20 metric tons; Can. $ per ton

	Open	High	Low	Settle	Change	Lifetime High	Lifetime Low	Open Interest
Dec	401.00	401.50	400.50	401.50	+ 4.00	482.00	242.10	342
Mr89	404.00	406.00	402.50	405.70	+ 1.50	485.00	266.00	4,024
May	403.50	406.00	402.00	405.50	+ 2.30	490.00	366.50	1,758
July	....	....	....	403.00	+ 4.00	492.00	368.00	379
Oct	362.00	362.00	361.00	361.00	....	394.50	345.00	446
Dec	361.00	361.50	360.10	360.10	+ .10	434.00	342.50	538

Est vol 460; vol Wed 587; open int 7,487, –6.

RAPESEED (WPG) 20 metric tons; Can. $ per ton

	Open	High	Low	Settle	Change	Lifetime High	Lifetime Low	Open Interest
Jan	353.00	355.50	352.70	355.00	+ 2.00	486.70	291.80	8,317
Mar	356.70	359.00	356.40	358.30	+ 1.60	489.50	300.70	12,676
June	366.00	367.50	365.10	366.10	+ 1.00	490.00	339.30	4,740
Sept	....	....	....	375.70	+ 1.00	390.50	349.00	1,744
Nov	378.00	380.00	377.50	378.40	+ .80	482.00	261.80	2,530

Est vol 1,370; vol Wed 3,236; open int 30,007, +257.

WHEAT (WPG) 20 metric tons; Can. $ per ton

	Open	High	Low	Settle	Change	Lifetime High	Lifetime Low	Open Interest
Dec	158.00	158.00	157.90	157.90	+ 1.20	167.00	94.00	278
Mr89	162.00	163.50	162.00	162.90	+ 1.20	170.50	103.50	8,853
May	161.50	162.00	161.40	161.50	+ .50	168.50	135.50	3,861
July	159.50	160.50	159.40	160.00	+ .70	166.50	144.30	990
Oct	....	....	....	153.00	+ .10	152.00	149.00	423

Est vol 1,595; vol Wed 262; open int 14,405, –13.

RYE (WPG) 20 metric tons; Can. $ per ton

	Open	High	Low	Settle	Change	Lifetime High	Lifetime Low	Open Interest
Dec	....	....	....	151.40	....	194.50	140.00	5
Mr89	156.80	157.50	156.80	157.50	....	178.00	149.90	1,360
May	....	....	....	158.70	....	171.50	156.00	606
July	....	....	....	161.00	....	164.00	157.50	156

Est vol 25; vol Wed 46; open int 2,127, +27.

LIVESTOCK & MEAT

CATTLE–FEEDER (CME) 44,000 lbs.; cents per lb.

	Open	High	Low	Settle	Change	Lifetime High	Lifetime Low	Open Interest
Jan	84.07	84.07	83.55	83.90	– .27	85.05	74.00	3,993
Mar	83.30	83.40	83.00	83.32	– .15	83.85	74.00	5,600
Apr	82.65	82.70	82.40	82.70	– .07	82.90	74.40	1,546
May	81.32	81.60	81.15	81.50	+ .07	81.80	76.00	1,368
Aug	80.25	80.25	79.90	80.25	+ .05	80.25	77.50	557

Est vol 1,571; vol Wed 1,480; open int 13,223, +125.

CATTLE–LIVE (CME) 40,000 lbs.; cents per lb.

	Open	High	Low	Settle	Change	Lifetime High	Lifetime Low	Open Interest
Feb	73.65	73.95	73.55	73.90	+ .10	75.60	65.10	34,369
Apr	75.20	75.32	74.90	75.30	– .02	76.47	67.20	24,561
June	73.80	73.85	73.55	73.72	– .15	75.20	68.75	7,078
Aug	71.25	71.35	71.00	71.32	– .02	73.20	69.35	7,451
Oct	70.35	70.50	70.35	70.35	– .12	74.00	68.60	1,896

Est vol 12,192; vol Wed 15,588; open int 75,429, +448.

HOGS (CME) 30,000 lbs.; cents per lb.

	Open	High	Low	Settle	Change	Lifetime High	Lifetime Low	Open Interest
Feb	46.25	46.65	46.12	46.57	+ .15	52.00	41.80	16,028
Apr	45.00	45.40	44.95	45.37	+ .17	51.65	40.60	8,469
June	49.20	49.42	49.10	49.20	– .25	56.25	42.50	2,487
July	49.50	49.65	49.15	49.47	– .17	56.00	46.10	2,304
Aug	49.00	49.10	48.70	49.00	– .02	51.00	45.05	676
Oct	45.20	45.40	45.20	45.30	– .07	47.00	42.30	419

Est vol 3,265; vol Wed 5,007; open int 30,441, –286.

PORK BELLIES (CME) 40,000 lbs.; cents per lb.

	Open	High	Low	Settle	Change	Lifetime High	Lifetime Low	Open Interest
Feb	43.90	44.50	43.50	44.07	– 1.10	67.00	41.80	9,476
Mar	44.50	45.00	44.02	44.65	– 1.10	66.35	42.50	3,746
May	46.50	46.65	45.65	46.32	– 1.00	65.50	44.25	2,414
July	47.75	47.95	47.05	47.47	– .97	64.50	45.50	3,239
Aug	47.25	47.35	46.27	46.40	– 1.25	58.25	44.52	776

Est vol 4,332; vol Wed2,622; open int 19,667, +62.

FOOD & FIBER

COCOA (CSCE) – 10 metric tons; $ per ton.

	Open	High	Low	Settle	Change	Lifetime High	Lifetime Low	Open Interest
Mar	1,510	1,518	1,485	1,500	– 16	2,088	1,125	16,331
May	1,490	1,502	1,480	1,489	– 8	2,088	1,152	7,898
July	1,497	1,500	1,480	1,491	– 5	1,985	1,172	3,784
Sept	1,496	1,498	1,493	1,495	– 5	1,850	1,206	1,601
Dec	1,493	1,504	1,493	1,495	– 13	1,735	1,240	4,511
Mr90	1,512	1,512	1,512	1,500	– 21	1,535	1,305	2,554
May	....	....	....	1,515	– 21	....	....	0

Est vol 3,613; vol Wed7,868; open int 36,879, –553.

COFFEE (CSCE) – 37,500 lbs.; cents per lb.

	Open	High	Low	Settle	Change	Lifetime High	Lifetime Low	Open Interest
Mar	149.50	154.00	149.00	149.39	– 6.55	159.00	112.44	13,019
May	151.50	151.50	146.50	147.12	– 6.38	158.00	112.13	5,480
July	150.00	150.50	146.25	146.50	– 5.75	154.39	114.00	2,145
Sept	148.00	149.50	145.33	145.63	– 5.70	152.30	114.00	970
Dec	147.00	147.00	143.50	144.50	– 5.00	148.50	118.00	183

Est vol 6,080; vol Wed10,271; open int 21,801, +640.

SUGAR–WORLD (CSCE) – 112,000 lbs.; cents per lb.

	Open	High	Low	Settle	Change	Lifetime High	Lifetime Low	Open Interest
Jan	9.25	9.25	9.25	7.75	– .13	15.00	7.50	30
Mar	10.98	11.28	10.95	11.09	+ .03	14.39	7.66	80,948
May	10.78	11.05	10.76	10.84	....	13.64	7.87	37,376
July	10.54	10.76	10.54	10.56	– .04	13.40	8.10	9,311
Oct	10.32	10.55	10.30	10.32	– .04	13.30	8.45	14,644
Mr90	10.10	10.15	10.10	10.08	– .09	10.62	8.75	1,494

Est vol 15,912; vol Wed11,124; open int 143,809, +608.

SUGAR–DOMESTIC (CSCE) – 112,000 lbs.; cents per lb.

	Open	High	Low	Settle	Change	Lifetime High	Lifetime Low	Open Interest
Mar	21.87	21.90	21.83	21.85	– .02	22.50	20.98	1,845
May	21.99	21.99	21.99	21.99	+ .01	22.60	21.80	2,066
July	22.20	22.20	22.20	22.20	+ .03	22.60	21.80	1,569
Sept	....	....	....	22.23	+ .03	22.60	21.95	1,586
Nov	....	....	....	22.04	+ .09	22.50	21.62	327

Est vol 126; vol Wed 199; open int 7,402, +64.

COTTON (CTN) – 50,000 lbs.; cents per lb.

	Open	High	Low	Settle	Change	Lifetime High	Lifetime Low	Open Interest
Mar	58.90	59.28	58.82	59.25	– .03	68.90	48.90	15,784
May	59.10	59.35	58.88	59.25	– .13	68.70	49.03	6,767
July	59.00	59.35	58.90	59.30	....	65.73	49.26	4,065
Oct	....	....	....	57.93	+ .13	65.50	50.35	814
Dec	57.30	57.59	57.20	57.58	+ .18	65.50	50.75	3,457

Est vol 2,100; vol Wed 3,120; open int 30,930, –356.

ORANGE JUICE (CTN) – 15,000 lbs.; cents per lb.

	Open	High	Low	Settle	Change	Lifetime High	Lifetime Low	Open Interest
Jan	163.00	163.50	162.60	163.20	+ .70	179.05	132.00	2,900
Mar	162.80	163.10	162.50	162.95	+ .60	175.50	152.90	3,656
May	163.00	163.50	162.50	163.50	+ .50	173.50	149.00	952
July	162.85	163.40	163.85	163.40	+ .05	171.80	162.25	723
Sept	163.00	163.00	163.00	162.95	+ .50	170.10	161.00	181

Est vol 800; vol Wed1,338; open int 8,478, –52.

METALS & PETROLEUM

COPPER-STANDARD (CMX) – 25,000 lbs.; cents per lb.

	Open	High	Low	Settle	Change	Lifetime High	Lifetime Low	Open Interest
Dec	159.70	160.00	158.10	159.40	– .80	164.75	64.70	1,886
Ja89	....	....	....	150.40	– .20	157.00	67.20	382
Mar	135.40	136.80	133.50	136.10	+ .50	142.00	66.50	22,089
May	125.00	126.40	124.50	126.10	+ .60	131.70	73.15	4,385
July	122.50	122.50	121.40	122.20	+ .50	126.70	76.00	2,514
Sept	....	....	....	119.20	+ .30	123.50	76.00	660
Dec	117.00	117.00	115.50	116.20	– .20	119.50	77.45	1,166

Est vol 7,500; vol Wed 10,204; open int 33,083, +232.

GOLD (CMX) – 100 troy oz.; $ per troy oz.

	Open	High	Low	Settle	Change	Lifetime High	Lifetime Low	Open Interest
Dec	416.00	418.50	416.00	418.00	+ 2.70	546.00	395.50	499
Fb89	419.20	421.60	418.80	421.30	+ 2.50	549.50	401.00	53,762
Apr	424.30	427.00	424.00	426.80	+ 2.50	550.00	407.00	17,312
June	430.00	432.60	430.00	432.30	+ 2.60	570.00	412.00	23,985
Aug	436.50	437.90	436.50	437.90	+ 2.60	575.00	419.30	10,353
Oct	....	....	....	443.60	+ 2.70	575.50	423.00	10,397
Dec	447.50	450.00	447.50	449.30	+ 2.80	514.50	428.00	15,028
Fb90	455.00	455.00	455.00	455.20	+ 2.90	516.00	439.70	4,476
Apr	....	....	....	461.20	+ 3.00	525.80	443.00	3,088
June	....	....	....	467.30	+ 3.10	497.00	447.00	3,237
Aug	....	....	....	473.60	+ 3.20	487.00	453.00	2,689
Oct	....	....	....	479.90	+ 3.30	....	....	535

Est vol 20,000; vol Wed 19,025; open int 145,361, +980.

PLATINUM (NYM) – 50 troy oz.; $ per troy oz.

	Open	High	Low	Settle	Change	Lifetime High	Lifetime Low	Open Interest
Dec	543.00	548.00	542.00	544.20	+ 1.80	575.00	510.00	433
Ja89	539.50	544.50	536.50	540.70	+ 2.30	646.00	459.00	8,524
Apr	534.00	539.00	533.50	538.20	+ 5.80	643.50	482.00	8,280
July	532.00	538.00	532.00	536.70	+ 7.30	640.00	501.00	2,254
Oct	532.00	539.00	532.00	537.70	+ 8.30	609.00	507.00	2,842

Est vol 7,258; vol Wed 6,394; open int 22,368, –714.

EXCHANGE ABBREVIATIONS
(for commodity futures and futures options)

CBT-Chicago Board of Trade; CME-Chicago Mercantile Exchange; CMX-Commodity Exchange, New York; CRCE-Chicago Rice & Cotton Exchange; CTN-New York Cotton Exchange; CSCE-Coffee, Sugar & Cocoa Exchange, New York; IPEL-International Petroleum Exchange of London; KC-Kansas City Board of Trade; MCE-MidAmerica Commodity Exchange; MPLS-Minneapolis Grain Exchange; NYM-New York Mercantile Exchange; PBOT-Philadelphia Board of Trade; WPG Winnipeg Commodity Exchange.

PALLADIUM (NYM) 100 troy oz.; $ per troy oz.

	Open	High	Low	Settle	Change	Lifetime High	Lifetime Low	Open Interest
Dec	150.00	150.00	143.00	145.00	– 3.30	155.95	104.50	114
Mr89	137.50	137.50	134.25	137.00	+ .70	145.25	115.50	3,965
June	131.50	133.00	129.00	131.50	+ 1.70	142.00	114.00	1,774
Sept	129.75	129.75	128.00	127.50	+ 2.20	140.25	119.00	764
Dec	128.30	128.30	128.30	125.50	+ 2.20	138.00	122.25	132

Est vol 409; vol Wed 414; open int 6,749, +332.

SILVER (CMX) – 5,000 troy oz.; cents per troy oz.

	Open	High	Low	Settle	Change	Lifetime High	Lifetime Low	Open Interest
Dec	611.5	615.0	611.5	616.0	+ 4.4	1082.0	598.0	105
Ja89	613.0	618.0	612.0	616.9	+ 3.8	1088.9	610.0	572
Mar	624.0	628.0	623.5	626.8	+ 3.8	1073.0	613.0	49,397
May	636.0	638.0	634.5	637.2	+ 3.8	948.0	622.0	7,454
July	644.0	647.0	644.0	647.9	+ 3.8	985.0	633.0	9,903
Sept	658.0	659.0	658.0	658.5	+ 3.8	861.0	640.0	6,991
Dec	672.0	673.5	672.0	673.9	+ 3.8	886.0	657.0	7,092
Mr90	....	....	....	689.5	+ 3.8	910.0	674.0	3,533
May	....	....	....	700.4	+ 3.8	910.0	700.0	2,720
July	....	....	....	711.4	+ 3.8	761.5	694.0	1,980

Est vol 6,000; vol Wed 4,705; open int 89,850, –147.

SILVER (CBT) – 1,000 troy oz.; cents per troy oz.

	Open	High	Low	Settle	Change	Lifetime High	Lifetime Low	Open Interest
Dec	612.0	615.0	612.0	615.0	+ 3.0	946.0	598.0	11
Fb89	620.0	623.0	619.0	622.0	+ 1.0	840.0	608.0	3,154
Apr	631.0	633.0	630.0	632.5	+ 3.0	855.0	619.0	1,434
June	641.0	644.0	640.0	643.0	+ 3.0	865.0	629.0	4,167
Dec	....	....	....	674.5	+ 2.0	735.0	660.0	853

Est vol 200; vol Wed 149; open int 9,792, +56.

CRUDE OIL, Light Sweet (NYM) 1,000 bbls.; $ per bbl.

	Open	High	Low	Settle	Change	Lifetime High	Lifetime Low	Open Interest
Feb	16.37	16.52	16.28	16.49	+ .19	18.10	12.30	75,162
Mar	15.93	16.08	15.85	16.07	+ .18	18.05	12.45	53,834
Apr	15.63	15.82	15.58	15.82	+ .20	18.25	12.60	23,450
May	15.54	15.71	15.45	15.70	+ .20	17.82	12.52	10,537
June	15.39	15.64	15.35	15.63	+ .22	16.80	12.60	10,139
July	15.35	15.60	15.25	15.58	+ .23	17.60	12.65	4,370
Aug	15.40	15.60	15.25	15.53	+ .24	16.40	12.60	2,107
Sept	15.38	15.38	15.38	15.48	+ .25	15.43	12.68	1,465

Est vol 39,115; vol Wed 75,522; open int 181,993, –6,074.

HEATING OIL NO. 2 (NYM) 42,000 gal.; $ per gal.

	Open	High	Low	Settle	Change	Lifetime High	Lifetime Low	Open Interest
Jan	.5185	.5250	.5170	.5248	+ .0056	.5250	.3825	12,550
Feb	.5070	.5125	.5050	.512	+ .0054	.5150	.3825	28,300
Mar	.4780	.4845	.4760	.4844	+ .0067	.5030	.3700	11,253
Apr	.4495	.4550	.4480	.4564	+ .0077	.5000	.3565	6,174
May	.4315	.4380	.4315	.4346	+ .0046	.4700	.3520	8,720
June	.4250	.4310	.4250	.4276	+ .0046	.4680	.3465	7,055
July	.4245	.4275	.4245	.4251	+ .0046	.4700	.3475	1,953
Aug	....	....	....	.4301	+ .0046	.4600	.3545	769
Sept	.4400	.4400	.4400	.4371	+ .0046	.4400	.3640	356
Oct	.4450	.4450	.4450	.4441	+ .0046	.4450	.3720	150
Dec	....	....	....	.4581	+ .0046	.4555	.3785	106

Est vol 16,318; vol Wed 23,954; open int 77,404, –196.

GASOLINE, Unleaded (NYM) 42,000 gal.; $ per gal.

	Open	High	Low	Settle	Change	Lifetime High	Lifetime Low	Open Interest
Jan	.4565	.4670	.4555	.4657	+ .0087	.4670	.3465	7,724
Feb	.4480	.4590	.4475	.4572	+ .0082	.4630	.3490	15,518
Mar	.4525	.4620	.4500	.4599	+ .0089	.4680	.3590	11,089
Apr	.4580	.4670	.4565	.4650	+ .0095	.4735	.3680	6,185
May	.4625	.4705	.4625	.4695	+ .0095	.4705	.3740	3,903
June	.4590	.4690	.4590	.4680	+ .0090	.4690	.3850	3,589
July	.4585	.4620	.4585	.4630	+ .0085	.4620	.4050	1,645
Aug	....	....	....	.4575	+ .0080	.4525	.4020	893
Sept	....	....	....	.4505	+ .0080	.4380	.4000	296

Est vol 8,841; vol Wed 8,848; open int 50,845, –1,166.

GAS OIL (IPEL) 100 metric tons; $ per ton

	Open	High	Low	Settle	Change	Lifetime High	Lifetime Low	Open Interest
Jan	148.25	149.50	148.25	149.25	+ .75	150.50	122.00	23,484
Feb	144.50	145.50	144.25	145.50	+ .75	147.00	119.00	15,176
Mar	139.50	140.25	139.50	139.75	....	142.00	117.25	3,101
Apr	133.00	134.25	133.50	133.75	+ .50	138.50	115.00	3,050
May	129.25	130.00	129.50	129.50	– 1.00	135.00	112.75	2,300
June	....	....	....	127.50	....	132.50	110.75	2,572
July	....	....	....	127.75	– .50	131.00	109.75	598

Actual Thur; vol 3,475; open int 50,281, +780.

WOOD

LUMBER (CME) – 150,000 bd. ft.; $ per 1,000 bd. ft.

	Open	High	Low	Settle	Change	Lifetime High	Lifetime Low	Open Interest
Jan	180.50	181.70	180.00	181.10	+ .10	187.60	160.00	1,883
Mar	184.80	185.70	184.30	184.70	....	187.00	171.00	2,592
May	186.80	188.10	186.70	187.20	+ .20	188.10	170.10	880
July	188.30	189.00	188.10	188.40	+ .30	189.50	175.10	821
Sept	188.50	188.90	188.50	188.80	+ .50	188.90	175.10	268

Est vol 667; vol Wed 1,453; open int 6,516, +171.

OTHER COMMODITY FUTURES

Settlement prices of selected contracts. Volume and open interest of all contract months.

Aluminum (CMX) 40,000 lbs.; cents per lb.
Mar 106.00 +1.00; Est. vol. 0; Open Int. 169
Cattle-Live (MCE) 20,000 lb. ¢ per lb.
Feb 73.90 +.10; Est. vol. 105; Open Int. 565
Corn (MCE) 1,000 bu.; cents per bu.
Mar 283¼ –1½; Est. vol. 700; Open Int. 5,871
Gold (CBT) 100 troy oz., $ per troy oz.
Feb 421.50 +2.70; Est. vol. 100; Open Int. 2,353
Gold (MCE) 33.2 fine troy oz.; $ per troy oz.
Jan 419.10 +2.50; Est. vol. 20; Open Int. 208
Gold-Kilo (CBT) 32.15 troy oz.; $ per troy oz.
Feb 421.50 +2.70; Est. vol. 100; Open Int. 706
Hogs-Live (MCE) 15,000 lb.; ¢ per lb.
Feb 46.57 +.15; Est. vol. 75; Open Int. 621
Propane (NYM) 42,000 gal.; ¢ per gal.
Jan 21.85 +.20; Est. vol. 31; Open Int. 864
Rice–Rough (CRCE) 2000 cwt; $ per cwt
Jan 6.56 +.02; Est. vol. 190; Open Int. 1,772
Silver (CBT) 5,000 troy oz., cents per troy oz.
Jan 617.0 +3.0; Est. vol. 0; Open Int. 94
Silver (MCE) 1,000 troy oz.; cents per troy oz.
Jan 616.9 +3.8; Est. vol. 20; Open Int. 646
Soybeans (MCE) 1,000 bu.; cents per bu.
Jan 792¼ –3¼; Est. vol. 3,000; Open Int. 5,934
Soybean Meal (MCE) 20 tons; $ per ton
Jan 255.10 –.60; Est. vol 15, Open Int. 570
Wheat (MCE) 1,000 bu.; cents per bu.
Mar 438¾ ; Est. vol. 400; Open Int. 9,499

FIGURE 4–13   MARKET TRANSACTIONS FROM *BARRON'S*

THE WEEK'S STATISTICS

NEW YORK STOCK EXCHANGE COMPOSITE LIST

These composite stock quotations include trades on the Midwest, Pacific, Philadelphia, Boston and Cincinnati stock exchanges, as reported by the National Association of Securities Dealers and Instinet.

Continued on Page 82

FIGURE 4–13   *(concluded)*

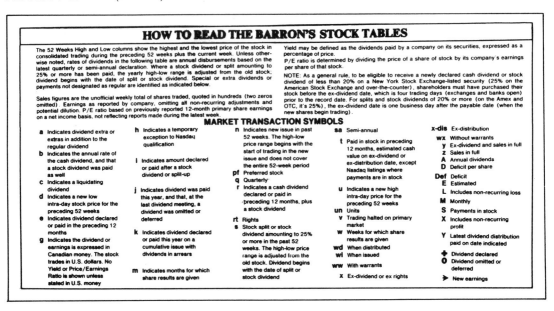

Source: *Barron's,* December 19, 1988, pp. 79, 84. Reprinted by permission of *Barron's,* © Dow Jones & Company, Inc., 1988. All rights reserved.

eight pages of each issue. Weekly data on major stock and bond markets are presented with the week's market statistics. Figures 4–14 and 4–15 show some of the tables from *Barron's* "Market Laboratory." Careful reading of this publication will turn up useful data in a compact summary form not found in other publications.

Other major papers would be the *Wall Street Transcript* (weekly) and the *Commercial and Financial Chronicle* (weekly). Media General's *Industriscope* is an exceptional source of fundamental and technical indicators for the professional manager. Over 3,400 common stocks are divided into 60 industrial groups and analyzed based on relative strength (whether they are leading or lagging the market), trends, earnings, and other variables that may be useful to the analyst.

Journals

Most journals are academic and, because of this, are more theoretical than practical or trade-oriented. However, several are industry-oriented, such as the *Financial Analysts Journal,* which is a publication of the Financial Analysts Federation. This journal has both academic and practitioner articles that deal mainly with analytical tools, new laws and regulations, and financial analysis. The *Journal of Portfolio Management* and the *Institutional Investor* are also well read by the profession. The more scholarly, research-oriented academic journals would include the *Journal of Finance,* the *Journal of Financial Economics,* and

FIGURE 4–14 MARKET LABORATORY—STOCKS FROM *BARRON'S*

Closing Tick

Daily	Dec. 19	Dec. 20	Dec. 21	Dec. 22	Dec. 23
NYSE	+91	−440	-156	−359	−32
Amex	−90	−151	−59	−57	+31
DJIA	+20	−8	+4	−8	+10

The tick shows the number of stocks whose last change in price was an increase, less the number whose last change was a downtick. It is computed for the NYSE, the American Stock Exchange and for the stocks in the Dow Jones Industrial Average. High positive figures indicate a strong market near the close, while negative ones indicate a weak one.

Arms Index

Daily	Dec. 19	20	21	22	23
NYSE	.41	1.25	.77	.95	.47
AMEX	.55	1.14	.92	.86	.47
NASDAQ	.61	.94	.90	.95	.46

The Arms index, also known as the short term trading index, is the average volume of declining issues divided by the average volume of advancing issues. It is computed separately for the NYSE, the American Stock Exchange and Nasdaq. A figure of less than 1.0 indicates more action in rising stocks.

Shearson Lehman Hutton Auction-Rate Preferred Index

	Last Week	Prev. Week	Yr. Ago Week
Total Index	7.454	7.245	7.200
Bank	7.418	7.213	7.143
Industrial	7.424	7.303	6.914
Insurance	7.159	6.906	6.724
Financial	7.341	7.130	7.075
Thrift	7.637	7.353	7.541
Utility	7.406	7.319	6.980

Weighted average of last week's auctions: 8.075

The dividend rates on auction-preferred issues are set by auction each week, with each issue's reset every seven weeks. The dividends in the index are the weighted average yield of all public issues rated A or better.

NYSE Odd-Lot Trading

Shares in thousands

Daily	Dec. 16	19	20	21	22
Purchases	435.2	338.6	307.0	240.0	232.2
Short Sales, z	9,442	2,738	2,311	6,381	8,423
Other sales	666.6	641.7	693.4	579.5	583.7
Total Sales	676.0	644.4	695.7	585.9	592.1

z-Actual sales.

World Stock Markets Indexes

	12/16/88 Close	Week's Change	−1987−'88 High	Low
Australia All-Ord.	1,484.10	+ 362.10	2,350.50	1,150.00
Belgium Cash	5,505.32	+ 98.68	5,414.50	3,508.26
Canada Composite	3,366.00	+ 64.04	N.A.	N.A.
France Agefi	365.01	+ 13.60	393.13	241.07
Hong Kong Hang Seng	2,656.59 *	+ 27.43	3,932.04	1,989.58
Italy Milan	1,215.00	+ 30.00	1,229.00	661.00
Japan Nikkei 225	29,686.26	+ 149.55	30,050.82	18544.05
Netherlands ANP-CBS	284.20	+ 4.00	327.50	192.20
Singapore Straits	N.A.	N.A.	1,502.77	778.94
Spain Madrid	273.71	-3.79	321.26	202.89
Sweden AffGen	1,008.50	+ 3.30	1,0085.20	N.A.
Switzerland CrSuisse	514.90	+ 9.80	639.10	406.50
U.K. FinTimes	1,436.20	+ 0.20	1,926.20	1,232.00
W. Germany DAX	1,328.46	+ 32.15	2,061.10	1,157.29

Indexes are based on local currencies.

IFC Emerging Market Price Indexes*

October 1988
(Dec. 1984 = 100)

	Latest Month	Previous Month	% Chg. Last Mo.	% Chg. Year Ago
Latin Amer.	138.82	145.84	−4.81	8.52
Argentina	204.28	255.44	−20.03	77.31
Brazil	79.97	82.13	−2.63	58.86
Chile	417.10	452.38	−7.80	5.94
Mexico	323.34	326.21	−0.88	−28.63
Asia	296.51	346.11	−14.33	68.20
Korea	377.52	348.09	8.46	61.58
Malaysia	106.79	102.97	3.71	14.89
Taiwan	807.79	1,077.50	−25.03	99.41
Thailand	236.31	246.82	−4.26	47.92

*Calculated in U.S. $ to permit comparison using a sample of actively traded stocks in each market. Source: IFC-Emerging Markets Data Base, World Bank, Washington, D.C.

Trading Activity

All numbers in thousands save percentages

	Last Week	Prev. Week	Year Ago
NYSE	702,886	722,205	686,394
30 Dow Inds	75,472	77,232	73,226
20 Dow Trans	20,190	22,345	16,462
15 Dow Utils	17,276	26,500	36,034
65 Dow Stks	112,938	126,077	125,723
Amex	53,960	49,190	52,870
OTC	637,080	575,894	537,610
NYSE 15 Most Active			
Average Price	44.06	42.22	38.09
% Tot Vol	12.92	14.07	15.55
Stock Offer ($000)	274,000	800,000	5,100
Barron's Low Price			
Stock Index	294.90	294.18	249.59
Vol (000)	9,259.7	6,920.1	2,012.6
% DJI Vol	9.58	11.21	1.91

Daily	Dec. 19	20	21	22	23
NYSE 15 Most Active					
% Tot Vol	19.72	15.15	11.53	18.33	13.42
Avg. Price	42.60	37.11	41.61	39.75	39.13

Daily Stock Volume

	Dec. 19	20	21	22	23
NYSE	162,250	161,080	147,250	150,510	81,700
30 Inds	17,649.5	18,981.6	16,036.6	16,804.7	5,980.5
20 Trans	5,148.2	4,389.7	3,911.6	4,355.8	2,384.6
15 Utils	2,878.4	2,008.2	3,087.5	5,083.9	2,948.2
65 Stks	25,676.1	26,089.5	23,015.7	26,844.4	11,332.3
Amex	11,710	12,080	9,550	11,620	8,980

Market Advance/Decline Volumes

	Dec. 19	20	21	22	23
NY Up	102,479	52,853	61,463	63,222	49,305
NY Down	30,068	85,363	57,227	64,087	13,178
% (QCHA)	+.25	−.10	−.16	−.02	+.48
Amex Up	5,900	4,091	3,187	4,513	5,129
Amex Down	3,212	4,904	3,359	3,597	1,617
% (QACH)	−.10	+.06	+.04	+.26	+.93
OTC Up	50,048	46,090	46,690	43,704	36,523
OTC Down	31,685	45,967	46,148	34,519	13,845

Supplied by Quotron, "QCHA" is the average percentage movement for all exchange listed stocks each day on an unweighted basis.

Indexes' P/Es & Yields

	Last Week	Prev. Week	Year Ago Week
DJ Ind.-P/E	12.0	11.9	15.8
Earns, $	181.04	181.04	126.23
Yield, %	3.70	3.73	3.46
Divs, $	80.19	80.19	69.19
Mkt to Book, %	214.97	213.16	202.71
Book Value, $	1008.95	1008.95	986.48
DJ Tran.-P/E	9.8	9.8	13.7
Earns, $	98.17	98.17	56.03
Yield, %	5.44	5.46	2.11
Divs, $	52.51	52.51	16.27
Mkt to Book, %	146.61	145.95	144.31
Book Value, $	658.42	658.42	533.76
DJ Util.-P/E	11.3	11.2	9.7
Earns, $	16.49	16.49	18.13
Yield, %	8.12	8.21	9.06
Divs, $	15.15	15.14	15.93
Mkt to Book, %	118.30	117.03	115.26
Book Value, $	157.66	157.66	152.52
S&P 500-P/E	12.20	12.11	15.97
Earns, $	22.73	22.73	15.86
Yield, %	3.68	3.70	3.59
Divs, $	10.21	10.19	9.09
Mkt to Book, %	207.20	205.65	199.62
Book Value, $	133.87	133.87	126.82
S&P Ind.-P/E	12.86	12.73	16.25
Earns, $	24.93	24.93	18.05
Yield, %	3.19	3.22	3.06
Divs, $	10.22	10.22	8.98
Mkt to Book, %	239.33	237.00	234.79
Book Value, $	133.93	133.93	124.87

DJ September 30 12-month earnings and 52-week dividends based on Friday close. S&P September 30 12-month earnings and indicated dividends based on Wednesday close. DJ and S&P book values latest available for FY December 1987 and 1986.

NYSE Half-Hourly Volume

Daily	Dec. 19	20	21	22	23
9:30-10:00	19,410	30,320	20,380	21,800	12,690
10:00-10:30	21,340	16,100	13,310	17,440	8,610
10:30-11:00	12,590	14,870	12,000	10,340	8,360
11:00-11:30	12,550	10,420	10,080	10,850	7,400
11:30-12:00	10,340	10,340	8,930	9,930	7,090
12:00-12:30	7,350	10,390	9,240	11,560	5,290
12:30- 1:00	7,540	8,330	9,530	8,530	6,320
1:00- 1:30	8,340	7,810	5,800	10,910	4,270
1:30- 2:00	5,900	7,400	7,300	7,020	4,380
2:00- 2:30	7,060	8,590	13,000	6,920	4,770
2:30- 3:00	11,620	7,790	9,840	9,880	4,530
3:00- 3:30	15,050	14,080	9,810	10,390	4,140
3:30- 4:00	23,100	14,590	16,830	14,930	3,910

Weekly Volume By Markets In NYSE-Listed Stocks

Shares in thousands

	Last Week	Prev. Week	Year Ago
NYSE	702,886	722,205	686,394
Midwest	58,544	49,750	49,380
Pacific	25,755	34,892	29,227
NASDAQ	28,170	24,171	14,686
Phila.	14,448	13,542	10,132
Boston	13,708	13,253	11,263
Cincinnati	13,282	5,225	8,943
Instinet	600	964	467
Total	857,393	864,002	790,492

Other Market Indexes

Daily	Dec. 19	20	21	22	23
NYSE Comp.	156.38	155.74	155.73	155.50	156.06
Ind.	189.13	188.48	188.52	188.23	189.07
Util.	75.47	75.05	75.12	74.93	74.88
Tran.	146.19	145.10	145.40	145.49	146.14
Fin.	128.52	127.78	127.29	127.35	127.86
Amex Index	298.70	299.67	299.71	300.23	302.22
S&P500 Index	278.91	277.47	277.38	276.87	277.87
Ind.	321.97	320.51	320.54	319.89	321.28
Trans.	229.43	227.36	227.09	227.38	228.34
Utils.	114.24	113.63	113.64	113.24	112.92
Fins.	24.76	24.51	24.39	24.43	24.57
OTC Comp.	376.39	376.05	375.60	376.50	377.34
Ind.	372.56	372.27	372.00	372.84	374.02
Insur.	424.84	422.20	422.75	426.20	424.45
Banks	434.64	434.18	433.41	433.95	433.97
NMS Comp.	163.45	163.33	163.12	163.49	163.86
Ind.	144.86	144.79	144.68	144.98	145.44
Value Line (A)	241.83	241.42	241.18	241.45	242.31
Value Line (G)	229.61	229.16	228.86	229.00	229.87
Wilshire 5000	2731.69	2722.72	2723.00	2721.07	2731.65
Russell 1000	147.07	146.50	146.43	146.25	146.78
Russell 2000	144.53	144.49	144.20	144.51	144.88
Russell 3000	157.64	157.08	156.99	156.83	157.39

(A)-Arithmetic Index. (G)-Geometric Index.

Market and Volume Reports

All numbers in thousands save percentages and ratios

New York Stock Exchange

	Week Dec. 9	Prev. Week	Year-Ago Week
TOTAL VOLUME			
Weekly	711,097.9	664,832.8	950,289.0
Average Daily	142,219.6	132,966.5	190,057.8
MEMBER ACTIVITY			
Specialists Buys (#†)	66,110.7	61,983.1	107,489.9
Specialists Sales (#†)	65,149.8	64,186.2	108,471.0
Floor Traders Buys	5.0	228.7	53.9
Floor Traders Sales	2.6	41.3	49.4
Other Member Buys (#)	105,194.4	85,898.3	121,833.9
Other Member Sales (#)	89,542.2	83,741.5	113,427.5
Total Member Buys	171,310.1	148,110.1	229,377.7
Total Member Sales	154,694.6	147,969.1	221,947.9
Net Member Buy/Sell	+16,615.5	+141.0	+7,429.8
Member volume as % of total	22.92	22.27	23.75
SHORT SALES			
Total	46,638.4	48,314.2	70,583.3
Public	15,156.6	14,273.5	15,926.2
Members Total	31,481.9	34,040.7	54,657.1
Specialists	20,325.5	19,093.6	37,440.3
Floor Traders	0	0	0
Other Members	11,156.4	14,947.2	17,216.8
Specialists/Public Short Ratio	1.3	1.3	2.3
Members/Public Short Ratio	2.1	2.4	3.4

Customers Odd-Lot Activity

NYSE	Week Dec. 9	Prev. Week	Year-Ago Week
Purchases, shares	2,055.2	1,688.0	2,100.3
Purchases $	76,292.2	58,402.3	75,393.3
Sales, shares	3,858.7	3,587.9	3,826.8
Sales $	145,258.4	139,322.8	123,229.7
Short Sales, shares	17.1	67.6	29.3
Short Sales $	601.5	2,905.8	1,472.4

American Stock Exchange

	Week Dec. 9	Prev. Week	Year-Ago Week
TOTAL VOLUME			
Weekly	51,212.4	59,722.7	61,607.7
Average Daily	10,242.5	11,944.5	12,321.5
MEMBER ACTIVITY			
Specialists Buys (#†)	5,115.0	4,922.4	7,229.3
Specialists Sales (#†)	5,097.2	5,147.3	7,225.3
Floor Traders Buys	76.1	55.8	42.3
Floor Traders Sales	60.0	67.4	79.6
Other Member Buys (#)	4,544.0	2,850.9	3,242.1
Other Member Sales (#)	3,095.7	2,716.2	3,147.2
Total Member Buys	9,735.1	7,829.2	10,513.7
Total Member Sales	8,252.8	7,931.0	10,452.1
Net Member Buy/Sell	+1,482.3	−101.8	+61.6
Member volume as % of total	17.56	13.19	17.02
SHORT SALES			
Total	569.0	1,047.5	1,260.6
Public	364.9	778.5	640.8
Member Total	204.9	269.0	619.8
Specialists	27.8	57.7	89.0
Floor Traders	33.3	13.5	0
Other Members	143.3	197.8	530.8
Specialists/Public Short Ratio	0.1	0.1	0.1
Members/Public Short Ratio	0.6	0.3	1.0

Customers Odd-Lot Activity

AMEX	Week Dec. 9	Prev. Week	Year-Ago Week
Purchases, shares	68.6	61.0	82.8
Sales, shares	202.0	167.8	213.8

#Includes transactions effected by members acting as Registered Competitive Market-Makers. †Including offsetting round-lot transactions arising from odd-lot dealer activity by specialists and other members. w-Shares and warrants.

Source: *Barron's*, December 26, 1988, p. 121. Reprinted by permission of *Barron's*,

FIGURE 4–15   MARKET LABORATORY—BONDS FROM *BARRON'S*

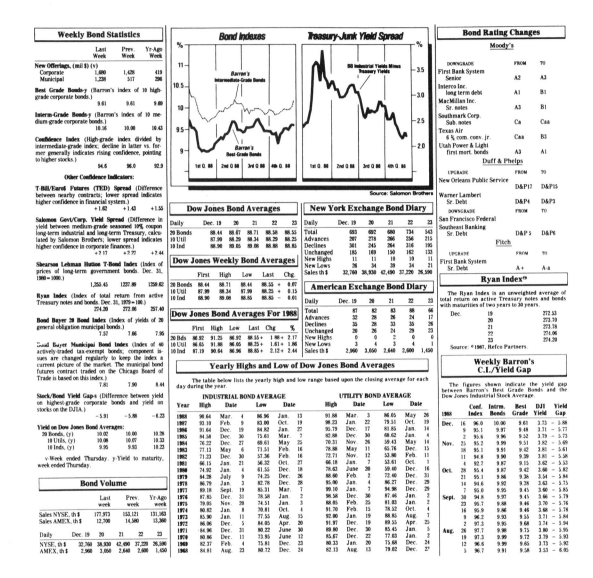

Source: *Barron's*, December 26, 1988, p. 123. Reprinted by permission of *Barron's*, © Dow Jones & Company, Inc., 1988. All rights reserved.

the *Journal of Financial and Quantitative Analysis.* These journals include information on the development and testing of theories such as the random walk and efficient market hypothesis, the capital asset pricing model, and portfolio theories and much empirical research on a variety of financial topics. The *Journal of Financial Education* includes articles on classroom topics and computer applications.

COMPUTER DATA BASES

More computer-accessible **data bases** have become available in the last several years as home computer usage has increased and data-based storage management has improved. Currently, there are several major sources of data that are available for use in large mainframe computers on magnetic tapes, or that are accessible on an interactive, time-sharing basis. Many of these data bases are now accessible from a personal computer.

The Use of Mainframe Computers

The following data bases are made to be used on large mainframe computers. Compustat is published by Investors Management Science Company, a subsidiary of Standard & Poor's Corporation. The **Compustat tapes** are very comprehensive, containing 20 years of annual financial data for over 3,000 companies. Each year's data for the industrial companies include over 120 balance-sheet, income-statement, and market-related items. Compustat has an industrial file that includes company data from the New York and American Stock Exchanges and the over-the-counter market. Also included is a file on utilities and banks. Besides the annual file, which is updated weekly, users can order tapes with quarterly data, also updated weekly.

A second data base created by Compustat is called the Price-Dividend-Earnings tape (PDE), which contains monthly data on per-share performance. These tapes are leased to financial institutions for a fairly large sum or to nonprofit educational institutions at a significant discount. The tapes may be paid for in cash or in soft dollars (commissions funneled through an S&P brokerage subsidiary).

These tapes are useful for analyzing large numbers of companies in a short time period. Ratios can be created, analyzed, and compared. Trends and regression analysis can be performed. Searches can be implemented for specific kinds of companies. For example, one could read through the tapes and screen for companies meeting certain parameters, such as:

1. Dividend yield greater than 6 percent.
2. Earnings growth greater than 15 percent per year.
3. Price-earnings ratio less than the Standard & Poor's 500 Index.
4. Market price less than book value.

It should be noted that Interactive Data Corporation also provides the same information as the Compustat tapes on a time-sharing basis.

The **CRSP tapes** are maintained by the University of Chicago in the Center for Research in Security Prices. The information provided is oriented to earnings, dividends, stock prices, and dates of mergers, stock splits, stock dividends, and so on. The tapes are extremely useful (data begin in 1926) for historical research on stock performance. They are widely used in academia for research on the efficient market hypothesis, the capital asset pricing model, and other portfolio questions.

Value Line also has made computer tapes of its 1,700 companies available. Again, these would have market price data as well as financial statement items. The Federal Trade Commission has aggregate industry data, and the Federal Reserve Bank of St. Louis has been known to make tapes of monetary data available for academic researchers.

The Use of Personal Computers

The last few years have brought a proliferation of data bases for the personal computer. The owner of a personal computer with communications ability and a modem (phone hookup) can now dial a data base such as the Dow Jones News Retrieval System. This data base is oriented to the business user and includes financial data, current and historical information on stock quotes, commodity quotes, access to Disclosure's SEC reports mentioned previously, and much more.[2] Other information outlets, such as The Source and CompuServe, also provide financial data, general information, government statistics, and electronic mail. Chase Econometrics and Nite-Line specialize in financial, business, and economic data, while Citishare Corporation offers U.S. economic statistics. Many old-line financial companies such as Value Line (Value/Screen, and ValuePak) and Standard & Poor's (Stockpak II) are offering their financial data on microcomputer floppy disks with monthly updates. One good place to look for more complete information on these sources is in a computer magazine such as *Personal Computing* or *Byte*.

In addition to the data bases available for the personal computer, new software to access and analyze the data is being created at an extremely rapid pace. The raw data can either be "downloaded" (quickly transferred) onto a floppy disk or into your computer memory to save time and be analyzed later, or it can be read directly into a software program designed to perform calculations on the raw data.

Some programs analyze and create charts of the technical behavior of price movements, and others evaluate the financial data from income statements and balance sheets. Using the Dow Jones Investment Evaluator, you can access the Dow Jones News Retrieval System to obtain information for stocks, bonds, warrants, options, mutual funds, or Treasury issues. Information related to 10-K statements, ratios, earnings growth rates, earnings per share forecasts, and so forth are available on 2,400 companies. The Dow Jones Market Analyzer, the Dow Jones Microscope, and the Dow Jones Investor Workshop all allow access to the Dow Jones information network. Once the correct data is entered into these software programs, they then create standardized analysis from preprogrammed instructions. Also, new programs are now able to transfer data from a news retrieval service straight into a spread sheet program such as Lotus 1-2-3 or Excel. This saves time and money and allows the individual flexibility to create his or her own financial analysis. Not all these programs are available for every personal computer. Most programs are for the IBM

---

[2]A monthly subscription fee is generally associated with this and other such services.

personal computer and compatible systems or for the Apple computer. Before buying a computer, check to make sure which software programs run on your computer.

INFORMATION ON NONTRADITIONAL MARKETS

For the purposes of this section, we define nontraditional as being out of the realm of stocks, bonds, and government securities. A major area that received increased attention during the last decade has been commodities and financial futures. A key source of information on commodities is the *Commodity Yearbook*.

Commodity Yearbook

This is a yearly publication which can be supplemented by the *Commodity Yearbook Statistical Abstract* three times a year. The *Commodity Yearbook* runs several feature articles of educational interest, covering commodities or situations that are currently in the forefront of commodity trading.

In addition to the featured articles, the *Yearbook* covers each traded commodity from alcohol to zinc. For example, corn is covered in six pages. The first page is a description of the corn crop and occurrences for the current year. The next five pages cover much data in tabular form for the last 13 years. The tables show world production of corn, acreage, and supply of corn in the United States, corn production estimates and disposition by value in the United States, corn supply and disappearance, distribution of corn in the United States, corn price support data, average price received by farmers for corn in the United States, and of course, the weekly high-low-close of the nearest month's futures price. Each commodity has a similarly detailed evaluation and statistical summary.

Other publications about commodities come from main-line brokerage houses and specialty commodity brokers. In addition, the commodities exchanges publish educational booklets and newsletters. The International Monetary Market publishes the *I.M.M. Weekly Report,* which discusses the interest rate markets, the foreign exchange markets, and gold. It also presents weekly prices for all interest rate futures, foreign exchange markets, gold, and selected cash market information such as the federal funds rate and the prime rate. The Chicago Board of Trade publishes the *Interest Rate Futures Newsletter.* As investors continue to become active in these markets, an investor (speculator) can be sure to find more available data.

Scott Publishing Company

The Scott Publishing Company has long been involved in the philatelic (stamp) market. They turn out annual catalogs with price data and pictures with descriptions. Recently, Scotts has added a *Stamp Market Update,* a quarterly report on current trends and prices. It features prices of major U.S. stamps and popular foreign stamps, information for specialized collectors, investment opportunities and strategies as stated by recognized experts, and special articles, statistical tables, and graphs.

APPENDIX 4–A: THE INDIVIDUAL INVESTOR'S GUIDE TO INVESTMENT INFORMATION

FOREWORD

An important aspect of investing is getting information when you need it. This can be a time-consuming process if you don't know where to look for it. This resource guide should aid you in finding the information you are most likely to need in managing your investment portfolio. While it is not exhaustive, the sources selected are those most commonly used by individual investors. The emphasis is to provide you with telephone numbers and addresses so that you can contact the sources directly.

Time is money, and information can be as well. This guide should help you in both regards.—*John Markese, Director of Research*

The American Association of Individual Investors is an independent non-profit corporation formed for the purpose of assisting individuals in becoming effective managers of their own assets through programs of education, information, and research.

MAJOR EXCHANGES

These exchanges have available brochures explaining how the exchange works, how the securities are traded, and a listing of the securities traded and their ticker symbols.

American Stock Exchange
86 Trinity Place—New York, N.Y. 10006
212/306-1000

Chicago Board of Trade
141 W. Jackson Blvd.—Chicago, Ill. 60604
312/435-3500

Chicago Board Options Exchange
400 S. LaSalle Street—Chicago, Ill. 60605
312/786-5600

Chicago Mercantile Exchange
30 S. Wacker Drive—Chicago, Ill. 60606
312/930-1000

Commodity Exchange, Inc. (COMEX)
4 World Trade Center—New York, N.Y. 10048
212/938-2900

Kansas City Board of Trade
4800 Main Street, Suite 303—Kansas City, Mo. 64112
816/753-7500

Mid-America Commodity Exchange
141 W. Jackson Blvd.—Chicago, Ill. 60604
312/341-3000

Midwest Stock Exchange
440 S. LaSalle Street—Chicago, Ill. 60605
312/663-2222

NASDAQ
1735 K Street, N.W.—Washington, D.C.
20006
202/728-8955 or 202/728-8055
(See below for more on NASD.)

New York Futures Exchange
20 Broad Street—New York, N.Y. 10005
212/656-4949 or 800/221-7722

New York Mercantile Exchange
4 World Trade Center, 8th Floor
New York, N.Y. 10048
212/938-2222

New York Stock Exchange
11 Wall Street—New York, N.Y. 10005
212/656-3000

Pacific Stock Exchange
301 Pine Street—San Francisco, Calif.
94104
415/393-4000

Philadelphia Stock Exchange
1900 Market Street—Philadelphia, Penn.
19103
215/496-5000

NATIONAL ASSOCIATION OF SECURITIES DEALERS, INC. (NASD)

The NASD is a self-regulatory organization operating under SEC oversight, with 6,400 member firms and 458,000 securities industry professionals registered. Its headquarters and District Offices answer investor questions, direct investors to appropriate services, and receive and resolve customer complaints.

NASD National Headquarters

1735 K Street, N.W.—Washington, D.C.
20006
202/728-8000

NASD District Offices

Alaska, Idaho, Mont., Ore., Wash.
1 Union Square, Suite 1911—600 University
Seattle, Washington 98101-3132
206/624-0790

N. Calif., Nev., Hawaii
425 California Street, 14th floor—
San Francisco, Calif. 94104
415/781-3434

Calif., Nev., Hawaii
300 S. Grand Ave., Suite 1600—
Los Angeles, Calif. 90071
213/627-2122

Ariz., Colo., N.M., Utah, Wyo.
1401 17th Street, Suite 700—Denver,
Colo. 80202
303/298-7234

Kan., Mo., Neb., Okla.
120 W. 12th Street, Suite 900—Kansas
City, Mo. 64105
816/421-5700

Ala., Ark., La., Miss., W. Tenn.
1100 Poydras Street, Suite 850—
New Orleans, La. 70163
504/522-6527

Texas
1999 Bryan Street, Suite 1450—Dallas,
Texas 75201
214/969-7050

Fla., Ga., S.C., E. Tenn., P.R., Canal Zone, Virgin Is.
3490 Piedmont Rd., N.E., Suite 500—
Atlanta, Ga. 30305
404/239-6100

Ill., Ind., Iowa, Mich., Minn., N.D., S.D., Wisc.
Three First National Plaza, Suite 1680—Chicago, Ill. 60602
312/899-4400

Ky., Ohio
1940 E. 6th Street—Cleveland, Ohio 44114
216/694-4545

D.C., Md., N.C., Va.
1735 K Street, N.W.—Washington, D.C. 20006
202/728-8400

Del., Penn., W. Va., N.J.
1818 Market Street, 14th Floor—Philadelphia, Pa. 19103
215/665-1180

N.Y. City (and adjacent N.Y. and N.J. counties)
NASD Financial Center—33 Whitehall Street
New York, N.Y. 10004
212/858-4000

Conn., Maine, Mass., N.H., R.I., Vt., N.Y.
260 Franklin Street, 20th floor—Boston, Mass. 02110
617/439-4404

SECURITIES AND EXCHANGE COMMISSION

Firms with securities traded on the exchanges and in the over-the-counter market are required to file a variety of documents with the SEC. Annual reports, registration statements, and other reports for all firms can be found in the Washington, New York, Chicago, and Los Angeles offices. Regional offices have most documents of exchange-listed firms in their region.

National Headquarters

450 5th Street, N.W.—Washington, D.C. 20549

Office of Public Affairs
202/272-2650

Office of Consumer Affairs
202/272-7440

Public Reference Room
202/272-7450

Forms and Publications
202/272-7040

Regional and Branch Offices

Atlanta Regional Office
1375 Peachtree Street, N.E., Suite 788—Atlanta, Ga. 30367
404/347-4768

Boston Regional Office
John W. McCormack Post Office and Courthouse Bldg.—90 Devonshire St., Suite 700—Boston, Mass. 02109
617/223-9900

Chicago Regional Office
Everett McKinley Dirksen Bldg.—219 S. Dearborn Street, Rm. 1204—Chicago, Ill. 60604
312/353-7390

Denver Regional Office
410 17th Street, Suite 700—Denver, Colo. 80202
303/844-2071

Fort Worth Regional Office
411 W. Seventh Street, 8th floor—Fort Worth, Texas 76102
817/334-3821

Houston Branch Office
7500 San Felipe, Suite 550—Houston, Texas 77063
713/266-3671

Los Angeles Regional Office
5757 Wilshire Blvd., Suite 500 East—
Los Angeles, Calif. 90036-3648
213/468-3098

Miami Branch Office
Dupont Plaza Center—300 Biscayne Blvd.
Way; Suite 500—Miami, Fla. 33131
305/536-5765

New York Regional Office
26 Federal Plaza, Room 1028—New York,
N.Y. 10278
212/264-1636

Philadelphia Branch Office
Federal Building—600 Arch Street, Room
2204—Philadelphia, Pa. 19106
215/597-3100

Salt Lake Branch Office
U.S. Post Office and Courthouse—350 S.
Main Street, Room 505—Salt Lake City,
Utah 84101
801/524-5796

San Francisco Branch Office
901 Market St., Suite 470—San Francisco,
Calif. 94103
415/995-5165

Seattle Regional Office
3040 Jackson Federal Building—915 Second
Avenue—Seattle, Wash. 98174
206/442-7990

COMMODITY FUTURES TRADING COMMISSION

2033 K Street, N.W.—Washington, D.C.
20581
202/254-8630

STATE SECURITIES REGULATORS

State regulators license brokerage firms and financial planners selling securities in their state and screen the offering documents of securities, mutual funds, and limited partnerships for compliance with state laws and fraud. Mutual funds and limited partnerships not registered with a state's regulatory agency are not allowed to be sold to residents of that state. State regulatory agencies often have literature discussing how to avoid fraud.

Alabama
Securities Commission—166 Commerce
Street, 2nd Floor—Montgomery, Ala.
36130
205/261-2984

Alaska
State of Alaska, Division of Banking and
Securities—P.O. Box D—Juneau, Alaska
99811
907/465-2521

Arizona
Securities Division, Corporation
Commission—1200 W. Washington, Suite
201—Phoenix, Ariz. 85007
602/542-4242

Arkansas
Securities Department—201 E. Markham,

3rd Floor—Heritage West Building—Little
Rock, Ark. 72201
501/371-1011

California
Department of Corporations—1230 J
Street—Sacramento, Calif. 95814
916/445-7205

Colorado
Division of Securities—1560 Broadway,
Suite 1450—Denver, Colo. 80202
303/894-2320

Connecticut
Dept. of Banking—44 Capitol Ave—
Hartford, Conn. 06106
203/566-4560

Delaware
*Department of Justice, Division of
Securities—820 N. French St., 8th floor—
Wilmington, Del. 19801*
302/571-2515

District of Columbia
*Public Service Commission, Securities
Division—450 5th Street, N.W., 8th
Floor—Washington, D.C. 20001*
202/626-5105

Florida
*Division of Securities, Office of the
Comptroller, LL22, Intake Unit—The
Capitol Building—Tallahassee, Fla. 32399-
0350*
904/ 488-9805

Georgia
*Business Services and Regulations—2
Martin Luther King Jr. Dr., S.E., Suite
306—West Tower—Atlanta, Ga 30334*
404/656-3920

Hawaii
*Securities Enforcement—P.O. Box 40—
Honolulu, Hawaii 96810*
808/548-6134

Idaho
*Securities Division—700 W. State Street—
Boise, Idaho 83720*
208/334-3684

Illinois
*Secretary of State, Securities Department—
900 S. Spring—Springfield, Ill. 62704*
217/782-2256

Indiana
*Securities—1 N. Capitol Street, Suite
560—Indianapolis, Ind. 46204*
317/232-6681

Iowa
*Securities Bureau—Lucas State Office
Building—Des Moines, Iowa 50319*
515/281-4441

Kansas
*Securities Commission—618 S. Kansas
Ave., 2nd floor—Topeka, Kan. 66603-
3804*
913/296-3307

Kentucky
*Financial Institutions Dept., Division of
Securities—911 Leawood Drive—Frankfurt,
Ky. 40601*
502/562-2180

Louisiana
*Securities Commission—315 Louisiana State
Office Bldg.—325 Loyola Avenue—New
Orleans, La. 70112*
504/568-5515

Maine
*Dept. of Professional & Financial
Regulation, Securities Division—State
House Station 121—Augusta, Maine 04333*
207/582-8760

Maryland
*Division of Securities, Office of the Attorney
General—7 N. Calvert Street—Baltimore,
Md. 21202*
301/576-6360

Massachusetts
*Securities Division, Secretary of State
Office—1 Ashburton Place, Suite 1719—
Boston, Mass. 02108*
617/727-3548

Michigan
*Enforcement Division, Corporations and
Securities Bureau—6546 Mercantile—P.O.
Box 30222—Lansing, Mich. 48909*
517/334-6209

Minnesota
*Registration and Licensing Division,
Department of Commerce—500 Metro
Square Building—St. Paul, Minn. 55101*
612/296-2594

Mississippi
*Securities Division, Office of Secretary of
State—P.O. Box 136—Jackson, Miss.
39205*
601/359-1350

Missouri
*Division of Securities, Office of Secretary of
State—301 W. High—8th Floor—Jefferson
City, Mo. 65102*
314/751-2302

Montana
*Securities Division, Office of State
Auditor—P.O. Box 4009—Helena, Mont.
59604-4009*
406/444-2040

Nebraska

Department of Banking and Finance,
Securities Bureau—P.O. Box 95006—301
Centennial Mall S.—Lincoln, Neb 68509-
5006
402/471-3445

Nevada

Secretary of State, Securities Division—
2501 E. Sahara Ave.—Suite 201—Las
Vegas, Nev. 89158
702/486-4400

New Hampshire

Office of Securities Regulation—157
Manchester Street—Concord, N.H. 03301
603/271-1463

New Jersey

Bureau of Securities, Department of Law
and Public Safety—Two Gateway Center—
Newark, N.J. 07102
201/648-2040

New Mexico

Securities Division, Regulation & Licensing
Department—Bataan Memorial Building,
Room 165—Santa Fe, N.M. 87503
505/827-7750

New York

Bureau of Investor Protection and
Securities—120 Broadway, 23rd Floor—
New York, N.Y. 10271
212/341-2222

North Carolina

Division of Securities, Office of Secretary of
State—300 N. Salisbury St., Suite 302—
Raleigh, N.C. 27611
919/733-3924

North Dakota

Securities Commissioner's Office—9th Floor,
State Capitol—Bismarck, N.D. 58505
701/224-2910

Ohio

Div. of Securities, Dept. of Commerce—
State Office Tower Two, 22nd Floor—77
South High Street—Columbus, Ohio
43266-0548
614/466-3001

Oklahoma

Department of Securities—P.O. Box
53595—Oklahoma City, Okla. 73152
405/521-2451

Oregon

Department of Insurance and Finance,
Securities Department—21 Labor and
Industries Bldg. Salem, Ore. 97310
503/378-4387

Pennsylvania

Securities Commissioner—1010 North
Seventh Street—Eastgate Office Building,
2nd Floor—Harrisburg, Penn. 17102
717/787-6828

Puerto Rico

Securities Office, Office of the Commissioner
of Financial Institutions—P.O. Box
70324—San Juan, Puerto Rico 00936
809/751-7837

Rhode Island

Securities Division, Dept. of Business
Regulation—233 Richmond Street—Suite
232—Providence, R.I. 02903-4232
401/277-3048

South Carolina

Secretary of State, Securities Division—
Edgar Brown Building—1205 Pendleton
St., Suite 501—Columbia, S.C. 29201
803/734-1087

South Dakota

Department of Commerce & Regulations,
Division of Securities—State Capitol
Bldg—
500 E. Capitol—Pierre, S.D. 57501
605/773-4823

Tennessee

Securities Division, Department of
Commerce and Insurance—500 James
Robertson Parkway—Nashville, Tenn.
37219
615/741-2947

Texas

Securities Board—P.O. Box 13167—
Capitol Station—Austin, Tex. 78711
512/474-2233

Utah

Securities Commissioner's Office, The
Department of Commerce—160 East 300
South—Heber Wells Building—Salt Lake
City, Utah 84111
801/530-6600

Vermont
Securities Commissioner, The Department of Banking and Insurance—38 State Street—Montpelier, Vt. 05602
802/828-3420

Virginia
Division of Securities and Retail Franchising, State Corporation Commissioner—P.O. Box 1197—Richmond, Va. 23209
804/786-7751

Virgin Island of the U.S.
Office of the Lieutenant Governor, Division of Banking and Insurance—Kongens Gade #18—St. Thomas, Virgin Islands 00802
809/774-2991

Washington
Securities Division, Department of

Licensing—P.O. Box 648—Olympia, Wash. 98504
206/753-6928

West Virginia
Securities Division, Office of State Auditor—State Capitol, Room W-118—Charleston, W. Va. 25305
304/348-2257

Wisconsin
Commissioner of Securities—P.O. Box 1768—Madison, Wis. 53701
608/266-3431

Wyoming
Securities Division, Secretary of State—State Capitol Building—Cheyenne, Wyo. 82002
307/777-7370

INVESTOR COMPLAINTS

These departments within the major exchanges and government agencies deal with securities transaction complaints. Complaints should be submitted in writing. You may also contact your state securities regulator.

Exchanges

New York Stock Exchange
Arbitration Dept.—11 Wall St.—New York, N.Y. 10005
212/656-2772

National Assoc. of Securities Dealers
Contact your district office or write to:
Surveillance Dept.—1735 K St.—Washington D.C. 20006

Chicago Board of Trade
Office of Investigation and Audit—141 W. Jackson Blvd., B Level—Chicago, Ill. 60604
312/435-3679

American Stock Exchange
Investor Inquiries—22 Thames Bldg., 7th floor—New York, N.Y. 10006
212/306-1691

Chicago Board of Options Exchange
Dept. of Market Regulation—400 S. LaSalle Street—Chicago, Ill. 60605
312/786-7705

Chicago Mercantile Exchange
Compliance Department—30 S. Wacker Drive—Chicago, Ill. 60606
312/930-1000

Government Agencies

Securities and Exchange Commission
Office of Consumer Affairs—450 5th Street, N.W.—Washington, D.C. 20549
202/272-7440

Commodity Futures Trading Commission
Division of Enforcement—2033 K Street, N.W.—Washington, D.C. 20581
202/254-7424

OTHER INVESTMENT ASSOCIATIONS

Financial Analysts Federation
*1633 Broadway, Suite 1602—New York,
N.Y. 10017*
212/957-2860

Futures Industry Association
*1825 Eye Street, N.W., Suite 1040—
Washington, D.C. 20006*
202/466-5460

**Investor Responsibility Research
Center**
*1755 Massachusetts Avenue, N.W.,
Suite 600—Washington, D.C. 20036*
202/939-6500

**National Association of Real Estate
Investment Trusts**
1129 20th Street, N.W., Suite 705—

Washington, D.C. 20036
202/785-8717

National Futures Association
*200 W. Madison Street, Suite 1600—
Chicago, Ill. 60606*
312/781-1300

**National Insurance Consumer
Organization**
*121 N. Payne Street—Alexandria, VA
22314*
703/549-8050

Securities Industry Association
120 Broadway—New York, N.Y. 10271
212/608-1500

FEDERAL RESERVE BANKS

These offices should be contacted if an investor is interested in buying U.S.
government securities (Treasury bills, notes, and bonds) directly, without any
brokerage costs. The district offices will provide forms and literature explaining the process. In addition, the district offices have pamphlets and information
on general economic conditions.

Atlanta
*Federal Reserve Bank of Atlanta—104
Marietta Street, N.W.—Atlanta, Ga.
30303*
404/521-8500

Boston
*Federal Reserve Bank of Boston—600
Atlantic Avenue—Boston, Mass. 02106*
617/973-3000

Chicago
*Federal Reserve Bank of Chicago—230 S.
LaSalle Street—Chicago, Ill. 60690*
312/322-5322

Cleveland
*Federal Reserve Bank of Cleveland—1455
E. Sixth Street—Cleveland, Ohio 44114*
216/579-2000

Dallas
*Federal Reserve Bank of Dallas—Station
K—Dallas, Tex. 75222*
214/651-6111

Kansas City
*Federal Reserve Bank of Kansas City—925
Grand Avenue—Kansas City, Mo. 64198*
816/881-2000

Minneapolis
*Federal Reserve Bank of Minneapolis—250
Marquette Avenue—Minneapolis, Minn.
55480*
612/340-2345

New York
*Federal Reserve Bank of New York—33
Liberty Street—New York, N.Y. 10045*
212/720-5000

Philadelphia
*Federal Reserve Bank of Philadelphia—
P.O. Box 66—Philadelphia, Penn. 19105*
215/574-6000

Richmond
*Federal Reserve Bank of Richmond—
701 E. Byrd St.—Richmond, Va. 23219*
804/697-8000

St. Louis
Federal Reserve Bank of St. Louis—P.O.
Box 442—St. Louis, Mo. 63166
314/444-8444

San Francisco
Federal Reserve Bank of San Francisco—
P.O. Box 7702—San Francisco, Calif.
94120
415/974-2000

INTERNAL REVENUE SERVICE

You can order free publications explaining the tax laws by writing the IRS distribution centers listed below, or by calling (toll-free): 1-800-424-3676. A full list of publications can be found in IRS Publication 910.

IRS Forms Distribution Centers

Connecticut, Delaware, Dist. of Columbia, Florida, Georgia, Maine, Maryland, Massachusetts, New Hampshire, New Jersey, New York, N. Carolina, Pennsylvania, Rhode Island, S. Carolina, Vermont, Virginia, W. Virginia
P.O. Box 25866—Richmond, Va. 23289

Alaska, Arizona, California, Colorado, Hawaii, Idaho, Montana,

Nevada, New Mexico, Oregon, Utah, Washington, Wyoming
Rancho Cordova, Calif. 95743-0001

Alabama, Arkansas, Illinois, Indiana, Iowa, Kansas, Kentucky, Louisiana, Michigan, Minnesota, Mississippi, Missouri, Nebraska, North Dakota, Ohio, Oklahoma, South Dakota, Tennessee, Texas, Wisconsin
P.O. Box 9903—Bloomington, Ill. 61799

FINANCIAL PLANNING ORGANIZATIONS

Financial planning has become an industry that is somewhat distinct from the investment industry. Listed below are educational institutions that offer courses and designations in the field and professional organizations that will provide select lists of planners in your area.

Educational Institutions

The following educational institutions provide designations or degrees specifically in financial planning. In addition, many colleges and universities offer adult education courses on financial planning that are designed for nonprofessionals.

College for Financial Planning: *9725 E. Hampden Ave., Denver, Colo. 80231, 303/755-7101.* Offers the Certified Financial Planner Professional Education Program that leads to the Certified Financial Planner (CFP) designation. The college also sponsors continuing education programs.

The American College: *270 Bryn Mawr Ave., Bryn Mawr, Penn. 19010, 215/526-1000.* Offers the Chartered Financial Consultant program that leads to the ChFC designation. It also offers continuing education.

Professional Organizations

International Association for Financial Planning: *2 Concourse Parkway, Suite 800, Atlanta, Ga. 30328, 404/395-1605.* This organization has 20,000 members who must be actively involved in the financial services industry and subscribe to its code of ethics. For referrals: Upon request, the IAFP will provide *The Registry,* a list (by location) of financial planners who have passed qualification requirements.

The Institute of Certified Financial Planners: *10065 E. Harvard Ave., Suite 320, Denver, Colo. 80231, 303/751-7600 (for referrals: 800-282-7526).* This organization has 7,600 members who are CFPs, who are full-time financial planners, and who subscribe to the group's code of ethics. For referrals: Upon request, the institute will send information on financial planners in a specified location who have the CFP designation. The list includes the planner's name, address and phone number, biographical data including educational background, specialties, organization memberships, and method of compensation.

LINC, Inc. (Licensed Independent Network of CPA Financial Planners): *404 James Robertson Parkway, Suite 1200, Nashville, Tenn. 37219, 615/242-7351.* This organization has 45 members who are major public accounting firms representing some 8,000 CPAs in the personal financial planning divisions of their firms. Members must be fee-only financial planners in a licensed firm engaged in the practice of public accounting. Upon request, a list of members in a specified location, including name, address and phone number, will be provided.

The National Association of Personal Financial Advisors: *1130 Lake Cook Road, Suite 105, Buffalo Grove, Ill. 60089, 312/537-7722.* This organization has 160 members who are fee-only financial planners. Members must be practicing financial planners, their compensation must be fee-only, and they must have certain educational designations or equivalent job experience. For referrals: Upon request, the association will send a list of members (by location) that includes the planner's name, address, education, number of years in the financial planning industry, and their professional affiliations. NAPFA will also provide a disclosure form to assist individuals when interviewing a prospective planner.

INVESTMENT DATA SOURCES

Firm Data: Listed by Publication

Barron's: Dow Jones & Co., 200 Liberty Street, New York, N.Y. 10281 (weekly). This publication contains articles discussing popular investment trends. The "Market Laboratory" section contains useful statistical data on major stock indexes, such as the Dow Jones industrials, S&P 500, etc.; the section also contains trading data for technical analysts and data on general economic indicators. The newspaper also provides data on individual stocks, bonds, mutual funds, futures, options, and government and agency securities.

Corporate reports: The annual report contains the balance sheet and income statement for recent years and a summary of earnings and dividends. In addition to this, it provides some background information on products; new developments are also frequently discussed. The 10-K is a report that most corporations must file annually with the SEC within 120 days after the close of their fiscal year. It incorporates the annual corporate report sent to shareholders, but it also includes other, more detailed information. Among the more useful information to investors are detailed financial statements and exhibits organized by lines of business. Both reports are available to the general public by writing to the firm; they may also be available through public and large university libraries and can be purchased from statistical service firms.

Directory of Companies Offering Dividend Reinvestment Plans: Evergreen Enterprises, P.O. Box 763-Dept. 5CVR, Laurel, Md. 20707. Provides names and addresses of companies offering dividend reinvestment plans, as well as a description of the plans.

Investor's Daily: Investor's Daily Inc., 1941 Armacost Ave., Los Angeles, Calif. 90025 (five days a week). Provides news coverage of investment trends and investment data on major indexes, groups, and individual stocks, bonds, mutual funds, futures, options, and government and agency securities. Information for each stock includes 52-week high and low; P/E ratio; earnings per share rank; relative price strength; daily high, low, and closing price; and net change in price. The paper also publishes information from recently released corporate earnings reports.

Media General Financial Weekly: Media General Financial Services, P.O. Box C-32333, Richmond, Va. 23293. This publication provides statistical information on major market indexes, technical indicators, market groups, and individual stocks. Stock data includes price trends, price-earnings ratios, earnings per share and growth rates, firm profitability (including return on equity), dividend yield, debt-equity ratio, and moving averages.

Moody's Bond Record: Moody's Investors Service, 99 Church St., New York, N.Y. 10007 (monthly). The Bond Record provides summary statistical information on corporate bonds and the Moody ratings for municipal bonds. Statistics on individual and corporate bonds include quality ratings, yield-to-maturity, recent and historical price ranges, and current yield.

Moody's Dividend Record: Moody's Investors Service, 99 Church St., New York, N.Y. 10007 (annual; twice weekly supplements). Provides information concerning dividend payments (including amounts, pay dates, splits, etc.) during the calendar year. Also includes a list of firms offering dividend reinvestment plans.

Moody's Handbook of Common Stocks: Moody's Investors Service, Inc., 99 Church Street, New York, N.Y. 10007 (quarterly). Ten-year statistics on over 1,600 common stocks. Data includes dividends per share, average yield, price range, and book value. Also included are price charts, Moody's valuation, and industry group stock price trends.

Moody's Manuals: Moody's Investors Service, 99 Church St., New York, N.Y. 10007 (annual; twice weekly supplements). Composed of six volumes:

Moody's Bank and Financial Manual, Moody's Industrial Manual, Moody's Municipal and Government Manual, Moody's OTC Industrial Manual, Moody's Public Utility Manual, Moody's Transportation Manual. One of the most comprehensive sources for information on American and some foreign companies listed on U.S. exchanges. Includes description of company's outstanding securities, price ranges, and dividends.

Standard & Poor's Bond Guide: Standard & Poor's Corp., 25 Broadway, New York, N.Y. 10004 (monthly). The Bond Guide provides summary statistical information on corporate and foreign bonds, including quality ratings, redemption provisions, recent price ranges, current yield, and yield to maturity. The Guide also provides the S&P ratings for the larger municipal bond issues.

Standard & Poor's Stock Guide: Standard & Poor's Corp., 25 Broadway, New York, N.Y. 10004 (monthly). For common stocks, the Guide gives a description of the securities and a summary of earnings, dividends, and balance sheet and income statement items along with a description of the business. Mutual fund information includes net asset value per share, minimum initial purchase required, maximum sales charge, price record, and yield from investment income.

Standard & Poor's Standard Corporation Records: Standard & Poor's Corp., 25 Broadway, New York, N.Y. 10004 (bimonthly). A two-page company report is found in the volume according to the exchange on which it is traded (New York, American, or over-the-counter). S&P opinion of the stock is included along with stock and bond information. Reports are periodically updated and information given is similar to Moody's. Kept up-to-date by the Daily News volume.

Standard & Poor's Industry Surveys: Standard & Poor's Corp., 25 Broadway, New York, N.Y. 10004 (quarterly). Provides data on about 34 industries and gives information on the leading companies including return on equity, debt relative to equity, and average P/E and dividend yields.

Standard & Poor's Register of Corporations, Directors, and Executives: Standard & Poor's Corp., 25 Broadway, New York, N.Y. 10004. Provides corporate addresses.

Value Line Investment Survey: Ratings and Reports and Selection and Opinion; 2 vols.; Value Line, Inc., 711 Third Avenue, New York, N.Y. 10017 (weekly updates). Analyzes over 1,600 common stocks. The *Ratings and Reports* volume devotes one page to each company. Information includes summary of the company's business, Value Line rating, beta, estimated future dividends and earnings, and a review of a stock's past developments and future prospects. Also includes lists of conservative, high-yielding, best-performing, and poorest-performing stocks.

Wall Street Journal: Dow Jones & Company, Inc., 200 Liberty Street, New York, N.Y. 10281 (five times per week). *The Wall Street Journal* is the most comprehensive daily source of information available to most investors. Investment data includes daily volume of shares traded; stock average indexes; bonds and futures indexes; dividend news; and prices of stocks, bonds, mutual funds, futures, options, and government and agency securities. Information for each stock includes 52-week high and low; dividend; dividend yield; P/E ratio; daily high, low, and closing price; and net change in price. The paper also publishes information from recently released corporate earnings reports.

Firm Data: Where to Find Stock Information

Information on specific stock data can be found in a variety of investment publications. Below, we list the publications by category of data. The addresses can be found in the previous section that lists publications.

Average P/E and dividend yields: Media General's *Financial Weekly, Moody's Handbook of Common Stocks, Standard & Poor's Stock Guide, Standard & Poor's Industry Surveys,* and *Value Line Investment Survey.*

Debt relative to equity: Annual corporate report, *Media General's Financial Weekly, Moody's Handbook of Common Stocks, Standard & Poor's Industry Surveys,* and *Value Line Investment Survey.*

Dividend reinvestment plans: Directory of Companies Offering Dividend Reinvestment Plans, Moody's Dividend Record.

Estimates earnings and dividends: Value Line Investment Survey.

Growth rate in earnings, five-year: Media General's *Financial Weekly* and *Value Line Investment Survey.*

Institutional stock holdings: Media General's *Financial Weekly, Moody's Handbook of Common Stocks, Standard & Poor's Stock Guide,* and *Value Line Investment Survey.*

Number of institutions holding stock: Standard & Poor's Stock Guide, Moody's Handbook of Common Stocks.

Price, high and low, earnings per share, dividends per share for the last five years: Moody's Handbook of Common Stocks, Standard & Poor's Stock Guide, and *Value Line Investment Survey.*

Return on equity: Media General's *Financial Weekly, Moody's Handbook of Common Stocks, Standard & Poor's Industry Surveys,* and *Value Line Investment Survey.*

Firm Data: Where to Find Bond Information

Coupon and maturity: Barron's, Standard & Poor's Bond Guide, Investor's Daily, Media General's *Market Data Graphics, Moody's Bond Record, Moody's Manuals* (municipal and government, bank and financial, industrial, OTC industrial, transportation, public utility), and *The Wall Street Journal.*

Interest payment dates: Standard & Poor's Bond Guide and *Moody's Bond Record.*

Rating: Standard & Poor's Bond Guide, Moody's Bond Record, and Moody's manuals.

Yield to maturity: Standard & Poor's Bond Guide and *Moody's Bond Record.*

Mutual Fund Data

Barron's: Dow Jones & Company, Inc., 200 Liberty Street, New York, N.Y. 10281. The "Quarterly Mutual Fund Record," a quarterly special report, gives

10-year statistics: Net asset value per share, 12-month dividends from income, and capital gains distributions (appears in the February, May, August, and November issues).

Business Week: McGraw-Hill Inc., 1221 Avenue of the Americas, New York, N.Y. 10020 (weekly). The annual issue on mutual funds discusses the best-performing funds (usually contained in one of the February issues).

CDA Mutual Fund Report: CDA Investment Technologies, Inc., 1355 Piccard Dr., Rockville, Md. 20850 (annual). This statistical service presents risk-adjusted return figures on all mutual funds listed in the financial media. Included among the statistics are fund performances for various periods and market cycles.

Changing Times: Kiplinger Washington Editors Inc., Editor's Park, MD. 20782 (monthly). The October issue contains mutual fund statistics and rankings.

Dow Jones-Irwin No-Load Mutual Funds: Dow Jones-Irwin; 1818 Ridge Rd., Homewood, Ill. 60430 (annual). Contains a description of most of the no-load mutual funds that are quoted in *The Wall Street Journal,* along with a performance summary. It also provides a method for analyzing how to diversify a portfolio among stocks, bonds, and money market instruments.

Forbes: Forbes Inc., 60 Fifth Avenue, New York, N.Y. 10011. Every year, one of the August issues gives statistics and ratings of mutual funds.

The Handbook for No-Load Fund Investors: The No-load Fund Investor, Inc., P.O. Box 283, Hastings-on-Hudson, N.Y. 10706 (annual). Provides an explanation of how to invest in mutual funds. In addition, it contains chapters and tables of mutual fund performance, and it provides a directory of no-load and closed-end funds.

ICI Guide to Mutual Funds: Investment Company Institute, 1600 M St., N.W., Suite 600, Washington, D.C. 20036 (annual). Provides a list of names and addresses of about 1,500 mutual funds, both loaded and no-load.

ICI Mutual Fund Fact Book: Investment Company Institute, 1600 M St., N.W., Suite 600, Washington, D.C. 20036 (annual). This short booklet, updated each year, provides statistical information on the mutual fund industry as a whole.

The Individual Investor's Guide to No-Load Mutual Funds: American Association of Individual Investors, 625 N. Michigan Avenue, Suite 1900, Chicago, Ill. 60611. All AAII members receive a comprehensive book with a detailed analysis of no-load mutual funds, including their historical performance, a statistical summary, fund objectives and services, the name of the portfolio manager, fund addresses and telephone numbers, and strategies for effective mutual fund investing. (Published annually in June. Free to members; $16 for each additional member copy; for nonmembers, $19.95.)

Money magazine: Time Inc., Rockefeller Center, New York, N.Y. 10020. One of the fall issues contains mutual fund rankings by category.

Mutual Funds Almanac: Box 540, Holliston, Mass. 01746. Published by William E. Donoghue (annual). The Almanac includes 10-year performance figures, fund objectives, sales charges, minimum investment, redemption fee, yield, year organized, and the address. It also includes informative articles and advice.

Mutual Fund Distributions: Internal Revenue Service, Publication #564. This IRS publication describes the tax implications of mutual fund ownership in full detail.

Mutual Fund Education Alliance Guide: Mutual Fund Education Alliance, 520 N. Michigan Ave., Suite 1632, Chicago, Ill. 60611. Published each year, this guide contains names and addresses of no-load and low-load mutual funds.

Mutual Fund Sourcebook: Morningstar Inc., 53 W. Jackson Blvd., Chicago, Ill. 60604. Published quarterly, this source provides performance and risk ratings on load and no-load mutual funds along with information on each fund.

Mutual Fund Values: Morningstar Inc., 53 W. Jackson Blvd., Chicago, Ill. 60604. Published every other week, this service provides reports on individual mutual funds much like what Value Line does for stocks.

Stock Guide: Standard & Poor's group (monthly). This stock manual includes some mutual fund information, such as: net asset value per share, minimum initial purchase of shares required, maximum sales charge, price record, and yield from investment income.

Wiesenberger Investment Companies Service: Warren, Gorham & Lamont, Inc., 210 South Street, Boston, Mass. 02111. This service publishes four mutual fund-related books. The annual report covers over 1,600 investment companies, including 700 mutual funds; a quarterly report provides the performance results of over 500 mutual funds and 51 closed-end companies; the "Panorama" is a quick mutual fund reference; and the "Current Performance & Dividend Record" provides monthly information.

Other Sources: Barron's, The Wall Street Journal, New York Times, local newspapers all provide daily and weekly quotes on mutual fund net asset values.

Part Two

ANALYSIS AND VALUATION OF EQUITY SECURITIES

■ OUTLINE

■ INTRODUCTION

While we often praise the investor who is fortunate enough to receive a hot tip and capitalize on it, in the real world, events do not normally follow this course. In the second section of the text, we examine the in-depth analytical process that the typical security analyst must pursue.

Initially, we look at key variables influencing the economy. The security analyst must consider the roles of fiscal and monetary policy and their impact on economic conditions in the near term and over a long period of time. The security analyst also should examine business cycles, their length, and their causation. An understanding of leading indicators and their ability to provide warnings about peaks and troughs in the economy is also important. We take a look at many of these items, although clearly we are drawing from a vast body of knowledge (exact and inexact) from which we can only consider the most relevant material.

As part of the consideration of economic movements, we also evaluate industry patterns. What industries peak with the economy; which go against the grain? Not only are industries influenced by the business cycle but also by their own life cycle which is related to the ability to adjust to technological change.

The evaluation of the individual firm is the next logical step in the valuation process. We first examine valuation procedures based on the present value of future dividends and earnings of the firm. The widely used concept of the price-earnings ratio (earnings multiplier) is also a major item for consideration.

In assessing value, the security analyst also devotes much time and attention to the examination of the financial statements of the firm. Key ratios must be computed and additional analysis done. Very little on the financial statements should be accepted at face value.

Finally, a key question for any security analyst is whether the security markets are assumed to be "efficient." In an efficient market environment, securities are assumed to be correctly priced at any point in time. All relevant information is thus presumed to be impounded into the value of the security at a given point in time. At the end of this section, we will consider the pros and cons of the arguments related to this efficient market hypothesis. We also present a discussion of technical analysis (the use of charting and key indicator series to predict stock prices) and its role in investment analysis.

5

ECONOMIC AND INDUSTRY ANALYSIS

T o determine the value of the firm, the process of fundamental analysis relies on long-run forecasts of the economy, the industry, and the company's financial prospects. Short-run changes in business conditions are also important in that they influence investors' required rates of return and expectations of corporate earnings and dividends. This chapter presents the basic information for analysis of the economy and industry, while the next chapter focuses specifically on the valuation of the individual firm. In Chapter 7, we extend our discussion to include financial statement and ratio analysis for the firm.

Figure 5–1 presents an overview of the valuation process as an inverted triangle. The process starts with a macroanalysis of the economy and then moves into industry variables. Next, common stocks are individually screened according to expected risk-return characteristics, and finally the surviving stocks are combined into portfolios of assets (portfolio management is discussed in Part Five). This figure is not inclusive of all variables considered by an analyst, but is intended to indicate representative areas applicable to most industries and companies.

ECONOMIC ACTIVITY AND THE BUSINESS CYCLE

An investor begins the valuation process with an economic analysis. The hope is that an accurate forecast and examination of economic activity will provide the basis for accurate stock market predictions and indicate which industries may prosper. The analyst needs information on present and expected interest rates, monetary and fiscal policy, government and consumer spending patterns, and other economic data. To be successful, investors must understand business cycles and be able to forecast accurately. Unfortunately, these are not easy tasks, but the rewards can be significant if the timing is right.

Whether an analyst uses statistical methods, such as regression analysis and probability theory, or simply seat-of-the-pants judgment, he or she is still basing the forecast on expectations related to past data and experiences. Past information usually is not extrapolated into the future without being adjusted to conform with the subjective beliefs of the decision maker. Even when highly sophisticated statistical methods are used, subjectivity enters into the decision in some fashion.

Most likely, past knowledge will be helpful, but modifications for the present effects of worldwide currency fluctuations, international debt obligations, and other factors, which were not so important previously, need to be included in any forecast now. Since most companies are influenced to some degree by the general level of economic activity, a forecast will usually start with an analysis of the government's economic program.

Federal Government Economic Policy

Government economic policy is guided by the Employment Act of 1946 and subsequent position statements by the Federal Reserve Board, the President's Council of Economic Advisors, and other acts of Congress. The goals estab-

FIGURE 5–1   OVERVIEW OF THE VALUATION PROCESS

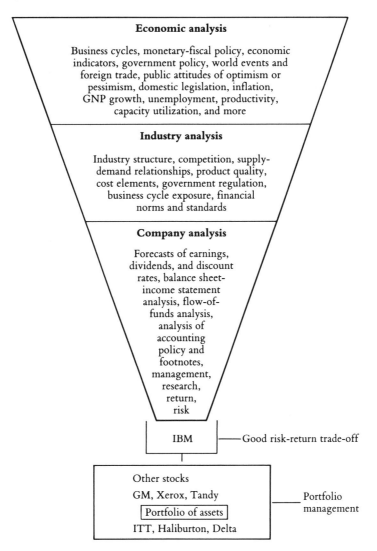

lished by the Employment Act still hold and cover four broad areas. These goals, the focus of monetary and fiscal policy, are as follows:

1. Stable prices.
2. Business stability at high levels of production and employment.
3. Sustained economic growth.
4. A balance in international payments.

These goals are often conflicting in that they do not all respond favorably to the same economic stimulus. Therefore, goal priorities and economic policies change to reflect current economic conditions. In the 1950s and early 1960s, the United States did not have an international trade problem or spiraling inflation, so the focus of economic policy was on employment and economic growth. The economy grew rapidly between 1961 and 1969, and because of the Vietnam War, unemployment reached very low levels. The demand for goods and competition for funds was very high during the war, and eventually war expenditures, large budget deficits, full employment, and large increases in the money supply caused many problems. Inflation accelerated to high levels, interest rates reached record heights, and an imbalance of international payments finally resulted in two devaluations of the U.S. dollar in the early 1970s.

By the time Jimmy Carter took office in January 1977, it was recognized that the primary goals were once again to reduce unemployment, control inflation, and create a moderate level of economic growth that could be sustained without causing more inflation (a very difficult task indeed!). The achievement of these goals was thrown into the hands of the Federal Reserve Board. The Fed's tight money policy caused a rapid increase in interest rates in order to control inflation and these high rates depressed common stock prices as the required rate of return by investors reached record levels. Ronald Reagan inherited most of the same problems as Carter but tried new ways of reaching the goals. As the 1980s began, Reagan relied more on fiscal policy than previous administrations in his desire to control inflation and increase economic growth. He instituted a three-year tax cut to increase disposable income and stimulate consumption and thus economic growth, and at the same time, he negotiated reductions in government spending. These policies were successful in sharply reducing inflation and creating strong growth in the gross national product (GNP), but they were accomplished with record government deficits.

By 1989, the economy had achieved the longest peacetime expansion in history (over six years). The expansion created record employment, reduced unemployment percentages, and lowered interest rates and inflation from the high levels of 1980 and 1981. The stock market began a major bull market in 1982 in response to these improved conditions but also sustained the biggest one day crash ever on October 19, 1987.

With the election of George Bush, a new team of economists and policy makers is now in charge. Many of the same deficit problems are waiting to be solved; only time will tell the outcome.

Fiscal Policy

Fiscal policy can be described as the government's taxing and spending policies. These policies can have a great impact on economic activity. One must realize at the outset that fiscal policy is cumbersome. It has a long implementation lag and is often motivated by political rather than economic considerations since Congress must approve budgets and develop tax laws. Figure 5–

FIGURE 5–2   FEDERAL BUDGET SEASONALLY ADJUSTED ANNUAL RATES
                  (Quarterly)

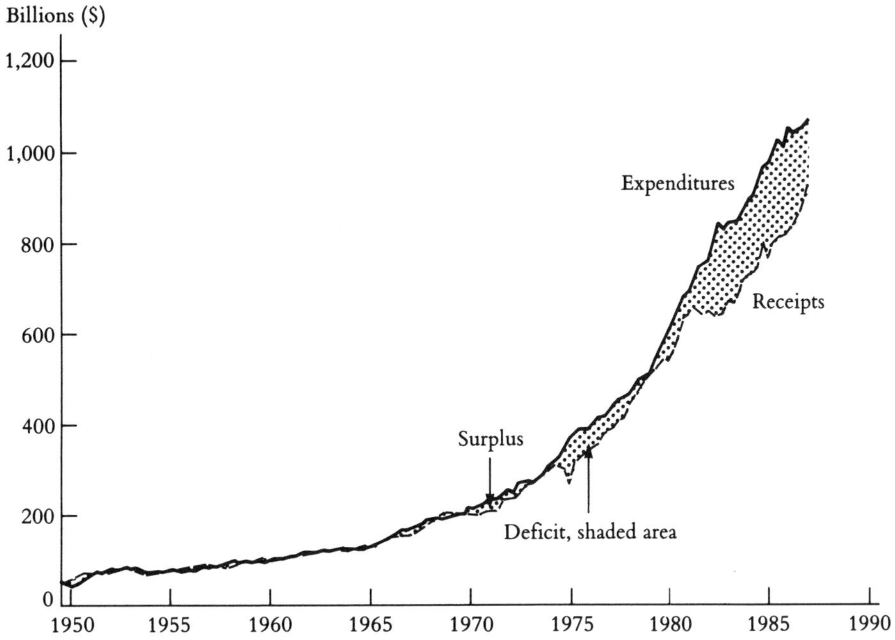

Source: *1987 Historical Chart Book* (Washington, D.C.: Board of Governors, Federal Reserve System, 1987).

2 presents a historical picture of government income and expenditures. When the government spends more than it receives, it runs a **deficit** which must be financed by the Treasury.

A forecaster must pay attention to the size of the deficit and how it is financed in order to measure its expected impact on the economy. If the deficit is financed by the Treasury selling securities to the Federal Reserve, it is very expansive. The money supply will increase without having any significant short-run effects on interest rates. If the deficit is financed by selling securities to individuals, there is not the same expansion in the money supply, and short-term interest rates will rise unless the Federal Reserve intervenes with open-market trading.

A look at Figure 5–2 shows that **surpluses** have occurred very infrequently from 1950 to 1988 and that the annual deficit increased dramatically during the 1980s. Surpluses have a tendency to reduce economic growth as the government slows its demand for goods and services relative to its income. In an analysis of fiscal policy, the important consideration for the investor is the determination of the flow of funds. In a deficit economy, the government usually stimulates GNP by spending on socially productive programs or by increasing spending on defense, education, highways, or other government programs. The Reagan administration instituted budget cuts in education and social programs at the same time that it reduced tax revenues through tax cuts. This strategy was one that attempted to shift GNP growth from the government sector into the private sector. The Bush administration appears to be following the same philosophy.

Monetary Policy

Monetary policy is conducted by the Federal Reserve Board of Governors through several methods of controlling the **money supply** and interest rates. Monetary policy can be implemented very quickly to reinforce fiscal policy or, when necessary, to offset the effects of fiscal policy.

The Federal Reserve has several ways to influence economic activity. First, it can raise or lower the **reserve requirements** on commercial bank time deposits or demand deposits. An increase in reserve requirements would contract the money supply. Why? The banking system would have to hold larger reserves for each dollar deposited and would not be able to loan as much money on the same deposit base. A reduction in reserve requirements would have the opposite effect. The Fed also changes the **discount rate** periodically to reflect its attitude toward the economy. This discount rate is the interest rate the Federal Reserve charges commercial banks on very short-term loans. The Fed does not make a practice of loaning funds to a single commercial bank for more than two or three weeks, and so this charge can influence an individual bank's willingness to borrow money for expansionary loans to industry. The Fed can also influence bank behavior by issuing policy statements, or jawboning.

Beyond these monetary measures, the tool most widely used is **open-market operations** in which the Fed buys and sells securities for its own portfolio. When the Fed sells securities in the open market, purchasers write checks to pay for their securities, and demand deposits fall, causing a contraction in the money supply. At the same time, the increase in the supply of Treasury bills sold by the Fed will force prices down and interest rates up to entice buyers to part with their money. The Fed usually accomplishes its adjustments by selling securities to commercial banks, government securities dealers, or individuals. If the Fed buys securities, exactly the opposite occurs; the money supply increases, and interest rates go down. As you will see in the next chapter on stock valuation, the interest rate is extremely important in determining the required rate of return, or discount rate for a stock. Many economists feel that Federal Reserve open-market activity and the resultant changes in the money supply and interest rates are good indicators of the policy position taken by the Fed. If the money supply increases and interest rates fall, the general consensus is that the Fed is encouraging economic expansion. As the money supply decreases or increases slowly and interest rates rise, the expectation is that the Fed is "tightening up" monetary policy to restrict economic growth and inflation. It should be pointed out that the Federal Reserve can not totally control the money supply. Money market funds, the resultant monetary expansion created by banks lending money, and changing spending patterns by the population all contribute to the difficulty in controlling the money supply.

In the early 1980s, the Federal Reserve began to direct substantially more attention to controlling steady growth in the money supply rather than attempting to control interest rates. Historically, the policy has been the opposite. Thus, the Fed, in recent times, has attempted to control the growth rate in the monetary aggregates of M1 (currency in circulation plus private checking deposits, including those in interest-bearing NOW accounts) and M2 (M1 plus savings accounts and money market mutual funds).

Many "pure monetarists" (those who think that money growth is the major economic driving force) think that the desired growth rates for the monetary aggregates should be very specific and constant such as 3 to 5 percent for M1 and 8 to 10 percent for M2. This is a very narrow range. Politicians often argue for much greater flexibility, particulary in election years. The Fed has often taken a middle ground by allowing for moderate growth ranges. For example, in 1984, the desired annual target growth in M1 was 4 to 8 percent, but the M2 target was 6 to 9 percent, which was 1 percent lower than the range in 1983. However, in 1987, the Fed stopped issuing growth targets for M1 and deemphasized growth targets for M2. This policy change came about as the Fed reversed its earlier strategy of focusing on money growth and took a more balanced approach between controlling interest rates and money growth.

Government Policy, Real Growth, and Inflation

The danger always exists that fiscal or monetary policy can be too stimulative. This can cause rapid economic growth, demand for goods greater than supply, rising inflation, and eventually, an economy that ends up in a recession.

Figure 5–3 depicts 37 years of GNP in current dollars and in inflation-adjusted 1982 dollars. In the bottom portion of the figure, we see changes in the annual growth rate of **real GNP**. This information needs to be looked at in context with Figure 5–4 which shows the annual percentage change in the consumer price index and is used as a proxy for inflation. Notice the inverse relationship between real GNP in the bottom half of Figure 5–3 and inflation in Figure 5–4. (For example, observe the 1960 and 1980 periods.) Since real GNP is the **"nominal" GNP** adjusted for inflation, it stands to reason that the change in real GNP is inversely related to the rate of inflation. As inflation rises, real GNP falls (as indicated in 1980), and as inflation subsides, as in 1981–83, real GNP rises. Since real GNP is the measure of economic output in real physical terms, it does not do any good to stimulate the economy only to have all the gains eroded by inflation.

BUSINESS CYCLES AND CYCLICAL INDICATORS

The economy expands and contracts through a cyclical process, and by measuring GNP and other economic data, we can develop a statistical picture of the economic growth pattern. The National Bureau of Economic Research (NBER) is the final authority in documenting cyclical turning points. The NBER defines recessions as two or more quarters of negative real GNP growth and documents the beginning and end of a recession. Table 5–1 presents an

FIGURE 5–3   GROSS NATIONAL PRODUCT SEASONALLY ADJUSTED ANNUAL
                  RATES (Quarterly)

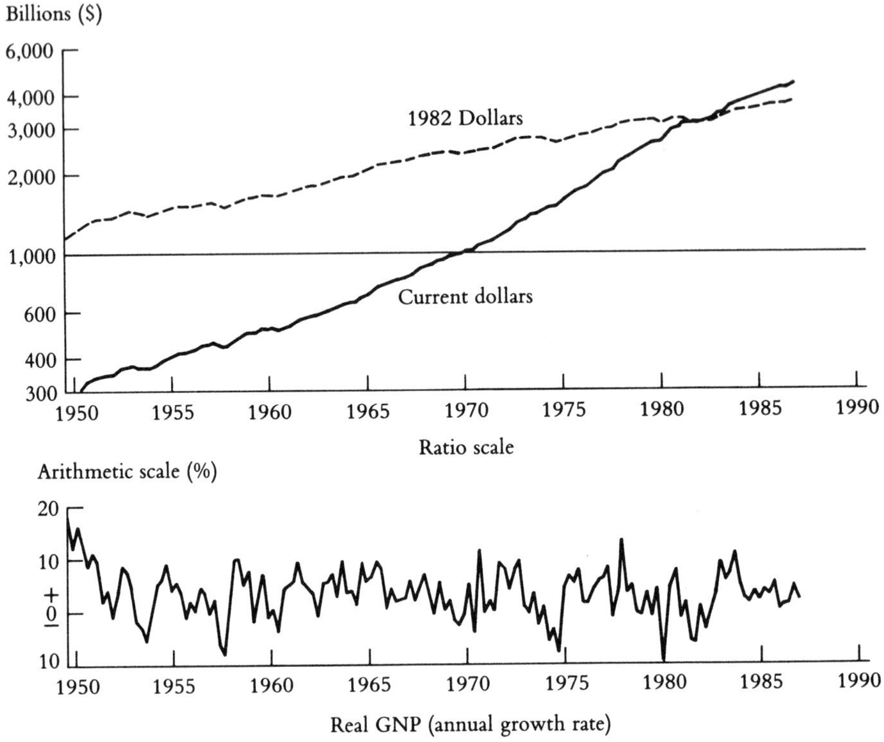

Billions ($)

Ratio scale

Arithmetic scale (%)

Real GNP (annual growth rate)

Source: *1987 Historical Chart Book* (Washington D.C.: Board of Governors, Federal Reserve System, 1987).

historical picture of business-cycle expansions and contractions in the United
States. While the modern day data may be more relevant, it is interesting to
see that economic cycles have existed and been defined for over 130 years.

Table 5–1 measures each contraction and expansion and then presents summary data at the bottom of the table for all business cycles and for cycles in
peacetime only. A **trough** represents the end of a recession and the beginning
of an expansion, and a **peak** represents the end of an expansion and the
beginning of a recession. In general, we see at the bottom of Table 5–1 that
during peacetime cycles between 1945 and 1982, contractions (recessions) have
lasted an average of 11 months, while expansions have averaged 34 months.
Thus, one *complete* **business cycle** during modern *peacetimes* lasts almost four
years whether measured from trough to trough or peak to peak. This has led
many to call the cycle politically induced by the four-year presidential elections.
While there may be some truth in this statement, there are many other theories
about what causes the economy to cycle. However, if investors can make some
forecast concerning the beginning and ending of the business cycle, they will

FIGURE 5–4   CONSUMER PRICE INDEX CHANGE IN ANNUAL RATES, SEASONALLY
                 ADJUSTED (Quarterly)

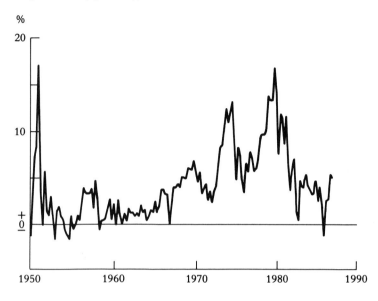

Source: *1987 Historical Chart Book* (Washington, D.C.: Board of Governors, Federal Reserve System, 1987).

be better able to choose what types of investments to hold over the various phases of the cycle.

The business cycle expansion that began in November 1982 is clearly the longest peacetime expansion on record. By April 1989, the expansion had reached 78 months in duration and was still going. This rather unusual expansion when compared to the average shown in Table 5–1 is more than twice as long as normal. It is not surprising that some economists and market analysts are in constant expectation of a recession. This makes sense if we assume that the past is a good measure of future expectations. However, if investors learned one thing during the late 1970s and early 1980s when inflation was outpacing all historical norms, it is that the past is not always a good predictor of the future.

So far we have discussed the government's impact on the economy. Fiscal policy and monetary policy both provide important clues to the direction and magnitude of economic expansions and contractions. Other measures are used to evaluate the direction of the business cycle. These measures, called economic indicators, are divided into leading, lagging, and coincident indicators. The National Bureau of Economic Research classifies indicators relative to their performance at economic peaks and troughs.

Leading indicators change direction in advance of general business conditions and are of prime importance to the investor who wants to anticipate rising corporate profits and possible price increases in the stock market. Coincident indicators move roughly with the general economy, and lagging in-

TABLE 5–1   BUSINESS CYCLE EXPANSIONS AND CONTRACTIONS IN THE
UNITED STATES

Business Cycle Reference Dates		Duration in Months		Cycle	
		Contraction (Trough from Previous Peak)	Expansion (Trough to Peak)	Trough from Previous Trough	Peak from Previous Peak
Trough	Peak				
December 1854	June 1857	—	30	—	—
December 1858	October 1860	18	22	48	40
June 1861	April 1865	8	_46_	30	_54_
December 1867	June 1869	_32_	18	_78_	50
December 1870	October 1873	18	34	36	52
March 1879	March 1882	65	36	99	101
May 1885	March 1887	38	22	74	60
April 1888	July 1890	13	27	35	40
May 1891	January 1893	10	20	37	30
June 1894	Decmeber 1895	17	18	37	35
June 1897	June 1899	18	24	36	42
December 1900	September 1902	18	21	42	39
August 1904	May 1907	23	33	44	56
June 1908	January 1910	13	19	46	32
January 1912	January 1913	24	12	43	36
December 1914	August 1918	23	_44_	35	_67_
March 1919	January 1920	_7_	10	_51_	17
July 1921	May 1923	18	22	28	40
July 1924	October 1926	14	27	36	41
November 1927	August 1929	13	21	40	34
March 1933	May 1937	43	50	64	93
June 1938	February 1945	13	_80_	63	_93_
October 1945	November 1948	_8_	37	_88_	45
October 1949	July 1953	11	_45_	48	_56_
May 1954	August 1957	_10_	39	_55_	49
April 1958	April 1960	8	24	47	32
February 1961	December 1969	10	106	34	116
November 1970	November 1973	_11_	36	_117_	47
March 1975	January 1980	16	58	52	74
July 1980	July 1981	6	12	64	18
November 1982		16	—	28	—
Average, all cycles:					
1854–1982 (30 cycles)		18	33	51	51★
1854–1919 (16 cycles)		22	27	48	49†
1919–1945 (6 cycles)		18	35	53	53
1945–1982 (8 cycles)		11	45	56	55‡
Average, peacetime cycles:					
1854–1982 (25 cycles)		19	27	46	46‡
1854–1919 (14 cycles)		22	24	46	47§
1919–1945 (5 cycles)		20	26	46	45
1945–1982 (6 cycles)		11	34	46	44

Note: Underscored figures are the wartime expansions (Civil War, World Wars I and II, Korean War, and Vietnam War), the postwar contractions, and the full cycles that include the wartime expansions.
★29 cycles.
†15 cycles.
‡24 cycles.
§13 cycles.
Source: *Business Conditions Digest* (U.S. Department of Commerce Bureau of Economic Analysis, July 1988).

dicators usually change directions after business conditions have turned around.

The National Bureau of Economic Research publishes its indicators in the monthly publication *Business Conditions Digest* (BCD). This publication includes moving averages, turning dates for recessions and expansions, cyclical indicators, composite indexes and their components, diffusion indexes,[1] and information on rates of change. Many of the series are seasonally adjusted and are maintained on a monthly or quarterly basis.

Figure 5–5 presents a summary of cyclical indicators by economic process and cyclical timing with the first part (Part A) of the figure presenting timing at business cycle peaks and the second part (Part B) showing timing at business cycle troughs. Thus, in the first part, we see the leading, coincident, and lagging indicators for business-cycle peaks and in the second part, similar indicators for the bottoming out of business cycles (troughs). While we would not expect you to study or learn all the leading or lagging indicators for a cyclical peak or trough, it is important that you know that they are heavily relied upon by economists and financial analysts. Let's look more specifically at how they are used.

Leading Indicators

Of the 108 leading indicators shown in Parts A and B of Figure 5–5, 61 lead at peaks and 47 lead at troughs. Of these, 11 basic indicators have been reasonably consistent in their relationship to the business cycle and are considered most important. These 11 leading indicators have been standardized and used to compute a composite index that is widely followed. It is a much smoother curve than each individual component since erratic changes in one indicator are offset by movements in other indicators. The same can be said for a similar index of four coincident indicators and six lagging indicators.

Figure 5–6 shows the performance of the composite index of leading, lagging, and coincident indicators over several past business cycles. The shaded areas are recessions as defined by the NBER. The minus figures indicate how many months the index preceded the economy. (Lagging indicators have plus signs.)

While the composite index of leading indicators (top of Figure 5–6) has been a better predictor than any single indicator, it has varied widely at peaks, with the longest lead time being 23 months before the peak in 1957 and the shortest being 3 months in 1981. At troughs, the longest lead has been eight months before the bottom in 1982, and the shortest, one month in 1974–75. Table 5–2 presents the components for the 11 leading, 4 roughly coincident, and 6 lagging indicators.

Studies have found that the 11 leading indicators do not exhibit the same notice at peaks as they do at troughs. The notice prior to peaks is quite long,

---

[1]A diffusion index shows the pervasiveness of a given movement in a series. If 100 units are reported in a series, the diffusion index will indicate what percentage followed a given pattern.

FIGURE 5–5   CROSS CLASSIFICATION OF CYCLICAL INDICATORS BY ECONOMIC PROCESS AND CYCLICAL TIMING

A. Timing at Business Cycle Peaks

Economic Process / Cyclical Timing	I. Employment and Unemployment (15 series)	II. Production and Income (10 series)	III. Consumption, Trade, Orders, and Deliveries (13 series)	IV. Fixed Capital Investment (19 series)	V. Inventories and Inventory Investment (9 series)	VI. Price, Costs, and Profits (18 series)	VII. Money and Credit (28 series)
Leading (L) Indicators (61 series)	Marginal employment adjustments (3 series) Job vacancies (2 series) Comprehensive employment (1 series) Comprehensive unemployment (3 series)	Capacity utilization (2 series)	Orders and deliveries (6 series) Consumption and trade (2 series)	Formation of business enterprises (2 series) Business investment commitments (5 series) Residential construction (3 series)	Inventory investment (4 series) Inventories on hand and on order (1 series)	Stock prices (1 series) Sensitive commodity prices (2 series) Profits and profit margins (7 series) Cash flows (2 series)	Money (5 series) Credit flows (5 series) Credit difficulties (2 series) Bank reserves (2 series) Interest rates (1 series)
Roughly Coincident (C) Indicators (24 series)	Comprehensive employment (1 series)	Comprehensive output and income (4 series) Industrial production (4 series)	Consumption and trade (4 series)	Business investment commitments (1 series) Business investment expenditures (6 series)			Velocity of money (2 series) Interest rates (2 series)
Lagging (Lg) Indicators (19 series)	Comprehensive unemployment (2 series)			Business investment expenditures (1 series)	Inventories on hand and on order (4 series)	Unit labor costs and labor share (4 series)	Interest rates (4 series) Outstanding debt (4 series)
Timing Unclassified (U) (8 series)	Comprehensive employment (3 series)		Consumption and trade (1 series)	Business investment commitments (1 series)		Sensitive commodity prices (1 series) Profits and profit margins (1 series)	Interest rates (1 series)

B. Timing at Business Cycle Troughs

Economic Process / Cyclical Timing	I. Employment and Unemployment (15 series)	II. Production and Income (10 series)	III. Consumption, Trade, Orders, and Deliveries (13 series)	IV. Fixed Capital Investment (19 series)	V. Inventories and Inventory Investment (9 series)	VI. Price, Costs, and Profits (18 series)	VII. Money and Credit (28 series)
Leading (L) Indicators (47 series)	Marginal employment adjustments (1 series)	Industrial production (1 series)	Orders and deliveries (5 series) Consumption and trade (4 series)	Formation of business enterprises (2 series) Business investment commitments (4 series) Residential construction (3 series)	Inventory investment (4 series)	Stock prices (1 series) Sensitive commodity prices (3 series) Profits and profit margins (6 series) Cash flows (2 series)	Money (4 series) Credit flows (5 series) Credit difficulties (2 series)
Roughly Coincident (C) Indicators (23 series)	Marginal employment adjustments (2 series) Comprehensive employment (4 series)	Comprehensive output and income (4 series) Industrial production (3 series) Capacity utilization (2 series)	Consumption and trade (3 series)	Business investment commitments (1 series)		Profits and profit margins (2 series)	Money (1 series) Velocity of money (1 series)
Lagging (Lg) Indicators (41 series)	Job vacancies (2 series) Comprehensive employment (1 series) Comprehensive unemployment (5 series)		Orders and deliveries (1 series)	Business investment commitments (2 series) Business investment expenditures (7 series)	Inventories on hand and on order (5 series)	Unit labor costs and labor share (4 series)	Velocity of money (1 series) Bank reserves (1 series) Interest rates (8 series) Outstanding debt (4 series)
Timing Unclassified (U) (1 series)							Bank reserves (1 series)

Source: *Business Conditions Digest* (U.S. Department of Commerce Bureau of Economic Analysis, July 1988).

FIGURE 5–6   COMPOSITE INDEXES (Leading, Lagging, and Coincident Indexes)

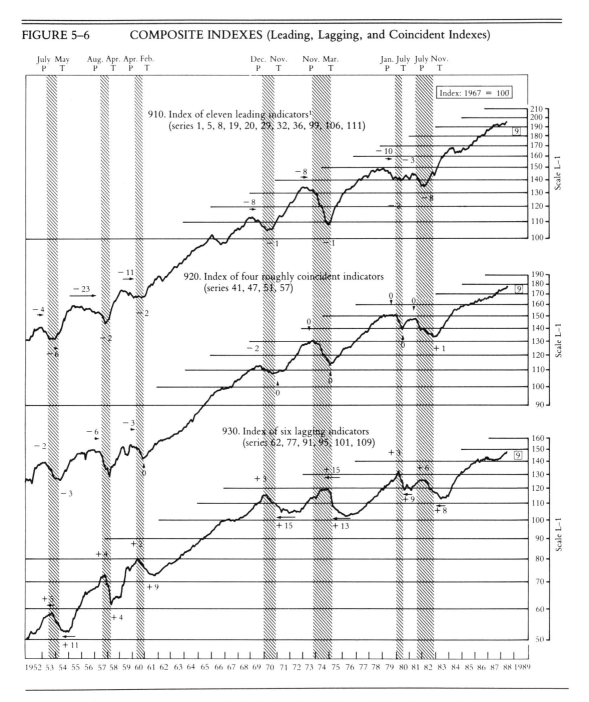

Note: Numbers entered on the chart indicate length of leads (−) and lags (+) in months from reference turning dates.
[1]Values of this index prior to January 1984 include a 12th component, series 12, which has been suspended from the current index.

Source: *Business Conditions Digest* (U.S. Department of Commerce Bureau of Economic Analysis, April 1988).

TABLE 5–2 COMPONENTS OF THE LEADING, COINCIDENT, AND LAGGING
INDICATORS (Series Title and Unit of Measure)

Leading indicators:

1. Average weekly hours of production or nonsupervisory workers, manufacturing (hours).
5. Average weekly initial claims for unemployment insurance, state programs (thous.).
8. Mfrs. new orders in 1982 dollars, consumer goods and materials industries (bil. dol).
32. Vendor performance, percent of companies receiving slower deliveries (percent).
20. Contracts and orders for plant and equipment in 1982 dollars (bil. dol.).
29. New private housing units authorized by local building permits (index: 1967 = 100).
36. Change in inventories on hand and on order in 1982 dol., smoothed (ann. rate, bil. dol.).
99. Change in sensitive materials prices, smoothed (percent).
19. Stock prices, 500 common stocks (index: 1941–43 = 10).
106. Money supply M2 in 1982 dollars (bil. dol.).
111. Change in business and consumer credit outstanding (ann. rate, percent).
910. Composite index of leading indicators (index: 1967 = 100).

Roughly Coincident Indicators:

41. Employees on nonagricultural payrolls (thous.).
51. Personal income less transfer payments in 1982 dollars (ann. rate, bil. dol.).
47. Industrial production (index: 1977 = 100).
57. Manufacturing and trade sales in 1982 dollars (mil. dol.).
920. Composite index of roughly coincident indicators (index: 1967 = 100).

Lagging indicators:

91. Average duration of unemployment (weeks).
77. Ratio, manufacturing and trade inventories to sales in 1982 dollars (ratio).
62. Labor cost per unit of output, manufacturing-actual data as a percent of trend (percent).
109. Average prime rate charged by banks (percent).
101. Commercial and industrial loans outstanding in 1982 dollars (mil. dol.).
95. Ratio, consumer installment credit outstanding to personal income (percent).
930. Composite index of lagging indicators (index: 1967 = 100).

Note: The net contribution of an individual component is that component's share in the composite movement of the group. It is computed by dividing the standardized and weighted change for the component by the sum of the weights for the available components and dividing that result by the index standardization factor. See the February 1983 *Business Conditions Digest* (pp. 108) or the 1984 *Handbook of Cyclical Indicators* (pp. 67–68) for the weights and standardization factors.
Source: *Business Conditions Digest* (U.S. Department of Commerce Bureau of Economic Analysis, July 1988).

but the warning prior to troughs is very short, which means that it is very easy to miss a turnaround to the upside, but on the downside, you can be more patient waiting for confirmation from other indicators. It should also be noted that the indicators occasionally give false signals. Sometimes the indicators give no clear signal at all, and with the large variability of leads and lags versus the average lead time, an investor is lucky to get close to predicting economic activity within three or four months of peaks and troughs. It becomes clear that despite economic indicators and forecasting methods, investors cannot escape uncertainty in an attempt to manage their portfolios of assets.

One very important fact is that the stock market is the most reliable and accurate of the 11 leading indicators. This, of course, presents a very real problem for us because our initial objective is to forecast (as well as we are able) changes in common stock prices. In order to do this, we are constrained by the fact that the stock market is anticipatory and, in fact, has worked on a lead time of nine months at peaks and five months at troughs.

FIGURE 5–7

MONEY SUPPLY, STOCK PRICES, CORPORATE PROFITS, AND CORPORATE NET CASH FLOW CYCLICAL INDICATORS (Leading Indicators)

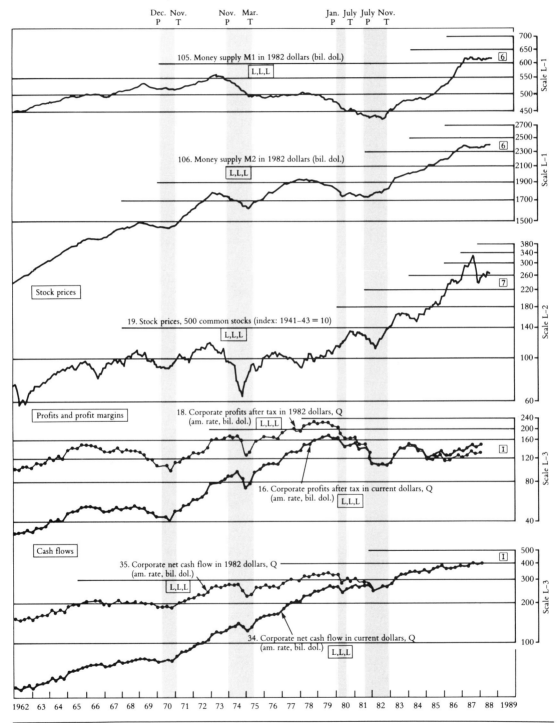

Source: *Business Conditions Digest* (U.S. Department of Commerce Bureau of Economic Analysis, July 1988).

MONEY SUPPLY AND STOCK PRICES

One variable that has been historically popular as an indicator of the stock market is the money supply. The money supply is supposed to influence stock prices in several ways. Studies of economic growth and the money supply by Milton Friedman and Anna Schwartz found a long-term relationship between these two variables.[2]

Why does money matter? If you are a **monetarist**, money explains much of economic behavior. The quantity theory of money holds that as the supply of money increases relative to the demand for money, people will make adjustments in their portfolios of assets. If they have too much money, they will first buy bonds (a modification of the theory would now include Treasury bills or other short-term monetary assets), stocks, and finally, real assets. This is the direct effect of money on stock prices sometimes referred to as the liquidity effect.

The indirect effect of money on stock prices would flow through the GNP's impact on corporate profits. As money influences economic activity, it will eventually influence corporate earnings and dividends and thus returns to the investors. Many studies have found that a significant relationship exists between the money supply variable and stock prices. However, even here, there have been some conflicting patterns in the last decade as shown in Figure 5–7. Note that in 1982, the money supply (M2) was increasing slightly while stock prices were declining sharply. This goes against the historical norm of comparable movements that can be seen in the same figure.

The point to be made is that there are many important predictors of economic patterns and stock market movements, but an investor must be flexible and consider as many variables as possible rather than simply relying on one or two factors. You may wish to acquaint yourself with many of the leading, coincident, and lagging indicators presented previously in Table 5–2 as you become active in the stock market.

BUSINESS CYCLES AND INDUSTRY ANALYSIS

Each industry may be affected by the business cycle differently. Industries where the underlying demand for the product is consumer-oriented will quite likely be sensitive to short-term swings in the business cycle. These industries would include durable goods such as washers and dryers, refrigerators, electric and gas ranges, and automobiles. Changes in the automobile industry will also be felt in the tire and rubber industry as well as by auto glass and other automobile component suppliers.

Figure 5–8 shows the automobile industry's sales from 1979 to mid-1987 relative to the real GNP's growth rate. Notice the similarity of the pattern. From the beginning of 1980 to the middle of 1980, both automobile sales and real GNP show sharp declines. This occurs again during 1981. At the beginning of 1982, real GNP recovers from its low point and is followed by automobile

---

[2]Milton J. Friedman and Anna J. Schwartz, "Money and Business Cycles," *Review of Economics and Statistics,* Supplement, February 1963.

FIGURE 5–8   NEW AUTO SALES AND REAL GNP, 1979–1987

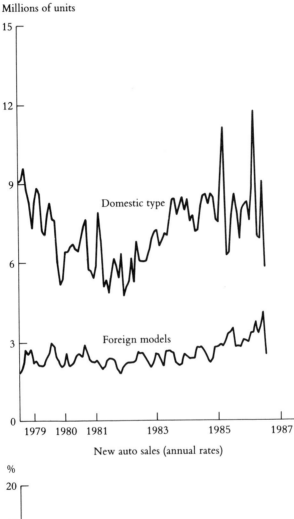

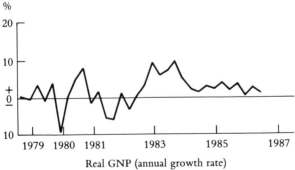

Source: *Federal Reserve Quarterly Chart Book* (Washington, D.C.: Board of Governors, Federal Reserve System, February 1987).

FIGURE 5–9   PERSONAL CONSUMPTION EXPENDITURES (Services, Nondurable Goods, and Durable Goods)

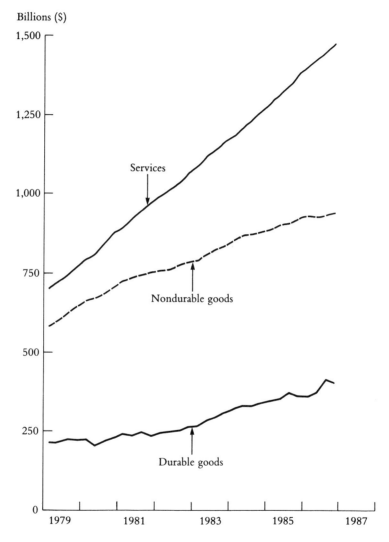

Source: *Federal Reserve Quarterly Chart Book* (Washington, D.C.: Board of Governors, Federal Reserve Systems, February 1987).

sales. This close relationship is why it is often said that the United States lives in an automobile economy. Automobile sales in the 1985–87 period show quite a bit of quarterly variation. The sharp spikes in this period are more a function of sales incentive programs in a healthy economy than a response to cyclical economic conditions.

Not all industries are so closely related to the business cycle. Necessity-oriented industries, such as food and pharmaceuticals, are consistent performers since people do have to eat, and illness is not dependent on the economy.

Industries that have products with low price elasticities[3] that are habitual in nature, such as cigarettes and alcohol, do not seem to be much affected by business cycles, either. In fact, some industries do better during a recession. The movie industry prospers during a recession as more people substitute low-cost entertainment for more expensive forms. This is one pattern that may not remain the same, however. As cable television and VCRs come into their own, people may find it even more convenient to stay at home than to go to the movies when money is tight. This is one thing that makes investments exciting—the ever-changing environment.

Housing is another example of an industry that historically has done well in recessionary environments. As the economy comes to a standstill, interest rates tend to come down, and prospective home purchasers are once again able to afford mortgage rates on a home. In the period of extremely high mortgage rates in the early 1980s, it was felt that a precipitous drop in mortgage rates would be necessary to once again stimulate growth in the housing market, and it did.

The Federal Reserve tracks data on various types of consumer expenditures. In Figure 5–9, we see the pattern for personal consumption expenditures. In this graph, we see the pattern for personal consumption expenditures on durable goods, nondurables, and services. Durable goods have fared relatively poorly during this period (1979–1987) and have been the most susceptible to mild downturns, while nondurables have done quite well, with services leading the growth for personal expenditures.

Sensitivity to the business cycle may also be evident in industries that produce *capital* goods for other business firms (rather than consumer goods). Examples would be manufacturers of business plant and equipment, machine tools, or pollution-control equipment. A lag often exists between the recovery from a recession and the increased purchase of capital goods, so recoveries within these industries may be delayed. Computers and other high-technology industries tend to be less cyclical in nature and not as sensitive to the ups and downs of the economy.

We do not mean to imply that cyclical industries are bad investments or that they should be avoided. We merely point out the cyclical influence of the economy. Often cyclical industries are excellent buys in the stock market because the market does not look far enough ahead to see a recovery and its impact on cyclical profits.

INDUSTRY LIFE CYCLES

Life cycles are created because of economic growth, competition, availability of resources, and the resultant market saturation by the particular goods and services offered. Life-cycle growth influences many variables considered in the valuation process. The particular phase in the life cycle of an industry or

---

[3]Price elasticity represents the sensitivity of quantity purchased to price.

FIGURE 5–10   INDUSTRY LIFE CYCLE

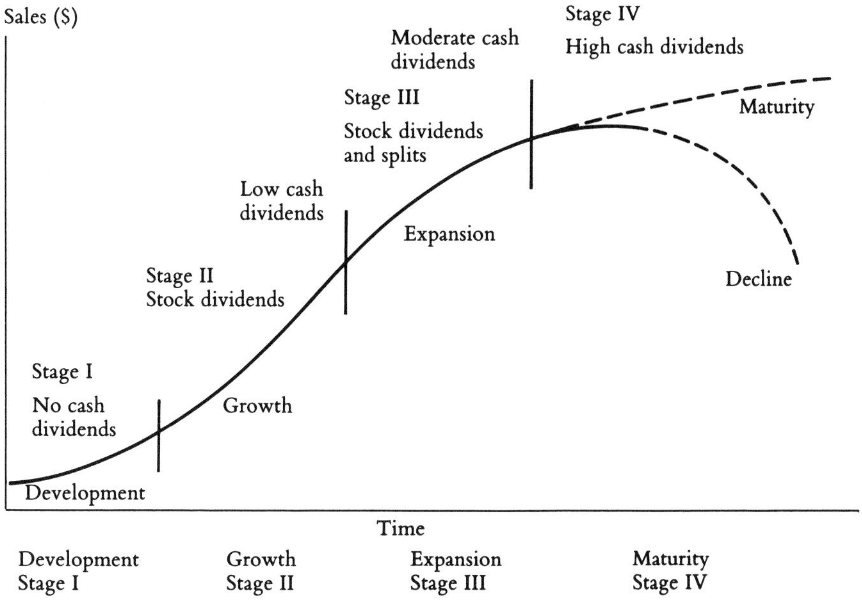

Source: Stanley Block and Geoffrey Hirt, *Foundations of Financial Management,* 5th ed. (Homewood, Ill.: Richard D. Irwin, 1989).

company determines the growth of earnings, dividends, capital expenditures, and market demand for products.

Figure 5–10 shows an industry life cycle (although it could very well be a company life cycle) and the corresponding dividend policy most likely to be found at each stage. A small firm in the initial stages of development (Stage I) pays no dividends because it needs all of its profits (if there are any) for reinvestment in new productive assets. If the firm is successful in the marketplace, the demand for its products will create growth in sales, earnings, and assets, and the industry will move into Stage II. At this stage, sales and returns on assets will be growing at an increasing rate, and earnings will still be reinvested. In the early part of Stage II, stock dividends (distributions of additional shares) may be instituted, and in the latter part of Stage II, *low* cash dividends may be started to inform investors that the firm is profitable.

Obviously, industries in Stage I or early Stage II are very risky, and the investor does not really know if growth objectives will be met or dividends will ever be paid. But if you want to have a chance to make an investment (after careful research) in a high-growth industry with large potential returns, then Stage I or II industries will provide you with opportunities for gains or losses. Since actual dividends are irrelevant in these stages, an investor will be purchasing shares for capital gains based on expected growth rather than current income. As the industry enters Stage III, the growth rate is still positive, but the rate of change starts declining. This is often the point where investors do not recognize that the growth rate has begun to decline, and they still pay large premiums over the regular market for stocks in these industries. However, when the market does realize that the growth rate in fact is diminishing, stock prices can take a sizable tumble.

In Stage III, the expansion of sales continues but at a decreasing rate, and returns on investment may decline as more competition enters the market and attempts to take away market share from existing firms. The industry has expanded to the point where asset expansion slows in line with production needs, and the firms in the industry are more capable of paying cash dividends. Stock dividends and stock splits are still common in Stage III, and the dividend payout ratio usually increases from a low level of 5 to 15 percent of earnings to a moderate level of 25 to 40 percent of earnings. Finally, at Stage IV, maturity, the firm maintains a stable growth rate in sales similar to that of the economy as a whole, and when risk premiums are considered, its returns on assets level out to those of the economy. Automobiles might be a good example of a mature industry.

In unfortunate cases, industries suffer declines in sales (for example, passenger railroads) if product innovation has not increased the product base over the years. In Stage IV, assuming maturity rather than decline, dividends might range from 40 to 60 percent of earnings. Of course, these percentages will be different from industry to industry depending on individual characteristics.

It is also important to realize that growth companies can exist in a mature industry and that not all companies within an industry experience the same growth path in sales, earnings, and dividends. Some companies are simply better managed, have better people, have more efficient assets, and have put more money into productive research and development that has created new products or improved products.

For example, electric utilities are generally considered mature, but some utilities exist in states like Florida and California that have undergone rapid population explosions over the last decade. These utilities would still have higher growth rates than the industry in general. Computer companies such as IBM were fast approaching maturity until technical innovations created new markets. Now personal computers and local area networks not only have added vitality to older markets but also created new industries of their own. You can trace the histories of many industries to see that this pattern repeats itself over and over.

The warning to the investor is to not become too enamored with a company just because it is in a "growth industry." Its time of glory may have passed. Other investors improperly ignore companies that are in the process of revitalization because they no longer carry the growth-stock tag. More will be said about growth stocks in the next chapter.

Other Industry Factors to Consider

A financial analyst may wish to evaluate other significant factors for a given industry. For example, is the industry structure monopolistic like a regulated utility, oligopolistic like the automobile or steel industry, partially competitive like the drug industry, or very competitive like the market for farm commodities? Questions of industry structure are very important in analyzing pricing structures and price elasticities that exist because of competition or lack of it.

Questions of supply and demand relationships are very important as they affect the price structure of the industry and its ability to produce quality products at a reasonable cost. The cost variable can be affected by many factors. For example, high relative hourly wages in basic industries such as steel, autos, and rubber, are somewhat responsible for the inability of the United States to compete in the world markets of these products. Availability of raw material is also an important cost factor. Industries like aluminum and glass have to have an abundance of low-cost bauxite and silicon to produce their products. Unfortunately, the aluminum industry uses very large amounts of electricity in the production process, and so the low cost of bauxite may be offset by the high cost of energy. Energy costs are of concern to all industries, but the availability of reasonably priced energy sources is particularly important to the airline and trucking industries. The list could go on and on, but as an analyst becomes familiar with a specific industry, he or she learns the crucial variables.

Most industries are also affected by government regulation. This applies to the automobile industry where safety and exhaust emissions are regulated and to all industries where air, water, and noise pollution are of concern. Many industries engaged in interstate commerce, such as utilities, railroads, and telephone companies, are strongly regulated by the government. On the other hand, many industries, such as airlines, trucking, and natural gas production companies, are being deregulated, and these industries are facing a new climate where the old game plan may no longer prove successful. Most industries are affected by government expenditures; this is especially true for industries involved in defense, education, and transportation.

These are but a few examples to alert you to the importance of having a thorough understanding of your industry. This is why in many large investment firms, trust departments, and insurance companies, analysts are assigned to only one industry or to several related industries so that they may concentrate their attention on a given set of significant factors. An example of an in-depth industry analysis is presented in Appendix 5–A.

APPENDIX 5–A: EXAMPLE OF AN INDUSTRY ANALYSIS BY THE STANDARD & POOR'S CORPORATION—THE HEALTH CARE INDUSTRY

JUNE 9, 1988 (Vol. 156, No. 23, Sec. 1)   Replaces Basic Analysis dated April 16, 1987

health care
hospitals, drugs and cosmetics
BASIC ANALYSIS

STANDARD & POOR'S

industry surveys

©1988 Standard & Poor's Corporation   USPS No. 517-780.

The Outlook

Drugs

Medical
Facilities

Medical Equipment
& Supplies

Cosmetics &
Personal Care Products

Industry References

Composite Industry Data

Comparative Company Analysis

U.S. health expenditures, by type
(In millions of dollars)

Type of Expenditure	1979	1980	1981	1982	1983	R1984	R1985	R1986	1987	E1990
Health Services and Supplies	204,500	237,100	273,500	308,300	341,800	375,400	407,200	442,000	479,300	626,500
Personal health care	188,900	219,400	254,600	286,900	314,800	341,900	371,300	404,000	438,900	573,500
Hospital care	86,100	100,400	118,000	135,500	148,800	156,300	167,200	179,600	192,600	250,400
Physician's services	40,200	46,800	54,800	61,800	68,400	75,400	82,800	92,000	101,400	132,600
Dentists' services	13,300	15,400	17,300	19,500	21,700	24,600	27,100	29,600	32,400	41,800
Other professional services	4,700	5,600	6,400	7,100	9,300	10,900	12,400	14,100	16,200	22,900
Drugs and medical sundries	17,200	19,300	21,300	22,400	24,500	26,500	28,700	30,600	32,800	42,100
Eyeglasses and appliances	4,600	5,100	5,700	5,700	6,200	7,000	7,500	8,200	8,800	11,200
Nursing home care	17,600	20,600	24,200	27,300	29,400	31,700	35,000	38,100	41,600	54,500
Other health services	5,100	6,000	6,900	7,600	8,400	9,400	10,800	11,900	13,100	18,000
Prepayment and administration	9,300	10,700	11,100	12,700	17,100	22,600	23,600	24,500	25,900	34,600
Government public health activities	6,200	7,000	7,700	8,600	10,000	11,000	12,300	13,400	14,400	18,500
Medical facilities	10,500	11,800	13,100	14,100	15,400	15,600	15,400	16,300	17,300	20,700
Research	4,800	5,300	5,700	5,900	6,200	6,800	7,400	8,200	9,000	11,500
Construction	5,700	6,500	7,500	8,200	9,200	8,900	8,100	8,000	8,300	9,300
Total health expenditures	215,000	249,000	286,600	322,400	357,200	391,100	422,600	458,200	496,600	647,300

R—Revised. E—Estimated.
Source: Health Care Financing Administration.

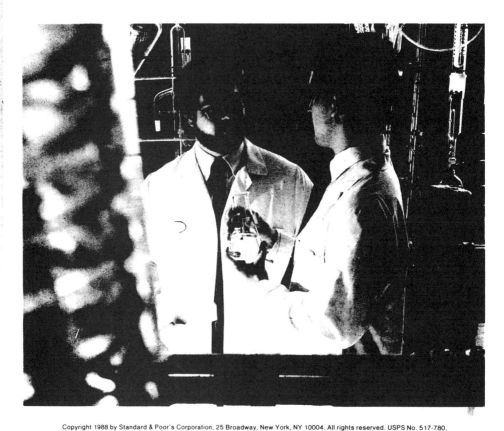

THE OUTLOOK

Costs continue to spiral

The U.S. health care system continues in a state of flux, as the nation grapples with the conflicting pressures of providing quality medical care to all citizens while at the same time controlling inflation in health care expenditures. Medical spending as a percentage of total GNP is higher in the U.S. than in any other country. Yet, some 37 million Americans are uninsured, and millions of others are without adequate coverage, especially for catastrophic-type illnesses. Resolving these matters without bankrupting the system remains a knotty problem for the nation's lawmakers and business leaders.

A fact of life in the U.S. economy for over half a century, "super inflation" in health care costs became especially pronounced during the 1970s. Total national health care expenditures grew at an annual compound rate of about 12% in the 20 years through 1987, compared with 8.9% in GNP over the same period. As a percentage of total GNP, health care expenditures rose from 6.3% in 1968 to an indicated 11.1% in 1987.

Reasons for this explosive growth are manifold. They include increased demand for health care services, spurred

Herman B. Saftlas, Health Care Analyst

by the creation of the Medicare and Medicaid programs in the mid-1960s; pressures from organized labor for ever-greater medical coverage; the steadily rising proportion of elderly in the general population (often referred to as the graying of America), who as a group spend more than 2.5 times the amount that younger persons spend on health care; inflation in the overall economy; and the growing sophistication of medical technology, which has spawned a plethora of expensive diagnostic and therapeutic equipment.

Efforts taken by government and industry to hold down medical cost inflation have yielded mixed results. The implementation several years ago of Medicare's prospective payment reimbursement system (PPS) and increasing cost consciousness among other third-party payers have resulted in declining inpatient utilization and a slowdown in the rate of growth of inpatient costs. On the other hand, the number of procedures carried out in physicians' offices and hospital outpatient settings has proliferated, pointing up what some observers have characterized as "the balloon effect." Just as squeezing a balloon on one side results in bulging on the other side, so sectors picked up slack caused by cutbacks in funding for conventional providers have forced people to seek alternatives in other sectors.

WHO PAYS FOR WHAT: NATIONAL HEALTH CARE EXPENDITURES BY SOURCE OF FUNDS
(In Percent)

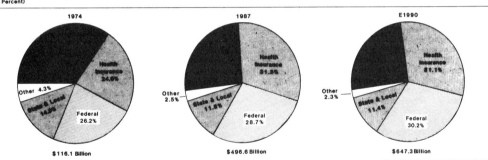

Source: Health Care Financing Administration

NATIONAL HEALTH EXPENDITURES
(In Percent)

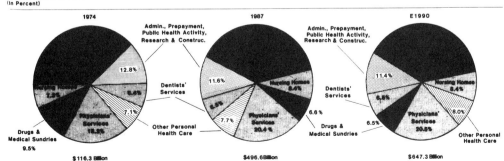

Source: Health Care Financing Administration

Outlays for hospital care rose 7.6% per year in the 1986–87 period, versus a compound annual rate of 12.7% over the 1972–85 period. However, annual increases in the cost of physicians' services and other professional services has abated only modestly in recent years from previous highs. The cost of prescription drugs has also continued to surge, rising 8.1% in 1987, compared with a 4.4% gain in the consumer price index (CPI).

On balance, however, cost-containment measures implemented by both government and the private sector have borne fruit, as seen by comparing trends in the rate of medical care inflation. Based on data provided by the Bureau of Labor Statistics, the spread between medical care inflation and the CPI declined to 3.1 percentage points in 1987 from 5.8 percentage points in 1986, and further narrowed to 2.5 percentage points in the first quarter of 1988, with the medical care component up 6.4%, versus a rise of 3.9% in the CPI.

Outlays to reach $1.5 trillion by 2000

Based on historical trends and relationships, the Health Care Financing Administration (HCFA) has projected national health care expenditures to reach the $1.5 trillion mark by the year 2000, equal to 15.0% of total GNP in that year. Health care spending per capita is expected to rise to $5,550 by the turn of the century, up from $1,837 in 1986. Continuing a trend begun with the imposition of the PPS system five years ago, HCFA expects per-capita inpatient utilization to continue to erode through the end of this decade and then experience modest growth, buoyed by the aging population. Outpatient volume is expected to show steady above-average growth through most of the 1986–2000 period, as new technology allows for an increasing number of procedures to be shifted from inpatient to less-expensive, outpatient settings. Demand for nursing care is also expected to mushroom from $38 billion in 1986 to $129 billion by 2000.

In mid-April, 1988 the Massachusetts State Legislature passed a controversial and costly new Universal Health Care program that would, in effect, guarantee health insurance to all residents by 1992. The bill provides that uninsured state residents be required to pay for health insurance, with premiums based on a sliding scale according to earnings. Employers not presently offering health coverage would be motivated to do so under the new law by a provision that would require them to pay a heavy surcharge per employee to a state risk pool. Governor Michael Dukakis, who sponsored that bill, has made universal health insurance a major issue of his campaign for the Democratic Presidential nomination. A somewhat similar bill proposed on the federal level by Senator Ted Kennedy (*D-Mass*) is presently under Congressional review.

Filling a gap in coverage for the elderly and disabled, Congress is expected to pass legislation soon that will provide medical insurance against "catastrophic illness" for Medicare's approximately 32 million beneficiaries. Under the new bill, hospital costs would be paid in full after a one-day deductible that will increase with average hospital costs. After deductibles are met, the new catastrophic plan, when fully phased in, will also cover all doctor bills and 80% of prescription drug costs. At present, Medicare covers only 80% of physicians' charges and provides coverage for only a few drugs that are considered extremely expensive. Part of the additional coverage, which will be completely phased in by 1993, will be paid for by extra monthly premiums paid for by Medicare enrollees.

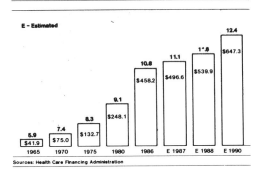

HEALTH CARE EXPENDITURES AS A % OF GNP
(In Billions of Dollars)

E - Estimated

								12.4
5.9	7.4	8.3	9.1	10.6	11.1	1*.6		$647.3
$41.9	$75.0	$132.7	$248.1	$458.2	$496.6	$539.9		
1965	1970	1975	1980	1986	E 1987	E 1988		E 1990

Sources: Health Care Financing Administration

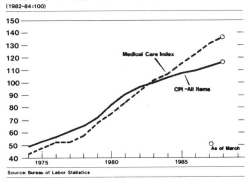

HEALTH CARE COSTS OUTSTRIP CPI
(1982–84=100)

Medical Care Index

CPI –All Items

As of March

Source: Bureau of Labor Statistics

Some notes on specific sectors

● **Hospitals**—Tightened reimbursement from Medicare and rising costs continue to batter this industry, and the American Hospital Association (AHA) estimates that more than half of all U.S. community hospitals sustain negative margins from inpatient care. Also according to the AHA, overall hospital admissions continued to slide in 1987, although some slight improvement was noted in 65-and-over utilization. Hospitals' operating costs accelerated last year, especially those related to labor. The latter was aggravated by a pervasive nurse shortage, a situation that is likely to worsen in the years ahead.

Competition in the inpatient hospital market has also intensified in recent years, as providers vied for patients in a contracted market. Increased competitive pressures have also come from HMO facilities, free-standing surgi-centers, physicians' offices, and other outpatient settings. Industry woes were behind investor-owned industry leader HOSPITAL CORPORATION OF AMERICA's decision to sell off about half of its acute care hospitals to an employee-owned firm last year. Following suit, AMERICAN MEDICAL INTERNATIONAL recently announced a similar plan, and major restructurings have been implemented at other hospital management firms.

● **Medical Suppliers**—Successfully adjusting to a contracted hospital market, earnings of most major medical products companies have recovered nicely from the depressed levels of the mid-1980s. Above-average growth is expected to continue over the foreseeable future, as demand from home health-care, independent physician practices and other non-hospital providers more than make up for sluggish trends in acute care markets. Industry results are also benefiting from new technology, which has spawned a bevy of new diagnostic and therapeutic products, many of which represent significant improvements over existing equipment both in terms of efficacy and cost savings. Bottom-line results are also being aided by cost reduction programs and expanding overseas penetration and favorable foreign exchange comparisons.

● **Drug producers**—The brightest sector in the health care universe in recent years, the drug group should continue to outshine the other sectors in the years ahead. With

most of their business essentially recession-proof, the industry's agressive new product research and development efforts are expected to generate a steady stream of new drug products which should translate into continued above average earnings growth in the years ahead. Results are also benefiting from stable raw material costs, foreign expansion, improved foreign exchange higher drug prices and the reduction in the corporate tax rate. One caveat, however, exists with the anticipated passage of the new Medicare catastrophic health insurance bill. The drug industry has opposed a drug amendment to that bill because of fears that it will mandate generic competition and impose strict pricing controls. However, additional volume generated from the new legislation may offset the effects of any pricing restrictions.

DRUGS

Industry has prescription for success

The brightest area of the health care universe in recent years, the drug group should continue to outshine other sectors of the industry in 1988 and beyond. With most of their businesses essentially recession-proof, the industry's aggressive new product research and development efforts are expected to generate a steady stream of new pharmaceutical products that should translate into continued above-average earnings growth in the years ahead. Besides an impressive lineup of new drugs, industry profits in 1988 will also be helped by higher pharmaceutical prices, stable raw material costs, a weaker dollar, and a reduced overall corporate tax rate. In addition, individual companies in the industry have made significant strides in cost reduction and margin improvement through the divestment of lower-margined nondrug businesses, cutbacks in industry employment, and other moves taken to improve productivity. Per-share comparisons of most of the leading drug producers are also benefiting from common share repurchase programs, many of which were instituted following the October 1987 stock market crash.

Despite heightened cost-consciousness throughout the all health care markets, long-term underlying fundamentals for the drug industry remain favorable. Strong demographic trends in the above-65 segment of the population, which accounts for about 30% of industry prescriptions, along with the rapidly expanding number of family physicians, should also spur drug demand. Drug sales are also receiving a boost from the cost-conscious environment now prevailing, since they usually represent the least-expensive form of medical therapy. Drugs that reduce the incidence of second heart attacks, prevent infection, and treat other ailments have saved the nation untold billions by avoiding or reducing expensive hospitalizations and physicians' services.

The industry's value of shipments totaled about $34 billion in 1987, based on data from the Department of Commerce. Of the total, pharmaceutical preparations accounted for about 80%, biological products (compounds from living organisms or products from living organisms such as vaccines) 10%, and medicinals and botanicals 10%.

According to the Department of Commerce, shipments of pharmaceutical preparations are projected to advance about 7.5% to approximately $29.1 billion in 1988, with higher drug prices accounting for the bulk of the gain. Total sales of pharmaceutical preparations of about $25 billion in 1986 (latest available) broke down by product classification

according to the Commerce Dept. as follows: drugs acting on the central nervous system 24%; preparations affecting parasitic and infective diseases, 16%; cardiovascular compounds, 14%; vitamins, nutrients and hematinic preparations, 11%; respiratory system drugs, 10%; pharmaceuticals affecting neoplasms, the endocrine system and metabolic diseases, 9%; gastrointestinal and genitourinary drugs, 8%; skin preparations, 5%; and veterinary items, 3%.

The drug industry is highly competitive, with no one firm accounting for more than 7% of the market. Based on the National Prescription Audit put out by IMS America, Ltd. the nation's four largest drug makers account for about 25% of industrywide sales, with the top eight firms accounting for less than half of the total market. A total of some 680 firms produce prescription and over-the-counter drugs in the U.S.

The U.S. also dominates the worldwide drug market, with 11 of the world's top 20 leading drug companies based in the U.S. The nine others were located in West Germany (three), Switzerland (three), and one each in the U.K., France, and Japan.

Firms consolidate operations

Reversing a trend aimed at horizontal diversification during the Sixties and Seventies, many large drug firms

Shipments of pharmaceutical preparations
(In millions of dollars)

Category	R1985 ship-ments	% of total	1986 ship-ments	% of total
Neoplasms, endocrine, metabolic diseases	2,110	9	2,132	9
Central nervous system	5,738	25	5,970	24
Cardiovascular system	3,171	14	3,529	14
Respiratory system	2,202	10	2,408	10
Digestive system	1,876	8	1,966	8
Dermatological	1,213	5	1,336	5
Vitamin, etc.	2,291	10	2,686	11
Parasitic and infective diseases	3,386	15	3,812	15
Veterinary	818	4	852	3
Total	$22,805		$24,691	

R—Revised.
Source: Dept. of Commerce

have been shedding lower-margined nondrug businesses in recent years in an effort to improve bottom-line results. In past years many drug firms made major investments in other health-care related fields, such as medical equipment and devices, hospital supplies, diagnostic products, as well as more diverse areas such as agricultural chemicals and cosmetics. However, over the past two years, many of those firms have divested non-pharmaceutical businesses. Some examples include ELI LILLY's sale of its Elizabeth Arden cosmetics division for $657 million in December 1987; SQUIBB's sale of its Charles of the Ritz cosmetics and fragrances unit in 1986 for $631 million; and WARNER LAMBERT's sale of three medical equipment businesses in 1986 for over $425 million.

Leading drug companies themselves have been the subject to renewed takeover interests, especially by large foreign pharmaceutical and chemical companies seeking entry or expansion in U.S. markets. Interest in the group has also come from its more-conservative market valuations following the October 1987 stock market crash and the weaker dollar, which has made domestic firms more attractive to foreign buyers. In January 1988 HOFFMAN-LA ROCHE, the giant Swiss pharmaceutical firm, made a $4.2 billion bid for Sterling Drug, representing the first bid in recent history by a major pharmaceutical company for another major non-bankrupt drug firm. While HOFFMAN'S bid was unsuccessful (Sterling was subsequently bought out by EASTMAN KODAK for close to $5 billion), it did point up the strong underlying interest in domestic drug firms.

Other potential overseas firms rumored to be interested in U.S. drug companies include HOECHST, BAYER, and IMPE-

RIAL CHEMICAL INDUSTRIES, as well as major U.S. chemical companies such as DU PONT and DOW CHEMICAL.

Profits to rise 20% in 1988

Buoyed by greater contributions from a spate of new drug products, improved volume in established pharmaceutical lines, further improvment in foreign exchange, higher prices, cost controls and a lower tax rate, industry earnings, as measured by the S&P drug stock price index, should advance close to 21% in 1988, following the 24% gain scored in 1987. As expressed in per-share statistics, index results will also benefit importantly from the many common share buyback programs which most major drug makers implemented in 1987.

The domestic pharmaceutical industry is one of the nation's most profitable business enterprises, both in terms of historical earnings performance and financial ratios. Pharmaceutical profits of the S&P drug stock price index expanded at a compound annual rate of 11.9% in the ten years through 1987, as compared with a growth record of only 5.8% for the overall market, as measured by the S&P 400 stock price index. In terms of operating margins and returns on capital, the drug industry also far surpasses industry norms. Based on data supplied by the Commerce Dept., the pharmaceutical industry had pretax and after-tax returns of 20.7% and 14.5% in 1986, as compared with 5.8% and 3.7% respectively, for all manufacturing industries. The drug industry's after-tax return on stockholders' equity was about 22.9% in the same year, versus an average of 9.6% for all manufacturing categories.

Underlying the high margins characteristic of the industry is the fact that fixed labor and production costs are relatively low and, after typically heavy new product development costs are amortized, a major chunk of revenues can be brought down to the bottom line. In addition, most of the leading domestic drug makers have taken advantage of significant tax incentives afforded by producing product at plants in Puerto Rico.

Industry revenue growth, which has averaged about 8% over the past ten years, has been largely due to higher selling prices as unit volume growth has been modest at best during much of the period. Partially due to larger dosing regimens (once-a-day doses, versus former three or four doses per day), market saturation in many product areas and generic competition, unit volume has been relatively stagnant over the past five years.

Drug prices accelerate

With unit volume relatively flat, the real key to industry profitability lies in pricing. Over the past five years, drug prices have risen steadily at a healthy clip, regardless of market conditions or general rates of inflation. During 1987, producer prices for ethical pharmaceuticals rose 9.5%, from the year-earlier level, as compared with a rise of only 2.2% in the overall producer price index. Consumers paid an average of 8.1% more for drug prescriptions last year, versus a rise of 4.4% in the consumer price index. In each of the past five years, the annual increase in the prescription drug price index also exceeded the comparable CPI by a wide margin. At the end of 1987, the prescription drug index was about 75% above its 1981 average, as compared with a gain of only 26% in the CPI over the same period.

Pharmaceutical pricing is extremely complicated, with numerous factors determining the price of each compound. Underlying the basic pricing structure is the need to recoup heavy research and development costs expended to bring the drug from the laboratory to pharmacy shelves. Relative market sizes for each compound and competitive market

Product line sales and profits for major pharmaceutical companies

Company	Product category	1987 Sales Mil. $	1987 Profits Mil. $
Amer. Home Prods.	Health care products	3,789	1,031
	Food & household prods.	1,240	180
Bristol-Myers	Pharmaceutical & medical prod.	2,217	484
	Toiletries & beauty products	1,189	199
	Non-prescription health	1,504	405
	Household items	491	71
Lilly (Eli)	Human health care	2,895	672
	Agricultural chemicals	748	-21
*Marion Laboratories	Pharmaceuticals & hospitals	597	459
Merck & Co. Inc.	Human / animal health prods.	4,630	1,315
	Environmental health	431	58
Pfizer Inc.	Health care	3,118	832
	Agricultural products	519	54
	Specialty chemicals	514	70
	Consumer products	396	63
	Materials science	374	29
Robins (A.H.) Co.	Ethical pharmaceuticals	426	100
	Consumer products	307	57
Rorer Group	Pharmaceuticals	929	54
Schering-Plough	Ethical pharmaceuticals	1,865	415
	Consumer products	835	136
SmithKline-Beckman	Therapeutics	2,640	689
	Diagnostic / analytical	1,135	121
Squibb Corp.	Pharmaceutical products	1,843	449
	Medical products	314	58
†Syntex Corp.	Human pharmaceuticals	926	322
	Agribusiness	86	3
	Dent., beauty care, diagn. prod.	118	10
Upjohn	Human health care	2,068	428
	Agricultural	453	40
Warner-Lambert	Ethical prods.	1,093	351
	Nonprescription prods.	1,195	256
	Gums & mints	777	173
	Other products	420	86

*For fiscal year ending June 30, 1987. †Fiscal year ending July 31, 1987.
Source: Company reports.

conditions also play important roles. Producers of drugs with strong patent protection and brand recognition are often able to push through hefty annual price hikes. In addition, consumers are not overly concerned with changes in drug prices, since much of the cost is often covered by medical insurance plans.

Drug companies also exploit the U.S. market by raising prices here to make up for frozen or only modestly higher allowable price hikes overseas. Drug pricing in Japan, England, France, and many other foreign countries is subject to strict regulatory scrutiny, with average realizations in those markets usually well below prices in unregulated markets.

Often, price increases are effected to offset patent expirations on branded drugs. Drug companies typically raise prices on drugs that have lost or are about to lose patent protection in an attempt to retain as much cash flow as possible after market share is lost to generic competition.

Comparing year-end 1987 prices with those of the year before, nearly all major drug segments showed gains, some in the double digit category. According to data supplied by the Bureau of Labor Statistics, prescription product prices in December 1987 were an average 9.5% above the year-earlier level, while prices for nonprescription or over-the-counter drugs were up 5.1%. Selected prescription categories showed the following increases: analgesics 13.3%; antiarthritics 9.2%; systemic antiinfectives (antibiotics and penicillins) 8.4%; antispasmodic/antisecretory (gastrointestinal drugs) 14.0%; bronchial therapy 8.5%; cancer therapy 8.5%; cardiovascular 8.1% (including antihypertensives, 14.4%); cough and cold preparations 8.0%; diuretics 11.8%,

Product	1983	1984	1985	1986	P1987
Ethical preparations	110.7	120.9	132.0	143.6	156.5
Systemic anti-infectives	105.8	111.5	115.8	119.4	125.7
Anti-arthritics	110.3	105.8	75.8	111.1	159.4
Cardiovascular therapy	111.5	126.5	145.1	160.1	172.5
Hormones	104.9	106.8	114.0	120.1	126.7
Diuretics	111.8	120.0	128.4	140.3	153.3
Analgesics, internal	107.9	116.4	128.1	141.8	158.4
Proprietary preparations	106.6	113.6	121.5	129.1	135.3
Vitamins	104.9	106.8	109.3	111.8	114.6
Cough and cold preparations	108.2	117.7	123.8	131.3	139.0
Laxatives	107.2	113.1	117.9	123.5	129.0
Analgesics, internal	108.1	115.4	127.5	139.7	150.3
External analgesics and counterirritants	99.9	101.1	101.7	101.9	100.9
Antacids	105.4	113.9	122.0	130.9	137.3
Dermatologicals	107.5	119.1	126.6	132.8	139.6

Producer price indexes for selected drug products
(1982 = 100)

P—Preliminary.
Source: Department of Labor.

and psychotherapeutics 18.4%.

Generally, segments showing the largest gains were those where therapeutic demand was the strongest and available product was limited. Last year saw two major breakthrough drugs come to market, each priced at heretofore unheard of levels. The first was Burroughs Wellcome's *Retrovir* or AZT compound for the treatment of AIDS, presently selling for about $7,800–$8,500 for a year's supply (after a recent 20% manufacturer's price reduction). The other was GENENTECH's *Activase* t-PA thrombolytic agent for dissolving blood clots. The latter, which is now being given to a good portion of heart attack victims, is priced at over $2,200 for one six-hour intravenous treatment.

One area where drug prices have been soft in recent years has been intravenous solutions sold to hospitals. That market has been severely squeezed by cutbacks in Medicare reimbursement and heightened competition. Average prices for hospital solutions at the end of 1987 were approximately 5.7% below year-earlier levels.

Congressional committees have periodically taken up the issue of hyperinflation in drug pricing over recent years under pressure from senior citizen groups (proportionately heavy users of prescription drugs) and other consumer organizations. Although the implementation of price controls is not likely, high drug prices are recognized as a matter of concern, and government agencies will at some future point probably move to increase competition and take other measures to bring down prices. For example, government-sponsored health programs are expected to promote greater usage of generic drugs, which are usually priced at steep discounts from those of branded drugs.

Industry fears new Medicare bill

While the Government's proposed catastrophic health insurance plan for the elderly will certainly help hospitals, nursing homes, and other health-care providers, it had been staunchly opposed by the branded prescription drug industry because price controls are likely to accompany it. It is feared that the drug amendment to the bill, which will provide for the payment of prescription drugs for Medicare enrollees, will mandate generic substitution and impose strict pricing controls similar to Medicare's DRG system which governs Medicare hospital care reimbursement. (see Hospitals section.) The proposed bill could affect about 35% of the prescription retail drug market. Some observers feel that additional business generated by the new bill will more than offset the effects of pricing restrictions.

PHARMACEUTICAL SALES* – U.S. & FOREIGN
(In Billions of Dollars)

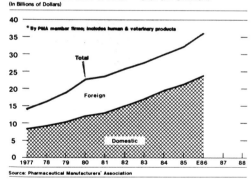

Source: Pharmaceutical Manufacturers' Association

PRODUCER PRICE INDEXES – DRUGS
(1982=100)

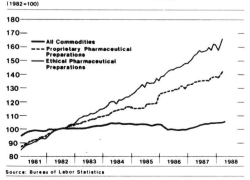

Source: Bureau of Labor Statistics

Drug sales to retail outlets, which account for about 80% of total industry volume, are much more profitable than sales to hospitals, where prices are subject to competitive bidding. Despite intense lobbying efforts last year, the drug industry was unsuccessful in its efforts to remove the prescription drug amendment from the catastrophic health care bill. Consumers' groups and many members of Congress concerned with spiraling drug prices have been strong supporters of the drug provision, while the drug industry continues its staunch opposition. A key fight is expected as the bill goes through Senate-House conference this year.

Foreign trade balance deteriorates

Despite the weaker dollar, the drug industry's balance of trade continued to decline in 1987, and a negative trade situation is forecast for 1988, the first one in many years. Based on data suplied by the Commerce Dept. net exports totaled $394 million in 1987, versus $764.2 million in 1986, with a balance of trade deficit of about $85 million estimated for 1988. Total exports rose 5.8% to $3.27 billion in 1987, while imports climbed nearly 23%, to $2.8 billion, mirroring growth patterns experienced in recent years. Extending those trends into 1988, the Commerce Dept. looks for exports of $3.49 billion to exceed imports of about $3.41 billion.

Steady erosion has taken place in the industry's trade surplus since it peaked at $1.24 billion in 1982, primarily reflecting strong gains in imports which more than doubled over the past four years. The principal factor in the burgeoning imports has been exceptionally strong demand for active ingredients (raw materials from which drugs are made), especially from the rapidly expanding domestic generic drug industry. Low production costs in Italy, Japan, Singapore, Switzerland, and other foreign countries have made these nations prime suppliers of active ingredients to U.S. drug manufacturers. Declining prices for medicinal chemicals especially from Eastern Europe, thus more than offset the weaker dollar.

Medicinals and botanicals (mostly active ingredients) accounted for about 88% of total imports and approximately 61% of total exports in 1987. Exports in 1988 should rise at a slightly higher rate than in 1986, aided by legislation passed in 1986 which allowed U.S. firms to export drugs still undergoing the Food & Drug Administration (FDA) approval process. During 1987, ten of the 24 applications to export drug products not approved for domestic sale were

cleared for foreign shipment. Exports should also benefit from an 11% increase in shipments of active ingredients from this country, aided by the growing trend to manufacture finished goods in the country where they are sold.

While the industry's balance of trade situation is important from the standpoint of the nation's overall competitive worldwide position, it is not that significant to domestic drug companies since most of them have important R&D and production operations based abroad. Industry leaders such as MERCK, PFIZER, SCHERING-PLOUGH SQUIBB, and WARNER LAMBERT derive close to half of their total sales from foreign operations.

Because of tariffs and other import barriers set up by nations to encourage native production capability, the establishment of manufacturing operations abroad is often the only way for American drug makers to do business there. Significant expansion of drug manufacturing facilities abroad has also been abetted by favorable tax treatment in those locations. According to the Pharmaceutical Manufacturers Association, U.S. drug sales abroad, both directly from exports and through foreign branches and subsidiaries, exceeded $10 billion in 1985 (latest available).

Profit rates from foreign operations, however, often vary appreciably because of local price restrictions and competitive factors. In many countries with socialized or semi-socialized health care systems, drug companies must live with price controls.

Fluctuations in the value of the dollar against foreign currencies also typically play an important role in reported foreign earnings. The sharp reversal in the value of the dollar vis-a-vis most other major world currencies beginning in early 1985 had a marked favorable impact on drug industry profits in 1986 and 1987, as year-to-year comparisons benefited from the translation of more dollars per unit of sales in local currency. The weaker dollar has also made U.S. exports more competitive abroad and imports relatively more expensive. The trade-weighted index of the dollar declined about 11% in 1987, and S&P expects it to continue to slide in 1988 and 1989.

R&D spending expanding

Representing the lifeblood of the pharmaceutical industry, research and development expenditures are expected to continue to expand at double-digit rates in the years ahead. Based on statistics published by the Pharmaceutical Manufacturers Association (PMA), total drug industry R&D expanded at a 16% annual compound rate in the ten years through 1987, with outlays in that year reaching a record $5.4 billion, including $4.4 billion spent in the U.S. and $1.0 billion spent abroad. Since the early 1940s, the industry has spent over $36 billion, generating more than 1,100 new drugs.

Industry R&D as a percentage of sales also ranks as one of the highest among the nation's major industries: it reached a record 15.1% in 1987, up from 11.3% ten years ago. Approximately 70% of drug R&D in this country is funded directly by domestic pharmaceutical manufacturers, 10% by colleges and universities (often in conjunction with leading drug companies), and 20% by government and other sources.

The share of U.S. company-funded R&D performed by foreign subsidiaries and related ventures abroad has shown exceptional growth in recent years, doubling to approximately $1 billion over the past five years, according to the PMA. Foreign-based work represented about 19% of total industry R&D outlays in 1987, up from 15% in 1983 and 10% in 1972. The rapid rise in foreign R&D can be attributed to lower costs abroad, as well as a shorter new-drug approval

Foreign sales of major U.S. drug companies

Company	1985		1986		1987	
	Foreign sales (mil. $)	% of total sales	Foreign sales (mil. $)	% of total sales	Foreign sales (mil. $)	% of total sales
Abbott	950	28	1,175	31	1,453	33
American Home Prod.	1,048	22	1,245	25	1,492	30
Bristol-Myers	1,315	38	1,501	31	1,754	32
Johnson & Johnson	2,431	38	3,031	43	3,485	48
Eli Lilly	1,005	34	1,234	37	1,455	40
Merck	1,689	48	2,141	52	2,698	53
Pfizer	1,682	42	1,993	45	2,268	46
Rorer Group	137	41	374	44	419	45
Schering-Plough	822	40	983	41	1,104	41
SmithKline	1,055	32	1,306	35	1,651	38
Squibb	736	52	865	48	1,038	48
†Syntex	275	32	316	32	370	33
Upjohn	676	34	826	36	963	38
Warner-Lambert	1,238	39	1,356	44	1,621	47

Note: Foreign sales are after interarea eliminations, where reported. †Fiscal year ends as of July 31, 1987.
Source: Annual reports.

processes. According to a recent PMA Survey, 58 of the 72 new molecular entities approved by the FDA between 1984 and 1986 were first approved in a foreign country.

Research directed towards new cardiovascular drugs represents the largest single category of R&D interest, accounting for about 26% of the R&D dollar in 1985 (latest available), according to the PMA. Other important categories included expenditures for pharmaceuticals to treat neoplasms and endocrine and metabolic diseases, 18% of R&D spending; infections 15% and central nervous system and related ailments 13%.

Increasing emphasis on new drug development has also contributed to the relatively high product turnover that now characterizes the industry. Based on a recent FDA Drug Utilization (which surveyed new drug performance) Study, the 14 new molecular entities introduced (first marketed) since 1980 for cardiovascular treatment accounted for nearly 25% of that category's 58.5 million prescriptions written in 1986. Two new anti-ulcer compounds—*Zantac* (GLAXO HOLDINGS) and *Carafate* (MARION LABORATORIES)—represented more than 26% of antispasmodic and GI/GU drug prescriptions in 1986. Two new bronchial agents accounted for roughly 25% of new bronchial prescriptions, while three new anti-diabetics and two new sedatives represented 34% and 47% of their respective markets in 1986.■

Ethical drugs

Prescription activity was relatively sluggish in 1987, with the total number of prescriptions dispensed at chain and independent pharmacies amounting to 1.508 billion, down 0.2% from the year-earlier level, according to Pharmaceutical Data Services (PDS), a market research firm in Phoenix, Ariz. While new prescriptions written totaled 769.7 million in 1987, up 1% year-to-year, refills held the total number of prescriptions down by falling 1%, to 738.5 million. The 1987 volume translated into about $16.5 billion at drugstore acquisition cost, up 7.8% from 1986's $15.3 billion, with all of the gain due to higher pharmaceutical prices.

The PDS prescription numbers do not include manufacturer's pipeline sales to distributors, nor do they reflect important drug sales to hospitals, outpatient and HMO pharmacies, mail order prescription services, and other end users. Strong growth in these outlets has cut into sales at traditional retail drug stores.

While still a miniscule part of the market, the mail order prescription drug business has been exhibiting strong growth in recent years, accounting for about 40 million prescriptions written last year, according to the Commerce Department. This market is expected to double within the next four years, as new players such as HOME SHOPPING NETWORK and others enter the market, and the idea becomes more acceptable to consumers.

Ethical, or prescription, drugs that are available only through medical practitioners account for about three-quarters of the value of all pharmaceutical preparations used in the U.S. Over-the-counter drugs comprise the balance. Sales to wholesale outlets account for about two-thirds of total U.S. prescription drug sales; retailers for about 16%; private hospitals, 9%; government hospitals, 5%; and other outlets, 3%.

Private and government programs have been picking up more of the tab for drug purchases in recent years than they had in the past. According to estimates by the Health Care Financing Administration, private health insurance paid 15% of the nation's total bill for drugs and medical sundries in 1987, up from 13% in 1983 and 5% in 1974, while the government's share was 11% in 1987, 9% in 1983, and 1% in

Research & development expenditures

Company	1985 Mil. $	1985 % of sales	1986 Mil. $	1986 % of sales	1987 Mil. $	1987 % of sales
Abbott	241	7	285	7	361	8
Bristol-Myers	273	6	311	8	342	8
Johnson & Johnson	471	7	521	7	617	8
Eli Lilly	R364	12	420	13	466	13
Merck	426	12	480	12	566	11
Pfizer	287	7	336	7	401	8
Rorer Group	R18	5	70	8	82	9
Schering-Plough	R189	9	212	9	251	9
SmithKline	310	10	377	10	424	10
Squibb	166	8	163	9	221	10
†Syntex	R123	14	143	15	175	16
Upjohn	284	16	314	14	356	14
Warner-Lambert	208	7	202	7	232	7

†Fiscal year ending July 31, 1987. R-Revised.
Source: Annual Reports.

*R&D outlays—pharmaceutical products
(In millions of dollars)

Year	R&D outlays	Year	R&D outlays	Year	R&D outlays
E1986	4,647	1981	2,340	1976	1,164
1985	4,078	1980	1,977	1975	1,062
1984	3,579	1979	1,627	1974	942
1983	3,218	1978	1,404	1973	825
1982	2,774	1977	1,276	1972	726

*By PMA member firms for human and veterinary products. The figures stated are "global" R&D outlays: ethical pharmaceutical R&D financed or conducted by U.S. firms in the U.S. and abroad, and in the U.S. only by U.S.-based subsidiaries of foreign-owned firms.
Source: Pharmaceutical Manufacturers Association.

Top drugs of 1987—retail market
(Ranked by total sales)

Product (company)	Function	1987 Sales Mil. dollars	1987 Sales % chg. from prev. yr.
Zantec (Glaxo)	Anti-ulcer	542	+29
Tagamet (SK&F)[1]	Anti-ulcer	423	−3
Cardizem (Marion)	Cardiovascular	291	+38
Naprosyn (Syntex)	Anti-arthritic	291	+13
Tenormin (Stuart)	Cardiovascular	256	+1
Dyazide (SK&F)[1]	Cardiovascular	252	−7
Xanax (Upjohn)	Tranquilizer	249	+28
Procardia (Pfizer)	Cardiovascular	234	+7
Capoten (Squibb)	Cardiovascular	230	+30
Ceclor (Lilly)	Antibiotic	220	+38

[1]Smith Kline & French, a subsidiary of SmithKline Beckman.
Source: Pharmaceutical Data Services.

1974. Conversely, direct patient outlays for drug and medical sundries have dropped to 74% of the total in 1987 from 78% in 1983, and 94% in 1974.

Three breakthrough drugs are approved

During 1987, the Food & Drug Administration (FDA) approved 27 new drugs, including 21 new molecular entities (NMEs) and six biologicals, versus 20 NMEs and four biologicals in the preceeding year. The number of NMEs approved each year has averaged about 20 since the mid-1970s. Of the 1987 approvals, three stand out as major breakthroughs—GENENTECH's *Activase* blood clot dissolving agent; MERCK's *Mevacor* cholesterol lowering drug; and BURROUGHS WELLCOME's *Retrovir* treatment for Acquired Immune Deficiency Syndrome (AIDS).

The new drug development & approval process

Searching for innovative products is a tough task in almost any industry, but it is especially difficult in pharmaceuticals because products involve the highly complex fields of molecular biology, biochemistry, and the intricate workings of the human body. Referred to as playing chess with nature, the quest for new pharmaceuticals combines an understanding of the complicated chemistry and physiology of the human organism with knowledge of all life sciences and a good dose of intuitive acumen in order to theorize and devise new therapeutic modalities.

Working from a set of hypotheses on how certain compounds might interact in the body, researchers begin to synthesize new compounds that, in theory at least, hold promise for combatting particular diseases. Often, genes isolated by molecular biologists or new chemicals discovered by analytical chemists form the basis for new drugs.

Once candidate drugs have been identified, they are studied by preclinical pharmacologists to determine their properties, while animal testing in mice and rats is conducted to determine possible side effects and efficacy. Most candidate drugs are eliminated at this stage because of unacceptable side effect profiles or because they do not function as expected.

Often, hundreds of compounds are tested before any are identified as promising enough to warrant human testing. When such trials are indicated, a company must submit to the FDA an Investigational New Drug (IND) application informing the agency that human studies will commence within 30 days unless the FDA objects.

Contrary to popular belief, the FDA does not perform clinical trials. All animal and human testing, which often lasts for years and costs millions of dollars, is borne by the manufacturer, often in conjunction with colleges or universities, the National Institutes of Health, and similar research institutions. Industry experts have speculated that the effort to move a drug from test tube to pharmacists' shelf can take close to ten years and cost over $100 million.

The clinical testing period in humans usually consists of three phases. During the first phase, the drug is given to a relatively small number of healthy people in order to test its safety. At first, very small doses of the drug are administered and dosage is slowly increased to determine its safety at higher levels. Phase II involves the administration of the drug to research subjects who have the

disease for which the drug is intended, involving a larger population of subjects and a lengthier test period than Phase I. Drugs that pass the first two hurdles then undergo Phase III, in which the most complex and rigorous tests are performed on still larger groups of ill patients in order to ascertain the drug's safety, effectiveness, and dosage regimens.

Usually, all Phase III procedures—and often Phase II—involve randomized, double-blind tests with placebo control. This means the one group of patients is given the drug and another control group is given a placebo, with neither the patients nor their doctors aware of which group is receiving what.

The FDA has said that out of an average of 20 drugs entering clinical testing, some 13 or 14 will successfully complete Phase I. Of those, about 9 will finish Phase II, and of that group, only one or two will complete Phase III. Only one of the original 20 will ultimately be approved for marketing.

When the basic research on the drug has been completed, the manufacturer then submits to the FDA a New Drug Application (NDA), reporting the research completed on the drug from the three phases, including full details of the product's formula, production, labeling, and intended use. Typically, NDAs are voluminous documents, with entries sometimes exceeding 50,000 pages. On average, about three years elapse between submission of an NDA and final approval.

Once an NDA is approved, the FDA continues to monitor the drug. Often, supplemental NDAs for the drug, requesting its use for additional indications, are submitted after marketing has begun. Sometimes, side effects or other unexpected developments come to light only after a drug is in wide use.

The FDA also determines a drug's labeling, which includes a detailed description of the drug, its chemical composition, indications, contraindications, and side effects. For drugs already on the market, the FDA can use several regulatory measures if a drug's safety and efficacy are in question. One of these measures is the drug recall. The recall may be used for any of wide range of problems, including defective packaging, misleading labeling, failure to meet disintegration tests, insterility, subpotency, a failure to meet content uniformity tests, or lack of evidence of effectiveness. ■

Promising new heart drugs approved

Tissue plasminogen activator (t-PA) and similar thrombolytic drugs, which were approved by the FDA for commercial marketing in November 1987, are revolutionizing the way we treat heart attacks and also hold much promise for the treatment of deep vein thrombosis, angina, and strokes. Cardiovascular disease is the No. 1 cause of death in the U.S., with an estimated 1.5 million Americans suffering heart attacks each year. Of the some 750,000 heart victims who survive the initial attack, about 600,000 could benefit from treatment with clot dissolving or thrombolytic agents such as t-PA.

GENENTECH's *Activase* t-PA drug, generically known as alteplase, is an enzyme produced naturally in the body, but in amounts too small to quickly dissolve blood clots in coronary arteries. Through genetic engineering techniques, however, GENENTECH has been able to produce the enzyme in quantities required for therapeutic use. The drug, which

is administered intravenously, triggers the body's own clot-dissolving mechanism in the vicinity of the arterial blockage, dissolving the clot and restoring blood flow through the artery.

Approved by the FDA in November, *Activase* had the most successful initial launch ever in U.S., racking up more than $58 million in sales during the last six weeks of the year. The drug represented a major advance from the first-generation thrombolytic agents, such as streptokinase (made by PHARMACIA and Hoechst-Roussell) and urokinase (ABBOTT LABORATORIES), in both efficacy and side effect profiles. In addition, t-PA is given intravenously, while the others can only be administered through intracoronary catheter. Some of the older thrombolytic agents have also been associated with allergic reactions.

Priced at more than $2,200 per treatment, t-PA cost considerably more than the streptokinase and urokinase. Considering, however, that t-PA does not require the intracoronary catheterizations as do the other two, the treatment is cost-competitive with the others. While *Activase* is expected to dominate the thrombolytic market in the near term, increasing competition from other clot-dissolving drugs, such as BEECHAM's *Eminase,* are expected to take away market share from t-PA. The worldwide market for clot-dissolving drugs is expected to surpass $1.5 billion within the next three years.

Another major breakthrough cardiovascular drug, *Mevacor,* received the green light from the FDA last year. *Mevacor,* which is manufactured by MERCK (which has brought to market more blockbuster drugs than any of its competitors over the past three years), has proven effective in controlling the body's production of cholesterol, the leading contributing factor in coronary heart disease. Generically known as lovastatin, the new drug is one of several new compounds called HMGCoa reductase inhibitors which can reduce levels of low-density lipoproteins, the culprits believed to form the plaque in coronary arteries.

Other cholesterol-regulating drugs now on the market include *Questran* (BRISTOL MYERS) and *Lopid* (WARNER-LAMBERT). Besides reducing dangerous low-density cholesterol, *Lopid* also increases high-density lipoprotein levels, which is believed to be beneficial in reducing cardiac risk. A major multi-year study in Helsinki, Finland, was completed in 1987, demonstrating *Lopid's* effectiveness in reducing the incidence of heart attacks.

Looking further down the road, several other cholesterol-reduction agents are anticipated, including another one from MERCK, called *Zocor,* and an entry from SQUIBB generically known as eptastatin. By the early 1990s, the anticholesterol market is expected to exceed $1 billion.

Accounting for about 14% of the total ethical pharmaceuticals market, cardiovascular drugs are expected to exhibit above-average sales growth in the years ahead, supported by a growing number of new products. Cardiovascular disease is still the leading cause of death in this country, although there has been a steady decline in the mortality rate from these disorders over the past twenty years (largely due to advancements in cardiac diagnostic techniques and new therapeutics). More than 42 million people are estimated to suffer from some form of heart or blood pressure problem, with coronary heart disease affecting about 4.5 million people.

Generic drugs

Increasing competition from generic drugs is probably the major worry for the leading manufacturers of branded pharmaceuticals. Essentially the bioequivalent of brand-name products, generic drugs are simply copies of brand-name drugs whose patent lives have expired. Unencumbered by the need to recover the heavy R&D, approval, and advertising expenditures incurred by primary producers, makers of generics are able to price their products at substantial discounts from the price of their branded cousins. Competition from generic drugs is expected to accelerate in the years ahead, reflecting an increasing number of major drugs coming off patent and efforts by the government and other third-party payers to reduce overall drug costs through mandatory generic substitution.

The total generic drug market is expected to expand to about $11 billion by 1991, up from some $5 billion in 1986, based on a recent study from Frost & Sullivan, a New York City based management consulting firm. According to the company, about 200 brand-name drugs will be coming off patent through 1995, representing about $14.4 billion in annual sales that will become vulnerable to generic substitution. Close to half of the nation's top 30 drugs are now subject to generic competition. Additionally, because they are priced lower than branded products, generics account for about 20% of the total prescription drug industry's value of shipments.

In addition to heightened cost-consciousness throughout the entire healthcare industry, makers of generics are also benefitting from the Waxman-Hatch Act passed by Congress in 1984, which simplified the FDA's generic drug approval process. Prior to the new legislation, the FDA had previously required manufacturers of generic drugs to repeat the lengthy and costly tests of safety and efficacy done by the original brand-name producers. Generic producers are now only required to demonstrate that their products are simply the bioequivalents of the branded products they aim to copy. As a tradeoff, primary producers were granted an additional five years of patent protection on their drugs. Substitution laws that mandate Medicare and Medicaid prescriptions be filled with cheaper generic products has fostered growth in the generics business. Retail pharmacists also often prefer to dispense generics rather than branded products because of the former's larger profit margins.

When a drug goes off patent, between 10 and 20 generic substitutions will typically become available, resulting in a highly competitive marketplace. Makers of branded products will often attempt to recover sales lost to generic competition by raising prices. SMITHKLINE increased the price of its popular *Dyazide* cardiovascular drug by roughly 18% following the appearance of competing generic products. Other major drugs that have witnessed substantial market erosion due to generics in recent years include *Inderal* (AMERICAN HOME PRODUCTS), *Aldomet* and *Indocin* (MERCK), *Keflex* (ELI LILLY), and *Valium* (HOFFMANN-LA ROCHE).

Approximately three-quarters of the generic market consists of "branded generics"—generic drugs produced by the large pharmaceutical companies under their own labels. Companies in this market include PFIZER, ELI LILLY, WARNER LAMBERT, and SMITHKLINE BECKMAN. Pure plays in the group are MYLAN LABORATORIES, ZENITH LABORATORIES, PAR PHARMACEUTICAL, BOLAR PHARMACEUTICAL, LYPHOMED, and BIOCRAFT LABORATORIES.

Proprietary drugs

Representing about one-third of the nation's total dollar shipments of pharmaceutical preparations, nonprescription drugs—often referred to as over-the-counter (OTC) or proprietary products—are expected to rise 6% to about $8.5 billion in 1988, roughly in line with their rate of growth in recent years. Essentially a slow-growth business, proprietary drug sales in recent years have been aided by higher prices and the switching of selected prescription products to over-the-counter status.

It has been estimated that only about one-third of American adults suffering from illness or injury seek professional help. The others self-diagnose or use nonprescription remedies. In light of this fact, the government has tried where possible to convert prescription products to OTC status. As a result of this policy, 30 former prescription drugs are presently available on an OTC basis.

The OTC market is divided roughly as follows: internal and external analgesics, 30%; cough and cold remedies, 25%; vitamins and related items, 20%; and antacids, skin medications, laxatives, and other medications, 25%. Sales are made through the following outlets: drugstores, about 40%; grocery stores, 45%; mass merchandisers and other outlets, 15%.

New study revitalizes aspirin market

After years of steadily losing market share in the $2 billion analgesic market, aspirin and aspirin-based products are expected to show vigorous growth over the next few years, thanks to the recent studies showing that the drug can prevent heart attacks. A study conducted by researchers at Harvard University and published in the New England Journal of Medicine last January found that taking a single aspirin every other day reduced the chances of a heart attack by 47%. Results of the five-year study that involved 22,000 men were so positive that it was concluded two years ahead of schedule. The Harvard study represented the first major experiment indicating aspirin's effect in preventing heart attacks in healthy men. Previous studies, in contrast, demonstrated its beneficial effects in preventing second heart attacks.

While the precise way that aspirin works on the heart is not yet fully understood, it is believed to aid in blocking the formation of blood clots, the primary cause of heart attacks. For this reason, aspirin is also believed to reduce the risk of ischemic strokes, which are those caused by clots in the blood vessels in the brain.

After several aspirin manufacturers began advertising campaigns using the Harvard study to promote their products, the FDA ordered an end to such claims on the basis that consumers may improperly medicate themselves based on incomplete information. The FDA was also concerned that for some people the risks involved may outweigh the benefits. Because aspirin interferes with blood clotting, it has been linked in certain instances with internal bleeding and brain hemorrhages. Aspirin has also been associated with Reye's syndrome, a rare but often fatal disease in children.

Although the $790 million aspirin market is fairly diversified with various formulas or strengths within branded and generic categories, three major brands account for slightly more than 40% of the market. These are Sterling Drug's *Bayer* (Sterling is now part of EASTMAN KODAK), the industry leader with estimated 1987 sales of $150 million; AMERICAN HOME PRODUCT's *Anacin*, with sales of $75 million; and BRISTOL MYERS' *Bufferin*, with sales of $75 million. Acet-

ESTIMATED OTC ANALGESIC MARKET—1987
(In Percent)

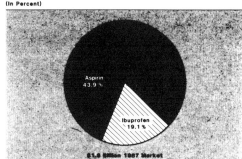

Source: Nielsen Marketing Research

aminophen, the active ingredient in *Tylenol* and similar pain relievers, does not affect clotting and, thus, does not offer protection against heart attacks.

The FDA is presently considering what to allow aspirin makers to claim in their advertising; chances are that some kind of qualified claims will be permitted. In any event, aspirin sales have been strong since the start of 1988 and are likely to more than double within the next four or five years.

Based on a study by Nielsen Marketing Research, sales of pain relievers totaled about $1.8 billion in 1987, of which aspirin accounted for about 44%; acetaminophen products, 37%; and ibuprofen products, 19%. Leading acetaminophen products are *Tylenol* (JOHNSON & JOHNSON), *Anacin 3* (AMERICAN HOME PRODUCTS), *Panadol* (Sterling), *Datril* (BRISTOL MYERS). Popular ibuprofen analgesics include *Advil* (AMERICAN HOME PRODUCTS), *Nuprin* (BRISTOL MYERS), and *Medipren* (JOHNSON & JOHNSON).

Biotechnology

The fledging biotechnology industry has finally delivered its first blockbuster drug with the FDA's approval of GENENTECH's *Activase* tissue plasminogen activator (t-PA) drug last November. Representing a major breakthrough in the treatment of heart attacks, t-PA dissolves the blood clots responsible for heart attacks in about 70% of the patients who receive it within six hours after the onset of the initial heart attack. The protein t-PA, which is the active ingredient in the drug, is naturally produced in the body in minute amounts. *Activase* contains larger quantities of the protein, which is produced through genetic engineering or gene-splicing techniques.

Based on Commerce Department estimates, shipments of products developed through recombinant DNA and monoclonal antibody technology totaled over $550 million in 1987, up from $400 million in 1986, $220 million in 1985, and $60 million in 1984. Despite this strong growth, the industry's overall success in bringing new products to market has been slower than earlier anticipated, especially in genetically engineered products; t-PA is the notable exception.

The industry is still in its infancy, and product sales are relatively small. As a result, most of its revenues, especially those of the smaller firms, have been derived from R&D contracts with larger firms. Based on government sources, R&D contracts of public biotech firms were valued at more than $350 million in 1987, while product sales of those firms amounted to only $150 million.

At present, most biotech firms are not profitable. Indeed,

Selected publicly owned biotech companies

Company	Stock symbol	1987 price range	*Recent price	Principal business
Amgen	AMGN	44¾ - 16	28½	Biologicals using DNA
Applied BioSystems	ABIO	44¼ - 13¾	23½	Biologicals & instruments
Biogen	BGENF	16 - 3¾	5⅝	R&D in recombinant DNA
Biotech Research	BTRL	13⅛ - 4⅜	7½	Biomed / DNA R&D
Bio-Technology General	BTGCC	18½ - 3	4⅝	Health prods. through biotech
Centocor	CNTO	48½ - 17	24¼	Develops diagnostic test kits
Cetus	CTUS	33¼ - 11½	11½	Genetic engineering
Damon Biochem	DBIO	9 - 2⅜	3¼	Monoclonal antibodies
Enzo Biochem	ENZO	12¾ - 3⅛	4⅛	Enzymes; DNA probes
Genentech	GNE	65¼ - 26	27¾	Gene splicing
Genex	GNEX	2⅝ - ½	¾	Genetic engineering
Immunex	IMNX	25⅝ - 9⅜	14⅝	Immunological bio products
Integrated Genetics	INGN	13⅝ - 4	4⅜	Diagnostic / therapeutic products
Molecular Genetics	MOGN	8¾ - 3	3⅜	R&D into vaccines
Monoclonal Antibodies	MABS	9 - 1⅝	3⅛	Hybridoma cells & monoclonal antibodies
Novo Industri	NVO	42½ - 17¼	28⅝	Enzymes & insulin
Pharmacia	PHABY	30¼ - 15	20⅝	Medical science prods.
Summa Medical	SUMA	3¼ - ⅞	1⅜	Radiopharmaceutical tracer drugs

*As of 6-2-88.

as a group, they are not likely to operate in the black until many more commercially successful products are approved—which is unlikely to occur before the next decade. In the interim, many biotech companies are going to have to rely on outside financing, which has become more difficult since the October 1987 stock market crash. The shares of nearly all publicly-traded biotech companies were particularly hard hit by the crash, since they lacked underlying earnings power to buoy them up. Some support, however, was afforded those companies with large cash positions.

Approximately 400 small biotechnology companies are operating in the U.S., with some 10%–15% publicly held. Most of these have established partnerships and joint ventures or product licensing agreements with large domestic and foreign pharmaceutical and chemical firms in order to gain access to their financial and marketing resources.

While reduced share prices should in theory make them attractive to outside suitors, most small biotech companies are not likely to be takeover targets because most of their promising R&D work on new products has been locked up in licensing agreements with larger drug and chemical firms. Another factor ruling out hostile takeovers is that the real value of these companies lies in their research scientists, who are under no obligation to remain with the acquiring company.

R&D crucial to future growth

Compared with the many billions of dollars in research and developed expended in recent years, industry shipments are relatively small. Similar to the pharmaceutical industry, new biotech compounds for either human therapeutics or agriculture involve large amounts of capital to fund lengthy review procedures. Based on government estimates, annual expenditures for industrial R&D in biotechnology range from more than $350 million for the group of publicly traded biotechnology companies to more than $1.6 billion for all firms engaged in biotechnology research. According to a National Science Foundation survey, total industrial R&D in biotechnology in 1985, segmented by industry application, broke down as follows: healthcare, 66%; plant agriculture, 13%; chemicals and foods, 11%; animal agriculture, 6%; and other areas, 4%.

Bolstered by t-PA and new diagnostic products based on monoclonal antibodies and DNA probes, sales of biotech products are expected to rise at least 50% in 1988. New diagnostic products include several more efficient tests for AIDS (see below) and a new monoclonal antibody product for in vivo imaging to detect damaged heart muscle. New

New product launches in U.S.—1987
(Retail drug market)

Product	Manufacturer	Use	1987 sales (thous. $)
Cipro	Miles	Antibiotic	383
Hytrin	Abbott	Antihypertensive	645
Keftab	Dista	Antibiotic	1,138
Mevacor	Merck Sharpe & Dohme	Cholesterol reducer	21,207
Retrovir	Burroughs-Wellcome	Antiviral	6,175

Source: Pharmaceutical Data Services

New drug filings with Food & Drug Administration

Year	Original INDs submitted	Original NDAs submitted	NDAs approved	New molecular entities
1986	1,623	120	98	20
1985	1,904	148	100	30
1984	2,112	217	142	22
1983	1,798	269	94	14
1982	1,467	202	116	28
1981	1,184	129	96	27
1980	1,087	162	114	12
1979	940	182	94	14
1978	925	121	86	22
1977	925	124	63	21

IND—Investigational new drug. NDA—New drug application.
Source: Pharmaceutical Manufacturers Association.

recombinant DNA pharmaceuticals likely to come to market within the next few years include erythropoietin, a hormone that induces production of red blood cells and used to treat anemia; superoxide dismutase, an enzyme used to limit tissue damage caused by the resumption of blood flow; epidermal growth factor, used in ophthalmic surgery; and interleukin-2 for the treatment of various cancers.

Looking further down the road, considerable promise is seen for a group of drugs called colony stimulating factors (CSFs) to increase blood cell production in patients suffering from cancer, AIDS, or kidney failure. CSFs are hormones produced by the body in minute amounts that regulate blood cell production. Through genetic engineering, biotech companies have been able to produce these substances in quantities needed for human therapeutic purposes. Leaders in this field are GENETICS INSTITUTE, which has licensed its rights to its product to SANDOZ AG; IMMUNEX, which has licensed its product to Behringwerke AG; and SCHERING PLOUGH.

Biotech products for AIDS

Although the ultimate cure for acquired immune deficiency syndrome (AIDS) will more than likely continue to elude medical science for some time, the biotech industry has positioned itself in the forefront in the battle against this dreaded disease with wide array of diagnostic and therapeutic products. Reflecting the urgency of the problem and its enormous market potential, numerous pharmaceutical, medical products, and biotechnology firms are working

feverishly on new AIDS products. According to Frost & Sullivan, a New York-based market research firm, the total market for AIDS therapeutics and diagnostic products is expected to expand to over $1 billion by 1991 from only $136 million last year. In addition, hospital care services to AIDS patients will expand to $3.5 billion in 1991 from $648 million in 1986, according to estimates made by the American Hospital Association.

Caused by one of a recently discovered group of viruses called retroviruses, the AIDS virus effects a catastrophic breakdown of the body's immune system, leaving it vulnerable to numerous opportunistic infections such as pneumonia, cancer, nervous system disorders, and other ailments. AIDS victims—which to date have largely consisted of homosexuals and intravenous drug abusers—usually do not survive more than 12–18 months after initial diagnosis, without drug therapy. An associated condition—AIDS Related Complex (ARC) affects patients with symptoms that are similar to AIDS but less severe.

According to the U.S. Public Health Services Center for Disease Control (CDC) in Atlanta, more than 31,000 of the nation's 53,400 reported AIDS cases have already died and an additional three million Americans may be infected with the virus, but as yet exhibit no symptoms. The government has projected 344,000 cases and more than 200,000 deaths caused by AIDS by 1991.

Diagnostic tests

Diagnostic tests for the AIDS virus were the biotech industry's first wave of products aimed at this market. Building on advances in monoclonal antibody technology and related work, several firms have been able to devise and bring to market a member of AIDS screening tests within a relatively short time after the virus was identified. Supplying AIDS tests to the American Red Cross—which typically screens between 15 million–20 million units of donated blood each year—ABBOTT LABORATORIES dominates the $100 million AIDS testing market at the present time.

AIDS tests fall into two categories:

● Indirect tests, which detect the antibodies or proteins called immunoglobulins that the body mobilizes to combat the virus.

● Tests that directly indicate the presence of the AIDS virus, either through its antigens (proteins in the cell which react to specific antibodies) or by detecting the virus's own genetic material.

The most popular antibody test is an enzyme-linked immunosorbent assay (ELISA) test, developed by ABBOTT and others to screen large numbers of blood samples. These tests are not infallible, however, and often yield false positive or negative readings. For more confirmatory results, a more rigorous and extensive test—the Western Blot—is employed. The Western Blot was developed by DUPONT in partnership with Biotech Research Laboratories of Rockville, MD. Other firms involved in marketing antibody tests include CELLULAR PRODUCTS, ELECTRO NUCLEONICS, CHIRON, DAMON, JOHNSON & JOHNSON, ENI Behring, and Wellcome, PLC.

A number of firms are also working on second-generation tests that detect the virus itself. ABBOTT LABORATORIES and CAMBRIDGE BIOSYSTEMS have both developed such antigen tests, which are presently under review by the FDA. Other companies working on similar tests include DUPONT in conjunction with MOLECULAR BIOSYSTEMS; Gene-Trak System—a joint venture between INTEGRATED GENETICS and AMOCO CORP.; and CETUS in collaboration with EASTMAN KODAK.

Therapeutic drugs

While no one has yet devised a cure for AIDS, a number of antiviral and immunodulating drugs have been developed and hold promise as potential therapeutic agents. As of early 1988, FDA commissioner Frank Young noted that his agency had received 128 applications for approval to test 75 new AIDS drugs, biologicals, and vaccines on humans, of which 90% had been approved for testing.

Although the FDA has cleared a large number of drugs for testing, only one has been approved for commercial sale. Approved in March 1987, in near-record time, zidovudine (formerly known as azidothymidine or AZT) has been found to be effective in retarding the progression of the disease and improving patients' vital clinical signs. The drug is sold by Burroughs Wellcome under the *Retrovir* name.

The National Institutes of Health (NIH), have also developed several chemical cousins of zidovudine, including dideoxycytidine (DDC), which has been licensed to HOFFMANN-LA ROCHE, and dideoxyinosine (DDI) and dideoxyadenosine (DDA), which have been licensed to BRISTOL MYERS.

Early in 1988, the FDA and the National Institute of Allergy and Infectious Diseases approved the sale of a new AIDS drug called trimetrexate. This is the first AIDS drug to be approved under the "treatment IND" rule that went into effect in June 1987. Under this new regulation, pharmaceutical companies are allowed to recover their costs by selling experimental drugs to patients with life-threatening or certain serious conditions before complete data on the drug's efficacy or toxicity are available. The new regulation was accepted following the highly successful use of a similar mechanism for early distribution of Retrovir to AIDS patients in 1986. Trimetrexate is produced by WARNER LAMBERT.

Other promising new antiviral AIDS compounds now undergoing testing include ampligen, peptide t, CD-4, and AL721. Formulated from double-stranded RNA, ampligen is another drug that inhibits HIV replication. The immune systems of ARC patients treated with the drug have stabilized or improved. The compound is being developed through a joint venture of HEM Research Inc. and DU PONT.

Developed by Dr. Candace Pert of the National Institute of Mental Health, peptide t is a protein believed to block infection. The Oncogen subsidiary of BRISTOL MYERS is developing this compound for treatment. The Salk polio vaccine is also being investigated for AIDS therapy. It is believed to neutralize the AIDS virus in a similar manner as peptide t. Some patients with difficulty in tolerating zidovudine have been treated with the Salk vaccine with favorable results. Much more testing is needed, however, before any definitive conclusions are reached.

Another protein, CD–4, which also mimics the immune system's T-cells, has also stirred much interest in recent months as a potential therapeutic agent. Scientists believe that injecting CD-4 into the body would cause the HIV virus would attack it instead of the immune system. Though the protein has not yet been approved for human testing, researchers at a number of hospitals and universities are studying it in conjunction with scientists at GENENTECH, SMITHKLINE-BECKMAN, and BIOGEN.

AIDS vaccine development

Although some scientists have questioned the feasibility of creating an AIDS vaccine because of the complex nature of the virus, most of the experts in the field believe that the development of an effective vaccine is possible and a considerable amount of research and development is now underway towards this end. Last August, the FDA gave the green light to MicroGeneSys Inc., a privately-held firm in West Haven, Conn,, to begin clinical testing of its AIDS vaccine at the NIH Clinical Center in Bethesda, MD. The tests are being conducted by researchers of the National Institute of Allergy and Infectious Diseases, the government agency overseeing federal AIDS research.

The classic methodology in vaccine development has been to stimulate cells to create antibodies against bacteria or viruses through the use of whole killed or weakened forms of the disease. The highly lethal nature of the virus, has led most experts to rule out traditional procedures; different approaches to the problem will have to be developed. Most alternative methods use genetic-engineering techniques to create vaccines out of parts of the virus, called "subunit" vaccines. The MicroGeneSys vaccine, for example, is based on purified protein from the HIV virus, while other firms are experimenting with the development of synthetic protein segments.

Other obstacles complicate vaccine developments: the mutating nature of the HIV virus, which in effect creates a moving target for the antibodies; the possibility that the virus may enter the body encapsulated in a cell that it had invaded and, thus, be undetectable by antibodies; and the lack of good animal surrogates on which to perform tests. In addition, two distinct AIDS viruses have been identified— HIV–I and HIV–II, further complicating vaccine development. HIV–I is presently the most common form of the virus. While HIV–II seems to be prevalent only in Africa, it can pose a threat of more widespread incidence in the years ahead.

Other firms involved in AIDS vaccine development include the Oncogen unit BRISTOL-MYERS, REPLIGEN (in conjunction with MERCK), CHIRON (with Ciba-Geigy), GENENTECH, Viral Technologies, CAMBRIDGE BIOSCIENCE, JOHNSON & JOHNSON, and Immune Response. Oncogen's vaccine, which is made from vaccinia virus (the virus from which smallpox

vaccine is made), was the second product to receive clearance from the FDA for human testing. In a widely publicized experiment, Dr. Daniel Zagury, a French physician, innoculated himself with this vaccine, which has resulted in limited antibody production and other immune responses. Oncogen is also working on a vaccine for HIV–II, which is now pending FDA review for approval to begin human testing.

The REPLIGEN/MERCK vaccine, which is based on genetically-engineered protein fragments of the AIDS surface coating, has shown promise in animal studies, although the FDA has not yet approved human testing of the vaccine. Studies involving chimpanzees have certain significant drawbacks: no chimp has yet developed AIDS after exposure to HIV, though they do come down with flu-like symptoms. Also, their positive reaction to the vaccine may not necessarily prove its efficiency in humans. Another approach being explored by some researchers involves what is known as "anti-idiotype" antibodies. In this technique, antibodies produced by animals are then inoculated into other animals in the hope that the second antibody can elicit an immune response.

Despite considerable efforts made by the government, science, and industry on the development of new AIDS vaccines, even the most optimistic experts in the field believe that it will take many years of intensive research and development before an effective vaccine is available for widespread use. ■

Industry references

Publication	Frequency of publication	Publisher	Content
American Druggist	Monthly	Brakely, John Price Jones, Inc. 1100 17th St. NW 10th Floor Washington, D.C. 20036 (202)-399-3081	Trends in prescription activities and general pharmacy and pharmaceutical issues.
Biomedical Business International	14 times a year	Biomedical Business Int'l. 17722 Irving Blvd., Suite 3 Tustin, CA 92680 714-838-8350	Technological developments and market analysis, data and forecasts for healthcare executives.
Drug Topics	Bimonthly	Drug Topics 680 Kinderkamack Road Oradell, NJ 07649 201-262-3030	Discussion of major issues affecting the pharmaceutical industry and pharmacies.
The Gray Sheet	Weekly	F-D-C Reports, Inc. 5550 Friendship Blvd. Chevy Chase, MD 20815	Covers the medical devices, diagnostics, and instrumentation industries.
Health Care Financing Review	Quarterly	Supt. of Doc., G.P.O. Washington, DC 20402 202-783-3238	Health statistics and industry trends.
Health U.S.	Annual	U.S. Dept. of Health 3700 East-West Hwy Hyattsville, MD 20782	Comprehensive compilation of national health statistics
Hospitals	Bimonthly	American Hospital Publishing, Inc. 211 E. Chicago Avenue Chicago, IL 60611 312-440-6800	General discussion on issues and trends in hospital management, plus government developments.
Journal of the American Medical Association	Weekly	American Medical Association 535 N. Dearborn Street Chicago, IL 60610 312-645-5000	General forum for matters relating to medicine and health care.
The Medical Business Journal	Bi-monthly	The Medical Business Journal 3461 Rte. 22 East Somerville, NJ 08876	News, data, information and analysis of development in the healthcare workplace.
Modern Healthcare	Monthly	Crain Communications Inc. 220 E. 42nd St. New York, NY 10017 212-649-5350	Issues concerning health care providers, including investor-owned chains.
New England Journal of Medicine	Weekly	Massachusetts Medical Society 1440 Main Street Waltham, MA 02254 617-890-8669	Articles on medical treatment and health issues.
PMA Newsletter	Weekly	Pharmaceutical Mfrs. Ass'n. 1155 Fifteenth Street Washington, DC 20005	News and information concerning pharmaceutical companies.
Product Marketing	Monthly	U.S. Business Press 11 W. 19th Street New York, NY 10011 212-741-7210	Developments, trends, and articles about cosmetic, fragrance, and beauty markets.
The Pink Sheet	Weekly	F-D-C Reports, Inc. 5550 Friendship Blvd. Chevy Chase, MD 20815	Reports on toiletries, fragrances, and skin care markets and on companies involved.
Review Magazine	Bimonthly	Federation of American Hospitals 1405 N. Pierce Street Little Rock, AR 72207	Trends in and perspectives on the investor-owned hospital industry.
The Rose Sheet	Weekly	F-D-C Reports, Inc. 5550 Friendship Blvd. Chevy Chase, MD 20815	Prescription and over-the-counter pharmaceutical industry news.

COMPOSITE INDUSTRY DATA

*Per-share data based on Standard & Poor's group stock price indexes

HOSPITAL MANAGEMENT

The companies used for this series of composite data are: American Medical Intl; Hospital Corp. of Amer.; Humana Inc.; National Medical Enterprises.

	1979	1980	1981	1982	1983	1984	R1985	1986
Sales	27.26	33.80	45.29	53.35	57.29	60.13	69.23	82.71
Operating Income	5.20	6.52	8.47	10.22	12.06	13.90	14.95	13.50
Profit Margins %	19.08	19.29	18.70	19.16	21.05	23.12	21.59	16.32
Depreciation	1.17	1.38	1.73	2.13	2.52	3.01	3.67	4.56
Taxes	1.25	1.66	2.14	2.53	3.10	3.53	3.30	0.58
Earnings	1.35	1.99	2.58	3.51	4.33	4.73	4.79	1.49
Dividends	0.28	0.41	0.54	0.71	0.88	1.09	1.30	1.44
Earnings as a % of Sales	4.95	5.89	5.70	6.58	7.56	7.87	6.92	1.80
Dividends as a % of Earnings	20.74	20.60	20.93	20.23	20.32	23.04	27.14	96.44
‡Price (1965 = 10) —High	19.63	39.58	52.06	64.96	81.90	68.21	76.59	62.06
—Low	11.85	18.90	35.98	29.26	54.04	52.65	49.73	45.20
Price-Earnings Ratios —High	14.54	19.89	20.18	18.51	18.92	14.42	15.99	41.66
—Low	8.78	9.50	13.95	8.33	12.48	11.13	10.38	30.34
Dividend Yield % —High	2.36	2.17	1.50	2.43	1.63	2.07	2.61	3.19
—Low	1.43	1.04	1.04	1.09	1.07	1.60	1.70	2.32
Book Value	7.70	10.09	14.26	17.39	21.67	26.32	30.17	29.15
Return on Book Value %	17.53	19.72	18.07	20.18	19.96	17.97	15.88	5.11
†Working Capital	2.40	3.11	4.72	4.86	4.51	5.74	6.35	6.36
Capital Expenditures	3.50	7.70	13.56	11.39	13.22	10.88	13.77	12.90

MEDICAL PRODUCTS & SUPPLIES

The companies used for this series of composite data are: Abbott labs. (added 2-7-79); Amer. Hospital Supply (deleted 11-20-85); Bard (C.R.); Baxter Travenol Labs; Becton, Dickinson; and Johnson & Johnson (added 2-7-79).

	1979	1980	1981	1982	1983	1984	1985	1986
Sales	36.21	41.12	46.59	48.79	52.52	55.36	53.10	71.54
Operating Income	5.65	6.25	7.36	7.92	8.87	9.29	10.28	13.51
Profit Margins %	15.60	15.20	16.11	16.23	16.89	16.78	19.36	18.88
Depreciation	0.94	1.10	1.25	1.50	1.74	2.03	2.36	3.27
Taxes	1.86	1.92	2.17	2.09	2.13	1.97	2.38	2.07
Earnings	2.97	3.32	3.79	4.30	4.51	4.51	5.19	4.83
Dividends	0.89	1.01	1.17	1.36	1.57	8.00	1.91	2.21
Earnings as a % of Sales	8.20	8.07	8.30	8.81	8.59	40.63	9.77	6.75
Dividends as a % of Earnings	29.97	30.42	30.87	31.63	34.81	1.80	36.80	45.76
‡Price (1965 = 10) —High	39.11	51.32	44.03	74.69	82.20	72.50	89.02	130.19
—Low	31.53	33.08	30.87	50.25	68.50	53.05	56.71	86.20
Price-Earnings Ratios —High	13.17	15.46	11.62	17.37	18.23	16.37	17.15	26.95
—Low	10.62	9.96	8.15	11.69	15.19	11.98	10.93	17.85
Dividend Yield % —High	2.82	3.05	3.79	2.71	2.29	3.39	3.37	2.56
—Low	2.28	1.97	2.66	1.82	1.91	2.48	2.15	1.70
Book Value	17.31	19.55	21.50	23.50	25.89	27.07	22.56	19.79
Return on Book Value %	17.16	16.98	17.63	18.30	17.56	16.37	23.01	24.41
†Working Capital	14.24	17.16	16.98	16.64	10.53	12.78	13.30	9.95
Capital Expenditures	2.26	2.99	3.33	3.92	3.88	3.79	3.71	5.30

COSMETICS

The companies used for this series of composite data are: Alberto-Culver; Avon Products; Cheesebrough-Pond's; Faberge Inc.; Intl. Flavors & Fragrances; Noxell Corp. (added 8-8-84); Faberge Inc deleted 8-8-84; and Revlon Inc deleted 11-20-85.

	1979	1980	1981	1982	1983	1984	1985	1986
Sales	61.24	69.34	73.87	71.21	71.95	71.97	74.89	77.83
Operating Income	11.12	12.01	11.88	10.38	10.16	11.13	11.45	12.37
Profit Margins %	18.16	17.32	16.08	14.58	14.12	15.46	15.29	15.89
Depreciation	0.87	1.14	1.35	1.42	1.89	1.91	2.55	1.97
Taxes	4.80	4.95	4.71	3.74	3.37	3.23	2.55	2.87
Earnings	5.59	5.80	5.53	4.30	4.19	4.47	3.95	3.74
Dividends	2.82	3.06	3.32	3.02	2.88	2.79	3.09	3.20
Earnings as a % of Sales	9.13	8.36	7.49	6.04	5.82	6.21	5.27	4.81
Dividends as a % of Earnings	50.45	52.76	60.04	70.23	68.74	62.42	78.23	85.56
‡Price (1941–43 = 10)—High	67.44	60.67	62.25	54.40	60.01	51.33	69.07	91.82
—Low	53.73	45.55	47.22	38.45	48.95	45.28	48.14	65.89
Price-Earnings Ratios —High	12.06	10.46	11.33	12.65	14.32	11.48	17.49	24.55
—Low	9.61	7.85	3.54	8.94	11.68	10.13	12.19	17.56
Dividend Yield % —High	5.25	6.73	7.03	7.85	5.88	6.16	6.42	4.87
—Low	4.18	5.04	5.55	4.80	5.44	4.47	4.47	3.49
Book Value	23.59	24.29	25.36	22.86	23.45	21.51	20.01	16.90
Return on Book Value %	23.70	23.88	21.81	18.81	17.87	20.78	19.74	22.13
†Working Capital	16.30	19.35	18.98	16.79	15.77	16.46	17.03	17.38
Capital Expenditures	3.08	3.39	3.44	4.32	2.56	2.82	4.06	3.91

DRUGS

The companies used for this series of composite data are: Abbott laboratories (deleted 2-7-79); American Home Products; Bristol-Myers; Johnson & Johnson (added 5-30-73 and deleted 2-7-79); Lilly (Eli); Merck; Pfizer, Inc.; Schering-Plough; Searle (deleted 9-25-85); SmithKline Beckman (added 2-7-79); Squibb; Sterling Drug; Syntex (added 9-25-85); UpJohn (added 4-23-80) and Warner-Lambert.

	1979	1980	1981	1982	1983	1984	1985	1986
Sales	139.06	159.21	170.31	175.92	181.72	190.64	200.30	223.94
Operating Income	28.96	31.45	32.76	35.25	39.22	42.37	45.51	52.73
Profit Margins %	20.84	19.75	19.24	20.04	21.58	22.23	22.72	23.55
Depreciation	3.12	3.53	4.01	4.51	5.14	5.52	6.18	7.09
Taxes	4.84	10.83	10.71	11.63	13.01	14.06	14.00	15.40
Earnings	14.95	16.94	16.48	18.90	21.12	23.34	22.76	30.64
Dividends	6.66	7.72	8.50	8.97	9.82	10.51	12.09	13.81
Earnings as a % of Sales	10.75	10.64	9.68	10.74	11.62	12.24	11.36	13.68
Dividends as a % of Earnings	44.55	45.57	51.58	47.46	46.50	45.03	53.12	45.07
‡Price (1941–43 = 10)—High	183.14	217.73	237.44	259.10	264.17	287.65	401.62	573.09
—Low	156.19	153.17	194.14	198.65	243.19	244.97	283.64	386.28
Price-Earnings Ratios —High	12.25	12.85	14.41	13.71	13.46	12.32	17.64	18.70
—Low	10.45	9.04	11.78	10.51	11.52	10.50	12.46	12.61
Dividend Yield % —High	4.26	5.04	4.38	4.52	4.04	4.29	4.26	3.58
—Low	3.64	3.55	3.58	3.46	3.46	3.65	3.01	2.41
Book Value	72.94	82.25	91.36	98.36	106.05	109.59	117.05	115.70
Return on Book Value %	20.50	20.60	18.04	19.22	19.92	22.10	19.45	26.48
†Working Capital	44.72	48.22	52.48	51.39	51.63	55.19	60.86	61.72
Capital Expenditures	6.91	9.09	11.73	12.05	11.45	11.13	10.91	11.98

*NOTE: Per-share data are expressed in terms of the S & P Stock Price Index, i.e., stock prices, 1941–43 = 10. Each of the items shown is first computed on a true per share basis for each company. Totals for each company are then reconstructed using the same number of shares outstanding as was used to compute our stock price index as of December 31st. This is done because the shares used on December 31st, although the latest known at the time, may differ from those reported in the annual reports which are not available for six or eight weeks after the end of the year. The sum of these reconstructed totals is then related to the base period value used to compute the stock price index. As a double check, we relate the various items to the dividends, as these are the most stable series. So, for example, if total sales amount to 15 times the total dividend payments, then, with per-share dividends at 3.50, the indicated per share sales will be (15 × 3.50) 52.50 in terms of the S & P Stock Price Index. For comparability between the various groups, all data are on a calendar year basis, corporate data being posted in the year in which most months fall. Fiscal years ending June 30 are posted in the calendar year in which the fiscal year ends. †Current assets less current liabilities, without allowance for long-term debt. ‡For cosmetics group 1957 = 10. R—Revised.

6

VALUATION OF THE INDIVIDUAL FIRM

*T*he analysis in Chapter 5 centered on economic activity and the resultant swings in the business cycle which affected industries and corporate profitability and influenced the purchase of common stocks. The valuation of the individual firm was depicted as the last major step of the valuation process (Figure 5–1).

Valuation is based upon economic factors, industry variables, and an analysis of the financial statements and the outlook for the individual firm. The purpose of valuation is to determine the long-run fundamental economic value of a specific company's common stock. In the process, we try to determine whether a common stock is undervalued, overvalued, or fairly valued relative to its market price. As will be indicated in Chapter 8, there is a continuing controversy in academic circles over the ability of security markets to correctly price securities. This has led to debate over the efficient market hypothesis, which states that all securities are correctly priced at any point in time (there is no secret information to be uncovered by the enterprising analyst). For purposes of this chapter, we shall not be fully bound by the limiting assumptions of the efficient market hypothesis—though they are carefully considered in Chapter 8. Furthermore, most of the orientation in this chapter is to long-run concepts of valuation rather than to the determination of short-term market pricing factors.

CHARACTERISTICS OF COMMON STOCK

Before we can put a price on a share of stock, we must understand the key features of common stock. Common stock is issued by the corporation to attract the necessary capital to finance the operations of the firm. While it is possible for the owners of smaller firms to provide the initial financing of the firm and to subsequently utilize bank loans to supplement their investment, eventually most truly successful firms look to the public markets to issue common stock to a wide range of investors.

The ultimate ownership of the firm resides in common stock, whether it is in the form of all outstanding shares of a closely held corporation or one share of IBM. In terms of legal distinctions, it is the common stockholder alone who directly controls the business. While control of the company is legally in the shareholders' hands, it is practically wielded by management on an everyday basis. It is also important to realize that large creditors may exert tremendous pressure on a firm to meet certain standards of performance, even though the creditor has no voting power.

Although there are over 45 million common stockholders in the United States, increasingly this ownership is being held by large institutional interests rather than the individual investor. As would be expected, management has become increasingly sensitive to these large stockholders who may side with corporate raiders in voting their shares for or against merger offers or takeover attempts. Mutual funds, pension funds, insurance companies, and bank trust accounts are all examples of institutional investors. To illustrate the importance of these large investors in the current decade, institutional investors own over 50 percent of the shares outstanding of such firms as Digital Equipment, Merck

& Co., Eastman Kodak, Sears, Johnson and Johnson, Atlantic Richfield, IBM, and Eli Lilly.

Let's look at two important rights that all common stockholders have.

Common Stockholders' Claim to Income

All income that is not paid out to creditors or preferred stockholders[1] automatically belongs to common stockholders. Thus, we say they have a residual claim to income. This is true regardless of whether these residual funds are actually paid out in dividends or retained in the corporation. A firm that earns $10 million before capital costs and pays $1 million in interest to bondholders and a like amount in dividends to preferred stockholders will have $8 million available for common stockholders.[2] Perhaps half of that will be paid out as common stock dividends, and the balance will be reinvested in the business for the benefit of stockholders, with the hope of providing even greater income, dividends, and price appreciation in the future.

Of course, it should be pointed out that the common stockholder does not have a legal or enforceable claim to dividends. Whereas a bondholder may force the corporation into bankruptcy for failure to make interest payments, the common stockholder must accept circumstances as they are or attempt to change management if a new dividend policy is desired.

Occasionally, a company will have several classes of common stock outstanding that carry different rights to dividends and income. For example, Wang Laboratories, a manufacturer of word processors and office computer systems, has Class B and Class C common stock outstanding, where the Class B stock is entitled to 5 cents per share per year more in dividends than the Class C stock. A more recent innovation, however, has come from General Motors Corporation through two acquisitions. In October of 1984, GM acquired Electronic Data Systems (EDS) for cash and General Motors Class E common stock (total value $2.5 billion), and in 1985, GM acquired Hughes Aircraft for cash and Class H common stock (total value $5.8 billion).

Both Class E and Class H common stock are distinct from the regular GM common shares in voting rights and dividend rights. The dividends on the Class E stock are based on the income generated by EDS, and the dividends on the Class H stock are based on the earnings of Hughes Aircraft. Both of these companies are now subsidiaries of General Motors. However, General Motors has distributed stock dividends of Class E and Class H shares to its regular GM stockholders and has thus created a minority-owned public group of shareholders for these subsidiaries. Both General Motors Class E and H shares are listed on the New York Stock Exchange.

As an example of a more standard dividend policy, note the Value Line data sheet for TRW Inc. In Figure 6–1. TRW is a diversified, high-technology

---

[1]Preferred stock is a hybrid form of security that falls somewhere in between debt and common stock. It receives dividends that have a lower priority for payment than interest on debt but a higher priority than dividends on common stock. See Chapter 9 for a more complete discussion of preferred stock.

[2]Tax consequences related to interest payments are ignored for the present.

FIGURE 6–1 TRW Inc. and Dividend Policy

TRW INC. NYSE-TRW

RECENT PRICE	51	
P/E RATIO	12.2	(Trailing: 12.5 / Median: 11.0)
RELATIVE P/E RATIO	0.92	
DIV'D YLD	3.6%	
VALUE LINE	579	

TIMELINESS 3 Average (Relative Price Performance Next 12 Mos.)

SAFETY 2 Above Average (Scale: 1 Highest to 5 Lowest)

BETA 1.00 (1.00 = Market)

1992-94 PROJECTIONS

	Price	Gain	Ann'l Total Return
High	105	(+105%)	22%
Low	75	(+45%)	13%

Insider Decisions

	M	A	M	J	J	A	S	O	N
to Buy	0	1	0	0	1	1	1	1	0
Options	0	0	1	1	0	1	0	0	0
to Sell	5	0	0	1	0	0	0	0	1

Institutional Decisions

	1Q'89	2Q'89	3Q'89
to Buy	60	60	67
to Sell	96	85	60
Hld's(000)	45244	38945	39357

High/Low prices by year:

	1974	1975	1976	1977	1978	1979	1980	1981	1982	1983	1984	1985	1986	1987	1988	1989	1990	1991
High	20.9	30.7	32.8	37.0	41.0	41.0	48.5	55.0	70.0	54.0	49.9							
Low	16.6	17.3	24.5	22.8	30.3	29.2	34.5	41.1	37.0	40.6	41.3							

Target Price Range 1992 1993 1994 1995

6.0 x "Cash Flow" p sh

2-for-1 split

Relative Price Strength

Options: ASE

© VALUE LINE, INC.

1974	1975	1976	1977	1978	1979	1980	1981	1982	1983	1984	1985	1986	1987	1988	1989	1990	1991		92-94E
46.74	47.04	53.01	57.91	66.32	77.00	77.85	79.46	72.63	75.54	82.33	101.92	102.45	114.32	115.92	120.15	131.15		Sales per sh	174.60
2.80	2.83	3.52	4.02	4.47	4.90	5.15	5.50	4.81	5.43	6.46	7.49	7.66	9.17	10.11	10.35	10.95		"Cash Flow" per sh	15.35
1.53	1.54	2.03	2.39	2.71	3.04	3.20	3.30	2.50	2.77	3.53	3.00	3.23	4.01	4.29	4.15	4.35		Earnings per sh (A)	7.05
.56	.60	.68	.78	.88	.98	1.08	1.18	1.28	1.33	1.43	1.50	1.55	1.60	1.66	1.72	1.84		Div'ds Decl'd per sh (B)	2.25
2.40	2.01	1.66	2.09	2.37	3.38	4.05	3.95	4.23	4.26	5.73	7.09	7.32	7.58	7.09	7.00	7.40		Cap'l Spending per sh	8.75
7.95	8.63	10.02	11.53	13.29	15.67	16.89	19.87	20.64	21.53	23.39	16.98	19.93	23.41	25.70	27.95	30.30		Book Value per sh (C)	41.70
53.19	54.96	55.26	56.36	57.11	59.22	64.02	66.51	70.66	72.72	73.62	58.06	58.91	59.67	60.23	60.75	61.00		Common Shs Outst'g (D)	63.00
5.0	7.1	8.5	7.5	6.7	6.1	7.2	8.7	11.0	13.0	9.7	12.9	14.7	13.1	10.6	13.3	Bold figures are Value Line estimates		Avg Ann'l P/E Ratio	13.0
.70	.95	1.09	.98	.91	.88	.96	1.06	1.21	1.10	.90	1.05	1.00	.88	.88	1.00			Relative P/E Ratio	1.10
7.4%	5.5%	3.9%	4.4%	4.8%	5.3%	4.7%	4.1%	4.7%	3.7%	4.2%	3.9%	3.3%	3.0%	3.6%	3.1%			Avg Ann'l Div'd Yield	2.5%

CAPITAL STRUCTURE as of 9/30/89

Total Debt $1410 mill. **Due in 5 Yrs** $721 mill.
LT Debt $873 mill. **LT Interest** $80 mill.
Incl. $19 mill. capit. leases. (LT interest earned: 6.0x; total int. coverage: 3.4x) (34% of Cap'l)
Leases, Uncapitalized Annual rentals $111 mill.
Pension Liability None in '88 vs. None in '87
Pfd Stock $18.0 mill. **Pfd Div'd** $1.0 mill.
99,926 shs. $4.40, cv. into 4.4 com. shs. Involuntary liq. price $104 ea. Redeemable at $104 ea.; 180,562 shs. $4.50, cv. into 3.724 com. shs. Involuntary liq. price $40 ea. Redeemable at $100 ea. (1% of Cap'l)
Common Stock 60,552,096 shares (65% of Cap'l)
(62.0 mill. fully diluted shs.)

	1980	1981	1982	1983	1984	1985	1986	1987	1988	1989	1990			
4984.0	5285.1	5131.9	5493.0	6061.7	5917.2	6036.0	6821.0	6982.0	7300	8000	Sales ($mill)	11000		
11.0%	11.0%	9.7%	10.2%	11.5%	10.7%	10.6%	12.0%	10.9%	12.0%	12.0%	Operating Margin	12.0%		
129.3	145.2	166.6	193.2	214.8	227.3	259.8	306.0	349.0	375	405	Depreciation ($mill) (F)	525		
211.9	228.8	178.7	205.2	263.6	210.0	193.4	243.0	261.0	255	265	Net Profit ($mill)	445		
42.6%	40.7%	44.6%	43.8%	45.0%	39.3%	44.0%	41.4%	37.9%	36.0%	36.5%	Income Tax Rate	37.0%		
4.3%	4.3%	3.5%	3.7%	4.3%	3.5%	3.2%	3.6%	3.7%	3.5%	3.3%	Net Profit Margin	4.0%		
783.4	889.9	716.9	638.6	608.0	254.6	397.2	490.0	709.0	325	440	Working Cap'l ($mill)	900		
386.4	350.0	324.6	255.6	256.5	698.0	786.1	870.0	863.0	895	945	Long-Term Debt ($mill)	760		
1287.1	1417.1	1519.5	1616.0	1758.3	1014.9	1197.9	1417.0	1566.0	1715	1865	Net Worth ($mill)	2645		
14.0%	14.2%	10.7%	11.8%	13.8%	13.5%	11.5%	12.3%	12.4%	11.5%	11.0%	% Earned Total Cap'l	14.0%		
16.5%	16.1%	11.8%	12.7%	15.0%	20.7%	16.1%	17.1%	16.7%	15.0%	14.0%	% Earned Net Worth	17.0%		
11.3%	10.7%	5.7%	6.6%	9.0%	11.1%	8.6%	10.5%	10.3%	9.0%	8.0%	% Retained to Comm Eq	11.5%		
38%	38%	54%	49%	41%	48%	48%	40%	39%	42%	43%	% All Div'ds to Net Prof	32%		

CURRENT POSITION ($MILL.)

	1987	1988	9/30/89
Cash Assets	145.0	127.0	70.0
Receivables	1233.0	1286.0	1356.0
Inventory (FIFO)	487.0	419.0	461.0
Other	121.0	273.0	187.0
Current Assets	1986.0	2105.0	2074.0
Accts Payable	411.0	461.0	425.0
Debt Due	306.0	120.0	537.0
Other	779.0	815.0	843.0
Current Liab.	1496.0	1396.0	1805.0

BUSINESS: TRW Inc. is a diversified, international company with a base in advanced technology. Makes engine valves, pistons, steering systems, and seat belt restraints; electronic components, spacecraft, fasteners, relays, and communications equip. Sold oilwell operations 1988. Prepares computer software. Provides credit and real estate information services. Government sales, 44% of total; foreign and export sales, 28%; R&D, 5.1%. 1988 depreciation rate: 9.3%. Estimated plant age: 6 years. Has 73,200 employees, 38,173 common stockholders. Insiders own 1.2% of common. Chairman, President & Chief Executive Officer: Joseph T. Gorman. Incorporated: Ohio. Address: 1900 Richmond Road, Cleveland, Ohio 44124. Telephone: 216-291-7000.

ANNUAL RATES

of change (per sh)	Past 10 Yrs.	Past 5 Yrs.	Est'd '86-'88 to '92-'94(E)
Sales	6.5%	8.0%	8.0%
"Cash Flow"	8.5%	11.5%	9.5%
Earnings	5.0%	6.0%	10.5%
Dividends	7.5%	5.0%	6.0%
Book Value	7.0%	2.0%	10.5%

QUARTERLY SALES ($ mill.)

Cal-endar	Mar.31	Jun.30	Sep.30	Dec.31	Full Year
1986	1488	1565	1433	1550	6036.0
1987	1687	1693	1701	1740	6821.0
1988	1799	1817	1654	1712	6982.0
1989	1785	1844	1792	1879	7300
1990	1925	2050	1975	2050	8000

EARNINGS PER SHARE (A)

Cal-endar	Mar.31	Jun.30	Sep.30	Dec.31	Full Year
1986	.97	1.04	.67	.55	3.23
1987	.83	1.04	1.04	1.10	4.01
1988	1.09	1.17	1.12	.91	4.29
1989	1.04	1.14	1.00	.97	4.15
1990	1.05	1.15	1.10	1.05	4.35

QUARTERLY DIVIDENDS PAID (B)■

Cal-endar	Mar.31	Jun.30	Sep.30	Dec.31	Full Year
1986	.375	.375	.375	.40	1.53
1987	.40	.40	.40	.40	1.60
1988	.40	.40	.40	.43	1.63
1989	.43	.43	.43	.43	1.72
1990					

Sales at TRW's automotive unit should hold up relatively well despite the sluggish industry environment. The company will probably register lower sales of its engine valves and steering and suspension systems. However, we think this will be more than offset by increased sales from its occupant restraint operations. Beginning with the 1990 model year, all new cars sold in the U.S. must be equipped with a passive restraint system (one that requires no action by the occupant) on the driver's side. By 1994, all new automobiles must have a passive restraint system on both the driver and passenger side. TRW is a leader in the production of airbags, a market that could grow to $3 billion in 1994 from $200 million in 1988. Last year's acquisition of Talley Industries' airbag business complements TRW's operations well. As shipments increase over the next couple of years, margins here should improve. Though sales should continue to rise, we expect startup and R&D expenses to limit bottom-line contributions for the next six months. **The focus is on cost control in the space and defense unit.** Governmental budgetary constraints have resulted in contract stretchouts that led to a two percent decrease in revenues over the first nine months of 1989. However, improved program performance lifted operating profit by three percent. Since TRW's products are used in command, control, communications and intelligence, it will probably be less affected by the defense scalebacks than the companies that supply hardware. We look for this unit to log a nominal operating profit gain on flat sales in 1990. **Information services is benefiting from the addition of Chilton.** Operating profits should continue their dramatic rise over the next couple of quarters since integration costs are expected to subside. We look for information services to log a solid year in 1990.

These shares have worthwhile capital appreciation potential for the pull to 1992-94. Though near-term earnings prospects suggest these shares are no better than an average choice in the year ahead, the growth of the airbag business should produce solid earnings growth supporting above-average share price gains.

Guy W. Woodlief — January 12, 1990

(A) Prim. egs. Excl. cap. gain: '82, 25¢; loss: '84, (27¢); '85, ($1.10); loss on disc. ops.: '85, ($2.03); nonrecurring gain: '84, 31¢; '86, 24¢; '89, 9¢. Next earnings report due mid-February. (B) Next div'd meeting about Jan. 26. Goes ex about Feb. 8. Payment dates: 15th of March, June, September, December. ■ Div'd reinvestment plan available. (C) Includes intangibles. In '88: $301 million, $5.00/sh. (D) In millions, adjusted for stock split. (E) Fully diluted 3 to 5 years hence. (F) On a partially accelerated basis.

Company's Financial Strength	A
Stock's Price Stability	85
Price Growth Persistence	45
Earnings Predictability	80

Factual material is obtained from sources believed to be reliable, but the publisher is not responsible for any errors or omissions contained herein.

company. On the fourth line from the top of the data in the table, observe that TRW paid out $1.72 in cash dividends in 1989. (This is actually labeled as dividends declared per share). Since earnings per share on the line above were $4.15 for the same year, the firm paid out 41.4 percent of its earnings ($1.72/$4.15) to common stockholders and retained 58.6 percent to reinvest for the benefit of stockholders.

Voting Right

Because the common stockholders are the owners of the firm, they are accorded the right to vote in the election of the board of directors and on all other major issues. Common stockholders may cast their ballots as they see fit on a given issue or assign a proxy, or "power to cast their ballot," to management or some outside contesting group. As mentioned in the previous section, some corporations have different classes of common stock with unequal voting rights. In the case of the Wang Laboratories Class B and Class C stock and General Motors Class E and Class H stock, not only are dividends unequal but voting rights are also unequal. Regular General Motors common stock is entitled to one vote per share, while each GM Class E share is entitled to 0.25 votes per share and each Class H share is entitled to 0.50 vote per share.

Of course, the more normal case is one vote per share for all shareholders. While the voting power is often overlooked by many stockholders, it can become critical when there is a battle for control of the corporation. This is likely to be the case when there is an unfriendly tender offer. A classic example is when T. Boone Pickens tried to take over Gulf Oil in the mid-1980s. Under these circumstances, it is critically important who owns the shares for voting purposes and what the nature of the voting system is. In the Gulf Oil example, the firm was able to thwart the advances by Pickens but ultimately had to sell out to Chevron to accomplish that end.

A key voting power also relates to the election of the board of directors. The board has primary responsibility for the stewardship of the corporation. If illegal or imprudent decisions are made, the board can be held legally accountable. Furthermore, members of the board of directors normally serve on a number of important subcommittees of the corporation, such as the audit committee, the long-range financial planning committee, and the salary and compensation committee. The board election process may take place through the familiar majority rule system or by cumulative voting. Under majority voting, any group of stockholders owning over 50 percent of the common stock may elect all of the directors. Under **cumulative voting,** it is possible for those who hold less than a 50 percent interest to elect some of the directors. The provision for some minority interests on the board is important to those who, at times, wish to challenge the prerogatives of management.

How does this cumulative voting process work? A stockholder gets one vote for each share of stock he or she owns times one vote for each director to be elected. The stockholder may then accumulate votes in favor of a specified number of directors.

Generally, a stockholder or unified group of stockholders with 10 percent of the shares outstanding can be assured of electing at least one director out of nine with cumulative voting.[3] With 20 percent, they can elect two, and so on. This, of course, provides much greater opportunity for representation on the board than under the majority rule system where those with over 50 percent of the votes totally control the board.

THE ACTUAL VALUATION OF STOCK

Having discussed some of the attributes and responsibilities of common stock ownership, we now are in a position to consider valuation concepts. While the common stockholder needs to know what legal rights and privileges he or she has, these are only important to the extent that they are collectively translated into recognizable value in the marketplace.

The most important components from a pragmatic investor's viewpoint are (a) the firm's price-earnings ratio and (b) it's present and future earnings per share. We shall take these in order and then look at some other valuation concepts as well. These include using assets as a basis for valuation and premium values associated with owning a control interest in the firm. In the appendix to the chapter, we also will examine the value of the firm based on the present value of future dividends. No doubt, in many instances it is a combination of all these various approaches that ultimately determines value.

THE PRICE-EARNINGS RATIO

Mathematically, the **price-earnings ratio (P/E)** is simply the price per share divided by earnings per share, and it is ultimately set by investors in the market as they bid the price of a stock up or down in relation to its earnings. Price-earnings ratios are often expressed in the financial press as historical numbers using today's price divided by the latest 12-month earnings.

For companies with cyclical earnings, a P/E using the latest 12-month earnings could be misleading because earnings could be high. If investors expect earnings to come back to a normal level, they will not bid the price up in relation to this short-term cyclical swing in EPS, and the P/E ratio will appear to be low. On the other hand, if earnings are severely depressed, investors will expect a return to normal higher earnings, so the price will not fall an equal percentage with earnings, and the P/E will appear to be high.

Even though the current P/E ratio for a stock in the market is known, investors may or may not agree that it is appropriate. In fact, stockbrokers and investors probably spend more time examing P/E ratios and assessing their appropriate level than any other variable.

What determines whether a stock should have a high or low P/E ratio? Let's

---

[3]Of course, not all boards have exactly nine directors. The point is that with 10 percent of the shares, 1/9th of the board can be elected, and this can be applied to any size board.

first talk about the market for stocks in general, and then we will look at individual securities.

Stocks generally trade at a relatively high P/E ratio (perhaps 15 or greater) when there are strong growth prospects in the economy. However, inflation also plays a key role in determining P/E ratios for the overall market.

To illustrate the latter point, Figure 6–2 presents the relationship between the year-end Standard & Poor's 500 composite P/E ratio and the annual rate of inflation measured by the change in the consumer price index (CPI). The graphical relationship between these two variables shows that they are inversely related. The price-earnings ratio goes down when the change in the CPI goes up, and the reverse is also true.

Of course, other factors besides inflationary considerations and growth factors influence the P/E ratio for the market in general. Federal Reserve policy and interest rates, federal deficits, the government's leading indicators, the political climate, the mood and confidence of the population, international considerations, and many other factors have an influence on the P/E ratio for the overall market. The astute analyst is constantly studying a multitude of variables in analyzing the future outlook for P/E ratios.

FIGURE 6–2   INFLATION AND PRICE-EARNINGS RATIOS

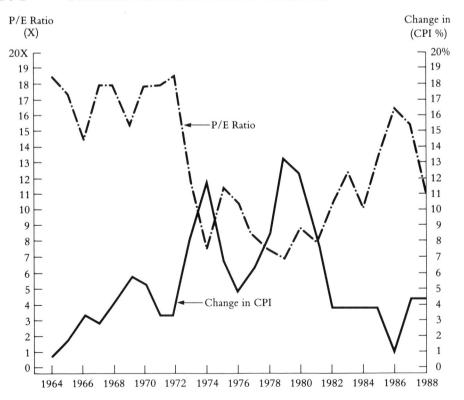

The P/E Ratio for Individual Stocks

Although the overall market P/E ratio is the collective average of individual P/Es, those factors that influence the market P/E do not necessarily impact P/E ratios of individual companies consistently from one industry to another. An individual firm's P/E ratio is heavily influenced by its growth prospects and the risk associated with its future performance. In Table 6–1, we see examples of growth rates and P/E ratios for different industries and firms. Generally, a strong expected future growth rate for 1988–93 (column 4) is associated with a reasonably high P/E for late 1988 (column 6). Obviously, the relationship can be complicated by other considerations. For example, the railroad company CSX shows an inordinately high P/E ratio of 56 in late 1988. This is associated with a modest 9 percent expected growth rate for EPS in 1988–93. The reason behind this inconsistency is that CSX suffered a major decline in EPS during 1988. Their slightly reduced price over an unusually low earnings base gives the appearance of a high P/E ratio. This high P/E ratio is phantom in nature and will work itself down as earnings improve, even if the stock price increases somewhat.

In addition to the future growth of the firm and the risk associated with that growth, investors and analysts also consider a number of other factors that influence a firm's P/E ratio. These cannot be easily quantified; nevertheless, they have an impact on a broad range of stocks. Included in this category are the debt-to-equity ratio and the dividend policy of the firm. All things being equal, the less debt that a firm has, the more likely it is to be highly valued in the marketplace.

The dividend policy is a more elusive matter. For firms that show superior internal reinvestment opportunities, low cash dividends may be acceptable. On the other hand, maturing companies may be expected to pay a high cash dividend. For the latter group, a reduction in cash dividends may be associated with a lower P/E ratio.

TABLE 6–1   P/E AND GROWTH IN EPS

(1) Industry	(2) Company	(3) 5-Year EPS Growth, 1984–1988	(4) Expected Growth in EPS, 1988–1993	(5) 1983–1987 Median P/E	(6) P/E Late 1988	(7) Expected Normal P/E
Appliances	Maytag	19.0%	8.5%	10.4x	11.0x	11.5x
Newspaper	Dow Jones	17.0	13.5	21.0x	13.0x	21.0x
Railroads	CSX	3.5	9.0	8.9x	56.0x	11.0x
Drugs	Bristol-Myers	−13.5	13.5	15.2x	15.0x	18.0x
Fast foods	McDonald's	14.5	15.5	13.1x	14.0x	15.0x
Trucking	Roadway	−1.5	11.5	15.7x	18.0x	16.0x
Tobacco	Philip Morris	19.0	18.0	8.2x	9.0x	10.0x
Brokerage	Merrill Lynch	2.0	10.5	14.0x	15.0x	11.0x
Market	S&P 500	8.0	9.0	N.A.	11.0x	12.0x

N.A. = Not available.
Source: *Value Line Investment Survey*, selected issues (Value Line Inc.)

Certain industries also traditionally command higher P/E ratios than others. Over the years, it would appear that investors have some preference for industries that have a high technology and research emphasis. Thus, firms in medical research and health care and sophisticated telecommunications often have higher P/E ratios than the market in general. This does not mean that firms in these industries represent superior investments but merely that investors value their earnings more highly.[4] Also, fads and other factors can cause a shift in industry popularity from time to time. For example, because Ronald Reagan emphasized military strength, defense-oriented stocks were popular during his administration. Jimmy Carter stressed the need for environmental control, and stocks dealing in air and water pollution control traded at high P/E ratios during his tenure in office. George Bush also appears to have picked up the banner on environmental control.

Another factor that influences a firm's P/E ratio is the quality of management as perceived by those in the marketplace. To the extent that management is viewed as being highly capable, clever, or innovative, the firm may carry a higher P/E ratio. Investors may look to magazines such as *Forbes* or *Business Week,* which highlight management strategies by various companies, or to management-oriented books such as *In Search of Excellence.*[5] Of course, it is entirely possible that today's trend setters may represent tomorrow's failures.

Not only is the quality of management important to investors in determining the firm's P/E ratio, but so is the quality of earnings. As, perhaps, you have studied in accounting and will observe further in the next chapter on financial statement analysis, there are many interpretations of a dollar's worth of earnings. Some companies choose to use very conservative accounting practices so that their reported earnings can be interpreted as being very solid by investors (in fact, they may even be understated). Other companies use more liberal accounting interpretations in order to report maximum earnings to their shareholders, and they, at times, overstate their true performance. It is easy to see that a dollar's worth of conservatively reported earnings may be valued at a P/E ratio of 13 to 15 times, whereas a dollar's worth of liberally reported earnings should be valued at a much lower multiple.

All of these factors impact a firm's P/E ratio. Thus, investors will consider growth in sales and earnings, future risk, the debt position, the dividend policy, the quality of management and earnings, and a multitude of other factors in eventually arriving at the P/E ratio. The P/E ratio, like the price of the stock, is set by the interaction of the forces of demand and supply for the security. Those firms which are expected to provide returns greater than the overall economy, with equal or less risk, generally have superior P/E ratios.

---

[4]William Kittrell, Geoffrey A. Hirt, and Roger Potter, "Price-Earnings Multiples, Investors' Expectations, and Rates of Return: Some Analytical and Empirical Findings" (Paper presented at the 1984 Financial Management Association meeting).

[5]Thomas J. Peters and Robert H. Waterman, Jr., *In Search of Excellence* (New York: Harper & Row, 1982).

Applying the P/E Ratio Concept

In 1989 K mart had earnings per share of $4.20 and an average P/E ratio of 11. This would yield a stock price of $46.20.

$$P_{1989} = EPS_{1989} \times P/E$$
$$= \$4.20 \times 11$$
$$P_{1989} = \$46.20$$

The question becomes: Is the P/E ratio and stock price reasonable? Lets look at some historical company data and compare K mart to the market in general. While you may have shopped in a K mart, you may not be familiar with the financial data expressed in Table 6–2. This table provides a summary of sales per share (SPS), dividends per share (DPS), earnings per share (EPS), book values per share (BVPS), the high and low stock prices, and high and low P/E ratios for the company. Also shown are the high and low P/E ratios for the Standard & Poor's 500 Stock Index over the same time. In the last two columns, the high and low P/E ratios for K mart are compared to the high and low P/E ratios for the S&P 500. For example, in 1979, K mart's high P/E ratio was 10.11, and the S&P 500 high P/E was 9.64. When K mart's high P/E is divided by the market's high P/E, a P/E relative of 1.05 is calculated in the high relative P/E column. This indicates that K mart's high P/E ratio was at 105 percent of the market or selling at a 5 percent premium to the market.

For each year, a high and low relative P/E ratio was calculated for K mart with the average high and low shown on the last line. We can see that K mart's high P/E relative averages 1.09, and its low P/E relative averages .87 percent of the market P/E. When we add the high and low and divide by two, we get an average of .98 which indicates that K mart historically sells at 98 percent of the S&P 500 P/E ratio.

At the time of the analysis, the S&P 500 Index was selling at a P/E ratio of 11.83 times earnings. We now compare the high, average, and low relative P/E ratios discussed in the previous paragraph to this value. The results are

TABLE 6–2												

K MART STOCK VALUATION DATA TABLE

Year	SPS	DPS	EPS	BVPS	Stock Price High	Low	Company P/E High	Low	S&P 500 P/E High	Low	Relative P/E High	Low
1979	$ 69.10	$0.56	$1.89	$11.86	$19.10	$15.00	10.11	7.94	9.64	8.13	1.05	0.98
1980	76.75	0.61	1.38	12.66	19.90	10.30	14.42	7.46	8.63	7.14	1.67	1.05
1981	88.87	0.64	1.17	13.20	15.90	10.30	13.59	8.80	9.38	6.69	1.45	1.32
1982	89.92	0.67	1.37	13.93	18.20	10.30	13.28	7.52	9.28	7.68	1.43	0.98
1983	98.47	0.72	2.53	15.57	26.20	14.50	10.36	5.73	10.36	6.92	1.00	0.83
1984	112.50	0.83	2.56	17.24	25.10	17.80	9.80	6.95	13.71	10.35	0.72	0.67
1985	118.62	0.93	2.42	17.32	27.70	20.40	11.45	8.43	12.65	9.77	0.90	0.86
1986	117.77	0.99	2.84	19.48	38.30	22.40	13.49	7.89	13.78	9.97	0.98	0.79
1987	125.92	1.16	3.40	21.66	48.40	21.60	14.24	6.35	15.64	12.53	0.91	0.51
1988	138.90	1.32	3.75	23.75	37.00	29.00	9.87	7.73	13.07	10.31	0.75	0.75
Average	$103.68	$0.84	$2.33	$16.67	$27.58	$17.16	12.06	7.48	11.61	8.95	1.09	0.87

TABLE 6–3	P/E RATIO MODEL, EARNINGS AND VALUATION					
		Relative P/E	S&P 500 Current P/E	K mart's Expected P/E	K mart's 1989 EPS	K mart's Estimated Value Based on Related P/E
Average high P/E		1.09 ×	11.83 =	12.89 ×	$4.20	$54.16
Average P/E		.98 ×	11.83 =	11.59 ×	$4.20	$48.68
Average low P/E		.87 ×	11.83 =	10.29 ×	$4.20	$43.22

shown in the first three columns of Table 6–3. When applied to the $4.20 EPS in 1989, we find that K mart should be selling in a range between $54.16 per share at its high price and $43.22 at its low price. Since K mart was selling in the mid-$40s at the time of this analysis, the relative P/E model indicates it may be a good buy.

Further analysis would also call for comparing K mart's P/E ratio at the time to other firms in the industry which have similar attributes in terms of growth, risk, quality of management, quality of earnings, and so forth. Comparisons could be made to Dillard's, Dayton Hudson, Family Dollar, J. C. Penney, Sears, Wal-Mart, and other such firms.

FORECASTING EARNINGS PER SHARE

The other side of choosing an appropriate P/E ratio is forecasting the earnings per share of a company with the proper growth rate. This is particularly important when you are applying P/E ratios not only to current earnings but to future earnings to evaluate future values. Investors can get earnings forecasts in several ways. They can rely on professional brokerage house research, investment advisory firms such as Value Line or Standard & Poor's, or financial magazines such as *Forbes* or *Business Week,* or they can do it themselves.

Least Squares Trendline

One of the most common ways of forecasting earnings per share is to use regression or **least squares trend analysis.** The technique involves a statistical method whereby a trendline is fitted to a time series of historical earnings. This trendline, by definition, is a straight line that minimizes the distance of the individual observations from the line. Figure 6–3 depicts a scattergram for the earnings per share of XYZ Corporation. The earnings of this company have been fairly consistent, so we get a good trendline with a minimum of variation. The compounded growth rate for the whole 10-year period was 16.5 percent, with 9.8 percent for the first 5 years and 20.4 for the last 5 years. This shows up in Figure 6–3 as two distinct five-year trendlines. Many companies have statistical programs that run regression analysis, and even hand-held calculators have the ability to compute a growth rate from raw data.

Whenever a mechanical forecast is made, subjectivity still enters the decision in choosing the data that will be considered in the regression plot.

FIGURE 6–3   LEAST SQUARES TRENDLINE FOR EPS OF XYZ CORPORATION

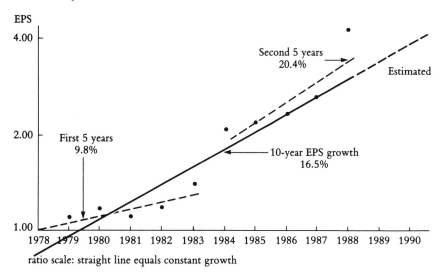

ratio scale: straight line equals constant growth

Using Nortek Inc., a cyclical company in building, aerospace, and electrical materials, and Merck & Company, a consistently growing drug company, we compare earnings-per-share trends in Table 6–4. Both companies have achieved strong growth over time. Nortek's earnings, however, are much more subject to the ups and downs in the economy.

The values are plotted in Figure 6–4. From that figure, it is clear that Merck & Company would provide the more reliable forecast based on past data. Its trendline is very consistent. In order to forecast Nortek, you would not start in 1982 and end in 1985 (trough to peak). Starting in 1981 and going to 1987 would probably also not provide a "true" trendline because the line would begin at a cyclical peak and end at a low point. Clearly, a Nortek forecast based on 10 or 12 years of data is more reliable than a three- or five-year

TABLE 6–4   GROWTH IN EARNINGS PER SHARE

Years	Earnings per Share Nortek Inc. (Past 10-Year EPS)	Earnings per Share Merck & Co. (Past 10-Year EPS)
1978	$ .86	$ .68
1979	.99	.84
1980	1.06	.92
1981	2.06	.89
1982	.78	.94
1983	1.02	1.02
1984	1.61	1.12
1985	1.98	1.26
1986	1.72	1.62
1987	1.43	2.23

FIGURE 6–4   NORTEK INC. AND MERCK & COMPANY EPS TRENDLINES

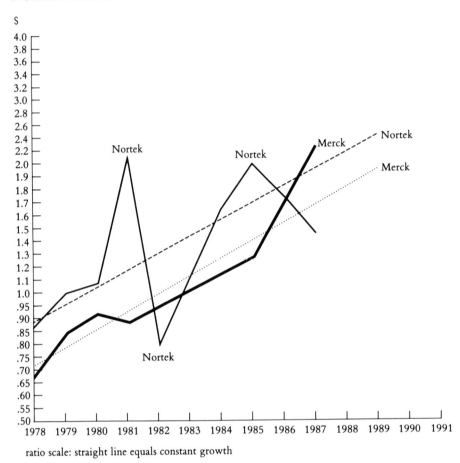

ratio scale: straight line equals constant growth

(based) forecast. With companies that follow economic cycles, the best forecasting period encompasses at least two peaks and two troughs or several
business cycles.

The Income Statement Method

A more process-oriented method of forecasting earnings per share is to start
with a sales forecast and create a standardized set of financial statements based
on historical relationships. Of course, the sales forecast must be accurate if the
earnings estimates are to have any significance. This method can be involved
and provides an analyst with a very integrated understanding of the relationships that go into the creation of earnings.

   Several important factors are included in this method of forecasting. The
analyst is forced to examine profitability and the resultant fluctuations in profit

TABLE 6–5   ABBREVIATED INCOME STATEMENT METHOD—HUTCHINS CORPORATION

Year	Sales ($000s)	×	After-Tax Profit Margin	=	Earnings ($000s)	÷	Shares (000s)	=	Earnings per Share
1983	$1,250,000		7.9%		$ 98,750		30,000		$3.29
1984	1,375,000		9.1		125,125		31,500		3.97
1985	1,512,500		8.5		128,562		33,200		3.87
1986	1,663,750		6.5		108,143		35,000		3.08
1987	1,830,125		8.3		151,900		35,200		4.31
1988	2,013,137		8.7		175,142		37,000		4.73
1989e	2,214,452		8.2		173,958		38,400		4.53
1990e	2,435,896		9.0		219,230		39,800		5.50

e = Estimated.

margins before and after taxes. The impact of short-term interest expense and any new bond financing can be factored into the analysis as well as any increase in shares of common stock from new equity financing.

Most analysts use an abbreviated method of forecasting earnings per share. They use a sales forecast combined with after-tax profit margins. For example, let us assume that the Hutchins Corporation has a sales and profit margin history as set forth in Table 6–5. The sales have been growing at a 10 percent growth rate, and so the forecast is a simple extrapolation. However, the profit margin has fluctuated between 6.5 percent and 9.1 percent, with 8.2 percent being the average. Common stock outstanding has also grown consistently by an average of 1.4 million shares per year. Given the cyclical nature of the profit margin, 8.2 percent was used for 1990, which is expected to be an average year. Nine percent was used for 1991, a year expected to be economically more robust. Multiplying the profit margin times the estimated sales for 1990 and 1991 produced an estimate of earnings that was divided by the number of shares outstanding to find the earnings per share. Once the EPS is found, it still must be plugged into a valuation model to determine an appropriate value.

GROWTH STOCKS AND GROWTH COMPANIES

In assessing the worth of an investment, stockholders, analysts, and investors often make reference to such terms as **growth stock** and **growth companies.** As part of the process of improving your overall valuation skills, you should have some familiarity with these terms.

A *growth stock* may be defined as the common stock of a company generally growing faster than the economy or market norm. These companies are usually predictable in their earnings growth. Many of the more popular growth stocks, such as 3M and McDonald's, are really in the middle-to-late stages of the expansion phase. They tend to be fully valued and recognized in the marketplace.

Growth companies, on the other hand, are those companies that exhibit rising returns on assets each year and sales that are growing at an increasing rate (growth phase of the life-cycle curve). Growth companies may not be as well known or recognized as growth stocks. Firms that may be considered to be growth companies might be in such industries as cable television, cellular telephones, personal computers, medical electronics, and so on. These companies are growing very rapidly, and extrapolations of growth trends can be very dangerous if you guess incorrectly. Growth companies have many things in common. Usually, they have developed a proprietary product that is patented and protected from competition like the original Xerox process (now other companies can use the dry process). This market protection allows a high rate of return and generates cash for new-product development.

One of the things that growth stocks and growth companies have in common is good research and development (R&D). Each company tries to prolong the growth and expansion phase of its life cycle as long as possible with new products or improved products. Value Line's November 13, 1981, issue of *Selection and Opinion* featured an article entitled "R&D: Key to Growth." Value Line took 409 companies over the 1978–80 period and measured research and development expenditures as a percentage of sales. They then ranked these 409 companies from the highest to lowest (R&D/sales) ratio. The top 10 R&D companies' average spending was 11 percent of sales dollars on research and development, which generated an earnings per share growth of 33.7 percent. The bottom 10 companies spent less than .12 percent on average, and EPS grew at only 8.3 percent. A further test with the top 100 companies showed R&D/sales averaged 5.6 percent with a resultant 15.2 percent growth in EPS, while the bottom 100 companies' R&D/sales averaged .44 percent with increased earnings of 11.3 percent.

Besides research and development, there are other indicators of growth potential. Companies should have sales growth greater than the economy by a reasonable margin. Increasing sales should be translated into similar earnings growth, which means consistently stable and high profit margins. Additionally, the earnings growth should show up in earnings per share growth (no dilution of earnings through unproductive stock offers). The firm should have a low labor cost as a percentage of total cost, since wages are prone to be inflexible on the downside and difficult to control on the upside.

The biggest error made in searching for growth-oriented companies is that the price may already be too high. By the time you identify the company, so has everyone else, and the price is probably inflated. If the company has one quarter where earnings do not keep up with expectations, the stock price could tumble. The trick, of course, is to find growth companies before they are generally recognized in the market, and this requires taking more risk in small companies trading over-the-counter.

ASSETS AS A SOURCE OF STOCK VALUE

Up until now, our emphasis has been primarily on earnings and perhaps dividends as the source of value. However, in certain industries, asset values may have considerable importance. These assets may take many forms—cash and marketable securities, buildings, land, timber, old movies, oil, and other natural resources. At times, any one of these assets may dominate a firm's value. Furthermore, companies with heavy cash positions are attractive merger and acquisition candidates because of the possibility that a firm with highly liquid assets could be taken over and have its own cash used to pay back debt incurred in the takeover. The emphasis here is not on book value as reported in the financial statements (which is often misleading) but on the true market value of the assets.

In the last two decades, natural resources also have had an important influence on value. Let's briefly examine this topic.

Natural Resources

Natural resources such as timber, copper, gold, and oil often give a company value even if the assets are not producing an income stream. This is because of the present value of the future income stream that is expected as these resources are used up. Companies like International Paper, Weyerhaeuser, and other forest-product companies have timberlands with market values far in excess of their book values and, and some cases, in excess of their common stock prices.

Oil companies with large supplies of oil under the ground may have to wait 20 years before some of it is pumped, but there may be substantial value there. In the case of natural gas pipeline companies, increasing reserves have changed the way these companies are viewed by the market. They used to be considered similar to utilities because of their natural gas transmission system, but now they are also being valued based on their **hidden assets** (energy reserves).

Investors should not overlook hidden assets because of naive extrapolation of past data or failure to understand an industry or company. Furthermore, assets do not always show up on the books of a company. They may be fully depreciated, like the movies *Sound of Music, Jaws,* or *Star Wars,* but still have substantial value in the television market.

STOCK VALUE ASSOCIATED WITH CONTROL

Up to this point we have been discussing the value of shares that trade daily on a stock exchange or over-the-counter. If you buy 100 or 1,000 shares, you will own an infinitesimal percentage of the stock outstanding.

What about the value of these same shares of the corporation when they represent a **control interest**? Perhaps, a merger tender offer is presented or a **leveraged buyout** is to be undertaken. In the latter case, the management of the company or some other investor group borrows the needed cash to repurchase all the shares of the company. As part of the leveraged buyout, the company is taken private. After a number of years, the firm may be taken public again when the new owners have increased its prospects for performance.

The important point associated with a merger or leveraged buyout is that it involves a control interest. That is, the purchaser now has the right to substantially change the operations of the company to enhance its value. This might include firing some incompetent managers, selling off unprofitable assets, increasing expenditures in other areas that are more profitable, better targeting research and development, and so on. Clearly, there are benefits associated with a control interest that are not present in the purchase of a minority interest (such as 100 or 1,000 shares). For these reasons, the common stock of companies that are "put into play" as merger or leveraged buyout candidates often increases in value by 60 percent or more.

Investors who can identify these situations in advance enjoy enormous returns. All of this does not mean that the merger or leveraged buyout candidate was improperly valued in the market before the tender offer. The added value is the result of new control and potentially better utilization of the assets.

Examples

As an example, Metromedia was bought and taken private in the mid-1980s for $1.1 billion. A few years later, the assets were sold for the following: seven TV stations for $2 billion; a cellular radio business for $1.1 billion; and other business units at $2.4 billion for a total of $5.5 billion. In another example, Leslie Fay, an apparal firm, was bought out for $58 million in April of 1982 and after changes in the firm were made and the overall stock market improved, resold to the public in 1986 for $360 million.

Of course, not all purchases work out this well. Many times the heavy debt burden associated with the purchase reduces the ability of the controlling firm to affect a successful turnaround. Every situation must be evaluated on its own merits. The important point for the reader to appreciate is that there are two types of value: control value and the more normal noncontrol value.

Some companies that do not want to be "put into play" actually devise protective measures to try to ensure that there will not be new control. The most prominent device of the last decade has been the **poison pill,** which makes it very difficult if not impossible for an unfriendly acquisition to take place. Perhaps, current stockholders must be paid a special premium over current value. (As an example, preferred stock has a par value of $100 but must be acquired at $200 per share). Another posion pill device is to allow current stockholders to buy new shares at an extremely low price so as to make it virtually impossible for another firm attempting to acquire a control position to accomplish its objective. Many poison pills go into effect when another firm has acquired a 20–25 percent interest in the target candidate. As you might guess, it is usually existing management and not stockholders that fight to put poison pills in the corporate bylaws.

APPENDIX 6–A: THE DIVIDEND VALUATION MODEL

The dividend valuation model is accepted in theory as an important explanation of common stock value. Though it lacks the wide application of the more pragmatic price-earnings ratio approach, it is often cited in the literature of finance.

The value of a share of stock may be interpreted by the shareholder as the present value of an expected stream of future dividends. Although in the short run, stockholders may be influenced by a change in earnings or other variables, the ultimate value of any asset rests with the distribution of earnings in the form of dividend payments. Though the stockholder may benefit from the retention and reinvestment of earnings by the corporation, at some point, the earnings must generally be translated into cash flow for the stockholder.

General Dividend Model

A generalized stock valuation model based on future expected dividends can be stated as follows:

$$P_0 = \frac{D_1}{(1 + K_e)^1} + \frac{D_2}{(1 + K_e)^2} + \frac{D_3}{(1 + K_e)^3} + \cdots + \frac{D_\infty}{(1 + K_e)^\infty}$$

$$(6A\text{--}1)$$

where:

P_0 = Present value of the stock price

D_i = Dividend for each year

K_e = Required rate of return (discount rate)

This model is very general and assumes that the investor can, in fact, determine the right dividend for each and every year as well as the annualized rate of return that an investor requires.

Constant Growth Model

Rather than predict the actual dividend each year, a more widely used model includes an estimate of the growth rate in dividends. This model assumes a constant growth rate in dividends to infinity.

If a constant growth rate in dividends is assumed, Formula (6A–1) can be expressed as:

$$P_0 = \frac{D_0(1 + g)^1}{(1 + K_e)^1} + \frac{D_0(1 + g)^2}{(1 + K_e)^2} + \frac{D_0(1 + g)^3}{(1 + K_e)^3} + \cdots + \frac{D_0(1 + g)^\infty}{(1 + K_e)^\infty}$$

$$(6A-2)$$

where:

$$D_0(1 + g)^1 = \text{Dividends in the initial year}$$
$$D_0(1 + g)^2 = \text{Dividends in year 2 and so on}$$
$$g = \text{Constant growth rate in the dividend}$$

The current price of the stock should equal the present value of the expected stream of dividends. If we can correctly predict the growth of future dividends and determine the discount rate, we can ascertain the value of the stock.

For example, assume we wanted to determine the present value of ABC Corporation common stock based on this model. We shall assume that ABC anticipates an 8 percent growth rate in dividends per share, and we use a 12 percent discount rate as the required rate of return. The required rate of return (discussed in Chapter 1) is intended to provide the investor with a minimum real rate of return, compensation for expected inflation, and a risk premium. Twelve percent is sufficient to fulfill that function in this example.

Rather than project the dividends for an extremely long period of time and then discount them back to the present, we can reduce Formula (6A–3) to a more usable form:

$$P_0 = D_1/(K_e - g)$$

$$(6A-3)$$

This formula is appropriate as long as two conditions are met. The first is that the growth rate must be constant in nature. For the ABC Corporation, we are assuming that to be the case. It is a constant 8 percent. Second, K_e (the required rate of return) must exceed g (the growth rate). Since K_e is 12 percent and g is 8 percent for the ABC Corporation, this condition is also met. Let's further assume D_1 (the dividend at the end of period 1) is $3.38.

Using Formula (6–3), we determine a stock value of:

$$P_0 = D_1/(K_e - g)$$
$$= \$3.38/(.12 - .08)$$
$$= \$3.38/.04$$
$$= \$84.50$$

This value, in theory, represents the present value of all future dividends. The meaning is further illustrated in Table 6A–1, in which we take the present value of the first 20 years of dividends ($43.71) and then add in a figure of $40.79 to arrive at the present value of all future dividends of $84.50 as previously determined by Formula (6A–3). The $40.79 value represents the present value of dividends occurring between 2010 and infinity (that is after the 20th year).

We must be aware that several things could be wrong with our analysis.

TABLE 6A–1   PRESENT VALUE ANALYSIS OF ABC CORPORATION

Year	Expected Dividends $g = 8\%$	Present Value Factor $K_e = 12\%$★	Present Value of Dividends
1990	$ 3.38	.893	$ 3.02
1991	3.65	.797	2.91
1992	3.94	.712	2.81
1993	4.26	.636	2.71
1994	4.60	.568	2.61
1995	4.97	.507	2.52
1996	5.37	.453	2.43
1997	5.80	.404	2.34
1998	6.26	.361	2.26
1999	6.76	.322	2.18
2000	7.30	.288	2.10
2001	7.88	.257	2.03
2002	8.51	.229	1.95
2003	9.19	.204	1.87
2004	9.93	.182	1.81
2005	10.72	.163	1.75
2006	11.58	.146	1.69
2007	12.51	.130	1.63
2008	13.51	.116	1.57
2009	14.59	.104	1.52
PV of dividends for years 1990–2009			43.71
PV of dividends for years 2010 to infinity			40.79
Total present value of ABC Common Stock			$84.50†

★Figures are taken from Appendix B at the end of this book.
†Notice that this value is the same as that found using Formula (6A–3).

First, our expectations of dividend growth may be too high for an infinite period of time. Perhaps 6 percent is a more realistic estimate of expected dividend growth. If we substitute our new estimate into Formula (6A–3), we can measure the price effect as dividend growth changes from an 8 percent rate to a 6 percent rate.

$$P_0 = \$3.38/(.12 - .06)$$
$$= \$3.38/.06$$
$$= \$56.33$$

A 6 percent growth rate cuts the present value down substantially from the prior value of $84.50.

We could also misjudge our required rate of return, K_e, which could be higher or lower. A lower K_e would increase the present value of ABC Corporation, whereas a higher K_e would reduce its value. We have made these points to show how sensitive stock prices are to the basic assumptions of the model. Even though you may go through the calculations, the final value is only as accurate as your inputs. This is where a security analyst's judgment and expertise are important—in justifying the growth rate and required rate of return.

A Nonconstant Growth Model

Many analysts do not accept the premise of a constant growth rate in dividends or earnings. As we examined in Chapter 5, industries go through a life cycle in which growth is nonlinear. Growth is usually highest in the infancy and early phases of the life cycle, and as expansion is reached, the growth rate slows until the industry reaches maturity. At maturity, a constant, long-run growth rate that approximates the long-run growth of the macro economy may be appropriate for a particular industry.

It should be remembered that some companies in an industry may not behave like the industry in general. Companies constantly try to avoid maturity or decline, and so they strive to develop new products and markets to maintain growth.

In situations where the analyst wants to value a company without the constant-growth assumption, a variation of the constant-growth model is possible. Growth is simply divided into several periods with each period having a present value. The present value of each period is summed to attain the total value of the firm's share price. An example of a two-period model may illustrate the concept. Assume that JAYCAR Corporation is expected to have the growth pattern shown in Figure 6A–1.

It is assumed that JAYCAR will have a dividend growth rate of 20 percent for the next 10 years of its life and an 8 percent perpetual growth rate after that. JAYCAR's dividend is expected to be $1 next year, and the appropriate required rate of return (discount rate) is 12 percent. Taking the present value for the first 10 years of dividends and then applying the constant dividend growth model for years 11 through infinity, we can arrive at an answer. First, we find the present value of the initial 10 years of dividends.

Year	Dividends (20 Percent Growth)	PV Factor (12 Percent)*	Present Value of Dividends First 10 Years
1	$1.00	.893	$ .89
2	1.20	.797	.96
3	1.44	.712	1.03
4	1.73	.636	1.10
5	2.07	.567	1.17
6	2.48	.507	1.26
7	2.98	.452	1.35
8	3.58	.404	1.45
9	4.29	.361	1.55
10	5.15	.322	1.66
			$12.42

*Figures are taken from Appendix B at the end of this book.

We then determine the present value of dividends after the 10th year. The dividend in year 11 is expected to be $5.56 or $5.15 (for year 10) compounded at the new, lower 8 percent growth rate ($5.15 × 1.08). Since the rest of the dividend stream will be infinite, Formula (6A–3) can provide the value of

FIGURE 6A–1   JAYCAR GROWTH PATTERN

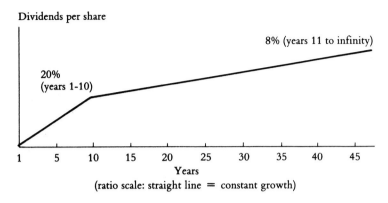

JAYCAR at the end of year 10, based on a discount rate of 12 percent and an expected growth rate of 8 percent.

$$P_{10} = D_{11}/(K_e - g)$$
$$= \$5.56/(.12 - .08)$$
$$= \$5.56/.04$$
$$= \$139$$

An investor would pay $139 at the end of the 10th year for the future stream of dividends from year 11 to infinity. To get the present value of the 10th-year price, the $139 must be discounted back to the present by the 10-year PV factor for 12 percent from Appendix B (.322). This part of the answer is $139.00 × .322, or $44.76. The two parts of this analysis can be combined to get the current valuation per share of $57.18.

Present value of the dividends from years 1 to 10	$12.42
Present value of 10th year price ($139.00 × .322)	44.76
Total present value of JAYCAR common stock	$57.18

Do Dividends Really Matter?

Dividend valuation models estimate the present value from an expected future stream of dividends. If the predictions are correct, the valuation will probably be reasonably accurate, but if the forecast is off its target, such would not be the case.

If a firm fails to pay dividends, then dividend valuation makes little sense. If a firm were never to pay a dividend, would the company cease to have value? Certainly not! As long as the expectation existed (borne out by reality) that retained earnings were being reinvested to increase the asset base of the company, the firm would have some value. Nevertheless, there has always

TABLE 6A–2   A DOZEN THAT PAID NO DIVIDENDS

| Company | Total Return to Investors, 1970–1980 | |
	Annual Average Compounded (Percent)	Rank in Fortune 500
NVF	41.7%	2
National Semiconductor★	33.3	7
Teledyne★	32.2	9
Tosco★	28.9	17
Data General★	25.3	34
Penn Central	19.9	78
Digital Equipment★	17.4	96
Lockheed	13.9	143
Median for 500	9.4	—
LTV	6.9	284
Crown Cork & Seal	4.6	342
DPF★	(5.7)	451
Memorex★	(13.9)	463

★Company has never paid a cash dividend.
Source: "Fresh Evidence that Dividends Don't Matter," *Fortune,* May 4, 1981, p. 351. *Fortune* Magazine Art Department. © 1981 Time Inc. All rights reserved.

TABLE 6A–3   GROWING DIVIDENDS DIDN'T SAVE THESE STOCKS

| Company | Growth in Cash Dividends, Average Annual Rate, Compounded 1971–1980 (Percent) | Decline in Stock Price 1970–1980 (Percent) | Total Return to Investors, 1970–1980 | |
			Annual Average Return, Compounded (Percent)	Rank in Fortune 500
Burroughs	26.6%	(1.4%)	1.2%	398
Brunswick	24.7	(17.3)	1.3	396
Economics Laboratory	16.7	(13.2)	.8	404
Jim Walter	16.3	(16.4)	1.9	386
Georgia-Pacific	14.0	(4.1)	2.4	381
Nashua	13.5	(16.8)	1.5	392
Coca-Cola	11.8	(21.2)	1.0	402
Brockway Glass	10.4	(36.4)	.7	411
Avon Products	10.0	(61.4)	(5.2)	449
Colgate-Palmolive	9.9	(8.1)	3.0	375
Quaker Oats	9.0	(6.4)	2.9	376
Warner-Lambert	8.7	(41.2)	(1.8)	432
ITT	8.5	(40.7)	.5	413
Owens-Illinois	8.4	(10.5)	3.3	370
Champion Spark Plug	8.0	(11.5)	4.2	350
Heublein	7.7	(38.3)	(1.3)	428
National Service Industries	7.3	(9.3)	5.0	324
Sybron	6.8	(45.4)	(1.7)	431
Squibb	4.9	(17.9)	.8	405

Source: "Fresh Evidence that Dividends Don't Matter," *Fortune,* May 4, 1981, p. 354, *Fortune* Magazine Art Department. © 1981 Time Inc. All rights reserved.

been the "bird-in-the-hand theory" that dividends are worth more than earnings because once paid to the stockholder, the company cannot take them away. While it is true that dividends do have information content and thus influence expectations, rising dividends are no guarantee that the common stock will also rise in the short run.

Fortune magazine compiled a list of companies with no dividends and companies with rising dividends for the period from 1970 to 1980. The results are not necessarily what one might expect. Table 6A–2 shows 12 companies that paid no dividends over the entire 10-year period. The median annual return to investors for these companies was 18.7 percent versus 9.4 percent for the Fortune 500 as a whole.

Table 6A–3 presents 19 companies with rising dividends over this decade. These 19 companies performed rather poorly on the basis of total return because of declining stock prices.

While increased dividends generally increase common stock value, we see that this is not always the case. If a company's overall performance is questionable, then raising dividends may not encourage investors. Although the examples in Table 6A–3 represent exceptions to the rule, they occur frequently enough to deserve investor caution.

7

FINANCIAL STATEMENT ANALYSIS

THE MAJOR FINANCIAL STATEMENTS

    Income Statement
    Balance Sheet
    Statement of Cash Flows

KEY FINANCIAL RATIOS FOR THE
SECURITY ANALYST

    Ratio Analysis
    Bankruptcy Studies
    Classification System

USES OF RATIOS

COMPARING LONG-TERM TRENDS

A GENERAL STUDY OF INDUSTRY
TRENDS

DEFICIENCIES OF FINANCIAL
STATEMENTS

    Inflation Effects
    Inventory Valuation
    Extraordinary Gains and Losses
    Pension Fund Liabilities
    Foreign Exchange Transactions
    Other Distortions

F | inancial statements present a numerical picture of a company's financial and operating health. Since each company is different, an analyst needs to examine the financial statements for industry characteristics as well as for differences in accounting methods. The major financial statements are the balance sheet, the income statement, and the statement of cash flows. A very helpful long-term financial overview also is provided by a 5- or 10-year summary statement found in the corporate annual report. One must further remember that the footnotes to these statements are an integral part of the statements and provide a wealth of in-depth explanatory information. More depth can often be found in additional reports such as the 10-K filed with the Securities and Exchange Commission and obtainable on request (free of charge) from most companies.

Fundamental analysis depends on variables internal to the company, and the corporate financial statements are one way of measuring fundamental value and risk. Financial-statement analysis should be combined with economic and industry analysis before a final judgment is made to purchase or sell a specific security. Chapter 6 presented methods of valuation that used forecasts of dividends and earnings per share. Earnings per share combined with an estimated price-earnings ratio was also used to get a future price. Careful study of financial statements provides the analyst with much of the necessary information to forecast earnings and dividends, to judge the quality of earnings, and to determine financial and operating risk.

THE MAJOR FINANCIAL STATEMENTS

In the first part of this chapter, we examine the three basic types of financial statements—the income statement, the balance sheet, and the statement of cash flows—with particular attention paid to the interrelationships among these three measurement devices. In the rest of the chapter, ratio analysis is presented in detail, and deficiencies of financial statements are discussed along with the role of the security analyst in interpreting financial statements.

Income Statement

The **income statement** is the major device for measuring the profitability of a firm over a period of time. An example of the income statement is presented in Table 7–1 for The Coca-Cola Company. First of all, note that the income statement is for a defined period of time, whether it be one month, three months, or a year. The statement is presented in a stair-step, or progressive, fashion so that we may examine the profit or loss after each type of expense item is deducted.

For 1987, the Coca-Cola Company had net operating revenues (sales) of $7,658,341,000. After subtracting the cost of goods sold, selling, administrative, and general expenses, and restructuring costs, the firm's operating income was $1,323,790,000. Because of a high level of cash and marketable securities during 1987, Coca-Cola had almost as much interest income as interest expense

TABLE 7–1   COCA-COLA INCOME STATEMENT
                   THE COCA-COLA COMPANY AND SUBSIDIARIES
                        Consolidated Statements of Income
                   For the Years Ended December 31, 1985, 1986, and 1987
                        (in thousands except per-share data)

	1987	1986 (Restated)	1985 (Restated)
Net operating revenue	$7,658,341	$6,976,558	$5,879,160
Cost of goods	3,633,159	3,453,891	2,909,496
Gross profit	4,025,182	3,522,667	2,969,664
Selling, administrative, and general expenses	2,665,022	2,445,602	2,162,991
Provisions for restructured operations and disinvestment	36,370	180,000	—
Operating income	1,323,790	897,065	806,673
Interest income	207,164	139,348	144,648
Interest expense	279,012	196,778	189,808
Equity income	118,533	155,804	164,385
Other income—net	34	33,014	66,524
Gain on sale of stock by former subsidiaries	39,654	375,000	—
Income from continuing operations before income taxes	1,410,163	1,403,453	992,422
Income taxes	494,027	469,106	314,856
Income from continuing operations	916,136	934,347	677,566
Income from discontinued operations (net of applicable income taxes of $7,870)	—	—	9,000
Gain on disposal of discontinued operations (net of applicable income taxes $20,252)	—	—	35,733
Net income	$ 916,136	$ 934,347	$ 722,299
Per-share data:			
Continuing operations	$ 2.43	$ 2.42	$ 1.72
Discontinued operations	—	—	.12
Net income	$ 2.43	$ 2.42	$ 1.84
Average shares outstanding	377,372	386,831	393,354

Source: *The Coca-Cola Company Annual Report*, 1987, p. 38.

(not a common occurrence). They also had income from 49 percent equity interests in three publicly held companies. Altogether, Coca-Cola reported income from continuing operations before taxes of slightly over $1.4 billion. Income after taxes from continuing operations is $916,136,000. Notice that The Coca-Cola Company disposed of some assets in 1985 and that income from discontinued operations is listed separately. While income from discontinued operation was not relatively material to the total results, the analyst still needs this information. The income statement indicates earnings per share from continuing operations, discontinued operations, and a total for the two, which is net income per share ($2.43 in 1987). It is the earnings per share from continuing operations that is relevant in making forecasts of expected growth.

Are these good income figures or bad? As we shall see later, the analyst's interpretation of the numbers will depend on historical figures, on industry data, and on the relationship of income to balance sheet items such as assets and net worth.

TABLE 7–2   COCA-COLA BALANCE SHEET

THE COCA-COLA COMPANY AND SUBSIDIARIES
Consolidated Balance Sheets
For the Years Ended December 31, 1986 and 1987
(in thousands except share data)

	1987	1986 (Restated)
Assets		
Current assets:		
Cash	$1,017,624	$ 606,848
Marketable securities, at cost (approximates market)	450,640	261,785
	1,468,264	868,633
Trade accounts receivable, less allowances of $13,429 in 1987 and $11,657 in 1986	672,160	672,568
Inventories	776,740	695,437
Prepaid expenses and other assets	674,148	932,630
Notes receivable—Columbia Pictures Entertainment, Inc.	544,889	—
Total current assets	4,136,201	3,169,268
Investments and other assets:		
Investments in affiliates:		
Columbia Pictures Entertainment, Inc.	989,409	1,436,707
Coca-Cola Enterprises Inc.	749,159	709,287
T.C.C. Beverages Ltd.	84,493	87,696
Other	435,484	212,194
Receivables and other assets	289,000	217,046
	2,547,545	2,662,930
Property, plant, and equipment:		
Land	112,741	98,842
Buildings and improvements	763,317	695,029
Machinery and equipment	1,488,464	1,390,689
Containers	275,120	287,672
	2,639,642	2,472.232
Less allowances for depreciation	1,041,983	934,679
	1,597,659	1,537,553
Goodwill and other intangible assets	74,155	114,377
Total assets	$8,355,560	$7,484,128
Liabilities and Shareholders' Equity		
Current liabilities:		
Accounts payable and accrued expenses	$1,430,193	$1,198,407
Loans and notes payable	1,685,408	697,743
Current maturities of long-term debt	213,609	4,628
Dividends payable in-kind	335,017	—
Accrued taxes—including income taxes	454,313	344,141
Total current liabilities	4,118,540	2,244,919
Long-term debt	803,352	907,676
Deferred income taxes	209,880	239,813
Due to Columbia Pictures Entertainment, Inc.	—	576,741
Shareholders' equity:		
Preferred stock, $1 par value:		
Authorized: 100,000,000 shares		
No shares issued and outstanding	—	—
Common stock, $1 par value:		
Authorized: 700,000,000 shares		
Issued: 415,977,479 shares in 1987 and 414,491,987 shares in 1986	415,977	414,492
Capital surplus	338,594	299,345
Reinvested earnings	3,783,625	3,624,046
Foreign currency translation adjustment	(5,047)	(118,087)
	4,533,149	4,219,796

TABLE 7–2	(concluded)		
		1987	1986 (Restated)
	Less treasury stock, at cost (43,621,336 shares in 1987; 29,481,220 shares in 1986)	1,309,361	704,817
		3,223,788	3,514,979
	Total liabilities and shareholders' equity	$8,355,560	$7,484,128

Source: *The Coca-Cola Company Annual Report*, 1987, pp. 36–37.

Balance Sheet

The **balance sheet** indicates what the firm owns and how these assets are financed in the form of liabilities or ownership interest. While the income statement purports to show the profitability of the firm, the balance sheet delineates the firm's holdings and obligations. Together, these statements are intended to answer two questions: How much did the firm make or lose, and what is a measure of its worth? A balance sheet for The Coca-Cola Company is presented in Table 7–2.

Note that the balance sheet is given at one point in time, in this case December 31, 1987. It does not represent the result of transactions for a specific month, quarter, or year but rather, is a cumulative chronicle of all transactions that have affected the corporation since its inception. This is in contrast to the income statement, which measures results only over a short, quantifiable period of time. Generally, balance sheet items are stated on an original cost basis rather than at market value.

The Coca-Cola Company was chosen for analysis because of its product diversification, its international scope, and its well-known soft drinks such as Coca-Cola, Tab, Sprite, and Diet Coke. Its food division's major product is Minute Maid orange juice, and this division accounted for 18.5 percent of revenues but only 5 percent of operating income in 1987. Coca-Cola has restructured its operations from 1985 through 1987 by spinning off wholly owned subsidiaries but retaining a 49 percent interest in the new publicly owned firms. These firms show up in the investment section of the balance sheet and are: Columbia Pictures Entertainment, Inc. (CPE); Coca-Cola Enterprises Inc. (CCE), a major bottler; and T.C.C. Beverages Ltd., a major Canadian bottler. The Coca-Cola Company reports the earnings of these companies using the equity method of reporting which means that 49 percent of their taxable income ($118 million) is included in Coca-Cola's income statement.

Statement of Cash Flows

In November 1987, the accounting profession designated the "**Statement of Cash Flows**" as the third required financial statement, along with the balance sheet and income statement. Referred to as Financial Accounting Standards

Board (FASB), *Statement No. 95,* it replaces the old statement of changes in financial position (and the sources and uses of funds statement).

The purpose of the new statement of cash flows is to emphasize the critical nature of cash flow to the operations of the firm. Cash flow generally represents cash or cash-equivalent items that can easily be converted into cash within 90 days (such as a money market fund).

The income statement and balance sheet we have studied thus far are normally based on the accrual method of accounting, in which revenues and expenses are recognized as they occur, rather than when cash actually changes hands. For example, a $100,000 credit sale may be made in December 1989 and shown as revenue for that year—in spite of the fact that the cash payment would not be received until March 1990. When the actual payment is finally received under accrual accounting, no revenue is recognized (it has already been accounted for previously). The primary advantage of accrual accounting is that it allows us to match revenues and expenses in the period in which they occur in order to appropriately measure profit; but a disadvantage is that adequate attention is not directed to the actual cash flow position of the firm.

One can think of situations in which a firm made a $1 million profit on a transaction but will not receive the actual cash payment for two years. Or perhaps, the $1 million profit is in cash, but the firm increased its asset purchases by $3 million (a new building). If you merely read the income statement, you might assume the firm is in a strong $1 million cash position; but if you go beyond the income statement to cash flow considerations, you would observe the firm is $2 million short of funds for the period.

As a last example, a firm might show a $100,000 loss on the income statement; but if it had a depreciation expense write-off of $150,000, the firm would actually have $50,000 in cash. Since depreciation is a noncash deduction, the $150,000 deduction in the income statement for depreciation can be added back to net income to determine cash flow.

The statement of cash flows addresses these issues by translating income statement and balance sheet data into cash flow information. A corporation that has $1 million in accrual-based accounting profits can determine whether it can actually afford to pay a cash dividend to stockholders, buy new equipment, or undertake new projects. In the low-profit and cash-tight era of the 1980s, cash flow analysis has taken on a very special meaning.

The three primary sections of the statement of cash flows are:

1. Cash flows from operating activities.
2. Cash flows from investing activities.
3. Cash flows from financing activities.

After each of these sections is completed, the results are added together to compute the net increase or decrease in cash flow for the corporation. An example of this process is shown in Figure 7–1. This statement informs us about how the cash was created (operations, investing, financing), where it was spent, and the net increase or decrease of cash for the entire year.

FIGURE 7–1   ILLUSTRATION OF CONCEPTS BEHIND STATEMENT OF CASH FLOWS

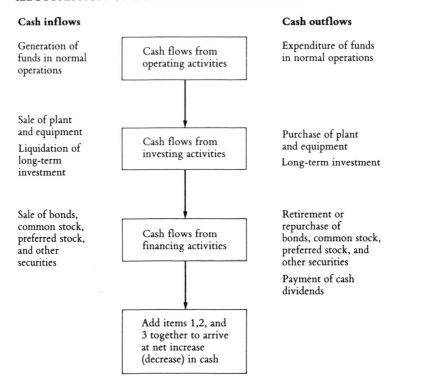

Since *FASB Statement No. 95* on the presentation of cash flows was not enacted until November 1987, Coca-Cola's 1987 annual report does not delineate the statement into the three major sections outlined above. They will follow this format in future years. However, the statement for 1987, as presented in Table 7–3, comes very close to the intent of *FASB Statement No. 95* because the firm knew the requirement was coming. The statement for 1987 separates cash flows from operations and financing activities and includes the cash flows from investing activities in the operations section. Cash provided from operations was $1,231.450 million in 1987, and net cash invested in operations (plant and equipment and subsidiaries) was $403.774 million. Cash provided from financing activities totaled $528.512 million. When we include all these cash flows plus dividends paid, Coca-Cola increased its cash balance by $599.631 million during 1987. The total cash and marketable securities on hand at the end of the year totaled $1.468 billion.

As we move down Table 7–3, we can see highlights of Coca-Cola's significant inflows and outflows of cash. For the year 1987, Coca-Cola created strong cash increases from income of $916 million and depreciation of $152 million. The major investing activities accounted for expenditures of $300 million for new plant and equipment and a significant investment in Columbia

TABLE 7–3 **COCA-COLA STATEMENT OF CHANGES IN FINANCIAL POSITION**

THE COCA-COLA COMPANY AND SUBSIDIARIES
Consolidated Statements of Changes in Financial Position
For the Years Ended December 31, 1985, 1986, and 1987
(in thousands)

	1987	1986 (Restated)	1985 (Restated)
Operations:			
Income from continuing operations:	$ 916,136	$ 934,347	$ 677,566
Depreciation	151,904	150,888	130,083
Amortization of goodwill	1,573	3,522	3,312
Deferred income taxes	(28,706)	42,300	61,185
Equity income, net of dividends	(79,701)	(126,768)	(155,438)
Gain on sale of stock by former subsidiaries	(39,654)	(375,000)	—
Provisions for restructured operations and disinvestment	36,370	180,000	—
Other	846	972	807
Discontinued operations	—	—	53,573
Working capital provided by operations	958,768	810,261	771,088
Decrease (increase) in net working capital	272,682	(69,384)	(77,221)
Cash provided by operations	1,231,450	740,877	693,867
Decrease (increase) in investments and other assets	234,741	196,204	(523,264)
Additions to property, plant, and equipment	(299,616)	(345,826)	(411,752)
Disposals of property, plant, and equipment	124,505	155,029	31,333
Decrease (increase) in temporary investments and other	323,209	(542,515)	33,221
Dividends payable in-kind	335,017	—	—
Notes receivable from and due to Columbia Pictures Entertainment, Inc.	(1,121,630)	(180,071)	876,243
Net cash obtained from (invested in) operations	(403,774)	(717,178)	5,718
Net cash available from operations	827,676	23,699	699,648
Financing activities:			
Increase (decrease) in loans and notes payable and current maturities of long-term debt	1,196,646	303,016	(197,387)
Increase in long-term debt	109,285	271,928	124,693
Decrease in long-term debt	(213,609)	(103,541)	(7,935)
Common stock issued (includes treasury)	41,300	51,249	194,190
Repurchase of common stock	(605,110)	(110,471)	(379,930)
Cash provided by (used for) financing activities	528,512	412,181	(266,369)
Discontinued operations:			
Net working capital	—	—	29,209
Net long-term assets (including property, plant, and equipment)	—	—	27,771
Resources provided by discontinued operations	—	—	56,980
Dividends:			
Cash	(421,540)	(402,556)	(388,939)
In-kind	(335,017)	—	—
Total dividends	(756,557)	(402,556)	(388,939)
Cash and current marketable securities:			
Net increase during the year	599,631	33,324	101,320
Balance at beginning of year	868,633	835,309	733,989
Balance at end of year	$1,468,264	$ 868,633	$ 835,309

Source: *The Coca-Cola Company Annual Report,* 1987, p. 40.

Pictures of $1.1 billion. Financing activities show that Coca-Cola borrowed $1.2 billion and used over $600 million to repurchase common stock.

An analysis of this statement can pinpoint many strengths or weaknesses in a company's cash flow. We can see that Coca-Cola has made some major moves within the last three years with the disposition of Columbia Pictures Entertainment, Inc., and the resultant 49 percent equity interest being one of the highlights of 1987. The company has a strong positive cash flow even after repurchasing large amounts of its common stock. Many companies are not so fortunate. For example, a number of hard-pressed firms in the energy industry in the 1980s had insufficient earnings to pay dividends or maintain or expand long-term asset commitments. In such cases, short-term borrowing is required to meet long-term needs. This can lead to a reduction of short-term working capital and a dangerous operating position.

KEY FINANCIAL RATIOS FOR THE SECURITY ANALYST

We have just summarized the three major financial statements that will be the basis of your analysis in this section emphasizing financial ratios. Ratio analysis brings together balance sheet and income statement data to permit a better understanding of the firm's past and current health which will aid you in forecasting the future outlook.

Ratio Analysis

Ratios are used in much of our daily life. We buy cars based on miles per gallon, we evaluate baseball players' earned run averages and batting averages and basketball players by field-goal and foul-shooting percentages, and so on. These are all ratios constructed to judge comparative performance. Financial ratios serve a similar purpose, but you must know what is being measured in order to construct a ratio and to understand the significance of the resultant number.

Financial ratios are used to weigh and evaluate the operating performance and capital structure of the firm. While an absolute value such as earnings of $50,000 or accounts receivable of $100,000 may appear satisfactory, its acceptability can only be measured in relation to other values.

For example, are earnings of $50,000 actually good? If a company earned $50,000 on $500,000 of sales (10 percent profit-margin ratio), that might be quite satisfactory, whereas earnings of $50,000 on $5 million could be disappointing (a meager 1 percent return.) After we have computed the appropriate ratio, we must compare our firm's results to the achievement of similar firms in the industry as well as to our own firm's past performance. Even then, this "number-crunching" process is not always adequate because we are forced to supplement our financial findings with an evaluation of company management, physical facilities, and numerous other factors.

Ratio analysis will not uncover "gold mines" for the analyst. It is more like a physical exam at the doctor's office. You hope you are all right, but if not, you may be content to know what is wrong and what to do about it. Just as with medical illness where some diseases are easier to cure than others, the same is true of financial illness. The analyst is the doctor. He or she determines the illness and keeps track of management to see if they can administer the cure. Sometimes ailing companies can be very good values. Penn-Central went into bankruptcy, and its common stock could have been purchased at $2 per share for several years. In 1988, Penn-Central traded in the $20–$25 range after a three-for-two stock split in 1982 and a two-for-one stock split in 1988. Chrysler and Lockheed were both on the brink of bankruptcy in the 1970s until the government made guaranteed loans available. At the time, Chrysler could have been bought at $3 per share and Lockheed at $1, but by 1988, Chrysler traded in a price range of $20–$28 after three-for-two stock splits in 1986 and 1987. Lockheed traded between $32–$48 in 1988 after a three-for-one split in 1983. These were sick companies that returned to health, and any investor willing to take such great risk would have been well rewarded.

Bankruptcy Studies

In a sense, ratio analysis protects an investor from picking losers more than it guarantees picking winners. Several studies have used ratios as predictors of financial failure. The most notable studies are by William Beaver and Edward Altman. Beaver found that ratios of failing firms signal failure as much as five years ahead of bankruptcy, and as bankruptcy approaches, the ratios deteriorate more rapidly, with the greatest deterioration in the last year. The Beaver studies also found that (a) "Investors recognize and adjust to the new solvency positions of failing firms," and (b) "The price changes of the common stocks act as if investors rely upon ratios as a basis for their assessments, and impound the ratio information in the market prices."[1]

The first Altman research study indicated that five ratios combined were 95 percent accurate in predicting failure one year ahead of bankruptcy and were 72 percent accurate two years ahead of failure, with the average lead time for the ratio signal being 20 months.[2] Altman developed a Z score which was an index developed through multiple discriminate analysis that could predict failure. Altman modified and improved his model's accuracy even further by increasing the number of ratios to seven.[3] This service is currently sold to institutional investors by Zeta Services Inc. The Z (zeta) score relies on the following variables:

1. Retained earnings/total assets (cumulative profitability).
2. Standard deviation of operating income/total assets (measure of earnings stability during last 10 years).
3. Earnings before interest and taxes/total assets (productivity of operating assets).

[1]William H. Beaver, "Market Prices, Financial Ratios, and the Prediction of Failure," *Journal of Accounting Research,* Autumn 1968, p. 192.

[2]Edward I. Altman, "Financial Ratios, Discriminant Analysis, and the Prediction of Corporate Bankruptcy," *Journal of Finance,* September 1968, pp. 589–609.

[3]Edward I. Altman, *Corporate Financial Distress* (New York: John Wiley & Sons, 1983).

4. Earnings before interest and taxes/interest (leverage ratio, interest coverage).
5. Current assets/current liabilities (liquidity ratio).
6. Market value of common stock/book value of equity (a leverage ratio).
7. Total assets (proxy for size of the firm).

The greater the firm's bankruptcy potential, the lower its Z score. The ratios were not equally significant, but together they separated the companies into a correct bankruptcy group and nonbankruptcy group a high percentage of the time. Retained earnings/total assets has the heaviest weight in the analysis, and leverage is also very important. In the next section, we present six classifications of ratios that ought to be helpful to the analyst. Many more could be used, but these represent the most widely used measures.

Classification System

We divide 20 significant ratios into six primary groupings:

A. Profitability ratios:
    1. Operating margin.
    2. After-tax profit margin.
    3. Return on assets.
    4. Return on equity.
B. Asset-utilization ratios:
    5. Receivables turnover.
    6. Inventory turnover.
    7. Fixed-asset turnover.
    8. Total asset turnover.
C. Liquidity ratios:
    9. Current ratio.
    10. Quick ratio.
    11. Net working capital to total assets.
D. Debt-utilization ratios:
    12. Long-term debt to equity.
    13. Total debt to total assets.
    14. Times interest earned.
    15. Fixed charge coverage.
E. Price ratios:
    16. Price to earnings.
    17. Price to book value.
    18. Dividends to price (dividend yield).
F. Other ratios:
    19. Average tax rate.
    20. Dividend payout.

The users of financial statements will attach different degrees of importance to the six categories of ratios. To the potential investor, the critical consideration is profitability and debt utilization. For the banker or trade creditor, the emphasis shifts to the firm's current ability to meet debt obligations. The bondholder, in turn, may be primarily influenced by debt to total assets—while also eyeing the profitability of the firm in terms of its ability to cover interest payments in the short term and principal payments in the long term. Of course, the shrewd analyst looks at all the ratios, with different degrees of attention.

A. Profitability Ratios.   The profitability ratios allow the analyst to measure the ability of the firm to earn an adequate return on sales, total assets, and invested capital. The profit-margin ratios (1, 2) relate to income statement items, while the two return ratios (3, 4) relate the income statement (numerator) to the balance sheet (denominator). Many of the problems related to profitability can be explained, in whole or in part, by the firm's ability to effectively employ its resources. We shall apply these ratios to Coca-Cola's income statement and balance sheet for 1987, which were previously presented in Tables 7–1 and 7–2. The values are further rounded for ease of computation (dollars in millions).

Profitability ratios (Coca-Cola, 1987—in millions):

1. Operating margin $= \dfrac{\text{Operating income}}{\text{Sales (revenue)}} = \dfrac{\$1,324}{\$7,658} = 17.29\%$

2. After-tax profit margin $= \dfrac{\text{Net income}}{\text{Sales}} = \dfrac{\$916}{\$7,658} = 11.96\%$

3. Return on assets

   (a) $\dfrac{\text{Net income}}{\text{Total assets}}$ $= \dfrac{\$916}{\$8,356} = 10.96\%$

   (b) $\dfrac{\text{Net income}}{\text{Sales}} \times \dfrac{\text{Sales}}{\text{Total assets}}$

   $11.96\% \times .9166 = 10.96\%$

4. Return on equity

   (a) $\dfrac{\text{Net income}}{\text{Stockholders' equity}^4}$ $= \dfrac{\$916}{\$3,224} = 28.41\%$

   (b) $\dfrac{\text{Return on assets}}{(1 - \text{Debt/Assets})}$ $= \dfrac{0.1096}{1 - .6142} = 28.41\%$

---

[4]A working definition of stockholders' equity is the common stock accounts plus retained earnings. Coca-Cola also has a few other adjustments. The total can be found on the second line from the bottom at the end of Table 7–2 on page 221.

FIGURE 7–2   DU PONT ANALYSIS

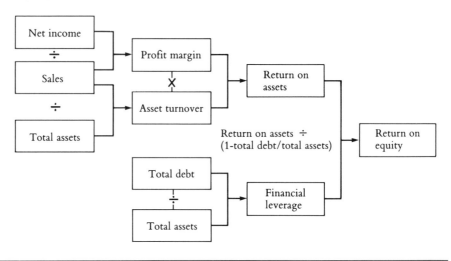

The profitability ratios indicate that Coca-Cola is quite profitable, but the analysis of its return on equity using 4(b) indicates that its high return on stockholders' equity is largely a result of heavy total debt to assets. The disparity between return on assets and return on equity is solely the result of financing 61 percent of assets with debt.

Du Pont Analysis—Notice that the return on assets and return on equity have parts (a) and (b), or two ways to determine the ratio. The methods employed in (b), which arise from the Du Pont Company's financial system, help the analyst see the relationship between the income statement and the balance sheet. The return on assets is generated by multiplying the after-tax profit margin (income statement) by the asset-turnover ratio (combination income statement–balance sheet ratio).

The Du Pont Company was a forerunner in stressing that satisfactory return on assets may be achieved through high profit margins or rapid turnover of assets, or a combination of both. The Du Pont system causes the analyst to examine the sources of a company's profitability. Since the profit margin is an income statement ratio, a high profit margin indicates good cost control, whereas a high asset turnover ratio demonstrates efficient use of the assets on the balance sheet. Different industries have different operating and financial structures. For example, in the heavy capital goods industry (machinery and equipment), the emphasis is on a high profit margin with a low asset turnover, while in food processing, the profit margin is low, and the key to satisfactory returns on total assets is a rapid turnover of assets.

Du Pont analysis further stresses that the return on equity stems from the return on assets adjusted for the amount of financial leverage by using the total debt-to-asset ratio. About 61 percent of The Coca-Cola Company's assets are financed by debt, and the return on equity reflects a high level of debt financing because the return on equity of 28.41 percent is two and one-half times as large as return on assets of 10.96 percent. As a detective, the financial analyst can judge how much debt a company employs by comparing these two measures of return. Of course, you will want to check this clue with the debt-utilization ratios. The total relationship between return on assets and return on equity under the Du Pont system is depicted in Figure 7–2.

In computing return on assets and equity, the analyst must also be sensitive to the age of the assets. Plant and equipment purchased 15 years ago may be carried on the books far below its replacement value in an inflationary economy. A 20 percent return on assets that were purchased in the late 60s or early 70s may be inferior to a 15 percent return on newly purchased assets.

B. Asset-Utilization Ratios. Under this heading, we measure the speed at which the firm is turning over accounts receivable, inventory, and longer-term assets. In other words, asset-utilization ratios measure how many times per year a company sells its inventory or collects its accounts receivable. For long-term assets, the utilization ratio tells us how productive the fixed assets are in terms of sales generation.

Asset-utilization ratios (Coca-Cola, 1987—in millions):

5. Receivables turnover $= \dfrac{\text{Sales}}{\text{Receivables}} = \dfrac{\$7,658}{\$672} = 11.40\times$

6. Inventory turnover $= \dfrac{\text{Sales}}{\text{Inventory}} = \dfrac{\$7,658}{\$777} = 9.86\times$

7. Fixed-asset turnover $= \dfrac{\text{Sales}}{\text{Fixed assets}} = \dfrac{\$7,658}{\$1,598} = 4.79\times$

8. Total asset turnover $= \dfrac{\text{Sales}}{\text{Total assets}} = \dfrac{\$7,658}{\$8,356} = 0.92\times$

The asset-utilization ratios relate the income statement (numerator) to the various assets on the balance sheet. Given that Coca-Cola's primary products are soft drinks and food, the receivables-turnover and inventory-turnover ratios reflect high turnover. Since most of the company's consumable products are not perishable, these ratios seem satisfactory. However the large amount of cash and marketable securities, as seen on the balance sheet, reduces the total asset turnover.

C. Liquidity Ratios. The primary emphasis of the liquidity ratios is a determination of the firm's ability to pay off short-term obligations as they come due. These ratios can be related to receivables and inventory turnover in that a faster turnover creates a more-rapid movement of cash through the company and improves liquidity. Again remember that each industry will be different. A jewelry store chain will have much different ratios than a grocery store chain.

Liquidity ratios (Coca-Cola, 1987—in millions):

9. Current ratio

$$\frac{\text{Current assets}}{\text{Current liabilities}} = \frac{\$4,136}{\$4,119} = 1.00$$

10. Quick ratio

$$\frac{\text{Current assets } - \text{ Inventory}}{\text{Current liabilities}} = \frac{\$3,359}{\$4,119} = 0.82$$

11. Net working capital to total assets

$$\frac{\text{Current assets } - \text{ Current liabilities}}{\text{Total assets}} = \frac{\$4,136 - \$4,119}{\$8,356} = .002$$

The first two ratios (current and quick) indicate whether the firm can pay off its short-term debt in an emergency by liquidating its current assets. The quick ratio looks only at the most-liquid assets, which include cash, marketable securities, and receivables. Cash and securities are already liquid, but receivables usually will be turned into cash during the collection period. If there is concern about the firm's liquidity, the analyst will want to cross-check the liquidity ratios with receivable turnover and inventory to determine how fast the current assets are turned into cash during an ordinary cycle.

The last liquidity ratio is a measure of the percentage of current assets (after short-term debt has been paid) to total assets. This indicates the liquidity of the assets of the firm. The higher the ratio, the greater the short-term assets relative to fixed assets and the safer a creditor. Net working capital to total assets is almost nonexistent for Coca-Cola. In some firms, a number this low would indicate serious trouble, but for Coca-Cola it is probably not a problem. The total borrowing power of the firm remains strong, but this ratio along with the low current ratio indicates a high reliance on short-term borrowing which could be a disadvantage to the firm if interest rates increase. The quick ratio probably indicates most correctly in Coca-Cola's case that liquidity is not a problem. Since the company holds $1.4 billion in cash and marketable securities, the quick ratio is adequate. Also consider that the firm generated net cash flow of $600 million after the repurchase of $600 million of common stock. Remember, ratios are pieces of the puzzle, and you cannot tell by looking at one piece whether the firm is healthy.

D. Debt-Utilization Ratios.   The debt-utilization ratios provide an indication of the way the firm is financed between debt (lenders) and equity (owners) and therefore helps the analyst determine the amount of financial risk present in the firm. Too much debt can not only impair liquidity with heavy interest payments but can also damage profitability and the health of the firm during an economic recession or industry slowdown.

Debt-utilization ratios (Coca-Cola, 1987—in millions):

12. Long-term debt to equity $= \dfrac{\text{Long-term debt}}{\substack{\text{Stockholders'} \\ \text{equity}}} = \dfrac{\$803}{\$3,224} = 24.9\%$

13. Total debt to total assets $= \dfrac{\text{Total debt}^5}{\text{Total assets}} = \dfrac{\$5,132}{\$8,356} = 61.4\%$

14. Times interest earned $= \dfrac{\text{Income before interest and taxes}^6}{\text{Interest}} = \dfrac{\$1,324}{\$279} = 4.75\times$

15. Fixed-charge coverage $= \dfrac{\text{Income before fixed charges and taxes}}{\text{Fixed charges}} = \dfrac{\$1,324}{\$279} = 4.75\times$

We have already discussed the impact of financial leverage on return on equity, and the first two ratios in this category indicate to the analyst how much financial leverage is being used by the firm. The more debt, the greater the interest payments and the more volatile the impact on the firm's earnings. Companies with stable sales and earnings such as utilities can afford to employ more debt than those in cyclical industries such as automobiles or airlines. Ratio 12, long-term debt to equity, provides information concerning the long-term capital structure of the firm. In the case of Coca-Cola, long-term liabilities represent 25 percent of the stockholders' equity base provided by the owners of the firm. Ratio 13, total debt to total assets, looks at the total assets and the use of borrowed capital. Each firm must consider its optimum capital structure, and the analyst should be aware of industry fluctuations in assessing the firm's proper use of leverage. Coca-Cola seems safe, given that its business is not subject to large swings in sales.

The last two debt-utilization ratios indicate the firm's ability to meet its cash payments due on fixed obligations such as interest, leases, licensing fees, or sinking-fund charges. The higher these ratios, the more protected the creditor's position. Use of the fixed-charge coverage is more conservative than interest earned since it includes all fixed charges. Now that most leases are capitalized and show up on the balance sheet, it is easier to understand that lease payments are similar in importance to interest expense. Charges after taxes such as sinking-fund payments must be adjusted to before-tax income. For example, if a firm is in the 40 percent tax bracket and must make a $60,000 sinking-fund payment, the firm would have had to generate $100,000 in before-tax income to meet that obligation. The adjustment would be as follows:

$$\text{Before-tax income required} = \frac{\text{After-tax payment}}{1 - \text{tax rate}}$$
$$= \frac{\$60,000}{1 - .40}$$
$$= \$100,000$$

Coca Cola's fixed-charge coverage is the same as its interest-earned ratio because it has no fixed charges other than interest expense.

---

[5]Total debt for Coca-Cola in 1987 represents total current liabilities plus long-term debt and deferred income taxes. See Table 7–2.

[6]This is the equivalent of operating income in Table 7–1.

E. Price Ratios.   Price ratios relate the internal performance of the firm to the external judgment of the marketplace in terms of value. What is the firm's end result in market value? The price ratios indicate the expectations of the market relative to other companies. For example, a firm with a high price-to-earnings ratio has a higher market price relative to $1 of earnings than a company with a lower ratio.

Price ratios (Coca-Cola, December 31, 1987—in millions):

16. Price to earnings $= \dfrac{\text{Common stock price}}{\text{Earnings per share}} = \dfrac{\$38.125}{\$2.43} = 15.7\times$

17. Price to book value $= \dfrac{\text{Common stock price}}{\text{Book value per share}} = \dfrac{\$38.125}{\$8.54} = 4.5\times$

18. Dividends to price (dividend yield)[7] $= \dfrac{\text{Dividends per share}}{\text{Common stock price}} = \dfrac{\$1.20}{\$38.125} = 3.15\%$

Coca-Cola's price-earnings ratio indicates that the firm's stock price represents $15.70 for every $1 of earnings. This number can be compared to that of other companies in the soft drink industry and/or related industries. As indicated in Chapter 6, the price-earnings ratio (or P/E ratio, as it is commonly called) is influenced by the earnings and the sales growth of the firm and also by the risk (or volatility in performance), the debt-equity structure of the firm, the dividend-payment policy, the quality of management, and a number of other factors. The P/E ratio indicates expectations about the future of a company. Firms that are expected to provide greater returns than those for the market in general, with equal or less risk, often have P/E ratios higher than the overall market P/E ratio.

Expectations of returns and P/E ratios do change over time, as Table 7–4 illustrates. Price-earnings ratios for a selected list of U.S. firms in 1975, 1981, and 1988 show that during this 13-year period price-earnings ratios fell for those companies between the first two periods and recovered for most companies between 1981 and 1988. This is true even though we are measuring P/E ratios after the crash of 1987.

P/E ratios are more complicated than they may appear at first glance. The level of the market is higher in 1988 as measured by the Standard & Poor's 500 Stock Index, but not all companies exhibit higher P/E ratios. The stable large industrial companies like Exxon seem to follow the market. Halliburton, an oil service company, has a P/E twice that of the market, not because of outstanding growth expectations but because of depressed earnings per share (which make the higher ratio deceiving). McDonald's, on the other hand, has a P/E 50 percent higher than 1981 but much lower than 1975. This relationship is due to the slower growth expectations for McDonald's in 1988 than were

---

[7]Dividends annualized at most recent quarterly rate.

TABLE 7-4   PRICE-EARNINGS RATIOS FOR SELECTED U.S. CORPORATIONS

Corporation	Industry	P/E Ratio* December 31, 1975	December 31, 1981	October 24, 1988
Exxon	International oil	8	5	12
Texas Utilities	Public utility	9	6	7
Union Carbide	Chemical	9	5	10
BankAmerica	Banking	10	7	9
CBS	Broadcasting	11	7	16
Halliburton	Oil service	12	11	26
Winn-Dixie	Retail	14	8	15
IBM	Computers	17	9	14
Upjohn	Ethical drugs	18	10	18
McDonald's	Restaurant franchises	26	10	15
Texas Instruments	Semiconductors	34	15	13
S&P 500	Market index	11	8	13

*P/E is calculated by taking the market price and dividing by the previous 12 months' earnings per share. Other calculations of P/E would include using the next 12 months' expected earnings per share.

present in 1975. Every company has to be examined carefully before making careless use of P/E ratios when computing stock values.

The price-to-book-value ratio relates the market value of the company to the historical accounting value of the firm. In a company that has old assets, this ratio may be quite high, but in one with new, undepreciated fixed assets, the ratio might be lower. This information needs to be combined with a knowledge of the company's assets and of industry norms.

The **dividend yield** is part of the total return that an investor receives along with capital gains or losses. It is usually calculated by annualizing the current quarterly dividend, since that is the cash value a current investor would receive over the next year.

The price-to-earnings and price-to-book-value ratios are often used in computing stock values. The simple view of these ratios is that when they are relatively low compared to a market index or company history, the stock is a good buy. In the case of the dividend yield, the opposite is true. When dividend yields are relatively high compared to the company's historical data, the stock may be undervalued. Of course, the application of these simple models is much more complicated because one has to determine if the company is performing the same as it was when the ratios were at what the analyst considers a normal level.

F. Other Ratios.   The other ratios presented in category F are to help the analyst spot special tax situations that impact the profitability of an industry or company and to determine what percentage of earnings are being paid to the stockholder and what is being reinvested for internal growth.

Other ratios (Cola-Cola, 1987—in millions):

19. Average tax rate $= \dfrac{\text{Income tax}}{\text{Taxable income}} = \dfrac{\$494}{\$1,410} = 35.0\%$

PICKING STOCKS BY THE BOOK IS A STANDBY SOME SWEAR BY

Investment fads come and go, but many successful investors still swear by one of the oldest and easiest ways to buy stocks.

Year in and year out, in bull markets and bear markets, they say, the best way to find undervalued companies and possible takeover candidates is to buy stocks that are selling below their book value.

Book value is generally defined as a company's net worth, its assets minus its liabilities. Those who use the buy-below-book strategy typically focus on "tangible" book value. This excludes such intangibles as patents and good will, which is a monetary value commonly placed on things such as reputation when one company acquires another.

"A price below book value is a beginning tool in the hunt for bargain stocks, not an end in itself," says Mark Keller, vice president of securities research at A. G. Edwards. For example, he says, "If you buy a company that sells below book value yet has a high debt, it may never recover."

Some of the biggest proponents of buying below book are the followers of the late Benjamin Graham, generally considered the father of modern security analysis.

In Mr. Graham's view, investors should concentrate on buying stocks below or close to their book value, or no more than 30 percent above that figure. "The greater the premium above the book value, the less certain the basis for determining intrinsic value, and the more this value depends on the changing moods and measurements of the stock market," Mr. Graham wrote in his 1949 book, *The Intelligent Investor*.

For a simulated test, one portfolio manager took 500 of the largest companies and "bought" 100 of the lowest price-to-book-ratio stocks at the first of the year and sold them at the end of the year. From 1969 to July 1988, this approach resulted in an average annual total return of 14.4 percent, including dividends, [compared to the average stock return of 10.8 percent for the S&P 500 Stock Index].

Source: Earl C. Gottschalk, Jr., *The Wall Street Journal*, November 3, 1988, p. C1. Reprinted by permission of *The Wall Street Journal*, © Dow Jones and Company, Inc., 1988. All rights reserved.

$$20. \quad \text{Dividend payout} = \frac{\text{Dividends per share}}{\text{Earnings per share}} = \frac{\$1.20}{\$2.43} = 49.3\%$$

These other ratios are calculated to provide the analyst with information that may indicate unusual tax treatment or reinvestment policies. For example, the tax ratio for forest products companies will be low because of the special tax treatment given timber cuttings. A company's tax rate may also decline in a given year due to special tax credits. Thus, earnings per share may rise, but we need to know if it is from operations or favorable tax treatment. If it is from operations, we will be more sure of next year's forecast, but if it is from tax benefits, we cannot normally count on the benefits being continued into the future.

The **dividend-payout ratio** provides data concerning the firm's reinvestment strategies. A high payout ratio tells the analyst that the stockholder is receiving a large part of the earnings and that the company is not retaining much income for investment in new plant and equipment. High payouts are usually found in industries that do not have great growth potential, while low payout ratios are associated with firms in growth industries.

TABLE 7-5 COCA-COLA'S LINES OF BUSINESS

Lines of Business. Information concerning operations in different lines of business at December 31, 1987, 1986, and 1985 and for the years then ended is presented below (in millions). The company operates principally in the soft drink industry. Citrus, fruit drinks, coffee, and other products are included in the Foods Business Sector.

Intercompany transfers between sectors are not material. Prior years' information has been restated to account for Columbia Pictures Entertainment, Inc., and T.C.C. Beverages Ltd. under the equity method.

	Soft Drinks		Foods	Corporate	Consolidated
	USA	International			
1987:					
Net operating revenues	$2,120.1	$4,109.2	$1,414.3	$ 14.7	$7,658.3
Operating income	323.6	1,108.9	66.6(a)	(175.3)	1,323.8
Identifiable assets	2,047.4	2,126.7	627.3	3,554.2(d)	8,355.6
Capital expenditures	78.0	92.3	55.4	73.9	299.6
Depreciation and amortization of goodwill	60.1	42.6	28.8	22.0	153.5
1986:					
Net operating revenues	2,016.3	3,628.6	1,319.8	11.9	6,976.6
Operating income	158.3(b)	843.0(c)	120.3	(224.5)	897.1
Identifiable assets	1,424.6	1,862.4	593.1	3,604.0(d)	7,484.1
Capital expenditures	73.7	102.3	71.8	98.0	345.8
Depreciation and amortization of goodwill	60.6	48.0	26.4	19.4	154.4
1985:					
Net operating revenues	1,864.7	2,676.7	1,326.5	11.3	5,879.2
Operating income	217.2	612.8	117.6	(140.9)	806.7
Identifiable assets	1,489.9	1,565.5	486.1	2,704.8(d)	6,246.3
Capital expenditures	112.3	101.5	113.8	84.2	411.8
Depreciation and amortization of goodwill	49.1	46.4	21.2	16.7	133.4

(a) Includes provisions for restructured operations aggregating $36 million. (b) Includes provisions for restructured operations aggregating $45 million. (c) Includes provisions for restructured operations aggregating $135 million. (c) Includes provisions for disinvestment aggregating $45 million. (d) Corporate identifiable assets are composed principally of marketable securities, investments, and fixed assets. At December 31, 1987, corporate assets included equity investments in Coca-Cola Enterprises Inc., Columbia Pictures Entertainment, Inc., and T.C.C. Beverages Ltd. of $749.2 million, $989.4 million, and $84.5 million, respectively. On a comparable basis, the amounts were $709.3 million, $1,436.7 million, and T.C.C. Beverages Ltd. at December 31, 1986; and $402.7 million, $1,442.8 million, and $74.1 million, respectively, at December 31, 1985.
Source: *The Coca-Cola Company Annual Report*, 1987, p. 48.

TABLE 7–6	SELECTED VALUES BY SEGMENT FOR THE COCA-COLA COMPANY, 1987		
	USA Soft Drinks	International Soft Drinks	Food
Revenue/assets	1.03×	1.93×	2.25×
Operating income/assets	15.77%	52.11%	10.62%
Operating income/sales	15.23%	26.98%	4.71%

USES OF RATIOS

The previous section presented 20 ratios that may be helpful to the analyst in evaluating a firm. How can we further use the data we have gathered to check the health of companies we are interested in analyzing?

One way is to compare the company to the industry. This is becoming more difficult as companies diversify into several industries. Twenty years ago, firms competed in one industry, and ratio comparisons were more reliable. Now companies have a wide range of products and markets.

Coca-Cola is no exception. Table 7–5 presents the business segments in which Coca-Cola operates. Soft drinks and foods comprise the business segments with soft drinks divided into USA and International. This additional information adds a new dimension to our analysis. The soft drink segment is by far the largest segment, accounting for almost 81 percent of the operating revenues and almost all of the operating income. The interesting fact is that the international soft drink division accounts for 54 percent of consolidated operating revenues and 84 percent of consolidated operating income. The foods division is not nearly as profitable as soft drinks. The corporate category is misleading since it holds the identifiable assets associated with the 49 percent equity interest in Columbia Pictures and the other investments. It also includes overhead and staff but generates no income.

Table 7–6 shows that while the food division dominates the asset-turnover ratio with a 2.25 turnover, its low operating profit margin of 4.71 percent drags down operating return on total assets. The soft drink portion shows an asset turnover of approximately 1 for the USA and, therefore, has little difference between operating return on assets and sales. The biggest contributor to Coca-Cola's bottom line is the international division. The company has much less investment internationally than domestically, and this shows up in higher ratios all the way down the column. While the food division is not a major contributor to The Coca-Cola Company currently, improvements in its operating performance and profitability could enhance the stock price. Coca-Cola evidently thinks that the food division is worth the investment since they continue to put capital expenditures into this area.

Companies in oligopolies such as Coca-Cola in the soft drink industry are hard to evaluate on a ratio basis because one or two firms (Pepsi and Coke) dominate the industry, and so industry ratios are not a helpful measure of performance. Since the last edition of this book, Dr Pepper, Royal Crown,

TABLE 7-7   SELECTED RATIO COMPARISONS FOR THE COCA-COLA COMPANY, 1987

		Industries	
	Coca-Cola	Food	Beverage
Operating margin	17.37%	10.6%	15.0%
After-tax profit margin	12.0%	4.1%	8.2%
Return on equity	28.4%	17.6%	19.3%
Long-term debt to equity	24.9%	48.1%	42.0%
Price-to-earnings ratio	15.7×	16.7×	15.4×
Dividend yield	3.2%	2.2%	2.3%
Average tax rate	35.0%	43.1%	32.0%
Payout ratio	49.3%	35.0%	32.0%

and MEI were removed as publicly traded companies. In the case of the food division of Coca-Cola, this would not be the case since this industry consists of many firms, and industry comparison would be helpful. Table 7-7 looks at Coca-Cola compared to the food industry, and since Coca-Cola dominates the soft drink industry, we compare its performance to another competitive industry, the beverage industry (beer).

Given the set of ratios above, Coca-Cola compares favorably with the ratios for both the food and beverage industries. The beverage industry is dominated by Budweiser, while the food industry is not dominated by any one company. Because Coca-Cola has low long-term debt, its interest expense may be lower than that of the food and beverage industries, allowing it to bring more of its operating profit down to the after-tax profit margin. The payout ratio for Coca-Cola is quite a bit higher than for the two industries, showing that these industries are reinvesting a larger percentage of their profits for growth. Coca-Cola has stated in its annual report that it is slowly moving toward a 40 percent payout ratio which indicates that it expects to grow faster in the future with reinvested earnings.

Coca-Cola's return on equity is higher than that of the comparative industries and reflects a better level of profitability. But the fact that the profitability ratios favor Coca-Cola has not been translated into the market in terms of a higher P/E ratio for Coca-Cola. Either the market thinks Coca-Cola will not grow any faster than the two industries or that there is more risk in buying Coca-Cola.

In general, after reviewing all the financial statements and ratios, Coca-Cola looks to be in good financial shape. The food division needs to improve profitability, and Coca-Cola needs to use more long-term debt in its capital structure to replace short-term borrowings that have more volatile interest rates and therefore may carry more risk as a financing vehicle.

It is important to realize that Coca-Cola is an international company that may be impacted by political and economic events abroad. Foreign revolts and a rising dollar can have a negative impact on Coca-Cola's earnings. Fortunately, its earnings during 1986–87 have benefited from a falling dollar. This

TABLE 7–8   COCA-COLA'S OPERATIONS IN GEOGRAPHIC AREAS

Operations in Geographic Areas. Information about the company's operations in different geographic areas at December 31, 1987, 1986, and 1985, and for the years then ended is presented below (in millions). Intercompany transfers between geographic areas are not material. Prior years' information has been restated to account for Columbia Pictures Entertainment, Inc., and T.C.C. Beverages Ltd. under the equity method.

	United States	Latin America	Europe and Africa	Pacific and Canada	Corporate	Consolidated
1987:						
Net operating revenues	$3,459.1	$558.0	$1,709.5	$1,917.0	$ 14.7	$7,658.3
Operating income	384.5 *(a)*	153.2	501.8	453.3	(175.3)	1,323.8
Identifiable assets	2,625.9	368.3	1,040.8	766.4	3,554.2 *(d)*	8,355.6
1986:						
Net operating revenues	3,277.9	555.5	1,628.9	1,502.4	11.9	6,976.6
Operating income	273.8 *(b)*	140.8	354.6 *(c)*	352.4	(224.5)	897.1
Identifiable assets	1,980.8	383.7	895.4	620.2	3,604.0 *(d)*	7,484.1
1985:						
Net operating revenues	3,147.2	452.4	1,240.8	1,027.5	11.3	5,879.2
Operating income	333.7	90.9	294.4	228.6	(140.9)	806.7
Identifiable assets	1,950.9	380.8	804.5	405.3	2,704.8 *(d)*	6,246.3

Identifiable liabilities of operations outside the United States amounted to approximately $949.6 million, $813.2 million, and $731.9 million at December 31, 1987, 1986, and 1985, respectively. (a) Includes provisions for restructured operations aggregating $36 million. (b) Includes provisions for restructured operations aggregating $135 million. (c) Includes provisions for disinvestment aggregating $45 million. (d) Corporate identifiable assets are composed principally of marketable securities, investments, and fixed assets. At December 31, 1987, corporate assets included equity investments in Coca-Cola Enterprises Inc, Columbia Pictures Entertainment, Inc., and T.C.C. Beverages Ltd. of $749.2 million, $989.4 million, and $84.5 million, respectively. On a comparable basis, the amounts were $709.3 million, $1,436.7 million, and $87.7 million, respectively, at December 31, 1986; and $402.7 million, $1,442.8 million, and $74.1 million, respectively, at December 31, 1985.

Source: *The Coca-Cola Company Annual Report,* 1987, p. 49.

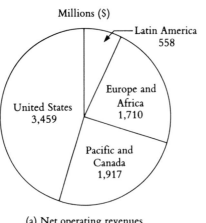

(a) Net operating revenues

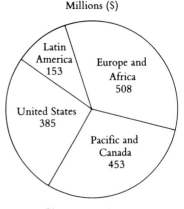

(b) Operating income

TABLE 7–9 **SELECTED FINANCIAL DATA FOR COCA-COLA** (In Millions Except Per-share Data)

	Year Ended December 31,		
	1987	1986	1985
Summary of operations (a,b):			
—Net operating revenues	$7,658	$6,977	$5,879
Cost of goods	3,633	3,454	2,909
Gross profit	4,025	3,523	2,970
Selling administrative, and general expenses	2,665	2,446	2,163
Provisions for restructured operations and disinvestment	36	180	—
Operating income	1,324	897	807
Interest income	207	139	145
Interest expense	279	197	190
Equity income	118	156	164
Other income (deductions)—net	—	33	66
Gain on sale of stock by former subsidiaries	40	375	—
Income from continuing operations before income taxes	1,410	1,403	992
Income taxes	494	469	314
Income from continuing operations	916	934	678
—Net income	$ 916	$ 934	$ 722
Per-share data (c):			
Income from continuing operations	$ 2.43	$ 2.42	$ 1.72
Net income	2.43	2.42	1.84
Dividends			
Cash	1.12	1.04	.99
In-kind	.90	—	—
—Year-end position:			
Cash and marketable securities	$1,468	$ 869	$ 835
Property, plant, and equipment—net	1,598	1,538	1,482
Total assets	8,356	7,484	6,246
Long-term debt	803	908	739
Total debt	2,702	1,610	1,139
Shareholders' equity	3,224	3,515	2,979
Total capital (d)	5,926	5,125	4,118
Financial ratios:			
Income from continuing operations to average shareholders' equity	27.2%	28.8%	23.5%
Total debt to total capital	45.6%	31.4%	27.7%
Cash dividend payout	46.0%	43.1%	53.7%
Other data:			
Average shares outstanding (c)	377	387	393
Capital expenditures	$ 300	$ 346	$ 412
Depreciation	$ 152	$ 151	$ 130
Market price per share at December 31 (c)	$38.13	$37.75	$28.17

Notes: (a) As a result of the December 1987 combination of the company's Entertainment Business Sector with Columbia Pictures Entertainment, Inc. (CPE), formerly known as Tri-Star Pictures, Inc., and the taxable, one-time dividend of CPE stock to the company's shareholders, the company's ownership interest in CPE has been reduced to approximately 49 percent and is reported under the equity method. In addition, T.C.C. Beverages Ltd., a Canadian bottling company, sold unissued shares of its common stock in an initial public

TABLE 7–9   (concluded)

			Year Ended December 31,				
1984	1983	1982	1981	1980	1979	1978	1977
$5,442	$5,056	$4,760	$4,836	$4,460	$3,895	$3,423	$2,753
2,738	2,580	2,472	2,675	2,594	2,101	1,854	1,531
2,704	2,476	2,288	2,161	2,046	1,794	1,569	1,222
1,855	1,648	1,515	1,441	1,366	1,150	967	694
—	—	—	—	—	—	—	—
849	828	773	720	680	644	602	528
131	90	119	85	56	46	41	32
127	77	76	34	30	10	7	6
117	84	46	20	14	18	17	19
12	2	11	(20)	(13)	(7)	(18)	(12)
—	—	—	—	—	—	—	—
982	927	873	771	707	691	635	561
360	374	379	339	313	305	284	251
622	553	494	432	394	386	351	310
$ 629	$ 559	$ 512	$ 482	$ 422	$ 420	$ 375	$ 331
$ 1.57	$ 1.35	$ 1.27	$ 1.17	$ 1.06	$ 1.04	$ .95	$ .84
1.59	1.37	1.32	1.30	1.14	1.13	1.01	.89
.92	.89	.83	.77	.72	.65	.58	.51
—	—	—	—	—	—	—	—
$ 734	$ 559	$ 254	$ 344	$ 235	$ 153	$ 325	$ 351
1,284	1,247	1,233	1,160	1,045	976	833	688
5,211	4,550	4,212	3,373	3,152	2,710	2,439	2,144
631	428	423	132	121	22	15	15
1,229	520	493	227	213	130	69	57
2,778	2,921	2,779	2,271	2,075	1,919	1,740	1,578
4,007	3,441	3,272	2,498	2,288	2,049	1,809	1,635
21.8%	19.4%	19.6%	19.9%	19.7%	21.2%	21.2%	20.6%
30.7%	15.1%	15.1%	9.1%	9.3%	6.3%	3.8%	3.5%
58.0%	65.3%	62.8%	59.5%	63.2%	57.6%	57.4%	57.5%
396	408	390	372	372	372	372	369
$ 300	$ 324	$ 273	$ 279	$ 241	$ 309	$ 234	$ 203
$ 119	$ 111	$ 104	$ 94	$ 87	$ 77	$ 61	$ 55
$20.79	$17.83	$17.33	$11.58	$11.13	$11.50	$14.63	$12.42

offering which reduced the company's ownership interest to 49 percent and is reported under the equity method of accounting. Prior years' information has been restated to conform to the current year's presentation. This change had no effect on previously reported net income or net income per share. (b) In 1982, the company adopted *FASB Statement No. 52,* "Foreign Currency Translation." (c) Adjusted for a three-for-one stock split in 1986 and a two-for-one stock split in 1977. (d) Includes shareholders' equity and total debt.

has made the translation of foreign profits more valuable in dollars and has aided Coca-Cola's earnings per share.

Table 7–8 shows the breakdown of the company's worldwide sales and profitability by region. While all U.S. products account for about 45 percent of sales, the two regions "Europe and Africa" and "Pacific and Canada" account for 22 percent and 25 percent of sales, respectively, but a much larger share of income on a smaller asset base. "Europe and Africa" accounts for about 38 percent of income, while "Pacific and Canada" accounts for 34 percent.

COMPARING LONG-TERM TRENDS

Over the course of the business cycle, sales and profitability may expand and contract, and ratio analysis for any one year may not present an accurate picture of the firm. Therefore, we look at trend analysis of performance over a number of years.

First, examine the 10-year summary of selected financial data for Coca-Cola in Table 7–9. One can see the overall growth in net operating revenues since 1977. However, net income has grown a little more slowly, partially due to increased competition from Pepsi during this time. Also, note under "Year-End Position," the large accumulation in cash and marketable securities by Coca-Cola over the last decade. This 10-year summary statement provides other in-depth perspectives on the company and its relative performance.[8]

A GENERAL STUDY OF INDUSTRY TRENDS

In this section, we expand the horizon by shifting our attention to four very diverse industries and look at their comparative trends over time based on their rates of return on equity and long-term debt to equity. The specially picked industries are airlines, brewing, chemicals, and drugs. By studying these important industries, the analyst develops a feel for comparative performance in our economy.

The return on equity for the four separate industries shown in Table 7–10 exhibits some wide differences in profitability. Table 7–10 is graphed in Figure 7–3, and the trends are more visible. It is clear that the drug industry has the highest and most-consistent returns on equity, with very little variation due to industry or economic effects. The brewing industry has the next highest returns but is more volatile than drugs. The chemical industry is next, followed by airlines, which show a cyclical character and very low returns.

Although it may be easy to generalize about industries and their relationship to economic cycles, individual companies within each industry seem to stand out. The benefit of looking at companies and the industry together is that the best and worst become apparent to the trained analyst.

In the brewing industry, Anheuser-Busch stands out as slightly better than

---

[8]A few of the ratios are slightly different from those shown earlier in the chapter due to different time periods for calculation.

TABLE 7–10	RETURN ON EQUITY (Selected Companies—in Percent)									
	1978	1979	1980	1981	1982	1983	1984	1985	1986	1987
Airline industry	16.6%	6.8%	1.0%	NMF	NMF	NMF	9.4%	4.1%	0.4%	1.0%
AMR (American)	16.2	9.8	NMF	2.0%	NMF	NMF	13.3	15.2	9.3	7.0
Delta	17.8	16.0	10.1	14.1	2.0	14.9%	16.7	20.2	3.6	13.6
NWA (Northwest)	7.8	8.5	0.8	1.3	0.6	5.9	9.7	7.7	7.0	6.8
Texas Air	19.6	51.0	5.2	105.2	55.8	NMF	NMF	23.0	8.6	49.1
UAL (United)	25.6	NMF	1.8	NMF	1.0	8.9	13.8	6.8	1.9	0.1
Brewing industry	10.3	12.7	12.8	11.6	11.9	15.6	16.4	16.3	17.2	19.3
Anheuser-Busch	14.7	15.8	16.6	18.0	15.1	17.0	17.5	18.0	19.9	21.3
Coors (Adolph)	9.2	10.4	9.1	6.9	5.1	10.4	5.0	5.7	6.0	4.7
Molson Cos. Ltd.	18.6	18.6	13.6	16.2	18.0	18.1	11.3	9.5	9.8	12.4
Labatt Ltd.	9.9	14.9	15.8	17.4	19.0	19.2	15.8	15.0	16.2	16.6
Chemical industry	13.6	15.0	13.0	11.9	7.1	8.5	10.9	8.1	11.9	14.2
Dow	16.9	20.1	18.1	11.5	4.4	5.8	9.6	9.2	14.3	21.6
Du Pont	16.5	17.7	12.6	10.3	8.5	9.3	11.6	9.7	11.5	11.9
Monsanto	11.7	11.9	5.3	13.4	9.4	10.6	12.1	6.3	9.2	10.7
Olin	9.1	9.6	4.5	11.7	7.8	8.5	10.0	5.8	8.9	11.1
Union Carbide	10.8	13.8	14.1	12.3	6.0	4.3	7.4	1.9	12.9	22.9
Drug industry	19.2	20.0	19.5	17.9	19.0	19.7	20.7	21.3	23.6	26.9
Lilly, Eli	20.1	21.0	19.7	19.8	20.0	21.6	22.1	21.7	20.4	20.6
Merck	21.1	22.9	22.3	19.9	18.8	18.5	19.4	20.5	26.3	42.8
Pfizer	16.5	16.8	16.2	13.0	16.9	20.5	20.4	19.8	19.3	17.8
SmithKline Beckman	29.9	32.8	31.2	30.2	24.7	23.6	21.8	22.7	42.4	36.0
Upjohn	20.2	20.1	19.7	18.8	13.0	15.2	15.3	15.7	17.2	18.2

NMF = not meaningful data.

FIGURE 7–3   RETURN ON EQUITY—AIRLINES, BREWING. CHEMICALS, AND DRUGS

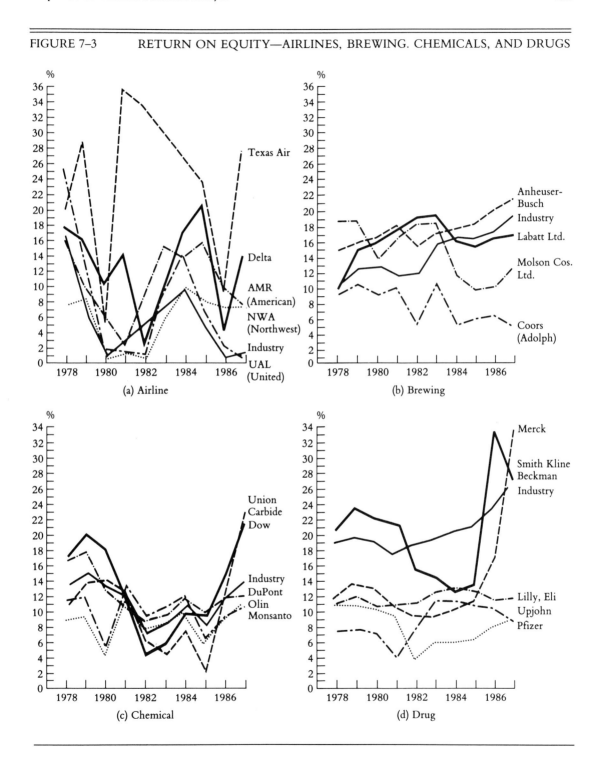

(a) Airline

(b) Brewing

(c) Chemical

(d) Drug

the Canadian brewer Labatt Ltd. While it appears that Coors has been struggling with low returns on equity, it should be noted that it uses no long-term debt in its capital structure. Use of debt at the same level of Anheuser-Busch would almost double Coors' return on equity but still leave it at the lowest level of the four firms. The chemical industry had a difficult time dealing with the recession in 1981–82, and the effects lingered into 1983. The industry as a whole is cyclical, but Du Pont and Monsanto exhibit the most consistency with Dow and Union Carbide showing the most variation of return. Union Carbide had a disaster in Bhopal, India, in 1985 when a gas leak in a chemical plant injured thousands of people. As the return-on-equity ratio shows, Union Carbide had barely recovered from the recession when this disaster lowered returns to 1.9 percent. By 1987, however, the company recovered to have the highest ROE in the industry. The drug industry has the highest and most-consistent performance, with SmithKline Beckman leading the pack in most years but with Lilly showing the most-stable returns over time. Airlines are the most-cyclical industry with NMF (not meaningful data) indicating losses. Northwest Airlines has at least kept from losing money, but its returns are less than desirable. On the other hand, Texas Air has so much debt that any profit at all is magnified into high returns on equity.

In Table 7–11 and Figure 7–4, the same four industries' long-term debt-to-equity ratios are given, which might explain the impact of financial leverage on the return on equity and possibly explain why some companies and industries are more volatile than others. In general, the airline industry has the most debt, followed by the chemical, brewing, and drug industries.

The basic business of airlines requires a large capital commitment in terms of airplanes, and therefore, a large amount of debt is needed to finance them because profitability is not sufficient to provide enough internal funds. Delta traditionally has had a low level of long-term debt, but in 1983, the firm increased its borrowing dramatically for the purchase of new equipment. Since that time, it has reduced its long-term debt-to-equity ratio to more reasonable levels. Even Northwest Airlines, which had maintained the lowest long-term debt ratios for years, got on the debt bandwagon in 1986 with its purchase of Republic Airlines. However given management's proclivity for a low-risk financial position, we can assume that Northwest will again reduce its long-term debt-to-equity ratio. The airline industry, in general, is burdened with debt, and the cyclical nature of the industry compounds earnings swings.

All the other industries are in safe territory. Coors has no long-term debt at all, while Molson has reduced its debt significantly in 1986 and 1987. Du Pont traditionally has had the lowest debt ratio in chemicals, but the purchase of Conoco Oil in 1981 caused long-term debt to rise significantly. The company has been reducing its debt burden and by 1987 was back to the level of the 1978–80 period of 20–24 percent. The Bhopal incident forced Union Carbide to increase its debt dramatically in 1986–87 to cover the expenses associated with this disaster. The drug industry has traditionally had the lowest long-term debt-to-equity ratio of the four industries, mostly because their consistently high returns allow internal generation of funds through retained earnings.

TABLE 7-11 LONG-TERM DEBT TO EQUITY (Selected Companies—in Percent)

	1978	1979	1980	1981	1982	1983	1984	1985	1986	1987
Airline industry										
AMR (American)	106.0%	118.6%	140.0%	150.8%	180.2%	139.2%	123.4%	128.3%	134.7%	127.5%
Delta	119.3	131.0	158.2	180.3%	160.2	98.8%	87.3	80.7	96.1	98.3
NWA	22.7	14.7	16.0	19.1	35.5	121.8	64.1	41.6	66.7	52.6
(Northwest)	12.6	11.8	7.5	1.5	0.0	11.7	11.2	52.2	125.4	62.5
Texas Air	265.0	207.4	230.9	1104.5	751.8	NMF	NMF	517.1	380.9	524.1
UAL (United)	97.2	106.3	100.0	107.4	160.1	82.1	52.1	147.4	90.0	48.8
Brewing industry										
Anheuser-Busch	32.0	32.7	39.4	37.0	38.7	35.6	29.3	32.2	42.9	42.0
—	55.7	55.2	71.0	67.7	53.5	46.8	37.5	35.0	43.3	48.3
Coors (Adolph)	0.0	0.0	0.0	0.0	0.0	0.0	0.0	0.0	0.0	0.0
Molson Cos. Ltd.	47.5	39.3	75.6	66.8	69.5	62.2	59.4	58.9	33.1	21.1
Labatt Ltd.	67.1	73.7	62.7	77.1	65.1	64.4	55.2	68.3	87.4	77.1
Chemical industry										
Dow	50.0	46.6	45.3	56.3	47.4	42.6	36.0	41.0	47.3	43.0
Du Pont	86.5	78.6	77.7	81.3	69.5	55.5	54.2	66.7	65.9	65.5
Monsanto	23.1	20.8	19.4	70.1	54.1	41.3	28.8	25.9	24.8	21.8
Olin	47.4	43.2	48.8	33.3	28.7	25.6	22.7	61.3	43.1	40.1
—	43.1	39.6	39.7	37.7	36.4	45.7	42.6	51.6	52.4	56.4
Union Carbide	40.7	43.9	38.9	39.9	47.1	48.4	48.0	43.5	304.2	229.6
Drug industry										
Lilly, Eli	22.5	20.2	18.9	18.3	17.1	15.7	11.5	11.0	19.8	16.8
Merck	0.3	0.2	1.9	2.8	2.4	4.3	5.3	10.0	14.4	12.0
Pfizer	14.5	12.8	11.3	12.0	15.3	15.8	7.0	6.5	6.5	7.9
SmithKline Beckman	42.8	40.0	37.1	40.7	26.3	22.2	13.6	11.1	8.4	6.4
—	20.4	16.1	12.4	11.4	10.6	4.3	3.8	4.5	98.4	45.1
Upjohn	33.6	29.8	35.3	47.5	47.4	51.9	33.7	29.1	28.8	26.1

NMF = not meaningful data.

FIGURE 7–4   TOTAL DEBT TO EQUITY—AIRLINES, BREWING, CHEMICALS, AND
                   DRUGS

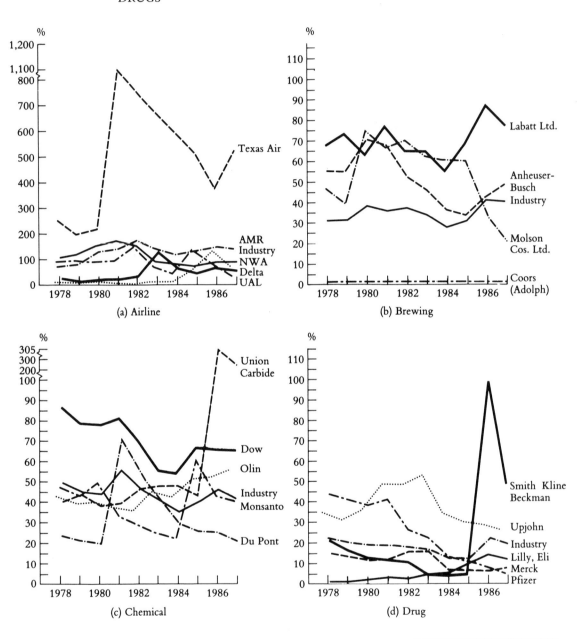

(a) Airline

(b) Brewing

(c) Chemical

(d) Drug

These tables only cover two ratios, but they should get across the point that industry comparisons allow one to pick the quality companies and find the potential losers. These two ratios (return on equity and long-term debt to equity) can be extremely important when making risk-return choices between common stocks. By comparing the two tables, we can see a distinct relationship between the ratios. The drug industry is in the lowest risk, highest return position by having the highest return on equity and at the same time having the lowest debt-to-equity ratio. On the other hand, the airline industry shows extremely high risk by having the highest debt-to-equity ratios and at the same time exhibiting lower and more volatile returns on equity.

DEFICIENCIES OF FINANCIAL STATEMENTS

Several differences occur between companies and industries, and inflation has additionally clouded the clarity of accounting statements. Some of the more-important difficulties occur in the area of inflation-adjusted accounting statements, inventory valuation, depreciation methods, pension funds liabilities, research and development, deferred taxes, and foreign exchange accounting. We do not have space to cover all of them, but we will touch on the most-important ones.

Inflation Effects

Inflation causes phantom sources of profit that may mislead even the most-alert analyst. The major problem is that revenue is almost always stated in current dollars, whereas plant and equipment or inventory may have been purchased at lower price levels. Thus, profit may be more a function of increasing prices than of satisfactory performance.

Inflation has decreased during the mid-1980s, but it is still running at about 4–5 percent annually, which, over time, can cause major distortions in the financial statements even if not as large as those experienced in the 1970s when inflation was in double digits for several years.

Much of the distortion of inflation shows up on the balance sheet since most of the values on the balance sheet are stated on a historical or original-cost basis. This may be particularly troublesome in the case of plant and equipment and inventory, which may now be worth two or three times the original cost or—from a negative viewpoint—may require many times the original cost for replacement.

The accounting profession has been groping with this problem for decades, and the discussion becomes particularly intense each time inflation rears its ugly head. In October 1979, the Financial Accounting Standards Board (FASB) issued a ruling that required about 1,300 large companies to disclose inflation-adjusted accounting data in their annual reports. The ruling was extended for five more years in 1984 but was later made optional. As inflation temporarily slowed, many companies chose not to disclose inflation-adjusted statements in addition to the historical-cost statements.

TABLE 7–12   COMPARISON OF REPLACEMENT-COST ACCOUNTING TO
HISTORICAL-COST ACCOUNTING

	Ten Chemical Companies		Eight Drug Companies	
	Replacement Cost	Historical Cost	Replacement Cost	Historical Cost
Increase in assets	28.4%	—	15.4%	—
Decrease in net income before taxes	(45.8)	—	(19.3)	—
Return on assets	2.8	6.2%	8.3	11.4%
Return on equity	4.9	13.5	12.8	19.6
Debt-to-assets ratio	34.3	43.8	30.3	35.2
Interest-coverage ratio (times interest earned)	7.1×	8.4×	15.4×	16.7

Note: Replacement cost is but one form of current cost. Nevertheless, it is widely used as a measure of current cost.

Source: Jeff Garnett and Geoffrey A. Hirt, "Replacement Cost Data: A Study of the Chemical and Drug Industry for Years 1976 through 1978" (Working paper).

Nevertheless, the impact of inflation cannot be ignored. From a study of 10 chemical firms and 8 drug companies using current-cost (replacement-cost) data found in the financial 10-K statements that these companies filed with the Securities and Exchange Commission, it was found that the changes shown in Table 7–12 occurred in their assets, income, and other selected ratios. The impact of these changes is still important as an example of the changes that take place on ratio analysis during periods of high inflation such as 1976–78.

The comparison of replacement-cost and historical-cost accounting methods in Table 7–12 shows that replacement cost increases assets but at the same time reduces income. This increase in assets lowers the debt-to-assets ratio since debt is a monetary asset that is not revalued because it is paid back in nominal dollars.

The decreased debt-to-assets ratio would indicate that the financial leverage of the firm is decreased, but a look at the interest-coverage ratio tells a different story. Because the interest-coverage ratio measures the operating income available to cover interest expense, the declining income penalizes the ratio, and the firm shows a decreased ability to cover its interest cost.

As long as prices continue to rise in an inflationary environment, profits appear to feed on themselves. The main objection is that when prices do level off, management and unsuspecting stockholders have a rude awakening as expensive inventory is charged against softening retail prices. A 15 to 20 percent growth rate in earnings may be little more than an "inflationary illusion." Industries most sensitive to inflation-induced profits are those with cyclical products, such as lumber, copper, rubber, and food products, as well as those in which inventory is a significant percentage of sales and profits. Reported profits for the lumber industry have been influenced as much as 50 percent by inventory pricing, and profits of a number of other industries have been influenced by 15 to 20 percent.

TABLE 7–13

RHOADES CORPORATION
First-Year Income Statement
Net Income for 1989

Sales	$20,000 (1,000 units at $20)
Cost of goods sold	10,000 (1,000 units at $10)
Gross profit	10,000
Selling and administrative expense	2,000
Depreciation	1,000
Operating profit	7,000
Taxes (40 percent)	2,800
Earnings after taxes	4,200
Operating margin	$7,000/20,000 = 35%
After-tax margin	$4,200/20,000 = 21%

Inventory Valuation

The income statement can show considerable differences in earnings, depending on the method of inventory valuation. The two basic methods are FIFO (first-in, first-out) and LIFO (last-in, first-out). In an inflationary economy, a firm could be reporting increased profits even though no actual increase in physical output took place. The example of the Rhoades Company will illustrate this point. We first observe their income statement for 1989 in Table 7–13. They sold 1,000 units for $20,000 and show earnings after taxes of $4,200 and an operating margin and after-tax margin of 35 percent and 21 percent, respectively.

Assume that in 1990 the number of units sold remains constant at 1,000 units. However, inflation causes a 10 percent increase in price, from $20 to $22 per unit. Total sales will go up to $22,000, but with no actual increase in physical volume. Further assume the firm uses FIFO inventory pricing, so that inventory first purchased will be written off against current sales. We will assume that 1,000 units of 1989 inventory at a cost of $10 per unit are written off against 1990 sales revenue. If Rhoades used LIFO inventory, and the cost of goods sold went up to 10 percent also, to $11 per unit, income will be less than under FIFO. Table 7–14 shows the 1990 income statement of Rhoades under both inventory methods.

Table 7–14 demonstrates the difference between FIFO and LIFO inventory methods. Under FIFO, Rhoades Corporation shows higher profit margins and more income even though no physical increase in sales occurs. This is because FIFO costing lags behind current prices, and the company generates "phantom profits" due to capital gains on inventory. Unfortunately, this inventory will need to be replaced next period at higher costs. When and if prices turn lower in a recessionary environment, FIFO will have the opposite effect and show a more negative performance. LIFO inventory costing, on the other hand, relates current costs to current prices, and although profits rise in dollar terms from 1989, the margins stay basically the same. The only problem with LIFO inventory accounting is that low-cost layers of inventory

TABLE 7–14

RHOADES CORPORATION
Second-Year Income Statement Using FIFO and LIFO
Net income for 1990

	FIFO	LIFO
Sales	$22,000 (1,000 at $22)	$22,000 (1,000 at $22)
Cost of goods sold	10,000 (1,000 at $10)	11,000 (1,000 at $11)
Gross profit	12,000	11,000
Selling and administrative expense	2,200 (10% of sales)	2,200 (10% of sales)
Depreciation	1,000	1,000
Operating profit	8,800	7,800
Taxes (40 percent)	3,520	3,120
Earnings after taxes	$ 5,280	4,680
Operating margin	$8,800/22,000 = 40%	$7,800/22,000 = 35.4%
After-tax margin	$5,280/22,000 = 24%	$4,680/22,000 = 21.2%

build up on the balance sheet of the company and understate inventory. This will cause inventory turnover to appear higher than under FIFO.

While many companies shifted to LIFO accounting by the 1980s, FIFO inventory valuation still exists in many industries, and the analyst must be ever alert to the consequences of both methods.

Extraordinary Gains and Losses

Nonrecurring gains or losses may occur from the sale of corporate fixed assets, lawsuits, or similar events that would not be expected to occur often, if ever again. Some analysts argue that such extraordinary events should be included in computing the current income of the firm, while others would leave them off in assessing operating performance. The choice can have a big impact on ratios that rely on earnings or earnings per share. Extraordinary gains can inflate returns and lower payout ratios if they are included in earnings. The analyst concerned about forecasting should only include those earnings from continuing operations; otherwise, the forecast will be seriously off its mark. Unfortunately, there is some inconsistency in the manner in which nonrecurring losses are treated in spite of determined attempts by the accounting profession to ensure uniformity of action.

Pension Fund Liabilities

One area of increasing concern among financial analysts is the unfunded liabilities of corporate pension funds. These funds eventually will have to pay workers their retirement income from the pension fund earnings and assets. If the money is not available from the pension fund, the company is liable to make the payments. These unfunded pensions may have to come out of earnings in future years, which would penalize shareholders and limit the corporation's ability to reinvest in new assets.

Foreign Exchange Transactions

During the 1980s, current values shifted dramatically as the dollar rose in the early part of the decade, fell in the middle part, and rose during the later part of the 1980s. The impact of foreign currency fluctuations has had a major impact on the earnings of those companies heavily involved in international trade. The drug industry is significantly affected. Coca-Cola, with 84 percent of operating income coming from foreign operations in 1987, is a prime example of a company greatly affected by swings in the currency markets. For example, when the dollar declines relative to foreign currencies, earnings from foreign subsidiaries get translated into more U.S. dollars and help the earnings of U.S. companies like Coca-Cola. In 1987, for example, Coca-Cola added $35 million to income from foreign currency transactions. Additionally, stockholders' equity increased by $113 million during 1987 due to foreign currency transactions. Since Coca-Cola is available in 155 countries, the firm has a diversification effect with some currencies rising and others falling. However, a major change in a given part of the world could cause this diversification effect to lose some of its meaning.

Other Distortions

Other problems exist in accounting statements and methods of reporting earnings. A mention of some of them might provide you with areas that require further investigation. Other areas for detective work are in accounting methods for the following: research and development expenditures, deferred taxes, tax credits, merger accounting, intangible drilling and development costs, and percentage depletion allowances. As you can see, many issues cause analysts to dig further and to be cautious about accepting bottom-line earnings per share.

8

A BASIC VIEW OF TECHNICAL ANALYSIS AND MARKET EFFICIENCY

In the preceding three chapters, we have followed a fundamental approach to security analysis. That is, we have examined the fundamental factors that influence the business cycle, the performance of various industries, and the operations of the individual firms. We have further examined the financial statements and tools of measurement that are available to the security analyst. In following a fundamental approach, one attempts to evaluate the appropriate worth of a security and perhaps ascertain whether it is under- or overpriced.

In this chapter, we shall examine a technical approach to investment timing. In this approach, analysts and market technicians examine prior price and volume data, as well as other market-related indicators, to determine past trends in the belief that they will help forecast future ones. Technical analysts place much more emphasis on charts and graphs of *internal market data* than on such fundamental factors as earnings reports, management capabilities, or new product development. They believe that even when important fundamental information is uncovered, it may not lead to profitable trading because of timing considerations and market imperfections.

We shall also devote much time and attention in this chapter to the concept of market efficiency; that is, the ability of the market to adjust very rapidly to the supply of new information in valuing a security. This area of study has led to the efficient market hypothesis, which states that all securities are correctly priced at any point in time.

At the outset, be aware that there are many disagreements and contradictions in the various areas that we will examine. As previously implied, advocates of technical analysis do not place much emphasis on fundamental analysis, and vice versa. Even more significant, proponents of the efficient market hypothesis would suggest that neither technical nor fundamental analysis is of any great value in producing superior returns.

In light of the various disagreements that exist, we feel it is important that the student be exposed to many schools of thought. For example, we devote the first part of the chapter to technical analysis and then later offer research findings that relate to the value of the technical approach as well as the fundamental approach. Our philosophy throughout the chapter is to recognize that there is a gap between practices utilized by brokerage houses (and on Wall Street) and beliefs held in the academic community, yet the student should be exposed to both.

TECHNICAL ANALYSIS

Technical analysis is based on a number of basic assumptions:

1. Market value is determined solely by the interaction of demand and supply.
2. Demand and supply are governed by both rational and irrational factors.
3. It is assumed that though there are minor fluctuations in the market, stock prices tend to move in trends that persist for long periods of time.
4. Reversals of trends are caused by shifts in demand and supply.

FIGURE 8–1   PRESENTATION OF THE DOW THEORY

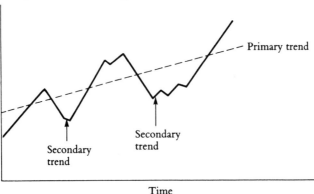

5. Shifts in demand and supply can be detected sooner or later in charts.
6. Many chart patterns tend to repeat themselves.[1]

For our purposes, the most-significant items to note are the assumptions that stock prices tend to move in trends that persist for long periods and that these trends can be detected in charts. The basic premise is that past trends in market movements can be used to forecast or understand the future. The market technician generally assumes that there is a lag between the time he perceives a change in the value of a security and when the investing public ultimately assesses this change.

In developing the tools of technical analysis, we shall divide our discussion between *(a)* the use of charting and *(b)* the key indicator series to project future market movements.

THE USE OF CHARTING

Charting is often linked to the development of the Dow theory in the late 1890s by Charles Dow.[2] Mr. Dow was the founder of the Dow Jones Company and editor of *The Wall Street Journal.* Many of his early precepts were further refined by other market technicians, and it is generally believed that the Dow theory was successful in signaling the market crash of 1929.

Essential Elements of the Dow Theory

The **Dow theory** maintains that there are three major movements in the market: daily fluctuations, secondary movements, and primary trends. Ac-

---

[1]R. D. Edwards and John Magee, Jr., *Technical Analysis of Stock Trends* (Springfield, Mass: John Magee, 1958).

[2]*The Wall Street Journal,* December 19, 1900.

FIGURE 8–2   MARKET REVERSAL AND CONFIRMATION

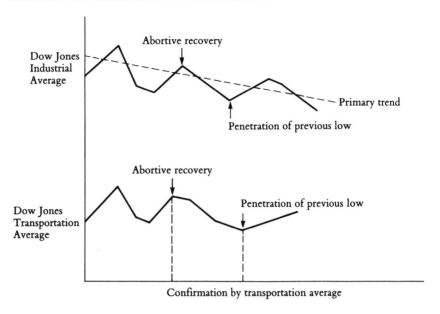

Confirmation by transportation average

cording to the theory, daily fluctuations and secondary movements (covering two weeks to a month) are only important to the extent they reflect on the long-term primary trend in the market. Primary trends may be characterized as either bullish or bearish in nature.

In Figure 8–1 we look at the use of the Dow theory to analyze a market trend. Note that the primary movement in the market is positive in spite of two secondary movements that are downward. The important facet of the secondary movements is that each low is higher than the previous low and each high is higher than the previous high. This tends to confirm the primary trend, which is bullish.

Under the Dow theory, it is assumed that this pattern will continue for a long period, and the analyst should not be confused by secondary movements. However, the upward pattern must ultimately come to an end. This is indicated by a new pattern in which a recovery fails to exceed the previous high (abortive recovery) and a new low penetrates a previous low as indicated in the top part of Figure 8–2. For a true turn in the market to take place, the new pattern of movement in the Dow Jones Industrial Average must also be confirmed by a subsequent movement in the Dow Jones Transportation Average as indicated on the bottom part of Figure 8–2.

A subsequent change from a bear to a bull market would require similar patterns of confirmation. While the Dow theory has proved helpful to market technicians, there is always the problem of false signals. For example, not every abortive recovery is certain to signal the end of a bull market. Further-

FIGURE 8–3   SUPPORT AND RESISTANCE

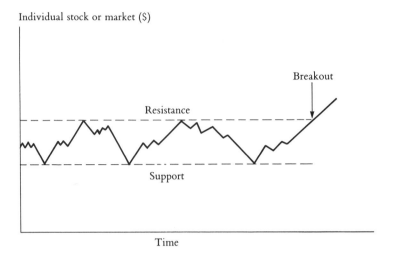

Support and Resistance Levels

Chartists attempt to define trading levels for individual securities (or the market) where there is a likelihood that price movements will be challenged. Thus, in the daily financial press or on television, the statement is often made that the next barrier to the current market move is at 2400 (or some other level). This assumes the existence of support and resistance levels. As indicated in Figure 8–3, a support level is associated with the lower end of a trading range and a resistance level with the upper end.

Support may develop each time a stock goes down to a lower level of trading because investors who previously passed up a purchase opportunity may now choose to act. It is a signal that new demand is coming into the market. When a stock reaches the high side of the normal trading range, **resistance** may develop because some investors who bought in on a previous wave of enthusiasm (on an earlier high) may now view this as a chance to get even. Others may simply see this as an opportunity to take a profit.

A breakout above a resistance point (as indicated in Figure 8–3) or below a support level is considered significant. The stock is assumed to be trading in a new range, and higher (lower) trading values may now be expected.

FIGURE 8–4   BAR CHART

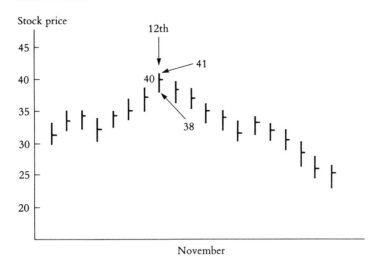

Volume

The amount of volume supporting a given market movement is also considered significant. For example, if a stock (or the market in general) makes a new high on heavy trading volume, this is considered to be bullish. Conversely, a new high on light volume may indicate a temporary move that is likely to be reversed.

A new low on light volume is considered somewhat positive because of the lack of investor participation. On the other hand, when a new low is established on the basis of heavy trading volume, this is considered to be quite bearish.

In the late-1980s, the New York Stock Exchange averaged a volume of 130 to 150 million shares daily. When the volume jumped to 200 to 250 million shares, analysts took a very strong interest in the trading pattern of the market.

Types of Charts

Until now, we have been using typical line charts to indicate market patterns. Technicians also use bar charts and point and figure charts. We shall examine each.

Bar Chart. A bar chart shows the high and low price for a stock with a horizontal dash along the line to indicate the closing price. An example is shown in Figure 8–4.

We see on November 12 the stock traded between a high of 41 and a low of 38 and closed at 40. Daily information on the Dow Jones Industrial Average

FIGURE 8–5   BAR CHART OF MARKET AVERAGE

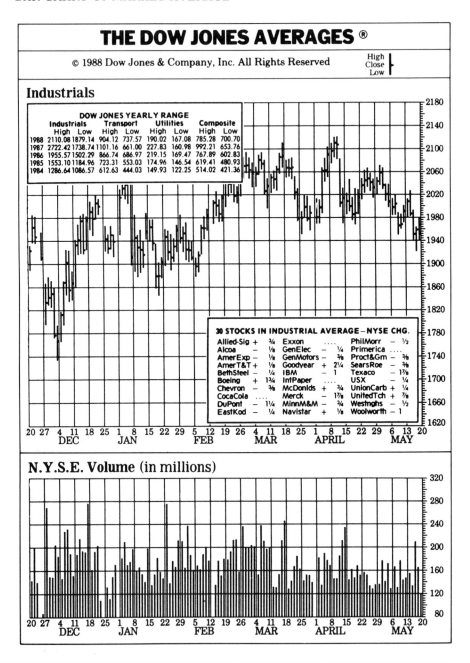

FIGURE 8–6   CHART REPRESENTATION OF MARKET BOTTOMS AND TOPS

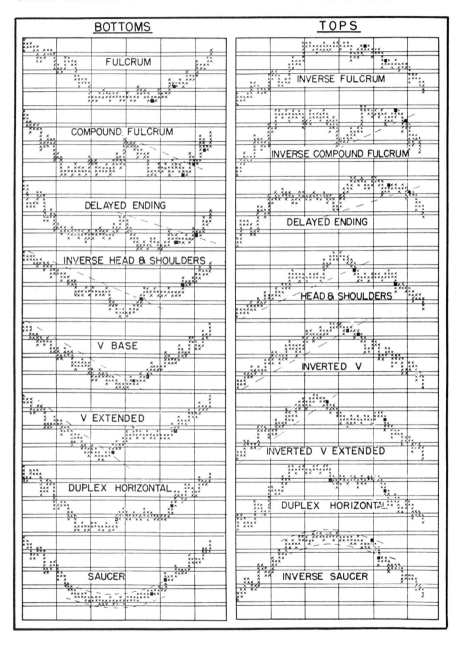

Source: Irwin Shishko, "Techniques of Forecasting Commodity Prices," *Commodity Yearbook* (New York: Commodity Research Bureau, 1965), p. 4.

is usually presented in the form of a bar chart, with daily volume shown at the bottom as indicated in Figure 8–5.

Trendline, published through a division of Standard & Poor's, provides excellent charting information on a wide variety of securities traded on the major exchanges and is available at many libraries and brokerage houses. Market technicians carefully evaluate the charts, looking for what they perceive to be significant patterns of movement. For example, the pattern in previously presented Figure 8–4 might be interpreted as a head-and-shoulder pattern (note the head in the middle) with a lower penetration of the neckline to the right indicating a sell signal. In Figure 8–6, we show a series of the price-movement patterns presumably indicating market bottoms and tops.

Though it is beyond the scope of this book to go into interpretation of chart formations in great detail, special books on the subject are suggested at the end of our discussion of charting.

Point and Figure Chart.   A point and figure chart (PFC) emphasizes significant price changes and the reversal of significant price changes. Unlike a line or bar chart, it has no time dimension. An example of a point and figure chart is presented in Figure 8–7.

The assumption is that the stock starts out at 30. Only moves of two points or greater are plotted on the graph (some may prefer to use one point). Advances are indicated by X's, and declines are shown by O's. A reversal from an advance to a decline or vice versa calls for a shift in columns. Thus, the stock initially goes from 30 to 42 and then shifts columns in its subsequent decline to 36 before moving up again in column 3. A similar pattern persists throughout the chart.

Chartists carefully read point and figure charts to observe market patterns (where there is support, resistance, breakouts, congestion, etc.). Students with a strong interest in charting may consult such books as Edwards and Magee, *Technical Analysis of Stock Trends*[3] and Zweig, *Understanding Technical Forecasting.*[4] The problem in reading charts has always been to analyze patterns in such a fashion that they truly predict stock market movements before they unfold. In order to justify the effort, one must assume that there are discernible trends over the long term.

KEY INDICATOR SERIES

In the television series "Wall Street Week," host Louis Rukeyser has a number of technical indicators that he watches on a weekly basis. He refers to them as his elves and compares the bullish and bearish indicators to determine what the next direction of the market might be.

In this section, we will examine similar bullish and bearish technical indi-

---

[3]R. D. Edwards and John Magee, Jr., *Technical Analysis of Stock Trends,* 5th ed. (Springfield, Mass: Stock Trends Service, 1966).

[4]Martin E. Zweig, *Understanding Technical Forecasting* (Princeton, N.J.: Dow Jones, 1978).

FIGURE 8–7   POINT AND FIGURE CHART

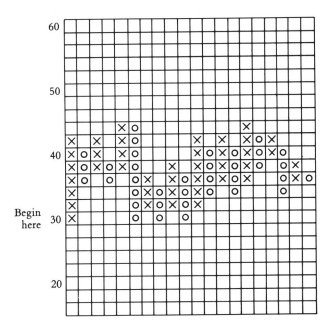

cator series. We will first look at contrary opinion rules, then smart money rules, and finally, overall market indicators.

Contrary Opinion Rules

The essence of a **contrary opinion rule** is that it is easier to figure out who is wrong than who is right. If you know your neighbor has a terrible sense of direction and you spot him taking a left at the intersection, you automatically take a right. In the stock market there are similar guidelines.

Odd-Lot Theory.   An odd-lot trade is one of less than 100 shares, and only small investors tend to engage in odd-lot transactions. The odd-lot theory suggests that you watch very closely what the small investor is doing and then do the opposite. *The Wall Street Journal* reports odd-lot trading on a daily basis, and *Barron's* reports similar information on a weekly basis. It is a simple matter to construct a ratio of odd-lot purchases to odd-lot sales. For example, on May 20, 1988, 233,850 odd-lot shares were purchased, and 478,703 shares were sold, indicating a ratio of .489. The ratio has historically fluctuated between .30 and 1.35, though in more recent times, it has been toward the lower end.

The odd-lot theory actually suggests that the small trader does all right most of the time but badly misses on key market turns. As indicated in Figure

FIGURE 8–8   COMPARING STANDARD & POOR'S 500 INDEX AND THE ODD-LOT
                    INDEX

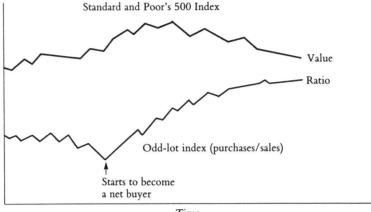

8–8, the odd-lot trader is on the correct path as the market is going up; that is, selling off part of the portfolio in an up market (the name of the game is to buy low and sell high). This net selling posture is reflected by a declining odd-lot index (purchase/sales ratio). However, as the market continues upward, the odd-lot trader suddenly thinks he or she sees an opportunity for a killing in the market and becomes a very strong net buyer. This precedes a fall in the market.

The odd-lot trader is also assumed to be a strong seller right before the bottom of a bear market. Presumably, when the small trader finally gets grandfather's 50 shares of AT&T out of the lockbox and sells them in disgust, it is time for the market to turn upward.

As if to add injury to insult, a corollary to the odd-lot theory says one should be particularly sensitive to what odd-lot traders do on Monday because odd-lotters tend to visit each other over the weekend, confirm each other's opinions or exchange hot tips, and then call their brokers on Monday morning. The assumption is that their chatter over the barbeque pit or in the bowling alley is even more suspect than their own individual opinions.

While the odd-lot theory appeared to have some validity in the 1950s and 1960s, it was not a particularly valuable tool in the 1970s and 1980s. For one thing, the odd-lotters outguessed many of the professional money managers in selling off before the stock market debacle of the mid-1970s and late 1980s, and they began buying in advance of a recovery. Another problem is that odd-lotters have been fairly consistent net sellers since the late 1960s, so there is not a balanced movement in the index.

Short Sales Position.   A second contrary opinion rule is based on the volume of short sales in the market. As you recall from Chapter 3, a short sale represents the selling of a security you do not own with the anticipation of purchasing the security in the future to cover your short position. An investor would only engage in a short sale transaction if he believed the security would, in fact, be going down in price in the near future so that he could buy back the security at a lower price to cover his short sale. When the aggregate number of short sellers is large (that is, they are bearish), this is thought to be a bullish signal.

The contrary opinion stems from two sources: first, short sellers are sometimes emotional and may overreact to the market; second and more important, there now is a built-in demand for stocks that have been sold short by investors who will have to repurchase the shares to cover their short positions.

Daily short sale totals for the New York Stock Exchange are recorded in *The Wall Street Journal.* Also once a month (around the 20th), *The Wall Street Journal* provides a report on total short sale figures for the two major exchanges as well as securities traded on those exchanges (based on mid-month data). This feature usually contains comments about current trends in the market.

Technical analysts compute a ratio of the total short sales positions on an exchange to average daily exchange volume for the month. The normal ratio is between 1.00 and 1.75. A ratio of 1.00 would indicate that the current short sales position is equal to one day's average trading volume.

As the short sales ratio (frequently called the short interest ratio) approaches the higher end of the normal trading range, this would be considered bullish (remember this is a contrary opinion trading rule). As is true with many other technical trading rules, its use in predicting future performance has produced mixed results.[5]

Investment Advisory Recommendations. A further contrary opinion rule states that you should watch the predictions of the investment advisory services and do the opposite. This has been formalized by Investors Intelligence (an investment advisory service itself) into the Index of Bearish Sentiment. Abraham W. Cohen, president of Investors Intelligence, suggests that when 42 percent or more of the advisory services are bearish, you should expect a market upturn. Conversely, when only 17 percent or fewer are bearish, you should expect a decline.[6]

Lest one take investment advisory services too lightly, however, observe the market impact of a recommendation by Joseph Granville, publisher of the *Granville Market Letter.* On Tuesday, January 6, 1981, Mr. Granville issued a late evening warning to his subscribers to "sell everything." He helped cause a $40 billion decline in market values the next day. Although subsequent events proved Mr. Granville wrong in his prediction of an impending bear market, the fact that one man could trigger such a reaction is an indication of the number of people who are influenced by the suggestions of advisory services.

---

[5]Randall Smith, "Short Interest and Stock Market Prices," *Financial Analysts Journal,* November–December 1968, pp. 151–54. Barton M. Briggs, "The Short Interest—A False Proverb," *Financial Analysts Journal,* July–August 1966, pp. 111–16.

[6]"How to Read Stock Market Indicators," *Business Week,* December 8, 1980, p. 14.

Mr. Granville has been followed by many other so-called gurus in the 1980s, most of whom have their day in the sun and then eventually fall into disrepute as they fail to call a major turn in the market or begin reversing their positions so often that investors lose confidence. No doubt a new series of such stars will appear in the 1990s.

Greed Index.   A final contrary opinion rule is represented by the **Greed Index**, which measures how greedy investors are. It is prepared by Lee H. Idleman, research director at Neuberger and Berman. Greed, as measured by the index, is synonymous with bullish sentiment, or optimism. The more greedy or optimistic investors are, the more likely the market is to fall under this contrary opinion rule. The Greed Index comprises 10 different factors that are assigned a value from 1 to 10. Among these factors are portfolio aggressiveness (high technology versus defensive stocks), acceptance of new ideas, ratio of positive to negative comments by investment analysts, willingness to invest in untested issues, and so on.

When the Greed Index exceeds 60, this is considered to be bearish. It got up to 69 in March 1983 before a market sell-off began. It got to an all-time high of 89 in December 1968 during the go-go days of a long-forgotten bull market. When the Greed Index goes below 30, this is interpreted as a buy signal. For example, the index was at 28 before the great market upturn of June 1982. It was also at an extremely high level before the Market Crash of October 1987.

Smart Money Rules

Market technicians have long attempted to track the pattern of sophisticated traders in the hope that they might provide unusual insight into the future. We shall briefly observe theories related to bond market traders and stock exchange specialists.

Barron's Confidence Index.   The *Barron's* Confidence Index is used to observe the trading pattern of investors in the bond market. The theory is based on the premise that bond traders are more sophisticated than stock traders and will pick up trends more quickly. The theory would suggest that a person who can figure out what bond traders are doing today may be able to determine what stock market investors will be doing in the near future.

Barron's Confidence Index is actually computed by taking the yield on 10 top-grade corporate bonds, dividing by the yield on 10 intermediate-grade bonds, and multiplying by 100.

$$\begin{matrix} Barron's \\ \text{Confidence} \\ \text{Index} \end{matrix} = \frac{\text{Yield on 10 top-grade corporate bonds}}{\text{Yield on 10 intermediate-grade bonds}} \times 100$$

(8–1)

The bonds in this index are presented in Table 8–1.

TABLE 8–1 ISSUES IN *BARRON'S* CONFIDENCE INDEX

Best-Grade Bonds

Name	Coupon	Age
AT&T	$8^3/_4\%$	2000
Balt G&E	$8^3/_8\%$	2006
Exxon Pipeline	$8^1/_4\%$	2001
Gen. Elec.	$8^1/_2\%$	2004
GMAC	$8^1/_4\%$	2006
IBM	$9^3/_8\%$	2004
Ill. Bell T	$7^5/_8\%$	2006
Pfizer	$9^1/_4\%$	2000
Proc. & G.	$8^1/_4\%$	2005
Sears Roe	$7^7/_8\%$	2007

Intermediate-Grade Bonds

Name	Coupon	Age
Ala Power	$9^3/_4\%$	2004
Beneficial	9%	2005
Cater Trac	8%	2001
Comwlth Ed	$9^1/_8\%$	2008
Crown Zell	$9^1/_4\%$	2005
Firestone	$9^1/_4\%$	2004
GTE	$9^3/_8\%$	1999
Union Carbide	$8^1/_2\%$	2005
USX Corp	$7^3/_4\%$	2001
Woolworth	9%	1999

The index is published weekly in the "Market Laboratory" section of *Barron's* magazine. What does it actually tell us? First, we can observe that the top-grade bonds in the numerator will always have a smaller yield than the intermediate-grade bonds in the denominator. The reason is that the higher-quality issues can satisfy investors with smaller returns. The bond market is very representative of a risk-return trade-off environment in which less risk requires less return and higher risk necessitates a higher return.

With top-grade bonds providing smaller yields than intermediate-grade bonds, the Confidence Index will always be less than 100 (percent). The normal trading range is between 80 and 95, and it is within this range that technicians look for signals on the economy. If bond investors are bullish about future economic prosperity, they will be rather indifferent between holding top-grade bonds and holding intermediate-grade bonds, and the yield differences between these two categories will be relatively small. This would indicate that the Confidence Index may be close to 95. An example is presented below in which top-grade bonds are providing 11.4 percent and intermediate-grade bonds are yielding 12 percent.

$$\begin{array}{l} \textit{Barron's} \\ \text{Confidence} \\ \text{Index} \end{array} = \frac{\text{Yield on 10 top-grade corporate bonds}}{\text{Yield on 10 intermediate-grade bonds}} \times 100$$

$$= \frac{11.4\%}{12\%} \times 100 = 95(\%)$$

Now let us assume that investors become quite concerned about the outlook for the future health of the economy. If events go poorly, some weaker corporations may not be able to make their interest payments, and thus, bond market investors will have a strong preference for top-quality issues. Some investors will continue to invest in intermediate- or lower-quality issues but only at a sufficiently high yield differential to justify the risk. We might assume that the *Barron's* Confidence Index will drop to 84 because of the increasing spread between the two yields in the formula.

$$\frac{Barron's}{Confidence} = \frac{\text{Yield on 10 top-grade corporate bonds}}{\text{Yield on 10 intermediate-grade bonds}} \times 100$$

$$= \frac{11.6\%}{13.8\%} \times 100 = 84(\%)$$

The yield on the intermediate-grade bonds is now 2.2 percent higher than that on the 10 top-grade bonds, and this is reflected in the lower Confidence Index reading. Of course, as confidence in the economy is once again regained, the yield spread differential will narrow, and the Confidence Index will go up.

Market technicians assume that there are a few months of lead time between what happens to the Confidence Index and what happens to the economy and stock market. As is true with other such indicators, it has a mixed record of predicting future events. One problem is that the Confidence Index is only assumed to consider the impact of investors' attitudes on yields (their demand pattern). We have seen in the late 1970s and 1980s that the supply of new bond issues can also influence yields. Thus, a very large bond issue by AT&T or General Motors may drive up high-grade bond yields even though investor attitudes indicate they should be going down.

Short Sales by Specialists.   Another smart money index is based on the short sales positions of specialists. Recall from Chapter 2 that one of the roles that specialists perform is to make markets in various securities listed on the organized exchanges. Because of the uniquely close position of specialists to the action on Wall Street, market technicians ascribe unusual importance to their decisions. One measure of their activity that is frequently monitored is the ratio of specialists' short sales to the total amount of short sales on an exchange.

When we previously mentioned short sales in this chapter, we suggested that a high incidence of short selling might be considered bullish because short sellers often overreact to the market and provide future demand potential to cover their short position. In the case of market specialists, this is not necessarily true. These sophisticated traders keep a book of limit orders on their securities so that they have a close feel for market activity at any given time, and their decisions are considered important.

The normal ratio of specialist short sales to short sales on an exchange is about 45 percent. When the ratio goes up to 50 percent or more, market technicians interpret this as a bearish signal. A ratio under 40 percent is considered bullish.

FIGURE 8–9   ADVANCE-DECLINE DATA ON THE NEW YORK STOCK EXCHANGE

Diaries		
NYSE	FRI	THUR
Issues traded	1,960	1,979
Advances	841	640
Declines	605	843
Unchanged	514	496
New highs	9	5
New lows	13	24
Adv Vol (000)	63,514	72,308
Decl Vol (000)	36,267	68,082
Total Vol (000)	120,600	165,160
Block trades	2,360	3,197

Source: *The Wall Street Journal,* May 23, 1988, p. 37. Reprinted by permission of *The Wall Street Journal,* ©
Dow Jones & Company, Inc. 1988. All rights reserved.

Overall Market Rules

Our discussion of key indicator series has centered on both contrary opinion
rules and smart money rules. We now briefly examine two overall market
indicators: the breadth of the market indicator series and the cash position of
mutual funds.

Breadth of the Market.   A breadth of the market indicator attempts to measure
what a broad range of securities is doing as opposed to merely examining a
market average. The theory is that market averages, such as the Dow Jones
Industrial Average of 30 stocks or the Standard & Poor's 500 Stock Average,
are weighted toward large firms and may not be representative of the entire
market. To get a broader perspective of the market, an analyst may examine
all stocks on an exchange. In Figure 8–9, we see an example of daily **advances**
and **declines** for all stocks on the New York Stock Exchange.

The technician often compares the advance-declines with the movement of
a popular market average to determine if there is a divergence between the
two. Advances and declines usually move in concert with the popular market
averages but may move in the opposite direction at a market peak or bottom.
One of the possible signals for the end of a bull market is when the Dow Jones
Industrial Average is moving up but the number of daily declines consistently
exceeds the number of daily advances. This indicates that conservative investors are investing in blue chip stocks, but there is a lack of broad-based confidence in the market. In Table 8–2, we look at an example of divergence
between the advance-decline indicators and the Dow Jones Industrial Average
(DJIA).

In column 4, we see the daily differences in advances and declines. In column
5, we look at the cumulative pattern by adding or subtracting each new day's
value from the previous total. We then compare the information in column 4
and column 5 to the Dow Jones Industrial Average (DJIA) in column 6. Clearly,
the strength in the Dow Jones Industrial Average is not reflected in the advance-

| TABLE 8–2 | COMPARING ADVANCE-DECLINE DATA AND THE DOW JONES INDUSTRIAL AVERAGE | | | | | |
| | (1) | (2) | (3) | (4) | (5) Cumulative | (6) |
Day	Advances	Declines	Unchanged	Net Advances or Declines	Advances or Declines	DJIA
1	850	750	350	+100	+100	+7.09
2	800	810	340	− 10	+ 90	+4.52
3	792	821	337	− 29	+ 61	+3.08
4	780	828	342	− 48	+ 13	+5.21
5	719	890	341	−171	−158	−2.02
6	802	812	336	− 10	−168	+5.43
7	783	824	343	− 41	−209	+3.01
8	692	912	340	−226	−435	+ .52

decline data, and this may be interpreted as signaling future weakness in the market.

Breadth of the market data can also be used to analyze upturns in the market. When the Dow Jones Industrial Average is going down but advances consistently lead declines, the market may be positioned for a recovery. Some market technicians develop sophisticated weighted averages of the daily advance-declines to go along with the data in Table 8–2.

While a comparison of advance-decline data to market averages can provide important insights, there is also the danger of false signals. Not every divergence between the two signals a turn in the market, so the analyst must be careful in his or her interpretation. The technical analyst generally looks at a wide range of variables.

Mutual Fund Cash Position.   Another overall market indicator is the cash position of mutual funds. This measure indicates the buying potential of mutual funds and is generally representative of the purchasing potential of other large institutional investors. The cash position of mutual funds, as a percentage of their total assets, generally varies between 5 percent and 20 to 25 percent.[7]

At the lower end of the boundary, it would appear that mutual funds are fully invested and can provide little in the way of additional purchasing power. As their cash position goes to 15 percent or higher, market technicians assess this as representing significant purchasing power that may help to trigger a market upturn. While the overall premise is valid, there are problems in identifying just what is a significant cash position for mutual funds in a given market cycle. It may change in extreme market environments.

EFFICIENT MARKET HYPOTHESIS

We shift our attention from technical analysis to that of examining market efficiency. As indicated at the beginning of the chapter, we shall now view any contradictions between the assumptions of fundamental or technical analysis and findings of the **efficient market hypothesis** (EMH).

---

[7]The cash dollars are usually placed in short-term credit instruments, as opposed to stocks and bonds.

We previously said that an efficient market is one in which new information is very rapidly processed so that securities are properly priced at any given time.[8] An important premise of an efficient market is that a large number of profit-maximizing participants are concerned with the analysis and valuation of securities. This would seem to describe the security market environment in the United States. Any news on IBM, AT&T, an oil embargo, or tax legislation is likely to be absorbed and acted upon very rapidly by profit-maximizing individuals. For this reason, the efficient market hypothesis assumes that no stock price can be in disequilibrium or improperly priced for very long. There is almost instantaneous adjustment to new information. The EMH applies most directly to large firms trading on the major security exchanges.

The efficient market hypothesis further assumes that information travels in a random, independent fashion and that prices are an unbiased reflection of all currently available information.

More generally, the efficient market hypothesis is stated and tested in three different forms: the weak form, the semistrong form, and the strong form. We shall examine each of these and the related implications for technical and fundamental analysis.

WEAK FORM OF THE EFFICIENT
MARKET HYPOTHESIS

The weak form of the efficient market hypothesis suggests that there is no relationship between past and future prices of securities. They are presumed to be independent over time. Because the efficient market hypothesis maintains that current prices reflect all available information and that information travels in a random fashion, it is assumed that there is little or nothing to be gained from studying past stock prices.

The weak form of the efficient market hypothesis has been tested in two different ways—tests of independence and trading rule tests.

Tests of Independence

Tests of independence have examined the degree of correlation between stock prices over time and have found the correlation to be consistently small (between $+.10$ and $-.10$) and not statistically significant. This would indicate stock price changes are independent.[9] A further test is based on the frequency and extent of runs in stock price data. A run occurs when there is no difference

---

[8]A slightly more precise definition is that securities are priced in an unbiased fashion at any given time. Because information is assumed to travel in a random, independent fashion, there is no consistent upside or downside pricing bias mechanism. Although the price adjustment is not always perfect, it is unbiased and cannot be anticipated in advance.

[9]Sidney S. Alexander, "Price Movements in Speculative Markets: Trends or Random Walks," *Industrial Management Review,* May 1961, pp. 7–26. Eugene F. Fama, "The Behavior of Stock Market Prices," *Journal of Business,* January 1965, pp. 34–105.

in direction between two or more price changes. An example of a series of data and some runs is presented below.

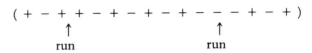

Runs can be expected in any series of data through chance factors, but an independent data series should not produce an unusual amount of runs. Statistical tests have indicated that security prices generally do not produce any more runs than would be expected through the process of random number generation.[10] This would also tend to indicate that stock price movements are independent over time.

Trading Rule Tests

A second method of testing the weak form of the efficient market hypothesis (that past trends in stock prices are not helpful in predicting the future) is through trading rule tests. Because practicing market technicians maintain that tests of independence (correlation studies and runs) are too rigid to test the assumptions of the weak form of the efficient market hypothesis, additional tests by academic researchers have been developed. These are known as trading rule or filter tests. The purpose of these tests is to determine whether a given trading rule based on past price data, volume figures, and so forth can be used to beat a naive buy-and-hold approach. The intent is to simulate the conditions under which a given trading rule is used and then determine if superior returns were produced after consideration of transaction costs and the risks involved.

As an example of a trading rule, if a stock moves up 5 percent or more, the rule might be to purchase it. The assumption is that this represents a breakout and should be considered bullish. Similarly, a 5 percent downward movement would be considered bearish and call for a sell strategy (rather than a buy-low/sell-high strategy, this is a follow-the-market-trend strategy). Other trading rule tests might be based on advance-decline patterns, short sales figures, and similar technical patterns. Research results have indicated that in a limited number of cases, trading rules may produce slightly positive returns, but after commission costs are considered, the results are neutral and sometimes negative in comparison to a naive buy-and-hold approach.[11]

Implications for Technical Analysis

The results of the *tests of independence* and *trading rules* would seem to uphold the weak form of the efficient market hypothesis. Security prices do appear to be independent over time or, more specifically, move in the pattern of a random walk.

[10]Ibid.

[11]Eugene F. Fama and Marshall Blume, "Filter Rules and Stock Market Trading Profits," *Journal of Business*, supplement, January 1966, pp. 226–41. George Pinches, "The Random Walk Hypothesis and Technical Analysis," *Financial Analysts Journal*, March–April 1970, pp. 104–10.

Some challenge the research on the basis that academic research in this area does not capture the personal judgment that an experienced technician brings forward in reading his charts. There is also the fact that there are an infinite number of trading rules, and not all of them can or have been tested.[12] Nevertheless, research on the weak form of EMH would seem to suggest that prices move independently over time, that past trends cannot be used to predict the future, and that charting and technical analysis may have limited value.

SEMISTRONG FORM OF THE EFFICIENT MARKET HYPOTHESIS

The **semistrong form of the efficient market hypothesis** maintains that all public information is already impounded into the value of a security, and therefore, one cannot use fundamental analysis to determine whether a stock is undervalued or overvalued.

Basically, the semistrong form of the efficient market hypothesis would support the notion that there is no learning lag in the distribution of public information. When a company makes an announcement, investors across the country assess the information with equal speed. Also, a major firm listed on the New York Stock Exchange could hardly hope to utilize some questionable accounting practice that deceptively leads to higher reported profits and not expect sophisticated analysts to pick it up. (This may not be equally true for a lesser known firm that trades over-the-counter and enjoys little investor attention.)

Researchers have tested the semistrong form of EMH by determining whether investors who have acted on the basis of newly released public information have been able to enjoy superior returns. If the market is efficient in a semistrong sense, this information is almost immediately impounded in the value of the security, and little or no trading profits would be available. The implications would be that one could not garner superior returns by trading on public information about stock splits, earnings reports, or other similar items.

Tests on the semistrong form of the efficient market hypothesis have generally been on the basis of risk-adjusted returns. Thus, the return from a given investment strategy must be compared to the performance of popular market indicators with appropriate risk adjustments. As will be described in Chapter 20, the risk measurement variable is usually the beta. After such adjustments are made, the question becomes: Are there abnormal returns that go beyond explanations associated with risk? If the answer is yes and can be shown to be statistically significant, then the investment strategy may be thought to refute the semistrong form of the efficient market hypothesis. The investor must also cover transaction costs in determining that a given strategy is superior.

---

[12]It has even been suggested that an investor observe the winning team in the Super Bowl and invest accordingly. If a National Football Conference team (or an original National Football League team such as the Steelers) wins, this is assumed to be bullish. If an American Football Conference team wins, this is considered bearish.

For example, assume a stock goes up 15 percent. The security is 20 percent riskier than the market. Further assume the overall market goes up by 10 percent. On a risk-adjusted basis, the security would need to go up in excess of 12 percent (the 10 percent market return × 1.2 risk factor) to beat the market.

The risk adjustment measure may be viewed as:

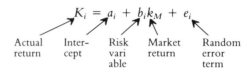

$$K_i = a_i + b_i k_M + e_i$$

Actual	Inter-	Risk	Market	Random
return	cept	vari	return	error
		able		term

Each of these items will receive further attention in Chapter 20. For now, our concern is whether an investment strategy can produce consistently superior, abnormal returns.

Tests examining the impact of such events as stock splits and stock dividends, corporate announcements, and changes in accounting policy have indicated that the market is generally efficient in a semistrong sense. For example, a study by Fama, Fisher, Jensen, and Roll indicated that almost all of the market impact of a stock split takes place before a public announcement.[13] There is little to be gained from acting on the announcement.

According to the semistrong form of the efficient market hypothesis, investors not only digest information very quickly, but they are able to see through mere changes in accounting information that do not have economic consequences. For example, the switching from accelerated depreciation to straight-line depreciation for financial reporting purposes (but not tax purposes) would tend to make earnings per share look higher but would provide no economic benefit for the firm. Research studies indicate this would have no positive impact on valuation.[14]

Similarly, investors are not deceived by mere accounting changes related to inventory policy, reserve accounts, exchange translations, or other items that appear to have no economic benefits. The corporate treasurer who switches from LIFO to FIFO accounting to make earnings look better in an inflationary economy will probably not see his or her firm's stock price rise as investors look at the economic consequences of higher taxes associated with the action and disregard the mere financial accounting consequences of higher reported profits.[15] Under this circumstance, the effect on stock may be neutral or negative.

[13]Eugene F. Fama, Lawrence Fisher, Michael G. Jensen, and Richard Roll, "The Adjustment of Stock Prices to New Information," *International Economic Review*, February 1969, pp. 2–21.

[14]T. Ross Archibald, "Stock Market Reaction to Depreciation Switch-Back," *Accounting Review*, January 1972, pp. 22–30. Robert S. Kaplan and Richard Roll, "Investor Evaluation of Accounting Information: Some Empirical Evidence," *Journal of Business*, April 1972, pp. 225–57.

[15]Shyam Sunder, "Stock Price and Risk Related to Accounting Changes in Inventory Valuation," *Accounting Review*, April 1975, pp. 305–15.

Implications for Fundamental Analysis

If stock values are already based on the analysis of all available public information, it may be assumed that little is to be gained from additional fundamental analysis. Under the semistrong form of the efficient market hypothesis, if General Motors is trading at $45, the assumption is that every shred of public information about GM has been collected and evaluated by thousands of investors, and they have determined an equilibrium price of $45. The assumption is that anything you read in *The Wall Street Journal* or Standard & Poor's publications has already been considered many times over by others and is currently impounded in the value of the stock. If you were to say that you think GM is really worth $47 because of some great new product, proponents of the semistrong form of the efficient market hypothesis would suggest that your judgment cannot be better than the collective wisdom of the marketplace in which everyone is trying desperately to come out ahead.

Ironically, although many would suggest that fundamental analysis may not lead to superior profits in an efficient market environment, it is fundamental analysis itself that makes the market so efficient. Because everyone is doing fundamental analysis, there is little in the way of unabsorbed or undigested information. Therefore, one extra person doing fundamental analysis is unlikely to achieve superior insight.

Although the semistrong form of the efficient market hypothesis has research support, there are exceptions. For example, Basu has found that stocks with low P/E ratios consistently provide better returns than stocks with high P/E ratios on both a nonrisk-adjusted and risk-adjusted basis.[16] Since a P/E ratio is publicly available information that may be used to generate superior returns, this flies in the face of the more-common conclusions on the semistrong form of the efficient market hypothesis. Banz[17] and Reinganum's[18] research indicates that small firms tend to provide higher returns than larger firms even after considering risk. Perhaps fewer institutional investors in smaller firms make for a less-efficient market and superior potential opportunities. Oppenheimer and Schlarbaum have also shown that investors can generate superior risk-adjusted returns by following widely disseminated rules by Graham and Dodd on such factors as dividends, capitalization, firm size and P/E ratios and by using only public information.[19] Additional evidence of this nature continues to accumulate, and in Chapter 14, on special situations, we present an extended discussion of some of the above items and other possible contradictions to the acceptance of the semistrong version of the efficient

---

[16]S. Basu, "Investment Performance of Common Stocks in Relation to Their Price-Earnings Ratios: A Test of the Efficient Market Hypothesis," *Journal of Finance,* June 1977, pp. 663–82. Also, S. Basu, "The Information Content of Price-Earnings Ratios," *Financial Management,* Summer 1975, pp. 53–64.

[17]Rolf W. Banz, "The Relationship between Returns and Market Value of Common Stocks," *Journal of Financial Economics,* March 1981, pp. 3–18.

[18]Marc R. Reinganum, "Misspecification of Capital Asset Pricing—Empirical Anomalies Based on Earnings Yield and Market Values," *Journal of Financial Economics,* March 1981, pp. 19–46.

[19]Henry R. Oppenheimer and Gary G. Schlarbaum, "Investing with Ben Graham: An Ex Ante Test of the Efficient Markets Hypothesis," *Journal of Financial and Quantitative Analysis,* September 1981, pp. 341–60.

market hypothesis. We also comment on measurement problems in that chapter.

Thus, even if the semistrong form of the efficient market hypothesis appears to be generally valid, exceptions can be noted. Also, it is possible that while most analysts may not be able to add additional insight through fundamental analysis, there are exceptions to every rule. It can be assumed that some analysts have such *extraordinary* insight and capability in analyzing publicly available information that they can perceive what others cannot. Also, if you take a very long-term perspective, the fact that a stock's value is in short-term equilibrium may not discourage you from taking a long-term position or attempting to find long-term value.

STRONG FORM OF THE EFFICIENT MARKET HYPOTHESIS

The **strong form of the efficient market hypothesis** goes beyond the semistrong form to state that stock prices reflect not only all public information but *all* information. Thus, it is hypothesized that insider information is also immediately impounded into the value of a security. In a sense, we go beyond the concept of a market that is highly efficient to one that is perfect.

The assumption is that no group of market participants or investors has monopolistic access to information. If this is the case, then no group of investors can be expected to show superior risk-adjusted returns under any circumstances.

Unlike the weak and semistrong forms of the efficient market hypothesis, major test results are not supportive of the strong form of the hypothesis. For example, specialists on security exchanges have been able to earn superior rates of return on invested capital.[20] The book they keep on unfilled limit orders would appear to provide monopolistic access to information. An SEC study actually found that specialists typically sell above their latest purchase 83 percent of the time and buy below their latest sell 81 percent of the time.[21] This implies wisdom that greatly exceeds that which would be available in a perfect capital market environment. Likewise, an institutional investor study, also sponsored by the SEC, indicated that specialists' average return on capital was over 100 percent.[22]

Another group that appears to use nonpublic information to garner superior returns is corporate insiders. As previously described, an insider is considered to be a corporate officer, member of the board of directors, or substantial stockholder. The SEC requires that insiders report their transactions to that regulatory body. A few weeks after reporting to the SEC, the information becomes public. Researchers can then go back and determine whether in-

[20]Victor Niederhoffer and M. F. M. Osborne, "Market-Making and Reversal on the Stock Exchange," *Journal of the American Statistical Association,* December 1966, pp. 897–916.

[21]Securities and Exchange Commission, *Report of the Special Study of the Security Markets,* part 2 (Washington, D.C.: U.S. Government Printing Office, 1965).

[22]Securities and Exchange Commission, *Institutional Investor Study Report* (Washington, D.C.: U.S. Government Printing Office, 1971).

vestment decisions made by investors appeared, on balance, to be wise. Did heavy purchases by insiders precede strong upward price movements, and did sell-offs precede poor market performance? The answer appears to be yes. Research studies indicate insiders consistently achieve higher returns than would be expected in a perfect capital market.[23] Although insiders are not allowed to engage in short-term trades (of six months or less) or illegal transactions to generate trading profits, they are allowed to take longer-term positions, which may well prove to be profitable. It has even been demonstrated that investors who follow the direction of inside traders after information on their activity becomes public may enjoy superior returns.[24] (This, of course, represents contrary evidence to the semistrong form of the efficient market hypothesis as well.)

Even though there is evidence on the activity of specialists and insiders that would cause one to reject the strong form of the efficient market hypothesis (or at least not to accept it), the range of participants with access to superior information is not large. For example, tests on the performance of mutual fund managers have consistently indicated that they are not able to beat the market averages over the long term.[25] Although mutual fund managers may get the first call when news is breaking, that is not fast enough to generate superior returns.

While the strong form of the efficient market hypothesis suggests more opportunity for superior returns than the weak or semistrong forms, the premium is related to monopolistic access to information rather than other factors.

It should also be pointed out that those who act *illegally* with insider information may initially achieve superior returns from their special access to information, but the price of their actions may be high indeed. For example, Ivan Boesky and Dennis Levine, convicted users of illegal insider information in the late 1980s, were forced to give up their gains, pay heavy fines, and serve jail sentences. In their particular cases, they traded on insider information about mergers well before the public was informed. Although they were not officers of the companies or on the boards, they had special fiduciary responsibilities as money managers that they violated.

---

[23]James H. Lorie and Victor Niederhoffer, "Predictive Statistical Properties of Insider Trading," *Journal of Law and Economics,* April 1966, pp. 35–53. Joseph E. Finnerty, "Insiders and Market Efficiency," *Journal of Finance,* September 1976, pp. 1141–48. Jeffrey Jaffe, "Special Information and Insider Trading," *Journal of Business,* July 1974, pp. 410–28. Shannon P. Pratt and Charles W. DeVere, "Relationship between Insider Trading and Rates of Return for NYSE Common Stocks, 1960–1966," in *Modern Developments in Investment Management,* ed. James H. Lorie and Richard Beasley (New York: Praeger Publishers, 1972), pp. 268–79.

[24]Pratt and DeVere, "Relationship," pp. 268–79.

[25]Michael Jensen, "The Performance of Mutual Funds in the Period 1945–1964," *Journal of Finance,* May 1968, pp. 389–416.

Part Three

FIXED-INCOME AND LEVERAGED SECURITIES

■ OUTLINE

■ INTRODUCTION

We now shift our attention from stocks to fixed-income and leveraged securities. Fixed-income securities include bonds, preferred stock, certificates of deposit, and even money market funds. In the high interest rate environment of the last decade, many investors have increased their emphasis on fixed-return investments. However, we shall see that fixed-income securities are not without risk or uncertainty as to outcome.

In Chapter 9, we look at the organization of the debt markets and the elements that define the basic debt instrument. The functions of the bond-rating agencies are also explored, along with the perceived efficiency of the bond market. In Chapter 10, we assume the role of the bond investor and examine a number of strategy considerations for optimizing return on investment. Chapter 11 moves to a discussion of duration, or weighted average life, of a bond. Since professional investors use duration concepts in designing their strategies, the student is given a basic description of these considerations. (The chapter is optional in nature and may be skipped without loss of continuity.)

The second half of this section covers leveraged securities, that is, securities with a magnified return or loss potential for a given level of investment (maximum "bang for the buck"). The discussion begins with convertibles and warrants in Chapter 12. We examine the valuation of these securities and the existence of speculative premiums (the difference between market value and intrinsic value). We also look at the advantages and disadvantages of convertibles and warrants to the investor as well as to the corporation. A recurring question is, are we dealing with fool's gold? While the answer is no, it is a qualified no that can only be fully understood after you have examined the ins and outs of investing in these securities.

The stock option became highly popular with the founding of the Chicago Board Options Exchange in 1973. Options allow the investor to buy and sell stock at a specified future price, and they may be used as a form of speculation or as a defensive tool. In Chapter 13, we examine the basic types of options (puts and calls), the operations of the options market, how option prices are established, and the use of leverage in the option contract. We also examine how option plays can be tailored to the overall objectives of the portfolio. We conclude with a discussion of some of the more-sophisticated option strategies. The Black-Scholes Option Pricing Model also is presented as an appendix to Chapter 13.

9

BOND AND FIXED-INCOME FUNDAMENTALS

A s the reader will observe in various sections of this chapter, bonds actually represent a more-substantial portion of new offerings in the capital markets than common stock. Some of the most financially rewarding jobs on Wall Street go to sophisticated analysts and dealers in the bond market.

In this chapter, we will examine the fundamentals of the bond instrument for both corporate and government issuers, with an emphasis on the debt contract and security provisions. We will also look at the overall structure of the bond market and the ways in which bonds are rated. The question of bond market efficiency is also considered. While most of the chapter deals with corporate and government bonds, other forms of fixed-income securities also receive attention. Thus, there is a brief discussion of short-term, fixed-income investments (such as certificates of deposit and commercial paper) as well as preferred stock.

In Chapter 10, we will shift the emphasis to actually evaluating fixed-income investments and devising strategies that attempt to capture profitable opportunities in the market. In Chapter 11, we will look at the interesting concept of *duration*. We begin our present discussion by considering the key elements that go into a bond contract.

THE BOND CONTRACT

A bond normally represents a long-term contractual obligation of the firm to pay interest to the bondholder as well as the face value of the bond at maturity. The major provisions in a bond agreement are spelled out in the **bond indenture,** a complicated legal document often over 100 pages in length, administered by an independent trustee (usually a commercial bank). We shall examine some important terms and concepts associated with a bond issue.

Par value—the face value of a bond. Most corporate bonds are traded in $1,000 units, while many federal, state, and local issues trade in units of $5,000 or $10,000.

Coupon rate—the actual interest rate on the bond, usually payable in semiannual installments. To the extent that interest rates in the market go above or below the coupon rate after the bond is issued, the market price of the bond will change from the par value. A bond initially issued at a rate of 8 percent will sell at a substantial discount from par value when 12 percent is the currently demanded rate of return. We will eventually examine how the investor makes and loses substantial amounts of money in the bond market with the swings in interest rates. A few corporate bonds are termed *variable-rate notes* or *floating-rate notes,* meaning that the coupon rate is only fixed for a short period of time and then varies with a stipulated short-term rate such as the rate on U.S. government Treasury bills. In this instance, the interest payment rather than the price of the bond varies up and down. This type of issue is likely to become increasingly popular in the future. In recent times, **zero-coupon bonds** have also been issued at values substantially below maturity value. The investor receives his or her return in the form of capital appreciation over the life of the bond since no semiannual cash interest payments are received.

Maturity date—the date on which final payment is due at the stipulated par value.

Methods of repayment—repayment of the bond can take place under many different arrangements. Some bonds are never paid off, such as selected **perpetual** bonds issued by the Canadian and British governments which have no maturity dates. A more-normal procedure would simply call for a single-sum lump payment at the end of the obligation. Thus, the issuer may make 40 semiannual interest payments over the next 20 years plus one lump-sum payment of the par value of the bond at maturity. There are also other significant means of repayment.

The first is the **serial** payment in which bonds are paid off in installments over the life of the issue. Each serial bond has its own predetermined date of maturity and receives interest only to that point. Although the total bond issue may span over 20 years, 15 to 20 maturity dates are assigned. Municipal bonds are often issued on this basis. Second, there may be a **sinking-fund** provision in which semiannual or annual contributions are made by a corporation into a fund administered by a trustee for purposes of debt retirement. The trustee takes the proceeds and goes into the market to purchase bonds from willing sellers. If no sellers are available, a lottery system may be used to repurchase the required number of bonds from among outstanding bondholders.

Third, debt may also be retired under a **call provision.** A call provision allows the corporation to call or force in all of the debt issue prior to maturity. The corporation usually pays a 5 percent to 10 percent premium over par value as part of the call provision arrangement. The ability to call is often *deferred* for the first five years of an issue (it can only take place after this time period).

The opposite side of the coin for a bond investor is a **put provision.** This provision enables the bondholder to have an option to sell a long-term bond back to the corporation at par value after a relatively short period of time (such as three to five years). This privilege can be particularly valuable if interest rates have gone up since the initial issuance, and the bond is currently trading at 75–80 percent of par. A put bond generally carries a lower interest rate than conventional bonds (perhaps 1 to 2 percent lower) because of this protective put privilege. If one buys a put bond and interest rates go down and bond prices up (perhaps to $1,200), the privilege is unnecessary and is merely ignored.

SECURED AND UNSECURED BONDS

We have discussed some of the important features related to interest payments and retirement of outstanding issues. At least of equal importance is the nature of the security provision for the issue. Bond market participants have a long-standing practice of describing certain issues by the nature of asset claims in liquidation. In actuality, only infrequently are pledged assets sold off and the proceeds distributed to bondholders. Typically, the defaulting corporation is reorganized, and existing claims are partially satisfied by issuing new securities to the participating parties. Of course, the stronger and *better secured* the initial claim, the higher the quality of the security to be received in a reorganization.

A number of terms are used to denote collateralized or **secured debt**. Under a *mortgage* agreement, real property (plant and equipment) is pledged as security for a loan. A mortgage may be *senior* or *junior* in nature, with the former requiring satisfaction of claims before payment is given to the latter. Bondholders may also attach an **after-acquired property clause** requiring that any new property be placed under the original mortgage.

A very special form of a mortgage or collaterialized debt instrument is the **equipment trust certificate** used by firms in the transportation industry (railroads, airlines, etc.). Proceeds from the sale of the certificate are used to purchase new equipment, and this new equipment, in turn, serves as collateral for the trust certificate.

Not all bond issues are secured or collateralized by assets. Certainly, most federal, state, and local government issues are unsecured. A wide range of corporate issues also are unsecured. There is a set of terminology referring to these unsecured issues. A corporate debt issue that is unsecured is referred to as a *debenture*. Even though the debenture is not secured by a specific pledge of assets, there may be priorities of claims among debenture holders. Thus, there are senior debentures and junior, or subordinated, debentures.

If liquidation becomes necessary because all other avenues for survival have failed, secured creditors are paid off first out of the disposition of the secured assets. The proceeds from the sale of the balance of the assets are then distributed among unsecured creditors, with those holding a senior ranking being satisfied before those holding a subordinate position (subordinated debenture holders).[1]

Unsecured corporate debt may provide slightly higher yields because of the greater suggested risk. However, this is partially offset by the fact that many unsecured debt issuers have such strong financial statements that security pledges may not be necessary.

Companies with less-favorable prospects may issue **income bonds.** These bonds specify that interest is to be paid only to the extent that it is earned as current income. There is no legally binding requirement to pay interest on a regular basis, and failure to make interest payments cannot trigger bankruptcy proceedings. These issues appear to offer the corporation the unusual advantage of paying interest as a tax-deductible expense (as opposed to dividends) combined with freedom from the binding contractual obligation of most debt issues. But any initial enthusiasm for these issues is quickly reduced by recognition of the fact that they have very limited appeal to investors. The issuance of income bonds is usually restricted to circumstances where new corporate debt is issued to old bondholders or preferred stockholders to avoid bankruptcy or where a troubled corporation is being reorganized.

---

[1]Those secured creditors that are not fully satisfied by the disposition of secured assets may also participate with the unsecured creditors in the remaining assets.

WALL STREET IS DEVISING THE TAKEOVER-PROOF BOND

With the leveraged buyout boom debasing the value of many corporate bonds, Wall Street investment bankers are scrambling to produce bonds with stronger investor safeguards.

Bonds carrying a new super "poison put," which would enable bondholders to get back their initial investment in the event of a takeover, merger, or buyout, already are on the drawing boards at several of Wall Street's biggest bond underwriting firms. Hundreds of industrial companies, faced with the possibility of much higher borrowing costs because of their perceived vulnerability to a takeover, now are considering proposals for tightening bondholders' protection.

The RJR Nabisco proposed buyout left the industrial sector of the corporate bond market in disarray. Prices of some RJR long-term bonds plunged 20 points ($200 per $1,000 bond).

Poison puts have been attached to many new bond offerings since 1986, when the leveraged buyout trend took off. But with the exception of a couple of issues, these "poison puts haven't been worth a bucket of warm spit," claims Richard Wilson, a Merrill Lynch executive. These covenants typically allowed bondholders to "put" their bonds back to the issuer at par value (the issue price) in the event of an unfriendly takeover. That made the put often worthless, since almost all takeovers ultimately become agreed-upon transactions.

"I think people now are finally waking up and willing to do something about the lack of bondholder protection," says Mr. Wilson of Merrill Lynch.

Note: By the time you read this, takeover-proof bonds may already be offered.
Source: The Wall Street Journal, November 3, 1988, p. C1. Reprinted by permission of The Wall Street Journal, © Dow Jones & Company, Inc., 1988. All rights reserved.

THE COMPOSITION OF THE BOND MARKET

Having established some of the basic terminology relating to the bond instrument, we are now in a position to take a more-comprehensive look at the bond market. Corporate issues must vie with offerings from the U.S. Treasury, federally sponsored credit agencies, and state and local governments (municipal offerings). The relative importance of the four types of issues is indicated in Figure 9–1.

Over the 18-year period presented in Figure 9–1, the two fastest growing users of funds (borrowers) were the U.S. government and corporations. The former's needs can be attributed to persistent federal deficits that must be financed by increased borrowing. In the case of corporations, low profitability, combined with internal expansions and mergers, have lead to tremendous borrowing needs. State and local governments have been the third most active participants with municipal bond issues used to finance local growth and cover local deficits. Finally, federally sponsored credit agencies must call on the long-term funds market, but to a lesser extent than the other participants. Please observe the explosive growth in long-term borrowing by all sectors of the economy since 1980.

FIGURE 9–1   LONG-TERM DEBT RAISED BY BUSINESS AND THE GOVERNMENT

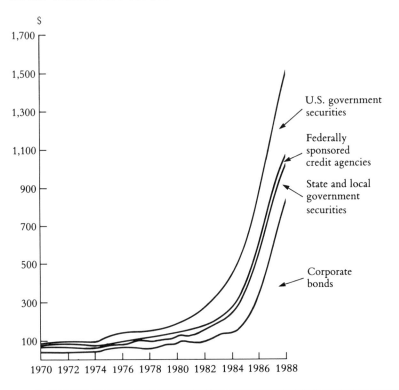

In the following section, we will briefly discuss the various forms of debt instruments available to the investor.

U.S. Government Securities

U.S. government securities take the form of **Treasury bills**, **Treasury notes**, and **Treasury bonds** (only the latter two are considered in the top part of Figure 9–1). The distinction between the three categories relates to the life of the obligation.

Treasury bills (*T-bills*) are short-term in nature, with a maximum maturity of one year and common maturities of 91 and 182 days. Treasury bills trade on a discount basis meaning that the yield the investor receives takes place as a result of the difference between the price paid and the maturity value (and no actual interest is paid). Thus, a $10,000 Treasury bill quoted to pay 10 percent annualized interest over a six-month period will initially sell for $9,500. The investor receives $500 on the $10,000 face amount, or 5 percent for six months, which is translated into a 10 percent annualized rate. Actually, the true rate is slightly higher than the 10 percent quoted rate. The investor is receiving $500 interest on the $9,500 discounted price ($500/$9,500) or 5.26 percent semiannually, which translates into 10.52 percent annually.

Treasury bills trade in minimum units of $10,000, and there is an extremely active secondary, or resale, market for these securities. Thus, an investor buying a Treasury bill from the government with an initial life of approximately six months would have no difficulty in selling it to another investor after two or three weeks. Since the T-bill now has a shorter time to run, its market value would be a bit closer to par.

A second type of U.S. government security is the *Treasury note,* which is considered to be of intermediate term and generally has a maturity of one to seven years. Finally, *Treasury bonds* are long term in nature and mature in 7 to 25 years or longer. Unlike Treasury bills, Treasury notes and bonds provide direct interest and trade in units of $1,000 and higher. Because there is no risk of default (unless the government stops printing money or the ultimate bomb explodes), U.S. government securities provide lower returns than other forms of credit obligations. Interest on U.S. government issues is fully taxable for IRS purposes, but is exempt from state and local taxes.

Some Treasury notes and bonds have been repackaged into zero-coupon bonds by major brokerage firms and investment bankers such as Merrill Lynch, Goldman Sachs, and A. G. Becker. These firms buy U.S. "governments" and put these securities in trust (usually a commercial bank acts as trustee). A security is divided into two parts—one generating a cash flow from the interest payments and the other providing principal at maturity. These two parts are then sold separately to investors with specific needs. The principal payment part is generically called a zero-coupon Treasury bond, but each investment banker labels his own product with names such as TIGRs (for Merrill Lynch's Treasury Investment Growth Receipts), COUGARs (for A. G. Becker's Zero-Coupon Certificates on Government Receipts); and RATs, CATs, and GATORs for other firms. For example, Merrill Lynch's TIGRs are called Principal TIGRs (the zero-coupon part) and Serial TIGRs (which pay interest at six-month intervals for up to 40 payments). In the mid-1980s, the U.S. Treasury also began trading zero-coupon bonds directly on its own.

Since zero-coupon bonds pay no interest, all returns to the investor come in the form of increases in the value of the investment. For example, 15-year zero-coupon bonds might initially sell for 18 percent of par value. You might buy a $1,000 instrument for $180.[2]

The Internal Revenue Service taxes zero-coupon bonds as if interest were paid annually even though no cash flow is received until maturity. The tax is based on amortizing the built-in gain over the life of the instrument. For tax reasons, zero-coupons are usually only appropriate for nontaxable accounts such as Individual Retirement Accounts, Keogh plans, or other nontaxable pension funds.

---

[2]On zero-coupon bonds, the yield to maturity is a true rate over the life of the security since the price paid includes the assumption of continuous compounding at the yield to maturity. Zero-coupon securities are the most price sensitive to a change in interest rates of any bond having the same maturity. This is fine when interest rates decline but can be disastrous when rates rise. A good deal more will be said about zero-coupon bonds in Chapter 11.

Federally Sponsored Credit Agency Issues

Referring back to Figure 9–1, the second category represents securities issued by federal agencies. While small in scope relative to the other three categories, these issues are still important to investors. The issues represent obligations of various agencies of the government such as the Federal Home Loan Bank and the Federal Housing Administration (FHA). Although these issues are authorized by an act of Congress and are used to finance federal projects, they are not direct obligations of the Treasury but rather of the agency itself.

Though the issues are essentially free of risk (there is always the implicit standby power of the government behind the issues), they carry a slightly higher yield than U.S. government securities simply because they are not directly issued by the Treasury. Agency issues have been particularly active as a support mechanism for the housing industry. The issues generally trade in denominations of $5,000 and up and have varying maturities of from 1 to 40 years, with an average life of approximately 15 years. Examples of some agency issues are presented below.

	Minimum Denomination	Life of Issue
Federal Home Loan Bank	$10,000	12–25 years
Federal Intermediate Credit Banks	5,000	Up to 4 years
Federal Housing Administration	50,000	1–40 years
Export-Import Bank	5,000	Up to 7 years
U.S. Postal Service	10,000	25 years

Interest on agency issues is fully taxable for IRS purposes and is generally taxable for state and local purposes although there are exceptions. (For example, interest on obligations issued by the Federal Housing Administration are subject to state and local taxes, but those of the Federal Home Loan Bank are not.)

One agency issue that is of particular interest to the investor because of its unique features is the GNMA (Ginnie Mae) pass-through certificate. These certificates represent an undivided interest in a pool of federally insured mortgages. Actually, GNMA, the Government National Mortgage Association, buys a pool of mortgages from various lenders at a discount and then issues securities to the public against these mortgages. Security holders in GNMA certificates receive monthly payments that essentially represent a pass through of interest and principal payments on the mortgages. These securities come in minimum denominations of $25,000, are long term in nature, and are fully taxable for federal, state, and local income tax purposes. A major consideration in this investment is that the investor has fully consumed his or her capital at the end of the investment. (Not only has interest been received monthly but all principal has been returned over the life of the certificate, and therefore, there is no lump-sum payment at maturity.)

State and Local Government Securities

Debt securities issued by state and local governments are referred to as **municipal bonds**. Examples of issuing agencies include states, cities, school districts, toll roads, or any other type of political subdivision. The most-important feature of a municipal bond is the tax-exempt nature of the interest payment. Dating back to the U.S. Supreme Court opinion of 1819 in *McCullough* v. *Maryland*, it was ruled that the federal government and state and local governments do not possess the power to tax each other. An eventual by-product of the judicial ruling was that income from municipal bonds cannot be taxed by the IRS. Furthermore, income from municipal bonds is also exempt from state and local taxes if bought within the locality in which one resides. Thus, a Californian buying municipal bonds in that state would pay no state income tax on the issue. However, the same Californian would have to pay state or local income taxes if the originating agency were in Texas or New York.

We cannot overemphasize the importance of the federal tax exemption that municipal bonds enjoy. The consequences are twofold. First, individuals in high tax brackets may find highly attractive investment opportunities in municipal bonds.[3] Some have referred to municipal bond investments as welfare for the rich. The formula used to equate interest on municipal bonds to other investments is:

$$Y = \frac{i}{(1 - t)}$$

(9–1)

where:

    Y = Equivalent before-tax yield on a taxable investment
    i = Yield on the municipal obligation
    t = Marginal tax rate of the investor

If an investor has a marginal tax rate of 33 percent and is evaluating a municipal bond paying 8 percent interest, the equivalent before-tax yield on a taxable investment would be:

$$\frac{8\%}{(1 - .33)} = \frac{8\%}{.67} = 11.94\%$$

Thus, the investor could choose between a *non*-tax-exempt investment paying 11.94 percent and a tax-exempt municipal bond paying 8 percent and be indifferent between the two. Table 9–1 presents examples of trade-offs between tax-exempt and nontax-exempt (taxable) investments at various interest rates and marginal tax rates. Clearly, the higher the marginal tax rate, the greater the advantage of tax-exempt municipal bonds.

---

[3]It should be noted, however, that any capital gain on a municipal bond is taxable as would be the case with any investment.

TABLE 9–1	MARGINAL TAX RATES AND RETURN EQUIVALENTS		
Yield on Municipal (Percent)	15 Percent Bracket	28 Percent Bracket	33 Percent Bracket
6%	7.1%	8.3%	9.0%
7	8.2	9.7	10.4
8	9.4	11.1	11.9
9	10.6	12.5	13.4
10	11.8	13.9	14.9
11	12.9	15.3	16.4
12	14.1	16.7	17.9

A second significant feature of municipal bonds is that the yield the issuing agency pays on municipal bonds is lower than the yield on taxable instruments. Of course, a municipal bond paying 8 percent may be quite competitive with taxable instruments paying more. Average differentials are presented in Table 9–2.

You should notice in Table 9–2 that the yield differences between municipal bonds and corporate bonds was normally 2–3 percent until after the passage of the Tax Reform Act in 1986. Starting in 1987, the differential has moved closer to 1 percent. This is because the marginal tax rates of investors are now lower, and thus, the relative tax advantages of municipal bonds have diminished. A major distinction that is also important to the bond issuer and investor is whether the bond is of a **general obligation** or **revenue** nature.

General Obligation versus Revenue Bonds.   A general obligation issue is backed by the full faith, credit, and "taxing power" of the governmental unit. For a revenue bond, on the other hand, the repayment of the issue is fully dependent on the revenue-generating capability of a specific project or venture, such as a toll road, bridge, or municipal colosseum.

Because of the taxing power behind most general obligation (GO) issues, they tend to be of extremely high quality. Approximately three fourths of all municipal bond issues are of the general obligation variety, and very few failures have taken place in the post–World War II era. Revenue bonds tend to be of more uneven quality, and the economic soundness of the underlying revenue-generating project must be carefully examined (though most projects are quite worthwhile).

Municipal Bond Guarantee.   A growing factor in the municipal bond market is the third-party guarantee. Whether dealing with a general obligation or revenue bond, a fee may be paid by the originating governmental body to a third-party insurer to guarantee that all interest and principal payments will be made. A number of states, including California and Michigan, now have provisions to guarantee payments on selected issues. There are also two large private insurers. The first is a consortium of four insurance companies that market their product under the name of the Municipal Bond Insurance As-

TABLE 9–2	COMPARABLE YIELDS ON LONG-TERM MUNICIPALS AND TAXABLE CORPORATES (Yearly Averages)		
Year	Municipals Aa	Corporates Aa	Yield Difference
1988	8.38%	9.66%	1.28%
1987	8.50	9.68	1.18
1986	7.35	9.47	2.12
1985	8.81	11.82	3.01
1984	9.95	12.25	2.30
1983	9.20	12.42	3.22
1982	11.39	14.41	3.02
1981	10.89	14.75	3.86
1980	8.06	12.50	4.44
1979	6.12	9.94	3.82
1978	5.68	8.92	3.24
1977	5.39	8.24	2.85
1976	6.12	8.75	2.63
1975	6.77	9.17	2.40
1974	6.04	8.84	2.80
1973	5.11	7.66	2.55
1972	5.19	7.48	2.29
1971	5.36	7.78	2.42

Source: *Moody's Municipal & Government Manual, Moody's Industrial Manual,* and *Moody's Bond Record* (published by Moody's Investors Service, Inc., New York, N.Y. selected issues).

sociation (MBIA). The second is the American Municipal Bond Assurance Corporation (AMBAC). Both will insure general obligation or revenue bonds.

A bond that carries a guarantee will have a slightly lower yield and a better secondary, or resale, market. This may be important because municipal bonds, in general, do not provide as strong a secondary market as U.S. government issues. The market for a given municipal issue is often small and fragmented, and high indirect costs are associated with reselling the issue.

Corporate Securities

While corporate bonds represent only 30–40 percent of the total bond market (which also includes U.S. government securities, federally sponsored credit agencies, and municipal bonds) as shown in previously presented Figure 9–1, they are the dominant source of new financing for the U.S. corporation. That is, corporate bonds have been the most-significant form of new financing for U.S. corporations as shown in Figure 9–2.

You can observe that bonds normally supply 75–80 percent of the firm's external financial needs. Even during the great bull stock market of 1982 to 1987, corporations looked as heavily as ever to the debt markets to provide financing (this, of course, was justified by the decreasing interest rates during this time period). Also, observe the sharp cutback in long-term financing in 1987 due to the market crash in October (which temporarily impacted all markets).

The corporate market may be broken down into a number of subunits, including *industrials, public utilities, rails* and *transportation,* and *financial issues*

FIGURE 9–2   LONG-TERM CORPORATE FINANCING

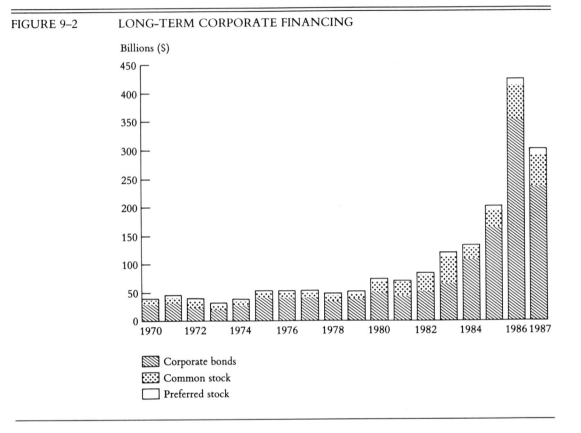

(banks, finance companies, etc.). The industrials are a catchall category that includes everything from high-technology companies to discount chain stores. Public utilities represent the largest segment of the market and have issues that run up to 40 years in maturity. Because public utilities are in constant need of funds to meet ever-expanding requirements for power generation, telephone services, and other essentials, they are always in the bond market to raise new funds. The needs associated with rails and transportation as well as financial issues tend to be less than those associated with public utilities or industrials. In Table 9–3, we see the comparative yields from three of the categories and for all corporations.[4]

The higher yields on public utility issues represent a supply-demand phenomenon more than anything else. A constant stream of new issues to the market can only be absorbed by a higher yield pattern. In other cases, the higher required return may also be associated with quality deterioration as measured by profitability and interest coverage. During 1983–84, the default of the Washington State Power Authority on bonds issued to construct power-

---

[4]Financial issues are generally not broken out of the published data.

TABLE 9–3	COMPARATIVE YIELDS ON Aa BONDS AMONG CORPORATE ISSUERS			
	Industrial	Public Utility	Rails and Transportation	All Corporations
1988	9.41%	10.20%	9.57%	9.66%
1987	9.73	9.83	9.33	9.68
1986	9.49	9.44	9.46	9.47
1985	11.57	12.02	11.62	11.82
1984	12.39	13.02	12.22	12.71
1983	11.94	12.74	11.24	12.35
1982	15.01	16.48	13.52	15.75
1981	13.01	14.03	11.40	13.52
1980	11.16	11.95	9.99	11.56
1979	9.24	9.70	8.33	9.48
1978	8.42	8.76	7.93	8.59
1977	7.90	8.41	7.52	8.16
1976	8.87	9.39	8.45	9.13
1975	8.81	9.45	8.70	9.13
1974	7.85	8.15	7.92	8.00

Source: *Moody's Bond Record* (published by Moody's Investors Service, Inc., New York, N.Y. selected issues).

generating facilities sent waves through the bond market. Again in 1984, when Public Service of Indiana canceled construction of a partially complete nuclear power plant, nuclear utility issues (both stocks and bonds) suffered severe price erosion, and the bond market demanded high risk premiums on bonds of almost all nuclear utilities.

Corporate bonds of all types generally trade in units of $1,000, and this is a particularly attractive feature to the smaller investor who does not wish to purchase in units of $5,000 to $10,000 (which is necessary for many Treasury, federally sponsored credit agency issues, and municipals). Because of higher risk relative to government issues, the investor will generally receive higher yields on corporates as well. All income from corporates is taxable for federal, state, and local purposes. Finally, corporate issues have the disadvantage of being subject to calls. When buying a bond during a period of high interest rates, the call provision must be considered a negative feature because the high-yielding bonds may be called in for early retirement as interest rates go down.

The list of innovative products in the corporate debt market is ever growing. Please see Appendix 9–A for an example of recent developments as presented by John D. Finnerty.

BOND MARKET INVESTORS

Having considered the issuer or supply side of the market, we now comment on the investor or demand side. The bond market is dominated by large institutional investors (insurance companies, banks, pension funds, mutual funds) even more than the stock market. Institutional investors account for 90 to 95 percent of the trading in key segments of the bond market. However, the presence of the individual investor is partially felt in the corporate and municipal bond market where the incentives of low denomination ($1,000) corporate bonds or tax-free municipal bonds have some attraction.

Institutional investors' preferences for various sectors of the bond market are influenced by their tax status as well as the nature of their obligations or liabilities to depositors, investors, or clients. For example, banks traditionally have been strong participants in the municipal bond market because of their substantial tax obligations. Their investments tend to be in short- to inter-mediate-term assets because of the short-term nature of their deposit obliga-tions (the funds supplied to the banks). One problem that banks find in their bond portfolios is that such investments are often preferred over loans to customers when the economy is weak and loan demand is sluggish. Not so coincidentally, this happens to be the time period when interest rates are low. When the economy improves, interest rates go up, and so does loan demand. In order to meet the loan demand of valued customers, banks liquidate portions of their bond portfolios. The problem with this recurring process is that banks are buying bonds when interest rates are *low* and selling them when interest rates are *high*. This can cause losses in the value of the bank portfolio.

The bond market investor must be prepared to deal in a relatively strong primary market (new issues market) and a relatively weak secondary market (resale market). While the secondary market is active for many types of Trea-sury and agency issues, such is not the case for corporate and municipal issues. Thus, the investor must look well beyond the yield, maturity, and rating to determine if a purchase is acceptable. The question that must be considered is: How close to the going market price can I dispose of the issue if that should be necessary? If a 5 or 10 percent discount is involved, that might be unac-ceptable. Unlike the stock market, the secondary market in bonds tends to be dominated by over-the-counter transactions (although there are listed bonds traded as well).

A significant development in the late 1980s has been the heavy participation of foreign investors in U.S. bond markets. Foreign investors now bankroll between 10 to 15 percent of the U.S. government's debt. While these investors have helped to finance the U.S. government's deficits, it is true that if at any point they decided to withdraw a major portion of their funds, the effects on the U.S. financial markets would be quite disruptive. For this reason, our government is quite sensitive to the demands and desires of its foreign cred-itors.

DISTRIBUTION PROCEDURES

In February 1982, the Securities and Exchange Commission began allowing a process called shelf registration under SEC Rule 415. Shelf registration per-mits large companies to file one comprehensive registration statement that outlines the firm's plans for future long-term financing. Then, when market conditions seem appropriate, the firm can issue the securities through an in-vestment banker without further SEC approval. Future issues are said to be sitting on the shelf, waiting for the most-advantageous time to appear. An example of bonds awaiting distribution on May 30, 1988, is presented from *Moody's Bond Survey* in Table 9–4.

Approximately half of the new public bond issues are distributed through the shelf registration process. The balance of the bonds is issued under more-traditional procedures in which the bonds are issued shortly after registration by a large syndicate of investment bankers in a highly structured process.

Private Placement

A number of bond offerings are sold to investors as a **private placement**. That is, they are sold privately to investors rather than through the public markets. Private placements are most popular with investors such as insurance companies and pension funds, and they are primarily offered in the corporate sector by industrial firms rather than public utilities. The lender can generally expect to receive a slightly higher yield than on public issues to compensate for the extremely limited or nonexistent secondary market and the generally smaller size of the borrowing firm in a private placement.

BOND RATINGS

Bond investors tend to place much more emphasis on independent analysis of quality than do common stock investors. For this reason, both corporate financial management and institutional portfolio managers keep a very close eye on bond rating procedures. The difference between an AA and an A rating may mean the corporation will have to pay $^1/_4$ percent more interest on the bond issue (perhaps 10 percent rather than $9^3/_4$ percent). On a $100 million, 20-year issue, this represents $250,000 per year (before tax), or a total of $5 million over the life of the bond.

The two major bond-rating agencies are Moody's Investors Service (a subsidiary of Dun & Bradstreet, Inc.) and Standard & Poor's (a subsidiary of McGraw-Hill, Inc.). They rank thousands of corporate and municipal issues as well as a limited number of private placements, commercial paper, preferred stock issues, and offerings of foreign companies and governments. U.S. government issues tend to be free of risk and therefore are given no attention by the bond-rating agencies. Moody's, founded in 1909, is the older of the two bond-rating agencies and covers twice as many securities as Standard & Poor's (particularly in the municipal bond area). Other less well known bond-rating agencies include Fitch Investors Service, Inc. (an old-line rating agency that specializes in bank securities) and Duff & Phelp, Inc.

The bond ratings, generally ranging from an AAA to a D category, are decided on a committee basis at both Moody's and Standard & Poor's.[5] There are no fast and firm quantitative measures that specify the rating that a new issue will receive. Nevertheless, measures pertaining to cash flow and earnings

---

[5]Irwin Ross, "Higher Stakes in the Bond Rating Game," *Fortune,* April 1976, pp. 133–42.

TABLE 9–4 EXAMPLES OF SHELF REGISTRATION

Prospective Offerings—Shelf Registrations Under SEC Rule 415

Date of Registration	Original Amount ($ Mill.)	Unsold Amount ($ Mill.)	Registrants	Listed Underwriters	Types of Securities Prospectively Rated	Page Nos.	Prospective Ratings
10/30/86	$1,000.0	$600.0	Australia (Commonwealth of)	To be determined	Debt securities	—	(P)Aa1
8/6/87	250.0	150.0	Austria (Republic of)	SB	Various debt securities	—	†
12/24/85	775.0	400.0	Avco Financial Services, Inc.	KP,MS,SB	Sr. debt (w/warrants)	7946	(P)A3
					Sr. sub. debt (w/warrants)	7946	(P)Baa2
					Jr. sub. debt (w/warrants)	7946	(P)Baa3
2/6/87	100.0	100.0	Avery International Corp.	To be determined	Various debt securities	7432	(P)A3
10/22/82	200.0	200.0	Avon Products, Inc.	MS	Various debt securities	688	(P)Baa1
12/22/82	100.0	100.0	Baker Hughes, Inc.	GS,SL	Sr. debt securities	3921	(P)Baa1
12/22/86	200.0 (1,000,000 shs.)	100.0	Baltimore Gas & Electric Company	To be determined	Preference stock	7306	(P)"aa3"
2/22/88	100.0	100.0	Baltimore Gas & Electric Company	To be determined	First mtge. bonds	7418	(P)Aa2
2/22/88	100.0	100.0	Baltimore Gas & Electric Company	To be determined	Unsecured debt securities	7418	(P)Aa3
7/9/87	300.0	100.0	Banc One Corporation	To be determined	Sr. debt securities	—	(P)Aa2
					Sub. debt securities	—	(P)Aa3
5/8/84	1,000.0	850.0	BankAmerica Corporation	To be determined	Sr. unsecured debt securities	6664	(P)Ba3
1/26/87	1,000.0	475.0	BankAmerica Corporation	SB	Preferred stock	—	(P)"b3"
					Sub. capital notes		(P)B2
1/3/86	500.0	133.120	Bank of Boston Corp.	FBC, GS, ML	Various debt securities	7776	(P)A1
5/15/87	500.0	500.0	Bank of Boston Corp.	To be determined	Debt securities (w/warrants)	—	(P)A1
2/5/86	250.0	100.0	Bank of New England Corp.	GS, KBW, ML, MS	Various debt securities	7594	(P)A2
4/7/86	295.3	.3	Bank of New York Co.	GS, MS	Various debt securities	6958	(P)A1
5/1/87	125.0	125.0	Bank of New York Co.	To be determined	Sub. capital notes	—	(P)A2
3/24/88	285.0	135.0	Bank of New York Co., Inc.	To be determined	Cum. pfd. stk.	—	(P)"a1"
					Noncum. pfd. stk.		(P)"a2"
4/17/86	500.0	102.0	Bankers Trust New York Corp.	To be determined	Sr. debentures	—	(P)A1
					Sub. debentures		(P)A2
4/9/87	400.0	250.0	Bankers Trust New York Corp.	To be determined	Sub. debentures	—	(P)A2

Date	Amount	Amount	Company	Underwriter	Type of Security	No.	Rating
6/26/87	102.0	102.0	Banner Industries, Inc.	To be determined	Jr. sub. debentures	—	(P)B3
6/26/87	160.0	160.0	Banner Industries, Inc.	To be determined	Intermediate sub. debentures	—	(P)B3
6/26/87	35.35	35.35	Banner Industries, Inc.	To be determined	8% Cum. Conv. Preferred	—	(P)"b3"
6/9/86	500.0	352.835	Barclays American Corporation	To be determined	Sr. sub. debt (w/warrants)	6159	(P)A1
11/27/87	800.0	500.0	Barclays North American Capital Corporation	To be determined	Various debt securities	4409	(P)Aa1
11/29/82	100.0	100.0	Barnett Banks of Florida, Inc.	FBC,SL,SB	Various debt securities	216	(P)A1
11/20/85	650.0	4.0	Baxter Travenol Laboratories, Inc.	To be determined	Sr. unsecured debt securities	1918	(P)A3
6/25/86	500.0	500.0	Baxter Travenol Laboratories, Inc.	To be determined	Sr. unsecured debt securities	5980	(P)A3
4/16/87	200.0	200.0	Becton, Dickinson & Co.	To be determined	Debt securities	6648	(P)A1
10/8/87	500.0	85.0	BellSouth Capital Funding Corporation	To be determined	Various debt securities	4778	(P)Aa2
5/3/88	300.0	300.0	Bell Telephone Company of Pennsylvania	To be determined	Various debt securities	6718	(P)Aa1
1/23/86	200.0	200.0	Beneficial Corporation	To be determined	Sr. debt securities	7724	(P)Baa2
	500.0	500.0			Sub. debt securities	7724	(P)Ba1
2/11/86	500.0	250.0	Boeing Company	FBC	Various debt securities	7409	(P)Aa3
5/15/86	250.0	200.0	Boise Cascade Corporation	FBC,LF,SB	Various debt securities	6542	(P)Baa1
3/28/86	400.0	160.0	Borden, Inc.	To be determined	Debt securities (w/warrants)	6943	(P)Aa3
12/14/87	315.0	315.0	Borden, Inc.	To be determined	Debt securities	4273	(P)Aa3
7/17/86	300.0	255.0	Borg-Warner Acceptance Corp.	To be determined	Debt securities (w/warrants)	5271	(P)A2
1/21/83	150.0	50.0	Borg-Warner Corporation	To be determined	Various debt securities	3682	(P)B1
2/26/88	1,950.0	1,950.0	BP America, Inc. (Gtd. by British Petroleum Company plc)	To be determined	Gtd. debt securities (w/warrants)	7173	(P)A1
6/17/83	500.0	500.0	BP North American Finance Corporation (Gtd. by British Petroleum Company plc)	To be determined	Gtd. debt securities	2386	(P)A1
7/9/86	200.0	65.0	Boston Edison Company	GS	First Mtge. Bonds	5962	(P)A2

Source: *Moody's Bond Survey* (published by Moody's Investor Service, Inc., New York, N.Y.), May 30, 1988, p. 6488.

generation in relationship to debt obligations are given strong consideration. Of particular interest are coverage ratios that show the number of times that interest payments, as well as all annual contractual obligations, are covered by earnings. A coverage of 2 or 3 may contribute to a low rating, while a ratio of 5 to 10 may indicate the possibility of a strong rating. Operating margins, return on invested capital, and returns on total assets are also evaluated along with debt-to-equity ratios.[6] Financial-ratio analysis makes up perhaps

TABLE 9–5	DESCRIPTION OF BOND RATINGS			
Quality	Moody's	Standard & Poor's	Description	
High grade	Aaa	AAA	Bonds that are judged to be of the best quality. They carry the smallest degree of investment risk and are generally referred to as "gilt edge." Interest payments are protected by a large or exceptionally stable margin, and principal is secure.	
	Aa	AA	Bonds that are judged to be of high quality by all standards. Together with the first group, they comprise what are generally known as high-grade bonds. They are rated lower than the best bonds because margins of protection may not be as large.	
Medium grade	A	A	Bonds that possess many favorable investment attributes and are to be considered as upper-medium-grade obligations. Factors giving security to principal and interest are considered adequate.	
	Baa	BBB	Bonds that are considered as medium-grade obligations—they are neither highly protected nor poorly secured.	
Speculative	Ba	BB	Bonds that are judged to have speculative elements; their future cannot be considered as well assured. Often the protection of interest and principal payments may be very moderate.	
	B	B	Bonds that generally lack characteristics of the desirable investment. Assurance of interest and principal payments or of maintenance of other terms of the contact over any long period of time may be small.	
Default	Caa	CCC	Bonds that are of poor standing. Such issues may be in default, or there may be elements of danger present with respect to principal or interest.	
	Ca	CC	Bonds that represent obligations which are speculative to a high degree. Such issues are often in default or have other marked shortcomings.	
	C		The lowest-rated class in Moody's designation. These bonds can be regarded as having extremely poor prospects of attaining any real investment standing.	
		C	Rating given to income bonds on which interest is not currently being paid.	
		D	Issues in default with arrears in interest and/or principal payments.	

Source: *Moody's Bond Record* (published by Moody's Investor's Service, Inc., New York, N.Y.), January 1989, p. 8.

---

[6]Similar appropriate measures can be applied to municipal bonds, such as debt per capita or income per capita within a governmental jurisdiction.

50 percent of the evaluation. Other factors of importance are the nature of the industry in which the firm operates, the relative position of the firm within the industry, the pricing clout that the firm has, and the quality of management.

Decisions are not made in a sterile, isolated environment. Thus, it is not unusual for corporate management or the mayor to make an actual presentation to the rating agency, and on-sight visitations to plants or cities may take place. Corporations or municipalities have been known to change their operating or financial policies in order to satisfy people at the rating agencies. Perhaps the size of the issue will be pared down to provide for better interest coverage, or an increase in cash dividends will be delayed to strengthen the internal financing position of the firm.

The overall quality of the work done by the bond-rating agencies may be judged by the agencies' acceptance in the business and academic community. In truth, their work is very well received. Although Paine Webber and some other investment houses have established their own analysts to shadow the activities of the bond-rating agencies and look for imprecisions in their classifications (and thus potential profits), the opportunities are not great. Academic researchers have generally found that accounting and financial data were well considered in the bond ratings and that rational evaluation appeared to exist.[7]

One item lending credibility to the bond-rating process is the frequency with which the two major rating agencies arrive at exactly the same grade for a given issue (and this occurs well over 50 percent of the time). When "split ratings" do occur (different ratings by different agencies), they are invariably of a small magnitude. A typical case might be AAA versus AA rather than AAA versus BBB. While one can question whether one agency is looking over the other's shoulder or "copying its homework," this is probably not the case in this skilled industry.

Nevertheless, there is room for criticism. While initial evaluations are quite thorough and rational, the monitoring process may not be wholly satisfactory. Subsequent changes in corporate or municipal government events may not trigger a rating change quickly enough in all cases. One sure way that a corporation or municipal government will get a reevaluation is for them to come out with a new issue. This tends to generate a review of all existing issues.

Actual Rating System

In Table 9–5 we see an actual listing of the designations used by Moody's and Standard & Poor's. Note that Moody's combines capital letters and small *a*'s, and Standard & Poor's uses all capital letters.

---

[7]James O. Horrigan, "The Determination of Long-Term Credit Standing with Financial Ratios," *Empirical Research in Accounting: Selected Studies,* supplement to *Journal of Accounting Research,* 4 (1966), pp. 44–62; Thomas F. Pogue and Robert M. Soldofsky, "What's in a Bond Rating?" *Journal of Financial and Quantitative Analysis,* June 1969, pp. 201–8; George E. Pinches and Kent A. Mingo, "A Multivariate Analysis of Industrial Bond Ratings," *Journal of Finance,* March 1973, pp. 1–18.

The first four categories are assumed to represent investment-grade quality (high or medium grades). Large institutional investors (insurance companies, banks, pension funds) generally confine their activities to these four categories. The next two B grades are considered speculative in nature, while C and D rated issues are generally in default and may trade flat (without interest). Moody's also modifies their basic ratings with numerical values for categories Aa through B. The highest in a category is 1, 2 is the mid-range, and 3 is the lowest. An Aa2 rating means the bond is in the mid-range of Aa. Standard & Poor's has a similar modification process with plusses and minuses applied, Thus, AA+ would be on the high end of a AA rating, AA would be in the middle, and AA− would be on the low end.

It is also possible for a corporation to have issues outstanding in more than one category. For example, highly secured mortgage bonds of a corporation may be rated AA, while unsecured issues carry an A rating.

The level of interest payment on a bond is inverse to the quality rating. If a bond rated AAA by Standard & Poor's pays 9.5 percent, an A quality bond might pay 10.5 percent; a BB, 12 percent; and so on. The spread between these yields changes from time to time and is watched closely by the financial community as a barometer of future movements in the financial markets. A relatively small spread between two rating categories would indicate investors generally have confidence in the economy. As the yield spread widens between higher and lower rating categories, this may indicate some loss of confidence. Investors are demanding increasingly higher yields for lower-rated bonds. Their loss of confidence indicates they will demand progressively higher returns for taking risks.

BOND QUOTES

The Wall Street Journal and a number of other sources publish bond values on a daily basis. In Table 9–6, we see an excerpt from the daily quote sheet for corporate bonds.

In the first column, note the company name followed by the annual coupon rate and the maturity date. For example, the eighth entry in the table shows Alabama Power with a coupon rate of $8^{7}/_{8}$ percent maturing in 03 (the year 2003). The current yield (Cur Yld) represents the annual interest or coupon payment divided by the price and is 9.6 percent (rounded). The volume (Vol) is indicated to be 5 bonds traded, and the closing price is $92^{1}/_{8}$. The bond quote does not represent actual dollars but percent of par value. Since corporate bonds trade in units of $1,000 par value, 92.125 percent represents $921.25. Other issues of Alabama Power also trade at different prices.

A student interested in further information on a bond could proceed to *Moody's Bond Record,* published by Moody's Investors Service, or the *Bond Guide,* published by Standard & Poor's. For example, using the aforementioned *Moody's Bond Record,* the reader could determine, in Table 9–7, that the American General Corporation 9.375s of 2008 have a Moody's bond rating of A1

TABLE 9–6   DAILY QUOTES ON CORPORATE BONDS

CORPORATION BONDS
Volume, $30,800,000

Bonds	Cur Yld	Vol	Close	Net Chg.
AVX 13½s00	12.9	4	105	+ ¾
AVX 8¼s12	cv	10	103	+ 1½
Advst 9s08	cv	30	82	— 1
AirPr 12¾s94	11.7	5	109	+ 4⅞
AirPr 11¾s15	...	10	107	+ 1
AlaP 9s2000	9.5	1	95	+ 1¼
AlaP 8½s01	9.3	7	91	— 1
AlaP 8⅞s03	9.6	5	92⅛	+ ⅛
AlaP 9¾s04	9.8	6	99½	+ 1⅜
AlaP 10½s05	10.4	5	101	+ ¾
AlaP 8¾s07	9.8	10	89⅛	— ⅞
AlaP 9½s08	9.8	11	96½	— ⅛
AlaP 9¾s08	10.0	5	96¼	+ ¾
AlaP 12⅝s10	11.8	30	106¾	+ ⅜
AlskH 16¼s99	14.3	44	114	...
AlskH 15¼s92	14.1	30	108	— ½
AlskH 11¾s92	11.2	21	105	+ ¾
vjAlgI 10¾s99†	...	71	60	— 2¾
vjAlgI 10.4s02†	...	40	60	...
AlldC zr92	...	10	68½	— ⅝
AlldC zr96	...	5	50½	+ ¾
AlldC zr2000	...	26	33⅝	+ 1½
AlldC dc6s88	6.1	5	98¹⁵⁄₁₆	+ ¹⁄₁₆
AlldC zr97	...	30	42	+ ¾
AlldC zr05	...	10	19¼	+ ¼
AlldC zr09	...	35	12⅞	+ ⅛
Alcoa 9s95	9.0	13	99¾	+ ⅛
AMAX 14½s94	12.4	10	117	+ ¼
ABrnd 8⅜s90	8.6	25	99⅞	+ ¼
AExC 11¼s00	10.6	1	105¼	...
AHosp 7⅞s07	9.9	5	79¾	— 1⅞
AmMed 9½s01	cv	31	100	+ ½
AmMed 8¼s08	cv	41	78¾	— ⅜
AmMed 11s98	10.9	6	100½	+ ½
ATT 3⅞s90	4.1	31	93½	— ⅛
ATT 5⅜s95	6.8	12	82⅜	— ⅞
ATT 7s01	8.1	45	74¼	— 1
ATT 8¾s00	9.1	206	96⅜	— ½
ATT 7s01	8.5	40	82⅜	+ ⅛
ATT 7⅛s03	8.7	45	82	+ ⅛
ATT 8.80s05	9.3	72	95⅛	— ⅜
ATT 8⅝s07	9.4	389	91⅞	+ ⅝
ATT 8⅝s26	9.7	130	89¼	+ ¼
Amoco 6s91	6.4	6	94⅜	+ ¼
Amoco 6s98	7.2	10	83¼	+ 1¼
Amoco 9.2s04	9.5	5	97¼	...
Amoco 8⅜s05	9.2	97	91	+ 2
Amoco 7⅞s96	8.2	15	95⅞	+ ⅞

Bonds	Cur Yld	Vol	Close	Net Chg.
ConnM 11½s90	11.4	3	100½	...
ConEd 9¾s00	9.4	9	99¾	— ¼
ConEd 7¾s03	9.0	25	86⅛	+ ⅝
ConEd 8.4s03	9.2	1	91	+ 1
ConEd 9⅛s04	9.5	15	95⅞	+ ⅜
CnPw 7⅝s99	9.1	9	83⅜	+ ⅜
CnPw 8⅛s01	9.5	1	85⅜	+ ⅜
CnPw 7½s01	9.2	1	81⅛	+ 1⅛
CnPw 7½s02J	9.3	8	80¾	+ 1⅞
CnPw 7½s02O	9.3	3	80⅜	— ⅞
CtlInf 9s06	cv	31	95	+ 2½
CtlOil 8⅞s01	9.4	34	94¾	+ ¾
CrayRs 6⅛s11	cv	50	113	— ¾
CrdF 12⅜s94	...	5	104½	— 1½
CritAc 12.3s13	12.1	13	102	— ¾
CritAc 13.10s14	12.7	5	103⅜	+ ⅜
CritAc 11¼s15	11.0	9	102¼	— ¾
CritAc 11.85s15	11.6	6	102⅛	— ¼
Culb 11½s05	11.6	3	99½	+ 1¼
Dana dc5⅞s06	cv	10	90½	+ ¼
Datpnt 8⅞s06	cv	10	58	+ ⅜
DaytH 10¾s13	10.8	96	99¾	— ⅞
Deere 9s08	cv	440	119	— 2¾
DetEd 6s96	7.8	25	77	+ 1¾
DetEd 9s99	9.7	4	92½	+ 1¼
DetEd 9.15s00	9.8	4	93⅜	+ ¾
DetEd 8.15s00	9.5	15	85⅞	— ¼
DetEd 7⅜s01	9.2	8	80⅛	+ 1⅛
DetEd 9⅞s04	10.2	8	96⅞	— ⅞
DetEd 10⅜s06	10.5	30	101	— ½
DiaSTel 7s08	9.6	2	73⅛	+ 5⅛
Divers 10½s91	10.7	1	98¾	— ½
Dow 8½s06	9.5	7	89⅞	+ ¼
duPnt 14s91	13.6	15	102¾	— ¼
duPnt dc6s01	7.9	3	76	+ 1⅛
duPnt 12⅞s92	12.1	40	106	...
DukeP 7¾s01	8.8	1	83⅜	+ ⅝
DukeP 7¾s03	9.0	44	86¼	...
DukeP 8⅛s03	9.3	5	87¼	— 1
DukeP 9¾s04	9.7	15	101	+ 1⅛
DukeP 9½s05	9.6	15	99	— ¼
DukeP 8⅛s07	9.4	15	86½	+ 1½
DukeP 9⅜s08	9.8	1	96⅛	+ 1⅛

Bonds	Cur Yld	Vol	Close	Net Chg
IFRB 7¼s05†	cv	302	23⅜	+ ..
IIIBel 7⅞s06	9.0	20	85	+ 1..
IIIBel 8s04	9.1	40	88	+
IIIPw 8⅞s06	10.2	15	84¼	—
IIIPw 10⅛s16	10.4	35	97	+ 1
IIIPw 9⅞s16	10.2	5	92	+ 3
Insilco 9s10	cv	21	118	+ ½
ItgRs 10¾s96	11.3	57	95½	— ¼
Intlgc 11.99s96	15.9	15	75⅜	
IBM 9¾s04	9.3	81	100½	+ ⅝
IBM 7⅞s04	cv	485	103⅛	+ ⅛
IBM 10¼s95	9.7	25	105⅞	+
IBM 9s98	9.0	205	100¼	+ ¼
IPap 8.85s95	8.9	2	99¼	+ 1⅛
IntRec 9s10	cv	19	73	+
JPInd 7¼s13	cv	27	101	+ ½
vjJnM 9.7s85mf	...	48	132¹⁄₃₂	— 17..
JohnCt 8½s15	cv	10	139	
vjJonsLi 6¾s94f	...	1	31	+
vjJonsLi 6⅛s88f	...	10	31	+
K Mart 8¾s17	9.9	21	84¾	—
Kenn 7⅞s01	8.8	20	89⅝	+ 17..
KerrGl 13s96	12.9	72	101	+
KerrMc 7¼s12	cv	22	104⅞	+
KimcI 11⅛s90	11.0	110	101¾	— ⅛
KogerP 9¼s03	cv	20	95	
Kraft 6⅞s96	7.9	4	87½	+ ⅛
vjLTV 5s88f	...	117	33¾	— ⅛
vjLTV 9¼s97f	...	34	47	
vjLTV 11s07f	...	148	32¾	— ⅞
vjLTV 13¾s02f	...	5	45	— 1½
vjLTV 14s04f	...	160	46⅛	— 1⅛
vjLTV 11½s97f	...	5	34⅜	+ ⅛
vjLTV 7⅞s98f	...	5	30	
vjLTV 8¼s98f	...	5	31¾	+ 1¼
LaQuin 10s02	cv	5	95½	— 1¼
Leget 6½s06	cv	16	99	+ 1
Litfon f1t00	...	2	98¾	
LomN zr01	...	30	29¾	— ¼
LomN 9s10	cv	20	91	
LgIsLt 12⅞s92	12.2	15	103⅝	— ⅜
LgIsLt 13½s13	12.5	2	108	+ ¾
LgIsLt 13¼s95	12.5	20	105¾	— 1½
LgIsLt 11¼s96	11.0	35	102¼	+ ¾
LgIsLt 11⅞s15	11.9	55	100	— 2
LgIsLt 11½s14	11.6	25	99½	
Loral 7¼s10	cv	39	101½	+ ½
Lorilld 6⅞s93	7.6	111	90⅜	+ 1..
vjLykes 7¼s94N f	...	10	31	—
vjLykes 7¼s94f	...	10	30⅜	— ¼

and a current call price of 105.18 percent of par, or $1,051.80. *Moody's Bond Record* further indicates that the bonds were initially issued on December 7, 1978, and interest is payable on June and December 15 of each year (first column, Interest Dates).

In Table 9–8, we turn our attention to quotes on U.S. government securities (as opposed to corporate issues). Treasury notes and bonds are traded on a price basis as a percentage of par value, similar to corporate bonds. Historically, price changes in the market have been rather small, and bonds are quoted in $1/32$ of a percentage point. For example, the price for the $8^3/_8$ Treasury note due April 1995 is quoted at 98.05 bid and 98.09 asked. These prices translate into $89\text{-}^5/_{32}$ and $89\text{-}^9/_{32}$ percent of $1,000. The bid price on a $1,000 bond would

TABLE 9–7 BACKGROUND DATA ON BOND ISSUES

Issue	Interest Dates	Current Call Price	Moody's Rating	Current Price		Yield to Mat.	Price 1988 High	Price 1988 Low	Range 1946-87 High	Range 1946-87 Low	Amt. Outst. Mil. $	Sink. Fund Prov.	Legal Status	Fed. Tax	Issued	Price	Yld.
American Express Credit sr.nts. 7.875 1993	M&N 1	N.C.	**Aa2 r**	93⅜	bid	9.61	96¼	93	100	92¾	200	No	-------	N	10-30-86	100.00	7.88
do sr.nts. 7.65 1993	M30&N30	[1] 100.00	**Aa2 r**			-----	---	---	100	99	50.0	No	-------	N	11-24-86	100.00	7.65
do sr.nts. 13.125 1994	F&A1	[2] 100.00	**Aa2 r**	106⅞	bid	11.42	113⅝	106⅞	112⅛	86	100	No	-------	N	8-2-84	99.88	13.15
do nts. 7.375 1994	F&A 1	N.C.	**Aa2 r**	90¼	bid	9.85	94½	90¼	90½	88⅞	200	No	-------	N	1-22-87	99.60	7.45
do sr.nts. 10.25 1995	J&D 15	[3] 100.00	**Aa2 r**	102¾	bid	9.65	105⅞	101⅞	105	99¼	100	No	-------	N	6-3-85	99.20	10.38
do sr.nts. 8.75 1995	F&A 1	N.C.	**Aa2 r**	95	bid	9.86	101	95	---	---	200	No	-------	N	1-27-88	99.60	8.83
do sr.nts. 8.45 1996 [4]	F&A15	N.C.	**Aa2 r**	96¼	bid	9.17	102⅛	96⅛	100	97⅞	100	No	-------	N	2-5-86	100.00	
do sr.nts. 8.125 1996	J&J 1	[5] 100.00	**Aa2 r**	90¼	bid	10.00	95½	89½	99⅜	88⅞	150	No	-------	N	6-18-86	99.35	8.22-
do sr.nts. 7.875 1996	J&D 1	N.C.	**Aa2 r**	88¾	bid	9.96	93⅞	87	99⅜	87⅛	250	No	-------	N	11-25-86	99.40	7.90
do sr.nts. 7.75 1997	M&S 1	N.C.	**Aa2 r**	87⅞	bid	9.95	92½	86½	99¾	86⅛	200	No	-------	N	2-24-87	99.80	7.78
do euroyen bonds 5.875 1993 [6]	MAY 8	N.C.	**Aa2**	104⅛	bid	4.81	104⅜	101½	102⅜	99½		No	-------	F	4-10-86	101.25	5.66
do euroyen bonds 8.00 1995 [7]			**Aa2**			-----	---	---	100½	100½		No	-------	F	8-6-85	100.50	
do euroyen bonds 8.00 1996 [8]	MAR 4	N.C.	**Aa2**			-----	---	---	101	101		No	-------	F	2-11-86	101.00	7.85
• do sub.deb. 7.80 1992	A&O1	101.84▲	**A1 r**	97	bid	8.88	100	95¾	105	56⅛	14.0	No	13	N	3-21-72	100.00	7.80
• do sub.deb. 11.25 2000	J&J 1	[9] 102.00▲	**A1 r**	102	bid	10.94	109	100	112	69	75.0	Yes	13	N	6-19-80	100.00	11.25
do euronts. 10.875 1990	MAY15	N.C.	**Aa2**	k 100⅞	bid	10.17	104¼	100⅞	111½	99⅞	200	No	-------	F	4-18-85	99.88	10.91
do euronts. 7.625 1993	[10] N.P.	N.C.	**Aa2**	k 91	bid	-----	93¾	91	100¾	86⅛	200	No	-------	F	9-17-86	100.75	7.49
do euronts. 11.95 1995		------	**Aa2**			-----	---	---	100	100	175	No	-------	F	12-28-84	100.00	11.95
• do sr.deb. 11.75 2012	M&N1	[11] 105.13▲	**Aa2 r**	108	bid	10.80	114⅞	104	116¼	84½	100	No	-------	N	11-2-82	98.00	12.00
• do sr.deb. 10.875 2013	M&N 15	[12] 105.44▲	**Aa2 r**	98½	bid	11.05	106	100⅝	104¾	71	100	No	1	N	5-6-83	99.34	10.86
American Express O/S euronts. 10.00 1991 [13]	JUL 20	N.C	**Aa2**	97	bid	11.39	101¼	97	---	---	50.0	No	-------	F	7-12-88	101.20	8.75
do euronts. 9.625 1993 [14]	MAY 11	N.C.	**Aa2**	93	bid	11.72	101¾	93	---	---	50.0	No	-------	F	4-14-88	101.75	9.39
American Financial deb. 9.50 A 1989 [15]	M&S14	100.00	**N.R. r**	100	bid	9.49	100⅝	94	100⅛	48	43.3	Yes	-------	N	Mar. 1974		
do deb. 10.00 1999	A&O20	100.00	**N.R. r**	86	bid	12.38	89¾	80½	92⅝	54¼	155	Yes	-------	N	1978		
do sub.deb. 9.50 1999 [15]	A&O22	101.40▲	**N.R. r**	83⅞	bid	12.30	100¼	74¾	89	44	9999	Yes	-------	N	1974		
• American Fructose Corp. sub.deb. 9.40 2000	J&D 15	[16] 100.00	**Ba2 r**	83¾	bid	12.05	87¼	83	90	72½	40.0	Yes	-------	N	6-7-85	75.00	13.29
American General Corp. nts. 9.625 2000	J&J 15	N.C.	**A1 r**	98⅝	bid	9.82	100¾	95⅞	---	---	200	No	-------	N	6-28-88	100.00	9.63
• do deb. 9.375 2008	J&D15	105.18▲	**A1 r**	94¾	bid	9.98	100¼	90¼	105	59	89.7	Yes	13	N	12-7-78	99.25	9.45
do s.f.deb. 9.625 2018	F&A 1	[17] 104.64▲	**A1 r**	96	bid	10.05	99⅝	90¼	---	---	150	Yes	-------	N	2-2-88	99.65	9.66
do nts. 9.50 1994	J&D 15	N.C.	**A1 r**			-----	---	---	99¾	99¾	150	No	-------	N	12-4-87	99.75	9.55
do euronts. 8.875 1991	AUG 5	N.C.	**A1**	k 97¼	bid	10.11	101¼	97¼	---	---	100	No	-------	F	8-5-88	101.25	8.39
do euronts. 10.00 1991 [13]	AUG 5	N.C.	**A1**	97½	bid	11.13	101¼	97½	---	---	125	No	-------	F	8-5-88	101.25	10.05
do euronts. 9.00 1994	OCT 15	N.C.	**A1**	k 98⅜	bid	9.37	101⅞	92½	100⅝	99¾	150	No	-------	F	9-23-87	100.63	8.88
do euronts. 9.75 1995	JUN 30	N.C.	**A1**			-----	101¼	101¼	---	---	100	No	-------	F	6-6-88	101.25	9.50
American Greetings nts. 8.375 1993	M&S 1	N.C.	**A2 r**			-----	100	100	---	---	100	No	-------	N	2-26-88	100.00	8.39
do nts. 8.125 1996	J&J 15	[18] 100.00	**A2 r**	90¾	bid	9.89	95½	89⅞	99¾	87½	100	No	-------	N	7-8-86	99.36	8.20
American Hosp. nts. 13.125 A 1992	M&S1	[19] 100.00	**A3 r**	101¾	bid	12.51	106⅝	101⅝	106⅛	99	50.0	No	1	N	9-2-82	99.10	13.29
• do deb. 7.875 2007 [20]	F&A15	104.24▲	**A3 r**	74½	bid	11.15	87	74	100⅝	54½	16.7	Yes	123	N	4-16-77	99.70	
American Int'l Group zero cpn.euronts. 2004	[21] N.P.	100.00	**Aaa**	24⅛	bid	9.31	24¾	20⅝	23¼	15⅞	63.9	No	-------	F	9-13-84		
American Investment Co. nts. 8.75 1989 [22]	F&A1	100.00	**Baa1r**	99⅝	bid	9.31	100½	99⅜	104	63	19.4	Yes	-------	N	8-6-69	99.50	8.80
• **AMERICAN MAIZE-PROD.** sr.sub.deb. 12.00 2006	J&D 15	[23] 104.35▲	**Ba2 r**			-----	---	---	---	---	40.0	Yes	-------	N	7-16-86		
Amer. Med. Int'l NV eurobonds 6.75 1997	NOV 18	------	**Baa2**	----		-----	---	---	---	---	124		-------	F	3-7-88	000.000	
AMER. MEDICAL INT'L. eurobonds 5.00 1996 [24]	MAR 18	[25] 101.50▲	**Baa2**			-----	101	101	---	---	100	No	-------	F	2-9-88	101.00	4.85
do nts. 6.75 1997	NOV 18	N.C.	**Baa2**			-----	---	---	---	---	63.52	No	-------	F	1982		
do eurobonds 9.875 2011 [26]	JUL 15	N.C.	**Baa2**			-----	88¼	88¼	---	---	50.0	No	-------	F	2-25-86	88.25	
do nts. 9.625 1991	J&J15	[27] 100.00	**Baa2r**	98⅛	bid	10.67	101½	98	101	99⅞	100	No	-------	N	1-14-86	99.88	9.66
do nts. 14.375 1992	F&A15	N.C.	**Baa2r**	109⅜	bid	11.15	118½	109⅜	118⅛	99½	100	No	1	N	8-17-82	100.00	14.38
do nts. 9.75 1993	F&A 1	[28] 100.00	**Baa2r**	96¼	bid	10.91	101½	96¼	101⅛	96	100	No	-------	N	2-1-86	99.35	
do nts. 12.25 1994	J&J15	[29] 100.00	**Baa2r**	101¾	bid	11.78	107½	101¾	107⅜	99⅝	96.31	No	-------	N	1-12-84	99.63	12.32
do nts. 13.125 1994	F&A15	[30] 100.00	**Baa2r**	106⅝	bid	11.49	116¼	105¾	113⅞	99⅜	99.45	No	-------	N	8-8-84	99.38	13.24
do nts. 11.375 1995	F&A1	N.C.	**Baa2r**	100⅝	bid	11.23	106½	99⅝	105⅞	99¼	99.32	No	-------	N	1-24-85	99.25	11.50
do nts. 10.25 1995	J&D 1	100.00	**Baa2r**	95⅞	bid	11.16	104	95⅜	102¼	98¼	99.59	No	-------	N	6-6-85	99.56	10.32
• **do** s.f.sub.deb. 11.00 1998 [31]	A&O 1	100.00	**Baa3r**	99½	bid	11.07	101	94½	105½	65⅛	5.0	Yes	-------	N	6-8-78		
do s.f.deb. 11.25 2015	J&D 1	§109.57▲	**Baa2r**	89¼	bid	12.66	104¾	88⅞	101⅝	98⅝	99.88	Yes	-------	N	Ref. fr. 6-1-95@ 105.63		
do eurobonds 5.00 1997	MAY 30	N.C.	**Baa2**			-----	---	---	---	---	47.7	No	-------	F	5-20-85		

Source: *Moody's Bond Record* (published by Moody's Investor's Service, Inc., New York, N.Y.), January 1989, p. 8.

be $891.5625, and the asked price, $892.8125, for a total spread between the bid and asked price of $1.25 per $1,000.

Note that while Treasury notes and bonds are quoted on the basis of price, Treasury bills are quoted on the basis of yield. Looking at the Treasury bills in the right-hand part of Table 9–8, notice that the bid and asked prices are quoted as a discount from the $10,000 par value. As a general example, a $10,000 Treasury bill quoted at 6 percent, with one year to maturity, would provide $600 in interest and would sell on a discount basis for $9,400. The effective yield would be 6.38 percent ($600/$9,400). The same 6 percent

TABLE 9–8   DAILY QUOTES ON GOVERNMENT ISSUES—TREASURY BONDS, NOTES AND BILLS

TREASURY BONDS, NOTES & BILLS

Tuesday, June 28, 1988

Representative Over-the-Counter quotations based on transactions of $1 million or more as of 4 p.m. Eastern time.

Hyphens in bid-and-asked and bid changes represent 32nds; 101-01 means 101 1/32. a-Plus 1/64. b-Yield to call date. d-Minus 1/64. k-Nonresident aliens exempt from withholding taxes. n-Treasury notes. p-Treasury note; nonresident aliens exempt from withholding taxes.

Source: Bloomberg Financial Markets

U.S. TREASURY BONDS AND NOTES

Rate	Mat. Date		Bid	Asked	Bid Chg.	Yld.
7	1988	Jun p.............	99-30	100-01	.....	1.27
13⅜	1988	Jun n.............	100	100-03	.....	2.11
6⅝	1988	Jul p.............	99-28	99-31	.....	6.80
14	1988	Jul n.............	100-07	100-10	− 01	6.46
6⅛	1988	Aug p.............	99-25	99-28	.....	6.73
9½	1988	Aug p.............	100-07	100-10	− 01	6.82
10½	1988	Aug n.............	100-11	100-14	.....	6.82
6¾	1988	Sep p.............	99-24	99-27	.....	6.89
11⅜	1988	Sep p.............	100-31	101-02	.....	6.93
15⅝	1988	Oct n.............	102-18	102-21	− 03	6.02
6⅜	1988	Oct p.............	99-21	99-24	.....	7.06
6¼	1988	Nov p.............	99-17	99-20	.....	7.13
8¾	1988	Nov n.............	100-16	100-19	.....	7.06
8⅝	1988	Nov n.............	100-14	100-17	.....	7.11
11¾	1988	Nov n.............	101-19	101-22	− 01	7.06
10⅝	1988	Dec n.............	101-14	101-18	− 01	7.40
6¼	1988	Dec p.............	99-10	99-14	.....	7.41
6⅛	1989	Jan n.............	99-06	99-10	.....	7.33
14⅜	1989	Jan n.............	104-01	104-05	+ 01	6.70
8	1989	Feb p.............	100-07	100-11		7.41
6¼	1989	Feb p.............	99-03	99-07	....	7.44
11⅜	1989	Feb n.............	102-07	102-11	....	7.46
11¼	1989	Mar p.............	102-17	102-21	....	7.52
6⅜	1989	Mar p.............	99-02	99-06	.....	7.48
7⅛	1989	Apr p.............	99-17	99-21	+ 01	7.54
14⅜	1989	Apr n.............	105-17	105-21	− 01	6.90
6⅞	1989	May p.............	99-08	99-12	+ 01	7.61

Rate	Mat. Date		Bid	Asked	Bid Chg.	Yld.
9	1994	Feb.............	101-26	101-30	+ 08	8.56
7	1994	Apr p.............	92-18	92-22	+ 05	8.63
4⅛	1989-94	May.............	94-01	94-19	+ 06	5.20
13⅛	1994	May p.............	120-14	120-18	+ 12	8.59
8	1994	Jul n.............	97	97-04	+ 10	8.62
8¾	1994	Aug.............	101-02	101-10	+ 10	8.47
12⅜	1994	Aug p.............	118-16	118-20	+ 12	8.64
9½	1994	Oct k.............	103-26	103-30	+ 10	8.67
10⅛	1994	Nov.............	106-27	106-31	+ 12	8.68
11⅝	1994	Nov.............	114-01	114-05	+ 06	8.68
8⅝	1995	Jan p.............	99-18	99-22	+ 09	8.69
3	1995	Feb.............	94-01	94-19	+ 06	3.93
10½	1995	Feb.............	108-27	108-31	+ 10	8.69
11¼	1995	Feb p.............	112-14	112-18	+ 10	8.71
8⅜	1995	Apr p.............	98-05	98-09	+ 10	8.71
10⅜	1995	May.............	108-15	108-19	+ 11	8.69
11¼	1995	May p.............	112-20	112-24	+ 07	8.74
12⅝	1995	May.............	120-04	120-08	+ 10	8.65
10½	1995	Aug p.............	108-31	109-03	+ 08	8.75
9½	1995	Nov p.............	103-25	103-29	+ 08	8.77
11½	1995	Nov.............	114-22	114-26	+ 07	8.73
8⅞	1996	Feb p.............	100-11	100-15	+ 11	8.79
7⅜	1996	May p.............	91-24	91-28	+ 11	8.83
7¼	1996	Nov p.............	90-19	90-23	+ 13	8.84
8⅝	1997	Aug k.............	98-07	98-11	+ 12	8.89
8½	1997	May k.............	97-19	97-23	+ 11	8.87
8⅞	1997	Nov p.............	99-23	99-27	+ 14	8.90
8⅛	1998	Feb p.............	94-31	95-03	+ 15	8.89
9	1998	May p.............	100-25	100-29	+ 14	8.86
7	1993-98	May.............	88-30	89-02	+ 17	8.67
3½	1998	Nov.............	94-03	94-21	+ 09	4.14
8½	1994-99	May.............	96-31	97-03	+ 16	8.92
7⅞	1995-00	Feb.............	92-04	92-08	+ 18	8.96
8⅜	1995-00	Aug.............	95-15	95-19	+ 24	8.98
11¾	2001	Feb.............	121	121-06	+ 23	8.92
13⅛	2001	May.............	131-19	131-25	+ 23	8.92
8	1996-01	Aug.............	94-12	94-18	+ 23	8.70
13⅜	2001	Aug.............	133-02	133-08	+ 06	9.00

U.S. Treas. Bills				U.S. Treas. Bills			
Mat. date	Bid	Asked	Yield Discount	Mat. date	Bid	Asked	Yield Discount
-1988-				10-20	6.58	6.51	6.74
6-30	4.01	3.49	3.54	10-27	6.65	6.59	6.83
7- 7	6.16	6.09	6.18	11- 3	6.66	6.60	6.85
7-14	5.63	5.56	5.65	11-10	6.69	6.63	6.89
7-21	6.00	5.93	6.03	11-17	6.73	6.67	6.94
7-28	6.04	5.97	6.08	11-25	6.79	6.73	7.02
8- 4	6.43	6.36	6.49	12- 1	6.75	6.69	6.98
8-11	6.40	6.33	6.47	12- 8	6.75	6.69	6.99
8-18	6.38	6.31	6.45	12-15	6.78	6.72	7.04
8-25	6.38	6.31	6.46	12-22	6.79	6.75	7.08
9- 1	6.54	6.50	6.67	-1989-			
9- 8	6.46	6.42	6.59	1-19	6.87	6.81	7.15
9-15	6.53	6.49	6.67	2-16	6.94	6.88	7.24
9-22	6.54	6.50	6.69	3-16	6.96	6.90	7.28
9-29	6.62	6.58	6.79	4-13	7.00	6.¹·	.55
10- 6	6.61	6.54	6.75	5-11	7.04	6.⁹8	7.42
10-13	6.59	6.52	6.74	6- 8	7.03	6.⁹9	7.46

Treasury bill with six months to maturity would provide $300 in interest and sell for $9,700. The effective yield would be 6.18 percent ($300/$9,700 times 2).

BOND MARKETS, CAPITAL MARKET THEORY, AND EFFICIENCY

In many respects, the bond market appears to demonstrate a high degree of rationality in recognition of risk and return. Corporate issues promise a higher yield than government issues to compensate for risk, and furthermore, federally sponsored credit agencies pay a higher return than Treasury issues for the same reason. Also, lower-rated bonds consistently trade at larger yields than higher quality bonds to provide a risk premium.

Taking this logic one step further, bonds should generally pay a lower return than equity investments. Why? The reason is that the equity holder is in a riskier position because of the absence of a contractual obligation to receive payment. As was pointed out in Chapter 1, Ibbotson and Sinquefield[8] and Fisher and Lorie[9] have attributed superior returns to equity investments relative to debt over the long term.

A number of studies have also investigated the efficiency of the bond market. A primary item under investigation was the extent of price change that was associated with a change in a bond rating. If the bond market is efficient, much of the information that led to the rating change was already known to the public and should have been impounded into the value of the bond before the rating change. Thus, the rating change should not have led to major price movements. Major research has generally been supportive of this hypothesis.[10] Nevertheless, there is evidence that the bond market may still be less efficient than the stock market (as viewed in terms of short-term trading profits.)[11] The reason behind this belief is that the stock market is heavily weighted toward being a secondary market in which *existing* issues are constantly traded back and forth between investors. The bond market is more of a primary market, with the emphasis on new issues. Thus, bond investors are not constantly changing their portfolios with each new action of the corporation. Many institutional investors, such as insurance companies, are not active bond traders in existing issues but, instead, buy and hold bonds to maturity.

---

[8]*Stocks, Bonds, Bills and Inflation, 1987 Yearbook* (Chicago: R. G. Ibbotson and Associates, Inc., 1987).

[9]Lawrence Fisher and James H. Lorie, *A Half Century of Returns on Stocks and Bonds* (Chicago: University of Chicago Graduate School of Business, 1977). Also, James H. Lorie and Lawrence Fisher, "Rates of Return on Investment in Common Stock," *Journal of Business,* January 1964, pp. 1–17; and Lawrence Fisher and James H. Lorie, "Rates of Return on Investment in Common Stock: The Year-by-Year Record 1926–1965," *Journal of Business,* July 1968, pp. 219–316.

[10]Steven Katz, "The Price Adjustment Process of Bonds to Rating Classifications: A Test of Bond Market Efficiency," *Journal of Finance,* May 1974, pp. 551–59; and George W. Hettenhouse and William S. Sartoris, "An Analysis of the Informational Content of Bond Rating Changes," *Quarterly Review of Economics and Business,* Summer 1976, pp. 65–78.

[11]George E. Pinches and Clay Singleton, "The Adjustment of Stock Prices to Bond Rating Changes," *Journal of Finance,* March 1978, pp. 29–44.

OTHER FORMS OF FIXED-INCOME SECURITIES

Our interest so far in this chapter has been on fixed-income securities, primarily in the form of bonds issued by corporations and various sectors of the government. There are other significant forms of debt instruments from which the investor may choose, and they are primarily short term in nature.

Certificates of Deposit (CDs).   These instruments are provided by commercial banks and savings and loans (or other thrift institutions) and have traditionally been issued in small amounts such as $1,000 or $10,000, or large amounts such as $100,000. The procedure is that the investor provides the funds and receives an interest-bearing certificate in return. The smaller CDs usually have a maturity of anywhere from six months to eight years, and the large CDs, 30 to 90 days.

The large CDs are usually sold to corporate investors, money market funds, pension funds, and so on, while the small CDs are sold to individual investors. One main difference between the two CDs, besides the dollar amount, is that there may be a secondary market for the large CDs which allows these investors to maintain their liquidity without suffering an interest penalty. Investors in the small CDs have no such liquidity. Their only option is to redeem the certificate before maturity to the borrowing institution and suffer an interest loss penalty.

Small CDs have been traditionally regulated by the government, with federal regulatory agencies specifying the maximum interest rate that can be paid and the life of the CD. In 1986, all such interest-rate regulations and ceilings were phased out, and the free market determines return. Any financial institution is able to offer whatever it desires. Almost all CDs are federally insured for up to $100,000 in the event of the collapse of the financial institution offering the instrument. This feature became particularly important in the late 1980s due to the problems in the savings and loan industry.

Commercial Paper.   Another form of a short-term credit instrument is commercial paper, which is issued by large business corporations to the public. Commercial paper usually comes in minimum denominations of $25,000 and represents an unsecured promissory note. Commercial paper will carry a higher yield than small CDs or government Treasury bills and will be in line with the yield on large CDs. The maturity is usually 30, 60, or 90 days (though up to six months is possible).

Bankers' Acceptance.   This instrument often arises from foreign trade. The acceptance is a draft drawn on a bank for approval for future payment and is subsequently presented to the bank for payment. The investor buys the bankers' acceptance from an exporter (or other third party) at a discount with the intention of presenting it to the bank at face value at a future date. Bankers' acceptances provide yields comparable to commercial paper and large CDs and have an active secondary or resale market.

Money Market Funds.   These funds are not a direct form of fixed-income security but, rather, represent a vehicle for individuals to buy short-term fixed-income securities through a mutual fund arrangement.[12] An individual with a small amount to invest may pool his or her funds with others to buy high-yielding large CDs and other similar instruments indirectly through the fund. There is a great deal of flexibility in withdrawing funds through check-writing privileges.

Money Market Accounts.   These accounts are similar to money market funds but are offered by financial institutions rather than mutual funds. Financial institutions introduced money market accounts in the early 1980s to compete with money market funds. These accounts pay rates generally competitive with money market funds and normally allow up to three withdrawals a month without penalty. One advantage of a money market account over a money market fund is that it is normally insured by the federal government for up to $100,000. However, due to the high quality of investments of *money market funds,* this advantage is not particularly important in most cases.

Both money market funds and money market accounts normally have minimum balance requirements of $500 to $1,000. Minimum withdrawal provisions of $250 to $500 may also exist. Each fund or account must be examined for its rules. In any event, either provides much more flexibility than a certificate of deposit in terms of access to funds with only a slightly lower yield.

PREFERRED STOCK AS AN ALTERNATIVE TO DEBT

Finally, we look at **preferred stock** as an alternative to debt because some investors may elect to purchase preferred stock to satisfy their fixed-income needs. A $50 par value preferred stock issue paying $4.40 in annual dividends would provide an annual yield of 8.8 percent.

Preferred stock as an investment falls somewhere between bonds and common stock as far as protective provisions for the investor. In the case of debt, the bondholders have a contractual claim against the corporation and may force bankruptcy proceedings if interest payments are not forthcoming. Common stockholders have no such claim, but are the ultimate owners of the firm and may receive dividends and other distributions after all prior claims have been satisfied. Preferred stockholders, on the other hand, are entitled to receive a stipulated dividend and must receive the dividend prior to any payment to common stockholders. However, the payment of preferred stock dividends is not compelling to the corporation as is true in the case of debt. In bad times, preferred stock dividends may be omitted by the corporation.

While preferred stock dividends are not tax deductible to the corporation, as would be true with interest on bonds, they do offer certain investors unique tax advantages. The tax law provides that any corporation which receives preferred or common stock dividends from another corporation must add only

---

[12]Most brokerage houses also offer money market fund options.

TABLE 9–9	YIELDS ON CORPORATE BONDS AND HIGH-GRADE PREFERRED STOCK		
Year	(1) High-Grade Bonds (Percent)	(2) High-Grade Preferred Stock (Percent)	(2) − (1) Spread
1988	9.75%	9.05%	−.70%
1987	9.68	8.37	−1.31
1986	9.47	8.76	−.71
1985	11.82	10.49	−1.33
1984	13.31	11.59	−1.72
1983	12.42	10.55	−1.87
1982	14.41	11.68	−2.73
1981	14.75	11.64	−3.11
1980	12.50	10.11	−2.39
1979	9.94	8.54	−1.40
1978	8.92	7.76	−1.16
1977	8.24	7.12	−1.12
1972	7.49	6.56	−.93
1967	5.66	5.13	−.53
1962	4.47	4.21	−.26
1957	4.03	4.36	.33
1952	3.04	3.75	.71
1947	2.70	3.51	.81

Source: *Moody's Industrial Manual* and *Moody's Bond Record* (published by Moody's Investor Service, Inc., New York, N.Y., selected issues).

30 percent of such dividends to its taxable income. Thus, if a $5 dividend is received, only 30 percent of the $5, or $1.50, would be taxable to the corporate recipient.[13]

Because of this tax feature, preferred stock may carry a slightly lower yield than corporate bond issues of similar quality as indicated in Table 9–9.

Features of Preferred Stock

Preferred stock may carry a number of features that are similar to a debt issue. For example, a preferred stock issue may be *convertible* into common stock. Also, preferred stock may be *callable* by the corporation at a stipulated price, generally slightly above par. The call feature of a preferred stock issue may be of particular interest in that preferred stock has no maturity date as such. If the corporation wishes to take preferred stock off the books, it must call in the issue or purchase the shares in the open market at the going market price.

An important feature of preferred stock is that the dividend payments are usually *cumulative* in nature. That is, if preferred stock dividends are not paid in any one year, they accumulate and must be paid before common stockholders can receive any cash dividends. If preferred stock carries a $6.40 dividend and dividends are not paid for three years, the full $19.20 must be paid

---

[13]An individual investor does not enjoy the same tax benefit.

TABLE 9–10   EXAMPLES OF OUTSTANDING PREFERRED STOCK ISSUES, MAY, 1988

Issuer	Moody's Rating*	Par Value	Call Price	Market Price	Yield (Percent)
Duke Power Co. 8.70% cumulative preferred	aa2	$100	$101.00	92 1/2	9.40%
Ohio Edison Co. 7.24% cumulative preferred	baa2	$100	$103.06	70 1/4	10.30
Interstate Power 9% cumulative preferred	a1	$50	$53.50	46 1/8	9.76

*Lowercase letters are used by Moody's to rate preferred stock.
Sources: *Moody's Bond Record* (published by Moody's Investor Service, Inc., New York, N.Y.) and *The Wall Street Journal*.

before any dividends go to common stockholders. This provides a strong incentive for the corporation to meet preferred stock dividend obligations on an annual basis even though preferred stock does not have a fixed, contractual obligation as is true of bonds. If the corporation gets behind in preferred stock dividends, it may create a situation that is quite difficult to get out of in the future. Being behind or in arrears on preferred stock dividends can make it almost impossible to sell new common stock because of the preclusion of common stock dividends until the preferred stockholders are satisfied.

An example of existing preferred stock issues is presented in Table 9–10. The issues are listed in *Moody's Bond Record*, and the daily price quotes may be found in the NYSE Composite Stock Transactions section of *The Wall Street Journal* or other newspapers.

APPENDIX 9-A: EVALUATION OF DEBT INNOVATIONS

Security	Distinguishing Characteristics	Yield Reduction or Risk Reallocation	Enhanced Liquidity	Reduction in Transaction Costs	Other Benefits
Zero-coupon bonds	Noninterest bearing. Payment in one lump sum at maturity.	Issuer assumes reinvestment risk. Issues sold in Japan carried below-market yields reflecting their tax advantage over conventional debt issues.			Straight-line amortization of original issue discount pre–TEFRA. Japanese investors realize significant tax savings.
Stripped Treasury securities	Coupons separated from corpus to create a series of zero-coupon bonds that can be sold separately.	Yield curve arbitrage; sum of the parts can exceed the whole.			
Adjustable-rate notes and floating-rate notes	Coupon rate floats with some index, such as the 91-day Treasury bill rate.	Issuer exposed to floating interest-rate risk, but initial rate is lower than for fixed-rate issue.	Price remains closer to par than the price of a fixed-rate note.		
Extendable notes	Interest rate adjusts every 2–3 years, at which time note holder has the option to put the notes back to the issuer if the new rate is unacceptable.	Coupon based on 2–3 year put date, not on final maturity.		Lower transaction costs than issuing 2- or 3-year notes and rolling them over.	
Puttable bonds and adjustable tender securities	Issuer can periodically reset the terms, in effect rolling over debt without having to redeem it for cash until the final maturity.	Coupon based on the type of interest-rate period selected, not on final maturity.		Lower transaction costs than having to perform a series of refundings.	

Security	Distinguishing Characteristics	Yield Reduction or Risk Reallocation	Enhanced Liquidity	Reduction in Transaction Costs	Other Benefits
Medium-term notes	Notes are sold in varying amounts and in varying maturities on an agency basis.			Agents' commissions are lower than underwriting spreads.	
Negotiable certificates of deposit	Certificates of deposit are registered and sold to the public on an agency basis.		More liquid than nonnegotiable CDs	Agents' commissions are lower than underwriting spreads.	
Mortgage pass-through certificates	Investor buys an undivided interest in a pool of mortgages.	Reduced yield due to the benefit to the investor of diversification and greater liquidity.	More liquid than individual mortgages.		
Collateralized mortgage obligations (CMOs)	Mortgage payment stream is divided into 3–5 classes which are prioritized in terms of their right to receive principal payments.	Reduction in prepayment risk to classes with prepayment priority. Designed to appeal to different classes of investors; sum of the parts can exceed the whole.	More liquid than individual mortgages.		
Receivable backed securities	Investor buys an undivided interest in a pool of receivables.	Reduced yield due to the benefit to the investor of diversification and greater liquidity. Significantly cheaper than pledging receivables to a bank.	More liquid than individual receivables.		
Euronotes and Euro-commercial paper	Euro-commercial paper is similar to U.S. commercial paper.	Elimination of intermediary brings savings that lender and borrower can share.		Corporations invest in each other's paper directly rather than through an intermediary.	

APPENDIX 9-A *(concluded)*

Security	Distinguishing Characteristics	Yield Reduction or Risk Reallocation	Enhanced Liquidity	Reduction in Transaction Costs	Other Benefits
Interest-rate swaps	Two entities agree to swap interest-rate-payment obligations, typically fixed rate for floating rate.	Weaker credits can borrow from banks and swap for fixed rate so as to achieve a lower fixed rate than they could by borrowing directly from traditional fixed-rate lenders.			
Credit-enhanced debt securities	Issuer's obligation to pay is backed by an irrevocable letter of credit or surety bond.	Stronger credit rating of the letter of credit or surety bond issuer leads to lower yield, which can more than offset letter of credit/surety bond fees.			Enables a privately held company to borrow publicly while preserving confidentiality.

Source: John D. Finnerty, *Financial Management Collection,* Financial Management Association, Winter 1988, p. 4.

10

PRINCIPLES OF BOND VALUATION AND INVESTMENT

T he old notion that a bond represents an inherently conservative investment can be quickly dispelled. A $1,000, 10 percent coupon rate bond with 25 years to maturity could rise $214.80 or fall $157.60 in response to a 2 percent change in interest rates in the marketplace. Investors enjoyed a total return of 43.79 percent on long-term high-grade corporate bonds in 1982 and 25.37 percent in 1985. However, the same bond investors would have had a positive total return in only 12 out of 20 years between 1968 and 1987. Losses that ranged up to 10 percent occurred in the other eight years.

In this chapter, we will examine the valuation process for bonds, the relationship of interest-rate changes to the business cycle, and various investment and speculative strategies related to bond maturity, quality, and pricing.

FUNDAMENTALS OF THE BOND VALUATION PROCESS

The price of a bond at any given time represents the present value of future interest payments plus the present value of the par value of the bond at maturity. We say that:

$$V = \sum_{t=1}^{n} \frac{C_t}{(1 + i)^t} + \frac{P_n}{(1 + i)^n}$$

(10–1)

where:

V = Market value or price of the bond
n = Number of periods
t = Each period
C_t = Coupon or interest payment for each period, t
P_n = Par or maturity value
i = Interest rate in the market

We can use logarithms and various mathematical calculations to find the value of a bond or simply use Table 10–1 and Table 10–2 to determine the present value of C_t and P_n and add the two together. (Expanded versions of these two tables are presented in appendixes at the end of the text.)

Assume a bond pays 10 percent interest or $100 (C_t) for 20 years (n) and has a par (P_n) or maturity value of $1,000. The interest rate (i) in the marketplace is assumed to be 12 percent. The present value of the bond, using annual compounding is shown to be $850.90 as follows:

Present Value of Coupon Payments (C_t) (from Table 10–1)	Present Value of Maturity Value (P_n) (from Table 10–2)
n = 20, i = 12%	n = 20, i = 12%
$100 × 7.469 = $746.90	$1,000 × .104 = $104.00

Present value of coupon payments	= $746.90
Present value of maturity value	= 104.00
Value of bond	= $850.90

TABLE 10–1	PRESENT VALUE OF AN ANNUITY OF $1 (Coupon Payments, C_t)					
Number of Periods (n)	Interest Rate (i)					
	4 Percent	5 Percent	6 Percent	8 Percent	10 Percent	12 Percent
1	0.962	0.952	0.943	0.926	0.909	0.893
2	1.886	1.859	1.833	1.783	1.736	1.690
3	2.775	2.723	2.673	2.577	2.487	2.402
4	3.630	3.546	3.465	3.312	3.170	3.037
5	4.452	4.329	4.212	3.993	3.791	3.605
10	8.111	7.722	7.360	6.710	6.145	5.650
20	13.590	12.462	11.470	9.818	8.514	7.469
30	17.292	15.373	13.765	11.258	9.427	8.055
40	19.793	17.160	15.046	11.925	9.779	8.244

TABLE 10–2	PRESENT VALUE OF A SINGLE AMOUNT OF $1 (Par or Maturity, Value P_n)					
Number of Periods (n)	Interest Rate (i)					
	4 Percent	5 Percent	6 Percent	8 Percent	10 Percent	12 Percent
1	.962	.952	.943	.926	.909	.893
2	.925	.907	.890	.857	.826	.797
3	.889	.864	.840	.794	.751	.712
4	.855	.823	.792	.735	.683	.636
5	.822	.784	.747	.681	.621	.567
10	.676	.614	.558	.463	.386	.322
20	.456	.377	.312	.215	.149	.104
30	.308	.231	.174	.099	.057	.033
40	.208	.142	.097	.046	.022	.011

Because the bond pays 10 percent of the par value when the competitive market rate of interest is 12 percent, investors will only pay $850.90 for the issue. This bond is said to be selling at a discount of $149.10 from the $1,000 par value. The discount is determined by several factors, such as the years to maturity, spread between the coupon and market rates, and the level of the coupon payment. While the $850.90 price was calculated using annual compounding, coupon payments on most bonds are paid semiannually. To adjust for this, we *divide* the annual coupon payment and required interest rate in the market by two and *multiply* the number of periods by two. Using the same example as before but with the appropriate adjustments for semiannual compounding, we show a slightly lower price of $849.30 as follows:

Present Value of Coupon Payments (C_t) (from Table 10–1)	Present Value of Maturity Value (P_n) (from Table 10–2)
$n = 40$, $i = 6\%$	$n = 40$, $i = 6\%$
$50 × 15.046 = $752.30	$1,000 × .097 = $97.00

Present value of coupon payments	= $752.30
Present value of maturity value	= 97.00
Value of bond	= $849.30

We see a minor adjustment in price as a result of using the more-exacting process. You should also be aware that expanded versions of Table 10–1 and Table 10–2 are presented as Appendix D and Appendix B at the end of the text. To check our answer, in Table 10–3 we present an excerpt from a bond table indicating prices for 10 percent and 12 percent annual coupon rate bonds at various market rates of interest (yields to maturity) and time periods. Though the values are quoted on an annual basis, the assumption is that semiannual discounting, such as that shown in our second example, was utilized. Note that for a bond with a 10 percent coupon rate, a 12 percent market rate (yield to maturity), and 20 years to run, the value in the table is 84.93. This is assumed to represent 84.93 percent of par value. Since the par value of the bond in our example was $1,000, the answer would be $849.30 ($1,000 × 84.93%). This is precisely the answer we got in our second example. A typical modern bond table may be 1,000 pages long and cover time periods up to 30 years and interest rates from $1/4$ to 30 percent. For professionals working with bonds on a continual basis, financial calculators and computers are replacing these tables, with quicker response time.

RATES OF RETURN

Bonds are evaluated on a number of different types of returns, including current yield, yield to maturity, yield to call, and anticipated realized yield.

Current Yield

The **current yield**, which is shown in *The Wall Street Journal* and many daily newspapers, is the annual interest payment divided by the price of the bond. An example might be a 12 percent coupon rate $1,000 par value bond selling for $900. The current yield would be:

$$\frac{\$120}{\$900} = 13.3\%$$

The 13.3 percent indicates the annual cash rate of return an investor would receive in interest payments on the $900 investment but does not include any adjustments for capital gains or losses as bond prices change in response to new market interest rates. Another problem with current yield is that it does not take into consideration the maturity date of a debt instrument. A bond with 1 year to run and another with 20 years to run would have the same current yield quote if interest payments were $120 and the price were $900. Clearly, the one-year bond would be preferable under this circumstance because the investor would not only get $120 in interest but also a gain in value of $100 ($1,000 − $900) within a one-year time period.

TABLE 10–3   EXCERPTS FROM BOND VALUE TABLE

Yield to Maturity (Percent)	Coupon Rate (10 Percent)				Coupon Rate (12 Percent)				Yield to Maturity (Percent)
	1 Year	5 Years	10 Years	20 Years	1 Year	5 Years	10 Years	20 Years	
8%	101.89%	108.11%	113.50%	119.79%	103.77%	116.22%	127.18%	139.59%	8%
9	100.94	103.96	106.50	109.20	102.81	111.87	119.51	127.60	9
10	100.00	100.00	100.00	100.00	101.86	107.72	112.46	117.16	10
11	99.08	96.23	94.02	91.98	100.92	103.77	105.98	108.02	11
12	98.17	92.64	88.53	84.93	100.00	100.00	100.00	100.00	12
13	97.27	89.22	83.47	78.78	99.09	96.41	94.49	92.93	13
14	96.38	85.95	78.81	73.34	98.19	92.98	89.41	86.67	14

Source: Reprinted by permission from the *Thorndike Encyclopedia of Banking and Financial Tables*, 1981, Copyright © 1981, Warren Gorham and Lamont Inc., 210 South Street, Boston, Mass. All rights reserved.

Yield to Maturity

Yield to maturity takes into consideration annual interest received, the difference between the current bond price and its maturity value, and the number of years to maturity. Returning to our earlier example, if a bond pays $100 in annual interest and sells for $849.30 with 20 years to maturity, the investor would be receiving $100 annually plus the $150.70 differential spread over 20 years, or $7.54 per year. This would indicate a total annual return of $107.54. We would also think of the investor's average investment as being approximately the mid-point between the initial investment of $849.30, and the ending value of $1,000. Actually, it is slightly different from this due to mathematical averaging procedures over time. The value for approximate yield to maturity can be found through using Formula 10–2.[1]

$$Y' = \frac{\text{Coupon payment } (C_t) + \dfrac{\text{Par value } (P_n) - \text{Market value } (V)}{\text{Number of periods } (n)}}{(0.6) \text{ Market value } (V) + (0.4) \text{ Par value } (P_n)}$$

(10–2)

On an annual basis, we indicate:

> Y' = Approximate yield to maturity
> Coupon payment = $100
> Par or maturity value = $1,000
> Market value = $849.30
> Number of periods = 20

[1] This formula is recommended by Gabriel A. Hawawini and Ashok Vora, "Yield Approximations: A Historical Perspective," *Journal of Finance*, March 1982, pp. 145–56. It tends to provide the best approximation.

$$Y' = \frac{\$100 + \dfrac{\$1,000 - \$849.30}{20}}{(0.6)\$849.30 + (0.4)\$1,000}$$

$$= \frac{\$100 + \dfrac{\$150.70}{20}}{\$509.58 + \$400}$$

$$= \frac{\$107.54}{\$909.58}$$

$$= 11.82\%$$

This answer is merely an approximation of exact yield to maturity. The precise answer can only be found mathematically by returning to Formula (10–1) and determining the precise interest rate (i) that allows us to discount back all future coupon payments (C_t) and the par or maturity value (P_n) at the end of n periods to arrive at the current price. The yield to maturity may be thought of as the internal rate of return or yield on the bond. Since computing the exact yield to maturity is a very involved, trial-and-error process, bond tables are readily available to allow us to determine this value. As a matter of fact, all we have to do is return to Table 10–3, the bond value table, and use it in a slightly different fashion. We pick our coupon rate, read across the table for number of years, look into the table for price (stated as a percent of par value of $1,000), and then read to the outside column to determine yield. A 10 percent coupon rate bond with 20 years to run, selling at $849.30 (84.93 in the table), provides the investor with a yield to maturity of 12 percent.[2] Financially oriented calculators or computer software may also be used to find approximate yield to maturity.

Note the exact answer in this case is .18 percent above the approximation (12 percent versus 11.82 percent). In the jargon of bond trading, each 1/100th of 1 percent is referred to as a **basis point**, so we say the difference is 18 basis points. The approximate-yield-to-maturity method tends to understate exact yield to maturity for issues trading at a discount (in this case, the bond is priced at $849.30). The opposite effect takes place for bonds trading at a premium (above par value).[3]

The concept of **yield to maturity** is used interchangeably with the term **market rate of interest.** When we say the market rate of interest is 12 percent, it is the equivalent of saying the required yield to maturity is 12 percent.

---

[2]Interpolation may also be used to find intermediate values in the table.

[3]It should be pointed out that in all our bond problems, we are assuming that we are buying the bond at the beginning of an interest payment period. To the extent there is accrued interest, we would have to modify our calculations slightly.

Yield to Call

As discussed in the preceding chapter on bond fundamentals, not all fixed-income securities are held to maturity. To the extent a debt instrument may be called in prior to maturity, a separate calculation is necessary to determine yield to the call date. Assume a 20-year bond was initially issued at a 13.5 percent interest rate, and after two years, rates have dropped. Let us assume the bond is currently selling for $1,180, and the yield to maturity on the bond is 11.15 percent. However, the investor who purchases the bond for $1,180 may not be able to hold the bond for the remaining 18 years because the issue can be called. Under these circumstances, yield to maturity may not be the appropriate measure of return over the expected holding period.

In the present case, we shall assume the bond can be called in five years after issue at $1,090. Thus, the investor who buys the bond two years after issue can have his bond called back after three more years at $1,090. To compute **yield to call**, we determine the approximate interest rate that will equate an $1,180 investment today with $135 (13.5 percent) per year for the next three years plus a payoff or call price value of $1,090 at the end of three years. We can adjust Formula (10–2) (approximate yield to maturity) to Formula (10–3) (approximate yield to call).

$$
Y'_c = \frac{\text{Coupon payment } (C_t) + \dfrac{\text{Call price } (P_c) - \text{Market price } (V)}{\text{Number of periods to call } (n_c)}}{(0.6)\,\text{Market value } (V) + (0.4)\,\text{Call price } (P_c)}
$$

(10–3)

On an annual basis, we show:

Y'_c = Approximate yield to call
Coupon payment = $135
Call price = $1,090
Market value = $1,180
Number of periods to call = 3

$$
\begin{aligned}
Y'_c &= \frac{\$135 + \dfrac{\$1,090 - \$1,180}{3}}{(0.6)\$1,180 + (0.4)\$1,090} \\[2ex]
&= \frac{\$135 + \dfrac{-\$90}{3}}{\$708 + \$436} \\[2ex]
&= \frac{\$135 - \$30}{\$1,144} \\[2ex]
&= \frac{\$105}{\$1,144} \\[2ex]
&= 9.18\%
\end{aligned}
$$

The yield to call figure of 9.18 percent is 264 basis points less than the yield to maturity figure of 11.82 percent. Clearly, the investor needs to be aware of the differential, which represents the decrease in yield that the investor would receive if the bond is called. Generally speaking, any time the market price of a bond is equal to or greater than the call price, the investor should do a separate calculation for yield to call.[4]

In the case where market interest rates are much lower than the coupon, there is always the chance that the company will call the bond. Because of this possibility, the call price often serves as an upper price limit, and further reductions in market interest rates will not cause this callable bond to increase in price. In other words, investors' capital gain potentials may be quite limited with bonds subject to a call.

Anticipated Realized Yield

Finally, we have the case where the investor purchases the bond with the intention of holding the bond for a period that is different from either the call date or the maturity date. Under this circumstance, we examine the **anticipated realized yield** for the holding period.

Assume an investor buys a 12.5 percent coupon bond for $900. Based on his forecasts of lower interest rates, he anticipates the bond will go to $1,050 in three years. The formula for the approximate realized yield is:

$$Y'_r = \frac{\text{Coupon payment } (C_t) + \dfrac{\text{Realized price } (P_r) - \text{Market price } (V)}{\text{Number of periods to realization } (n_r)}}{(0.6)\text{Market value } (V) + (0.4)\text{Realized price } (P_r)}$$

(10–4)

The terms are:

Coupon payment = $125
Realized price = $1,050
Market price = $900
Number of periods to realization = 3

$$Y'_r = \frac{\$125 + \dfrac{\$1,050 - \$900}{3}}{(0.6)\$900 + (0.4)\$1,050}$$

$$= \frac{\$125 + \dfrac{\$150}{3}}{\$540 + \$420}$$

$$= \frac{\$125 + \$50}{\$960}$$

---

[4]Bond tables may also be used to find the exact value for yield to call. A source is *Thorndike Encyclopedia of Banking and Financial Tables* (Boston: Warren, Gorham & Lamont, 1981).

$$= \frac{\$175}{\$960}$$

$$= 18.23\%$$

The anticipated return of 18.23 percent would not be unusual in periods of falling interest rates.

Reinvestment Assumption

Throughout our analysis, when we have talked about yield to maturity, yield to call, and anticipated realized yield, we have assumed that the determined rate also represents an appropriate rate for reinvestment of funds. If yield to maturity is 11 percent or 12 percent, then it is assumed that coupon payments, as they come in, can also be reinvested at that rate. To the extent that this is an unrealistic assumption, the investor will wish to temper his thinking. For example, if it is anticipated that returns can be reinvested at a higher rate in the future, this increases true yield, and the opposite effect would be present for a decline in interest rates. The reinvestment topic is more fully developed in Chapter 11.

THE MOVEMENT OF INTEREST RATES

In developing our discussion of bond valuation and investments, we have observed that lower interest rates bring higher bond prices and profits. A glance back at Table 10–3 (right-hand portion) indicates that a 12 percent coupon rate, 20-year bond will sell for $1,171.60 if yields to maturity on competitive bonds decline to 10 percent and for $1,276.00 when yields decline to 9 percent. The maturity of the bond is also important, with the impact on price being much greater for longer-term obligations.

The investor who wishes to make a substantial profit in the bond market must make an attempt to anticipate the turns and directions of interest rates. While much of the literature on efficient markets would indicate this is an extremely difficult task,[5] Wall Street economists, bank economists, and many others rely on interest-rate forecasts to formulate financial strategies. The fact that short-term and long-term rates do not necessarily move in the same direction or move with the same magnitude makes the task even more formidable. Nevertheless, some historical analysis and knowledge of interest-rate patterns over the business cycle are useful in making investment decisions.

Interest rates have long been viewed as a coincident indicator in our economy; that is to say, they are thought to move in concert with industrial production, gross national product, and similar measures of general economic

---

[5]Michael J. Prell, "How Well Do the Experts Forecast Interest Rates?" Federal Reserve Bank of Kansas City, *Monthly Review,* September–October, 1973, pp. 3–13; Oswald D. Bowlin and John D. Martin, "Extrapolations of Yields over the Short Run: Forecast or Folly?" *Journal of Monetary Economics,* 1975, pp. 275–88; and Richard Roll. *The Behavior of Interest Rates* (New York: Basic Books, 1970).

health. This is generally true, although in the recessions of 1969–70, 1973–75, 1980–81 and also 1981–1982, the change in interest rates actually lagged behind the decline in industrial production.

This pattern of lag between interest-rate changes and the business cycle, witnessed since the mid-1960s, can be explained in terms of inflationary expectations. In earlier time periods, the occurrence of a recession tended to immediately break off inflationary expectations. Since the mid-60s, a decline in inflationary rates has only taken place well into the recession, deferring the drop-off of interest rates.

While inflationary expectations have their greatest influence on long-term rates, a number of other factors also influence overall interest rates. The demand for funds by individuals, business, and the government represent one side of the equation, with the desire for savings and Federal Reserve policy influencing the supply side. A classic study by Feldstein and Eckstein found that bond yields were inversely related to the money supply (the slower the growth, the higher the interest rates) and directly related to economic activity, the demand for loanable funds by the government, the level of inflation, and changes in short-term interest rate *expectations*.[6]

Term Structure of Interest Rates

Of general importance to understanding the level of interest rates is the development of an appreciation for the relationship between the level of interest rates and the maturity of the debt obligation. There is no one single interest rate but, rather, a whole series of interest rates associated with the given maturity of bonds.

The **term structure of interest rates** depicts the relationship between maturity and interest rates. It is sometimes called a yield curve because yields on existing securities having maturities from three months to 30 years are plotted on a graph to develop the curve. To eliminate any business risk consideration, the securities analyzed are usually U.S. Treasury issues. Examples of four different types of term structures are presented in Figure 10–1.

In panel (a) we see an ascending term structure pattern in which interest rates increase with the lengthening of the maturity dates. When the term structure is in this posture, it is a general signal that interest rates will rise in the future. In panel (b) we see a descending pattern of interest rates, with this pattern generally predictive of lower interest rates. Panel (c) is a variation of panel (b), with the hump representing intermediate-term interest rates. This particular configuration is an even stronger indicator that interest rates may be declining in the future. Finally, in panel (d) we see a flat-term structure indicating investor indifference between debt instrument maturity. This generally indicates there is no discernible pattern for the future of interest rates. Several theories of interest rates are used to explain the particular shape of the yield curve. We shall review three of these theories.

---

[6]Martin Feldstein and Otto Eckstein, "The Fundamental Determinants of the Interest Rate," *The Review of Economics and Statistics,* November 1970, pp. 363–75.

FIGURE 10–1   TERM STRUCTURE OF INTEREST RATES

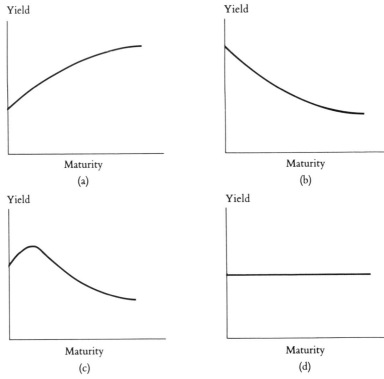

Expectations Hypothesis.   The dominant rationale for the shape of the term structure of interest rates rests on a phenomenon called the **expectations hypothesis**. The hypothesis is that any long-term rate is an average of the expectations of future short-term rates over the applicable time horizon. Thus, if lenders expect short-term rates to be continually increasing in the future, they will demand higher long-term rates. Conversely, if they anticipate short-term rates to be declining, they will accept lower long-term rates. An example may be helpful. Suppose that the interest rate on a one-year Treasury bill is 10 percent, and that after one year, it is assumed a new one-year Treasury bill may be bought to yield 12 percent. At the end of year 2 it is assumed that a third one-year Treasury bill may be bought to yield 14 percent. In other words, the investor can buy (this is sometimes called roll over) three one-year Treasury bills in yearly succession, each with an expected one-year return.

But what about the investor who buys one-, two-, or three-year securities today? The yield he will require will be based on expectations about the future. For the one-year security, there is no problem. The 10 percent return will be acceptable. But the investor who buys a two-year security now will want the average of the 10 percent he could expect in the first year and the 12 percent expected in the second year, or 11 percent.[7] An investor who buys a three-year security will demand an average of 10, 12, and 14 percent, or a 12 percent return. Higher expected interest rates in the future will mean that longer maturities will carry higher yields than will shorter maturities. The reverse would be true if interest rates were expected to go down.

The expectations hypothesis tends to be reinforced by lender/borrower strategies. If investors (lenders) expect interest rates to increase in the future, they will attempt to lend short-term and avoid long-term obligations so as to diminish losses on long maturity obligations when interest rates go up. Borrowers have exactly the opposite incentive. When interest rates are expected to go up, they will attempt to borrow long-term now to lock in the lower rates. Thus, the desire of lenders to lend short-term (and avoid long-term) and the desire of borrowers to borrow long term (and avoid short-term) accentuates the expected pattern of rising interest rates. The exact opposite motivations are in effect when interest rates are expected to decline.

Liquidity Preference Theory.   The second theory used to explain the term structure of interest rates is called the **liquidity preference theory**. The shape of the term structure curve tends to be upward sloping more than any other pattern. This reflects a recognition of the fact that long maturity obligations are subject to greater price-change movements when interest rates change. Because of the increased risk of holding longer-term maturities, investors demand a higher return to hold long-term securities relative to short-term securities. This is called the liquidity preference theory of interest rates. Since short-term securities are more easily turned into cash without the risk of large price changes, investors will pay a higher price for short-term securities and thus receive a lower yield.

Market Segmentation Theory.   The third theory related to the term structure of interest rates is called the **market segmentation theory** and focuses on the demand side of the market. There are several large institutional participants in the bond market, each with its own maturity preference. Banks tend to prefer short-term liquid securities to match the nature of their deposits, whereas life insurance companies prefer long-term bonds to match their long-run obligations. The behavior of these two institutions, as well as of savings and loans, often creates pressure on short-term or long-term rates but very little in the intermediate market of five-to-seven year maturities. This theory helps to focus on the accumulation or liquidation of securities by institutions during the different phases of the business cycle and the resultant impact on the yield curve.

As stated earlier, the expectations hypothesis is probably the most-dominant theory, but all three theories have some part in the creation of the term structure of interest rates. Also, as we discussed, the curve takes on many different

---

[7]The expectations hypothesis actually uses the geometric mean (compound growth rate) rather than the arithmetic mean (simple average) used in the example. For a short number of years, the two means would be quite similar.

FIGURE 10–2   YIELD CURVE PATTERNS

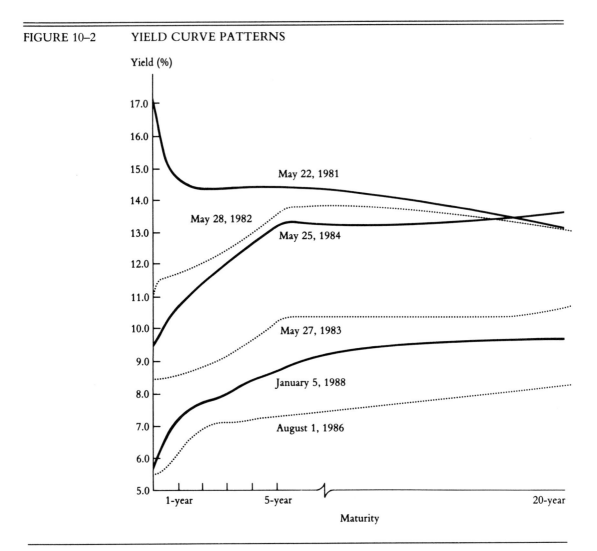

shapes over time. For example, as viewed in Figure 10–2, in May 1981, the yield curve had reached new high levels and was steeply downsloping in anticipation of lower interest rates. Lower rates came, and by May 1982, short-term rates had fallen sharply, but long-term rates were still relatively high, as investors had fears of high continued inflation. The term structure at this point was slightly humped, but by May 1983 (fourth line), the curve had shifted down significantly for all maturities and was now presenting a more-normal upsloping yield curve. Over the two-year period from May 1981 to May 1983, three-month Treasury bills dropped from 16.99 percent to 8.48 percent, for a total decline of 851 basis points. Long-term Treasuries went from 13.26 percent to 10.75 percent over the same two-year period for a decline of only 251 basis points. One year later, by May 1984, interest rates had started to

FIGURE 10–3   RELATIVE VOLATILITY OF SHORT-TERM AND LONG-TERM INTEREST
                     RATES

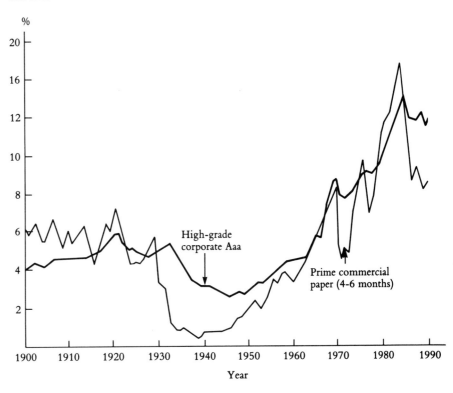

Source: *Federal Reserve Historical Chart Book* (Washington, D.C.: Federal Reserve Board of Governors) 1988.

rise on fears that large government deficits would rekindle rampant inflation.
What happened between May 1983 and May 1984 was that long-term rates
rose to 13.49 percent, or a change of 274 basis points, more than wiping out
the previous decrease.

Two years later, the yield curve in August 1986 had bottomed out with
three-month rates at 5.9 percent and 20-year rates at 8.2 percent. Rates rose
through 1987 and peaked before the market crash of October 19, 1987. The
Federal Reserve Board brought rates down over 100 basis points in the following months, but by January 1988 (second line from the bottom), rates
were still significantly higher than 17 months earlier. This pattern of interest-
rate advances and declines depicted by the yield curves in Figure 10–2 no doubt
will continually offer bond speculators opportunities for trading profits (or
losses).

Before concluding our discussion of the term structure of interest rates and
proceeding to the development of investment strategies, one final observation
is significant. Short-term rates, which are most influenced by Federal Reserve
policy in attempting to regulate the money supply and economy, are much

more volatile in nature than long-term rates. An examination of Figure 10–3 indicates that *short-term* prime commercial paper rates move much more widely than *long-term*, high-grade corporate bond rates.

INVESTMENT STRATEGY—INTEREST-RATE CONSIDERATIONS

Thus far in this chapter, we have examined the different valuation procedures for determining the price or yield on a bond and the methods for evaluating the future course of interest rates. We now bring this knowledge together in the form of various investment strategies.

When the bond investor believes that interest rates are going to fall, he will take a bullish position in the market by buying long-term bonds and try to maximize the price movement pattern associated with a change in interest rates. He can do this by considering the *maturity, coupon rate,* and *quality* of the issue.

Because the impact of an interest-rate change is much greater on long-term securities, the investor will generally look for extended maturities. The impact of various changes in yields on bond prices for a 12 and a 6 percent coupon-rate bond can be examined in Table 10–4. For example, looking at the −2% line for the 12 percent coupon bond, we see a 2% drop in competitive yields would cause a 1.86 percent increase in value for a bond with 1 year to maturity but an 18.93 percent increase in value for a bond with 30 years to maturity. For the same 2% drop in rates, the 6 percent coupon bond would increase

| TABLE 10–4 | CHANGE IN MARKET PRICES OF BONDS FOR SHIFTS IN YIELDS TO MATURITY |

12 percent coupon rate

Yield Change (Percent)	Maturity (Years)				
	1	5	10	20	30
+3%	−2.69%	−10.30%	−15.29%	−18.89%	−19.74%
+2	−1.81	−7.02	−10.59	−13.33	−14.04
+1	−0.91	−3.57	−5.01	−7.08	−7.52
−1	+0.92	+3.77	+5.98	+8.02	+8.72
−2	+1.86	+7.72	+12.46	+17.16	+18.93
−3	+2.81	+11.87	+19.51	+27.60	+30.96

6 percent coupon rate

Yield Change (Percent)	Maturity (Years)				
	1	5	10	20	30
+3%	−2.75%	−11.67%	−19.25%	−27.39%	−30.82%
+2	−1.85	−7.99	−13.42	−19.64	−22.52
+1	−0.94	−4.10	−7.02	−10.60	−12.41
−1	+0.95	+4.33	+7.72	+12.46	+15.37
−2	+1.92	+8.90	+16.22	+27.18	+34.59
−3	+2.91	+13.74	+25.59	+44.63	+58.80

1.92 percent (1 year to maturity) and 34.59 percent (30 years to maturity). The relationship between these two bonds further shows that the lower 6 percent coupon bond is more price sensitive than the higher 12 percent coupon bond.

We can also observe that the effect of interest-rate changes is not symmetrical. Drops in interest rates will cause proportionally greater gains than increases in interest rates will cause losses, particularly as we expand the maturity. An evaluation of the 30-year column in Table 10–4 confirms that both bonds are more price sensitive to a decline in yields than to a rise in yields.[8]

Though we have emphasized the need for long maturities in maximizing price movement, the alert student will recall that short-term interest rates generally move up and down more than long-term interest rates as was indicated in Figure 10–3. What if short-term rates are more volatile—even though long-term rates have a greater price impact—which then do we choose? The answer is fairly direct. The mathematical impact of long maturities on price changes far outweighs the more-volatile feature of short-term interest rates. A one-year, 12% debt instrument would need to have an interest-rate *change* of almost 9 *percent* to have the equivalent impact of a 1 percent change in a 30-year debt obligation.

Bond-Pricing Rules

The relationships we have presented in this section can be summarized in a set of bond-pricing rules. Prices of existing bonds have a relationship to maturities, coupons, and market yields for bonds of equal risk. These relationships are evident from an examination of previously presented Table 10–4. If you look at the change in bond prices in Table 10–4, you may be able to describe many of the relationships presented in the list below.

1. Bond prices and interest rates are inversely related.
2. Prices of long-term bonds are more sensitive to a change in yields to maturity than short-term bonds.
3. Bond price sensitivity increases at a decreasing rate as maturity increases.
4. Bond prices are more sensitive to a decline in market yields to maturity than to a rise in market yields to maturity.
5. Prices of low-coupon bonds are more sensitive to a change in yields to maturity than high-coupon bonds.
6. Bond prices are more sensitive when yields to maturity are low than when yields to maturity are high.

---

[8]A sophisticated investor would also consider the concept of *duration*. Duration is defined as the weighted average time to recover interest and principal. For a bond that pays interest (which includes most cases except zero-coupon bonds), duration will be shorter than maturity in that interest payments start almost immediately. Portfolio strategy may call for maximizing duration rather than maturity in order to achieve maximum movement. A complete discussion of this topic is presented in Chapter 11.

HOW TO TAKE A "JUNK" BOND PLUNGE

Junk bonds are bonds rated below Baa-3 by Moody's Investor Service, Inc., or below triple-B-minus by Standard & Poor's Corp. Often issued by some of America's most heavily indebted companies, they can be a mine field for the unsophisticated. Wall Street brokerage houses consider them so risky they don't want to take responsibility for selling them to individuals. "Unless you consider yourself fairly sophisticated and willing to spend some time, avoid it," warns a spokesman for Drexel Burnham Lambert, Inc., the firm that more or less created the junk bond market.

Professionals typically place junk bonds into three categories: First are the so-called fallen angel bonds, issued by companies that once had high credit ratings but now face hard times. Second are the "emerging growth" companies, relatively young or small concerns that don't have the track record, the cash flow, or the diversification that would bring investment-grade ratings. Third, the bulk of the junk bond market is made up of companies undergoing a restructuring, usually a leveraged buyout that would take the company private in a transaction financed largely through debt. In these cases, bonds are usually paid off by sales of assets rather than by the company's cash flow.

For people who just can't say no, here are some ways investment professionals recommend to make venturing into the junk bond market at least a little less risky:

Safeguards for Junk Bond Investors

Diversify

- Consider junk bond mutual funds for diversity and professional management.
- Do-it-yourself types should spread their investment among at least 10 separate bonds, selecting issues from each of three principal types of junk.

Buy

- Bonds listed on stock exchanges.
- Bonds with covenants that promise preferential treatment or other protections to bondholders.

Avoid

- Bonds that are part of small issues (under $75 million), which can be illiquid.
- Bonds with the highest yields, often sold by the most troubled companies.

Source: Alexandra Peers, *The Wall Street Journal*, January 14, 1988. Reprinted by permission of *The Wall Street Journal*, © Dow Jones & Company, Inc., 1988. All rights reserved.

Understanding these six bond-pricing relationships is at the heart of creating bond trading and investment strategies. The next chapter on duration provides a more-comprehensive analysis of price sensitivity, coupon rates, maturity, market rates, and their combined impact on bond prices.

Bond Prices and Junk Bonds

Another consideration in bond-price sensitivity is the quality of the offering. High-quality securities are more sensitive to *pure* interest-rate changes than are lower-quality issues. Most of the movement in Treasury securities or Aaa utilities is a function of interest rates, whereas lower-grade corporates may also be influenced by GNP, industry projections, and corporate profits. To take advantage of a perceived interest-rate move, quality should be stressed.

For other investment strategies related to a perceived improvement in business conditions, lower-quality corporates may be an ideal investment outlet.

Actually, some investment managers put together portfolios of high-risk, low-grade bonds. The headline in a *Wall Street Journal* article of May 16, 1984, read "Merrill Lynch Seeks 'Junk-Bond' Buyers for Cash to Finish Seabrook Nuclear Unit." These so-called **junk bonds** are extremely speculative and carry high yields with a relatively high risk of default. These bonds may behave more like common stock than bonds and rally on good news, actual interest payments, or improving business conditions. Several institutions such as Drexel Burnham Lambert, Merrill Lynch, and Fidelity Investments manage mutual funds with a junk bond emphasis.

Since junk bonds are quite risky, you can imagine what happened to the market for them after the October 1987 stock market crash. Yields to maturity soared as the prices collapsed on fears of a recession or even worse. Financing dried up for this segment of the bond market as investors moved away from high-risk bonds into low-risk governments and short-term Treasury bills. The collapse caused sales of new junk bonds issues to decline to $36 billion in 1987 from the $45 billion sold in 1986. By the late 1980s junk bond investors were returning to the market, and there were indications that junk bond offerings would continue on.

For those willing to accept the risk of junk bonds in a diversified bond portfolio, the rewards can be quite beneficial. Junk bond yields can be as much as 300 to 800 basis points higher than yields on high-grade AAA corporate securities or U.S. Treasury securities. Also, if the bond rating improves, additional return will result from the increase in price as quality improves. The financial analysis involved in analyzing junk bonds is similar to that employed in stock analysis rather than in AAA bond decisions. Since we have no experience on the performance of junk bonds during severe recessions, junk bond investors could be in for a surprise if bankruptcies and bond defaults are the result of an extended recession. For now, let's return to a more-conventional approach to bond investments and look at an investment example based on an anticipated change in interest rates.

Example of Interest-Rate Change

Assume we buy 20-year, $1,000 Aaa utility bonds at par providing a 12 percent coupon rate. Further assume that interest rates on these bonds in the market fall to 10 percent. Based on Table 10–5, the new price on the bonds would be $1,171.60 ($1,000 × 117.16).

Though we have assumed the gain in price from $1,000 to $1,171.60 took place very quickly, even if the time horizon were one year, the gain is still 17.16 percent annually. This is only part of the picture. An integral part of many bond-interest-rate strategies is the use of margin or borrowed funds. For government securities, it is possible to use margin as low as 5 percent, and on high-quality utility or corporate bonds, the requirement is generally

TABLE 10–5

BOND VALUE TABLE (Coupon Rate 12 Percent)

Yield to Maturity (Percent)	Number of Years		
	10	20	30
8%	127.18%	139.59%	145.25%
10	112.46	117.16	118.93
12	100.00	100.00	100.00
14	89.41	86.55	85.96

Source: Reprinted by permission from the *Thorndike Encyclopedia of Banking and Financial Tables*, 1981, copyright © 1981, Warren, Gorham and Lamont Inc., 210 South Street, Boston, Mass. All rights reserved.

30 percent. In the above case, if we had put down 30 percent cash and borrowed the balance, the rate of return on invested capital would have been 57.2 percent.

$$\frac{\text{Return}}{\text{Investment}} = \frac{\$171.60}{\$300.00} = 57.2\%$$

Though we would have had to pay interest on the $700 we borrowed, the interest on the bonds (which belongs to the borrower/investor) would have partially or fully covered this expense. Also, if interest rates drop down to 8 percent, our leveraged return could be over 100 percent on our original investment.

Lest the overanxious student sell all his or her worldly possessions to participate in this impressive gain, there are many admonitions. Even though we think interest rates are going down, they may do quite the opposite. A two percent *increase* in interest rates would cause a $134.50 loss or a negative return on a leveraged investment of $300 (or 44.8 percent). At the very time it appears that interest rates should be falling due to an anticipated or actual recession, the Federal Reserve may generate the opposite effect by tightening the money supply as an anti-inflation weapon as it did in 1970, 1974, 1979, and 1981.

Deep Discount versus Par Bonds

Another feature in analyzing a bond is the current pricing of the bond in regard to its par value. Bonds that were previously issued at interest rates significantly lower than current market levels may trade at deep discounts from par. The long-term secular upward trend in interest rates since World War II has made the **deep discount bond** very common. As an example, consider the pricing pattern for a number of American Telephone & Telegraph bonds in mid-1988.

Coupon Rate (Percent)	Maturity Year	Price
5.50%	1997	$761.25
5.125	2001	661.25
7.125	2003	786.25

Deep discount bonds generally trade at a lower yield to maturity than bonds selling at close to par. There are two reasons for this. First, a deep discount bond has almost no chance to be called away. Even if prices go up because of falling interest rates, the price is still likely to be below par value. Because of this protection against a call, the investor in deep discount bonds accepts a lower yield. Also, investors in deep discount bonds have the potential for higher percentage price increases (because of the low price base at which the investment is made).

Yield Spread Considerations

As discussed in the previous chapter, different types or grades of bonds provide different yields. For example, the yield on Baa corporate bonds is always above that of corporate Aaa obligations to compensate for risk. Similarly, Aaa corporates pay a higher yield than long-term government obligations. In Figure 10–4, we observe the actual yield spread between Moody's corporate Baa's, Moody's corporate Aaa's, and long-term government securities.

Let's direct our attention to total spread between corporate Baa bonds and government securities (corporate Aaa's fall somewhere in between). Over the long term, the spread appears to be between 75 and 100 basis points.[9] Nevertheless, at certain phases of the business cycle, the yield spread changes. For example, in the early phases of a recession, confidence tends to be at a low ebb, and as a consequence, investors will attempt to shift out of low-grade securities into stronger instruments. The impact on the yield spreads can be observed in the recessions of 1969–70, 1973–74, and 1981–82. In all cases, the yield spread between corporate Aaa's and government securities went over 200 basis points, only to narrow again during the recovery. Remember that in Chapter 8, on technical analysis, one of the market indicators was the *Barron's* Confidence Index which measured the ratio of high-grade bonds to medium-grade bonds. The closer the confidence index is to 1.00, the smaller the spread between rates and the more optimistic investors are about the economy. The further the index is below 1.00, the greater the spread in yields and the less the confidence.

The individual investor must determine how the yield spread affects his strategy. If he does not need to increase the quality of his portfolio during the low-confidence periods of a recession, he can enjoy unusually high returns on lower-grade instruments relative to higher grades.

BOND SWAPS

The term **swap** refers to the procedure of selling out of a given bond position and immediately buying into another one with similar attributes in an attempt to improve overall portfolio return or performance.

Often there are bonds that appear to be comparable in every respect with

---

[9]The concept of higher yields on Baa bonds should not be confused with that of junk bonds. In the latter case, the yield is substantially higher, but so is the risk of default.

FIGURE 10–4   YIELD SPREAD DIFFERENTIALS ON LONG-TERM BONDS

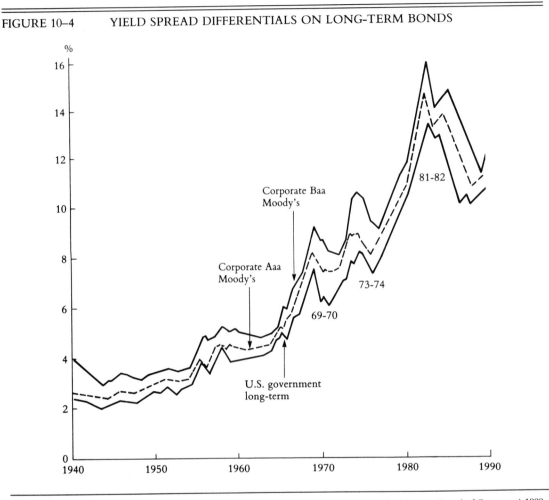

Source: *Federal Reserve Historical Chart Book* (Washington, D.C.: Federal Reserve Board of Governors) 1988.

the exception of one characteristic. For example, newly issued bonds that are the equivalent in every sense to outstanding issues generally trade at a slightly higher yield.

Swaps may also be utilized for tax-adjustment purposes and are very popular at the end of the year. Assume that you own a AAA rated AT&T bond that you bought five months ago and are currently sitting on a 20 percent capital loss because of rising interest rates. You can sell the bond and claim the loss (up to $3,000) against other income.[10] This will save you taxes equal to the loss times your marginal tax rate. You can then take the proceeds from the sale and reinvest in a bond of equal risk, and you will have increased your total cash returns because of tax benefits.

[10]Losses above $3,000 can be carried forward to future years.

Another common swap is the **pure pickup yield swap** where a bond owner thinks he can increase the yield to maturity by selling a bond and buying a different bond of equal risk. The key to this swap is that the bond price of one or both bonds has to be in disequilibrium. This, of course, assumes the market is less than totally efficient. By selling the bond that is overpriced and purchasing the bond that is underpriced, the investor is increasing the yield on his investment. If by chance the true quality and risk of the two bonds are different, the bond trader may have swapped for nothing or may even end up losing on the trade. Other types of swaps exist for arbitrages associated with interest-payment dates, call transactions, conversion privileges, or any quickly changing factor in the market.

11

DURATION AND REINVESTMENT CONCEPTS

REVIEW OF BASIC BOND VALUATION CONCEPTS

In Chapter 10, we discussed the principles of bond valuation. The value of a bond was established in Formula (10–1) as follows:

$$V = \sum_{t=1}^{n} \frac{C_t}{(1 + i)^t} + \frac{P_n}{(1 + i)^n}$$

$$(10\text{–}1)$$

where:

V = Market value or price of the bond

n = Number of periods

t = Each period

C_t = Coupon or interest payment for each period, t

P_n = Par or maturity value

i = Interest rate in the market

Based on this equation, as interest rates in the market rise, the price of the bond will decline because the present value of the cash flows is worth less at a higher discount rate. The opposite is true if interest rates decline. We also demonstrated in Table 10–4 that bonds with long-term maturities were generally more sensitive to changes in interest rates than were short-term bonds. In the reproduction of part of Table 10–4 below, it can be seen that a 30-year bond exhibits larger price changes in response to a change in yield than do shorter-term obligations. For example, a 2 percent drop in interest rates would cause a 1.86 percent increase in value for a bond with one year to maturity, but an 18.93 percent increase in value for a bond with 30 years to maturity. Given the relationship between the life of a bond and the price sensitivity just described, it is particularly important that we have an appropriate definition of the life or term of a bond.

(REPRODUCTION OF TABLE 10–4)   CHANGE IN MARKET PRICES OF BONDS FOR SHIFTS IN YIELDS TO MATURITY (12 Percent Coupon Rate)

Yield Change (Percent)	Maturity (Years)				
	1	5	10	20	30
+3%	−2.69%	−10.30%	−15.29%	−18.89%	−19.74%
+2	−1.81	− 7.02	−10.59	−13.33	−14.04
+1	− .91	− 3.57	− 5.01	− 7.08	− 7.52
−1	+ .92	+ 3.77	+ 5.98	+ 8.02	+ 8.72
−2	+1.86	+ 7.72	+12.46	+17.16	+18.93
−3	+2.81	+11.87	+19.51	+27.60	+30.96

The first inclination is to say the term of a bond is an easily determined matter. One supposedly merely needs to look up the maturity date (such as 1995 or 2004) in a bond book, and the matter is settled. However, the notion of effective life of a bond is more complicated than this. The situation is somewhat analogous to the quoted coupon rate on the bond, not really conveying the true yield on the obligation. Similarly, the maturity date on a bond may not convey all important information about the life of a bond.

In studying the true characteristics about the life of a bond, not only must the final date and amount of the maturity payment be considered but also the pattern of coupon payments that takes place in the interim. If you were to receive $1,000 after 20 years and no interest payments during the term of the obligation, clearly the effective life is 20 years. But suppose in addition to the $1,000, you were also to receive $100 per year for the next 20 years. Part of the payment is coming early and part of the payment is coming late, and the weighted average term of the payout is certainly less than 20 years. The higher the coupon payments relative to the maturity payment, the shorter the weighted average life of the payout. In the next section, we shall go through the simple mathematics of computing the weighted average life of the payout; for now it is enough to know that such a concept exists.

The important consideration is that **bond price sensitivity** can be more appropriately related to **weighted average life** than to just the maturity date. While many bond analysts simply relate price sensitivity to maturity (and we did that also in Chapter 10), there is a more-sophisticated approach related to weighted average life.

Before we move on to determining weighted average life, there is an investment decision we wish you to consider. Assume you have to decide whether to invest in an 8 percent coupon rate bond with a 20-year maturity or a 12 percent coupon rate bond with a 25-year maturity. Which bond will have the larger increase in price if interest rates decline? You may choose the 25-year, 12 percent coupon rate bond because it has the longer maturity, but don't answer too quickly on this. Let's consider weighted average life and then eventually come back to this question of price sensitivity.

DURATION

The concept of weighted average life of a bond falls under the general topic of duration. We shall first of all do a simple example of weighted average life and then more formally look at duration. Assume we have a five-year bond that provides $80 per year for the next five years plus $1,000 at the end of five years. For ease of calculation, we are using annual coupon payments in our analysis. Semiannual analysis would change the answer only slightly. An approach to computing weighted average life is presented in Table 11–1.

First, we see the weighted average life of the bond, based on the annual cash flows, is 4.4290 years. Let's see how this is calculated. In column (1) is the year in which each cash flow falls, and in column (2) is the size of the cash flow for each year plus the total cash flow. Column (3) calls for dividing the annual cash flow in column (2) by the total cash flow at the bottom of column (2) to determine what percentage of the total it represents. For example, the annual cash flow of $80 on the first line of column (2) represents .0571 of the total cash flow of $1,400. ($80 ÷ $1,400 = .0571.) The same basic procedure

TABLE 11–1   SIMPLE WEIGHTED AVERAGE LIFE

(1)	(2)	(3) Annual Cash Flow (2) ÷ by Total Cash Flow	(4) Year × Weight (1) × (3)
Year, t	Cash Flow		
1	$ 80	.0571	.0571
2	80	.0571	.1142
3	80	.0571	.1713
4	80	.0571	.2284
5	80	.0571	.2855
5	1,000	.7145	3.5725
	Total cash → $1,400 flow	1.0000	4.4290

is followed for all subsequent years. In column (4), each year is multiplied by the weights (percentages) developed in column (3). For example, year 1 is multiplied by .0571 to arrive at .0571 in column (4). Year 2 is multiplied by .0571 to arrive at .1142 in column (4). This procedure is followed for each year and each weight. The final answer is 4.4290 for the weighted average life of the bond.

If you can understand the approach presented in Table 11–1, you should have no difficulty in following a more formal and appropriate definition of weighted average life called duration. **Duration** represents the weighted average life of a bond where the weights are based on the *present value* of the individual cash flows relative to the *present value* of the total cash flows. An example of duration is presented in Table 11–2. Present value calculations are based on the market rate of interest (yield to maturity) for the bond, which in this case, we shall assume to be 12 percent.

The only difference between Table 11–1 and Table 11–2 is that in Table 11–2, the cash flows are present valued before the weights are determined. Thus the cash flows (2) are multiplied by the present value factors at 12 percent (3) to arrive at the present value of cash flows (4). The total present value of cash flows at the bottom of column (4) is also the same as the price of the bond. In column (5), weights for each year are determined by dividing the present value of each annual cash flow (4) by the total present value of cash flows (bottom of column 4). For example in year 1, the present value of the cash flow is $71.44, and this is divided by the total present value of cash flows of $855.40 to arrive at .0835 in column (5). Similarly, the weight in year 2, as shown in column (5), is determined by dividing $63.76 by $855.40 to arrive at .0745. In column (6), each year is multiplied by the weights developed in column (5). For example, year 1 is multiplied by .0835 to arrive at .0835 in column (6). Year 2 is multiplied by .0745 to arrive at .1490. This procedure is followed for each year, and the values are then summed. The final answer for duration (the weighted average life based on present value) is 4.2498. Duration, once determined, is the most-representative value for effective bond life and the measure against which bond price sensitivity should be evaluated.

TABLE 11–2		DURATION CONCEPT OF WEIGHTED AVERAGE LIFE				
(1)	(2)	(3)	(4)	(5) PV of Annual Cash Flow (4) ÷ by Total PV of Cash Flows	(6) Year × Weight (1) × (5)
Year, t	Cash Flow (CF)	PV Factor at 12 Percent	PV of Cash Flow (CF)		
1	$ 80	.893	$ 71.44	.0835	.0835
2	80	.797	63.76	.0745	.1490
3	80	.712	56.96	.0666	.1998
4	80	.636	50.88	.0595	.2380
5	80	.567	45.36	.0530	.2650
5	$1,000	.567	567.00	.6629	3.3145
			Total PV of → $855.40 cash flows (V)	1.000	4.2498 ↑ Duration

The formula for duration can be formally stated as:

$$\text{Duration} = \underbrace{\frac{CF\ PV}{V}}_{\uparrow\ \text{Weight}}\ \underbrace{(1)}_{\uparrow\ \text{Year}} + \underbrace{\frac{CF\ PV}{V}}_{\uparrow\ \text{Weight}}\ \underbrace{(2)}_{\uparrow\ \text{Year}} + \underbrace{\frac{CF\ PV}{V}}_{\uparrow\ \text{Weight}}\ \underbrace{(3)}_{\uparrow\ \text{Year}}$$

$$+ \cdots + \underbrace{\frac{CF\ PV}{V}}_{\uparrow\ \text{Weight}}\ \underbrace{(n)}_{\uparrow\ \text{Year}} \qquad (11\text{–}1)$$

where:

CF = The yearly cash flow for each time period

PV = The present value factor for each time period (from Appendix B at the end of the book)

V = The total present value or market price of the bond

n = Number of periods to maturity[1]

In Table 11–3, we observe durations for an 8 percent coupon rate bond with maturities of 1, 5, and 10 years. The discount rate is 12 percent. The procedure used to compute duration in Table 11–3 is precisely the same as that employed in Table 11–2. Although many calculations are involved, you

---

[1]Using the symbols from Formula (10–1), duration can also be stated as:

$$\text{Duration} = \sum_{t=1}^{n} \frac{C_t \frac{1}{(1+i)^t}}{V}(t) + \frac{P_n \frac{1}{(1+i)^n}}{V}(n)$$

If semiannual analysis is used throughout the calculation, the answer should be divided by two to convert the figure to annual terms.

TABLE 11–3   DURATION FOR AN 8 PERCENT COUPON RATE BOND WITH
              MATURITIES OF 1, 5, AND 10 YEARS DISCOUNTED AT 12 PERCENT

1-Year Bond

(1)	(2)	(3)	(4)	(5)	(6)
				PV of Annual Cash Flow (4) ÷ by Total *PV* of Cash Flows	Year × Weight
Year, *t*	Cash Flow (*CF*)	*PV* Factor at 12 Percent	*PV* of Cash Flow (*CF*)		(1) × (5)
1	$ 80	.893	$ 71.44	.0741	.0741
1	1,000	.893	893.00	.9259	.9259
		Total *PV* of → cash flows	$964.44	1.0000	1.0000 ↑ Duration

5-Year Bond

1	$ 80	.893	$ 71.44	.0835	.0835
2	80	.797	63.76	.0745	.1490
3	80	.712	56.96	.0666	.1998
4	80	.636	50.88	.0595	.2380
5	80	.567	45.36	.0530	.2650
5	1,000	.567	567.00	.6629	3.3145
		Total *PV* of → cash flows	$855.40	1.0000	4.2498 ↑ Duration

10-Year Bond

1	$ 80	.893	$ 71.44	.0923	.0923
2	80	.797	63.76	.0824	.1648
3	80	.712	56.96	.0736	.2208
4	80	.636	50.88	.0657	.2628
5	80	.567	45.36	.0586	.2930
6	80	.507	40.56	.0524	.3144
7	80	.452	36.16	.0467	.3269
8	80	.404	32.32	.0418	.3344
9	80	.361	28.88	.0373	.3357
10	80	.322	25.76	.0333	.3330
10	1,000	.322	322.00	.4160	4.1600
		Total *PV* of → cash flows	$774.08	1.0000	6.8381 ↑ Duration

should primarily direct your attention to the last value presented in column (6) for each of the three bonds. This value, of course, represents the duration of the issue.

We see in Table 11–3 that the duration for a one-year bond is 1.0. Since all cash flows are paid at the end of year 1, duration equals the maturity.[2] As maturity increases (to 5 and 10 years), duration increases but less than the maturity of the bond. With a 5-year bond, duration is 4.2498, and with a

---

[2]If semiannual analysis were used, the duration would be slightly less than the maturity in the first year.

10-year bond, duration is 6.8381. Duration is increasing at a decreasing rate because the principal repayment in the last year becomes a smaller percentage of the total present value of cash flow, and the annual coupon payments become more important.[3]

DURATION AND PRICE SENSITIVITY

Once duration is computed, its most-important use is in determining the price sensitivity of a bond. In Table 11–4, we consider the maturity, duration, and percentage price change for an 8 percent coupon rate bond based on a 2 percent decrease and on a 2 percent increase in interest rates. The *market* rate of interest for computing duration in Table 11–4 is 8 percent. One quick point before examining Table 11–4, duration is related not only to maturity but also to coupon rate and market rate of interest. For example, in Table 11–3, the coupon rate of interest was 8 percent and the market rate of interest was 12 percent. In the calculations in Table 11–4, the coupon rate is 8 percent and the market rate of interest is assumed to be 8 percent. Because of the different market rates of interest in Tables 11–3 and 11–4, the duration for a given maturity (such as 5 or 10 years) will be different. The point just discussed will be further clarified later in the chapter, so even if you do not fully understand it, you should still continue to read on.

We see in Table 11–4 that the longer the maturity or duration, the greater the impact of a 2 percent change in interest rates on price. However, we shall also observe how much more closely the percentage change in price parallels the change in duration as compared to maturity. For example, between 25 and 50 years, duration increases very slowly (column 2) and the same can be said for the increase in the percentage impact that a 2 percent decline in interest rates has on price (column 3). This is true in spite of the fact that the maturity period has increased by 100 percent, from 25 to 50 years.

As a rough measure of price sensitivity, one can multiply duration times the change in interest rates to determine the percentage change in the value of a bond.

$$\begin{matrix} \text{Percentage} \\ \text{change in the} \\ \text{value of a} \\ \text{bond} \end{matrix} \ldots \begin{matrix} \text{Approximately} \\ \text{equals} \end{matrix} \rightarrow \text{Duration} \times \begin{matrix} \text{Change in} \\ \text{interest rates} \end{matrix}$$

The sign in the final answer is reversed because interest-rate changes and bond prices move in opposite directions. For example, if a bond has a duration of 7.2470 years, and interest rates go down by 2 percent, a rough measure of bond value appreciation is +14.494 percent (7.2470 × 2). Columns (2) and (3) in Table 11–4, across from 10 years maturity, indicate that this is a reasonably good approximation. That is, when duration was 7.2470, a 2 percent

---

[3]A sinking-fund provision can also have an effect on duration, causing the weighted average life of the bond to be shorter.

TABLE 11–4	DURATION AND PRICE SENSITIVITY (8 Percent Coupon Rate Bond)			
	(1)	(2)	(3) Impact of a 2 Percent Decline in Interest Rates on Price	(4) Impact of a 2 Percent Increase in Interest Rates on Price
	Maturity	Duration		
	1	1.0000	+ 1.89%	− 1.81%
	5	4.3121	+ 8.42	− 7.58
	10	7.2470	+14.72	−12.29
	20	10.6038	+22.93	−17.03
	25	11.5290	+25.57	−18.50
	30	12.1585	+27.53	−18.85
	40	12.8787	+30.09	−19.55
	50	13.2123	+31.15	−19.83

drop in interest rates produced a 14.72 percent increase in bond prices (not too many basis points away from our formula value of +14.494 percent). The approximation gets progressively rougher as the term of the bond is extended.[4] It is also a less-valid measure for interest-rate increases (and the associated price decline). Even with these qualifications, one can observe a more-useful relationship between price changes and duration than between price changes and maturity.

It is for this reason that the analyst must have a reasonable feel for the factors that influence duration. It is apparent that the length of the bond affects duration, but as previously mentioned, it is not the only variable. Duration is also influenced by market rate of interest and the coupon rate on the bond. In fact, it is theoretically possible for these two factors to outweigh maturity in determining duration. That is to say, it is possible that a bond with a shorter maturity than another bond may actually have a longer duration and be more price sensitive to interest rate changes.

Duration and Market Rates

Market rates of interest (yield to maturity) and duration are inversely related. The higher the market rate of interest, the lower the duration. This is because of the present-valuing effect that is part of duration. Higher market rates of interest mean lower present values. For example, in Table 11–2, if the market rate of interest in column (3) had been 16 percent instead of 12 percent, the final answer for duration would have been 4.1859. The new value is actually computed in Table 11–5. Clearly, it is less than the 4.2498 duration value in Table 11–2.

---

[4]The approximation can be slightly improved by using modified duration instead of actual duration. Modified duration is defined as: Duration ÷ (1 + Market rate of interest/Number of coupon payments per period). For more information, see Michael H. Hopewell and George C. Kaufman, "Bond Price Volatility and Term to Maturity: A Generalized Respecification," *American Economic Review*, September 1973, pp. 749–53.

TABLE 11–5   DURATION OF AN 8 PERCENT COUPON RATE BOND WITH A
16 PERCENT MARKET RATE OF INTEREST

(1)	(2)	(3)	(4)	(5) PV of Annual Cash Flow (4) ÷ by Total PV of Cash Flows	(6)
Year, t	Cash Flow (CF)	PV Factor at 16 Percent	PV of Cash Flow (CF)		Year × Weight (1) × (5)
1	$ 80	.862	$ 68.96	.0935	.0935
2	80	.743	59.44	.0806	.1612
3	80	.641	51.28	.0695	.2085
4	80	.552	44.16	.0598	.2392
5	80	.476	38.08	.0516	.2580
5	1,000	.476	476.00	.6451	3.2255
			Total PV of → $737.92 cash flows	1.0000	4.1859 ↑ Duration

To expand our analysis, in Table 11–6 we see the duration values for an 8 percent coupon rate bond at different market rates of interest. As market rates of interest increase, duration decreases. This can be easily seen in the 20-year row (reading across). At a 4 percent market rate of interest, duration for the 8 percent coupon rate bond is 12.3995. At 8 percent, it is 10.6038, and at 12 percent, 8.9390.

Also note in Table 11–6 that an equal change in market rates of interest will have a bigger impact on duration when rates move down than when they move up. For example, in the 50-year row, a 4 percent decrease in market rates of interest (say, from 8 percent to 4 percent) causes duration to increase by 7.0358 years, from 13.2123 to 20.2481 years. A similar increase of 4 percent from 8 percent to 12 percent would only cause duration to decrease by 3.8407 years, from 13.2123 to 9.3716 years.

Duration and Coupon Rates

In the previous section, we learned that duration is inversely related to market rate of interest. We now look at the relationship between duration and the coupon rate on a bond. As the coupon rate rises, duration decreases. Why? The answer is that high coupon rate bonds tend to produce higher annual cash flows prior to maturity and thus tend to weight duration toward the earlier to middle years. On the other hand, low coupon rate bonds produce less annual cash flows prior to maturity and have less influence on duration. Duration is weighted more heavily toward the final payment at maturity, and duration tends to be somewhat closer to the actual maturity on the bond. At the extreme, a zero-coupon bond has the same maturity and duration.

The relationship between duration and coupon rates can be seen in Table 11–7. Here three different coupon rate bonds are presented. Each bond is assumed to have a maturity of 25 years. The best way to read the table is to pick a market rate of interest in the first column and then read across the table

| TABLE 11–6 | DURATION VALUES AT VARYING MARKET RATES OF INTEREST (Based on 8 Percent Coupon Rate Bond) |

Maturity (Years)	Market Rates of Interest				
	4 Percent	6 Percent	8 Percent	10 Percent	12 Percent
1.	1.00	1.00	1.00	1.00	1.00
5.	4.3717	4.3423	4.3121	4.2814	4.2498
10.	7.6372	7.4450	7.2470	7.0439	6.8381
→20	12.3995	11.4950	10.6038	9.7460	8.9390
25.	14.2265	12.8425	11.5290	10.3229	9.2475
30.	15.7935	13.8893	12.1585	10.6472	9.3662
40.	18.3274	15.3498	12.8787	10.9176	9.3972
50.	20.2481	16.2494	13.2123	10.9896	9.3716

to determine the duration at various coupon rates. For example, at an 8 percent market rate of interest, duration is 13.2459 at a 4 percent coupon rate, 11.5290 at an 8 percent coupon rate, and 10.8396 at a 12 percent coupon rate. Clearly, the higher the coupon rate, the lower the duration (and vice versa).

The impact of coupon rates on duration is also demonstrated in Figure 11–1. Note that with a zero-coupon bond, the line is at a 45-degree angle; that is, duration and years to maturity are always the same value. There is only one payment, and it is at maturity.

You can also observe in Figure 11–1 that progressively higher coupon rates lead to a lower duration. As an example, go to point N on the horizontal axis and observe duration for 4 percent, 8 percent, and 12 percent interest. Clearly the higher the coupon rate, the lower the duration value.

Because the higher the duration, the greater the price sensitivity, it follows that an investor desiring maximum price movements will look toward lower coupon rate bonds. As previously demonstrated, low coupon rate and high duration go together, and high duration leads to maximum price sensitivity. The relationship of low coupon rates to price sensitivity was briefly discussed in Chapter 10 under investment strategy. We now see that the unnamed explanatory variable at that point was duration.

| TABLE 11–7 | DURATION AND COUPON RATES (25-Year Bonds) |

Market Rate of Interest	Coupon Rates		
	4 Percent	8 Percent	12 Percent
4%	16.2470	14.2265	13.3278
6	14.7455	12.8425	12.0407
8	13.2459	11.5290	10.8396
10	11.8112	10.3229	9.7501
12	10.4912	9.2475	8.7844

BRINGING TOGETHER THE INFLUENCES ON DURATION

The three factors that determine the value of duration are the maturity of the bond, the market rate of interest, and the coupon rate. Duration is positively correlated with maturity but moves in the opposite direction of market rates of interest and coupon rates; that is, the higher the coupon rate, the lower the duration. Earlier in this chapter, you were asked to consider whether you should invest in an 8 percent coupon rate, 20-year bond or a 12 percent coupon rate, 25-year bond. Since we were assuming interest rates were going to go down, you were looking for maximum price volatility. Had you not studied duration, you probably would have selected the bond with the longer maturity. This would generally be a valid assumption as indicated in Chapter 10. However, the primary emphasis to the sophisticated bond investor when assessing price volatility, or sensitivity, is duration.

Note that the bond with the longer maturity (25 years versus 20 years) also has a higher coupon rate (12 percent versus 8 percent). The first factor (longer maturity) would indicate higher duration, but the second factor (higher coupon rate) would indicate a lower duration. What is the net effect? The answer can be found in earlier tables in this chapter. Let's assume that the *market rate* of interest is 12 percent for both bonds. Table 11–6 presented information on 8 percent coupon rate bonds for varying maturities and market rates of interest. To determine the duration on the 8 percent coupon rate, 20-year bond, assuming a 12 percent market rate of interest, we read across the 20-year row to the last column in the table and see the answer is 8.9390. (Note that all bonds in Table 11–6 have an 8 percent coupon rate, so we must identify the value associated with 20 years and a 12 percent market rate of interest.)

To determine the duration for the 12 percent coupon rate, 25-year bond with a 12 percent market rate of interest, we must go to Table 11–7. Note that all bonds in this table have a 25-year maturity, so read down to a market rate of interest of 12 percent and across to a coupon rate of 12 percent. The value for duration on this bond is 8.7844.

Based on the above analysis, the answer to the question posed earlier in the chapter is that the bond with the shorter maturity (8 percent coupon rate for 20 years) has a longer duration than the bond with the greater maturity (12 percent for 25 years) and thus is the most price sensitive.[5]

Bond	Duration
8%, 20 years	8.9390 ← greater price sensitivity
12%, 25 years	8.7844

In actuality, if interest rates went down by 2 percent, the 8 percent, 20-year bond would go up by 18.5 percent, while the 12 percent, 25-year bond would only increase by 17.9 percent.

---

[5]As previously indicated, if we vary the market rate of interest, we can also influence the outcome to our question.

FIGURE 11–1   THE EFFECT OF COUPON RATES ON DURATION

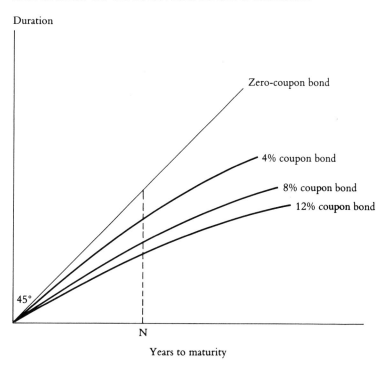

DURATION AND ZERO-COUPON BONDS

Characteristics of **zero-coupon bonds** were briefly described in Chapter 9. As previously mentioned, Figure 11–1 depicts the duration of zero-coupon bonds as a 45-degree line relative to years to maturity. This graphically indicates that the duration of a zero-coupon bond equals the number of years it has to maturity. For all bonds of equal risk and maturity, the zero-coupon bond has the greatest duration and therefore the greatest price sensitivity. This price risk is one that is often lost in the image of safety that CATs, RATs, TGRs, COUGARs, and other zero-coupons have when backed by U.S. government securities.

A headline in *The Wall Street Journal* on June 1, 1984, appeared as follows: "Zero-Coupon Bonds' Price Swings Jolt Investors Looking for Security."[6] It was reported that between March 31, 1983, and March 31, 1984, Salomon Brothers' 30-year CATs declined 25 percent in price, while returns on conventional 30-year government bonds declined only a few percentage points.

---

[6]Randall Smith, "Zero-Coupon Bonds' Price Swings Jolt Investors Looking for Security," *The Wall Street Journal*, June 1, 1984, p. 19. Reprinted by permission of *The Wall Street Journal*, © Dow Jones & Company, Inc. All rights reserved.

TABLE 11–8	DURATION OF ZERO-COUPON VERSUS 8 PERCENT COUPON BONDS (Market Rate of Interest Is 12 Percent)			
(1)	(2)	(3)	(4)	
Years to Maturity	Duration of Zero-Coupon Bond	Duration of 8 Percent Coupon Bond	Relative Duration of Zero-Coupon to 8 Percent Coupon Bonds (2) ÷ (3)	
10	10	6.8374	1.4625	
20	20	8.9390	2.2374	
30	30	9.3662	3.2030	
40	40	9.3972	4.2566	
50	50	9.3716	5.3353	

The article cited one client buying $100,000 of zero coupons, thinking they were similar to short-term Treasury bill investments, only to find out four weeks later that his zero-coupon bonds had declined in value by $24,000.

To put the volatility of a zero-coupon bond into better perspective, we compare the duration of a zero-coupon bond to that of an 8 percent coupon bond for several maturities in Table 11–8.

The far right column in Table 11–8 indicates the ratio of duration between zero-coupon and 8 percent coupon rate bonds. As stressed throughout the chapter, duration represents a measure of price sensitivity. Thus, for a 10-year maturity period, a zero-coupon bond is almost 1½ times as price sensitive as an 8 percent coupon rate bond (the ratio in the last column is 1.4625). For a 20-year maturity period, it is over two times more price sensitive (2.2374), and for 50 years the duration, or price sensitivity ratio, is over five times greater (5.3353). This might explain why zero-coupons were much more sensitive to rising interest rates during 1983–84 as described in the story in *The Wall Street Journal*. Of course, tremendous profits can be made in zero-coupon bonds when there is a sharp drop in interest rates as in early 1985.

THE USES OF DURATION

Duration is primarily used as a measure to judge bond price sensitivity to interest-rate changes. Since duration includes information on several variables (maturity, coupon rate, and market rate of interest), it captures more information than any one of them. It therefore allows more accurate decisions for complex bond strategies. One such strategy involves the timing of investment inflows to provide a needed cash outlay at a known future date. Perhaps $1 million is needed after five years. Everything is tailored to this five-year time horizon. If interest rates go up, there will be a decline in the value of the portfolio but a higher reinvestment rate opportunity for inflows. Similarly, if interest rates go down, there will be capital appreciation for the portfolio but a lower reinvestment rate opportunity. By tying all the investment decisions to a duration period, the portfolio manager can take advantage of these counter

TABLE 11–9   A SAMPLE OF 20 BONDS FROM MOODY'S INVESTMENT-GRADE
CORPORATE BOND INDEX
(As of May 5, 1988)

Issuer	Coupon	Maturity	Rating	Duration	Price	Yield To Maturity
Alabama Power	8.875	01–Aug–2003	A	8.13	91.259	10.00
American Tel & Tel	7.125	01–Dec–2003	A	8.59	80.158	9.61
American Tel & Tel	7.000	15–Feb–2001	A	8.00	81.207	9.58
American Tel & Tel	8.625	01–Apr–2026	A	10.21	86.107	10.06
American Tel & Tel	5.500	01–Jan–1997	A	6.57	77.250	9.40
American Tel & Tel	4.375	01–Oct–1996	A	6.80	71.683	9.30
Amoco Corp	7.875	01–Aug–2007	Aaa	9.23	84.455	9.67
Atlantic Richfield Co	10.875	15–Jul–2005	A	8.19	107.778	9.92
Atlantic Richfield Co	10.375	15–Jul–1995	A	5.15	105.521	9.30
Atlantic Richfield Co	9.875	01–Mar–2016	A	9.72	99.740	9.90
Atlantic Richfield Co	9.125	01–Mar–2011	A	9.40	93.011	9.90
B P North America	9.500	01–Jan–1998	A	6.32	99.666	9.55
Boise Cascade Corp	8.375	15–Aug–1994	Baa	4.88	94.861	9.47
Capital Cities Communications	11.625	15–Aug–2015	A	9.01	108.579	10.65
Capital Cities/ABC Finance Co	8.750	15–Mar–2016	A	9.74	86.968	10.16
Capital Cities/ABC Finance Co	8.250	15–Mar–1996	A	5.79	92.907	9.55
Caterpillar Inc	8.000	01–Nov–2001	A	8.15	88.456	9.54
Champion International Corp	8.500	15–Aug–1993	Baa	4.27	97.000	9.22
Chase Manhattan Corp	7.375	01–Feb–1994	Baa	4.63	90.226	9.63
Chevron Corp	8.750	01–Jul–2005	Aa	8.61	92.690	9.63

Source: Moody's Investment-Grade Corporate Bond Index, May 5, 1988.

forces to ensure a necessary outcome. This strategy is called **immunization** and is used by insurance companies, pension funds, and other institutional money managers to protect their portfolios against swings in interest rates. For a more-comprehensive discussion of immunization strategies, an article by Fisher and Weil is an appropriate source.[7] For an excellent criticism of duration and immunization strategy, see Yawitz and Marshall.[8] One of the problems with duration analysis is that it often assumes a parallel shift in yield curves. Although long-duration bonds are clearly more price sensitive than shorter-duration bonds, there is no assurance that long- and short-term interest rates will move by equal amounts.

More and more duration data is becoming available for use by all bond investors. Each week *Moody's Bond Survey* presents data on the 80 bonds included in Moody's Investment-Grade Corporate Bond Index. These data include the bond issuer, coupon, maturity, rating, duration, price, yield to maturity, weekly price change, and the weekly change in yield to maturity. While all 80 bonds are not listed in Table 11–9, the reader can see from the sample that duration varies according to the bond-pricing factors presented in Chapter 10 and more fully developed in this chapter.

[7]Lawrence Fisher and Roman L. Weil, "Coping with Risk of Interest Rate Fluctuations: Returns to Bondholders from Naive and Optimal Strategies," *Journal of Business*, October 1971, pp. 408–31.

[8]Jess B. Yawitz and William J. Marshall, "The Shortcomings of Duration as a Risk Measure for Bonds," *The Journal of Financial Research*, Summer 1981, pp. 91–101.

BOND REINVESTMENT ASSUMPTIONS
AND TERMINAL WEALTH ANALYSIS

Reinvestment Assumptions

As indicated in the previous section, one concern an investor may have when purchasing bonds is that the interest income will not be reinvested to earn the same return that the coupon payment represents. This may not be a problem for an individual consuming the interest payments, but it could be a serious concern for individuals building a retirement portfolio or a pension fund manager accumulating funds for future payout to retirees. The crucial issue is the amount of money accumulated at the time the retirement fund will be used to cover living expenses. And of course, one major determinant of the ending value of a retirement fund is the rate of return on coupon payments as they are reinvested.

Since the late 1960s, interest rates have been much higher and more volatile than during the previous time periods. This has caused more emphasis on the management of fixed-income securities, not only in the selection of maturity but also in the switching from short- to long-term securities. These volatile high rates have caused more emphasis on concepts like duration to measure bond price sensitivity and on total return as a measure of bond management success. Given that interest rates change daily and by large amounts over the period of a year, what impact would a lower or higher **reinvestment assumption** have on the outcome of your retirement nest egg?

First, let us look at a partial reproduction of Appendix A at the back of the text (reproduced in Table 11–10). The material covers the compound sum of $1. Appendix A assumes that all interest is reinvested at the stated rate in order to find the ending value of $1 invested to maturity. For our current analysis, we are assuming annual interest (though the answer only changes slightly if we use semiannual interest).

The table values are given in $1 amounts, so for a $1,000 bond we would just move the decimal three places to the right. A $1,000 bond having a 12 percent coupon rate with interest being reinvested at 12 percent would compound to $93,051 over 40 years, while a 7 percent coupon bond reinvested at 7 percent would only compound to $14,974 over a similar time period. A difference of 5 percent in the rates creates a total difference of $78,077. This is quite a large difference. Notice that the longer the compounding period, the larger the difference. From further inspection of Table 11–10, other comparisons can be made between years and total ending values.

The importance of the reinvestment assumption can also be viewed from the perspective of its contribution to total wealth. For example, an investor owning a 40-year bond with a 12 percent coupon rate and an assumed reinvestment rate of 12 percent will have an accumulated value of $93,051. In terms of payout, $4,800 (40 × $120) comes directly from 40 years of 12 percent interest payments, $1,000 comes from principal, and the balance of $87,251 comes from interest that is earned on the annual interest payments. In this case, interest on interest represents 93.8 percent of the overall return ($87,251/ $93,051).

TABLE 11–10	COMPOUND SUM OF $1.00 (From Appendix A)					
	Period	7 Percent	8 Percent	9 Percent	10 Percent	11 Percent	12 Percent
	10	$ 1.967	$ 2.159	$ 2.367	$ 2.594	$ 2.839	$ 3.106
	20	3.870	4.661	5.604	6.727	8.062	9.646
	30	7.612	10.063	13.268	17.449	22.892	29.960
	40	14.974	21.725	31.409	45.259	65.001	93.051

Terminal Wealth Analysis

Now, we will assume a reinvestment assumption different from the coupon rate. Take the two extreme values from Table 11–10 of 12 percent and 7 percent. Assume that you buy a bond having a 12 percent coupon rate, but the interest can only be reinvested at 7 percent. To find the ending value of this investment, we will need to use a **terminal wealth table**.

Table 11–11 is called a terminal wealth table because it generates the ending value of the investment at the end of each year, assuming that the bond has a *maturity* date corresponding to that year. Let's use 10 years as an example in examining Table 11–11. If the bond matures in 10 years, the $1,000 principal in column (2) will be recovered. Also the investor will receive $120 in annual interest (12 percent of $1,000) in year 10 as indicated in column (3). In column (4), the accumulated interest up to the beginning of year 10 is shown. The reinvestment rate on this previously accumulated interest is a mere 7 percent as indicated in column (5). The interest on the previously accumulated interest is $100.62 (.07 × $1,437.38). Finally, the total interest for year 10 is shown in column (7). This consists of the coupon interest of $120 and the interest on interest of $100.62 and totals to $220.62. The total ending value of the portfolio is shown in column (8). The ending value consists of the recovered principal of $1,000 plus the accumulated interest of $1,437.38 up to the beginning of year 10 plus the total interest paid in year 10 of $220.62. The ending wealth value (portfolio sum) thus shown in column (8) is $2,658.00. The value is summarized below.

Recovered principal	$1,000.00	Column (2)
Accumulated interest (beginning of year 10)	1,437.38	Column (4)
Total annual interest (during year 10)	220.62	Column (7)
Ending wealth value (portfolio sum)	$2,658.00	Column (8)

A $1,000 investment that grows to $2,658.00 after 10 years is the equivalent of a $1 investment that grows to 2.65800 as indicated in column (9). The annual percentage return for a $1 investment that grows to 2.65800 after 10 years is 10.26 percent as indicated in column (10).

A similar analysis can be done for all other maturity periods running from 1 to 40 years. One thing to notice from Table 11–11 is that the longer the maturity period of the bond, the greater the effect the low 7 percent reinvestment rate has on the bond. For 5 years, the annual percentage return

TABLE 11–11		TERMINAL WEALTH TABLE (12 Percent Coupon with 7 Percent Reinvestment Rate on Interest)							
(1)	(2)	(3)	(4)	(5)	(6)	(7)	(8)	(9)	(10)
Years to Maturity	Principal	Annual Coupon Interest	Accumulated Interest★	Reinvestment Rate on Interest	Interest on Interest	Total Annual Interest	Portfolio Sum	Compound Sum Factor	Annual Percentage Return
0.0	$1,000.00								
1.0	1,000.00	$120.00	$ 0.00			$ 120.00	$ 1,120.00	1.12000	12.00%
2.0	1,000.00	120.00	120.00	.07	$ 8.40	128.40	1,248.40	1.24840	11.73
3.0	1,000.00	120.00	248.40	.07	17.39	137.39	1,385.79	1.38579	11.48
4.0	1,000.00	120.00	385.79	.07	27.01	147.01	1,532.80	1.53280	11.26
5.0	1,000.00	120.00	532.80	.07	37.30	157.30	1,690.10	1.69010	11.06
6.0	1,000.00	120.00	690.10	.07	48.31	168.31	1,858.41	1.85841	10.86
7.0	1,000.00	120.00	858.41	.07	60.09	180.09	2,038.50	2.03850	10.71
8.0	1,000.00	120.00	1,038.50	.07	72.70	192.70	2,231.20	2.23120	10.55
9.0	1,000.00	120.00	1,231.20	.07	86.18	206.18	2,437.38	2.43738	10.40
10.0	1,000.00	120.00	1,437.38	.07	100.62	220.62	2,658.00	2.65800	10.26
11.0	1,000.00	120.00	1,658.00	.07	116.06	236.06	2,894.06	2.89406	10.14
12.0	1,000.00	120.00	1,894.06	.07	132.58	252.58	3,146.64	3.14664	10.02
13.0	1,000.00	120.00	2,146.64	.07	150.26	270.26	3,416.90	3.41690	9.91
14.0	1,000.00	120.00	2,416.90	.07	169.18	289.18	3,706.08	3.70608	9.80
15.0	1,000.00	120.00	2,706.08	.07	189.43	309.43	4,015.51	4.01551	9.71
16.0	1,000.00	120.00	3,015.51	.07	211.09	331.09	4,346.60	4.34660	9.61
17.0	1,000.00	120.00	3,346.60	.07	234.26	354.26	4,700.86	4.70086	9.54
18.0	1,000.00	120.00	3,700.86	.07	259.06	379.06	5,079.92	5.07992	9.44
19.0	1,000.00	120.00	4,079.92	.07	285.59	405.59	5,485.51	5.48551	9.37
20.0	1,000.00	120.00	4,485.51	.07	313.99	433.99	5,919.50	5.91950	9.29
21.0	1,000.00	120.00	4,919.50	.07	344.37	464.37	6,383.87	6.38387	9.22
22.0	1,000.00	120.00	5,383.87	.07	376.87	496.87	6,880.74	6.88074	9.16
23.0	1,000.00	120.00	5,880.74	.07	411.65	531.65	7,412.39	7.41239	9.09
24.0	1,000.00	120.00	6,412.39	.07	448.87	568.87	7,981.26	7.98126	9.04
25.0	1,000.00	120.00	6,981.26	.07	488.69	608.69	8,589.95	8.58995	8.98
26.0	1,000.00	120.00	7,589.95	.07	531.30	651.30	9,241.25	9.24125	8.92
27.0	1,000.00	120.00	8,241.25	.07	576.89	696.89	9,938.14	9.93814	8.87
28.0	1,000.00	120.00	8,938.14	.07	625.67	745.67	10,683.81	10.68381	8.82
29.0	1,000.00	120.00	9,683.81	.07	677.87	797.87	11,481.68	11.48168	8.78
30.0	1,000.00	120.00	10,481.68	.07	733.72	853.72	12,335.40	12.33540	8.73
31.0	1,000.00	120.00	11,335.40	.07	793.48	913.48	13,248.88	13.24888	8.69
32.0	1,000.00	120.00	12,248.88	.07	857.42	977.42	14,226.30	14.22630	8.65
33.0	1,000.00	120.00	13,226.30	.07	925.84	1,045.84	15,272.14	15.27214	8.61
34.0	1,000.00	120.00	14,272.14	.07	999.05	1,119.05	16,391.19	16.39119	8.57
35.0	1,000.00	120.00	15,391.19	.07	1,077.38	1,197.38	17,588.57	17.58857	8.53
36.0	1,000.00	120.00	16,588.57	.07	1,161.20	1,281.20	18,869.77	18.86977	8.50
37.0	1,000.00	120.00	17,869.77	.07	1,250.88	1,370.88	20,240.65	20.24065	8.46
38.0	1,000.00	120.00	19,240.65	.07	1,346.85	1,466.85	21,707.50	21.70750	8.43
39.0	1,000.00	120.00	20,707.50	.07	1,449.53	1,569.53	23,277.03	23.27703	8.40
40.0	1,000.00	120.00	22,277.03	.07	1,559.39	1,679.39	24,956.42	24.95642	8.37

★At beginning of year.

(column 10) is 11.06 percent; for 15 years, 9.71 percent; and for 40 years, 8.37 percent.

What is the actual difference between the ending value for a 40-year, 12 percent coupon rate bond assuming a *12 percent* reinvestment rate and the 40-year, *7 percent* reinvestment rate just presented in Table 11–11? Earlier in this section we saw in using Table 11–10 that a 12 percent coupon rate bond with an assumed 12 percent reinvestment rate for 40 years would grow to $93,051. In Table 11–11, we see a 12 percent coupon rate bond with a 7 percent reinvestment rate will only grow to $24,956.42 after 40 years. It should be evident that it is not only the coupon rate that matters but the reinvestment rate as well.

If the bond were not held to maturity in our analysis, then we would have to rely on the realized rate of return analysis developed in Chapter 10. The realized rate of return approach would assume that the bond is not held to maturity and that it is sold at either a gain or a loss. In the case of the bond analyzed in the terminal wealth table (11–11), we know that since interest rates are assumed to decline, any sale of the bond before maturity should result in a capital gain. How large that capital gain would be will be dependent on its duration. Terminal wealth analysis is a way of analyzing the reinvestment assumption when bonds are held to maturity, while the realized yield approach assumes that bonds are actively traded to take advantage of interest-rate swings.

Zero-Coupon Bonds and Terminal Wealth

One of the benefits of **zero-coupon bonds** is that they lock in a compound rate of return (or reinvestment rate) for the life of the bond *if held to maturity*. There are no coupon payments during the life of the bond to be reinvested, so the originally quoted rate holds throughout if held to maturity. If a $1,000 par value, 15-year zero-coupon bond is quoted at a price of $183 to yield 12 percent, you truly have locked in a 12 percent reinvestment rate. Some would say you have not only locked in 12 percent but have thrown away the key. In any event, zero-coupon bonds allow you to predetermine your reinvestment rate.

Of course, if a zero-coupon bond is sold before maturity, there could be large swings in the sales price of the bond because of its high duration characteristics. Under this circumstance, the locked-in reinvestment concept for the zero-coupon bond loses much of its meaning. It is only valid when the zero-coupon bond is held to maturity.

12

CONVERTIBLE SECURITIES AND WARRANTS

A n investment in convertible securities or warrants offers the market participant special opportunities to meet investment objectives. For conservative investors, convertible securities can offer regular income and potential downside protection against falling stock prices. Convertibles also offer capital gains opportunities for an investor desiring the appreciation potential of an equity investment. Warrants are more speculative securities and offer the chance for leveraged returns.

These securities have been used as financing alternatives by corporations in periods of high interest rates or tight money. Also, convertibles have been utilized as a medium of exchange for acquiring other companies' stock in mergers and acquisitions. Convertibles and warrants have advantages to the corporation and to the owner of the security. It is important to realize as we go through this chapter that what is an advantage to the corporation is often a disadvantage to the investor, and vice versa. These securities involve trade-offs between the buyer and the corporation that are taken into consideration in the pricing of each security.

CONVERTIBLE SECURITIES

A **convertible security** is a bond or share of preferred stock that can be converted into common stock at the option of the holder. Thus, the owner has a fixed-income security that can be transferred to common stock if and when the affairs of the firm indicate that such a conversion is desirable. For purposes of our discussion, we will use a Tandy Corporation $6^1/_2$ percent convertible bond (debenture) rated Aa by Moody's as an example. While this Tandy bond was called for redemption on September 10, 1980, we feel that it still serves as one of the best examples of the benefits and perils of owning convertible bonds. During the 23 months this bond was outstanding, an investor could have had a change in price of between -35 percent and $+270$ percent.

In general, the best time to buy convertible bonds is when interest rates are high (bond prices are depressed) and when stock prices are relatively low. A purchase at times like these increases the probability of a successful investment because rising stock prices and falling interest rates both exert upward pressure on the price of a convertible security. This will become more apparent as we proceed through the chapter.

CONVERSION PRICE AND CONVERSION RATIO

The following quote from the footnotes to Tandy's 1979 Annual Report indicates the kind of information available to the bond- or stockholder.

On October 31, 1978, the Company issued $100,000,000 of $6^1/_2$ percent convertible subordinated debentures due 2003. These debentures are convertible at the option of the holder into common stock of the Company at $29 per share, unless previously redeemed. The debentures may be redeemed, at the Company's option, at any time in whole or in part on not less than 30 nor more than 60 days notice at 106.50 percent of their principal amount on or before December

31, 1979. The redemption price declines annually to 100.00 in 1998. Mandatory sinking fund payments are required, beginning in 1989, sufficient to redeem on December 31 of each year $5,000,000 principal amount of debentures at par.

Most of the terms contained in the quote are simply a review of your knowledge on bonds. However, one question is not answered directly. How many shares of common stock are you entitled to receive upon conversion? Notice that the debentures are convertible at $29 per share. This is called the **conversion price.** The face value ($1,000) or par value never changes (the market price does), so by dividing the face value by the conversion price, we get the number of shares received upon conversion of one $1,000 bond. This is called the **conversion ratio.**

$$\frac{\text{Face value}}{\text{Conversion price}} = \text{Conversion ratio}$$

$$(12\text{--}1)$$

For the Tandy convertible bond, an investor would receive 34.4827 shares for each bond.

$$\frac{\$1,000 \text{ (face value)}}{\$29 \text{ share (conversion price)}} = \frac{34.4827 \text{ shares}}{\text{(conversion ratio)}}$$

Value of the Convertible Bond

Let us follow the October 31, 1978, issue of Tandy's $6\frac{1}{2}$ percent convertible bond through conversion on September 10, 1980. The bond was originally sold at $1,000, and the common stock price on the day of this offering closed at $23\frac{1}{8}$ on the New York Stock Exchange. If the bondholder converted the bond into 34.48 shares of common stock, what would be the market value of the common stock received? We can find this by multiplying the conversion ratio by the market price per share of the common stock, and we get a value of $797.35.

$$\begin{array}{ccc}
\text{Conversion ratio} \times \text{Common stock price} & = & \text{Conversion value} \\
34.48 \text{ shares} \times \quad \$23.125 & = & \$797.35 \text{ (round to \$797)}
\end{array}$$

$$(12\text{--}2)$$

This value is called the **conversion value** and indicates the value of the underlying shares of common stock each bond represents.

The convertible bond also has what is called a **pure bond value.** This represents its value as a straight bond (nonconvertible). In the case of Tandy Corporation, there was also a straight debenture outstanding, carrying a coupon rate of 10 percent and a market price of $960. Based on this information, the yield to maturity on a nonconvertible Tandy bond would be 10.45 percent at the time the convertible bond was issued. If the $6\frac{1}{2}$ percent Tandy bond were valued as a straight debenture at this 10.45 percent yield to maturity, it

FIGURE 12–1   TANDY CONVERTIBLE BOND ON DAY OF ISSUE, OCTOBER 31, 1978

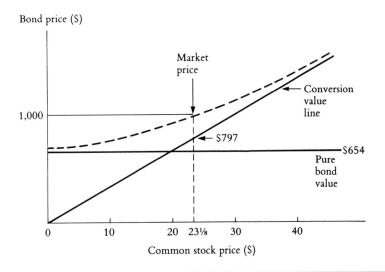

would have a pure bond value of $654.[1] This is considered the **floor price or minimum value** of the bond. The conversion value and the pure bond value can be seen in Figure 12–1, which depicts the Tandy convertible bond. As a side point, the reader should be aware that it is possible for the pure bond value to change if interest rates in the market change. This point, of course, is not reflected in Figure 12–1.

Bond Price and Premiums

You may wonder how a company can originally sell a bond for $1,000 when the conversion value is $797 and the pure bond value is $654. Let's examine these values. The difference between the bond's market price ($1,000) and the conversion value ($797) is a premium of $203; it is usually expressed as a percentage of the conversion value and thus is called the **conversion premium.** In this case, the conversion premium at issue was 25.47 percent.

$$\text{Conversion premium} = \frac{\text{Market price of bond} - \text{Conversion value}}{\text{Conversion value}}$$

$$= \frac{\$1,000 - \$797}{\$797} = \frac{\$203}{\$797}$$

$$= 25.47 \text{ percent}$$

(12–3)

[1]Using present value procedures from Chapter 10, the interest payment of $65 per year for 25 years would have a present value at 10.45 percent of $570.17, and the principal of $1,000 would have a present value of 83.34 for a total value of $653.51. We round to $654.

The $203 premium indicates the extra amount paid for the 34.48 shares of stock. Remember, in essence, you paid $29 per share for 34.48 shares by purchasing the bond, but you could have had the same number of shares purchased on the NYSE for 23$^1/_8$.

People pay the conversion premium for several reasons. In the case of Tandy's bond, the premium is somewhat larger than the usual 15 to 20 percent. First, at the time, Tandy common stock paid no dividend, while the bond paid $65 per year in interest. If the bondholder owns the bond for a little over three years, he recovers almost all the premium through the $65 yearly differential between interest and dividend income. Many companies do pay dividends on their common stock, and an analysis of interest income versus dividend income is always important in comparing a stock purchase to a convertible bond purchase.

Additionally, the bond price will rise as the stock price rises because of the convertible feature, but there is a downside limit if the stock should decline in price. This downside limit is established by the pure bond value, which in this case is $654. This downside protection is further justification for the conversion premium. One way to compute this downside protection is to calculate the difference between the market price of the bond and the pure bond value as a percentage of the market price.

$$\text{Downside risk} = \frac{\text{Market price of bond } - \text{ Pure bond value}}{\text{Market price of bond}}$$

$$= \frac{\$1,000 - \$654}{\$1,000} = \frac{\$346}{\$1,000}$$

$$= 34.6 \text{ percent}$$

(12–4)

In the case of Tandy, there is a downside limit of 34.6 percent. This is the maximum percentage the bond will decline in value if the stock price falls. One important warning is necessary—the pure bond value is sensitive to market interest rates. As competitively rated Aa bond interest rates rise, the pure bond value will decline. Therefore, downside risk can vary with changing interest rates.

The conversion premium is also affected by several other variables. The more volatile the stock price as measured by beta or standard deviation of returns, the higher the conversion premium. This occurs because the potential for capital gains is larger than on less-volatile stocks. The longer the term to maturity, the higher the premium—because there is a greater chance that the stock price could rise, making the bond more valuable.

Figure 12–2 presents a graph of the Tandy convertible bond and depicts the conversion premium in panel (a) and the downside risk in panel (b). Each is shaded. Point P in both panels represents the parity point where the conversion value equals the pure bond value. Notice that the market price follows the conversion value to the right of point P and is more influenced by the pure bond value to the left of point P. As the common stock price rises, the conversion value rises accordingly, and the bond market price also rises. Fur-

FIGURE 12–2   TANDY CONVERTIBLE BOND—6¹/₂ PERCENT, 2003 MATURITY
(Convertible into 34.4827 Shares of Common Stock as of October 31, 1978)

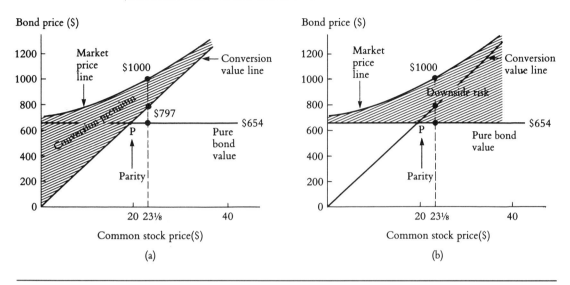

(a)   (b)

thermore, the conversion premium shrinks, and the downside risk increases, which gives the bondholder less downside protection should the stock decline. As the stock declines, the conversion value falls, and the conversion premium increases, but the downside risk declines as the pure bond value acts as a "floor value."

Let us track the Tandy bond from issue to conversion. As previously mentioned, Tandy Corporation also had a debenture (nonconvertible) outstanding with a 10 percent coupon. The debenture maintained a relatively stable price, and the yield to maturity hovered around 10.45 percent during the 22 months the convertible bond was outstanding. Given that the convertible bond would have approximately the same yield to maturity as the debenture, we assume that the pure bond value of the convertible bond stayed the same in all three panels in Figure 12–3. In panel (a), we see the original information on the convertible issue. Approximately seven months later, as shown in panel (b), Tandy common stock had declined to 18⁵/₈ and the bond to $880, creating a conversion value of $642 and a conversion premium of 37 percent. The downside risk had declined from 34.6 percent on October 31, 1978, to 25.7 percent by May 16, 1979. In retrospect, this would have been a good price at which to buy the bond. By September 10, 1980, we see in panel (c) that the stock skyrocketed to 71³/₄, and the bond had a conversion value of $2,474. This was exactly equal to the market price, as there was no conversion premium. On this date, the Tandy Corporation also called the bond at $1,061.60. Thus, the investor could allow the bond to be redeemed for cash and receive a check for $1,061.60 or convert it into 34.48 common shares worth $2,474. Because the company knows that the investor will take the higher of the two values

FIGURE 12–3   TANDY 6½ CONVERTIBLE BOND CLOSING PRICES

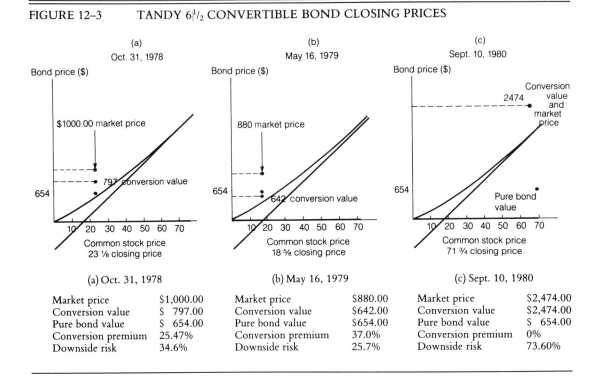

(a) Oct. 31, 1978		(b) May 16, 1979		(c) Sept. 10, 1980	
Market price	$1,000.00	Market price	$880.00	Market price	$2,474.00
Conversion value	$ 797.00	Conversion value	$642.00	Conversion value	$2,474.00
Pure bond value	$ 654.00	Pure bond value	$654.00	Pure bond value	$ 654.00
Conversion premium	25.47%	Conversion premium	37.0%	Conversion premium	0%
Downside risk	34.6%	Downside risk	25.7%	Downside risk	73.60%

between the call price and conversion value, the call serves to force conversion of the bond into shares of common stock.

Comparison to Common Stock

Would you have been better off putting $1,000 in Tandy stock on October 31, 1978, or $1,000 into the convertible bond? One thousand dollars in Tandy stock at 23$^1/_8$ would have purchased 43.24 shares, while $1,000 invested in the bond got the investor 34.48 shares. On the day of redemption (September 10, 1980), a stock investment would have been worth $3,103 and the convertible bond, $2,474 plus $128 in interest over the life of the issue, or $2,602. The common stock investor would have been better off, but if the stock had gone down sharply, then the convertible with its floor value would have been the better investment. Table 12–1 shows the comparison between a stock investment and a convertible bond investment.

Actually, we have picked one of the more-successful convertible bond offerings in recent years. If the convertible bondholder had taken common shares on the call date, these 34.48 shares would have increased to 137.93 shares by June 1981 through several two-for-one stock splits. During 1983, Tandy common stock reached $64.50 per share, which would have created a total value of $8,896.00 on the original $1,000 investment. However, by July 1984, the shares fell to $25.25 ($3,483), and in June 1988, the shares were $45 ($6,207),

TABLE 12–1	COMPARATIVE TANDY CORPORATION INVESTMENTS							
	Amount Invested October 31, 1978	Shares	Stock Prices September 10, 1980	Ending Value	Total Dividends	Total Interest	Total Value
Stock	$1,000	43.24	71 ³/₄	$3,103	$0	—	$3,103
Convertible bond	$1,000	34.48	71 ³/₄	2,474	—	$128	2,602

which shows that timing is important in taking advantage of price movements. The danger in using an example with such a large percentage increase is that you may think convertible bonds are always a good investment.

Table 12–2 presents a selection of convertible bonds and preferred stock and helps to illustrate several basic points. First, notice that there are no bonds rated A, Aa, or Aaa. While an occasional convertible bond may have a rating of A or higher, in general, convertible bonds are usually lower-quality subordinated debentures. Notice that the Alliant Computer and Arrow Electronics bonds have conversion premiums of approximately 200 percent. This indicates that the stock price has fallen since the original issue and that the bond price is trading based on its pure bond value (investment value) or interest-paying ability rather than the stock price. The conversion value is extremely low relative to the bond price, and the common stock would have to at least double in value before an investor would begin to benefit from an increased bond price. The Potlach B convertible *preferred stock* has a low conversion premium which indicates that the price of the preferred is selling based on the underlying common stock price.

Disadvantages to Convertibles

It has been said that everything has a price, and purchasing convertible securities at the wrong price can eliminate one of their main advantages. For example, once convertible debentures begin going up in value, the downside protection becomes pretty meaningless. In the case of Bergen Brunswig in Table 12–2, the market price is $1,003.75, while the pure bond value is $650. If the investor buys the bond at this price and the common stock declines significantly, the investor is exposed to a potential decline of $353.75 (hardly adequate protection for a true risk averter). Also, don't forget that if market yields rise, the floor price or pure bond value could decline from $650, thus creating even greater downside risk.

Another drawback with convertible bonds is that the purchaser is invariably asked to accept below-market yields on the debt instrument. The interest rate on convertibles is generally one third below that for instruments in a similar risk class (perhaps 8 percent instead of 12 percent). Figure 12–4 (upper part) illustrates the yield spreads between corporate BBB bonds, corporate AAA bonds, 6-month Treasury bills, and the Value Line's Convertible Index. As indicated in the bottom panel of the figure, the yield spread between corporate

TABLE 12-2 SELECTED CONVERTIBLE BONDS AND PREFERRED STOCK

Selected Convertible Bonds—June 1988

Issue	Coupon	Maturity	Moody's Bond Rating	Bond Price	Conversion Price/Ratio	Common Stock Price	Conversion Value	Conversion Premium	Pure Bond Value	Stock Dividend Yield	Bond Current Yield	Call Price★
AMR (American Airlines)	6.25%	1996	Ba	$932.40	$61.76/16.19sh.	$42.75	$692.12	35%	$760.00	nil.	6.7%	105.00
Alliant Computer	7.25	2012	B3	545.00	39.75/25.16	6.62	166.56	227	480.00	nil.	13.3	105.075
Arrow Electronics	9.00	2003	B2	725.00	34.80/28.73	8.63	247.94	192	620.00	nil.	12.3	104.5
Bally Manufacturing	10.00	2006	B1	897.50	32.68/30.60	16.00	489.60	83	790.00	1.3%	11.1	105.98
Bergen Brunswig Corp.	7.625	2010	Baa3	1,003.75	33.33/30.00	26.50	795.00	26	650.00	1.2	7.6	106.10

Selected Convertible Preferred Stocks—June 1988

	Dividend	Call Date	Preferred Stock Price	Common Stock Price	Conversion Ratio	Conversion Value	Conversion Premium	Pure Value†	Common Stock Dividend Yield	Preferred Stock Dividend Yield
Arrow Electronics	$1.9375	4/30/89	$16.50	$ 8.625	1.524	$13.14	23%	NMF	nil.	11.7%
Baxter Intl. B.	3.50	11/25/90	68.00	20.25	2.976	60.26	13	$36.00	2.5%	5.1
Northern Trust B	3.125	11/14/89	50.25	42.00	1.018	42.76	18	32.00	2.4	6.2
PaineWebber	1.375	3/14/89	14.88	15.00	.567	8.51	75	12.00	3.5	9.2
Potlach B	3.75	4/15/89	61.50	29.50	1.886	55.64	11	35.00	3.1	6.1

★Percent of par value of $1,000.
†Value based strictly on dividend-paying level of the preferred stock.

FIGURE 12–4   YIELD SPREADS

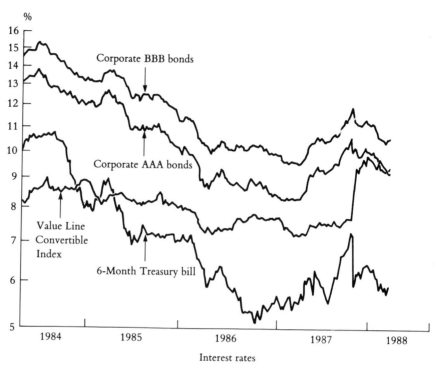

Interest rates

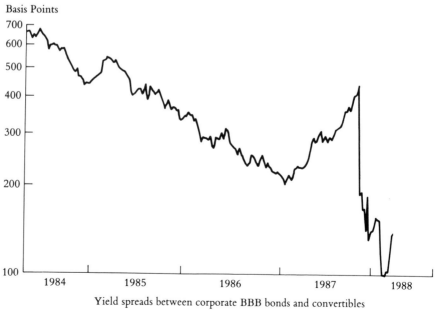

Yield spreads between corporate BBB bonds and convertibles

BBB and convertibles was between 200 and 700 basis points between 1984 and 1987, but the crash of 1987 forced up the yields on convertibles to within 100 basis points of BBB bonds. This relationship is quite unusual because convertible bonds are usually priced to yield substantially less than straight corporate bonds. Since convertibles are generally high-risk bonds, the fear generated by the crash caused the normal yield relationships to vanish as investors refused to hold convertibles at substantially lower yields.

The student will also recall that the purchaser of a convertible bond pays a premium over the conversion value. For example, if a $1,000 bond were convertible into 20 shares of common at $45 per share, a $100 conversion premium would be involved initially. If the same $1,000 were invested directly in common stock at $45 per share, 22.2 shares could be purchased. If the shares go up in value, we have 2.2 more shares on which to garner a profit.

From the institutional investor's standpoint, many convertible securities lack liquidity because of small trading volume or even the small amount of convertibles issued by one company. The institutions tend to stick with convertible issues of $100 million or more when they can be found.

When to Convert into Common Stock

Convertible securities generally have a call provision, such as the Tandy bond had (in the earlier description), which gives the corporation the option of redeeming the bond at a specified price before maturity. The call price is usually at a premium over par value ($1,000) in the early years of callability, and it generally declines over time to par value. We know that as the price of the common stock goes up, the convertible security will rise along with the stock so that the investor has no incentive to convert his bonds into stock. However, the corporation may use the call privilege to force conversion before maturity. Companies usually force conversion when the conversion value is well above the call price, like the Tandy offer which forced conversion on September 10, 1980, when the conversion value was $2,474 and the call price was $1,061.60. Investors will take the shares rather than the call price since the shares are worth more. This enables the company to turn debt into equity on its balance sheet and makes new debt issues a better risk for future lenders because of higher interest coverage and a lower debt-to-equity ratio.

Corporations may also encourage voluntary conversion by using a step-up in the conversion price over time. When the bond is issued, the contract may specify the following conversion provisions.

	Conversion Price	Conversion Ratio
First five years	$40	25.0 shares
Next three years	45	22.2 shares
Next two years	50	20.0 shares
Next five years	55	18.2 shares

At the end of each time period, there is a strong inducement to convert rather than accept an adjustment to a higher conversion price and a lower conversion ratio. This is especially true if the bond's conversion value is the dominating influence on the market price of the bond. In the case where the conversion value is below the pure bond value and where the interest income is greater than the dividend income, an investor will most likely not be induced to convert through the step-up feature.

About the only other reason for voluntarily converting is if the dividend income received on the common stock is greater than the interest income on the bond. Even in this case, risk-averse investors may want to hold the bond because interest is guaranteed, whereas dividends may be reduced. As with most investment decisions, investors must consider their expectations of future corporate and market conditions. Hard-and-fast rules are difficult to find, and different investors may react according to their own risk aversion and objectives.

ADVANTAGES AND DISADVANTAGES TO THE ISSUING CORPORATION

Having established the fundamental characteristics of the convertible security from the investor viewpoint, let us now turn the coin over and examine the factors a corporate financial officer must consider in weighing the advisability of a convertible offer for the firm.

It has been established that the interest rate paid on convertible issues is lower than that paid on a straight debt instrument. Also, the convertible feature may be the only device for allowing smaller corporations access to the bond market. In this day of debt-ridden corporate balance sheets, investor acceptance of new debt may be contingent upon a special sweetener, such as the ability to convert to common stock.

Convertible debentures are also attractive to a corporation that feels its stock is currently undervalued. For example, assume a corporation's $1,000 bonds are convertible into 20 shares of common stock at a conversion price of $50. Also assume the company's common stock has a current price of $45, and new shares of stock might be sold at only $44.[2] Thus, the corporation will effectively receive $6 over current market price, assuming future conversion. Of course, one can also argue that if the firm had delayed the issuance of common stock or convertibles for a year or two, the stock might have gone up from $45 to $60 or $65, and new common stock might have been sold at this lofty price.

To translate this to overall numbers for the firm, if a corporation needs $10 million in funds and offers straight stock now at a new price of $44, it must issue 227,272 shares ($10 million/$44 per share). With convertibles, the number of shares potentially issued is only 200,000 shares ($10 million/$50 per share). Finally, if no stock or convertible bonds are issued now and the stock goes up to a level at which new shares can be offered at a price of $60, only 166,667 will be required ($10 million/$60).

---

[2]There is always a bit of underpricing to ensure the success of a new offering.

Another matter of concern to the corporation is the accounting treatment accorded to convertibles. In the funny-money days of the 1960s' conglomerate merger movement, corporate management often chose convertible securities over common stock because the convertibles had a nondilutive effect on earnings per share. As is indicated in the following section on reporting earnings for convertibles, the rules were changed in 1969, and this practice is no longer followed.

ACCOUNTING CONSIDERATIONS
WITH CONVERTIBLES

Prior to 1969, the full impact of the conversion privilege as it applied to convertible securities, warrants (long-term options to buy stock), and other dilutive securities was not adequately reflected in reported earnings per share. Since all of these securities may generate additional common stock in the future, the potential effect of **dilution** should be considered. Let us examine the unadjusted (for conversion) financial statements of the XYZ Corporation in Table 12–3.

An analyst would hardly be satisfied in accepting the unadjusted earnings per share figure of $1 for the XYZ Corporation. In computing earnings per share, we have not accounted for the 400,000 additional shares of common stock that could be created by converting the bonds. How then do we make this full disclosure? According to *APB Opinion No. 15,* issued by the American Institute of Certified Public Accountants in 1969, we need to compute earnings per share using two different methods when there is potential dilution; **primary earnings per share** and **fully diluted earnings per share**.

1. Primary earnings per share

$$= \frac{\text{Adjusted earnings after taxes}}{\text{Shares outstanding} + \text{Common stock equivalents}}$$

(12–5)

Common stock equivalents include warrants, other options, and any convertible securities that paid less than two thirds of the going interest rate at time of issue.[3]

2. Fully diluted earnings per share

$$= \frac{\text{Adjusted earnings after taxes}}{\begin{array}{c}\text{Shares outstanding} + \text{Common stock equivalents} \\ + \text{All convertibles regardless of the interest rate}\end{array}}$$

(12–6)

The intent in computing both primary and fully diluted earnings per share is to consider the effect of potential dilution. Common stock equivalents rep-

---

[3]The going interest rate was initially defined as the prime interest rate in *APB Opinion No. 15* (1969). In 1982, the Financial Accounting Standards Board defined the going interest rate as the average Aa bond yield at the time of issue.

TABLE 12–3	XYZ CORPORATION

1. Capital section of balance sheet:

Common stock (1 million shares at $10 par)	$10,000,000
4.5% convertible debentures (10,000 debentures of $1,000; convertible into 40 shares per bond, or a total of 400,000 shares)	10,000,000
Retained earnings	20,000,000
Net worth	$40,000,000

2. Condensed income statement:

Earnings before interest and taxes	$ 2,950,000
Interest (4.5% of $10 million of convertibles)	450,000
Earnings before taxes	$ 2,500,000
Taxes (40%)	1,000,000
Earnings after taxes	$ 1,000,000

3. Earnings per share (unadjusted):

$$\frac{\text{Earnings after taxes}}{\text{Shares of common stock}} = \frac{\$1,000,000}{1,000,000} = \$1$$

resent those securities that are capable of generating new shares of common stock in the future. Note that convertible securities may or may not be required in computing primary earnings per share depending on rates, but they must be included in computing fully diluted earnings per share.

In the case of the XYZ Corporation in Table 12–3, the convertibles pay 4.5 percent interest. We assume that the going interest rate was 9 percent at the time they were issued, so they are considered as common stock equivalents and are included in both primary and fully diluted earnings per share.

We get new earnings per share for the XYZ Corporation by assuming that 400,000 new shares will be created from potential conversion, while at the same time, allowing for the reduction in interest payments that would take place as a result of the conversion of the debt to common stock. Since before-tax interest payments on the convertibles are $450,000, the after-tax interest cost ($270,000) will be saved and can be added back to income. After-tax interest cost is determined by multiplying interest payments by one minus the tax rate or $450,000 (1 − .4) = $270,000. Making the appropriate adjustments to the numerator and denominator, we show adjusted earnings per share.

$$\frac{\text{Primary earnings}}{\text{per share}^4} = \frac{\text{Adjusted earnings after taxes}}{\text{Shares outstanding} + \text{Common stock equivalents}}$$

$$= \frac{\overset{\substack{\text{Reported} \\ \text{earnings}}}{\$1,000,000} + \overset{\substack{\text{Interest} \\ \text{savings}}}{\$270,000}}{1,000,000 + 400,000} = \frac{\$1,270,000}{1,400,000} = \$.91$$

---

[4]Same as fully diluted in this instance.

TABLE 12-4   SELECTED WARRANTS AS OF JUNE 3, 1988

(1) Name of Firm, Place of Warrant Listing, and Stock Listing*	(2) Warrant Price	(3) Per- Share Stock Price	(4) Per- Share Option Price	(5) Intrinsic Value† [(3) − (4)]	(6) Speculative Premium [(2) − (5)]	(7) Percent Stock Must Rise to Break Even	(8) Number of Shares per Warrant	(9) Due Date
1. Atlas Corp., ASE, NYSE	$12.625	$35.00	$31.25	$ 3.75	$ 8.88	25.37%	1.00	Perpetual
2. Bristol-Myers, NYSE, NYSE	8.25	41.25	16.42	8.25	.00	0	.332	12/31/94
3. Cetus Corp., OTC, OTC	3.50	11.25	30.00	−18.75	22.25	197.78	1.00	6/30/93
4. Intel Corp., OTC, OTC	13.875	32.00	26.67	8.00	5.88	18.38	1.50	5/15/95
5. Navistar Intl., NYSE, NYSE	3.75	6.875	5.00	1.875	1.875	27.20	1.00	12/15/93
6. Pan Am Corp., NYSE, NYSE	.625	2.625	8.00	−5.38	6.01	228.95	1.00	5/01/93
7. Turner Broadcasting, OTC, ASE	8.00	14.50	11.25	6.50	1.50	10.34	2.00	12/15/91
8. Wickes Companies, OTC, NYSE	3.75	10.375	22.15	−11.78	15.53	149.69	1.00	1/26/92

*OTC = Over-the-counter market, NYSE = New York Stock Exchange; AMEX = American Stock Exchange.

†Even though the intrinsic value is negative in several cases, a warrant may not have an actual value of less than zero. The negative values are given so that the speculative premium may be calculated easily. Although the intrinsic value is normally the stock price (3) minus the option price (4), some adjustment may have to be made for number of shares per warrant as shown in column (8).

We see a 9-cent reduction from the earnings per share figure of $1 in Table 12–3. The new figure is the value that a sophisticated security analyst would utilize.

INNOVATIONS IN CONVERTIBLE SECURITIES

Not all convertible securities are convertible into the common stock of the company issuing the convertible. Some convertibles are convertible into bonds, preferred stock, stock of another company, or another type of asset.

Another type of new convertible security bears mentioning. For many companies recovering from years of losses and having tax-loss carryforwards, "convertible exchangeable preferred stock" is a security that can improve the firm's balance sheet and provide high returns to investors. A firm with losses does not need tax-deductible interest expenses but does need balanced financing. Since no taxes are due, preferred dividends are no different than interest expenses to the issuing company. When the issuing firm becomes taxable again, it can exchange the preferred stock for debt with the same conversion ratio and then can utilize the tax savings from the deductible interest expense. The exchange takes place without the cost of new underwriting fees.

SPECULATING THROUGH WARRANTS

A warrant is an option to buy a stated number of shares of stock at a specified price over a given time period. A list of eight warrants is presented in Table 12–4 that demonstrates the relationships discussed in the following sections. For example, Pan Am Corp. (Pan American Airlines—number 6 in the table) has a warrant outstanding that allows the owner to buy one share of common stock at $8 per share (column 4) until May 1, 1993. Pan Am has been struggling to stay alive in the airline competition, and the stock price as of June 1988 was $2.625. If Pan Am can return to profitability, the common stock could rise above $8 per share, and the warrants could become valuable. If the stock does not eventually rise above the option price, it is possible that Pan Am could extend the expiration date of the warrant. Some investors are willing to pay $.625 (column 2) for each warrant with the hope that the stock price will be over $8 before the warrant expires. This could happen if the airline turns itself around or if some competitor makes a purchase offer for the company above $8 per share.

Warrants are usually issued as a sweetener to a bond offering, and they may enable the firm to issue debt when this would not be feasible otherwise. The warrants allow the bond issue to carry a lower coupon rate and are usually detachable from the bond after the issue date. After being separated from the bond, warrants have their own market price and may trade on a different market than the common stock. After the warrants are exercised, the initial debt with which they were sold remains in existence.

The financial company Bache Group (now Prudential Bache) had a bond offering October 30, 1980. They offered 35,000 units of $1,000 debentures due in the year 2000 with a coupon interest rate of 14 percent. To each bond,

30 warrants were attached. Each warrant allowed the holder to buy one share of stock at $18.50 until November 1, 1985. At the time of issue, the warrant had no true value since the common stock was selling below $18.50. During 1981, however, the stock went up as several merger offers were made for retail brokerage companies. On May 29, 1981, Bache common stock was selling at $31\frac{1}{2}$, and each warrant traded at $13\frac{5}{8}$. The 30 warrants received with each bond were now worth $408.75 and provided the sweetener every bondholder had hoped for.

Because a warrant is dependent on the market movement of the underlying common stock and has no "security value" as such, it is highly speculative in nature. If the common stock of the firm is volatile, the value of the warrants may change dramatically.

Valuation of Warrants

Because the value of a warrant is closely tied to the underlying stock price, we can develop a formula for the minimum or intrinsic value of a warrant.

$$I = (M - OP) \times N$$

$$(12–7)$$

where:

I = The intrinsic or minimum value of the warrant

M = The market value of the common stock

OP = The **option** or **exercise price** of the warrant

N = The number of shares each warrant entitles the holder to purchase

Assume that the common stock of the Graham Corporation is $25 per share, and each warrant carries an option to purchase one share at $20 over the next 10 years. Using Formula (12–7), the minimum value is $5 [($25 − $20) × 1]. Since the warrant has 10 more years to run and is an effective vehicle for speculative trading, it may well trade for over $5. If the warrant were selling for $9, we would say that it had an **intrinsic or formula value** of $5 and a **speculative premium** of $4.

Even if the stock were trading at less than $20 (the option price on the warrant), the warrant might still have some value in the market. Speculators might purchase the warrant in the hope that the common stock value would increase sufficiently in the future to make the option provision valuable. If the common stock were selling for $15 per share, thus giving the warrant a negative intrinsic value of $5, the warrant might still command a value of $1 or $2 in anticipation of increased common stock value.

Observe in previously presented Table 12–4 the intrinsic values (column 5) and speculative premiums (column 6). In many cases, firms with negative intrinsic values still have large speculative premiums.

As an example of an extreme case, Cetus Corporation's common stock was trading $18.75 below the exercise price on the warrant, and yet the warrant still traded for $3.50. This lead to a speculative premium of $22.25. Cetus

FIGURE 12–5   MARKET PRICE RELATIONSHIPS FOR A WARRANT

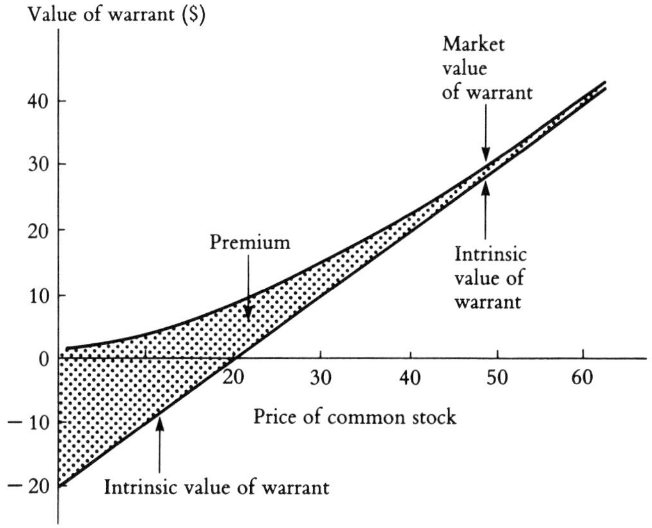

warrants are due to expire on June 30, 1993. Because Cetus is in the biotech-nology field, one new drug that cures cancer (it is working on Interleukin 2) could cause the stock to soar.

The typical relationship between the market price and the intrinsic value of a warrant is depicted in Figure 12–5. We assume the warrant entitles the holder to purchase one new share of common stock at $20.

Although the intrinsic value of the warrant is theoretically negative at a common stock price between 0 and $20, the warrant still carries some value in the market. Also, observe that the difference between the market price of the warrant and its intrinsic value is diminished at the upper ranges of value. Two reasons may be offered for this declining premium.

First, the speculator loses the ability to use leverage to generate high returns as the price of the stock goes up. When the price of the stock is relatively low, say, $25, and the warrant is in the $5 to $10 range, a 10-point movement in the stock could mean a 200 percent gain in the value of the warrant, as indicated in part (A) of Table 12–5. At the upper levels of stock value, much of this leverage is lost, as indicated in part (B) of the same table. At a stock value of $50 and a warrant value of approximately $30, a 10-point movement in the stock would produce only a 33 percent gain in the warrant.

Another reason why speculators pay a very low premium at higher stock prices is that there is less downside protection. A warrant selling at $30 when the stock price is $50 is more vulnerable to downside movement than is a $5 to $10 warrant when the stock is in the 20s.

Warrant premiums are also influenced by the same factors that affect con-vertible bond premiums. More volatile common stocks will have greater

TABLE 12–5	LEVERAGE IN VALUING WARRANTS

(A)	(B)
Stock price, $25; warrant price, $5* + 10-point movement in stock price. New warrant price, $15 (10-point gain)	Stock price, $50; warrant price, $30 + 10-point movement in stock price. New warrant price, $40 (10-point gain)
$$\text{Percentage gain in warrant} = \frac{\$10}{\$5} \times 100 = 200\%$$	$$\text{Percentage gain in warrant} = \frac{\$10}{\$30} \times 100 = 33\%$$

*The warrant price would, of course, be greater than $5 because of a premium. Nevertheless, we use $5 for ease of computation.

potential to create short-run profits for warrant speculators, so the higher the price volatility, the greater the premium. Also, the longer the option has before expiration, the higher the premium will be. This "time premium" is worth more the longer the common stock has to reach and surpass the option price of the warrant.

Use of Warrants by Corporations

As previously indicated, warrants may allow for the issuance of debt under difficult circumstances. While a straight debt issue may not be acceptable or may be accepted only at extremely high rates, the same security may be well received because detachable warrants are included. Warrants may also be included as an add-on in a merger or acquisition agreement. A firm might offer $20 million in cash plus 10,000 warrants in exchange for all the outstanding shares of the acquisition candidate.

The use of warrants has traditionally been associated with such aggressive, "high-flying" firms as real estate investment trusts, airlines, and conglomerates.

As a financing device for creating new common stock, warrants may not be as desirable as convertible securities. A corporation with convertible bonds outstanding may force the conversion of debt to common stock through a call, while no similar device is available to the firm with warrants. The only possible inducement might be a step-up in the option price—whereby the warrant holder must pay a progressively higher option price if he does not exercise by a given date.

The capital structure of the firm after the exercise of a warrant also is somewhat different from that created after the conversion of a debenture. In the case of a warrant, the original debt outstanding remains in existence after the detachable warrant is exercised, whereas the conversion of a debenture extinguishes the former debt obligation.[5]

---

[5]It should be pointed out that a number of later financing devices can blur this distinction. See Jerry Miller, "Accounting for Warrants and Convertible Bonds," *Management Accounting*, January 1973, pp. 36–38.

ACCOUNTING CONSIDERATIONS WITH WARRANTS

As with convertible securities, the potential dilutive effect of warrants must be considered. Warrants are generally included in computing both primary and fully diluted earnings per share.[6] The accountant must compute the number of new shares that could be created by the exercise of all warrants, with the provision that the total can be reduced by the assumed use of the cash proceeds to purchase a partially offsetting amount of shares at the market price. Assume that warrants to purchase 10,000 shares at $20 are outstanding and that the current price of the stock is $50. We show the following:

1. New shares created 10,000
2. Reduction of shares from cash proceeds (computed below) 4,000

   Cash proceeds—10,000 shares at $20 = $200,000
   Current price of stock—$50
   Assumed reduction in shares outstanding from cash proceeds
      = $200,000/$50 = 4,000
3. Assumed net increase in shares from exercise of warrants
      (10,000 − 4,000) 6,000

In computing earnings per share, we will add 6,000 shares to the denominator with no adjustment to the numerator, which will lower earnings per share. If earnings per share had previously been $1 based on $100,000 in earnings and 100,000 shares outstanding, EPS would now be reduced to $.943.

$$\frac{\text{Earnings}}{\text{Shares}} \frac{\$100,000}{106,000} = \$.943$$

With warrants included in computing both primary and fully diluted earnings per share, their impact on reported earnings is important from both the investor and corporate viewpoints.

---

[6]Under some circumstances, where the market price is below the option price, dilution need not be considered (*APB Opinion No. 15*).

13

PUT AND CALL OPTIONS

OPTIONS MARKETS

Listed Options Exchanges

THE OPTIONS CLEARING CORPORATION

OPTION PREMIUMS

Intrinsic Value
Speculative Premium

BASIC OPTION STRATEGIES

Buying Call Options
Writing Call Options
Buying Put Options

USING OPTIONS IN COMBINATIONS

Spreads
Straddles

OTHER OPTION CONSIDERATIONS

APPENDIX 13–A: OPTIONS AVAILABLE ON COMPANIES' COMMON STOCK

APPENDIX 13–B: THE BLACK-SCHOLES PRICING MODEL

T he word **option** has many different meanings, but most of them include the ability or right to choose a certain alternative. One definition provided by *Webster's* is "the right, acquired for a consideration, to buy or sell something at a fixed price within a specified period of time." This definition is very general and applies to puts, calls, warrants, real estate options, or any other contracts entered into between two parties where a choice of action or decision can be put off for a limited time at a cost. The person acquiring the option pays an agreed-upon sum to the person providing the option. For example, someone may want to buy your house for its sale price of $75,000. The buyer does not have the money but will give you $2,000 in cash if you give him the right to buy the house for the next 60 days at $75,000. If you accept, you have given the buyer an option and have agreed not to sell the house to anyone else for the next 60 days. If the buyer raises $75,000 within the 60-day limit, he may buy the house, giving you the $75,000. Perhaps he finds the $75,000 but also finds another house he likes better for $72,000. He will not buy your house, but you have $2,000 and must now find someone else to buy your house. By selling the option, you tied up the sale of your house for 60 days, and if the option is unexercised, you have foregone an opportunity to sell the house to someone else.

The most widely known options are **puts** and **calls** on common stock. A put is an option to sell 100 shares of common stock at a specified price for a given period of time. Calls are the opposite of puts and allow the owner the right to buy 100 shares of common stock from the option seller (writer). Contracts on listed puts and calls have been standardized and can be bought on several different exchanges.

OPTIONS MARKETS

Before the days of options trading on exchanges, puts and calls were traded over-the-counter by the Put and Call Dealers Association. These dealers would buy and sell puts and calls for their own accounts for stocks traded on the New York Stock Exchange and then try to find an investor, hedger, or speculator to take the other side of the option. For example, if you owned 1,000 shares of General Motors and you wanted to write a call option giving the buyer the right to buy 1,000 shares of General Motors at $42 per share for six months, the dealer might buy the calls and look for someone who would be willing to buy them from him.

This system had several disadvantages. Dealers had to have contact with the buyers and sellers, and the financial stability of the option writer had to be endorsed (guaranteed) by a brokerage house. The option writer either had to keep the shares on deposit with the brokerage firm or put up a cash margin. Options in the same stock could exist in the market at various strike prices (price at which the option could be exercised) and scattered expiration dates. This meant that when an option buyer wanted to exercise or terminate the contract before expiration, he or she would have to deal directly with the option writer. This does not make for an efficient, liquid market. Unlisted options also reduced the striking price of a call by any dividends paid during the option period, which did not benefit the writer of the call.

Listed Options Exchanges

The **Chicago Board Options Exchange** was established in 1973 as the first exchange for call options. The market response was overwhelming, and within three years, the American, Pacific, and Philadelphia exchanges were also trading call options. By 1988, the list of stocks with available option contracts increased dramatically from the original list of 16 companies to 560 companies, and puts as well as calls were traded for many companies. Appendix 13–A at the end of the chapter presents a comprehensive list of available options as well as the principal trading exchange for the option. On many days, the number of underlying shares of stock represented by options traded on the option exchanges is greater than the number of actual shares traded on the NYSE in those same issues.

Table 13–1, from the *Chicago Board Option Exchange's Market Statistics*, shows the growth in options trading since 1973. Besides the Chicago Board Options Exchange (CBOE), the American Exchange (AMEX), the Philadelphia Exchange (PHLX), the Pacific Coast Exchange (PSE), and the New York Stock Exchange (NYSE) currently trade options.

One can now also buy a put or call option on *stock indexes*. For example, the Standard & Poor's 500 Stock Index or the S&P 100 Stock Index are traded on the CBOE; options on the New York Stock Exchange Index are traded on the NYSE; and Value Line Index Options, the National O-T-C Index Options, and the Utilities Index Options are all traded on the Philadelphia Exchange. Options on stock indexes are covered in detail in Chapter 16, while this chapter concentrates on options on individual common stocks.

There are several reasons why the listed options markets are so desirable compared to the previous method of over-the-counter trading for options. The contract period was standardized with three-, six-, and nine-month expiration dates on three calendar cycles.

Cycle 1: January/April/July/October.

Cycle 2: February/May/August/November.

Cycle 3: March/June/September/December.

As one month's expiration date comes up, another month in the cycle is added. For example, as the January option expires, the October nine-month option is added, and the cycle is continued. The use of three cycles spreads out the expiration dates for the options so that not all contracts come due on the same day. Each contract expires at 11:59 P.M. Eastern time on the Saturday immediately following the third Friday of the expiration month. For all practical purposes, any closing out of positions must be done on that last Friday while the markets are open.

In addition to the three calendar cycles, the Chicago Board Options Exchange and other exchanges began offering sequential options in 1986 to take

TABLE 13–1		TOTAL OPTIONS CONTRACT VOLUME BY EXCHANGE (For Individual Stocks)						
	CBOE	AMEX	PHLX	PSE	NYSE	MSE*	NASD	Total
1987	182,112,636	70,988,990	29,155,308	19,410,875	3,499,095	—	—	305,166,904
1986	180,357,774	65,440,500	24,467,468	14,075,872	4,823,782	—	45,239	289,210,635
1985	148,889,091	48,559,122	18,134,575	12,793,451	4,426,855	—	107,453	232,910,547
1984	123,273,736	40,104,605	16,109,050	11,366,056	4,093,816	—	—	194,947,263
1983	82,468,750	38,967,725	16,808,125	11,155,906	656,480	—	—	150,056,986
1982	75,735,739	38,790,852	13,466,652	9,309,563	—	—	—	137,302,806
1981	57,584,175	34,859,475	10,009,565	6,952,567	—	—	—	109,405,782
1980	52,916,921	29,048,323	7,758,101	5,486,590	—	1,518,611	—	96,728,546
1979	35,379,600	17,467,018	4,952,737	3,856,344	—	2,609,164	—	64,264,863
1978	34,277,350	14,380,959	3,270,378	3,289,968	—	2,012,363	—	57,231,018
1977	24,838,632	10,077,578	2,195,307	1,925,031	—	600,780	—	39,637,328
1976	21,498,027	9,035,767	1,274,702	550,194	—	15,237	—	32,373,927
1975	14,431,023	3,530,564	140,982	—	—	—	—	18,102,569
1974	5,682,907	—	—	—	—	—	—	5,682,907
1973	1,119,177	—	—	—	—	—	—	1,119,177

*The Midwest Stock Exchange Options Program was consolidated with the CBOE on June 2, 1980.
Source: *The Chicago Board Option Exchange's Market Statistics*, 1987, p. 27.

advantage of the high liquidity found in options having short-term maturities. The sequential options program created one-month and two-month options to be added to the January/April/July/October cycle. This allows more options to be available with maturities of between one and four months.

The exercise price (striking price) is also standardized. This is the price which the contract specifies for a buy or sell. For all stocks over $25 per share, the striking price changes by $5 intervals, and for stocks selling under $25 per share, the strike price changes by $2.50 a share. As the underlying stocks change prices in the market, options with new striking prices are added. For example, a stock selling at $30 per share when the January option is added will have a striking price of 30, but if the stock gets to $32\frac{1}{2}$ (half way to the next striking price), the exchange may add another option (to the class of options) with a 35 strike price.

This standardization of expiration dates and strike prices creates more certainty when buying and selling options in a changing market and allows more-efficient trading strategies because of better coordination between stock prices, strike prices, and expiration dates. Dividends no longer affect the option contract as they did in the unlisted market. Transactions occur at arm's length between the buyer and seller without any direct matchmaking needed on the part of the broker. The ultimate result of these changes in the option market is a highly liquid, efficient market where speculators, hedgers, and arbitrageurs all operate together.

General Electric put and call options are presented in Table 13–2 as an example of different strike prices (35, 40, 45) and expiration months. The expiration months demonstrate the third expiration cycle of June/September/December combined with the sequential option program of adding the month of July to get more short-term liquid options. General Electric common stock closed at $42\frac{5}{8}$ on June 5, 1988. The values within Table 13–2, such as

TABLE 13–2		JUNE 27, 1988, GENERAL ELECTRIC OPTIONS							
Stock Price Close	Strike Price	Calls—Last				Puts—Last			
		June	July	September	December	June	July	September	December
Gen El.									
$42^5/_8$	35	$7^5/_8$	$7^3/_8$	$7^7/_8$	$8^3/_8$	Not traded	$^1/_8$	$^3/_{16}$	$^9/_{16}$
$42^5/_8$	40	$2^5/_8$	3	$3^7/_8$	$4^5/_8$	$^1/_4$	$^5/_8$	$1^1/_{16}$	$1^5/_8$
$42^5/_8$	45	$^3/_{16}$	$^5/_8$	$1^5/_{16}$	$2^1/_8$	$2^3/_4$	$3^1/_2$	$3^3/_4$	$3^7/_8$

$7^5/_8$ or $2^5/_8$, reflect the price of the various option contracts. This information will take on greater meaning as we go through the chapter.

THE OPTIONS CLEARING CORPORATION

Much of the liquidity and ease of operation of the option exchanges is due to the role of the **Options Clearing Corporation**, which functions as the issuer of all options listed on the five exchanges—the CBOE, the AMEX, the Philadelphia Exchange, the Pacific Coast Exchange, and the NYSE. Investors who want to trade puts and calls need to have an approved account with a member brokerage firm; upon opening an account, they receive a prospectus from the Options Clearing Corporation detailing all aspects of option trading.

Options are bought and sold through a member broker the same as other securities. The exchanges allow special orders, such as limit, market, and stop orders, as well as orders used specifically in options trading, like spread orders and straddle orders. The order process originates with the broker and is transacted on the floor of the exchange. Remember that for every order there must be a buyer and seller (writer) so that the orders can be "matched." Once the orders are matched, they are filed with the Options Clearing Corporation, which then issues the necessary options or closes the position. There are four basic transactions handled:

Opening purchase transaction—A transaction in which an investor intends to become the holder of an option.

Opening sale transaction—A transaction in which an investor intends to become the writer of an option.

Closing purchase transaction—A transaction in which an investor who is obligated as a writer of an option intends to terminate his obligation as a writer. This is accomplished by "purchasing" an option in the same series as the option previously written. Such a transaction has the effect, upon acceptance by the Options Clearing Corporation, of canceling the investor's preexisting position as a writer.

Closing sale transaction—A transaction in which an investor who is the holder of an outstanding option intends to liquidate his position as a holder. This is accomplished by "selling" an option in the same series as the option previously purchased. Such a transaction has the effect, upon acceptance by the Options Clearing Corporation, of liquidating the investor's preexisting position as a holder of the option.

What occurs in a transaction is that holders and writers of options are not contractually linked together but are committed to the Options Clearing Corporation. Since there are no certificates issued for options, a customer must maintain a brokerage account as long as he or she holds an option position and must liquidate the option through the broker originating the transaction unless a brokerage transfer is completed before an ensuing transaction. If an option is traded on more than one exchange, it may be bought, sold, or closed out on any exchange and cleared through the Options Clearing Corporation. Basically, the aggregate obligation of the option holders is backed up by the aggregate obligation of the option writers. If holders choose to exercise their options, they must do so through the Clearing Corporation, which randomly selects a writer from all Clearing member accounts in the same option series.[1] This would be true whether the holder chooses to exercise early or at expiration. Upon notice from the Options Clearing Corporation, a call writer must sell 100 shares of the underlying common stock at the exercise price, while the put writer must buy 100 shares from the holder exercising the put.

All option contracts are adjusted for stock splits, stock dividends, or other stock distributions. For example, a two-for-one stock split for a stock selling at 60, with options available at 70, 60, and 50 strike prices, would cause the stock to trade at 30 and the strike prices to be 35, 30, and 25.

OPTION PREMIUMS

Before an investor or speculator can understand various option strategies, he or she must be able to comprehend what creates option premiums (prices). Look at Table 13–3. Using Texaco (on the upper right-hand side) as an example, we can see that the common stock closed at $48.50 per share on the NYSE and that calls and puts are available for the following strike prices— 40, 45, 50, and 55. The October 45 call closed at $6^1/_8$ ($612.50 for one call on 100 shares), while the October 50 call closed at $3^3/_8$. The 40 and 45 call options are said to be **in-the-money** because the market price ($48^1/_2$) is above the strike (or purchase) price of 40 or 45. The 50 and 55 calls are out-of-the-money since the strike price is above the market price. If Texaco common were trading at 50, the 50 call and put would be at-the-money. Let's once again assume the stock is selling for $48^1/_2$. Since a put allows you to sell the stock at the strike price, in-the-money puts would be the 50 and 55 strike prices, and out-of-the-money puts would be 40 and 45.

---

[1]Actually, very few option holders choose to exercise their options and take possession of securities. During the 1980s, approximately 15 percent of all call options were exercised while only 7 percent of put options were exercised. Assuming that the option holder does not want to exercise his option, he may choose to close out his position on the open market through a closing sale transaction.

TABLE 13–3

LISTED OPTIONS QUOTATIONS

Friday, June 24, 1988

Options closing prices. Sales unit usually is 100 shares.
Stock close is New York or American exchange final price.

Option & NY Close	Strike Price	Calls—Last			Puts—Last		
		Jul	Aug	Sep	Jul	Aug	Sep
74 7/8	80	3/4	1 1/2	2	r	r	r
NiagMP	12 1/2	r	r	r	r	r	1/16
15 3/8	15	3/8	1/2	r	r	r	r
PacGE	12 1/2	r	r	3 5/8	r	r	r
16	15	1	1 1/4	1 3/8	1/8	1/4	3/8
16	17 1/2	1/8	r	5/16	r	r	r
Pfizer	50	1 7/8	3 1/8	3 1/8	3/4	1 1/4	1 3/4
51 3/8	55	1/4	13/16	15/16	r	4 1/2	4 1/2
51 3/8	60	s	s	1/4	s	s	r
Ph Mor	80	6	7 3/8	7 3/8	5/16	r	1 3/8
85 1/2	85	2 1/4	3 7/8	4 3/4	1 1/4	2 1/8	3
85 1/2	90	1/2	1 5/8	2 1/8	4 5/8	r	r
85 1/2	95	r	r	13/16	r	r	r
85 1/2	100	s	s	3/8	s	s	r
PrimeC	15	1	1 3/16	r	r	1/2	9/16
15 3/8	17 1/2	1/8	3/16	1/2	r	r	r
PSEG	25	r	r	5/8	r	r	r
QuakSt	20	3 7/8	4 1/8	4 3/8	r	3/8	1/2
23 3/8	22 1/2	1 1/2	2 1/2	2 3/4	3/4	1 1/4	1 5/8
23 3/8	25	5/8	1 3/8	1 1/2	1 13/16	3/8	2 7/8
23 3/8	30	1/8	3/8	5/8	r	r	r
SFeSP	15	6 5/8	s	7	r	s	r
21 5/8	17 1/2	4 3/4	5 1/4	5 1/2	1/16	r	r
21 5/8	20	2 3/8	2 3/4	3	11/16	7/8	1 9/16
21 5/8	22 1/2	7/8	1 1/2	1 3/4	1 1/2	2	2 3/8
SFe o	20	s	s	7 1/2	s	s	1/4
	25	s	s	3 1/4	s	s	1 1/4
Seagte	15	2	r	3 1/8	1/8	3/8	r
17 3/8	17 1/2	3/4	1 1/16	1 1/4	7/8	1 1/4	r
17 3/8	20	r	7/16	5/8	r	3 1/8	3 1/4
17 3/8	22 1/2	s	s	1/4	s	s	5 1/2
SnapOn	40	3	r	r	1/2	3/4	r
43	45	1/2	r	r	2 7/8	r	r
Valero	5	r	3 5/8	r	r	r	r
8 3/8	7 1/2	1 1/8	r	1 5/8	r	r	5/8
8 3/8	10	1/4	1/2	11/16	r	r	1 7/8
		Jul	Aug	Oct	Jul	Aug	Oct
Aetna	40	6 1/8	r	6 3/8	r	r	1/4
45 1/2	45	1 5/16	1 7/8	2 5/8	1/2	r	r
45 1/2	50	r	r	3/4	r	r	r
Ahman	12 1/2	r	s	4	r	s	r
16 3/8	15	1 11/16	r	r	r	r	r
16 3/8	17 1/2	3/16	r	3/4	1 1/4	r	1 3/4
AlaskA	15	r	r	4 1/2	r	r	r
18 7/8	17 1/2	1 9/16	r	2 1/4	1/4	r	1
18 7/8	20	3/8	7/8	1 1/4	r	r	r
ABrrck	20	r	r	2 3/4	r	r	r
21 3/4	22 1/2	r	1	1 1/2	1 1/8	r	r
21 3/4	25	r	r	r	3 1/4	r	r
Am Cya	40	r	s	15 1/2	r	s	r
54 5/8	45	9 1/2	r	12	1/8	5/8	1 1/4
54 5/8	50	6	7	8 1/8	5/8	1 3/4	3
54 5/8	55	3	4 1/4	6	3	3 3/4	4 1/2
54 5/8	60	1 9/16	s	3 1/2	r	s	r
Am Exp	25	2 3/8	2 3/4	3	r	1/2	1
27 1/8	30	1/8	3/8	13/16	r	r	3 3/4
Am Hom	75	1 3/8	2 3/4	3 1/2	r	2	r

Option & NY Close	Strike Price	Calls—Last			Puts—Last		
		Jul	Aug	Oct	Jul	Aug	Oct
47 3/4	50	7/16	1 3/16	2 1/4	r	r	r
Tandem	15	4 7/8	s	r	r	s	r
19 3/4	17 1/2	2 5/8	r	3 5/8	r	r	1/2
19 3/4	20	11/16	1 1/4	1 3/4	7/8	r	1 1/2
19 3/4	22 1/2	r	r	1	2 3/4	r	r
TeleCm	25	r	7/8	r	r	r	r
Texaco	40	8 5/8	s	9 5/8	1/8	s	r
48 1/2	45	4 1/8	4 3/4	6 1/8	3/8	1 7/16	2
48 1/2	50	1 1/8	2 1/16	3 3/8	2 7/16	3 1/2	4 1/2
48 1/2	55	1/4	7/8	1 5/8	6 3/4	r	r
U Carb	17 1/2	5 3/8	s	6	r	s	r
23 3/8	20	3 3/8	3 1/4	4	1/16	r	1/2
23 3/8	22 1/2	1 1/4	1 3/4	2 3/8	3/8	7/8	1 1/2
23 3/8	25	1/4	11/16	1 1/4	2 1/2	r	2 1/2
23 3/8	30	r	s	5/16	r	s	r
Unisys	30	r	r	7 7/8	r	r	r
37	35	2 1/2	r	r	3/8	r	r
37	40	1/8	5/8	1 3/16	r	r	r
USX	30	3	3 1/4	4	3/16	1/2	1 1/16
32 5/8	35	5/16	5/8	1 7/16	2 1/2	r	3 3/8
USWst	55	2 3/8	r	r	r	r	1 1/2
56 1/2	60	r	1/4	r	r	r	r
Walgrn	35	r	1 3/4	r	1/2	r	r
Wrn Lm	65	3 1/8	r	r	r	r	r
66 3/4	70	r	r	3 1/8	3 3/8	r	r
66 3/4	75	1/4	s	r	r	s	r
WellsF	60	r	r	2 3/8	r	r	r
Westng	50	5 7/8	r	r	1/16	r	r
55 3/4	55	1 3/4	2 5/8	3 3/4	1	r	r
55 3/4	60	5/16	5/8	1 1/4	r	r	r
WyseTc	17 1/2	2 1/4	r	3 1/2	r	r	r
20 1/8	20	11/16	1 1/4	2	3/4	r	r
20 1/8	22 1/2	3/16	1/2	7/8	r	r	r
20 1/8	25	r	s	5/8	r	s	r
		Jul	Aug	Nov	Jul	Aug	Nov
A M R	40	9 1/4	r	10 3/4	r	1/16	r
48 7/8	45	4 1/4	5 1/4	r	r	11/16	r
48 7/8	50	1	2 1/4	r	1 3/4	r	r
A S A	40	r	4	5 1/8	1/4	11/16	1 11/16
43 1/8	45	7/16	1 1/4	2 1/2	2 1/8	3	4
43 1/8	50	r	5/16	1 1/16	r	r	r
AFamly	12 1/2	r	1 5/8	r	r	r	r
13 5/8	15	3/16	7/16	7/8	r	1 1/2	r
13 5/8	17 1/2	s	r	r	s	r	3 5/8
Arkla	20	1/8	3/8	r	r	r	r
Avnet	25	1 3/8	2	r	r	3/4	r
Bally	15	3 7/8	r	4 3/4	r	r	r
18 7/8	17 1/2	1 5/8	2	2 5/8	r	r	r
18 7/8	20	3/8	7/8	1 5/8	r	r	r
CaesrW	25	2 3/4	3 1/2	r	r	1/2	r
27 3/4	30	5/16	1	r	2 3/8	r	r
Caterp	60	r	7 3/4	9 1/2	r	1/2	r
66 1/2	65	3 7/8	4	6	7/8	1 5/8	r
66 1/2	70	9/16	1 1/2	3 3/8	3 3/4	r	5
CitzSo	25	r	r	3	r	r	r
ColuGs	30	r	2 1/2	r	r	r	r
32 1/2	35	r	r	1	r	r	r

r-Not Traded. s-No Option.

Texaco options. Closing price of common stock—48 1/2

Strike price for Caterpillar. Stock price at which the option may be exercised. (100 shares for $70 per share)

Source: *The Wall Street Journal,* June 27, 1988, p. 26. Reprinted by permission of *The Wall Street Journal,*

Intrinsic Value

In-the-money *call* options have an **intrinsic value** equal to the market price minus the strike price. In the case of the Texaco October 45 call, the intrinsic value is $3^1/_2$ as indicated by Formula (13–1).

$$\text{Intrinsic value (call)} = \text{Market price} - \text{Strike price}$$
$$\text{Intrinsic value} = 48^1/_2 - 45$$
$$(\text{Texaco 45 Oct call}) = 3^1/_2$$

(13–1)

Options that are out-of-the-money have no positive intrinsic value. In fact, if we use Formula 13–1 for the Texaco 50 call, we calculate a negative $1.50 intrinsic value. When the market price minus the strike price is negative, the negative value represents the amount the stock price must increase to have the option at-the-money where the strike price and market price are equal.

The intrinsic value for in-the-money *put* options equals the strike price minus the market price. In the case of the Texaco October 55 put, the intrinsic value is $6^1/_2$ as indicated by Formula (13–2).

$$\text{Intrinsic value (put)} = \text{Strike price} - \text{Market price}$$
$$\text{Intrinsic value} = 55 - 48^1/_2$$
$$(\text{Texaco 55 Oct put}) = 6^1/_2$$

(13–2)

Since puts allow the owner to sell stock at the strike price, in-the-money put options exist where the strike price is above the market price of the stock. Out-of-the-money puts have market prices for common stock above the strike price.

Speculative Premium

Returning to the Texaco 45 October call, we see in Table 13–3 that the total premium is $6^1/_8$, while the previously computed intrinsic value is $3^1/_2$. This call option has an additional **speculative premium** of $2^5/_8$ due to other factors. The total premium (option price) is a combination of the intrinsic value plus a speculative premium. This relationship is indicated in Formula 13–3 and in Figure 13–1.

$$\text{Total premium} = \text{Intrinsic value} + \text{Speculative premium}$$
$$6^1/_8 = 3^1/_2 + 2^5/_8$$

(13–3)

Generally, the higher the volatility of the common stock—as measured by its stock price's standard deviation or by its beta—and the lower the dividend yield, the greater the speculative premium.[2] The longer the exercise period, the higher the speculative premium, especially if market expectations over the

---

[2]Some people refer to the speculative premium as the time premium because time may be the overriding factor affecting the speculative premium.

FIGURE 13–1   COMPONENTS OF THE TOTAL PREMIUM ON A CALL OPTION

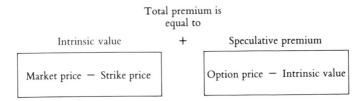

duration of the option are positive. Finally, the deeper the option is in-the-money, the smaller the leverage potential and therefore the smaller the speculative premium. Most often, we examine the speculative premium separately to see if it is a reasonable premium to pay for the possible benefits.

The speculative premium can be expressed in dollars or as a percentage of the common stock price. A speculative premium expressed in percent indicates the increase in the stock price needed for the purchaser of a call option to break even on the expiration date. Table 13–4 shows this point.[3] Notice that the Texaco October 40 call option, which is deep in-the-money, has the lowest speculative premium, while the 55 call option has the highest. Realize that the 55 call option only has a cash value of $1^5/_8$ (the total premium), and that the other $6^1/_2$ represents the required increase in the stock price for the market price and strike price to be equal. The 16.75 percent speculative premium represents the percentage movement in stock price by the expiration date for a break-even position. Remember that at expiration there will be no speculative premium. The option will only reflect the intrinsic value and possibly even a discount because of commission expenses incurred upon exercise.

Speculative Premiums and the Time Factor.   Table 13–5 provides a look at premiums for in-the-money and out-of-the-money call options with varying times to expiration. Since the quotes are as of June 24, the July options will expire first, then the August options, and finally, the October options. You should notice how the option premiums increase with more time to expiration.

Texaco's speculative premiums in Table 13–5 demonstrate the basic point that percentage speculative premiums increase with time across all series of strike prices. The speculative premiums are lowest with the in-the-money 40 and 45 calls because of the low leverage potential and the downside risk if the stock declines. The 50 and 55 call options have high speculative premiums, but an option writer would *not reap much cash inflow*. Generally speaking, out-of-the-money call options have high speculative premiums, but little of the premium may be in the form of cash. For example, the Texaco July 55 call has a total premium of $^1/_4$ and a speculative premium of of $6^3/_4$, which consists

TABLE 13–4		SPECULATIVE PREMIUMS ON JUNE 24, 1988, FOR TEXACO OPTIONS				
Market Price	Texaco Strike Price	Total Premium (Price)	Intrinsic − Value	Speculative = Premium	Speculative Premium as a Percent of Stock Price
48^1/_2$	40 Oct Call	$9^5/_8$	− $8^1/_2$	= $1^1/_8$	2.32%
$48^1/_2$	45 Oct Call	$6^1/_8$	− $3^1/_2$	= $2^5/_8$	5.41
$48^1/_2$	50 Oct Call	$3^3/_8$	− $(1^1/_2)$	= $4^7/_8$	10.05
$48^1/_2$	55 Oct Call	$1^5/_8$	− $(6^1/_2)$	= $8^1/_8$	16.75

of the $6^1/_2$ difference between the market price of $48^1/_2$ and the strike price of 55. The fact that the cash premium is only 25 cents is an important consideration for an option writer.

Speculative Premiums, Betas, and Dividend Yields.   Table 13–6 demonstrates the relationship of betas and dividend yields to the speculative premium. The four options listed are all October calls from Table 13–3. Aetna and American Home are slightly in-the-money, and American Cyanamid and Tandem Computer are slightly out-of-the-money. It would be better to have all of them at-the-money so that the comparison would not be biased by differences between the strike price and market price. Notice that in general, the speculative premiums (in percent) are higher for the high-beta, low-dividend yield stocks, and lower for the low-beta, high-dividend stocks.

High-beta stocks have a greater probability of participating in a market upturn, and so speculators will pay a higher speculative premium on a call for the chance to participate in an up market. High-dividend-yield stocks are the ones favored by call writers, and therefore, the speculative premiums are lower because there is a larger number of call writers for these stocks. Other factors, such as market attitudes or individual company conditions, can also have a strong bearing on the speculative premium.

Speculative Premiums per Day.   Speculative premiums can be deceiving. The novice may attempt to write the options with the highest total premium or speculative premium, while the buyer may think the smallest dollar investment provides the greatest advantage. These are not usually true if we look at speculative premiums on a per-day basis. For example, the Texaco 50 calls in Table 13–5 have the following speculative premiums per day. Note the speculative premium per day is divided by the number of days to expiration.

Month	Strike	Speculative Premium	Days to Expiration	Speculative Premium per Day
July	50	5.41% /	21 days	= .2576% per day
August	50	7.35 /	56 days	= .1313 per day
October	50	10.05 /	119 days	= .0845 per day

An examination of daily premiums would suggest that call writers should write short-lived calls on a continuous basis to get a maximum return. On

TABLE 13-5 SPECULATIVE PREMIUMS OVER TIME (Texaco Calls, June 24, 1988)

Market Price	Strike Price	**July** Total Premium* (Price)	Speculative Premium Dollars	Speculative Premium Percent	**August** Total Premium† (Price)	Speculative Premium Dollars	Speculative Premium Percent	**October** Total Premium‡ (Price)	Speculative Premium Dollars	Speculative Premium Percent
$48.50	$40	8^{5}/_{8}$	$ $^{1}/_{8}$	.25%	Not traded	—	—	9^{5}/_{8}$	11^{1}/_{8}$	2.32%
48.50	45	4$^{1}/_{8}$	$^{5}/_{8}$	1.29	4^{3}/_{4}$	1^{1}/_{4}$	2.58%	6$^{1}/_{8}$	2$^{5}/_{8}$	5.41
48.50	50	1$^{1}/_{8}$	2$^{5}/_{8}$	5.41	2$^{1}/_{16}$	3$^{9}/_{16}$	7.35	3$^{3}/_{8}$	4$^{7}/_{8}$	10.05
48.50	55	$^{1}/_{4}$	6$^{3}/_{4}$	13.92	$^{7}/_{8}$	7$^{3}/_{8}$	15.21	1$^{5}/_{8}$	8$^{1}/_{8}$	16.75

*July—21 days to expiration.
†August—56 days to expiration.
‡October—119 days to expiration.

TABLE 13–6	SPECULATIVE PREMIUMS RELATED TO BETAS AND DIVIDEND YIELDS						
	October Strike	Market Price	Total Premium	Speculative Premium		Beta	Expected Dividend Yield
				Dollars	Percent		
Aetna	$45	$45$1/2$	$2$5/8$	$2$1/8$	4.67%	.95	6.9%
American Home	75	75$5/8$	3$1/2$	2$7/8$	3.80	.90	5.1
American Cyanamid	55	54$5/8$	6	5$3/8$	9.84	1.15	2.6
Tandem Computer	20	19$3/4$	1$3/4$	2	10.13	1.60	0.0

the other hand, call buyers get more time for less premium by purchasing long-lived calls.

Understanding option premiums is important in order to make sense out of options strategies. Various strategies involving calls and puts are covered in the next section. Appendix 13–B presents the Black-Scholes option pricing model, a much more sophisticated way of analyzing option prices and their time premiums and speculative premiums. This appendix is primarily designed for those who wish to achieve a more-advanced understanding of the theoretical basis for option pricing and is not essential for the standard reading of the text.

BASIC OPTION STRATEGIES

Option strategies can be very aggressive and risky, or they can be quite conservative and used as a means of reducing risk. Option buyers and writers both attempt to take advantage of the option premiums discussed in the preceding section. In theory, many option strategies can be created, but in practice, the market must be liquid in order to execute these strategies. After a decade of explosive growth, option volume on individual common stocks has not expanded as much in the mid- to late-1980s as in the first 10 years of the Chicago Board Options Exchange. Although volume on the underlying common stock has continued to increase, much of the option activity has been absorbed by options on the Standard & Poor's 100 and 500 Stock Indexes, where large institutional investors can transact portfolio strategies on the market rather than on individual stocks. A reduction of individual option trading reduces the ability to create workable strategies for specific companies. For example, the lack of a liquid market can keep institutional investors from executing hedging strategies involving several hundred thousand shares. Even with these limitations in mind, the average investor can still find many opportunities for option strategies. In this section, we discuss the possible uses of calls and puts to achieve different investment goals. Table 13–7 provides option quotes at three separate time periods for our examples. We have ignored commissions in most examples, but we do advise that commissions can be a significant hidden cost in some types of option strategies.

TABLE 13–7 CHICAGO BOARD LISTED OPTIONS QUOTATIONS
(Closing prices of all options. Sales unit usually is 100 shares. Security description includes exercise price. Stock close is New York or American exchange final price.)

April 28, 1988

Option & NY Close	Strike Price	Calls – Last			Puts – Last		
		May	Jun	Sep	May	Jun	Sep
Apache	10	r	r	1/4	r	r	r
BrisMy	35	r	6	r	r	1/4	r
40 3/4	40	1 1/2	2 1/8	3 1/4	3/4	1 1/8	2
40 3/4	45	1/16	3/8	1 1/4	r	4 5/8	r
40 3/4	50	r	1/8	r	r	r	r
Bruns	15	s	8	r	s	r	r
23 3/8	17 1/2	r	6	r	r	r	r
23 3/8	20	3 1/2	3 3/4	4 1/2	1/8	r	1
23 3/8	22 1/2	1 3/8	1 3/4	3	1/2	1	r
23 3/8	25	5/16	3/4	1 5/8	r	r	r
23 3/8	30	s	1/4	s	s	r	s
Chamln	35	3/4	1 3/8	r	r	r	r
CompSc	45	7/8	1 3/4	3 7/8	r	2 3/4	3 7/8
Dow Ch	70	s	r	s	s	1/2	s
82 3/4	75	r	9	r	3/8	13/16	2 1/4
82 3/4	80	4 1/4	5 1/4	r	1 1/8	2	r
82 3/4	85	1 1/2	2 1/2	5	3 3/8	r	6
82 3/4	90	1/4	1 1/8	3	7 3/4	r	r
82 3/4	95	r	7/16	r	r	r	r
FBost	25	2	r	3 1/2	r	r	r
Ford	35	s	13 1/4	13 1/4	s	1/16	r
47 3/4	37 1/2	s	r	s	s	1/8	s
47 3/4	40	7 5/8	8 1/8	8 7/8	1/16	3/16	3/4
47 3/4	42 1/2	s	5 3/4	s	s	3/8	s
47 3/4	45	3 1/8	3 7/8	5 1/8	3/8	7/8	1 15/16
47 3/4	47 1/2	s	2 1/4	s	s	1 3/4	s
47 3/4	50	9/16	1 3/16	2 7/16	3	3 1/4	4 1/2
Gap	17 1/2	r	6	r	r	r	r
23 1/2	20	r	r	r	r	1/2	r
23 1/2	22 1/2	1 5/8	r	3 1/2	r	r	r
23 1/2	25	9/16	1 3/16	2 1/8	r	2 7/8	r
23 1/2	30	r	1/4	r	r	r	r
Gencp	17 1/2	1	r	r	r	r	r
Gen El	35	5 5/8	5 3/4	6 3/4	1/16	1/4	3/4
40 3/8	40	15/16	1 15/16	3 1/8	13/16	1 1/2	2 1/8
40 3/8	45	1/8	3/8	1 3/16	4 5/8	5	5 3/8
40 3/8	50	r	r	3/8	r	r	9 3/4
G M	65	11 1/8	10 3/4	11 1/4	1/8	3/8	1 1/8
75 1/2	70	6	6 1/8	7 7/8	1/2	15/16	2 1/2
75 1/2	75	1 3/4	2 3/4	4 1/4	1 15/16	2 7/8	4 1/2
75 1/2	80	1/4	3/4	2	5 3/4	6	7 1/2
Glf Wn	75	r	3 5/8	r	1	r	r
75 7/8	80	1/4	1 15/16	r	r	r	r
75 7/8	85	r	1/2	2	r	r	r
Hanson	12 1/2	r	3/8	r	r	3/4	r
12	15	r	r	1/8	r	r	r
Heinz	40	r	3	r	r	1	r
41 5/8	45	r	7/16	1 3/8	r	r	r
ICX Ind	30	5 5/8	6	r	r	7/16	1 3/8
35 5/8	35	1 1/2	2 3/8	4	3/4	1 7/8	r
35 5/8	40	1/4	7/8	2	r	r	r
I T T	45	2	2 1/2	r	1/2	1 1/8	r
46 5/8	50	r	1/2	1 11/16	r	r	r
46 5/8	55	s	1/8	s	s	r	s
K mart	30	r	4 3/8	5 1/8	1/16	r	1 1/8
33 5/8	35	1/2	1 1/4	2 1/4	r	2 3/8	r
33 5/8	40	1/16	r	7/8	r	r	r
Litton	70	s	13 7/8	r	s	r	r
82 5/8	75	r	r	r	r	r	2 1/8
82 5/8	80	r	r	7 3/4	1 1/8	r	r
82 5/8	85	r	r	5	r	r	r
Loews	60	s	r	11 3/8	s	r	r
69 1/4	65	r	6 3/4	r	r	r	r
69 1/4	70	1 1/4	2 5/8	r	r	r	3 7/8
69 1/4	75	r	3/4	2 1/4	r	r	r
69 1/4	80	r	3/8	r	r	r	r
MayDS	30	5	r	r	r	r	r
34 7/8	35	1 1/8	2 1/8	3 1/2	r	2 1/4	3 1/8
34 7/8	40	1/4	3/4	1 9/16	r	r	r
34 7/8	45	r	r	3/4	r	r	r
Mc Don	40	r	3 3/4	4 7/8	1/4	11/16	r
43	45	7/16	1	2 1/4	2 1/8	2 3/4	r
43	50	r	1/4	7/8	r	r	r
Mid SU	10	3/16	1/2	1	r	1 1/8	1 1/2
9 1/4	12 1/2	r	1/8	5/16	r	r	r
N C R	50	s	r	r	s	3/16	r
61 3/4	55	6 3/4	8	r	r	r	r
61 3/4	60	3	4	6	1 1/8	r	r
61 3/4	65	5/8	1 5/8	3 1/2	r	r	5 1/4
61 3/4	70	s	3/4	2 1/4	s	r	9
61 3/4	75	s	5/16	s	s	r	s
61 3/4	80	s	r	s	s	18 1/4	s

May 26, 1988

Option & NY Close	Strike Price	Calls – Last			Puts – Last		
		Jun	Jul	Sep	Jun	Jul	Sep
BrisMy	35	5 3/4	r	6	1/8	r	r
40 1/2	40	1 5/16	1 11/16	2 1/2	11/16	1 1/4	1 3/4
40 1/2	45	1/8	1/4	11/16	r	r	r
40 1/2	50	r	s	r	r	s	10
Bruns	20	2	r	3 1/8	r	r	r
21 1/2	22 1/2	9/16	r	1 5/8	r	r	r
21 1/2	25	1/8	r	5/8	r	r	r
Chamln	35	1/4	1/2	1 1/16	2 1/2	r	r
32 1/2	40	r	s	3/16	r	s	r
CompSc	40	r	r	r	3/4	r	2
Dow Ch	75	6	r	8	1/2	1 1/4	2
80	80	2 1/4	3 1/2	5 1/4	2	3 1/8	4 1/4
80	85	5/8	1 3/8	3 1/4	5 1/2	r	7 1/4
80	90	1/8	s	1 5/8	r	s	r
80	95	r	s	7/8	r	s	r
80	105	1/16	s	s	r	s	s
FBost	20	r	s	s	1/16	s	s
28 7/8	25	r	4 3/4	r	r	r	r
28 7/8	30	7/8	1 3/4	2 3/4	r	r	3
28 7/8	35	7/16	5/8	1 1/4	r	r	r
28 7/8	40	1/8	s	s	r	s	s
FireFd	30	r	r	1	r	r	r
Ford	35	r	s	r	r	s	3/16
46 1/4	40	6 3/4	7 1/8	7 1/8	r	r	5/8
46 1/4	42 1/2	4 3/8	s	s	3/16	s	s
46 1/4	45	2 1/4	2 7/8	3 3/4	11/16	1	2
46 1/4	47 1/2	13/16	s	s	1 3/4	s	s
46 1/4	50	1/4	11/16	1 1/2	3 3/4	r	r
Gap	17 1/2	r	s	r	1/16	s	r
23 7/8	20	3 3/4	r	r	1/16	r	5/8
23 7/8	22 1/2	1 1/2	r	r	3/8	r	1 1/2
23 7/8	25	1/2	7/8	1 7/8	1 3/4	r	2 3/4
23 7/8	30	1/8	[illegible]	r	r	s	r
Gencp	17 1/2	r	1 1/2	2 1/16	r	r	r
17 3/4	20	r	1/2	r	2 1/2	r	r
Gen El	35	5	5 1/8	6	1/16	3/16	9/16
40	40	1	1 9/16	2 1/2	1	1 1/2	2 1/8
40	45	1/8	1/4	3/4	5 1/2	5 1/4	5 1/2
40	50	1/16	s	1/4	r	s	r
G M	55	18	s	s	r	s	s
72 7/8	65	8 1/2	s	9	3/16	s	1
72 7/8	70	3 5/8	5	5 1/4	9/16	1 1/4	2 1/2
72 7/8	75	7/8	1 7/8	3	2 3/4	3 1/4	4 1/2
72 7/8	80	3/16	1/2	1 3/8	7	7 7/8	r
GlfWn	37 1/2	r	s	4 1/4	r	s	r
39 1/2	40	1 1/8	1 7/8	r	r	r	r
39 1/2	42 1/2	5/16	s	r	r	s	r
Heinz	40	7/8	1 1/4	2 1/2	r	1 1/2	r
40 1/8	45	1/8	r	7/8	r	r	5 3/4
ICX Ind	30	2 1/8	r	3 1/2	9/16	r	1 3/4
31 5/8	35	1/4	5/8	1 1/2	r	r	r
31 5/8	40	1/16	s	1/2	r	s	r
I T T	40	r	r	r	1/16	r	r
47	45	2 1/4	2 3/4	3 5/8	3/8	r	1 1/4
47	50	5/16	1/2	1 3/8	r	r	r
K mart	30	2 5/8	r	4	1/4	r	7/8
32 3/4	35	1/4	3/8	1 1/4	2 5/8	r	r
32 3/4	40	1/16	s	r	r	s	r
Litton	80	5 1/8	r	r	r	r	r
83 1/8	85	1 3/4	r	r	r	4 3/8	r
Loews	65	r	2 1/4	r	r	r	r
63 1/2	70	1/8	s	r	r	s	r
63 1/2	75	1/16	s	1/2	r	s	r
63 1/2	80	r	s	1/4	r	s	r
63 1/2	85	1/16	s	s	r	s	s
MayDS	25	5 1/4	r	r	r	r	r
30	30	1 1/4	1 3/4	2 3/4	1	1 1/2	r
30	35	1/4	1/2	1 1/4	r	r	r
30	40	1/8	s	7/16	r	s	r
Mc Don	40	3	r	r	1/4	r	r
42 7/8	45	5/16	11/16	1 5/8	r	r	r
42 7/8	50	r	s	1/2	r	s	r
Mid SU	7 1/2	r	r	2 1/2	r	r	r
9 3/4	10	3/8	15/16	1 1/8	7/8	r	1 7/16
9 3/4	12 1/2	1/16	r	3/8	r	r	r
N C R	50	10 1/8	s	r	r	s	r
60	55	5 1/2	r	7 5/8	r	r	r
60	60	1 7/8	2 1/2	r	1 3/4	2 1/2	r
60	65	9/16	1 1/4	2 1/4	r	r	r
60	70	3/16	s	1 3/16	r	s	r

June 27, 1988

Option & NY Close	Strike Price	Calls Last			Puts Last		
		Jul	Aug	Sep	Jul	Aug	Sep
Apache	5	r	r	2 5/8	r	r	r
7 3/8	7 1/2	r	r	3/4	r	r	r
BrisMy	35	r	r	5 5/8	1/16	r	r
39 3/4	40	15/16	1 5/8	2 1/16	1	1 1/2	1 3/4
39 3/4	45	1/16	3/16	7/16	r	r	5 5/8
39 3/4	50	s	s	1/16	s	s	r
Bruns	20	1 5/8	2 1/8	2 3/8	5/16	1/2	3/4
21 1/4	22 1/2	5/16	3/4	1 1/16	1 1/8	r	r
21 1/4	25	1/8	r	3/8	r	r	r
Chamln	35	1 1/2	2	2 3/4	1/2	r	r
35 3/4	40	r	3/8	3/4	r	3 7/8	4 1/4
CompSc	40	r	r	5 3/8	r	r	r
43 3/4	45	1/2	r	2 1/4	1 5/8	r	2 5/8
Dow Ch	75	r	s	r	1/16	s	r
87 1/4	80	r	s	9 5/8	r	s	7/8
87 1/4	85	3 1/2	5 1/2	6 1/4	7/8	1 3/4	2 1/2
87 1/4	90	1 1/16	2 3/4	3 7/8	3 1/2	r	5
87 1/4	95	3/8	1 1/4	2 1/8	r	r	r
FBost	25	r	s	12	r	s	1/4
36 1/2	30	7	7 1/4	7 5/8	3/16	1/2	3/4
36 1/2	35	3	3 1/2	4 3/4	1 1/8	2 1/4	2 1/2
36 1/2	40	1 1/8	1 3/4	2 3/8	3 1/2	r	r
FireFd	30	2 1/2	r	r	r	r	r
Ford	35	s	s	17 1/8	s	s	r
51 3/4	45	7 1/4	s	7 5/8	r	s	1/2
51 3/4	50	2 11/16	3 1/4	3 3/4	5/8	1 1/2	1 3/4
51 3/4	55	7/16	1 5/16	1 5/8	3 1/2	4	4 1/2
Gap	25	r	r	6 3/4	1/8	r	5/8
30 3/4	30	1 3/4	r	3 3/8	15/16	r	1 7/8
30 3/4	35	5/16	1	1 7/16	r	r	r
Gencp	20	5/8	1 1/4	1 5/8	1 3/8	r	r
19 1/4	22 1/2	r	r	9/16	r	r	r
Gen El	35	r	s	9 1/8	r	s	r
42 1/2	40	2 7/8	4	3 7/8	3/16	1/2	3/4
42 1/2	45	5/16	15/16	1 1/4	2 1/2	2 5/8	2 3/4
42 1/2	50	1/16	1/8	1/4	r	6 1/2	6 7/8
G M	60	s	s	r	s	s	1/8
78 3/8	65	s	s	r	s	s	3/8
78 3/8	70	r	r	9 1/2	1/16	3/8	5/8
78 3/8	75	4 1/4	5 1/4	4 7/8	5/8	1 1/8	1 7/8
78 3/8	80	1 1/8	2	2 9/16	2 3/8	3 1/2	4 1/4
78 3/8	85	3/16	9/16	1	6 1/2	r	r
GlfWn	40	r	4 3/4	5 1/4	r	r	r
43 1/2	45	3/4	1 1/2	2	r	r	r
Hanson	10	r	r	2 5/8	r	r	r
12 1/4	12 1/2	r	r	r	5/16	r	r
Heinz	40	1	r	2	3/4	r	1 3/8
39 1/2	45	r	r	9/16	r	r	r
39 1/2	50	s	s	3/16	s	s	r
ICX Ind	30	2 1/8	r	3 1/8	r	1/2	3/4
31 7/8	35	3/16	9/16	15/16	r	r	r
I T T	45	r	7	6 3/8	r	r	r
50 7/8	50	2	2 1/2	3	7/16	1	r
50 7/8	55	1/4	7/8	1 1/4	r	r	r
K mart	25	r	s	10 1/4	r	s	r
34 1/4	30	r	r	5	r	r	3/8
34 1/4	35	1/2	1 1/8	1 3/4	1	7/8	1 1/2
34 1/4	40	r	1/8	1/4	r	r	r
Litton	85	r	r	1 3/4	r	r	r
Loews	60	6 1/2	r	8	r	r	r
66 1/8	65	2 3/4	r	4 1/4	r	r	r
66 1/8	70	1/2	r	1 11/16	r	r	r
MayDS	25	r	s	9 3/4	r	s	r
33 1/4	30	3 5/8	r	4 1/2	r	r	r
33 1/4	35	7/16	1 1/16	1 3/4	r	3	2 5/8
33 1/4	40	r	r	1/2	r	r	r
Mc Don	40	5 1/8	r	r	r	r	5/16
44 3/4	45	1 1/16	1 3/4	2 3/8	r	1 1/2	1 3/4
44 3/4	50	1/16	1/4	1/2	r	r	4 7/8
Mid SU	7 1/2	6	r	6 3/8	r	r	1/16
13 5/8	10	3 5/8	3 5/8	4	1/16	r	1/16
13 5/8	12 1/2	1 1/4	1 1/2	1 11/16	1/16	5/8	3/8
13 5/8	15	3/16	3/8	9/16	1 1/4	r	1 5/8
N C R	55	r	s	r	1/16	s	r
64 5/8	60	5	6 1/2	r	1/2	r	1 15/16
64 5/8	65	1 3/8	3 1/4	4 3/4	2	r	r
64 5/8	70	9/16	1 1/2	2 1/4	5 3/4	r	r
64 5/8	75	1/4	s	1	r	s	r

Source: *The Wall Street Journal,* April 29, May 27, June 28, 1988. Reprinted by permission of *The Wall Street Journal,*

Buying Call Options

The Leverage Strategy.   Leverage is a very common reason for buying call options when the market is expected to rise during the exercise period. The use of calls in this way is similar to warrants discussed in Chapter 12, but calls have shorter lives and lower premiums. The call option is priced much lower than the common stock, and the leverage is derived from a small percentage change in the price of the common stock that can cause a large percentage change in the price of the call option. For example, on May 26, 1988, Dow Chemical (Dow Ch.) common stock closed at $80 per share and the 85 July call closed at $1^3/_8$ (see Table 13–7). One month later, on June 27, the stock closed at $87^1/_4$ for a $7^1/_4$ point gain of 9.06 percent. The 85 July call closed at $3^1/_2$ for a $2^1/_8$ gain of 154.55 percent. The call option increased by more than 17 times the percentage move in the common stock. The relationship is indicated below.

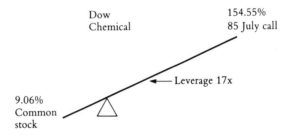

Figure 13–2 depicts the relationship between profit and loss opportunities for the Dow Chemical 85 July call option, assuming that the option is held until the day of expiration (no speculative premium exists at expiration).

As long as the common stock closes under 85, the call buyer loses the whole premium of $1^3/_8$ (or 100 times $1.375 equals $137.50). At a price of $86^3/_8$, the call buyer breaks even as the option is worth an intrinsic value of $1^3/_8$. As the stock increases past $86^3/_8$, the profit starts accumulating. At a price of $91^3/_8$, the profit equals $500 at expiration. If the option is sold before expiration, a speculative premium may alter the profit potential.

An investor striving for maximum leverage will generally buy options that are out-of-the-money or only slightly in the money. Buying high-priced options for $10 or $15 that are well in-the-money definitely limits the potential for leverage. You may have to invest almost as much in the options as you would have in the stock.

Playing the leverage game doesn't always work out. If a speculator on April 28 had assumed that Dow Chemical would go up and bought the June 80 call for $5^1/_4$, one month later on May 26, the 80 call option would have been worth $2^1/_4$. A three point loss has taken place. The decline in Dow common stock from $82^3/_4$ to 80 would have caused a $300 loss (100 × $3 = $300) for the option buyer. Although the stock declined only $2^3/_4$, or 3.32 percent, the call declined 3 points or 57.14 percent. This is a significant decline. If the stock

FIGURE 13–2   DOW CHEMICAL 85 JULY CALL BUY 1 OPTION (Excludes Commissions)

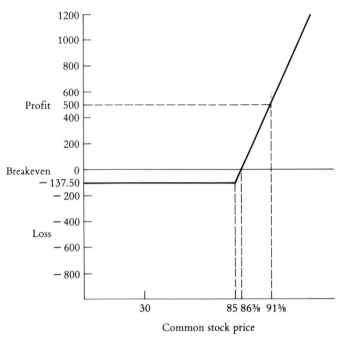

Common stock price

price stays at 80 until expiration, the owner of the 80 call can expect to lose the current call premium of $2^1/_4$ because the intrinsic value at a market price of 80 is zero. It is not hard to lose all your money under these circumstances—leverage works in reverse, too.

Call Options Instead of Stock.   Many people do not like to risk losing large amounts of money and view call options as a way of controlling 100 shares of stock without a large dollar commitment. For example, using Table 13–7 for the April 28, 1988, prices, May Department Stores (May DS) common stock could have been purchased at $34^7/_8$ or $3,487.50 for 100 shares. A September 35 call purchased on April 28, 1988, could also be bought for $3^1/_2$ ($350), which would leave $3,137.50 leftover cash ($3,487.50 − $350) for an investment elsewhere while still controlling 100 shares of May Department Stores at 35 through the option.

Assume the call is purchased for $350 and the $3,137.50 is left to be invested in a money market fund at 7 percent until May 26. The interest income would be about $17 for slightly less than one month.[4]

During this time, the stock declined from $34^7/_8$ to 30 for a loss of $4^7/_8$ or $487.50. This was partially offset by a $32 dividend for a net loss of $455.50

---

[4]The approximate calculation is: $3,137.50 × 7% × (28 days/365) = $16.85.

TABLE 13–8	COMPARISON OF CALL OPTION TO STOCK PURCHASE (May Department Stores)	
	Buy Stock: Receive Dividend	Buy Call: Receive Interest
	April 28, 1988: − $3,487.50 (100 × $34⁷/₈) investment	April 28, 1988: − $350 (100 × $3¹/₂) investment
	May 26, 1988, value: + $3,000.00 (100 × $30) value of stock + ____32.00 dividend $3,032.00 total value $455.50 loss ($3,032.00 − $3,487.50)	May 26, 1988, value: + $125 (100 × $1¹/₄) value of option + ____17 interest $142 total value $208 loss ($142 − $350)

on the 100 shares of stock. As would be expected, the call option also went down from 3¹/₂ ($350) to 1¹/₄ ($125). That's a loss of $225 which was partially offset by the $17 of interest income from the investment of leftover cash in a money market fund. The net loss associated with the call option is $208 ($225 − $17). The net loss on the call option of $208 is certainly less than the net loss of $455.50 on the stock purchase. The overall effect is demonstrated in Table 13–8. An additional unspecified cost consideration is that the investor probably saved another $25 to $50 in commissions since stock trading is more expensive than option trading.

Had the stock really declined in value, say to 20, the advantage of the limited dollar loss exposure of the option would be even more apparent. The purchaser of 100 shares of stock would have lost $1,487.50 as the stock declined from 34⁷/₈ to 20. This loss is only slightly reduced by the receipt of $32 in dividends. On the other hand, the purchaser of the option cannot lose more than the initial purchase price of $350 ($3¹/₂ × 100). Even this loss is slightly offset by the $17 of interest from the investment of leftover cash in a money market account.

Of course, if the stock does the opposite and goes way up to 50 or 60, both the stock purchaser and option buyer will show substantial profits.

Protecting a Short Position.   Calls are often used to cover a short sale against the risk of rising stock prices. This is called hedging your position; by purchasing a call, the short seller guarantees a loss of no more than a fixed amount while at the same time reducing any potential profit by the total premium paid for the call. Again refer to Table 13–7 and assume you had sold 100 shares of Ford Motor short at 46¹/₄ on May 26, 1988, and bought a September 45 call for 3³/₄ as protection against a rise in the price of the stock. By June 27, the stock has risen to 51³/₄ for a 5¹/₂ loss on the short position. This loss has been partially offset by an increase in the call option price on June 27 to 7⁵/₈, or a 3⁷/₈ gain. Instead of losing 5¹/₂, the short position is only out 1⁵/₈ so far (5¹/₂ − 3⁷/₈). This is the loss of 5¹/₂ on the short position less the gain of 3⁷/₈ on the call option. This strategy has locked in a maximum loss potential of 2¹/₂ plus commissions. The 2¹/₂ is the speculative premium paid for the September 45 call; as the stock rises, the speculative premium evaporates at expiration, but otherwise, the call goes up dollar for dollar with the stock. If the investor thinks Ford is a good short at $51^3/_4$ on June 27, he may sell the September 45 call for $7^5/_8$ on June 27 and be left with an unprotected short position hoping that the stock will eventually decline from its current price.

Consider the initial $3^3/_4$ call premium insurance. If the stock goes up, it limits your loss, but if the stock goes down as expected, your profit on the short position is reduced by the call premium. In the case of Ford, the stock would have to decline to $42^1/_2$ ($46^1/_4 - 3^3/_4$) before the short seller with call protection would break even. In other words, a decline of more than 8 percent in the stock price would have to occur before the short seller would begin to profit, and this ignores commissions. As is true of most option plays, there are advantages and disadvantages to most strategies.

Guaranteed Price.   Often, an investor thinks a stock will rise over the long term but does not currently have the cash available to purchase the stock. The important point for this strategy is that the investor wants to own this stock eventually but does not want to miss out on a good buying opportunity now (based on his or her expectations). Perhaps the oil stocks are depressed or semiconductors have hit bottom. A call option can be utilized. The investor could be anticipating a cash inflow at a specific time in the future when he plans to exercise the call option with a tax refund, a book royalty, or even the annual Christmas bonus.

For example, on May 26, 1988, Susan Davis buys a September 40 General Electric call option for $2^1/_2$, which is all speculative premium since GE is selling for $40 per share on that date. By the third Friday in September, she has received her $4,000 royalty check and exercises the option to buy the stock when the stock is selling at $45. For tax purposes, the cost or basis of this 100 shares of General Electric is the strike price (40) plus the option premium ($2^1/_2$), or $42^1/_2$ per share. Since most investors will not pursue this strategy if they expect prices to fall, they will usually seek out the deepest in-the-money option they can afford because it is likely to have the lowest speculative premium. For example, Ms. Davis could have bought the September 35 call with a price of 6, and the final cost would be 41 rather than $42^1/_2$ per share.

Writing Call Options

Writers of call options take the opposite side of the market from the buyers. The writer is similar to a short seller in that he or she expects the stock to decline or stay the same. In order for short sellers to profit, prices may decline, but since writers of call options receive a premium, they can make a profit if prices stay the same or even rise less than the speculative premium. Option writers can write covered options, meaning they own the underlying common stock, or they can write naked call options, meaning they do not own the underlying stock.

Writing covered call options is often considered a hedged position because if the stock price declines, the writer's loss on the stock is partially offset by the option premium. A potential writer of a covered call must decide if he is

TABLE 13–9	K MART JUNE STRIKE PRICES			
April 28, 1988		Market Price	June Strike Price	June Option Price
K mart		$33^5/_8$	30	$4^3/_8$
K mart		$33^5/_8$	35	$1^1/_4$
K mart		$33^5/_8$	40	Not traded

willing to sell the underlying stock if it closes above the strike price and the option is exercised.

Returning to Table 13–7 for another set of option quotes, find K mart options on April 28, 1988. The market price of the common stock is $33^5/_8$, and the writer for a June call option can choose from the strike prices reprinted in Table 13–9.

Remember, the writer agrees to sell 100 shares at the strike price for the consideration of the premium. The 30 strike price has the highest premium and would be a good write if the stock closed at less than 30 because the call would not get exercised and the writer would profit by the amount of the premium, $4^3/_8$. If the stock closed above 30, then the call could get exercised, and the writer would have to deliver 100 shares at 30. More likely, the option writer would buy back the option for its price in the market to avoid having the option exercised. For example, if the ending value of the stock were 34, the option writer could buy back the 30 call option for 4 and still have a $^3/_8$ profit before commissions. If the stock closed at more than $34^3/_8$, the call writer would buy back the option at a loss. Figure 13–3 shows this relationship between profit and loss and the common stock price in writing an option.

By June 17, the date of expiration, K mart stock closed at 33, and the 30 option was worth 3. Both a covered and a naked option would have made a profit. The covered option writer is assumed to have bought 100 shares at $33^5/_8$ at the time he wrote the option for $4^3/_8$ in April. The naked option writer merely sold the option for $4^3/_8$. It is further assumed the covered option writer received a $32 quarterly cash dividend between April and June. The analysis is presented below.

Covered Writer		Naked Writer	
− Initial investment (100 @ $33^5/_8$)	($3,362.50)	− Margin (30 percent of stock price)	($1,008.75)
+ Option premium ($4^3/_8$)	437.50	+ Option premium ($4^3/_8$)	437.50
+ Dividend	32.00	(no dividends received)	—
+ Ending value stock (33)	3,300.00	+ Ending value margin	1,008.75
− Repurchase of option (3)	(300.00)	− Repurchase of option (3)	(300.00)
Profit	$ 107.00	Profit	$ 137.50
Percent return on initial investment	2.45%	Percent return on initial margin investment	13.63%

The covered writer hedged the loss on his stock from $33^5/_8$ to 33 through profits from the option and a dividend. The naked option writer also made

FIGURE 13–3   K MART 30 JUNE CALLS WRITE 1 CALL (Excludes Commissions)

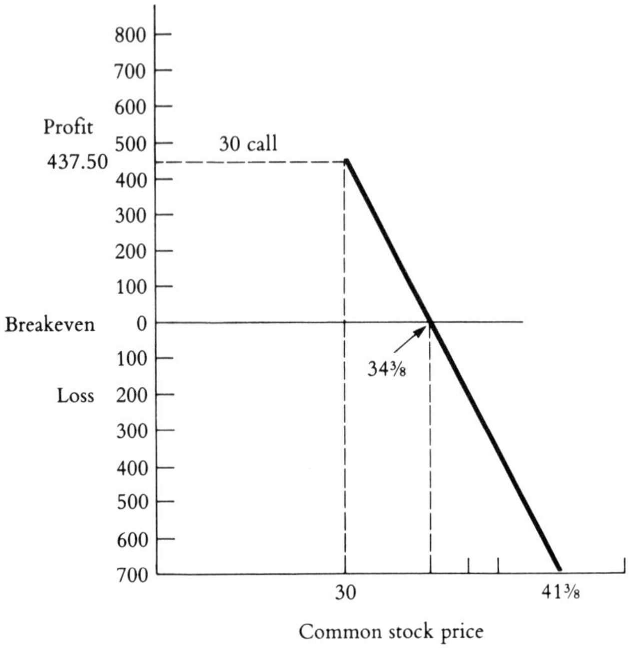

Common stock price

money and a high percentage return on his initial margin (13.63 percent) for less than a two-month investment or close to a 100 percent annualized return. The naked writer was required to put up margin on 30 percent of the value of the stock to ensure his ability to close out the option write if the stock should rise significantly. The capital was returned to him when it was no longer needed as collateral. To avoid exercise of the option, the call writer in both cases is assumed to enter the market with a closing transaction to repurchase the 30 call at 3 before expiration. If the stock price had risen, the naked writer was exposed to unlimited risk as he either had to close out his position at a loss or purchase the stock above the strike price and deliver it at a loss. The covered writer had limited risk because he owned the stock and can deliver it or close out his position before it is called.

Another critical decision for a call writer is the choice of months. In the section on option premiums, we examined percentage premiums per day and found that the shortest expiration dates provided the highest daily speculative premium. In most cases, the call writer will choose the short-term options and, as they expire, write another short-term option. *Annualized* returns of 10 to 15 percent are not uncommon for continuously covered writing strategies.

Buying Put Options

The owner (buyer) of a put may sell 100 shares of stock to the put writer at the strike price. The strategy behind a put is similar to selling short or writing a call except losses are limited to the total investment (premium), and no more risk exposure is possible if the stock rises. Buying a put in anticipation of a price decline is one method of speculating on market price changes. The same factors influencing call premiums also apply to put premiums except that expectations for the direction of the market are the opposite.

On April 28, 1988, Dow Chemical common stock price was $82^3/_4$, and an 85 September put could be purchased for 6 (see Table 13–7 and remember to look for put prices rather than call prices). The put was in the money by $2^1/_4$ ($85–82^3/_4$). Four and one-half months remained until expiration. The buyer of the put would expect a price decline with the idea that the intrinsic value of the put would increase. By May 26, Dow Chemical declined to 80 with the September 85 put trading at $7^1/_4$. The intrinsic value was now 5 ($85 - 80$), and the speculative premium was $2^1/_4$. At this time, the owner of the put had a $1^1/_4$ point gain on a $6 investment (or a 20.8 percent return) while the stock had declined only 3.44 percent.

Puts can make money in a down market and also possibly help offset a loss in the value of the common stock. As an example of the latter case, an owner of 100 shares of Dow Chemical could have bought a put to hedge against a loss in the value of the stock. Dow Chemical dropped $2^3/_4$ ($82^3/_4 - 80$), and the gain of $1^1/_4$ on the put would have offset some of the loss suffered on the common stock.

Hedges do not always work out as expected. For example, assume on May 26, an owner of Dow Chemical stock felt that the stock was going to decline because of expectations of rising interest rates, but he did not want to sell the stock and pay a capital gains tax on these shares held for many years. Instead, he bought an at-the-money September 80 put for $4^1/_4$ when the stock was trading at 80. One month later (June 27), Dow Chemical was up $7^1/_4$ (the decline never materialized), and the September put was worth $^7/_8$, providing a loss of $3^3/_8$ ($337.50) on the put. This $337.50 loss partially offset the $725 ($7^1/_4$) gain on the stock and reduced the total profit. Of course, one can think of the $337.50 loss as insurance against a price decline that never happened—much like auto insurance, we pay a premium for something we hope never happens.

USING OPTIONS IN COMBINATIONS

Spreads

Now that you have studied puts and calls from both the buyer's and writer's perspective, we proceed with a discussion of **spreads**. Most combinations of options are called spreads and consist of buying one option (going long) and writing an option (going short) on the same underlying stock. Spreads are for

TABLE 13–10	SPREADS (Call options)					
	Vertical spreads				*Option prices*	
		Market Price	Strike Price	Oct.	Jan.	April
XYZ		$36^3/_8$	35	4	6	$6^1/_2$
		$36^3/_8$	40	2	$3^3/_8$	4
		$36^3/_8$	45	$^{11}/_{16}$	$1^1/_2$	6
	Horizontal spread					
		Market Price	Strike Price	Oct.	Jan.	April
XYZ		$36^3/_8$	35	4	6	$6^1/_2$
		$36^3/_8$	40	2	$3^3/_8$	4
		$36^3/_8$	45	$^{11}/_{16}$	$1^1/_2$	6
	Diagonal Spread					
		Market Price	Strike Price	Oct.	Jan.	April
XYZ		$36^3/_8$	35	4	6	$6^1/_2$
		$36^3/_8$	40	2	$3^3/_8$	4
		$36^3/_8$	45	$^{11}/_{16}$	$1^1/_2$	6

the sophisticated investor and involve many variations on a theme. Vertical spreads involve buying and writing two contracts at different striking prices with the same month of expiration. Horizontal spreads consist of buying and writing two options with the same strike price but different months, and a diagonal spread is a combination of the vertical and horizontal spread. Table 13–10 presents an example of XYZ Corporation demonstrating the options, months, and strike prices involved in each type of spread. There are more complicated spreads than these, such as the butterfly spread, variable spread, and domino spread. We cannot attempt to explain all of these spreads in the space available, and so we will concentrate on vertical bull spreads and vertical bear spreads.

Since spreads require the purchase of one option and the sale of another option, a speculator's account will have either a debit or credit balance. If the cost of the long option position is greater than the revenue from the short option position, the speculator has a net cash outflow and a debit in his account. When your spread is put on with a debit, it is said that you have "bought the spread." You have "sold the spread" if the receipt from writing the short option position is greater than the cost of buying the long option position and you have a credit balance. For example, the difference between the option prices for a vertical spread on XYZ Corporation in Table 13–10 with October strike prices of 35 and 40 is $2 ($4 − $2). The $2 difference between these two option prices could be either a debit or credit, depending on whether a bull or bear spread is used. In either case, the profit or loss from a spread position results in the change between the two option prices over time as the price of the underlying stock goes up or down.

Vertical Bull Spread.   In a bull spread, the expectation is that the common stock price will rise. The speculator can buy the common stock outright, or if he wants to profit from an expected price increase but reduce his risk of

TABLE 13–11	PROFIT ON VERTICAL BULL SPREAD				
	XYZ October 35		XYZ October 40		Price Spread
	Bought at	4	Sold at	2	2
	Sold at	$7^1/_2$	Bought at	$4^1/_2$	3
	Gain	$3^1/_2$	(Loss)	$(2^1/_2)$	1
			Net gain	$100	
			Investment	$200	
			Return	50%	

loss, he can enter into a bull spread. Vertical bull spreads limit both the maximum gain and maximum loss available. They are usually debit positions because the spreader buys the higher-priced, in-the-money option and shorts (writes) an inexpensive, out-of-the-money option. Using Table 13–10 for an XYZ October vertical bull spread, we would buy the October 35 at 4 and sell the October 40 at 2 for a debit of 2 (price spread). This represents a $200 investment. Assume that three weeks later, XYZ stock rises from $36^3/_8$ to 42 with the October 35 selling at $7^1/_2$ (previously purchased at 4) and the October 40 at $4^1/_2$ (previously sold at 2). Table 13–11 shows the result of closing out the spread.

Because the investment was only $200, the total return of $100 provided a 50 percent return. However, returns on spreads can be greatly altered by commissions. If the following spread incurred commissions of $25 in and $25 out, the percentage return could be cut in half to 25 percent.

The maximum profit at expiration is equal to the difference in strike prices ($5 in this case) minus the initial price spread ($2 in this case). For the XYZ vertical bull spread, the maximum profit is $300, and the maximum loss is the original debit of $200. At expiration, all speculative premiums are gone, and each option sells at its intrinsic value. Table 13–12 shows maximum profit and loss at various closing market prices at expiration. Remember, our initial investment is $200.

As Table 13–12 indicates, profit does not increase after the stock moves through the 40 price range. Every dollar of increased profit on the long position is offset by $1 of loss on the short position after the stock passes a price of 40. One of the important but difficult aspects of spreading is forecasting a range of prices rather than just the direction prices will move. If a speculator is bullish, he or she may buy a call instead of spreading. The potential loss is higher with the call but still limited, while the possible gain is unlimited. The relationship between long calls and bull spreads starts in the *bottom* of Figure 13–4. Note the maximum loss with the bull spread is $200 and $400 with a long call. The break-even point is also $2 less for the bull spread ($37 versus $39). However, the long call has unlimited profit potential, and the bull spread is locked in at $300 at a stock price of $40 or higher. The spread position lowers the break-even point by $2 per share but also limits potential returns— a classic case of risk-return trade-off.

TABLE 13-12 XYZ VERTICAL BULL SPREAD

XYZ Stock Price at Expiration 35

October 35		October 40	
Bought at	4	Sold at	2
Expired at*	0	Expired at*	0
(Loss)	(4)	Gain	2

(Net loss) (2)
$(200) 100 percent loss

XYZ Stock Price at Expiration 40

October 35		October 40	
Bought at	4	Sold at	2
Sold at*	5	Expired at*	0
Gain	1	Gain	2

Net gain 3
$300 150 percent gain

XYZ Stock Price at Expiration 45

October 35		October 40	
Bought at	4	Sold at	2
Sold at*	10	Bought at*	5
Gain	6	Loss	(3)

Net gain 3
$300 150 percent gain

*All call options on date of expiration equal their intrinsic value.

FIGURE 13–4   PROFIT AND LOSS RELATIONSHIPS ON SPREADS AND CALLS

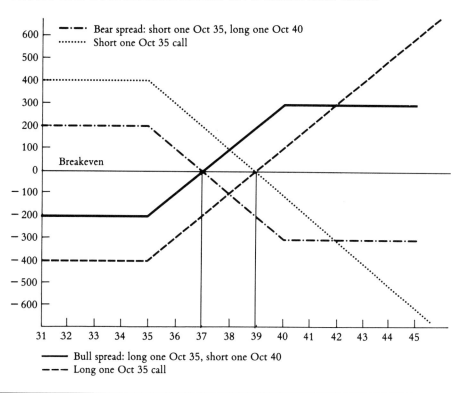

Vertical Bear Spread.   The speculator enters a bear spread anticipating a decline in stock prices. Instead of selling short or writing a call with both having
unlimited risk, he spreads by selling short the call with the lower strike price
(highest premium) and covers the upside risk with the purchase of a call having
a higher strike price. This creates a credit balance. In a sense, the bear spread
does the opposite of the vertical bull spread as seen in Table 13–13 in which
we show profits and losses from the strategy if XYZ ends up at 35 or at 40.
With a bear spread, the price spread of 2 is the maximum gain if the stock
closes at 35 or less at expiration, while the maximum loss equals 3, the difference between the exercise prices minus the price spread. The relationship
between bear spreads and writing a call option is also demonstrated in Figure
13–3 (the comparison starts at the *top* of the figure).

Straddles

A straddle is a combination of a put and call on the same stock with the same
strike price and expiration date. It is used to play wide fluctuations in stock
prices and is usually applied to individual stocks with high betas and a history
of large, short-term fluctuations in price. The speculator using a straddle may

TABLE 13–13   XYZ VERTICAL BEAR SPREAD

XYZ Stock Price at Expiration 35			XYZ Stock Price at Expiration 40		
October 35		October 40	October 35		October 40
Sold at	4	Bought at 2	Sold at	4	Bought at 2
Expired at	0	Expired at 0	Bought at	5	Expired at 0
Gain	4	(Loss) (2)	(Loss)	1	(Loss) 2
	Net gain 2			Net loss (3)	
	$200			$(300)	

be unsure of the direction of the price movement but may be able to make a large enough profit on one side of the straddle to cover the cost of both options even if one option expires worthless.

For example, assume a put and a call can be bought for $5 apiece on an ABC October 50 when ABC Corporation is selling at 50 with six months to expiration. The total investment is 10 ($1,000). If the stock should rise from 50 to 65 at expiration, the call would provide a profit of 10 (15 value − 5 cost), and the put would be left to expire worthless for a loss of 5. This would provide a net gain of 5, or $500. The same type of example can be drawn if the price goes way down. Some who engage in spreads or straddles might attempt to close out one position before the other. This expands the profit potential but also increases the risk.

OTHER OPTION CONSIDERATIONS

Many factors have not been covered in detail because of their changing nature over time. Tax laws relating to options are constantly changing, and some items, such as capital gains, have been revised several times in the last few years. We do know that the tax laws have a significant impact on spread positions and also on the tax treatment where put options are involved. Since the Tax Reform Act of 1986 made short-term and long-term capital gains taxed at the same rate as dividend income, some of the tax complications have been eliminated. However, the recognition of the year in which a gain or loss is declared can still be affected by option strategies in combination with stock positions. The best advice we can give is to check the tax consequences of any option strategy with your accountant or stockholder.

Commissions vary between different brokerage houses and are not easy to pinpoint for option transactions since quantity discounts exist. We can assure you that because many option positions involve small dollar investment outlays, commissions of $25 to $50 for buying and selling can significantly alter your returns and even create losses. Commissions on acquiring common stock through options are higher than the transaction costs of options, and this is a motivating force in closing out option transactions before expiration. Overall, commissions on options tend to be more significant than commissions on commodities or other highly leveraged investments.

APPENDIX 13–A: OPTIONS AVAILABLE ON COMPANIES' COMMON STOCK

EQUITY OPTIONS

Symbol	Name	Exchange[1]	Cycle[2]	Industry
ABT	Abbott Labs	PH	2	Drug/medical care
AMD	Advanced Micro Devices	P	1	Electronics
AET	Aetna Life	A	1	Insurance and finance
AHM	Ahmanson (H.F.) & Co.	A	1	Insurance and finance
APD	Air Products & Chemicals	PH	3	Chemicals
ALK	Alaska Air Group	A	1	Transportation
AL	Alcan Aluminum	A	3	Metals and mining
AAL	Alexander & Alexander Services	C	2	Insurance and finance
AEG	Allegis	C	2	Transportation
ALD	Allied Signal	PH	3	Chemicals
AA	Aluminum Co. of America	C	1	Metals and mining
AZA	ALZA	P	1	Drug/medical care
AMX	Amax	A	3	Metals and mining
AMH	Amdahl	C	2	Data process/computer
AHC	Amerada Hess	PH	2	Integrated oil
ABX	American Barrick Resources	A	1	Metals and mining
AMB	American Brands	A	3	Foods and beverage
ACY	American Cyanamid	A	1	Chemicals
AEP	American Electric Power	C	2	Utilities
AXP	American Express	C,A	1	Insurance and finance
AFL	American Family	A	2	Insurance and finance
AGC	American General	C	1	Insurance and finance
AGQ	American Greetings	C	1	Building materials
AHP	American Home Products	A	1	Drug/medical care
AIG	American International Group	C	2	Insurance and finance
AMI	American Medical International	P	3	Drug/medical care
APS	American President Companies, Ltd.	P	1	Transportation
AST	American Standard	NY	1	Building materials
T	American Telephone & Telegraph	C	1	Utilities
AIT	Ameritech	C	1	Insurance and finance
ADD	Ames Department Stores	P	1	Retail/merchandising
AMQ	Amgen	A	1	Drug/medical care
AN	Amoco	C	2	Integrated oil
AMP	AMP	C	2	Electronics
AMR	AMR	A	2	Transportation
APC	Anadarko Petroleum	C	2	Nonintegrated oil
ADI	Analog Devices	PH	3	Data process/computer
BUD	Anheuser-Busch	PH	3	Foods and beverage
APA	Apache	C	3	Nonintegrated oil
APQ	Apollo Computer	A	1	Data process/computer
AAQ	Apple Computer	C,A	1	Data process/computer
ABQ	Applied Biosystems	P	1	Drug/medical care
ADM	Archer-Daniels-Midland	PH	3	Foods and beverage
ALG	Arkla	A	2	Nonintegrated oil

[1]A—AMEX; P—Pacific; C—CBOE; PH—Philadelphia; NY—NYSE.
[2]Expiration cycle: 1—January cycle; 2—February cycle; 3—March cycle.

EQUITY OPTIONS (*continued*)

Symbol	Name	Exchange[1]	Cycle[2]	Industry
AS	Armco	PH	2	Metals and mining
ACK	Armstrong World Industries	PH	3	Building materials
ASA	ASA Ltd.	A	2	Metals and mining
AR	ASARCO	A	3	Metals and mining
ASH	Ashland Oil	PH	1	Integrated oil
TAQ	Ashton Tate	P	1	Data process/computer
ARC	Atlantic Richfield	C	1	Integrated oil
ADQ	Autodesk	P	1	Data process/computer
AUD	Automatic Data Processing	PH	2	Data process/computer
AVQ	Avantek	P	1	Electronics
AVT	Avnet	A	2	Electronics
AVP	Avon	C	1	Consumer goods
BHI	Baker Hughes	P	1	Oil services
BLY	Bally Manufacturing	C,A	2	Leisure and entertainment
BKB	Bank of Boston	PH	2	Insurance and finance
BAC	BankAmerica	C	1	Insurance and finance
BT	Bankers Trust New York	P	1	Insurance and finance
BCR	Bard (C.R.)	PH	1	Drug/medical care
BMG	Battle Mountain Gold	C,A	1	Metals and mining
BOL	Bausch & Lomb	A	1	Drug/medical care
BAX	Baxter Travenol Labs	C	2	Drug/medical care
BSC	Bear Stearns Companies	C	1	Insurance and finance
BDX	Becton Dickinson & Co.	PH	3	Drug/medical care
BEL	Bell Atlantic	C	1	Utilities
BLS	BellSouth	A	1	Utilities
BNL	Beneficial	P	1	Insurance and finance
BS	Bethlehem Steel	C	1	Metals and mining
BEV	Beverly Enterprises	P	3	Drug/medical care
BDK	Black & Decker	C	2	Tool/industrial machine
BA	Boeing	C	2	Aerospace
BCC	Boise Cascade	C	2	Building materials
BN	Borden	P	1	Foods and beverage
BOW	Bowater	P	3	Consumer goods
BMY	Bristol-Myers	C	3	Drug/medical care
BP	British Petroleum	P	1	Integrated oil
BFI	Browning-Ferris Industries	A	3	Tool/industrial machine
BC	Brunswick	C	3	Leisure and entertainment
BNI	Burlington Northern	C	1	Transportation
CAW	Caesars World	A	2	Leisure and entertainment
CAL	CalFed	P	1	Insurance and finance
CPB	Campbell Soup	NY	2	Foods and beverage
CP	Canadian Pacific	PH	1	Transportation
CCB	Capital Cities Communications	C	2	Leisure and entertainment
CHH	Carter Hawley Hale	P	2	Retail/merchandising
CKE	Castle & Cooke	P	3	Foods and beverage
CAT	Caterpillar	A	2	Tool/industrial machine
CBS	CBS	C	2	Leisure and entertainment
CX	Centerior Energy	P	2	Utilities
CTQ	Cetus	A	1	Drug/medical care
CHA	Champion International	C	3	Building materials
CSQ	Charming Shoppes	PH	1	Retail/merchandising
CMD	Charter Medical	P	1	Drug/medical care
CMB	Chase Manhattan	A	3	Insurance and finance
CHL	Chemical New York	A	3	Insurance and finance
CHW	Chemical Waste Management	A	3	Tool/industrial machine

[1]A—AMEX; P—Pacific; C—CBOE; PH—Philadelphia; NY—NYSE.
[2]Expiration cycle: 1—January cycle; 2—February cycle; 3—March cycle.

EQUITY OPTIONS (*continued*)

Symbol	Name	Exchange[1]	Cycle[2]	Industry
CHV	Chevron	A	3	Integrated oil
CHQ	Chi-Chi's	A	1	Leisure and entertainment
CNW	Chicago & Northwestern	C	1	Transportation
CCN	Chris-Craft Industries	C	1	Leisure and entertainment
C	Chrysler	C	1	Automotive and tire
CB	Chubb	NY	1	Insurance and finance
CHU	Church's Fried Chicken	PH	3	Leisure and entertainment
CI	CIGNA	C	1	Insurance and finance
CMZ	Cincinnati Milacron	PH	2	Tool/industrial machine
CKP	Circle K	P	1	Retail/merchandising
CC	Circuit City Stores	P	1	Retail/merchandising
CIR	Circus Circus Enterprises	A	3	Leisure and entertainment
CCI	Citicorp	C	1	Insurance and finance
CLX	Clorox	PH	1	Consumer goods
CGP	Coastal	C,A	3	Nonintegrated oil
KO	Coca-Cola	C	2	Foods and beverage
CCE	Coca-Cola Enterprises	C	2	Foods and beverage
CLO	Coleco Industries	PH	1	Leisure and entertainment
CL	Colgate Palmolive	C	2	Consumer goods
COT	Colt Industries	PH	2	Tool/industrial machine
CSP	Combustion Engineering	P	3	Tool/industrial machine
CCQ	Comcast (Class A)	PH	1	Leisure and entertainment
CDO	Comdisco	P	1	Data process/computer
CCC	Commercial Credit Company	PH	3	Insurance and finance
CBU	Commodore International	PH	2	Data process/computer
CWE	Commonwealth Edison	C	2	Utilities
CQ	Communications Satellite	PH	1	Utilities
CMY	Community Psychiatric Centers	PH	1	Drug/medical care
CPQ	Compaq Computer	P	1	Data process/computer
CMQ	Comprehensive Care	PH	1	Drug/medical care
CA	Computer Associates International	C	1	Data process/computer
CSC	Computer Sciences	C	3	Data process/computer
CAG	ConAgra	A	3	Foods and beverage
ED	Consolidated Edison	A	2	Utilities
CNF	Consolidated Freightways	NY	3	Transportation
CNG	Consolidated Natural Gas	A	1	Nonintegrated oil
CRR	Consolidated Rail	PH	1	Transportation
CTC	Contel	A	1	Utilities
CIC	Continental	PH	2	Insurance and finance
CDA	Control Data	C	2	Data process/computer
CVQ	Convergent Technologies	P	1	Data process/computer
COO	Cooper Companies	A	2	Drug/medical care
CBE	Cooper Industries	A	1	Tool/industrial machine
GLW	Corning Glass	C	2	Automotive and tire
CPC	CPC International	P	1	Retail/merchandising
CYR	Cray Research	P	3	Data process/computer
CSX	CSX	P	2	Transportation
CUL	Cullinet Software	C	1	Data process/computer
COQ	CVN Companies	A	1	Retail/merchandising
DAQ	Daisy Systems	P	1	Data process/computer
DCN	Dana	NY	1	Automotive and tire
DGN	Data General	P	3	Data process/computer
DPC	Dataproducts	P	1	Data process/computer
DH	Dayton Hudson	P	1	Retail/merchandising
DIC	Decision Industries	A	1	Data process/computer
DE	Deere	A	3	Tool/industrial machine
DAL	Delta Airlines	C	1	Transportation

[1]A—AMEX; P—Pacific; C—CBOE; PH—Philadelphia; NY—NYSE.
[2]Expiration cycle: 1—January cycle; 2—February cycle; 3—March cycle.

EQUITY OPTIONS (*continued*)

Symbol	Name	Exchange[1]	Cycle[2]	Industry
DLX	Deluxe Check Printer	P	1	Consumer goods
DTE	Detroit Edison	PH	1	Utilities
DBD	Diebold	C	2	Data process/computer
DEC	Digital Equipment	C,A	1	Data process/computer
D	Dominion Resources	PH	1	Utilities
DNY	Donnelley (R.R) and Sons	A	3	Leisure and entertainment
DOW	Dow Chemical	C	3	Chemicals
DJ	Dow Jones & Company	PH	3	Lesiure and entertainment
DI	Dresser Industries	PH	1	Oil services
DRY	Dreyfus	C	1	Insurance and finance
DIQ	DSC Communications	A	1	Electronics
DUK	Duke Power	PH	1	Utilities
DNB	Dun & Bradstreet	A	2	Insurance and finance
DD	duPont, (E.I. de Nemours)	C,A	1	Chemicals
ESY	E-Systems	P	2	Electronics
EFU	Eastern Gas & Fuel	PH	1	Misc/conglomerates
EK	Eastman Kodak	C	1	Consumer goods
ETN	Eaton	C	1	Electronics
ECH	Echlin	P	3	Automotive and tire
ECO	Echo Bay Mines	P	1	Metals and mining
AGE	Edwards (A.G.) & Sons	C	2	Insurance and finance
EGG	EG & G	PH	3	Electronics
EMR	Emerson Electric	A	3	Electronics
EAF	Emery Air Freight	PH	3	Transportation
EC	Engelhard	C	1	Metals and mining
ENE	Enron	C	1	Nonintegrated oil
ENS	ENSERCH	P	2	Nonintegrated oil
EY	Ethyl	P	1	Chemicals
XON	Exxon	C	1	Integrated oil
FGQ	Farmer's Group	PH	2	Insurance and finance
FDX	Federal Express	C	1	Transportation
FNM	Federal National Mortgage Assoc.	PH	3	Insurance and finance
FDS	Federated Department Stores	PH	2	Retail/merchandising
FIN	Financial Corp. of America	PH	3	Insurance and finance
FFC	Fireman's Fund	C	3	Insurance and finance
FIR	Firestone Tire & Rubber	A	2	Automotive and tire
FBC	First Boston	C	3	Insurance and finance
FNB	First Chicago	C	1	Insurance and finance
FEQ	First Executive	PH	1	Insurance and finance
I	First Interstate Bancorp	C	1	Insurance and finance
FLE	Fleetwood Enterprises	A	2	Automotive and tire
FLP	Floating Point Systems	A	2	Data process/computer
FLR	Fluor	C	1	Oil services
FMC	FMC	NY	2	Tool/industrial machine
F	Ford Motor	C	3	Automotive and tire
FRX	Forest Laboratories	C	2	Drug/medical care
FHP	Fort Howard Paper	PH	3	Consumer goods
FWC	Foster Wheeler	P	1	Tool/industrial machine
FPL	FPL Group	PH	3	Utilities
FBH	Frank B. Hall & Co.	A	2	Insurance and finance
FTX	Freeport-McMoRan	C	2	Metals and mining
GAF	GAF	PH	1	Building materials
GCI	Gannett	P	1	Leisure and entertainment
GPS	Gap, The	C	3	Retail/merchandising
GY	GenCorp	C	3	Nonintegrated oil
GEQ	Genentech	C,P	1	Drug/medical care

[1]A—AMEX; P—Pacific; C—CBOE; PH—Philadelphia; NY—NYSE.
[2]Expiration cycle: 1—January cycle; 2—February cycle; 3—March cycle.

EQUITY OPTIONS (continued)

Symbol	Name	Exchange[1]	Cycle[2]	Industry
GCN	General Cinema	C	2	Leisure and entertainment
GD	General Dynamics	C	2	Aerospace
GE	General Electric	C	3	Electronics
GRL	General Instrument	PH	3	Electronics
GIS	General Mills	P	1	Foods and beverage
GM	General Motors	C	3	Automotive and tire
GME	General Motors Class E Cmn.	PH	3	Data process/computer
GRN	General Re	A	3	Insurance and finance
GEN	Genrad	PH	3	Electronics
GPC	Genuine Parts	P	2	Automotive and tire
GP	Georgia-Pacific	PH	1	Building materials
GEB	Gerber Products Company	A	1	Foods and beverage
GRB	Gerber Scientific	PH	3	Data process/computer
GS	Gillette	A	3	Consumer goods
GLX	Glaxco Holdings	A	2	Drug/medical care
GLN	Glenfed Inc.	A	1	Insurance and finance
GNG	Golden Nugget	A	2	Leisure and entertainment
GDW	Golden West Financial	PH	2	Insurance and finance
GR	Goodrich (B.F.)	C	2	Automotive and tire
GT	Goodyear Tire & Rubber	A	1	Automotive and tire
GLD	Gould	A	1	Electronics
GRA	Grace (W.R.)	A	2	Misc./conglomerates
GNN	Great Northern Nekoosa	C	1	Consumer goods
GWF	Great Western Financial	C	1	Insurance and finance
G	Greyhound	A	1	Transportation
GQ	Grumman	C	1	Aerospace
GTE	GTE	A	3	Utilities
GW	Gulf + Western	C	3	Miscellaneous/conglomerates
HAL	Halliburton	C	1	Oil services
HAN	Hanson Trust	C	3	Miscellaneous/conglomerates
HBJ	Harcourt Brace Jovanich	A	1	Leisure and entertainment
HRS	Harris	C	2	Tool/industrial machine
HAS	Hasbro	P	1	Retail/merchandising
HBQ	HBO & Company	P	1	Drug/medical care
HL	Hecla Mining	A	3	Metals and mining
HNZ	Heinz (H.J.)	C	3	Foods and beverage
HP	Helmerich & Payne	NY	3	Oil services
HPC	Hercules	A	3	Chemicals
HSY	Hershey Foods	A	2	Food and beverage
HWP	Hewlett-Packard	C	2	Electronics
HLT	Hilton Hotels	P	1	Leisure and entertainment
HIT	Hitachi	C	1	Tool/industrial machine
HIA	Holiday Inns	C	2	Leisure and entertainment
HD	Home Depot	PH	2	Building materials
HFD	Home Federal Savings & Loan	C	1	Insurance and finance
HSN	Home Shopping Network	C	1	Retail/merchandising
HM	Homestake Mining	C	1	Metals and mining
HMC	Honda Motor	PH	1	Automotive and tire
HON	Honeywell	C	2	Data process/computer
HCA	Hospital Corp. of America	P	1	Drug/medical care
HI	Household International	A	1	Insurance and finance
HOU	Houston Industries	NY	3	Utilities
HUM	Humana	C	2	Drug/medical care
EFH	Hutton (E.F.) Group	A	1	Insurance and finance
ICX	IC Industries	C	3	Transportation
ICI	Imperial Chemical Industries	NY	1	Chemicals
N	Inco Limited	A	1	Miscellaneous/conglomerates

[1]A—AMEX; P—Pacific; C—CBOE; PH—Philadelphia; NY—NYSE.
[2]Expiration cycle: 1—January cycle; 2—February cycle; 3—March cycle.

EQUITY OPTIONS (*continued*)

Symbol	Name	Exchange[1]	Cycle[2]	Industry
IR	Ingersoll-Rand	NY	3	Tool/industrial machine
INQ	Intel	A	1	Data process/computer
IGQ	Intergraph	A	1	Data process/computer
IBM	International Business Machines	C	1	Data process/computer
IFF	International Flavors & Fragrances	C	2	Consumer goods
IGL	International Minerals and Chemical	C	1	Chemicals
IP	International Paper	C	1	Building materials
ITX	International Technology	P	3	Chemicals
IPG	Interpublic Group of Companies	NY	1	Leisure and entertainment
V	Irving Bank	NY	1	Insurance and finance
ITT	ITT	C	3	Misc./conglomerates
STN	J.P. Stevens	P	2	Consumer goods
JR	James River	NY	3	Building materials
JEQ	Jerrico	P	1	Leisure and entertainment
JLQ	Jiffy Lube	P	1	Retail/merchandising
JNJ	Johnson & Johnson	C	1	Drug/medical care
KM	K mart	C	3	Retail/merchandising
KB	Kaufman & Broad	PH	3	Building materials
K	Kellogg	A	3	Food and beverage
KEQ	Kemper	PH	1	Insurance and finance
KMG	Kerr-McGee	C	1	Intergrated oil
KMB	Kimberly Clark	A	1	Consumer goods
KNQ	Kinder-Care Learning Centers	P	1	Consumer goods
KWP	King World Productions	P	2	Leisure and entertainment
KRI	Knight Ridder	PH	1	Leisure and entertainment
KRA	Kraft	A	1	Food and beverage
KR	Kroger (The) Company	A	1	Retail/merchandising
LAC	Lac Minerals	C	1	Metals and mining
LEM	Lehman	PH	2	Insurance and finance
LLY	Lilly (Eli)	A	1	Drug/medical care
LTD	Limited	C	2	Retail/merchandising
LNQ	LIN Broadcasting	PH	2	Leisure and entertainment
LIT	Litton Industries	C	3	Miscellaneous/conglomerates
LIQ	Liz Claiborne	C	1	Retail/merchandising
LK	Lockheed	P	3	Aerospace
LTR	Loews	C	3	Miscellaneous/conglomerates
LNF	Lomas & Nettleton Financial	PH	3	Insurance and finance
LOR	Loral	C	1	Electronics
LT	Lorimar-Telepictures	C	1	Leisure and entertainment
LOQ	Lotus Development	A	1	Data process/computer
LLX	Louisiana Land & Explor.	PH	2	Nonintegrated oil
LPX	Louisiana-Pacific	A	2	Building materials
LOW	Lowe's Companies	PH	1	Building materials
LSQ	LSI Logic	C	1	Electronics
LZ	Lubrizol	PH	2	Chemicals
LKS	Lucky Stores	P	1	Retail/merchandising
LMQ	LyphoMed	A	1	Drug/medical care
MAI	M/A Com	A	2	Electronics
MLL	Macmillan	A	3	Leisure and entertainment
MNR	Manor Care	PH	1	Drug/medical care
MHC	Manufacturers Hanover	A	1	Insurance and finance
MDA	Mapco	P	1	Nonintegrated oil
MKC	Marion Labs	P	1	Drug/medical care
MHS	Marriott	PH	1	Leisure and entertainment
MMC	Marsh McLennan	P	1	Insurance and finance
ML	Martin Marietta	PH	3	Aerospace
MAS	Masco	A	1	Building materials

[1]A—AMEX; P—Pacific; C—CBOE; PH—Philadelphia; NY—NYSE.
[2]Expiration cycle: 1—January cycle; 2—February cycle; 3—March cycle.

EQUITY OPTIONS (*continued*)

Symbol	Name	Exchange[1]	Cycle[2]	Industry
MAT	Mattel	A	1	Retail/merchandising
MAQ	Maxicare Health Plans	P	1	Drug/medical care
MXQ	Maxtor	P	1	Data process/computer
MXS	Maxus Energy	P	1	Chemicals
MA	May Department Stores	C	3	Retail/merchandising
MYG	Maytag	NY	1	Tool/industrial machine
MCA	MCA	PH	2	Leisure and entertainment
MDR	McDermott International	PH	2	Oil services
MCD	McDonald's	C	3	Leisure and entertainment
MD	McDonnell Douglas	P	2	Aerospace
MHP	McGraw Hill	PH	2	Leisure and entertainment
MCP	MCI Communications	C	1	Electronics
MEA	Mead	C	1	Consumer goods
MDT	Medtronic	C	2	Electronics
MEL	Mellon Bank	NY	3	Insurance and finance
MES	Melville	P	2	Retail/merchandising
MNQ	Mentor	A,P	1	Drug/medical care
MGQ	Mentor Graphics	A	1	Data process/computer
MRK	Merck	C	1	Drug/medical care
MER	Merrill Lynch	C,A	1	Insurance and finance
MLP	Mesa Ltd. Partnership Deposit. Units	A	1	Nonintegrated oil
MSQ	Microsoft	A,P	1	Data process/computer
MSU	Middle South Utilities	C	3	Utilities
MYQ	Miniscribe	A	2	Data process/computer
MMM	Minnesota Mining & Mfg.	C	1	Consumer goods
MIQ	Minnetonka	P	1	Consumer goods
MND	Mitchell Energy & Devel.	P	3	Nonintegrated oil
MOB	Mobil	C	2	Integrated oil
MTC	Monsanto	C	1	Chemicals
JPM	Morgan (J.P.)	PH	3	Insurance and finance
MTI	Morton Thiokol	PH	1	Chemicals
MOT	Motorola	A	1	Electronics
MUR	Murphy Oil	P	2	Integrated oil
MYL	Mylan Laboratories	A	1	Drug/medical care
NME	National Medical Enterprises	A	2	Drug/medical care
NPD	National Patent Development	P	3	Drug/medical care
NSM	National Semiconductor	C,A	2	Electronics
NBI	NBI	C	2	Data process/computer
NCR	NCR	C	3	Data process/computer
NSQ	Network Systems	A	1	Electronics
NGC	Newmont Gold	PH	2	Metals and mining
NEM	Newmont Mining	PH	3	Metals and mining
NMK	Niagara Mohawk Power	A	3	Utilities
NIQ	Nike (Class B)	P	1	Consumer goods
NBL	Noble Affiliates	A	2	Nonintegrated oil
NOQ	Nordstrom	A	1	Retail/merchandising
NSC	Norfolk Southern	C	3	Transportation
NT	Northern Telecom	C	3	Electronics
NOC	Northrop	C	2	Aerospace
NWA	Northwest Airlines	C	1	Transportation
NVO	Novo Industri A/S	A	2	Drug/medical care
NYT	NY Times (Class A)	P	1	Leisure and entertainment
NYN	NYNEX	NY	1	Utilities
OXY	Occidental Petroleum	C	2	Nonintegrated oil
ODR	Ocean Drilling & Exploration	A	2	Oil services
OG	Ogden	C	2	Building materials

[1]A—AMEX; P—Pacific; C—CBOE; PH—Philadelphia; NY—NYSE.
[2]Expiration cycle: 1—January cycle; 2—February cycle; 3—March cycle.

EQUITY OPTIONS (*continued*)

Symbol	Name	Exchange[1]	Cycle[2]	Industry
OLN	Olin	A	2	Insurance and finance
ORQ	Oracle Systems	C	3	Data process/computer
OCF	Owens-Corning Fiberglas	PH	3	Building Materials
PCG	Pacific Gas & Electric	A	3	Utilities
PLT	Pacific Lighting	A	1	Utilities
PAC	Pacific Telesis	P	1	Utilities
PWJ	PaineWebber	C	1	Insurance/finance
PLL	Pall	C	3	Tool/industrial machine
PEL	Panhandle Eastern	PH	1	Nonintegrated oil
PH	Parker Hannifin	PH	2	Tool/industrial machine
PCI	Payless Cashways	C	1	Retail/merchandising
PC	PennCentral	PH	3	Miscellaneous/conglomerates
JCP	Penney (J.C.)	A	2	Retail/merchandising
PZL	Pennzoil	C	1	Nonintegrated oil
PEP	PepsiCo	C	1	Food and beverage
PKN	Perkin-Elmer	P	3	Electronics
PST	Petrie Stores	PH	3	Retail merchandising
PFE	Pfizer	A	3	Drug/medical care
PD	Phelps Dodge	A	1	Metals and mining
PE	Philadelphia Electric	P	1	Utilities
MO	Philip Morris	A	3	Food and beverage
PHG	Philips NV	NY	1	Tool/industrial machine
P	Phillips Petroleum	A	2	Integrated oil
PHM	PHM Holding	PH	1	Building materials
PIQ	Pic' N Save	P	1	Retail/merchandising
PBI	Pitney Bowes	A	1	Data process/computer
PCO	Pittston	PH	2	Metals and mining
PDG	Placer Dome	PH	3	Metals and mining
PNC	PNC Financial	PH	2	Insurance and finance
PRD	Polaroid	C,P	1	Consumer goods
PPG	PPG Industries	PH	2	Chemicals
PCQ	Price	P	1	Retail/merchandising
PRM	Prime Computer	A	3	Data process/computer
PDQ	Prime Motor Inns	P	1	Leisure and entertainment
PA	Primerica	A	2	Insurance/finance
PG	Procter & Gamble	A	1	Consumer goods
PEG	Public Service Enterprise Group	A	3	Utilities
OAT	Quaker Oats	PH	1	Food and beverage
KSF	Quaker State	A	3	Integrated oil
CUE	Quantum Chemical	A	2	Food and beverage
RAL	Ralston Purina	C	3	Food and beverage
RYC	Raychem	P	1	Chemicals
RTN	Raytheon	C	2	Electronics
RBK	Reebok International Ltd.	A,P	1	Retail/merchandising
RLM	Reynolds Metals	P	2	Metals and mining
RAD	Rite Aid	PH	1	Drug/medical care
RJR	RJR Nabisco	C	2	Food and beverage
ROK	Rockwell International	C	1	Aerospace
ROH	Rohm and Hass	A	1	Chemicals
RHR	Rohr Industries	PH	3	Tool/industries machine
REN	Rollins Environmental Services	P	1	Misc./conglomerates
ROR	Rorer Group	A	1	Drug/medical care
R	Rothschild (L.F.) Holdings	PH	2	Insurance and finance
RD	Royal Dutch Petroleum	A	2	Integrated oil
RBD	RubberMaid	P	2	Consumer goods
RYQ	Ryans Family Steakhouse	P	1	Leisure and entertainment

[1]A—AMEX; P—Pacific; C—CBOE; PH—Philadelphia; NY—NYSE.
[2]Expiration cycle: 1—January cycle; 2—February cycle; 3—March cycle.

EQUITY OPTIONS (*continued*)

Symbol	Name	Exchange[1]	Cycle[2]	Industry
RDR	Ryder Systems	P	2	Transportation
SAB	Sabine	C	1	Nonintegrated oil
SFQ	SafeCard Services	P	1	Insurance and finance
SAQ	Safeco	NY	2	Insurance and finance
SB	Salomon	PH	1	Insurance and finance
SFX	Santa Fe Southern Pacific	A	3	Transportation
SLE	Sara Lee	A	1	Food and beverage
SGP	Schering-Plough	P	2	Drug/medical care
SLB	Schlumberger Ltd.	C	2	Oil services
SFA	Scientific Altanta	P	3	Electronics
SPP	Scott Paper	PH	1	Consumer goods
SGQ	Seagate Technology	A	3	Data process/computer
VO	Seagram	P	2	Food and beverage
S	Sears, Roebuck	C	1	Retail/merchandising
SPC	Security Pacific	PH	3	Insurance and finance
SMQ	Service Merchandise	PH	1	Retail/merchandising
SHC	Shaklee	A	1	Leisure and entertainment
SDQ	Shared Medical Systems	P	1	Drug/medical care
SLH	Shearson Lehman Brothers Holdings	NY	3	Insurance/finance
SC	Shell Transport & Trading	C	2	Miscellaneous/conglomerates
SHW	Sherwin-Williams	C	3	Consumer goods
SHQ	Shoneys	P	1	Leisure and entertainment
SMF	Singer	A	2	Tool/industrial machine
SKY	Skyline	C	2	Automotive and tire
SKB	SmithKline-Beckman	P	3	Drug/medical care
SNA	Snap-on Tools	A	3	Retail/merchandising
SNT	Sonat	A	1	Nonintegrated oil
SNE	Sony	P	1	Electronics
SO	Southern	C	2	Utilities
SCE	Southern California Edison	P	1	Utilities
LUV	Southwest Airlines	C	3	Transportation
SBC	Southwestern Bell	P	1	Utilities
SQB	Squibb	C	1	Drug/medical care
SPQ	St. Paul Companies	C	1	Insurance and finance
STA	Staley Continental	C	2	Food and beverage
STO	Stone Container	P	3	Consumer goods
SHP	Stop and Shop	PH	2	Retail/merchandising
STQ	Stratus Computer	P	1	Data process/computer
SLM	Student Loan Marketing	C	1	Insurance and finance
SBQ	Subaru of America	PH	3	Automotive and tire
SUN	Sun	PH	2	Integrated oil
SUQ	Sun Microsystems	P	1	Data process/computer
SVU	Super Valu Stores	PH	1	Food and beverage
SYN	Syntex	C	3	Drug/medical care
TMB	Tambrands	NY	1	Consumer goods
TDM	Tandem Computers	A	1	Data process/computer
TAN	Tandy	C,A	1	Retail/merchandising
YOQ	TCBY Enterprises	P	1	Leisure and entertainment
TEK	Tektronix	C	3	Electronics
TCQ	Tele-Communications	A	1	Utilities
TDY	Teledyne	C,P	1	Miscellaneous/conglomerates
TLR	Telerate	NY	1	Insurance/finance
TGT	Tenneco	A	2	Nonintegrated oil
TER	Teradyne	P	1	Data process/computer
TSO	Tesoro Petroleum	PH	2	Nonintegrated oil

[1]A—AMEX; P—Pacific; C—CBOE; PH—Philadelphia; NY—NYSE.
[2]Expiration cycle: 1—January cycle; 2—February cycle; 3—March cycle.

EQUITY OPTIONS (*continued*)

Symbol	Name	Exchange[1]	Cycle[2]	Industry
TX	Texaco	A	1	Integrated oil
TET	Texas Eastern	PH	1	Nonintegrated oil
TXN	Texas Instruments	C	1	Electronics
TXU	Texas Utilities	P	1	Utilities
TXT	Textron	PH	3	Miscellaneous/conglomerates
CG	The Columbia Gas System	A	2	Utilities
THQ	3Com	P	1	Data process/computer
TL	Time	PH	3	Leisure and entertainment
TMC	Times Mirror	NY	3	Leisure and entertainment
TMK	Torchmark	A	2	Insurance/finance
TOY	Toys "R" Us	C	3	Retail/merchandising
TA	Transamerica	PH	2	Insurance and finance
E	Transco Energy	NY	2	Nonintegrated oil
TIC	Travelers	P	2	Insurance and finance
TY	Tri-Continental	PH	3	Insurance and finance
TRB	Tribune	C	2	Leisure and entertainment
TRW	TRW	A	1	Aerospace
TYC	Tyco Laboratories	PH	1	Consumer goods
TYQ	Tyson Foods	P	1	Food and beverage
USW	U S WEST	A	1	Utilities
HCQ	U.S. Health Care	A	1	Drug/medical care
USR	U.S. Shoes	PH	1	Retail/merchandising
UN	Unilever N.V.	A	2	Consumer goods
UCC	Union Camp	C	3	Chemicals
UK	Union Carbide	A	1	Chemicals
UNP	Union Pacific	PH	2	Transportation
UIS	Unisys	C, A	1	Data process/computer
UTX	United Technologies	C	2	Aerospace
UT	United Telecommunications	PH	2	Utilities
UCL	Unocal	P	1	Integrated oil
UPJ	Upjohn	C	1	Drug/medical care
U	USAirGroup	P	3	Transportation
FG	USF & G	PH	1	Insurance and finance
USG	USG	C	3	Building materials
UST	UST	C	2	Consumer goods
X	USX	A	1	Metals and mining
VLO	Valero Energy	A	3	Nonintegrated oil
VAR	Varian Associates	A	2	Electronics
VEE	Veeco Instrument	P	3	Electronics
VFC	VF	NY	2	Retail/merchandising
WMT	Wal-Mart Stores	C	3	Retail/merchandising
WAG	Walgreen	A	1	Drug/medical care
DIS	Walt Disney Company	C, A	1	Leisure and entertainment
WAN	Wang Labs (Class B)	P	1	Data process/computer
WCI	Warner Communications	C	2	Leisure and entertainment
WLA	Warner-Lambert	A	1	Drug/medical care
WMX	Waste Management	PH	2	Miscellaneous/conglomerates
WFC	Wells Fargo and Company	A	1	Insurance/finance
WEN	Wendy's International	P	3	Leisure and entertainment
WDC	Western Digital	P	1	Data process/computer
WX	Westinghouse Electric	A	1	Electronics
WY	Weyerhaeuser	C	1	Building materials
WHR	Whirlpool	C	3	Tool/industrial machine
WKR	Whittaker	A	3	Miscellaneous/conglomerates
WMB	Williams	C	2	Chemicals

[1] A—AMEX; P—Pacific; C—CBOE; PH—Philadelphia; NY—NYSE.
[2] Expiration cycle: 1—January cycle; 2—February cycle; 3—March cycle.

EQUITY OPTIONS (*concluded*)

Symbol	Name	Exchange[1]	Cycle[2]	Industry
WGO	Winnebago Industries	C	1	Automotive and tire
Z	Woolworth (F.W.)	PH	2	Retail/merchandising
WOQ	Worlds of Wonder	A	2	Retail/merchandising
WYQ	Wyse Technology	A	1	Data process/computer
XRX	Xerox	C,P	1	Data process/computer
XIQ	Xidex	P	1	Data process/computer
YLQ	Yellow Freight	C	3	Transportation
ZY	Zayre	C	1	Retail/merchandising
ZEN	Zenith Labs	P	1	Drug/medical care
ZE	Zenith Radio	A	2	Electronics

[1]A—AMEX; P—Pacific; C—CBOE; PH—Philadelphia; NY—NYSE.
[2]Expiration cycle: 1—January cycle; 2—February cycle; 3—March cycle.
Source: *Exchange Traded Options* (Chicago: Chicago Board Options Exchange, March, 1988), pp. 1–14.

APPENDIX 13–B: THE BLACK-SCHOLES OPTION PRICING MODEL*

THEORY

In 1973, Fischer Black and Myron Scholes published their derivation of a theoretical option pricing model. They started with three securities: riskless bonds, shares of common stock, and call options. The shares of common stock and call options were combined to form a riskless hedge which, by definition, had to duplicate the return of a discount bond with the same maturity length as the option. Using the riskless-hedge concept as a basis, Black and Scholes then proceeded with their model derivation.

Black and Scholes made the following assumptions:

1. Markets are frictionless. This means that there are no taxes or transactions costs; all securities are infinitely divisible; all market participants may borrow and lend at the known and constant riskless rate of interest; there are no penalties for short selling.
2. Stock prices are lognormally distributed, with a constant variance for the underlying returns.
3. The stock neither pays dividends nor makes any other distributions.
4. The option may be exercised only at maturity.

Given the above assumptions and the riskless hedging strategy, Black and Scholes derived a call option pricing model which may be expressed as:

$$c = (S)(N(d_1)) - (X)(e^{-rt})(N(d_2))$$

(13B–1)

where:

$$d_1 = \frac{ln(S/X) + (r + (\sigma^2/2))(T)}{(\sigma)(\sqrt{T})}$$

(13B–2)

$$d_2 = d_1 - (\sigma)(\sqrt{T})$$

(13B–3)

---

*This appendix was developed by Professor Carl Luft of DePaul University in consultation with the authors.

The terms are defined as follows:

c = The price of the call option
S = The prevailing market price of a share of common stock on the date the call option is written
X = The call option's striking price (exercise price)
r = The annualized prevailing short-term riskless rate of interest
T = The length of the option's life expressed in annual terms
σ^2 = The annualized variance associated with the underlying security's price changes
$N(\cdot)$ = The cumulative normal density function

At maturity ($T = 0$), so the call option must sell for either its intrinsic value or zero, whichever is greater. This boundary condition may be expressed mathematically as:

$$c = \text{Max}\ (0,\ S - X)$$

(13B–4)

It can be shown that given a put option and a call option, with the same striking price, and one share of the underlying stock, one can form a portfolio which will earn an amount equal to the option's striking price no matter what value the stock takes at expiration. From this relationship, the value of a put option can be determined mathematically as:

$$p = (X)(e^{-rt}) - S + c$$

(13B–5)

with the boundary condition,

$$p = \text{Max}(0,\ X - S)$$

(13B–6)

Equation 13B–5 is known as the put-call parity relationship, and Equation 13B–6 shows that at maturity the put must sell for either its intrinsic value or zero.

Inspection of Equations (13B–1) through (13B–6) reveals that both the call and put option prices are a function of only five variables: S, the underlying stock's market price; X, the striking price; T, the length of the option's life; σ^2, the volatility of the stock price changes; and r, the riskless rate of interest. All of these variables are easily observed or estimated. Previously developed option pricing models relied on variables that were based on individual investor risk preferences or on expected values of the stock price. Since the Black-Scholes model does not rely on such variables, it is superior to prior models.

To understand the behavior of options, it is necessary to examine the relationship of the option price to each of the five inputs. For call options, the price is positively related to the stock's price, the riskless rate of interest, the volatility, and the time to maturity, whereas an inverse relationship exists between the call option price and the striking price. Put options exhibit positive relationships with the striking price and volatility, negative relationships with the underlying stock price and riskless rate, and either a positive or negative relationship with time.

These relationships are easy to grasp if one realizes that options will not be exercised unless they have an intrinsic value. Consider first the price of the underlying stock. As it increases, calls go in-the-money and gain intrinsic value while puts fall out-of-the-money and lose intrinsic value. If the stock price declines, then the reverse is true. This explains the positive relationship between the call price and the stock price and the inverse relationship between the put price and stock price. Higher striking prices cause lower intrinsic values for call options but result in greater intrinsic values for put options. In this case, the loss of intrinsic value causes the inverse relationship between the call option and striking price, while the gain in intrinsic value causes the positive relationship between the put price and the striking price. The positive relationship of both put and call prices to the volatility can be explained by the fact that options written on higher-volatility stocks have a relatively better chance of being in the money at expiration than do options written on lower-volatility stocks. The positive relationship of the call price to the risk-free rate reflects the fact that the intrinsic value increases because the present value of the exercise price decreases as the risk-free rates rises. For put options, such rate increases and declining present values of exercise prices cause a loss of intrinsic value and account for the inverse relationship between the put option price and risk-free rate. Finally, the positive relationship of the call price to time is caused by an increasing intrinsic value due to lower present values of the exercise price for longer time periods. A more-complex relationship exists for put options.

Intuitively, one might expect a strictly positive relationship between the put option price and time. Such a relationship will occur if the put is at-the-money or out-of-the-money, while a negative relationship can exist for deep in-the-money puts. The reason for this inverse relationship lies embedded in the stock's price behavior. Since stock prices cannot be less than zero, the put option has a maximum value which equals the strike price. Investors who own deep in-the-money put options which are close to their maximum value because of extremely low stock prices are prohibited from exercising these options by assumption 4. Thus, time is working against these investors since they run the risk of losing intrinsic value if the stock price rises prior to expiration.

After deriving the model, Black and Scholes subjected it to empirical testing. They implemented the riskless-hedging strategy by combining options and stock in proportions dictated by the model and comparing these hedged returns to observed Treasury bill returns. They hypothesized that if the model provided equilibrium, or fair option prices, then the hedged returns should equal the returns generated by the investment in riskless securities. In effect, they attempted to create a synthetic Treasury bill by combining options and stock. If the returns from the option-stock hedge were not equal to the Treasury bill return, it meant that the model was unable to provide equilibrium option prices. On the other hand, if there was no significant difference between the hedge and Treasury bill returns, then it could be concluded that the model did indeed provide equilibrium prices. The results of the Black-Scholes empirical test showed no significant difference between the option-stock hedged returns and the Treasury bill returns. Thus, Black and Scholes concluded that the model did provide equilibrium prices.

The theoretical derivation and empirical justification of an option pricing model by Black and Scholes was an extremely important accomplishment with far-reaching implications. Basically, it meant that model-generated prices could be considered being the equilibrium, or correct, prices. Thus, an investor could use the model to determine whether the market had mispriced an option. Mispriced options spawn arbitrage opportunities. Given such an opportunity, the most-obvious way to benefit is to form a riskless hedge by combining options and stock and then maintaining the hedge until the option's market price adjusts to the equilibrium model price. This strategy will provide arbitrage profits since the level of risk that is being assumed equals that of a Treasury bill, but the profits earned when the mispriced option adjusts to the equilibrium, or model price, will exceed the profits earned from investing in a Treasury bill.

APPLICATION

The data in Table 13B–1 are used to illustrate the mechanics of the Black-Scholes Option Pricing Model.

Column (1) simply denotes the stock's ticker symbol, while columns (2) through (7) provide the required inputs for the model. Notice that the option maturity is expressed in calendar days and that the volatility is given as the standard deviation of returns. The call and put option prices (for both stocks) implied by the data will now be computed.

When the values from Table 13B–1 for CFL stock are used in equations (13B–2) and (13B–3), we obtain the following answers for d_1 and d_2:

$$d_1 = \frac{\ln(33/35) + (.09 + (.04/2))(.4932)}{(.2)(\sqrt{.4932})}$$

$$= \frac{-.0588 + .0543}{.1405}$$

$$= -.032$$

$$d_2 = -.032 - .1405$$

$$= -.1725$$

To obtain values for $N(d_1)$ and $N(d_2)$, the Standard Normal Distribution Function Table (Table 13B–2) must be used. The $N(d_1)$ and $N(d_2)$ values are found by first locating the row and column entries in the table which correspond to the computed d_1 and d_2 values. For CFL stock, the row entry is $-.0$, and the column entry is 3. This value of $-.03$ approximates the computed d_1

TABLE 13B–1   ILLUSTRATIVE DATA FOR BLACK-SCHOLES OPTION MODEL

(1)	(2)	(3)	(4)	(5)	(6)	(7)
	(S)	(X)	(T) Days to	(r)	(σ) Standard	(σ^2) Variance
Stock Symbol	Stock Price	Strike Price	Maturity Divided by Days in Year	Risk-Free Rate	Deviation of Returns	of Stock Returns
CFL	33	35	180/365	.09	.20	.04
GAH	42	40	50/365	.10	.23	.0529

value of $-.032$. For d_2, the row entry is $-.1$, and the column entry is 7, yielding a value of $-.17$, approximating the computed value of $-.1725$ for d_2.

Locating the d_1 and d_2 values yield the table entries which define the values of $N(d_1)$ and $N(d_2)$. For CFL stock, the $N(d_1)$ value is .4880, while the $N(d_2)$ value is .4325. In this example, these values are only approximations, since $-.03$ and $-.17$ are approximations. If one desires more precise ($N(d_1)$ and $N(d_2)$ values, they can be obtained through interpolation. For these examples, the approximations are sufficient.

At this point, all the necessary values for computing the option price have been found. Determining the options' prices via Equations (13B–1) and (13B–5) is all that remains to be done. Thus, the CFL call option price is:

$$
\begin{aligned}
c &= (33)(.4880) - (35)(e^{-(.09)(.4932)})(.4325) \\
&= 16.1040 - (35)(.9566)(.4325) \\
&= 16.1040 - 14.4805 \\
&= 1.6235
\end{aligned}
$$

and the CFL put option price is:

$$
\begin{aligned}
p &= (35)(e^{-(.09)(.4932)}) - 33 + 1.6235 \\
&= (35)(.9566) - 33 + 1.6235 \\
&= 2.1045
\end{aligned}
$$

Since each option controls 100 shares of stock, the theoretical call price is $162.35, while the put's theoretical price is $210.45.

A second example (using GAH stock) again uses the variables from Table 13B–1 and substitutes them into Equations (13B–2) and (13B–3) to derive d_1 and d_2 as follows:

$$
\begin{aligned}
d_1 &= \frac{\ln(42/40) + (.10 + (.0529/2))(.1370)}{(.23)(\sqrt{.1370})} \\
&= \frac{.0488 + .0173}{.0851} \\
&= .7767
\end{aligned}
$$

$$
\begin{aligned}
d_2 &= .7767 - .0851 \\
&= .6916
\end{aligned}
$$

TABLE 13B–2   STANDARD NORMAL DISTRIBUTION FUNCTION

t	0	1	2	3	4	5	6	7	8	9
.0	.5000	.5040	.5080	.5120	.5160	.5199	.5239	.5279	.5319	.5359
.1	.5398	.5438	.5478	.5517	.5557	.5596	.5636	.5675	.5714	.5753
.2	.5793	.5832	.5871	.5910	.5948	.5987	.6026	.6064	.6103	.6141
.3	.6179	.6217	.6255	.6293	.6331	.6368	.6406	.6443	.6480	.6517
.4	.6554	.6591	.6628	.6664	.6700	.6736	.6772	.6808	.6844	.6879
.5	.6915	.6950	.6985	.7019	.7054	.7088	.7123	.7157	.7190	.7224
.6	.7257	.7291	.7324	.7357	.7389	.7422	.7454	.7486	.7517	.7549
.7	.7580	.7611	.7642	.7673	.7704	.7734	.7764	.7794	.7823	.7852
.8	.7881	.7910	.7939	.7967	.7995	.8023	.8051	.8079	.8106	.8133
.9	.8159	.8186	.8212	.8238	.8264	.8289	.8315	.8340	.8365	.8389
1.0	.8413	.8438	.8461	.8485	.8508	.8531	.8554	.8577	.8599	.8621
1.1	.8643	.8665	.8686	.8708	.8729	.8749	.8770	.8790	.8810	.8830
1.2	.8849	.8869	.8888	.8907	.8925	.8944	.8962	.8980	.8997	.9015
1.3	.9032	.9049	.9066	.9082	.9099	.9115	.9131	.9147	.9162	.9177
1.4	.9192	.9207	.9222	.9236	.9251	.9265	.9279	.9292	.9306	.9319
1.5	.9332	.9345	.9357	.9370	.9382	.9394	.9406	.9418	.9429	.9441
1.6	.9452	.9463	.9474	.9484	.9495	.9505	.9515	.9525	.9535	.9545
1.7	.9554	.9564	.9573	.9582	.9591	.9599	.9608	.9616	.9625	.9633
1.8	.9641	.9649	.9656	.9664	.9671	.9678	.9686	.9693	.9700	.9706
1.9	.9713	.9719	.9726	.9732	.9738	.9744	.9750	.9756	.9761	.9767
2.0	.9773	.9778	.9783	.9788	.9793	.9798	.9803	.9808	.9812	.9817
2.1	.9821	.9826	.9830	.9834	.9838	.9842	.9846	.9850	.9854	.9857
2.2	.9861	.9864	.9868	.9871	.9875	.9878	.9881	.9884	.9887	.9890
2.3	.9893	.9896	.9898	.9901	.9904	.9906	.9909	.9911	.9913	.9916
2.4	.9918	.9920	.9922	.9925	.9927	.9929	.9931	.9932	.9934	.9936
2.5	.9938	.9940	.9941	.9943	.9945	.9946	.9948	.9949	.9951	.9952
2.6	.9953	.9955	.9956	.9957	.9959	.9960	.9961	.9962	.9963	.9964
2.7	.9965	.9966	.9967	.9968	.9969	.9970	.9971	.9972	.9973	.9974
2.8	.9974	.9975	.9976	.9977	.9978	.9978	.9979	.9979	.9980	.9981
2.9	.9981	.9982	.9982	.9983	.9984	.9984	.9985	.9985	.9986	.9986
3.	.9987									

t	0	1	2	3	4	5	6	7	8	9
-3.	.0013									
-2.9	.0019	.0018	.0017	.0017	.0016	.0016	.0015	.0015	.0014	.0014
-2.8	.0026	.0025	.0024	.0023	.0023	.0022	.0021	.0021	.0020	.0019
-2.7	.0035	.0034	.0033	.0032	.0031	.0030	.0029	.0028	.0027	.0026
-2.6	.0047	.0045	.0044	.0043	.0041	.0040	.0039	.0038	.0037	.0036
-2.5	.0062	.0060	.0059	.0057	.0055	.0054	.0052	.0051	.0049	.0048
-2.4	.0082	.0080	.0078	.0075	.0073	.0071	.0069	.0068	.0066	.0064
-2.3	.0107	.0104	.0102	.0099	.0096	.0094	.0091	.0089	.0087	.0084
-2.2	.0139	.0136	.0132	.0129	.0125	.0122	.0119	.0116	.0113	.0110
-2.1	.0179	.0174	.0170	.0166	.0162	.0158	.0154	.0150	.0146	.0143
-2.0	.0227	.0222	.0217	.0212	.0207	.0202	.0197	.0192	.0188	.0183
-1.9	.0287	.0281	.0274	.0268	.0262	.0256	.0250	.0244	.0239	.0233
-1.8	.0359	.0351	.0344	.0336	.0329	.0322	.0314	.0307	.0300	.0294
-1.7	.0446	.0436	.0427	.0418	.0409	.0401	.0392	.0384	.0375	.0367
-1.6	.0548	.0537	.0526	.0516	.0505	.0495	.0485	.0475	.0465	.0455
-1.5	.0668	.0655	.0643	.0630	.0618	.0606	.0594	.0582	.0571	.0559
-1.4	.0808	.0793	.0778	.0764	.0749	.0735	.0721	.0708	.0694	.0681
-1.3	.0968	.0951	.0934	.0918	.0901	.0885	.0869	.0853	.0838	.0823
-1.2	.1151	.1131	.1112	.1093	.1075	.1056	.1038	.1020	.1003	.0985
-1.1	.1357	.1335	.1314	.1292	.1271	.1251	.1230	.1210	.1190	.1170
-1.0	.1587	.1562	.1539	.1515	.1492	.1469	.1446	.1423	.1401	.1379
-.9	.1841	.1814	.1788	.1762	.1736	.1711	.1685	.1660	.1635	.1611
-.8	.2119	.2090	.2061	.2033	.2005	.1977	.1949	.1921	.1894	.1867
-.7	.2420	.2389	.2358	.2326	.2297	.2266	.2236	.2206	.2177	.2148
-.6	.2743	.2709	.2676	.2643	.2611	.2578	.2546	.2514	.2483	.2451
-.5	.3085	.3050	.3015	.2981	.2946	.2912	.2877	.2843	.2810	.2776
-.4	.3446	.3409	.3372	.3336	.3300	.3264	.3228	.3192	.3156	.3121
-.3	.3821	.3783	.3745	.3707	.3669	.3632	.3594	.3557	.3520	.3483
-.2	.4207	.4168	.4129	.4090	.4052	.4013	.3974	.3936	.3897	.3859
-.1	.4602	.4562	.4522	.4483	.4443	.4404	.4364	.4325	.4286	.4247
-.0	.5000	.4960	.4920	.4880	.4840	.4801	.4761	.4721	.4681	.4641

The $N(d_1)$ and $N(d_2)$ values from the Standard Normal Distribution Table (13B–2) are .7823 and .7549, respectively. As mentioned in the previous example, greater precision is possible through interpolation.

Given the above values, the GAH call and put prices are computed as:

$$c = (42)(.7823) - (40)(e^{-(.10)(.1370)})(.7549)$$
$$= 32.8566 - (40)(.9864)(.7549)$$
$$= 32.8566 - 29.7853$$
$$= 3.0713$$
$$p = (40)(e^{-(.10)(.1370)}) - 42 + 3.0713$$
$$= (40)(.9864) - 42 + 3.0713$$
$$= .5273$$

These calculations indicate that the theoretically correct price (for 100 shares) for the call is $307.13 and that $52.73 is the theoretically correct price for the put.

Suppose the market had priced the GAH call at $262.50. How would you be able to earn arbitrage profits? According to Black and Scholes, you would buy the undervalued calls at $262.50 and sell shares of GAH stock at $42 per share to form a riskless hedge and thus obtain arbitrage profits when equilibrium is established. However, to implement such a strategy, an investor must know how many shares to combine with each option in order to form the riskless hedge. This information is provided by $N(d_1)$ and is known as the hedge ratio or delta.

Since each option controls 100 shares of stock, the appropriate arbitrage activity in this example is to sell .7823 shares of GAH stock for every option purchased. Practically speaking, one cannot buy and sell fractional shares. Thus, 78 shares should be sold for each option that is purchased. If the market had overpriced the option, then the arbitrageur would sell options and purchase 78 shares for each option sold. In either case, the hedge's risk level will equal that of a Treasury bill, but the hedge's returns will exceed the Treasury bill's return, thus generating arbitrage profits.

Part Four

BROADENING THE INVESTMENT PERSPECTIVE

■ OUTLINE

■ INTRODUCTION

In this section, we expand the investment horizon to consider many different types of investment strategies.

We begin in Chapter 14 with a consideration of special situations that at times exist in the stock market. Empirical research has indicated that some of these investment alternatives may provide superior returns on a risk-adjusted basis. Topics for consideration include investing in mergers and acquisitions, in new stock issues, in securities that are initially listed on major exchanges, and in firms that are repurchasing their own shares in the market. Also, the possible advantage of investing in small firms or those with low P/E ratios is considered along with other similar topics. Many of these special situations may indicate that the market is less efficient than was generally thought a decade ago.

Another consideration for the investor expanding the investment horizon is that of commodity and financial futures (discussed in Chapter 15). Commodities include such items as wheat, copper, and pork bellies, whereas financial futures include such categories as currencies and Treasury securities. In the chapter, we consider the mechanics of various trading and hedging strategies and the risks that are involved.

As a follow-up to Chapter 15, we expand the discussion to stock index futures and options in Chapter 16. It is currently possible to hedge the risk of an entire stock portfolio by going short (selling futures or writing options) on such indexes as the S&P 500, S&P 100, NYSE Index, and so on. Speculative strategies for upward markets are also considered. Furthermore, the relationship of these so-called derivative products to the market crash of 1987 is also considered.

The emphasis in Chapter 17 is on real assets, which include real estate, gold and silver, precious gems, collectibles, and many other forms of tangible assets. Real assets are thought to represent a strong inflation hedge; however, they also have drawbacks in terms of illiquidity and high transaction costs. In this chapter, we also go through a detailed analysis of a real estate investment project with special attention to the effects of the Tax Reform Act of 1986 on real estate deals.

For those who might wish to add an international dimension to their investment strategy, Chapter 18 may be of interest. Not only are there risk reduction benefits through international diversification but, in some cases, superior return potential as well. After pointing out some of the difficulties of foreign investments, the authors indicate how most of these can be overcome.

In the last chapter of this section, mutual funds are considered. We indicate the different types of funds (open-end versus closed-end, load versus no-load, and so forth). We also discuss the various services that are provided to mutual fund shareholders and important sources of information to potential investors.

14

INVESTMENTS IN SPECIAL SITUATIONS

MERGERS AND ACQUISITIONS

    Premiums for Acquired Companies
    Acquiring Company Performance
    Form of Payment
    Leveraged Buyouts

NEW STOCK ISSUES

    Performance of Investment Bankers
    Factors to Consider in a New Issue

EXCHANGE LISTINGS

STOCK REPURCHASE

    Reasons for Repurchase
    Actual Market Effect

THE SMALL FIRM AND LOW P/E RATIO EFFECTS

OTHER STOCK-RELATED SPECIAL SITUATIONS

I n a previous discussion of market efficiency in Chapter 8, we suggested that while the security markets were generally efficient in the valuing of securities, there were still opportunities for special returns in a limited number of circumstances. Just what these circumstances are is subject to debate as not all researchers agree.

In most instances, special or **abnormal returns** refer to gains beyond what the market would normally provide after adjustment for risk. In this chapter, we will explore such topics as market movements associated with mergers and acquisitions, the underpricing of new stock issues, the impact of an exchange listing on a stock's valuation, the stock market impact of a firm repurchasing its own shares, and the small-firm and low P/E effects.

We will attempt to separate some of the market folklore from significant analysis. Furthermore, when a valid investment opportunity is perceived to exist, we attempt to suggest under what circumstances it is most likely to prove profitable. Let's begin our analysis with a discussion of investment opportunities in mergers and acquisitions.

MERGERS AND ACQUISITIONS

Many stocks that were leaders in daily volume and price movement in the late 1970s and 1980s represented firms that were merger candidates; that is, companies that were being acquired or anticipated being acquired by other firms. The stocks of these acquisition candidates often increased by 60 percent or more over a relatively short period of time. The list of acquired companies include such well-known names as Conoco, Gulf Oil, Avis, EDS, Seven-Up, and Anaconda Copper.

Premiums for Acquired Company

The primary reason for the upward market movement in the value of the acquisition candidate is the high **premium** that is offered over current market value in a merger or acquisition. The premium represents the difference between the offering price per share and the market price per share for the candidate (before the impact of the offer). For example, a firm that is selling for $25 per share may attract a purchase price of $40 per share. Quite naturally, the stock will go up in response to the offer and the anticipated consummation of the merger.

As expected, researchers have consistently found that there are abnormal returns for acquisition candidates.[1] A study has indicated that the average

[1]Gershon Mandelker, "Risk and Return: The Case of Merging Firms," *Journal of Financial Economics*, December 1974, pp. 303–35; Donald R. Kummer and J. Ronald Hoffmeister, "Valuation Consequences of Cash Tender Offers," *Journal of Finance*, May 1978, pp. 505–16; and Peter Dodd, "Merger Proposals, Management Discretion and Stockholder Wealth," *Journal of Financial Economics*, December 1980, pp. 105–38.

TABLE 14–1   PREMIUMS PAID IN MERGERS AND ACQUISITIONS

Acquiring Firm	Acquired Firm	Price Paid in Cash for Acquired Company's Stock	Value of Acquired Firm three Months Before Announcement	Premium Paid (Percent)
Chevron	Gulf Oil	$80.00	$38.00	110.53%
Beatrice Food Co	Harmon International Industries	35.25	20.00	76.25
Parker Pen Co.	Manpower, Inc.	15.20	11.50	32.18
Colt Industries	Menaso Man.	26.60	15.00	77.33
Pepsico, Inc.	Pizza Hut, Inc.	38.00	22.375	69.83
Walter Kidde & Co.	Victor Comptometer	11.75	7.375	59.32
Dana Corporation	Weatherford Co.	14.00	9.375	49.33
Allis Chalmers Corporation	American Air Filter	34.00	19.50	74.36
Time, Inc.	Inland Containers	35.00	20.75	68.67
Chemical Bank	Texas Commerce Bank	32.75	20.25	61.73

premium paid in a recent time period was approximately 60 percent, and there was an associated upward price movement of a similar magnitude.[2] This is a much larger average premium than in prior time periods and may be attributed to the recognition of high replacement value in relationship to current market value. The premium was based on the difference between the price paid and the value of the acquisition candidate's stock *three months* before announcement of the merger. Some examples of premiums paid during the 1980s are presented in Table 14–1.

The only problem from an investment viewpoint is that approximately two thirds of the price gain related to large premiums takes place before public announcement. It is clear that people close to the situation are trading on information leaks. In the early 1980s, the highly prestigious investment banking house of Morgan Stanley was actually embarrassed by charges brought by the U.S. Attorney's Office that two of its former merger and acquisition specialists were conspiring to use privileged information on takeovers to make profits on secret trading accounts.[3] Later on in the 1980s, notorious insider traders Ivan Boesky and Dennis Levine actually served jail sentences for their misuse of information related to unannounced mergers.

Those who attempt to legitimately profit by investing in mergers and acquisitions can follow a number of routes. First of all, some investors try to identify merger candidates before public announcement to capture maximum profits. This is a difficult process. While researchers have attempted to identify financial and operating characteristics of acquisition candidates, the information

---

[2]Henry Oppenheimer and Stanley Block, "An Examination of Premiums and Exchange Ratios Associated with Merger Activity during the 1975–78 Period" (Financial Management Association Meeting, 1980).

[3]"Two Former Morgan Stanley Executives Accused of Plot Involving Takeover Data," *The Wall Street Journal*, February 4, 1981, p.2.

is often contradictory and may even change over time.[4] In prior time periods (such as the 1960s), acquisition candidates were often firms with sluggish records of performance, whereas many of the current acquirees are high-quality companies that have unusually good records of performance (Alcon Labs, Coca-Cola Bottling of Los Angeles, Steak and Ale, and EDS).

Some alert analysts do keep a close eye on such sources as *Industriscope's* "Stocks in the Spotlight," which pinpoints securities that are undergoing unusual volume or pricing patterns (of course, this could be for any number of reasons). Other investors identify industries where companies are being quickly absorbed and attempt to guess which firm will be the next to be acquired. Prime examples of such industries in recent times were natural resource firms being acquired by multinational oil companies, and food companies being absorbed by tobacco companies or other firms in the food or consumer product industry.

While trying to guess an acquisition candidate prior to public announcement can be potentially profitable, it requires that an investor tie up large blocks of capital in betting on an event that may never come to pass. Others prefer to invest at the time of announcement of a merger or acquisition. A gain of the magnitude of 20 percent or more may still be available (over a few months' time period). Perhaps a stock that was $25 before any consideration of merger is up to $34 on announcement. If the actual price is $40, there may still be a nice profit to be made. The only danger is that the announced merger may be called off, in which case the stock may sharply retreat in value, perhaps all the way back down to $25 (that is, assuming another potential acquiring company does not come into the picture). Examples of price drops associated with merger cancellations are shown in Table 14–2.

TABLE 14–2	STOCK MOVEMENT OF POTENTIAL ACQUIREES IN CANCELLED MERGERS		
Acquirer—Potential Acquiree	Preannouncement	One Day After Announcement	One Day After Cancellation
Mead Corporation—Occidental Petroleum	$20^3/_8$	$33^1/_4$	$23^1/_4$
Olin Corp.—Celanese	16	$23^3/_4$	$16^3/_4$
Chicago Rivet—MITE	$20^3/_4$	$28^1/_8$	$20^3/_4$

The wise investor must carefully access the likelihood of cancellation. Special attention must be given to such factors as the possibility of antitrust action, the attitude of the target company's management toward the merger, the possibility of unhappy stockholder suits, and the likelihood of poor earnings reports or other negative events. In a reasonably efficient market environment,

---

[4]Robert J. Monroe and Michael A. Simkowitz, "Investment Characteristics of Conglomerate Targets: A Discriminant Analysis," *Southern Journal of Business,* November 1971, pp. 1–15; and Donald J. Stevens, "Financial Characteristics of Merger Firms: A Multivariate Analysis," *Journal of Financial and Quantitative Analysis,* March 1973, pp. 149–58.

the potential price gain that exists at announcement may be well correlated with the likelihood of the merger being successfully consummated. That is to say, if it appears that the merger is almost certain to go through, the stock may be up to $37.50 at announcement based on an anticipated purchase price of $40. If a serious question remains, the stock may only be at $33. When a merger becomes reasonably certain, arbitrageurs come in and attempt to lock in profits by buying the acquisition candidate at a small spread from the purchase price.

One of the most interesting features of the current merger movement has been the heavy incidence of **unfriendly takeovers**; that is, the bidding of one company for another against its will. This strategy has occurred in 20 to 25 percent of announced mergers.[5] Such events often lead to the appearance of a third company on the scene, referred to as a **"white knight,"** whose function is to save the target company by buying them out, thus thwarting the undesired suitor. The new suitor is generally deemed to be friendly to the interests of the target company and may be specifically invited by it to partake in the process. Examples of white knights occurred when Gulf Oil thwarted an offer from Mesa Petroleum and went with Standard Oil of California (renamed Chevron) in 1984. Similarly, Marathon Oil rejected an offer from Mobil to merge with U.S. Steel in 1982.

As one might guess, these multiple-suitor bidding wars often lead to unusually attractive offers. A 40 to 60 percent premium may ultimately parlay into an 80 to 100 percent gain or more. For example, the bidding for Gulf Oil sent the stock from 38 to 80.

Acquiring Company Performance

What about the acquiring company's stock in the merger and acquisition process? Is this a special situation; that is, does this stock also show abnormal market gains associated with the event? A study by Mandelker has indicated that it does not.[6] Long-term economic studies have indicated that many of the anticipated results from mergers may be difficult to achieve.[7] There is often an initial feeling of optimism that is not borne out in reality. The **synergy**, or "$2 + 2 = 5$," effect associated with broadening product lines or eliminating overlapping functions may be offset by the inability of management to mesh divergent philosophies. However, companies do appear to be more adept at the process than in prior time periods; now, conservatively managed firms, such as General Motors, Du Pont, and Atlantic Richfield, are replacing the funny-money conglomerate gunslingers of the 1960s. Nevertheless, most investors would prefer to position themselves with the acquired firm, which

---

[5]Anna Merjos, "Costly Propositions—Some Big Mergers Have Lately Fallen through," *Barron's*, May 14, 1979, p. 9.

[6]Gershon Mandelker, "Risk and Return: The Case of Merging Firms," *Journal of Financial Economics*, December 1974, pp. 303–35.

[7]T. Hogarty, "The Profitability of Corporate Managers," *Journal of Business*, July 1970, pp. 317–27.

is certain to receive a high premium, rather than with the acquiring firm, which has to pay it.

Form of Payment

Another consideration in a merger is the form of payment. Cash offers usually carry a slightly higher premium than stock offers because of the immediate tax consequences to the acquired firm's shareholders. When stock is offered, the tax obligation usually may be deferred by the acquired company's stockholders until the stock of the acquiring firm is actually sold. This may occur relatively soon or many years in the future.

The merger movement of the late 1970s and the 1980s has seen a much heavier utilization of cash as a medium of payment than in prior time periods (in the 50 percent range as opposed to 25 percent in the 1960s). Many of the old accounting advantages associated with stock or residual stock items (convertibles, warrants) in mergers have been diminished by accounting rule changes.

Leveraged Buyouts

Some corporations are also taken over through **leveraged buyouts** (LBOs). Here, either the management of the company or some other investor group borrows the needed cash to repurchase all the shares of the company. The balance sheet of the company serves as the collateral base to make the borrowing possible. After the leveraged buyout, the company may be taken private for a period of time, in which unprofitable assets are sold off and reduction of debt takes place. The intent is then to bring the company to the public market once again (or resell it to another company) at a large profit over the initial purchase price. Successful leverage buyouts in the 1980s, in which profits of 50 percent or more were made, include those of Blue Bell, Leslie Fay, Metromedia, SFN, and Uniroyal. The largest leveraged buyoff (or financial transaction of any kind) involved RJR Nabisco in 1988. The price tag was in excess of $25 billion. Even larger deals may take place in the future.

NEW STOCK ISSUES

Another form of a special situation is the initial issuance of stock by a corporation. There is a belief in the investment community that securities may be underpriced when they are issued to the public for the first time. That is to say, when a company **goes public** by selling formerly privately held shares to new investors in the over-the-counter market, the price may not fully reflect the value of the security.

Why does this so-called **underpricing** take place, and what is the significance to the investor? The underpricing may be the result of the firm commitment to buy the shares that an investment banker makes in distributing the issue. That is, the investment banker agrees to buy the stock from company A at a set price and then resells it to the public (along with other investment bankers, dealers, and brokers). The investment banker must be certain that the issue will be fully subscribed to at the initial public market price or he (and others) will absorb losses or build up unwanted inventory. In order to protect his position, the investment banker may underprice the issue by 5 to 10 percent to ensure adequate demand.

Studies by Reilly,[8] McDonald and Fisher,[9] Ibbotson[10] and others have indicated there are positive abnormal returns in the new issues market for one week and one month after issue. Reilly, for example, observed positive excess returns of 10.9 percent of one week after issue and 11.6 percent one month after issue. However, the efficiency of the market comes into play after the stock is actively trading on a regular basis, and any excess returns begin to quickly disappear. The lesson to be learned here is that, on average, the best time to buy a new, **unseasoned** issue is on initial distribution from the underwriting syndicate (investment bankers, dealers, brokers), and the best time to sell is shortly thereafter.

Participating in the distribution of a new issue is not always as easy as it sounds. A really hot new issue may be initially oversubscribed, and only good customers of a brokerage house may be allocated shares. Such was the case in the feverish atmosphere that surrounded the initial public trading of Apple Computer and Genentech. Genentech actually went from $35 to $89 in the first 20 minutes of trading (only to quickly come back down). For the most part, customers with a regular brokerage account and a desire to participate in the new-issues market can find adequate opportunities for investment, though perhaps in less-spectacular opportunities than those described above.

Performance of Investment Bankers

Research studies indicate that large, prestigious investment banking houses do not generally provide the highest initial returns to investors in the new issues they underwrite.[11] The reason for this is that the upper-tier investment bankers tend to underwrite the issues of the strongest firms coming into the market. These firms generally shop around among the many investment bankers that are interested in their business and eventually negotiate terms that would allow for very little underpricing when they reach the market. (They want most of the benefits to go to the corporation, not to the initial stockholders.)

[8]Frank K. Reilly, "New Issues Revisited," *Financial Management,* Winter 1977, pp. 28–42.

[9]J. G. McDonald and A. K. Fisher, "New Issue Stock Price Behavior," *Journal of Finance,* March 1974, pp. 97–102.

[10]Roger G. Ibbotson, "Price Performance of Common Stock New Issues," *Journal of Financial Economics,* September 1975, pp. 235–72.

[11]Brian M. Neuberger and Carl T. Hammond, "A Study of Underwriters' Experience with Unseasoned New Issues," *Journal of Financial and Quantitative Analysis,* March 1974, pp. 165–74. Also, see Dennis E. Logue, "On the Pricing of Unseasoned New Issues, 1965–1969," *Journal of Financial and Quantitative Analysis,* January 1973, pp. 91–103; and Brian M. Neuberger and Chris A. La Chapelle, "Unseasoned New Issue Price Performance on Three Tiers: 1975–1980," *Financial Management,* Autumn 1983, pp. 23–28.

Factors to Consider in a New Issue

First, the investor should consider the management of the firm and their prior record of performance. In most cases, a firm that is going public will have past sales and profit figures that can be compared to others in the industry. In one study, the average sales volume for a firm approaching the new issues market was $22.9 million with $1.8 million in after-tax profits and $14.6 million in assets.[12]

The investor also should take a close look at the intended use of funds from the public distribution. There are many legitimate purposes, such as the construction of new plant and equipment, the expansion of product lines, or the reduction of debt. The investor should be less enthusiastic about circumstances in which funds are being used to buy out old stockholders or to acquire property from existing shareholders.

EXCHANGE LISTINGS

A special situation of some interest to investors is an **exchange listing**, in which a firm trading over-the-counter now lists its shares on an exchange (such as the American or New York Stock Exchange). Another version of a listing is for a firm to step up from an American Stock Exchange listing to a New York Stock Exchange listing.

An exchange listing may well generate interest in a security (particularly in reference to moving up from the over-the-counter market to an organized exchange). The issue will now be assigned a specialist who has responsibility for maintaining a continuous and orderly market.[13] Furthermore, there may be greater marketability for the issue as well as more readily available price quotes (particularly in small-town newspapers). An exchange listing may also make the issue more acceptable for margin trading and short selling. Large institutional investors and foreign investors may also consider a listed security more appropriate for inclusion in their portfolios.

Listed firms must meet certain size and performance criteria provided in Table 14–3 (and previously mentioned in Chapter 2 for the NYSE). Although the criteria are not highly restrictive, meeting these standards may still signal a favorable message to investors.

A number of research studies have specifically examined the stock market impact of exchange listings. As might be expected, a strong upward movement is associated with securities that are to be listed, but there is also a strong, sell-

---

[12]Stanley Block and Marjorie Stanley, "The Financial Characteristics and Price Movement Patterns of Companies Approaching the Unseasoned Securities Market in the Late 1970's," *Financial Management*, Winter 1980, pp. 30–36.

[13]This is not always a superior arrangement to having multiple market makers in the over-the-counter market. It depends on how dedicated the specialist is to maintaining the market. Some banks and smaller industrial firms may choose the competitive dealer system in the over-the-counter market in preference to the assigned specialist.

TABLE 14–3   MINIMUM REQUIREMENTS FOR EXCHANGE LISTING

1. Demonstrated earning power under competitive conditions of: *either* $2.5 million before Federal income taxes for the most recent year and $2 million pre-tax for each of the preceding two years, *or* an aggregate for the last three fiscal years of $6.5 million *together with* a minimum in the most-recent fiscal year of $4.5 million. (All three years must be profitable.)

2. Net tangible assets of $18 million, but greater emphasis is placed on the aggregate market value of the common stock.

3. Market value of publicly held shares, subject to adjustment depending on market conditions, within the following limits:

Maximum	$18,000,000
Minimum	$ 9,000,000
Present (2/13/84)	$18,000,000

4. A total of 1,100,000 common shares publicly held.

5. *Either* 2,000 holders of 100 shares or more, *or* 2,200 total stockholders *together with* average monthly trading volume (for the most recent six months) of 100,000 shares.

off after the event has taken place. Research by Van Horne,[14] Fabozzi,[15] and others[16] indicates that the total effect may be neutral. Research by Ying, Lewellen, Schlarbaum, and Lease (YLSL) would tend to indicate an overall gain.[17]

The really significant factor is that regardless of whether a stock has a higher net value a few months after listing as opposed to a few months before listing, there still may be profits to be made. This would be true if the investor simply bought the stock four to six weeks before listing and sold it upon listing. Because an application approval for listing is published in the weekly bulletin of the American Stock Exchange or the New York Stock Exchange well before the actual date of listing, this is often possible. The study by YLSL, cited above, indicates there may be an opportunity for abnormal returns on a risk-adjusted basis in the many weeks between announcement of listing and actual listing (between 4.40 percent and 16.26 percent over normal market returns, depending on the time period involved). In this case, YLSL actually reject the semistrong form of the efficient market hypothesis by suggesting there are substantial profits to be made even after announcement of a new listing. The wise investor may wish to sell on the eventual date of listing because sometimes a loss in value may take place at that point.

The reader should also be aware of the potential impact of delisting on a security; that is, the formal removal from New York Stock Exchange or

[14]James C. Van Horne, "New Listings and Their Price Behavior," *Journal of Finance,* September 1970, pp. 783–94.

[15]Frank J. Fabozzi, "Does Listing on the AMEX Increase the Value of Equity?" *Financial Management,* Spring 1981, pp. 43–50.

[16]Richard W. Furst, "Does Listing Increase the Market Value of Common Stock?" *Journal of Business,* April 1970, pp. 174–80; and Waldemar M. Goulet, "Price Changes, Managerial Accounting and Insider Trading at the Time of Listing," *Financial Management,* Spring 1974, pp. 303–6.

[17]Louis K. W. Ying, Wilbur G. Lewellen, Gary G. Schlarbaum, and Ronald C. Lease, "Stock Exchange Listing and Securities Returns," *Journal of Financial and Quantitative Analysis,* September 1977, pp. 415–32.

American Stock Exchange listing, and a resumption of trading over-the-counter. This may take place because the firm has fallen substantially below the requirements of the exchange.[18] As you would expect, this has a large negative effect on the security. Merjos found that 48 of the 50 firms in her study declined between the last day of trading on an exchange and the resumption of trading over-the-counter.[19] The average decline was 17 percent. While the value was not risk adjusted, it is large enough to indicate the clear significance of the event.

STOCK REPURCHASE

The **repurchase** by a firm of its own shares provides for an interesting special situation. The purchase price is generally over current market value and tends to increase the demand for the shares while decreasing the effective supply. Before we examine the stock market effects of a repurchase, we will briefly examine the reasons behind the corporate decision.

Reasons for Repurchase

In some cases, management believes their stock is undervalued in the market. Prior research studies have indicated that repurchased securities have generally underperformed the popular market averages before announcement of repurchase.[20] Thus, management or the board of directors may perceive this to be an excellent opportunity because of depressed prices. Others, however, might see the repurchase as a sign that management is not creative or that it lacks investment opportunities for the normal redeployment of capital.[21] Empirical study indicates that firms that engage in repurchase transactions often have lower sales and earnings growth and lower return on net worth than other, comparable firms.[22] There also tends to be a concentration of these firms in the lower-growth areas, such as apparels, steel, food products, tobacco, and aerospace.

Another reason for the repurchase of shares is the acquisition of treasury stock to be used in future mergers and acquisitions or to fulfill obligations under an employee stock option plan. Shares may also be acquired to reduce the number of voting shares outstanding and thus diminish the vulnerability of the corporation to an unwanted or unsolicited takeover attempt by another corporation. Finally, the repurchase decision may be closely associated with

---

[18]Firms may also be delisted because they have been acquired in a merger or acquisition, in which case the shares are no longer traded.

[19]Anna Merjos, "Stricken Securities," *Barron's,* March 4, 1963, p. 9.

[20]Richard Norgaard and Connie Norgaard. "A Critical Evaluation of Share Repurchase," *Financial Management,* Spring 1974, pp. 44–50; and Larry Y. Dann, "Common Stock Repurchases: An Analysis of Returns to Bondholders and Stockholders," *Journal of Financial Economics,* June 1981, pp. 113–38.

[21]Charles D. Ellis and Allen E. Young, *The Repurchase of Common Stock* (New York: The Ronald Press, 1971), p. 61.

[22]Norgaard and Norgaard, "A Critical Evaluation."

a desire to reduce stockholder servicing cost; that is, to eliminate small stockholder accounts that are particularly unprofitable for the corporation to maintain.

Actual Market Effect

From the viewpoint of a special situation, the key question is, What is the stock market impact of the repurchase? Is there money to be made here or not? Much of the earlier research said no.[23] However, more recent research would tend to indicate there might well be positive returns to investors in a repurchase situation.[24] Most of the higher returns are confined to formal tender offers to repurchase shares (perhaps 10 to 20 percent of the shares outstanding) rather than the use of informal, unannounced, open-market purchases. Under a formal tender offer, the corporation will specify the purchase price, the date of purchase, and the number of shares it wishes to acquire.

Of particular interest is the fact that most of the positive market movement comes *on* and *after* the announcement rather than before it. The implications are that there may be trading profits to be made here.

Dann determined that the average premium paid over the stock price (the

TABLE 14–4	SUMMARY STATISTICS FOR THE TENDER OFFER SAMPLE, 1962–1976 (143 Observations)		
	Characteristic of Offers	Mean (Percent)	Median (Percent)
	Tender offer premium relative to closing market price one *day* prior to announcement	22.46%	19.40%
	Tender offer premium relative to closing market price one *month* prior to announcement	20.85	18.83
	Percentage of outstanding shares sought	15.29	12.57
	Percentage of outstanding shares acquired	14.64	11.93
	Percentage of outstanding shares tendered	18.04	14.27
	Number of shares tendered ÷ number of shares sought	142.30	115.63
	Number of shares acquired ÷ number of shares sought	111.35	100.00
	Value of proposed repurchase relative to pre-offer market value of equity	19.29	15.28
	Value of actual repurchase relative to pre-offer market value of equity	18.63	13.90
	Duration of offer	22 days	20 days

Source: Larry Y. Dann, "Common Stock Repurchases: An Analysis of Returns of Bondholders and Stockholders," *Journal of Financial Economics*, June 1981, p. 122.

---

[23]A good example is Ellis and Young, *The Repurchase of Common Stock*, p. 156.

[24]Terry E. Dielman, Timothy J. Nantell, and Roger L. Wright, "Price Effects of Stock Repurchasing: A Random Coefficient Regression Approach," *Journal of Financial and Quantitative Analysis*, March 1980, p. 175–89; Larry Y. Dann, "Common Stock Repurchases: An Analysis of Returns to Bondholders and Stockholders," *Journal of Financial Economics*, June 1981, pp. 113–38; Theo Vermaelen, "Common Stock Repurchases and Market Signaling: An Empirical Study," *Journal of Financial Economics*, June 1981, pp. 139–83; and R. W. Masulis, "Stock Repurchase by Tender Offer: An Analysis of the Causes of Common Stock Price Changes," *Journal of Finance*, May 1980, pp. 305–19.

TABLE 14–5	COMMON STOCK RATES OF RETURN OVER A 121-DAY PERIOD AROUND ANNOUNCEMENT OF COMMON STOCK REPURCHASE TENDER OFFER

Trading Day	Mean Rate of Return (Percent)	Trading Day	Mean Rate of Return (Percent)
−60	.217%	0	8.946%
−50	−.034	1	6.832
−40	.058	2	.908
−30	−.562	3	−.041
−25	−.125	4	.133
−20	−.071	5	.158
−19	.026	6	.230
−18	−.346	7	.129
−17	−.317	8	.051
−16	−.413	9	−.211
−15	.377	10	.213
−14	−.228	11	.172
−13	−.738	12	−.024
−12	.051	13	.181
−11	−.424	14	−.143
−10	−.578	15	.497
−9	.188	16	−.105
−8	−.391	17	−.236
−7	.107	18	.148
−6	.417	19	.141
−5	−.169	20	−.057
−4	.943	25	−.003
−3	.239	30	−.025
−2	.490	40	.133
−1	.959	50	−.069
		60	.161

Source: Larry Y. Dann, "Common Stock Repurchases: An Analysis of Returns to Bondholders and Stockholders," *Journal of Financial Economics*, June 1981, p. 124.

day prior to announcement) was 22.46 percent as indicated on the top line of Table 14–4.

This high premium helps to generate a return of 8.946 percent on the day of announcement and 6.832 percent one day after announcement as indicated in Table 14–5. This represents a two–day return of approximately 15.8 percent.[25] Dann further indicated that the price movements shortly *before* announcement (time period 0) were negligible, as indicated in Table 14–5.

The predominant argument for the beneficial effects of the repurchase is that management knows what they are doing when they purchase their *own* shares. In effect, they are acting as insiders for the benefit of the corporation, and we previously observed in Chapter 8 that insiders tend to be correct in their investment decisions. This factor, combined with the high premium, may provide positive investment results. Of course, these are merely average results over many transactions, and not all tender offers will prove to be beneficial events. The investor must carefully examine the premium offered,

[25]Professor Dann's observations are based on raw data rather than normalized returns. However, they are of sufficient magnitude to be important.

TABLE 14–6   BIGGEST ANNOUNCED STOCK BUYBACKS OF 1987

Company	Common Shares (in Millions)	Value	Company	Common Shares (in Millions)	Value
General Motors	64.0	$4.72 billion	Procter & Gamble	10.0	810.0 million
Sante Fe Southern			Salomon	21.3	808.7 million
Pacific	60.0	3.38 billion	Hewlett-Packard	15.3	750.0 million
Ford	27.9	2.00 billion	Nynex	10.0	736.3 million
Coca-Cola	40.0	1.80 billion	Chrysler	27.0	729.0 million
Henley Group	64.5	1.76 billion	Burlington Industries	8.0	640.0 million
Gencorp	12.5	1.63 billion	Monsanto	8.0	627.0 million
IBM	12.9	1.57 billion	ITT	10.0	625.0 million
American Express	40.0	1.35 billion	Hospital Corp.		
Allied-Signal	25.0	1.11 billion	of America	12.0	612.0 million
Owens-Illinois	20.0	1.11 billion	Atlantic Richfield	8.3	600.0 million
J. C. Penney	20.0	1.04 billion	Schlumberger	20.0	595.0 million
Hercules	15.0	1.02 billion	Tektronix	15.6	593.2 million
IC Industries	30.8	1.00 billion	Boeing	15.0	592.5 million
Merck	5.4	1.00 billion	Kimberly-Clark	9.0	547.5 million
Philip Morris	10.0	933.5 million	Kraft	10.0	547.5 million
Bristol-Myers	25.0	925.0 million	Eaton	8.5	500.0 million
NCR	14.0	825.3 million	K mart	17.9	500.0 million

Note: Figures represent announcements, not actual purchases, and may include more than one announcement. Values are actual dollar amounts when available or estimates based on closing prices before announcements.
Source: Merrill Lynch & Co.

the number of shares to be repurchased, the reasons for repurchase, and the future impact on earnings and dividends per share.

One of the major developments of 1987 (the year of the crash) was the unusually large number of stock repurchases. More than 1,400 companies announced plans to buy back over $80 billion in stock. Many of these buybacks came after the Dow Jones Industrial Average declined 508 points on Black Monday, October 19, 1987. As one example, Citicorp sold $1.2 billion in new stock in September 1987 at $58.25 a share only to buy back almost $200 million on October 20 at a mere $37.50 a share. The largest announced stock buybacks for the historic year of 1987 are shown in Table 14–6.

THE SMALL-FIRM AND LOW P/E RATIO EFFECT

Two University of Chicago doctoral studies in the early 1980s have contended that the true key to superior risk-adjusted rates of return rests with investing in firms with small **market capitalizations**. (Market capitalization refers to shares outstanding times stock price.) In a study of New York Stock Exchange firms, covering from 1936 to 1975, Banz indicates that the lowest quintile (one fifth) firms in terms of market capitalization provide the highest returns even after adjusting for risk. Banz suggests, "On average, small NYSE firms have had significantly larger risk-adjusted returns than larger NYSE firms over a 40-year period."[26]

Some criticized Banz for using only NYSE firms in his analysis and for using a time period that included the effects of both a depression and a major war. Small firms had incredibly high returns following the depression. A similar type study, produced by Reinganum[27] at about the same time, overcame these criticisms. Reinganum examined 2,000 firms that were traded on the New York Stock Exchange or the American Stock Exchange between 1963 and 1980. He annually divided the 2,000 firms into 10 groupings based on size, with the smallest category representing less than $5 million in market capitalization and the largest grouping representing a billion dollars or more.

A synopsis of the results from the Reinganum study are presented in Table 14–7.

TABLE 14–7	SYNOPSIS OF RESULTS—REINGANUM STUDY		
(1) Grouping*	(2) Median Market Value (Capitalization, in Millions)	(3) Median Share Price	(4) Average Annual Return
MV 1	$ 4.6	$ 5.24	32.77%
MV 2	10.8	9.52	23.51
MV 3	19.3	12.89	22.98
MV 4	30.7	16.19	20.24
MV 5	47.2	19.22	19.08
MV 6	74.2	22.59	18.30
MV 7	119.1	26.44	15.64
MV 8	209.1	30.83	14.24
MV 9	434.6	34.43	13.00
MV 10	1,102.6	44.94	9.47

*MV = Market value.
Source: Marc R. Reinganum, "Portfolio Strategies Based on Market Capitalization," *The Journal of Portfolio Management,* Winter 1983, pp. 29–36.

Column (2) indicates the median value of the market capitalization for the firms in each group. Column (3) is the median stock price for firms in each group, while column (4) indicates average annual return associated with that category.

As observed in column (4), the smallest capitalization group (MV 1) outperformed the largest capitalization group (MV 10) by over 23 percent per year. Although not included in the table, in 14 out of the 18 years under study, the MV 1 group showed superior returns to the MV 10 group. In another similar analysis, Reinganum found that $1 invested in the smallest capitalization group would have grown to $46 between 1963 and 1980, while the same dollar

---

[26]Rolf W. Banz, "The Relationship between Returns and Market Value of Common Stocks," *Journal of Financial Economics,* March 1981, pp. 3–18.

[27]Marc R. Reinganum, "Misspecification of Capital Asset Pricing—Empirical Anomalies Based on Earnings Yield and Market Values," *Journal of Financial Economics,* March 1981, pp. 19–46. Also, "A Direct Test of Roll's Conjecture on the Firm Size Effect," *Journal of Finance,* March 1982, pp. 27–35; and "Portfolio Strategies Based on Market Capitalization," *The Journal of Portfolio Management,* Winter 1983, pp., 29–36.

invested in the largest capitalization group would have only grown to $4. As did Banz, Reinganum adjusted his returns for risk and continued to show superior risk-adjusted returns.

Such superior return evidence drew criticisms from different quarters. Roll suggested that small-capitalization studies underestimate the risk measure (beta) by failing to account for the infrequent and irregular trading patterns of stocks of smaller firms.[28] Stoll and Whaley maintained that transaction costs associated with dealing in smaller capitalization firms might severely cut into profit potential.[29] They indicated that the average buy-sell spread on small-capitalized, low-priced stocks might be four or five times that of large-capitalization firms. Reinganum has maintained that even after accounting for these criticisms, small-capitalization firms continue to demonstrate superior risk-adjusted returns.[30]

Given that there might be advantages to investing in smaller firms, why haven't professional money managers picked up on the strategy. This, in part, is a catch-22. Part of the reason for the inefficiency in this segment of the market that allows for superior returns is the absence of institutional traders. This absence means that less information is generated on the smaller firms, and the information that is generated is reacted to in a less-immediate fashion. Studies suggest an important linkage between the absence of organized information and superior return potential.[31]

Advocates of the small-firm effect argue that it is this phenomenon alone, rather than others, such as the low-P/E-ratio effect, that leads to superior risk-adjusted returns. Peavy and Goodman would argue that the low-P/E-ratio effect is also important.[32] In following up on the earlier work of Basu[33] on the importance of P/E ratios, they compensated for other factors that may have resulted in superior returns, such as the small size of the firm, the infrequent trading of stock, and the overall performance of an industry. They did this by using firms that had a market capitalization of at least $100 million, that had an active monthly trading volume of at least 250,000 shares, and were in the same industry. Thus, none of these factors was allowed to be an intervening variable in the relationship between returns and the level of P/E ratios.

After following these parameters, Peavy and Goodman showed a significant relationship between the firm's P/E ratios and risk-adjusted returns. Firms were broken down into quintiles based on the size of their P/E ratios. Quintile 1 con-

[28]Richard Roll, "A Possible Explanation of the Small Firm Effect," *Journal of Finance,* September 1981, pp. 879–88.

[29]H. A. Stoll and R. E. Whaley, "Transaction Costs and the Small Firm Effect," *Journal of Financial Economics,* March 1985, pp. 121–43.

[30]Marc R. Reinganum, "Misspecification of Capital Asset Pricing—Empirical Anomalies Based on Earnings Yield and Market Values," *Journal of Financial Economics,* March 1981, pp. 19–46.

[31]Avner Arbel and Paul Strebel, "Pay Attention to Neglected Firms," *The Journal of Portfolio Management,* Winter 1983, pp., 37–42.

[32]John W. Peavy III and David A. Goodman, "The Significance of P/Es for Portfolio Returns," *The Journal of Portfolio Management,* Winter 1983, pp. 43–47.

[33]S. Basu, "Investment Performance of Common Stocks in Relation to Their Price-Earnings Ratios: A Test of the Efficient Market Hypothesis," *Journal of Finance,* June 1977, pp. 663–82.

TABLE 14–8   P/E RATIOS AND PERFORMANCE: THE ELECTRONICS INDUSTRY
                    (1970–1980)

Quintile	Average P/E	Average Quarterly Return (Risk-Adjusted)	Average Beta
1	7.1	8.53	1.15
2	10.3	4.71	1.12
3	13.4	4.34	1.13
4	17.4	2.53	1.19
5	25.5	1.86	1.29

Source: John W. Peavy III and David A. Goodman, "The Significance of P/Es for Portfolio Returns," *The Journal of Portfolio Management,* Winter 1983, pp. 43–47.

tained firms with the lowest P/E ratios, quintile 2 had the next lowest P/E ratios, and so on up the scale. A portion of their results is presented in Table 14–8.

Note that lower P/E stocks have higher risk-adjusted returns. While Table 14–8 only shows data for the electronics industry, a similar pattern was found for other industries.

In summarizing this section, some researchers such as Banz and Reinganum argue that small size is the primary variable leading to superior returns, while others argue that it is the low-P/E-ratio effect. Perhaps it is a bit of both. Some would argue the existence of even a third or forth variable that is even more important than small size or low P/E ratio (such as dividend yield or low volume).[34] What is important is that smaller firms with low P/E ratios that are often neglected by major investors seem to provide a superior risk-adjusted return.

OTHER STOCK-RELATED SPECIAL SITUATIONS

Although the authors have attempted to highlight the major special situations related to stocks in the preceding pages, there are other opportunities as well. While only brief mention will be made in this section, the student may choose to follow up the footnoted references for additional information.

The January Effect.   Because stockholders may sell off their losers in late December to establish tax losses, these stocks are often depressed in value in early January and may represent bargains and an opportunity for high returns.[35]

The Weekend Effect.   Research evidence indicates that stocks tend to peak in value on Friday and generally decline in value on Monday. Thus, the theory

---

[34]Solveig Jansson, "The Big Debate over Little Stocks," *Institutional Investor,* June 1982, pp. 141–48.

[35]Ben Branch and J. Ryan, "Tax-Loss Trading: An Inefficiency Too Large to Ignore," *Financial Review,* Winter 1980, pp. 20–29.

IT'S THE "JANUARY EFFECT," BUT WILL IT OCCUR IN JANUARY?

Something mysterious happens every January in stock and bond markets around the world.

Small-company stocks rise sharply—overwhelming increases in large-company stocks for that month. High-yield, high-risk "junk" bonds also get a large hunk of their yearly appreciation in January.

Why it happens still isn't understood. One thing is known, however: A growing number of traders and speculators believe it's possible to make a short-term profit by playing the January Effect.

The strategy is simple. Around mid-December, investors buy small-company stocks selling for depressed prices or a mutual fund that invests in small-company stocks. After prices surge in early January, these investors lock in their gains by selling the stocks or switching out of their mutual fund and into a money market fund. Some investors take a similar approach with mutual funds that invest in junk bonds.

Still, it is possible to lose money trying to play the January Effect. In bear markets like the Januaries of 1978 and 1982, small stocks lost money.

"Even though they outperform large stocks, they can't fight the tape," says one trader.

One problem for investors trying to capitalize on the January Effect is transaction costs. Brokers' commissions, poor prices from wide bid-and-asked spreads on thinly traded over-the-counter stocks, and taxes can all erode returns, points out Robert Haugen, co-author of *The Incredible January Effect*. "Still, historically, the force is with you," he says.

Since the effect first got wide notice in 1981, Goldman, Sachs & Co. says the performance difference between small stocks and large stocks in January has been narrowing. Since 1982, small stocks rose an average of 4.2 percent in January, compared with 3.8 percent for large stocks. That's not nearly as significant as the 7.4 percent versus 1.4 percent comparison for 1926 to 1981.

Earl C. Gottschalk, Jr., *The Wall Street Journal*, December 14, 1988, pp. C1, C16. Reprinted by permission of *The Wall Street Journal,* © Dow Jones & Co., Inc., 1988. All rights reserved.

is that the time to buy is on late Monday and the time to sell is on late Friday. While over many decades this observation is valid,[36] generally the price movement is too small to profitably cover transaction costs. However, if you *know* you are going to sell a stock that you have held for a long time, you may prefer to do so later in the week rather than early in the week.

The Value Line Ranking Effect. *The Value Line Investment Survey* contains information on approximately 1,700 stocks (see Chapter 4). Using a valuation model, each company is rated from 1 through 5 for profitable market performance over the next 12 months. One is the highest possible rating, and 5 is the lowest. One hundred stocks are always in category 1. Researchers have generally indicated that category 1 stocks provide superior risk-adjusted returns

---

[36]Frank Cross, "The Behavior of Stock Prices on Fridays and Mondays," *Financial Analysts Journal,* November–December, 1973, pp. 67–69; Kenneth R. French, "Stock Returns and the Weekend Effect," *Journal of Financial Economics,* March 1980, pp. 55–69; and Lawrence Harris, "A Transaction Data Study of Weekly and Interdaily Patterns in Stock Returns," *Journal of Financial Economics,* May 1986, pp. 99–117.

over the other four categories and the market in general.[37] Of course, frequent trading may rapidly cut into these profits.

The Surprise-Earnings Effect.   As indicated in Chapter 8 in the discussion of efficient markets, accounting information tends to be quickly impounded in the value of a stock, and there appears to be little opportunity to garner superior returns from this data. Even if a firm reports a 20 percent increase in earnings, there is likely to be little market reaction to the announcement if the gain was generally anticipated. However, an exception to this rule may relate to truly *unexpected* earnings announcements.[38] If they are very positive, the stock may go up for a number of days after the announcement and thus provide a superior investment opportunity. The opposite would be true of a totally unexpected negative announcement.

---

[37]Fisher Black, "*Yes*, Virginia, There is Hope: Test of the Value Line Ranking System," *Financial Analysts Journal,* September–October 1973, pp. 10–14; Clark Holloway, "A Note on Testing an Aggressive Strategy Using Value Line Ranks," *Journal of Finance,* June 1981, pp. 711–19; and Scott E. Stickel, "The Effect of *Value Line Investment Survey* Rank Changes on Common Stock Prices," *Journal of Financial Economics,* March 1985, pp. 121–43.

[38]Richard Rendleman, Charles Jones, and Henry A. Latane, "Empirical Anomalies Based on Unexpected Earnings and the Importance of Risk Adjustments," *Journal of Financial Economics,* November 1982, pp. 269–87.

15

COMMODITIES AND FINANCIAL FUTURES

W hat do pork bellies, soybeans, Japanese yen, and Treasury bills have in common? They are all items on which contracts may be traded in the commodities and financial futures markets.

A **futures contract** is an agreement that provides for the delivery of a specific amount of a commodity at a designated time in the future at a given price. An example might be a contract to deliver 5,000 bushels of corn next September at $3 per bushel. The person who sells the contract does not need to have actual possession of the corn, nor does the purchaser of the contract need to plan on taking possession of the corn. Almost all commodity futures contracts are closed out or reversed before the actual transaction is to take place. Thus, the seller of a futures contract for the delivery of 5,000 bushels of corn may simply later buy back a similar contract for the purchase of 5,000 bushels and close out his position. The initial buyer also reverses his position. Over 97 percent of all contracts are closed out in this fashion rather than through actual delivery. The commodities futures market is similar to the options market in that there is a tremendous volume of activity, but very few actual items ever change hands.

The futures markets were originally set up to allow grain and livestock producers and processors to **hedge** their positions in a given commodity. For example, a wheat producer might have a five-month lead time between the planting of his crop and the actual harvesting and delivery to the market. While the current price of wheat might be $4 a bushel, there is a tremendous risk that the price might change before delivery to the market. The wheat producer can hedge his position by offering to sell futures contracts for the delivery of wheat. Even though he will probably close out or reverse these futures contracts prior to the call for actual delivery, he will still have effectively hedged his position. Let's see how this works. If the price of wheat goes down, he will have to sell his crop for less than he anticipated when he planted the wheat, but he will make up the difference on the wheat futures contracts. That is, he will be able to buy back the contracts for less than he sold them. Of course, if the price of the wheat goes up, the extra profit he makes on the crop will be lost on the futures contracts as he now has to buy back the contracts at a higher price.[1]

A miller who uses wheat as part of his processing faces the opposite dilemma in terms of pricing. The miller is afraid the price of wheat might go up and ultimately cut into his profit margin when he takes actual delivery of his product. He can hedge his position by buying futures contracts in wheat. If the actual price of wheat does go up, the extra cost of producing his product will be offset by the profits he makes on his futures contracts.

The commodities market allows the many parties in need of hedging opportunities to acquire contracts. While some of this could be accomplished on a private basis (one party in Kansas City calls another party in Chicago on the advice of his banker), this would be virtually impossible to handle on a large-

---

[1]The hedger not only reduces risk of loss but also eliminates additional profit opportunities. This may be appropriate for farmers since they are not in the risk-taking business but rather in agriculture.

FIGURE 15–1   COMMODITY RESEARCH BUREAU FUTURES PRICE INDEX (Monthly
                High, Low, and Close)

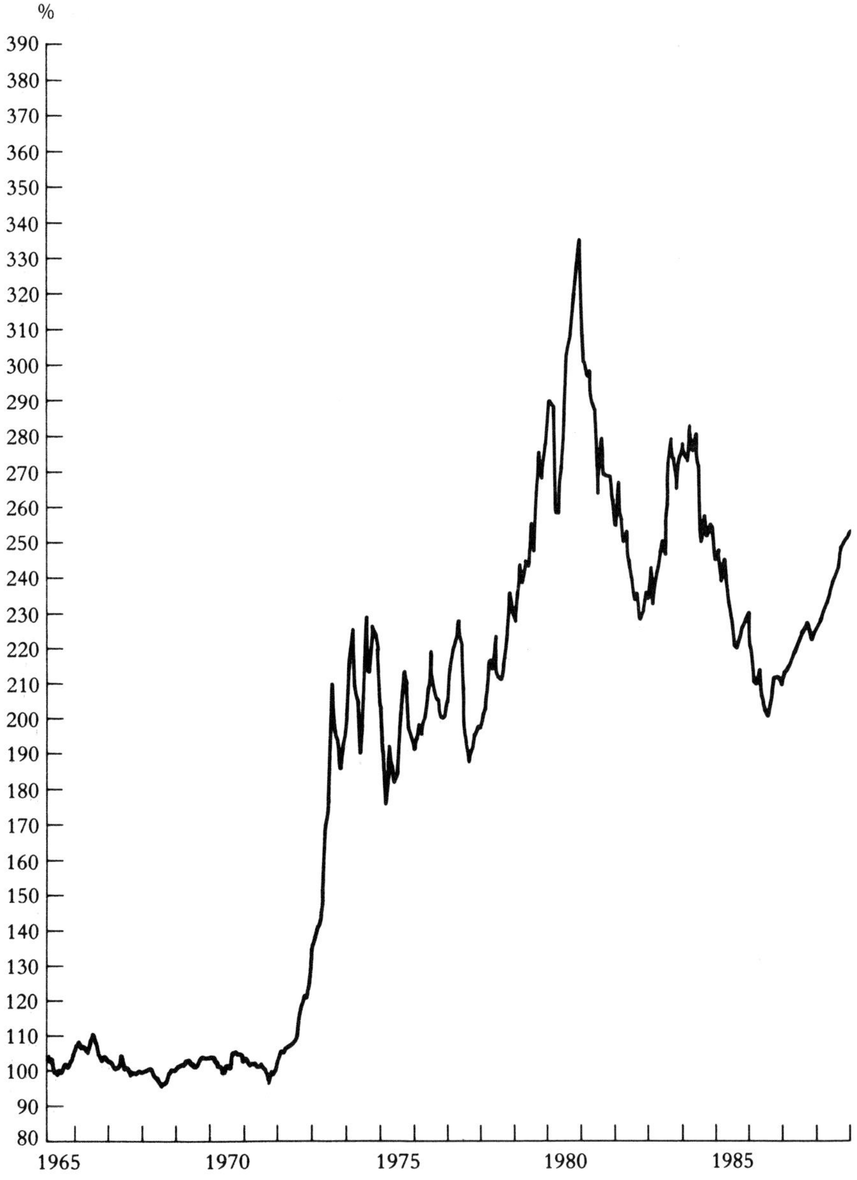

Source: *Commodity Yearbook* (New York Commodity Research Bureau, 1987), p. 7 (updated).

scale basis. Liquid, fluid markets such as those provided by the commodity exchanges are necessary to accomplish this function.

While the hedgers are the backbone and basic reason for existence of the commodity exchanges, they are not the only significant participants. We also have the speculators who take purely long or short positions without any intent to hedge actual ownership. Thus, there is the speculator in wheat or silver who believes that the next major price move can be predicted to such an extent that a substantial profit can be made. Because commodities are purchased on the basis of a small investment in the form of **margin** (usually running 5 to 15 percent of the value of the contract), there is substantial leverage on the investment, and percentage returns and losses are greatly magnified. The typical commodities trader often suffers many losses with the anticipation of a few very substantial gains. Commodities speculation, as opposed to hedging, represents somewhat of a gamble, and stories have been told of reformed commodities speculators who gave up the chase to spend the rest of their days merely playing the slot machines.

The volatility of commodity prices can be seen in Figure 15–1. While the price trend for the 27 commodities in the index has been upward, note the up and down patterns, particularly in the 1980s.

TYPES OF COMMODITIES AND EXCHANGES

Commodities and financial futures can be broken down into a number of categories based on their essential characteristics. As indicated in Table 15–1, there are six primary categories. In each case, we show representative items that fall under the category.

The first five categories represent traditional commodities, but category six came into prominence in the 1970s and 1980s, with foreign exchange futures originating in 1972, interest rate futures beginning in 1975, and stock index futures in 1982. Because many financial futures have tremendous implications for financial managers, we will give them special attention in a later section of this chapter. We will defer discussion of stock index futures to Chapter 16 so that they can be given *complete coverage* as a separate topic.

The commodities listed in Table 15–1 trade on various commodity exchanges in the United States and Canada (see Table 15–2). While the exchanges are well organized and efficient in their operation, they are still run by an open auction complete with outcries of bids and various hand-signal displays.

The largest commodity exchange is the Chicago Board of Trade (CBT) with the Chicago Mercantile Exchange (CME) in second place. While some exchanges are highly specialized, such as the New York Cotton Exchange, most exchanges trade in a wide number of securities. For example, the Chicago Board of Trade deals in such diverse products as corn, oats, soybeans, wheat, plywood, and Treasury bonds.

The activities of the commodity exchanges are primarily regulated by the Commodity Futures Trading Commission (CFTC), a federal regulatory agency established by Congress in 1975. The CFTC has had a number of jurisdictional disputes with the SEC over the regulation of financial futures.

TABLE 15–1	CATEGORIES OF COMMODITIES AND FINANCIAL FUTURES	
(1)	(2)	(3)

Grains and oilseeds:
  Corn
  Oats
  Soybeans
  Wheat
  Barley
  Rye
	Livestock and meat:
	  Cattle—feeder
	  Cattle—live
	  Hogs—live
	  Pork bellies
	  Turkeys
	  Broilers
		Food and fiber:
		  Cocoa
		  Coffee
		  Cotton
		  Orange juice
		  Potatoes
		  Sugar
		  Rice
		  Butter

(4)	(5)	(6)

Metals and petroleum:
  Copper
  Gold
  Platinum
  Silver
  Mercury
  Heating oil no. 2
	Wood:
	  Lumber
	  Plywood
		Financial futures:
		  a. Foreign exchange:
		     Pound, yen, franc,
		      etc.
		  b. Interest rate futures:
		     Treasury bonds
		     Treasury bills
		     Certificates of
		      deposit
		     Municipal bonds
		     Eurodollars
		  c. Stock index futures:
		     S&P 500
		     Value Line

Types of Commodities Contracts

The commodity contract lists the type of commodity and the denomination in which it is traded (bushels, pounds, troy ounces, metric tons, percentage points, etc.). The contract will also specify the standardized unit for trade (5,000 bushels, 30,000 pounds, etc.). A further designation will indicate the month in which the contract ends, with most commodities having a whole range of months from which to choose. Typically, contracts run as far as a year into the future, but some interest rate futures contracts extend as far as three years.

Examples of the sizes of futures contracts are presented in Table 15–3. Be aware that there may be many different forms of the same commodity (such as spring wheat or amber/durum wheat).

ACTUAL COMMODITIES CONTRACT

To examine the potential gain or loss in a commodities contract, let's go through a hypothetical investment. Assume we are considering the purchase of a December wheat contract (it is now May 1). The price on the futures contract is $4 per bushel. Since wheat trades in units of 5,000 bushels, the total price is $20,000. As we go through our example, we will examine many important features associated with commodity trading—beginning with margin requirements.

| TABLE 15–2 | MAJOR UNITED STATES AND CANADIAN COMMODITY EXCHANGES |

American Commodities Exchange (ACE)
Chicago Board of Trade (CBT)
Chicago Mercantile Exchange (CME)
   Also controls International Monetary Market (IMM)
Commodity Exchange (CMX)
Kansas City Board of Trade (KC)
Minneapolis Grain Exchange (MPLS)
New Orleans Commodity Exchange
New York Coffee, Sugar, and Cocoa Exchange (CSCE)
New York Cotton Exchange (CTN)
New York Futures Exchange (NYFE)
   Subsidiary of the New York Stock Exchange
New York Mercantile Exchange (NYM)
Pacific Commodities Exchange (PCE)
Winnipeg Grain Exchange (WPG)

Margin Requirements

Commodity trading is based on the use of margin rather than on actual cash dollars. Margin requirements are typically 5 to 15 percent of the value of the contract and may vary over time or even from exchange to exchange for a given commodity. For our example, we will assume a $2,100 margin requirement. This would represent 10.5 percent of the value of the contract ($20,000).

Margin requirements on commodities contracts are much lower than those on common stock transactions, where 50 percent of the purchase price has been the requirement since 1974. Furthermore, in the commodities market,

| TABLE 15–3 | SIZE OF COMMODITY CONTRACTS |

Contract	Trading Units	Size of Contract Based on Mid-1988 Prices
Corn	5,000 bushels	$ 16,200
Oats	5,000 bushels	17,600
Wheat	5,000 bushels	20,000
Pork bellies	38,000 pounds	13,400
Coffee	37,500 pounds	48,750
Cotton	50,000 pounds	32,000
Sugar	112,000 pounds	14,560
Copper	25,000 pounds	25,000
Gold	100 troy ounces	45,000
Silver	5,000 troy ounces	33,250
Treasury bonds	$100,000	88,100
Treasury bills	$1,000,000	933,000

the margin payment is merely considered to be a good-faith payment against losses. There is no actual borrowing or interest to be paid.[2]

In addition to the initial margin requirements, there are also **margin maintenance requirements** (minimum maintenance standards) that run 70 to 90 percent of the value of the initial margin. In the case of the wheat contract, the margin maintenance requirement might be $1,800 (86% × $2,100). If our initial margin of $2,100 is reduced by $300 due to losses on our contract, we will be required to replace the $300 to cover our margin position. If we do not do so, our position will be closed out, and we will take our losses.

The margin requirement, relative to size, is even less for financial futures. For example, on a $1 million Treasury bill contract, the investor generally must only post an initial margin of $2,500. Similar requirements exist for other types of financial futures.

Note that the high risk inherent in a commodities contract is not so much a function of volatile price movements as it is the impact of high leverage made possible by the low initial margin requirements. A 10 percent price move may equal or exceed the size of our initial investment in the form of the margin deposit. This is similar to the type of leverage utilized in the options market as described in Chapter 13. However, the action in the commodities market is much quicker. You can be asked to put up additional margin within hours after you establish your initial position.

Market Conditions

Because the price of every commodity moves in response to market conditions, each investor must determine the key market variables that influence the value of his or her contract. In the case of wheat, the investor may be particularly concerned about such factors as weather and crop conditions in the Midwest, the price of corn as a substitute product, the carryover of wheat supply from the previous year, and the potential wheat sales to the Soviet Union and other foreign countries. A rumor about an impending transaction with the Soviet Union has often caused market prices to change radically.

Gains and Losses

In the present example, assume we guessed right in our analysis of the wheat market; we purchased a December futures contract for $4.00 per bushel, and the price goes to $4.42 per bushel (recall that the contract was for 5,000 bushels). With a 42-cent increase per bushel, we have established a dollar gain of $2,100 (5,000 bushels × $.42 per bushel profit). With an initial margin requirement of $2,100, we have made a percentage profit of 100 percent as indicated in the following formula.[3]

---

[2] It should also be pointed out that we may need a minimum account balance of $5,000 or greater to open a commodity account.

[3] This does not include commissions, which are generally less than $100 for a complete transaction (buy and sell).

$$\frac{\text{Dollar gain}}{\text{Amount of margin deposit}} = \frac{\$2,100}{\$2,100} \times 100 = 100\%$$

If this transaction took place over a one-month time period, the annualized gain would be 1,200 percent (100% × 12 = 1,200%). Note that this was all accomplished by a 42-cent movement in the price of a December wheat contract from $4.00 to $4.42, a percentage change of 10.5 percent ($.42/$4.00).

Actually, the investor may choose to close out his contract or attempt to let his profits run. He also may use his profits to establish the basis for margin on additional futures contracts. A paper gain of $2,100 is enough to provide the $2,100 margin on another wheat contract.

The investor is now in a position to use an **inverse pyramid** to expand his position. With two contracts outstanding, a mere 21-cent price change will provide $2,100 in profits.

$$
\begin{array}{rl}
\$ & .21 \text{ Price change} \\
\times & 10,000 \text{ Bushels (two contracts)} \\
\hline
& \$2,100 \text{ Profits (can be applied} \\
& \text{to third contract)}
\end{array}
$$

The $2,100 in profits can be used to purchase a third contract, and now with 15,000 bushels under control, a 14-cent price change will generate enough profits for a fourth contract.

$$
\begin{array}{rl}
\$ & .14 \text{ Price change} \\
\times & 15,000 \text{ Bushels (three contracts)} \\
\hline
& \$2,100 \text{ Profits (can be applied} \\
& \text{to fourth contract)}
\end{array}
$$

The process of inverse pyramiding begins to sound astounding since eventually a 1-cent or $1/2$-cent change in the price of wheat will trigger off enough profits for a new contract. Of course, there are great risks associated with such a process. It is like building a house with playing cards. If one tumbles, the whole house comes down. The investor can become so highly leveraged that any slight reversal in price can trigger off margin calls. While it is often wise to let profits run and perhaps do some amount of pyramiding, prudence must be exercised.

Our primary attention up to this point has been on contracts that are making money. What are the implications if there is an immediate price reversal after we have purchased our December wheat contract? You will recall there was a margin maintenance requirement of $1,800 based on our initial margin of $2,100. In this case, a $300 loss would call for an additional deposit to bring our margin position up to $2,100. How much would the price of wheat have to decline for us to get this margin call to increase our deposit? With a 5,000-bushel contract, we are talking about a mere decline of 6 cents per bushel.

$$\frac{\$300 \text{ loss}}{5,000 \text{ bushels}} = \$.06 \text{ per bushel}$$

This could happen in a matter of hours or days after our initial purchase. When we get the margin call, we can either elect to put up the additional $300 and continue with the contract or tell our commodities broker to close out our contract and take our losses. If we put up the $300, our broker could still be on the phone two hours later asking for more margin because the price has shown further deterioration. Because investors often buy multiple contracts, such as 10 December wheat contracts, the process can be all the more intense. In the commodities market, the old adage of "cut your losses short and let your profits run" probably has its greatest significance. Even a seasoned commodities trader might determine that he is willing to lose 80 percent of the time and only win 20 percent of the time, but those victories will represent home runs and the losses mere outs.

Price Movement Limitations

Because of the enormous opportunities for gains and losses in the commodities markets, the commodity exchanges do place some broad limitations on maximum daily price movements in a commodity. Some examples are shown in Table 15–4.

TABLE 15–4	MAXIMUM DAILY PRICE CHANGES		
Commodity	Exchange	Normal Price Range	Maximum Daily Price Change (from Previous Close)★
Corn	CBT	$2.30—$4.00	$.15 per bushel
Oats	CBT	$1.25–$2.40	$.15 per bushel
Wheat	CBT	$3.00–$5.50	$.20 per bushel
Pork bellies	CBT	$.30–$.60	$.02 per pound
Copper	CME	$.60–$1.50	$.03 per pound
Silver	CBT	$6.00–$50.00	$1.00 per ounce
Tresury bills	IMM of CME	85% of par and up	no limit

★These values may change slightly from exchange to exchange and are often temporarily altered in response to rampant speculation.

These daily trading limits obviously must affect the efficiency of the market somewhat. If market conditions indicate the price of wheat should decline by 30 cents and the daily limit is 20 cents, then obviously the price of wheat is not in equilibrium as it opens the following morning. However, the desire to stop market panics tends to override the desire for total market efficiency in the commodity markets. Nevertheless, the potential intraday trading range is still large. Recall, for example, that a 20-cent change in the price of wheat, which is the daily limit, is more than enough to place tremendous pressure on the investor to repeatedly increase his margin position. On the typical 5,000-bushel contract, this would represent a daily loss of $1,000.

DON'T DISCOUNT THIS SECTOR OF COMMODITY BROKERS

They aren't household names; most of them have been in business only a few years, and the services they provide are spare.

But, as a growing number of individual investors are learning, discount brokerage firms that specialize in commodity trading can make a big difference in the bottom line. While the standard commission for trading soybeans, pork bellies, financial futures and other commodities is $75 to $130 per contract at a big, full-service Wall Street firm, the cost at one of the handful of discount brokers is generally less than $30.

Discounts can be important in commodity trading. While many individual investors buy or sell stocks only three or four times a year, commodity investors may trade 20 times a month. By paying

$29 a contract at a discounter instead of $95 at a full-service firm, an average customer saves $15,840 a year.

Saving on commissions isn't everything, however. Commodity traders who depend on fundamentals appreciate the insights and information they can get from a full-service broker's research department. Merrill Lynch & Co. has its own weather forecaster. That sort of support is crucial for some investors. So is individual attention.

Even discounters concede that their bare-bones services aren't for everyone. But for customers who feel the need of extra help, most offer "broker-assisted" services at rates that are generally between $35 and $65 a contract—still less than what a full-service house charges.

HOW THE MAJOR DISCOUNTERS COMPARE

Firm (Phone)	Day Trade	Over- Night Trade	Exchange Fees Extra	Commission per Contract Clearing Member	Trades Securities	24-Hour Trading	Minimum Account Size
E. David Stephens (800-421-0190; in N.Y. 516-248-6900)	$25	$25	No	No	No	No	$5,000
First American (800-621-4415)	22	22	Yes	No	No	No	None
Futures Discount Group (800-872-6673)	23	26	Yes	No	No	Yes	5,000
Ira Epstein & Co. (800-284-6000)	22	26	No	No	Yes	Yes	5,000
Jack Carl/312 Futures (800-621-3424)	27	30	Yes	Yes	Yes	Yes	5,000
J.F. Dalton Associates (800-362-8117)	27	29	No	Yes	No	Yes	5,000
Lachman Co. (800-446-3400)	25	25	Yes	No	No	Yes	4,500
Lind-Waldock Co. (800-621-0762)	30	30	No	Yes	No	Yes	5,000

Source: Stanley W. Angrist, *The Wall Street Journal*, October 13, 1988, p. C1. Reprinted by permission of *The Wall Street Journal*, © Dow Jones & Co., Inc., 1988. All rights reserved.

READING MARKET QUOTES

We turn our attention to interpreting market quotes in the daily newspaper. In Figure 15–2, we show an excerpt from the June 9, 1988, edition of *The Wall Street Journal* covering 18 different types of contracts (this represents about one third of the contracts reported for that day).

In each case, we see a wide choice of months for which a contract may be purchased. For example, oats, which trade on the Chicago Board of Trade (CBT), have futures contracts for July, September, December and March. Some commodities offer a contract for virtually every month. In order to directly examine some of the terms in Figure 15–2, we produce the portion related to the oats contract (CBT) in Table 15–5.

TABLE 15–5	PRICE QUOTES FOR OAT CONTRACTS							
						Lifetime		Open Interest
(1)	Open	High	Low	Settle	Change	High	Low	
(2) Oats (CBT)—5,000 bu.; cents per bu.								
July	$217^1/_2$	$236^1/_2$	$217^1/_2$	235	$+13^1/_2$	$236^1/_2$	144	3,338
Sept	222	240	222	$238^1/_2$	$+13$	240	143	3,508
Dec	229	247	229	241	$+9$	247	162	2,374
Mar '89	228	245	228	235	$+5$	$245^1/_2$	171	578

Source: *The Wall Street Journal*, June 9, 1988, p. 40. Reprinted by permission of *The Wall Street Journal*, © Dow Jones & Company, Inc., 1988. All rights reserved.

We initially read the second line in the table that indicates we are dealing in oats traded on the CBT. We then note that oats are traded in 5,000-bushel units and quoted in cents per bushel. Quotations in cents per bushel require some mental adjustment. For example, 200 cents per bushel would actually represent two dollars ($2) per bushel. We generally move the decimal point two places to the left and read the quote in terms of dollars. For example, the July 1988 opening price was $217^1/_2$, or $2.1750 per bushel.

Across the top of the table we observe that we are given information on the open, high, low, settle (close), and change from the previous day's close as well as the lifetime high and low for that particular contract. The last column represents the open interest, or the number of actual contracts presently outstanding for that delivery month.

THE CASH MARKET AND THE FUTURES MARKET

Many commodity futures exchanges provide areas where buyers and sellers can negotiate **cash** (or **spot**) prices. The cash price is the actual dollar value paid for the immediate transfer of a commodity. Unlike a futures contract, there must be a transfer of the physical possession of the goods. Prices in the cash market are somewhat dependent on prices in the futures market. Thus, it is said that the futures markets provide an important service as a price discovery mechanism. By cataloging price trends in everything from corn to

FIGURE 15–2   EXAMPLES OF PRICE QUOTES ON COMMODITY FUTURES

FUTURES PRICES

Wednesday, June 8, 1988.

Open Interest Reflects Previous Trading Day.

—GRAINS AND OILSEEDS—

	Open	High	Low	Settle	Change	Lifetime High	Lifetime Low	Open Interest
CORN (CBT) 5,000 bu.; cents per bu.								
July	252	256	246½	251	− 6¼	259½	174	62,869
Sept	260	265	256¼	260½	− 5½	268½	180¾	28,077
Dec	272	276	267	272	− 4¾	281¼	184	87,500
Mr89	278	282	275	279¼	− 4½	287½	193½	11,976
May	283	285½	279¼	283½	− 4½	291½	207½	3,791
July	284	287	281½	284	− 5	293	233	2,304
Sept				266	− 1	275	245	201
Dec	250	259	250	251	− 4	270	235	1,443
Est vol 50,000; vol Tues 90,454; open int 198,161, +4,302.								
OATS (CBT) 5,000 bu.; cents per bu.								
July	217½	236½	217½	235	+13½	236½	144	3,338
Sept	222	240	222	238½	+13	240	143	3,508
Dec	229	247	229	241	+ 9	247	162	2,374
Mr89	228	245	228	235	+ 5	245½	171	578
Est vol 4,000; vol Tues 4,130; open int 9,815, +896.								
SOYBEANS (CBT) 5,000 bu.; cents per bu.								
July	870	880	859	860½	−21½	909	488½	59,144
Aug	869	885	863	865½	−21½	911	512	16,572
Sept	870	882	861	861½	−25	913	503	7,804
Nov	870	886	861	862	−28½	918	499¼	78,064
Ja89	880	891	866	866½	−30	924	553	9,117
Mar	885	895	872	872½	−28¾	925	579	4,018
May	875	883	864	866	−23½	914	647	1,594
July	865	873	855	855	−20½	900	684	2,236
Nov	708	722	708	708	− 8	734¼	677	1,419
Est vol 75,000; vol Tue 103,847; open int 179,969, +548.								
SOYBEAN MEAL (CBT) 100 tons; $ per ton.								
July	276.00	280.50	273.00	273.50	− 7.00	287.70	148.00	28,657
Aug	272.00	278.50	271.00	271.20	− 7.00	285.40	148.00	14,099
Sept	271.00	275.50	268.50	268.50	− 7.50	284.70	153.00	7,117
Oct	269.50	273.50	265.50	265.70	− 9.00	284.00	159.00	6,167
Dec	268.00	271.50	265.00	265.20	−7.30	277.50	159.00	15,852
Ja89	266.00	270.00	263.50	263.50	− 6.50	277.00	177.00	3,405
Mar	265.00	267.00	260.00	260.20	− 6.80	274.00	193.50	2,157
May	265.00	266.00	258.00	260.50	− 5.50	274.00	200.50	1,103
July	264.00	264.00	260.00	260.00	− 5.00	268.00	229.00	247
Aug	263.50	263.50	256.00	257.00	− 8.00	268.50	256.00	142
Est vol 35,000; vol Tues 41,500; open int 78,946, +466.								
SOYBEAN OIL (CBT) 60,000 lbs.; cents per lb.								
July	25.15	25.79	25.15	25.23	− .73	27.47	16.65	35,727
Aug	25.55	26.00	25.45	25.46	− .71	27.69	16.71	16,269
Sept	25.90	26.25	25.68	25.69	− .66	28.05	16.55	10,563
Oct	26.15	26.45	25.85	25.87	− .65	28.24	17.25	7,218
Dec	26.55	26.80	26.20	26.21	− .69	28.55	18.30	19,277
Ja89	26.55	26.85	26.20	26.20	− .75	28.75	20.75	1,997
Mar	26.85	27.00	26.30	26.30	− .90	29.00	21.35	1,537
May	27.20	27.20	26.65	26.65	−1.00	28.95	22.95	1,014
July	27.20	27.20	26.50	26.50	−1.00	28.95	23.00	323
Aug	26.60	26.60	26.60	26.60	− .97	28.60	26.00	150
Est vol 30,000; vol Tues 31,006; open int 94,075, +2,213.								
WHEAT (CBT) 5,000 bu.; cents per bu.								
July	370½	378	368½	369¾	− 8¼	382¾	253½	23,422
Sept	380	386	377½	379	− 5½	392¾	272	11,672
Dec	388	395	387	388½	− 7	403½	289	17,747
Mr89	391	398	390	391	− 8	407	323	1,564
May	379	382	375	376	− 7	397	330	157
July	345	347	340	342½	− 7½	362	335	320
Est vol 25,000; vol Tues 19,686; open int 54,882, +343.								
WHEAT (KC) 5,000 bu.; cents per bu.								
July	368	375½	367	367¼	+ 8¾	386	272	12,778
Sept	378	383	375	375	− 9	397	304½	7,995
Dec	383½	389¼	380	381	− 8	403	301½	4,286
Mr89	388	393	380	380	−16	404½	322¾	284
Est vol 6,036; vol Tues 6,848; open int 26,353, +526.								
WHEAT (MPLS) 5,000 bu.; cents per bu.								
July	380	398	380	395½	+10	402½	292½	n.a.
Sept	390	400	388	405¾	+11½	412¾	296	n.a.
Dec	400	415	400	410	+ 7½	421½	308¾	n.a.
Mr89				402		378	347	n.a.
Est vol n.a.; vol Tues n.a.; open int n.a., n.a..								
BARLEY (WPG) 20 metric tons; Can. $ per ton								
July	100.50	102.60	100.00	100.00	− 5.00	115.00	71.00	7,412
Oct	105.70	108.70	105.70	105.70	− 5.00	120.00	75.00	14,347
Nov	108.10	108.40	107.00	107.00	− 5.00	119.50	78.50	1,154
Dec	107.50	109.50	107.50	107.50	− 5.00	120.50	78.90	5,080
Mar	112.00	112.00	110.00	110.00	− 5.00	123.50	105.00	238
Est vol 4,400; vol Tues 8,774; open int 28,231, +816.								
FLAXSEED (WPG) 20 metric tons; Can. $ per ton								
July	294.20	298.00	294.00	294.00	−10.00	312.00	229.70	3,584
Oct	307.00	309.50	305.90	305.90	−10.00	322.80	237.20	2,067
Dec	312.00	313.50	310.70	310.70	−10.00	328.50	242.10	810
Est vol 2,120; vol T̲ ̲̲434; open int 6,532, +̲̲								

	Open	High	Low	Settle	Change	Lifetime High	Lifetime Low	Open Interest
Mr89	63.35	63.50	62.05	62.07	− 1.95	67.90	54.70	2,264
May	63.30	63.50	62.10	62.10	− 1.80	65.15	56.40	500
July				62.15	− 1.80	64.08	56.50	205
Est vol 6,500; vol Tues 7,414; open int 31,689, −1,245.								
ORANGE JUICE (CTN)—15,000 lbs.; cents per lb.								
July	174.10	174.10	172.80	173.25	− 1.25	178.25	124.00	4,913
Sept	168.10	168.30	166.80	167.10	− 1.35	177.00	125.00	3,014
Nov	158.75	158.75	157.95	158.15	− 1.00	172.75	132.00	2,024
Ja89	154.50	154.60	153.50	154.00	− .50	171.25	132.00	943
Mar	153.35	153.35	153.05	153.10	− .95	167.90	152.90	289
Est vol 1,000; vol Tues 2,025; open int 11,200, +221.								
SUGAR—WORLD (CSCE)—112,000 lbs.; cents per lb.								
July	9.99	10.00	9.80	9.85	− .31	10.38	6.79	28,765
Oct	9.90	9.95	9.71	9.76	− .28	10.35	7.00	79,891
Mr89	9.86	9.88	9.66	9.70	− .25	10.32	7.66	51,335
May	9.86	9.89	9.67	9.71	− .24	10.20	7.87	5,293
July	9.94	9.95	9.72	9.74	− .24	10.12	8.10	890
Oct	9.90	9.90	9.72	9.72	− .26	10.19	8.98	645
Est vol 30,483; vol Tues 22,712; open int 166,829, +843.								
SUGAR—DOMESTIC (CSCE)—112,000 lbs.; cents per lb.								
July	22.35	22.35	22.30	22.32	+ .01	22.40	21.55	925
Sept	22.26	22.26	22.26	22.25	+ .01	22.26	21.52	2,618
Nov	22.08	22.08	22.08	22.08		22.08	21.50	2,086
Ja89	21.93	21.93	21.93	21.93		21.93	21.70	322
Mar	21.88	21.88	21.88	21.88	− .01	21.88	21.75	145
Est vol 85; vol Tues 1,323; open int 6,131, −581.								

—METALS & PETROLEUM—

	Open	High	Low	Settle	Change	Lifetime High	Lifetime Low	Open Interest
COPPER (CMX)—25,000 lbs.; cents per lb.								
June	110.00	110.00	109.00	110.00	− 1.50	111.60	87.50	370
July	106.30	107.00	104.50	105.15	− 1.35	107.00	62.30	17,205
Sept	97.20	97.70	96.00	96.00	− 1.20	97.70	59.45	8,066
Dec	89.50	89.60	88.30	88.40	− 1.30	96.50	64.70	5,571
Mr89	83.50	83.70	82.30	82.50	− 1.40	93.00	66.50	1,296
May				80.10	− 1.40	89.00	73.15	141
July				78.90	− 1.30	80.00	77.50	173
Sept				77.90	− 1.30	82.00	76.00	116
Dec				77.90	− 1.30	82.20	77.45	177
Est vol 6,500; vol Tues 9,885; open int 33,133, +152.								
GOLD (CMX)—100 troy oz.; $ per troy oz.								
June	457.50	459.70	456.30	456.10	− 3.90	523.00	399.00	2,688
July	460.00	460.00	460.00	457.50	− 4.10	467.50	458.40	305
Aug	464.10	464.40	460.50	460.70	− 4.10	527.00	425.00	62,648
Oct	468.00	469.50	465.50	465.80	− 4.20	533.50	429.00	11,366
Dec	473.00	475.00	470.50	471.10	− 4.30	546.00	430.00	24,322
Fb89	478.70	479.80	478.00	476.40	− 4.40	549.50	446.00	10,109
Apr	484.00	484.00	484.00	481.80	− 4.50	550.00	451.00	7,134
June	490.50	490.50	490.50	487.40	− 4.60	570.00	455.50	10,425
Aug				493.30	− 4.70	575.00	482.20	6,299
Oct				499.60	− 4.80	575.50	466.30	7,080
Dec				506.00	− 4.90	514.50	472.50	5,569
Fb90				512.40	− 5.00	516.00	502.00	2,323
Apr				518.90	− 5.10	525.80	525.80	346
Est vol 40,000; vol Tues 33,720; open int 150,614, +508.								
PLATINUM (NYM)—50 troy oz.; $ per troy oz.								
June				573.00	−23.50	619.00	580.00	18
July	592.50	594.00	574.10	575.50	−23.50	667.50	443.00	13,628
Oct	597.50	600.00	579.80	581.20	−23.60	667.50	452.00	6,492
Ja89	604.20	606.00	586.80	588.20	−23.60	646.00	459.00	3,221
Apr	614.50	614.50	598.00	595.20	−23.60	643.50	482.00	754
Est vol 11,618; vol Tues 9,971; open int 24,118, +886.								
PALLADIUM (NYM) 100 troy oz.; $ per troy oz.								
June	130.50	130.50	129.90	130.00	− 2.25	160.50	103.65	568
Sept	130.50	131.50	128.00	128.25	− 2.75	142.25	103.65	4,284
Dec	130.00	130.00	127.50	127.75	− 2.75	139.50	104.50	1,989
Mr89	127.50	128.50	127.50	127.25	− 2.75	137.00	115.50	281
Est vol 592; vol Tues 581; open int 7,124, +39.								
SILVER (CMX)—5,000 troy oz.; cents per troy oz.								
June	716.0	716.0	709.0	709.0	−14.7	731.0	635.0	29
July	720.0	728.5	711.0	713.0	−15.0	1053.0	580.0	46,639
Sept	730.0	738.0	720.5	722.8	−15.0	1064.0	588.0	13,233
Dec	747.0	753.0	736.0	737.7	−15.5	1082.0	606.0	11,146
Mr89	762.0	771.0	754.0	753.4	−15.8	1073.0	660.0	4,726
May	770.0	770.0	768.0	764.4	−16.0	948.0	675.0	1,60?
July	780.0	792.0	780.0	775.8	−16.2	985.0	688.0	1,161
Sept				787.3	−16.4	820.0	698.0	918
Dec				804.4	−16.7	834.0	722.0	549
Mr90				821.7	−17.0	840.0	770.0	494
...ol 35,000;...int 80,522, ...69								

cattle, the producers, processors, and handlers of over 50 commodities are able to observe price trends in categories of interest.

THE FUTURES MARKET FOR FINANCIAL INSTRUMENTS

The major event in the commodities markets for the last decade has been the development of financial futures contracts. With the great volatility in the foreign exchange markets and in interest rates, corporate treasurers, investors, and others have felt a great need to hedge their positions. Financial futures also have an appeal to speculators because of their low margin requirements and wide swings in value.

Financial futures may be broken down into three major categories, currency futures, interest rate futures, and stock index futures (the latter is covered in depth in Chapter 16). Trading in currency futures began in May of 1972 on the International Monetary Market (part of the Chicago Mercantile Exchange). Interest rate futures started trading on the Chicago Board of Trade in October of 1975 with the GNMA certificate. Trading in financial futures, regardless of whether they are currency or interest rate futures, is very similar to trading in traditional commodities such as corn, wheat, copper, or pork bellies. There is a stipulated contract size, month of delivery, margin requirement, and so on. We will first look at currency futures and then shift our attention to interest rate futures.

CURRENCY FUTURES

Futures are generally available in the currencies listed below.

British pound	Swiss franc
Australian dollar	West German mark
Canadian dollar	French franc
Japanese yen	Mexican peso

The **futures market in currencies** provides many of the same functions as the older and less formalized market in foreign exchange operated by banks and specialized brokers, who maintain communication networks throughout the world. In either case, one can speculate or hedge. The currency futures market, however, is different in that it provides standardized contracts and a strong secondary market.

Let's examine how the currency futures market works. Assume you wish to purchase a currency futures contract in Japanese yen. The standardized contract is 12.5 million yen. The value of the contract is quoted in cents per yen. Assume that you purchase a December futures contract in May, and the price on the contract is $.007932 per yen. The total value of the contract is $99,150 (12.5 million yen × $.007932). The typical margin on a yen contract is $2,100.

We will assume that the yen strenghtens relative to the dollar. This might happen because of decreasing U.S. interest rates, declining inflation in Japan, or any number of other reasons. Under these circumstances, the currency might rise to $.00806 per yen (the yen is now equivalent to more cents than it was previously). The value of the contract has now risen to $100,750 (12.5 million × $.00806). This represents an increase in value of $1,600.

$$\begin{array}{r} \$100,750 \\ -\ \underline{99,150} \\ \$\ \ \ 1,600 \end{array}$$

With an original margin requirement of $2,100, this represents a return of 76.2 percent.

$$\frac{\$1,600}{\$2,100} \times 100 = 76.2\%$$

On an annualized basis, it would even be higher. Of course, the contract could produce a loss if the yen weakens against the dollar as a result of higher interest rates in the United States or increasing inflation in Japan. With a normal margin maintenance requirement of $1,700, a $400 loss on the contract will call for additional margin.

Corporate treasurers often try to hedge an exposed position in their foreign exchange dealings through the currency futures market. Assume a treasurer closes a deal today to receive payment in two months in Japanese yen. If the yen goes down relative to the dollar, he will have less value than he anticipated. One solution would be to sell a yen futures contract (go short). If the value of the yen goes down, he will make money on his futures contract that will offset the loss on the receipt of the Japanese yen in two months.

In Table 15–6, we see the typical size of contracts for four other foreign currencies that trade on the International Monetary Market (part of the Chicago Mercantile Exchange).

TABLE 15–6	CONTRACTS IN CURRENCY FUTURES		
Currency		Trading Units	Size of Contract Based on Mid-1988 Prices
British pound		25,000	$45,000
Canadian dollar		100,000	81,800
Swiss franc		125,000	87,500
West German mark		125,000	73,750

INTEREST RATE FUTURES

Since the inception of **the interest rate futures contract** with GNMA certificates in October 1975, the market has been greatly expanded to include Treasury bonds, Treasury bills, Treasury notes, commercial paper, certificates of deposit, and Eurodollars. There is almost unlimited potential for futures contracts on interest-related items.

FIGURE 15–3   EXAMPLES OF PRICE QUOTES ON INTEREST RATE FUTURES

					Yield		Open
	Open	High	Low Settle	Chg	Settle Chg		Interest
TREASURY BONDS (CBT)–$100,000; pts. 32nds of 100%							
June	87-22	88-23	87-19	88-20 +	30	9.259 –	.115	56,439
Sept	86-24	87-24	86-20	87-22 +	30	9.374 –	.117	267,817
Dec	86-00	86-30	85-31	86-27 +	30	9.479 –	.119	34,345
Mr89	85-13	86-03	85-11	86-02 +	30	9.578 –	.120	24,986
June	84-22	85-12	84-22	85-10 +	30	9.674 –	.122	13,232
Sept	....	....	....	84-20 +	30	9.763 –	.124	405
Dec	....	....	....	83-31 +	30	9.849 –	.125	794
Mr90	82-28	83-12	82-28	83-12 +	30	9.928 –	.122	166
Est vol 330,000; vol Tues 319,920; op int 398,331, +20,553.							
TREASURY NOTES (CBT)–$100,000; pts. 32nds of 100%							
June	93-10	93-29	93-10	93-29 +	21	8.934 –	.106	30,584
Sept	92-17	93-07	92-16	93-06 +	21	9.050 –	.106	57,660
Dec	92-03	92-16	92-01	92-16 +	19	9.161 –	.097	1,046
Est vol 22,000; vol Tues 26,107; open int 89,417, +4,539.							
5 YR TREAS NOTES (FINEX) $100,000; pts. 32 of 100%							
June	97-16	97-21	97-21	97-285 +13.5		8.53 –	.10	2,385
Sept	96-28	97-09	96-28	97-085 +14.0		8.69 –	.11	5,370
Dec	96-12	96-245	96-12	96-245 + 9.0		8.81 –	.08	2,498
Est vol 3,400; vol Tues 4,542; open int 10,263, –223.							
TREASURY BONDS (MCE)–$50,000; pts. 32nds of 100%							
June	87-22	88-25	87-22	88-20 +	29	9.259 –	.111	1,110
Sept	86-25	87-26	86-23	87-22 +	29	9.374 –	.113	4,598
Est vol 5,400; vol Tues 4,951; open int 5,766, –327.							
TREASURY BILLS (IMM)–$1 mil.; pts. of 100%							
						Discount	Open
	Open	High	Low Settle	Chg	Settle Chg		Interest
Sept	93.32	93.46	93.31	93.46 +	.13	6.54 –	.13	14,668
Dec	93.09	93.24	93.09	93.22 +	.13	6.78 –	.13	3,098
Mr89	93.01	93.06	93.01	93.06 +	.12	6.94 –	.12	381
June	....	....	....	92.86 +	.11	7.14 –	.11	163
Sept	....	....	....	92.74 +	.10	7.26 –	.10	89
Est vol 4,328; vol Tues 1,948; open int 18,487, –93.							

Interest rate futures trade on a number of major exchanges, including the Chicago Board of Trade, the International Monetary Market of the Chicago Mercantile Exchange, and the New York Futures Exchange. There is strong competition between Chicago and New York City for dominance in this business, with Chicago being not only the historical leader but also the current leader.

Figure 15–3 shows examples of quotes on interest rate futures. Direct your attention to the first category, Treasury bonds (CBT), trading on the Chicago Board of Trade.

The bonds trade in units of $100,000, and the quotes are in percent of par taken to 32nds of a percentage point. Although it is not shown in this data, the bonds on which the futures are based are assumed to be new, 15-year instruments paying 8 percent interest. Since long-term rates tend to be above 8 percent, the quoted price is usually at a discount from $100,000. In the first column for the September contract for Treasury bonds, we see a price of 86–24. This indicates a value of $86^{24}/_{32}$ percent of stated (par) value. We thus show a contract value of $86,750 ($86^{24}/_{32} \times $100,000$). This represents the opening value. The entire line in Figure 15–3 would read as follows:

	Open	High	Low	Settle	Chg.	Yield Settle	Chg.	Open Interest
Sept	86–24	87–24	86–20	87–22	+30	9.374	– .117	267,817

We see the **settle**, or closing price is 87–22, which represents a change (chg.) of $^{30}/_{32}$ from the close for the previous day. The reader should be aware that the close for the previous day is not always the same as the open for the current day.[4] We also see what yield the settle (closing) price represents on a 15-year bond paying an 8 percent coupon rate. In this case, it is 9.374 percent, which is a decline in yield from the previous day of .117 percent. The decline in yield is consistent with the increase in settle price (and vice versa). Finally, we see there is an open interest of 268,817 indicating the number of contracts that are presently outstanding for September.

Assume we buy a September futures contract for $87^{22}/_{32}$ or $87,687.50 ($87^{22}/_{32} \times$ $100,000). The margin requirement for this contract on the Chicago Board of Trade is $2,500 with a $2,000 margin maintenance requirement. In this case, it may be that we have bought the futures contract because we anticipate easier monetary policy by the Federal Reserve, which will trigger a decline in interest rates and an increase in bond prices. If interest rates decline by .6 percent (60 basis points), Treasury bond prices will increase by approximate $1^{17}/_{32}$.[5] On a $100,000 par value futures contract, this would represent a gain of $1,531.25 as indicated below.

$$\begin{array}{r} \$ 100,000 \\ \times \quad \underline{1^{17}/_{32}\% \; (1.53125\%)} \\ \$1,531.25 \end{array}$$

With a $2,500 initial margin, the $1,531.25 profit represents an attractive return of 61.25 percent. Note, however, that if interest rates go up by even a small amount, our Treasury bond futures contract value will fall, and there may be a margin call.

As is true of other commodities, when we trade in interest rate futures, we do not take actual title or possession of the commodity unless we fail to reverse our initial position. The contract merely represents a bet or hedge on the direction of future interest rates and bond prices.

Quotes on Treasury Bill Futures

One type of interest rate futures contract that requires special attention is the Treasury bill future. Particular reference in this case is made to the 90–day, $1 million, T-bill futures contract that trades on the International Monetary Market of the Chicago Mercantile Exchange and is shown on the bottom portion of Figure 15–3. We reproduce the first line below.

						Discount		Open
	Open	High	Low	Settle	Chg.	Settle	Chg.	Interest
Sept	93.32	93.46	93.31	93.46	+.13	6.54	−.13	14,668

---

[4]A number of overnight events can cause the difference. In this case, we can assume the close for the previous day was, in fact, 86-24 as shown in the table.

[5]This is derived from a standard bond table and not explicitly calculated in the example.

The items of particular interest are the settle price of 93.46 and the settle discount of 6.54 percent. Unlike other interest rate futures, such as Treasury bonds, we cannot simply multiply the settle price of 93.46 (percent) times the par value of $1 million to get the value of the contract. Why? Because this Treasury bill represents a 90-day instrument, and the annual yield of 6.54 percent must be converted to a 90-day rate in order to determine value. We thus take the annual rate of 6.54 percent and multiply it by $^{90}/_{360}$ to get an equivalent 90-day yield of 1.64%.

$$6.54 \times \frac{90}{360} = 1.64\%$$

We then subtract this value from 100 percent to get the appropriate percentage to multiply times par value to get the value of the contract. For the $1 million Treasury bill, the actual converted price is:

$$(100\% - 1.64\%) \times \$1,000,000$$
$$98.36\% \times \$1,000,000 = \$983,600$$

Each time the yield on a Treasury bill changes by .01 percent ($^1/_{100}$ of 1 percent or 1 basis point), the price of the T-bill future will change by $25 as indicated in the two steps below:

$$.01\% \text{ of } \$1,000,000 = \$100$$

we convert this from an annual rate to a 90-day rate by multiplying by $^{90}/_{360}$.

$$\$100 \times {}^{90}/_{360} = \$25$$

Thus, if you buy a Treasury bill futures contract and interest rates on Treasury bills change by .50 percent (50 basis points), you will gain or lose $1,250.

$25 For each .01% or basis point

$\underline{\times \ 50}$ Basis points

$1,250

The initial margin requirement for a $1 million Treasury bill on the International Money Market of the Chicago Mercantile Exchange is only $1,000, with a $700 margin maintenance requirement. A 50 basis point move would provide a return or loss on the initial margin of 125 percent.

Hedging with Interest Rate Futures

Interest rate futures have opened up opportunities for hedging that can only be compared to the development of the traditional commodities market over a century ago. Consider the following potential hedges against interest rate risks.

a. A corporate treasurer is awaiting a new debt issue that will take place in 60 days. The underwriters are still putting the final details together. The great fear is that interest rates will rise between now and then. The treasurer could hedge his or her position in the futures market by selling a Treasury bond, Treasury bill, or other similar security short. If interest rates go up, the price to buy back the interest rate futures will go down, and a profit will be made on the short position. This will partially or fully offset the higher interest costs on the new debt issue.

b. A corporate treasurer is continually reissuing commercial paper at new interest rates or borrowing under a floating prime agreement at the bank. He or she fears that interest rates will go up and make a big dent in projected profits. By selling (going short) certificates of deposit or other interest rate futures, the corporate treasurer can make enough profit on interest rate futures if interest rates go up to compensate for the higher costs of money.[6]

c. A mortgage banker has made a forward commitment to provide a loan at a set interest rate one month in the future. If interest rates go up, the resale value of the mortgage in the secondary market will go down. He or she can hedge the position by selling or going short on an interest rate futures contract.

d. A pension fund manager has been receiving a steady return of eight percent on his short-term portfolio in 90-day Treasury bills. He is afraid that interest rates will go down and he will have to adjust to receiving lower returns on the managed funds. His strategy might be to buy (go long on) a Treasury bill futures contract. If interest rates go down, he will make a profit on his futures contract that will partially or fully offset his decline in interest income. Of course, if he is heavily invested in long-term securities and fearful of an interest rate rise, a sell or short position that would provide profits on an interest rate rise would be advisable. This, of course, would offset part of the loss in the portfolio value due to increasing interest rates.

e. A commercial banker has most of his loans on a floating prime basis, meaning that the rate that he charges will change with the cost of funds. However, some of the loans have a fixed rate associated with them. If the cost of funds goes up, the fixed-rate loans will become unprofitable. By selling or going short interest rate futures, the danger of higher interest rates can be hedged away by the profits he will make on the interest rate futures. Similarly, a banker may make a commitment to pay a set amount of interest on certificates of deposit for the next six months. If interest rates go down, the banker may have to loan the funds at a lower rate than he is currently paying. If he buys a futures contract in certificates of deposit, then lower interest rates will increase the value of the contract and provide a profit. This will offset the possible negative profitability spread described above.

---

[6]Commercial paper futures are not presently traded, so CD futures are probably the best substitute.

An Actual Example

Assume an industrial corporation has a $10 million, 15-year bond to be issued in 60 days. Long-term rates for such an issue are currently 10.75 percent, and there is concern that interest rates will go up by $1/4$ percent to 11 percent by the time of the issue. The corporate treasurer has figured out that the extra $1/4$ percent would have a present value cost of $179,775 over the life of the issue (on a before-tax basis).

$$
\begin{array}{r}
\$10,000,000 \\
\times \quad 1/4\% \\
\hline
\$25,000 \\
\times \quad 7.191 \\
\hline
\$179,775
\end{array}
$$

Present value factor for 15 years at 11 percent

Present value of futures costs

To establish a hedge position, he sells 118 Treasury bond futures short. We assume they are currently selling at 85 (85 percent of $100,000), equaling $85,000 each. The total value of the hedge would be $10,030,000. This is roughly the equivalent to the $10 million size of the corporate bond issue. If interest rates go up by $1/4$ percent, the profit on the Treasury bond futures contract (due to falling prices with a short position) will probably offset the present value of the increased cost of the corporate bond issue.

Of course, we do not suggest that both rates (on Treasury bonds and corporate bonds) would move exactly together. However, the general thrust of the example should be apparent. We are actually establishing a **cross-hedging** pattern by using one form of security (Treasury bonds) to hedge another form of security (corporate bonds). This is often necessary. Even when the same security is used, there may be differences in maturity dates or quality characteristics so that a perfect hedge is difficult to establish.

Many financial managers prefer **partial hedges** to complete hedges. They are willing to take away part of the risk but not all of it. Others prefer no hedge at all because it locks in their position. While a hedge ensures them against loss, it precludes the possibility of an abnormal gain.

Nevertheless, in a risk-averse financial market environment, most financial managers can gain by hedging their position as described in the many examples in this section. Companies such as Burlington Northern, Esmark, and Stauffer Chemical have established reputations for just such actions. Others have not yet joined the movement because of a lack of appreciation or understanding of the highly innovative financial futures market. Much of this will change with the passage of time.

OPTIONS AS WELL AS FUTURES

In late 1982, many exchanges began offering options on financial instruments and commodities. For example, the Chicago Board Options Exchange began listing put and call options on Treasury bonds. Also the American Stock Exchange started trading options on Treasury bills and Treasury notes, and the Philadelphia Exchange offered foreign currency options. The Chicago Board of Trade, the Chicago Mercantile Exchange, and the Comex have also attached options to commodity plays. The relationship, similarities, and dissimilarities between option contracts and futures contracts is given much greater attention in the following chapter, Stock Index Futures and Options. For now it will suffice to say that the futures contract requires an initial margin, which can be parlayed into large profits or immediately wiped out, whereas an option requires the payment of an option premium, which represents the full extent of an option purchaser's liability. In Chapter 16, we will also see there are options to purchase futures, which combine the elements of both types of contracts.

16

STOCK INDEX FUTURES AND OPTIONS

I n February of 1982, the Kansas City Board of Trade began trading futures on a stock index, the Value Line Index. This event ushered in a whole new era of futures and options trading.

A future or option on an index allows the investor to participate in the movement of an entire index rather than an individual security. Currently, futures and options relate to such indexes as the Standard & Poor's 500 Stock Index, the Standard & Poor's 100 Stock Index, the New York Stock Exchange Composite Index, the Major Market Index, the Value Line Index, and many other old and new market measures.[1]

If an investor purchases a **futures contract on a stock market index**, he puts down the required margin and gains or loses on the transaction based on the movement of the index. For example, an investor may purchase a futures contract on the Standard & Poor's 500 Stock Index with $20,000 in margin. The actual contract value is based on the index value times 500. If the S&P 500 Futures Index were at 270 the initial contract value would be $135,000 (500 × 270). If the index went up or down by 2 points, the investor would gain or lose $1,000 (500 × ± 2). Because the initial investment is $20,000 in margin, we see a gain or loss of 5 percent (5 percent = $1,000/$20,000). Since this might happen over a one- or two-day time period, the annualized return or loss could be high.

If the investor is trading in **stock index options** instead of futures, he may choose to participate in the Standard & Poor's 100 Stock Index. The S&P 100 Index is a smaller version of the S&P 500 Index and is composed of 100 blue-chip stocks on which the Chicago Board Options Exchange currently has individual option contracts. Included in the S&P 100 Index are such firms as IBM, General Motors, AT&T, and so on. The value of the S&P 100 Index tends to be about 10 points lower than the S&P 500 Index. If the S&P 100 Index were at 260 at a given time, an option to purchase the index at a strike price of 260 in two months might carry a premium (option price) of $5. The option price is multiplied by 100 to get a total value for the option of $500 (100 × $5). If the S&P 100 Index closed out at 269 on expiration, the option price will be $9, and a profit of $400 will be achieved over the two-month period.

Final value (100 × $9)	$900
Purchase price (100 × $5)	− 500
Profit	$400

As we go further into the chapter, you will see there are not only futures and options on stock market indexes, but also **"options to purchase futures"** on stock market indexes.

Stock index futures have grown faster than any new futures trading outlet in history. In their first six months of trading, the average daily volume was 4.5 times as great as the volume on Treasury bond futures during a comparable

---

[1]To date, there is no contract on the Dow Jones Industrial Average because Dow Jones & Company has resisted having their venerable index used for this purpose.

period of infancy. The same sort of pattern has taken place in index option trading.

THE CONCEPT OF DERIVATIVE PRODUCTS

It should be pointed out that trading in stock index futures and options has had a tremendous impact on the financial markets in the United States. Stock index futures and options are sometimes referred to as **derivative products** because they derive their existence from actual market indexes, but have no intrinsic characteristics of their own. These derivative products are thought to make market movements more volatile. The primary reason is that enormous amounts of securities can be controlled by relatively small amounts of margin payments or option premiums. Also, these derivative products are often used as part of **program trading**. As discussed in Chapter 2, program trading means that computer-based trigger points are established in which large volume trades are initiated by institutional investors. Stock index futures and options facilitate program trading because a large volume of securities can be controlled. The presence of program trading, as supported by the use of stock index futures and options, was blamed by many for the market crash of 508 points in the Dow Jones Industrial Average on October 19, 1987. It was thought that too many institutional investors were moving in the same direction (to sell) at one time. Increased stock price volatility since the market crash has also been blamed on program trading and the use of stock index futures and options.

Actually, these are somewhat controversial topics. A study by the Chicago Mercantile Exchange suggests that program trading and the use of derivative products has no negative effect on the market per se. These trading tools merely help the market reach a new equilibrium level (in terms of value) more quickly.[2]

It is the contention of the authors that stock index futures and options have many useful purposes, which we will cover throughout the chapter. We will also try to point out potential negatives where they exist.

Before going into further discussion of futures and options on stock market indexes, the student should have read Chapter 13, Put and Call Options, and Chapter 15, Commodities and Financial Futures.

TRADING STOCK INDEX FUTURES

As indicated in Table 16–1, there are four key stock index futures contracts. They relate to the S&P 500 Index traded on the Chicago Mercantile Exchange (CME), the NYSE (New York Stock Exchange) Composite Index traded on the New York Futures Exchange (NYFE),[3] the Value Line Index traded on

---

[2]*Report of the Committee of Inquiry Appointed by the Chicago Mercantile Exchange to Examine the Events Surrounding October 19, 1987* (Chicago: The Chicago Mercantile Exchange, December 17, 1987).

[3]The NYFE is a division of the New York Stock Exchange.

TABLE 16–1   STOCK INDEX FUTURES (June 14, 1988, Prices)

```
                                                          Open
                    Open High  Low Settle Chg  High   Low Interest
S&P 500 INDEX (CME) 500 times index
June  275.50 277.90 272.90 274.60 + 2.90 347.90 190.00  43,716
Sept  277.00 280.00 275.10 276.70 + 3.05 343.50 193.00  80,022
Dec   279.00 282.10 277.10 278.70 + 3.10 282.10 252.20   1,284
Mr89  282.50 283.50 279.20 280.15 + 3.10 283.50 253.90     100
   Est vol 81,834; vol Mon 46,817; open int 125,122,  − 4,478.
   Indx prelim High 276.14; Low 271.58; Close 274.31  + 2.88
NYSE COMPOSITE INDEX (NYFE) 500 times index
June  155.55 156.70 153.95 154.85 + 1.55 194.60 113.00   3,604
Sept  156.30 158.10 155.30 156.20 + 1.60 158.10 128.50   4,043
Dec   158.00 159.20 157.10 157.20 + 1.60 159.20 137.95     887
Mr89  ....   ....   ....   158.20 + 1.60 156.20 144.25     230
   Est vol 11,610; vol Mon 5,089; open int 8,684, − 192.
   The index: High 155.36; Low 153.00; Close 154.52 + .150
KC VALUE LINE INDEX (KC) 500 times index
June  241.25 241.50 237.60 238.85 + 1.15 287.00 177.20   1,749
xSept 248.00 249.50 245.70 246.65 + 1.25 247.60 225.00   1,074
xDec  ....   ....   ....   249.25 + 1.35 240.00 237.25      10
   Est vol 700; vol Mon 338; open int 2,833, +11.
   X- New index: High 243.66; Low 241.48; Close 243.02
   +1.56
MAJOR MKT INDEX (CBT) $250 times index
June  414.00 416.50 411.00 412.95 + 4.45 478.00 373.00   5,445
July  416.80 418.00 412.80 414.30 + 4.20 418.00 376.70     389
Sept  418.00 418.50 413.50 415.10 + 4.40 543.30 249.00     132
   Est vol 9,000; vol Mon 2,400; open int 5,982, − 24.
   The index: High 415.70; Low 408.09; Close 413.03 + 4.94
```

Source: *The Wall Street Journal*, June 15, 1988, p. 36. Reprinted by permission of *The Wall Street Journal*, © Dow Jones & Company, Inc. All rights reserved.

the Kansas City Board of Trade, and the Major Market Index traded on the Chicago Board of Trade.

We have previously mentioned all these indexes in earlier chapters with the exception of the Major Market Index. It is a price-weighted index composed of 20 of the largest firms in the United States. It is actually a convenient way to imitate movements in the Dow Jones Industrial Average and has a 97 percent correlation with that average (although its price movements are from a different base). As previously indicated in footnote 1, Dow Jones & Company has prohibited the use of the Dow Jones Industrial Average for futures and options trading, so this is an alternative way to play the same game. Sixteen of the 20 firms in the Major Market Index are part of the Dow Jones Industrial Average.

You will note in Table 16–1 that the title line for each contract (such as the S&P 500 Index) indicates an appropriate multiple times the value in the table. For the first three contracts, the multiplier is 500, while for the Major Market Index, it is 250 ($250). Looking at the June settle prices in each of the four indexes, we see the value of the contracts in Table 16–2.

With a margin requirement ranging from $6,000 on the New York Futures Exchange to $20,000 on the Chicago Mercantile Exchange, the investor can engage in a futures trade. (These margin values apply to June 1988 and change from time to time).

If the investor thinks the market is going up, he will purchase a futures contract. If he thinks the market is going down, he will sell a futures contract and hope that the market will decline so that the contract can be closed out

TABLE 16–2	VALUE OF CONTRACTS			
		June Settle Price	Multiplier	Contract Value
S&P 500 Index		274.60	500	$137,300
NYSE Composite Index		154.85	500	77,425
KC Value Line Index		238.85	500	119,425
Major Market Index		412.95	250	103,238

(repurchased) at a lower value than the sales price. Selling futures contracts can also be used to hedge a large stock portfolio. If the market goes down, what you lose on your portfolio you recoup in your futures contract.

In the example in Table 16–2, the investor has four indexes from which to choose. You should be aware that the S&P 500 Index, the NYSE Composite Index, and the Major Market Index are heavily influenced by large corporations (IBM, Exxon, etc.). The KC (Kansas City) Value Line Index is more broadly based, being composed of 1,700 firms, and furthermore, each stock in this index is equal-weighted, which means that IBM has no greater price influence than a smaller firm trading on the American Stock Exchange or over-the-counter. Institutional investors generally prefer indexes influenced by large stocks, while smaller investors may prefer the Value Line Index for hedging or speculating. Since institutional investors tend to dominate these markets, the S&P 500 Index futures contract is the most widely used as can be seen in the open interest (outstanding contract) data in the last column of Table 16–1.

We shall direct our attention for now to the S&P 500 Index futures contract (though the same basic principles would apply to other indexes). Part of the material from Table 16–1 that pertains to the S&P 500 Index futures contract is reproduced in Table 16–3 so that we can examine a number of key features related to the contract.

Trading Cycle

The trading cycle is made up of the four months of June, September, December, and March. The last day of trading for a contract is the third Thursday of the ending month. The reader will observe that the contracts in Table 16–3 extend nine months into the future.

Margin Requirement

As previously mentioned, the basic margin requirement for buying or selling an S&P 500 Index futures contract on the Chicago Mercantile Exchange was $20,000 in mid-1988. Based on the June 1988 contract settle value of $137,300 (found in Table 16–2) this represents a margin requirement of 14.57 percent ($20,000 ÷ $137,300). There is also a margin maintenance requirement of $10,000. Thus, if the initial margin or equity in the account falls to this level,

TABLE 16–3   S&P 500 INDEX FUTURES CONTRACT (CME), 500 MULTIPLIER
                   (June 14, 1988)

Contract Month	Open	High	Low	Settle	Change
June, 88	275.50	277.90	272.90	274.60	+2.90
Sept	277.00	280.00	275.10	276.70	+3.05
Dec	279.00	282.10	277.10	278.70	+3.10
March, 89	282.50	283.50	279.20	280.15	+3.10

Value of S&P 500 Stock Index (June 14, 1988) = 274.31.

the investor will be required to supply sufficient cash or securities to bring the account back up to the $20,000 level. Since the contract trades at 500 times the index, a decline of 20 points in the S&P contract value would cause a loss of $10,000. In this instance, the margin position would be reduced from $20,000 to $10,000, and the investor would be called upon to supply $10,000 in funds.

Actually, if the investor can prove that he is hedging a long position, the margin requirement will be less. For example, if an investor owns a portfolio of stocks that roughly equals the value of the index futures contract ($137,300 in this case), the initial margin requirement is only $10,000 (though the margin maintenance requirement remains at $10,000). Since a hedged position is not as risky as a speculative position, less initial margin is required. Of course, it is sometimes difficult to prove that a truly hedged position is in place.[4]

One of the developments following the market crash of October 1987 was to raise the margin requirements on stock index futures contracts. For example, in the prior edition of this book written in mid-1985, the initial margin requirement for the S&P Index futures contract was only $6,000 (7.54 percent of the value of the contract at that time). In mid-1988, it was $20,000, or 14.57 percent of the contract value.[5] Although the margin requirement will undoubtedly change again many times in the future, there is a definite intent by the exchanges and regulatory authorities to keep the margin on stock index futures relatively high as compared to the margin on interest rate futures and many other commodities. This once again pertains to a fear that stock index futures have contributed to new trading patterns that have increased the volatility of stock prices and driven some small investors from the marketplace.

Minimum Price Change

The minimum price change per trade for the S&P 500 Futures Index contract is .05. Thus, if the June futures contract is at 274.60, the smallest possible price move would be down to 274.55 or up to 274.65. Since the contract is

---

[4]For an investor initiating a spread position (buying and selling comparable but somewhat different contracts at the same time), the margin requirement is even lower.

[5]During the June 1988 time period, the initial margin requirement on the Value Line Index futures contract (Kansas City Board of Trade) was $7,500. For the Major Market Index (Chicago Board of Trade), it was $15,000, and for the New York Stock Exchange Composite Index (New York Financial Exchange), the value was $6,000. However, one should keep in mind that the majority of volume is done on the Standard & Poor's 500 Index futures contract on the Chicago Mercantile Exchange.

multiplied by 500 to determine value, an index movement of .05 represents $25 (500 × .05 = $25). Therefore, the smallest possible price change is $25.

Cash Settlement

In traditional commodity futures markets, the potential for physical delivery exists. One who is trading in wheat could actually decide to deliver the commodity to close out the contract. As discussed in Chapter 15, this only happens a very small percentage of the time, but it is possible. The stock index futures market, on the other hand, is purely a **cash-settlement** market. There is never the implied potential for future delivery of the Standard & Poor's 500 Stock Index. An investor simply closes out (or reverses) his position prior to the settlement date. If he does not, his account is automatically credited with his gains or debited with his losses, and the transaction is completed.[6]

One of the advantages of a cash-settlement arrangement is that it makes it impossible for a "short squeeze" to develop. A short squeeze takes place when an investor attempts to corner a market in a commodity, such as silver, so that it is not possible for those who have short positions to make physical delivery. Clearly, with a cash-settlement position, this can never happen.

Basis

The term **basis** represents the difference between the stock index futures price and the value of the actual underlying index.[7] We can now turn back to Table 16–3 to see a numerical example of basis. On the date of the table, the S&P 500 futures contract for June was quoted at a settle (closing) price of 274.60 (second item from the right in the first row). The actual S&P 500 Stock Index, as shown at the bottom of Table 16–3, closed at 274.31. The basis, or difference, between the futures price and the actual underlying index was .29.

Stock index futures price	274.60
Actual underlying index	− 274.31
Basis	.29

Moving to the September 1988 contract in Table 16–3, the basis is the difference between the September contract settle value of 276.70 and the value of the underlying index which, of course, is still 274.31. The difference is 2.39. For the data in Table 16–3, the basis indicates a premium is being paid over the actual underlying index value, and furthermore, the premium expands with the passage of time. This is generally thought to be a positive sign. If the index futures price is below the actual underlying index, there is a negative basis.

An excellent discussion of the ability of stock index futures to forecast the

---

[6]Actually, the account is adjusted daily to reflect the gains and losses. This is known as marking the customer's position to market.

[7]The same concept can be applied to other types of futures contracts.

actual underlying index is presented in an article by Zeckhauser and Nieder-hoffer in the January–February 1983 issue of the *Financial Analysts Journal*.[8] A part of their thesis is that futures contracts move instantaneously to reflect market conditions, whereas the actual underlying index moves more slowly. If the market makes an important move, some of the stocks that are part of the actual underlying index will not yet have reacted. Thus, initial, significant, and potentially predictive information may be found in the futures market quotes.

Also, at times, futures or options markets stay open later or begin trading earlier than the actual underlying stock markets. This can be very beneficial not only in providing lead time information on market movements, but also in giving the trader an opportunity to take a position prior to the opening or after the closing of the stock market.

Overall Features

Many of the important features related to stock index futures on the various exchanges are presented in Table 16–4. This table can serve as a ready reference guide to trading commodities in various markets.

USE OF STOCK INDEX FUTURES

There are a number of actual and potential users of stock index futures. As is true of most commodity futures contracts, the motivation may be either speculation or the opportunity to hedge.

Speculation

The speculator may use stock index futures in an attempt to profit from major movements in the market. He or she may have developed a conviction about the next move in the market through utilizing fundamental or technical analysis. For example, those who utilize fundamental analysis may determine that P/E ratios are at a 10-year low or that earnings performance should be extremely good in the next two quarters, so they wish to bet on the market moving upward. Market technicians might observe that a resistance or support position in the market is being penetrated and that it is time to take a position based on the anticipated consequences of that penetration.

While the market participant could put his or her money in individual stocks, it might be more efficient and less time-consuming to simply invest in stock index futures. In buying futures on the S&P 500 Index, the investor is capturing the performance of 500 securities; with the New York Stock Exchange Index over 1,500 securities; and with the Value Line Index, 1,700 securities.

As discussed in Chapter 1, two types of risks are associated with investments: systematic or market-related risks, and unsystematic or firm-related

---

[8]Richard Zeckhauser and Victor Niederhoffer, "The Performance of Market Index Futures Contracts," *Financial Analysts Journal*, January–February 1983, pp. 59–65.

TABLE 16–4   SPECIFICATIONS FOR STOCK INDEX FUTURES CONTRACTS

Index and Exchange	Trading Hours	Index	Contract Size and Value	Contract Months
S&P 500 Index Index and Options Market (IOM) of Chicago Mercantile Exchange (CME)	10:00 A.M. to 4:15 P.M. (NYT)*	Value of 500 selected stocks traded on NYSE, AMEX, and OTC, weighted to reflect market value of issues	$500 × the S&P 500 Index	March, June, September, December
NYSE Composite Index New York Futures Exchange (NYFE) of the New York Stock Exchange	10:00 A.M. to 4:15 P.M. (NYT)*	Total value of NYSE Market: 1550 listed common stocks, weighted to reflect market value of issues	$500 × the NYSE Composite Index	March, June, September, December
Value Line Index Kansas City Board of Trade (KCBT)	10:00 A.M. to 4:15 P.M. (NYT)*	Equally-weighted average of 1,700 NYSE, AMEX, OTC, and regional stock prices expressed in index form	$500 × the Value Line Index	March, June, September, December
Major Market Index Chicago Board of Trade (CBT)	10:00 A.M. to 4:15 P.M (NYT)*	Price-weighted average of 20 blue-chip companies	$250 × MMI Index	March, June, September, December

*NYT = New York time.

risks. Since only systematic risk is assumed to be rewarded in an efficient capital market environment (unsystematic risk can be diversified away), the investor may only wish to be exposed to systematic risk. Stock index futures represent an efficient approach to only taking systematic, market-related risk.

Another advantage of stock index futures is that there is less manipulative action and insider trading than with individual securities. While it is possible (though not legal) for "informed" insider trading to cause an individual stock to move dramatically in the short-term, such activity is not as likely for an entire index. This advantage, however, should not be overstated. Unusual trading activity of stock index futures does come under the scrutiny of federal regulators from time to time.

Stock index futures also offer leverage potential. A $135,000 to $140,000 S&P futures contract can be established for $20,000 in margin and with no interest on the balance.[9] If you were investing $140,000 in actual stocks through

---

[9]As mentioned in Chapter 15, margin on futures contracts merely represents good-faith money, and there is never any interest on the balance.

margin, you would have to put up a minimum of $70,000 (50 percent) in margin and pay interest on the balance. While we previously said that the margin on stock index futures is relatively high in comparison to interest rate futures (and other commodities), and was raised following the market crash in October 1987, we see the margin requirement is still considerably lower than that on an outright stock purchase. Also, the commissions on a stock index futures contract are miniscule in comparison to commissions on securities of comparable value.

Volatility and Profits or Losses.   Prior to the market crash of 1987, the average daily move on the S&P 500 Index was approximately .50 (one half of a point per day). Since the crash, the average daily movement has been in the .75 to 1.00 range. A .90 upward move in a futures contract (say from 270 to 270.90) means a daily gain of $450 (recall the contract has a multiplier of 500). With a margin requirement of $20,000, that's a 2.25 percent one-day return on your money.

Gain in futures contract	$ .90
Multiplier	× 500
Dollar gain	$450
Margin	$20,000
Percentage gain	2.25%

This translates into an 810 percent annualized return (2.25 percent × 360). By contrast if the $20,000 were invested in an 8 percent certificate of deposit, only $4.44 in interest would accrue on a daily basis. The difference here, of course, is that the $450 average daily movement related to the index may be up or down, whereas the $4.44 is only up.

Actually, from January 1 to early October 1987, the S&P 500 Index (and futures contracts) went up by almost 100 points as indicated in Figure 16–1. That represents a gain of $50,000 (500 × 100) on a typical margined investment of $20,000. However, the S&P 500 Index fell 57.86 points on October 19th, 1987 and related futures contracts declined by 80 points (that meant an incredible negative basis of 22.14 points). An investor in an S&P 500 contract lost $40,000 (500 × 80) in one day if he held his position. Based on $20,000 margin, that's a 200 percent loss in one day.[10] To view the extent of declines in key individual stocks, the reader may wish to observe Figure 16–2.

Needless to say, the market crash of October 19, 1987, represents the most-extreme example one could discuss. However, it does help to indicate that stock index futures are a two-edged sword.

When a stock index futures contract starts to run against an investor, he or she can bail out and cut losses. If the contract value is going down rapidly, the investor will be continually called upon to put up more margin as the

---

[10]This, of course, assumes the investor continued to maintain margin and did not close out his or her position.

FIGURE 16–1   PRICE MOVEMENTS IN THE S&P 500 INDEX

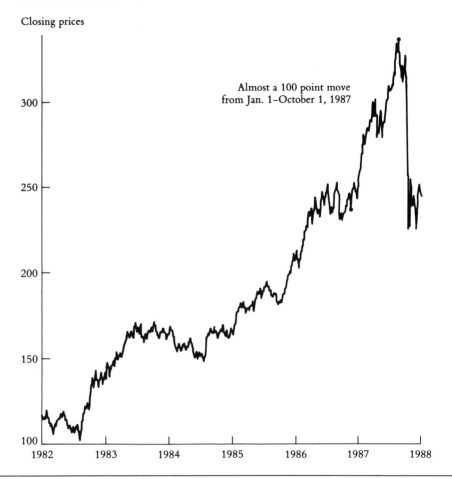

Source: *Report of the Presidential Task Force on Market Mechanisms* (Washington, D.C.: U.S. Government Printing Office, January 1988), p. 10.

margin position is being depleted. That puts tremendous pressure on the investor. He or she must decide whether to put up more margin and hold the position in hopes of a comeback or close out the position and take a loss.

It should also be pointed out that not all speculation in stock index futures must necessarily be based on the market going up. Quite obviously, you can also speculate that the market will go down. You simply sell a contract with the anticipation of repurchasing it at a lower price at a later point in time. Margin requirements are similar, and gains come from a declining market and losses from an increasing market. If the index goes up rapidly, the investor will be called on to put up more margin.

FIGURE 16–2   CHANGE IN VALUE OF DOW JONES INDUSTRIAL STOCKS ON THE
                   DAY OF THE MARKET CRASH (October 19, 1987)

	Closing Price	Change in Price
Alcoa	$42.50	− $13.50
Allied	$28.00	− $11.125
Am Exp	$21.50	− $9.625
AT&T	$24.00	− $6.125
Beth Steel	$11.00	− $5.50
Boeing	$38.50	− $5.125
Chevron	$41.25	− $8.25
Coca-Cola	$30.00	− $9.75
Du Pont	$80.00	− $18.50
Est Kodak	$63.50	− $26.00
Exxon	$35.00	− $8.50
Gen Elec	$41.875	− $8.875
Gen Motors	$50.00	− $16.00
Goodyear	$42.00	− $17.50
IBM	$103.25	− $31.25
Itl Paper	$34.25	− $11.50
McDonalds	$35.75	− $8.00
Merck	$151.00	− $33.00
Mn Mining	$51.00	− $19.75
Navistar	$4.50	− $1.50
Philip Morris	$87.50	− $15.125
Primerica	$34.125	− $10.50
P&G	$61.00	− $23.25
Sears	$30.75	− $10.25
Texaco	$30.875	− $5.625
USX	$21.00	− $13.00
Un Carb	$22.50	− $4.875
Utd Tech	$39.00	− $9.75
Wsthouse	$40.00	− $20.50
Woolwrth	$36.25	− $6.125

Hedging

Up to now our discussion of stock index futures has mainly related to speculating (or anticipating the next major move in the market). Perhaps the most-
important use of stock index futures is for hedging purposes. One who has a
large diversified portfolio may feel the market is about to decline. A portfolio
manager who suffers a 20 percent decline in his or her portfolio actually requires
a 25 percent gain from the new lower base just to break even.

A portfolio manager faced with the belief that a declining market is im-
minent may be inclined to sell off part or all of the portfolio. The question
becomes, is this realistic? First of all, large transaction costs are associated with
selling off part or all of a portfolio and then repurchasing it at a later time.
Second, it may be difficult to liquidate a position in certain securities that are
thinly traded. For example, a mutual fund or pension fund that tries to sell

10,000 shares of a small over-the-counter stock may initially find a price quote of $25, but only be able to close out its relatively large position at $23.50. A $15,000 loss would be suffered. Furthermore, the fund might find the same type of problem in reacquiring the stock after the overall market decline is over. This problem could be multiplied by 25 or 50 times, depending on the number of securities in the portfolio. Though larger, more-liquid holdings would be easier to trade, significant transactions costs are still involved.

A more easily executed defensive strategy would be to sell one or more stock index futures as a hedge against the portfolio. If the stock market does go down, the loss on the portfolio will be partially or fully offset by the profit on the stock index futures contract(s) because they are bought back at a lower price than the initial sales price.

As an example, assume a corporate pension fund has $20 million in stock holdings. The investment committee for the fund is very bearish in its outlook, fearing that the overall market could go down by 20 percent in the next few months and a $4 million loss would be suffered. The pension fund decides to fully hedge its position.

The fund is going to use S&P 500 Index futures for the hedge. We shall assume the futures can be sold for 274, with a settlement date in three months. Before the number of contracts for execution is determined, the portfolio manager must consider the relative volatility of his portfolio. If the portfolio is more volatile than the market, this must be factored into the decision-making process. As discussed in Chapter 1, the beta coefficient indicates how volatile a stock is relative to the market. If a stock has a beta of 1.20, it is 20 percent more volatile than the market (or market index). We shall assume the $20 million portfolio discussed above has a weighted average beta of 1.15 (that is, the portfolio is 15 percent more volatile than the market).

In order to determine the number of contracts necessary to hedge the position, we use the following formula:

$$\frac{\$ \text{ Value of portfolio}}{\$ \text{ Value of contract}} \times \frac{\text{Weighted beta}}{\text{of portfolio}} = \frac{\text{Number of}}{\text{contracts}}$$

$$(16\text{--}1)$$

In the example under discussion, we would show:

$$\frac{\$20,000,000}{274 \times 500} \times 1.15 = \text{Number of contracts}$$

In the first term of the formula, the numerator is the size of the portfolio being hedged. The denominator is the size of each contract and, in this example, is found by multiplying the S&P futures contract value of 274 by 500. The first term is then multiplied by the weighted beta value of 1.15. The answer works out as:

$$\frac{\$20,000,000}{\$137,000} \times 1.15 = 145.99 \times 1.15 = 168 \text{ contracts}$$

The portfolio can be effectively hedged with 168 contracts.

Assume the market does go down but only by 10 percent instead of the 20 percent originally anticipated. Let's demonstrate that the hedge has worked. Since the portfolio has a beta of 1.15, its decline would be 11.5 percent (10 percent × 1.15). With a $20 million portfolio, the loss would be $2.3 million. To offset this loss, we will have a gain on 168 contracts. The gain is shown as follows:

S&P Index futures contract (sales price)	274.0
Decline in price on the futures contract (10% × 274)	− 27.4
Ending value (purchase price)	246.6

The 27.4 point decline on the index futures contract indicates the profit made on each contract.[11] They were sold for 274.0 and repurchased for 246.6. With 168 contracts, the profit on the stock index futures contracts comes out as $2,301,600.

Profit per contract (27.4 × 500)	$13,700
Number of contracts	× 168
Total profit	$2,301,600

The gain of $2,301,600 on the stock index futures contracts offsets the loss of $2.3 million on the portfolio. The small difference between the two values represents a rounding procedure. Actually, executing a perfect hedge may be further complicated by a number of other factors such as the lack of an appropriate index to match against the portfolio and the change in basis over time. Also, the portfolio may not move exactly in accordance with the beta. No doubt, many real-world factors can complicate any hedge.

While a stock index futures hedge offers the advantage of protecting against losses, it, of course, takes away the upside potential. If the market goes up by 10 percent instead of down, the gain on the portfolio may be wiped out by the loss on the stock index futures contracts. The investor could be forced to buy back the futures for 10 percent more than the selling price. Because some portfolio managers are afraid of losing all their upside potential in a hedged position, they may only wish to hedge a fourth or a half of their position.

While the hedging procedure just described can be potentially beneficial to portfolio managers, it can be potentially detrimental to the market in general if overused. Actually, protecting a large portfolio against declines is sometimes referred to as **portfolio insurance.**[12] It is potentially a good strategy, but what if a large number of investors initiate their portfolio-insurance strategies at the same time? Perhaps they are worried because there has been an increase in the prime rate or a bad report on inflation. An overload of stock index

---

[11]Note that the futures contract is assumed to move on a one-to-one basis with the market. The actual relationship may not be this precise.

[12]Portfolio insurance also refers to the process of insuring a minimum return on a portfolio. For example, if the minimum return is 6 percent, in a down market, stocks may be sold off and the funds converted to CDs to insure the desired results.

futures sales hitting the market at the same time has the effect of driving down not only stock index futures prices but the stocks in the indexes as well (such as those in the S&P 500 Stock Index). An overall panic can set in. The chain reaction is that a whole new round of portfolio-insurance-induced sales are triggered. Since there is so much selling of futures contracts and so little buying, there may be a large negative basis. Perhaps the actual index is 270, and the futures contract can now only be sold at 260 or less. This type of occurrence was a key element in the market crash of 1987.

The point is that the concept of hedging and portfolio insurance works well when used in moderation, but if large-scale selling starts, the results may be counterproductive.

Other Uses of Hedging. Hedging with stock index futures has a number of other uses besides attempting to protect the position of a long-term investment portfolio. These include:

Underwriter Hedge. As described in Chapter 14, the investment banker (underwriter) has a risk exposure from buying stock from the issuing corporation with the intention of reselling it in the public markets. If there is weakness during the distribution period, the potential resale price could fall below the purchase price, and the underwriter's profit would be wiped out. In order to protect against this market risk, the underwriter could sell stock index futures contracts. If the market goes down, presumably, the loss on the stock will be compensated for by the gain on the stock index futures contract as a result of being able to repurchase it at a lower price. This, of course, is not a perfect hedge. It is entirely possible that the stock could go down while the market is going up, and losses on both the stock and stock index futures contract would take place (writing options directly against the stock might be more efficient, but in many cases such options are not available).

Specialist or Dealer Hedge. As indicated in Chapter 2, a specialist on an exchange or a dealer in the over-the-counter market buys and sells stocks for his own inventory for temporary holding. He may, at times, assume a larger temporary holding than desired, with all the risks associated with that exposure. Stock index futures can reduce the market (or systematic) risk, although the futures cannot reduce the specific risk associated with a security.

Retirement or Estate Hedge. As we move into the next two or three decades, large retirement funds will be accumulated from voluntary retirement plans. A retirement plan participant who has accumulated a large sum in an equity fund may feel a need to hedge his or her position in certain time periods in the economy (where liquidation is neither legal or possible). A futures contract may provide that hedge. Also, a person with responsibility for an estate may be locked into a portfolio during the period of probate (validation of the will process) and wish to hedge his or her position with a stock index futures contract.

Tax Hedge.   An investor may have accumulated a large return on a diversified portfolio in a given year. In order to maintain the profitable position but defer the taxable gains until the next year, futures contracts may be employed.

Arbitraging

While stock index futures started out as a major tool for speculating and hedging, they are now also widely used for purposes of arbitraging. Basically, an **arbitrage** is set up when a simultaneous trade (a buy and a sell) takes place in two different markets and a profit is locked in. Assume the S&P 500 Stock Index has a value of 272 based on the market value of all the stocks in the index. Also, assume the S&P 500 Stock Index futures contract, due to expire in two months, is selling for 273. There is a one-point positive basis between the futures contract and the underlying index. A sophisticated institutional investor may decide to arbitrage based on this difference. He or she will simultaneously sell a futures contract for 273 and buy a basket of stocks that matches the S&P 500 Stock Index for 272.[13] Because at expiration, the futures contract and underlying index will have the same value, a one-point profit is locked in at the time of arbitraging. For example, if at expiration, the S&P 500 Stock Index has a value of 270, a gain of three will take place on the sale, and a loss of two will be associated with the purchase for a net profit of one. If thousands of such contracts are involved, the profits can be substantial, and the potential for losses in a true arbitrage are nonexistent.

As you might assume, index arbitraging is in the exclusive providence of wealthy, sophisticated investors. For this reason, many smaller investors are somewhat resentful of the process and claim it tends to disrupt the normal operations of the marketplace. While there is nothing inherently wrong with the process of arbitraging and it may even make the markets more efficient, it is sometimes a target for criticism by regulators. This is because it involves the process of program trading, discussed earlier in the chapter.

TRADING STOCK INDEX OPTIONS

Stock index options also allow the market participant to speculate or hedge against major market movements, though there is no opportunity for arbitraging. Stock index options are similar in many respects to the standard put and call options on individual stocks discussed in Chapter 13. The purchaser of an option pays an initial premium and then closes out the option at a given price in the future. One essential difference between stock index options and options on individual securities is that in the former case, there is only a cash settlement of the position, whereas in the latter case (individual securities), you can force the option writer to deliver the securities.

Examples of stock index options are presented in Table 16–5.

---

[13]Actually, arbitraging has become sufficiently sophisticated through mathematics and computer analysis that all 500 stocks do not actually have to be purchased. Perhaps 10 or 15 key stocks bought in large quantities will be sufficient to adequately represent the S&P 500 Index. Commissions on such transactions tend to be extremely small.

TABLE 16–5 INDEX OPTIONS

Tuesday, June 14, 1988

Chicago Board

S&P 100 INDEX

Strike Price	Calls—Last Jun	Calls—Last Jul	Calls—Last Aug	Puts—Last Jun	Puts—Last Jul	Puts—Last Aug
220	....	....	....		⅜	1 5/16
225	37¾	....	39¾	1/16	9/16	1⅝
230	33	....	....	1/16	⅞	2¼
235	26¼		30	1/16	1¼	2⅞
240	21¼	22	24½	1/16	1 11/16	3¾
245	16¼	18	21⅜	⅛	2⅜	4⅝
250	11¼	14½	18½	¼	3¼	6
255	6½	10¾	13¾	11/16	4⅝	7½
260	2⅝	7⅝	10¾	1 13/16	6¾	10
265	¾	5¼	8¼	4⅞	9⅜	11¾
270	3/16	3⅜	5¾	10½	12½	16
275	1/16	1 15/16	4	....	16½	

Total call volume 173,909 Total call open int. 340,881
Total put volume 128,145 Total put open int. 397,104
The index: High 262.98; Low 258.04; Close 261.20, +3.16

S&P 500 INDEX

Strike Price	Calls—Last Jun	Calls—Last Jul	Calls—Last Sep	Puts—Last Jun	Puts—Last Jul	Puts—Last Sep
195	....	....	....		....	7/16
200	76⅜	....	....	....	....	
215	....	....	....	....	....	⅞
220	54¾	....	....	1/16	....	....
225	....	....		....	....	
230	....	....		....	⅜	....
235	41¼	....		1/16	½	....
240	....			1/16	11/16	....
250	25	27	....	1/16	1½	3⅝
255	19⅜	22½		1/16	1⅞	4½
260	14	17	23¼	3/16	2⅝	5⅞
265	9¼	13¼	18¾	½	4	7¼
270	5¼	10⅛	16½	1 1/16	4½	8
275	1 13/16	8	13	2⅞	6⅝	10⅝
280	½	5¾	10⅜	4⅞	9⅜	10½
285	¼	3⅜	8	....	....	
290		2⅛	5¼	....	....	19⅝
295	....	....	4¼	....	....	21¼
300	....	....	2⅞		....	25
305	....	....	2¼	....	....	
310	....	....	2⅜	....	....	
315	....	....	....	....	....	40
325	....	....	⅜	....	....	

Total call volume 24,720 Total call open int. 241,750
Total put volume 20,910 Total put open int. 245,766
The index: High 276.14; Low 271.43; Close 274.30, +2.87

American Exchange

MAJOR MARKET INDEX

Strike Price	Calls—Last Jun	Calls—Last Jul	Calls—Last Aug	Puts—Last Jun	Puts—Last Jul	Puts—Last Aug
350	....	....	....		⅝	....
355	....	....	....		¾	....
360	....	....	....		1	....
365		....	....	1/16	1⅛	....
370			....	1/16	1 7/16	....
375	39⅜	....	....		1¾	4¼
380	33¼	38	....	1/16	2⅜	5
385	31	31½	....	⅛	3	5⅞
390	23	30	....	¼	3⅝	6⅞
395	18	23¼		½	4⅞	
400	13¾	19½	....	⅞	6	9⅝
405	9⅜	16⅝		1½	7½	
410	5⅜	13	17	2½	9⅛	14¾
415	2 9/16	10⅜	16¼	4⅝	12⅛	....
420	1	8⅜	13¾	8	14½	....
425	7/16	6⅛	....	11¾	16¼	....
430	⅛	4⅝	9¼	....	21⅛	
435	⅛	3½		....		
440	1/16	2½	5¼	....	27	....
445	1/16	....	....	....	....	....

Total call volume 23,589 Total call open int. 30,893
Total put volume 15,034 Total put open int. 32,389
The index: High 415.70; Low 408.09; Close 413.03, +4.94

COMPUTER TECHNOLOGY INDEX

Strike Price	Calls—Last Jun	Calls—Last Jul	Calls—Last Aug	Puts—Last Jun	Puts—Last Jul	Puts—Last Aug
110	4¾		....	....	....	....
115	1	3¾	....	....		....

Total call volume 20 Total call open int. 350
Total put volume 0 Total put open int. 265
The index: High 116.34; Low 114.03; Close 114.74, +0.71

OIL INDEX

Strike Price	Calls—Last Jun	Calls—Last Jul	Calls—Last Aug	Puts—Last Jun	Puts—Last Jul	Puts—Last Aug
175			....	....	1 11/16	....

Total call volume 0 Total call open int. 205
Total put volume 5 Total put open int. 743
The index: High 185.84; Low 183.39; Close 183.98, +0.06

INSTITUTIONAL INDEX

Strike Price	Calls—Last Jun	Calls—Last Jul	Calls—Last Aug	Puts—Last Jun	Puts—Last Jul	Puts—Last Aug
250	....	....	....	1/16		....
255	....	....	....	⅛		....

Strike Price	Calls—Last Jun	Calls—Last Jul	Calls—Last Aug	Puts—Last Jun	Puts—Last Jul	Puts—Last Aug
260	11	....	....	¼	2⅞	....
265	6½	....	....	9/16	4	....
270	3	....	....	1¾		....
275	⅞	....	....	5		....
280	⅛		....	....	....	....
285	1/16	2¼		....	....	....
290	....	....	2 13/16	....	....	....
295	....	⅞	....	....	....	....
300	....	....	....	27½	....	....

Total call volume 2,487 Total call open int. 43,182
Total put volume 1,486 Total put open int. 44,926
The index: High 273.01; Low 268.34; Close 271.21, +2.87

N.Y. Stock Exchange

NYSE INDEX OPTIONS

Strike Price	Calls—Last Jun	Calls—Last Jul	Calls—Last Aug	Puts—Last Jun	Puts—Last Jul	Puts—Last Aug
130	....	....	....	....	3/16	⅝
135	....	....	....	....	5/16	....
140	16	....	....	....	9/16	....
142½	....	....	....	....	¾	....
145	11¼	....	13⅜		1 5/16	2⅜
147½	8½	....	....			....
150	4¾	8⅝	9¼	3/16	2¼	3¾
152½	3	6¼	....	5/16	2½	....
155	⅞	4	5⅝	1⅜	3⅞	5 9/16
157½	¼	3⅛	....	....	....	....
160	⅛	1⅝		4 7/16	6¼	....
165	1/16	¾	2⅛	....	....	11½

Total call volume 5,630. Total call open int. 11,967.
Total put volume 2,798. Total put open int. 12,191.
The index: High 155.36; Low 153.00; Close 154.52, +1.50

Philadelphia Exchange

GOLD/SILVER INDEX

Strike Price	Calls—Last Jun	Calls—Last Jul	Calls—Last Aug	Puts—Last Jun	Puts—Last Jul	Puts—Last Aug
100			....	1/16	⅞	
105	....	....	....	....	2⅜	....
110	⅞		....	....	....	....
115	1/16		....		....	....

Total call volume 76 Total call open int. 525
Total put volume 121 Total put open int. 1,069
The index: High 110.40; Low 108.78; Close 109.23, +0.50

VALUE LINE INDEX OPTIONS

Strike Price	Calls—Last Jun	Calls—Last Jul	Calls—Last Aug	Puts—Last Jun	Puts—Last Jul	Puts—Last Aug
220	....			....	....	1⅞
240	7	10	....	....	....	....
245	3	....	....	....	....	....
250	....	4¼	....	....	....	....
255	....	2	....	....	....	....

Total call volume 380 Total call open int. 1,319
Total put volume 50 Total put open int. 843
The index: High 243.66; Low 241.48; Close 243.02, +1.54

NATIONAL O-T-C INDEX

Strike Price	Calls—Last Jun	Calls—Last Jul	Calls—Last Aug	Puts—Last Jun	Puts—Last Jul	Puts—Last Aug
235	....	....	....	1/16		....
245	....	....	....	1/16	....	....
255	5¼	....	....	....	....	....

Total call volume 10 Total call open int. 114
Total put volume 13 Total put open int. 123
The index: High 259.52; Low 256.42; Close 258.31, +1.87

UTILITIES INDEX

Strike Price	Calls—Last Jun	Calls—Last Jul	Calls—Last Aug	Puts—Last Jun	Puts—Last Jul	Puts—Last Aug
170	18⅛	17½	....	....		....
180	7⅝	8	....	....	½	....
185	1¾	3⅞	....	....	....	....
190	....	1⅝	....	....	....	....

Total call volume 863 Total call open int. 2,844
Total put volume 10 Total put open int. 1,704
The index: High 188.13; Low 186.33; Close 187.18, +1.61

Pacific Exchange

FINANCIAL NEWS COMPOSITE INDEX

Strike Price	Calls—Last Jun	Calls—Last Jul	Calls—Last Sep	Puts—Last Jun	Puts—Last Jul	Puts—Last Sep
160	28⅝	....	31¼	....	....	....
165		....	26⅛	....	....	....
170	18⅝	....	....	....		....
175	13½	....	....	1/16	1 5/16	....
180	8		14⅝			....
185	3⅞	7⅞	11¼	7/16	3½	....
190	13/16	4¾	....	2 7/16		....
195	⅛	3	....	7⅛	7⅝	....
200		1 5/16	....	11⅛	....	....
205	....	....	....		15½	....

Total call volume 1,565 Total call open int. 7,612
Total put volume 1,059 Total put open int. 4,175
The index: High 189.64; Low 186.42; Close 188.54, +2.12

Actually, Table 16–5 contains a wide variety of stock index options, some covering broad stock market indexes and others covering industry averages. For now, we will look at options on broad stock market indexes and then shift to industry indexes.

The key option contracts on broad market indexes relate to:

Standard & Poor's 100 Index (Chicago Board Options Exchange).

Standard & Poor's 500 Index (Chicago Board Options Exchange).

Major Market Index (American Stock Exchange).

Institutional Index (American Stock Exchange).

New York Stock Exchange Composite Index (New York Stock Exchange).

Value Line Index (Philadelphia Stock Exchange).

National O-T-C Index (Philadelphia Stock Exchange).

Financial News Composite Index (Pacific Coast Stock Exchange).

We have discussed many of these indexes either in Chapter 3 or in this chapter. One item to observe is that the stock index option contract often trades on a different exchange than the previously discussed stock index futures contract. For example, the Standard and Poor's 500 Index *option* contract trades on the Chicago Board Options Exchange where the *futures* contract on the same index trades on the Chicago Mercantile Exchange (CME). Similarly, the option contract on the Major Market Index trades on the American Stock Exchange, and the futures contract trades on the Chicago Board of Trade (CBT). Other examples could also be cited. The point is that some exchanges have greater expertise in options (such as the Chicago Board Options Exchange and the American Stock Exchange), while others specialize in futures (the Chicago Mercantile Exchange and the Chicago Board of Trade). There is tremendous competition to find the appropriate niche in stock index futures and options.

Actual Trade in the S&P 100 Index

Let's take a closer look at the most popular of the stock index options, the Standard and Poor's 100 Index options trading on the Chicago Board Options Exchange. We reproduce a part of Table 16–5 covering this index in Table 16–6. You will recall from an earlier discussion that the S&P 100 Index is composed of 100 blue-chip stocks on which the Chicago Board Options Exchange currently has individual option contracts. It is a smaller version of the S&P 500 Index and generally has a value of about 10 points less (though it closely parallels the overall movements of the S&P 500). Both indexes are value-weighted.

Note at the bottom of Table 16–6 that the S&P 100 Index closed on June 14, 1988, at 261.20. With this value in mind, we can examine the strike prices and premiums for the various contracts. The premium in each case is multiplied by 100 to determine the total cash value involved.[14] Let's read down to the

TABLE 16–6   S&P 100 INDEX STOCK OPTIONS (Chicago Board Options Exchange, June 14, 1988)

Strike Price	Calls			Puts		
	June	July	August	June	July	August
220	—	—	—	—	$3/8$	$1^{15}/16$
225	$37^3/4$	—	$39^3/4$	$1/16$	$9/16$	$1^5/8$
230	33	—	—	$1/16$	$7/8$	$2^1/4$
235	$26^1/4$	—	30	$1/16$	$1^1/4$	$2^7/8$
240	$21^1/2$	22	$24^1/2$	$1/16$	$1^{11}/16$	$3^3/4$
245	$16^1/4$	18	$21^3/8$	$1/8$	$2^3/8$	$4^5/8$
250	$11^1/4$	$14^1/2$	$18^1/2$	$1/4$	$3^1/4$	6
255	$6^1/2$	$10^3/4$	$13^3/4$	$11/16$	$4^5/8$	$7^1/2$
260	$2^5/8$	$7^5/8$	$10^3/4$	$1^{13}/16$	$6^3/4$	10
265	$3/4$	$5^1/4$	$8^1/4$	$4^7/8$	$9^3/8$	$11^3/4$
270	$3/16$	$3^3/8$	$5^3/4$	$10^1/2$	$12^1/2$	16
275	$1/16$	$1^{15}/16$	4	—	$16^1/2$	—

The multiplier times the premium is 100.
Value of the S&P 100 Index (June 14, 1988) = 261.20.

260 strike price and across to the July call option (second monthly column). The premium is $7^5/8$ (7.625).

Assume an investor bought a July 260 contract for a 7.625 premium on June 14, 1988, and that when the July contract expired, the S&P 100 Index was 278 under our optimistic assumption, and that under our pessimistic assumption it was 242. At an index value of 278, the option value is 18 (278 − 260). The ending or expiration price is 18 points higher than the strike price. Keep in mind the option cost of 7.625. The profit is shown below to be $1,037.50. At an ending value of 242 (pessimistic assumption), the option is worthless, and there is a loss of 762.50. Remember there are July 260 call options.

278 Optimistic Assumption		242 Pessimistic Assumption	
Final value (100 × 18)	$1,800.00		$ 0.00
Purchase price (100 × 7.625)	−762.50		− 762.50
Profit or loss	+ $1,037.50		− $762.50

We have been working with call options. Now, let's shift our attention to put options. If a 260 July put option (the option to sell at 260 rather than buy at 260) had been acquired on June 14, we can see in Table 16–6 (July put column, fourth row from the bottom) that the initial price of the put option would be $6^3/4$. Let's assume that when the July put contract expired, the S&P 100 Index was 278 under what is now our pessimistic assumption and 242 under what is now our optimistic assumption.

---

[14]The 100 multiplier applies to all the other option contracts listed in Table 16–5 as well.

At an index value of 278, no value is associated with a put option that allows you to sell at only 260. Since the put option cost $6^3/_4$, there is a $675 loss. At a final value of 242, the put option to sell at 260 has a value of 18. With a cost of $6^3/_4$, a profit of $1,125 takes place. The profit and losses are indicated below.

278 Pessimistic Assumption		242 Optimistic Assumption	
Final value	$ 0	$(100 \times \$18)$	$1,800
Purchase price $(100 \times 6^3/_4)$	− 675	$(100 \times 6^3/_4)$	− 675
Profit or loss	− $675		+ $1,125

HEDGING WITH STOCK INDEX OPTIONS

The discussion of stock index options thus far has pertained to speculation about market moves. Stock index options can also be used for hedging. Like stock index futures, stock index options can be used to protect a portfolio or for special purposes by underwriters, specialists, dealers, tax planners, and others.

At times, options may offer a hedging advantage over futures to investors who are limited by law from purchasing futures contracts. On the other hand, futures generally allow for a more-efficient hedge than options. If the market goes down by 20 or 25 percent, chances are good that a completely hedged short futures position (selling futures contracts) will compensate fully, or to a reasonable degree, losses in a portfolio. An option write, used to hedge a portfolio, may prove to be inadequate. Perhaps the option premium income represents 10 percent of the portfolio, but the market goes down by 25 percent. Fifteen percent of the loss will be unprotected. Buying a put option may overcome this problem, but the cash outflow to purchase the put option could involve substantial funds. Clearly, both futures and options have their advantages and disadvantages.

Stock Index Options for Industries

There are also option contracts tailor-designed for industries. Thus, one who wishes to speculate on a given industry's performance, or hedge against holdings in that industry, can use industry index options. The options are similar to those previously discussed in that put and call options are traded at various strike prices. The industry index options trade at a value equal to 100 times the premium.

Examples of industry index options are presented below.

Computer Technology Index (American Stock Exchange).

Oil Index (American Stock Exchange).

Gold/Silver Stock Index (Philadelphia Stock Exchange).

Utilities Index (Philadelphia Stock Exchange).

TABLE 16–7	STOCKS IN THE COMPUTER TECHNOLOGY INDEX ON THE AMERICAN STOCK EXCHANGE

Advanced Micro Devices, Inc.
Amdahl Corporation
Automatic Data Processing, Inc.
Commodore International Limited
Computer Sciences Corporation

Computervision Corporation
Control Data Corporation
Cray Research, Inc.
Data General Corporation
Datapoint Corporation

Digital Equipment Corporation
Hewlett-Packard Company
Honeywell, Inc.
International Business Machines Corporation
Mohawk Data Sciences Corp.

Motorola, Inc.
National Semiconductor Corporation
NBI, Inc.
NCR Corporation
Paradyne Corporation

Prime Computer Inc.
Storage Technology Corporation
Tandy Corporation
Telex Corporation (The)
Texas Instruments Incorporated

Uccel Corporation
Unisys Corporation
Wang Laboratories, Inc. (Cl. B)
Xerox Corporation

These indexes generally provide value-weighted measures based on key firms in the industry. For example, the Computer Technology Index on the American Stock Exchange contains such firms as IBM, Control Data, Digital Equipment, NCR, Unisys, and so on. A complete listing is shown in Table 16–7. Each firm is weighted in terms of its total market value in relationship to the total market value of the other firms in the industry. If a portfolio manager is bullish on the market in general but bearish on computer technology stocks, he may buy put options or sell call options on the computer technology index. Other market strategies can also be devised.

OPTIONS ON STOCK INDEX FUTURES

We have discussed *stock index futures* and *stock index options,* so a natural extension of our discussion is to consider the third form of stock index trading, **options on stock index futures.** The three forms of index trading are listed below for future reference.

1. Stock index futures.

2. Stock index options.

3. Options on stock index futures.

An option on a stock index future (item 3 above) gives the holder the right
to purchase the stock index *futures contract* at a specified price over a given time
period. This is slightly different from the stock index option (item 2) that
gives the holder the right to purchase the *underlying index* at a specified price
over a given time period.[15] The contrast is shown in Figure 16–3.

The primary topic for discussion in this section is represented by the lefthand
column in Figure 16–3, an option on a stock index futures contract. The value
of an option to purchase a stock index futures contract will depend on the
outlook for the futures contract. Quotes on options to purchase stock index
futures are shown in Table 16–8.[16]

As indicated in Table 16–8, options on stock index futures trade on the
NYSE Composite Index (at the NYFE—New York Futures Exchange) and
on the S&P 500 Stock Index (at the CME—Chicago Mercantile Exchange).
Let's look at the quotes on the S&P 500 Stock Index at the bottom half of the
table. A call option to buy a June S&P 500 Stock Index futures contract at a
strike price of 275 has a premium of 1.95.[17] On these option contracts, the

---

FIGURE 16–3   COMPARISON OF OPTION CONTRACTS

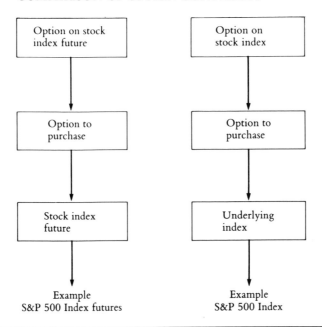

<table>
<tr><td>Option on stock index future</td><td>Option on stock index</td></tr>
<tr><td>Option to purchase</td><td>Option to purchase</td></tr>
<tr><td>Stock index future</td><td>Underlying index</td></tr>
<tr><td>Example
S&P 500 Index futures</td><td>Example
S&P 500 Index</td></tr>
</table>

---

[15]Because of cash-settlement procedures, the actual index will never actually be purchased, and the gain
or loss will be settled for cash.

[16]These quotes generally appear in the futures section of *The Wall Street Journal* rather than in the options
section. This can be potentially confusing to the reader.

[17]With the option expiring toward the end of the third week of June, there are only a few days
remaining so the premium is small.

TABLE 16–8   OPTIONS ON STOCK INDEX FUTURES (June 14, 1988)

NYSE COMPOSITE INDEX (NYFE) $500 times premium						
Strike	Calls – Settle			Puts – Settle		
Price	Jun-c	Jly-c	Sep-c	Jun-p	Jly-p	Sep-p
152	3.15	6.30	8.65	0.30	2.55	4.95
154	1.55	5.05	7.45	0.80	3.25	5.70
156	0.55	3.90	6.35	1.75	4.05	6.50
158	0.40	3.00	5.35	3.15	5.15	7.50
160	0.15	2.20	4.40	5.15	6.30	8.55
162	0.05	1.60	3.65	7.15	7.70	9.70
Est. vol. 131, Mon vol. 20 calls, 29 puts						
Open interest Mon 679 calls, 836 puts						
S&P 500 STOCK INDEX (CME) $500 times premium						
Strike	Calls – Settle			Puts – Settle		
Price	Jun-c	Jly-c	Sp-c	Jun-p	Jly-p	Sep-p
265	9.80	15.05	18.65	0.20	3.35	7.20
270	5.35	11.40	15.50	0.75	4.70	8.95
275	1.95	8.30	12.55	2.35	6.60	10.90
280	0.45	5.75	9.95	5.85	9.05	13.15
285	0.05	3.80	7.65	10.45	12.10	....
290	0.05	2.50	5.75	....	....	18.80
Est. vol. 9,074; Mon vol. 1,199 calls; 1,078 puts						
Open interest Mon; 24,830 calls; 25,834 puts						

Source: *The Wall Street Journal,* June 15, 1988, p. 37. Reprinted by permission of *The Wall Street Journal,* © Dow Jones & Company, Inc., 1988. All rights reserved.

premium is multiplied by 500 to get the value of the contract. Thus, the cost of the contract is $975 (500 × 1.95).

In examining Table 16–8, note that the premiums on the call options increase substantially with the passage of time from June to September. This gain in value is not only a function of the extended time period associated with the option but is also due to the fact that the S&P 500 futures contract has a higher value in September than June. On June 14, 1988, the June S&P 500 futures contract traded at 274.60, while the September S&P contract traded at 276.70. Thus, options on stock index futures not only have a time premium (as all options do) but may also have an additional premium (or discount) depending on the relationship of the far-term futures market to the near-term futures market.

Options on stock index futures may be settled on a cash basis, or the holder of a call option may actually exercise the option and force the option writer to produce a specified future contract.

17

INVESTMENTS IN REAL ASSETS

I n this chapter, we turn our attention to **real assets**; that is, tangible assets that may be seen, felt, held, or collected. Examples of such assets are real estate, gold, silver, diamonds, coins, stamps, and antiques. This is no small area from which to consider investments. For example, the total market value of all real estate holdings in the United States in the late 1980s was in excess of $5 trillion.

As further evidence of value, in the late 1980s, a Van Gogh painting sold for $40 million, and a 132-carat diamond earring set sold for $6.6 million. Coins and stamps also sold for values well into the hundreds of thousands.

A number of the traditional stock brokerage houses have moved into the area of real estate. Likewise, Citicorp of New York has an art investment program. No less than 25 million people in the United States are stamp collectors, and 8 million collect and invest in coins.

As was pointed out in Chapter 1, in inflationary environments, real assets have at times outperformed financial assets (such as stocks and bonds). With this in mind, the reader is well advised to become familiar with these investment outlets—not only to take advantage of the investment opportunities but to be well aware of the pitfalls. A money manager who is challenged by clients to include real assets in a portfolio (such as real estate or precious metals) must be conversant not only with the opportunities but also with the drawbacks.

ADVANTAGES AND DISADVANTAGES OF REAL ASSETS

As previously mentioned, real assets may offer an opportunity as an inflation hedge because inflation means higher replacement costs for real estate, precious metals, and other physical items. Real assets also serve as an investment hedge against the unknown and feared. When people become concerned about world events, gold and other precious metals may be perceived as the last safe haven for investments.

Real assets also may serve as an effective vehicle for portfolio diversification. Since financial and real assets at times move in opposite directions, some efficient diversification may take place. A study by Robichek, Cohn, and Pringle in the *Journal of Business* actually indicates that movements between various types of real and monetary assets are less positively correlated than are those for monetary assets alone.[1] The general findings indicate that enlarging the universe of investment alternatives would benefit the overall portfolio construction in terms of risk–return alternatives.

A final advantage of an investment in real assets is the psychic pleasure that may be provided. One can easily relate to a beautiful painting in the living room, a mint gold coin in a bank lockbox, or an attractive real estate development.

There are many disadvantages to consider as well. Perhaps the largest drawback is the absence of large, liquid, and relatively efficient markets. Whereas

---

[1]Alexander A. Robichek, Richard A. Cohn, and John J. Pringle, "Return on Alternative Media and Implications for Portfolio Construction," *Journal of Business*, July 1972, pp. 427–43.

stocks or bonds can generally be sold in a few minutes at a value close to the latest quoted trade, such is not likely to be the case for real estate, diamonds, art, and other forms of real assets. It may take many months to get the desired price for a real asset, and even then, there is an air of uncertainty about the impending transaction until it is consummated.

Furthermore, there is the problem of dealer spread or middleman commission. Whereas in the trading of stocks and bonds, spreads or commissions are very small (usually 1 or 2 percent), dealer spreads for real assets can be as large as 20 to 25 percent or more. This is particularly true for small items that do not have great value. On more valuable items, such as rare paintings, valuable jewels, or mint gold coins, the dealer spread tends to be smaller (perhaps 5 to 10 percent) but still more than that on securities.

The investor in real assets generally receives no current income (with the possible exception of real estate) and may in fact incur storage and insurance costs. Furthermore, there may be the problem of high unit cost for investments. You cannot easily acquire multiple art masterpieces.

A final drawback or caveat in real assets is the hysteria or overreaction that tends to come into the marketplace from time to time. Gold, silver, diamonds, and coins may be temporarily bid all out of proportion to previously anticipated value. The last buyer, who arrives too late, may end up owning a very unprofitable investment. The trick is to get into the recurring cycle early enough to take advantage of the large capital gains opportunities that regularly occur for real assets. Also, you should buy items of high enough quality so that you can ride out the setbacks if your timing is incorrect.

In the remainder of this chapter, we will examine real estate, gold, silver, diamonds, and other collectibles as investment outlets. Because real estate lends itself more directly to analytical techniques familiar to students of finance, it will receive a proportionately larger share of our attention.

REAL ESTATE AS AN INVESTMENT

Approximately one half of the households in the United States own real estate as a home or investment. Also, many firms in the brokerage and investment community have also moved into the real estate sector. As examples, Merrill Lynch and Shearson Lehman Hutton have acquired real estate affiliates to broker property, conduct mortgage banking activities, or package real estate syndications. While only 2–3 percent of pension fund assets are currently in real estate, the number may grow to 10 percent or more in the 1990s.

Some insight into changing real estate values may be gained from viewing Figure 17–1. We see the gain for a dollar invested in real estate in 1946 (as compared to fixed-income investments).

In Table 17–1 we see the change in conventional mortgage rates and median home prices in the United States. The gain in home prices is over fourfold.

Real estate investments may include such outlets as your own home, duplexes and apartment buildings, office buildings, shopping centers, industrial buildings, hotels and motels, as well as raw land. The investor may participate as an individual, as part of a limited partnership real estate syndicate, or through

FIGURE 17–1   GROWTH IN VALUE, 1946–1988 ($1 of Investment)

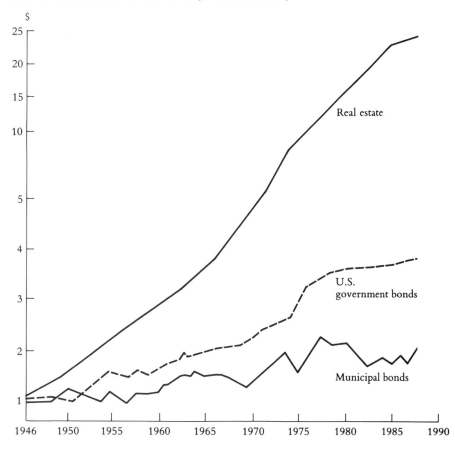

a real estate investment trust. These forms of ownership will receive further coverage toward the end of this section.

Throughout the rest of the section, we will consider the effect of tax reform on real estate projects, evaluate a typical real estate investment, consider new methods of real estate financing, and examine limited partner syndicates and real estate investment trusts.

Tax Reform and Real Estate Investments

With tax reform, the life over which a real estate investor can write off his or her depreciation deduction for tax purposes was extended from 19 years to $27^1/_2$ years for residential rental property and to $31^1/_2$ years for commercial property. This means you have to wait longer to take full advantage of tax deductions. Furthermore, the lowering of the marginal tax rate has reduced

TABLE 17–1   MORTGAGE RATES AND HOME PRICES

Year	Average Conventional Mortgage Rate	Median Price of A New Home
1970	8.40	$23,258
1971	7.71	24,998
1972	7.56	27,110
1973	7.98	30,823
1974	8.97	34,055
1975	9.11	37,237
1976	9.05	42,200
1977	8.80	47,900
1978	9.30	55,100
1979	10.48	64,000
1980	12.25	72,700
1981	14.16	78,000
1982	14.47	80,400
1983	12.20	82,500
1984	13.75	86,300
1985	11.98	88,390
1986	10.18	92,167
1987	9.78	93,200
1988	9.67	95,818

the incentive to invest in real estate as a tax shelter. A maximum tax rate of 33 percent gives much less incentive to go for tax write-offs than a 50 percent rate. Finally, real estate investors not actively involved in the management of property are very limited in writing off paper losses created through limited partnerships against other forms of income.

The effect of tax reform is to make real estate a less-attractive investment, at least for the present. Because of the loss of many traditional tax benefits for real estate, some existing properties have less value, and new construction is proceeding at a slower pace. Over the long term, however, real estate may still be a good investment. Why? With fewer new properties being developed as a result of tax reform, the glut in office space and apartments in certain sections of the country (Houston, Atlanta, Denver, and other areas) will eventually disappear. Furthermore, with fewer new properties brought to the market, rents will eventually go up on existing properties. The increased rents will also be necessary to provide adequate cash returns to investors who previously received a large portion of their total return from tax-shelter benefits but no longer do. The eventual impact of higher rents will be higher valuation, perhaps by the early 1990s.

The above comments about real estate apply primarily to real estate investments (apartments, shopping centers, and so on) as opposed to homeownership. All the benefits of homeownership basically remain in effect after tax reform. There is no depreciation deduction on your personal residence, so this is really not an issue. The only slight disadvantage to homeownership as a result of tax reform is that marginal tax rates are now lower so there is somewhat less benefit in taking tax deductions. Nevertheless, the overall tax advantages of owning your own home still remain firmly in place. Homeownership was simply too much a part of the American way of life to be attacked by tax reformers in Congress.

Let's now look at a real estate investment.

An Actual Example

Assume we are considering investing $170,000 in a new fourplex (four-unit apartment housing project). The land costs will be $30,000, and the actual physical structure will cost $140,000. This latter amount will be the value to be depreciated. We will assume that we will borrow 75 percent of the total property value of $170,000, which represents a loan of $127,500. Though we are dealing with relatively small numbers for ease of computation, the same types of considerations would apply to a multimillion-dollar shopping center or office building. Before we actually evaluate our cash inflows and outflows, we will consider tax and accounting factors related to depreciation in real estate.

Depreciation Effects

In the present case, we can write off depreciation on residential real estate property over $27^1/_2$ years. You will recall the depreciation period for commercial property (shopping centers, for example) is $31^1/_2$ years. Furthermore, under the Tax Reform Act of 1986, only **straight-line depreciation** can be applied to any form of real estate investment. There is no potential for accelerated depreciation as there was before the passage of this act.

Returning to our example, the $140,000 physical structure would be depreciated over $27^1/_2$ years using straight-line depreciation.[2] The annual depreciation charge would be $5,091.

$$\frac{\$140,000}{27.5} = \$5,091 \text{ annual depreciation}$$

Prior to tax reform, you could have depreciated 8.8 percent of the $140,000 physical structure in the first year, or $12,320. This was based on using accelerated depreciation over a 19-year life. The effect of pre- and post-tax reform is shown in Figure 17–2.

Cash Flow Considerations

The only aspect of our investment we have considered so far is depreciation. We have established the fact that on a $170,000 investment with $30,000 in land and $140,000 in the building, we could take annual depreciation of $5,091. Depreciation is a noncash tax-deductible item that is used to lower tax obli-

---

[2]The time period may vary slightly from this due to mid-month conventions. The impact is too small to be considered.

FIGURE 17–2   DEPRECIATION BEFORE AND AFTER TAX REFORM (Residential Real
                   Estate)

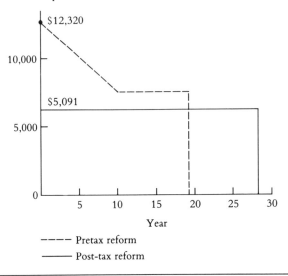

Depreciation Base = $140,000.

gations. We now must consider various cash flow items, such as the receipt
of the rent, the payment of interest, property taxes, insurance, maintenance
expenses, and so on. An overall example of cash flow analysis is presented in
Table 17–2. This is assumed to represent the first year of the investment.

We see in Table 17–2 that we have a loss of $1,797 for federal income tax
purposes and that this provides a tax-shelter benefit of $593 against other
income.[3] We also add depreciation of $5,091 back in to get cash flow because
although it was subtracted out, it is really a noncash item. The negative and
two positive values at the bottom of the table provide a positive cash flow of
$3,887.

In terms of investor return in the first year, the initial cash investment is
$42,500. This is based on the total value of the property of $170,000 minus
the initial loan of $127,500, requiring the investor to put up $42,500 in cash.
With a cash inflow of $3,887 in the first year, the cash-on-cash return in the
first year is 9.15 percent ($3,887/$42,500).

However, we should point out that in considering the cost of the loan in
Table 17–2, we have only evaluated interest payments. We might wish to

---

[3]The assumption in this case is that we have an active participation in the property and are allowed to
deduct the tax loss. This is a tricky matter in real estate because all real estate losses are considered to be
passive in nature and nondeductible. However, there are exceptions. If the investor is actively involved in
the management of the property and has adjusted gross income of $100,000 or less, up to $25,000 in losses
can be claimed. For income over $100,000, the $25,000 write-off is phased out up to income levels of
$150,000. In a later discussion on limited partnerships, we will examine circumstances in which tax losses on
real estate cannot be claimed on an individual's tax return regardless of income level.

TABLE 17–2	CASH FLOW ANALYSIS FOR AN APARTMENT (FOURPLEX) INVESTMENT

Gross annual rental (4 units at $490 per month
  or $5,880 per year for each unit) $23,520
Less 5 percent vacancy .... __1,176__
Net rental income $22,344

Interest expense on a loan
    of 75 percent of property
    value at 12 percent interest:
    (75%) × $170,000 = $127,500
    (12%) × $127,500 = $15,300 ...... $15,300
Property taxes 2,000
Insurance 750
Maintenance 1,000
Depreciation .... __5,091__

        Total expenses $24,141
Before-tax income or (loss) .... (1,797)
Tax benefit
    (assumes 33 percent tax rate) 593
Depreciation .... __5,091__
Cash flow .... $ 3,887

consider repayment of principal as well. In the present case, we are assuming that in the first year we are paying 12 percent interest on a loan balance of $127,500, or $15,300 (as shown in Table 17–2). Assuming a 20-year loan (it is not unusual for the life of the loan to be different from the depreciation period), the total first-year payment for interest and principal is $17,070, indicating that $1,770 is applied toward the repayment of principal.

$$\text{Payment} - \text{Interest} = \text{Repayment of principal}$$
$$\$17,070 - \$15,300 = \$1,770$$

On this basis, our net cash flow figure will be reduced to $2,117.

$$\text{Cash flow} - \text{Repayment of principal} = \text{Net cash flow}^4$$
$$\$3,887 - \$1,770 = \$2,117$$

With a net cash flow of $2,117 (after repayment of principal), the cash-on-cash return in the first year is 4.98 percent ($2,117/$42,500). This value will change from year to year as rental income, expenses, and repayment of principal changes.

While the return appears to be low, it should be pointed out that the investor will build up his or her equity or ownership interest by the amount of repayment toward principal each year as well as any increase in property value resulting from inflation. If the property increases by 5 percent in the

----

[4]One could argue that we are building up equity or ownership interest through the repayment of principal. However, our focus for now is simply on the amount of cash flow going in and out. We will consider buildup in equity in a subsequent discussion.

first year, this represents an added benefit of $8,500 (5 percent times the $170,000 value of the property). Actually, return benefits associated with price appreciation may exceed all other considerations. An investor may be willing to accept relatively low cash flow if he or she can enjoy inflation-related gains. Note in the present case, the $8,500 gain from price appreciation alone would represent a first-year return on cash investment of 20 percent ($8,500/$42,500).

This gain is particularly relevant because most of the tax advantages of real estate have been largely reduced, so there is a dependence on cash generation and *inflation*.

You can readily see the twin factors that make real estate attractive are depreciation write-offs and appreciation in value due to price appreciation. Apartments, office buildings, warehouses, and shopping centers have served particularly well as good performers in inflationary environments. In low-inflationary environments, the benefits of real estate are substantially reduced as there is less price appreciation potential.

FINANCING OF REAL ESTATE

One of the essential considerations in any real estate investment analysis is the cost of financing. In the prior example, we said a loan for $127,500 over 20 years at 12 percent interest would have yearly payments of $17,070. Note in Table 17–3 the effects of various interest rates on annual payments.

We see the difference in annual payments ranges from $12,986 at 8 percent up to $21,504 at 16 percent. Even more dramatic is the increase in total interest paid over the life of the loan; it goes from $132,220 at 8 percent to $302,580 at 16 percent. (Keep in mind that the total loan was only $127,500.)

An investor who has the unlikely opportunity to shift out of the loan at 16 percent into one at 8 percent might be willing to pay as much as $83,692.72 for the privilege. (Tax effects are not specifically considered here.)

16 percent interest − 8 percent interest = Dollar difference in annual
                                                     payments
       $21,504 − $12,986   = $8,518

The present value of $8,518 over 20 years assuming an 8 percent discount rate (see Appendix D at the end of the book) is:

$$\$8,518 \times 9.818 = \$83,629.72$$

Thus, it is easy to appreciate the role of interest rates in a real estate investment decision. No industry is more susceptible to the impact of changing interest rates than real estate. Each time the economy overheats and interest rates skyrocket, the real estate industry comes to a standstill. With the eventual easing of interest-rate pressures, the industry once again enjoys a recovery.

TABLE 17–3	INTEREST RATES AND ANNUAL REPAYMENT OBLIGATIONS FOR A 20-YEAR LOAN (Principal Amount Equals $127,500)				
	8 Percent	10 Percent	12 Percent	14 Percent	16 Percent
Annual payment	$ 12,986	$ 14,975	$ 17,070	$ 19,251	$ 21,504
Total interest over the life of the loan	132,220	172,000	213,900	257,520	302,580

This pattern continued throughout the 1980s. It is within this environment that many traditional lenders hesitated to commit themselves to long-term lending on a fixed-interest-rate basis. A 20-year loan commitment at a fixed rate of 10 percent can be both embarrassing and expensive to the lender when interest rates advance to 14 or 15 percent.

New Types of Mortgages

In actuality, a whole new set of mortgage arrangements have appeared as alternatives to the fixed-interest-rate mortgage (particularly for home mortgages). The borrower must now be prepared to consider such alternative lending arrangements as the **adjustable rate mortgage,** the **graduated payment mortgage,** and the **shared appreciation mortgage.**

Adjustable Rate Mortgage (ARM).   Under this mortgage arrangement, the interest rate is adjusted regularly. If interest rates go up, borrowers may either increase their normal payments or extend the maturity date of the loan at the same fixed-payment level to fully compensate the lender. Similar downside adjustments can also be made if interest rates fall. Generally, adjustable rate mortgages are initially made at rates 1 to 2 percent below fixed-interest-rate mortgages because the lender enjoys the flexibility of changing interest rates and is willing to share the benefits with the borrower. Adjustable rate mortgages currently account for over half of the residential mortgage market. Although adjustable rate mortgages usually have an upper boundary (such as 15 or 18 percent), there is a real possibility of default for many borrowers if interest rates reach high levels.

Graduated Payment Mortgage (GPM).   Under this type of financial arrangement, the payments start out on a relatively low basis and increase over the life of the loan. This type of mortgage may be well suited to the young borrower who has an increasing repayment capability over the life of the loan. An example would be a 30-year, $50,000 loan at 12 percent which would normally require monthly payments of $503.20 under a standard fixed-payment mortgage. With a graduated payment mortgage, monthly payments might start out as $350 or $400 and eventually progress to over $600. The GPM plan has been referred to by a few of its critics as the "gyp em" plan, in that early payments may not be large enough to cover interest, and therefore, later payments must cover not only the amortization of the loan but also interest on the accumulated, unpaid, early interest. This is not an altogether fair criticism, but merely an interpretation of what the graduated payment stream represents.

Shared Appreciation Mortgage (SAM).   Perhaps the newest and most innovative of the mortgage payment plans is the shared appreciation mortgage. This provides the lender with a hedge against inflation because he directly participates in any increase in value associated with the property being mortgaged. The lender may enjoy as much as 30 to 40 percent of the appreciation in value over a specified time period, such as 10 years. The lender may take his return from the selling of the property or from the refinancing of the appreciated property value with a new lender. In return for this appreciation-potential privilege, the lender may advance funds at well below current market rates (perhaps at three quarters of current rates). The shared appreciation mortgage is not yet legal in all states.

Other Forms of Mortgages.   Somewhat similar to the shared appreciation mortgage is the concept of **equity participation** that is popular in commercial real estate. Under an equity participation arrangement, the lender not only provides the borrowed capital but part of the equity or ownership funds as well. A major insurance company or savings and loan thus may acquire an equity interest of 10 to 25 percent (or more). This financing arrangement becomes popular each time inflation rears its head. Some lenders are simply unwilling to commit capital for long time periods without a participation feature.

Borrowers may also look toward a *second mortgage* for financing. Here, a second lender provides additional financing beyond the first mortgage in return for a secondary claim or lien. The second mortgage is generally for a shorter period of time than the initial mortgage. Primary suppliers of second mortgages in recent times have been sellers of property. Quite often, in order to consummate a sale, it is necessary for the seller to supplement the financing provided by a financial institution. Sellers providing second mortgages generally advance the funds at rates below the first mortgage rate to facilitate the sale, whereas other second mortgage lenders (nonsellers) will ask for a few percentage points above the first mortgage rate to compensate for the extra risk of being in a secondary claim position.

In some cases, sellers may actually provide all the financing to the buyer. Usually the terms of the mortgage are for 20–30 years, but the seller has the right to call in the loan after three to five years if he so desires. The assumption is that the buyer may have an easier time finding his own financing at that point in time. This may or may not turn out to be true.

FORMS OF REAL ESTATE OWNERSHIP

Ownership of real estate may take many forms. The investor may participate as an individual, in a regular partnership, through a real estate syndicate (generally a limited partnership), or through a real estate investment trust (REIT).

Individual or Regular Partnership

Investing as an individual or with two or three others in a regular partnership offers the simplest way of getting into real estate from a legal viewpoint. The investors pretty much control their own destinies and can take advantage of personal knowledge of local markets and changing conditions to enhance their returns.

As is true with most smaller and less-complicated business arrangements, there is a well-defined center of responsibility that often leads to quick corrective action. However, there may be a related problem of inability to pool adequate capital to engage in large-scale investments as well as the absence of expertise to develop a wide range of investments. Furthermore, there is unlimited liability to the investor(s).

Syndicate or Limited Partnership

In order to expand the potential for investor participation, a syndicate or **limited partnership** has traditionally been formed.[5] The limited partnership works as follows: A general partner forms the limited partnership and has unlimited liability for the partnership liabilities. The general partner then sells participation units to the limited partners whose liability is generally limited to the extent of their initial investment (such as $5,000 or $10,000). Limited liability is particularly important in real estate because mortgage debt obligations may exceed the net worth of the participants. The general partner is generally responsible for managing the property, while the limited partners are merely investors.

Although the restricted liability feature of the limited partnership remains attractive, the Tax Reform Act of 1986 generally restricted the use of limited partnerships as tax shelters. Historically, real estate limited partnerships generated large paper losses through accelerated depreciation (though not cash losses), and these paper losses were used to shelter other forms of income (such as a doctor's salary) from taxation. Under the Tax Reform Act of 1986, a taxpayer is no longer allowed to use passive losses to offset other sources of income such as salary or portfolio income. Such losses can only be used to offset income from other passive investments.

It is easy to see why the Tax Reform Act of 1986 had a damaging effect

---

[5]A syndicate may take the form of a corporation, but this is not common. The term *real estate syndicate* has become virtually synonymous with the limited partnership form of operation.

on real estate values. Investors who had bought into real estate limited partnerships a number of years before the act was passed had their tax write-off privileges rapidly phased out after the passage of the act. All of a sudden, investors in existing real estate limited partnerships were bailing out. They were refusing to make required annual payments into the partnership, and as a result, many of the limited partnerships (as well as their investors) were disposing of property at fire-sale prices.

As previously mentioned, the initial impact of the act has already taken place, so real estate does have the potential to be a bargain in the future. Real estate limited partnerships still exist but more for limited liability than for tax reasons. The successful partnerships stress strong cash flow generation and capital appreciation potential. In the analysis in Table 17–2, a limited partnership was not involved, and the investor actively participated in managing the property. Some small tax write-offs were allowed, but note that the success of the project was much more dependent on cash flow and potential capital appreciation.

If you decide to invest in a limited partnership, you should follow certain guidelines. You must be particularly sensitive to the front-end fees and commissions that the general partner might charge. These can vary anywhere from 5 to 10 percent to as large as 20 to 25 percent. The investor must also be sensitive to any double-dealing that the general partner might be doing. An example would be selling property back and forth between different partnerships that the general partner has formed and taking a commission each time. The inflated paper profits may prove quite deceptive and costly to the uninformed limited partner.

In assessing a general partner and his associated real estate deal, the investor should look at a number of items. First of all, he should review the prior record of performance of the general partner. Is this the 1st or 10th deal that the general partner has put together? The investor will also wish to be sensitive to any lawsuits against the general partner that might exist. The investor might also wish to ascertain whether he or she is investing in a **blind pool** arrangement where funds are provided to the general partner to ultimately select properties for investment or if specific projects have already been identified and analyzed.

Finally the investor may have to decide whether to invest in a limited partnership/syndication that is either *public* or *private* in nature. A public offering generally involves much larger total amounts and has gone through the complex and rigorous process of SEC registration. Of course, SEC registration only attempts to ensure that full disclosure has taken place—it does not judge the prudence of the venture. A private offering of a limited partnership syndication is usually local in scope and restricted to a maximum of 35 investors.

Secondary (resale) markets for both public and private limited partnerships exist, but the dealer spreads and commissions tend to be very high. The spreads on desirable property are perhaps 10–15 percent; on less desirable property, 20–30 percent or more. Really bad property may approach total illiquidity. As you might anticipate, a public limited partnership has much more resale potential than a private one.

GETTING OUT OF A LIMITED PARTNERSHIP CAN MEAN GETTING LITTLE BACK

Despite their popularity, limited partnerships have presented a major shortcoming for many investors. Unlike stocks and mutual funds, most partnerships aren't easy to get out of.

But lately a fledgling secondary market has been developing. The market is made up of a growing number of small investment firms that buy limited partnership interests from investors, either for their own accounts or for resale to new investors.

Many partnership syndicators say the low prices in the secondary market shouldn't come as a surprise and that the secondary market firms are vultures preying on distressed sellers. Fundamentally, limited partnerships are long-term investments that weren't intended to trade.

The secondary market can be a treacherous place for the unwary. "Everyone who's a buyer is fairly sophisticated, and everyone who's a seller is just trying to get out," says an Ernst & Whinney representative.

In addition to being a place where investors who want to get out of partnerships can sell their interests, the secondary market gives new investors the opportunity to get in for a lot less than the original offering prices. However, they sometimes pay significantly more than the previous owners got when they sold, with the secondary-market firms pocketing the difference.

Partnership investors who are unhappy don't always have to rely on the secondary market if they want to get out. Some partnerships themselves have limited redemption features. And the major brokerage firms that syndicated or at least sold many of the biggest partnerships say they help investors find buyers for their unwanted interests.

Real Estate Investment Trust

Another form of real estate investment is the **real estate investment trust (REIT)**. REITs are similar to mutual funds or investment companies and trade on organized exchanges or over-the-counter. They pool investor funds, along with borrowed funds, and invest them directly in real estate or use them to make construction or mortgage loans to investors.

The advantage to the investor of an REIT is that he or she can participate in the real estate market for as little as $5 to $10 per share. Furthermore, this is the most-liquid type of real estate investment because of the large secondary market for the shares.

REITs were initiated under the Real Estate Investment Trust Act of 1960. Like other investment companies, they enjoy the privilege of single taxation of income (only the stockholder pays and not the trust). In order to qualify for the tax privilege of a REIT, a firm must pay out at least 90 percent of its income to shareholders, have no less than 75 percent of its assets in real estate, and concurrently obtain at least 75 percent of its income from real estate.

REITs may take any of three different forms or combinations thereof. **Equity trusts** buy, operate, and sell real estate as an investment; **construction**

FIGURE 17–3 DATA SHEET FOR AN REIT

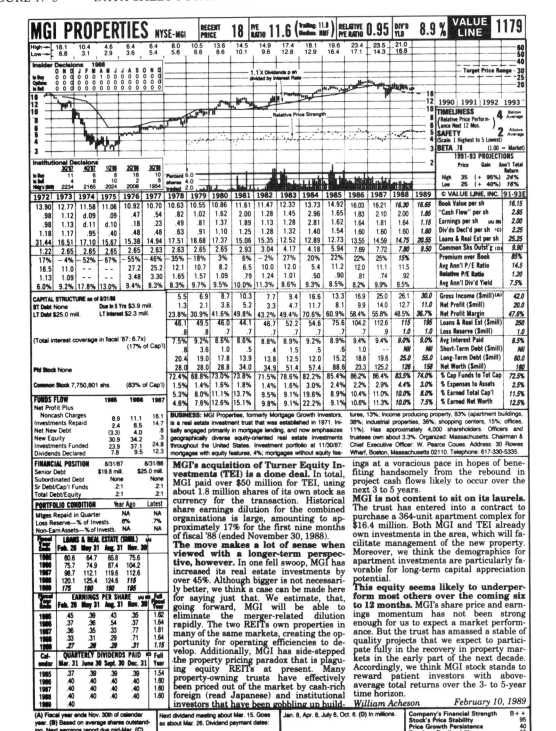

and development trusts make short-term loans to developers during their construction period; and **mortgage trusts** make long-term loans to real estate investors. REITs are generally formed and advised by affiliates of commercial banks, insurance companies, mortgage bankers, and other financial institutions. Representative issues include Bank American Realty, Continental Illinois Property, and Connecticut General Mortgage.

Although REITs were enormously popular investments during the 1960s and early 1970s, the bottom fell out of the REIT market in the mid-1970s. Many had made questionable loans that came to the surface in the tight money, recessionary period of 1973–75. Nevertheless, REITs have now regained some of their earlier popularity. Many investors look at the equity trust, which owns real estate directly, as a hedge against inflation. Somewhat less popular are the construction and development trusts and mortgage trusts (many REITs combine these various functions). The investor in REITs hopes to receive a reasonably high yield because 90 percent of income must be paid out in the form of dividends plus a modest capital appreciation in stock value. In some cases, outside investors have taken over REITs with the intention of liquidating assets at higher than current stock market values.

There are over 200 REITs from which the investor may choose. Further information on REITs may be acquired from the National Association of Real Estate Investment Trusts, 1101 17th St., N.W., Washington, D.C. 20036. In Figure 17–3, a Value Line data sheet is presented for MGI Properties, an example of a reasonably successful REIT.

GOLD AND SILVER

We now examine a number of other forms of real asset investments. Precious metals represent the most volatile of the investment alternatives. Gold and silver tend to move up in troubled times and show a decline in value during stable, predictable periods. Observe the movement in the price of gold between January 1976 and June 1988 in Figure 17–4.

Gold

Major factors that tend to drive up gold prices are fear of war, political instability, and inflation (these were particularly evident in 1979 with the takeover of U.S. embassies and double-digit inflation). Conversely, moderation in worldwide tensions and lower inflation cause a decline in gold prices. High interest rates are also a negative influence on gold prices. When interest rates are high, it may be very expensive to carry gold as an investment.

Gold may be owned in many different forms, and a survey by *Changing Times* indicated that 30 percent of the U.S. population with incomes over $30,000 per year owned gold (directly or indirectly) or other forms of precious metals. Let's examine the different forms of gold ownership.

Gold Bullion.   Gold bullion includes gold bars or wafers. The investor may own anywhere from 1 troy ounce to 10,000 troy ounces (valued at approxi-

FIGURE 17–4   DOLLAR PER TROY OUNCE

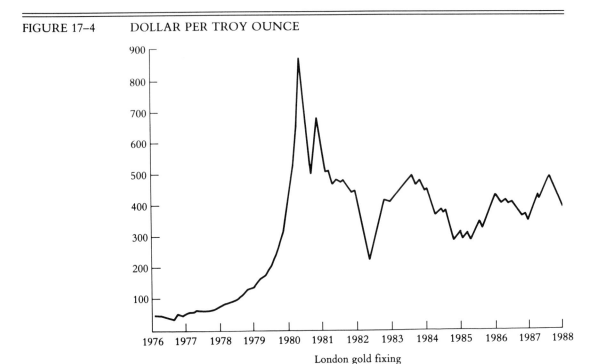

London gold fixing

mately $4.5 million in 1988). Smaller bars generally trade at a 6 to 8 percent premium over pure gold bullion value, with larger bars trading at a 1 to 2 percent premium. Gold bullion may provide storage problems, and unless the gold bars remain in the custody of the bank or dealer who initially sells them, they must be reassayed before being sold.

Gold Coins.   Many of the storing and assaying costs associated with gold bullion can be avoided by investing directly in gold coins. There are three basic outlets for investing in gold coins. First, there are *gold bullion coins,* such as the South African Krugerrand, the Mexican 50 peso, and the Canadian Maple Leaf. These coins trade at a small premium of 2 to 3 percent over pure bullion value and afford the investor an excellent outlet for taking a position in the market. A second form is represented by *common date gold coins* that are no longer minted, such as the U.S. double eagle, the British sovereign, or the French Napoleon. These coins may trade at as much as 50 to 100 times their pure gold bullion value. Finally, there are gold coins that are *old* and *rare* and that may trade at a numismatic value into the thousands or hundreds of thousands of dollars.

Gold Stocks.   In addition to gold bullion and gold coins, the investor may choose to take a position in gold by simply buying common stocks that have heavy gold-mining positions. Examples of companies listed on U.S. exchanges include Battle Mountain (U.S. based), Placer Dome Inc. (Canadian based), and Homestake Mining (U.S. based). Because these securities often move in the opposite direction of the stock market as a whole, they may provide excellent portfolio diversification.

Gold Futures Contracts.   Finally, the gold investor may consider trading in futures contracts. Gold futures are traded on five different U.S. exchanges and on many foreign exchanges.[6]

Silver

Silver has many of the same investment characteristics as gold in terms of being a hedge against inflation and a safe haven for investment during troubled times. Silver moved from $4 a troy ounce in 1976 to over $50 an ounce in early 1980 and then back to $6 an ounce in the mid- to late-1980s.

More so than gold, silver has heavy industrial and commercial applications. Areas of utilization include photography, electronic and electrical manufacturing, electroplating, dentistry, and silverware and jewelry. It is estimated that industrial uses of silver exceed annual production by 150 million ounces per year. Furthermore, the supply of silver does not necessarily increase with price because silver is a byproduct of copper, lead, zinc, and gold. Because of the undersupply factor, many consider silver to be appropriate for long-term holding.

Investment in silver can also take many different forms. Some may choose to buy *silver bullion* in the form of silver bars. Because the price of silver generally is $1/_{20}$th to $1/_{40}$th the price of gold and larger bulk is involved for an equivalent dollar size investment, the storage and carrying costs can be quite high. Second, *silver coins* may be bought in large bags or as rare coins for their numismatic value. Keep in mind that dimes, quarters, and half-dollars minted during and prior to 1965 were 90 percent pure silver. As a third outlet, the investor may wish to consider *silver futures contracts*. Finally, the investor may purchase *stocks* of firms that have interests in silver mining, such as Callahan Mining, Hecla Mining, or Sunshine Mining.

PRECIOUS GEMS

Precious gems include diamonds, rubies, sapphires, and emeralds. Diamonds and other precious gems have appeal to investors because of their small size, easy concealment, and great durability. They are particularly popular in Europe because of a long-standing distrust of paper currencies as a store of value.

The reason diamonds are so valuable can be best understood by considering the production process. It is estimated that 50 to 200 *tons* of rock or sand is required to uncover one carat ($1/_{142}$ of an ounce) of quality diamonds.

The distribution of diamonds is under virtual monopolistic control by De

---

[6]There are also options on gold futures on the Comex.

Beers Consolidated Mines of South Africa, Ltd. They control the distribution of approximately 80 percent of the world's supply and have a stated policy of maintaining price control. Diamonds have generally enjoyed a steady, somewhat spectacular movement in price. For example, the price of a "D" color, one-carat, flawless, polished diamond increased over tenfold between 1974 and 1980.

Of course, not all diamonds have done so well. Furthermore, there have been substantial breaks in the market, such as in 1974 and 1980–82 when diamond prices declined by one fourth and more. Even with large increases in value, the diamond investor does not automatically come out ahead. Dealer markups may be anywhere from 10 percent to 100 percent so that three to five years of steady gain may be necessary to show a substantial profit.

In no areas of investment is product and market knowledge more important. Either you must be an expert yourself or know that you are dealing with an "honest" expert. Diamonds are judged on the basis of the four c's (color, clarity, carat weight, and cut), and the assessment of any stone should be certified by the Gemological Institute of America. As is true of most valuable items, the investor is well advised to purchase the highest quality possible. You are considerably better off using the same amount of money to buy a higher-quality, smaller-carat diamond than a lesser-quality, high-carat diamond.

OTHER COLLECTIBLES

A listing of other collectibles for investment might include art, antiques, stamps, Chinese ceramics, rare books, baseball cards, and other items that appeal to various sectors of our society. Each offers psychic pleasure to the investor as well as the opportunity for profit.

Anyone investing in a collectible should have some understanding of current market conditions and of the factors that determine the inherent worth of the item. Otherwise, you may be buying someone else's undesirable holding at a premium price. It is important not to get swept away in a buying euphoria. The best time to buy art, antiques, or stamps is when the bloom is off the market and dealers are overburdened with inventory, not when there is a weekly story in *The Wall Street Journal* or *Business Week* about overnight fortunes being made. There seems to be a pattern or cycle in the collectibles market the same as in other markets (arts, antiques, and stamps actually do move together). The market was very strong in the 1970s with a pause in the mid-1970s caused by the recession. The market gained tremendous momentum from 1975 to 1980, with a sell-off in late 1980 and early 1981. A moderate recovery took place in the mid- to late-1980s.

As is true of other markets, the wise investor in the collectibles market must be sensitive to dealer spreads. A price guide that indicates a doubling in value every two or three years may be meaningless if the person with whom you are dealing sells for $100 and buys back for $50. The wise investor/collector can best maintain profits by dealing with other collectors or investors and eliminating the dealer or middleman from the transaction where possible.

BASEBALL CARDS FOR SERIOUS INVESTORS

Although we most often associate baseball cards with the 10-year-old child who coaxes 50 cents from his parents to buy a pack of cards in the drug store, there's actually a $200 million-a-year industry out there. A July 4, 1988 *Sports Illustrated* story estimates there are 100,000 serious baseball card collectors and millions of child arbitragers doing business on a daily basis.

And why not? In 1988, a Honus Wagner card (Pittsburgh Pirate shortstop at the turn of the century) sold for $110,000. It seems old Honus did not approve of smoking and when his card appeared in a tobacco-related set around 1910, he forced the American Tobacco Company to pull all but 100 of his cards off the market. The law of demand and supply has clearly set in over the decades.

For other collectors, a Mickey Mantle Topps card purchased for one cent in 1952 had a going value of $6,500 in 1989. A 1967 Topps Tom Seaver rookie card has increased in value from a penny to approximately $600. All the while, former teenage collectors were asking mom about the old shoe box of cards they left in the attic when they went off to college.

For the modern day collector, it's such stars as Don Mattingly, Dwight Gooden, and Roger Clemens that promise potential appreciation in value. In fact, any hot rookie prospect will do.

Not only baseball cards, but other forms of sports memorabilia have value as well. A clearly autographed Babe Ruth baseball is worth about $1,200. A truly enterprising collector went so far as to pay $500 for the dental records of Eddie Cicotte, a long-deceased pitcher for the infamous Chicago Black Sox of 1919.

1952 Topps card

Such periodicals as *Money* magazine and the *Collector/Investor* provide excellent articles on the collectibles market. Specialized periodicals, such as *American Arts and Antiques, Coin World, Linn's Stamp News, The Sports Collectors Digest,* and *Antique Monthly,* also are helpful. The interested reader can find books on almost any type of collectible in a public library or large bookstore.

18

INTERNATIONAL SECURITIES MARKETS

I n Chapter 1, we discussed the advantage of diversification in terms of risk reduction. In order to reduce risk exposure, the investor may desire a broad spectrum of securities from which to choose. An investor who lives in California would hardly be expected to limit all his investments to that geographic boundary. The same might be said for an investor living in the United States or Germany or Japan. The advantages of crossing international boundaries may be substantial in terms of diversification benefits.

Companies operating in different countries will be affected differently by international events such as crop failures, energy prices, wars, tariffs, trade between countries, and the value of local currencies relative to other currencies, especially the U.S. dollar. Furthermore, in spite of the up and down markets in the United States, there is almost certain to be a bull market somewhere in the world for the investor who likes to keep his chips on the table at all times.

The main drawback to investing in international securities would appear to be the more-complicated nature of the investment. Currently, one cannot simply pick up the phone and ask his broker to buy 100 shares of Banco Bilbao on the Spanish Stock Exchange (this may change some day in the future). Nevertheless, the difficulties of participating in international securities are not as great as one might initially expect. As will be later suggested in this chapter, an investor has a number of feasible and easily executed routes to follow in participating in the international markets.

The primary attention in this chapter is to international equities, although investments may certainly include fixed-income securities and real assets. We shall examine the composition of world equity markets, the diversification and return benefits that can be derived from foreign investments, the obstacles that are present, and finally, the methods of participating in foreign investments, directly and indirectly.

THE WORLD EQUITY MARKET

The world markets have grown dramatically since the last edition of this book in 1986, and Japan has emerged as the country having the largest value of securities traded. The New York Stock Exchange is now in second place. Figure 18–1 indicates the relative value of the major *international* equity markets.

The crash of 1987 was an international phenomenon where 19 out of 23 markets declined more than 20 percent. This is quite unusual given the low degree of correlation between the historical returns of different countries. Many worried that an international panic was in the making, but since that time, international markets have performed quite differently, with the Tokyo Stock Exchange reaching new highs in 1988. One thing became evident, and that was that international equity markets were becoming more sophisticated with

FIGURE 18–1   MARKET VALUES OF NON-U.S. EQUITIES AT THE END OF 1980 (In
                  Billions of U.S. Dollars; Non-U.S. Equity Total = $1,049.3 Billion)

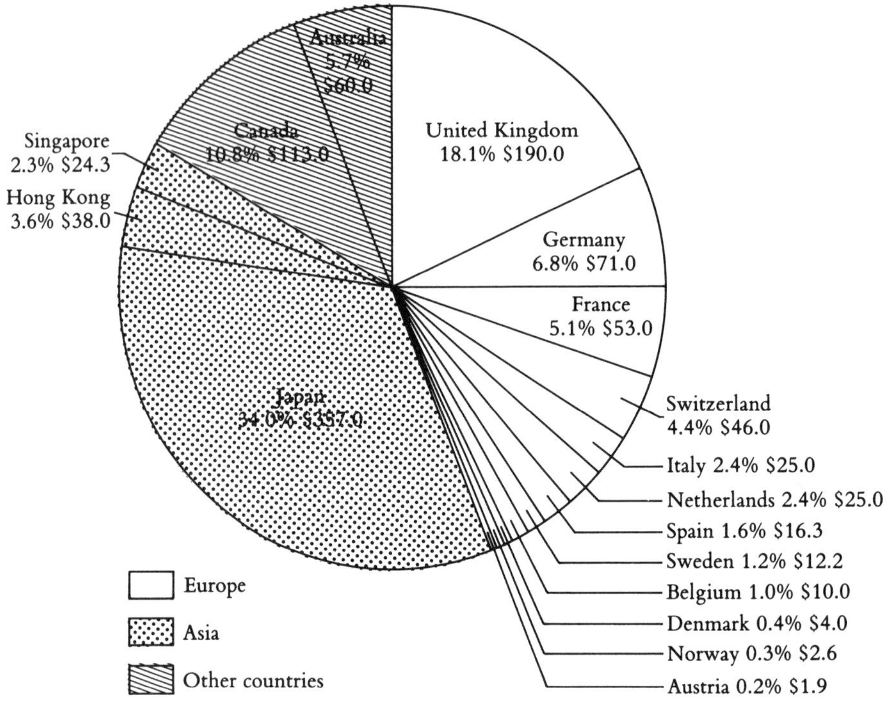

Source: Roger G. Ibbotson, Richard C. Carr, and Anthony W. Robinson, "International Equity and Bond
Returns," *Financial Analysts Journal,* July–August 1982, p. 63. Updated.

the use of computerized trading systems and the use of options and futures
contracts in several major markets.

Table 18–1 shows the institutional arrangements in world markets. The
breakdown is quite interesting with continuous auction markets (second column) the standard in markets like the United States, Japan, United Kingdom,
Germany, Canada, Hong Kong, and others. Table 18–1 also summarizes the
use of specialists, the use of forward contracts, automated quotations, com-
puter-directed trading, the use of options and futures, price limits, transactions
taxes, margin requirements, and trading off the exchange (called the third
market in the United States). This comprehensive table was produced by
Richard Roll in his analysis of the world market crash of October 1987. The
most-significant factor relating to the size of the market decline in each country
was the beta of that market to the world market index.

TABLE 18–1 INSTITUTIONAL ARRANGEMENTS IN WORLD MARKETS

Country	Auction	Official Special- ists	Forward Trading on Ex- change	Auto- mated Quota- tions	Computer- Directed Trading	Options/ Futures Trading	Price Limits	Transac- tion Tax (Round Trip)	Margin Require- ments	Trading Off Exchange
Australia	Continuous	No	No	Yes	No	Yes	None	0.6%	None	Infrequent
Austria	Single	Yes	No	No	No	No	5%	0.3%	100%	Frequent
Belgium	Mixed	No	Yes	No	No	No^a	10%/ None^b	0.375%/ 0.195%	100%/ 25%^{b}	Occasional
Canada	Continuous	Yes	No	Yes	Yes	Yes	None^c	0	50%^{d}	Prohibited
Denmark	Mixed	No	No	No	No	No	None	1%	None	Frequent
France	Mixed	Yes	Yes	Yes	Yes	Yes	4%/7%^{e}	0.3%	100%/ 20%^{f}	Prohibited
Germany	Continuous	Yes	No	No	No	Options	None	0.5%	None	Frequent
Hong Kong	Continuous	No	No	Yes	No	Futures	None^g	0.6% +	None	Infrequent
Ireland	Continuous	No	No	Yes	No	No	None	1%	100%	Frequent
Italy	Mixed	No	Yes	No	No	No	10–20%^{h}	0.3%	100%	Frequent
Japan	Continuous	Yes	No	Yes	Yes	No^i	−10%	0.55%	70%^{j}	Prohibited
Malaysia	Continuous	No	No	Yes	No	No	None	0.03%	None	Occasional
Mexico	Continuous	No	Yes	No	No	No	10%^{k}	0	None	Occasional
Netherlands	Continuous	Yes	No	No	No	Options	Variable^l	2.4%^{m}	None	Prohibited
New Zealand	Continuous	No	No	No	No	Futures	None	0	None	Occasional
Norway	Single	No	No	No	No	No	None	1%	100%	Frequent
Singapore	Continuous	No	No	Yes	No	No^n	None	0.5%	71%	Occasional
South Africa	Continuous	No	No	Yes	No	Options	None	1.5%	100%	Prohibited
Spain	Mixed^o	No	No	No	No	No	10%^{p}	0.11%	50%^{p}	Frequent
Sweden	Mixed	No	No	Yes	No	Yes	None	2%	40%	Frequent
Switzerland	Mixed	No	Yes	Yes	No	Yes	5%^{q}	0.9%	None	Infrequent
United Kingdom	Continuous	No	No	Yes	Yes	Yes	None	0.5%	None	Occasional
United States	Continuous	Yes	No	Yes	Yes	Yes	None	0	Yes	Occasional

^{a}Calls only on just five stocks.
^{b}Cash/forward
^{c}None on stocks; 3–5% on index futures.
^{d}10% (5%) for uncovered (covered) futures.
^{e}Cash/forward, but not always enforced.
^{f}Cash/forward; 40% if forward collateral is stock rather than cash.
^{g}"Four Spread Rule": offers not permitted more than four ticks from current bids and asks.
^{h}Hitting limit suspends auction; auction then tried a second time at end of day.
^{i}Futures on the Nikkei Index are traded in Singapore.
^{j}Decreased to 50% on October 21, 1987, "to encourage buyers."

^{k}Trading suspended for successive periods, 15 and then 30 minutes; effective limit: 30–40%.
^{l}Authorities have discretion. In October, 2% limits every 15 minutes used frequently.
^{m}For nondealer transactions only.
^{n}Only for Nikkei Index (Japan).
^{o}Groups of stocks are traded continuously for 10 minutes each.
^{p}Limits raised to 20% and margin to 50% on October 27.
^{q}Hitting limit causes 15-minute trading suspension. Limits raised to 10–15% in October.
Source: Richard Roll, "The International Crash of October 1987," *Financial Analysts Journal*, September–October 1988, p. 29.

DIVERSIFICATION BENEFITS

As previously mentioned, not all foreign markets move in the same direction at any point in time. In Table 18–2, we see the stock market movements for a number of key countries over a 21-year period. Sharply contrasting movements are noted in such years as 1973 and 1977. In 1973, U.S. equities were down by 18.68 percent, while equities in Norway gained 128.52 percent, those

TABLE 18–2 WORLD EQUITIES: YEAR-BY-YEAR ADJUSTED TOTAL RETURNS (in Percent)*

Year	U.S. Total	Europe Austria	Bel- gium	Den- mark	France	Ger- many	Italy	Nether- lands	Nor- way	Spain	Sweden	Swit- zer- land	United King- dom	Hong Kong	Japan	Singa- pore	Can- ada	Aus- tralia
1960	0.83	52.28	−7.99	3.77	6.72	42.32	46.18	3.24	12.24	10.14	5.51	43.82	0.13		38.50		−1.16	−0.07
1961	27.52	41.14	22.84	3.81	13.62	2.14	14.73	12.49	18.14	36.42	5.57	54.89	12.56		−13.03		39.03	14.86
1962	−9.29	−12.76	−1.99	8.12	11.38	−21.70	−10.44	−5.39	−15.43	19.65	12.47	−8.51	4.76		4.68		−6.84	0.95
1963	21.04	−4.28	18.06	17.77	−14.77	14.87	−12.71	17.71	0.42	0.15	12.92	−14.49	22.80		8.78		14.39	24.92
1964	16.71	3.78	8.04	11.88	−1.17	4.70	−26.43	9.61	10.22	10.44	23.17	−7.16	−5.14		10.93		24.36	5.17
1965	15.26	−1.16	−2.65	11.93	−4.10	−12.63	30.16	−10.00	0.37	16.12	11.00	−11.74	12.66		21.39		4.81	−9.75
1966	−8.21	−4.88	−15.82	5.63	−8.18	−15.06	8.89	−14.54	−7.61	11.87	−23.93	−12.91	−2.07		9.04		−9.24	4.87
1967	30.45	0.97	13.35	−11.88	0.46	51.80	−2.51	38.97	1.09	−8.48	7.69	52.39	16.57		−4.85		7.18	44.70
1968	14.95	2.95	13.63	17.81	14.81	13.61	4.23	37.58	21.55	31.42	45.52	30.44	51.34		26.43		26.61	28.62
1969	−9.86	6.90	7.18	3.36	18.39	23.42	15.19	−4.42	24.75	46.87	1.75	5.05	−12.52		34.15		3.21	16.10
1970	−1.00	13.49	9.66	−6.47	−5.14	−23.76	−17.52	−6.50	39.53	−3.68	−18.92	−13.17	−5.72	21.31	−6.35	−5.43	15.81	−19.14
1971	18.16	8.44	25.00	10.18	1.66	24.61	−12.34	1.76	14.13	26.26	36.12	27.41	47.99	59.52	46.55	65.52	14.13	−1.59
1972	17.71	37.65	32.69	112.20	24.83	18.54	15.33	29.56	9.03	42.30	16.82	28.61	3.93	161.66	126.56	211.04	33.12	21.06
1973	−18.68	25.09	18.16	5.44	3.83	−4.44	10.18	−4.74	28.52	24.03	2.86	−3.75	−23.44	−39.01	−20.13	−34.58	−3.11	−12.06
1974	−27.77	15.00	−11.74	−10.74	−22.43	17.20	−33.43	−15.56	−39.98	−8.49	11.72	−12.37	−50.33	−60.33	−15.65	−46.69	−26.52	−32.97
1975	37.49	−2.90	17.45	23.96	45.08	30.09	−8.69	50.23	−15.14	0.05	21.00	41.18	115.06	99.56	19.84	63.57	15.07	50.71
1976	26.68	15.58	13.00	7.23	−20.03	6.57	−26.55	16.94	14.98	−36.00	6.37	10.42	−12.55	40.55	25.80	13.83	9.71	−10.00
1977	−3.03	−3.76	11.02	1.74	5.07	23.08	−18.92	14.65	−23.83	−19.66	−21.64	25.49	56.49	−11.58	15.70	4.60	−1.37	11.25
1978	8.53	15.68	33.27	9.47	73.19	26.96	46.37	20.83	6.81	7.86	23.96	21.82	14.63	18.61	53.33	45.31	20.55	22.24
1979	24.18	19.43	21.08	−2.18	28.90	−1.93	17.39	19.95	183.01	5.51	2.64	12.21	22.20	83.50	−11.69	28.58	52.26	43.44
1980	33.22	−11.90	−11.40	15.80	−1.30	−8.20	78.40	11.90	−17.30	4.60	21.00	−7.10	38.80	69.90	29.70	61.20	22.00	52.20

*U.S.–dollar-adjusted.

Source: Roger G. Ibbotson, Richard C. Carr, and Anthony W. Robinson, "International Equity and Bond Returns," *Financial Analysts Journal*, July–August 1982, p. 69.

in Austria appreciated by 25.09 percent, and those in Spain gained 24.03 percent. In 1977, U.S. equities showed a slightly bearish posture with a 3.03 percent decline, while equities in the United Kingdom were up 56.49 percent, and stocks in Switzerland appreciated 25.49 percent.

Another way to consider **diversification benefits** is to measure the extent of correlation of stock movements. Such a measure is presented in Table 18–3, in which stock movements of a number of foreign countries are compared to those of the United States. Two sets of correlation coefficients are presented, one long-term set from 1960 through 1980 and a more-current short-term set of data from June 1981 through September 1987. The countries are listed from the highest correlation to the lowest based on 1960–80 data. By comparing the two sets of correlations, we can see that there is not a great amount of stability between the two time periods, with some countries like Hong Kong going from the top of the list to the bottom. However, correlations of returns with the U.S. market are still quite low on average with the median correlation being .389 in the first period and .328 in the second period.

The best risk-reduction benefits can be found by combining U.S. securities with those from countries having low correlations such as Spain and Austria in both periods. Countries with high correlations provide the least benefit from diversification. Even though countries like Germany and Italy have fairly stable correlations between the two periods, Hong Kong and France display a switching of rankings between the two periods. According to one researcher, Bruno Solnik, a well-diversified international portfolio can achieve the same risk-reduction benefits as a pure U.S. portfolio that is twice the size in terms

TABLE 18–3   CORRELATION OF FOREIGN STOCK MOVEMENTS WITH U.S. STOCK MOVEMENTS

Country	Correlation 1960–1980		Correlation June 1981– September 1987	
United States	1.000		1.000	
Hong Kong	.814	(1)	.114	(17)
Netherlands	.730	(2)	.473	(4)
Canada	.710	(3)	.720	(1)
Australia	.699	(4)	.328	(9) median
United Kingdom	.617	(5)	.513	(2)
Singapore	.579	(6)	.377	(6)
Switzerland	.454	(7)	.500	(3)
Sweden	.398	(8)	.279	(11)
Belgium	.389	(9) median	.250	(12)
Denmark	.243	(10)	.351	(8)
Japan	.216	(11)	.326	(10)
France	.214	(12)	.390	(5)
Germany	.210	(13)	.209	(15)
Italy	.208	(14)	.224	(13)
Norway	.009	(15)	.356	(7)
Austria	−.076	(16)	.138	(16)
Spain	−.115	(17)	.214	(14)

Source: Roger G. Ibbotson, Richard C. Carr, and Anthony W. Robinson, "International Equity and Bond Returns," *Financial Analysts Journal,* July–August 1982, p. 71; and Richard Roll, "The International Crash of 1987," *Financial Analysts Journal,* September–October 1988, pp. 20–21.

of securities.[1] Chapter 20 presents a much more detailed discussion on the importance of correlation considerations to risk reduction. We have merely touched the surface for now.

RETURN POTENTIAL IN INTERNATIONAL MARKETS

Actually, risk reduction through effective international diversification is only part of the story. Not only does the investor have less risk exposure, but there is also the potential for higher returns in many foreign markets. Why? A number of countries have had superior growth rates to that of the United

TABLE 18–4	WORLD EQUITIES: SUMMARY STATISTICS, 1960–1980				
	Annual Returns in U.S. Dollars			Year-End Wealth Index (1959 = 1.00)	1980 Year-End Value in Billions U.S. Dollars
Asset	Compound Return (Percent)	Arithmetic Mean (Percent)	Standard Deviation (Percent)		
Non-U.S. equities:					
Europe					
Austria	9.1%	10.3%	16.9%	6.23	$ 1.9
Belgium	9.2	10.1	13.8	6.39	10.0
Denmark	9.5	11.4	24.2	6.72	4.0
France	6.2	8.1	21.4	3.56	53.0
Germany	8.3	10.1	19.9	5.32	71.0
Italy	2.4	5.6	27.2	1.63	25.0
Netherlands	9.3	10.7	17.8	6.45	25.0
Norway	10.3	17.4	49.0	7.81	2.6
Spain	8.4	10.4	19.8	5.49	16.3
Sweden	8.4	9.7	16.7	5.40	12.2
Switzerland	10.2	12.5	22.9	7.74	46.0
United Kingdom	10.0	14.7	33.6	7.39	190.0
Europe total	8.4	9.6	16.2	5.47	457.0
Asia					
Hong Kong★	24.6	40.3	61.3	11.24	38.0
Japan	15.6	19.0	31.4	20.86	357.0
Singapore★	23.2	37.0	66.1	9.96	24.3
Asia total	15.9	19.7	33.0	22.29	419.3
Other					
Australia	9.8	12.2	22.8	7.12	60.0
Canada	10.7	12.1	17.5	8.47	113.0
Other total	10.6	11.9	17.1	8.24	173.0
Non-U.S. total equities	10.6	11.8	16.3	8.23	1049.3
—U.S. total equities	8.7	10.2	17.7	5.78	1380.6
World total equities	9.3	10.5	15.8	6.47	2429.9

★1970–1980.
Source: Roger G. Ibbotson, Richard C. Carr, and Anthony W. Robinson, "International Equity and Bond Returns," *Financial Analysts Journal,* July–August 1982, p. 65.

---

[1]Bruno H. Solnik, "Why Not Diversify Internationally Rather than Domestically?" *Financial Analysts Journal,* July–August 1974, pp. 48–54.

States in terms of real GNP. These would include Japan, Norway, Singapore, and Hong Kong. Second, many countries have become highly competitive in traditional U.S. products such as automobiles, steel, and consumer electronics. A classic example is Japan. Third, many nations (Germany, Japan, France, Canada) enjoy higher individual savings rates than the United States, and this leads to capital formation and potential investment opportunity. This, of course, is not to imply that the United States does not have the strongest and best regulated security markets in the world. It clearly does. However, it is a more-mature market than many others, and there may be abundant opportunities for superior returns in a number of foreign markets.

In Table 18–4 we can see the compound rate of return for 18 different countries over a long time period. While the return for U.S. equities during this time frame was 8.7 percent (column one, second item from the bottom),

---

FIGURE 18–2   U.S.-DOLLAR-ADJUSTED CUMULATIVE WEALTH INDEXES OF WORLD
               EQUITIES, 1960–1980 (Year-End 1959 = 1.00)

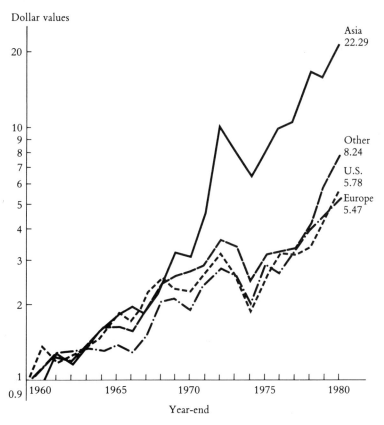

Source: Roger C. Ibbotson, Richard C. Carr, and Anthony W. Robinson, "International Equity and Bond Returns," *Financial Analysts Journal,* July–August 1982, p. 66.

Hong Kong, Japan, and Singapore enjoyed annualized returns of between 15 and 25 percent. If you examine the next-to-last column in Table 18–4, you can observe the value that a one-unit investment would have grown to over this 21-year period. If it had been invested in U.S. equities, the ending value would be 5.78. The same one-unit investment in Asian securities (referred to as "Asia total" and including Hong Kong, Japan, and Singapore) would have grown to 22.29. If invested in the category of "Other" securities (including Australia and Canada), the accumulation is to 8.24.

It should be pointed out that Table 18–4 represents a relatively long-term perspective. There are, of course, time periods when the United States out-performs foreign markets. A diagram of the accumulated values previously discussed is presented in Figure 18–2.

We bring together two main points of this chapter in Table 18–5. Here we see a listing of a number of foreign countries whose returns are superior to those of the United States and whose correlation values with U.S. equity markets are less than .5 (providing high returns and risk reduction at the same time). Japan, with its strong returns and low correlation, appears particularly attractive. More recent data on the following pages further confirm these patterns.

Current Quotations on Foreign Market Performance

In order to track the current performance of selected world markets, *The Wall Street Journal* provides daily quotes of price movements, while *Barron's* presents a weekly summary of the major global markets. The closing quotes of November 27, 1988, from *Barron's* are presented in Table 18–6.

The quotes are shown in local currencies as well as in the U.S. dollars. For a U.S. investor, the returns in U.S. dollars are the best comparative measure for an investment in U.S. stocks. Under the U.S.-dollars columns, you can first observe the percentage change from the last weekly quote. Next observe the index values shown under the 11/24/88 column for U.S.-dollar values. The

TABLE 18–5	ANNUAL COMPOUND RETURNS AND CORRELATION VALUES WITH U.S. SECURITY MARKETS, 1960–1980		
	Country	Compound (Percent) Return	Correlation with U.S. Security Market
	Japan	15.6%	.216
	Norway	10.3	.009
	Switzerland	10.2	.454
	Denmark	9.5	.243
	Belgium	9.2	.389
	Austria	9.1	−.076
	United States	8.7	1.000

Source: Roger C. Ibbotson, Richard C. Carr, and Anthony W. Robinson, "International Equity and Bond Returns," *Financial Analysts Journal,* July–August 1982, pp. 65 and 71.

TABLE 18–6   GLOBAL STOCK MARKETS

Index	In Local Currencies			In U.S. Dollars[1]		
	Percent Change	11/24/88	52-Week Range	Percent Change	11/24/88	52-Week Range
The World	1.3%	370.5	370.7–300.7	2.5%	491.1	491.1–381.9
E.A.F.E.[2]	1.2	552.7	553.3–423.7	2.7	963.2	963.2–716.0
Australia	0.3	293.8	327.1–227.9	1.7	227.9	236.9–144.8
Austria	0.1	239.7	244.0–193.0	2.5	516.8	518.3–415.5
Belgium	1.3	424.1	426.6–248.2	2.2	586.2	586.2–357.6
Canada	2.1	352.7	377.8–320.7	5.4	319.1	337.8–264.7
Denmark	3.1	495.4	497.0–335.1	4.7	561.7	561.7–393.3
Finland	1.6	119.2	126.9– 94.8	2.9	115.3	118.0– 91.4
France	0.6	416.0	421.3–258.1	1.8	393.4	393.4–253.0
Germany	1.4	199.5	204.7–145.6	2.7	425.5	425.5–317.9
Hong Kong	4.4	1,992.9	2,030.5–1,348.7	4.3	1,417.3	1,442.3–962.0
Italy	1.4	461.4	469.6–333.8	2.7	226.3	226.3–166.5
Japan	1.3	1,372.5	1,376.4–1,000.1	3.0	4,095.3	4,095.3–2,880.6
Netherlands	0.8	255.2	275.2–204.2	2.0	477.7	482.1–395.1
New Zealand	–2.0	89.5	111.9– 79.4	–1.1	88.8	108.2– 79.3
Norway	1.5	511.8	513.6–380.8	3.0	563.5	576.0–420.6
Singapore/ Malaysia	2.6	588.0	670.1–405.6	3.1	931.7	1,008.5–612.5
Spain	–0.7	248.7	271.1–193.7	0.8	154.7	166.3–120.1
Sweden	1.9	1,009.8	1,016.8–668.4	3.1	871.9	873.2–576.6
Switzerland	1.1	167.3	170.9–137.2	2.4	499.6	499.6–424.8
U.K.	0.6	558.5	566.9–471.3	1.8	427.7	429.7–355.2
U.S.A.	1.6	248.6	261.4–208.8	1.6	248.6	261.4–208.8
Mexico[3]	na	na	na	2.8	169.9	na

Base: January 1, 1970 = 100.
[1]Adjusted for foreign exchange fluctuations relative to the U.S. dollar.
[2]Europe, Australia, Far East Index.
[3]Mexico is no longer included in the global index.
na-Not available.
Source: Morgan Stanley Capital International Perspective, Geneva; Source: *Barron's,* November 28, 1988, p. 64. Reprinted by permission of *Barron's,* © Dow Jones & Company, Inc., 1988. All rights reserved.

base period for the index is 1970. Over the 18-year period, the indexes of Japan (4095.3) and Hong Kong (1417.3) have substantially outperformed the United States (248.6). The wide disparity in index values over time indicates the differing movements in foreign markets.

At the top of Table 18–6 is the **World Index,** which is a value-weighted index of the performance in 19 major countries as compiled by Capital International, S.A., of Geneva, Switzerland.

The *Institutional Investor,* a magazine used by professional portfolio managers, also tracks the performance of world markets on a regular basis. Quotes for June 30, 1987 (from the August 1987 issue) are shown in Table 18–7. Table 18–7 is of interest because it shows price-earnings ratios and yields, as well as price changes, for foreign markets.

TABLE 18–7   WORLD STOCK MARKETS

Rank		3 Months Percent Change	6 Months Percent Change	9 Months Percent Change	12 Months Percent Change	Price-Earnings Ratio	Yield
1	Mexico	85.0%	265.0%	465.2%	906.8%	22.4	0.6%
2	Singapore/Malaysia	19.8	43.7	67.9	80.9	40.3	1.2
3	Hong Kong	18.0	28.0	58.7	90.3	17.7	2.8
4	United Kingdom	15.2	37.9	49.4	39.3	15.7	3.2
5	Netherlands	11.3	19.5	20.7	19.9	12.9	3.9
6	Spain	8.2	10.2	11.3	24.4	16.7	3.9
7	Belgium	7.6	13.4	21.9	26.2	11.9	5.9
8	Japan	7.3	28.6	31.9	56.9	58.2	0.5
9	Norway	7.3	23.4	21.4	19.4	27.7	2.4
10	Australia	6.4	25.1	46.7	52.7	16.1	3.1
11	Germany	4.3	−10.8	−7.0	−6.0	14.7	3.1
12	Denmark	4.2	7.1	7.4	−0.9	27.5	2.4
13	Sweden	4.1	7.3	9.5	11.5	14.4	2.2
14	United States	4.0	24.4	30.0	19.8	17.8	3.0
15	Canada	1.1	24.7	29.4	26.8	27.8	2.5
16	Switzerland	0.9	−5.3	3.2	0.6	19.0	2.0
17	Italy	−2.9	−5.6	−5.7	5.7	18.9	2.1
18	Austria	−5.7	−19.1	−20.8	−20.0	19.1	2.4
19	France	−10.0	0.7	5.1	12.8	16.3	2.6
	The World Index	5.9	23.0	28.2	31.2	22.7	2.2

This is a recap of the performance of 19 stock markets in leading countries around the world as of June 30, 1987, based on data supplied by Morgan Stanley Capital International Perspective-Geneva. It should be noted that the percentage changes are in local currencies and are calculated from Morgan Stanley Capital International's market indexes.

Source: *Institutional Investor,* August 1987, p. 75.

Note the extremes in price-earnings ratios for certain countries such as Japan (58.2) and Singapore (40.3). The analyst must be careful when making conclusions about price-earnings ratios, however, since each country has its own accounting conventions, and reported earnings per share are not necessarily comparable from country to country. For example, in Japan, companies are allowed to set up reserve accounts against earnings. These accounts reduce earnings and lower taxes but still maintain cash flow. If adjusted for accounting variations, the Japanese P/E ratios might only be 40–50 percent higher than U.S. P/E ratios instead of over 300 percent higher. Also note the difference in dividend yields, with Belgium having the highest average yield of 5.6 percent and Japan having the lowest average yield of 0.5 percent.

Less-Developed Countries

Our discussion thus far has primarily centered on what are considered as developed countries (DCs). While many of these countries are considerably smaller than the United States, they still have reasonably well organized economies and financial markets. There are also potential investment opportunities in **less-developed countries** that have not been previously mentioned. These include such nations as Chile, Jordan, Korea, Thailand, and Zimbabwe. A number of these less-developed countries may represent superior investment opportunities in terms of return and risk-reduction opportunities. In fact, most have low or negative correlations with the United States. While this chapter will not explicitly cover the less-developed markets, the reader who has an interest in this subject is encouraged to read an article by Vihang Errunza in the September–October 1983 issue of the *Financial Analysts Journal*—"Emerging Markets: A New Opportunity for Improving Global Portfolio Performance."[2]

CURRENCY FLUCTUATIONS AND RATES OF RETURN

We must explicitly consider the effect of **currency fluctuations** as well as rates of return in different countries. For example, assume an investment in France produces a 10 percent return. But suppose at the same time the French franc declines in value by 5 percent against the U.S. dollar. The French franc profits are thus worth less in dollars. In the present case, the gain on the investment would be shown as follows:

110%	(Investment with 10% profit)
× .95	(Adjusted value of French franc relative to U.S. dollar)
104.5%	Percent of original investment

The actual return in U.S. dollars would be 4.5 percent instead of 10 percent. Of course, if the French franc appreciated by 5 percent against the dollar, the French franc profits converted to dollars would be worth considerably more than 10 percent. The values are indicated below.

110%	(Investment with 10% profit)
× 1.05	(Adjusted value of French franc relative to U.S. dollar)
115.5%	Percent of original investment

The 10 percent gain in the French franc investment has produced a 15.5 percent gain in U.S. dollars. It is apparent that a U.S. investor in foreign securities must consider not only the potential trend of security prices but also the trend of foreign currencies against the dollar. This point will become more apparent as we examine Table 18–8.

Let's examine currency effects in London. In this instance, the one-year return in the local currency was 15.2 percent (second column), but the currency (British pound) declined 16.9 percent (5th column) against the U.S. dollar for

---

[2]Vihang R. Errunza, "Emerging Markets: A New Opportunity for Improving Global Portfolio Performance," *Financial Analysts Journal*, September–October 1983, p. 51–58.

TABLE 18–8   RETURN ON WORLD STOCK MARKETS (through March 1983)

	Return in Each Currency (Percent)			Currency Valuation (Percent)			Return in U.S. Dollars (Percent)		
	3 Months	1 Year	5 Years	3 Months	1 Year	5 Years	3 Months	1 Year	5 Years
New York	8.8%	36.6%	11.4%	0.0%	0.0%	0.0%	8.8%	36.6%	11.4%
Tokyo	4.0	15.7	8.7	−2.0	3.5	−1.7	1.9	19.8	6.8
—London	9.8	15.2	7.2	−8.3	−16.9	−4.5	0.6	−4.3	2.4
Toronto	10.1	36.6	15.2	−0.7	−0.8	−1.7	9.3	35.5	13.2
Frankfurt	19.1	26.5	2.7	−2.2	−0.7	−3.9	16.5	25.6	−1.3
Sydney	5.6	11.0	10.8	−11.9	−17.7	−5.4	−6.9	−8.7	4.8
Paris	20.5	10.8	8.6	−7.4	−13.9	−9.1	11.6	−4.5	−1.3
Zurich	9.0	22.4	1.3	−3.7	−7.2	−2.6	5.0	13.7	−1.3
Hong Kong	27.1	14.6	17.3	−3.7	−13.0	−7.2	22.4	−25.7	8.8
Milan	28.5	4.8	28.5	−5.3	−8.4	−10.1	21.7	−4.0	15.6
Amsterdam	29.4	49.9	7.1	4.0	−2.0	−4.6	24.1	47.0	2.2
Singapore	18.5	19.3	24.9	1.1	2.3	2.1	19.8	22.0	27.5

the one-year period, causing an overall *loss* on the investment of 4.3 percent (second column from the right for London). The values are computed as follows:

115.2%	(Investment with 15.2% profit)
	(Adjusted value of British pound to the U.S. dollar)
× .831	1.000 − .169 decline in currency)
95.7%	Percent of original investment

The ending value of 95.7 percent indicates a loss of 4.3 percent from the initial value of 100 percent.[3] If one were merely to subtract the foreign currency loss of 16.9 percent from the 15.2 percent profit, the answer would be a loss of 1.7 percent, but this is not the correct procedure. The reason is that the gain of 15.2 percent was on an initial base of 100 percent, but the foreign currency loss of 16.9 percent was on an ending value of 115.2 percent (which comes out to an actual loss in currency value of 19.5 percent).

Actually, those who track the performance in foreign markets usually make adjustments so that the reported returns are in U.S. dollars that have already been adjusted for **foreign currency effects**. For example, most of the returns in prior tables of this chapter have already been adjusted for the foreign currency effect.

One might justifiably ask, how important is the foreign currency effect in relation to the overall return performance in the foreign currency? Do events

[3]Due to rounding and other statistical adjustments, not all values adjusted to U.S. dollars come out as precisely as this.

in foreign exchange markets tend to overpower actual returns achieved in specific investments in foreign countries? Normally, the foreign current effect is only about 10–20 percent as significant as the actual return performance in the foreign currency.[4] However, when the dollar is rising or falling rapidly over a short period of time, the impact can be much greater. For example, the return to U.S. investors in Japanese securities between 1985 and 1988 were increased by 50 percent from the gain in the yen against the dollar.

In a well-diversified international portfolio, the changes in foreign currency values in one part of the world normally tend to cancel out changes in other parts of the world. Also, those who do not wish to have foreign currency exposure of any sort may use forward exchange contracts, futures market contracts, or put options on foreign currency to hedge away the risk. Finally, there are those who believe in parity theories that suggest that one should get additional compensation in local returns to make up for potential losses in foreign currency values. This latter point is a purely theoretical matter that provides little comfort in the short run.

The authors would suggest that those considering international investments be sensitive to the foreign currency effect, but not be overly discouraged by it. The superior return potential from foreign investments previously shown in Figure 18–2 (and most other places in this chapter) are constructed *after* taking into consideration the foreign exchange effect on U.S. dollar returns. While foreign currency swings have been *wider* in recent times, they are still not a major deterrent to an internationally diversified portfolio.

OTHER OBSTACLES TO INTERNATIONAL INVESTMENTS

Some other problems are peculiar to international investments. Let us consider some of them.

Political Risks

Many firms operate in foreign political climates that are more volatile than that of the United States (such as Mexico). There is the danger of nationalization of foreign firms or the blockage of capital flows to investors. There also may be the danger of a violent overthrow of the political party in power. Furthermore, many countries have been unable to meet their foreign debt obligations, and this has important political implications.

The informed investor must have some feel for the political/economic climate of the foreign country in which he or she invests. Of course, problems sometimes create opportunities. It is entirely possible that local investors may overreact to political changes that are taking place in their environment. Because all their eggs are in one basket, they may engage in an oversell in regard

---

[4]Bertrand Jacquillat and Bruno Solnik, "Multinationals are Poor Tools for Diversification," *Journal of Portfolio Management,* Winter 1978, pp. 8–12.

to political changes. It is possible that a less-impassioned outside investor may actually identify an opportunity for profit.

Nevertheless, political risk represents a potential deterrent to foreign investment. The best solution for the investor is to be sufficiently diversified around the world so that a political or economic development in one foreign country does not have a major impact on his or her portfolio (this can be accomplished through a mutual fund or through other means discussed later in the chapter).

Tax Problems

Many major foreign countries may impose a 7.5 percent to 15 percent withholding tax against the dividends or interest paid to nonresident holders of equity or debt securities. However, it is often possible for *tax-exempt* U.S. investors to secure an exemption or rebate on part or all of the withholding tax. Also, taxable U.S. investors can normally claim a U.S. tax credit for taxes paid in foreign countries. The problem is more likely to be one of inconvenience and paper shuffling rather than loss of funds.[5]

Lack of Market Efficiency

U.S. capital markets tend to be the most liquid and efficient in the world. Therefore, an investor who is accustomed to trading on the New York Stock Exchange may have some difficulties in adjusting to foreign markets. A larger spread between the bid (sell) and asked (buy) price in foreign countries is likely. Also, an investor may have more difficulty in handling a large transaction (the seller may have to absorb a larger discount in executing the trade). Furthermore, as a general rule, commission rates are higher in foreign markets than in the United States.

Administrative Problems

There can also be administrative problems in dealing in foreign markets in terms of adjusting to the various local systems. For example, in the Hong Kong, Swiss, and Mexican stock markets, you must settle your account one day after the transaction; in London, there is a two-week settlement procedure; and in France, there are different settlement dates for cash and forward markets. The different administrative procedures of foreign countries simply add up to an extra dimension of difficulty in executing trades. (As implied throughout this chapter, there are ways to avoid most of these difficulties by going through mutual funds and other investment outlets.)

---

[5]Gary L. Bergstrom, John K. Koeneman, and Martin J. Siegel, "International Securities Market," in *Readings in Investment Management,* ed. Frank J. Fabozzi (Homewood, Ill.: Richard D. Irwin, 1983).

Information Difficulties

The U.S. security markets are the best in the world at providing investment information. The Securities and Exchange Commission, with its rigorous requirements for full disclosure, is the toughest national regulator of investment information. Also, the United States has the Financial Accounting Standard Board (FASB) continually providing pronouncements on generally accepted accounting principles for financial reporting. Publicly traded companies are required to provide stockholders with fully audited annual reports. In the United States, we are further spoiled by the excellent evaluative reports and ratings generated by Moody's, Standard & Poor's, Value Line, and other firms. We also have extensive economic data provided by governmental sources such as the Department of Commerce and the Federal Reserve System.

Many international firms, trading in less-sophisticated foreign markets, simply do not provide the same quantity or quality of data. This would be particularly true of firms trading in some of the smaller foreign markets. Even when the information is available, there may be language problems for the analyst who does not speak German, French, Portuguese, and so on.

Also, the analyst must be prepared to analyze the firm in light of the standards that are generally accepted in the foreign market in which the company operates. For example, Japanese companies often have much higher debt ratios than U.S. firms. A debt-to-equity ratio of three times is not unusual in Japan, whereas in the United States, the standard is closer to 1 : 1. The analyst may be inclined to "mark down" the Japanese firm for high debt unless he or she realizes the different features at play in the Japanese economy. For example, in Japan there are normally very close relationships between the lending bank and the borrower, with the lender perhaps having an equity position in the borrower and with interlocking boards between the two. This diminishes the likelihood of the lender calling in the loan in difficult economic periods. Also, the Japanese make extensive use of reserve accounts which tend to give the appearance of a smaller asset or equity base than actually exists. This pattern of understatement is further aided by a strict adherence to historical cost valuation even though Japanese land values have increased more rapidly than almost anywhere else in the world. When appropriate adjustments are made for these effects on financial reporting, a Japanese debt-to-equity ratio of 3 : 1 may not be a matter of any greater concern than a U.S. debt-to-equity ratio 1 : 1.

METHODS OF PARTICIPATING IN FOREIGN INVESTMENTS

The avenues to international investment include investing in firms in their own foreign markets, purchasing the shares of foreign firms trading in the United States, investing in mutual funds and closed-end funds with a global orientation, buying the shares of multinational corporations, and entrusting funds to private money managers who specialize in international equities. We shall examine each of these alternatives.

FOREIGN PERILS: LANGUAGE, CUSTOMS, AND CURRENCY SHIFTS TAX THE WITS OF GLOBAL-FUND MANAGERS

Mutual-fund trader Madis Senner thought he had found one of the world's best bond markets—in Ireland. In January 1987, yields on Irish government securities were a robust 12 percent. What's more, the Irish pound, as part of the European Monetary System, seemed likely to benefit from a dollar slump. As head bond trader at New York-based Clemente Capital Inc., Mr. Senner bought about $5 million of Irish bonds. He largely cashed out a few months later at a profit. But what he kept gave him fits.

A surge in global interest rates sent the Irish market into a tailspin. Mr. Senner tried to sell, but "there were no bids," he recalls. "Although the Irish government is the marketmaker for bonds, it would have taken two days to sell a million of them," Mr. Senner says. So he had to hang on in a market he would have preferred to be out of.

Such is the life of a global trader. Mutual funds that invest abroad have soared in popularity, particularly when dollar weakness has helped foreign stocks and bonds. Small U.S. investors in effect rely on pros like Mr. Senner to help them invest in foreign markets without having to sort out all the different time zones, languages, and customs.

For the folks at Clemente Capital, however, there's no escaping the quirks of dozens of overseas markets, none of which functions quite according to U.S. rules. English brokers, for instance, "don't show us their whole hand because . . . they see us as the competition, not as the client," says Mr. Senner. And in Asian markets, getting into the early stages of the rumor mill counts for a lot more than the detailed number-crunching that's practiced on public data in the United States.

Clemente's $148 million Freedom Global Income Plus mutual fund, which Mr. Senner helps manage, has been a standout among long-term bond funds. Competing mutual funds in 1988 averaged small losses while Freedom Global has a 4.32 percent gain over a nine-month period.

Source: Matthew Winkler, *The Wall Street Journal*, September 23, 1988, p. 23R. Reprinted by permission of *The Wall Street Journal*, © Dow Jones & Company, Inc., 1988. All rights reserved.

Direct Investments

The most obvious but least likely alternative would be to directly purchase the shares of a firm in its own foreign market through a foreign broker or an overseas branch of a U.S. broker. The investor might consider such firms as Toshiba or Fanuc on the Tokyo Stock Exchange, Consolidated Rutile on the Sydney Stock Exchange, or Hoechst on the Frankfort Stock Exchange. This approach is hampered by all the difficulties and administrative problems associated with international investments. There could be information-gathering problems, tax problems, stock-delivery problems, capital-transfer problems, and communication difficulties in executing orders. Only the most sophisticated money manager would probably follow this approach (though this may change somewhat in the future as foreign markets become better coordinated).

A more-likely route to direct investment would be to purchase the shares of foreign firms that actually trade in U.S. security markets. Actually, hundreds of foreign firms actively trade their securities in the United States. A listing of some key participants is presented in Table 18–9.

TABLE 18–9   FOREIGN FIRMS TRADING ON THE NEW YORK STOCK EXCHANGE

Stocks of Foreign Corporate Issuers, December 31, 1987

Country	Company	Industry
Australia	Broken Hill Proprietary Co. Ltd.★	Petroleum; minerals; steel
	News Corporation Ltd.★	Publishing; broadcasting
British W.I.	Club Med, Inc.	Hotel, resort operator
Canada	Abitibi-Price Inc.	Newsprint, uncoated papers
	Alcan-Aluminium Ltd.	Aluminum producer
	AMCA International Limited	Industrial products; construction services
	American Barrick Resources Corporation	Gold mining
	Bell Canada Enterprises Inc.	Holding company—telecommunications services
	Campbell Resources Inc.	Holding company—diversified natural resources
	Canadian Pacific Limited	Transportation; telecommunications; oil; mining
	Cineplex Odeon Corporation	Motion pictures theatres operator
	Domtar Inc.	Pulp, paper, packaging; construction products
	Inco Ltd.	Nickel, copper producer
	LAC Minerals Ltd.	Gold mining
	McIntyre Mines Ltd.	Coal mining
	Mitel Corporation	Telecommunications equipment manufacturer
	Moore Corporation Ltd.	Business forms manufacturer
	Northern Telecom Ltd.	Telecommunications equipment manufacturer
	Northgate Exploration Limited	Holding company—metal producer
	Placer Dome Inc.	Gold, silver, copper mining
	Ranger Oil Limited	Oil and gas exploration, production
	Seagram Co. Ltd.	Distilled spirits producer
	TransCanada PipeLines Ltd.	Natural gas transmission
	Varity Corporation (2 issues)	Farm equipment producer
	Westcoast Transmission Co., Ltd.	Natural gas distributor
Denmark	Novo Industri A/S★	Industrial enzymes; pharmaceuticals
England	Barclays PLC★	Holding company—bank
	BET Public Limited Company★	Industrial; transportation; construction services
	British Airways Pic★	Passenger airline
	British Gas PLC★	Natural gas distributor
	British Petroleum Company Ltd.★ (2 issues)	Holding company—integrated international oil company
	British Telecommunications PLC★	Telecommunications services and products
	Dee Corporation plc★	Food; sporting goods retailer
	Dixons Group plc★	Consumer electronics, appliances retailer
	Glaxo Holdings p.l.c.★	Pharmaceuticals
	Hanson Trust PLC★	Consumer goods; building products
	Imperial Chemical Industries PLC★	Diversified chemical producer
	National Westminster Bank PLC★	Holding company—bank
	Plessey Company Ltd.★	Telecommunications and electronic equipment
	Saatchi & Saatchi Company PLC★	Advertising; consulting
	"Shell" Transport and Trading Co., PLC★	Holding company—integrated international oil company
	Tricentrol PLC★	Oil and gas production, oil trading
	Unilever PLC★	Holding company—branded foods
Hong Kong	Universal Matchbox Group Ltd. Inc.	Designs and manufactures toys
Israel	Elscint Ltd.	Diagnostic medical imaging equipment
Italy	Montedison S.p.A.★ (2 issues)	Diversified chemicals
Japan	Hitachi, Ltd.★	Electronic equipment; machinery; consumer products
	Honda Motor Co., Ltd.★	Motor vehicle manufacturer
	Kubota, Ltd.★	Agricultural equipment; pipe manufacturer
	Kyocera Corp.★	Ceramic products; electronic equipment
	Matsushita Electric Industrial Co., Ltd.★	Consumer electronic manufacturer
	Pioneer Electronic Corporation★	Consumer electronic manufacturer
	Sony Corporation★	Consumer electronic manufacturer
	TDK Corporation★	Electronic components; magnetic tape producer
Netherlands	Ausimont N.V.	Chemicals
	KLM Royal Dutch Airlines†	Air transportation

TABLE 18–9   (concluded)

Stocks of Foreign Corporate Issuers, December 31, 1987

Country	Company	Industry
Netherlands	Philips N.V.†	Electronics; appliances; professional products
	Royal Dutch Petroleum Co.†	Holding company—integrated international oil company
	Unilever N.V.†	Holding company—branded foods
Netherlands Antilles	Erbamont N.V.	Pharmaceuticals
	Schlumberger Limited	Oilfield services; electronics
Norway	Norsk Hydro a.s.★	Agriculture; oil and gas
Philippines	Benguet Corporation	Mining; industrial construction
South Africa	ASA Limited	Closed-end investment company—gold mining
Spain	Banco Central, S.A.★	Holding company—bank
	Banco de Santander, Sociedad Anonima de Credito★	Banking, financial services
	Compania Telefonica Nacional de Espana, S.A.★	Telephone service—Spain

★American depository receipts/shares.
†N.Y. shares and/or guilder shares.
Source: *New York Stock Exchange Fact Book* (New York: New York Stock Exchange, 1988), p. 26–27.

Firms such as Alcan Aluminium Ltd., Campbell Resources Inc., and Ranger Oil Limited trade their stocks *directly* on the New York Stock Exchange. Most of the other firms in the table (as well as other large foreign firms) trade their shares in the United States through *American Depository Receipts* (ADRs). In Table 18–9, such firms have an asterisk after their names. The ADRs represent the ownership interest in a foreign company's common stock. The process is as follows: The shares of the foreign company are purchased and put in trust in a foreign branch of a New York branch. The bank, in turn, receives and can issue depository receipts to the American shareholders of the foreign firm. These ADRs (that is, depository receipts) allow foreign shares to be traded in the United States.

When you call your broker and ask to purchase Sony Corporation or Honda Motor Co., Ltd. (which are represented by ADRs), you will notice virtually no difference between this transaction and buying shares of General Motors or Eastman Kodak. You can receive a certificate that looks very much like a U.S. stock certificate. You'll receive your dividends in dollars and get your reports about the company in English. Generally, you will pay your normal commission rates.

In Table 18–10, you see a page from *Standard & Poor's Stock Guide* that includes Sony Corporation's ADRs. Note the financial information is basically the same as that for other U.S. corporations trading on a major exchange or over-the-counter. The Sony ADRs also receive coverage from Value Line and other reporting services. *The Wall Street Journal* has daily quotes just as it would have for any company. Since these ADRs trade on the New York Stock Exchange, the quote would be found in that section of the paper.

TABLE 18–10 SAMPLE PAGE FROM *STANDARD & POOR'S STOCK GUIDE*

198 SKI-SOU Standard & Poor's Corporation

¶S&P 500 •Options Index	Ticker Symbol	Name of Issue (Call Price of Pfd. Stocks)	Market	Com. Rank. & Pfd. Rating	Par Val.	Inst. Hold Cos	Inst. Hold Shs. (000)	Principal Business	Price Range 1971-87 High	1971-87 Low	1988 High	1988 Low	1989 High	1989 Low	Feb. Sales in 100s	February, 1989 Last Sale Or Bid High	Low	Last	%Div Yield	P-E Ratio
1	SKIP	Skipper's Inc[51]	OTC	↓B−	10¢	13	282	Seafood restaurants	15½	2⅞	7⅛	4⅜	10½	6⅜	10369	10½	7¾	8⅛B	1.2	d
2	SKN	Skolniks Inc	AS	NR	.001	1	.5	Owns/operates restaurants	....	....	4¾	2½	3¼	2¾	532	3¼	2¾	2¾	...	18
3	WS	Wrrts(Pur 1com at[52]$7.50)([53]50)	AS	....	..	1	17		....	....	¾	⅛	⅜	¼	60	⅜	¼	⅜	...	..
¶4•[1]	SKY	Skyline Corp	NY,B,M,P,Ph	B+	.0277	89	5783	Mob homes, recreat'n'l veh	74	8½	16⅝	12½	18⅛	15	7393	18⅛	16⅝	16⅞	2.8	13
5	SKYW	SkyWest Inc	OTC	NR	No	18	1394	Regional airline service	11	3⅜	7	3½	6⅜	5	1267	6⅜	5½	6⅛B	0.9	51
6	SL	SL Industries	NY,B,Ph	B+	20¢	27	1413	Specialty ind'l prod & svs	11⅞	½	10	7	8⅝	7¾	2435	8⅝	7¾	8	s2.1	d
7	SSI	Slater Indus Cl'A'	To	B−	No	5	238	Steel: pole line hardware	15⅝	3⅜	6¾	4⅞	8½	6¼	60	8	7⅜	7⅜B	...	16
8	SGI	Slattery Group	NY,M	B−	10	17	381	Construction: cement mfr	32	5⅞	31½	17	32½	29	95	32½	29½	31¾	3.1	9
9	SMC.A	Smith (A.O.) Cl'A'	AS,M	B−	5	35	1151	Auto & truck eq: farm eq	32⅛	4⅛	18¾	14	22⅜	16½	245	22⅜	20⅛	21¼B	3.8	11
10	SMC.B	Class'B'(1/10 vtg)	AS	B−	5	33	1883	electric motors	29⅝	3¼	17⅛	12	18½	14¾	351	18½	17⅜	17⅝	4.5	9
11	Pr C	$2.125cm Cv[58]Exch Pfd([59]26.488)	AS	BB+	1	16	1153		37⅞	19½	24¾	20¾	25⅛	22⅜	116	25⅛	24¼	24¼	8.8	..
12	SII	Smith Int'l	NY,B,M,P,Ph	C	No	50	6512	Varied line drill,boring eq	70¼	1¼	10⅞	5¾	10	8½	7800	10	8½	9¾	...	d
13	SMLB	Smith Laboratories	OTC	C	No	18	1512	Drug mfr-chymopapain	25¾	1 5/16	2⅝	1 5/16	2⅞	2 5/16	6767	2¾	2½	2⅝B	...	66
14	SFDS	Smithfield Foods	OTC	B+	1	30	2481	Fresh pork,processed meats	13¾	⅛	20½	11½	16¼	13	2949	15	13	13¾B	...	9
¶15•[2]	SKB	SmithKline Beckman	NY,B,C,M,P,Ph	↓A	25¢	593	81896	Ethical drugs:analyt'l instr	72¾	3¾	59⅞	40⅞	53⅝	46¼	155588	53	48¼	50	3.7	27
16	SJM	Smucker (J.M.)	NY,M,Ph	A	No	86	3431	Preserves: jellies & fillings	60	2 1/16	62¾	46¾	61⅜	59¼	1426	61¼	59¼	•59¼	1.5	16
¶17•[3]	SNA	Snap-On Tools	NY,B,M,P,Ph	A	1	261	19396	Hand tools: auto/ind'l maint	46½	3⅝	44⅞	32⅝	38¾	33⅝	14127	38¾	36⅜	36⅝	2.7	13
18	SOI	Snyder Oil Partners[61]	NY,M,Ph	NR	No	23	2638	Mgmt of oil & gas prop	16¾	6½	9⅜	3	4½	3⅞	8957	4⅜	3⅞	4⅛	14.5	d
19	Pr A	Cm[64]Cv'A'Pref Units	NY	NR	No	7	281		22¾	13⅝	18¾	9¼	11⅞	11	554	11¾	11	11⅝	18.0	..
20	SOCI	Society Corp	OTC	A	1	136	8712	Commercial bkg,Ohio	40	4¼	37¾	31	35½	33¼	4186	35½	33⅞	34¼B	4.7	8
21	SOCS	Society For Svg Bancorp	OTC	NR	1	22	3588	Savings bank,Connecticut	23⅝	3⅝	20½	12	20½	15⅜	4951	20½	17¾	20B	3.0	7
22	SOFT	SofTech Inc	OTC	B−	10¢	19	1376	Devel software svcs & prod	25⅛	5¼	8½	3⅞	5	4⅜	774	4¾	4⅜	4⅝B	...	14
23	SOFS	Softsel Computer Prod	OTC	NR	1¢	..	...	Wholesale computer products	....	....	6⅜	5	6⅞	5½	10384	6⅞	5½	5¾B	...	8
24	SPCO	Software Publishing	OTC	NR	No	63	4110	Mkts pkgd applicat'n software	16½	4⅝	26¾	8	21½	16	23305	21½	16	16¾B	...	9
25	SOD	Solitron Devices	NY,B,M,P,Ph	B−	1	14	727	Semiconductors-microwave	19⅜	¾	7¼	3⅜	3¾	2⅝	1517	3½	2⅞	3	...	d
26	SOMR	Somerset Group	OTC	NR	No	10	431	Concrete,radio,svgs bank	18	5½	11	6	7¼	6¼	145	7¼	6½	7¼B	...	7
¶27•[4]	SNT	Sonat, Inc	NY,B,C,M,P,Ph	↓B+	1	256	22277	Nat'l gas P.L.: drill'g o&g	43⅛	6¾	31¼	23⅛	32¾	28⅝	52499	32⅜	29⅛	30	6.7	14
28•[5]	SONO	Sonoco Products	OTC	A	No	130	11373	Industrial paper products	30¾	1 3/16	35	19½	38½	32½	15364	38½	33¾	36½B	†2.0	17
29	SONNF	Sonora Gold	OTC	NR	No	24	3164	Gold&mineral explor,dvlp	11⅝	3¾	6⅝	1⅜	2	1⅜	1856	2	1½	2B		
30•[5]	SNE	Sony Corp ADR..	NY,B,C,M,P,Ph,Mo,To	NR	50Y	45	4558	Color TV sets,tape rec,radio	40¼	3	58½	35⅜	59⅞	53⅞	13124	56⅛	53⅞	54⅝	0.5	31
31	SOO	Soo Line Corp	NY,M	C	3⅓	33	2276	R.R. hldg:contr by Canad Pac	36⅞	5⅝	26⅜	14	23½	20¾	1490	22¾	20⅞	22	...	13
32	SFOK	Sooner Fed'l Sv & Ln	OTC	C	1¢	10	212	Svg & loan,Oklahoma,TX	35½	5½	19½	6½	7	1	8444	4	1	1B	...	d
33	SRG	Sorg Inc	AS	B−	1	11	338	Fin'l & corporate printing	24½	⅞	11¾	5¾	9	6⅜	742	9	7⅝	7⅞	...	d
34	BID	Sotheby's Holdings'A'	AS	NR	10¢	30	1305	Worlds largest art auctioneer	....	....	20⅞	15⅜	25⅝	19⅝	6550	25⅝	22⅞	23	e1.1	15
35	SUND	Sound Advice	OTC	NR	1¢	9	224	Retails consumer electr prod	7¾	2⅝	7⅜	2¾	8½	6⅝	1849	8½	8	8¼B	...	9
36	SWHI	Sound Warehouse[69]	OTC	NR	1¢	19	812	Retails records,tapes,videos	31⅛	7½	22¼	9	25¼	20⅞	1499	25¼	24⅞	25¼B	...	28
37	SOR	Source Capital	NY,M	NR	1	11	65	Closed-end invest:divers	45⅞	5⅝	39⅜	32¾	38½	36⅜	590	37⅞	36⅜	37	9.5	..
38	Pr	$2.40 cm Pfd(27.50)vtg	NY	NR	3	1	30		27½	16	25⅞	24	24¾	24	123	24¾	24	24	10.0	..
39	SAC Pr	So.Carolina E&G 5%cmPfd(52 1/2)..	NY	A	50	..	...	Subsid of SCANA Corp	39½	16¼	29½	26⅛	27⅝	26¾	8	27⅝	27¼	27B	9.3	..
40	SCNC	South Carolina Nat'l	OTC	A	5	66	5723	Comm'l bkg,South Carolina	27⅝	2½	23⅝	18⅜	23⅝	20⅝	2977	22⅝	20⅝	21B	3.0	8
41	SJI	South Jersey Indus	NY,B,M,Ph	A−	1.25	32	1471	Hldg co: gas, fuel oil, sand	22⅞	4⅝	19⅛	16⅝	19¼	18⅛	1004	19⅛	18⅜	18¾	7.1	10
42	SDW	Southdown, Inc	NY,M,Ph	↓B	1¼	92	8744	Cement mfr & dstr: oil & gas	25½	1⅜	24¼	17	21¾	19¼	12095	20⅞	19¼	19⅝	2.6	8
43	STB	Southeast Banking	NY,B,M,Ph	A−	5	129	18270	Commercial bkg,Florida	31⅜	5¾	26¼	18⅜	24⅜	21½	16638	24⅜	23¼	23⅝	4.7	10
44	Pr C	10%cm Cv C Pfd([74]52.22)	NY	NR	1	5	70		85½	55	71	54	67	60	20	67	64	64½B	7.8	..
45	SMGS	Southeast'n Mich Gas Ent	OTC	↑A−	1	11	346	Integrated natural gas sys	16¼	3	17½	12⅞	17¾	15½	624	17½	15½	15½B	s5.2	14

Uniform Footnote Explanations-See Page 1. Other: [1]CBOE:Cycle 2. [2]P:Cycle 3. [3]ASE:Cycle 3. [4]ASE:Cycle 1. [5]P:Cycle 1. [51]Nat'l Pizza co offer,$9.25 to Feb 28: rejected. [52]Wrrts exerciseable fr 4-21-89. [53]Fr 4-21-89. [54]Fiscal Mar'86 & prior. [55]12 Mo Dec,'87. [56]Special divd. [57]®$1.84,'88. [58]Co opt exch for $25 amt 8½%Cv 2015. [59]Thru 8-14-89,scale to $25 in'95. [60]□$0.06,'84. [61]Units Ltd Partnership Int. [62]Return of capital. [63]100% non-taxable,'88. [64]Hldr may Cv 12-31-89 into 2 com. [65]9 Mo Dec'86. [66]$d0.34,3 Mo Dec,'87. [67]Fiscal Oct.'86 & prior,est 11 Mo Mar,'87 $0.61. [68]®$1.15,'88. [69]Shamrock Hldgs plan mgr, $25.65. [70]®$2.43,'88. [71]Subsid Pfd. [72]®$2.06,'88. [73]®$2.26,'88. [74]Thru 12-31-89,scale to $50 in'93.

Source: *Standard & Poor's Stock Guide,* March 1989, p. 198.

The *Standard & Poor's Stock Guide* is a good place to start in determining whether a foreign company has ADRs trading in the United States. As previously indicated, hundreds of ADRs trade in U.S. markets.

Indirect Investments

The forms of indirect investments in the international securities include *(a)* purchasing shares of multinational corporations, *(b)* purchasing mutual funds or closed-end investment funds specializing in worldwide investments, and *(c)* engaging the services of a private firm specializing in foreign investment portfolio management.

Purchasing Shares of Multinational Corporations. **Multinational corporations**, that is, firms with operations in a number of countries, represent an opportunity for international diversification. For example, the major oil companies have investments and operations throughout the world. The same can be said for large banking firms and mainframe computer manufacturers. When one buys Exxon, to some extent he or she is buying exposure to the world economy (75.1 percent of sales are foreign for this firm). A list of the 20 largest U.S. multinational firms is presented in Table 18–11. Of particular interest is the third column from the left, which represents foreign revenue as a percentage of total revenue, and the fourth column from the right, which represents foreign profit as a percentage of total profit.

Although buying shares in a U.S. multinational firm is an easy route to take in order to experience worldwide economic effects, some researchers maintain that multinationals do not provide the major *investment* benefits that are desired. Jacquillat and Solnik found that multinationals provide very little risk reduction over and above purely domestic firms (perhaps only 10 percent).[6] The prices of multinational shares tend to move very closely with U.S. financial markets in spite of their worldwide investments. Thus, U.S. multinationals may not do well in a U.S. bear market even if they have investments in strong markets in other countries. This leaves us to turn to mutual funds and closed-end investment companies as potential international investments.

Mutual Funds and Closed-End Investment Companies. As will be described in Chapter 19, mutual funds offer the investor an opportunity for diversification as well as professional management. Nowhere is the mutual-fund concept more important than in the area of international investments. Those who organize the funds usually have extensive experience in investing overseas and are prepared to deal with the administrative problems. This, of course, does not necessarily lead to superior returns, but the likelihood for inexperienced blunders is reduced.

One may also invest in closed-end investment companies specializing in international equity investments. As later described in Chapter 19, a closed-

---

[6]Jacquillat and Solnik, "Multinationals Are Poor Tools for Diversification," pp. 8–12.

TABLE 18–11 LARGE U.S. MULTINATIONAL CORPORATIONS

1987 Rank	Company	Foreign Revenue (Millions)	Total Revenue (Millions)	Foreign Revenue as Percent of Total	Foreign Operating Profit (Millions)	Total Operating Profit (Millions)	Foreign Operating Profit as Percent of Total	Foreign Assets (Millions)	Total Assets (Millions)	Foreign Assets as Percent of Total
1	Exxon	$57,375	$76,416[1]	75.1%	$3,301[1]	$4,840[1]	68.2%	$37,742	$74,042	51.0%
2	Mobil	31,633[2]	52,256[2]	60.5	1,238[3]	2,033[3]	60.9	20,110	41,140	48.9
3	IBM	29,280	54,217	54.0	3,330[1]	5,258[1]	63.3	34,468	63,688	54.1
4	General Motors	24,091	101,782	23.7	1,919[1]	3,551[1]	54.0	20,389	87,241	23.4
5	Ford Motor[4]	23,955	73,145	32.8	1,184[1]	4,625[1]	25.6	24,077	61,090	39.4
6	Texaco	17,120	34,372	49.8	863	−1,128	P-D	10,550	33,962	31.1
7	Citicorp	13,314	27,519	48.4	−2,293[1]	−1,138[1]	201.5	89,675[5]	198,683[5]	45.1
8	E.I. du Pont de Nemours	11,651[6]	30,468[6]	38.2	682[7]	2,100[7]	32.5	7,757	28,209	27.5
9	Dow Chemical	7,431	13,377	55.6	1,278	2,315	55.2	7,037	14,356	49.0
10	Chevron	5,905	26,015	22.7	2,006	3,313	60.5	6,947	34,465	20.2
11	Procter & Gamble	5,524	17,000	32.5	95[1]	327[1]	29.1	3,849	13,715	28.1
12	Eastman Kodak	5,265	13,305	39.6	815	2,132	38.2	5,014	14,451	34.7
13	Chase Manhattan	5,021	10,745	46.7	−1,438[1]	−895[1]	160.7	37,280	99,130	37.6
14	ITT[4]	4,891	19,525	25.0	384	1,278	30.0	5,908	39,983	14.8
15	Xerox[4]	4,852[2]	15,125[2]	32.1	182	575	31.7	5,691	23,462	24.3
16	United Technologies	4,713	17,170	27.4	252[1]	592[1]	42.6	3,913	11,929	32.8
17	Philip Morris	4,544	22,279	20.4	436	4,067	10.7	3,774	19,145	19.7
18	Amoco	4,400[2]	20,477[2]	21.5	517[1]	1,360[1]	38.0	5,734	24,827	23.1
19	Digital Equipment	4,373	9,389	46.6	913	1,672	54.6	3,089	8,407	36.7
20	Unisys	4,237	9,713	43.6	400	1,432	27.9	2,865	9,958	28.8

[1]Net income.
[2]Includes other income.
[3]Net income before corporate and net financing expenses.
[4]Includes proportionate interest in unconsolidated subsidiaries and affiliates.
[5]Average assets.
[6]Includes excise taxes.
[7]Operating income after taxes.
P-D = Profit over deficit.
Source: *Forbes*, July 25, 1988, p. 248. Excerpted by permission. © Forbes Inc., 1988.

end investment company has a fixed supply of shares outstanding and trades on a national exchange or over-the-counter, much as an individual company does. It may trade at a premium or discount from its net asset value. An example is the Japan Fund.

A listing of internationally oriented funds is presented in Table 19–3 of the next chapter. The addresses of these funds can be found in *Forbes* magazine or the Wiesenberger Investment Companies Service (also discussed in the next chapter).

Specialists in International Securities.   The large investor may consider the option of engaging the services of selected banks and investment counselors with specialized expertise in foreign equities. Major firms include Morgan Guaranty Trust Co., State Street Bank and Trust Co., Batterymarch Financial Management, and Fidelity Trust Company of New York. These firms provide a total range of advisory and management services. However, they often require a minimum investment well in excess of $100,000 and are tailored to the needs of the large institutional investor.

19

MUTUAL FUNDS

O f over 40 million investors in the United States, approximately one third participate through the purchase of **mutual funds** rather than directly through the ownership of common stock or other securities.

The concept of a mutual fund is best understood by an example. Suppose that you and your friends are too busy to develop the expertise needed to manage your own assets. One of your neighbors, however, has studied investments and security markets extensively. He has also had years of hands-on experience as a trustee of his company's pension fund. You and your friends decide to pool your money and have this experienced investor act as your investment adviser. He will be compensated by receiving a small percentage of the average amount of assets under his management during the forthcoming year.

By common agreement, the pooled money is to be invested in the common stock of large, stable companies with the objective of capital appreciation and moderate dividend income; funds not so invested are to be placed in short-term T-bills to earn interest. Group members collectively contribute $100,000 and decide to issue shares in the fund at a rate of one share for each $10 contributed—a total of 10,000 shares. Since you put in $10,000, you receive 1,000 shares of the fund—or 10 percent of the fund's shares. Over the next few weeks, your investment adviser uses $90,000 to purchase common stock in a number of companies representing several different industries and puts $10,000 in T-bills. The portfolio looks like this:

Common stocks grouped by industry:
    Computers:
        Hewlett-Packard
        IBM
        Digital Equipment
    Financial services:
        Chemical Bank
        Merrill Lynch
        Northwestern National Life Insurance Co.
    Consumer retail:
        K mart
        Toys R Us
        Dayton Hudson
    Treasury bills:
        $10,000

Since you own 10 percent of this portfolio, you are entitled to 10 percent of all income paid out to shareholders and 10 percent of all realized capital gains or losses.

The initial value of the portfolio is $100,000, or $10 per share. Assume your investment manager picked some winning stocks, and the portfolio rises to $115,000. Now each share is worth $11.50 per share.

Your group of investors has many characteristics of a mutual fund: ownership interest represented by shares, professional management, stated investment objectives, and a diversified portfolio of assets. A billion dollar mutual fund would operate with many of the same concepts and principles—only the magnitude of the operation would be thousands of times larger.

ADVANTAGES AND DISADVANTAGES OF MUTUAL FUNDS

Mutual funds offer an efficient way to diversify your investments. For many small investors, diversification may be difficult to achieve. The normal trading unit for listed stocks—the "round lot"—is 100 shares. If proper diversification required a portfolio of at least 10 different stocks, the investor should purchase 100 shares of each of them. If each stock had a market value of $30, cost would be (excluding commission) $30,000 ($30 × 100 × 10). That's a big bite for most individuals just to get started.

With a mutual fund, you are also buying the expertise of the fund management. In many cases, fund managers have a long history of investment experience and may be specialists in certain areas such as international securities, gold stocks, or municipal bonds. By entrusting your funds to capable hands, you are freeing up your time for other pursuits. This may be particularly important to people such as doctors or lawyers who may be capable of earning $150 to $200 an hour in their normal practice but are novices in the market.

As will be demonstrated throughout the chapter, you have a multitude of funds from which to choose to satisfy your needs. Thus, another advantage of mutual funds is that they can be used to buy not only stocks, but also U.S. government bonds, corporate bonds, municipal securities, and so on. Also, they represent a particularly efficient way to invest in foreign securities.

With many of these advantages in mind, it is not surprising that mutual funds have enjoyed an enormous growth in the last decade. The amount of funds in existence grew from 300 in the 1970s to over 1,500 in 1988. The amount of assets being managed increased tenfold.

Having stated some of the advantages of mutual funds, let's look at the disadvantages. First of all, mutual funds, on average, do not outperform the market. That is to say, over long periods of time, they do no better than the Standard & Poor's 500 Stock Index, the Dow Jones Industrial Average, and so on. Nevertheless, they do provide an efficient means for diversifying your portfolio. Also, a minority of funds have had exceptional returns over time (many of these have had exposure to international investments).

Some mutual funds can be expensive to purchase. However, this factor should not overly concern you because a high commission can often be avoided. As you read further into the chapter, you will become very proficient at identifying the absence or presence of a commission and whether it is justified.

An investor in mutual funds must also be sensitive to the excessive claims that are sometimes made by mutual fund salespeople. Oftentimes, potential returns to the investor are emphasized without detailing the offsetting risks. The fact that a fund made 20–25 percent last year in no way ensures such a return in the future. Although the Securities and Exchange Commission has begun clamping down on false or overly enthusiastic advertising practices by members of the industry, the buyer still needs to beware. We will also help develop your skills in measuring actual performance as we progress through the chapter.

A final potential drawback to mutual funds is actually a reverse view of an advantage. With over 1,500 mutual funds from which to choose, an investor has almost as much of a problem in selecting a mutual fund as a stock. For example, there are approximately 1,500 stocks on the New York Stock Exchange, about equal the number of mutual funds in existence. Nevertheless, if you sharpen your goals and objectives, you will be able to focus in on a handful of funds that truly meet your needs.

Having discussed the general nature of mutual funds and some of the potential advantages and disadvantages, we now examine the actual mechanics. In the remainder of this chapter, we shall discuss closed-end versus open-end funds, load versus no-load funds, fund objectives, considerations in selecting a fund, and measuring the return on a fund. There is also a brief description of unit investment trusts (UITs) in Appendix 19–A. UITs have some attributes similar to mutual funds.

CLOSED-END VERSUS OPEN-END FUNDS

There are basically two types of investment funds, the **closed-end fund** and the **open-end fund.** We shall briefly discuss the closed-end fund and then move on to the much more important type of arrangement, the open-end fund.

Actually, these terms refer to the manner in which shares are distributed and redeemed. A closed-end fund has a fixed number of shares, and purchasers and sellers of shares must trade with each other. You cannot buy the shares directly from the fund (except at the inception of the fund) because of the limitation on shares outstanding. Furthermore, the fund does not stand ready to buy the shares back from you.

As we shall eventually see, an open-end fund represents exactly the opposite concept. The open-end fund stands ready at all times to sell you new shares or buy back your old shares. Having made this distinction, let's stay with the closed-end fund for now. The shares of closed-end funds trade on security exchanges or over-the-counter just as any other stock might. Instead of the firm being involved in the manufacturing of automobiles or the discovery of new drugs, it is involved in the investment and management of a security portfolio. An example of a closed-end fund that trades on a security exchange is shown in Figure 19–1. Note the Blue Chip Value Fund, which is a closed-end fund specializing in high-grade equities, is presented the same as any other common stock, such as Boeing (airplanes, missiles) shown directly below it. If you wish to buy or sell shares in the Blue Chip Value Fund, you call your broker and place your order.

One of the most important considerations in purchasing a closed-end fund is whether it is trading at a discount or premium from **net asset value.** First, let's look at the formula for net asset value.

$$\text{Net asset value (NAV)} = \frac{\text{Total value of securities} - \text{Liabilities}}{\text{Shares outstanding}}$$

(19–1)

FIGURE 19–1   A CLOSED-END FUND QUOTE ON THE NEW YORK STOCK
                EXCHANGE

| 52 Weeks | | | Yld | P-E | Sales | | | | Net |
High	Low	Stock	Div.	%	Ratio	100s	High	Low	Close	Chg.
25½	12¾	Bemis s	.44	1.9	18	62	23¾	23¼	23¼	– ⅜
62¾	28½	BenfCp	2.00	4.5	8	134	44⅜	44	44	– ¼
47⅞	38	Benef pf	4.30	9.7	...	10	44¼	43½	44¼	+ 1½
49	41	Benef pf	4.50	10.6	...	z80	42½	42½	42½	...
8	2¼	BengtB	.12r	2.7	15	98	4½	4⅜	4⅜	...
6⅛	½	vlBerkey	...	...	...	979	1	⅞	1	+ ⁷⁄₁₆
20½	5¾	BestBy s	...	...	24	92	8⅛	8	8⅛	...
15	6	BestPd	...	...	17	870	14¾	14⅜	14⅝	– ¼
25½	9⅛	BethStl	...	...	10	2710	24⅜	24¼	24¼	– ¼
55¼	29	BethSt pf	5.00	9.4	...	5	53⅜	53⅜	53⅜	+ ¼
27½	13½	BthS pfB	2.50	9.5	...	26	26⅜	26	26⅜	...
15½	4⅛	Bevrly	.05j	...	...	560	6¾	6⅝	6⅝	...
22¾	12¼	BevlP	2.33e	15.9	9	175	14¾	14⅝	14⅝	– ⅛
28⅜	10⅞	Biocft	...	...	10	272	11	d 10⅜	10½	– ⅜
23¼	10⅜	BirStl s	.30	1.4	11	161	21½	21¾	21½	...
26½	13	BlackD	.40	1.8	15	786	22	21¾	22	+ ⅛
28⅛	19½	BlkHC s	1.40	5.2	11	57	27½	27	27⅛	– ⅛
10	10	Blkstn n	...	...	...	936	10	10	10	...
34⅜	20	BlkHR s	1.04	4.0	15	486	26⅛	25⅝	26	+ ¼
22¾	17⅞	BlueAr n	.14e	.8	...	106	17⅞d	17⅝	17¾	– ¼
9	4⅝	BlueChp	.20e	3.5	...	95	5⅞	5¾	5¾	...
59⅝	33⅝	Boeing .	1.60	2.7	18	7949	59½	58⅛	59	+ ¾
51⅛	28¾	BoiseC s	1.20	2.8	8	2281	43½	42¾	43⅜	– ⅝
24⅞	11¾	BoltBr s	.06	.4	...	353	17	16⅝	16¾	– ⅛
19⅝	9¾	BordC n	1.13e	6.0	...	1382	18⅞	18⅜	18¾	+ ¼
63⅞	31¼	Borden	1.56	3.1	14	2557	50⅞	50½	50⅝	+ ¼
21	8¼	Bormns	.05j	...	...	12	11⅛	11	11	...
13⅞	10⅜	BCelts	1.40	10.7	10	30	13⅜	13⅛	13⅛	...
22	12½	BostEd	1.82	12.3	9	2354	15	14¾	14¾	– ¼
16	13½	BosE pr	1.46	10.0	...	60	14⅞	14⅝	14⅝	– ¼
44½	22	Bowatr	.92	3.0	9	1078	30⅝	29⅞	30½	+ ⅝
14¼	8¾	Brazil n	...	...	...	56	9⅛	9	9	– ⅛
41⅞	20¼	BrigSt	1.60	4.9	15	56	32¾	32	32⅜	+ ½
54⅛	28¼	BristMy	1.68	4.0	15	5093	41⅝	40⅞	41½	+ ½
37½	22⅛	BritAir	1.44e	5.7	6	210	25⅜	25⅛	25⅛	– ¼
34½	30½	BritGas	1.82e	5.8	90	252	32	31½	31⅝	– ⅝
4½	1⅜	BritLnd	...	...	...	16	4½	4⅜	4⅜	– ⅛
77¼	44⅞	BritPt	3.13e	5.9	12	1286	53¾	53⅛	53⅜	– ⅜
19	6½	BritP wt	...	...	...	48	7½	7¼	7¼	– ¼
18⅞	12	BrtPt pp	2.03e	16.7	...	395	12⅜	12	12⅛	– ¼
32½	16½	BHP n	.96e	3.6	14	7	27	26⅞	26⅞	– ⅛
26⅞	18⅝	BklyUG	1.72	7.1	10	185	24¼	23⅞	24¼	+ ⅜
29	26½	BkUG pf	2.47	8.9	...	3	27⅝	27⅝	27⅝	+ ⅜
27¼	12½	B	.40h	2.7	...	4		14¾	14¾	+ ¼

The net asset value (NAV) is equal to the current value of the securities
owned by the fund minus any liabilities divided by the number of shares
outstanding. For example, assume a fund has securities worth $140 million,
liabilities of $5 million, and 10 million shares outstanding. The NAV is $13.50.

$$\text{NAV} = \frac{\$140 \text{ million} - \$5 \text{ million}}{10 \text{ million shares}} = \frac{\$135 \text{ million}}{10 \text{ million}} = \$13.50$$

The NAV is computed at the end of each day for a fund.

Intuitively, one would expect a closed-end fund to sell at its net asset value,
but that is not the case. Many funds trade at a discount from NAV because
they have a poor record of prior performance or are heavily invested in an
unpopular industry. A few trade at a premium because of the known quality
of their management, the nature of their investments, or the fact they have
holdings in nonpublicly traded securities that are believed to be undervalued

FIGURE 19–2   PREMIUMS OR DISCOUNTS FROM NET ASSET VALUE

Diversified Common Stock Funds									
Fund Name	Stock Exchg.	N.A. Value	Stock Price	% Diff.	Fund Name	Stock Exchg.	N.A. Value	Stock Price	% Diff.
Adams Express	NYSE	17.52	15⅞	− 9.39	Liberty All-Star	NYSE	8.34	6⅞	− 17.60
Baker Fentress-n	OTC	51.22	42½	− 17.03	Niagara Share	NYSE	16.43	13⅝	− 17.07
Blue Chip Value	NYSE	7.34	6	− 18.26	Nicholas App Gr Eq	NYSE	8.82	7⅝	− 13.55
Clemente-Gbl	NYSE	b8.73	6⅝	− 24.11	Quest Value Cap	NYSE	10.53	7¾	− 26.40
Gemini II Cap	NYSE	16.70	12¼	− 26.64	Quest Value Inc	NYSE	11.80	10	− 15.25
Gemini II Inc	NYSE	9.63	13¼	+ 37.59	Royce Value	NYSE	9.63	8⅝	− 10.43
Gen'l Amer Inv	NYSE	19.23	15½	− 19.40	Schafer Value	NYSE	8.90	7⅜	− 17.13
GlobalGr Cap	NYSE	8.73	8⅛	− 6.93	Source Cap	NYSE	38.71	38⅛	− 1.51
GlobalGr Inc	NYSE	9.34	9⅝	+ 3.05	Tri-Continental	NYSE	24.90	21⅞	− 12.10
GSO Trust	NYSE	9.78	9	− 8.00	Worldwd Value	NYSE	19.58	15	− 23.39
Lehman Corp.	NYSE	14.54	12¾	− 12.31	Zweig Fund	NYSE	a10.32	10⅞	+ 5.38

Source: *Barron's*, July 11, 1988, p. 120. Reprinted by permission of *Barron's*, © Dow Jones & Company, Inc., 1988. All rights reserved.

on their books. Note in Figure 19–2 the predominance of common stock funds that were trading at discounts from NAV in July 1988. This has normally been the case over the last decade. Some researchers even use the fact that closed-end funds do not sell for what they are worth (in terms of their holdings) as evidence that the market is something less than truly efficient in valuing securities.

INVESTING IN OPEN-END FUNDS

We now shift our discussion to open-end funds. As previously indicated, an open-end fund stands ready at all times to sell new shares or buy back old shares from investors. You do not deal with other shareholders. Over 95 percent of the investment funds in the United States are open-ended in nature. Actually the term *mutual fund* applies specifically to *open-end* investment companies, although closed-end funds are sometimes loosely labeled as mutual funds as well. We shall be careful to make the distinction where appropriate.

Transactions with open-end funds are made at net asset value as described in Formula 19–1 (though there may be an added commission). If the fund has 100 million shares outstanding at a NAV of $10 per share ($1 billion) and sells 20 million more shares at $10 per share, the new funds ($200 million) are redeployed in investments worth $200 million, and the NAV remains unchanged. The only factor that changes the NAV is the up and down movement of the securities in the fund's portfolio. The primary distinctions between closed-end and open-end funds are presented in Table 19–1. All of our subsequent discussion will be about open-end (mutual) funds. These include such

TABLE 19–1	DISTINCTIONS BETWEEN CLOSED-END AND OPEN-END FUNDS		
	Method of Purchase	Number of Shares Outstanding	Shares Traded at Net Asset Value
Closed-end fund	Stock exchange or over-the-counter	Fixed	No—there may be a discount or premium from NAV
Open end fund (mutual fund)	Direct from fund or fund salesperson	Fluctuates	Yes—but there may be a commission

established names as Fidelity, Dreyfus, Vanguard, IDS, T. Rowe Price, and Templeton.

Load versus No-Load Funds

Some funds have established selling agreements with stockbrokers, financial planners, insurance agents, and others licensed to sell securities. Because fund managers' compensation is a percentage of all the money they manage, they are eager to enlarge their pool of money and are willing to pay a commission to selling agents. These funds are *load* funds. The commission, or load, is paid to the selling agent directly from the investor's capital. The typical stock mutual fund has a load of 8.5 percent for investments under $15,000. Bond funds usually charge 3 to 4 percent. In both cases, the commission percentage normally decreases with larger purchases (see Table 19–2).

Several stock funds are referred to as low-load funds because their sales charges are 3 to 4 percent instead of the more-normal 8 to 8.5 percent. In recent years, a few investment companies have introduced a number of end-load funds. This type of fund has no sales charge on purchases, but imposes a redemption charge of 5 percent that declines by 1 percent per year. After five years, the fund can be sold without charge.

No-Load Funds

No-load funds do not charge commissions and are sold directly by the investment company through advertisements, prospectuses, and 800-number telephone orders. As of mid-1988, no-load funds made up about 30 percent of all mutual fund assets. Some wonder how no-load funds justify their existence since they charge no commission to purchase their shares. The answer is because of the management fee they charge to manage the assets in the fund. This normally totals about 1 percent. On a billion dollar fund, this represents $10 million a year and can be more than adequate to compensate the fund managers. It should also be pointed out that load funds also have similar management fees.

TABLE 19–2	TYPICAL SALES CHARGES FOR LOAD STOCK FUND	
	Purchase Amount	As Percent of Offering Price
	Less than $15,000	8.5%
	$15,000–$24,999	7.5
	$25,000–$49,999	6.25
	$50,000–$99,999	4.75
	$100,000–$149,999	3.50
	$250,000–$499,999	2.75
	$5,000,000 and .... over	0.25

The question then becomes, why pay the load (commission)? Studies indicate that there is no significant statistical difference in the investment performance of load and no-load funds. Consequently, most astute investors shop around for a no-load fund to fit their needs rather than pay a commission. This statement is not intended to dismiss the possibility that apprehensive or uncomfortable investors may benefit from the consultation and advice of a competent mutual fund salesman or financial adviser, and thus receive a commensurate service from paying the commission. However, many other investors are better off using the typical 8.5 percent commission toward the purchase of new shares rather than the payment of a sales fee.

If you invest $1,000 in a mutual fund and pay an 8.5 percent commission, only 91.5 percent will go toward purchasing your shares. A $1,000 investment will immediately translate into a holding of $915. This means the fund must go up by $85, or 9.29 percent, just for you to break even.

$$\frac{\$85}{\$915} = 9.29 \text{ percent}$$

With these thoughts in mind, you should become proficient in recognizing funds that are charging a load and those that are not. In order to accomplish this goal, observe Figure 19–3, which is an excerpt on mutual fund quotations from *The Wall Street Journal*.

The bold letters in the table represent the name of the mutual fund sponsor. For example, AARP (the second listed group) has six different mutual funds dedicated to serving diverse needs ranging from Capital Growth (Cap Grw) to Tax-Free Short-Term investments (TXF Shrt). The table has three primary headings: NAV, Offer Price, and NAV Chg. It is by observing the first two columns that we can tell whether a fund is a load or a no-load. As examples of load funds, observe the AAL Mutual Funds at the top of the table or the American Capital Group at the bottom of the first column. In each case, the NAV (net asset value) is different from the offer price. This means a commission must be paid. For example, in the first fund in the American Capital Group, the NAV is $13.09, and the offer price is $14.31. This means that the fund has a net asset value of 13.09 per share, but it is offered to the public for $14.31. The difference between $14.31 and $13.09 of $1.22 represents the commission.

Offer price	$14.31
NAV (net asset value)	13.09
Commission	$ 1.22

In this case, the commission represents 8.53 percent of the offer price ($1.22/ $14.31 = 8.53%).[1] You will buy a fund valued at $13.09 for $14.31 because of the sales charge.[2] What if you decided to sell the fund on the same day you bought it for an unanticipated reason? You would receive the net asset value of $13.09 and be out $1.22.

Contrast this with no-load funds. With no-load funds, you buy and sell at the same price.[3] You can identify no-load funds by the symbol NL under the offer price column in Figure 19–3. For example, the AARP group (second listed funds) are primarily no-loads, and you will generally see NL (no-load) under the offer price column. Looking at the Capital Growth (Cap Grw) fund under the AARP group, the offering price is the same as the NAV of $23.21 because there is no commission. Observe the next group of no-loads in the table is sponsored by Advest Advantage. (Incidently, the third column in the table indicates whether the NAV changed for the day.)

Another way to determine whether a fund is load or no-load is by examining the *Forbes* annual mutual fund survey published in September of each year. A two-page excerpt from approximately 50 pages of data is presented in Figure 19–4. Observe the maximum sales charge is shown in the second column from the right. Clearly, the term *none* indicates a no-load.

As you can see, you will get a great deal of other information from Figure 19–4 as well. This can be important if you are trying to pick an appropriate no-load fund because you will have to select the fund and initiate the action on your own. Remember, there is no salesmen to call on you with a no-load fund. (But opening up a no-load fund is an easy, routine process.)

Some of the information from *Forbes* in Figure 19–4 will be discussed later in the chapter, but note for now that you get a rating on performance in up and down markets (left margin), average annual return data for 10 years (1978–1988), returns for the latest 12 months, yield, size of total assets, maximum sales charges, and annual expenses per $100. Although not specifically listed,

---

[1] It also represents 9.32 percent of the net asset value ($1.22/$13.09 = 9.32%).

[2] On large-scale purchases, some volume discount may be possible.

[3] An exemption would be if there is a hidden end load. This is not very common.

FIGURE 19–3   MUTUAL FUND QUOTATIONS

MUTUAL FUND QUOTATIONS

Tuesday, July 26, 1988

Price ranges for investment companies, as quoted by the National Association of Securities Dealers. NAV stands for net asset value per share; the offering includes net asset value plus maximum sales charge, if any.

	Offer NAV	
	NAV	Price Chg.

AAL Mutual Fds:
Cap Gro p8.42 8.84+ .01
Income p9.50 9.97 ...
Muni Bd p9.74 10.23 ...
AARP Invest Program:
Cap Grw 23.21 N.L.− .03
Gen Bnd 14.67 N.L. ...
Ginnie M 15.03 N.L.− .01
Gro Inc x20.61 20.61− .23
TxFr Bd 15.75 N.L.+ .01
TxF Shrt 15.37 N.L.− .03
ABT Funds:
Emrg Gr 8.50 8.92− .10
Growth I 10.21 10.72+ .01
Sec Inc 8.83 9.28+ .16
Util Inc 13.38 14.05 ...
AcornFd r 38.72 N.L.+ .02
Addsn Cp p14.09 14.53 ...
Adtek Fd 9.14 N.L.+ .01
Advnt Gv p9.39 9.81− .01
Advest Advantage:
Govt r p8.59 N.L.− .01
Growth r p11.26 N.L.+ .03
Income r p9.69 N.L.− .01
Specl r p9.41 N.L.− .03
Afuture Fd 9.68 N.L.− .01
AIM Funds:
Charter p5.18 5.44+ .01
Constel 7.44 7.81− .01
Conv Yld p9.44 9.91+ .01
Grnway p8.73 9.29+ .02
HiYld Sc p8.56 8.99 ...
LMTr p9.85 10.03 ...
Summit 6.61 (z) +.01
Weingr 8.97 9.42+ .01
AlgrGP r 9.87 9.87+ .03
Alliance Capital:
Allnc p5.87 5.93 ...
Balanc p12.51 13.24+ .06
Canada p6.92 7.32+ .01
Convert p9.26 9.80 ...
Cntrpt p14.56 15.41+ .01
Divdnd p2.89 3.06+ .01
Govt p8.43 8.92 ...
HB TxF p9.09 9.47+ .01
HI Yld p8.56 9.06+ .01
HI TxFr 9.19 9.57+ .01
Ins Cal 11.72 12.21+ .02
Intl p16.42 17.38+ .03
Mnthly 11.69 12.37 ...
Mrtge p9.06 9.59 ...
Quasr p17.73 18.76− .04
Survyr p11.16 11.81− .02
Technol p21.53 22.78+ .18
AMA Funds:
Class Gr p8.87 N.L.+ .02
Globl Gr p19.51 N.L.− .03
Glob Inc p20.03 N.L.− .07
Glob ST p10.17 N.L. ...
Grw+ I p18.07 N.L.+ .03
Class In p8.82 N.L.+ .01
EMT p28.88 13.52− .01
Med Tec p10.13 N.L.− .03
American Capital Group:
Comstk 13.09 14.31+ .01
Corp Bd 7.16 7.52+ .01
Enterpr 10.21 11.16+ .04
Exch Fd 63.54 (z) +.18
Fed Mtg p12.75 13.39− .01
Fd Amer 10.82 11.83+ .01
Govt Sec p10.13 10.86+ .01
Growth 15.38 (z) +.04
Harbor 12.30 13.44 ...
Yld 9.27 9.94+ .01

CommonSense Trust:
Govt 11.00 11.80 ...
Growth 10.45 11.42+ .02
Gro Inc 10.07 11.01− .01
Commonwealth Trust:
A & B 1.40 1.51+ .01
C 1.94 2.10 ...
Composite Group:
Bond Stk p9.97 10.39+ .02
Growth p10.63 11.07+ .03
Income p8.92 9.29 ...
NW Pt p14.35 14.95− .06
Tax Ex p7.16 7.46 ...
US Gov p9.90 10.31 ...
Value p11.07 11.54+ .02
Conn Mutual:
Govt 10.21 10.89+ .01
Growth 10.61 11.32 ...
Totl Ret 11.40 12.16 ...
Concord In 6.88 7.17 ...
Concrd TE 6.93 7.22+ .01
Continental Equities:
Equity r p8.99 9.22− .03
OptInc r p8.67 8.89 ...
US Gov r p9.05 9.28 ...
Copley F 10.89 10.89+ .03
Corp Pfd 40.83 41.88+ .03
Counsellors Funds:
Cap App 9.21 N.L.− .01
Fxd Inc 9.95 N.L. ...
NY Muni 9.63 N.L.+ .01
Coutry Cap 14.68 15.87+ .04
CownIG r p9.59 9.59+ .03
Cowen Op p9.49 9.97− .01
Criterion Funds:
Cm IncS p8.87 9.31+ .02
CvSecs r p9.29 9.29 ...
GlblGr r p10.78 10.78− .02
Gov Inst p8.67 8.89 ...
Inv Qual p9.03 9.48 ...
Lowry M p8.73 9.17+ .02
Pilot Fd p7.68 8.06 ...
Qlty TF p9.72 10.20+ .01
Sunblt G p16.77 17.61+ .13
Techni p18.00 18.90+ .04
US Govt p8.67 9.10+ .01
Cmbrind G 9.92 N.L. ...
Dean Witter:
AmVal r p12.72 12.72+ .02
Cal TxFr p11.38 11.38+ .01
Convrt r p8.73 8.73+ .01
DevlGr r p9.74 9.74− .01
DivGro r p18.80 18.80+ .05
GPlus r p8.99 8.99 ...
High Yld 12.18 12.89 ...
Mngd r p9.90 9.90+ .02
NatRes r p9.59 9.59− .01
NYTxF r p10.68 10.68 ...
OptionI r p7.97 7.97+ .01
Sears Tx 10.84 10.84+ .02
Tax Adv p9.36 N.L.+ .04
Tax Ex 10.70 11.15+ .01
USGovt r p9.61 9.61 ...
Util r p10.14 10.14+ .03
Val Ad p12.04 12.04+ .01
WWIT r p14.19 14.19− .05
Delaware Group:
Dectr I 16.18 17.68+ .01
Dectr II p10.80 11.34+ .01
Del Cap p13.59 14.27− .01
Delch II p7.75 8.14 ...
7.75 8.31 ...

SelElec r 7.82 7.98− .01
SelEng r 12.75 13.01− .04
SelEn r 7.83 7.99− .11
SelEUt r 8.84 9.02+ .01
SelFd r 16.65 16.99+ .05
SelFnS r 27.75 28.32+ .02
SelHlth r 33.64 34.33+ .15
Sel Hs r (z) (z) ...
SelInd r 13.52 13.80+ .01
SelLesr r 22.93 23.40− .06
SelMD r 7.46 7.61− .05
SelMetl r 12.85 13.11 ...
SelPap r 12.05 12.30+ .03
SelPrp r 10.52 10.73+ .03
SelReg r 9.60 9.80+ .01
SelRetl r 11.93 12.17 ...
SelSL r 9.09 9.28+ .04
SelSoft r 14.11 14.40 ...
SelTec r 17.94 18.31− .06
SelTele r 17.20 17.55− .05
SelUtil r 24.95 25.46+ .07
Fidelity Plymouth Fds:
Agg Inc 9.98 10.40 ...
Grw Opp 13.85 14.43+ .06
Gov Sec 9.17 9.55− .01
Inc Gwth p10.83 11.28− .02
Spec Sit p15.30 15.94+ .07
St Bd 9.93 10.08 ...
Fidu CapG 15.16 N.L.− .06
Financial Programs:
Dynam 6.75 N.L.+ .01
Hi Yield 8.08 N.L.+ .01
Industl 3.57 N.L.+ .02
Income 7.81 N.L.+ .02
Select 6.49 N.L. ...
Tax Free 13.85 N.L.+ .02
FBS Gov 6.94 N.L. ...
FSP Bay p9.27 N.L.+ .03
FSP Eur 8.41 N.L.− .02
FSP Fin 7.53 N.L. ...
FSP Gld 5.79 N.L.− .04
FSP HS 13.72 N.L.+ .09
FSP Ls 11.40 N.L.+ .01
FSP PaB 12.50 N.L.− .11
FSP Tc 10.57 N.L.+ .05
FSPUt 8.27 N.L.+ .01
FstEagl r 11.33 N.L.+ .06
First Investors Fund:
Bond Ap 10.82 11.67 ...
Discovr p9.05 9.89− .02
Govt Fd p10.96 11.82 ...
Growth p5.46 5.97+ .01
High Yld p13.58 14.64+ .02
Income p5.32 5.81+ .01
Intl Sec p4.28 4.68− .02
NY TxFr p13.30 14.34+ .03
Optn Fd p4.24 4.57 ...
Spec Bd 13.60 14.66+ .01
Tx Exmt p9.76 10.52+ .01
Value 11.14 12.17+ .02
FstTr US 10.06 10.56 ...
Flag Investors Fds:
Corp Cs p9.62 N.L.+ .01
Int .49− .03
.06

Omega p13.32 14.52+ .07
Investment Portfolios:
GvtPl r p7.58 7.58 ...
HiYd r p9.49 9.49 ...
Optn r p6.02 6.02 ...
Eqit r p10.75 10.75− .01
TR r p9.16 9.16+ .01
ITB Group:
InvT Bos 10.36 11.14+ .01
InvT Hip 11.88 12.74 ...
InT MTF 16.00 16.71 ...
IDS Group:
Bond p4.63 4.87 ...
CA TE p4.73 4.97+ .01
Discov p6.70 7.05− .03
Eq Plus p8.46 8.91− .01
Extr Inc p4.70 4.95 ...
Fed Inc p4.99 5.26 ...
Growth p17.21 18.12− .06
HiYd TE p4.38 4.62 ...
Insr TE p4.77 5.03 ...
Intrntl p8.40 8.85− .05
Mgd Ret p7.60 8.00+ .01
MN TE p4.81 5.06+ .01
Mutual p11.73 12.35− .01
NY TE p4.63 4.87+ .01
New D p8.15 8.58− .04
Prec Mtl p7.30 7.68− .12
Progres p6.39 6.72 ...
Select p8.41 8.85 ...
Stock p17.49 18.41+ .05
TE Bd p3.95 4.16 ...
StrAgg r p9.11 9.11 ...
StrEq r p7.58 7.58+ .02
StrInc r p5.64 5.64 ...
StrPan r p4.13 4.13− .02
Intl Cash (z) (z) ...
Inv Resrch 4.99 5.45− .01
IRI Stock p6.93 7.26− .01
Istel Fund p12.34 N.L.− .01
Ivy Funds:
Grwth 12.98 N.L.+ .04
Inst 105.01 N.L.+ .05
Intl 15.01 N.L.− .02
JP Growth 12.06 13.11+ .05
JP Income 9.05 9.84 ...
Janus Funds:
Jan Fnd 11.27 11.27+ .02
Janus VI 9.83 9.83+ .02
Jans Vn 28.06 28.06− .05
Japan Fd 18.07 N.L.+ .01
John Hancock Funds:
Bond Fd 14.59 15.95+ .01
Globl Tr 14.72 16.09− .04
Growth 13.22 14.45+ .03
High Inc 9.27 9.73+ .01
Fed Pl 9.47 9.94+ .01
Pac Bas 10.47 10.99− .06
Spcl Eqt 5.09 5.56− .01
Tax Ex 10.30 10.81+ .01
Gtd Mtg 9.89 10.81+ .01
US Govt 8.73 9.54 ...
KaufF r 1.02 1.02 ...
Kemper Funds:
Blue Chp ...

Sector r p8.04 8.04 ...
MidAmer Funds:
Mid Am 5.23 5.72+ .02
MdA HG 3.83 4.19+ .01
MdA HY 9.97 10.55+ .03
Midas Gld p2.90 3.09 ...
Midwest Funds:
FI Gwth 11.86 12.45− .01
FI Govt 10.01 10.43 ...
FI Treas 9.01 9.39 ...
Int Govt 10.08 10.29 ...
TF Ltd 10.12 10.33 ...
MIMLIC:
Asst All 10.42 10.97 ...
Inv I 10.33 10.87 ...
Mtg Secs 9.90 10.42 ...
Monitrd p15.95 16.53− .01
MorKg SC 11.13 11.47 ...
Morison p5.09 5.49 ...
MSB Fund 18.57 N.L.− .02
Mutl BnFd 13.88 15.17− .01
Mutual of Omaha Funds:
Amer 9.83 9.83 ...
Growth 7.24 7.87− .01
Income 8.93 9.71 ...
Tax Free 10.96 11.91+ .02
Mutual Series Fund:
Qual In 23.11 N.L.+ .02
Mtl Bcn 23.54 N.L.+ .01
Share 69.80 N.L.+ .07
NtlAvia Tc 10.11 10.61 ...
Natl Ind 11.89 N.L.+ .01
National Securities Funds:
Bond 2.47 2.66 ...
Cal TEx 12.33 12.91+ .02
Fed Sec 9.14 9.80− .01
Income 7.59 8.18+ .02
Preferd 7.49 8.08+ .04
Prem p10.58 11.35+ .05
Real Est 8.62 9.34 ...
RE Incm 10.25 11.11+ .02
Stock 7.54 8.13+ .02
Str p10.64 11.53+ .02
Tax ExB 9.66 10.12+ .01
Totl Ret 6.98 7.53+ .02
Grwth 10.26 11.06− .11
Fairfld 7.36 8.04− .09
Natl Telcm 14.92 15.66− .08
Nationwide Funds:
Fund 12.80 13.84+ .03
Growth 8.27 8.94 ...
Bond 9.11 9.85+ .02
TaxFr r 9.12 N.L.+ .01
New England Funds:
Equity x9.30 9.95− .12
Glob Gv x11.79 12.61− .01
Grwth 7.67 8.20+ .01
Income x10.95 11.71− .07
Gvt Sec xd11.95 12.78− .10
Ret Eqty p6.18 6.61+ .01
Tax Ex x6.89 7.21− .03
Neuberger Berman Mngt:
Energy 17.23 N.L.− .01
Guardn 38.68 N.L.− .04
Liberty 4.22 N.L.+ .01
Ltd Mat 9.83 N.L. ...
Manhtn 8.71 N.L.+ .01
MM Plus 9.85 N.L. ...
Partner 16.47 N.L.− .01
Newton Gr p20.62 N.L.− .09
Newtn Inc p8.00 N.L.+ ...
Muni p1.05 N.L. ...

most of these funds have an initial minimum investment of $500 to $1,000, but the amount may vary from fund to fund (later additional contributions may be smaller).

Assume you pick out a number of funds that interest you from the over 1,500 funds listed in *Forbes* or some other source. The next step is to contact the fund by mail or telephone (most have toll-free numbers). You can then ask any questions, and you will receive a detailed prospectus describing the fund.

The same September *Forbes* issue that provided financial information on funds in Figure 19–4 also supplies information about mailing addresses and telephone numbers for all major funds. An excerpt is presented in Figure 19–5. Other sources of similar mutual fund information include *Consumer Reports, Business Week, Financial World,* and *Money* magazine. For more-comprehensive information to use in screening a fund, you may wish to consult the *Wiesenberger Investment Companies Service* publication (produced annually by Warren, Gorham and Lamont, Boston). This hardback, oversized book has a complete page of information on all mutual funds and can be found in most libraries. An excerpt is presented in Figure 19–6. This presents data on the T. Rowe Price New Era Fund, Inc.

DIFFERING OBJECTIVES AND THE DIVERSITY OF MUTUAL FUNDS

Recognizing that different investors have different objectives and sensitivities to risk, the mutual fund industry offers a large group of funds from which to choose. In 1988, there were over 1,500 mutual funds, each unique in terms of stated objectives, investment policies, and current portfolio. To make some sense out of this much variety, funds can be classified in terms of their stated objectives.

Money Market Funds.   Money market funds were the phenomenon of the late 1970s and 1980s (Forbes Mutual Fund Survey lists over 150). Money market mutual funds invest in short-term securities, such as U.S. Treasury bills and Eurodollar deposits, commercial paper, jumbo bank certificates of deposit (CDs), and repurchase agreements.

Money market funds are no-load, and most require minimum deposits of $500 to $1,000. Most have check-writing privileges, but usually the checks must be written for at least $250 to $500.

Because the maturities of assets held in money market portfolios generally range from 20 to 50 days, the yields of these funds closely track short-term market interest rates. Money market funds give small investors an opportunity to invest in securities that were once out of reach.

FIGURE 19–4 FORBES MUTUAL FUND INFORMATION

Performance			Total Return			Assets			
In Up Markets	In Down Markets	Fund/Distributor	Annual Average 1978 to 1988	Last 12 Months	Yield	6/30/88 (Millions)	Percent change 1988 versus 1987	Maximum Sales Charge	Annual Expenses per $100
		Standard & Poor's 500 Stock Average Forbes stock fund composite	16.9% 16.4%	−6.9% −5.6%	3.3% 2.7%				$1.49
•C	•A	Dean Witter Div Grow Secs/Dean Witter	—★	−3.4%	3.8%	$1,781	−13%	5.00%r	$1.55
•D	•C	Dean Witter Natural Res Dev/Dean Witter	—★	−3.5	2.0	165	−8	5.00r	1.81
		Dean Witter Option Income/Dean Witter	—★	−7.5	2.0	341	−37	5.00r	1.94
C	A	Delaware Group Decatur Fund—I/Delaware	17.8%	−3.9	5.7	1,536	−6	8.50	0.69
		Delaware Group Decatur Fund—II/Delaware	—★	−5.0	3.4	185	38	4.75	1.27p
		Delaware Group DelCap—Concept I/Delaware	—★	7.1	3.0	118	29	4.75	1.49
C	B	Delaware Group Trend Fund2/Delaware	16.5	−10.9	None	60	−24	8.50	1.20
		Depositors Fund of Boston/‡	15.1	−6.7	1.6	55	−17	None	0.81
B	D	Depositors Invest—Capital Grow/Putnam	—★	−8.3	1.0	13	−15	None	1.33
B	C	Diversification Fund/‡	16.3	−5.6	1.3	62	−16	None	0.75
•D	•B	Dividend/Growth—Dividend/Dividend Growth	—★	−11.6	3.2	4	−27	None	1.99
A	B	Dodge & Cox Stock Fund/Dodge & Cox	19.5	−0.8	3.0	75	6	None	0.65
		Dover Regional Financial Shares/closed end	—★	0.8	1.6	7	−3	NA	1.80
C	B	Drexel Burnham Fund/Drexel	17.3	−2.0	4.3	204	−11	5.00	1.00
		Drexel Series—Convertible Secs/Drexel	—★	−10.8	5.5	25	−38	5.00r	2.10

Grade	Fund							
	Drexel Series—Emerging Growth/Drexel	—★	-25.1	None	15	-56	5.00r	*2.36*
	Drexel Series—Growth/Drexel	—★	-3.0	1.8	33	-22	5.00r	*2.10*
	Drexel Series—Option Income/Drexel	—★	-3.2	3.0	33	-30	5.00r	*2.01*
	Dreyfus Capital Value Fund/Dreyfus	—★	11.1	1.2	488	NM	4.50	*1.65*
D	Dreyfus Fund/Dreyfus	16.7	-2.5	5.2	2,648	-2	None	0.71
B	Dreyfus General Aggressive Grow/Dreyfus	—★	-1.0	1.0	45	-9	None	*1.63*
A	Dreyfus Growth Opportunity Fund/Dreyfus	17.5	-2.1	3.9	599	8	None	0.91
D	Dreyfus Index Fund/Dreyfus	—★	-6.4	2.4	33	47	None	NA
B	Dreyfus Leverage Fund/Dreyfus	17.5	-9.0	2.9	497	-16	4.50	*1.23*
C	Dreyfus New Leaders Fund/Dreyfus	—★	-3.6	0.4	120	2	None	*1.41*
	Dreyfus Strategic Aggres Inv LP/Dreyfus	—★	17.3	None	155	NM	3.00	NA
B	Dreyfus Strategic Investing/Dreyfus	—★	-3.3	1.2	117	3	4.50	*1.59p*
D	Dreyfus Third Century Fund/Dreyfus	16.0	-3.9	6.0	156	-11	None	1.02
D	Eagle Growth Shares/Fahnestock	10.9	7.9	None	2	-31	8.50	*2.26p*
B	Eaton & Howard Stock Fund/Eaton Vance	14.8	-2.6	3.5	79	-10	7.25	0.95
B	Eaton Vance Growth Fund/Eaton Vance	17.9	-5.7	0.8	89	-12	4.75	1.02
D	Eaton Vance Special Equities/Eaton Vance	16.6	-2.6	None	35	-14	7.25	1.16
•C	Eaton Vance Total Return Trust/Eaton Vance	—★	-11.4	9.4	516	-26	4.75	*1.03*
	Eclipse Equity Fund/Eclipse	—★	4.4	4.7	160	5	None	*1.09p*
	Emerging Medical Technology/AMA	—★	-20.1	None	7	-43	4.75	*3.61*
C	Energy Fund/Neuberger	15.0	-8.6	3.4	389	-18	None	0.86

A stock fund is added to this list if it has at least $5 million in net assets and, if open-end, is at least 12 months old; a fund is dropped when its assets fall below $2 million. Stock funds are graded only if in operation since 7/31/82. Long-term average total return is for 2/28/78 to 6/30/88. Yield is last 12 months' income dividends divided by 6/30/88 net asset value; it may differ from "yield" as defined by the SEC. *Expense ratio is in italics if the fund has a shareholder-paid 12b-1 plan exceeding 0.1% (hidden load) pending or in force.* • Fund rated for two periods only; maximum allowable grade A. ★Fund not in operation for full period. ‡Exchange fund, not currently selling new shares. p: Net of partial absorption of expenses by fund sponsor. b: Includes back-end load that reverts to fund. r: Includes back-end load that reverts to distributor. NA: Not applicable or not available. NM: Not meaningful. [1]Formerly Decatur Fund-Series I. [2]Formerly Delta Trend Fund. Source: Reprinted by permission of *Forbes* Magazine, September 5, 1988, p. 178, © Forbes Inc., 1988.

FIGURE 19–5   ADDRESSES OF MUTUAL FUNDS (Fund Distributors)

Distributor	Type of Fund	Distributor	Type of Fund
Country Capital Management Co P.O. Box 2222 Bloomington, IL 61701 (309) 557-2444 (local) Exchange privilege: Yes		Dean Witter/Sears Tax-Free Daily Inc Dean Witter/Sears US Govt MM Dean Witter Tax-Exempt Secs Dean Witter US Govt Securities Dean Witter World Wide Investment	MM MM MU BD FO
Country Capital Growth Fund Country Capital Income Fund	ST BA	Delaware Distributors Ten Penn Center Plaza Philadelphia, PA 19103 (215) 988-1333 (local) (800) 523-4640 (nationwide) Exchange privilege: Yes	
Cowen & Co. Financial Square New York, NY 10005 (212) 495-6000 (local) (800) 221-5616 (out of state) Exchange privilege: Yes		Delaware Group Cash Reserve Delaware Group Decatur Fund-I Delaware Group Decatur Fund-II Delaware Group Delaware Fund Delaware Group DelCap—Concept I Delaware Group Delchester Hi Yld-I Delaware Group Government—Inc Delaware Group Tax-Free—Money Delaware Group Tax-Free—USA Delaware Group Tax-Free—USA Ins Delaware Group Treasury Res—Inv Delaware Group Trend Fund DMC Tax-Free Income Trust-PA	MM ST ST BA ST BD BD MM MU MU BD ST MU
Cowen Income + Growth Fund Standby Tax-Exempt Reserve Fund	ST MM		
Craig-Hallum 701 Fourth Avenue South Minneapolis, MN 55415 (800) 331-4923 (nationwide) Exchange privilege: No			
General Securities	ST	Diversified Securities P.O. Box 357 Long Beach, CA 90801 (213) 595-7711★ (local) Exchange privilege: No	
Criterion Distributors 1000 Louisiana Houston, TX 77002-5098 (800) 999-3863 (local) (800) 231-4645 (out of state) Exchange privilege: Yes		Investors Research Fund	ST
Criterion Bond-Investment Quality Criterion Bond-US Govt High Yield Criterion Income-Commerce Inc Shs Criterion Lowry Market Timing Criterion Pilot Fund Criterion Special Convertible Secs Criterion Special Global Growth Criterion Sunbelt Growth Fund Criterion Technology Fund Current Interest—Money Market Current Interest—Tax-Free	BD BD BA ST ST BA FO ST ST MM MM	Dividend Growth Fund 107 North Adams Street Rockville, MD 20850 (301) 251-1002★ (local) (800) 638-2042 (out of state) Exchange privilege: Yes	
		Dividend/Growth-Dividend	ST
Dean Witter Reynolds One World Trade Center New York, NY 10048 (212) 938-4554 (local) (800) 221-2685 (out of state) Exchange privilege: Yes		Dodge & Cox One Post Street 35th Floor San Francisco, CA 94104 (415) 434-0311 (local) Exchange privilege: Yes	
Active Assets Money Trust Active Assets Tax-Free Trust Dean Witter American Value Fund Dean Witter Calif Tax-Free Income Dean Witter Convertible Secs Dean Witter Developing Growth Secs Dean Witter Dividend Growth Secs Dean Witter Government Secs Plus Dean Witter High Yield Secs Dean Witter Natural Resource Dev Dean Witter NY Tax-Free Income Dean Witter Option Income Trust Dean Witter/Sears Liquid Asset	MM MM ST MU BA ST ST BD BD ST MU ST MM	Dodge & Cox Balanced Fund Dodge & Cox Stock Fund	BA ST
		Dolphin FRIC Convertible Fund 10900 Wilshire Boulevard Los Angeles, CA 90024 (213) 824-7609 (local) Exchange privilege: No	
		Dolphin FRIC Convertible Fund	BA
		Drexel Burnham Lambert 60 Broad Street New York, NY 10004	

FIGURE 19–5   (concluded)

Distributor	Type of Fund	Distributor	Type of Fund
(212) 480-6000★ (local)		Dreyfus New York Tax-Exempt MM	MM
(800) 221-3290 (out of state)		Dreyfus Short-Intermediate Tax-Ex	MU
Exchange privilege: Yes		Dreyfus Strategic Aggressive Inv LP	ST
		Dreyfus Strategic Income	BD
DBL Cash Fund—Money Market	MM	Dreyfus Strategic Investing	ST
DBL Tax-Free Fund—Limited Term	MU	Dreyfus Strategic World Investing LP	FO
DBL Tax-Free Fund—Long-Term	MU	Dreyfus Tax-Exempt Bond Fund	MU
DBL Tax-Free Fund—Money Market	MM	Dreyfus Tax-Exempt Money Market	MM
Drexel Burnham Fund	ST	Dreyfus Third Century Fund	ST
Drexel Series—Convertible Secs	ST	Dreyfus US Govt Intermed Secs LP	BD
Drexel Series—Emerging Growth	ST	First Lakeshore Diversified Asset	BA
Drexel Series—Government Securities	BD	First Lakeshore T-E Money Market	MM
Drexel Series—Growth	ST	General Money Market Fund	MM
Drexel Series—Option Income	ST	General NY Tax-Ex Intermed Bond	MU
Fenimore International Fund Equity	FO	General Tax-Exempt Money Market	MM
		Westwood Fund	ST
		Eaton Vance Distributors	
		24 Federal Street	
		Boston, MA 02110	
Dreyfus Service Corp		(617) 482-8260 (local)	
600 Madison Avenue		(800) 225-6265 (out of state)	
New York, NY 10022		Exchange privilege: Yes	
(718) 895-1206 (local)			
(800) 645-6561 (out of state)		Eaton & Howard Stock Fund	ST
Exchange privilege: Yes		Eaton Vance California Municipals	MU
		Eaton Vance Government Oblig	BD
Dreyfus A Bonds Plus	BD	Eaton Vance Growth Fund	ST
Dreyfus California Tax-Exempt Bond	MU	Eaton Vance High Income Trust	BA
Dreyfus California Tax-Exempt MM	MM	Eaton Vance High Yield	BD
Dreyfus Capital Value Fund	ST	Eaton Vance High Yield Municipals	MU
Dreyfus Convertible Securities Fund	BA	Eaton Vance Income Fund of Boston	BA
Dreyfus Fund	ST	Eaton Vance Investors Fund	BA
Dreyfus General Aggressive Growth	ST	Eaton Vance Muni Bond Fund	MU
Dreyfus General Calif Tax-Ex Money	MM	Eaton Vance Special Equities Fund	ST
Dreyfus General NY Tax-Ex Money	MM	Eaton Vance Tax-Free Reserves	MM
Dreyfus General Tax-Exempt Bond	MU	Eaton Vance Total Return Trust	ST
Dreyfus GNMA Fund	BD	Leverage Fund of Boston	ST
Dreyfus Growth Opportunity Fund	ST	Nautilus Fund	ST
Dreyfus Index Fund	ST	Vance, Sanders Special Fund	ST
Dreyfus Insured Tax-Exempt Bond	MU	Eclipse Financial Services	
Dreyfus Intermediate Tax-Ex Bond	MU	P.O. Box 2196	
Dreyfus Leverage Fund	ST	Peachtree City, GA 30269	
Dreyfus Liquid Assets	MM	(404) 631-0414 (local)	
Dreyfus Massachusetts Tax-Ex Bond	MU	(800) 872-2710 (out of state)	
Dreyfus MM Instruments—Govt Secs	MM	Exchange privilege: No	
Dreyfus New Leaders Fund	ST		
Dreyfus New York Insured T-E Bond	MU	Eclipse Equity Fund	ST
Dreyfus NY Tax-Exempt Bond Fund	MU		
Dreyfus NY Tax-Ex Intermed Bond	MU		

★Will accept collect calls.
Source: Reprinted by permission of *Forbes* Magazine, September 5, 1988, p. 254, © Forbes Inc., 1988.

Growth Funds.   The pursuit of capital appreciation is the emphasis here. This class of funds includes those called aggressive growth funds and those concentrating on more-stable and predictable growth. Both types invest primarily in common stock. Aggressive funds concentrate on speculative issues, emerging small companies, and "hot" sectors of the economy and frequently use financial leverage to magnify returns. Regular growth funds generally invest

FIGURE 19–6   WIESENBERGER INVESTMENT COMPANIES SERVICE REPORTS

T. ROWE PRICE NEW ERA FUND, INC.

The investment objective of the fund is long-term growth of capital. It may seek this in any industry, but its current portfolio consists largely of securities of companies in the energy sources area, forest products, precious metals and other metals and minerals; other basic commodities, and companies which own or develop land. Investments in companies which provide consumer products and services are included, as well as companies operating in technological areas, such as the manufacture of labor-saving machinery and instruments.

At the 1986 year-end, the fund had 85.1% of its assets in common stocks, of which the major portion was in five industry groups: science & technology (14.6% of assets), diversified resources (10.5%), integrated petroleum (10.4%), diversified metals (8.5%) and precious metals (7.6%). The five largest common stock holdings were Salomon (4.6% of assets), IBM (4.4%), Newmont Mining (4.1%), Dow Chemical (3.5%) and Digital Equipment (3.4%). The rate of portfolio turnover during the latest fiscal year was 32.4% of average assets. Unrealized appreciation amounted to 25.7% of year-end total net assets.

Statistical History

				AT YEAR-ENDS					ANNUAL DATA			
			Net Asset		——— % of Assets in ———			Income	Capital			
	Total Net	Number of	Value Per		Cash &	Bonds &	Com-	Div-	Gains	Expense		
	Assets	Share-	Share	Yield	Equiv-	Pre-	mon	idends	Distribu-	Ratio	Offering Price ($)	
Year	($)	holders	($)	(%)	alent	ferreds	Stocks	($)	tion ($)	(%)	High	Low
1986	496,242,331	39,248	17.76	2.4	15	—	85	0.50	3.25	0.73	20.84	17.45
1985	529,469,479	42,102	18.67	3.4	8	—	92	0.68	1.41†	0.72	18.87	15.67
1984	471,995,371	45,828	17.13	3.3	10	—	90	0.61	1.29†	0.68	18.94	15.14
1983	485,072,775	47,214	18.44	4.4	12	6	82	0.81	0.072	0.68	18.60	14.97
1982	411,506,259	46,422	15.53	4.6	11	—	89	0.863	3.045	0.71	19.35	11.38
1981	436,197,041	44,712	19.34	3.4	20	—	80	0.672	1.489	0.64	25.53	17.87
1980	571,568,790	41,463	25.27	1.9	10	1*	89	0.47	0.362	0.63	27.23	14.58
1979	330,817,793	30,172	17.45	2.3	15	—	85	0.38	0.388	0.67	17.45	11.15
1978	189,827,658	28,600	11.66	2.7	7	—	93	0.316	0.254	0.73	12.79	9.66
1977	198,186,550	32,680	11.00	2.2	8	—	92	0.244	0.03	0.67	11.66	10.25
1976	245,158,364	35,574	11.74	2.4	6	3*	91	0.279	—	0.68	11.74	10.00

* Includes a substantial proportion in convertible issues.
† Includes short-term capital gains of $0.45 in 1984; $0.67 in 1985.

An assumed investment of $10,000 in this fund, with capital gains accepted in shares and income dividends reinvested, is illustrated below. The explanation in the introduction to this section must be read in conjunction with this illustration.

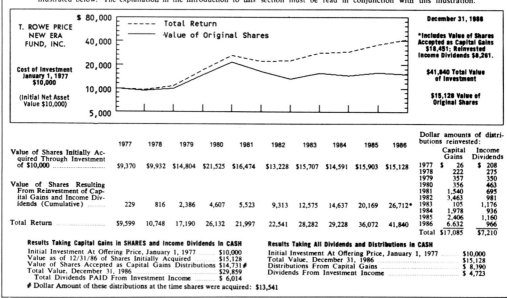

T. ROWE PRICE NEW ERA FUND, INC.

Cost of Investment January 1, 1977 $10,000

(Initial Net Asset Value $10,000)

December 31, 1986

*Includes Value of Shares Accepted as Capital Gains $18,451; Reinvested Income Dividends $8,261.

$41,840 Total Value of Investment

$15,128 Value of Original Shares

	1977	1978	1979	1980	1981	1982	1983	1984	1985	1986
Value of Shares Initially Acquired Through Investment of $10,000	$9,370	$9,932	$14,804	$21,525	$16,474	$13,228	$15,707	$14,591	$15,903	$15,128
Value of Shares Resulting From Reinvestment of Capital Gains and Income Dividends (Cumulative)	229	816	2,386	4,607	5,523	9,313	12,575	14,637	20,169	26,712*
Total Return	$9,599	10,748	17,190	26,132	21,997	22,541	28,282	29,228	36,072	41,840

Dollar amounts of distributions reinvested:

	Capital Gains	Income Dividends
1977	$ 26	$ 208
1978	222	275
1979	357	350
1980	356	463
1981	1,540	695
1982	3,463	981
1983	105	1,176
1984	1,978	936
1985	2,406	1,160
1986	6,632	966
Total	$17,085	$7,210

Results Taking Capital Gains in SHARES and Income Dividends In CASH

Initial Investment At Offering Price, January 1, 1977 ...... $10,000
Value as of 12/31/86 of Shares Initially Acquired $15,128
Value of Shares Accepted as Capital Gains Distributions $14,731#
Total Value, December 31, 1986 ...... $29,859
 Total Dividends PAID From Investment Income ...... $ 6,014
Dollar Amount of these distributions at the time shares were acquired: $13,541

Results Taking All Dividends and Distributions In CASH

Initial Investment At Offering Price, January 1, 1977 ...... $10,000
Total Value, December 31, 1986 ...... $15,128
Distributions From Capital Gains ...... $ 8,390
Dividends From Investment Income ...... $ 4,723

in common stocks of more-stable firms. They are less inclined to stay fully invested in stocks during periods of market decline, seldom use aggressive techniques like leverage, and tend to be long-term in orientation.

The best way to determine the type of growth fund is to carefully examine the fund's prospectus and current portfolio.

Growth with Income.   A number of large, growing firms pay steady dividends. Their stocks are attractive to investors interested in capital growth potential with a base of dividend or interest income. Funds that invest in such stocks are less volatile and risky than growth funds investing in small companies paying low or no dividends.

Balanced Funds.   These funds combine investments in common stock and bonds and often preferred stock. They try to provide income plus some capital appreciation. Funds that invest in convertible securities are also considered balanced, since the convertible security is a hybrid fixed-income security with the opportunity for appreciation if the underlying common stock rises.

Bond Funds.   Income-oriented investors have always been attracted to bonds. Because bonds represent a contractual obligation on the part of the issuer to the bondholder, they normally offer a certain return. But as pointed out in Chapter 10, rising interest rates can undercut the market value of all classes of fixed-income securities. During the 1970s and early 1980s, a time of intense interest-rate fluctuations, many bondholders watched the principal value of even their "safe" government bonds drop to 75 percent of face value. Bonds held in mutual funds were affected by the same market forces. Returns from bonds are historically lower than those from stocks, and bond funds are no exception.

Bond mutual funds can be roughly subdivided into corporate, government, and municipal funds.

Some corporate bond funds are particularly targeted to low-rated, high-yielding bonds. These funds are termed *junk bond funds*. They may have a yield 4 or 5 percent over the typical corporate bond fund but also possess greater risk in terms of potential default by the securities in the bond portfolio.

Because municipal bond funds buy only tax-exempt securities, interest income to shareholders is free of federal tax. Special tax-exempt funds also have been established for the benefit of investors in states with high state and local income taxes. For example, fund managers of New York municipal bond funds establish portfolios of tax-exempt securities issued within the boundaries of that state. Under current tax law, interest income from these funds is exempt from federal, state, and local taxes for New York residents—a very appealing feature to high-bracket taxpayers.

Sector Funds.   Special funds have been created to invest in specific sectors of the economy. Sector funds exist for such areas as energy, medical technology, computer technology, leisure, and defense.

Because stock performance of companies within a particular industry, or sector, tend to be positively correlated, these funds offer investors less diversification and higher loss/reward potential.

Investors should be cautious of the initial offering of new sector funds. An initial offering usually occurs after the sector has already been the subject of intense interest based on recent spectacular performance. As a result, stocks in that sector are often fully priced or overpriced.

Foreign Funds.   As noted in Chapter 18, investors seeking participation in foreign markets and foreign securities confront a number of obstacles, but the rewards can be remarkable. The mutual fund industry has made overseas investing convenient by establishing funds whose policies mandate investing on a global basis (Templeton World Fund), within the markets of a particular locale (Canadian Fund, Inc.), or within a region (Merrill Lynch Pacific). One fund even specializes in Third World countries.

Foreign funds as a group outperformed all other kinds of mutual funds in the 1980s. A listing of some important international funds is presented in Table 19–3.

Specialty Funds.   Some mutual funds have specialized approaches that do not fit neatly into any of the preceding categories. Their names are often indicative of their investment objectives or policies: the Sunbelt Fund, the Phoenix Fund (rising from the ashes?), the Calvert Social Investment Fund, and United Services Gold Shares, to name just a few.

There is even a "fund of funds" (FundTrust) that manages a portfolio of different mutual fund shares.

Owing to some fund managers' poor record in attempting to outperform the market, a number of funds have taken up the maxim that "if you can't beat 'em, join 'em!" Calling themselves index funds, these mutual funds establish portfolios that replicate some major market index, such as the S&P 500. Fund performance is almost exactly correlated with performance of "the market."

Matching Investment Objectives with Fund Types

Investors must consider how much volatility of return they can tolerate. Investors who require safety of principal with very little deviation of returns should choose money market funds first and bond funds second. They should also expect to receive lower returns based on historical evidence. While aggressive growth stock funds provide the highest return, they also have the biggest risk.

Liquidity objectives are met by all mutual funds since redemption can take place any time. If investors need income, bond funds provide the highest annual current yield, while aggressive growth funds provide the least. Growth-income and balanced funds are most appropriate for investors who want growth of principal with moderate current income.

TABLE 19–3 INTERNATIONALLY ORIENTED FUNDS

Name of Fund	Open- or Closed-End	Load (L) No-Load (NL)	Where Invested
Canadian Fund, Inc.	Open	L	Canada
International Investors Incorporated	Open	L	Gold mines
G. T. Pacific Fund, Inc.	Open	NL	Asia (Japan, Hong Kong, etc.)
Fidelity Overseas Fund	Open	L	Worldwide
Kemper International Fund, Inc.	Open	L	Worldwide
Merrill Lynch Pacific	Open	L	Far East
Merrill Lynch International Holdings	Open	L	Worldwide
Putnam International Equities Fund	Open	L	Worldwide
Research Capital Fund, Inc.	Open	L	Foreign mining
T. Rowe Price International Fund, Inc.	Open	NL	Worldwide
Scudder International Fund, Inc.	Open	NL	Worldwide
Strategic Investments Fund, Inc.	Open	L	South African gold mines
Templeton World Fund, Inc.	Open	L	Worldwide
Transatlantic Fund, Inc.	Open	NL	Worldwide
United International Growth Fund	Open	L	Worldwide
ASA Limited	Closed	Commission	South African gold mines
Japan Fund	Closed	Commission	Japan
U.S. and Foreign Securities	Closed	Commission	Worldwide

Many investors diversify by fund type. For example, at one stage in the business cycle, an investor may want to have 50 percent of his assets in common stocks, 35 percent in bonds, 10 percent in money market funds, and 5 percent in an international stock fund. These percentages could change as market conditions change. If interest rates are expected to decline, it would be better to have a higher percentage of bonds and fewer money market securities. Investing with a "family of funds" allows the investor a choice of many different types of funds and the privilege of switching between funds at no or low cost. Some of the larger families of funds are managed by American Capital, Dreyfus Group, Federated Funds, Fidelity Investments, T. Rowe Price Funds, and the Vanguard Group. In addition, most major retail brokerage firms, such as Merrill Lynch, Dean Witter, Prudential-Bache, and Shearson Lehman Hutton have families of mutual funds.

Each mutual fund has a unique history and management team. There is no guarantee that past performance will be repeated in the future. Investors should check on a fund's longevity of management, historical returns, trading history, and management expenses. A very key instrument in providing information in this regard is the fund prospectus.

THE PROSPECTUS

The Investment Companies Act of 1940, which established the standard of practice for all investment companies, requires that the purchaser of fund shares be provided with a current **prospectus**. This document is furnished to the SEC for its inspection prior to public distribution. It contains information deemed essential by the SEC in providing "full disclosure" to potential investors regarding the fund's investment objectives and policies, risks, management, expenses, and current portfolio. The prospectus also provides information on how shares can be purchased and redeemed, sales and redemption charges (if any), and shareholders' services. Other fund documents are available to the public on request including the Statement of Additional Information and the fund's annual and quarterly reports.

While it is beyond the scope of this chapter to provide a complete discourse on interpreting a prospectus, investors need to understand the following essentials.

Investment Objectives and Policies.   This section is always found in the beginning of the prospectus. It usually describes the fund's basic objectives:

> The Fund will invest only in securities backed by the full faith and credit of the U.S. Government. At least 70% of the Fund's assets will be invested in certificates issued by the Government National Mortgage Association (GNMA). It may also purchase other securities issued by the U.S. Government, its agencies, or instrumentalities as long as these securities are backed by the full faith and credit of the U.S. Government.

The prospectus normally goes on to detail investment management policies under which it intends to operate—typically with regard to the use of borrowed money, lending of securities, or something like the following:

> The Fund may, under certain circumstances, sell covered call options against securities it is holding for the purpose of generating additional income.

Portfolio (or "Investment Holdings").   This section lists the securities held by the fund as of the date indicated. Since investment companies are only required to publish their prospectuses every 16 months, the information is probably dated. Still, the portfolio should be compared to the stated objectives of the fund to see if they are consistent.

Management Fees and Expenses.   Besides sales and redemption charges, the prospectus also provides information and figures on fund managers' reimbursement and the fund's housekeeping expenses. Annual fees for the investment advisor are expressed as a percentage of the average daily net assets during the year (usually 0.50 percent). Other expenses include legal and auditing fees, the cost of preparing and distributing annual reports and proxy statements, directors' fees, and transaction expenses. When lumped together with investment advisory fees, a fund's total yearly expenses typically range from 1 to 1.2 percent of fund assets. Experienced mutual fund investors cast a jaundiced eye on funds with expense ratios that exceed this figure.

A controversial SEC ruling—Rule 12b-1—allows mutual funds to use fund assets for marketing expenses. Since marketing expenses have nothing to do with advancing shareholders' interests and everything to do with increasing the managers' fees, investors should be alert to this in the prospectus.

Turnover Rate.   A portion of the expense ratio results from commissions paid when the fund manager trades securities. A number of mutual funds trade aggressively in pursuit of profits; others do just the opposite. In one year, the Fidelity Contrafund had a 243 percent turnover rate; the rate for the Oppenheimer Special Fund was 9 percent.

In reality, transaction costs amount to more than just commissions, and they are not always accounted for in the expense ratio. When fund assets are traded over-the-counter, the dealer's spread between the bid and asked price is not considered. Nor is the fact that large block trades—the kind mutual funds usually deal in—are made at less-favorable prices than are smaller volume transactions.

The prospectus contains audited data on the turnover rate, the expense ratio, and other important data in the section on per-share income and capital changes.

DISTRIBUTION AND TAXATION

The selling of securities by a mutual fund's portfolio results in capital losses or gains for the fund. After netting losses against gains, most mutual funds distribute capital gains to shareholders annually.

Funds with securities that pay dividends or interest also have a source of investment income. The fund, in turn, distributes such income to shareholders either quarterly or annually.

A fund that distributes at least 90 percent of its net investment income and capital gains is not subject, as an entity, to federal income tax. It is simply acting as a "conduit" in channeling taxable sources of income from securities held in the portfolio to the fund's shareholders. Most funds operate this way. But while the mutual fund may not be subject to taxation, its shareholders are.

At the end of every calendar year, each fund shareholder receives a Form 1099-DIV. This document notifies the shareholder of the amount and tax status of his or her distributions.

When the investor actually sells (redeems) his or her shares in a mutual fund, another form of taxable event takes place. It is precisely the same as if stocks or bonds or other securities were sold. The investor must consider the cost basis, the selling price, and any gain or loss and appropriately report the tax consequences on his or her tax form.

SHAREHOLDER SERVICES

Most mutual funds offer a number of services to their shareholders. Some can be used in the investor's strategy. Common services include:

Automatic reinvestment. The fund reinvests all distributions (usually without sales charge). Shares and fractional shares are purchased at the net asset value. Purchases are noted on annual and periodic account statements.

Safekeeping. While shareholders are entitled to receive certificates for all whole shares, it is often convenient to let the fund's transfer agent hold the shares.

Exchange privilege. Many large management companies sponsor a family of funds. They may have five or more funds, each dedicated to a different investment objective. Within certain limits, shareholders are free to move their money between the different funds in the family on a net asset value basis. Transfers can often be done by telephone; a minimal charge is common to cover paperwork. These exchanges are taxable events.

Pre-authorized check plan. Many people lack the discipline to save or invest regularly. Those who recognize this trait in themselves can authorize a management company to charge their bank account for predetermined amounts on a regular basis. The amounts withdrawn are used to purchase new shares.

Systematic withdrawal plan. Every shareholder plans to convert his shares into cash at some time in the future. The investor who wants to receive a regular amount of cash each month or quarter can do so by arranging for such a plan. The fund sells enough shares on a periodic basis to meet the shareholder's cash requirement.

Checking privileges. Most money market mutual funds furnish shareholders with checks that can be drawn against the account, provided that the account balance is above a minimum amount (usually $1,000). A per-check minimum of $250 to $500 is commonplace.

INVESTMENT FUNDS, LONG-TERM PLANNING, AND DOLLAR-COST AVERAGING

Perhaps more than anything else, the liquidity and conveniences inherent in mutual funds lend themselves best to financial-planning activities. The most-important of these is the gradual accumulation of capital assets.

Using the pre-authorized check plan, investors can have fixed amounts regularly withdrawn from their checking accounts to purchase fund shares. Just as savers can have their banks channel a specific amount from their pay-checks into savings accounts, so too can investors make regular, lump-sum

SOME FUNDS LIKE QUICK-CHANGE ARTISTS

A few mutual funds are starting to embrace the troublesome clients that most people in the industry regard as Fund Enemy No. 1.

These pesky customers are the market timers—money managers who dash in and out of mutual funds with the aim of catching broad market swings.

The chief complaint about timers is that their frenzied switching forces funds to buy and sell huge blocks of securities, penalizing other, often smaller, shareholders. Many fund groups have accelerated their anti-timer campaigns in recent months by imposing limits and fees on switches.

Timers are drawn most often to no-load fund groups—which don't levy an upfront sales charge—because they offer the fastest and cheapest way to switch in and out of stocks.

Fund operators over the years have abruptly kicked out a number of timers who have failed to heed pleas to curb switching. Fidelity Investments of Boston has responded with a series of ever-tighter restrictions on switches. They now are limited to four a year for most funds and five a month for its select funds, which usually invest in one industry and are intended to handle much faster turnover.

The timers' strategy continues to pose a basic dilemma. Says the president of one firm: "If we trade too often, we get kicked out by the funds. And if we don't perform, we get kicked out by our clients."

Source: *The Wall Street Journal*, November 22, 1988, p. C1. Reprinted by permission of *The Wall Street Journal*, © Dow Jones & Company, Inc., 1988. All rights reserved.

fund share purchases on an "out of sight, out of mind" basis. Reinvestment of distributions enhances this strategy.

What distinguishes the mutual fund from the bank savings strategy is the fact that fund shares are purchased at different prices. The investor can even use a passive strategy known as **dollar-cost averaging**. It applies to the acquisition of individual stocks, mutual fund shares, or other assets. Under dollar-cost averaging, the investor buys a fixed dollar's worth of a given security at regular intervals regardless of the security's price or the current market outlook. By using such a strategy, investors concede that they cannot outsmart the market. The intent of dollar-cost averaging is to avoid the common practice of buying high and selling low. In fact, investors are forced to do the opposite. Why? They commit a fixed-dollar amount each month (or year) and buy shares at the current market price. When the price is high, they are buying relatively fewer shares; when the price is low, they are accumulating more shares. An example is presented in Table 19–4. Suppose we use the pre-authorized check plan to channel $200 per month into a mutual fund. The price ranges from a low of $12 and a high of $19.

Note that when the share price is relatively low, such as in January, we purchased a larger number of shares than when the share prices were high, as in April. In this case, the share price ended in June at the same price it was in January ($12).

TABLE 19–4	DOLLAR-COST AVERAGING			
	(1)	(2)	(3)	(4)
	Month	Investment	Share Price	Shares Purchased
	January	$200	$12	16.66
	February	200	14	14.28
	March	200	16	12.50
	April	200	19	10.52
	May	200	15	13.33
	June	200	12	16.66
	Totals	1,200	88	83.95

What would happen if the price merely ended up at the average price over the six-month period? The values in column 3 total $88, so the average price over six months is $14.67 ($88/6). Actually, we would still make money under this assumption because the average *cost* is less than this amount. Consider that we invested $1,200 and purchased 83.95 shares. This translates to an average cost of only $14.29.

$$\frac{\text{Investment}}{\text{Shares purchased}} = \frac{\$1,200}{83.95} = \$14.29$$

The reason that the average cost ($14.29) is less than the average price ($14.67) is that we bought relatively more shares at the lower price levels, and they weighed more heavily in our calculations. Thus, under dollar-cost averaging, investors can come out ahead over a period of investing fixed amounts, even if the share price ends up less than the average price paid on each transaction.[4]

The only time investors lose money is if the eventual price falls below the average cost ($14.29) and they sell at that point. While dollar-cost averaging has its advantages, it is not without criticism. Clearly, if the share price continues to go down over a long period of time, it is hard to make a case for continued purchases. However, the long-term performances of most diversified mutual funds has been positive, and long-term investors may find this strategy useful in accumulating capital assets for retirement, childrens' education funds, or other purposes.

---

[4]This does not consider any sales charges or commissions, which could be important.

EVALUATING FUND PERFORMANCE

Throughout this chapter, we have made reference to mutual fund performance. We will now consider the issue more directly by actually comparing mutual fund performance to the market in general.

A good place to start the current discussion is to return to Figure 19–4, which covers *Forbes* mutual fund information. Direct your attention to total returns in the middle two columns of the table. The first column shows the average annual total return over a 10-year period (1978–1988).[5] This total return figure is composed of capital appreciation plus dividend income. Notice at the top of the table that the S&P 500 Stock Average (a measure of the total market) had an average annual return of 16.9 percent, while the Forbes Stock Fund Composite (a measure of mutual funds) had a value of 16.4 percent.

The next column shows return data for the most recently reported 12 months. While both the S&P 500 Stock Average and the Forbes Stock Fund Composite were both negative, the funds slightly outperformed the market in that their losses were less (minus 5.6 percent versus minus 6.9 percent). As you can infer from the data, sometimes mutual funds do better than the market and sometimes they do not. If we were to look at many other 10-year and 1-year periods, we would reach similar conclusions.

You can also identify the performance of individual funds over comparable time periods. Examples of strong performers are the Dodge and Cox Stock Fund and Eaton Vance Growth Fund. Underperformers include many of the Drexel Series funds.

You should also notice that grades are assigned to fund performance in the first two columns on the far left-hand side of Figure 19–4. The grades are based on how the funds performed in up and down markets over the last 10 years. The grades theoretically range from A + to F (though there are no A +'s or F's in the particular funds in this exhibit). Most investors like funds that do reasonably well in both types of markets. Of course, if you feel strongly that the market is about to move in one direction rather than another, you will adjust your emphasis accordingly.

One warning: Past performance in no way guarantees future performance. A fund that did well in the past may do poorly in the future and vice versa. Nevertheless, all things being equal, investors generally prefer funds that have a prior record of good performance. Investors do not know whether the funds can reproduce the performance, but at least the funds have indicated the capacity for good returns in the past. The same cannot be said for underperformers.

Lipper Mutual Fund Performance Averages

As you can see in Figure 19–7, mutual fund performance can also be broken down by type of fund (this information was previously presented in Chapter 3 under the discussion of stock market index and averages, but now takes on

---

[5]Actually, the period covers mid-1978 to mid-1988.

greater meaning in the current context of mutual fund evaluation). You can observe how certain types of funds did better or worse and how their performance changed with differing periods for measurement. Overall in this example, small growth companies and science and technology funds appeared to do well. The Lipper Mutual Fund Performance Averages are published weekly in *Barron's*.

Computing Total Return on Your Investment

Assume you own a fund for a year and want to determine the total return on your investment. There are three potential sources of return:

Change in net asset value (NAV).

Dividends distributed.

Capital gains distributed.[6]

FIGURE 19–7   LIPPER MUTUAL FUND PERFORMANCE AVERAGES (Managed Indexes Total Reinvested Cumulative Performance)

Number of Current Funds	Type of Fund	12/03/87–4/14/88		8/20/87–4/14/88		4/16/87–4/14/88		Year-to-Date 12/31/87–4/14/88		Weekly 4/07/88–4/14/88	
154	Capital appreciation	+	19.29%	−	16.85%	−	8.05%	+	8.16%	−	1.18%
245	Growth funds	+	19.53	−	17.33	−	7.36	+	8.19	−	1.33
62	Small company growth	+	29.28	−	15.70	−	10.07	+	14.50	−	0.79
174	Growth and income	+	15.55	−	14.14	−	4.09	+	7.39	−	1.23
49	Equity income	+	9.21	−	10.98	−	4.47	+	5.22	−	1.04
684	General equity funds average	+	18.56	−	15.81	−	6.71	+	8.32	−	1.20
8	Health funds	+	21.75	−	20.70	−	13.53	+	8.32	−	1.61
14	Natural resources	+	22.82	−	15.51	−	4.26	+	12.19	−	0.36
26	Science and technology	+	24.38	−	19.97	−	12.29	+	8.46	−	1.01
10	Utility funds	+	6.96	−	5.66	−	1.05	+	5.53	−	0.97
43	Specialty funds	+	18.21	−	17.35	−	10.26	+	9.93	−	0.91
33	Global funds	+	17.82	−	11.51	−	2.51	+	9.03	+	0.82
55	International funds	+	20.63	−	4.27	+	4.05	+	11.98	+	2.20
25	Gold-oriented funds	−	10.80	−	26.10	−	23.26	−	8.74	+	0.00
4	Option growth funds	+	6.56	−	1.00	+	10.37	+	1.58	−	0.67
20	Option income funds	+	15.25	−	12.59	−	3.77	+	6.88	−	1.57
922	All equity funds average	+	17.81	−	15.28	−	6.62	+	8.15	−	0.86
26	Conv. sec funds	+	13.60	−	10.23	−	5.54	+	8.66	+	0.08
39	Balanced funds	+	11.46	−	8.39	−	1.11	+	5.46	−	0.84
19	Income funds	+	7.31	−	1.30	+	1.77	+	5.37	−	0.46
25	World income funds	+	5.47	+	13.09	+	12.91	+	1.35	+	0.68
416	Fixed income funds	+	4.62	+	4.27	+	4.32	+	3.54	−	0.11
1447	All funds average	+	13.46	−	8.93	−	3.08	+	6.62	−	0.60
1447	All funds-median	+	13.20	−	10.73	−	2.51	+	5.65	−	0.58
	Number of funds in universe		1,406		1,346		1,284		1,419		1,428

Source: *Barron's* April 18, 1988, p. 131. Reprinted by permission of *Barron's*, © Dow Jones & Company, Inc., 1988. All rights reserved.

[6]This represents net capital gains that the fund actually had as a result of selling securities. They are distributed to shareholders.

Assume the following:

Beginning NAV	$14.05
Ending NAV	15.10
Change in NAV (+)	1.05
Dividends distributed	.40
Capital gains distributed	.32
Total return	$ 1.77

In this instance, there is a total return of $1.77. Based on a beginning NAV of $14.05, the return is 12.60 percent.

$$\frac{\text{Total return}}{\text{Beginning NAV}} = \frac{\$\,1.77}{\$14.05} = 12.60 \text{ percent}$$

As a further consideration, assume that instead of taking dividends and capital gains income in cash, you decide to automatically reinvest the proceeds to purchase new mutual fund shares. To compute the percentage return in this instance, you must compare the total value of your ending shares to the total value of your beginning shares. Assume you owned 100 shares to start, and you received a total of 72 cents in dividends plus capital gains per share (see prior example). This would allow you to reinvest $72 (100 shares × $.72 per share). Further assume you bought new shares at an average price of $14.40 per share. This would provide you with five new shares.[7]

$$\frac{\text{Dividends and capital gains allocated to the account}}{\text{Average purchase price of new shares}} =$$

$$\frac{\$72}{\$14.40} = 5 \text{ new shares}$$

In comparing the ending and beginning value of the investment based on the example in this section, we show the following:

$$\text{Total return} = \frac{\left(\begin{array}{c}\text{Number of}\\\text{ending shares}\\\times \text{ Ending price}\end{array}\right) - \left(\begin{array}{c}\text{Number of}\\\text{beginning shares}\\\times \text{ Beginning price}\end{array}\right)}{\text{Number of beginning shares} \times \text{ Beginning price}}$$

$$= \frac{(105 \times \$15.10) - (100 \times \$14.05)}{(100 \times \$14.05)}$$

$$= \frac{\$1,585.50 - \$1,405}{\$1,405}$$

---

[7]In this case, the number of new shares came out to be a whole number. It is also possible to buy fractional shares in a mutual fund.

$$= \frac{\$180.50}{\$1,405} = 12.85\%$$

$$(19\text{--}2)$$

In determining whether the returns computed in this section are adequate, you must compare your returns to the popular market averages and to the returns on other mutual funds. You must also consider the amount of risk you are taking. While the returns might be considered quite good for a conservative fund, such might not be the case for an aggressive, growth-oriented fund.

APPENDIX 19–A: UNIT INVESTMENT TRUSTS (UITS)

Unit investment trusts (UITs) are investment companies organized for the purpose of purchasing a pool of securities—usually tax-exempt municipal bonds. UITs issue units to investors, representing a proportionate interest in the assets of the trust. Investors also receive a proportionate share in the interest or dividends received by the trust.

Unit investment trusts are passive investments. They normally purchase assets and hold them for the benefit of owners for a specified period of time.

To understand UITs better, consider the following hypothetical example. Nuveen, Inc.—a prominent firm in this field—announces the formation of the next in their series of tax-exempt unit trusts: Nuveen Series 200. Through advertising and selling agents, Nuveen will raise $4 million; investors will pay approximately $1,000 per unit. After deducting 3 to 4 percent for sales commissions, Nuveen will use the remaining cash to purchase large blocks of municipal securities from 10 to 20 different issuers. Once this diversified pool of bonds is acquired, Nuveen will play a passive role. It will collect and pass on to unit holders all interest payments received and all principal repayments resulting from maturing or recalled bonds. While UITs usually hold bonds until maturity, the trust custodian may sell off bonds whose future ability to pay interest and principal is altered by events.

The majority of UITs formed in the past decade have invested in tax-exempt securities. Often, trusts are formed to purchase tax-exempt securities from issuers in specific, high-tax states, such as New York, Massachusetts, and Minnesota. Unit holders residing in these states expect to receive a stream of income exempt from federal, state, and local taxation.

Even unit investment trusts dedicated to tax-exempt bonds have different investment objectives. Some deal strictly in long-term, high-rated issues. Others seek higher yields by purchasing issues with low ratings.

Units of a trust are redeemable under terms set forth in the prospectus. In most cases, this means that a unit holder can sell units back to the trust at their net asset value, which is the current market value of each trust unit.

A secondary market for unit trusts is evolving among broker-dealers. Investors seeking to acquire or sell units can sometimes find a better deal in this market. However, most investors in UITs do not intend to redeem early.

Investors in UITs benefit by professional selection of securities, by diversification, and by avoiding the housekeeping chores of collecting coupon payments. As a large buyer, a UIT can usually purchase securities at a better price than the individual who buys in small lots.

Essential Difference between a Unit Investment Trust and a Mutual Fund

There is an important difference between UITs and mutual funds. UITs are formed with the intention of keeping all the initially purchased assets until maturity. The investment strategy, as described above, is strictly passive. A UIT of $4 million with a 10-year life will draw interest over that time period, while only cashing in bonds as they mature and returning the funds to the investors. The UIT will cease to exist after 10 years. Because of the features just described, there is very little interest-rate risk associated with UITs. Since all bonds are intended to be held until maturity, the investor can be reasonably well assured of recovering his initial investment (plus interest). The fact that interest rates and bond prices are changing at any point in time during the life of the UIT makes little difference.[1]

A bond-oriented mutual fund has no such assurance of recovering the initial investment. First, mutual funds have no stipulated life. Second, the bonds in the portfolio are actively managed and frequently sold off before their maturity dates at large profits or losses. Thus, the purchaser of a bond-oriented mutual fund may experience large capital gains or losses as well as receiving interest income.

The message is that if preservation of capital is of paramount importance to the investor, the UIT may be a better investment than a mutual fund. Of course, if one thinks interest rates are going down and bond prices up, the bond-oriented mutual fund would be a better investment.

---

[1]Of course, if the investor needs to redeem his shares before the end of the life of the trust, there will be fluctuations in value.

APPENDIX 19B: MUTUAL FUND ADDRESSES

AAL Mutual Funds
*222 West College Ave.—Appleton, WI
54919-0007*
Telephone: (414) 734-5721
AAL Capital Growth Fund
AAL Income Fund

Accrued Equities
*295 Northern Boulevard—Great Neck, NY
11021*
(516) 466-0808★ (local)
New Alternatives Fund

Acorn Fund
*2 North LaSalle Street—Suite 500—
Chicago, IL 60602-3790*
(312) 621-0630★ (local)
(800) 922-6769 (out of state)
Acorn Fund

Adtek Fund
*4920 West Vliet Street—Milwaukee, WI
53208*
(414) 257-1842 (local)
Adtek Fund

Advest Group
280 Trumbull Street—Hartford, CT 06103
(800)842-3807 (local)
(800)243-8115 (out of state)
Advantage Government securities★
Advantage Growth Fund
Advantage Income Fund

AFA Distributors
50 Broad Street—New York, NY 10004
(212) 482-8100★ (local)
National Aviation & Technology
National Telecom & Technology

Afuture Fund
*617 Willowbrook Lane—West Chester, PA
19382*
(215) 344-7910★ (local)

(800) 523-7594 (Out of state)
Afuture Fund

AIM Advisors, Inc.
*Eleven Greenway Plaza, Suite 1919—
Houston, TX 77046*
*Telephone: (800) 231-0803 or
(800) 392-9681*
AIM Charter Fund
AIM Constellation Fund
AIM High Yield Securities
AIM Limited Maturity Treasury Shares
AIM Summit Fund
AIM Weingarten Fund

Fred Alger & Co.
75 Maiden Lane—New York, NY 10038
(800) 992-3863 (nationwide)
Alger Fund-Growth
Alger Fund-Small Capitalization

ALPS Securities, Inc.
*600 17th Street, Suite 1605 South—
Denver, CO 80202*
*Telephone: (303) 623-2577 or
(800) 666-0367*
Westcore Basic Value Fund
Westcore Intermediate-Term Bond Fund

AMA Group
*5 Sentry Parkway West, Suite 120—
Blue Bell, PA 19422*
*Telephone: (215)825-0400 or
(800) 523-0864*
AMA Growth Fund Global Growth
   Portfolio
AMA Income Fund US Government
   Income Plus Portfolio

AMEV Advisers, Inc.
P.O. Box 64284—St Paul, MN 55164
*Telephone: (612) 738-4000 or
(800) 872-2638*

★Funds with asterisks will accept collect calls.

AMEV Capital Fund
AMEV Growth Fund
AMEV U.S. Government Securities
  Fund

Advest, Inc.
One Commercial Plaza—Hartford, CT
06103
Telephone: (203) 525-1421 or
(800) 243-8115

Advantage Government Securities Fund
Advantage Income Fund

Alliance Capital Mgt
P.O. Box 4089—Secaucus, NJ 07094
Telephone: (201) 319-4000 or
(800) 227-4618

Alliance Balanced Shares
Alliance Bond Fund High Yield
  Portfolio
Alliance Bond Fund Monthly Income
  Portfolio
Alliance Bond Fund U.S. Government
  Portfolio
Alliance Convertible Fund
Alliance Counterpart Fund
Alliance Dividend Shares
Alliance Fund
Alliance International Fund
Alliance Mortgage Securities Income
  Fund
Alliance Quasar Fund
Alliance Short-Term Multi-Market
Alliance Technology Fund
Surveyor Fund

American Capital—Asset Mgt
2800 Post Oak Blvd—Houston, TX 77056
Telephone: (713) 993-0500 or
(800) 421-5666

American Capital Comstock Fund
American Capital Corporate Bond Fund
American Capital Enterprise Fund
American Capital Federal
  Mortgage Trust
American Capital Government Securities
American Capital Harbor Fund
American Capital High Yield
  Investments
American Capital Over-The-Counter
  Securities
American Capital Pace Fund

American Capital Venture Fund
Fund of America
Provident Fund for Income

American Fund Advisors, Inc.
50 Broad Street—New York, NY 10004
Telephone: (212) 482-8100 or
(800) 654-0001

National Aviation & Technology
  Corporation
National Telecommunications &
  Technology Fund

American Funds
333 South Hope Street—Los Angeles, CA
90071
Telephone: (213) 486-9200 or
(800) 421-0180

AMCAP Fund
American High Income Trust
American Mutual Fund
Bond Fund of America
Capital Income Builder
EuroPacific Growth Fund
Intermediate Bond Fund of America
Investment Company of America
New Economy Fund
New Perspective Fund
US Government Guaranteed Securities
Washington Mutual Investors Fund

American Funds
Four Embarcadero Center, Suite 1800—
San Francisco, CA 94111
Telephone: (415) 421-9360 or
(800) 421-0180

American Balanced Fund
Fundamental Investors
Growth Fund of America
Income Fund of America

American Growth Fund Sponsors
410 17th Street—Suite 800—Denver, CO
80202
Telephone: (303) 623-6137★ (local)
(800) 525-2406 (out of state)

American Growth Fund

American Investors
PO Box 2500—Greenwich, CT 06836
Telephone: (203) 531-5000★ (local)
(800) 243-5353 (out of state)

American Investors Growth Fund

American Pension Distributors
PO Box 2529—Lynchburg, VA 24501
Telephone: (800) 533-4115★ (local)
(800) 544-6060 (out of state)

API Trust—Growth

AMEV Investors
PO Box 64284—St Paul, MN 55164
Telephone: (612) 738-4000★ (local)
(800) 872-2638 (out of state)

AMEV Advantage—Asset Allocation
AMEV Advantage—Capital Apprec
AMEV Capital Fund
AMEV Fiduciary Fund
AMEV Growth Fund
AMEV US Govt Securities Fund

Amway Management Co
7575 East Fulton Road—Ada, MI 49355
Telephone: (800) 346-2670 (nationwide)

Amway Mutual Fund

Analytic Inv't Mgt
2222 Martin Street, #230—Irvine, CA 92715
Telephone: (714) 833-0294

Analytic Optioned Equity Fund

Angeles Securities
10301 West Pico Boulevard—Los Angeles, CA 90064
Telephone: (213) 277-4900★ (local) or
(800) 421-4374 (out of state)

FPA Capital Fund
FPA Paramount Fund
FPA Perennial Fund

Aquila Distributors
200 Park Avenue—Suite 4515—
New York, NY 10017
(212) 697-6666★ (local)
(800) 228-4227 (out of state)

Churchill Tax-Free Fund of Kentucky
Hawaiian Tax-Free Trust
Tax-Free Fund of Colorado
Tax-Free Trust of Arizona
Tax-Free Trust of Oregon

Armstrong Associates
1445 Ross Avenue LB 212—Dallas, TX 75202
(214) 720-9101 (local)

Armstrong Associates

Arnhold and S. Bleichroeder
45 Broadway—New York, NY 10006
Telephone: (212) 943-9200 or
(800) 451-3623

First Eagle Fund of America

Arnold Inv't Counsel
700 N. Water Street—Milwaukee, WI 53202
Telephone: (414) 271-7870 or
(800) 443-6544

Primary Trend Fund

Associated Planners Security
1925 Century Park East—Suite 1900—
Los Angeles, CA 90067
(213) 553-6740★ (local)
(800) 950-2748 (out of state)

Associated Planners Stock Fund

Axe-Houghton Mgt
400 Benedict Ave—Tarrytown, NY 10591
Telephone: (914) 631-8131 or
(800) 366-0444

Axe-Houghton Fund B
Axe-Houghton Income Fund
Axe-Houghton Stock Fund

Bailard, Biehl & Kaiser
2755 Campus Drive, Suite 300—San Mateo, CA 94403
Telephone: (415) 571-6002 or (800) 882-8383

Bailard, Biehl & Kaiser Diversa Fund

Robert W Baird & Co
777 East Wisconsin Avenue—Milwaukee, WI 53202
(414) 765-3500★ (local)
(800) 792-2473 (out of state)

Baird Blue Chip Fund
Baird Capital Development Fund

Baron Asset Fund
450 Park Avenue—New York, NY 10022
(212) 759-7700 (local)
(800) 992-2766 (out of state)

Baron Asset Fund

Bartlett Capital Trust
36 East Fourth Street—Cincinnati, OH 45202
(800) 327-4363 (local)
(800) 543-0863 (out of state)

Bartlett Capital Trust-Basic Value
Bartlett Capital Trust-Fixed Income

Baxter Financial Corp
3380 N.E. 29th Avenue—Light House Point, FL 33064
Telephone: (212) 425-9655 or (800) 221-5588
Philadelphia Fund

Beacon Hill Mutual Fund
75 Federal Street—Boston, MA 02110
(617) 482-0795 (local)
Beacon Hill Mutual Fund

Benham Capital Management
755 Page Mill Road—Palo Alto, CA 94304
(800) 982-6150 (local)
(800) 227-8380 (out of state)
Benham Calif Tax-Free—High Yield
Benham Calif Tax-Free—Insured
Benham Calif Tax-Free—Intermediate
Benham Calif Tax-Free—Long-Term
Benham Calif Tax-Free—MM
Benham Government Inc—GNMA
Benham National Tax-Free—MM
Benham Target Maturities—2015
Benham Treasury Note Fund
Capital Preservation Fund
Capital Preservation Fund II

Berger Associates
899 Logan Street—Suite 211—Denver, CO 80203
(303) 837-1020★ (local)
(800) 333-1001 (out of state)
One Hundred Fund

Berwyn Fund
1189 Lancaster Avenue—Berwyn, PA 19312
(215) 640-4330★ (local)
Berwyn Fund

Boston Co Funds Distributor
One Boston Place—Boston, MA 02108
(800) 225-5267 (nationwide)
Boston Co Capital Appreciation Fund
Boston Co Tax-Free Muni-Mass MM
Boston Co Special Growth Fund
Boston Co Tax-Free Muni-Money

Boston Company Managed Income Fund
Boston Company Special Growth Fund

Boston Co Advisors
One Boston Place—Boston, MA 02108
Telephone: (617) 573-9300 or (800) 441-7379
Galaxy Bond Fund
Galaxy Equity Fund

Brandywine Fund
PO Box 4166—Greenville, DE 19807
(302) 656-6200 (local)
Brandywine Fund

Bridges Investment Fund
8401 West Dodge Road—Omaha, NE 68114
(402) 397-4700 (local)
Bridges Investment Fund

Alex Brown & Sons
135 East Baltimore Street—Baltimore, MD 21202
(301) 727-1700 (local)
(800) 638-2596 (out of state)
Alex Brown Cash Reserve—Prime
Flag Investors Corporate Cash Trust
Flag Investors Emerging Growth
Flag Investors International Trust
Flag Investors T-F Cash Reserve Shs
Flag Investors Telephone Income

Bruce Fund
20 North Wacker Drive—Suite 1425—Chicago, IL 60606
(312) 236-9160 (local)
Bruce Fund

Bull & Bear Group, Inc
11 Hanover Square—New York, NY 10005
Telephone: (212) 363-1100 or (800) 847-4200
Bull & Bear Capital Growth Fund
Bull & Bear Gold Investors
Bull & Bear High Yield Fund
Bull & Bear U.S. Government
   Guaranteed Securities Fund

Burnham Securities, Inc
25 Broadway, 12th Floor—New York, NY 10004

Telephone: (212) 483-1461 or
(800) 223-4522

Burnham Fund
Fenimore International Fund Equity
  Series

Calamos Financial Services
2001 Spring Road—Suite 750—Oakbrook,
IL 60521
(312) 571-7115 (local)
(800) 323-9943 (out of state)

Calamos Convertible Income

California Investment Trust
44 Montgomery Street—Suite 2200—
San Francisco, CA 94104
(800) 225-8778 (local)
(800) 826-8166 (out of state)

California Tax-Free Income
California Tax-Free MM

Calvert Group
1700 Pennsylvania Avenue NW—
Washington, DC 20006
(301) 951-4800★ (local)
(800) 368-2748 (out of state)

Calvert Ariel Growth Fund
Calvert Fund—Equity
Calvert—Washington Area Growth
Calvert Social Inv—Equity
Calvert Tax-Free Reserves—Limited
Calvert Social Inv—Managed Growth
Calvert Tax Free Reserves—Limited
Calvert Tax-Free Reserves—MM
Money Management Plus—Tax Free

Capstone Asset Planning Co
PO Box 3167—Houston, TX 77253-3167
(713) 750-8000 (local)
(800) 262-6631 (out of state)

Capstone Equity Guard
Cashman Farrell Value Fund
Fund of the Southwest
PBHG Growth Fund
US Trend Fund

Cardinal Mgt Corp
155 East Broad Street, 11th Floor—
Columbus, OH 43215
Telephone: (614) 464-6817 or
(800) 848-7734

Cardinal Fund
Cardinal Government Guaranteed Fund

Carnegie Capital Mgt Co.
1100 The Halle Building, 1228 Euclid
Avenue—Cleveland, OH 44115-1831
Telephone: (216) 781-4440 or
(800) 321-2322

Carnegie Cappiello Trust Growth Series
Carnegie Cappiello Trust Total Return
  Series
Carnegie Government Securities Trust
High Yield Government

Centennial Capital Corp
3410 South Galena Street—Denver, CO
80201
(800) 356-3556 (local)
(800) 525-7048 (out of state)

Centennial Tax-Exempt Trust
Daily Cash Accumulation Fund

Century Shares Trust
One Liberty Square—Boston, MA 02109
(617) 482-3060★ (local)
(800) 321-1928 (out of state)

Century Shares Trust

Cigna Securities
1350 Main Street—Springfield, MA 01103
(413) 784-0100 (local)

Cigna Aggressive Growth Fund
Cigna Growth Fund
Cigna High Yield Fund
Cigna Income Fund
Cigna Municipal Bond Fund
Cigna Tax-Exempt Cash Fund
Cigna Utilities
Cigna Value Fund

CJ Lawrence, Morgan Grenfell
1290 Avenue of the Americas—
New York, NY 10104-0101
Telephone: (301) 727-1700 or
(800) 334-1898

C.J. Lawrence Total Return US
Treasury Fund Shares

Clayton Brown & Assoc. Inc.
500 W. Madison Suite 3000—Chicago, IL
60606
Telephone: (312) 559-3000

First Trust Fund U.S. Government
  Series

Colonial Mgt Assoc.
One Financial Center—Boston, MA 02111-2690
Telephone: (617) 426-3750 or (800) 345-6611

Colonial Advanced Strategies Gold
  Trust
Colonial Corporate Cash Trust I
Colonial Corporate Cash Trust II
Colonial Diversified Income Fund
Colonial Fund
Colonial Government Securities
  Plus Trust
Colonial Growth Shares Trust
Colonial High Yield Securities Trust
Colonial Income Plus Fund
Colonial Income Trust
Colonial Small Stock Index Trust
Colonial U.S. Government Trust
Colonial VIP High Income Fund

Colorado Tax Exempt
717 17th Street—Suite 2500—Denver, CO 80202
(303) 292-0300 (local)

Colorado Double Tax Exempt Fund

Columbia Funds Management Co
PO Box 1350—Portland, OR 97207-1350
(800) 452-4512 (local)
(800) 547-1707 (out of state)

Columbia Daily Income Co
Columbia Fixed Income Securities
Columbia Growth Fund
Columbia Municipal Bond Fund
Columbia Special Fund

Command Money Market Funds
115 Broadway—16th Floor—New York, NY 10006
(212) 306-0521 (local)
(800) 222-4321 (out of state)

Command Money Fund
Command Tax-Free Fund

Common Sense Distributors
3100 Breckenridge Boulevard—Building 400—Duluth, GA 30199-0001
(404) 381-2668 (local)
(800) 888-3863 (out of state)

Common Sense—Growth
Common Sense—Growth & Income

Composite Research & Mgt Co.
W. 601 Riverside Avenue, 9th Floor—Spokane, WA 99201
Telephone: (509) 353-3400 or (800) 543-8072

Composite Bond & Stock Fund
Composite Growth Fund
Composite Income Fund
Composite U.S. Government Securities

Concord Financial Group
156 West 56th Street—Suite 1902—New York, NY 10019
(212) 492-1600★ (local)
(800) 332-3863 (out of state)

Pacific Horizon—Aggressive Growth
Pacific Horizon—Calif Tax-Ex Bond
Pacific Horizon—Government MM
Pacific Horizon—Money Market
Pacific Horizon—Tax-Exempt MM

Connecticut Mutual Financial Services
140 Garden Street—MS 240—Hartford, CT 06154
(203) 727-6500★ (local)
(800) 243-2501 (out of state)

Connecticut Mutual—Growth
Connecticut Mutual—Total Return

Conway, Luongo, Williams
3000 Sand Hill Road—Menlo Park, CA 94025
(415) 854-9150★ (local)

Adam Investors

Copley Financial Services Corp
PO Box 3287—Fall River, MA 02722
(508) 674-8459★ (local)

Copley Fund

Cortland Distributors
315 State Street—Hackensack, NJ 07601
(201) 342-6066 (local)
(800) 433-1918 (out of state)

Aim General Money Market
Aim Tax-Free Money Market

Counsellors Securities
466 Lexington Avenue—New York, NY 10017-3147
(212) 878-0600 (local)
(800) 888-6878 (out of state)

Counsellors Capital Appreciation
Counsellors Emerging Growth Fund
Counsellors New York Tax-Exempt

Country Capital Management Co
PO Box 2222—Bloomington, IL 61701
(309) 557-2444 (local)

Country Capital Growth Fund
Country Capital Income Fund

Cowen & Co
Financial Square—New York, NY 10005
(212) 495-6000 (local)
(800) 221-5616 (out of state)

Cowen Income + Growth Fund
Cowen Opportunity Fund
Standby Tax-Exempt Reserve Fund

Craig-Hallum
701 Fourth Avenue South-10th Floor—
Minneapolis, MN 55415
(612) 332-1212 (local)
(800) 331-4923 (out of state)

General Securities

D.H. Blair Advisors, Inc.
777 West Putnam Ave.—Greenwich, CT
06836
Telephone: (203) 531-5000 or
(800) 243-5353

American Investors Growth Fund

DFA Investment Dimensions Group
1299 Ocean Avenue, Suite 650—
Santa Monica, CA 90401
Telephone: (213) 395-8005

DFA Five-Year Government Fixed
Income Portfolio

Dain Bosworth
790 North Milwaukee Street—Milwaukee,
WI 53202
(414) 347-7276 (local)
(800) 432-7856 (out of state)

Heartland Group-Value Fund

Dean Witter Reynolds
One World Trade Center—New York, NY
10048
(212) 392-2500 (local)
(800) 869-3863 (out of state)

Active Assets Money Trust
Active Assets Tax-Free Trust

Dean Witter American Value Fund
Dean Witter Calif Tax-Free Income
Dean Witter Convertible Secs
Dean Witter Developing Growth Secs
Dean Witter Dividend Growth Secs
Dean Witter Government Secs Plus
Dean Witter High Yield Secs
Dean Witter Managed Assets
Dean Witter Natural Resource Dev
Dean Witter NY Tax-Free Income
Dean Witter Option Income Trust
Dean Witter/Sears Liquid Asset
Dean Witter/Sears Tax-Free Daily Inc
Dean Witter/Sears US Govt MM
Dean Witter Tax-Exempt Secs
Dean Witter US Govt Securities
Dean Witter Utilities Fund
Dean Witter Value-Added Mkt
Dean Witter World Wide Investment

Delaware Distributors
10 Penn Center Plaza—Philadelphia, PA
19103
(215) 988-1333 (local)
(800) 523-4640 (out of state)

Delaware Group Cash Reserve
Delaware Group Decatur Fund—I
Delaware Group Decatur Fund—II
Delaware Group Delaware Fund
Delaware Group Delcap Fund—I
Delaware Group Delchester H-Y—I
Delaware Group Govt—Govt Income
Delaware Group Tax-Free Fund—USA
Delaware Group Tax-Free— Money
Delaware Group Treasury—Investors
Delaware Group Trend Fund
Delaware Group Value Fund
DMC Tax-Free Income Trust—PA

Delfi Mgt, Inc.
3801 Kennett Pike, Greenville Center
C-200—Wilmington, DE 19807
Telephone: (302) 652-3091 or
(800) 441-9490

ISI Trust
Sigma Capital Shares
Sigma Income Shares
Sigma Investment Shares
Sigma Trust Shares
Sigma Venture Shares

Dillon, Read Capital, Inc.
535 Madison Avenue—New York, NY
10022
Telephone: (212) 906-7658 or
(800) 356-6454
DR Equity Fund

Diversified Securities
PO Box 357—Long Beach, CA 90801
(213) 595-7711★ (local)
Investors Research Fund

Dividend Growth Fund
107 North Adams Street—Rockville, MD
20850
(301) 251-1002★ (local)
(800) 638-2042 (out of state)
Dividend/Growth—Dividend

Dodge &Cox
One Post Street—35th Floor—
San Francisco, CA 94104
(415) 434-0311 (local)
Dodge & Cox Balanced Fund
Dodge & Cox Stock Fund

Dolphin FRIC Convertible Fund
10900 Wilshire Boulevard—Suite 1050—
Los Angeles, CA 90024
(213) 824-7609 (local)
Dolphin FRIC Convertible Fund

Drexel Burnham Lambert
25 Broad Street—New York, NY 10004
(212) 480-6000★ (local)
(800) 221-3290 (out of state)
DBL Cash Fund—Money Market
DBL Tax-Free Fund—Money Market
Drexel Burnham Fund
Drexel Series—Convertible Secs
Drexel Series—Emerging Growth
Drexel Series—Government Securities
Drexel Series—Growth
Drexel Series—Option Income
Drexel Series—Priority Selection
Fenimore International Fund Equity

Dreyfus Service Corp
600 Madison Avenue—New York, NY
10022
(718) 895-1206 (local)
(800) 645-6561 (out of state)
Dreyfus A Bonds Plus
Dreyfus California Tax-Exempt Bond

Dreyfus California Tax-Exempt MM
Dreyfus Capital Value Fund
Dreyfus Convertible Securities Fund
Dreyfus Fund
Dreyfus GNMA Fund
Dreyfus Growth Opportunity Fund
Dreyfus Index Fund
Dreyfus Insured Tax-Exempt Bond
Dreyfus Intermediate Tax-Ex Bond
Dreyfus Leverage Fund
Dreyfus Liquid Assets
Dreyfus Massachusetts Tax-Ex Bond
Dreyfus MM Instruments—Govt Secs
Dreyfus New Jersey Tax-Ex Bond
Dreyfus New Leaders Fund
Dreyfus New York Insured T-E Bond
Dreyfus NY Tax-Exempt Bond Fund
Dreyfus NY Tax-Ex Intermed Bond
Dreyfus New York Tax-Exempt MM
Dreyfus Strategic Aggressive Inv LP
Dreyfus Strategic Investing
Dreyfus Strategic World Investing LP
Dreyfus Tax-Exempt Bond Fund
Dreyfus Tax-Exempt Money Market
Dreyfus Third Century Fund
First Prairie Diversified Asset Fund
First Prairie T-E Money Market
General Aggressive Growth
General Calif Tax-Exempt Money
General Money Market Fund
General NY T-E Intermed Bond
General NY Tax-Exempt Money
General Tax-Exempt Money Market
Premier Calif Tax-Exempt Bond
Premier Tax-Exempt—Maryland
Premier Tax-Exempt—Connecticut
Premier Tax-Exempt—Massachusetts
Premier Tax-Exempt—Ohio
Westwood Fund

Eaton Vance Distributors
24 Federal Street—Boston, MA 02110
(617) 482-8260 (local)
(800) 225-6265 (out of state)
Eaton Vance California Municipals
Eaton Vance Government Oblig
Eaton Vance Growth Fund
Eaton Vance High Income Trust
Eaton Vance High Yield Municipals
Eaton Vance Income Fund of Boston
Eaton Vance Investors Fund
Eaton Vance Special Equities Fund

Eaton Vance Stock Fund
Eaton Vance Tax-Free Reserves
Eaton Vance Total Return Trust
Nautilus Fund
Vance, Sanders Special Fund

Eclipse Financial Services
PO Box 2196—Peachtree City, GA 30269
(404) 631-0414★ (local)
(800) 872-2710 (out of state)

Eclipse Equity Fund

Empire of America Adv Serv
320 Empire Tower—Buffalo, NY 14202
Telephone: (716) 855-7890 or
(800) 221-1238

Big E Pathfinder Government Plus Fund

Enterprise Fund Distributors
1200 Ashwood Parkway—Suite 290—
Atlanta, GA 30338
(404) 396-8118★ (local)
(800) 432-4320 (out of state)

Enterprise Group—Growth
Enterprise Group—Growth & Income
Enterprise Group—International Grow

EQSF Advisers
767 Third Avenue—5th Floor—New York,
NY 10017
(212) 888-6685 (local)
(800) 834-3400 (out of state)

Equity Strategies Fund

Equitable Funds
1755 Broadway—Location 3D—New York,
NY 10019
(212) 641-8100 (local)
(800) 541-2150 (nationwide)

Equitable Funds—Balanced Fund
Equitable Funds—Growth

Equitec Securities
PO Box 2470—7677 Oakport Street—
Oakland, CA 94614
(800) 869-8008 (nationwide)

Equitec Siebel Aggressive Growth
Equitec Siebel Total Return Fund
Equitec Siebel US Government Secs

Equity Services
National Life Drive—Montpelier, VT
05604
(802) 229-3900★ (local)
(800) 233-4332 (out of state)

Sentinel Balanced Fund
Sentinel Bond Fund
Sentinel Common Stock Fund
Sentinel Growth Fund

Evergreen Asset Management
2500 Westchester Avenue—Purchase, NY
10577
Telephone: (914) 694-2020

Evergreen Fund
Evergreen Total Return Fund

Excel Advisors
16955 Via Del Campo—Suite 120—
San Diego, CA 92127
(618) 485-9400 (local)
(800) 333-9235 (out of state)

Excel Midas Gold Shares & Bullion
Excel Value Fund

Fahnestock & Co
50 Broad Street—Suite 237—New York,
NY 10004
(212) 425-9655 (local)
(800) 221-5588 (out of state)

Eagle Growth Shares
Philadelphia Fund

Fairfield Group
200 Gibraltar Road—Horsham, PA 19044
(800) 222-3429 (local)
(800) 441-3885 (out of state)

St Clair Equity—Capital Growth Fund
St Clair Tax-Free—Money Market
Viking Equity Index Fund—General

Fairmont Fund
1346 South Third Street—Louisville, KY
40208
(502) 636-5633 (local)
(800) 262-9936 (out of state)

Fairmont Fund

FBL Investment Advisory Services
5400 University Avenue—
West Des Moines, IA 50265
(800) 422-3175 (local)
(800) 247-4170 (out of state)

FBL—Growth Common Stock

Federated Securities Corp
Federated Tower—Pittsburgh, PA
15222-3779
(412) 288-1900★ (local)
(800) 245-2423 (out of state)

American Leaders Fund
Convertible Securities & Income
Federated GNMA Trust
Federated Growth Trust
Federated High Income Securities
Federated High Quality Stock Fund
Federated High Yield Trust
Federated Income Trust
Federated Intermediate Government
Federate Short-Intermed Govt
Federated Stock & Bond Fund
Federate Stock Trust
Federated Tax-Free Income Fund
Federated Tax-Free Trust
Federated Utility Trust
FT International
Fund for US Govt Securities
Government Income Securities
Liberty US Govt Money Market
AT Ohio Tax-Free Money Fund
Progressive Income Equity
Tax-Free Instruments Trust

Fidelity Distributors Corp

82 Devonshire Street—Boston, MA 02109
(800) 544-6666 (nationwide)

Fidelity Balanced Fund
Fidelity Blue Chip Growth Fund
Fidelity Calif Tax-Free—High Yield
Fidelity Calif Tax-Free—Insured
Fidelity Calif Tax-Free—MM
Fidelity Canada Fund
Fidelity Capital Appreciation
Fidelity Cash Reserves
Fidelity Connecticut Tax-Free
Fidelity Contrafund
Fidelity Convertible Securities Fund
Fidelity Daily Income Trust
Fidelity Destiny Portfolio I
Fidelity Destiny Portfolio II
Fidelity Equity Income Fund
Fidelity Europe Fund
Fidelity Flexible Bond Fund
Fidelity Freedom Fund
Fidelity Fund
Fidelity Ginnie Mae
Fidelity Global Bond Fund
Fidelity Government Securities Fund
Fidelity Growth & Income
Fidelity Growth Company
Fidelity High Income Fund

Fidelity Intermediate Bond Fund
Fidelity International Growth & Inc
Fidelity Magellan Fund
Fidelity Mass Tax-Free—High Yield
Fidelity Mass Tax-Free—MM
Fidelity Mortgage Securities
Fidelity New Jersey Tax-Free—MM
Fidelity NY Tax-Free—High Yield
Fidelity NY Tax-Free—Insured
Fidelity NY Tax-Free—Money Market
Fidelity OTC Portfolio
Fidelity Overseas Fund
Fidelity Pacific Basin Fund
Fidelity Pennsylvania T-F—Hi Yld
Fidelity Pennsylvania Tax-Free—MM
Fidelity Plymouth—Growth Oppor
Fidelity Plymouth—Income & Grow
Fidelity Puritan Fund
Fidelity Real Estate Investment
Fidelity Select—Air Transportation
Fidelity Select—American Gold
Fidelity Select—Biotechnology
Fidelity Select—Broadcast & Media
Fidelity Select—Brokerage & Inv
Fidelity Select—Capital Goods
Fidelity Select—Chemicals
Fidelity Select—Computers
Fidelity Select—Electric Utilities
Fidelity Select—Electronics
Fidelity Select—Energy
Fidelity Select—Energy Service
Fidelity Select—Financial Services
Fidelity Select—Food & Agriculture
Fidelity Select—Health Care
Fidelity Select—Industrial Materials
Fidelity Select—Leisure
Fidelity Select—Medical Delivery
Fidelity Select—Money Market
Fidelity Select—Paper & Forest Prod
Fidelity Select—Prec Metals & Mins
Fidelity Select—Prop & Casualty
Fidelity Select—Regional Banks
Fidelity Select—Retailing
Fidelity Select—Savings & Loan
Fidelity Select—Software & Computer
Fidelity Select—Technology
Fidelity Select—Telecommunications
Fidelity Select—Utilities
Fidelity Short-Term Bond
Fidelity Short-Term Government
Fidelity Special Situations—Initial

Fidelity Special Situations—Plymouth
Fidelity State-Tax Free—Michigan
Fidelity State-Tax Free—Minnesota
Fidelity State-Tax Free—Ohio
Fidelity Tax-Exempt—Money Market
Fidelity Tax-Free—Aggressive
Fidelity Tax-Free—High Yield
Fidelity Tax-Free—Insured
Fidelity Tax-Free—Ltd Term Munis
Fidelity Tax-Free—Municipal Bond
Fidelity Texas Tax-Free
Fidelity Trend Fund
Fidelity US Government Reserves
Fidelity Utilities Income
Fidelity Value Fund

Fiduciary Investment Co
230 South Tryon Street—Suite 345—
Charlotte, NC 28202
(704) 331-0710★ (local)
(800) 527-1578 (out of state)

Salem Funds—Growth

Fiduciary Management
225 East Mason Street—Milwaukee, WI
53202
(414) 226-4556★ (local)
(800) 338-1579 (out of state)

Fiduciary Capital Growth Fund

Financial Programs
PO Box 2040—Denver, CO 80201
(303) 779-1233 (local)
(800) 525-8085 (out of state)

Financial Dynamics Fund
Financial Industrial Fund
Financial Industrial Income Fund
Financial Strategic—Energy
Financial Strategic—European
Financial Strategic—Gold
Financial Strategic—Health Science
Financial Strategic—Leisure
Financial Strategic—Pacific Basin
Financial Strategic—Technology
Financial Strategic—Utilities
Financial Tax-Free Income Shares
Financial Tax-Free Money Fund

First Eagle Fund of America
45 Broadway—New York, NY 10006
(212) 943-9200★ (local)
(800) 451-3623 (out of state)

First Eagle Fund of America

First Investors Management Co
10 Woodbridge Center Drive—Woodbridge,
NJ 07095
(212) 208-6000 (local)
(800) 423-4026 (out of state)

First Investors Bond Appreciation
First Investors Discovery Fund
First Investors Fund for Growth
First Investors Fund for Income
First Investors Government Fund
First Investors High Yield Fund
First Investors International Secs
First Investors New York Tax-Free
First Investors Tax-Exempt Fund
First Investors Tax-Exempt MM
First Investors Value Fund

First Pacific Advisors
10301 West Pico Boulevard—Los Angeles,
CA 90064
Telephone: (213) 277-4900 or
(800) 421-4374

FPA Capital Fund
FPA Paramount Fund
FPA Perennial Fund

Flag Investors Funds
P.O. Box 515—Baltimore, MD 21203
Telephone: (301) 727-1700 or
(800) 767-3524

Flag Investors Emerging Growth Fund
Flag Investors Telephone Income Fund
Flag Investors Total Return US
   Treasury Shares

Flagship Financial
One First National Plaza—Suite 910—
Dayton, OH 45402
(800) 354-7447 (local)
(800) 227-4648 (out of state)

Flagship Tax-Ex—Arizona Double
Flagship Tax-Exempt—Conn Double
Flagship Tax-Ex—Georgia Double
Flagship Tax-Ex—Kentucky Triple
Flagship Tax-Exempt—Mich Triple
Flagship Tax-Exempt—NC Triple
Flagship Tax-Exempt—Ohio Double
Flagship Tax-Exempt—Penn Triple
Flagship Tax-Exempt—Tenn Double
Flagship Tax-Exempt—Va Double

Flex Funds
PO Box 7177—Dublin, OH 43017
(614) 766-7000★ (local)
(800) 325-3539 (out of state)

Flex-funds—Growth Fund
Flex-funds—Income & Growth Fund

44 Securities
26 Broadway—Suite 205—New York, NY 10004
(212) 248-8080 (local)
(800) 543-2620 (out of state)

44 Wall Street Equity Fund
44 Wall Street Fund

Founders Asset Management
3033 East First Avenue—Suite 810—Denver, CO 80206
(303) 394-4404 (local)
(800) 525-2440 (out of state)

Founders Blue Chip
Founders Equity Income Fund
Founders Frontier Fund
Founders Growth Fund
Founders Special Fund

Franklin Distributors
777 Mariner's Island Boulevard—San Mateo, CA 94404-1585
(800) 342-5236 (local)
(800) 632-2180 (out of state)

Franklin AGE High Income Fund
Franklin Arizona Tax-Free Income
Franklin Calif Insured Tax-Free Inc
Franklin Calif Tax-Exempt Money
Franklin Calif Tax-Free Income
Franklin DynaTech Fund
Franklin Equity Fund
Franklin Federal Tax-Free Income
Franklin Florida Tax-Free Income
Franklin Gold Fund
Franklin Growth Fund
Franklin High Yield Tax-Free Income
Franklin Income Fund
Franklin Insured Tax-Free Income
Franklin Managed Trust Rising Divs
Franklin Mass Insured Tax-Free Inc
Franklin Mich Insured Tax-Free Inc
Franklin Minn Insured Tax-Free Inc
Franklin Money Fund
Franklin New Jersey Tax-Free Inc
Franklin New York Tax-Ex Money

Franklin New York Tax-Free Income
Franklin Ohio Insured Tax-Free Inc
Franklin Option Fund
Franklin Oregon Tax-Free Income
Franklin Pennsylvania Tax-Free Inc
Franklin PR Tax-Free Income Fund
Franklin Tax-Exempt Money Fund
Franklin US Government Securities
Franklin Utilities Fund

Freedom Capital Management Corp
One Beacon Street—4th Floor—Boston, MA 02108
(800) 392-6037 (local)
(800) 225-6258 (out of state)

Freedom Cash Management
Freedom Equity Value Fund
Freedom Inv—Gold & Government
Freedom Inv—Government Plus
Freedom Inv—Regional Bank
Freedom Inv II—Global Fund
Freedom Inv II—Global Income +
Freedom Tax-Exempt Money
Tocqueville Fund

Friess Associates
3908 Kennett Pike—Greenville, DE 19807
Telephone: (302) 656-6200 or
(800) 338-1579

Brandywine Fund

Fund Source
230 Park Avenue., 13th Floor—New York, NY 10169
Telephone (212) 309-8400 or
(800) 845-8406

Fund Source International Equity

Fund Trust
P.O. Box 1641—Hartford, CT 06144-1641
Telephone (800) 344-9033

Fund Trust Growth & Income Fund
Fund Trust Income Fund

Fundamental Services
111 Broadway—Suite 1107—New York, NY 10006
(212) 608-6864★ (local)
(800) 225-6864 (out of state)

New York Muni Fund

Furman Selz Mager Dietz & Birney
230 Park Avenue—New York, NY 10169
(212) 309-8400★ (local)
(800) 845-8406 (out of state)
FFB Tax-Free Money Market Fund
Fund Source—International Equity
FundTrust—Aggressive Growth
FundTrust—Growth
FundTrust—Growth & Income
Olympus California Tax-Exempt
Olympus Equity Plus Fund
Olympus Option Income Plus Fund

G. R. Phelps & Co, Inc
140 Garden Street—Hartford, CT 06154
Telephone: (203) 727-6500 or
(800) 243-2501
Connecticut Mutual Total Return
  Account

GNA Investors Trust
Two Union Square, Suite 5600—Seattle,
WA 98111-0490
Telephone: (206) 625-1755 or
(800) 433-0684
GNA US Government Securities Fund

Gabelli & Co
PO Box 1634—Grand Central Station—
New York, NY 10163
(212) 490-3670 (local)
(800) 422-3554 (out of state)
Gabelli Asset Fund
Gabelli Growth Fund

GAM Funds
PO Box 2798—Boston, MA 02208
(617) 482-9300★ (local)
(800) 356-5740 (out of state)
GAM Global Fund
GAM International Fund
GAM Pacific Basin Fund

Gateway Investment Advisers
PO Box 458167—Cincinnati, OH 45245
(513) 248-2700★ (local)
(800) 354-6339 (out of state)
Gateway Growth Plus Fund
Gateway Option Index Fund

Gintel & Co
Greenwich Office Park 6—Greenwich, CT
06830
(203) 622-6400 (local)
(800) 243-5808 (out of state)
Gintel Capital Appreciation Fund
Gintel Erisa Fund
Gintel Fund

GIT Investment Services
1655 North Fort Myer Drive—Arlington,
VA 22209
(703) 528-6500 (local)
(800) 336-3063 (out of state)
GIT Equity Trust—Special Growth

Gradison & Co
580 Walnut Street—Cincinnati, OH 45202
(800) 582-7062 (local)
(800) 543-1818 (out of state)
Gradison Cash Reserves Trust
Gradison Established Growth Fund
Gradison Opportunity Growth Fund

Greenspring Fund
Suite 322, The Quadrangle—Village of
Cross Keys—Baltimore, MD 21210
(301) 435-9000★ (local)
Greenspring Fund

Growth Industry Shares
135 South LaSalle Street—Chicago, IL
60603
(312) 346-4830 (local)
(800) 635-2886 (out of state)
Growth Industry Shares

GT Global Financial Services
50 California Street—Suite 2700—
San Francisco, CA 94111-4624
(415) 392-6181★ (local)
(800) 824-1580 (out of state)
GT Global Growth—Europe
GT Global Growth—Intl
GT Global Growth—Japan
GT Global Growth—Pacific
GT Global Growth—Worldwide
GT Investment—Global Bond

Guardian Investor Services Corp
201 Park Avenue South—New York, NY
10003
(800) 221-3253 (nationwide)
Guardian Park Ave Fund

John Hancock Advisors

*101 Huntington Avenue—Boston, MA
02199*
(617) 375-1800 (local)
(800) 225-5291 (out of state)

John Hancock Bond Trust
John Hancock Global Trust
John Hancock Growth Trust
John Hancock Special Equities Trust
John Hancock Tax-Exempt Income
John Hancock US Govt Guar Mort
John Hancock US Govt Securities

Hartwell Funds

*515 Madison Avenue—31st Floor—New
York, NY 10022*
(212) 309-8400★ (local)
(800) 624-3863 (out of state)

Hartwell Emerging Growth
Hartwell Growth Fund

HCA Securities

One SeaGate—Toledo, OH 43666
(419) 247-2477 (local)
(800) 422-1050 (out of state)

Harbor Growth Fund
Harbor International
Harbor US Equities
Harbor Value

Heine Management Group

PO Box 830—Westport, CT 06881
(800) 522-2564 (local)
(800) 422-2564 (out of state)

LMH Fund

Heine Securities

*51 John F Kennedy Parkway—Short Hills,
NJ 07078*
(201) 912-2100★ (local)
(800) 448-3863 (out of state)

Mutual Series Fund—Beacon
Mutual Series Fund—Mutual Shares
Mutual Series Fund—Qualified

Heritage Asset Management

*880 Carillon Parkway—St Petersburg, FL
33716*
(800) 421-4184 (nationwide)

Heritage Capital Appreciation
Heritage Convertible Income—Grow

HT Insight Funds

345 Park Avenue—New York, NY 10154
(212)326-6656 (local)
(800) 854-8525 (out of state)

HT Insight—Convertible Fund
HT Insight—Equity Fund
HT Insight—Tax-Free MM Fund

Wayne Hummer & Co

*175 West Jackson Boulevard—Chicago, IL
60604*
(800) 972-5566 (local)
(800) 621-4477 (out of state)

Wayne Hummer Growth Fund

Huntington Investments

*251 South Lake Avenue—Suite 600—
Pasadena, CA 91101*
(818) 440-9688★ (local)
(800) 232-3310 (out of state)

International Cash—Global

IAI Funds

PO Box 357—Minneapolis, MN 55440
(612) 371-2884 (local)

IAI Apollo
IAI Bond Fund
IAI International Fund
IAI Regional Fund
IAI Stock Fund

IDEX Management

PO Box 5068—Clearwater, FL 34618
(813) 585-6565 (local)
(800) 237-3055 (out of state)

IDEX Fund
IDEX II
IDEX Fund 3

IDS Financial Services

IDS Tower 10—Minneapolis, MN 55440
(612) 372-3733 (local)
(800) 328-8300 (out of state)

IDS Bond Fund
IDS California Tax-Exempt Fund
IDS Cash Management Fund
IDS Discovery Fund
IDS Equity Plus
IDS Extra Income Fund
IDS Federal Income Fund
IDS Growth Fund
IDS High Yield Tax-Exempt Fund

IDS International Fund
IDS Managed Retirement Fund
IDS Minnesota Tax-Exempt Fund
IDS Mutual
IDS New Dimensions Fund
IDS New York Tax-Exempt Fund
IDS Precious Metals Fund
IDS Progressive Fund
IDS Selective Fund
IDS Stock Fund
IDS Strategy—Aggressive Equity
IDS Strategy—Equity
IDS Strategy—Income
IDS Strategy—Pan Pacific Growth
IDS Tax-Exempt Bond Fund
IDS Tax-Free Money Fund

Integrated Resources Asset Mgmt
10 Union Square East—New York, NY 10003
(212) 551-7125 (local)
(800) 821-5100 (out of state)

Home Investors Govt Guaranteed Inc
Integrated Capital Appreciation Fund
Integrated Equity—Aggressive Growth
Integrated Equity—Growth
Integrated Income—Convertible Secs
Integrated Multi-Asset—Total Return
Integrated Tax-Free—Money Market
Integrated Tax-Free—Stripes

Investment Research Corp.
410 17th Street, Suite 800—Denver, CO 80202
Telephone: (303) 623-6137 or
(800) 525-2406

American Growth Fund

Investors Research Fund, Inc.
P.O. Box 30—
Santa Barbara, CA 93102
Telephone: (805) 569-1011

Investors Research Fund

Investment Trust of Boston
399 Boylston Street—Boston, MA 02117
(617) 578-1388★ (local)
(800) 888-4823 (out of state)

Inv Trust of Boston Grow Opp
Inv Trust of Boston—Mass T-F

Investors Management Group
418 Sixth Avenue—720 Liberty Building—Des Moines, IA 50309
(515) 244-5426 (local)

IMG Stock Accumulation Fund

Investors Security Trust
110 Bank Street—Suffolk, VA 23434
(804) 539-2396★ (local)

Old Dominion Investors' Trust

Ivy Fund
40 Industrial Park Road—Hingham, MA 02043
(800) 235-3322 (nationwide)

Ivy Growth Fund
Ivy International Fund

Janus Capital
100 Fillmore Street—Suite 300—Denver, CO 80206
(303) 333-3863★ (local)
(800) 525-3713 (out of state)

Janus Fund
Janus Twenty Fund
Janus Venture Fund

Jefferson-Pilot Investor Services
PO Box 22086—Greensboro, NC 27420
(919) 378-2448 (local)
(800) 458-4498 (out of state)

JP Growth Fund

Jones & Babson
2440 Pershing Road—Kansas City, MO 64108
(816) 471-5200★ (local)
(800) 422-2766 (out of state)

Babson Bond Trust—Long Term
Babson Enterprise Fund
Babson Growth Fund
Babson Value Fund
Shadow Stock Fund
UMB Stock Fund
UMB Tax-Free Money Market

Edward D Jones & Co
201 Progress Parkway—Maryland Heights, MO 63043
(314) 851-2000★ (local)
(800) 441-0100 (out of state)

ED Jones Daily Passport Cash Trust

Kaufmann
17 Battery Place—Suite 2624—New York,
NY 10004
(212) 344-2661 (local)
(800) 237-0132 (out of state)

Kaufmann Fund

Keffer Capital Management
50 Monument Square—465 Congress
Street—Portland, ME 04101
(207) 879-1900 (local)

Warburg International Fund

Kemper Financial Services
120 South LaSalle Street—Chicago, IL
60603
(312) 781-1121★ (local)
(800) 621-1048 (out of state)

Cash Equivalent Fund—Govt
Cash Equivalent Fund—MM
Cash Equivalent Fund—T-E MM
Investment Portfolios—Divers Inc
Investment Portfolios—Equity
Investment Portfolios—Govt Plus
Investment Portfolios—High Yield
Investment Portfolios—Total Return
Kemper Blue Chip Fund
Kemper California Tax-Free Income
Kemper Diversified Income Fund
Kemper Growth Fund
Kemper High Yield Fund
Kemper Income & Capital Preserv
Kemper International Fund
Kemper Money Market—MM
Kemper Municipal Bond Fund
Kemper Summit Fund
Kemper Technology Fund
Kemper Total Return Fund
Kemper US Government Securities
Tax-Exempt California MM

Keystone Distributors
99 High Street—Boston, MA 02110
(617) 338-3400 (local)
(800) 343-2898 (out of state)

Keystone America Equity Income
Keystone America Fund of Grow Stk
Keystone America High Yield Bond
Keystone America Omega
Keystone America Tax-Free Income
Keystone Custodian B-1
Keystone Custodian B-2

Keystone Custodian B-4
Keystone Custodian K-1
Keystone Custodian K-2
Keystone Custodian S-1
Keystone Custodian S-3
Keystone Custodian S-4
Keystone International Fund
Keystone Precious Metals
Keystone Tax-Exempt Trust
Keystone Tax-Free Fund

Kidder, Peabody & Co
20 Exchange Place—New York, NY 10005
(212) 510-5351★ (local)

Kidder, Peabody California T-E MM
Kidder, Peabody Equity Income
Kidder, Peabody Government Income
Kidder, Peabody Premium Account
Kidder, Peabody Special Growth Fund
Kidder, Peabody Tax-Exempt MM
Kidder, Peabody MarketGuard I
Webster Cash Reserve Fund

Kleinwort Benson
200 Park Avenue—24th Floor—New York,
NY 10166
(212) 687-2515 (local)
(800) 237-4218 (out of state)

Kleinwort Benson——Intl Equity

Landmark Funds Broker Dealer Svcs
6 St James Avenue—9th Floor—Boston,
MA 02116
(617) 423-1679★ (local)
(800) 223-4447 (out of state)

Landmark Capital Growth Fund
Landmark Growth & Income Fund
Landmark New York T-F Reserves
Landmark Tax-Free Reserves

Lazard Freres & Co
One Rockefeller Plaza—New York, NY
10020
Telephone: (212) 489-6600 or
(800) 228-0203

Lazard Special Equity Fund

Legg Mason Wood Walker
PO Box 1476—Baltimore, MD 21203
(301) 539-3400 (local)
(800) 822-5544 (out of state)

Legg Mason Cash Reserve Trust
Legg Mason Special Investment Trust

Legg Mason Tax-Exempt Trust
Legg Mason Total Return Trust
Legg Mason Value Trust

Lehman Mgt Co

55 Water Street—New York, NY 10041
Telephone: (212) 668-8578 or
(800) 221-5350

Lehman Capital Fund
Lehman Investors Fund
Lehman Opportunity Fund

Lepercq-Istel Fund

345 Park Avenue—23rd Floor—New York,
NY 10154
(212) 702-0174★ (local)

Lepercq-Istel Fund

Lexington Management Corp

PO Box 1515—Saddle Brook, NJ 07662
(201) 845-7300★ (local)
(800) 526-0057 (out of state)

Lexington Corp Leaders Trust Fund
Lexington Global Fund
Lexington GNMA Income Fund
Lexington Goldfund
Lexington Growth Fund
Lexington Research Fund
Lexington Tax-Free Money Fund
Lexington Technical Strategy Fund

Liberty Asset Management Co

600 Atlantic Avenue—Boston, MA
02210-2214
Telephone: (617) 722-6000 or
(800) 872-5426

Liberty Advantage Trust US
Government Securities Fund

Lieber & Co

550 Mamaroneck Avenue—Harrison, NY
10528
(914) 698-5711★ (local)
(800) 235-0064 (out of state)

Evergreen American Retirement
Evergreen Fund
Evergreen Limited Market Fund
Evergreen Total Return Fund
Evergreen Value Timing Fund

Lincoln Investment Planning

218 Glenside Avenue—Wyncote, PA
19095-1595

(800) 222-3317 (local)
(800) 242-1421 (out of state)

Rightime Fund
Rightime Fund—Blue Chip
Rightime Fund Growth

Lindner Management Corp

PO Box 11208—St Louis, MO 63105
(314) 727-5305 (local)

Lindner Dividend Fund
Lindner Fund

Lord Abbett & Co

767 Fifth Avenue—11th Floor—New York,
NY 10153
(212) 848-1800★ (local)
(800) 223-4224 (out of state)

Affiliated Fund
Lord Abbett Bond-Debenture Fund
Lord Abbett California Tax-Free Inc
Lord Abbett Developing Growth
Lord Abbett Fundamental Value
Lord Abbett Tax-Free—National
Lord Abbett Tax-Free—New York
Lord Abbett US Government Secs
Lord Abbett Value Appreciation

Lutheran Brotherhood Securities

625 Fourth Avenue South—Minneapolis,
MN 55419
(800) 752-4208 (local)
(800) 328-4552 (out of state)

Lutheran Brotherhood Fund
Lutheran Brotherhood High Yield
Lutheran Brotherhood Income Fund
Lutheran Brotherhood Muni Bond

MacKay-Shields Financial Corp.

51 Madison Avenue—New York, NY
10010
Telephone: (800) 522-4202

MacKay Shields Mainstay Series
  Government Plus Fund
MacKay Shields Mainstay Series High
  Yield Corporate Bond Fund

Mackenzie Investment Management

PO Box 5007—Boca Raton, FL 33431
(800) 456-5111 (nationwide)

Mackenzie American Fund
Mackenzie Canada Fund
Mackenzie No Amer Total Return

Madison Investment Advisors

6411 Mineral Point Road—Madison, WI
53705
(608) 273-2020★ (local)
(800) 767-0300 (out of state)

Bascom Hill Balanced Fund
Bascom Hill Investors

Mairs & Power

W-2062 First National Bank Building—
St Paul, MN 55101
(612) 222-8478 (local)

Mairs & Power Growth Fund
Mairs & Power Income Fund

Horace Mann Growth Fund

One Horace Mann Plaza—Springfield, IL
62715
(217) 789-2500 (local)
(800) 999-1030 (out of state)

Horace Mann Growth Fund

Mass Mutual Integrity Funds

1295 State Street—Springfield, MA 01111
Telephone: (800) 252-6643

Mass Mutual Investment Grade
  Bond Fund

Massachusetts Financial Services

500 Boylston Street—Boston, MA 02116
(617) 954-5000★ (local)
(800) 225-2606 (out of state)

Mass Capital Development Fund
Mass Cash Management—Prime
Mass Financial Bond Fund
Mass Financial Development Fund
Mass Financial Emerging Growth
Mass Financial High-Income—Series I
Mass Financial Intl-Bond
Mass Financial Special Fund
Mass Financial Total Return Trust
Mass Investors Growth Stock Fund
Mass Investors Trust
MFS Government Guaranteed Secs
MFS Government Securities Hi Yld
MFS Lifetime Capital Growth Trust
MFS Lifetime Dividends Plus Trust
MFS Lifetime Emerging Growth
MFS Lifetime Global Equity Trust
MFS Lifetime Government Inc Plus
MFS Lifetime High Income Trust
MFS Lifetime Managed Muni Bond

MFS Lifetime Managed Sectors Trust
MFS Managed California Tax-Exempt
MFS Managed High Yield Muni Bond
MFS Managed M-S Tax-Exempt—Md
MFS Managed M-S Tax-Ex—Mass
MFS Managed M-S Tax-Exempt—NC
MFS Managed M-S Tax-Exempt—SC
MFS Managed M-S Tax-Exempt—Va
MFS Managed M-S Tax-Ex—W Va
MFS Managed Muni Bond Trust
MFS Managed Sectors Trust

Mathers Fund

100 Corporate North—Suite 201—
Bannockburn, IL 60015
(312) 295-7400★ (local)
(800) 962-3863 (out of state)

Mathers Fund

McDonald & Co Securities

2100 Society Building—Cleveland, OH
44114
(216) 443-2300 (local)
(800) 553-2240 (out of state)

McDonald Tax-Exempt MM

Meeschaert & Co

28 Hill Farm Road—St Johnsbury, VT
05819
(802) 748-2400 (local)

Meeschaert Capital Accumulation
Meeschaert Gold and Currency

Meridian Fund

60 East Sir Francis Drake Boulevard—
Suite 306—Larkspur, CA 94939
(800) 445-5553 (local)
(800) 446-6662 (out of state)

Meridian Fund

Merrill Lynch Funds Boston

One Financial Center—15th Floor—
Boston, MA 02111
(617) 357-1434★ (local)
(800) 225-1576 (out of state)

Merrill Lynch Government Fund
Merrill Lynch Institutional Fund

Merrill Lynch Funds Distributor

PO Box 9011—Princeton, NJ 08543-9011
(609) 282-2800★ (local)
(800) 637-3863 (out of state)

CBA Money Fund
Merrill Lynch Basic Value Fund-A
Merrill Lynch California Tax-Exempt
Merrill Lynch Capital Fund
Merrill Lynch Corp—High Income
Merrill Lynch Corp—High Quality
Merrill Lynch Corp—Intermediate
Merrill Lynch Equi-Bond I Fund
Merrill Lynch EuroFund-B
Merrill Lynch Federal Securities
Merrill Lynch Fund for Tomorrow-B
Merrill Lynch Global Convertible-B
Merrill Lynch International Holdings
Merrill Lynch Muni—High Yield-A
Merrill Lynch Muni—Insured-A
Merrill Lynch Muni Ltd Maturity-A
Merrill Lynch Municipal Income
Merrill Lynch Natural Resources
Merrill Lynch NY Muni Bond-B
Merrill Lynch Pacific Fund
Merrill Lynch Phoenix Fund-A
Merrill Lynch Ready Assets Trust
Merrill Lynch Retire Benefit Inv-B
Merrill Lynch Retire Globe Bond-B
Merrill Lynch Retire Equity
Merrill Lynch Retire/Income Fund
Merrill Lynch Retire Reserves Money
Merrill Lynch Special Value-A
Merrill Lynch Strat Div-B
Sci/Tech Holdings-A
Summit Cash Reserves Fund

Merrill Lynch, Pierce, Fenner & Smith
One Liberty Plaza—165 Broadway—
New York, NY 10080
(212) 637-5730 (local)
CMA Government Securities Fund
CMA Money Fund
CMA Tax-Exempt Fund

Mesirow Investment Services
350 North Clark Street—Chicago, IL 60610
(312) 670-6035 (local)
(800) 458-5222 (out of state)
Skyline Fund—Balanced
Skyline Fund—Special Equities

MetLife State Street Investment
One Financial Center—30th Floor—Boston, MA 02111

(617) 348-2000 (local)
(800) 882-0052 (out of state)
MetLife-State Street Cap Apprec
MetLife-State Street Equity Income
MetLife-State Street Equity Inv
MetLife-State Street Government Inc
MetLife-State Street High Income

MGF Distributors
700 Dixie Terminal Building—Cincinnati, OH 45202
(513) 629-2000 (local)
(800) 543-8721 (out of state)
Financial Independence—Growth
Midwest Group Tax-Free—MM
Midwest Group T-T—Ohio MM
Midwest Income—Intermediate Govt

MidAmerica Management
4333 Edgewood Road NE—Cedar Rapids, IA 52499
(800) 288-2346 (local)
(800) 288-2346 (out of state)
MidAmerica High Growth Fund
MidAmerica Mutual Fund

Midvale Securities Corp
11601 Wilshire Boulevard—24th Floor—Los Angeles, CA 90025
(800) 233-6483 (local)
(800) 225-9655 (out of state)
RNC Convertible Securities
RNC Income Fund
RNC Regency Fund
RNC Westwind Fund

Midwest Advisory Serv.
700 Dixie Terminal Building—Cincinnati, OH 45202
Telephone: (513) 629-2000 or
(800) 354-0436
Financial Independence US Treasury
  Allocation Fund
Midwest Income Trust Intermediate
  Term Government Fund

Miller, Anderson & Sherrerd
2 Bala Plaza—Bala Cynwyd, PA 19004
Telephone: (215) 668-0850 or
(800) 762-1155
MAS Pooled Trust Fund Equity
  Portfolio

MAS Pooled Trust Fund Fixed Income
  Portfolio
MAS Pooled Trust Fund International
  Equity Portfolio
MAS Pooled Trust Fund Select Fixed
  Income Portfolio
MAS Pooled Trust Fund Select Value
  Portfolio
MAS Pooled Trust Fund Small
  Capitalization Value Portfolio
MAS Pooled Trust Fund Value Portfolio

Mimlic Sales Corp
PO Box 64132—St Paul, MN 55101
(612) 228-4833 (local)
(800) 443-3677 (out of state)
Mimlic Asset Allocation Fund
Mimlic Investors Fund I

MML Investor Services
1350 Main Street—Springfield, MA 01103
(800) 854-9100 (local)
(800) 542-6767 (out of state)
MassMutual Integrity—Balanced Fund
MassMutual Integrity—Cap Apprec
MassMutual Integrity—Valued Stock

Morgan Keegan & Co
50 North Front Street—Memphis, TN
38103
(901) 524-4100 (local)
(800) 238-7127 (out of state)
Morgan Keegan Southern Capital

Morgan Stanley & Co
1221 Avenue of the Americas—30th
Floor—New York, NY 10020
(212) 398-2900 (local)
(800) 366-7426 (out of state)
Pierpont Capital Appreciation Fund
Pierpont Equity Fund
Pierpont Money Market
Pierpont Tax-Exempt Bond Fund
Pierpont Tax-Exempt Money Market

Morison Asset Management
1201 Marquette Avenue—Suite 400—
Minneapolis, MN 55403
(612) 332-1588 (local)
(800) 325-9244 (out of state)
Morison Asset Allocation Fund

Murphey Favre
West 601 Riverside Avenue—Spokane, WA
99201
(509) 353-3400 (local)
(800) 543-8072 (out of state)
Composite Bond & Stock Fund
Composite Growth Fund
Composite Income Fund
Composite Northwest 50 Index
Composite Tax-Exempt Bond Fund

Mutual Benefit Financial Services Co
290 Westminster Street—Providence, RI
02903
(401) 751-8600★ (local)
(800) 333-4726 (out of state)
Mutual Benefit Fund

Mutual of Omaha Fund Management
10235 Regency Circle—Omaha, NE 68114
(800) 642-8112 (local)
(800) 228-9596 (out of state)
Mutual of Omaha America Fund
Mutual of Omaha Growth Fund
Mutual of Omaha Income Fund
Mutual of Omaha Tax-Free Income

Mutual Series Fund, Inc.
51 John F. Kennedy Parkway—Short Hills,
NJ 07078
Telephone: (201) 912-2100 or
(800) 448-FUND
Mutual Beacon Fund
Mutual Qualified Fund
Mutual Shares Fund

National Financial Data Service
PO Box 26070—Kansas City, MO
64916-7070
(816) 283-1700 (local)
(800) 225-8011 (out of state)
Neuwirth Fund
Pine Street Fund
Winthrop Focus Funds—Growth

National Securities & Research Corp
2 Pickwick Plaza—Greenwich, CT 06830
(203) 863-5600★ (local)
(800) 223-7757 (out of state)
California Tax-Exempt Bonds
Fairfield Fund
National Bond Fund

National Federal Securities Trust
National Growth Fund
National Real Estate—Stock Fund
National Stock Fund
National Strategic Allocation Fund
National Total Income Fund
National Total Return Fund

Nationwide Financial Services
One Nationwide Plaza—Columbus, OH 43216
(800) 848-0920 (nationwide)

Nationwide Bond Fund
Nationwide Fund
Nationwide Growth Fund

Neuberger & Berman Management
342 Madison Avenue—New York, NY 10173
(212) 850-8300★ (local)
(800) 877-9700 (out of state)

Neuberger & Berman Guardian Fund
Neuberger & Berman Ltd Mat Bond
Neuberger & Berman Manhattan
Neuberger & Berman Muni Money
Neuberger & Berman Partners Fund
Neuberger & Berman Select Energy

New England Securities
399 Boylston Street—Boston, MA 02116
(617)267-6600 (local)
(800) 343-7104 (out of state)

Loomis-Sayles Capital Development
Loomis Sayles Mutual Fund
New England Bond Income Fund
New England Cash Mgmt—MM
New England Equity Income Fund
New England Government Securities
New England Growth Fund
New England Retirement Equity
New England Tax-Exempt Income
New England Tax-Exempt MM

Newton Fund
PO Box 1348—Milwaukee, WI 53201
(414) 347-1141 (local)
(800) 247-7039 (out of state)

Newton Growth Fund

Nicholas Co
700 North Water Street—Milwaukee, WI 53202
(414) 272-6133 (local)

Nicholas Fund
Nicholas II
Nicholas Income Fund
Nicholas Limited Edition

Noddings and Associates
Two MidAmerica Plaza—Suite 920—Oakbrook Terrace, IL 60181
(312) 954-1322★ (local)
(800) 544-7785 (out of state)

Noddings Convertible Strategies

Nomura Capital Management
180 Maiden Lane—New York, NY 10038
(212) 208-9300 (local)
(800) 833-0018 (out of state)

Nomura Pacific Basin Fund

Northeast Investors Trust
50 Congress Street—Boston, MA 02109
(617) 523-3588 (local)
(800) 225-6704 (out of state)

Northeast Investors Growth
Northeast Investors Trust

John Nuveen & Co
333 West Wacker Drive—Chicago, IL 60606
(312) 917-7844★ (local)
(800) 621-7227 (out of state)

Nuveen California T-F—Ins Bond
Nuveen California Tax-Free—MM
Nuveen California T-F—Spec Bond
Nuveen Insured Tax-Free Bond—Natl
Nuveen Municipal Bond Fund
Nuveen Tax-Exempt Money Market
Nuveen Tax-Free Bond—Ohio
Nuveen Tax-Free MM—Mass
Nuveen Tax-Free MM—New York
Nuveen Tax-Free Reserves

NYLife Securities
51 Madison Avenue—New York, NY 10010
(800) 522-4202 (nationwide)

Mackay-Shields Gold & Prec Met
MacKay-Shields MainStay—Cap App
MacKay-Shields MainStay—Convert
MacKay-Shields MainStay—Global
MacKay-Shields MainStay—Govt +
MacKay-Shields MainStay—H-Y Corp
MacKay-Shields MainStay—T-F Bond

MacKay-Shields MainStay—Value
MacKay-Shields Total Return Fund

Oberweis Emerging Growth
30 North LaSalle Street—Chicago, IL 60602
(800) 942-0850 (local)
(800) 323-6166 (out of state)
Oberweis Emerging Growth

Ohio Company
155 East Broad Street—Columbus, OH 43215
(614) 464-6852 (local)
(800) 848-7734 (out of state)
Cardinal Fund
Cardinal Government Guaranteed
Cardinal Government Securities
Cardinal Tax-Exempt Money Trust

Olympic Trust
800 West Sixth Street—Suite 540—Los Angeles, CA 90017
(213) 623-7833 (local)
(800) 346-7301 (out of state)
Olympic Trust—Balanced Income
Olympic Trust—Equity Income
Olympic Trust—Small Cap Fund

Oppenheimer Fund Management
PO Box 300—Denver, CO 80201
(303) 671-3200 (local)
(800) 525-7048 (out of state)
Champion High Yield Fund
Oppenheimer Blue Chip Fund
Oppenheimer Directors Fund
Oppenheimer Equity Income Fund
Oppenheimer Fund
Oppenheimer Global Fund
Oppenheimer Gold & Special Mins
Oppenheimer High Yield Fund
Oppenheimer Money Market Fund
Oppenheimer New York Tax-Exempt
Oppenheimer Ninety Ten Fund
Oppenheimer OTC Fund
Oppenheimer Premium Income
Oppenheimer Regency Fund
Oppenheimer Special Fund
Oppenheimer Target Fund
Oppenheimer Tax-Free Bond Fund
Oppenheimer Time Fund
Oppenheimer Total Return Fund
Oppenheimer US Government Trust

Ostrander Capital Mgt LP
10 Liberty Square—Boston, MA 02109
Telephone: (617) 426-0182 or
(800) 548-1921
Ostrander High Income Reserve Fund

Pacific Financial Research
9601 Wilshire Boulevard, Suite 828—Beverly Hills, CA 90210
Telephone: (213) 278-5033
Clipper Fund

Pacific Inv't Mgt Co
840 Newport Center Drive, Suite 360—Newport Beach, CA 92660
Telephone: (800) 443-6915
Pacific Investment Management
   Institutional Trust—Low Duration
Pacific Investment Mgmt Institutional
   Trust Total Return Portfolio

PaineWebber
1285 Avenue of the Americas—18th Floor, Mutual Funds Finance Dept—New York, NY 10019
(800) 544-9300 (local)
PaineWebber Asset Allocation
PaineWebber Calif Tax-Exempt Inc
PaineWebber Cashfund
PaineWebber Classic Atlas Fund
PaineWebber Classic Growth & Inc
PaineWebber Classic Growth Fund
PaineWebber Fixed Inc—GNMA
PaineWebber Fixed Inc—High Yield
PaineWebber Fixed Inc—Invest Grade
PaineWebber Master Energy-Util
PaineWebber Master Global Income
PaineWebber Master Growth
PaineWebber Master Income
PaineWebber RMA—Money Market
PaineWebber RMA—Tax-Free
PaineWebber Tax-Exempt Income

Pallas Financial Corp
2325 Crestmoor Road—Suite P200—Nashville, TN 37215
(615) 298-1000
(800) 251-1970 (out of state)
Monitrend Value Fund

Palm Beach Capital Management
205 Royal Palm Way—Palm Beach, FL 33480

(407) 655-7255 (local)
(800) 289-2281 (out of state)
ABT Growth & Income Trust
ABT Invest—Emerging Growth
ABT Invest—Security Income
ABT Utility Income Fund

Paribas Asset Management
787 Seventh Avenue—30th Floor—
New York, NY 10019
(212) 841-3245★ (local)
Paribas Trust—Quantus Equity

Parnassus Financial Management
244 California Street—
San Francisco, CA 94111
(415) 362-3505★ (local)
(800) 999-3505 (out of state)
Parnassus Fund

Pasadena Funds
600 North Rosemead Boulevard—Pasadena,
CA 91107-2101
(818) 351-9286★ (local)
(800) 882-2855 (out of state)
Pasadena Growth Fund

Pax World Fund
224 State Street—Portsmouth, NH 03801
(603) 431-8022 (local)
Pax World Fund

Penn Square Management
2650 Westview Drive—Wyomissing, PA
19610
(800) 222-7506 (local)
(800) 523-8440 (out of state)
Penn Square Mutual Fund

Pennsylvania Mutual Fund
1414 Avenue of the Americas—New York,
NY 10019
(212) 355-7311★ (local)
(800) 221-4268 (out of state)
Pennsylvania Mutual Fund

Permanent Portfolio
PO Box 5847—Austin, TX 78763
(512) 453-7558 (local)
(800) 355-7311 (out of state)
Permanent Portfolios—Permanent

Phoenix Equity Planning Corp
100 Bright Meadow Boulevard—Enfield,
CT 06082
(203) 278-8050★ (local)
(800) 243-4361 (out of state)
Phoenix Balanced Fund
Phoenix Convertible Fund
Phoenix Growth Fund
Phoenix High Yield Fund
Phoenix Stock Fund
Phoenix Total Return

Pilgrim Group
10100 Santa Monica Boulevard—21st
Floor—Los Angeles, CA 90067
(213) 551-1833 (local)
(800) 334-3444 (out of state)
Pilgrim GNMA Fund
Pilgrim High Yield Trust
Pilgrim MagnaCap Fund
Pilgrim Preferred Fund

Pioneer Group
60 State Street—Boston, MA 02109
(617) 742-7825★ (local)
(800) 225-6292 (out of state)
Pioneer Bond Fund
Pioneer Fund
Pioneer II
Pioneer III

Piper Capital Management
Piper Jaffray Tower—222 South 9th
Street—Minneapolis, MN 55402
(612) 342-6384 (local)
(800) 333-6000 (out of state)
Piper Jaffray Balanced Fund
Piper Jaffray Money Market
Piper Jaffray Sector Performance
Piper Jaffray Value Fund

Plymouth Investments
82 Devonshire Street—Boston, MA 02109
Telephone: (800) 522-7297
Fidelity Special Situations Fund
Plymouth Class Shares
Plymouth Income & Growth Portfolio

Prescott, Ball & Turben
230 West Monroe Street—Suite 2800—
Chicago, IL 60606
(312) 641-7862 (local)
(800) 553-5533 (out of state)

Selected American Shares
Selected Special Shares

T Rowe Price Associates
100 East Pratt Street—Baltimore, MD
21202
(301) 547-2308★ (local)
(800) 638-5660 (out of state)
T Rowe Price Calif T-F Inc—Bond
T Rowe Price Calif T-F Inc—Money
T Rowe Price Capital Appreciation
T Rowe Price Equity Income Fund
T Rowe Price GNMA Fund
T Rowe Price Growth & Income
T Rowe Price Growth Stock Fund
T Rowe Price High Yield Fund
T Rowe Price International Bond
T Rowe Price International Stock
T Rowe Price Maryland T-F Bond
T Rowe Price New America Growth
T Rowe Price New Era Fund
T Rowe Price New Horizons Fund
T Rowe Price New Income Fund
T Rowe Price New York T-F Bond
T Rowe Price New York T-F Money
T Rowe Price Prime Reserve Fund
T Rowe Price Science & Technology
T Rowe Price Short-Term Bond Fund
T Rowe Price Small-Cap Value Fund
T Rowe Price Tax-Exempt Money
T Rowe Price Tax-Free High Yield
T Rowe Price Tax-Free Income Fund
T Rowe Price T-F Short Intermed

Primary Trend Fund
First Financial Centre—4th Floor—700
North Water Street—Milwaukee, WI 53202
(800) 443-6544 (nationwide)
Primary Trend Fund

Princor Financial Services Corp
711 High Street—Des Moines, IA 50309
(515) 247-5711 (local)
(800) 247-4123 (out of state)
Princor Aggressive Growth Fund
Princor Capital Accumulation Fund
Princor Growth Fund
Princor Managed Fund
Princor World Fund

Provident Financial Processing
466 Lexington Avenue—New York, NY
10017-3147

Telephone: (302) 479-1827 or
(800) 878-0600
Counsellors Capital Appreciation Fund
Counsellors Fixed Income Fund

Prudent Speculator Group
4023 West Sixth Street—Los Angeles, CA
90020
(213) 252-9000★ (local)
(800) 444-4778 (out of state)
Prudent Speculator Leveraged Fund

Prudential-Bache
One Seaport Plaza—Mutual Funds-18th
Floor—New York, NY 10292
(800) 225-1852 (nationwide)

Pru-Bache Bond—Insured
Pru-Bache California Municipal
Pru-Bache Equity Fund
Pru-Bache Equity Income
Pru-Bache FlexiFund—Aggressive
Pru-Bache FlexiFund—Conservative
Pru-Bache Global Fund
Pru-Bache Global Genesis
Pru-Bache Global Natural Resources
Pru-Bache GNMA Fund
Pru-Bache Government Plus
Pru-Bache Government Plus II
Pru-Bache Govt Secs—Intermediate
Pru-Bache Govt Secs—Money Market
Pru-Bache Growth Opportunity
Pru-Bache High Yield Fund
Pru-Bache Income Vertible Plus
Pru-Bache Moneymart Assets
Pru-Bache Muni—Arizona
Pru-Bache Muni—Georgia
Pru-Bache Muni—High Yield
Pru-Bache Muni—Maryland
Pru-Bache Muni—Massachusetts
Pru-Bache Muni—Michigan
Pru-Bache Muni—New Jersey
Pru-Bache Muni—New York
Pru-Bache Muni—New York MM
Pru-Bache Muni—North Carolina
Pru-Bache Muni—Ohio
Pru-Bache Muni—Pennsylvania
Pru-Bache National Municipals
Pru-Bache Option Growth Fund
Pru-Bache Research Fund
Pru-Bache Tax-Free Money Fund
Pru-Bache Utility Fund

Putnam Financial Services
One Post Office Square—12th Floor—
Boston, MA 02109
(617) 292-1000 (local)
(800) 225-1581 (out of state)

Depositors Invest—Capital Growth
Putnam California Tax-Exempt Inc
Putnam California Tax-Exempt MM
Putnam Convertible Income—Growth
Putnam Daily Dividend Trust
Putnam Energy-Resources Trust
Putnam Fund for Growth & Income
George Putnam Fund of Boston
Putnam Global Governmental Trust
Putnam GNMA Plus Trust
Putnam Health Sciences Trust
Putnam High Income Government
Putnam High Yield Trust
Putnam High Yield Trust II
Putnam Income Fund
Putnam Information Sciences Trust
Putnam International Equities Fund
Putnam Investors Fund
Putnam Massachusetts Tax-Ex Inc
Putnam Michigan Tax-Exempt Inc
Putnam Minnesota Tax-Exempt Inc
Putnam New York Tax-Exempt Inc
Putnam New York Tax-Exempt MM
Putnam Ohio Tax-Exempt Income
Putnam Option Income Trust
Putnam Option Income Trust II
Putnam OTC Emerging Growth Fund
Putnam Tax-Exempt Income Fund
Putnam Tax-Exempt Money Market
Putnam Tax-Free Income—High Yield
Putnam Tax-Free Income—Insured
Putnam US Govt Guaranteed Secs
Putnam Vista Basic Value
Putnam Voyager Fund

Quest Distributors
1414 Avenue of the Americas—New York,
NY 10019
(212) 355-7311★ (local)
(800) 221-4268 (out of state)

Royce Fund—Total Return
Royce Fund—Value

Quest for Value
200 Liberty Street—World Financial
Center—New York, NY 10281

(212) 667-7587 (local)
(800) 232-3863 (out of state)

Quest for Value Cash Management
Quest for Value Fund

James B Rea
10966 Chalon Road—Los Angeles, CA
90077
(213) 208-2282★ (local)
(800) 433-1998 (out of state)

Rea-Graham Fund

Reich & Tang LP
100 Park Avenue—28th Floor—New York,
NY 10017
(212) 370-1240★ (local)
(800) 221-3079 (out of state)

California Daily Tax-Free Income
Connecticut Daily Tax-Free Income
Daily Income Fund
Daily Tax-Free Income Fund
Empire Tax-Free Money Market
Michigan Daily Tax-Free Income
Reich & Tang Equity Fund
Short-Term Income—Money Market
Sound Shore Fund

Resrv Partners
810 Seventh Avenue—35th Floor—
New York, NY 10019
(800) 633-7890★ (local)
(800) 223-5547 (out of state)

Reserve Equity—Contrarian
Reserve Fund—Government
Reserve Fund—Primary
Reserve New York Tax-Exempt—NY
Reserve Tax-Exempt—Connecticut
Reserve Tax-Exempt—Interstate

Review Management Corp
PO Box 1537—Suite 228—
Fort Washington, PA 19034-1537
(215) 643-2510★ (local)
(800) 523-2578 (out of state)

Over-the-Counter Securities Fund

Rochester Fund Distributors
379 Park Avenue—Rochester, NY 14607
(716) 442-5500★ (local)

Rochester Convertible—Growth
Rochester Convertible—Income
Rochester Tax Managed Fund

Ruane, Cunniff & Co
1370 Avenue of the Americas—New York, NY 10019
(212) 245-4500 (local)

Sequoia Fund

Rushmore Group
4922 Fairmont Avenue—Bethesda, MD 20814
(301) 657-1500★ (local)
(800) 343-3355 (out of state)

Fund for Govt Investors
Fund for Tax-Free Inv—Money Market
Rushmore—OTC Index Plus
Rushmore—Stock Market Index Plus

Safeco Securities
PO Box 34890—Seattle, WA 98124
(206) 545-5530 (local)
(800) 426-6730 (out of state)

Safeco California Tax-Free Income
Safeco Equity Fund
Safeco Growth Fund
Safeco Income Fund
Safeco Municipal Bond Fund
Safeco Tax-Free Money Market

SBSF Funds
45 Rockefeller Plaza—New York, NY 10111
(212) 903-1200 (local)
(800) 422-7273 (out of state)

SBSF-Growth Fund

SEI Financial Mgt Corp
680 East Swedesford Road—Wayne, PA 19087
Telephone: (617) 227-9500 or
(800) 345-1151

SEI Cash + Plus Trust Intermediate-
   Term Government
SEI Index Funds/S&P 500
SEI Institutional Managed Trust/Value

Salem Funds
99 High Street—Boston, MA 02110
Telephone: (704) 331-0710 or
(800) 527-1578

The Salem Funds—Growth Portfolio

Sanford C. Bernstein & Co
767 Fifth Avenue—New York, NY 10153
Telephone: (212) 486-8434

Bernstein Government Short Duration
   Portfolio
Bernstein Intermediate Duration
   Portfolio
Bernstein Short Duration Plus Portfolio

Sass-Southmark Mutual Funds
1270 Avenue of the Americas—New York, NY 10020
Telephone: (212) 956-7030 or
(800) 872-8052

Hidden Strength Funds Moderate Asset
   Allocation Portfolio
Hidden Strength Funds U.S.
   Government High Yield Portfolio

Schield Portfolios Series
390 Union Boulevard—Suite 410—Denver, CO 80228
(800) 233-4971 (local)
(800) 826-8154 (out of state)

Shield—Aggressive Growth
Shield—Value

Scudder Fund Distributors
160 Federal Street—Boston, MA 02110
(800) 225-2470 (local)

AARP Growth Trust—Capital Growth
AARP Growth—Growth & Income
AARP Income Trust—General Bond
AARP Income—GNMA & US Treas
AARP Insured T-F Inc—Genl Bond
Japan Fund
Scudder California Tax Free Fund
Scudder California Tax-Free Money
Scudder Cash Investment Trust
Scudder Development Fund
Scudder Equity—Capital Growth
Scudder Equity—Equity Income
Scudder Fund—Lazard Equity
Scudder Fund—Managed Tax-Free
Scudder GLBL—Global Fund
Scudder GNMA Fund
Scudder Growth & Income Fund
Scudder High Yield Tax Free Fund
Scudder Income Fund
Scudder International Fund
Scudder Managed Municipal Bonds
Scudder Massachusetts Tax Free
Scudder NY Tax Free Fund
Scudder NY Tax-Free Money Fund
Scudder Tax-Free Money Fund

Securities Management & Research

Two Moody Plaza—Galveston, TX 77550
(800) 392-9753 (local)
(800) 231-4639 (out of state)

American National Growth Fund
American National Income Fund
Triflex Fund

Security Distributors

700 Harrison Street—Topeka, KS 66636
(800) 888-2461 (nationwide)

Security Action Fund
Security Equity Fund
Security Income—Corporate Bond
Security Investment Fund
Security Omni Fund
Security Ultra Fund

Selected Funds Group

1331 Euclid Ave.—Cleveland, OH 44115
Telephone: (312) 641-7862 or
(800) 553-5533

Selected American Shares

Seligman Marketing

One Bankers Trust Plaza—New York, NY 10006
(800) 522-6869 (local)
(800) 221-2450 (out of state)

Seligman Calif Tax-Exempt—High Yld
Seligman Calif Tax-Exempt—Quality
Seligman Capital Fund
Seligman Common Stock Fund
Seligman Commun & Inform
Seligman Growth Fund
Seligman Income Fund
Seligman New Jersey Tax-Exempt
Seligman Penn Tax-Exempt—Quality
Seligman Tax-Exempt—Colorado
Seligman Tax-Exempt Louisiana
Seligman Tax-Exempt—Maryland
Seligman Tax-Exempt—Mass
Seligman Tax-Exempt—Michigan
Seligman Tax-Exempt—Minnesota
Seligman Tax-Exempt—Missouri
Seligman Tax-Exempt—National
Seligman Tax-Exempt—New York
Seligman Tax-Exempt—Ohio
Seligman Tax-Exempt—Oregon
Seligman Tax-Exempt—SC

Sentinel Advisors, Inc

National Life Dr.—Montpelier, VT 056405
Telephone: (802) 229-3761 or
(800) 233-4322

Sentinel Balanced Fund
Sentinel Common Stock Fund
Sentinel Growth Fund

Sentry Equity Services

1800 North Point Drive—A3/32—
Stevens Point, WI 54481
(800) 533-7827 (nationwide)

Sentry Fund

Shearson Lehman Hutton

One Western Union Plaza—15th Floor—
New York, NY 10004
(212) 528-2744 (local)

American Telecom—Growth
Lehman Capital Fund
Lehman Investors Fund
Lehman Opportunity Fund
SLH Aggressive Growth Fund
SLH Appreciation Fund
SLH California Daily Tax-Fund
SLH California Municipals Fund
SLH Convertible Securities Fund
SLH Daily Dividend
SLH Daily Tax-Free Dividend
SLH Equity—Growth & Opportunity
SLH Equity—International
SLH Equity—Sector Analysis
SLH Equity—Strategic Investors
SLH Fundamental Value Fund
SLH Global Opportunities
SLH Government & Agencies
SLH High Yield Fund
SLH Income—Convertible Secs
SLH Income—Global Bond
SLH Income—High Income
SLH Income—Option Income
SLH Income—Tax-Exempt
SLH Income—Utilities
SLH Investment—Basic Value
SLH Investment—Global Equity
SLH Investment—Government Secs
SLH Investment—Growth
SLH Investment—High Grade
SLH Investment—Prec Metals
SLH Investment—Spec Equities
SLH Managed Government

SLH Managed Municipals
SLH Multi Opportunities LP
SLH NJ Municipals
SLH NY Daily Tax-Free
SLH New York Municipals
SLH Precious Metals & Mins
SLH Small Capitalization

Sheffield Investments
*41 Madison Avenue—New York, NY
10010*
(212) 779-7979★ (local)
(800) 922-7771 (out of state)
Blanchard Precious Metals Fund
Blanchard Strategic Growth

Sherman, Dean Fund
*6061 NW Expressway—Suite 465—
San Antonio, TX 78201*
(512) 735-7700 (local)
(800) 247-6375 (out of state)
Sherman, Dean Fund

Sigma Investor Services
*Greenville Center C-200—3801 Kennett
Pike—Wilmington, DE 19807*
(302) 652-3091★ (local)
(800) 441-9490 (out of state)
ISI Growth Fund
ISI Trust Fund
Sigma Capital Shares
Sigma Income Shares
Sigma Investment Shares
Sigma Pennsylvania Tax-Free Trust
Sigma Special Fund
Sigma Trust Shares
Sigma Value Shares
Sigma Venture Shares
Sigma World Fund

Sit Investment Associates
*90 South 7th Street—Minneapolis, MN
55402*
(612) 323-3223 (local)
(800) 332-5580 (out of state)
Sit New Beginning Growth Fund
Sit New Beginning Income & Growth

Smith Barney, Harris Upham & Co
*1345 Avenue of the Americas—New York,
NY 10105*
(212) 698-5349 (local)
(800) 544-7835 (out of state)

Muni Bond Funds—California
Muni Bond Funds—National
National Liquid Reserves—Cash
National Liquid Reserves—Retire
Smith Barney Equity Fund
Smith Barney—Income & Growth
Smith Barney—US Government
Tax-Free Money Fund
Vantage Money Market—Cash

Sogen Securities Corp
*50 Rockefeller Plaza—New York, NY
10111*
(212) 832-6363 (local)
(800) 334-2143 (out of state)
SoGen International Fund

Southeastern Asset Management
*860 Ridgelake Boulevard—Suite 301—
Memphis, TN 38119*
(901) 761-2474★ (local)
(800) 445-9469 (out of state)
Southeastern Asset Mgmt Value

Sovereign Advisers
*985 Old Eagle School Road—Suite 515A—
Wayne, PA 19087*
(215) 254-0703★ (local)
Sovereign Investors

State Bond Sales Corp
*8500 Normandale Lake Boulevard—
Minneapolis, MN 55437*
(507) 354-2144★ (local)
(800) 328-4735 (out of state)
State Bond Common Stock Fund
State Bond Diversified Fund
State Bond Progress Fund

State Street Research & Management
One Financial Center—Boston, MA 02111
(617) 482-3920★ (local)
State Street Investment Trust

Steadman Security Corp
*1730 K Street NW—Suite 904—
Washington, DC 20006*
(202) 223-1000 (local)
(800) 424-8570 (out of state)
Steadman American Industry Fund
Steadman Associated Fund
Steadman Investment Fund
Steadman Oceanographic Tech & Gr

Stein Roe & Farnham

PO Box 1131—Chicago, IL 60690
(800) 338-2550 (nationwide)

SteinRoe—Capital Opportunities
SteinRoe—Growth & Income
SteinRoe—High Yield Bonds
SteinRoe—High Yield Municipals
SteinRoe—Income—Cash Reserves
SteinRoe—International Growth
SteinRoe—Managed Bonds
SteinRoe—Managed Municipals
SteinRoe—Prime Equities
SteinRoe—Special Fund
SteinRoe—Stock Fund
SteinRoe—Tax-Exempt Income—
  Money
Stein Roe—Total Return Fund

Stonebridge Capital

1801 Century Park East—Suite 1800—
Los Angeles, CA 90067
(213) 277-1450 (local)

National Industries Fund

Strategic Distributors

2030 Royal Lane—Dallas, TX 75229
(214) 484-1326★ (local)
(800) 527-5027 (out of state)

Strategic Gold/Minerals Fund
Strategic Investments Fund
Strategic Silver Fund

Stratton Management

610 West Germantown Pike—Suite 361—
Plymouth Meeting, PA 19462
(215) 941-0255★ (local)
(800) 634-5726 (out of state)

Stratton Growth Fund
Stratton Monthly Dividend Shares

Strong/Corneliuson Capital Management

PO Box 2936—Milwaukee, WI
53201-2936
(414) 359-1400★ (local)
(800) 368-3863 (out of state)

Strong Discovery Fund
Strong Income Fund
Strong Investment Fund
Strong Money Market Fund
Strong Tax-Free Money Market Fund
Strong Opportunity Fund
Strong Total Return Fund

Templeton Funds Distributors

700 Central Avenue—St Petersburg, FL
33701-3628
(813) 823-8712 (local)
(800) 237-0738 (out of state)

Templeton Foreign Fund
Templeton Global I
Templeton Growth Fund
Templeton Income Fund
Templeton World Fund

Thompson, Unger & Plumb

PO Box 55320—Madison, WI 53705
(608) 231-1676★ (local)

Thompson, Unger & Plumb Fund

Thomson McKinnon Asset Management

One State Street Plaza—New York, NY
10004
(212) 482-5894 (local)
(800) 628-1236 (out of state)

Cash Accumulation—National MM
Cash Accumulation—National Tax-Ex
Thomson McKinnon—Global
Thomson McKinnon—Growth
Thomson McKinnon—Income
Thomson McKinnon—Oppor
Thomson McKinnon—US Govt

Thornburg Securities

119 East Marcy Street—Suite 202—
Santa Fe, NM 87501
(505) 984-0200 (local)
(800) 847-0200 (out of state)

Limited Term Municipal—National

Transamerica

1000 Louisiana—Suite 6000—Houston,
TX 77002-5098
(800) 999-3863 (local)
(800) 231-4645 (out of state)

Lowry Market Timing Fund
Transamerica Bond—US Govt Hi Yld
Transamerica Growth & Income
Transamerica Inv Quality Bond
Transamerica Special Blue Chip Fund
Transamerica Special Convert Secs
Transamerica Special Emerging Grow
Transamerica Special Global Growth
Transamerica Sunbelt Growth Fund
Transamerica Technology Fund

Trinity Capital Management
183 East Main Street—Suite 1135—
Rochester, NY 14604
(716) 262-4080 (local)
(800) 456-7780 (out of state)
Trinity Liquid Assets Trust

Trusteed Funds
One Winthrop Square—Boston, MA 02110
(800) 462-1199 (local)
(800) 343-2902 (out of state)
Commonwealth Indenture A & B
Commonwealth Indenture C
GPM Fund

Twentieth Century Investors
4500 Main Street—Kansas City, MO 64111
(816) 531-5575 (local)
(800) 345-2021 (out of state)
20th Century Cash Reserve
20th Century Giftrust Investors
20th Century Growth Investors
20th Century Heritage Investors
20th Century Select Investors
20th Century Ultra Investors
20th Century US Governments
20th Century Vista Investors

Unified Management Corp
PO Box 6110—Indianapolis, IN 46206-6110
(317) 634-3300 (local)
(800) 862-7283 (out of state)
Unified Growth Fund
Unified Income Fund
Unified Mutual Shares

United Services Advisors
PO Box 29467—
San Antonio, TX 78229-0467
(512) 696-1234★ (local)
(800) 873-8637 (out of state)
United Services—Gold Shares Fund
United Services—Good & Bad
United Services—Growth Fund
United Services—Income Fund
United Services—New Prospector
United Services—Prospector Fund

US Boston Investment
6 New England Executive Park—
Burlington, MA 01803
(617) 272-6420 (local)
US Boston Inv—Growth & Income
US Boston Inv—Foreign G&I

USAA Investment Management Co
PO Box 33338—Mutual Fund Accounting—
San Antonio, TX 78265
(512) 498-8000 (local)
(800) 531-8000 (out of state)
USAA Investment—Cornerstone Fund
USAA Investment—Gold Fund
USAA Mutual—Aggressive Growth
USAA Mutual—Growth Fund
USAA Mutual—Income Fund
USAA Mutual—Income Stock Fund
USAA Mutual—Money Market
USAA Tax-Exempt Fund—High Yield
USAA Tax-Exempt—Intermediate
USAA Tax-Exempt Fund—MM
USAA Tax-Exempt Fund—Short-Term

UST Securities
555 South Flower Street—Suite 2710—
Los Angeles, CA 90071
(213) 488-0666 (local)
(800) 233-1136 (out of state)
UST Master Funds—Equity
UST Master Funds—Income & Grow
UST Master Funds—International
UST Master Tax-Exempt—Short-Term

Valley Forge Fund
PO Box 262—Valley Forge, PA 19481
(215) 688-6839 (local)
(800) 548-1942 (out of state)
Valley Forge Fund

Value Line Securities
711 Third Avenue—New York, NY 10017
(800) 223-0818 (local)
Value Line Cash Fund
Value Line Convertible Fund
Value Line Fund
Value Line Income Fund
Value Line Leveraged Growth Inv
Value Line New York Tax-Exempt
Value Line Special Situations Fund
Value Line Tax-Exempt—High Yield

Value Line Tax-Exempt—MM
Value Line US Government Secs

Van Eck Securities Corp
122 East 42nd Street—42nd Floor—
New York, NY 10168
(212) 687-5200★ (local)
(800) 221-2220 (out of state)

Van Eck Gold/Resources Fund
Van Eck International Investors
Van Eck World Trends Fund

Van Kampen Merritt
1001 Warrenville Road—Lisle, IL 60532
(312) 719-6000 (local)
(800) 225-2222 (out of state)

Van Kampen Merritt Cal Ins Tax-Free
Van Kampen Merritt Growth & Inc
Van Kampen Merritt High Yield
Van Kampen Merritt Insured T-F
Van Kampen Merritt Penn T-F Inc
Van Kampen Merritt T-F Hi Inc
Van Kampen Merritt T-F Money
Van Kampen Merritt US Government

Vanguard Group of Investment Cos
PO Box 2600—MS 136—Valley Forge,
PA 19482
(215) 648-6000 (local)
(800) 662-7447 (out of state)

Vanguard California T-F—Ins L-T
Vanguard California Tax-Free—MM
Vanguard Convertible Securities
Vanguard Equity Income Fund
Vanguard Explorer Fund
Vanguard Explorer II
Vanguard Fixed Income—GNMA
Vanguard Fixed Income—High Yield
Vanguard Fixed Income—Invest Grade
Vanguard Fixed Income—Short Term
Vanguard Fixed Income—US Govt S-T
Vanguard Fixed Income—US Treasury
Vanguard High Yield Stock
Vanguard Index—500 Portfolio
Vanguard Index—Extended Market
Vanguard MM Reserves—Federal
Vanguard MM Reserves—Prime
Vanguard WL Morgan Growth Fund
Vanguard Muni Bond—High Yield
Vanguard Muni Bond—Insured L-T
Vanguard Muni Bond—Intermediate
Vanguard Muni Bond—Limited Term

Vanguard Muni Bond—Long Term
Vanguard Muni Bond—Money Market
Vanguard Muni Bond—Short-Term
Vanguard Naess & Thomas Special
Vanguard NJ Tax-Free—Insured
Vanguard NJ Tax-Free—MM
Vanguard New York Insured T-F
Vanguard Penn Tax-Free—Insured L-T
Vanguard Preferred Stock Fund
Vanguard Primecap Fund
Vanguard Quantitative Portfolios
Vanguard Special—Energy
Vanguard Spec—Gold & Prec
Vanguard Special—Health Care
Vanguard Special—Service Economy
Vanguard Special—Technology
Vanguard STAR Fund
Vanguard Trustees Comm—Intl
Vanguard Trustees Commingled—US
Vanguard Wellesley Income Fund
Vanguard Wellington Fund
Vanguard Windsor Fund
Vanguard Windsor II
Vanguard World—International Grow
Vanguard World—US Growth

Variable Stock Fund
One Monarch Place—12th Floor—
Springfield, MA 01144
(413) 781-3000 (local)
(800) 343-2902 (out of state)

Variable Stock Fund

Venture Advisers
PO Box 1688—
Santa Fe, NM 87504-1688
(505) 983-4335 (local)
(800) 545-2098 (out of state)

New York Venture Fund
RPF of America—Equity Fund
Venture Income (+) Plus

Voyageur Asset Management
100 South Fifth Street—Suite 2200—
Minneapolis, MN 55402
(800) 247-1576 (local)
(800) 553-2143 (out of state)

Double Exempt Flex Fund

Waddell & Reed
2400 Pershing Road—PO Box 418343—
Kansas City, MO 64141-9343

(816) 283-4122 (local)
(800) 366-5465 (out of state)
United Accumulative Fund
United Bond Fund
United Continental Income Fund
United Gold & Government Fund
United Government Securities
United High Income Fund
United High Income Fund II
United Income Fund
United International Growth
United Municipal Bond Fund
United Municipal High Income
United New Concepts Fund
United Retirement Shares
United Science & Energy Fund
United Vanguard Fund

Wall Street Management Corp
641 Lexington Avenue—21st Floor—
New York, NY 10022
(212) 319-9400★ (local)
Wall Street Fund

Washington Funds Distributors
1101 Vermont Avenue NW—Washington,
DC 20005
(202) 842-5300 (local)
(800) 972-9274 (out of state)
Growth Fund of Washington

Wealth Monitors Fund
1001 East 101st Terrace—Suite 220—
Kansas City, MO 64131
(816) 941-7990★ (local)
Wealth Monitors Fund

Weiss, Peck & Greer
One New York Plaza—New York, NY
10004
(212) 908-9582★ (local)
(800) 223-3332 (out of state)
Tudor Fund
WPG Dividend Income Fund
WPG Fund
WPG Growth Fund
WPG Tax-Free Money Market Fund

Weitz Value Fund
9290 West Dodge Road—Suite 405—
Omaha, NE 68114-3323

(402) 391-1980★ (local)
Weitz Value Fund

Westchester Capital Management
11 High Meadows—Mount Kisco, NY
10549
(914) 241-3360★ (local)
The Merger Fund

Wheat First Securities
PO Box 1357—Richmond, VA 23211
(804) 649-2311 (local)
(800) 999-4328 (out of state)
Southeastern Growth Fund

Winsbury Company
1900 E. Dublin, Granville Road—
Columbus, OH 43229
Telephone: (614) 461-4141 or
(800) 554-3862
Helmsman Disciplined Equity Portfolio
Helmsman Fund Income Portfolio
Parkstone Bond Fund
Parkstone Equity Fund
Parkstone High Income Equity Fund
Parkstone Intermediate Government
   Obligations Fund
Parkstone Limited Maturity Bond Fund
Parkstone Small Capitalization Value
   Fund
Seagate Intermediate Government
   Obligations Fund

Wood, Struthers & Winthrop Mgt
140 Broadway—New York, NY 10005
Telephone: (816) 283-1700 or
(800) 225-8011
Pine Street Fund
Winthrop Focus Growth Fund

Wood Logan
1455 East Putnam Avenue—
Old Greenwich, CT 06870
(800) 334-4437 (local)
Hidden Strength—Conserve Asset
Hidden Strength—Growth
Hidden Strength—Mod Asset

Yamaichi Capital Mgt., Inc.
Two World Trade Center—New York, NY
10048
Telephone: (212) 912-6400
Yamaichi Global Fund

BC Ziegler & Co

215 North Main Street—West Bend, WI 53095

(414) 334-5521 (local)

(800) 826-4600 (out of state)

Principal Preservation—Div Achievers

Principal Preservation—S&P 100 Plus

Zweig/Glaser Advisers

25 Broadway—New York, NY 10004

Telephone: (212) 361-9612 or (800) 272-2700

Zweig Series Trust Government Securities Series

Part Five

INTRODUCTION TO PORTFOLIO MANAGEMENT

■ OUTLINE

■ INTRODUCTION

The contemporary portfolio manager is continually called on to assess the nature of his or her performance over a period of time. A couple of decades ago, an analysis that merely indicated the extent of gains and losses would have been sufficient. This is no longer the case. There are at least two dimensions to every modern portfolio evaluation: the rate of return that was earned and the amount of risk that was taken. Many of the earlier concepts related to risk, introduced in Chapter 1, will now be more formally developed.

In Chapter 20 we evaluate the risk measurement tools for an individual asset as well as a portfolio of assets. We also review the concept that most investors are risk-averse. This implies that higher returns will have to be expected in order to induce investors to accept higher risks.

If we accept the concept of a premium return for risk, we must then consider what type of risk should be rewarded. Portfolio theory suggests that much of the risk in individual assets can be diversified away in a cross section or portfolio of investments and that only risk that cannot be diversified is likely to receive a higher return in a competitive marketplace. We examine the performance of institutional investors at the end of Chapter 20.

Chapter 20 brings together many of the risk-return concepts discussed in the previous chapters. The concept of asset allocation is discussed with an emphasis on portfolios allocated as a percentage of common stocks, bonds, Treasury bills, real estate, and international securities. This helps to tie together the concepts of risk-return trade-offs for each different security when viewed in a context of a portfolio.

20

PORTFOLIO MANAGEMENT

I n this chapter, we develop a more complete understanding of how the investor perceives risk and demands compensation for it. We eventually build toward a theory of portfolio management that incorporates many of these concepts. While some mathematics must be used to develop the concepts, we have attempted as much as possible to simplify the mathematical presentation, instead focusing on conceptual understanding rather than computational competency.

PORTFOLIO GOALS REVIEWED

Any portfolio manager must start with a set of goals and objectives and some planned strategy for meeting those goals. The investor's basic consideration is to decide between several conflicting goals. Should the investor pursue income or growth? Can growth be compatible with safety of principal? How much liquidity is needed in the portfolio? Is the investor in a high enough tax bracket to pursue tax-advantaged investments? Should the investment orientation be long-term or short-term? (These issues were discussed more fully in Chapter 1.)

Of course, one goal common to all investors is an expected rate of return. The higher the desired rate of return, however, the greater the assumed risk. Investors have not always thought this way; they often neglected risk considerations and focused only on return.

THE RETURN TRAP

In the bull market days of the 1950s and part of the 1960s, many portfolio managers turned in performances that were vastly superior to the market averages. High returns were often achieved by taking larger than normal risks through investing in small growth companies or concentrating in a limited number of high-return industries. These portfolio managers or their representatives proclaimed their superior ability in managing money and often extrapolated past returns to tempt investors with their image of the future. There was very little attempt to relate rate of return directly to risk exposure or to provide caveats about the likelihood of replicating past performance. They projected an image that in terms of generating returns, people were either superior money managers or they were not.

Nevertheless, with the end of the bull market era of the 1960s, a new mentality developed. Many of the gunslinging super performers of the past were the worst performers in a bear market. Their high returns of the past were probably not so much a result of unusual insight but rather that they utilized unusually high risk. Actually some portfolio managers began to welcome the notion of risk-adjusted returns. A mutual fund manager or bank trust department head could rationally explain to a client, "Although a competitor had a 2 percent higher return, it was actually inferior to our performance on a risk-adjusted basis." With the return to a bull market mentality in the 1980s and early 1990s, investors must be careful not to fall into the return trap; they should continue looking at return on a risk-adjusted basis.

A BASIC LOOK AT RISK-RETURN TRADE-OFFS

As indicated in Chapter 1, risk is generally associated with uncertainty about future outcome. The greater the range of possible outcomes, the greater the risk. We also observed in Chapter 1 that most investors tend to be risk-averse; that is, all things being equal, investors prefer less risk to more risk and will only increase their risk-taking position if a premium for risk is involved. Each investor has a different attitude toward risk. The inducement one investor needs to withdraw his funds from a savings account to drill an oil well may be quite different from that required by another. For some, only a very small premium for risk is necessary; others won't participate unless there are exceptionally high rewards.

The first 19 chapters cover many types of investments. The individual features of stocks, bonds, convertible bonds, Treasury bills, real estate, options, and futures have been presented and discussed. Figure 20–1 lists these investments in a risk-return trade-off graph. While some may take exception to the placement of one or two investment types, the general concept of higher risk holds in moving from left to right along the horizontal axis. This graph is relatively true for large portfolios of these asset types. But there are always exceptions. While an Eastern Airlines bond may be more risky than IBM stock, stocks in general are more risky than corporate bonds in general. As we move into the next section, we will present some basic quantitative methods

---

FIGURE 20–1   RISK-RETURN TRADE-OFFS FOR SELECTED INVESTMENTS

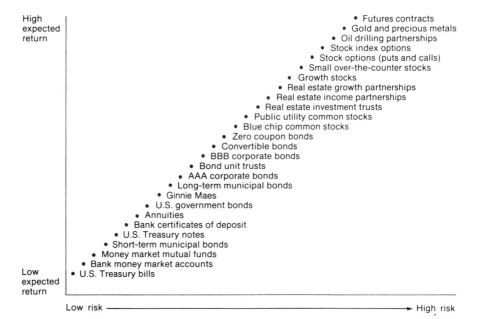

---

of measuring risk so that Figure 20–1 can be quantified as well as concep-
tualized.

Expected Value

To determine the expected value, we multiply each possible outcome by its
probability of occurence. Assume we are considering two investment proposals
where K represents a possible outcome and P represents the probability of that
outcome based on the state of the economy. The total probability always
equals 1.00 or 100 percent. If we were dealing with common stocks, K would
represent the price appreciation potential plus the dividend yield (total return).
Assume that we are examining two potential investments (investments i and
j) and that the potential returns are based on the following data.

Economic Possibilities	Probability P	Investment i Potential Returns K_i	Investment j Potential Returns K_j
Recession	.20	5%	20%
Slow growth	.30	7	8
Semistrong economy	.30	13	8
Strong economy	.20	15	6

Given the data for the economy and potential returns, an expected return value
$\bar{K}$ can be calculated for each investment. The expected value $\bar{K}$ is equal to the
sum (Σ) of K times P. In the case of both investments, the expected return is
10 percent. The calculation is as follows:

$$\bar{K} = \Sigma KP \qquad\qquad (20\text{--}1)$$

Economic Possibilities	Probability P	K	Investment i Potential Returns KP	K	Investment j Potential Returns KP
Recession	.20	5%	1.0%	20%	4.0%
Slow growth	.30	7	2.1	8	2.4
Semistrong economy	.30	13	3.9	8	2.4
Strong economy	.20	15	$\dfrac{3.0}{10\% = \bar{K}_i}$	6	$\dfrac{1.2}{10\% = \bar{K}_j}$

While both investments have the same expected rate of return, they may not
necessarily have the same risk characteristics. We use the standard deviation
as one measure of risk.

Standard Deviation

The commonly used measure of dispersion (variability) is the standard deviation denoted by the symbol (σ). The standard deviation measures the spread

of the outcomes around the expected value and is represented by Formula (20–2).

$$\sigma_i = \sqrt{\Sigma(K - \bar{K}_i)^2 P} \qquad (20\text{–}2)$$

Let's determine the standard deviation for investment i around the expected value ($\bar{K}_i$) of 10 percent.

K	$\bar{K}_i$	P	$(K - \bar{K}_i)$	$(K - \bar{K}_i)^2$	$(K - \bar{K}_i)^2 P$
5%	10%	.20	−5%	25%	5.0%
7	10	.30	−3	9	2.7
13	10	.30	+3	9	2.7
15	10	.20	+5	25	5.0
					15.4% $= \Sigma(K - \bar{K}_i)^2 P$

$$\sigma_j = \sqrt{\Sigma(K - \bar{K}_i)^2 P} = \sqrt{15.4\%} = 3.9\% \text{ (rounded)}$$

The standard deviation for investment j is:

$$\sigma_j = \sqrt{\Sigma(K - K_j)^2 P}$$

K	$\bar{K}_i$	P	$(K - \bar{K}_i)$	$(K - \bar{K}_i)^2$	$(K_j - \bar{K}_i)^2 P$
20%	10%	.20	+10%	100%	20.0%
8	10	.30	−2	4	1.2
8	10	.30	−2	4	1.2
6	10	.20	−4	16	3.2%
					25.6% $= \Sigma(K - \bar{K}_i)^2 P$

$$\sigma_j = \sqrt{\Sigma(K - \bar{K}_j)^2 P} = \sqrt{25.6\%} = 5.1\% \text{ (rounded)}$$

The standard deviation of investment i is 3.9 percent (rounded), while that of investment j is 5.1 percent (rounded). We assume that investment j is a countercyclical investment. It does well during a recession and poorly in a strong economy. Perhaps it represents a firm in the housing industry that is most profitable when the economy is sluggish and interest rates are low. Under these circumstances, people will avail themselves of low-cost financing to purchase a new home, and the firm's stock will do well. In a booming economy, interest rates will advance rapidly, and the financing of housing will become quite expensive. Thus, we have a countercyclical investment.

Even though both investments have an expected value of 10 percent, investment i has less risk because its standard deviation of 3.9 percent is smaller than the standard deviation of 5.1 percent for investment j. The bigger the standard deviation, the greater the risk for two securities that have the same expected returns. The standard deviation measures dispersion of outcomes around the mean of a normal distribution and statistically tells us that 68.26 percent of the outcomes should be within one standard deviation from the expected value. Two standard deviations includes 95.45 percent of the expected outcomes. If we show investments i and j in a normal distribution with a

FIGURE 20–2   INVESTMENTS i AND j—NORMALLY DISTRIBUTED RETURNS

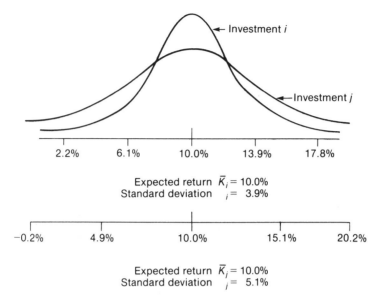

range of expected returns based on the standard deviation, the potential riskiness of both investments can be compared. As shown in Figure 20–2, approximately 68 percent of the time, investment *i* will have returns between 13.9 percent and 6.1 percent, while investment *j* will have returns between 15.1 percent and 4.9 percent. On the basis of two standard deviations (95.45 percent of the time), investment i will have returns between 17.8 percent and 2.2 percent, while investment *j* will be between 20.2 percent and −0.2 percent. The chance for bigger gains or losses is clearly higher (and therefore more risky) for investment *j*.

The above example demonstrates one measure of risk—the standard deviation of returns. The second basic measure of risk that we will discuss is called beta. The concept of beta is developed in the capital asset pricing model, which is presented in the next section.

THE CAPITAL ASSET PRICING MODEL

The capital asset pricing model (CAPM) relates the risk-return trade-offs of individual assets to market returns. Common stock returns over time have generally been used to test this model since stock prices are widely available and efficiently priced, as are market indexes of stock performance. In theory the CAPM encompasses all assets, but in practice it is difficult to measure returns on all types of assets or to find an all-encompassing market index. For our purposes, we will use common stock returns to explain the model, and occasionally we will generalize to other assets.

The basic form of the CAPM is a linear relationship between returns on individual stocks and the market over time. By using least squares regression analysis, the return on an individual stock, K_j, is expressed in Formula (20–3).

$$K_j = \alpha + \beta_j K_m + e \qquad (20\text{–}3)$$

where

K_j = Return on individual common stock of a company
α = Alpha, the intercept on the y-axis
B_j = Beta, the coefficient
K_m = Return on the market (usually an index of stock prices is used)
e = Error term of the regression equation

As indicated in Table 20–1 and Figure 20–3, this equation uses historical data to generate the beta coefficient (β_j), a measurement of the return performance of a given stock versus the return performance of the market. Assume that we want to calculate a beta for Parts Associates, Inc. (PAI), and that we have the performance data for that company and the market shown in Table 20–1. The relationship between PAI and the market appears graphically in Figure 20–3.

The alpha term in Figure 20–3 is 2.8 percent, and the beta term is .9. The alpha term is the expected return on PAI stock if returns on the market are zero. However, if the returns on the market are expected to approximate the historical rate of 12.4 percent, the expected rate return on PAI would be $K_j = 2.8 + 0.9(12.4) = 14.4$ percent. This maintains the historical relationship. If the returns on the market are expected to rise to 18 percent next year, expected returns on PAI would be $K_j = 2.8 + 0.9 (18.0) = 19$ percent.

Notice that we are talking in terms of equations. The CAPM is an expectational (ex ante) model, and there is no guarantee that historical data will recur. One area of empirical testing involves the stability and predictability of the beta coefficient based on historical data. Research has indicated that betas are more useful in a portfolio context (for groupings of stocks) because the

TABLE 20–1	PERFORMANCE OF PAI AND THE MARKET	
	Rate of Return on Stock	
Year	PAI	Market
1	12.0%	10.0%
2	16.0	18.0
3	20.0	16.0
4	16.0	10.0
5	6.0	8.0
Mean return	14.0%	12.4%
Standard deviation	4.73%	3.87%

FIGURE 20–3   LINEAR REGRESSION OF RETURNS BETWEEN PAI AND THE MARKET

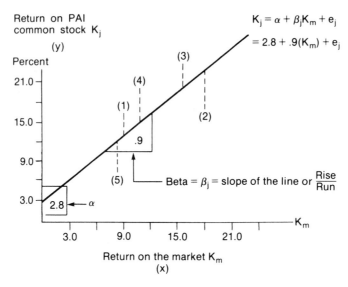

betas of individual stocks are less stable from period to period than portfolio betas. In addition, there seems to be a tendency for individual betas to approach 1.0 over time.

Systematic and Unsystematic Risk

Previously we mentioned that there are two major types of risk associated with a stock. One is the market movement or beta (β_j) risk. If the market moves up or down, a stock is assumed to change in value. This type of risk is referred to as *systematic* risk and was first introduced in Chapter 1. The second type of risk is represented by the error term (e_j) and indicates changes in value not associated with market movement. It may represent the temporary influence of a competitor's new product, changes in raw material prices, or unusual economic and government influences on a given firm. These changes are peculiar to an individual security or industry at a given point in time and are not directly correlated with the market. This second type of risk is referred to as *unsystematic* risk.

Recall that one type of risk is assumed to be compensated for under the capital asset pricing model while another is not. The investor is presumed to receive a risk premium for the beta (or systematic) risk but not for unsystematic risk. Since the latter is associated with an individual company or industry, it may be diversified away in a large portfolio and is not a risk inherent in investing in common stock. Thus, by picking stocks that are less than perfectly correlated, unsystematic risk may be eliminated. For example, the inherent risks of investing in semiconductor stocks may be diversified away by investing in the countercyclical housing stocks. Researchers have indicated that all but 15 percent of unsystematic risk may be eliminated with a carefully selected portfolio of 10 stocks and all but 11 percent with a portfolio of 20 stocks.[1] We thus can describe total risk as:

$$\text{Total risk} = \text{Systematic risk} + \text{Unsystematic risk}$$

But unsystematic risk can be diversified away, so that systematic risk (β_j) is the only relevant risk under the capital asset pricing model for which the investor can expect to receive compensation.

The Security Market Line (SML)

The capital asset pricing model evolved from Formula (20–3) into a risk premium model where the basic assumption is that in order for investors to take more risk they must be compensated by larger expected returns. Investors should also not accept returns that are less than they get from a riskless asset. For CAPM purposes, it is assumed that short-term U.S. Treasury bills may be considered a riskless asset.[2] When viewed in this context, an investor must achieve an extra return above that obtainable from a Treasury bill in order to induce the assumption of more risk. This brings us to the more common and theoretically useful model:

$$K_j = R_j + \beta_j(K_m - R_j) \qquad (20\text{–}4)$$

where

$$R_f = \text{Risk-free rate of return}$$
$$\beta_j = \text{Beta coefficient from Formula (20–3)}$$
$$K_m = \text{Return on the market index}$$
$$K_m - R_f = \text{Equity-risk premium or excess return of the market}$$
versus the risk-free rate (since the market is riskier than R_f, the assumption is that the expected K_m will be greater than R_f)
$$\beta_j(K_m - R_f) = \text{Expected return above the risk-free rate for}$$
the stock of company j, given the level of risk.

The model centers on beta, the coefficient of the premium demanded by an investor to invest in an individual stock. For each individual security, beta measures the sensitivity (volatility) of the security's return to the market. By definition, the market has a beta of 1.0, so that if an individual company's beta is 1.0, it can expect to have returns as volatile as the market and total returns equal to the market. A company with a beta of 2.0 would be twice as

---

[1]Wagner and Lau, "The Effect of Diversification on Risk," *Financial Analysts Journal,* November–December 1971.

[2]A number of studies have also indicated that longer term government securities may appropriately represent R_f, or the risk-free rate.

volatile as the market and would be expected to generate more returns, whereas a company with a beta of 0.5 would be half as volatile as the market.

Since the beta factor is deemed to be important in analyzing potential risk and return, there is much emphasis placed on knowing the beta for a given security. Merrill Lynch, Value Line, and various brokerage houses and investment services publish information on beta for a large number of securities. A representative list is presented in the table below.

Corporation	Beta (February 1990)
Liz Claiborne	1.55
Limited Inc.	1.40
Polaroid Corp.	1.25
Highland Superstores	1.00
Mobile Corp.	0.85
Homestake Mining	0.60

In order to practically apply the model to determine expected returns, the investor must have some estimate of the market risk premium $(K_m - R_f)$. While R_f, the one-year Treasury bill yield, is easily obtainable from *The Wall Street Journal* or other daily financial publications, estimating the expected market return, K_m, is not so easy. More often than not analysts will estimate the expected risk premium rather than K_m. A long-term study of security returns is updated each year by Ibbotson and Associates. This study provides useful insights into long-term risk premiums and the annual returns on stocks, bonds, and Treasury bills.

The Ibbotson-Sinquefield data ending the year 1988 shows that from 1926 through 1988 common stocks provided an annualized return of 10 percent while Treasury bills returned 3.5 percent annually over that same time period. If we substitute these values into the risk premium equation $(K_m - R_f)$, we get a premium of 6.5 percent over the last 62 years. Using more current data from 1948 to 1988, common stocks returned 12 percent while Treasury bills returned 4.9 percent for a 40-year equity-risk premium of 7.1 percent. This data is shown in Table 20–2. The risk premium for the last 20 years is quite low because of low annual stock returns and high Treasury bill yields. Both were the victims of high rates of inflation. This is a good time to remember that the capital asset pricing model is expectational and that we should not be blind slaves to past data. While history is important in setting expectations, we should not be so myopic that we use only the recent past to set our

TABLE 20–2	ANNUAL RETURNS—COMMON STOCK AND TREASURY BILLS		
Ibbotson-Sinquefield Data	Common Stock Returns K_m	One-Year T Bills R_j	Risk Premium $(\overline{K}_m - R_j)$
1926–1988	10.00%	3.50%	6.50%
1948–1988	12.00	4.90	7.10
1968–1988	9.60	7.40	2.20

expectations. The equity risk premium calculated on an annual basis is extremely volatile having a standard deviation of almost 20 percent. The market
does not always provide positive returns on an annual basis, and as far as risk
premiums are concerned, the long-term experience is a better measure of what
our expectations should be. For example, the recent past performance of the
stock market between 1982 and 1989 has increased the reported long-term risk
premiums as stock returns rose and Treasury bill yields fell. The risk premium
over longer periods is more stable; many analysts expect the average premium
should be between 5.5 percent and 6.5 percent. For illustrative purposes, we
will use an expected risk premium of 6.0 percent in the return equation.

For example, assuming that the risk-free rate is 7 percent and that the risk
premium is 6 percent, the following returns would occur with stocks having
betas of 0.5, 1.0, and 2.0.

$$K_j = R_f + B_j(K_m - R_f)$$

$$K_5 = 7.0\% + .5(6.0\%) = 10.0\%$$

$$K_{1.0} = 7.0\% + 1.0(6.0\%) = 13.0\%$$

$$K_{2.0} = 7.0\% + 2.0(6.0\%) = 19.0\%$$

Basically, beta measures the riskiness of an investment relative to the market.
In order to outperform the market, we would have to assume more risk by
selecting assets with betas greater than 1.0. Another way of looking at the
risk-return trade-off would be that if less risk than the market is desired, an
investor should choose assets with a beta of less than 1.0. Beta is a good
measure of a stock's risk when the stock is added to a diversified portfolio.

In Figure 20–3 individual stock returns were compared to market returns,
and the beta Formula (20–3) was shown. From Formula (20–4), the risk premium model, a generalized risk-return graph called the security market line
(SML), can be constructed that identifies the risk-return trade-off of any
common stock (asset) relative to the company's beta. This is shown in
Figure 20–4.

The required return for all securities can be expressed as the risk-free rate
plus a premium for risk. Thus, we see that a stock with a beta of 1.0 would
have a risk premium of 6.0 percent added to the risk-free rate of 7.0 percent
to provide a required return of 13 percent. Since a beta of 1.0 implies risk
equal to the market, the return is also at the overall market rate. If the beta is
2.0, twice the market risk premium of 6.0 percent must be earned, and we
add 12 percent to the risk-free rate of 7.0 percent to determine the required
return of 19 percent. For a beta of 0.5, the required return is 10 percent.

Using the SML for Risk–Return Analysis

The primary usefulness in examining the model in Figure 20–4 or similar risk-
return trade-off models is to provide some reasonable basis for relating return
opportunity with risk on the investment. Portfolio managers find risk-return
models helpful in explaining their performance or the performance of their
competitors to clients. A competitor's portfolio that has unusually high returns

FIGURE 20–4   THE SECURITY MARKET LINE (SML)

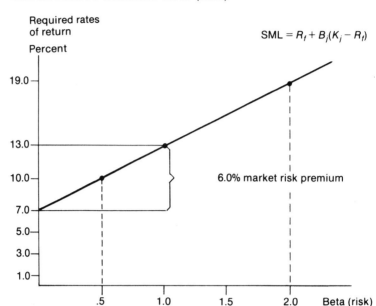

may have been developed primarily on the basis of high-risk assets. To the extent that this can be explained on the basis of capital market theory, the competitors' performance may look less like superior money management and more like a product of high risk taking. Many of the techniques for assessing portfolio performance on Wall Street are explicitly or implicitly related to the risk-return concepts discussed in this chapter.

Though empirical tests have somewhat supported the capital asset pricing model, a number of testing problems remain. In order to develop the SML in which stock returns (vertical axis) can be measured against beta (horizontal axis), an appropriate line must be drawn. Researchers have some disagreement about R_f. (Is it represented by short-term or long-term Treasury rates?) There is also debate about what is the appropriate K_m, or market rate of return. Some suggest the market proxy variable will greatly influence beta and that difficulties in dealing with this problem can bring the whole process under attack.[3]

When empirical data is compared to theoretical return expectations, there is some discrepancy in that the theoretical SML may have a slightly greater

[3]Richard Roll, "A Critique of the Asset Pricing Theory's Test," *Journal of Financial Economics,* March 1977, pp. 129–76. Also, "Ambiguity when Performance Is Measured by the Securities Market Line," *Journal of Finance,* September 1978, pp. 1051–69.

FIGURE 20–5   TEST OF THE SECURITY MARKET LINE

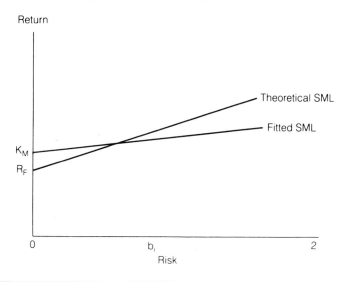

There may also be a possible problem in that betas for individual securities are not necessarily stable over time (rather than remaining relatively constant at 1.3 or perhaps .7, they tend to approach 1 over time). Thus, a beta based on past risk may not always reflect current risk.[5] Because the beta for a portfolio may be more stable than an individual stock's beta, portfolio betas are also used as a systematic risk variable.

By examining portfolio betas rather than individual stock betas, we overcome part of the criticism leveled at the instability of betas in the capital asset pricing model. Many of the other criticisms have also evoked new research that may provide different approaches or possible solutions to past deficiencies in the model. In any event, the capital asset pricing model is likely to remain relatively important in the future.

The major advantage of beta as a measure of risk is that the mathematical calculation to calculate the risk of a portfolio is much simpler than using the standard deviation as a portfolio risk measure. A portfolio beta is simply the weighted average of the betas of the individual stocks that make up the portfolio. The expected portfolio return is also a weighted average of the expected

The prose above "There may also be a possible problem..." begins:

slope than the actual line fitted of the basis on real-world data as shown in Figure 20–5.[4]

---

[4]Franco Modigliani and Gerald A. Pogue, "An Introduction to Risk and Returns," *Financial Analysts Journal,* March–April 1971, pp. 68–86, and May–June 1974, pp. 69–86.

[5]Robert A. Levy, "On the Short-Term Stationary of Beta Coefficients," *Financial Analysts Journal,* November–December 1971, pp. 55–62. Also, Marshall E. Blume, "Betas and Their Regression Tendencies," *Journal of Finance,* June 1975, pp. 785–95.

TABLE 20–3   PORTFOLIO RETURNS AND BETAS

Stock	Shares	Stock Price	Amount	Percent of Portfolio X	Expected Return K	Weighted Return XK_j	Beta B_j	XB_j
Beginning portfolio:								
OWU	100	$20	$ 2,000	10%	10%	1.0%	1.00	.10
ISU	100	30	3,000	15	12	1.8	1.20	.15
UOI	100	40	4,000	20	14	2.8	1.50	.30
DPU	100	50	5,000	25	15	3.75	2.00	.50
TCU	100	60	6,000	30	9	2.7	.80	.24
		Total portfolio =	$20,000		$K_p =$ 12.05%		$B_p =$ 1.32	
Restructured Portfolio:								
OWU	250	$20	$ 5,000	25.0%	10%	2.5 %	1.00	.25
ISU	150	30	4,500	22.5	12	2.7	1.20	.27
UOI	50	40	2,000	10.0	14	1.4	1.50	.15
DPU	50	50	2,500	12.5	15	1.875	2.00	.25
TCU	100	60	6,000	30.0	9	2.7	.80	.24
	Total portfolio value =		$20,000		$K_p =$ 11.175%		$B_p =$ 1.16	

return for each stock. These relationships are expressed in Formulas (20–5) and (20–6):

$$B_p \text{ (portfolio beta)} = XB_j \qquad (20\text{–}5)$$

$$K_p = R_f + B_p(K_m - R_f) \qquad (20\text{–}6)$$

where the subscript p represents the portfolio, X is the percentage of the portfolio invested in each stock, and j represents each individual stock in the portfolio. Perhaps a more practical way of presenting these concepts is to look at an actual portfolio of individual stocks. The first panel of Table 20–3 shows a five-stock portfolio where the expected return is 12.55 percent and the beta of the portfolio is 1.32. The second panel assumes that the same stocks are held in the portfolio but the percentage weights are changed to reduce the beta (risk) of the portfolio. As expected, the return also declines as risk decreases.

MEASUREMENT OF RETURN IN RELATION TO RISK

In examining the performance of fund managers, the return measure commonly used is excess returns. Though the term *excess returns* has many definitions, the one most commonly used is: total return on a portfolio (capital appreciation plus dividends) minus the risk-free rate:

Excess returns = Total portfolio return − Risk-free rate

Thus, excess returns represent returns over and above what could be earned on a riskless asset. The rate of U.S. government Treasury bills is often used to represent the risk-free rate of return in the economy (though other definitions are possible). Thus, a fund that earns 12 percent when the Treasury bill rate is 6 percent has excess returns of 6 percent.

Once computed, excess returns are then compared to risk. We look at three different approaches to comparing excess returns to risk: the Sharpe approach, the Treynor approach, and the Jensen approach.

Sharpe Approach

In the Sharpe approach,[6] the excess returns on a portfolio are compared to the portfolio standard deviation.

$$\text{Sharpe measure} = \frac{\text{Total portfolio return} - \text{Risk-free rate}}{\text{Portfolio standard deviation}}$$

$$(20\text{--}7)$$

The portfolio manager is thus able to view his or her excess returns per unit of risk. If a portfolio has a total return of 10 percent, the risk-free rate is 6 percent, and the portfolio standard deviation is 18 percent, the Sharpe measure is .22.

$$\text{Sharpe measure} = \frac{10\% - 6\%}{18\%} = \frac{4\%}{18\%} = .22$$

This measure can be compared to other portfolios or to the market in general to assess performance. If the market return per unit of risk is greater than .22, then the portfolio manager has turned in an inferior performance. Assume there is a 9 percent total market return, a 6 percent risk-free rate, and a market standard deviation of 12 percent. Then the Sharpe measure for the overall market is:

$$\frac{9\% - 6\%}{12\%} = \frac{3\%}{12\%} = .25$$

The portfolio measure of .22 is less than the market measure of .25 and represents an inferior performance. Of course, a portfolio measure above .25 would have represented a superior performance.

Treynor Approach

The formula for the second approach for comparing excess returns to risk (developed by Treynor[7]) is:

$$\text{Treynor measure} = \frac{\text{Total portfolio return} - \text{Risk-free rate}}{\text{Portfolio beta}}$$

$$(20\text{--}8)$$

The only difference between the Sharpe and Treynor approaches is in the denominator. While Sharpe uses the portfolio standard deviation—Formula

---

[6]William F. Sharpe, "Mutual Fund Performance," *Journal of Business,* January 1966, pp. 119–38.

[7]Jack L. Treynor, "How to Rate Management of Investment Funds," *Harvard Business Review,* January–February 1965, pp. 63–74.

(20–7), Treynor uses the portfolio beta—Formula (20–8). Thus, Sharpe uses total risk, while Treynor uses only the systematic, or beta, risk. Implicit in the Treynor approach is the assumption that portfolio managers have diversified away unsystematic risk, and only systematic risk remains.

If a portfolio has a total return of 10 percent, the risk-free rate is 6 percent, and the portfolio beta is .9, the Treynor measure would be:

$$\frac{10\% - 6\%}{.9} = \frac{4\%}{.9} = \frac{.04}{.9} = .044$$

This measure can be compared to other portfolios or to the market in general to determine whether there is a superior performance in terms of return per unit of risk. Assume that the total market return is 9 percent, the risk-free rate is 6 percent, and the market beta (by definition) is 1; then the Treynor measure as applied to the market is 0.3.

$$\frac{9\% - 6\%}{1.0} = \frac{3\%}{1.0} = \frac{.03}{1.0} = .03$$

This would imply that the portfolio has turned in a superior return to the market (.044 versus .03). Not only is the portfolio return higher than the market return (10 percent versus 9 percent), but the beta is less (.9 versus 1.0). Clearly, there is more return per unit of risk.

In the Sharpe and Treynor measures, we find that as long as the portfolios are well diversified, they usually provide the same rankings. The correlation coefficient R_{pm} is introduced in Table 20–4. It (R_{pm}) indicates how closely the market and the portfolio move together in generating returns. If a portfolio has a correlation coefficient of 1.00, the market and the portfolio have a perfect relationship with each other. In practice, as a portfolio becomes larger and more diversified, the correlation coefficient will usually be above .75 and move

TABLE 20–4	PORTFOLIO RISK-RETURN COMPARISONS USING SHARPE AND TREYNOR RISK MEASURES (Risk-Free Rate R_f = 7.0%)					
Portfolio Number	Returns K_p	Standard Deviation σ_p	Beta B_p	Sharpe $\frac{(K_p - R_i)}{\sigma_p}$	Treynor $\frac{(K_p - R_j)}{B_p}$	Correlation Coefficient R_{pm}
1	10%	11.8%	.68	.2542(7)	.0441(7)	.7492
2	10	12.1	.78	.2479(8)	.0385(8)	.8380
Market	12	13.0	1.00	.3846(6)	.0500(6)	1.0000
4	13	14.2	1.00	.4225(3)	.0600(2)	.9155
5	13	15.0	1.15	.4000(5)	.0522(5)	.9967
6	14	15.0	1.10	.4667(1)	.0636(1)	.9533
7	14	17.2	1.30	.4070(4)	.0538(4)	.9826
8	15	18.9	1.40	.4233(2)	.0571(3)	.9630

Note: Numbers in parentheses indicate the ranking of the portfolio on a risk-return basis.
Sharpe measures total risk versus excess returns, while Treynor assumes a diversified portfolio and measures systematic risk versus excess returns

closer to 1.00. Table 20–4 demonstrates this point. Using both the Sharpe and Treynor measures, portfolios 4, 5, 6, 7, and 8 all outperform the market.

Jensen Approach

In the third approach, Jensen also emphasizes using certain aspects of the capital asset pricing model to evaluate portfolio managers.[8] He compares their actual excess returns (total portfolio return − risk-free rate) to what should be required in the market, based on their portfolio beta.

The required rate of excess returns in the market for a given beta is shown in Figure 20–6 as the market line. If the beta is 0, the investor should expect to earn no more than the risk-free rate of return since there is no systematic risk. If the portfolio manger earns only the risk-free rate of return, the excess returns will be 0. Thus, with a beta of 0, the expected excess returns on the market line is 0. With a portfolio beta of 1, the portfolio has a systematic risk equal to the market, and the expected portfolio excess returns should be equal to market excess returns. If the market return (K_m) is 9 percent and the risk-

FIGURE 20–6   RISK-ADJUSTED PORTFOLIO RETURNS

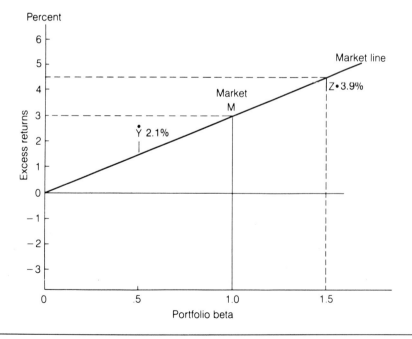

[8]Michael C. Jensen, "The Performance of Mutual funds in the Period 1945–1964," *Journal of Finance,* May 1968, pp. 389–416.

free rate (R_f) is 6 percent, the market excess returns are 3 percent. A portfolio with a beta of 1 should expect to earn the market rate of excess returns ($K_m - R_f$) equal to 3 percent. Other excess returns expectations are shown for beta ranging from 0 to 1.5. For example, a portfolio with a beta of 1.5 should provide excess returns of 4.5.

Adequacy of Performance

Using the Jensen approach, the adequacy of a portfolio manager's performance can be judged against the market line. Did he fall above or below the line? While it would appear that portfolio manager Y in Figure 20–6 had inferior excess returns in comparison to portfolio manager Z (2.1 percent versus 3.9 percent), this notion is quickly dispelled when one considers risk. Actually, portfolio manager Y performed above risk-return expectations as indicated by the market line, while portfolio manager Z was below his risk-adjusted expected level. The vertical difference from a fund's performance point to the market line can be viewed as a measure of performance. This value, termed *alpha* or *average differential return*, indicates the difference between the return on the fund and a point on the market line that corresponds to a beta equal to the fund. In the case of fund Z, the beta of 1.5 indicated an excess return of 4.5 percent along the market line, and the actual excess return was only 3.9 percent. We thus have a negative alpha of .6 percent (3.9% − 4.5%). Clearly, a positive alpha indicates a superior performance, while a negative alpha leads to the opposite conclusion.

A key question for portfolio managers in general is: Can they consistently perform at positive alpha levels? Can they generate returns better than those that are available along the market line, which are theoretically available to anyone? The results of a study conducted by John McDonald on 123 mutual funds are presented in Figure 20–7.

The upward-sloping line is the market line, or anticipated level of performance based on risk. The small dots represent performance of the funds. About as many funds underperformed (negative alpha below the line) as overperformed (positive alpha above the line). Although a few high-beta funds had an unusually strong performance on a risk-adjusted basis, there is no consistent pattern of superior performance.

DIVERSIFICATION

An important service that a money manager can provide is effective diversification of asset holdings. Once we accept the fact that superior performance on a risk-adjusted basis is a difficult achievement, we begin to look hard at other attributes that money managers may possess. We can ask: Are mutual fund managers effective diversifiers of their holdings?

As previously discussed, there are two measures of risk: systematic and unsystematic. Systematic risk is measured by the portfolio (or individual stock's)

FIGURE 20–7   EMPIRICAL STUDY OF RISK-ADJUSTED PORTFOLIO RETURNS—
                   SYSTEMATIC RISK AND RETURN

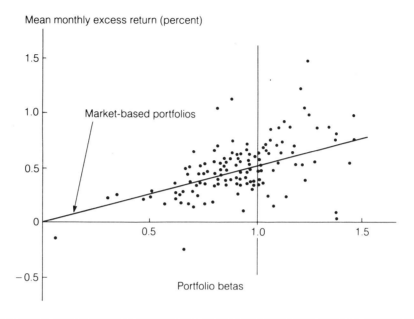

Source: John G. McDonald, "Objectives and Performance of Mutual Funds, 1960–1969," *Journal of Financial and Quantitative Analysis,* June 1974, p. 321.

beta. Under the capital asset pricing model, higher betas are rewarded with relatively high returns, and vice versa. As the market goes up 10 percent, our portfolio might go up 12 percent (beta of 1.2), and a similar phenomenon may occur on the downside. Unsystematic risk is random or nonmarket related and may be generally diversified away by the astute portfolio manager. Under the capital asset pricing model, there is no market reward for unsystematic risk since it can be eliminated through diversification.

The question for a portfolio manager then becomes: How effective have you been at diversifying away the nonrewarded, unsystematic risk? Put another way, to what extent can a portfolio's movements be described as market related rather than random in nature? If we plot a portfolio's excess returns over an extended period of time against market excess returns, we can determine the joint movement between the two as indicated in Figure 20–8. In panel (a) we plot our basic points. In panel (b) we draw a regression line through these points. Of importance to the present discussion is the extent to which our line fits the data. If the points of observation fall very close to the line, the independent variable, excess market returns, is largely responsible for describing the dependent variable, excess returns for portfolio X.

The degree of association between the independent and dependent variables

FIGURE 20–8   RELATIONSHIP OF PORTFOLIO'S EXCESS RETURNS TO MARKET
                    EXCESS RETURNS

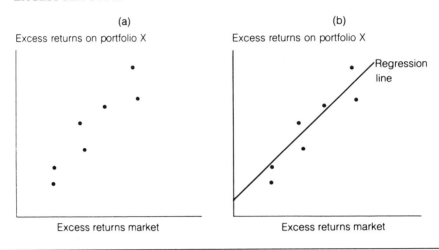

is measured by R^2 (coefficient of determination).[9] R^2 may take on a value anywhere between 0 and 1. A high degree of correlation between the independent and dependent variables will produce an R^2 of .7 or better. In panel (b) it is assumed to be .90.

In Figure 20–9 the points do not fall consistently close to the regression line, and the R^2 value is assumed to be only .55. In this instance, we say that the independent variable (excess market returns) was not the only major variable in explaining changes in the dependent variable (excess returns for portfolio Y).

The points in Figure 20–9 imply that the portfolio manager for portfolio Y may have not been particularly effective in his diversification efforts. Many other factors besides market returns appear to be affecting the portfolio returns of portfolio Y, and these could have been diversified away rather than allowed to influence returns. In this instance, we say there is a high degree of unsystematic, or nonmarket-related, risk. Since unsystematic risk is presumed to go unrewarded in the marketplace under the capital asset pricing model, there is evidence of inefficient portfolio diversification.

What does empirical data tell us about the effectiveness of portfolio managers in achieving diversification? How have they stacked up in terms of R^2 values

---

[9] R^2 also represents the correlation coefficient squared. Another statement is

$$R^2 = 1 - \frac{\Sigma(y - y_i)^2/n}{\Sigma(y - \bar{y})^2/n}$$

where y_i represents points along the regression line and y is the average value of the independent variable.

FIGURE 20–9   EXAMPLE OF LOWER CORRELATION

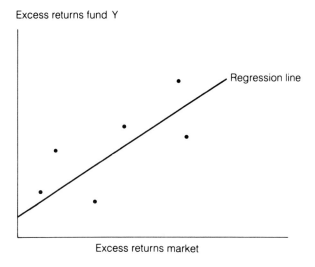

FIGURE 20–10   QUARTERLY RETURNS ATTRIBUTABLE TO MARKET FLUCTUATIONS: 100 MUTUAL FUNDS, 1970–1974

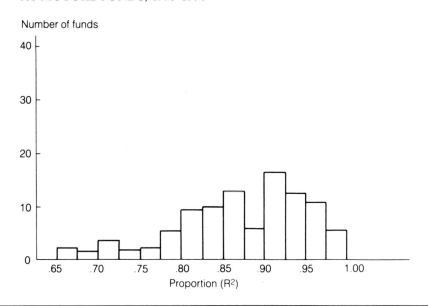

Source: Merrill Lynch, Pierce, Fenner & Smith, *Investment Performance Analysis, Comparative Survey, 1970–1974.*

TABLE 20–5   REDUCTION IN PORTFOLIO RISK THROUGH DIVERSIFICATION

Number of Securities in Portfolio	Standard Deviation of Portfolio Returns σ_p (percent per month)	Correlation with Return on Market Index★
1	7.0	0.54
2	5.0	0.63
3	4.8	0.75
4	4.6	0.77
5	4.6	0.79
10	4.2	0.85
15	4.0	0.88
20	3.9	0.89

★The market here refers to an unweighted index of all NYSE stocks.
Source: W. H. Wagner and C. S. Lau, "The Effect of Diversification on Risk," *Financial Analysts Journal,* November–December 1971, p. 53.

for their portfolios? As indicated in Figure 20–10, their record is generally quite good.

The Merrill Lynch study of 100 mutual funds depicted in Figure 20–10 shows an average R^2 value of approximately .90 with very few funds falling below .70. The actual range is between .66 and .98. Studies by McDonald, Jensen, Gentry, and Williamson have led to similar conclusions.

Although many mutual funds invest in 80 to 100 securities to achieve effective diversification, this is often more than is necessary. A high degree of diversification can be achieved with between 10 and 20 efficiently selected stocks, as is indicated in Table 20–5. The Wagner and Lau study shows the number of securities in the portfolio, the portfolio standard deviation, and correlation with return on the market index (R^2).

ASSET ALLOCATION: A PRACTICAL APPROACH TO DIVERSIFICATION

Asset allocation is an extension of the practical application of diversification. The concept of diversification used to be primarily concerned with buying common stocks from different industries so that a decline in one industry would not cause the whole equity portfolio to suffer. The rise of a more mathematical portfolio theory in the 1960s led to the concept of diversification by investing in common stocks that were not highly correlated. This was an extension of the commonsense industry diversification concept since stocks in the same industry were likely to be highly correlated while stocks in different industries might have unequal economic effects that would cause them to be not as highly correlated.

In the 1970s with the publication of *Stocks Bonds Bills and Inflation* by Ibbotson and Sinquefield, portfolio managers began giving more attention to the way these different asset classes were related in terms of risk, return, and correlation of returns. In the 1980s world equity markets began to become more viable capital markets as private ownership of companies became more popular throughout the world. This made investing in international securities easier than had previously had been the case.

Also during the bull market that began in 1982, mutual fund investing became very popular, and the number of funds dramatically increased during this decade. This was accompanied by a large growth in money market mutual funds as well as the concept of "families of funds." In a family of funds an investor could shift assets between a stock fund, a bond fund, and a money market fund in the same mutual fund family (such as Vanguard Funds or Fidelity Funds) without paying a commission each time.

As we enter the 1990s, the portfolio management trend has focused on allocating an investor's assets between a diversified mix of various financial, real, and monetary assets. This is the continued logical development of the diversification concept combined with the efficient market concept. Research studies indicate that markets are so efficient it is very difficult for even professional managers to outperform average market returns on a continuous basis. Statistical analysis of professionally managed mutual fund returns supports this conclusion.

Studies such as the one by Ibbotson and Sinquefield identify the risk-return characteristics of different asset classes over time. This information as well as studies on foreign investment returns and real estate returns allow an investor to choose a risk level and allocate a percentage of assets to the various asset categories to achieve a desired risk-return goal.

Allocating assets across asset classes by percentages reduces the importance of the individual asset selection process and focuses instead on the asset mix. By focusing on the mix of assets, the importance of timing is not eliminated, but its importance is reduced. Instead of being 100 percent right or wrong, an investor is likely to have some percentage of assets invested in each asset category at all times. However, if stock prices seem high, the percentage invested in stock could be reduced while the amount invested in money market funds could be increased. If foreign stocks are expected to perform better than domestic stocks, then the asset mix can be tilted more in favor of foreign equity investments.

The data provided by the Ibbotson study is shown in Table 20–6. Returns and the risk of each asset from 1926 to 1988 are given, and we can see that small stocks are the most risky and have the highest return. Small stocks are followed in descending order of risk and return by common stock, corporate bonds, U.S. government bonds, U.S. Treasury bills, and inflation as measured by the consumer price index. To put 100 percent of an investor's assets in small stocks would involve accepting the largest risk but over time the expected highest return.

Unfortunately, high returns cannot be counted on each and every year, and so to avoid suffering a 40–50 percent loss in a bad year, the investor might want to diversify into other assets. By combining securities with correlations of returns of less than one, the investor reduces his or her risk and can create portfolios with higher returns than otherwise might be the case without considering the return correlations between asset types. If the investor combines 100 shares of General Motors with 100 shares of Ford, the correlation between

TABLE 20–6   SUMMARY STATISTICS OF ANNUAL RETURNS, 1926–1988

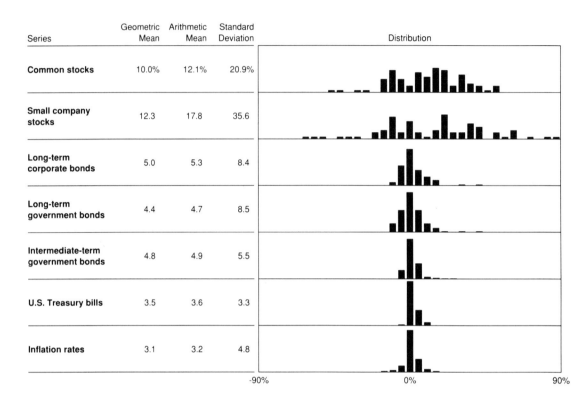

Series	Geometric Mean	Arithmetic Mean	Standard Deviation	Distribution
Common stocks	10.0%	12.1%	20.9%	
Small company stocks	12.3	17.8	35.6	
Long-term corporate bonds	5.0	5.3	8.4	
Long-term government bonds	4.4	4.7	8.5	
Intermediate-term government bonds	4.8	4.9	5.5	
U.S. Treasury bills	3.5	3.6	3.3	
Inflation rates	3.1	3.2	4.8	

Source: *Stocks, Bonds, Bills and Inflation, 1989 Yearbook: Market Results for 1926–1988,* Chicago: Ibbotson Associates, Inc., 1989, p. 29.

these two companies is likely to be close to one, and little risk reduction is likely to occur. On the other hand, if the investor combines 100 shares of General Motors with 100 shares of Philip Morris, some risk reduction will occur because the correlation of returns between these two stocks is less than one and not as high as that of GM and Ford.

If we carry this example a bit further, we could also reduce the risk of a portfolio by combining our 100 shares of General Motors with another asset type such as U.S. Treasury bills, which have even a lower correlation of returns with common stocks. Table 20–7, from the Ibbotson data, shows the correlations of returns between common stocks, small stocks, long-term corporate bonds, long-term government bonds, intermediate government bonds, U.S. Treasury bills, and inflation. Examination of the column titled "Common Stocks" shows the relationship between returns on common stocks and all the other assets. For example, common stocks have a negative correlation with U.S. Treasury bills of − .07. This makes sense because over longer time periods as interest rates go up, returns on Treasury bills go up but common stock

TABLE 20–7			SERIAL AND CROSS CORRELATIONS OF HISTORICAL YEARLY RETURNS (1926–1988)				
	Common Stocks	Small Stocks	Long-Term Corporate Bonds	Long-Term Government Bonds	Intermediate Government Bonds	U.S. Treasury Bonds	Inflation
Common stocks	1.00						
Small stocks	0.82	1.00					
Long-term corporate bonds	0.19	0.08	1.00				
Long-term government bonds	0.11	−0.01	0.93	1.00			
Intermediate government bonds	0.03	−0.07	0.89	0.89	1.00		
U.S. Treasury bills	−0.07	−0.08	0.19	0.22	0.50	1.00	
Inflation	−0.02	0.06	−0.17	−0.17	0.01	0.41	1.00
Serial correlations	0.01	0.10	0.16	0.09	0.28	0.92	0.64

Note: The standard error for all estimates is 0.13.
Source: *Stocks, Bonds, Bills and Inflation, 1989 Yearbook: Market Results for 1926–1988,* Chicago: Ibbotson Associates, Inc., 1989. p. 99.

prices generally go down. Stock returns are also negatively correlated to inflation and not very highly correlated with the returns of bonds in general.

Allocating assets between those assets classes shown in Table 20–7 will definitely reduce the risk faced by an investor. Most investors would assume that it will also reduce the risk over a portfolio invested entirely in common stock. To conceptualize the impact of various asset strategies without actually putting numbers on the returns, we have indicated some possible asset allocation strategies with estimated risk-return labels.

Portfolio A—Low Risk, Low Return

U.S. Treasury bills	20%
U.S. government bonds	40
U.S. corporate bonds	20
U.S. common stocks	20

Portfolio B—Medium Risk, Medium Return

U.S. Treasury bills	5%
U.S. government bonds	15
U.S. corporate bonds	20
U.S. common stocks	60

Portfolio C—High Risk, High Returns

U.S. Treasury bills	2%
U.S. corporate bonds	13
U.S. common stock	55
U.S. small stock	30

If one refers back to Tables 20–6 and 20–7 for the risk-return data, it is easy to see that portfolios B and C increase in risk and return. This happens as we increase the percentage of riskier high-return assets and reduce the percentage of lower risk, low-return assets to portfolios B and C. These portfolios would be very typical of a U.S. domestic portfolio with portfolio B representing a normal asset allocation that might be found in a U.S. pension fund portfolio. Portfolio A might be the asset allocation for a very conservative investor or the portfolio configuration for an investor who is trying to time the market and is expecting a decline in stock prices. Portfolio C could represent the asset allocation for an aggressive investor who expects to benefit from the long-term trend of high-return small stocks. If the investor has a long time horizon of 10 years or more before needing the income or principal from the portfolio, then it might pay to be aggressive because he or she would be less likely to be forced to sell the assets in a bad market. For investors with a short time horizon, the increased risk of portfolio C might not be warranted unless there were enough assets that selling in a bad market would not negatively impact the ability to maintain one's standard of living.

In addition to the three portfolios listed above, many investment managers would include two other categories of assets in an asset allocation strategy. First would be real estate which would at least represent the value of an investor's home or could represent other real estate assets such as rental property, real estate mutual funds, or real estate investment trusts. In addition, a

TABLE 20–8	THE BENEFITS OF DIVERSIFICATION (Stock Market and Bond-Market Returns Compared with Returns for Three Diversified Portfolios)				
Year	Stocks*	Bonds†	60% Stocks, 40% Bonds	1/3 Stocks, 1/3 Bonds, 1/3 Cash	BB&K Index‡
1970	4.01%	12.10%	7.52%	7.98%	4.7%
1971	14.31	13.23	14.14	10.83	13.7
1972	18.98	5.68	13.54	9.38	15.1
1973	− 14.66	− 1.11	− 9.11	− 3.03	− 2.2
1974	− 26.47	4.35	− 14.88	− 5.44	− 6.6
1975	37.20	9.19	25.65	17.04	19.6
1976	23.84	16.75	21.18	15.19	11.5
1977	− 7.18	− 0.67	− 4.57	− 0.94	6.1
1978	6.56	− 1.16	3.65	4.40	13.0
1979	18.44	− 1.22	10.28	9.14	11.5
1980	32.42	− 3.95	17.45	13.17	17.9
1981	− 4.91	1.85	− 1.99	4.06	6.4
1982	21.41	40.35	28.98	23.97	14.4
1983	22.51	0.68	13.43	10.52	15.4
1984	6.27	15.43	10.11	10.75	10.4
1985	32.16	30.97	31.85	23.38	25.4
1986	18.47	24.44	21.11	16.61	23.3
1987	5.23	− 2.69	3.59	3.92	8.6
1988	16.81	9.67	13.97	11.01	13.2
1989	31.49	18.11	26.24	19.22	14.3
Compound annual return	11.55	9.00	10.89	9.78	11.54

*Standard & Poor's 500 index
†Long-Term Treasury Bonds
‡20% U.S. stocks, 20% bonds, 20% cash, 20% real estate, 20% foreign stocks
Sources: Bailard, Biehl & Kaiser: Ibbotson Associates Inc.

category for foreign investments could include foreign stocks, foreign corporate bonds, and foreign government securities. Since foreign securities usually are not highly correlated to U.S. securities, diversifying into foreign securities should reduce the overall risk of the portfolio. If expected returns are higher than expected U.S. returns, inclusion of foreign assets could increase returns and at the same time lower portfolio risk. Adding foreign securities does open the portfolio to the foreign exchange risk. If the dollar rises against foreign currencies, the value of the foreign holdings will be worth less dollars. Any rise in the dollar would have to be offset by an equal percentage in foreign returns to simply maintain a zero adjusted return.

In an article that appeared in *The Wall Street Journal,* different asset allocation strategies were applied over the period 1970 to 1989. The results, which appear in Table 20–8, were rather surprising. Five asset allocation strategies were employed:

		Compound Annual Return
1.	100% common stock	11.55%
2.	100% long-term U.S. Treasury bonds	9.00
3.	60% stocks and 40% bonds	10.89
4.	1/3 stocks, 1/3 bonds, and 1/3 cash	9.78
5.	Bailard, Biehl & Kaiser Index	11.54
	(20% each in stocks, bonds, cash, real estate, and foreign stocks)	

Note: In the cases where cash is listed, the money is invested in U.S. Treasury bills.

The lowest risk strategy based on full diversification would be number 5 (equal weights between five asset classes). The interesting results are that the returns are about equal on portfolio 5 and portfolio 1. If you look closely at the annual returns in Table 20–8, you also notice that the returns are generally less volatile for portfolio 5 than portfolio 1. Additionally, strategy 5 had negative returns in only two years, and these were relatively small.

The overriding issue in asset allocation goes back to the concept of diversification. Research indicates that most investors, even professional ones, are not smart enough to always be in the right asset at the right time. Allocating your investment capital between different assets requires the investor to go back to the basics of setting goals, defining how much risk you will accept, having a time frame, and accepting the appropriate return for your risk. If your asset allocation strategy does not match your basic requirements, you are not being realistic with yourself or your investment advisor. Successful investors have a plan, stick to it, and know how to balance their risk-return requirements.

GLOSSARY

A

Abnormal Return Gains beyond what the market would normally provide after adjustment for risk.

Adjustable Rate Mortgage A mortgage in which the interest rate is adjusted regularly to current market conditions. It is sometimes referred to as a variable rate mortgage.

Advances Increases in the prices of various stocks as measured between two points in time. Significant advances in a large number of stocks indicate a particular degree of market strength. Also see *Declines*.

After-Acquired Property Clause The stipulation in a mortgage bond indenture requiring all real property subsequently obtained by the issuing firm to serve as additional bond security.

After-Market Performance The price experience of new issues in the market.

Alpha The value representing the difference between the return on a portfolio and a return on the market line that corresponds to a beta equal to the portfolio. A portfolio manager who performs at positive alpha levels would generate returns better than those available along the market line.

American Depository Receipts (ADRs) These securities represent the ownership interest in a foreign company's common stock. The process is as follows: The shares of the foreign company are purchased and put in trust in a foreign branch of a New York bank. The bank, in turn, receives and can issue depository receipts to the American shareholders of the foreign firm. These ADRs (depository receipts) allow foreign shares to be traded in the United States much like any other security. Through ADRs, one can purchase the stock of Sony Corporation, Honda Motor Co., Ltd., and hundreds of other foreign corporations.

Anticipated Realized Yield The return received on a bond held for a period other than that ending on the call date or the maturity date. In computing the anticipated realized yield, the investor considers both coupon payments and expected capital gains.

Arbitrage An arbitrage is instituted when a simultaneous trade (a buy and a sale) takes place in two different markets and a profit is locked in.

Arbitrage Pricing Theory A theory for explaining stock prices and stock returns. While the capital asset pricing model bases return solely on one form of systematic risk (market risk), arbitrage pricing theory can utilize several sources of risk (GNP, unemployment, etc.). Under this theory, it is assumed that the investor will not be allowed to earn a return greater than that dictated by the various sensitivity factors affecting returns. To the extent that he does, arbitrageurs will eliminate the extra returns by selling the security and buying other comparable securities—thus the term *arbitrage pricing theory*. Unlike the capital asset pricing model, there is no necessity to define K_M (the market rate of return).

Asset Utilization Ratios Ratios that indicate the number of times per year that assets are turned over. They show the activity in the various asset accounts.

Automatic Reinvestment Plan A plan offered by a mutual fund in which the fund automatically reinvests all distributions to a shareholder account.

Average Differential Return The alpha value which indicates the difference between the return on a portfolio or fund and a return on the market line that corresponds to a beta equal to the portfolio or fund.

B

Balance Sheet A financial statement that indicates, at a given point in time, what the firm owns and how these assets are financed in the form of liabilities and ownership interest.

Balanced Funds Mutual funds that combine investments in common stock, bonds, and preferred stock. Many balanced funds also invest in convertible securities as well. They try to provide income plus some capital appreciation.

Banker's Acceptance A short-term debt instrument usually issued in conjunction with a foreign trade transaction. The acceptance is a draft that is drawn on a bank for approval for future payment and is subsequently presented to the payer.

Barron's *Confidence Index* An indicator utilized by technical analysts who follow smart money rules. Movements in the index measure the expectations of bond investors whom some technical analysts see as astute enough to foresee economic trends before the stock market has time to react.

Barron's *Group Stock Averages* *Barron's* publishes stock averages covering 32 industry groups. These averages are especially useful to the analyst who is following the performance of a specific industry relative to the general market.

Basis The difference between the futures price and the value of the underlying item. Thus, on a stock index futures contract, basis represents the difference between the stock index futures price and the value of the underlying index. The basis may be either positive or negative, with the former indicating optimism and the latter signifying pessimism.

Basis Point The unit of measure of change on interest bearing instruments. One basis point is equal to .01 percent.

Best Efforts The issuing firm, rather than the investment banker, assumes the risk for a distribution. The investment banker merely agrees to provide his best effort to sell the securities.

Beta A measurement of movement of a security with the market in general. It measures volatility. A high beta coefficient indicates high amounts of systematic risk.

Beta-Related Hedge A stock index futures hedge in which the relative volatility of the portfolio to the market is considered in determining the number of contracts necessary to offset a given dollar level of exposure. If a portfolio has a beta greater than 1, then extra contracts may be necessary to compensate for high volatility.

Beta Stability The amount of consistency in beta values over time. Instability means prior beta values may not be reflective of future beta values.

Black-Scholes Option Pricing Model A formal model used to determine the theoretical value of an option. Such factors as the riskless interest rate, the length of the option, and the volatility of the underlying security are considered. For a more complete discussion, see Appendix 13–B.

Blind Pool A form of limited partnership for real estate investments in which funds are provided to the general partner to select properties for investment.

Bond Price Sensitivity The sensitivity of a change in bond prices to a change in interest rates. Bond price sensitivity is influenced by the duration of the bond in that the longer the duration of a bond, the greater the price sensitivity. A less-sophisticated but acceptable approach is to tie price sensitivity to the maturity of the bond rather than the duration.

Bond Swaps The term refers to selling out of a given bond position and immediately buying into another one with similar attributes in an attempt to improve overall portfolio return or performance.

Breadth of Market Indicators Overall market rules used by technical analysts in comparing broad market activity with trading activity in a few stocks. By comparing all advances and declines in NYSE-listed stocks, for example, with the Dow Jones Industrial Average, analysts attempt to judge when the market has changed directions.

Bull Spread An option strategy utilized when the expectation is that the stock price will rise. The opposite strategy is a bear spread.

Business Cycle Swings in economic activity encompassing expansionary and recessionary periods and, on average, occurring over four-year periods.

Buying the Spread A term indicating the cost from writing the call is more than the revenue of the short position. The opposite results in "selling the spread."

C

Call An option to buy 100 shares of common stock at a specified price for a given period of time.

Call Provision A mechanism for repaying funds advanced through a bond issue. A provision of the bond indenture allows the issuer to retire bonds prior to maturity by paying holders a premium above principal.

Capital Appreciation A growth in the value of a stock or other investments as opposed to income from dividends or interest.

Capital Asset Pricing Model A model by which assets are valued based on their risk characteristics. The required return for an asset is related to its beta.

Capital Market Line The graphic representation of the relationship of risks and returns with various portfolios of assets. The line is part of the capital asset pricing model.

Cash Settlement Closing out a futures or options contract for cash rather than calling for actual delivery of the underlying item specified in the contract—for example, pork bellies and T-bills. The stock index futures markets and stock index options markets are *purely* cash-settlement markets. There is never even the implied potential for future delivery of the S&P 500 Stock Index or other indexes.

CBOE Chicago Board Options Exchange, the first exchange for call options.

Certificates of Deposit Savings certificates which entitle the holder to the receipt of interest. These instruments are issued by commercial banks and savings and loans (or other thrift institutions)

Certified Financial Planner (CFP) A financial planner who has been appropriately certified by the College for Financial Planning in Denver. He or she must demonstrate skills in risk management, tax planning, retirement and estate planning, and other similar areas.

Chartered Financial Analyst (CFA) A security analyst or portfolio manager who has been appropriately certified through experience requirements and testing.

Charting The use by technical analysts of charts and graphs to plot past stock price movements which are used to predict future prices.

Closed-End Fund A closed-end investment fund has a fixed number of shares, and purchasers and sellers of shares must deal directly with each other rather than with the fund. Close-end funds trade on an exchange or over-the-counter.

Closing Purchase Transactions A transaction in which an investor who is a writer of an option intends to terminate his obligation.

Closing Sale Transaction A transaction in which an investor who is the holder of an outstanding security intends to liquidate his position as a holder.

Combined Earnings and Dividend Model A model combining earnings per share and an earnings multiplier with a finite dividend model. Value is derived from both the present value of dividends and the present value of the future price of the stock based on the earnings multiplier (P/E).

Commercial Paper A short-term credit instrument which is issued by large business corporations to the public. Commercial paper usually comes in minimum denominations of $25,000 and represents an unsecured promissory note.

Commission Broker An individual who represents a stock brokerage firm at an exchange and who executes sales and purchases stocks for the firm's clients across the nation.

Commodities Such tangible items as livestock, farm produce, and precious metals. Users and producers of commodities hedge against future price fluctuations by transferring risks to speculators through futures contracts.

Constant-Dollar Method Adjusting for inflation in the financial statements by using the consumer price index.

Constant-Growth Model A dividend valuation model that assumes a constant growth rate for dividends.

Construction and Development Trust A type of REIT that makes short-term loans to developers during their construction period.

Consumer Price Index An index used to measure the changes in the general price level.

Contrary Opinion Rules Guidelines, based on such factors as the odd-lot or the short sales position, used by technical analysts who predict stock market activity on the assumption that such groups as small traders or short sellers are often wrong. Also see *Smart Money Rules*.

Control Value The value of a company based on having control of the firm through a merger or leveraged buyout. It may be 50 percent or more than the then current value.

Conversion Premium The amount, expressed as a dollar value or as a percentage, by which the price of the convertible security exceeds the current market value of the common stock into which it may be converted.

Conversion Price The face value of a convertible security divided by the conversion ratio, gives the price of the underlying common stock at which the security is convertible. An investor would usually not convert the security into common stock unless the market price was greater than the conversion prices.

Conversion Ratio The number of shares of common stock an investor receives in exchanging convertible bonds or shares of convertible preferred stock for shares of common stock.

Conversion Value The value of the underlying common stock represented by convertible bonds or convertible preferred stock. This dollar value is obtained by multiplying the conversion ratio by the per-share market price of the common stock.

Convertible Security A corporate bond or a share of preferred stock which, at the option of the holder, can be converted into shares of common stock of the issuing corporation.

Correlation Coefficient The measurement of joint movement between two variables.

Coupon Rate The stated, fixed rate of interest paid on a bond.

Covered Writer A writer of an option who owns the stock on which the option is written. If the stock is not owned, the writer is deemed naked.

Creditor Claims Claims represented by debt instruments offered by financial institutions, industrial corporations, or the government.

Cross Hedge A hedging position in which one form of security is used to hedge another form of security (often because differences in maturity dates or quality characteristics make a perfect hedge difficult to establish).

Cumulative Voting The stockholder gets one vote for each share of stock he or she owns times one vote for each director to be elected. The stockholder may then accumulate votes in favor of a specified director or number of directors. Cumulative voting tends to allow the minority interest to have some representation on the board.

Currency Fluctuations Changes in the relative value of one currency to another. For example, the French franc may advance or decline in relation to the dollar. To the extent a foreign currency appreciates relative to the dollar, returns on foreign investments will increase in terms of dollars. The opposite would be true for declining foreign currencies.

Currency Futures Futures contracts for speculation or hedging in different nations' currencies.

Current-Cost Method Adjusting for inflation in the financial statements by revaluing assets at their current cost.

Current Ratio Current assets divided by current liabilities.

Current Yield The annual dollar amount of interest paid on a bond divided by the price at which the bond is currently trading in the market.

Cyclical Indicators Factors that economists can observe to measure the progress of economic cycles. Leading indicators move in a particular direction in advance of the movement of general business conditions, while lagging indicators change direction after general conditions, and coincident indicators move in unison with the economy.

Cyclical Industry An industry, such as automobiles, whose financial health is closely tied to the condition of the general economy. Such industries tend to make the type of products whose purchase can be postponed until the economy improves.

D

Data Base A form of organized, stored data. It is usually fed into the computer for additional analysis.

Debenture An unsecured corporate bond.

Debt-Utilization Ratios Ratios that indicate how the firm is financed between debt (lenders)and equity (owners) and the firm's ability for meeting cash payments due on fixed obligations, such as interest, lease payments, licensing fees, or sinking-fund charges.

Declines Decreases in the prices of various stocks as measured between two points in time. Significant declines in a large number of stocks indicate a particular degree of market weakness. Also see *Advances*.

Deep Discount Bond A bond that has a coupon rate far below rates currently available on investments and which consequently can be traded only at a significant discount from par value. It may offer an opportunity for capital appreciation.

Defined-Benefit Plan Under a defined-benefit plan, the employee can calculate his or her pension based on a formula using such factors as years of service and average earnings.

Defined-Contribution Plan Under a defined-contribution plan, retirement benefits are a function of total contributions over the life of the plan and are not based on such factors as years of service or average earnings.

Derivative Products Securities that derive their existence from other items. Stock index futures and options are sometimes thought of as derivatives because they derive their existence from actual market indexes but have no intrinsic characteristics of their own.

Diagonal Spread A combination of a vertical and horizontal spread.

Dilution The reduction in earnings per share that occurs when earnings remain unchanged yet the number of shares outstanding increases, as in the conversion of convertible bonds or preferred stock into common stock.

Direct Equity Claim Representation of ownership interests through common stock or other instruments to purchase common stock, such as warrants and options.

Discount Rate The interest rate at which future cash flows are discounted to a present value.

Dispersion The distribution of values or outcomes around an expected value.

Diversification Lack of concentration in any one item. A portfolio composed of many different securities is diversified.

Diversification Benefits Risk reduction through a diversification of investments. Investments that are negatively correlated or that have low positive correlation provide the best diversification benefits. Such benefits may be particularly evident in an internationally diversified portfolio.

Dividend Valuation Model Any one of a number of stock valuation models based on the premise that the value of stock lies in the present value of its future dividend stream.

Dividend Yield Annual dividends per share divided by market place.

Dollar Cost Averaging The inventor buys a fixed dollar's worth of a given security at regular intervals regardless of the security's price or the current market outlook. This provides a certain degree of discipline and also means that more shares will be purchased at low prices rather than high prices since the amount of the regular investment is fixed and only the number of shares purchased varies.

Dow Jones Industrial Average An index of stock market activity based on the price movements of 30 large corporations. The average is price-weighted, which means that each stock is effectively weighted by the magnitude of its price.

Dow Theory The theory, developed by Charles Dow in the late 1890s and still in use today, states that the analysis of long-term (primary) stock market trends can yield accurate predictions for future price movements.

Downside Protection The protection that a convertible bond investor enjoys during a period of falling stock prices. While the underlying common stock and the convertible bond may both fall in value, the bond will fall only to a particular level because it has a fundamental, or pure, bond value based on its assured income stream.

Downside Risk The possibility that an asset, such as a security, may fall in value as a result of fundamental factors or external market forces. The limit of the downside risk for a convertible bond can be computed as the difference between the bond's market price and its pure bond value divided by the market price.

Du Pont Analysis A system of analyzing return on assets through examining the profit margin and asset turnover. Also, the value of return on equity is analyzed through evaluating return on assets and the debt/total assets ratio. Figure 7–2 summarizes the major components of the Du Pont system of analysis.

Duration The weighted average life of a bond. The weights are based on the present values of the individual cash flows relative to the present value of the total cash flows. Duration is a better measure than maturity when assessing the price sensitivity of bonds; that is, the impact of interest-rate changes on bond prices can be more directly correlated to duration than to maturity.

E

Earnings per Share The earnings available to holders of common stock divided by the number of common stock shares outstanding.

Earnings Valuation Model Any one of a number of stock valuation models based on the premise that a stock's value is some appropriate multiple of earnings per share.

Effective Diversification The diversification of a portfolio to remove unsystematic risk.

Efficient Frontier A set of portfolios of investments in which the investor receives maximum return for a given level of risk or a minimum risk for a given level of return.

Efficient Hedge A hedge in which one side of the transaction effectively covers the exposed side in terms of movement.

Efficient Market The capacity of the market to react to new information, to avoid rapid price fluctuations, and to engage in increased or reduced trading volume without realizing significant price changes. In an efficient market environment, securities are assumed to be correctly priced at any point in time.

Efficient Market Hypothesis The concept that there are many participants in the securities markets who are profit maximizing and alert to information so that there is almost instant adjustment to new information. The weak form of this hypothesis suggests that there is no relationship between past and future prices. The semistrong form maintains that all forms of public information are already reflected in the price of a security, so fundamental analysis cannot determine under- or overvaluation. The strong form suggests that all information, insider as well as public, is impounded in the value of a security.

Efficient Portfolio A portfolio that combines assets so as to minimize the risk for a given level of return.

Equal-Weighted Index Each stock, regardless of total market value or price, is weighted equally. It is as if there were $100 invested in each and every

stock in the index. The Value Line Index is a prime example of an equal-weighted index.

Equipment Trust Certificate A secured debt instrument used by firms in the transportation industry that provides for bond proceeds to purchase new equipment, which in turn is collateral for the bond issue.

Equity Participation The lender also participates in an ownership interest in the property.

Equity Trust A type of REIT that buys, operates, and sells real estate as an investment as opposed to construction and development trusts and mortgage trusts.

Excess Returns Returns in excess of the risk-free rate or in excess of a market measure such as the S&P 500 Stock Index.

Exchange Listing A firm lists its shares on an exchange (such as the American or New York Stock Exchange).

Exchange Privilege A feature offered by a mutual fund sponsor in which a shareholder is able to move his or her money between various funds under the management of the sponsor at a very minimal processing charge and without a commission.

Exercise Price (Warrant) The price at which the stock can be bought using the warrant.

Expectations Hypothesis The hypothesis which explains the term structure of interest rates, stating that a long-term interest rate is the average of expected short-term interest rates over the applicable time period. If, for example, long-term rates are higher than short-term rates, then according to the expectations hypothesis, investors must expect that short-term rates will be increasing in coming periods.

Expected Value The sum of possible outcomes times their probability of occurrence.

Extraordinary Gains and Losses Gains or losses from the sale of corporate fixed assets, lawsuits, or similar events that would not be expected to occur often, if ever again.

F

Fed The Federal Reserve serves as the central banking authority for the United States. The Fed enacts monetary policy, and it plays a major role in regulating commercial banking operations and controlling the money supply.

Federal Deficit A situation in which the federal government spends more money than it receives through taxes and other revenue sources.

Federal Surplus A situation in which taxes and other government revenues provide more money than is needed to cover government expenditures.

FIFO A method of inventory valuation in which it is assumed that inventory purchased first is sold first (first-in, first-out).

Financial Asset A financial claim on an asset (rather than physical possession of a tangible asset) usually documented by a legal instrument, such as a stock certificate.

Financial-Service Companies Firms that provide a broad range of financial services in order to diversify their consumer base. Services may include brokerage activities, insurance, banking, and so forth.

Fiscal Policy Government spending and taxing practices designed to promote or inhibit various economic activities.

Floor Broker An independent stockbroker who is a member of a stock exchange and who executes trades, for a fee, for commission brokers experiencing excessive volumes of trading.

Floor Value A value which an income-producing security will not fall below because of the fundamental value attributable to its assured income stream.

Flow-of-Funds Analysis Analysis of the pattern of financial payments between business, government, and households.

Foreign Currency Effects To the extent a foreign currency appreciates relative to the dollar, returns on foreign investments will increase in terms of dollars. The opposite would be true for declining foreign currencies.

Foreign Political Risks The risks associated with investing in firms operating in foreign countries. There is the danger of nationalization of foreign firms or the blockage of capital flows to investors. There also may be the danger of violent overthrow of the political party in power, with all the associated implications. Punitive legislation against foreign firms or investors is another political risk.

Fourth Market The direct trading between large institutional investors in blocks of listed stocks. The participants avoid paying brokerage commissions.

Fully Diluted Earnings per Share The value of earnings per share that would be realized if all outstanding securities convertible into common stock were, in fact, converted.

Fundamental Analysis The valuation of stocks based on fundamental factors, such as company earnings, growth prospects, and so forth.

Funded Pension Plan Current income is charged with pension liabilities in advance of the actual payment, and funds are set aside.

Futures Contract An agreement that provides for sale or purchase of a specific amount of a commodity at a designated time in the future at a given price.

G

General Obligation Bonds A municipal bond backed by the full faith, credit, and "taxing power" of the issuing unit rather than the revenue from a given project.

GNMA Pass-Through Certificates These securities represent an undivided interest in a pool of federally insured mortgages. Actually, GNMA (the Government National Mortgage Association) buys a pool of mortgages from various lenders at a discount and then issues securities to the public against the mortgages. They are pass-through securities in that the holder of a GNMA certificate receives the interest and principal payment on the mortgages on a monthly basis.

Going Public Selling privately held shares to new investors on the over-the-counter market for the first time.

Government Securities Bonds issued by federal, state, or local governmental units or government agencies. Whereas corporate securities' returns are paid through company earnings, government securities are repaid through taxes or the revenues from projects financed by the bonds.

Graduated-Payment Mortgage A type of mortgage in which payments start out on a relatively low basis and increase over the life of the loan.

Greed Index A contrary opinion index that measures how "greedy" investors are. Greed is thought to be synonymous with bullish sentiment, or optimism. Under the assumptions of the greed index, the more greedy or optimistic investors are, the more likely the market is to fall and vice versa.

Gross National Product Implicit Price Deflator A calculation made by the Department of Commerce which adjusts the prices of all goods and services in the GNP estimate for the effects of price change. It's a measure of inflation.

Growth Company A company that exhibits rising returns on assets each year and sales that are growing at an increasing rate (growth phase of the life-cycle curve). Growth companies may not be as well known as growth stocks.

Growth Funds Mutual funds with the primary objective of capital appreciation.

Growth Stock The stock of a firm generally growing faster than the economy or market norm.

Growth-with-Income Funds Mutual funds that combine a strategy of capital appreciation with income generation.

H

Hedging A process for lessening or eliminating risk by taking a position in the market opposite to your original position. For example, someone who owns wheat can sell a futures contract to protect against future price declines.

Horizontal Spread Buying and writing two options with the same strike price but maturing in different months.

I

Ibbotson and Sinquefield Study A University of Chicago study examining comparative returns on stocks and fixed-income securities from the mid-1920s to the present.

Immunization Immunizing or protecting a bond portfolio against the effects of changing interest rates on the ending value of the portfolio. The process is usually tied to a time horizon. In the process, if interest rates go up, there will be a decline in the value of the portfolio, but a higher reinvestment rate opportunity for inflows. Conversely, if interest rates go down, there will be capital appreciation for the portfolio, but a lower reinvestment rate opportunity. By tying all the investment decisions to a specified duration period, the portfolio manager can take advantage of these counter forces to ensure a necessary outcome.

Income Bond A corporate debt instrument on which interest is paid only if funds are available from current income.

Income Statement A financial statement that shows the profitability of a firm over a given period of time.

Income-Statement Method A method of forecasting earnings per share based on a projected income statement.

Indenture A lengthy, complicated legal document which spells out the borrowing firm's responsibilities to the individual lenders in a bond issue.

Index Fund A fund investing in a portfolio of corporate stocks, the composition of which is determined by the Standard & Poor's 500 Index or some other index.

Indirect Equity Claim An indirect claim on common stock such as that achieved by placing funds in investment companies.

Individual Retirement Account (IRA) An IRA allows a taxpayer to deduct $2,000 from taxable income and invest the funds at a bank, savings and loan, brokerage house, mutual fund, or other financial institution. The funds are normally placed in interest-bearing instruments, or perhaps in other securities, such as common stock. Not only is the $2,000 allowed to be deducted from earned income to reduce current taxes, but the income on the funds is allowed to grow tax-free until withdrawn at retirement.

Industry Factors The unique attributes that must be considered in analyzing a given industry or group of industries. Examples include industry structure, supply/demand of labor and materials, and government regulation.

Industry Life Cycle The movement of a firm or industry through stages of development, growth, expansion, and maturity.

Inflation A general increase in the prices of goods and services.

Inflation-Adjusted Accounting Restating financial statements to show the effect of inflation on the balance sheet and income statement. This is supplemental to the normal presentation based on historical data.

Inflationary Expectations A value representing future expectations about the rate of inflation. This value, combined with the real rate of return, provides the risk-free required return for the investor.

Insider Trading Trading by those who had special access to unpublished information. If the information is used to illegally make a profit, there may be large fines and possible jail sentences.

Institutional Investor A type of investor (as opposed to individual investors) representing organizations responsible for bringing together large pools of capital for investment. Institutional investors include investment companies, pension funds, life insurance companies, bank trust departments, and endowments and foundations.

In the Money A term that indicates when the market price of a stock is above the striking price of the option. When the strike price is above the market price, the option is out of the money.

Interest Rate Futures Futures contracts involving Treasury bills, Treasury bonds, Treasury notes, commercial paper, certificates of deposit, and GNMA certificates.

International Tax Problems Many foreign countries impose a 7.5 percent to 15 percent withholding tax against the dividends or interest paid to nonresident holders of equity or debt securities. However, it is often possible for tax-exempt U.S. investors to secure an exemption or rebate on part or all of the withholding tax. Also, taxable U.S. investors can normally claim a U.S. tax credit for taxes paid in foreign countries. The problem is more likely to be one of inconvenience and paper shuffling rather than loss of funds.

Internationally Oriented Funds Mutual funds and closed-end investment companies that invest in worldwide securities. Some funds specialize in Asian holdings, others in South African, and so on.

Intrinsic Value Value of an option equal to market price minus the strike price.

Inverse Pyramiding A process of leveraging to control commodities contracts in which the profits from one contract are used to purchase another contract on margin, and profits on this contract are applied to a third, and so on.

Investment The commitment of current funds in anticipation of the receipt of an increased return of funds at some point in the future.

Investment Banker One who is primarily involved in the distribution of securities from the issuing corporation to the public. An investment banker also advises corporate clients on their financial strategy and may help to arrange mergers and acquisitions.

Investment Banking The underwriting and distribution of a new security issue in the primary market. The investment banker advises the issuing concern on price and other terms and normally guarantees sale while overseeing distribution of the securities through the selling brokerage houses.

Investment Companies A type of financial institution that takes proceeds of individual investors and reinvests them in securities according to their specific objectives. A popular type of investment company is the mutual fund.

J

Jensen Measure of Portfolio Performance Jensen compares excess returns (total portfolio returns minus the risk-free rate) to what should be required in the market based on the portfolio beta. For example, if the portfolio beta is 1, the portfolio has a systematic risk equal to the market, and the expected portfolio excess returns should be equal to market excess returns (the market rate of return minus the risk-free rate). The question then becomes: Did the portfolio manager do better or worse than what is expected? The portfolio manager's excess returns can be compared to the market line of expected excess returns for any beta level.

Junk Bonds High-risk, low-grade bonds rated below BBB. They often perform like common stock and may provide interesting investment opportunities.

K

K_e The term representing anticipated rate of return equal to dividend yield plus expected growth in earnings and dividends. It is the discount rate applied to future dividends.

Key Indicators Various market observations used by technical analysts to predict the direction of future market trends. Examples include the contrary opinion and smart money rules.

L

Least Squares Trendline A statistically developed linear trendline that minimizes the distance of the individual observations from the line.

Less-Developed Countries Foreign countries that have not fully developed their economic system and productive capacity. Examples might include Chile, Jordan, Korea, Thailand, and Zimbabwe. A number of these less-developed countries may represent good risk-reduction potential for U.S. investors because the factors that influence their economic welfare may be quite different from critical factors in the United States. Investments in these countries, at times, may also provide high returns.

Leveraged Buy-Outs The management of the company or some other investor group borrows the needed cash to repurchase all the shares of an existing company. The balance sheet of the company serves as the collateral base to make the borrowing possible. After the leveraged buy-out, the company may be taken private for a period of time in which unprofitable assets are sold off and reduction of debt takes place. The intent is then to bring the company to the public market once again (or resell it to another company) at a large profit over the initial purchase price.

LIFO A method of inventory valuation in which it is assumed that inventory purchased last is sold first (last-in, first-out).

Limit Order A condition placed on a transaction executed through a stockbroker to assure that securities will be sold only if a specified minimum price is received or purchased only if the price to be paid is no more than a given maximum.

Limited Partnership A business arrangement in which there is the limited liability protection of a corporation with the tax provisions of a regular partnership. All profits or losses are directly assigned to the partners for tax purposes. The general partner has unlimited liability.

Lipper Mutual Fund Investment Performance Averages Lipper publishes indexes for growth funds, growth-with-income funds, and balanced funds. Lipper also shows year-to-date and weekly performance for many other categories of funds.

Liquidity The capacity of an investment to be retired for cash in a short period of time with a minimum capital loss.

Liquidity Preference Theory A theory related to the term structure of interest rates. The theory states that the term structure tends to be upward sloping more than any other pattern. This reflects a recognition of the fact that long maturity obligations are subject to greater price change movements than short maturity obligations when interest rates change. Because of increased risk of holding longer-term maturities, investors demand a higher return to hold such securities. Thus, they have a preference for short-term liquid obligations.

Liquid Ratios Ratios that demonstrate the firm's ability to pay off short-term obligations as they come due.

Long Position A market transaction in which an investor purchases securities with the expectation of holding the securities for cash income or for resale at a higher price in the future. See also *Short Position*.

Lorie and Fisher Study A University of Chicago study indicating comparative returns on financial assets over half a decade. It is similar to the Ibbotson and Sinquefield study in many respects.

M

Margin Account A trading account maintained with a brokerage firm on which the investor may borrow a percentage of the funds for the purchase of securities. The broker loans the fund at interest slightly above the prime rate.

Margin Maintenance Requirement The amount of money that must be "deposited" to hold a margin position if losses reduce the initial margin that was put up.

Margin Requirements The amount of money that must be "deposited" to purchase a commodity contract or shares of stock on margin.

Market A mechanism for facilitating the exchange of assets through buyer-seller communication. The communication, and not a central negotiating location, is the requisite condition for a market to exist, though some transactions (for example, trades at the various stock exchanges) do involve a direct meeting of buyers and sellers or their agents.

Market Capitalization The total market value of the firm. It is computed by multiplying shares outstanding times stock price.

Market Line On a graph, excess returns are shown on the vertical axis, the portfolio beta is shown on the horizontal axis, and the market line describes the relationship between the two.

Market Rate of Interest The coupon rate of interest paid on bonds currently issued. Of course, a previously issued bond which is currently traded may be sold at a discount or a premium so that the buyer in effect receives the market rate even if the coupon rate on this older bond is substantially higher or lower than market rates. The market rate is also known as the yield to maturity.

Market-Segmentation Theory A theory related to the term structure of interest rates that focuses on the demand side of the market. There are several large institutional participants in the bond market, each with its own maturity preferences. Banks tend to prefer short-term liquid securities to match the nature of their deposits, whereas life insurance companies prefer long-term bonds to match their long-run obligations. The behavior of these two institutions and of savings and loans often creates pressure on short-term or long-term rates but very little on the intermediate market of five- to seven-year maturities. This theory helps to focus on the accumulation or liquidation of securities by institutions during the different phases of the business cycle and the resultant impact on the yield curve.

Maturity Date The date at which outstanding principal must be repaid to bondholders.

Merger Price Premium The difference between the offering price per share and the market price per share of the merger candidate (before the impact of the offer).

Monetarist An economic analyst who feels that monetary policy tools, and not fiscal policy, can best provide a stable environment of sustained economic growth.

Monetary Policy Direct control of interest rates or the money supply undertaken by the Federal Reserve to achieve economic objectives. Used in some cases to augment or offset the use of fiscal policy.

Money Market Account Accounts offered by financial institutions to compete with money market funds. The minimum deposit is $500 to $1,000, with a maximum of three checks drawn per month.

Money Market Fund A type of mutual fund which invests in short-term government securities, commercial paper, and repurchase agreements. Most offer check-writing privileges.

Money Supply The level of funds available at a given time for conducting transactions in our economy. The Federal Reserve can influence the money supply through its monetary policy tools. There are many different definitions of the money supply. For example, M1 is currency in circulation plus private checking deposits, including those in interest-bearing NOW accounts. M2 adds in savings accounts and money market mutual funds, and so on.

Mortgage Trust A form of REIT in which long-term loans are made to real estate investors.

Multinational Corporations Firms that have operations in a number of foreign countries. Multinationals are frequently found in such industries as oil, mainframe computers, and banking.

Municipal Bonds Tax-exempt debt securities issued by state and local governments (including special political subdivisions).

Mutual Fund A pooling of funds by investors for reinvestment. The funds are administered by professional managers. Technically, only an open-end (see definition) investment fund is considered to be a mutual fund.

Mutual Fund Cash Position An overall market rule which asserts that by examining the level of uncommitted funds held by large institutional investors, analysts can measure the potential demand for stocks and thereby anticipate market movements.

N

NASDAQ OTC Indexes Index measures for components of the over-the-counter market. The OTC Indexes are value-weighted.

National Association of Securities Dealers Automated Quotations System (NASDAQ) A computerized system that provides up-to-the-minute price quotations on about 5,000 of the more actively traded OTC stocks.

Net Asset Value The net asset value (NAV) represents the current value of an investment fund. It is computed by taking the total value of the securities, subtracting out the liabilities, and dividing by the shares outstanding.

Net Debtor-Creditor Hypothesis Since inflation makes each dollar worth less, it is often argued that a person or firm that is a net debtor gains from inflation because payments of interest and return of principal are made with continually less-valuable dollars. Conversely, a net creditor loses real capital because the loans are repaid in less-valuable dollars.

Net Working Capital Current assets minus current liabilities.

New York Stock Exchange Index A market value-weighted measure of stock market changes for all stocks listed on the NYSE.

No-Load Mutual Fund A mutual fund on which no sales commission must be paid. The funds' shares are sold, not through brokers, but rather through the mail or other direct channels.

Nominal GNP Gross national product expressed in current, noninflation-adjusted dollars.

Nominal Return A return that has not been adjusted for inflation.

Nonconstant Growth Model A dividend valuation model that does not assume a constant growth rate for dividends.

O

Odd-Lot Dealer A member of a stock exchange who maintains an inventory of a particular firm's stock in order to sell odd lots (trades of less than 100 shares) to customers of the exchange.

Odd-Lot Theory The contrary opinion rule stating that small traders (who generally buy or sell odd lots) often misjudge market trends, selling just before upturns and buying before downturns. The theory has not been useful in predicting trends observed in recent years.

Open-End Fund An open-end investment fund stands ready at all times to sell or redeem shares from stockholders. There is no limit to the number of shares. Technically, a mutual fund is considered to be an open-end investment fund. Also see *Closed-End-Fund*.

Open-Market Operations The Federal Reserve's action of buying or selling government securities in order to expand or contract the amount of money in the economy.

Opening Purchase Transaction A transaction in which an investor intends to become the holder of an option.

Opening Sale Transaction A transaction in which an investor intends to be a writer of an option.

Operating Margin Operating income divided by sales.

Option The right acquired for a consideration to buy or sell something at a fixed price within a specified period of time.

Option Premium The intrinsic value plus a speculative premium.

Option Price The specified price at which the holder of a warrant may buy the shares to which the warrant entitles purchase.

Options Clearing Corporation Issues all options listed on the exchanges which trade in options.

Options on Industry Indexes An option index contract specifically tailored to a given industry. Thus, one who wishes to speculate on a given industry's performance or hedge against holdings in that industry can use industry index options (sub-indexes).

Options on Stock Index Futures An option to purchase a stock index futures contract at a specified price over a given time period. This security combines the options concept with the futures concept.

Organized Exchanges Institutions, such as the New York Stock Exchange, the American Stock Exchange, or any of the smaller regional exchanges, that provide a central location for the buying and selling of securities.

OTC National Market System A segment of the OTC stock market made up of stocks that have a diversified geographical stockholder base and relatively large activity in their securities. Stocks in the National Market System receive enhanced market activity reporting through the NASDAQ system.

Overall Market Rules Guidelines, such as breadth of market indicators or mutual fund cash positions, used by technical analysts who predict stock market activity based on past activity.

Over-the-Counter Market Not a specific location but rather a communications network through which trades of bonds, nonlisted stocks, and other securities take place. Trading activity is overseen by the National Association of Securities Dealers (NASD).

P

Par Bonds Bonds that are selling at their par or maturity values rather than at premium or discounted prices. Par value on a corporate bond is generally $1,000.

Par Value (Bond) The face value of a bond, generally $1,000 for corporate issues, with higher denominations for many government issues.

Partial Hedge A hedge position in which only part of the risk is eliminated or lessened.

Payout Ratio Annual dividends per share divided by annual earnings per share.

Peak The point in an economic cycle at which expansion ends and a recession begins.

Perpetual Bond A bond with no maturity date.

Personal Savings/Personal Disposable Income The rate at which people are saving their disposable income. This has implications for the generation of funds to modernize plant and equipment and increase productivity.

Poison Pill A provision that makes it very difficult for a firm to be taken over in a merger or acquisition against its will. The potential purchaser may have to pay a prohibitive price for existing securities or perhaps current stockholders are allowed to buy new shares at a very low price to dilute the anticipated ownership of the intended acquirer.

Portfolio The term applied to a collection of securities or investments.

Portfolio Effect The effect obtained when assets are combined into a portfolio. The interaction of the assets can provide risk reduction such that the portfolio standard deviation may be less than the standard deviation of any one asset in it.

Portfolio Insurance Protecting a large portfolio against a decline. A common strategy is to sell stock index futures contracts in anticipation of a decline.

Portfolio Manager One who has responsibility for managing large pools of funds. Portfolio managers may be employed by insurance companies, mutual funds, bank trust departments, pension funds, and other institutional investors.

Preferred Stock A hybrid security that generally provides fixed returns. Preferred stockholders are paid returns after bondholder claims are satisfied but before any returns are paid to common stockholders. Though preferred stock returns are fixed in amount, they are classified as dividends (not interest) and are not tax-deductible to the issuing firm.

Price-Earnings Ratio The multiplier applied to earnings per share to determine current value. The P/E ratio is influenced by the earnings and sales growth of the firm, the risk or volatility of its performance, the debt-equity structure, and other factors.

Price Ratios Ratios that relate the internal performance of the firm to the external judgment of the marketplace in terms of value.

Price-Weighted Average Each stock in the average is weighted by its price. The higher the price, the greater the relative weighting. The Dow Jones Industrial Average represents a price-weighted average.

Primary Earnings Per Share A firm's adjusted earnings after taxes divided by the number of shares of common stock outstanding plus common stock equivalents. Common stock equivalents include warrants and other options along with convertible securities that are paying low returns at the time of issue compared to other comparable securities.

Primary Market A market in which an investor purchases an asset (via an investment banker) from the issuer of that asset. The purchase of newly issued shares of corporate stock is an example of primary market activity. Subsequent transfers of the particular asset take place in the secondary market.

Private Placement The company sells its securities to private investors such as insurance companies, pension funds, and so on rather than through the public markets. Investment bankers may also aid in a private placement on a fee basis. Most private placements involve debt rather than common stock.

Profitability Ratios Ratios that allow the analyst to measure the ability of the firm to earn an adequate return on sales, total assets, and invested capital.

Program Trading Computer-based trigger points are established in which large volume trades are indicated. The technique is used by institutional investors.

Prospectus A document that must accompany a new issue of securities. It contains the same information appearing in the registration statement, such as a list of directors and officers, financial reports certified by a CPA, the underwriters, the purpose and use for the funds, and other reasonable information that investors need to know.

Public Placement Public distribution of securities through the financial markets.

Pure Bond Value The fundamental value of a bond that represents a floor price below which the bond's value should not fail. The pure bond value is computed as the present value of all future interest payments added to the present value of the bond principal.

Pure Pickup Yield Swap A bond swap where a bond owner thinks that he or she can increase the yield to maturity by selling a bond and buying a different bond of equal risk. This implies market disequilibrium.

Put An option to sell 100 shares of common stock at a specified price for a given period of time.

Put Provision This provision enables a bond investor to have an option to sell a long-term bond back to the corporation at par value after a relatively short period of time (such as three to five years). This privilege can be particularly valuable if interest rates have gone up and bond prices have gone down.

Q

Quick Ratio Current assets minus inventory (i.e., cash, marketable securities, and accounts receivables) divided by current liabilities.

R

R^2—The Coefficient of Determination It measures the degree of association between the independent variable(s) and the dependent variable. It may take on a value anywhere between 0 and 1.

Real Asset A tangible piece of property that may be seen, felt, held, or collected, such as real estate, gold, diamonds, and so on.

Real Estate Investment Trust (REIT) An organization similar to a mutual fund where investors pool funds that are invested in real estate or used to make construction or mortgage loans.

Real GNP Gross national product expressed in dollars that have been adjusted for inflation.

Real Rate of Return The return that investors require for allowing others to use their money for a given time period. This is the value that investors demand for passing up immediate consumption and allowing others to use their savings until the funds are returned. Because the term *real* is employed, this means it is a value determined *before* inflation is added.

Registered Trader A member of a stock exchange who trades for his or her own account rather than for the client of a brokerage firm.

Reinvestment Assumption with Bonds The assumed rate of reinvestment for inflows from a bond investment. It is normally assumed that inflows can be reinvested at the yield to maturity of the bond. This, however, may not be valid. Interest rates may go up or down as inflows from coupon payments come in and need to be reinvested. A more-valid approach is to assign appropriate reinvestment rates to inflows and then determine how much the total investment will be worth at the end of a given time period. This process is known as terminal wealth analysis.

Reported Income versus Adjusted Earnings Reported income is generally based on historical cost accounting, whereas adjusted earnings have been modified for the effect of inflation (on inventory and plant and equipment).

Reserve Requirements Percentages of bank deposit balances stipulated by the Federal Reserve as unavailable for lending. By increasing or reducing reserve requirements, the Fed can contract or expand the money supply.

Resistance Level The technical analysts' view that as long as a given long-term trend continues, prices of a particular stock or of the market as a whole will not rise above the upper end of the normal trading range (the resistance level) because at that point, investors sell in an attempt to get even or take a profit.

Return on Equity Net income divided by stockholder's equity.

Revenue Bond A municipal bond supported by the revenue from a specific project, such as a toll, road, bridge, or municipal coliseum.

Risk Uncertainty concerning the outcome of an investment or other situation. It is often defined as variability of returns from an investment. The greater the range of possible outcomes, the greater the risk.

Risk-Adjusted Return The amount of return after adjustment for the level of risk incurred to achieve the return.

Risk-Free Rate The required rate of return before risk is explicitly considered. It is composed of the real rate of return plus a rate equivalent to inflationary expectations. It is referred to as R_F.

Risk Premium A premium assumed to be paid to an investor for the risk inherent in an investment. It is added to the risk-free rate to get the overall required return on an investment.

S

Secondary Market A market in which an investor purchases an asset from another investor rather than the issuing corporation. The activity of secondary markets sets prices and provides liquidity. Also see *Primary Market*.

Sector Funds Mutual funds that specialize in a given segment of the economy such as energy, medical technology, computer technology, and so forth. While they may offer the potential for high returns, they are clearly less diversified and more risky than a typical mutual fund.

Secured Bond A bond which is collateralized by the pledging of assets.

Securities Act of 1933 Enacted by Congress to curtail abuses by securities issuers, the law requires full disclosure of pertinent investment information and provides for penalties to officers of firms that do not comply.

Securities Acts Amendments of 1975 Enacted to increase competition in the securities markets, this legislation prohibits fixed commissions on public offerings of securities and directs the Securities and Exchange Commission to develop a single, nationwide securities market.

Securities and Exchange Commission (SEC) The federal government agency created in 1934 to enforce securities laws. Issuers of securities must register detailed reports with the SEC, and the SEC polices such activities as insider trading, investor conspiracies, and the functionings of the securities exchanges.

Securities Exchange Act of 1934 Created the Securities and Exchange Commission to regulate the securities markets. The act further empowers the Board of Governors of the Federal Reserve System to control margin requirements.

Securities Investor Protection Corporation Created under the Securities Investor Protection Act of 1970, this agency oversees the liquidation of insolvent brokerage firms and provides insurance on investors' trading accounts.

Security Analyst One who studies various industries and companies and provides research reports and valuation studies.

Security Market Line The graphic representation of risk (as measured by beta) and return for an individual security.

Selling Short against the Box A short sale of securities with the objective of deferring the payment of taxes. This requires a short sale against shares already owned so that shares owned are delivered to cover the short position as the transaction is completed.

Semistrong Form of Efficient Market Hypothesis The hypothesis states that all public information is already impounded into the value of a security, so fundamental analysis cannot determine under- or overvaluation.

Serial Bond A mechanism for repaying funds advanced through a bond issue. Regular payments systematically retire individual bonds with increasing maturities until, after many years, the entire series has been repaid.

Settle Price The term for the closing price on futures contracts.

Shared-Appreciation Mortgage A type of mortgage in which the lender participates in any increase in value associated with the property being mortgaged.

Sharpe Measure of Portfolio Performance Total portfolio return minus the risk-free rate divided by the portfolio standard deviation. It allows the portfolio manager to view his or her excess returns in relation to total risk. Comparisons between various portfolios can be made based on this relative risk measure.

Short Position (Short Sale) A market transaction in which an investor sells borrowed securities in anticipation of a price decline. The investor's expectation is that the securities can be repurchased (to replace the borrowed shares) at a lower price in the future. Also see the definition for *Long Position*.

Short Sales Position Theory The contrary opinion rule stating that large volumes of short sales can signal an impending market upturn because short sales must be covered and thereby create their own demand. Also, the average short seller is often thought to be wrong.

Sinking Fund A mechanism for repaying funds advanced through a bond issue. The issuer makes periodic payments to the trustee, who retires part of the issue by purchasing the bonds in the open market.

Small-Firm Effect A market theory that suggests that small firms produce superior returns compared to larger firms on both an absolute and risk-adjusted basis.

Smart Money Rules Guidelines, such as *Barron's* Confidence Index, used by technical analysts who predict stock market activity based on the assumption that sophisticated investors will correctly predict market trends and that their lead should be followed. Also see *Contrary Opinion Rules*.

Specialist or Dealer Hedge A specialist on an exchange or dealer in the over-the-counter market buys and sells stocks for his own inventory for temporary holding (as a part of his market-making function). At times, he may assume a larger temporary holding than desired with all the risks associated with that exposure. Stock index futures or options can reduce the market, or systematic, risk, although they cannot reduce the specific risk associated with a security.

Speculative Premium The difference between an option or warrant's price and its intrinsic value. That an investor would pay something in excess of the intrinsic value indicates a speculative desire to hold the security in anticipation of future increases in the price of the underlying stock.

Spot Market The term applied to the cash price for immediate transfer of a commodity as opposed to the futures market where no physical transfer takes place immediately.

Spreads A combination of options which consists of buying one option (going long) and writing an option (going short) on the same stock.

Standard & Poor's 500 Stock Index An index of 500 major U.S. Corporations. There are 400 industrial firms, 20 transportation firms, 40 utilities, and 40 financial firms. This index is value-weighted.

Standard & Poor's 400 Industrial Index An index which measures price movements in the stocks of 400 large industrial corporations listed on the New York Stock Exchange.

Standard & Poor's International Oil Index A value-weighted index of oil firms. Options on the index have been traded on the Chicago Board Options Exchange.

Standard Deviation A measure of dispersion that considers the spread of outcomes around the expected value.

Statement of Cash Flows Formally established by the Financial Accounting Standards Board in 1987, the purpose of the statement of cash flows is to emphasize the critical nature of cash flows to the operations of the firm. The statement translates accrual-based net income into actual cash dollars.

Stock Dividend A dividend paid by issuing more stock which results in retained earnings being capitalized.

Stock Index Futures A futures contract on a specific stock index, such as the Standard & Poor's 500 Stock Index or the NYSE Composite Index.

Stock Index Options An option contract to purchase (call) or sell (put) a stock index. Popular contracts include the S&P 100 Index, the American Exchange Major Market Index, and others. The purchaser of a stock index option pays an initial premium and then closes out the option at a given price in the future.

Stock Repurchase A purchase by a firm of its own shares in the marketplace.

Stock Split The result of a firm dividing its shares into more shares with a corresponding decrease in par value.

Stop Order A mechanism for locking in gains or limiting losses on securities transactions. The investor is not assured of paying or receiving a particular price but rather agrees to accept the price prevailing when the broker is able to execute the order after prices have reached some predetermined figure.

Straddle A combination of a put and call on the same stock with the same strike price and expiration date.

Straight-Line Depreciation A method of depreciation in which the project cost is divided by the project life to calculate each year's depreciation amount.

Strong Form of the Efficient Market Hypothesis A hypothesis that says that all information, insider as well as public, is reflected in the price of a security.

Support Level The technical analyst's view that as long as a given long-term trend continues, prices of a particular stock or of the market as a whole will not fall below the lower end of a normal trading range (the support level) because at that point, low prices stimulate demand.

Swaps The procedure of selling out of a given bond position and immediately buying into another one with similar attributes in an attempt to improve overall portfolio return or performance.

Syndicate A group of investment bankers which jointly shares the underwriting and distribution responsibilities in a large offering of new securities. Each participant is responsible for a predetermined sales volume. One or a few firms serve as the managing underwriters.

Synergy A more-than-proportionate increase in performance from the combination of two or more parts.

Systematic Risk Risk inherent in an investment related to movements in the market that cannot be diversified away.

Systematic Withdrawal Plan A plan offered by a mutual fund in which the investor receives regular monthly or quarterly payments from his or her investment in the fund.

T

Tax Hedge An investor may have accumulated a large return on a diversified portfolio in a given year. In order to maintain the profitable position but defer the taxable gains until the next year, stock index future or options contracts may be employed. Of course, for individual securities, individual stock options may be used when available.

Tax Swaps Selling out of one bond position and buying into a similar one in order to take advantage of a tax situation. For example, one might sell a bond that has a short-term capital loss in order to take the deduction and replace it with a similar bond.

Technical Analysis An analysis of price and volume data as well as other related market indicators to determine past trends that are believed to be predictable into the future. Charts and graphs are often utilized.

Term Structure of Interest Rates This depicts the relationship between maturity and interest rates for up to 30 years.

Terminal Wealth Table A table that indicates the ending or terminal wealth from a bond investment based on the reinvestment of the inflows at a specified rate (which may be different from the coupon rate). The initial investment can then be compared to the terminal wealth (compound interest plus principal) and an overall rate of return computed.

Third Market The trading between dealers and institutional investors, through the over-the-counter market, of NYSE-listed stocks. The third market accounts for an extremely small share of total trading activity.

Trading Range The spread of prices that a stock normally sells within.

Treasury Bill A short-term U.S. government obligation. A Treasury bill is purchased at a discount and is readily marketable.

Treasury Bond A long-term U.S. government bond.

Treasury Note An intermediate-term (one to seven years) U.S. government bond.

Treasury Stock Stock issued but not outstanding by virtue of being held (after it is repurchased) by the firm.

Trend Analysis Comparable analysis of performance over time.

Treynor Measure of Portfolio Performance Total portfolio return minus the risk-free rate divided by the portfolio beta. Unlike the Sharpe Measure, which uses the portfolio standard deviation in the denominator, the risk measure here is the beta, or systematic risk. It enables the portfolio manager to view his or her excess return in relation to nondiversifiable risk. The assumption is that all other types of risk have been diversified away. Once computed, the Treynor Measure allows for comparisons between different portfolios.

Trough The point in an economic cycle at which recession ends and expansion begins.

U

Underpricing In selling formerly privately held shares to new investors in the over-the-counter market, the price might not fully reflect the value of the issue. Underpricing is used to attempt to ensure the success of the initial distribution.

Underwriter Hedge A hedge, based on stock index futures or options contracts, used to offset the risk exposure associated with the underwriting of new securities by an investment banker. If the market goes down, presumably the loss on the stock being underwritten will be compensated for by the gain on the stock index futures or options contract as a result of being able to repurchase it at a lower price. This, of course, is not a perfect hedge. It is possible that the stock could go down while the market is going up, and losses on both the stock and stock index contract would take place (writing options directly against the stock may be more efficient, but in many cases such options are not available).

Unfriendly Takeover A merger or acquisition in which the firm acquired does not wish to be acquired.

Unfunded Pension Plan Payments to retirees are made out of current income and not out of prior funding.

Unit Investment Trusts (UITs) These are formed by investment companies with the intention of acquiring a portfolio of fixed income to be passively managed over a fixed period of time. The trust is then terminated.

Unseasoned Issue An issue that has not been formerly traded in the public markets.

Unsystematic Risk Risk of an investment that is random in nature. It is not related to general market movements. It may represent the temporary influence of a competitor's new product, changes in raw material prices, or unusual economic or government influences on a firm. It may generally be diversified away.

V

Valuation The process of attributing a value to a security based on expectations of the future performance of the issuing concern, the relevant industry, and the economy as a whole.

Valuation Model A representation of the components that provide the value of an investment, such as a dividend valuation model used to determine the value of common stock.

Value Line Index The index represents 1,700 companies from the New York and American Stock Exchanges and the over-the-counter market. Many individual investors use the Value Line Index because it more closely corresponds to the variety of stocks the average investor may have in his or her portfolio. It is an equal-weighted index, which means that each of the 1,700 stocks, regardless of market price or total market value, is weighted equally.

Value-Weighted Index Each company in the index is weighted by its own total market value as a percentage of the total market value for all firms in the index. Most major indexes such as the S&P 500, S&P 400, and the NYSE Index, are value-weighted. With value-weighted indexes, large firms tend to be weighted more heavily than smaller firms.

Variability The possible different outcomes of an event. As an example, an investment with many different levels of return would have great variability.

Variable Rate Mortgage A mortgage in which the interest rate is adjusted regularly.

Vertical Spread Buying and writing two contracts at different striking prices with the same month of expiration.

Vesting A legal term meaning that pension benefits or rights cannot be taken away.

W

Warrant A right or option to buy a stated number of shares of stock at a specified price over a given time period. It is usually of longer duration than a call option.

Warrant Break-Even The price movement in the underlying stock necessary for the warrant purchaser to break even, that is, recover the initial purchase price of the warrant.

Weak Form of Efficient Market Hypothesis A hypothesis suggesting there is no relationship between past and future prices of securities.

Weighted Average Life The weighted average time period over which the coupon payments and maturity payment on a bond are recovered.

White Knight A firm that "rescues" another firm from an unfriendly takeover by a third firm.

Wiesenberger Financial Services An advisory service that provides important information on mutual funds.

Wilshire 5,000 Equity Index A stock market measure comprising 5,000 equity securities. It includes all New York Stock Exchange and American Stock Exchange issues and the most active over-the-counter issues. The index represents the *total dollar value* of all 5,000 stocks. By measuring total dollar value, it is, in effect, a value-weighted measure.

World Index A value-weighted index of the performance in 19 major countries as compiled by Capital International, S.A., of Geneva, Switzerland.

Y

Yield Curve A curve that shows interest rates at a specific point in time for all securities having equal risk but different maturity dates. Usually, government securities are used to construct such curves. The yield curve is also referred to as the term structure of interest rates.

Yield Spread The difference between the yields received on two different types of bonds, or bonds with different ratings. It is important to investment strategy because during periods of economic uncertainty, spreads increase because investors demand larger premiums on risky issues to compensate for the greater chance of default.

Yield to Call The interest yield that will be realized on a callable bond if it is held from a given purchase date until the date when it can be called by the issuer. The yield to call reflects the fact that lower overall returns may be realized if the issuer avoids some later payments by retiring the bonds early.

Yield to Maturity The annualized rate of return that an investor will receive if a bond is held until its maturity date. It is the market rate of return. The yield-to-maturity formula includes any capital gains or losses that arise because the par value is greater or less than the current market price.

Ying, Lewellen, Schlarbaum, and Lease Study A research study that indicates there may be an opportunity for abnormal returns on a risk-adjusted basis in the many weeks between announcement of listing and actual listing of a security.

Z

Zero–Coupon Bonds Bonds that are designed to pay no interest, in which the return to the investor is in the form of capital appreciation over the life of the issue.

APPENDIXES

■ OUTLINE

APPENDIX A   COMPOUND SUM OF $1

Compound sum of $1

Period	1%	2%	3%	4%	5%	6%	7%	8%	9%	10%	11%
1	1.010	1.020	1.030	1.040	1.050	1.060	1.070	1.080	1.090	1.100	1.110
2	1.020	1.040	1.061	1.082	1.103	1.124	1.145	1.166	1.188	1.210	1.232
3	1.030	1.061	1.093	1.125	1.158	1.191	1.225	1.260	1.295	1.331	1.368
4	1.041	1.082	1.126	1.170	1.216	1.262	1.311	1.360	1.412	1.464	1.518
5	1.051	1.104	1.159	1.217	1.276	1.338	1.403	1.469	1.539	1.611	1.685
6	1.062	1.126	1.194	1.265	1.340	1.419	1.501	1.587	1.677	1.772	1.870
7	1.072	1.149	1.230	1.316	1.407	1.504	1.606	1.714	1.828	1.949	2.076
8	1.083	1.172	1.267	1.369	1.477	1.594	1.718	1.851	1.993	2.144	2.305
9	1.094	1.195	1.305	1.423	1.551	1.689	1.838	1.999	2.172	2.358	2.558
10	1.105	1.219	1.344	1.480	1.629	1.791	1.967	2.159	2.367	2.594	2.839
11	1.116	1.243	1.384	1.539	1.710	1.898	2.105	2.332	2.580	2.853	3.152
12	1.127	1.268	1.426	1.601	1.796	2.012	2.252	2.518	2.813	3.138	3.498
13	1.138	1.294	1.469	1.665	1.886	2.133	2.410	2.720	3.066	3.452	3.883
14	1.149	1.319	1.513	1.732	1.980	2.261	2.579	2.937	3.342	3.797	4.310
15	1.161	1.346	1.558	1.801	2.079	2.397	2.759	3.172	3.642	4.177	4.785
16	1.173	1.373	1.605	1.873	2.183	2.540	2.952	3.426	3.970	4.595	5.311
17	1.184	1.400	1.653	1.948	2.292	2.693	3.159	3.700	4.328	5.054	5.895
18	1.196	1.428	1.702	2.206	2.407	2.854	3.380	3.996	4.717	5.560	6.544
19	1.208	1.457	1.754	2.107	2.527	3.026	3.617	4.316	5.142	6.116	7.263
20	1.220	1.486	1.806	2.191	2.653	3.207	3.870	4.661	5.604	6.727	8.062
25	1.282	1.641	2.094	2.666	3.386	4.292	5.427	6.848	8.623	10.835	13.585
30	1.348	1.811	2.427	3.243	4.322	5.743	7.612	10.063	13.268	17.449	22.892
40	1.489	2.208	3.262	4.801	7.040	10.286	14.974	21.725	31.409	45.259	65.001
50	1.645	2.692	4.384	7.107	11.467	18.420	29.457	46.902	74.358	117.39	184.57

Percent

COMPOUND SUM OF $1 (concluded)

Compound sum of $1

Period	12%	13%	14%	15%	16%	17%	18%	19%	20%	25%	30%
1	1.120	1.130	1.140	1.150	1.160	1.170	1.180	1.190	1.200	1.250	1.300
2	1.254	1.277	1.300	1.323	1.346	1.369	1.392	1.416	1.440	1.563	1.690
3	1.405	1.443	1.482	1.521	1.561	1.602	1.643	1.685	1.728	1.953	2.197
4	1.574	1.630	1.689	1.749	1.811	1.874	1.939	2.005	2.074	2.441	2.856
5	1.762	1.842	1.925	2.011	2.100	2.192	2.288	2.386	2.488	3.052	3.713
6	1.974	2.082	2.195	2.313	2.436	2.565	2.700	2.840	2.986	3.815	4.827
7	2.211	2.353	2.502	2.660	2.826	3.001	3.185	3.379	3.583	4.768	6.276
8	2.476	2.658	2.853	3.059	3.278	3.511	3.759	4.021	4.300	5.960	8.157
9	2.773	3.004	3.252	3.518	3.803	4.108	4.435	4.785	5.160	7.451	10.604
10	3.106	3.395	3.707	4.046	4.411	4.807	5.234	5.696	6.192	9.313	13.786
11	3.479	3.836	4.226	4.652	5.117	5.624	6.176	6.777	7.430	11.642	17.922
12	3.896	4.335	4.818	5.350	5.936	6.580	7.288	8.064	8.916	14.552	23.298
13	4.363	4.898	5.492	6.153	6.886	7.699	8.599	9.596	10.699	18.190	30.288
14	4.887	5.535	6.261	7.076	7.988	9.007	10.147	11.420	12.839	22.737	39.374
15	5.474	6.254	7.138	8.137	9.266	10.539	11.974	13.590	15.407	28.422	51.186
16	6.130	7.067	8.137	9.358	10.748	12.330	14.129	16.172	18.488	35.527	66.542
17	6.866	7.986	9.276	10.761	12.468	14.426	16.672	19.244	22.186	44.409	86.504
18	7.690	9.024	10.575	12.375	14.463	16.879	19.673	22.091	26.623	55.511	112.46
19	8.613	10.197	12.056	14.232	16.777	19.748	23.214	27.252	31.948	69.389	146.19
20	9.646	11.523	13.743	16.367	19.461	23.106	27.393	32.429	38.338	86.736	190.05
25	17.000	21.231	26.462	32.919	40.874	50.658	62.669	77.388	95.396	264.70	705.64
30	29.960	39.116	50.950	66.212	85.850	111.07	143.37	184.68	237.38	807.79	2.620.0
40	93.051	132.78	188.88	267.86	378.72	533.87	750.38	1.051.7	1.469.8	7.523.2	36.119.
50	289.00	450.74	700.23	1.083.7	1.670.7	2.566.2	3.927.4	5.988.9	9.100.4	70.065.	497.929.

Percent

Source: Maurice Joy, *Introduction to Financial Management* (Homewood, Ill.: Richard D. Irwin, 1977).

APPENDIX B   PRESENT VALUE OF $1

Present value of $1

Percent

Period	1%	2%	3%	4%	5%	6%	7%	8%	9%	10%	11%	12%
1	0.990	0.980	0.971	0.962	0.952	0.943	0.935	0.926	0.917	0.909	0.901	0.893
2	0.980	0.961	0.943	0.925	0.907	0.890	0.873	0.857	0.842	0.826	0.812	0.797
3	0.971	0.942	0.915	0.889	0.864	0.840	0.816	0.794	0.772	0.751	0.731	0.712
4	0.961	0.924	0.885	0.855	0.823	0.792	0.763	0.735	0.708	0.683	0.659	0.636
5	0.951	0.906	0.863	0.822	0.784	0.747	0.713	0.681	0.650	0.621	0.593	0.567
6	0.942	0.888	0.837	0.790	0.746	0.705	0.666	0.630	0.596	0.564	0.535	0.507
7	0.933	0.871	0.813	0.760	0.711	0.665	0.623	0.583	0.547	0.513	0.482	0.452
8	0.923	0.853	0.789	0.731	0.677	0.627	0.582	0.540	0.502	0.467	0.434	0.404
9	0.914	0.837	0.766	0.703	0.645	0.592	0.544	0.500	0.460	0.424	0.391	0.361
10	0.905	0.820	0.744	0.676	0.614	0.558	0.508	0.463	0.422	0.386	0.352	0.322
11	0.896	0.804	0.722	0.650	0.585	0.527	0.475	0.429	0.388	0.350	0.317	0.287
12	0.887	0.788	0.701	0.625	0.557	0.497	0.444	0.397	0.356	0.319	0.286	0.257
13	0.879	0.773	0.681	0.601	0.530	0.469	0.415	0.368	0.326	0.290	0.258	0.229
14	0.870	0.758	0.661	0.577	0.505	0.442	0.388	0.340	0.299	0.263	0.232	0.205
15	0.861	0.743	0.642	0.555	0.481	0.417	0.362	0.315	0.275	0.239	0.209	0.183
16	0.853	0.728	0.623	0.534	0.458	0.394	0.339	0.292	0.252	0.218	0.188	0.163
17	0.844	0.714	0.605	0.513	0.436	0.371	0.317	0.270	0.231	0.198	0.170	0.146
18	0.836	0.700	0.587	0.494	0.416	0.350	0.296	0.250	0.212	0.180	0.153	0.130
19	0.828	0.686	0.570	0.475	0.396	0.331	0.277	0.232	0.194	0.164	0.138	0.116
20	0.820	0.673	0.554	0.456	0.377	0.312	0.258	0.215	0.178	0.149	0.124	0.104
25	0.780	0.610	0.478	0.375	0.295	0.233	0.184	0.146	0.116	0.092	0.074	0.059
30	0.742	0.552	0.412	0.308	0.231	0.174	0.131	0.099	0.075	0.057	0.044	0.033
40	0.672	0.453	0.307	0.208	0.142	0.097	0.067	0.046	0.032	0.022	0.015	0.011
50	0.608	0.372	0.228	0.141	0.087	0.054	0.034	0.021	0.013	0.009	0.005	0.003

Present value of $1

Percent

Period	13%	14%	15%	16%	17%	18%	19%	20%	25%	30%	35%	40%	50%
1	0.885	0.877	0.870	0.862	0.855	0.847	0.840	0.833	0.800	0.769	0.741	0.714	0.667
2	0.783	0.769	0.756	0.743	0.731	0.718	0.706	0.694	0.640	0.592	0.549	0.510	0.444
3	0.693	0.675	0.658	0.641	0.624	0.609	0.593	0.579	0.512	0.455	0.406	0.364	0.296
4	0.613	0.592	0.572	0.552	0.534	0.515	0.499	0.482	0.410	0.350	0.301	0.260	0.198
5	0.543	0.519	0.497	0.476	0.456	0.437	0.419	0.402	0.320	0.269	0.223	0.186	0.132
6	0.480	0.456	0.432	0.410	0.390	0.370	0.352	0.335	0.262	0.207	0.165	0.133	0.088
7	0.425	0.400	0.376	0.354	0.333	0.314	0.296	0.279	0.210	0.159	0.122	0.095	0.059
8	0.376	0.351	0.327	0.305	0.285	0.266	0.249	0.233	0.168	0.123	0.091	0.068	0.039
9	0.333	0.300	0.284	0.263	0.243	0.225	0.209	0.194	0.134	0.094	0.067	0.048	0.026
10	0.295	0.270	0.247	0.227	0.208	0.191	0.176	0.162	0.107	0.073	0.050	0.035	0.017
11	0.261	0.237	0.215	0.195	0.178	0.162	0.148	0.135	0.086	0.056	0.037	0.025	0.012
12	0.231	0.208	0.187	0.168	0.152	0.137	0.124	0.112	0.069	0.043	0.027	0.018	0.008
13	0.204	0.182	0.163	0.145	0.130	0.116	0.104	0.093	0.055	0.033	0.020	0.013	0.005
14	0.181	0.160	0.141	0.125	0.111	0.099	0.088	0.078	0.044	0.025	0.015	0.009	0.003
15	0.160	0.140	0.123	0.108	0.095	0.084	0.074	0.065	0.035	0.020	0.011	0.006	0.002
16	0.141	0.123	0.107	0.093	0.081	0.071	0.062	0.054	0.028	0.015	0.008	0.005	0.002
17	0.125	0.108	0.093	0.080	0.069	0.060	0.052	0.045	0.023	0.012	0.006	0.003	0.001
18	0.111	0.095	0.081	0.069	0.059	0.051	0.044	0.038	0.018	0.009	0.005	0.002	0.001
19	0.098	0.083	0.070	0.060	0.051	0.043	0.037	0.031	0.014	0.007	0.003	0.002	0
20	0.087	0.073	0.061	0.051	0.043	0.037	0.031	0.026	0.012	0.005	0.002	0.001	0
25	0.047	0.038	0.030	0.024	0.020	0.016	0.013	0.010	0.004	0.001	0.001	0	0
30	0.026	0.020	0.015	0.012	0.009	0.007	0.005	0.004	0.001	0	0	0	0
40	0.008	0.005	0.004	0.003	0.002	0.001	0.001	0.001	0	0	0	0	0
50	0.002	0.001	0.001	0.001	0	0	0	0	0	0	0	0	0

Source: Maurice Joy, *Introduction to Financial Management* (Homewood, Ill.: Richard D. Irwin, 1977).

APPENDIX C COMPOUND SUM OF AN ANNUITY OF $1

Compound sum of an annuity of $1

Percent

Period	1%	2%	3%	4%	5%	6%	7%	8%	9%	10%	11%
1	1.000	1.000	1.000	1.000	1.000	1.000	1.000	1.000	1.000	1.000	1.000
2	2.010	2.020	2.030	2.040	2.050	2.060	2.070	2.080	2.090	2.100	2.110
3	3.030	3.060	3.091	3.122	3.153	3.184	3.215	3.246	3.278	3.310	3.342
4	4.060	4.122	4.184	4.246	4.310	4.375	4.440	4.506	4.573	4.641	4.710
5	5.101	5.204	5.309	5.416	5.526	5.637	5.751	5.867	5.985	6.105	6.228
6	6.152	6.308	6.468	6.633	6.802	6.975	7.153	7.336	7.523	7.716	7.913
7	7.214	7.434	7.662	7.898	8.142	8.394	8.654	8.923	9.200	9.487	9.783
8	8.286	8.583	8.892	9.214	9.549	9.897	10.260	10.637	11.028	11.436	11.859
9	9.369	9.755	10.159	10.583	11.027	11.491	11.978	12.488	13.021	13.579	14.164
10	10.462	10.950	11.464	12.006	12.578	13.181	13.816	14.487	15.193	15.937	16.722
11	11.567	12.169	12.808	13.486	14.207	14.972	15.784	16.645	17.560	18.531	19.561
12	12.683	13.412	14.192	15.026	15.917	16.870	17.888	18.977	20.141	21.384	22.713
13	13.809	14.680	15.618	16.627	17.713	18.882	20.141	21.495	22.953	24.523	26.212
14	14.947	15.974	17.086	18.292	19.599	21.015	22.550	24.215	26.019	27.975	30.095
15	16.097	17.293	18.599	20.024	21.579	23.276	25.129	27.152	29.361	31.772	34.405
16	17.258	18.639	20.157	21.825	23.657	25.673	27.888	30.324	33.003	35.950	39.190
17	18.430	20.012	21.762	23.698	25.840	20.213	30.840	33.750	36.974	40.545	44.501
18	19.615	21.412	23.414	25.645	28.132	30.906	33.999	37.450	41.301	45.599	50.396
19	20.811	22.841	25.117	27.671	30.539	33.760	37.379	41.446	46.018	51.159	56.939
20	22.019	24.297	26.870	29.778	33.066	36.786	40.995	45.762	51.160	57.275	64.203
25	28.243	32.030	36.459	41.646	47.727	54.865	63.249	73.106	84.701	98.347	114.41
30	34.785	40.588	47.575	56.085	66.439	79.058	94.461	113.28	136.31	164.49	199.02
40	48.886	60.402	75.401	95.026	120.80	154.76	199.64	259.06	337.89	442.59	581.83
50	64.463	84.579	112.80	152.67	209.35	290.34	406.53	573.77	815.08	1,163.9	1,668.8

APPENDIX C COMPOUND SUM OF AN ANNUITY OF $1 *(concluded)*

Compound sum of an annuity of $1

Period	12%	13%	14%	15%	16%	17%	18%	19%	20%	25%	30%
1	1.000	1.000	1.000	1.000	1.000	1.000	1.000	1.000	1.000	1.000	1.000
2	2.120	2.130	2.140	2.150	2.160	2.170	2.180	2.190	2.200	2.250	2.300
3	3.374	3.407	3.440	3.473	3.506	3.539	3.572	3.606	3.640	3.813	3.990
4	4.779	4.850	4.921	4.993	5.066	5.141	5.215	5.291	5.368	5.766	6.187
5	6.353	6.480	6.610	6.742	6.877	7.014	7.154	7.297	7.442	8.207	9.043
6	8.115	8.323	8.536	9.754	8.977	9.207	9.442	0.683	9.930	11.259	12.756
7	10.089	10.405	10.730	11.067	11.414	11.772	12.142	12.523	12.916	15.073	17.583
8	12.300	12.757	13.233	13.727	14.240	14.773	15.327	15.902	16.499	19.842	23.858
9	14.776	15.416	16.085	16.786	17.519	18.285	19.086	19.923	20.799	25.802	32.015
10	17.549	18.420	19.337	20.304	21.321	22.393	23.521	24.701	25.959	33.253	42.619
11	20.655	21.814	23.045	24.349	25.733	27.200	28.755	30.404	32.150	42.566	56.405
12	24.133	25.650	27.271	29.002	30.850	32.824	34.931	37.180	39.581	54.208	74.327
13	28.029	29.985	32.089	34.352	36.786	39.404	42.219	45.244	48.497	68.760	97.625
14	32.393	34.883	37.581	40.505	43.672	47.103	50.818	54.841	59.196	86.949	127.91
15	37.280	40.417	43.842	47.580	51.660	56.110	60.965	66.261	72.035	109.69	167.29
16	42.753	46.672	50.980	55.717	60.925	66.649	72.939	79.850	87.442	138.11	218.47
17	48.884	53.739	59.118	65.075	71.673	78.979	87.068	96.022	105.93	173.64	285.01
18	55.750	61.725	68.394	75.836	84.141	93.406	103.74	115.27	128.12	218.05	371.52
19	63.440	70.749	78.969	88.212	98.603	110.29	123.41	138.17	154.74	273.56	483.97
20	72.052	80.947	91.025	102.44	115.38	130.03	146.63	165.42	186.69	342.95	630.17
25	133.33	155.62	181.87	212.79	249.21	292.11	342.60	402.04	471.98	1,054.8	2,348.80
30	241.33	293.20	356.79	434.75	530.31	647.44	790.95	966.7	1,181.9	3,227.2	8,730.0
40	767.09	1,013.7	1,342.0	1,779.1	2,360.8	3,134.5	4,163.21	5,529.8	7,343.9	30,089.	120,393.
50	2,400.0	3,459.5	4,994.5	7,217.7	10,436.	15,090.	21,813.	31,515.	45,497.	280,256	165,976.

Percent

Source: Maurice Joy, *Introduction to Financial Management* (Homewood, Ill.: Richard D. Irwin, 1977).

APPENDIX D PRESENT VALUE OF AN ANNUITY OF $1

Present value of an annuity of $1

Percent

Period	1%	2%	3%	4%	5%	6%	7%	8%	9%	10%	11%	12%
1	0.990	0.980	0.971	0.962	0.952	0.943	0.935	0.926	0.917	0.909	0.901	0.893
2	1.970	1.942	1.913	1.886	1.859	1.833	1.808	1.783	1.759	1.736	1.713	1.690
3	2.941	2.884	2.829	2.775	2.723	2.673	2.624	2.577	2.531	2.487	2.444	2.402
4	3.902	3.808	3.717	3.630	3.546	3.465	3.387	3.312	3.240	3.170	3.102	3.037
5	4.853	4.713	4.580	4.452	4.329	4.212	4.100	3.993	3.890	3.791	3.696	3.605
6	5.795	5.601	5.417	5.242	5.076	4.917	4.767	4.623	4.486	4.355	4.231	4.111
7	6.728	6.472	6.230	6.002	5.786	5.582	5.389	5.206	5.033	4.868	4.712	4.564
8	7.652	7.325	7.020	6.733	6.463	6.210	5.971	5.747	5.535	5.335	5.146	4.968
9	8.566	8.162	7.786	7.435	7.108	6.802	6.515	6.247	5.995	5.759	5.537	5.328
10	9.471	8.983	8.530	8.111	7.722	7.360	7.024	6.710	6.418	6.145	5.889	5.650
11	10.368	9.787	9.253	8.760	8.306	7.887	7.499	7.139	6.805	6.495	6.207	5.938
12	11.255	10.575	9.954	9.385	8.863	8.384	7.943	7.536	7.161	6.814	6.492	6.194
13	12.134	11.348	10.635	9.986	9.394	8.853	8.358	7.904	7.487	7.103	6.750	6.424
14	13.004	12.106	11.296	10.563	9.899	9.295	8.745	8.244	7.786	7.367	6.982	6.628
15	13.865	12.849	11.939	11.118	10.380	9.712	9.108	8.559	8.061	7.606	7.191	6.811
16	14.718	13.578	12.561	11.652	10.838	10.106	9.447	8.851	8.313	7.824	7.379	6.974
17	15.562	14.292	13.166	12.166	11.274	10.477	9.763	9.122	8.544	8.022	7.549	7.102
18	16.398	14.992	13.754	12.659	11.690	10.828	10.059	9.372	8.756	8.201	7.702	7.250
19	17.226	15.678	14.324	13.134	12.085	11.158	10.336	9.604	8.950	8.365	7.839	7.366
20	18.046	16.351	14.877	13.590	12.462	11.470	10.594	9.818	9.129	8.514	7.963	7.469
25	22.023	19.523	17.413	15.622	14.094	12.783	11.654	10.675	9.823	9.077	8.422	7.843
30	25.808	22.396	19.600	17.292	15.372	13.765	12.409	11.258	10.274	9.427	8.694	8.055
40	32.835	27.355	23.115	19.793	17.160	15.046	13.332	11.925	10.757	9.779	8.951	8.244
50	39.196	31.424	25.730	21.482	18.256	15.762	13.801	12.233	10.962	9.915	9.042	8.304

Present value of an annuity of $1

							Percent						
Period	13%	14%	15%	16%	17%	18%	19%	20%	25%	30%	35%	40%	50%
1	0.885	0.877	0.870	0.862	0.855	0.847	0.840	0.833	0.800	0.769	0.741	0.714	0.667
2	1.668	1.647	1.626	1.605	1.585	1.566	1.547	1.528	1.440	1.361	1.289	1.224	1.111
3	2.361	2.322	2.283	2.246	2.210	2.174	2.140	2.106	1.952	1.816	1.696	1.589	1.407
4	2.974	2.914	2.855	2.798	2.743	2.690	2.639	2.589	2.362	2.166	1.997	1.849	1.605
5	3.517	3.433	3.352	3.274	3.199	3.127	3.058	2.991	2.689	2.436	2.220	2.035	1.737
6	3.998	3.889	3.784	3.685	3.589	3.498	3.410	3.326	2.951	2.643	2.385	2.168	1.824
7	4.423	4.288	4.160	4.039	3.922	3.812	3.706	3.605	3.161	2.802	2.508	2.263	1.883
8	4.799	4.639	4.487	4.344	4.207	4.078	3.954	3.837	3.329	2.925	2.598	2.331	1.922
9	5.132	4.946	4.772	4.607	4.451	4.303	4.163	4.031	3.463	3.019	2.665	2.379	1.948
10	5.426	5.216	5.019	4.833	4.659	4.494	4.339	4.192	3.571	3.092	2.715	2.414	1.965
11	5.687	5.453	5.234	5.029	4.836	4.656	4.486	4.327	3.656	3.147	2.752	2.438	1.977
12	5.918	5.660	5.421	5.197	4.988	4.793	4.611	4.439	3.725	3.190	2.779	2.456	1.985
13	6.122	5.842	5.583	5.342	5.118	4.910	4.715	4.533	3.780	3.223	2.799	2.469	1.990
14	6.302	6.002	5.724	5.468	5.229	5.008	4.802	4.611	3.824	3.249	2.814	2.478	1.993
15	6.462	6.142	5.847	5.575	5.324	5.092	4.876	4.675	3.859	3.268	2.825	2.484	1.995
16	6.604	6.265	5.954	5.668	5.405	5.162	4.938	4.730	3.887	3.283	2.834	2.489	1.997
17	6.729	6.373	6.047	5.749	5.475	5.222	4.988	4.775	3.910	3.295	2.840	2.492	1.998
18	6.840	6.467	6.128	5.818	5.534	5.273	5.033	4.812	3.928	3.304	2.844	2.494	1.999
19	6.938	6.550	6.198	5.877	5.584	5.316	5.070	4.843	3.942	3.311	2.848	2.496	1.999
20	7.025	6.623	6.259	5.929	5.628	5.353	5.101	4.870	3.954	3.316	2.850	2.497	1.999
25	7.330	6.873	6.464	6.097	5.766	5.467	5.195	4.948	3.985	3.329	2.856	2.499	2.000
30	7.496	7.003	6.566	6.177	5.829	5.517	5.235	4.979	3.995	3.332	2.857	2.500	2.000
40	7.634	7.105	6.642	6.233	5.871	5.548	5.258	4.997	3.999	3.333	2.857	2.500	2.000
50	7.675	7.133	6.661	6.246	5.880	5.554	5.262	4.999	4.000	3.333	2.857	2.500	2.000

Source: Maurice Joy, *Introduction to Financial Management* (Homewood, Ill.: Richard D. Irwin, 1977).

Tables of squares and square roots

N	N²	√N	√10N	N	N²	√N	√10N
				50	2 500	7.071 068	22.36068
1	1	1.000 000	3.162 278	51	2 601	7.141 428	22.58318
2	4	1.414 214	4.472 136	52	2 704	7.211 103	22.80351
3	9	1.732 051	5.477 226	53	2 809	7.280 110	23.02173
4	16	2.000 000	6.324 555	54	2 916	7.348 469	23.23790
5	25	2.236 068	7.071 068	55	3 025	7.416 198	23.45208
6	36	2.449 490	7.745 967	56	3 136	7.483 315	23.66432
7	49	2.645 751	8.366 600	57	3 249	7.549 834	23.87467
8	64	2.828 427	8.944 272	58	3 364	7.615 773	24.08319
9	81	3.000 000	9.486 833	59	3 481	7.681 146	24.28992
10	100	3.162 278	10.00000	60	3 600	7.745 967	24.49490
11	121	3.316 625	10.48809	61	3 721	7.810 250	24.69818
12	144	3.464 102	10.95445	62	3 844	7.874 008	24.89980
13	169	3.605 551	11.40175	63	3 969	7.937 254	25.09980
14	196	3.741 657	11.83216	64	4 096	8.000 000	25.29822
15	225	3.872 983	12.24745	65	4 225	8.062 258	25.49510
16	256	4.000 000	12.64911	66	4 356	8.124 038	25.69047
17	289	4.123 106	13.03840	67	4 489	8.185 353	25.88436
18	324	4.242 641	13.41641	68	4 624	8.246 211	26.07681
19	361	4.358 899	13.78405	69	4 761	8.306 824	26.26785
20	400	4.472 136	14.14214	70	4 900	8.366 600	26.45751
21	441	4.582 576	14.49138	71	5 041	8.426 150	26.64583
22	484	4.690 416	14.83240	72	5 184	8.485 281	26.83282
23	529	4.795 832	15.16575	73	5 329	8.544 004	27.01851
24	576	4.898 979	15.49193	74	5 476	8.602 325	27.20294
25	625	5.000 000	15.81139	75	5 625	8.660 254	27.38613
26	676	5.099 020	16.12452	76	5 776	8.717 798	27.56810
27	729	5.196 152	16.43168	77	5 929	8.774 964	27.74887
28	784	5.291 503	16.73320	78	6 084	8.831 761	27.92848
29	841	5.385 165	17.02939	79	6 241	8.888 194	28.10694
30	900	5.477 226	17.32051	80	6 400	8.944 272	28.28427
31	961	5.567 764	17.60682	81	6 561	9.000 000	28.46050
32	1 024	5.656 854	17.88854	82	6 724	9.055 385	28.63564
33	1 089	5.744 563	18.16590	83	6 889	9.110 434	28.80972
34	1 156	5.830 952	18.43909	84	7 056	9.165 151	28.98275
35	1 225	5.916 080	18.70829	85	7 225	9.219 544	29.15476
36	1 296	6.000 000	18.97367	86	7 396	9.273 618	29.32576
37	1 369	6.082 763	19.23538	87	7 569	9.327 379	29.49576
38	1 444	6.164 414	19.49359	88	7 744	9.380 832	29.66479
39	1 521	6.244 998	19.74842	89	7 921	9.433 981	29.83287
40	1 600	6.324 555	20.00000	90	8 100	9.486 833	30.00000
41	1 681	6.403 124	20.24846	91	8 281	9.539 392	30.16621
42	1 764	6.480 741	20.49390	92	8 464	9.591 663	30.33150
43	1 849	6.557 439	20.73644	93	8 649	9.643 651	30.49590
44	1 936	6.633 250	20.97618	94	8 836	9.695 360	30.65942
45	2 025	6.708 204	21.21320	95	9 025	9.746 794	30.82207
46	2 116	6.782 330	21.44761	96	9 216	9.797 959	30.98387
47	2 209	6.855 655	21.67948	97	9 409	9.848 858	31.14482
48	2 304	6.928 203	21.90890	98	9 604	9.899 495	31.30495
49	2 401	7.000 000	22.13594	99	9 801	9.949 874	31.46427
50	2 500	7.071 068	22.36068	100	10 000	10.00000	31.62278

Tables of squares and square roots

N	N^2	$\sqrt{N}$	$\sqrt{10N}$	N	N^2	$\sqrt{N}$	$\sqrt{10N}$
100	10 000	10.00000	31.62278	150	22 500	12.24745	38.72983
101	10 201	10.04988	31.78050	151	22 801	12.28821	38.85872
102	10 404	10.09950	31.93744	152	23 104	12.32883	39.98718
103	10 609	10.14889	32.09361	153	23 409	12.36932	39.11521
104	10 816	10.19804	32.24903	154	23 716	12.40967	39.24283
105	11 025	10.24695	32.40370	155	24 025	12.44990	39.37004
106	11 236	10.29563	32.55764	156	24 336	12.45000	39.49684
107	11 449	10.34408	32.71085	157	24 649	12.52996	39.62323
108	11 664	10.39230	32.86335	158	24 964	12.56981	39.74921
109	11 881	10.44031	33.01515	159	25 281	12.60952	39.87480
110	12 100	10.48809	33.16625	160	25 600	12.64911	40.00000
111	12 321	10.53565	33.31666	161	25 921	12.68858	40.12481
112	12 544	10.58301	33.46640	162	26 244	12.72792	40.24922
113	12 769	10.63015	33.61547	163	26 569	12.76715	40.37326
114	12 996	10.67708	33.76389	164	26 896	12.80625	40.49691
115	13 225	10.72381	33.91165	165	27 225	12.84523	40.62019
116	13 456	10.77033	34.05877	166	27 556	12.88410	40.74310
117	13 689	10.81665	34.20526	167	27 889	12.92285	40.86563
118	13 924	10.86278	34.35113	168	28 224	12.96148	40.98780
119	14 161	10.90871	34.49638	169	28 561	13.00000	41.10961
120	14 400	10.95445	34.64102	170	28 900	13.03840	41.23106
121	14 641	11.00000	34.78505	171	29 241	13.07670	41.35215
122	14 884	11.04536	34.92850	172	29 584	13.11488	41.47288
123	15 129	11.09054	35.07136	173	29 929	13.15295	41.59327
124	15 376	11.13553	35.21363	174	30 276	13.19091	41.71331
125	15 625	11.18034	35.35534	175	30 625	13.22876	41.83300
126	15 876	11.22497	35.49648	176	30 976	13.26650	41.95235
127	16 129	11.26943	35.63706	177	31 329	13.30413	42.07137
128	16 384	11.31371	35.77709	178	31 684	13.34166	42.19005
129	16 641	11.35782	35.91657	179	32 041	13.37909	42.30839
130	16 900	11.40175	36.05551	180	32 400	13.41641	42.42641
131	17 161	11.44552	36.19392	181	32 761	13.45362	42.54409
132	17 424	11.48913	36.33180	182	33 124	13.49074	42.66146
133	17 689	11.53256	36.46917	183	33 489	13.52775	42.77850
134	17 956	11.57584	36.60601	184	33 856	13.56466	42.89522
135	18 225	11.61895	36.74235	185	34 225	13.60147	43.01163
136	18 496	11.66190	36.87818	186	34 596	13.63818	43.12772
137	18 769	11.70470	37.01351	187	34 969	13.67479	43.24350
138	19 044	11.74734	37.14835	188	35 344	13.71131	43.35897
139	19 321	11.78983	37.28270	189	35 721	13.74773	43.47413
140	19 600	11.83216	37.41657	190	36 100	13.78405	43.58899
141	19 881	11.87434	37.54997	191	36 481	13.82027	43.70355
142	20 164	11.91638	37.68289	192	36 864	13.85641	43.81780
143	20 449	11.95826	37.81534	193	37 249	13.89244	43.93177
144	20 736	12.00000	37.94733	194	37 636	13.92839	44.04543
145	21 025	12.04159	38.07887	195	38 025	13.96424	44.15880
146	21 316	12.08305	38.20995	196	38 416	14.00000	44.27189
147	21 609	12.12436	38.34058	197	38 809	14.03567	44.38468
148	21 904	12.16553	38.47077	198	39 204	14.07125	44.49719
149	22 201	12.20656	38.60052	199	39 601	14.10674	44.60942
150	22 500	12.24745	38.72983	200	40 000	14.14214	44.72136

Tables of squares and square roots

N	N²	√N	√10N	N	N²	√N	√10N
200	40 000	14.14214	44.72136	250	62 500	15.81139	50.00000
201	40 401	14.17745	44.83302	251	63 001	15.84298	50.09990
202	40 804	14.21267	44.94441	252	63 504	15.87451	50.19960
203	41 209	14.24781	45.05552	253	64 009	15.90597	50.29911
204	41 616	14.28296	45.16636	254	64 516	15.93738	50.39841
205	42 025	14.31782	45.27693	255	65 025	15.96872	50.49752
206	42 436	14.35270	45.38722	256	65 536	16.00000	50.59644
207	42 849	14.38749	45.49725	257	66 049	16.03122	50.69517
208	43 264	14.42221	45.60702	258	66 564	16.06238	50.79370
209	43 681	14.45683	45.71652	259	67 081	16.09348	50.89204
210	44 100	14.49138	45.82576	260	67 600	16.12452	50.99020
211	44 521	14.52584	45.93474	261	68 121	16.15549	51.08816
212	44 944	14.56022	46.04346	262	68 644	16.18641	51.18594
213	45 369	14.59452	46.15192	263	69 169	16.21727	51.28353
214	45 796	14.62874	46.26013	264	69 696	16.24808	51.38093
215	46 225	14.66288	46.36809	265	70 225	16.27882	51.47815
216	46 656	14.69694	46.47580	266	70 756	16.30951	51.57519
217	47 089	14.73092	46.58326	267	71 289	16.34013	51.67204
218	47 524	14.76482	46.69047	268	71 824	16.37071	51.76872
219	47 961	14.79865	46.79744	269	72 361	16.40122	51.86521
220	48 400	14.83240	46.90415	270	72 900	16.43168	51.96152
221	48 841	14.86607	47.01064	271	73 441	16.46208	52.05766
222	49 284	14.89966	47.11688	272	73 984	16.49242	52.15362
223	49 729	14.93318	47.22288	273	74 529	16.52271	52.24940
224	50 176	14.96663	47.32864	274	75 076	16.55295	52.34501
225	50 625	15.00000	47.43416	275	75 625	16.58312	52.44044
226	51 076	15.03330	47.53946	276	76 176	16.61325	52.53570
227	51 529	15.06652	47.64452	277	76 729	16.64332	52.63079
228	51 984	15.09967	47.74935	278	77 284	16.67333	52.72571
229	52 441	15.13275	47.85394	279	77 841	16.70329	52.82045
230	52 900	15.16575	47.95832	280	78 400	16.73320	52.91503
231	53 361	15.19868	48.06246	281	78 961	16.76305	53.00943
232	53 824	15.23155	48.16638	282	79 524	16.79286	53.10367
233	54 289	15.26434	48.27007	283	80 089	16.82260	53.19774
234	54 756	15.29706	48.37355	284	80 656	16.85230	53.29165
235	55 225	15.32971	48.47680	285	81 225	16.88194	53.38539
236	55 696	15.36229	48.57983	286	81 796	16.91153	53.47897
237	56 169	15.39480	48.68265	287	82 369	16.94107	53.57238
238	56 644	15.42725	48.78524	288	82 944	16.97056	53.66563
239	57 121	15.45962	48.88763	289	83 521	17.00000	53.75872
240	57 600	15.49193	48.98979	290	84 100	17.02939	53.85165
241	58 081	15.52417	49.09175	291	84 681	17.05872	53.94442
242	58 564	15.55635	49.19350	292	85 264	17.08801	54.03702
243	59 049	15.58846	49.29503	293	85 849	17.11724	54.12947
244	59 536	15.62050	49.39636	294	86 436	17.14643	54.22177
245	60 025	15.65248	49.49747	295	87 025	17.17556	54.31390
246	60 516	15.68439	49.59839	296	87 616	17.20465	54.40588
247	61 009	15.71623	49.69909	297	88 209	17.23369	54.49771
248	61 504	15.74802	49.79960	298	88 804	17.26268	54.58938
249	62 001	15.77973	49.89990	299	89 401	17.29162	54.68089
250	62 500	15.81139	50.00000	300	90 000	17.32051	54.77226

Tables of squares and square roots

N	N²	√N	√10N	N	N²	√N	√10N
300	90 000	17.32051	54.77226	350	122 500	18.70829	59.16080
301	90 601	17.34935	54.86347	351	123 201	18.73499	59.24525
302	91 204	17.37815	54.95453	352	123 904	18.76166	59.32959
303	91 809	17.40690	55.04544	353	124 609	18.78829	59.41380
304	92 416	17.43560	55.13620	354	125 316	18.81489	59.49790
305	93 025	17.46425	55.22681	355	126 025	18.84144	59.58188
306	93 636	17.49288	55.31727	356	126 736	18.86796	59.66574
307	94 249	17.52142	55.40758	357	127 449	18.89444	59.74948
308	94 864	17.54993	55.49775	358	128 164	18.92089	59.83310
309	95 481	17.57840	55.58777	359	128 881	18.94730	59.91661
310	96 100	17.60682	55.67764	360	129 600	18.97367	60.00000
311	96 721	17.63519	55.76737	361	130 321	19.00000	60.08328
312	97 344	17.66352	55.85696	362	131 044	19.02630	60.16644
313	97 969	17.69181	55.94640	363	131 769	19.05256	60.24948
314	98 596	17.72005	56.03670	364	132 496	19.07878	60.33241
315	99 225	17.74824	56.12486	365	133 225	19.10497	60.41523
316	99 856	17.77639	56.21388	366	133 956	19.13113	60.49793
317	100 489	17.80449	56.30275	367	134 689	19.15724	60.58052
318	101 124	17.83255	56.39149	368	135 424	19.18333	60.66300
319	101 761	17.86057	56.48008	369	136 161	19.20937	60.74537
320	102 400	17.88854	56.56854	370	136 900	19.23538	60.82763
321	103 041	17.91647	56.65686	371	137 641	19.26136	60.90977
322	103 684	17.94436	56.74504	372	138 384	19.28730	60.99180
323	104 329	17.97220	56.83309	373	139 129	19.31321	61.07373
324	104 976	18.00000	56.92100	374	139 876	19.33908	61.15554
325	105 625	18.02776	57.00877	375	140 625	19.36492	61.23724
326	106 276	18.05547	57.09641	376	141 376	19.39072	61.31884
327	106 929	18.08314	57.18391	377	142 129	19.41649	61.40033
328	107 584	18.11077	57.27128	378	142 884	19.44222	61.48170
329	108 241	18.13836	57.35852	379	143 641	19.46792	61.56298
330	108 900	18.16590	57.44563	380	144 000	19.49359	61.64414
331	109 561	18.19341	57.53260	381	145 161	19.51922	61.72520
332	110 224	18.22087	57.61944	382	145 924	19.54483	61.80615
333	110 889	18.24829	57.70615	383	146 689	19.57039	61.88699
334	111 556	18.27567	57.79273	384	147 456	19.59592	61.96773
335	112 225	18.30301	57.87918	385	148 225	19.62142	62.04837
336	112 896	18.33030	57.96551	386	148 996	19.64688	62.12890
337	113 569	18.35756	58.05170	387	149 769	19.67232	62.20932
338	114 224	18.38478	57.13777	388	150 544	19.69772	62.28965
339	114 921	18.41195	58.22371	389	151 321	19.72308	62.36986
340	115 600	18.43909	58.30952	390	152 100	19.74842	62.44998
341	116 281	18.46619	58.39521	391	152 881	19.77372	62.52999
342	116 694	18.49324	58.48077	392	153 664	19.79899	62.60990
343	117 649	18.52026	58.56620	393	154 449	19.82423	62.68971
344	118 336	18.54724	58.65151	394	155 236	19.84943	62.76942
345	119 025	18.57418	58.73670	395	156 025	19.87461	62.84903
346	119 716	18.60108	58.82176	396	156 816	19.89975	62.92853
347	120 409	18.62794	58.90671	397	157 609	19.92486	63.00794
348	121 104	18.65476	58.99152	398	158 404	19.94994	63.08724
349	121 801	18.68154	59.07622	399	159 201	19.97498	63.16645
350	122 500	18.70829	59.16080	400	160 000	20.00000	63.24555

Tables of squares and square roots

N	N²	√N	√10N	N	N²	√N	√10N
400	160 000	20.00000	63.24555	450	202 500	21.21320	67.08204
401	160 801	20.02498	63.32456	451	203 401	21.23676	67.15653
402	161 604	20.04994	63.40347	452	204 304	21.26029	67.23095
403	162 409	20.07486	63.48228	453	205 209	21.28380	67.30527
404	163 216	20.09975	63.56099	454	206 116	21.30728	67.37952
405	164 025	20.12461	63.63961	455	207 025	21.33073	67.45369
406	164 836	20.14944	63.71813	456	207 936	21.35416	67.52777
407	165 649	20.17424	63.79655	457	208 849	21.37756	67.60178
408	166 464	20.19901	63.87488	458	209 764	21.40093	67.67570
409	167 281	20.22375	63.95311	459	210 681	21.42429	67.74954
410	168 100	20.24846	64.03124	460	211 600	21.44761	67.82330
411	168 921	20.27313	64.10928	461	212 521	21.47091	67.89698
412	169 744	20.29778	64.18723	462	213 444	21.49419	67.97058
413	170 569	20.32240	64.26508	463	214 369	21.51743	68.04410
414	171 396	20.34699	64.34283	464	215 296	21.54066	68.11755
415	172 225	20.37155	64.42049	465	216 225	21.56386	68.19091
416	173 056	20.39608	64.49806	466	217 156	21.58703	68.26419
417	173 889	20.42058	64.57554	467	218 089	21.61018	68.33740
418	174 724	20.44505	64.65292	468	219 024	21.63331	68.41053
419	175 561	20.46949	64.73021	469	219 961	21.65641	68.48357
420	176 400	20.49390	64.80741	470	220 900	21.67948	68.55655
421	177 241	20.51828	64.88451	471	221 841	21.70253	68.62944
422	178 084	20.54264	64.96153	472	222 784	21.72556	68.70226
423	178 929	20.56696	65.03845	473	223 729	21.74856	68.77500
424	179 776	20.59126	65.11528	474	224 676	21.77154	68.84706
425	180 625	20.61553	65.19202	475	225 625	21.79449	68.92024
426	181 476	20.63977	65.26808	476	226 576	21.81742	68.99275
427	182 329	20.66398	65.34524	477	227 529	21.84033	69.06519
428	183 184	20.68816	65.42171	478	228 484	21.86321	69.13754
429	184 041	20.71232	65.49809	479	229 441	21.88607	69.20983
430	184 900	20.73644	65.57439	480	230 400	21.90800	69.28203
431	185 761	20.76054	65.65059	481	231 361	21.93171	69.35416
432	186 624	20.78461	65.72671	482	232 324	21.95450	69.42622
433	187 489	20.80865	65.80274	483	233 280	21.97726	69.50820
434	188 356	20.83267	65.87868	484	234 256	22.00000	69.57011
435	189 225	20.85665	65.95453	485	235 225	22.02272	69.64194
436	190 096	20.88061	66.03030	486	236 196	22.04541	69.71370
437	190 969	20.90454	66.10598	487	237 169	22.06808	69.78530
438	191 844	20.92845	66.18157	488	238 144	22.09072	69.85700
439	192 721	20.95233	66.25708	489	239 121	22.11334	69.92853
440	193 600	20.97618	66.33250	490	240 100	22.13594	70.00000
441	194 481	21.00000	66.40783	491	241 081	22.15852	70.07139
442	195 364	21.02380	66.48308	492	242 064	22.18107	70.14271
443	196 249	21.04757	66.55825	493	243 049	22.20360	70.21396
444	197 136	21.07131	66.63332	494	244 036	22.22611	70.28513
445	198 025	21.09502	66.70832	495	245 025	22.24860	70.35624
446	198 916	21.11871	66.78323	496	246 016	22.27106	70.42727
447	199 809	21.14237	66.85806	497	247 009	22.29350	70.49823
448	200 704	21.16601	66.93280	498	248 004	22.31519	70.56912
449	201 601	21.18962	67.00746	499	249 001	22.33831	70.63993
450	202 500	21.21320	67.08204	500	250 000	22.36068	70.71068

Tables of squares and square roots

N	N²	√N	√10N	N	N²	√N	√10N
500	250 000	22.36068	70.71068	550	302 500	23.45208	74.16198
501	251 001	22.38303	70.78135	551	303 601	23.47339	74.22937
502	252 004	22.40536	70.85196	552	304 704	23.49468	74.29670
503	253 009	22.42766	70.92249	553	305 809	23.51595	74.36397
504	254 016	22.44994	70.99296	554	306 916	23.53720	74.43118
505	255 025	22.47221	71.06335	555	308 025	23.55844	74.49832
506	256 036	22.49444	71.13368	556	309 136	23.57965	74.56541
507	257 049	22.51666	71.20393	557	310 249	23.60085	74.63243
508	258 064	22.53886	71.27412	558	311 364	23.62202	74.69940
509	259 081	22.56103	71.34424	559	312 481	23.64318	74.76630
510	260 100	22.58318	71.41428	560	313 600	23.66432	74.83315
511	261 121	22.60531	71.48426	561	314 721	23.68544	74.89993
512	262 144	22.62742	71.55418	562	315 844	23.70654	74.96666
513	263 169	22.64950	71.62402	563	316 969	23.72762	75.03333
514	264 196	22.67157	71.69379	564	318 096	23.74686	75.09993
515	265 225	22.69361	71.76350	565	319 225	23.76973	75.16648
516	266 256	22.71563	71.83314	566	320 356	23.79075	75.23297
517	267 289	22.73763	71.90271	567	321 489	23.81176	75.29940
518	268 324	22.75961	71.97222	568	322 624	23.83275	75.36577
519	269 361	22.78157	72.04165	569	323 761	23.85372	75.43209
520	270 400	22.80351	72.11103	570	324 900	23.87467	75.49834
521	271 441	22.82542	72.18033	571	326 041	23.89561	75.56454
522	272 484	22.84732	72.24957	572	327 184	23.91652	75.63068
523	273 529	22.86919	72.31874	573	328 329	23.93742	75.69676
524	274 576	22.89105	72.38784	574	329 476	23.95830	75.76279
525	275 625	22.91288	72.45688	575	330 625	23.97916	75.82875
526	276 676	22.93469	72.52586	576	331 776	24.00000	75.89466
527	277 729	22.95648	72.59477	577	332 929	24.02082	75.96052
528	278 784	22.97825	72.66361	578	334 084	24.04163	76.02631
529	279 841	23.00000	72.73239	579	335 241	24.06242	76.09205
530	280 900	23.02173	72.80110	580	336 400	24.08319	76.15773
531	281 961	23.04344	72.86975	581	337 561	24.10394	76.22336
532	283 024	23.06513	72.93833	582	338 724	24.12468	76.28892
533	284 089	23.08679	73.00685	583	339 889	24.14539	76.35444
534	285 156	23.10844	73.07530	584	341 056	24.16609	76.41989
535	286 225	23.13007	73.14369	585	342 225	24.18677	76.48529
536	287 296	23.15167	73.21202	586	343 396	24.20744	76.55064
537	288 369	23.17326	73.28028	587	344 569	24.22808	76.61593
538	289 444	23.19483	73.34848	588	345 744	24.24871	76.68116
539	290 521	23.21637	73.41662	589	346 921	24.26932	76.74634
540	291 600	23.23790	73.48469	590	348 100	24.28992	76.81146
541	292 681	23.25941	73.55270	591	349 281	24.31049	76.87652
542	293 764	23.28089	73.62056	592	350 464	24.33105	76.94154
543	294 849	23.30236	73.68853	593	351 649	24.35159	77.00649
544	295 936	23.32381	73.75636	594	352 836	24.37212	77.07140
545	297 025	23.34524	73.82412	595	354 025	24.39262	77.13624
546	298 116	23.36664	73.89181	596	355 216	24.41311	77.20104
547	299 209	23.38803	73.95945	597	356 409	24.43358	77.26578
548	300 304	23.40940	74.02702	598	357 604	24.45404	77.33046
549	301 401	23.43075	74.09453	599	358 801	24.47448	77.39509
550	302 500	23.45208	74.16198	600	360 000	24.49490	77.45967

Tables of squares and square roots

N	N²	√N̄	√10N	N	N²	√N̄	√10N
600	360 000	24.49490	77.45967	650	422 500	25.49510	80.62258
601	361 201	24.51530	77.52419	651	423 801	25.51470	80.68457
602	362 404	24.53569	77.58868	652	425 409	25.53240	80.80130
603	363 609	24.55606	77.65307	653	426 409	25.55386	80.80842
604	364 816	24.57641	77.71744	654	427 716	25.57342	80.87027
605	366 025	24.59675	77.78175	655	429 025	25.59297	80.93207
606	367 736	24.61707	77.84600	656	430 336	25.61250	80.99383
607	368 449	24.63737	77.91020	657	431 649	25.63201	81.05554
608	369 664	24.65766	77.97435	658	432 964	25.65151	81.11720
609	370 881	24.67793	78.03845	659	434 281	25.67100	81.17881
610	372 100	24.69818	78.10250	660	435 600	25.69047	81.24038
611	373 321	24.71841	78.16649	661	436 921	25.70992	81.30191
612	374 544	24.73863	78.23043	662	438 244	25.72936	81.36338
613	375 769	24.75884	78.29432	663	439 569	25.74879	81.42481
614	376 996	24.77902	78.35815	664	440 896	25.76820	81.48620
615	378 225	24.79919	78.42194	665	442 225	25.78759	81.54753
616	379 456	24.81935	78.48567	666	443 556	25.80698	81.60882
617	380 689	24.83948	78.54935	667	444 889	25.82634	81.67007
618	381 924	24.85961	78.61298	668	446 224	25.84570	81.73127
619	383 161	24.87971	78.67655	669	447 561	25.86503	81.79242
620	384 400	24.89980	78.74008	670	448 900	25.88436	81.85353
621	385 641	24.91987	78.80355	671	450 241	25.90367	81.91459
622	386 884	24.93993	78.86698	672	451 584	25.92296	81.97561
623	388 129	24.95997	78.93035	673	452 929	25.94224	82.03658
624	389 376	24.97999	78.99367	674	454 276	25.96151	82.09750
625	390 625	25.00000	79.05694	675	455 625	25.98076	82.15838
626	391 876	25.01999	79.12016	676	456 976	26.00000	82.21922
627	393 129	25.03997	79.18333	677	458 329	26.01922	82.28001
628	394 384	25.05993	79.24645	678	459 684	26.03843	82.34076
629	395 641	25.07987	79.30952	679	461 041	26.05763	82.40146
630	396 900	25.09980	79.37254	680	462 400	26.07681	82.46211
631	398 161	25.11971	79.43551	681	463 761	26.09598	82.52272
632	399 424	25.13961	79.49843	682	465 124	26.11513	82.58329
633	400 689	25.15949	79.56130	683	466 489	26.13427	82.64381
634	401 956	25.17936	79.62412	684	467 856	26.15339	82.70429
635	403 225	25.19921	79.68689	685	469 225	26.17250	82.76473
636	404 496	25.21904	79.74961	686	470 596	26.19160	82.82512
637	405 769	25.23886	79.81228	687	471 969	26.21068	82.88546
638	407 044	25.25866	79.87490	688	473 344	26.22975	82.94577
639	408 321	25.27845	79.93748	689	474 721	26.24881	83.00602
640	409 600	25.29822	80.00000	690	476 100	26.26785	83.06624
641	410 881	25.31798	80.06248	691	477 481	26.28688	83.12641
642	412 164	25.33772	80.12490	692	478 864	26.30589	83.18654
643	413 449	25.35744	80.18728	693	480 249	26.32489	83.24662
644	414 736	25.37716	80.24961	694	481 636	26.34388	83.30666
645	416 025	25.39685	80.31189	695	483 025	26.36285	83.36666
646	417 316	25.41653	80.37413	696	484 416	26.38181	83.42661
647	418 609	25.43619	80.43631	697	485 809	26.40076	83.48653
648	419 904	25.45584	80.49845	698	487 204	26.41969	83.54639
649	421 201	25.47548	80.56054	699	488 601	26.43861	83.60622
650	422 500	25.49510	80.62258	700	490 000	26.45751	83.66600

Tables of squares and square roots

N	N²	√N	√10N	N	N²	√N	√10N
700	490 000	26.45751	83.66600	750	562 500	27.38613	86.60254
701	491 401	26.47640	83.72574	751	564 001	27.40438	86.66026
702	492 804	26.49528	83.78544	752	565 504	27.42262	86.71793
703	494 209	26.51415	83.84510	753	567 009	27.44085	86.77557
704	495 616	26.53300	83.90471	754	568 516	27.45906	86.83317
705	497 025	26.55184	83.96428	755	570 025	27.47726	86.89074
706	498 436	26.57066	84.02381	756	571 536	27.49545	86.94826
707	499 849	26.58947	84.08329	757	573 049	27.51363	87.00575
708	501 264	26.60827	84.14274	758	574 564	27.53180	87.06320
709	502 681	26.62705	84.20214	759	576 081	27.54995	87.12061
710	504 100	26.64583	84.26150	760	577 600	27.56810	87.17798
711	505 521	26.66458	84.32082	761	579 121	27.58623	87.23531
712	506 944	26.68333	84.38009	762	580 644	27.60435	87.29261
713	508 369	26.70206	84.43933	763	582 169	27.62245	87.34987
714	509 796	26.72078	84.49852	764	583 696	27.64055	87.40709
715	511 225	26.73948	84.55767	765	585 225	27.65863	87.46428
716	512 656	26.75818	84.61578	766	586 756	27.67671	87.52143
717	514 089	26.77686	84.67585	767	588 289	27.69476	87.57854
718	515 524	26.79552	84.73488	768	589 824	27.71281	87.63561
719	516 961	26.81418	84.79387	769	591 361	27.73085	87.69265
720	518 400	26.83282	84.85281	770	592 900	27.74887	87.74964
721	519 841	26.85144	84.91172	771	594 441	27.76689	87.80661
722	521 284	26.87006	84.97058	772	595 984	27.78489	87.86353
723	522 729	26.88866	85.02941	773	597 529	27.80288	87.92042
724	524 176	26.90725	85.08819	774	599 076	27.82086	87.97727
725	525 625	26.92582	85.14693	775	600 625	27.83882	88.03408
726	527 076	26.94439	85.20563	776	602 176	27.85678	88.09086
727	528 529	26.96294	85.26429	777	603 729	27.87472	88.14760
728	529 984	26.98148	85.32294	778	605 284	27.89265	88.20431
729	531 411	27.00000	85.38150	779	606 841	27.91057	88.26098
730	532 900	27.01851	85.44004	780	608 400	27.92848	88.31761
731	534 361	27.03701	85.49854	781	609 961	27.94638	88.37420
732	535 824	27.05550	85.55700	782	611 524	27.96426	88.43076
733	537 289	27.07397	85.61542	783	613 089	27.98214	88.48729
734	538 756	27.09243	85.67380	784	614 656	28.00000	88.54377
735	540 225	27.11088	85.73214	785	616 225	28.01785	88.60023
736	541 696	27.12932	85.79044	786	617 796	28.03569	88.65664
737	543 169	27.14774	85.84870	787	619 369	28.05352	88.71302
738	544 644	27.16616	85.90693	788	620 944	28.07134	88.76936
739	546 121	27.18455	85.96511	789	622 521	28.08914	88.82567
740	547 600	27.20294	86.02325	790	624 100	28.10694	88.88194
741	549 081	27.22132	86.08136	791	625 681	28.12472	88.93818
742	550 564	27.23968	86.13942	792	627 264	28.14249	88.99438
743	552 049	27.25803	86.20745	793	628 849	28.16026	89.05055
744	553 536	27.27636	86.25543	794	630 436	28.17801	89.10668
745	555 025	27.29469	86.31338	795	632 025	28.19574	89.16277
746	556 516	27.31300	86.37129	796	633 616	28.21347	89.21883
747	558 009	27.33130	86.42916	797	635 209	28.23119	89.27486
748	559 504	27.34959	86.48609	798	636 804	28.24889	89.33085
749	561 001	27.36786	86.54479	799	638 401	28.26659	89.38680
750	562 500	27.38613	86.60254	800	640 000	28.28427	89.44272

Tables of squares and square roots

N	N²	√N	√10N	N	N²	√N	√10N
800	640 000	28.28427	89.44272	850	722 500	29.15476	92.19544
801	641 601	28.30194	89.49860	851	724 201	29.17190	92.24966
802	643 204	28.31960	89.55445	852	725 904	29.18904	92.30385
803	644 809	28.33725	89.61027	853	727 609	29.20616	92.35800
804	646 416	28.35489	89.66605	854	729 316	29.22328	92.41212
805	648 025	28.37252	89.72179	855	731 025	29.24038	92.46621
806	649 636	28.39014	89.77750	856	732 736	29.25748	92.52027
807	651 249	28.40775	89.83318	857	734 449	29.27456	92.57429
808	652 864	28.42534	89.88882	858	736 164	29.29164	92.62829
809	654 481	28.44293	89.94443	859	737 881	29.30870	92.68225
810	656 100	28.46050	90.00000	860	739 600	29.32576	92.73618
811	657 721	28.47806	90.05554	861	741 321	29.34280	92.79009
812	659 344	28.49561	90.11104	862	743 044	29.35984	92.84396
813	660 969	28.51315	90.16651	863	744 769	29.37686	92.89779
814	662 596	28.53069	90.22195	864	746 496	29.39388	92.95160
815	664 225	28.54820	90.27735	865	748 225	29.41088	93.00538
816	665 856	28.56571	90.33272	866	749 956	29.42788	93.05912
817	667 489	28.58321	90.38805	867	751 689	29.44486	93.11283
818	669 124	28.60070	90.44335	868	753 424	29.46184	93.16652
819	670 761	28.61818	90.49862	869	755 161	29.47881	93.22017
820	672 400	28.63564	90.55385	870	756 900	29.49576	93.27379
821	674 041	28.65310	90.60905	871	758 641	29.51271	93.32738
822	675 684	28.67054	90.66422	872	760 384	29.52965	93.38094
823	677 329	28.68798	90.71935	873	762 129	29.54657	93.43447
824	678 976	28.70540	90.77445	874	763 876	29.56349	93.48797
825	680 625	28.72281	90.82951	875	765 625	29.58040	93.54143
826	682 276	28.74022	90.88454	876	767 376	29.59730	93.59487
827	683 929	28.75761	90.93954	877	769 129	29.61419	93.64828
828	685 584	28.77499	90.99451	878	770 884	29.63106	93.70165
829	687 241	28.79236	91.04944	879	772 641	29.64793	93.75500
830	688 900	28.80972	91.10434	880	774 400	29.66479	93.80832
831	690 561	28.82707	91.15920	881	776 161	29.68164	93.86160
832	692 224	28.84441	91.21403	882	777 924	29.69848	93.91486
833	693 889	28.86174	91.26883	883	779 689	29.71532	93.96808
834	695 556	28.87906	91.32360	884	781 456	29.73214	94.02027
835	697 225	28.89637	91.37833	885	783 225	29.74895	94.07444
836	698 896	28.91366	91.43304	886	784 996	29.76575	94.12757
837	700 569	28.93095	91.48770	887	786 769	29.78255	94.10868
838	702 244	28.94823	91.54234	888	788 544	29.79933	94.23375
839	703 921	28.96550	91.59694	889	790 321	29.81610	94.28680
840	705 600	28.98275	91.65151	890	792 100	29.83287	94.33981
841	707 281	29.00000	91.70605	891	793 881	29.84962	94.39280
842	708 964	29.01724	91.76056	892	795 664	29.86637	94.44575
843	710 649	29.03446	91.81503	893	797 449	29.88311	94.49868
844	712 336	29.05168	91.86947	894	799 236	29.89983	94.55157
845	714 025	29.06888	91.92388	895	801 025	29.91655	94.60444
846	715 716	29.08608	91.97826	896	802 816	29.93326	94.65728
847	717 409	29.10326	92.03260	897	804 609	29.94996	94.71008
848	719 104	29.12044	92.08692	898	806 404	29.96665	94.76286
849	720 801	29.13760	92.14120	899	808 201	29.98333	94.81561
850	722 500	29.15476	92.19544	900	810 000	30.00000	94.86833

Tables of squares and square roots

N	N²	√N	√10N	N	N²	√N	√10N
900	810 000	30.00000	94.86833	950	902 500	30.82207	97.46794
901	811 801	30.01666	94.92102	951	904 401	30.83829	97.51923
902	813 604	30.03331	94.97368	952	906 304	30.85450	97.57049
903	815 409	30.04996	95.02631	953	908 209	30.87070	97.62172
904	817 216	30.06659	95.07891	954	910.116	30.88689	97.67292
905	819 025	30.08322	95.13149	955	912 025	30.90307	97.72410
906	820 836	30.09938	95.18403	956	913 936	30.91925	97.77525
907	822 649	30.11644	95.23655	957	915 849	30.93542	97.82638
908	824 464	30.13304	95.28903	958	917 764	30.95158	97.87747
909	826 281	30.14963	95.34149	959	919 681	30.96773	97 92855
910	828 100	30.16621	95.39392	960	921 600	30.98387	97.97959
911	829 921	30.18278	95.44632	961	923 521	31.00000	98.03061
912	831 744	30.19934	95.49869	962	925 444	31.01612	98.08160
913	833 569	30.21589	95.55103	963	927 369	31.03224	98.13256
914	835 396	30.23243	95.60335	964	929 296	31.04835	98.18350
915	837 225	30.24897	95.65563	965	931 225	31.06445	98.23441
916	839 056	30.26549	95.70789	966	933 156	31.08054	98.28530
917	840 889	30.28201	95.76012	967	935 089	31.09662	98.33616
918	842 724	30.29851	95.81232	968	937 024	31.11270	98.38699
919	844 561	30.31501	95.86449	969	938 961	31.12876	98.43780
920	846 400	30.33150	95.91663	970	940 900	31.14482	98.48858
921	848 241	30.34798	95.96874	971	942 841	31.16087	98.53933
922	850 084	30.36445	96.02083	972	944 784	31.17691	98.59006
923	851 929	30.38092	96.07289	973	946 729	31.19295	98.64076
924	853 776	30.39735	96.12492	974	948 676	31.20897	98.69144
925	855 625	30.41381	96.17692	975	950 625	31.22499	98.74209
926	857 476	30.43025	96.22889	976	952 576	31.24100	98.79271
927	859 329	30.44667	96.28084	977	954 529	31.25700	98.84331
928	861 184	30.46309	96.33276	978	956 484	31.27299	98.89388
929	863 041	30.47950	96.38465	979	958 441	31.28898	98.94443
930	864 900	30.49590	96.43651	980	960 400	31.30495	98.99495
931	866 761	30.51229	96.48834	981	962 361	31.32092	99.04544
932	868 624	30.52868	96.54015	982	964 324	31.33688	99.09591
933	870 489	30.54505	96.59193	983	966 144	31.34021	99.10321
934	872 356	30.56141	96.64368	984	968 256	31.36877	99.19677
935	874 225	30.57777	96.69540	985	970 225	31.38471	99.24717
936	876 096	30.59412	96.74709	986	972 196	31.40064	99.29753
937	877 969	30.61046	96.79876	987	974 169	31.41656	99.34787
938	879 844	30.62679	96.85040	988	976 144	31.43247	99.39819
939	881 721	30.64311	96.90201	989	978 121	31.44837	99.44848
940	883 600	30.65942	96.95360	990	980 100	31.46427	99.49874
941	885 481	30.67572	97.00515	991	982 081	31.48015	99.54898
942	887 364	30.69202	97.05668	992	984 064	31.49603	99.54920
943	889 249	30.70831	97.10819	993	986 049	31.51190	99.64939
944	891 136	30.72458	97.15966	994	988 036	31.52777	99.69955
945	893 025	30.74085	97.21111	995	990 025	31.54362	99.74969
946	894 916	30.75711	97.26253	996	992 016	31.55947	99.79980
947	896 809	30.77337	97.31393	997	994 009	31.57531	99.84989
948	898 704	30.78961	97.36529	998	996 004	31.59114	99.89995
949	900 601	30.80584	97.41663	999	998 001	31.60696	99.94999
950	902 500	30.82207	97.46794	1000	1 000 000	31.62278	100.00000

Source: Donald H. Sanders, A. Franklin Murph, Robert J. Eng, *Statistics, A Fresh Approach* (New York: McGraw Hill, 1976).

APPENDIX F   FINANCIAL AND ECONOMIC DATA BASES
Part I
Stock Market Data, p. 643.

Part II
Interest Rate Data, p. 662.

Part III
Economic Data, p. 674.

Part I: Stock Market Data

QUARTERLY DOW JONES INDUSTRIAL STOCK AVERAGE

The table below lists the earnings (losses) of the Dow Jones Industrial Average based on generally accepted accounting principles. The price-earnings ratio for the DJI correctly reflects deficit/negative earnings for the 1982 September and December quarters. The 1985 December quarter and year-end dividend reflects $2.00 GM dividend distribution value of one share of class H common for each 20 shares of common held. The 1984 December quarter and year-end dividend reflects $1.87½ GM dividend distribution value of one share of class E common for each 20 shares of common held. N.A.-Not available. d-Indicates deficit/negative earnings for the quarter.

Year	Quarter Ended		Clos. Avg.	Qtrly Chg.		% Chg.		Qtrly Earns	12-Mth Earns	P/E Ratio	Qtrly Divs	12-Mth Divs	Divs Yield	Payout Ratio
1988	Dec.	30	2168.57	+	55.66	+	2.63	50.96	215.46	10.1	20.79	79.53	3.67	.3691
	Sept.	30	2112.91	−	28.80	−	1.34	57.27	181.04	11.7	20.54	76.41	3.62	.4221
	June	30	2141.71	+	153.65	+	7.73	60.20	168.54	12.7	20.18	73.92	3.45	.4386
	Mar.	31	1988.06	+	49.23	+	2.54	47.03	144.45	13.8	18.02	71.85	3.61	.4974
1987	Dec.	31	1938.83	−	657.45	−	25.32	16.54	133.05	14.6	17.67	71.20	3.67	.5351
	Sept.	30	2596.28	+	177.75	+	7.34	44.77	137.99	18.8	18.05	70.62	2.72	.5117
	June	30	2418.53	+	113.84	+	4.94	36.11	126.23	19.2	18.11	69.36	2.87	.5494
	Mar.	31	2304.69	+	408.74	+	21.56	35.63	126.49	18.2	17.37	68.19	2.96	.5391
1986	Dec.	31	1895.95	+	128.37	+	7.26	21.48	115.59	16.4	17.09	67.04	3.54	.5800
	Sept.	30	1767.58	−	125.14	−	6.61	33.01	118.80	14.9	16.79	67.14	3.80	.5652
	June	30	1892.72	+	74.11	+	4.08	36.37	103.39	18.3	16.94	65.37	3.45	.6323
	Mar.	31	1818.61	+	271.94	+	17.58	24.73	96.43	18.9	16.22	63.38	3.49	.6573
1985	Dec.	31	1546.67	+	218.04	+	16.41	24.69	96.11	16.1	17.19	62.03	4.01	.6454
	Sept.	30	1328.63	−	6.83	−	0.51	17.60	90.78	14.6	15.02	61.83	4.65	.6811
	June	28	1335.46	+	68.68	+	5.14	29.41	102.26	13.1	14.95	61.53	4.61	.6017
	Mar.	29	1266.78	+	55.21	+	4.56	24.41	107.87	11.7	14.87	61.56	4.86	.5707
1984	Dec.	31	1211.57	+	4.86	+	0.40	19.36	113.58	10.7	16.99	60.63	5.00	.5338
	Sept.	28	1206.71	+	74.31	+	6.56	29.08	108.11	11.2	14.72	58.41	4.84	.5403
	June	29	1132.40	−	32.49	−	2.79	35.02	102.07	11.1	14.98	57.67	5.09	.5650
	Mar.	30	1164.89	−	93.75	−	7.45	30.12	87.38	13.3	13.94	56.39	4.84	.6453
1983	Dec.	30	1258.64	+	25.51	+	2.07	13.89	72.45	17.4	14.77	56.33	4.47	.7775
	Sept.	30	1233.13	+	11.17	+	0.91	23.04	56.12	22.0	13.98	54.59	4.43	.9727
	June	30	1221.96	+	91.93	+	8.13	20.33	11.59	105.4	13.70	54.05	4.42	4.6635
	Mar.	31	1130.03	+	83.49	+	7.98	15.19	9.52	118.7	13.88	54.10	4.79	5.6828
1982	Dec.	31	1046.54	+	150.29	+	16.77	d2.44	9.15	114.4	13.03	54.14	5.17	5.9169
	Sept.	30	896.25	+	84.32	+	10.38	d21.49	35.15	25.5	13.44	55.55	6.20	1.5804
	June	30	811.93	−	10.84	−	1.32	18.26	79.90	10.2	13.75	55.84	6.88	.6989
	Mar.	31	822.77	−	52.23	−	5.97	14.82	97.13	8.5	13.92	56.28	6.84	.5794
1981	Dec.	31	875.00	+	25.02	+	2.94	23.56	113.71	7.7	14.44	56.22	6.42	.4944
	Sept.	30	849.98	−	126.90	−	12.99	23.26	123.32	6.9	13.73	56.18	6.61	.4539
	June	30	976.88	−	26.99	−	2.69	35.49	128.91	7.6	14.19	55.98	5.73	.4266
	Mar.	31	1003.87	+	39.88	+	4.14	31.40	123.60	8.1	13.86	54.99	5.48	.4449
1980	Dec.	31	963.99	+	31.57	+	3.39	33.17	121.86	7.9	14.40	54.36	5.64	.4461
	Sept.	30	932.42	+	64.50	+	7.43	28.85	111.58	8.4	13.53	53.83	5.77	.4824
	June	30	867.92	+	82.17	+	10.46	30.18	116.40	7.5	13.20	52.81	6.08	.4537
	Mar.	31	785.75	−	52.99	−	6.32	29.66	120.77	6.5	13.23	52.10	6.63	.4314
1979	Dec.	31	838.74	−	39.93	−	4.54	22.89	124.46	6.7	13.87	50.98	6.08	.4096
	Sept.	28	878.67	+	36.69	+	4.36	33.67	136.26	6.4	12.51	51.45	5.85	.3776
	June	29	841.98	−	20.20	−	2.34	34.55	128.99	6.5	12.49	50.35	5.98	.3903
	Mar.	30	862.18	+	57.17	+	7.10	33.35	124.10	6.9	12.11	49.48	5.74	.3987
1978	Dec.	29	805.01	−	60.81	−	7.02	34.69	112.79	7.1	14.34	48.52	6.03	.4302

RETURN ON DOW JONES INDUSTRIAL AVERAGE

The table below lists the earnings (losses) of the Dow Jones Industrial Average based upon generally accepted accounting principles. The 1984 dividend reflects $1.87½ GM dividend distribution value of one share of class E common for each 20 shares of common held. Book value is total assets minus total liabilities, including the par value of the preferred stock, divided by the number of shares outstanding. The industrial average's book value is the total of the book values of each of its 30 components.

Year	Market First	Closing High	Date	Closing Low	Date	D.J.I. Close	Change	% Change	Book Value	Earns	P/E	Divs	Divs Yield, %
1988	2015.25	2183.50	Oct. 21	1879.14	Jan. 20	2168.57	+ 229.74	+ 11.85	N.A.	215.46	10.1	79.53	3.67
1987	1927.31	2722.42	Aug. 25	1738.74	Oct. 19	1938.83	+ 42.88	+ 2.26	1008.95	133.05	14.6	71.20	3.67
1986	1537.73	1955.57	Dec. 2	1502.29	Jan. 22	1895.95	+ 349.28	+ 22.58	986.48	115.59	16.4	67.04	3.54
1985	1198.87	1553.10	Dec. 16	1184.96	Jan. 4	1546.67	+ 335.10	+ 27.66	944.97	96.11	16.1	62.03	4.01
1984	1252.74	1286.64	Jan. 6	1086.57	July 24	1211.57	− 47.07	− 3.74	916.70	113.58	10.7	60.63	5.00
1983	1027.04	1287.20	Nov. 29	1027.04	Jan. 3	1258.64	+ 212.10	+ 20.27	888.21	72.45	17.4	56.33	4.47
1982	882.52	1070.55	Dec. 27	776.92	Aug. 12	1046.54	+ 171.54	+ 19.60	881.51	9.15	114.4	54.14	5.17
1981	972.78	1024.05	Apr. 27	824.01	Sept. 25	875.00	− 88.99	− 9.23	975.59	113.71	7.7	56.22	6.42
1980	824.57	1000.17	Nov. 20	759.13	Apr. 21	963.99	+ 15.25	+ 14.93	928.50	121.86	7.9	54.36	5.64
1979	811.42	897.61	Oct. 5	796.67	Nov. 7	838.74	+ 33.73	+ 4.19	859.41	124.46	6.7	50.98	6.08
1978	817.74	907.74	Sept. 8	742.12	Feb. 28	805.01	− 26.16	− 3.15	890.69	112.79	7.1	48.52	6.03
1977	999.75	999.75	Jan. 3	800.85	Nov. 2	831.17	− 173.48	− 17.27	841.76	89.10	9.3	45.84	5.51
1976	858.71	1014.79	Sept. 21	858.71	Jan. 2	1004.65	+ 152.24	+ 17.86	798.20	96.72	10.4	41.40	4.12
1975	632.04	881.81	July 15	632.04	Jan. 2	852.41	+ 236.17	+ 38.32	783.61	75.66	11.3	37.46	4.39
1974	855.32	891.66	Mar. 13	577.60	Dec. 6	616.24	− 234.62	− 27.57	746.95	99.04	6.2	37.72	6.12
1973	1031.68	1051.70	Jan. 11	788.31	Dec. 5	850.86	− 169.16	− 16.58	690.23	86.17	9.9	35.33	4.15
1972	889.30	1036.27	Dec. 11	889.15	Jan. 26	1020.02	+ 129.82	+ 14.58	642.87	67.11	15.2	32.27	3.16
1971	830.57	950.82	Apr. 28	797.97	Nov. 23	890.20	+ 51.28	+ 6.11	607.61	55.09	16.2	30.86	3.47
1970	809.20	842.00	Dec. 29	631.16	May 26	838.92	+ 38.56	+ 4.82	573.15	51.02	16.4	31.53	3.76
1969	947.73	968.85	May 14	769.93	Dec. 17	800.36	− 143.39	− 15.19	542.25	57.02	14.0	33.90	4.24
1968	906.84	985.21	Dec. 3	825.13	Mar. 21	943.75	+ 38.64	+ 4.27	521.08	57.89	16.3	31.34	3.32
1967	786.41	943.08	Sept. 25	786.41	Jan. 3	905.11	+ 119.42	+ 15.20	476.50	53.87	16.8	30.19	3.33
1966	968.54	995.15	Feb. 9	744.32	Oct. 7	785.69	− 183.57	− 18.94	475.92	57.68	13.6	31.89	4.06
1965	869.78	969.26	Dec. 31	840.59	June 28	969.26	+ 95.13	+ 10.88	453.27	53.67	18.1	28.61	2.95
1964	766.08	891.71	Nov. 18	766.08	Jan. 2	874.13	+ 111.18	+ 14.57	417.39	46.43	18.8	31.24	3.57
1963	646.79	767.21	Dec. 18	646.79	Jan. 2	762.95	+ 110.85	+ 17.00	425.90	41.21	18.5	23.41	3.07
1962	724.71	726.01	Jan. 3	535.76	June 26	652.10	− 79.04	− 10.81	400.97	36.43	17.9	23.30	3.57
1961	610.25	734.91	Dec. 13	610.25	Jan. 3	731.14	+ 115.25	+ 18.71	385.82	31.91	22.9	22.71	3.11
1960	679.06	685.47	Jan. 5	566.05	Oct. 25	615.89	− 63.47	− 9.34	369.87	32.21	19.1	21.36	3.47
1959	587.59	679.36	Dec. 31	574.46	Feb. 9	679.36	+ 95.71	+ 16.40	339.02	34.31	19.8	20.74	3.05
1958	439.27	583.65	Dec. 31	436.89	Feb. 25	583.65	+ 147.96	+ 33.96	310.97	27.95	20.9	20.00	3.43
1957	496.03	520.77	July 12	419.79	Oct. 22	435.69	− 63.78	− 12.77	298.69	36.08	12.1	21.61	4.96
1956	485.78	521.05	Apr. 6	462.35	Jan. 23	499.47	+ 11.07	+ 2.27	284.78	33.34	15.0	22.99	4.60
1955	408.89	488.40	Dec. 30	388.20	Jan. 17	488.40	+ 84.01	+ 20.77	271.77	35.78	13.7	21.58	4.42
1954	282.89	404.39	Dec. 31	279.87	Jan. 11	404.39	+ 123.49	+ 43.96	248.96	28.18	14.4	17.47	4.32
1953	292.14	293.79	Jan. 5	255.49	Sept. 14	280.90	− 11.00	− 3.77	244.26	27.23	10.3	16.11	5.73
1952	269.86	292.00	Dec. 30	256.35	May 1	291.90	+ 22.67	+ 8.42	213.39	24.78	11.8	15.43	5.29
1951	239.92	276.37	Sept. 13	238.99	Jan. 3	269.23	+ 33.82	+ 14.37	202.60	26.59	10.1	16.34	6.07
1950	198.89	235.47	Nov. 24	196.81	Jan. 13	235.41	+ 35.28	+ 17.63	194.19	30.70	7.7	16.13	6.85
1949	175.03	200.52	Dec. 30	161.60	June 13	200.13	+ 22.83	+ 12.88	170.12	23.54	8.5	12.79	6.39
1948	181.04	193.16	June 15	165.39	Mar. 16	177.30	− 3.86	− 2.13	159.67	23.07	7.7	11.50	6.49
1947	176.39	186.85	July 24	163.21	May 17	181.16	+ 3.96	+ 2.23	149.08	18.80	9.6	9.21	5.08
1946	191.66	212.50	May 29	163.12	Oct. 9	177.20	− 15.71	− 8.14	131.40	13.63	13.0	7.50	4.23
1945	152.58	195.82	Dec. 11	151.35	Jan. 24	192.91	+ 40.59	+ 26.65	122.74	10.56	18.3	6.69	3.47
1944	135.92	152.53	Dec. 16	134.22	Feb. 7	152.32	+ 16.43	+ 12.09	118.33	10.07	15.1	6.57	4.31
1943	119.93	145.82	July 14	119.26	Jan. 8	135.89	+ 16.49	+ 13.81	113.03	9.74	14.0	6.30	4.64
1942	112.77	119.71	Dec. 26	92.92	Apr. 28	119.40	+ 8.44	+ 7.61	107.50	9.22	13.0	6.40	5.36
1941	130.57	133.59	Jan. 10	106.34	Dec. 23	110.96	− 20.17	− 15.38	102.33	11.64	9.5	7.59	6.84
1940	151.43	152.80	Jan. 3	111.84	June 10	131.13	− 19.11	− 12.72	98.75	10.92	12.0	7.06	5.38
1939	153.64	155.92	Sept. 12	121.44	Apr. 8	150.24	− 4.52	− 2.92	95.58	9.11	16.5	6.11	4.07

Dow Jones Industrial Average
Earnings, Dividends and Price-Earnings Ratio

		Price	Earnings (by qtrs)	Preceding 12 mos. earnings	Price Earnings Ratio (col. 1 ÷ col. 3)	Dividends
1987	December 31	1938.83	. . . .	. . . .	. . . .	17.67
	September 30	2596.28	44.77	137.99	18.8	18.05
	June 30	2418.53	36.11	126.23	19.2	18.11
	March 31	2304.69	35.63	126.49	18.2	17.37
			. . . .			71.20
1986	December 31	1895.95	21.48	115.59	16.4	17.09
	September 30	1767.58	33.01	118.80	14.9	16.79
	June 30	1892.72	36.37	103.39	18.3	16.94
	March 31	1818.61	24.73	96.43	18.9	16.22
			115.59			67.04
1985	December 31	1546.67	24.69	96.11	16.1	17.19
	September 30	1328.63	17.60	90.78	14.6	15.02
	June 28	1335.46	29.41	102.26	13.1	14.95
	March 29	1266.78	24.41	107.87	11.7	14.87
						62.03
1984	December 31	1211.57	19.36	113.58	10.7	16.99
	September 28	1206.71	29.08	108.11	11.2	14.72
	June 29	1132.40	35.02	102.07	11.1	14.98
	March 30	1164.89	30.12	87.38	13.3	13.94
			113.58			60.63
1983	December 30	1258.94	13.89	72.45	17.4	14.77
	September 30	1233.13	23.04	56.12	30.0	13.98
	June 30	1221.96	20.33	11.59	105.4	13.70
	March 31	1130.03	15.19	9.52	118.7	13.88
			72.45			56.33
1982	December 31	1046.54	d2.44	9.15	114.4	13.03
	September 30	896.25	d21.49	35.15	25.5	13.44
	June 30	811.93	18.26	79.90	10.2	13.75
	March 31	822.77	14.82	97.13	8.5	13.92
			9.15			54.14

Earnings and Price-Earnings Ratio

Earnings on the Dow Jones industrial average are computed by adding the per share results of the latest quarter of each of the 30 components. This total is then divided by the then-current divisor. Having obtained the figure for the quarter, the four most recent quarterly figures are totaled to give the 12-month figure.

The industrial average stood at 2596.28 on September 30, 1987, for instance (see above). The 12-month earnings for that date were 137.99, being the sum of the four previous quarters ended September.

To obtain the price-earnings ratio on the industrials, the industrial average on a given date is divided by the 12-month earnings of the same date.

Source: Phyllis Pearce, *The Dow Jones Investor's Handbook* (Homewood, Ill.: Dow Jones-Irwin, 1988).

Dow Jones Industrial Average
Earnings, Dividends and Price-Earnings Ratio

		Price	Earnings (by qtrs)	Preceding 12 mos. earnings	Price Earnings Ratio (col. 1 ÷ col. 3)	Dividends
1981	December 31	875.00	23.56	113.71	7.7	14.44
	September 30	849.98	23.26	123.32	6.9	13.73
	June 30	976.88	35.49	128.91	7.6	14.19
	March 31	1003.87	31.40	123.60	8.1	13.86
			113.71			56.22
1980	December 31	963.99	33.17	121.86	7.9	14.40
	September 30	932.42	28.85	111.58	8.4	13.53
	June 30	867.92	30.18	116.40	7.5	13.20
	March 31	785.75	29.66	120.77	6.5	13.23
			121.86			54.36
1979	December 31	838.74	22.89	124.46	6.7	13.87
	September 28	878.67	33.67	136.26	6.4	12.51
	June 29	841.98	34.55	128.99	6.5	12.49
	March 30	862.18	33.35	124.10	6.9	12.11
			124.46			50.98
1978	December 29	805.01	34.69	112.79	7.1	14.34
	September 29	865.82	26.40	101.59	8.5	11.41
	June 30	818.95	29.66	91.37	9.0	11.62
	March 31	757.36	22.04	89.23	8.5	11.15
			112.79			48.52
1977	December 30	831.17	23.49	89.10	9.3	13.24
	September 30	847.11	16.18	89.86	9.4	10.73
	June 30	916.30	27.52	97.18	9.4	11.41
	March 31	919.13	21.91	95.51	9.6	10.46
			89.10			45.84
1976	December 31	1004.65	24.25	96.72	10.4	12.13
	September 30	990.19	23.50	95.81	10.3	9.85
	June 30	1002.78	25.85	90.68	11.1	10.19
	March 31	999.45	23.12	81.87	12.2	9.23
			96.72			41.40
1975	December 31	852.41	23.34	75.66	11.3	9.63
	September 30	793.88	18.37	75.47	10.5	9.05
	June 30	878.99	17.04	83.83	10.5	8.97
	March 31	768.15	16.91	93.47	8.2	9.81
			75.66			37.46
1974	December 31	616.24	23.15	99.04	6.2	10.45
	September 30	607.87	26.73	99.73	6.1	9.43
	June 28	802.41	26.68	93.26	8.6	8.87
	March 29	846.68	22.48	89.46	9.5	8.97
			99.04			37.72

Source: Phyllis Pearce, *The Dow Jones Investor's Handbook* (Homewood, Ill.: Dow Jones-Irwin, 1988).

Dow Jones Industrial Average
Earnings, Dividends and Price-Earnings Ratio

		Price	Earnings (by qtr)	Preceding 12 mos. earnings	Price Earnings Ratio (col. 1 ÷ col. 3)	Dividends
1973	December 31	850.86	23.84	86.17	9.9	10.62
	September 28	947.10	20.26	82.09	11.5	8.36
	June 29	891.71	22.88	77.56	11.5	8.27
	March 30	951.01	19.19	71.98	13.2	8.08
			86.17			35.33
1972	December 29	1020.02	19.76	67.11	15.2	8.99
	September 29	953.27	15.73	62.15	15.3	7.76
	June 30	929.03	17.30	58.87	15.8	7.87
	March 30	940.70	14.32	56.76	16.6	7.65
			67.11			32.27
1971	December 31	890.20	14.80	55.09	16.2	7.85
	September 30	887.19	12.45	53.43	16.6	7.51
	June 30	891.14	15.19	53.45	16.7	7.80
	March 31	904.37	12.65	52.36	17.3	7.70
			55.09			30.86
1970	December 31	838.92	13.14	51.02	16.4	8.25
	September 30	760.68	12.47	51.83	14.7	7.80
	June 30	683.53	14.10	53.18	12.8	7.80
	March 31	785.57	11.31	54.07	14.5	7.68
			51.02			31.53
1969	December 31	800.36	13.95	57.02	14.0	8.63
	September 30	813.09	13.82	59.60	13.6	7.82
	June 30	873.19	14.99	59.47	14.7	8.08
	March 28	935.48	14.26	59.34	15.8	9.37
			57.02			33.90
1968	December 31	943.75	16.53	57.89	16.3	8.59
	September 30	935.79	13.69	57.05	16.4	7.73
	June 28	897.80	14.86	55.71	16.1	7.73
	March 29	840.67	12.81	53.98	15.6	7.29
			57.89			31.34
1967	December 29	905.11	15.69	53.87	16.8	8.03
	September 29	926.66	12.35	52.73	17.6	7.25
	June 30	860.26	13.13	54.27	15.8	7.36
	March 31	865.98	12.70	56.67	15.3	7.55
			53.87			30.19
1966	December 30	785.69	14.55	57.68	13.6	10.01
	September 30	774.22	13.89	57.36	13.5	7.18
	June 30	870.10	15.53	56.23	15.5	7.26
	March 31	924.77	13.71	55.05	16.8	7.44
			57.68			31.89

Source: Phyllis Pearce, *The Dow Jones Investor's Handbook* (Homewood, Ill.: Dow Jones-Irwin, 1988).

Dow Jones Industrial Average
Earnings, Dividends and Price-Earnings Ratio

		Price	Earnings (by qtrs)	Preceding 12 mos. earnings	Price Earnings Ratio (col. 1 ÷ col. 3)	Dividends
1965	December 31	969.26	14.23	53.67	18.1	8.54
	September 30	930.58	12.76	52.74	17.6	6.58
	June 30	868.03	14.35	50.84	17.1	6.79
	March 31	889.05	12.33	48.55	18.3	6.70
			53.67			28.61
1964	December 31	874.13	13.30	46.43	18.8	10.46
	September 30	875.37	10.86	45.88	19.1	5.79
	June 30	831.50	12.06	44.46	18.7	7.16
	March 31	813.29	10.21	42.60	19.1	7.83
			46.43			31.24
1963	December 31	762.95	12.75	41.21	18.5	7.39
	September 30	732.79	9.44	40.18	18.2	5.35
	June 28	706.68	10.20	38.71	18.3	5.52
	March 29	682.52	8.82	37.35	18.3	5.15
			41.21			23.41
1962	December 31	652.10	11.72	36.43	17.9	7.66
	September 28	578.98	7.97	35.52	16.3	5.26
	June 29	561.28	8.84	34.74	16.2	5.23
	March 30	706.95	7.90	34.11	20.7	5.15
			36.43			23.30
1961	December 29	731.13	10.81	31.91	22.9	7.57
	September 29	701.21	7.19	29.03	24.2	5.09
	June 30	683.96	8.21	29.29	23.4	5.05
	March 30	676.63	5.70	29.53	22.9	5.00
			31.91			22.71
1960	December 31	615.89	7.93	32.21	19.1	6.55
	September 30	580.14	7.45	31.64	18.3	4.86
	June 30	640.62	8.45	31.26	20.5	4.83
	March 31	610.59	8.38	33.82	18.2	5.12
			32.21			21.36
1959	December 31	679.36	7.36	34.31	19.8	6.73
	September 30	631.68	7.07	35.70	17.7	4.53
	June 30	643.60	11.01	35.71	18.0	4.59
	March 31	601.71	8.87	31.04	19.4	4.89
			34.31			20.74
1958	December 31	583.65	8.75	27.95	20.9	5.83
	September 30	532.09	7.08	27.97	19.0	4.59
	June 30	478.18	6.34	29.41	16.3	4.62
	March 31	446.76	5.78	32.56	13.7	4.96
			27.95			20.00

Source: Phyllis Pearce, *The Dow Jones Investor's Handbook* (Homewood, Ill.: Dow Jones-Irwin, 1988).

Dow Jones Industrial Average
Earnings, Dividends and Price-Earnings Ratio

		Price	Earnings (by qtrs)	Preceding 12 mos. earnings	Price Earnings Ratio (col. 1 ÷ col. 3)	Dividends
1957	December 31	435.69	8.78	36.08	12.1	6.91
	September 30	456.30	8.51	36.70	12.4	4.91
	June 28	503.29	9.49	34.82	14.4	4.79
	March 29	474.81	9.30	34.30	13.8	5.00
			36.08			21.61
1956	December 31	499.47	9.40	33.34	15.0	8.17
	September 28	475.25	6.63	33.65	14.1	4.83
	June 29	492.78	8.97	35.51	13.9	4.98
	March 29	511.79	8.34	36.02	14.2	5.01
			33.34			22.99
1955	December 30	488.40	9.71	35.78	13.7	8.13
	September 30	466.62	8.49	34.41	13.6	4.25
	June 30	451.38	9.48	32.11	14.1	4.24
	March 31	409.70	8.10	29.65	13.8	4.96
			35.78			21.58
1954	December 31	404.39	8.34	28.18	14.4	5.76
	September 30	360.46	6.19	26.99	13.4	3.75
	June 30	333.53	7.02	27.52	12.1	3.92
	March 31	303.51	6.63	27.20	11.2	4.04
			28.18			17.47
1953	December 31	280.90	7.15	27.23	10.3	4.86
	September 30	264.04	6.72	27.63	9.6	3.53
	June 30	268.26	6.70	26.93	10.0	3.95
	March 31	279.87	6.66	25.78	10.9	3.77
			27.23			16.11
1952	December 31	291.90	7.55	24.78	11.8	4.62
	September 30	270.61	6.02	24.37	11.1	3.55
	June 30	274.35	5.55	24.06	11.4	3.55
	March 31	269.46	5.66	25.11	10.7	3.71
			24.78			15.43
1951	December 31	269.23	7.14	26.59	10.1	5.25
	September 28	271.16	5.71	29.02	9.3	3.72
	June 29	242.64	6.60	31.83	7.6	3.48
	March 31	247.94	7.14	32.40	7.7	3.89
			26.59			16.34

d-Deficit.

Source: Phyllis Pearce, *The Dow Jones Investor's Handbook* (Homewood, Ill.: Dow Jones-Irwin, 1988).

YEARLY HIGHS AND LOWS OF DOW JONES AVERAGES

	—Industrials—		—Transportation—		—Utilities—	
	High	Low	High	Low	High	Low
1987	2722.42	1738.74	1101.16	661.00	227.83	160.98
1986	1955.57	1502.29	866.74	686.97	219.15	169.47
1985	1553.10	1184.96	723.31	553.03	174.96	146.54
1984	1286.64	1086.57	612.63	444.03	149.93	122.25
1983	1287.20	1027.04	612.57	434.24	140.70	119.51
1982	1070.55	776.92	464.55	292.12	122.83	103.22
1981	1024.05	824.01	447.38	335.48	117.81	101.28
1980	1000.17	759.13	425.68	233.69	117.34	96.04
1979	897.61	796.67	271.77	205.78	109.74	98.24
1978	907.74	742.12	261.49	199.31	110.98	96.35
1977	999.75	800.85	246.64	199.60	118.67	104.97
1976	1014.79	858.71	237.03	175.69	108.38	84.52
1975	881.81	632.04	174.57	146.47	87.07	72.02
1974	891.66	577.60	202.45	125.93	95.09	57.93
1973	1051.70	788.31	228.10	151.97	120.72	84.42
1972	1036.27	889.15	275.71	212.24	124.14	105.06
1971	950.82	797.97	248.33	169.70	128.39	108.03
1970	842.00	631.16	183.31	116.69	121.84	95.86
1969	968.85	769.93	279.88	169.03	139.95	106.31
1968	985.21	825.13	279.48	214.58	141.30	119.79
1967	943.08	786.41	274.49	205.16	140.43	120.97
1966	995.15	744.32	271.72	184.34	152.39	118.96
1965	969.26	840.59	249.55	187.29	163.32	149.84
1964	891.71	766.08	224.91	178.81	155.71	137.30
1963	767.21	646.69	179.46	142.03	144.37	129.19
1962	726.01	535.76	149.83	114.86	130.85	103.11
1961	734.91	610.25	152.92	131.06	135.90	99.75
1960	685.47	566.05	160.43	123.37	100.07	85.02
1959	679.36	574.46	173.56	146.65	94.70	85.05
1958	583.65	436.89	157.91	99.89	91.00	68.94
1957	520.77	419.79	157.67	95.67	74.61	62.10
1956	521.05	462.35	181.23	150.44	71.77	63.03
1955	488.40	388.20	167.83	137.84	66.68	61.39
1954	404.39	279.87	146.23	94.84	62.47	52.22
1953	293.79	255.49	112.21	90.56	53.88	47.87
1952	292.00	256.35	112.53	82.03	52.64	47.53
1951	276.37	238.99	90.08	72.39	47.22	41.47
1950	235.47	196.81	77.89	51.24	44.26	37.40
1949	200.52	161.60	54.29	41.03	41.31	33.36
1948	193.16	165.39	64.95	48.13	36.04	31.65
1947	186.85	163.21	53.42	41.16	37.55	32.28
1946	212.50	163.12	63.31	44.69	43.74	33.20
1945	195.82	151.35	64.89	47.03	39.15	26.15

Source: Phyllis Pearce, *The Dow Jones Investor's Handbook* (Homewood, Ill.: Dow Jones-Irwin, 1988).

YEARLY HIGHS AND LOWS OF DOW JONES AVERAGES

	—Industrials—		—Transportation—		—Utilities—	
	High	Low	High	Low	High	Low
1944	152.53	134.22	48.40	33.45	26.37	21.74
1943	145.82	119.26	38.30	27.59	22.30	14.69
1942	119.71	92.92	29.28	23.31	14.94	10.58
1941	133.59	106.34	30.88	24.25	20.65	13.51
1940	152.80	111.84	32.67	22.14	26.45	18.03
1939	155.92	121.44	35.90	24.14	27.10	20.71
1938	158.41	98.95	33.98	19.00	c25.19	c15.14
1937	194.40	113.64	64.46	28.91	37.54	19.65
1936	184.90	143.11	59.89	40.66	36.08	28.63
1935	148.44	96.71	41.84	27.31	29.78	14.46
1934	110.74	85.51	52.97	33.19	31.03	16.83
1933	108.67	50.16	56.53	23.42	37.73	19.33
1932	88.78	41.22	41.20	13.23	36.11	16.53
1931	194.36	73.79	111.58	31.42	73.40	30.55
1930	294.07	157.51	157.94	91.65	108.62	55.14
1929	381.17	198.69	189.11	128.07	144.61	64.72
1928	300.00	191.33	b152.70	b132.60	....	....
1927	202.40	152.73	144.82	119.92	....	....
1926	166.64	135.20	123.23	102.41	....	....
1925	159.39	115.00	112.93	92.82	....	....
1924	120.51	88.33	99.50	80.23	....	....
1923	105.38	85.76	90.63	76.78	....	....
1922	103.43	78.59	93.99	74.43	....	....
1921	81.50	63.90	77.56	65.52	....	....
1920	109.88	66.75	85.37	67.83	....	....
1919	119.62	79.15	91.13	73.63	....	....
1918	89.07	73.38	92.91	77.21	....	....
1917	99.18	65.95	105.76	70.75	....	....
1916	110.15	84.96	112.28	99.11	....	....
1915	99.21	54.22	108.28	87.85	....	....
1914	a83.43	a71.42	a109.43	a89.41	....	....
1913	88.57	72.11	118.10	100.50	....	....
1912	94.15	80.15	124.35	114.92	....	....

a—The high and low figures for the industrials and transportation are for the period ended July 31, 1914. The industrial average was composed of 12 stocks when the New York Stock Exchange closed in July 1914 because of World War I. In September 1916, a new list of 20 stocks was adopted and computed back to the opening of the Exchange on December 12, 1914. On October 1, 1928, the stocks comprising the industrial average was increased to 30. The high and low for the industrial average for December 1914 was 56.76 and 53.17, respectively. The high and low for transportation for December 1914 was 92.29 and 86.40.

b—On March 7, 1928, transportation components were increased to 20 from 12.

c—Since June 2, 1938, the utility average has been based on 15 stocks instead of 20.

Source: Phyllis Pearce, *The Dow Jones Investor's Handbook* (Homewood, Ill.: Dow Jones-Irwin, 1988).

COMPOSITE—500 STOCKS

Per Share Data—Adjusted to stock price index level. Average of stock price indexes, 1941-1943=10

	Earnings Per Share	Dividends Per Share	Dividends % of Earn.	Price 1941-1943=10 High	Price 1941-1943=10 Low	Price/Earn. Ratio High	Price/Earn. Ratio Low	Div. Yields % High	Div. Yields % Low	Book Value Per Share	Book Value % Return	Equity Per Share	Equity % Return
1957	3.37	1.79	53.12	49.13	38.98	14.58	11.57	4.59	3.64	...	...	...	...
1958	2.89	1.75	60.55	55.21	40.33	19.10	13.96	4.33	3.17	...	...	...	...
1959	3.39	1.83	53.98	60.71	53.58	17.91	15.81	3.42	3.01	...	...	...	...
1960	3.27	1.95	59.63	60.39	52.30	18.47	15.99	3.73	3.23	...	...	...	...
1961	3.19	2.02	63.32	72.64	57.57	22.77	18.05	3.51	2.78	...	...	...	...
1962	3.67	2.13	58.04	71.13	52.53	19.38	14.26	4.07	2.99	...	...	...	...
1963	4.02	2.28	56.72	75.02	62.69	18.66	15.59	3.64	3.04	...	...	...	...
1964	4.55	2.50	54.95	86.28	75.43	18.96	16.58	3.31	2.90	...	...	...	...
1965	5.19	2.72	52.41	92.63	81.60	17.85	15.72	3.33	2.94	...	...	...	...
1966	5.55	2.87	51.71	94.06	73.20	16.95	13.19	3.92	3.05	...	...	...	...
1967	5.33	2.92	54.78	97.59	80.38	18.31	15.08	3.63	2.99	...	...	...	...
1968	5.76	3.07	53.30	108.37	87.72	18.81	15.23	3.50	2.83	...	...	...	...
1969	5.78	3.16	54.67	106.16	89.20	18.37	15.43	3.54	2.98	...	...	...	...
1970	5.13	3.14	61.21	93.46	69.29	18.22	13.51	4.53	3.36	...	...	...	...
1971	5.70	3.07	53.86	104.77	90.16	18.38	15.82	3.41	2.93	...	...	...	...
1972	6.42	3.15	49.07	119.12	101.67	18.55	15.84	3.10	2.64	...	...	...	...
1973	8.16	3.38	41.42	120.24	92.16	14.74	11.29	3.67	2.81	...	...	...	...
1974	8.89	3.60	40.49	99.80	62.28	11.23	7.01	5.78	3.61	...	...	...	...
1975	7.96	3.68	46.23	95.61	70.04	12.01	8.80	5.25	3.85	...	...	...	...
1976	9.91	4.05	40.87	107.83	90.90	10.88	9.17	4.46	3.76	...	...	...	...
1977	10.89	4.67	42.88	107.00	90.71	9.83	8.33	5.15	4.36	79.07	13.77	81.23	13.41
1978	12.33	5.07	41.12	106.99	86.90	8.68	7.05	5.83	4.74	85.35	14.45	87.84	14.04
1979	14.86	5.65	38.02	111.27	96.13	7.49	6.47	5.88	5.08	94.27	15.76	97.00	15.32
1980	14.82	6.16	41.57	140.52	98.22	9.48	6.63	6.27	4.38	102.48	14.46	105.08	14.10
1981	15.36	6.63	43.16	138.12	112.77	8.99	7.34	5.88	4.80	109.43	14.04	112.44	13.66
1982	12.64	6.87	54.35	143.02	102.42	11.31	8.10	6.71	4.80	112.46	11.24	115.74	10.92
1983	14.03	7.09	50.54	172.65	138.34	12.31	9.86	5.13	4.11	116.93	12.00	120.24	11.67
1984	16.64	7.53	45.25	170.41	147.82	10.24	8.88	5.09	4.42	122.47	13.59	127.19	13.08
1985	14.61	7.90	54.07	212.02	163.68	14.51	11.20	4.83	3.73	125.20	11.67	133.40	10.95
R1986	14.48	8.28	57.18	254.00	203.49	17.54	14.05	4.07	3.26	126.82	11.43	138.82	10.45
P1987	17.50	8.81	50.34	336.77	223.92	19.24	12.80	3.93	2.62	133.87	13.01	147.09	11.84

Source: *Standard & Poor's Analyst's Handbook* (New York: Standard & Poor's Corporation, 1988).

400 INDUSTRIALS*

Per Share Data—Adjusted to stock price index level. Average of stock price indexes, 1941-1943—10

	Sales	Oper. Profit	Profit Margin %	Depr.	Income Taxes	Earnings Per Share	Earnings % of Sales	Dividends Per Share	Dividends % of Earn.	Price 1941-1943—10 High	Price Low	Price/Earn. Ratio High	Price/Earn. Ratio Low	Div. Yields % High	Div. Yields % Low	Book Value Per Share	Book Value % Return	Working Capital	Capital Expenditures
1957	55.81	8.79	15.75	2.41	2.87	3.53	6.33	1.94	54.96	53.25	41.98	15.08	11.89	4.62	3.64	29.44	11.99	13.50	4.84
1958	53.48	7.70	14.40	2.38	2.40	2.95	5.52	1.86	63.05	58.97	43.20	19.99	14.64	4.31	3.15	30.66	9.62	14.27	3.58
1959	57.83	8.84	15.29	2.47	2.99	3.47	6.00	1.95	56.20	65.32	57.02	18.82	16.43	3.42	2.99	32.26	10.76	14.93	3.65
1960	59.47	8.73	14.68	2.56	2.87	3.40	5.72	2.00	58.82	65.02	55.34	19.12	16.28	3.61	3.08	33.74	10.08	15.29	4.23
1961	59.51	8.75	14.70	2.66	2.80	3.37	5.66	2.07	61.42	76.69	60.87	22.76	18.06	3.40	2.70	34.85	9.67	15.84	3.97
1962	64.63	9.81	15.18	2.89	3.16	3.83	5.93	2.20	57.44	75.22	54.80	19.64	14.31	4.01	2.92	36.37	10.53	16.85	4.41
1963	68.50	10.73	15.66	3.04	3.51	4.24	6.19	2.36	55.66	79.25	65.48	18.69	15.44	3.60	2.98	38.17	11.11	17.64	4.41
1964	73.19	11.67	15.94	3.24	3.70	4.85	6.63	2.58	53.20	91.29	79.74	18.82	16.44	3.24	2.83	40.23	12.06	18.07	5.71
1965	80.69	13.11	16.25	3.52	4.14	5.50	6.82	2.82	51.27	98.55	86.43	17.92	15.71	3.26	2.86	43.50	12.64	18.80	6.87
1966	88.46	14.48	16.37	3.87	4.35	5.87	6.64	2.95	50.26	100.60	77.89	17.14	13.27	3.79	2.93	45.59	12.88	19.48	8.26
1967	91.86	14.28	15.55	4.25	4.11	5.62	6.12	2.97	52.85	106.15	85.31	18.89	15.18	3.48	2.80	47.78	11.76	20.74	8.35
1968	101.49	16.08	15.84	4.56	5.14	6.16	6.07	3.16	51.30	118.03	95.05	19.16	15.43	3.32	2.68	50.21	12.27	21.08	8.65
1969	108.53	16.63	15.32	4.87	5.14	6.13	5.65	3.25	53.02	116.24	97.75	18.96	15.95	3.32	2.80	51.70	11.86	21.05	9.70
1970	109.85	15.54	14.15	5.17	4.23	5.41	4.92	3.20	59.15	102.87	75.58	19.01	13.97	4.23	3.11	52.65	10.28	20.70	10.25
1971	118.23	17.22	14.56	5.45	4.98	5.97	5.04	3.16	52.93	115.84	99.36	19.40	16.64	3.18	2.73	55.28	10.80	22.61	9.96
1972	128.79	19.39	15.06	5.76	5.90	6.83	5.30	3.22	47.14	132.95	112.19	19.47	16.43	2.87	2.42	58.34	11.71	24.41	10.08
1973	149.22	23.64	15.84	6.25	7.59	8.89	5.96	3.46	38.92	134.54	103.37	15.13	11.63	3.35	2.57	62.84	14.15	26.49	11.65
1974	182.10	27.97	15.36	6.86	10.22	9.61	5.28	3.71	38.61	111.65	69.53	11.62	7.24	5.34	3.32	67.81	14.17	28.47	14.65
1975	185.16	26.63	14.38	7.36	9.40	8.58	4.63	3.72	43.36	107.40	77.71	12.52	9.06	4.79	3.46	70.84	12.11	30.47	14.43
1976	202.66	29.23	14.42	7.58	10.21	10.69	5.27	4.22	39.48	120.89	101.64	11.31	9.51	4.15	3.49	76.26	14.02	31.89	14.92
1977	224.24	32.20	14.36	8.53	11.14	11.45	5.11	4.95	43.23	118.92	99.88	10.39	8.72	4.96	4.16	82.21	13.93	33.28	17.02
1978	251.32	36.19	14.40	9.64	12.14	13.04	5.19	5.37	41.18	118.71	95.52	9.10	7.33	5.63	4.53	89.34	14.60	34.88	19.70
1979	292.38	42.01	14.37	10.82	14.02	16.29	5.57	5.92	36.34	124.49	107.08	7.64	6.57	5.53	4.76	98.71	16.50	36.32	26.44
1980	327.36	43.08	13.16	12.37	13.67	16.12	4.92	6.49	40.26	160.96	111.09	9.99	6.89	5.84	4.03	108.33	14.88	36.52	29.86
1981	344.31	44.50	12.92	13.82	12.95	16.74	4.86	7.01	41.88	157.02	125.93	9.38	7.52	5.57	4.46	116.06	14.42	35.98	33.03
1982	333.86	42.67	12.78	15.30	10.95	13.20	3.95	7.13	54.02	159.66	114.08	12.10	8.64	6.25	4.47	118.60	11.13	34.41	31.30
1983	334.07	45.57	13.64	15.67	12.12	14.77	4.42	7.32	49.56	194.84	154.95	13.19	10.49	4.72	3.76	122.32	12.07	36.55	25.24
1984	379.70	51.50	13.56	16.31	14.15	18.11	4.77	7.51	41.47	191.48	167.75	10.57	9.26	4.48	3.92	123.99	14.61	38.94	30.08
1985	398.42	53.23	13.36	18.19	13.68	15.28	3.84	7.87	51.51	235.75	182.24	15.43	11.93	4.32	3.34	125.89	12.14	39.32	31.42
R1986	387.76	51.02	13.16	19.41	11.01	14.53	3.75	8.14	56.02	282.77	224.88	19.46	15.48	3.62	2.88	124.87	11.64	40.30	29.58
P1987	431.92	58.81	13.62	20.17	14.07	20.48	4.74	8.78	42.87	393.17	255.43	19.20	12.47	3.44	2.23	133.93	15.29	47.32	27.33

NOTE: 1983 data incls. results of "old" A.T. & T.; excls. $5.5 bil. charge; 1984 data reflect A.T. & T. divestiture.

*Based on 70 individual groups.

Stock Price Indexes for this group extend back to 1918.

Source: *Standard & Poor's Analyst's Handbook* (New York: Standard & Poor's Corporation, 1988).

S & P INDUSTRIAL INDEX

Per Share Data - Adjusted to Stock Price Index Level
Average of Stock Price Indexes, 1941 - 1943 = 10

Income Account —

	1987	1986	1985	1984	1983	1982
Sales	421.26	387.76	398.42	379.70	334.00	333.86
Costs & expenses	363.51	336.74	345.19	328.21	288.44	291.19
Operating income	57.75	51.02	53.22	51.50	45.56	42.67
Other income	6.95	6.51	7.06	6.75	5.69	5.74
Total income	64.70	57.53	60.28	58.25	51.25	48.41
Depreciation	19.81	19.41	18.19	16.31	15.67	15.30
Interest	9.92	9.75	9.24	8.54	7.62	8.23
Special items	-0.81	-2.41	-3.42	-0.62	-0.57	-0.32
Minority interest	0.23	0.17	0.16	0.18	0.21	0.19
Income taxes	13.72	11.01	13.68	14.15	12.12	10.95
Net income	20.21	14.79	15.60	18.45	15.07	13.41
Preferred dividends	0.26	0.28	0.35	0.36	0.34	0.26
Savings fr. com. stk. equiv.	0.03	0.03	0.03	0.03	0.03	0.04
Common earnings	19.98	14.54	15.28	18.11	14.76	13.20
Common dividends	9.72	9.05	7.87	7.51	7.32	7.13
Balance after dividends	10.26	5.48	7.41	10.60	7.45	6.06

Balance Sheet

Assets —

	1987	1986	1985	1984	1983	1982
Cash & equivalent	NA	27.07	22.76	21.01	20.52	15.67
Receivables	55.52	47.81	47.78	47.39	45.36	41.90
Income tax refund	0.20	0.40	0.22	0.14	0.29	0.34
Inventories	56.95	55.75	57.85	51.68	41.89	44.99
Other current assets	8.60	8.41	7.95	6.18	4.99	5.21
Total current assets	NA	NA	NA	NA	NA	NA
Net property, plant, & equipment	157.76	154.64	150.20	138.79	142.26	144.06
Inv. & adv. to uncons. subs.	19.42	17.19	16.44	16.62	13.13	12.58
Intangibles	16.86	14.95	9.63	5.94	3.98	3.76
Other assets	46.13	37.42	33.86	24.30	16.94	15.72
Total assets	391.14	363.64	346.68	312.04	289.35	284.22

Liabilities —

	1987	1986	1985	1984	1983	1982
Notes payable	28.31	25.86	27.53	19.90	13.40	13.94
Current portion of long term debt	3.63	4.77	3.64	3.79	2.52	2.44
Accounts payable	37.29	33.29	34.47	30.07	27.41	25.16
Income tax payable	9.05	8.28	8.25	7.82	6.84	6.70
Accrued expenses	25.74	23.00	22.28	18.31	15.68	15.12
Other current liabilities	13.86	12.24	11.07	10.27	9.09	9.12
Total current liabilities	NA	NA	NA	NA	NA	NA
Long term debt	68.23	66.89	59.22	53.25	50.08	52.72
Deferred income tax	22.75	21.34	19.99	17.85	18.49	17.74
Investment tax credit	0.69	0.78	0.81	0.78	1.83	1.86
Minority interest	2.26	1.71	1.56	1.47	1.84	1.95
Other liabilities	26.85	21.87	18.09	14.33	12.10	10.96
Preferred stock	2.85	2.92	3.51	3.56	3.21	3.48
Common stock	11.56	10.52	9.85	10.29	9.53	11.33
Capital surplus	25.56	25.49	20.30	17.30	20.71	16.20
Retained earnings	126.56	115.01	106.13	103.07	96.64	95.50
Treasury cost	14.15	10.29	CF	CF	CF	CF
Total liabilities	391.14	363.64	346.68	312.04	289.35	284.22

Financial Ratios —

	1987	1986	1985	1984	1983	1982
Current ratio	NA	NA	NA	NA	NA	NA
Quick ratio	NA	NA	NA	NA	NA	NA
Debt to total assets (%)	17	18	17	17	17	19
Debt to total equity (%)	45	47	42	40	39	42
Debt to total capital (%)	28	29	27	26	25	26
Times interest earned	4.4	3.6	4.2	4.8	4.6	4.0
Inventory turnover	7.4	7.0	6.9	7.3	8.0	7.4
Total assets turnover	1.1	1.1	1.2	1.2	1.2	1.2
Profit margin (%)	13.71	13.16	13.36	13.56	13.64	12.78
Return on total assets (%)	5.11	4.00	4.41	5.80	5.10	4.64

NA - Not Available
NM - Not Meaningful
CF - Combined Figure

Source: *Standard & Poor's Analyst's Handbook* (New York: Standard & Poor's Corporation, 1988).

STOCK PRICE INDEXES—COMPOSITE†

(*500 Stocks)

1941–1943 = 10

Monthly Averages of Daily Indexes

	Jan.	Feb.	Mar.	Apr.	May	June	July	Aug.	Sept.	Oct.	Nov.	Dec.	Avg.
1930	21.71	23.07	23.94	25.46	23.94	21.52	21.06	20.79	20.78	17.92	16.62	15.51	21.03
1931	15.98	17.20	17.53	15.86	14.33	13.87	14.33	13.90	11.83	10.25	10.39	8.44	13.66
1932	8.30	8.23	8.26	6.28	5.51	4.77	5.01	7.53	8.26	7.12	7.05	6.82	6.93
1933	7.09	6.25	6.23	6.89	8.87	10.39	11.23	10.67	10.58	9.55	9.78	9.97	8.96
1934	10.54	11.32	10.74	10.92	9.81	9.94	9.47	9.10	8.88	8.95	9.20	9.26	9.84
1935	9.26	8.98	8.41	9.04	9.75	10.12	10.65	11.37	11.61	11.92	13.04	13.04	10.60
1936	13.76	14.55	14.86	14.88	14.09	14.69	15.56	15.87	16.05	16.89	17.36	17.06	15.47
1937	17.59	18.11	18.09	17.01	16.25	15.64	16.57	16.74	14.37	12.28	11.20	11.02	15.41
1938	11.31	11.04	10.31	9.89	9.98	10.21	12.24	12.31	11.75	13.06	13.07	12.69	11.49
1939	12.50	12.40	12.39	10.83	11.23	11.43	11.71	11.54	12.77	12.90	12.67	12.37	12.06
1940	12.30	12.22	12.15	12.27	10.58	9.67	9.99	10.20	10.63	10.73	10.98	10.53	11.02
1941	10.55	9.89	9.95	9.64	9.43	9.76	10.26	10.21	10.24	9.83	9.37	8.76	9.82
1942	8.93	8.65	8.18	7.84	7.93	8.33	8.64	8.59	8.68	9.32	9.47	9.52	8.67
1943	10.09	10.69	11.07	11.44	11.89	12.10	12.35	11.74	11.99	11.88	11.33	11.48	11.50
1944	11.85	11.77	12.10	11.89	12.10	12.67	13.00	12.81	12.60	12.91	12.82	13.10	12.47
1945	13.49	13.94	13.93	14.28	14.82	15.09	14.78	14.83	15.84	16.50	17.04	17.33	15.16
1946	18.02	18.07	17.53	18.66	18.70	18.58	18.05	17.70	15.09	14.75	14.69	15.13	17.08
1947	15.21	15.80	15.16	14.60	14.34	14.84	15.77	15.46	15.06	15.45	15.27	15.03	15.17
1948	14.83	14.10	14.30	15.40	16.15	16.82	16.42	15.94	15.76	16.19	15.29	15.19	15.53
1949	15.36	14.77	14.91	14.89	14.78	13.97	14.76	15.29	15.49	15.89	16.11	16.54	15.23
1950	16.88	17.21	17.35	17.84	18.44	18.74	17.38	18.43	19.08	19.87	19.83	19.75	18.40
1951	21.21	22.00	21.63	21.92	21.93	21.55	21.93	22.89	23.48	23.36	22.71	23.41	22.34
1952	24.19	23.75	23.81	23.74	23.73	24.38	25.08	25.18	24.78	24.26	25.03	26.04	24.50
1953	26.18	25.86	25.99	24.71	24.84	23.95	24.29	24.39	23.27	23.97	24.50	24.83	24.73
1954	25.46	26.02	26.57	27.63	28.73	28.96	30.13	30.73	31.45	32.18	33.44	34.97	29.69
1955	35.60	36 79	36.50	37.76	37.60	39.78	42.69	42.43	44.34	42.11	44.95	45.37	40.49
1956	44.15	44.43	47.49	48.05	46.54	46.27	48.78	48.49	46.84	46.24	45.76	46.44	46.62
1957	45.43	43.47	44.03	45.05	46.78	47.55	48.51	45.84	43.98	41.24	40.35	40.33	44.38
1958	41.12	41.26	42.11	42.34	43.70	44.75	45.98	47.70	48.96	50.95	52.50	53.49	46.24
1959	55.62	54.77	56.15	57.10	57.96	57.46	59.74	59.40	57.05	57.00	57.23	59.06	57.38
1960	58.03	55.78	55.02	55.73	55.22	57.26	55.84	56.51	54.81	53.73	55.47	56.80	55.85
1961	59.72	62.17	64.12	65.83	66.50	65.62	65.44	67.79	67.26	68.00	71.08	71.74	68.27
1962	69.07	70.22	70.29	68.05	62.99	55.63	56.97	58.52	58.00	56.17	60.04	62.64	66.27
1963	65.06	65.92	65.67	68.76	70.14	70.11	69.07	70.98	72.85	73.03	72.62	74.17	69.87
1964	76.45	77.39	78.80	79.94	80.72	80.24	83.22	82.00	83.41	84.85	85.44	83.96	81.37
1965	86.12	86.75	86.83	87.97	89.28	85.04	84.91	86.49	89.38	91.39	92.15	91.73	88.17
1966	93.32	92.69	88.88	91.60	86.78	86.06	85.84	80.65	77.81	77.13	80.99	81.33	85.26
1967	84.45	87.36	89.42	90.96	92.59	91.43	93.01	94.49	95.81	95.66	92.66	95.30	91.93
1968	95.04	90.75	89.09	95.67	97.87	100.5	100.3	98.11	101.3	103.8	105.4	106.5	98.69
1969	102.0	101.5	99.30	101.3	104.6	99.14	94.71	94.18	94.51	95.52	96.21	91.11	97.84
1970	90.31	87.16	88.65	85.95	76.06	75.59	75.72	77.92	82.58	84.37	84.28	90.05	83.22
1971	93.49	97.11	99.60	103.0	101.6	99.72	99.00	97.24	99.40	97.29	92.78	99.17	98.29
1972	103.3	105.2	107.7	108.8	107.7	108.0	107.2	111.0	109.4	109.6	115.1	117.5	109.2
1973	118.4	114.2	112.4	110.3	107.2	104.8	105.8	103.8	105.6	109.8	102.0	94.78	107.4
1974	96.11	93.45	97.44	92.46	89.67	89.79	82.82	76.03	68.12	69.44	71.74	67.07	82.85
1975	72.56	80.10	83.78	84.72	90.10	92.40	92.49	85.71	84.67	88.57	90.07	88.70	86.16
1976	96.86	100.6	101.1	101.9	101.2	101.8	104.2	103.3	105.5	101.9	101.2	104.7	102.0
1977	103.8	101.0	100.6	99.05	98.76	99.29	100.2	97.75	96.23	93.74	94.28	93.82	98.20
1978	90.25	88.98	88.82	92.71	97.41	97.66	97.19	103.9	103.9	100.6	94.71	96.11	96.02
1979	99.71	98.23	100.1	102.1	99.73	101.7	102.7	107.4	108.6	104.5	103.7	107.8	103.0
1980	110.9	115.3	104.7	103.0	107.7	114.6	119.8	123.5	126.5	130.2	135.7	133.5	118.8
1981	133.0	128.4	133.2	134.4	131.7	132.3	129.1	129.6	118.3	119.8	122.9	123.8	128.1
1982	117.3	114.5	110.8	116.3	116.4	109.7	109.4	109.7	122.4	132.7	138.1	139.4	119.7
1983	144.3	146.8	151.9	157.7	164.1	166.4	167.0	162.4	167.2	167.7	165.2	164.4	160.4
1984	166.4	157.3	157.4	157.6	156.6	153.1	151.1	164.4	166.1	164.8	166.3	164.5	160.5
1985	171.6	180.9	179.4	180.6	184.9	188.9	192.5	188.3	184.1	186.2	197.5	207.3	186.8
1986	208.2	219.4	232.3	238.0	238.5	245.3	240.2	245.0	238.3	237.4	245.1	248.6	236.3
1987	264.5	280.9	292.5	289.3	289.1	301.4	310.1	329.4	318.7	280.2	245.0	241.0	286.8

Annual Range, and Close, of Daily Indexes

Year	High	Low	Close	Year	High	Low	Close	Year	High	Low	Close
1928	24.35	16.95	24.35	1948	17.06	13.84	15.20	1968	108.4	87.72	103.9
1929	31.92	17.66	21.45	1949	16.79	13.55	16.76	1969	106.2	89.20	92.06
1930	25.92	14.44	15.34	1950	20.43	16.65	20.41	1970	93.46	69.29	92.15
1931	18.17	7.72	8.12	1951	23.85	20.69	23.77	1971	104.8	90.16	102.1
1932	9.31	4.40	6.89	1952	26.59	23.09	26.57	1972	119.1	101.7	118.1
1933	12.20	5.53	10.10	1953	26.66	22.71	24.81	1973	120.2	92.16	97.55
1934	11.82	8.36	9.50	1954	35.98	24.80	35.98	1974	99.80	62.28	68.56
1935	13.46	8.06	13.43	1955	46.41	34.58	45.48	1975	95.61	70.04	90.19
1936	17.69	13.40	17.18	1956	49.74	43.11	46.67	1976	107.8	90.90	107.5
1937	18.68	10.17	10.55	1957	49.13	38.98	39.99	1977	107.0	90.71	95.10
1938	13.79	8.50	13.21	1958	55.21	40.33	55.21	1978	107.0	86.90	96.11
1939	13.23	10.18	12.49	1959	60.71	53.58	59.89	1979	111.3	96.13	107.9
1940	12.77	8.99	10.58	1960	60.39	52.30	58.11	1980	140.5	98.22	135.8
1941	10.86	8.37	8.69	1961	72.64	57.57	71.55	1981	138.1	112.8	122.6
1942	9.77	7.47	9.77	1962	71.13	52.32	63.10	1982	143.0	102.4	140.6
1943	12.64	9.84	11.67	1963	75.02	62.69	75.02	1983	172.7	138.3	164.9
1944	13.29	11.56	13.28	1964	86.28	75.43	84.75	1984	170.4	147.8	167.2
1945	17.68	13.21	17.36	1965	92.63	81.60	92.43	1985	212.0	163.7	211.3
1946	19.25	14.12	15.30	1966	94.06	73.20	80.33	1986	254.0	203.5	242.2
1947	16.20	13.71	15.30	1967	97.59	80.38	96.47	1987	336.8	223.9	247.1

INDUSTRIAL STOCKS†

(*400 Stocks)

1941–1943 = 10

Monthly Averages of Daily Indexes

	Jan.	Feb.	Mar.	Apr.	May	June	July	Aug.	Sept.	Oct.	Nov.	Dec.	Avg.
1930	17.13	18.06	18.73	19.93	18.60	16.68	16.41	16.33	16.21	13.84	12.97	12.17	16.42
1931	12.34	13.27	13.45	12.18	10.97	10.56	10.95	10.72	9.15	7.91	8.09	6.54	10.51
1932	6.39	6.33	6.35	4.83	4.27	3.80	4.00	5.94	6.39	5.49	5.45	5.18	5.37
1933	5.35	4.74	4.93	5.75	7.41	8.61	9.40	9.15	9.37	8.49	8.92	9.16	7.61
1934	9.56	10.11	9.63	9.86	8.88	8.96	8.60	8.41	8.22	8.31	8.70	8.81	9.00
1935	8.88	8.72	8.19	8.67	9.40	9.64	10.14	10.71	11.01	11.39	12.43	12.38	10.13
1936	12.96	13.71	14.12	14.20	13.44	13.93	14.66	14.96	15.17	16.04	16.69	16.41	14.69
1937	16.87	17.51	17.52	16.45	15.74	15.26	16.18	16.45	14.12	12.04	10.82	10.68	14.97
1938	11.10	10.89	10.22	9.81	9.78	10.07	12.12	12.29	11.81	12.98	12.96	12.63	11.39
1939	12.30	12.12	12.09	10.56	10.91	11.11	11.37	11.15	12.56	12.60	12.35	12.06	11.77
1940	11.95	11.87	11.84	11.94	10.28	9.34	9.55	9.79	10.26	10.39	10.73	10.34	10.69
1941	10.30	9.64	9.73	9.43	9.27	9.66	10.19	10.14	10.21	9.81	9.41	8.86	9.72
1942	8.95	8.67	8.24	7.93	8.01	8.47	8.82	8.76	8.84	9.45	9.56	9.68	8.78
1943	10.22	10.81	11.13	11.44	11.87	12.14	12.29	11.66	11.91	11.78	11.25	11.42	11.49
1944	11.78	11.63	11.95	11.75	11.98	12.58	12.90	12.67	12.47	12.76	12.67	12.90	12.34
1945	13.23	13.63	13.63	13.94	14.44	14.58	14.23	14.39	15.43	16.03	16.41	16.73	14.72
1946	17.34	17.38	16.85	18.02	18.04	17.85	17.42	17.12	14.65	14.35	14.20	14.58	16.48
1947	14.69	15.31	14.73	14.23	14.02	14.58	15.48	15.15	14.76	15.19	15.15	14.93	14.85
1948	14.60	13.88	14.07	15.19	15.92	16.65	16.21	15.74	15.53	16.02	15.16	15.11	15.34
1949	15.23	14.57	14.72	14.66	14.51	13.69	14.55	15.04	15.20	15.62	15.86	16.29	15.00
1950	16.56	16.90	17.03	17.58	18.27	18.68	17.31	18.47	19.18	20.06	20.05	19.92	18.33
1951	21.38	22.22	21.84	22.24	22.29	21.88	22.31	23.35	23.98	23.80	23.09	23.83	22.68
1952	24.61	24.05	24.04	23.96	23.94	24.66	25.49	25.53	25.06	24.48	25.24	26.29	24.78
1953	26.45	26.07	26.18	24.84	25.01	24.12	24.41	24.44	23.26	23.96	24.51	24.85	24.84
1954	25.55	26.12	26.72	27.97	29.21	29 43	30.64	31.26	32.20	33.17	34.56	36.14	30.25
1955	36.79	38.06	37.65	39.04	38.88	41.45	44.94	44.56	46.88	44.52	47.78	48.25	42.40
1956	46.88	47.13	50.59	51.38	49.64	49.38	52.27	51.89	50.15	49.52	48.92	49.79	49.80
1957	48.43	46.10	46.86	48.06	50.10	51.30	52.54	49.51	47.52	44.43	43.41	43.29	47.63
1958	43.98	44.01	44.97	45.09	46.51	47.62	48.96	51.00	52.40	54.55	56.11	57.09	49.36
1959	59.30	58.33	59.79	60.92	62.09	61.75	64.23	63.74	61.21	61.04	61.46	63.56	61.45
1960	62.27	59.60	58.71	59.46	58.84	61.06	59.25	59.96	57.96	56.90	58.89	60.22	59.43
1961	63.20	65.71	67.83	69.64	70.34	69.48	69.15	71.69	70.89	71.42	74.72	75.81	69.99
1962	72.99	74.22	74.22	71.64	66.32	58.32	59.61	61.29	60.67	58.66	62.90	65.59	65.54
1963	68.00	68.91	68.71	72.17	73.60	73.61	72.45	74.43	76.63	77.09	76.69	78.38	73.39
1964	80.85	81.96	83.64	84.92	85.79	85.13	88.19	86.70	88.27	89.75	90.36	88.71	86.19
1965	91.04	91.64	91.75	93.08	94.69	90.19	89.92	91.68	94.93	97.20	98.02	97.66	93.48
1966	99.56	99.11	95.04	98.17	92.85	92.14	91.95	86.40	83.11	82.01	86.10	86.50	91.08
1967	89.88	93.35	95.86	97.54	99.59	98.61	100.4	102.1	103.8	104.2	100.9	103.9	99.18
1968	103.1	98.33	96.77	104.4	107.0	109.7	109.2	106.8	110.5	113.3	114.8	116.0	107.5
1969	111.0	110.2	108.2	110.7	114.5	108.6	103.7	103.4	104.0	105.1	105.9	100.5	107.2
1970	99.40	95.73	96.95	94.01	83.16	82.96	83.00	85.40	90.66	92.85	92.58	98.72	91.29
1971	102.2	106.6	109.6	113.7	112.4	110.3	109.1	107.3	109.9	107.3	102.2	109.7	108.4
1972	114.1	116.9	119.7	121.3	120.2	120.8	120.0	124.4	122.3	122.4	128.3	131.1	121.8
1973	132.6	127.9	126.1	123.6	120.0	117.2	118.7	116.8	118.5	123.4	114.6	106.2	120.5
1974	107.2	104.1	109.0	103.7	101.2	101.6	93.54	85.51	76.54	77.57	80.17	74.80	92.91
1975	80.50	89.29	93.90	95.27	101.5	103.7	103.8	96.21	94.96	99.29	100.9	99.31	96.56
1976	108.5	113.0	113.7	114.7	113.8	114.5	117.0	115.6	118.2	114.0	113.0	116.3	114.3
1977	115.2	112.1	111.9	109.9	109.1	109.5	110.1	107.5	105.9	103.2	103.7	103.1	108.4
1978	99.34	97.95	97.65	102.1	107.7	108.0	107.4	115.0	115.1	111.6	105.2	106.9	106.2
1979	111.2	109.5	111.7	114.0	111.2	113.0	113.6	118.9	121.1	117.0	116.1	120.8	114.8
1980	124.7	130.9	118.7	115.6	120.8	128.8	135.2	140.2	143.7	148.4	155.1	152.2	134.5
1981	151.1	145.7	151.0	152.3	149.1	148.7	145.4	146.0	132.7	134.0	136.8	138.4	144.3
1982	131.1	127.6	122.9	129.2	129.7	122.6	122.5	122.3	137.1	148.1	153.9	156.0	133.6
1983	162.0	165.2	170.3	176.8	184.1	187.4	188.3	183.2	188.6	189.0	185.9	185.2	180.5
1984	187.5	177.1	177.9	178.6	177.6	174.2	171.7	186.9	188.1	185.4	186.6	183.6	181.3
1985	191.6	202.1	200.4	201.1	204.8	208.5	212.9	209.4	205.2	207.7	219.4	230.3	207.8
1986	230.4	241.9	256.3	263.9	266.4	274.6	266.2	270.2	263.6	263.1	272.8	276.7	262.2
1987	296.1	318.2	334.7	335.4	336.1	349.6	362.4	384.9	372.5	323.1	280.1	277.7	330.9

Annual Range, and Close, of Daily Indexes

Year	High	Low	Close	Year	High	Low	Close	Year	High	Low	Close
1928	20.85	14.05	20.85	1948	16.93	13.58	15.12	1968	118.0	95.05	113.0
1929	25.38	14.18	16.99	1949	16.52	13.23	16.49	1969	116.2	97.75	101.5
1930	20.32	11.33	11.90	1950	20.60	16.34	20.57	1970	102.9	75.58	100.9
1931	14.07	6.02	6.32	1951	24.33	20.85	24.24	1971	115.8	99.36	112.7
1932	7.26	3.52	5.18	1952	26.92	23.30	26.89	1972	133.0	112.2	131.9
1933	10.25	4.24	9.26	1953	26.99	22.70	24.87	1973	134.5	103.4	109.1
1934	10.54	7.63	9.12	1954	37.24	24.84	37.24	1974	111.7	69.53	76.47
1935	12.84	7.90	12.77	1955	49.54	35.66	48.44	1975	107.4	77.71	100.9
1936	17.02	12.67	16.50	1956	53.28	45.71	50.08	1976	120.9	101.6	119.5
1937	18.10	9.73	10.26	1957	53.25	41.98	42.86	1977	118.9	99.88	104.7
1938	13.66	8.39	13.07	1958	58.97	43.20	58.97	1978	118.7	95.52	107.2
1939	13.08	9.92	12.17	1959	65.32	57.02	64.50	1979	124.5	107.1	121.0
1940	12.42	8.70	10.37	1960	65.02	55.34	61.49	1980	161.0	111.1	154.5
1941	10.62	8.47	8.78	1961	76.69	60.87	75.72	1981	157.0	125.9	137.1
1942	9.94	7.54	9.93	1962	75.22	54.80	66.00	1982	159.7	114.1	157.6
1943	12.58	10.00	11.61	1963	79.25	65.48	79.25	1983	194.8	155.0	186.2
1944	13.18	11.43	13.05	1964	91.29	79.74	89.62	1984	191.5	167.8	186.4
1945	17.06	12.97	16.79	1965	98.55	86.43	98.47	1985	235.8	182.2	234.6
1946	18.53	13.64	14.75	1966	100.6	77.89	85.24	1986	282.8	224.9	269.9
1947	15.83	13.40	15.18	1967	106.2	85.31	105.11	1987	393.2	255.4	285.9

Source: *Standard & Poor's Statistics Handbook* (New York: Standard & Poor's Corporation, 1988).

PREFERRED STOCK PRICE INDEXES

Dollars per $100 par value

The indexes are based upon one price weekly (as of Wednesday's close), the monthly index being an average of the four or five weekly indexes of the month. These indexes have been based upon ten high-grade non-callable issues, the yield for each being determined and the average of the four median yields representing the group yield. The average yield has, in turn, been converted into an equivalent price basis (7%) for the composite price index.

Monthly Averages of Weekly Indexes

	Jan.	Feb.	Mar.	Apr.	May	June	July	Aug.	Sept.	Oct.	Nov.	Dec.	Avg.
1935	142.8	144.5	145.6	149.2	153.5	153.8	153.9	154.4	153.5	152.6	154.6	157.9	151.4
1936	159.2	160.8	162.6	162.7	161.4	161.7	162.4	163.1	162.1	161.4	160.9	164.5	161.9
1937	167.6	166.5	159.0	154.8	153.1	155.3	155.2	157.1	156.6	155.2	153.8	156.5	157.6
1938	157.2	158.2	156.0	154.3	157.2	158.8	160.9	163.6	165.5	166.9	169.7	168.9	161.4
1939	170.1	170.6	169.4	168.3	169.1	170.7	172.8	172.0	156.1	156.9	165.3	169.0	167.5
1940	172.2	171.0	169.6	170.5	166.5	159.9	166.1	167.0	168.6	170.8	171.6	176.2	169.2
1941	177.9	172.9	171.5	170.8	168.9	168.9	173.1	174.3	173.4	172.1	170.5	168.7	171.9
1942	166.3	165.1	159.8	154.8	156.3	159.2	162.0	164.0	164.0	165.5	165.4	166.9	162.4
1943	168.0	170.8	171.5	171.5	172.1	173.8	175.9	176.4	175.9	175.1	172.6	169.1	172.7
1944	171.2	172.7	173.4	174.1	173.2	175.8	177.6	176.9	177.4	177.4	178.5	180.9	175.8
1945	183.3	185.5	187.7	190.9	191.2	190.9	189.6	188.1	186.7	188.0	192.2	195.3	189.1
1946	197.9	200.5	203.1	204.9	201.9	202.4	204.1	203.4	196.2	191.6	189.3	186.2	198.5
1947	187.3	189.0	188.1	186.5	186.2	186.2	188.4	188.7	188.3	181.2	174.5	172.1	184.7
1948	169.5	167.5	170.1	169.8	171.6	172.8	169.5	166.9	166.5	163.8	166.2	168.7	168.6
1949	171.4	173.2	172.2	172.2	173.2	176.1	176.6	179.5	182.1	180.3	179.8	180.6	176.4
1950	182.8	182.4	183.8	183.5	183.1	182.0	178.5	181.9	181.7	180.5	180.7	179.9	181.7
1951	180.9	180.9	174.9	170.4	168.9	167.9	166.7	169.4	168.5	167.0	165.4	163.7	170.4
1952	164.2	165.9	168.2	172.2	173.4	173.3	171.1	169.9	170.2	168.3	169.8	170.3	169.7
1953	168.4	166.3	165.7	161.7	160.0	156.8	160.1	163.1	162.8	167.3	168.8	166.5	164.0
1954	168.7	171.8	173.3	174.3	173.8	172.9	173.3	174.7	175.8	178.1	178.9	178.3	174.5
1955	175.8	175.0	174.6	176.0	175.6	175.7	176.7	174.4	172.7	173.5	174.7	172.9	174.8
1956	173.9	175.7	174.5	168.7	166.0	167.8	168.2	165.1	159.6	158.5	153.7	151.4	165.3
1957	155.1	156.7	157.2	156.8	154.6	149.5	147.3	145.1	146.2	145.9	146.5	156.0	151.4
1958	160.7	159.9	158.3	160.4	162.4	163.5	160.5	157.5	153.0	150.8	150.7	151.1	157.4
1959	154.4	155.1	156.3	155.0	149.7	146.0	147.2	149.0	146.0	145.6	145.6	144.3	149.5
1960	143.8	145.3	147.1	148.6	147.3	147.7	148.9	151.9	149.2	147.5	146.3	144.8	147.4
1961	148.0	149.8	150.2	150.1	151.0	150.2	149.4	149.2	149.3	151.6	152.7	150.9	150.2
1962	152.6	155.0	156.2	157.2	157.3	155.0	152.7	154.0	155.7	155.8	157.4	158.3	155.6
1963	161.3	164.1	164.9	162.4	163.4	163.2	161.4	162.7	162.9	164.5	163.6	161.9	163.0
1964	162.4	162.6	161.2	160.1	158.8	158.9	160.3	163.5	164.8	164.8	164.7	165.6	162.3
1965	167.5	166.1	164.2	163.7	162.8	159.7	159.8	161.3	162.2	159.8	158.9	156.6	161.9
1966	155.2	151.1	144.8	146.5	145.0	142.1	139.9	135.3	133.8	132.7	134.5	133.5	141.2
1967	138.3	140.7	138.9	139.2	135.5	132.0	131.1	131.0	129.4	125.3	120.8	117.8	131.7
1968	122.9	123.9	130.8	119.5	118.0	118.7	121.9	125.2	124.4	121.6	120.3	118.1	121.3
1969	118.2	117.9	115.0	114.0	113.0	110.6	109.1	108.6	106.1	103.1	102.3	97.4	109.6
1970	99.8	99.3	100.6	100.3	96.5	92.4	92.0	94.6	95.8	95.6	95.9	101.7	97.0
1971	107.3	110.7	108.1	106.4	102.7	100.1	99.6	99.5	101.5	103.7	103.4	102.9	103.8
1972	106.7	105.0	103.6	101.3	101.4	101.0	100.1	101.5	100.0	99.5	101.2	101.2	101.9
1973	102.1	101.4	99.5	98.6	98.1	96.7	95.3	94.2	94.9	97.6	94.6	90.2	96.9
1974	92.2	93.7	92.7	89.5	86.3	84.9	83.3	81.4	78.4	79.8	81.4	79.7	85.3
1975	84.1	86.8	87.1	84.7	82.2	83.9	85.0	83.2	81.8	81.6	82.4	82.8	83.8
1976	85.8	87.5	86.8	87.1	86.9	86.4	86.7	87.7	88.6	89.9	89.8	90.9	87.8
1977	92.9	92.7	92.6	92.1	91.8	91.9	93.3	92.7	92.4	91.9	91.2	89.2	92.1
1978	88.35	87.66	86.80	86.88	86.37	84.23	83.26	84.76	85.02	84.50	83.02	79.27	85.01
1979	79.61	79.87	79.80	80.01	79.33	78.94	78.40	77.62	76.67	74.01	70.42	69.60	77.02
1980	68.84	66.40	61.57	62.83	68.63	71.59	71.40	69.76	69.02	65.84	61.72	58.63	66.35
1981	60.62	59.19	59.27	59.26	56.94	57.23	56.30	55.45	53.82	53.50	54.88	54.58	56.75
1982	53.06	53.02	53.98	54.30	55.67	54.03	52.86	54.80	56.41	59.83	62.60	62.55	56.09
1983	62.37	62.92	64.45	64.84	65.72	64.75	63.32	63.27	63.32	63.82	62.94	60.96	63.56
1984	61.72	62.74	61.50	60.04	59.72	58.16	57.73	59.50	60.11	60.26	61.65	62.47	60.47
1985	62.90	64.36	63.80	65.10	66.06	69.67	70.56	68.98	68.27	67.62	69.21	69.69	67.19
1986	71.07	72.82	76.70	78.07	77.78	78.77	80.84	83.17	86.43	85.68	86.78	85.53	80.26
1987	88.48	88.31	93.07	88.21	83.21	84.29	84.79	84.11	80.99	77.93	76.89	77.08	83.95

Annual Range, and Close, of Weekly Indexes

Year	High	Low	Close	Year	High	Low	Close	Year	High	Low	Close
1933	128.7	113.5	120.3	1952	173.8	161.6	169.6	1970	103.0	89.3	101.2
1934	141.4	121.3	140.9	1953	169.6	156.2	166.7	1971	112.2	98.5	103.6
1935	159.1	141.4	159.1	1954	179.1	167.0	177.5	1972	107.9	99.2	101.0
1936	165.5	158.7	165.5	1955	177.4	172.0	172.6	1973	102.7	88.6	88.6
1937	168.3	152.5	156.6	1956	176.4	150.7	151.9	1974	94.7	77.6	78.7
1938	170.7	153.5	167.5	1957	158.2	144.2	157.7	1975	88.4	80.4	82.5
1939	173.7	152.5	168.7	1958	164.4	150.0	151.7	1976	91.5	83.1	91.5
1940	178.1	159.1	178.1	1959	157.3	142.7	142.8	1977	94.5	89.0	89.3
1941	179.5	166.7	166.7	1960	153.1	143.5	146.4	1978	89.42	78.32	78.52
1942	167.1	152.5	166.7	1961	153.0	146.4	150.7	1979	80.90	68.93	69.03
1943	176.4	167.1	169.9	1962	159.1	151.0	159.1	1980	72.16	57.96	57.88
1944	181.9	170.7	181.9	1963	165.2	159.1	161.2	1981	61.04	52.62	52.62
1945	196.7	182.3	196.7	1964	166.2	158.0	166.0	1982	65.35	52.43	61.47
1946	205.3	185.7	185.7	1965	168.7	155.2	155.2	1983	66.10	60.02	60.02
1947	189.2	167.9	167.9	1966	155.6	131.2	135.3	1984	63.26	57.52	62.59
1948	173.7	163.6	169.5	1967	141.5	116.7	118.4	1985	71.11	61.32	62.23
1949	183.3	169.1	181.4	1968	125.8	116.3	116.5	1986	87.61	70.61	85.26
1950	184.2	178.1	179.8	1969	118.9	95.6	97.7	1987	93.31	75.86	75.86
1951	181.7	161.9	161.9								

PREFERRED STOCK YIELD INDEXES

Yield in percent.

The indexes are based upon one price weekly (as of Wednesday's close), the monthly index being an average of the four or five weekly indexes of the month. These indexes have been based upon ten high-grade non-callable issues, the yield for each being determined and the average of the four median yields representing the group yield. The average yield has, in turn, been converted into an equivalent price basis (7%) for the composite price index.

Monthly Averages of Weekly Indexes

	Jan.	Feb.	Mar.	Apr.	May	June	July	Aug.	Sept.	Oct.	Nov.	Dec.	Avg.
1933	5.75	5.81	6.07	6.12	5.95	5.68	5.53	5.50	5.47	5.55	5.74	5.78	5.75
1934	5.66	5.46	5.40	5.33	5.28	5.24	5.16	5.18	5.28	5.32	5.16	4.99	5.29
1935	4.90	4.85	4.81	4.69	4.56	4.55	4.55	4.54	4.56	4.59	4.53	4.43	4.63
1936	4.40	4.36	4.31	4.30	4.34	4.33	4.31	4.29	4.32	4.34	4.35	4.26	4.33
1937	4.18	4.21	4.40	4.52	4.57	4.51	4.51	4.46	4.47	4.51	4.55	4.47	4.45
1938	4.45	4.43	4.49	4.54	4.46	4.43	4.35	4.28	4.23	4.20	4.12	4.15	4.34
1939	4.12	4.11	4.13	4.16	4.14	4.10	4.05	4.07	4.49	4.47	4.24	4.14	4.19
1940	4.07	4.10	4.13	4.11	4.21	4.38	4.22	4.19	4.15	4.10	4.08	3.97	4.14
1941	3.94	4.05	4.08	4.10	4.15	4.15	4.05	4.02	4.04	4.07	4.01	4.15	4.08
1942	4.21	4.24	4.38	4.52	4.48	4.40	4.32	4.27	4.27	4.23	4.23	4.19	4.31
1943	4.17	4.10	4.08	4.08	4.07	4.03	3.98	3.97	3.98	4.00	4.06	4.14	4.06
1944	4.09	4.06	4.04	4.02	4.04	3.98	3.94	3.96	3.95	3.95	3.92	3.87	3.99
1945	3.82	3.78	3.73	3.67	3.66	3.67	3.69	3.72	3.75	3.72	3.64	3.59	3.70
1946	3.54	3.49	3.45	3.42	3.47	3.46	3.43	3.44	3.57	3.65	3.70	3.76	3.53
1947	3.74	3.71	3.72	3.75	3.76	3.76	3.72	3.71	3.72	3.86	4.01	4.07	3.79
1948	4.13	4.18	4.12	4.12	4.08	4.05	4.13	4.20	4.20	4.28	4.21	4.15	4.15
1949	4.09	4.04	4.07	4.07	4.04	3.98	3.97	3.90	3.85	3.88	3.89	3.88	3.97
1950	3.83	3.84	3.81	3.82	3.82	3.85	3.92	3.85	3.85	3.88	3.88	3.89	3.85
1951	3.87	3.87	4.00	4.11	4.15	4.17	4.20	4.13	4.16	4.19	4.23	4.28	4.11
1952	4.26	4.22	4.16	4.07	4.04	4.04	4.09	4.12	4.12	4.16	4.12	4.11	4.13
1953	4.16	4.21	4.23	4.33	4.38	4.47	4.37	4.30	4.30	4.19	4.15	4.20	4.27
1954	4.15	4.08	4.04	4.02	4.03	4.05	4.04	4.01	3.98	3.93	3.92	3.93	4.02
1955	3.98	4.00	4.01	3.98	3.99	3.98	3.96	4.01	4.06	4.04	4.01	4.05	4.01
1956	4.03	3.99	4.01	4.15	4.22	4.17	4.16	4.24	4.39	4.42	4.56	4.63	4.25
1957	4.51	4.47	4.46	4.47	4.53	4.69	4.75	4.83	4.79	4.80	4.78	4.49	4.63
1958	4.36	4.38	4.42	4.37	4.31	4.28	4.36	4.45	4.58	4.64	4.65	4.63	4.45
1959	4.54	4.52	4.48	4.51	4.68	4.79	4.75	4.70	4.80	4.81	4.81	4.85	4.69
1960	4.87	4.82	4.76	4.71	4.75	4.74	4.70	4.61	4.69	4.75	4.78	4.84	4.75
1961	4.73	4.68	4.66	4.67	4.63	4.66	4.69	4.69	4.69	4.62	4.59	4.64	4.66
1962	4.59	4.52	4.48	4.45	4.45	4.52	4.59	4.55	4.50	4.49	4.45	4.42	4.50
1963	4.34	4.27	4.24	4.31	4.29	4.29	4.34	4.30	4.30	4.26	4.28	4.32	4.30
1964	4.31	4.31	4.34	4.37	4.41	4.41	4.37	4.29	4.25	4.25	4.25	4.23	4.32
1965	4.18	4.22	4.26	4.28	4.30	4.38	4.38	4.34	4.32	4.38	4.41	4.47	4.33
1966	4.51	4.63	4.83	4.78	4.83	4.93	5.00	5.18	5.23	5.28	5.21	5.24	4.87
1967	5.07	4.98	5.04	5.03	5.17	5.30	5.34	5.35	5.41	5.59	5.79	5.95	5.34
1968	5.70	5.65	5.80	5.86	5.92	5.90	5.74	5.59	5.63	5.76	5.82	5.93	5.78
1969	5.93	5.94	6.09	6.14	6.20	6.33	6.42	6.45	6.61	6.79	6.84	7.19	6.41
1970	7.02	7.04	6.97	6.98	7.26	7.57	7.62	7.41	7.31	7.33	7.30	6.88	7.22
1971	6.53	6.32	6.48	6.59	6.82	6.99	7.03	7.04	6.90	6.75	6.78	6.81	6.75
1972	6.57	6.67	6.76	6.91	6.90	6.93	6.99	6.90	7.00	7.03	6.93	6.92	6.88
1973	6.85	6.91	7.03	7.11	7.13	7.25	7.35	7.43	7.38	7.18	7.40	7.76	7.23
1974	7.60	7.47	7.56	7.83	8.11	8.25	8.40	8.61	8.93	8.78	8.60	8.78	8.24
1975	8.33	8.07	8.04	8.27	8.51	8.34	8.24	8.41	8.56	8.58	8.50	8.46	8.36
1976	8.16	8.00	8.07	8.04	8.06	8.10	8.08	7.99	7.90	7.80	7.80	7.70	7.98
1977	7.54	7.55	7.56	7.60	7.63	7.62	7.51	7.55	7.58	7.62	7.67	7.85	7.61
1978	7.92	7.99	8.07	8.06	8.11	8.31	8.42	8.26	8.24	8.29	8.43	8.84	8.25
1979	8.79	8.77	8.77	8.75	8.82	8.87	8.93	9.02	9.13	9.46	9.95	10.06	9.11
1980	10.17	10.55	11.37	11.16	10.20	9.78	9.81	10.04	10.14	10.64	11.35	11.94	10.60
1981	11.55	11.83	11.81	11.81	12.30	12.23	12.43	12.63	13.01	13.09	12.76	12.83	12.36
1982	13.79	13.20	12.97	12.90	12.58	12.96	13.24	12.78	12.41	11.71	11.18	11.20	12.53
1983	11.23	11.13	10.86	10.80	10.65	10.81	11.06	11.07	11.06	10.97	11.12	11.49	11.02
1984	11.35	11.16	11.39	11.66	11.72	12.04	12.13	11.77	11.65	11.62	11.36	11.21	11.59
1985	11.13	10.88	10.97	10.75	10.60	10.05	9.92	10.15	10.26	10.35	10.12	10.05	10.44
1986	9.85	9.62	9.13	8.97	9.00	8.89	8.66	8.42	8.10	8.17	8.07	8.18	8.76
1987	7.91	7.93	7.52	7.94	8.41	8.31	8.25	8.32	8.64	8.99	9.11	9.08	8.37

Annual Range, and Close, of Weekly Indexes

Year	High	Low	Close	Year	High	Low	Close	Year	High	Low	Close
1933	6.17	5.44	5.82	1952	4.33	4.03	4.13	1970	7.84	6.79	6.89
1934	5.77	4.95	4.97	1953	4.48	4.13	4.20	1971	7.10	6.24	6.76
1935	4.95	4.40	4.40	1954	4.19	3.91	3.95	1972	7.06	6.49	6.93
1936	4.41	4.23	4.23	1955	4.07	3.96	4.06	1973	7.90	6.82	7.90
1937	4.59	4.16	4.47	1956	4.65	3.97	4.61	1974	9.02	7.39	8.89
1938	4.56	4.10	4.18	1957	4.86	4.42	4.44	1975	8.70	7.92	8.48
1939	4.59	4.03	4.15	1958	4.67	4.26	4.62	1976	8.42	7.65	7.65
1940	4.40	3.93	3.93	1959	4.90	4.45	4.90	1977	7.87	7.41	7.84
1941	4.20	3.90	4.20	1960	4.88	4.57	4.81	1978	8.94	7.83	8.92
1942	4.59	4.19	4.20	1961	4.78	4.58	4.65	1979	10.16	8.71	10.14
1943	4.19	3.97	4.12	1962	4.64	4.40	4.40	1980	12.09	9.57	12.09
1944	4.10	3.85	3.85	1963	4.40	4.24	4.34	1981	13.30	11.47	13.30
1945	3.84	3.56	3.56	1964	4.41	4.21	4.22	1982	13.35	10.71	11.39
1946	3.77	3.41	3.77	1965	4.51	4.15	4.51	1983	11.66	10.59	11.66
1947	4.17	3.70	4.17	1966	5.34	4.50	5.17	1984	12.17	11.07	11.18
1948	4.28	4.03	4.13	1967	6.00	4.95	5.91	1985	11.42	9.84	10.11
1949	4.14	3.82	3.86	1968	6.02	5.57	6.01	1986	9.91	7.99	8.21
1951	4.32	3.85	4.32	1969	7.33	5.88	7.16	1987	9.23	7.50	9.23

Source: *Standard & Poor's Statistics* (New York: Standard & Poor's Corporation, 1988).

HIGH GRADE COMMON STOCKS

(*25 Stocks)

1941–1943 = 10

Monthly Averages of Weekly Indexes

	Jan.	Feb.	Mar.	Apr.	May	June	July	Aug.	Sept.	Oct.	Nov.	Dec.	Avg.
1936	11.70	11.80	11.83	11.60	11.56	12.12	12.36	12.35	12.50	12.67	13.13	12.97	12.22
1937	13.10	13.23	13.46	13.08	12.64	12.59	12.90	13.10	12.02	10.81	10.54	10.38	12.32
1938	10.83	10.96	10.69	10.54	11.00	11.27	12.06	12.19	11.60	12.35	12.38	12.26	11.51
1939	12.37	12.31	12.37	11.51	11.99	12.39	12.44	12.44	11.85	12.09	12.42	12.44	12.22
1940	12.66	12.58	12.55	12.62	11.37	10.36	10.69	10.69	11.12	11.07	10.81	10.58	11.43
1941	10.72	10.18	10.11	9.93	9.72	9.99	10.42	10.43	10.59	10.35	9.71	9.33	10.12
1942	9.51	9.03	8.37	7.89	8.04	8.72	8.90	8.85	8.99	9.24	9.38	9.66	8.88
1943	10.07	10.49	10.62	10.76	11.03	11.29	11.60	11.34	11.49	11.33	10.99	10.94	11.00
1944	11.30	11.19	11.36	11.24	11.41	11.75	11.96	11.97	11.94	12.17	12.10	12.04	11.70
1945	12.16	12.40	12.38	12.60	13.06	13.16	12.93	12.97	13.55	14.26	14.55	14.68	13.23
1946	15.30	15.21	15.14	15.93	15.98	15.88	15.55	15.38	13.79	13.64	13.52	13.96	14.94
1947	14.11	14.23	14.01	13.60	13.23	13.61	14.12	13.95	13.64	13.71	13.66	13.51	13.78
1948	13.49	13.00	13.15	13.81	14.11	14.43	14.16	13.95	14.00	14.04	13.75	13.95	13.82
1949	14.41	14.24	14.47	14.54	14.65	14.13	14.68	15.18	15.40	15.70	15.97	16.60	15.00
1950	17.24	17.44	17.52	17.53	17.61	17.41	15.92	16.16	16.69	17.17	17.23	17.05	17.08
1951	17.63	17.94	17.61	17.53	17.62	17.44	17.50	18.07	18.34	17.94	17.24	17.77	17.72
1952	18.14	17.78	17.61	17.52	17.64	18.11	18.68	18.64	18.44	18.31	18.78	19.34	18.25
1953	19.66	19.57	19.90	19.59	19.88	19.17	19.46	19.79	19.48	20.03	20.52	20.79	19.82
1954	21.14	21.39	22.11	22.85	23.61	24.05	24.93	24.70	24.58	24.66	26.10	27.06	23.92
1955	26.75	27.05	27.32	28.78	28.69	29.51	29.66	29.19	30.10	28.63	29.47	29.97	28.76
1956	29.83	29.82	31.72	32.63	32.57	33.47	35.48	35.12	33.51	32.95	33.14	33.28	32.79
1957	34.11	33.34	34.32	34.37	34.92	34.89	35.59	34.76	34.13	33.06	32.78	33.81	34.19
1958	35.23	35.66	36.29	36.89	38.01	38.84	39.83	40.39	41.37	42.32	44.59	45.64	39.59
1959	46.50	46.46	47.86	47.25	47.47	47.40	48.64	48.88	47.31	47.51	48.69	49.52	47.79
1960	49.14	48.30	48.48	49.48	50.43	54.49	55.53	56.57	56.07	56.10	58.67	62.18	53.79
1961	62.99	66.72	70.27	71.90	71.87	72.44	73.88	77.29	78.12	80.17	84.43	83.32	74.45
1962	78.15	78.22	78.08	76.46	70.98	62.26	63.40	64.71	64.02	61.51	65.05	67.89	69.23
1963	69 88	70.30	69.83	71.83	72.91	73.05	72.42	74.63	76.30	75.73	74.81	75.53	73.10
1964	76.86	77.62	78.45	79.02	79.51	79.76	82.05	81.90	82.64	83.69	84.66	83.44	80.80
1965	85.55	85.66	86.04	86.62	88.00	84.10	83.50	83.68	84.62	84.98	85.26	84.46	85.21
1966	84.37	82.33	78.36	79.41	77.31	76.54	76.24	72.46	70.64	70.97	74.66	74.39	76.47
1967	74.75	78.11	78.54	79.88	79.72	78.96	80.85	82.28	81.90	79.54	76.96	78.64	79.26
1968	80.00	77.03	76.00	80.90	83.87	86.67	87.00	85.14	87.86	89.64	90.99	92.02	84.72
1969	87.63	88.52	86.69	88.53	91.92	87.11	83.21	82.37	83.56	84.31	85.48	82.07	85.93
1970	81.86	79.41	81.87	79.71	70.09	70.51	70.66	71.71	75.18	76.51	77.24	82.96	76.48
1971	86.25	87.74	89.46	91.67	89.86	88.52	88.53	86.95	88.29	86.76	83.39	87.73	87.93
1972	90.47	90.08	92.13	93.92	92.82	92.78	92.24	94.92	93.56	94.53	99.39	100.8	93.97
1973	101.4	96.88	96.75	94.36	92.93	91.98	93.05	91.02	92.62	95.22	87.93	80.63	92.90

	Jan.	Feb.	Mar.	Apr.	May	June	July	Aug.	Sept.	Oct.	Nov.	Dec.	Avg.
1974	84.08	83.21	87.36	83.35	81.17	82.38	75.63	68.12	61.09	61.29	63.34	60.25	74.27
1975	64.16	70.23	72.67	73.84	78.14	79.08	78.70	72.32	71.00	74.14	76.68	75.26	73.85
1976	80.55	82.05	82.61	83.55	82.21	82.46	83.44	81.10	82.17	79.20	77.55	79.17	81.34
1977	77.95	75.43	74.46	72.83	72.21	72.65	73.59	73.36	72.88	70.42	70.08	69.21	72.92
1978	67.39	66.28	65.21	68.21	71.62	72.29	71.93	76.41	75.95	74.53	70.87	72.29	71.08
1979	74.30	72.79	74.13	75.23	73.68	74.88	72.83	75.98	75.82	73.46	73.03	74.71	74.24
1980	75.96	80.65	73.78	74.02	77.15	81.75	83.99	86.12	88.78	88.38	89.95	88.47	82.42
1981	90.58	89.25	93.71	95.18	94.33	96.87	91.31	90.09	84.48	84.33	85.81	86.68	90.22
1982	84.51	85.20	84.34	88.42	88.60	85.89	86.69	87.55	97.03	107.1	110.5	111.6	93.13
1983	112.4	113.4	119.1	124.5	127.7	126.8	128.1	125.2	128.6	131.7	131.1	127.7	124.7
1984	126.2	119.5	119.8	119.6	119.9	117.5	115.5	123.1	125.2	124.6	126.6	124.9	121.9
1985	129.2	135.1	135.1	136.2	137.6	142.4	144.4	141.6	138.5	139.5	147.0	154.7	140.1
1986	153.6	161.7	176.7	184.5	186.3	189.2	186.7	190.3	183.6	180.2	187.7	190.4	180.9
1987	202.2	213.2	222.4	221.1	216.9	219.3	224.0	239.0	228.2	194.0	168.6	168.2	209.8

Annual Range, and Close, of Weekly Indexes

Year	High	Low	Close	Year	High	Low	Close	Year	High	Low	Close
1934	9.17	7.57	8.78	1952	19.65	17.35	19.65	1970	85.21	67.56	85.21
1935	11.58	8.98	11.56	1953	20.91	19.02	20.74	1971	92.86	81.47	90.52
1936	13.38	11.08	12.91	1954	27.25	20.85	27.13	1972	101.7	89.05	101.1
1937	13.64	10.01	10.06	1955	30.54	26.42	30.13	1973	103.3	78.85	84.08
1938	12.64	9.78	12.39	1956	36.11	29.43	34.48	1974	88.77	55.92	60.77
1939	12.94	11.41	12.45	1957	35.81	32.17	34.30	1975	81.44	61.35	75.71
1940	12.80	10.00	10.70	1958	46.26	34.82	46.26	1976	85.77	75.96	81.30
1941	10.90	9.03	9.43	1959	50.18	46.09	50.18	1977	78.95	67.92	70.39
1942	9.79	7.54	9.77	1960	62.79	47.96	62.52	1978	77.97	64.22	72.48
1943	11.75	9.94	11.02	1961	85.85	61.77	82.71	1979	77.05	71.14	74.52
1944	12.24	11.04	11.96	1962	81.35	58.57	68.03	1980	91.28	70.21	90.93
1945	14.75	12.05	14.69	1963	76.37	67.90	76.12	1981	98.31	83.16	86.78
1946	16.33	12.83	13.98	1964	85.54	76.70	84.15	1982	113.9	82.36	112.5
1947	14.41	13.07	13.61	1965	88.81	82.18	84.57	1983	133.0	110.2	125.5
1948	14.55	12.82	14.08	1966	84.49	68.21	72.58	1984	128.6	114.1	126.2
1949	17.00	14.01	17.00	1967	83.51	72.42	80.47	1985	157.3	124.9	157.3
1950	17.74	15.37	17.15	1968	95.45	75.10	89.15	1986	196.0	150.0	185.9
1951	18.43	17.19	17.76	1969	93.13	78.95	83.93	1987	244.6	160.9	169.6

LOW PRICED COMMON STOCKS

(*20 Stocks)

1941–1943 = 10

Monthly Averages of Weekly Indexes

	Jan.	Feb.	Mar.	Apr.	May	June	July	Aug.	Sept.	Oct.	Nov.	Dec.	Avg.
1936	17.86	20.65	21.38	18.83	16.51	16.11	16.20	16.54	17.07	17.36	18.87	20.88	18.19
1937	24.24	26.03	28.58	24.22	21.53	19.70	21.78	22.27	17.17	12.48	12.32	10.87	20.10
1938	11.95	11.10	9.58	9.38	8.92	9.16	12.39	11.52	10.51	12.71	12.87	11.23	10.94
1939	11.44	10.47	9.89	8.08	8.64	8.67	8.57	8.40	15.14	14.24	13.04	11.92	10.71
1940	11.40	11.19	11.26	12.19	9.65	8.67	8.24	8.23	9.20	9.20	9.88	9.26	9.86
1941	9.41	8.36	8.79	7.93	7.75	8.11	9.22	9.98	9.68	8.67	8.04	7.31	8.60
1942	9.32	9.15	8.44	7.91	7.38	7.77	8.00	7.81	8.17	9.31	9.22	8.57	8.42
1943	9.65	11.39	13.08	13.91	15.19	14.93	14.49	13.12	13.34	13.12	12.00	11.77	13.00
1944	13.04	12.97	13.41	13.05	13.05	14.93	18.12	18.64	17.48	18.22	17.78	18.08	15.74
1945	19.99	21.91	20.25	20.09	20.85	23.55	23.48	22.72	24.73	27.74	31.52	36.80	24.47
1946	39.88	42.32	39.09	40.12	39.14	37.58	35.78	32.58	25.82	24.78	24.74	25.27	33.93
1947	24.74	26.50	24.37	21.70	18.42	19.61	21.41	20.27	20.05	21.26	20.38	20.30	21.58
1948	19.87	18.08	18.12	19.83	21.42	22.24	21.76	20.70	19.86	19.95	18.24	17.36	19.79
1949	17.57	16.09	16.56	17.12	16.30	15.06	15.93	16.50	16.70	18.04	18.19	18.38	16.87
1950	19.84	19.99	20.51	21.99	23.34	22.86	21.42	23.30	24.39	24.82	25.10	26.61	22.85
1951	30.99	31.76	29.24	28.82	29.19	27.47	26.42	27.92	31.63	32.95	30.30	30.73	29.79
1952	30.93	29.90	29.27	28.40	27.88	27.65	27.80	27.61	26.93	25.94	26.53	27.00	27.99
1953	28.25	28.68	29.21	27.99	27.90	26.10	25.70	25.53	22.94	22.67	22.28	21.86	25.76
1954	23.53	23.76	23.79	24.09	24.30	25.13	25.45	27.29	27.04	27.40	27.71	31.87	25.95
1955	34.37	36.10	36.57	38.42	36.69	37.21	37.78	38.56	39.59	37.46	38.56	39.30	37.55
1956	39.66	39.20	40.43	41.19	40.87	39.76	40.95	41.93	41.32	40.14	40.09	40.18	40.48
1957	41.78	39.72	40.65	41.44	41.83	41.51	41.84	40.09	39.09	34.89	33.29	32.84	39.08
1958	35.71	36.53	36.18	37.14	39.67	40.37	41.95	45.84	49.27	54.61	61.00	65.41	45.31
1959	69.78	71.45	75.57	77.30	74.17	71.57	73.58	73.53	71.41	70.35	70.34	69.75	72.40
1960	71.91	68.05	66.97	65.12	61.95	60.77	59.71	60.47	59.72	56.15	55.66	55.10	61.80
1961	60.60	64.51	69.34	71.45	74.24	72.56	69.29	69.54	68.90	68.79	70.48	70.78	69.21
1962	72.37	73.21	73.25	69.95	62.43	53.20	54.77	56.75	56.01	51.91	54.17	56.55	61.21
1963	59.27	61.77	61.48	62.98	65.43	65.63	64.93	65.66	67.46	68.73	67.48	68.40	64.94
1964	72.27	72.73	75.54	79.60	79.91	76.45	79.82	79.38	79.67	82.66	83.38	81.92	78.61
1965	86.92	90.49	90.86	92.66	94.40	88.08	85.71	90.11	94.76	105.9	111.7	120.3	96.00
1966	124.2	126.6	127.0	134.8	119.5	116.9	118.4	109.9	103.4	98.05	103.7	107.7	115.8
1967	115.3	133.2	141.8	142.3	147.5	156.0	170.1	176.7	177.4	179.6	168.7	185.1	157.8
1968	213.1	206.6	193.1	202.5	216.9	234.6	234.0	229.6	240.9	245.8	245.3	259.6	226.8
1969	247.5	238.8	220.8	220.4	226.0	202.6	180.5	169.0	168.7	176.2	179.3	155.0	198.7
1970	160.7	153.0	154.0	139.1	111.1	111.1	99.41	101.9	118.5	125.4	118.8	122.9	126.3
1971	140.6	160.9	164.0	166.6	165.1	156.2	152.6	146.4	146.6	141.0	126.7	132.4	150.0
1972	149.7	156.8	158.8	154.3	145.4	140.0	137.7	139.3	132.9	126.5	129.8	129.4	141.7
1973	124.8	114.3	110.6	106.7	95.54	86.87	91.61	93.13	95.61	104.3	92.99	76.54	99.42

	Jan.	Feb.	Mar.	Apr.	May	June	July	Aug.	Sept.	Oct.	Nov.	Dec.	Avg.
1974	87.76	91.48	94.12	91.79	85.23	82.85	77.76	77.36	67.78	68.73	66.47	55.71	78.92
1975	71.56	85 68	96.14	100.6	104.8	112.6	117.3	102.7	100.6	97.63	96.01	92.54	98.16
1976	108.1	125.8	134.7	128.8	124.6	126.3	137.8	133.2	133.6	125.9	123.2	129.6	127.6
1977	137.8	136.7	135.1	146.5	150.8	148.8	153.1	149.4	144.9	141.9	143.9	145.4	144.5
1978	143.4	151.2	159.5	177.7	198.3	207.9	204.8	231.7	238.5	221.9	168.9	172.1	189.8
1979	192.6	191.4	203.7	217.0	212.5	221.3	225.0	243.7	235.9	207.4	205.3	225.6	215.1
1980	242.1	259.0	216.2	198.7	214.2	218.3	238.4	260.8	277.9	266.6	261.2	246.1	241.6
1981	252.7	256.0	267.9	290.2	285.6	301.5	278.4	269.5	235.1	238.3	247.3	253.4	264.7
1982	252.6	259.0	253.3	266.1	273.2	252.1	256.0	250.6	278.2	309.0	359.1	380.8	282.5
1983	404.0	432.7	462.1	477.0	534.8	581.8	596.4	551.8	554.6	543.3	533.3	540.6	517.7
1984	566.0	505.8	499.3	486.3	467.0	447.6	430.0	458.6	477.9	475.4	469.8	458.9	478.5
1985	500.2	528.8	517.3	531.7	523.6	526.3	531.8	511.7	483.8	475.4	485.6	507.6	510.3
1986	517.4	544.6	621.6	641.0	629.9	645.4	621.6	606.5	567.7	570.1	590.8	570.4	593.9
1987	618.3	659.8	672.7	657.8	649.5	653.8	686.4	702.7	683.9	555.2	452.0	437.7	619.2

Annual Range, and Close, of Weekly Indexes

Year	High	Low	Close	Year	High	Low	Close	Year	High	Low	Close
1934	19.60	10.60	11.70	1952	31.25	25.53	27.09	1970	167.0	95.25	128.6
1935	15.72	8.93	15.54	1953	29.55	21.25	21.25	1971	169.4	118.6	139.8
1936	21.74	14.95	21.35	1954	34.82	22.93	34.82	1972	162.4	123.2	124.9
1937	28.81	9.53	9.53	1955	40.42	33.60	39.78	1973	131.2	75.75	76.67
1938	13.91	7.19	10.83	1956	42.36	38.58	41.40	1974	95.14	53.23	53.23
1939	15.36	7.65	11.55	1957	42.46	32.12	32.64	1975	120.7	65.50	95.87
1940	12.38	7.94	9.18	1958	66.16	34.55	65.68	1976	141.7	101.1	134.5
1941	10.60	6.88	7.42	1959	78.62	67.56	70.71	1977	157.9	133.5	144.9
1942	9.76	7.12	8.40	1960	72.88	54.11	55.19	1978	245.8	138.5	169.3
1943	15.52	9.06	11.73	1961	75.77	56.41	70.91	1979	247.5	179.4	225.9
1944	19.57	12.62	17.91	1962	73.68	49.40	55.38	1980	284.8	190.2	248.9
1945	37.48	19.31	37.48	1963	69.33	55.74	68.19	1981	304.5	221.5	257.2
1946	45.33	22.60	24.27	1964	84.50	70.45	81.82	1982	392.3	236.1	378.1
1947	27.89	17.59	20.33	1965	122.6	83.59	121.2	1983	608.7	391.4	536.1
1948	23.31	17.00	17.36	1966	136.8	97.28	104.5	1984	576.2	399.2	470.6
1949	18.91	14.70	18.28	1967	195.9	106.8	195.9	1985	538.6	466.7	524.0
1950	28.48	19.14	28.48	1968	262.3	191.0	259.8	1986	657.1	505.0	562.2
1951	33.82	26.11	30.38	1969	249.8	149.4	152.9	1987	707.6	403.6	446.1

New York Stock Exchange

Composite Stock Index

Year	Open	High	Low	Close	Chg.
1987	138.58	187.99	125.91	138.23	— .35
1986	121.58	145.75	117.75	138.58	+17.00
1985	96.38	121.90	94.60	121.58	+25.20
1984	95.18	98.12	85.13	96.38	+ 1.3
1983	79.79	99.63	79.79	95.18	+14.15
1982	81.33	82.35	58.80	81.03	+ 9.92
1981	78.26	79.14	64.96	71.11	— 6.75
1980	60.69	81.02	55.30	77.86	+15.91
1979	53.93	63.39	53.88	61.95	+ 8.33
1978	51.82	60.38	48.37	53.62	+ 1.12
1977	57.69	57.69	49.78	52.50	— 5.38
1976	48.04	57.88	48.04	57.88	+10.24
1975	37.06	51.24	37.06	47.64	+11.51
1974	51.98	53.37	32.89	36.13	—15.69
1973	65.06	65.48	49.05	51.82	—12.66
1972	56.23	65.14	56.23	64.48	+ 8.05
1971	49.73	57.76	49.60	56.43	+ 6.20
1970	52.10	52.36	37.69	50.23	— 1.30
1969	58.94	59.32	49.31	51.53	— 7.37
1968	53.68	61.27	48.70	58.90	+ 5.07
1967	43.74	54.16	43.74	53.83	+10.11
1966	49.86	51.06	39.37	43.72	— 6.28
1965	45.37	50.00	43.64	50.00	+ 4.35
1964	40.47	46.49	40.47	45.65	+ 5.73
1963	34.41	39.92	34.41	39.92	+ 6.11
1962	37.34	38.02	28.20	33.81	— 4.58
1961	31.17	38.60	31.17	38.39	+ 7.45
1960	31.99	31.99	28.38	30.94	— 1.21
1959	29.54	32.39	28.94	32.15	+ 3.30
1958	21.71	28.85	21.45	28.85	+ 7.74
1957	24.43	26.30	20.92	21.11	— 3.24
1956	23.56	25.90	22.55	24.35	+ 0.64
1955	19.05	23.71	19.05	23.71	+ 4.31
1954	13.70	19.40	13.70	19.40	+ 5.80
1953	14.65	14.65	12.62	13.60	— 0.89
1952	13.70	14.49	13.31	14.49	+ 0.89
1951	12.28	13.89	12.28	13.60	+ 1.59

The New York Stock Exchange composite stock index has been computed on a daily basis since June 1, 1964. Prior to that date it was on a weekly basis. December 31, 1965, equals 50.

Source: Phyllis Pearce, *The Dow Jones Investor's Handbook* (Homewood, Ill.: Dow Jones-Irwin, 1988).

New York Stock Exchange

Cash Dividends and Yields on Common Stocks

Calendar Year	Number of Issues Listed at Year End	Number Paying Cash Dividends During Year	Estimated Aggregate Cash Payments (Millions)	a-Median Yield (%) *Dividend Yield	Calendar Year	Number of Issues Listed at Year End	Number Paying Cash Dividends During Year	Estimated Aggregate Cash Payments (Millions)	a-Median Yield (%) *Dividend Yield
1987	1,606	N.A.	N.A.	*3.4	1963	1,194	1,032	$12,096	a3.6
1986	1,536	1,180	76,161	*3.4	1962	1,168	994	11,203	a3.8
1985	1,503	1,206	74,237	*3.6	1961	1,145	981	10,430	a3.3
1984	1,511	1,243	68,215	a3.8	1960	1,126	981	9,872	a4.2
1983	1,518	1,259	67,102	a3.5	1959	1,092	953	9,337	a3.8
1982	1,499	1,287	62,224	a4.1	1958	1,086	961	8,711	a4.1
1981	1,534	1,337	60,628	a5.0	1957	1,098	991	8,807	a6.1
1980	1,540	1,361	53,072	a4.6	1956	1,077	975	8,341	a5.2
1979	1,536	1,359	46,937	a5.0	1955	1,076	982	7,488	a4.6
1978	1,552	1,373	41,151	a4.8	1954	1,076	968	6,439	a4.7
1977	1,549	1,360	36,270	a4.5	1953	1,069	964	5,874	a6.3
1976	1,550	1,340	30,608	a4.0	1952	1,067	975	5,595	a6.0
1975	1,531	1,273	26,901	a5.0	1951	1,054	961	5,467	a6.5
1974	1,543	1,308	25,662	a7.4	1950	1,039	930	5,404	a6.7
1973	1,536	1,276	23,627	a5.0	1949	1,017	887	4,235	a7.0
1972	1,478	1,195	21,490	a3.0	1948	986	883	3,806	a7.8
1971	1,399	1,132	20,256	a3.2	1947	964	851	3,255	a6.3
1970	1,330	1,120	19,781	a3.7	1946	933	798	2,669	a4.8
1969	1,290	1,121	19,404	a3.6	1945	881	746	2,275	a3.6
1968	1,253	1,104	18,124	a2.6	1944	864	717	2,223	a5.0
1967	1,255	1,116	16,866	a3.2	1943	845	687	2,063	a6.1
1966	1,267	1,127	16,151	a4.1	1942	834	648	1,997	a7.8
1965	1,254	1,111	15,300	a3.2	1941	834	627	2,281	a9.3
1964	1,227	1,066	13,555	a3.3	1940	829	577	2,099	a6.1

*Dividend yield based on common stocks of NYSE Composite Index.

a-Based on cash payments during the year and price at end of year for dividend-paying stocks only. N.A.-Not available.

Source: NYSE Fact Book.

Source: Phyllis Pearce, *The Dow Jones Investor's Handbook* (Homewood, Ill.: Dow Jones-Irwin, 1988).

NASDAQ Index Comparisons, 1973–1987

1973–87 Yearly Highs, Lows, Closes & Percent Changes for the Year

Index		1973		1974		1975		1976		1977	
Composite	High	136.84	1/11	96.53	3/15	88.00	7/15	97.88	12/31	105.05	12/30
	Low	88.67	12/24	54.87	10/03	60.70	1/02	78.06	1/02	93.66	4/05
	Close	92.19		59.82		77.62		97.88		105.05	
	% Change	−31.1		−35.1		+29.8		+26.1		+ 7.3	
Industrial	High	136.97	1/11	89.78	3/15	93.79	7/15	100.12	12/31	109.43	12/30
	Low	80.15	12/24	54.21	10/03	57.22	1/02	81.44	1/02	96.29	4/26
	Close	83.57		56.46		80.95		100.12		109.43	
	% Change	−36.9		−32.4		+43.4		+23.7		+9.3	
Other Finance	High	151.93	1/11	111.60	1/23	88.47	6/24	101.57	12/31	105.65	7/25
	Low	102.93	12/24	57.16	10/03	64.70	1/02	79.36	1/02	97.04	4/06
	Close	107.50		63.43		79.02		101.57		105.53	
	% Change	−27.8		−41.0		+24.6		+28.5		+3.9	
Insurance	High	149.69	1/03	113.46	1/17	91.19	7/15	105.21	12/31	115.01	11/25
	Low	103.22	5/21	57.57	10/03	73.47	9/17	81.60	1/02	96.14	4/04
	Close	110.15		74.69		80.90		105.21		114.51	
	% Change	−26.1		−32.2		+8.3		+30.0		+8.8	
Bank	High	123.57	1/22	105.11	1/17	82.76	7/15	92.72	12/31	96.02	12/05
	Low	96.50	12/05	59.43	10/04	62.22	1/02	72.73	1/02	89.64	5/31,6/06
	Close	100.42		61.49		72.37		92.72		95.28	
	% Change	−15.7		−38.8		+17.7		+28.1		+2.8	
Utility	High	101.30	2/20	76.55	3/06	69.52	6/30	86.91	12/31	101.68	12/23
	Low	69.85	12/05	48.22	12/24	50.44	1/02	66.15	1/02	87.04	1/03
	Close	72.07		49.60		65.95		86.91		101.03	
	% Change	−26.9		−31.2		+33.0		+31.8		+16.2	
Transportation	High	124.95	1/12	96.66	3/15	90.92	7/14	105.78	4/20	104.40	7/22
	Low	77.65	12/21	61.24	12/23	66.67	1/06	85.97	1/02	91.60	4/25
	Close	81.04		65.79		85.52		101.28		97.68	
	% Change	−31.00		−18.8		+30.0		+18.4		−3.6	

Index		1978		1979		1980		1981		1982		1983	
Composite	High	139.25	9/13	152.29	10/05	208.15	11/28	223.47	5/29	240.70	12/08	328.91	06/24
	Low	99.09	1/11	117.84	1/02	124.09	3/27	175.03	9/28	159.14	8/13	230.59	01/03
	Close	117.98		151.14		202.34		195.84		232.41		278.60	
	% Change	+12.3		+28.1		+33.9		−3.2		+18.7		+19.9	
Industrial	High	155.79	9/12	175.18	12/31	274.70	11/28	283.03	5/29	281.64	12/08	408.42	06/24
	Low	101.91	1/11	126.88	1/02	145.03	3/27	204.62	9/25	177.70	8/13	270.55	01/03
	Close	126.85		175.18		261.36		229.29		273.58		323.68	
	% Change	+15.9		+38.1		+49.2		−12.3		+19.3		+18.3	
Other Finance	High	129.85	9/13	139.50	8/24	154.07	12/31	182.10	6/25	216.40	12/08	284.39	09/26
	Low	101.11	1/16	114.18	1/02	106.35	3/27	154.61	1/02	152.45	8/13	206.86	01/04
	Close	114.43		130.92		154.07		176.20		207.50		227.53	
	% Change	+8.4		+14.4		+17.7		+14.4		+17.8		+33.7	
Insurance	High	144.14	9/11	166.31	10/05	184.71	9/23	204.77	6/15	236.76	12/06	287.34	05/10
	Low	106.71	1/16	126.58	1/02	128.74	3/27	166.10	2/13	163.78	8/13	257.63	01/24
	Close	127.24		162.03		166.81		194.31		226.40		257.63	
	% Change	+11.1		+27.3		+3.0		+16.5		+16.5		+13.8	
Bank	High	111.56	10/13	115.81	8/31	118.58	12/24	144.06	12/01	160.73	11/12	203.75	12/30
	Low	93.96	1/11	102.09	1/03	91.99	3/27	118.59	1/02	127.84	8/13	155.68	01/12
	Close	102.33		108.24		118.39		143.13		156.37		203.75	
	% Change	+7.4		+5.8		+9.4		+20.9		+9.3		+30.3	
Utility	High	116.73	9/13	130.41	12/31	165.92	11/28	191.18	11/30	316.17	12/08	293.76	11/30
	Low	93.23	1/20	106.27	1/02	106.01	3/27	148.69	2/04	168.02	3/12	194.27	01/04
	Close	106.04		130.41		165.70		181.67		286.23		280.80	
	% Change	+5.0		+23.0		+27.1		+9.1		+57.6		+43.6	
Transportation	High	128.71	9/13	133.42	10/04	179.20	10/10	201.71	6/15	205.81	11/05	391.37	06/16
	Low	92.92	1/23	100.76	1/02	100.55	3/27	155.99	1/08	145.26	3/16	257.12	10/12
	Close	100.53		118.47		164.19		167.77		195.48		269.39	
	% Change	+2.9		+17.8		+39.0		+2.2		+16.5		−5.9	

NASDAQ INDEX COMPARISONS, 1973–1987 (concluded)

Index		1984		1985		1986		1987	
Composite	High	287.90	1/06	325.16	12/16	411.16	7/03	455.26	8/26
	Low	225.30	7/25	245.91	1/02	323.01	1/09	291.88	10/28
	Close	247.35		324.93		348.83		330.47	
	% Change	− 11.2		31.4		7.4		− 5.3	
Industrial	High	336.16	1/06	330.17	12/31	414.45	7/03	488.92	10/05
	Low	250.18	7/25	258.85	1/02	326.56	1/09	288.30	10/28
	Close	260.73		330.17		349.33		338.94	
	% Change	− 19.4		26.6		5.8		− 3.0	
Other Finance	High	298.62	12/31	423.52	12/16	553.42	7/03	542.04	3/20
	Low	252.34	5/30	298.20	1/02	424.52	1/02	382.43	12/07
	Close	298.62		423.49		460.64		406.96	
	% Change	7.6		41.8		8.8		− 11.7	
Insurance	High	283.91	12/26	385.45	12/17	467.05	3/19	475.78	8/21
	Low	226.87	7/19	276.33	1/08	381.59	1/09	333.66	10/28
	Close	283.11		382.07		404.14		351.06	
	% Change	9.9		35.0		5.8		− 13.1	
Bank	High	229.77	12/31	350.08	12/23	457.59	7/03	526.64	3/20
	Low	192.99	6/01	230.23	1/02	346.35	1/09	366.75	12/07
	Close	229.77		349.36		412.53		390.66	
	% Change	12.8		52.0		18.1		− 5.3	
Utility	High	280.54	1/06	303.84	12/20	362.86	7/03	441.61	8/21
	Low	194.33	7/26	234.87	1/02	295.97	1/09	301.51	10/28
	Close	238.66		301.57		316.09		355.30	
	% Change	− 11.4		26.4		4.8		12.4	
Transportation	High	290.70	1/09	296.91	12/13	365.81	6/20	436.53	8/21
	Low	194.33	7/25	236.20	1/04	288.13	1/09	276.03	10/28
	Close	239.29		291.59		348.84		319.21	
	% Change	− 14.8		21.9		19.6		− 8.5	

Source: NASDAQ 1988 *Fact Book*, National Association of Security Dealers, Inc.

Part II: Interest Rate Data

Moody's U.S. Government Bond Yield Averages (Monthly Data)
1941–87	3–5 Year Maturities, p. 663.
1941–87	Long-term Bonds, p. 663.
1943–87	3-Year Treasury, p. 664.
1943–87	5-Year Treasury, p. 664.
1943–87	10-year Treasury, p. 665.
1941–87	91-day T-Bill Rate—Average for Last Offering of Month, p. 665.

Moody's Corporate and Industrial Bond Yields (Monthly Data)
1919–88	Average of Yields on Aaa Corporate Bonds, p. 666.
1919–88	Average of Yields on Aa Corporate Bonds, p. 667.
1919–88	Average of Yields on A Corporate Bonds, p. 668.
1919–88	Average of Yields on Baa Corporate Bonds, p. 669.
1919–88	Average of Yields on Aaa Industrial Bonds, p. 670.
1919–88	Average of Yields on Aa Industrial Bonds, p. 671.
1919–88	Average of Yields on A Industrial Bonds, p. 672.
1919–88	Average of Yields on Baa Industrial Bonds, p. 673.

MOODY'S GOVERNMENT BOND YIELD AVERAGES
3-5 YEAR MATURITY, SELECTED ISSUES[1]

	Annual	Jan.	Feb.	Mar.	Apr.	May	June	July	Aug.	Sept.	Oct.	Nov.	Dec.
1941	.73	.76	.81	.84	.81	.72	1.41	.67	.62	.62	.72	.98	1.10
1942	1.46	1.05	1.02	1.02	1.06	1.11	1.32	1.45	1.47	1.47	1.48	1.49	1.48
1943	1.34	1.43	1.41	1.40	1.39	1.36	.68	1.30	1.29	1.31	1.31	1.29	1.30
1944	1.33	1.30	1.32	1.36	1.36	1.35	1.34	1.31	1.30	1.31	1.35	1.34	1.35
1945	1.18	1.31	1.22	1.18	1.14	1.16	1.16	1.16	1.17	1.19	1.17	1.14	1.13
1946	1.16	1.06	.99	.96	1.10	1.16	1.15	1.15	1.19	1.29	1.29	1.28	1.30
1947	1.32	1.26	1.26	1.24	1.24	1.27	1.29	1.33	1.31	1.28	1.35	1.47	1.54
1948	1.62	1.63	1.63	1.60	1.58	1.51	1.49	1.56	1.65	1.69	1.71	1.69	1.64
1949	1.43	1.59	1.57	1.54	1.53	1.49	1.42	1.26	1.26	1.34	1.38	1.37	1.37
1950	1.50	1.39	1.44	1.45	1.45	1.45	1.47	1.45	1.45	1.55	1.65	1.62	1.64
1951	1.93	1.66	1.67	1.86	2.03	2.04	2.00	1.94	1.89	1.93	2.00	2.01	2.09
1952	2.13	2.08	2.07	2.02	1.93	1.95	2.04	2.14	2.29	2.28	2.26	2.25	2.30
1953	2.56	2.39	2.42	2.46	2.61	2.86	2.92	2.72	2.77	2.69	2.38	2.32	2.22
1954	1.82	2.04	1.84	1.80	1.71	1.78	1.79	1.69	1.74	1.80	1.85	1.90	1.94
1955	2.50	2.11	2.18	2.30	2.39	2.40	2.42	2.54	2.73	2.72	2.58	2.72	2.83
1956	3.12	2.74	2.65	2.83	3.11	3.04	2.87	2.97	3.36	3.43	3.29	3.49	3.65
1957	3.62	3.40	3.33	3.38	3.48	3.60	3.77	3.89	3.91	3.93	3.99	3.63	3.04
1958	2.90	2.77	2.67	2.50	2.33	2.25	2.25	2.34	3.11	3.57	3.63	3.60	3.65
1959	4.33	3.86	3.85	3.88	4.03	4.16	4.33	4.40	4.45	4.78	4.69	4.74	4.95
1960	3.99	4.87	4.66	4.24	4.23	4.42	4.06	3.71	3.50	3.50	3.61	3.68	3.51
1961	3.60	3.53	3.54	3.43	3.39	3.28	3.70	3.69	3.80	3.77	3.64	3.68	3.82
1962	3.57	3.84	3.77	3.55	3.48	3.53	3.51	3.71	3.57	3.56	3.46	3.46	3.44
1963	3.72	3.47	3.48	3.50	3.56	3.57	3.67	3.78	3.81	3.88	3.91	3.97	4.04
1964	4.06	4.06	4.02	4.15	4.18	4.07	4.03	3.99	3.99	4.03	4.04	4.04	4.07
1965	4.22	4.06	4.08	4.12	4.12	4.11	4.09	4.10	4.19	4.24	4.33	4.46	4.77
1966	5.16	4.89	5.02	4.94	4.86	4.94	5.01	5.22	5.58	5.62	5.38	5.43	5.43
1967	5.05	4.71	4.73	4.52	4.46	4.69	4.96	5.17	5.28	5.40	5.52	5.73	5.07
1968	5.60	5.52	5.58	5.77	5.69	5.95	5.71	5.44	5.32	5.31	5.42	5.47	5.99
1969	6.86	6.04	6.16	6.33	6.16	6.32	6.64	7.02	7.07	7.58	7.47	7.58	7.98
1970	7.34	8.14	7.80	7.20	7.49	7.97	7.86	7.58	7.56	7.24	7.06	6.36	5.87
1971	5.74	5.73	5.32	4.74	5.42	6.02	6.30	6.69	6.33	5.89	5.63	5.43	5.32
1972	5.77	5.28	5.43	5.64	5.92	5.58	5.65	5.74	5.84	6.09	6.07	5.96	5.98
1973	6.84	6.21	6.54	6.78	6.67	6.72	6.69	7.41	7.62	7.67	7.09	6.73	6.88
1974	7.73	6.87	6.70	7.26	7.92	8.16	8.06	8.32	8.57	8.31	7.91	7.58	7.15
1975	7.46	7.22	6.78	6.91	7.66	7.39	7.16	7.62	8.03	8.14	7.73	7.42	7.41
1976	6.83	7.08	7.09	7.14	6.87	7.23	7.30	7.13	6.90	6.75	6.40	6.23	5.85
1977	6.79	6.44	6.62	6.67	6.52	6.70	6.53	6.60	6.83	6.87	7.18	7.21	7.33
1978	8.23	7.64	7.69	7.71	7.84	8.02	8.24	8.46	8.24	8.32	8.53	8.91	9.13
1979	9.52	9.30	9.10	9.20	9.27	9.24	8.85	8.82	9.03	9.48	10.67	10.90	10.35
1980	11.29	10.67	12.48	13.31	11.50	9.44	8.97	9.34	10.63	11.44	11.77	12.83	13.12
1981	14.06	12.59	13.25	13.23	13.80	14.57	13.75	14.63	15.41	15.81	15.24	13.03	13.45
1982	12.83	14.39	14.38	13.77	13.77	13.45	14.12	13.81	12.64	12.17	10.81	10.32	10.27
1983	10.52	9.98	10.19	10.03	9.92	9.85	10.45	10.99	11.33	11.15	10.96	10.07	11.33
1984	12.10	11.15	11.24	11.77	12.12	12.85	13.34	13.05	12.50	12.35	12.96	11.08	10.89
1985	9.95	10.72	10.87	11.33	10.74	10.18	9.44	9.63	9.53	9.66	9.51	9.11	8.67
1986	7.36	8.63	8.39	7.55	7.12	7.63	7.78	7.23	6.84	6.98	6.83	6.69	6.61
1987	7.83	6.59	6.72	6.74	7.47	8.15	7.95	7.87	8.13	8.78	8.97	8.22	8.33

LONG-TERM BONDS[2]

	Annual	Jan.	Feb.	Mar.	Apr.	May	June	July	Aug.	Sept.	Oct.	Nov.	Dec.
1941	2.05	2.12	2.22	2.12	2.07	2.04	2.01	1.98	2.01	2.02	1.98	2.34	2.47
1942	2.46	2.48	2.48	2.46	2.44	2.45	2.43	2.46	2.47	2.46	2.45	2.47	2.49
1943	2.47	2.46	2.46	2.48	2.48	2.46	2.45	2.45	2.46	2.48	2.48	2.48	2.49
1944	2.48	2.49	2.49	2.48	2.48	2.49	2.49	2.49	2.48	2.47	2.48	2.48	2.48
1945	2.37	2.44	2.38	2.40	2.39	2.39	2.35	2.34	2.36	2.37	2.35	2.33	2.33
1946	2.19	2.21	2.12	2.09	2.08	2.19	2.16	2.18	2.23	2.28	2.26	2.25	2.24
1947	2.25	2.21	2.21	2.19	2.19	2.19	2.22	2.25	2.24	2.24	2.27	2.36	2.39
1948	2.44	2.45	2.45	2.44	2.44	2.42	2.41	2.41	2.45	2.45	2.45	2.44	2.44
1949	2.31	2.42	2.39	2.38	2.38	2.38	2.38	2.27	2.24	2.22	2.22	2.20	2.19
1950	2.32	2.20	2.24	2.27	2.30	2.31	2.33	2.34	2.33	2.36	2.38	2.38	2.39
1951	2.57	2.39	2.40	2.47	2.56	2.63	2.65	2.63	2.57	2.56	2.61	2.66	2.70
1952	2.68	2.74	2.71	2.70	2.64	2.57	2.61	2.61	2.70	2.71	2.74	2.71	2.75
1953	2.94	2.80	2.83	2.89	2.97	3.12	3.13	3.04	3.05	3.01	2.87	2.86	2.79
1954	2.55	2.69	2.62	2.53	2.48	2.54	2.55	2.47	2.48	2.52	2.54	2.57	2.59
1955	2.84	2.68	2.77	2.78	2.82	2.81	2.82	2.91	2.95	2.92	2.87	2.89	2.91
1956	3.08	2.88	2.85	2.93	3.07	2.97	2.93	3.00	3.17	3.21	3.20	3.30	3.40
1957	3.47	3.34	3.22	3.26	3.32	3.40	3.58	3.60	3.63	3.66	3.73	3.57	3.30
1958	3.43	3.24	3.26	3.25	3.12	3.14	3.19	3.36	3.60	3.75	3.76	3.70	3.80
1959	4.07	3.90	3.92	3.92	4.01	4.08	4.09	4.11	4.10	4.26	4.11	4.12	4.27
1960	4.01	4.37	4.22	4.08	4.17	4.16	3.99	3.86	3.79	3.82	3.91	3.93	3.88
1961	3.90	3.89	3.81	3.78	3.80	3.73	3.88	3.90	4.00	4.02	3.98	3.98	4.06
1962	3.95	4.08	4.09	4.01	3.89	3.88	3.90	4.02	3.97	3.94	3.89	3.87	3.87
1963	4.00	3.88	3.92	3.93	3.97	3.97	4.00	4.01	3.99	4.04	4.07	4.10	4.14
1964	4.15	4.15	4.14	4.18	4.20	4.16	4.13	4.13	4.14	4.16	4.16	4.12	4.14
1965	4.21	4.14	4.16	4.15	4.15	4.14	4.14	4.15	4.19	4.25	4.28	4.34	4.43
1966	4.65	4.43	4.61	4.63	4.55	4.57	4.63	4.75	4.80	4.79	4.70	4.74	4.65
1967	4.85	4.40	4.47	4.45	4.51	4.76	4.86	4.86	4.95	4.98	5.18	5.43	5.36
1968	5.26	5.17	5.15	5.38	5.28	5.39	5.23	5.09	5.04	5.10	5.24	5.36	5.66
1969	6.12	5.74	5.86	6.05	5.86	5.85	6.06	6.07	6.02	6.32	6.27	6.51	6.81
1970	6.58	6.86	6.44	6.39	6.53	6.94	6.99	6.58	6.75	6.63	6.59	6.25	5.98
1971	5.70	5.93	5.85	5.73	5.77	6.00	5.88	5.80	5.68	5.47	5.36	5.40	5.53
1972	5.54	5.53	5.58	5.57	5.65	9.54	5.50	5.49	5.51	5.61	5.60	5.42	5.53
1973	6.21	5.80	5.99	6.11	6.02	6.18	6.24	6.45	6.76	6.32	6.16	6.24	6.25
1974	6.88	6.45	6.46	6.70	6.92	6.98	6.92	7.07	7.21	7.19	7.11	6.82	6.67
1975	6.96	6.58	6.51	6.65	6.94	6.94	6.85	6.93	7.13	7.29	7.28	7.20	7.16
1976	6.79	6.92	6.92	6.86	6.72	6.98	6.93	6.88	6.86	6.72	6.66	6.62	6.37
1977	7.53	7.35	7.53	7.57	7.50	7.57	7.43	7.45	7.50	7.45	7.60	7.67	7.77
1978	8.40	8.02	8.10	8.10	8.22	8.37	8.45	8.61	8.38	8.37	8.60	8.68	8.84
1979	9.26	8.93	8.94	8.99	9.03	9.11	8.84	8.85	8.89	9.14	9.93	10.38	10.08
1980	11.23	10.54	12.01	12.26	11.22	10.15	9.74	10.20	10.94	11.36	11.63	12.30	12.35
1981	13.31	12.05	12.68	12.59	13.08	13.44	12.82	13.49	14.05	14.59	14.59	13.08	13.28
1982	12.61	14.16	14.07	13.37	13.24	13.05	13.75	13.40	12.54	11.86	10.84	10.46	10.60
1983	11.17	10.64	10.89	10.65	10.49	10.52	10.95	11.44	11.78	11.62	11.55	11.68	11.81
1984	12.36	11.65	11.81	12.28	12.58	13.43	13.43	13.24	12.63	12.34	12.00	11.55	11.51
1985	10.89	11.46	11.56	11.92	11.55	11.08	10.48	10.62	10.70	10.78	10.66	10.19	9.68
1986	8.19	9.59	9.26	8.15	7.62	8.09	8.27	7.88	7.74	8.01	8.06	7.82	7.66
1987	8.70	7.62	7.71	7.64	8.35	8.85	8.67	8.77	9.06	9.67	9.73	9.10	9.23

[1]Selected notes and bonds maturing within 3 to 5 years. [2]Long-term: due or callable after 15 years, Jan. 1941-March 1952; after 12 years, Apr. 1952-Mar. 1953; 10 years or more, beginning Apr. 1953.

Source: *Moody's Municipal & Government Manual*, vol. 2 (New York: Moody's Investor's Service, Inc., 1988).

3-YEAR TREASURY*

	Jan.	Feb.	Mar.	Apr.	May	June	July	Aug.	Sept.	Oct.	Nov.	Dec.
1943	1.22	1.22	1.23	1.27	1.19	1.16	1.15	1.18	1.20	1.20	1.20	1.19
1944	1.22	1.24	1.27	1.23	1.21	1.24	1.20	1.19	1.17	1.23	1.25	1.30
1945	1.23	1.17	1.19	1.16	1.18	1.14	1.19	1.22	1.20	1.15	1.10	1.07
1946	0.96	0.92	1.00	1.10	1.12	1.09	1.11	1.13	1.23	1.22	1.23	1.20
1947	1.15	1.18	1.13	1.19	1.23	1.23	1.26	1.22	1.24	1.37	1.44	1.49
1948	1.45	1.49	1.47	1.47	1.39	1.46	1.49	1.56	1.61	1.63	1.60	1.54
1949	1.49	1.51	1.47	1.48	1.43	1.37	1.25	1.22	1.25	1.25	1.28	1.26
1950	1.33	1.33	1.36	1.41	1.39	1.43	1.39	1.45	1.59	1.64	1.62	1.68
1951	1.70	1.71	1.97	2.00	2.05	2.08	1.93	1.87	1.95	2.07	2.04	2.11
1952	2.06	2.10	2.04	1.94	1.96	2.07	2.20	2.34	2.30	2.24	2.25	2.34
1953	2.30	2.31	2.37	2.59	2.68	2.62	2.52	2.60	2.39	2.20	2.24	1.96
1954	1.88	1.57	1.52	1.43	1.60	1.43	1.44	1.49	1.66	1.75	1.73	1.79
1955	1.95	2.19	2.24	2.40	2.29	2.42	2.56	2.73	2.54	2.56	2.76	2.90
1956	2.62	2.68	2.88	3.14	2.93	2.94	3.20	3.42	3.43	3.39	3.66	3.66
1957	3.33	3.42	3.44	3.54	3.67	3.82	3.93	3.95	4.04	4.00	3.43	2.78
1958	2.65	2.41	2.32	2.12	1.97	2.15	2.43	3.33	3.65	3.57	3.56	3.70
1959	3.93	3.85	4.02	4.10	4.24	4.54	4.59	4.77	4.93	4.68	4.86	5.17
1960	4.86	4.83	4.14	4.32	4.37	3.98	3.47	3.42	3.41	3.52	3.71	3.34
1961	3.46	3.42	3.38	3.29	3.36	3.56	3.51	3.62	3.63	3.55	3.60	3.64
1962	3.75	3.57	3.40	3.35	3.34	3.48	3.66	3.41	3.34	3.26	3.35	3.38
1963	3.39	3.38	3.44	3.51	3.57	3.56	3.76	3.77	3.81	3.88	3.88	4.00
1964	3.99	4.00	4.16	4.10	4.02	3.96	3.93	3.95	3.99	4.01	4.07	4.09
1965	4.15	4.20	4.18	4.17	4.14	4.08	4.12	4.19	4.33	4.36	4.48	4.88
1966	4.89	5.04	4.92	4.91	5.05	5.04	5.21	6.11	5.72	5.38	5.42	4.93
1967	4.62	4.76	4.29	4.41	4.55	5.10	5.24	5.29	5.45	5.64	5.64	5.71
1968	5.83	5.69	5.81	5.95	6.05	5.87	5.52	5.53	5.46	5.61	5.73	6.51
1969	6.17	6.38	6.34	6.31	6.61	6.88	7.32	7.34	8.06	7.41	7.79	8.41
1970	8.20	7.62	7.20	7.73	8.14	7.72	7.57	7.43	7.01	6.90	5.71	5.75
1971	5.60	5.08	4.48	5.13	5.89	6.20	6.59	6.18	5.74	5.46	5.21	5.14
1972	5.00	5.19	5.45	5.78	5.38	5.54	5.65	5.69	5.95	5.89	5.82	5.89
1973	6.15	6.46	6.86	6.76	6.83	6.73	7.43	7.85	7.27	6.74	6.96	6.75
1974	6.87	6.66	7.20	7.97	8.16	8.09	8.33	8.64	8.40	7.91	7.62	7.20
1975	7.03	6.51	6.87	7.65	7.13	7.28	7.78	8.02	8.24	7.41	7.51	7.01
1976	6.91	6.93	6.95	6.84	7.37	7.10	7.05	6.74	6.62	6.36	5.80	5.61
1977	6.49	6.52	6.49	6.28	6.46	6.22	6.49	6.68	6.91	7.27	7.10	7.36
1978	7.52	7.66	7.67	7.82	8.12	8.37	8.39	8.34	8.50	8.76	9.04	9.55
1979	9.18	9.45	9.33	9.48	9.34	8.95	9.03	9.50	9.60	11.60	10.58	10.72
1980	11.06	13.79	13.76	10.32	8.92	9.27	9.44	11.64	12.44	12.49	13.19	12.43
1981	13.01	13.29	13.36	14.24	14.66	14.12	15.03	16.21	16.03	15.40	12.67	13.97
1982	14.74	13.87	14.39	13.67	13.67	14.90	13.82	12.45	12.04	10.81	10.31	10.03
1983	10.12	9.68	10.09	9.82	10.25	10.58	11.04	11.23	10.73	10.92	10.89	10.93
1984	10.69	11.16	11.74	12.09	13.21	13.30	12.72	12.50	12.33	11.55	10.62	10.38
1985	10.23	10.83	10.70	10.44	9.44	9.43	9.60	9.23	9.31	9.34	8.93	8.31
1986	8.39	8.10	7.29	7.28	7.52	7.19	7.14	6.37	6.83	6.63	6.34	6.54
1987	6.46	6.53	6.86	7.75	7.94	7.71	7.84	8.19	8.78	8.09	8.06	8.19

5-YEAR TREASURY*

	Jan.	Feb.	Mar.	Apr.	May	June	July	Aug.	Sept.	Oct.	Nov.	Dec.
1943	1.63	1.66	1.68	1.69	1.63	1.55	1.56	1.60	1.61	1.61	1.63	1.61
1944	1.62	1.61	1.62	1.62	1.62	1.64	1.64	1.62	1.62	1.64	1.64	1.66
1945	1.54	1.48	1.47	1.36	1.40	1.37	1.39	1.40	1.40	1.36	1.26	1.24
1946	1.14	1.11	1.15	1.29	1.31	1.27	1.29	1.33	1.43	1.43	1.46	1.44
1947	1.36	1.40	1.35	1.38	1.39	1.41	1.42	1.37	1.40	1.51	1.61	1.76
1948	1.76	1.77	1.74	1.73	1.62	1.68	1.73	1.83	1.84	1.86	1.81	1.74
1949	1.69	1.69	1.63	1.63	1.58	1.51	1.41	1.36	1.40	1.40	1.41	1.39
1950	1.45	1.45	1.48	1.54	1.50	1.57	1.49	1.55	1.68	1.72	1.71	1.76
1951	1.78	1.79	2.03	2.09	2.14	2.15	2.00	1.96	2.04	2.14	2.12	2.20
1952	2.14	2.19	2.12	2.04	2.13	2.22	2.33	2.42	2.44	2.34	2.34	2.39
1953	2.42	2.45	2.49	2.70	2.80	2.74	2.65	2.74	2.49	2.36	2.43	2.16
1954	2.09	1.98	1.85	1.75	1.95	1.80	1.85	1.87	1.95	2.05	2.07	2.13
1955	2.32	2.39	2.50	2.57	2.51	2.63	2.79	2.88	2.76	2.71	2.89	2.95
1956	2.74	2.75	3.00	3.17	2.95	3.03	3.24	3.48	3.40	3.46	3.65	3.58
1957	3.33	3.37	3.39	3.57	3.71	3.85	3.98	3.88	4.03	4.00	3.42	2.84
1958	2.76	2.66	2.54	2.38	2.38	2.54	2.88	3.48	3.77	3.78	3.60	3.87
1959	4.04	3.87	4.02	4.19	4.32	4.50	4.55	4.72	4.87	4.70	4.72	5.10
1960	4.85	4.78	4.24	4.38	4.43	4.07	3.65	3.64	3.64	3.72	3.96	3.60
1961	3.73	3.63	3.60	3.57	3.55	3.80	3.80	3.91	3.79	3.78	3.84	3.89
1962	4.00	3.83	3.64	3.62	3.61	3.72	3.87	3.65	3.64	3.55	3.62	3.56
1963	3.61	3.65	3.71	3.73	3.75	3.79	3.88	3.88	3.92	3.98	3.96	4.08
1964	4.07	4.08	4.21	4.16	4.11	4.04	4.06	4.06	4.09	4.12	4.14	4.14
1965	4.17	4.21	4.19	4.19	4.17	4.14	4.16	4.24	4.33	4.38	4.49	4.83
1966	4.87	5.04	4.90	4.91	5.03	5.04	5.21	5.98	5.38	5.21	5.37	4.88
1967	4.64	4.77	4.45	4.57	4.72	5.22	5.29	5.34	5.46	5.69	5.67	5.69
1968	5.55	5.70	5.83	5.92	6.04	5.86	5.55	5.58	5.52	5.67	5.77	6.45
1969	6.19	6.38	6.38	6.34	6.62	6.80	7.02	7.04	7.97	7.31	7.58	8.33
1970	8.14	7.56	7.24	7.82	8.10	7.79	7.61	7.50	7.18	7.15	6.18	6.05
1971	6.03	5.73	5.13	5.69	6.32	6.61	6.88	6.48	6.04	5.86	5.73	5.64
1972	5.48	5.63	5.88	6.14	5.80	5.88	5.94	6.00	6.25	6.15	6.06	6.12
1973	6.30	6.59	6.89	6.71	6.88	6.60	7.25	7.59	7.01	6.70	6.87	6.75
1974	6.83	6.75	7.22	7.87	7.99	7.88	8.15	8.50	8.25	7.88	7.63	7.32
1975	7.33	6.95	7.28	7.82	7.48	7.55	7.84	8.01	8.35	7.67	7.80	7.38
1976	7.35	7.32	7.27	7.24	7.60	7.46	7.46	7.19	7.08	6.82	6.25	6.19
1977	6.91	6.96	6.94	6.80	6.86	6.62	6.81	6.93	7.09	7.41	7.28	7.56
1978	7.70	7.83	7.85	8.00	8.23	8.43	8.47	8.26	8.42	8.65	8.81	9.24
1979	8.96	9.17	9.15	9.20	8.97	8.75	8.86	9.19	9.25	11.07	10.43	10.40
1980	10.85	13.43	12.90	10.22	9.28	9.58	9.79	11.84	12.28	12.21	12.71	12.09
1981	12.66	13.20	13.24	14.08	14.17	13.78	14.62	16.05	16.06	15.63	12.99	13.96
1982	14.50	13.54	14.17	13.34	13.32	14.55	13.50	12.20	12.22	11.31	10.99	10.51
1983	10.69	10.19	10.56	10.30	10.70	11.00	11.43	11.70	11.28	11.41	11.36	11.36
1984	11.37	11.63	12.14	12.51	13.55	13.56	12.90	12.70	12.47	11.78	11.03	11.17
1985	10.72	11.43	11.85	11.01	9.96	10.02	10.18	9.83	9.89	9.86	9.40	8.75
1986	8.81	8.17	7.45	7.54	7.85	7.57	7.62	6.75	7.28	7.09	6.66	6.83
1987	6.77	6.81	7.11	8.04	8.45	8.04	8.21	8.21	9.11	8.42	8.50	8.53

Source: *Moody's Municipal & Government Manual*, vol. 2 (New York: Moody's Investor's Service, Inc., 1988).

10-YEAR TREASURY*

	Jan.	Feb.	Mar.	Apr.	May	June	July	Aug.	Sept.	Oct.	Nov.	Dec.
1943	2.08	2.06	2.09	2.08	2.02	2.02	2.00	2.03	2.03	2.05	2.08	2.09
1944	2.09	2.06	2.05	2.06	2.06	2.07	2.07	2.05	2.05	2.07	2.06	2.06
1945	1.96	1.87	1.85	1.75	1.75	1.71	1.70	1.71	1.74	1.75	1.79	1.70
1946	1.38	1.43	1.45	1.58	1.61	1.59	1.64	1.71	1.74	1.75	1.79	1.70
1947	1.68	1.70	1.67	1.70	1.69	1.72	1.70	1.65	1.66	1.78	1.87	2.17
1948	2.17	2.17	2.12	2.08	1.96	2.08	2.07	2.16	2.15	2.19	2.11	2.05
1949	2.00	1.98	1.91	1.89	1.86	1.79	1.73	1.66	1.70	1.70	1.70	1.66
1950	1.74	1.73	1.74	1.79	1.76	1.82	1.75	1.80	1.91	1.95	1.93	1.96
1951	1.96	2.01	2.20	2.27	2.26	2.29	2.15	2.19	2.25	2.27	2.28	2.35
1952	2.31	2.35	2.29	2.20	2.35	2.37	2.42	2.51	2.64	2.52	2.50	2.52
1953	2.61	2.66	2.74	2.87	3.02	2.92	2.85	2.87	2.62	2.56	2.63	2.41
1954	2.37	2.37	2.41	2.33	2.37	2.39	2.36	2.43	2.45	2.44	2.49	2.51
1955	2.59	2.64	2.65	2.73	2.65	2.76	2.94	2.94	2.83	2.80	2.89	2.92
1956	2.80	2.83	2.99	3.13	2.90	2.99	3.14	3.37	3.26	3.39	3.53	3.51
1957	3.29	3.30	3.30	3.50	3.60	3.84	3.87	3.75	3.88	3.78	3.62	2.96
1958	2.92	2.88	2.79	2.67	2.69	2.92	3.23	3.52	3.79	3.76	3.62	3.86
1959	4.06	3.88	4.00	4.12	4.32	4.38	4.41	4.54	4.68	4.46	4.47	4.87
1960	4.78	4.57	4.31	4.37	4.29	4.09	3.80	3.79	3.76	3.92	4.10	3.81
1961	3.86	3.72	3.76	3.75	3.76	3.91	3.91	3.96	3.88	3.93	4.05	4.15
1962	4.19	4.09	3.91	3.86	3.91	3.97	4.03	3.92	3.94	3.89	3.95	3.85
1963	3.85	3.94	3.96	3.98	3.95	3.99	3.99	3.99	4.05	4.13	4.09	4.14
1964	4.16	4.14	4.22	4.22	4.20	4.15	4.21	4.21	4.18	4.19	4.18	4.18
1965	4.18	4.22	4.21	4.21	4.21	4.21	4.22	4.26	4.33	4.37	4.50	4.64
1966	4.70	4.96	4.84	4.85	4.89	4.89	5.05	5.53	5.12	4.94	5.13	4.72
1967	4.51	4.73	4.50	4.65	4.80	5.16	5.21	5.26	5.33	5.59	5.64	5.65
1968	5.51	5.63	5.78	5.70	5.93	5.70	5.37	5.45	5.40	5.56	5.72	6.18
1969	6.00	6.24	6.33	6.05	6.34	6.50	6.54	6.60	7.35	6.97	7.34	7.99
1970	7.64	7.10	7.00	7.77	8.20	7.66	7.28	7.35	7.16	7.30	6.29	6.46
1971	6.02	6.03	5.42	5.81	6.26	6.78	6.66	6.26	5.96	5.82	5.74	5.70
1972	5.88	5.66	6.01	6.11	5.96	5.96	5.82	6.21	6.37	6.31	6.29	6.40
1973	6.51	6.74	6.73	6.59	6.78	6.78	7.31	7.00	6.52	6.58	6.71	6.67
1974	6.91	6.85	7.16	7.61	7.72	7.53	7.75	8.19	7.89	7.59	7.35	7.12
1975	6.96	6.93	7.05	7.55	7.14	7.28	7.31	7.41	7.92	7.66	7.81	7.36
1976	7.24	7.26	7.12	7.18	7.34	7.26	7.23	7.05	6.98	6.77	6.45	6.22
1977	7.33	7.44	7.44	7.34	7.31	7.09	7.11	7.21	7.30	7.58	7.49	7.77
1978	7.93	8.00	8.04	8.15	8.33	8.49	8.52	8.29	8.45	8.67	8.72	9.02
1979	8.86	9.11	9.08	9.12	8.92	8.90	9.00	9.22	9.29	10.74	10.24	10.33
1980	11.10	13.07	12.50	10.53	9.88	9.97	10.31	11.48	11.97	12.06	12.34	11.82
1981	12.48	13.11	13.02	13.75	13.70	13.34	14.13	15.37	15.51	15.19	12.96	14.00
1982	14.57	13.83	14.11	13.25	13.21	14.30	13.54	12.45	11.80	10.78	10.53	10.32
1983	10.64	10.10	10.35	10.08	10.53	10.84	11.28	11.52	11.27	11.44	11.37	11.43
1984	11.32	11.74	12.26	12.64	13.82	13.72	13.00	12.73	12.44	11.87	11.20	11.51
1985	11.11	11.73	11.80	11.37	10.38	10.34	10.68	10.23	10.35	10.31	9.78	9.05
1986	9.22	8.38	7.61	7.60	7.83	7.62	7.74	7.06	7.54	7.44	7.10	7.26
1987	7.08	7.17	7.37	8.33	8.72	8.35	8.57	8.96	9.52	8.83	8.97	8.91

*Taken from a line, commonly called a yield curve, on last Tuesday of month.

91-DAY BILL RATE-AVG. FOR LAST OFFERING OF MONTH

	Jan.	Feb.	Mar.	Apr.	May	June	July	Aug.	Sept.	Oct.	Nov.	Dec.
1941	NEG.	.086	.055	.097	.107	.087	.094	.090	.062	.151	.242	.310
1942	.220	.222	.221	.335	.365	.360	.372	.367	.373	.373	.368	.357
1943	.369	.369	.374	.373	.374	.375	.374	.375	.375	.375	.375	.373
1944	.374	.375	.375	.374	.375	.375	.375	.375	.375	.375	.375	.373
1945	.375	.375	.376	.375	.375	.375	.375	.375	.375	.375	.375	.373
1946	.375	.375	.375	.375	.376	.376	.376	.375	.375	.376	.376	.374
1947	.376	.376	.376	.376	.376	.376	.740	.766	.817	.895	.944	.952
1948	.990	.997	.996	.997	.997	.998	.997	1.072	1.109	1.120	1.147	1.157
1949	1.160	1.164	1.162	1.156	1.159	1.158	1.017	1.031	1.076	1.036	1.052	1.087
1950	1.103	1.132	1.145	1.166	1.167	1.172	1.174	1.285	1.324	1.316	1.383	1.382
1951	1.589	1.390	1.507	1.506	1.600	1.527	1.591	1.645	1.647	1.593	1.609	1.865
1952	1.589	1.563	1.592	1.616	1.728	1.682	1.877	1.899	1.635	1.757	1.931	2.228
1953	1.961	2.070	2.036	2.243	2.084	1.954	2.157	2.001	1.634	1.220	1.488	1.574
1954	0.998	0.986	1.030	0.886	0.718	0.635	0.800	0.983	0.984	1.007	0.897	1.175
1955	1.349	1.355	1.374	1.697	1.471	1.401	1.720	1.875	2.122	2.231	2.440	2.688
1956	2.245	2.429	2.422	2.788	2.573	2.535	2.303	2.832	2.986	2.907	3.174	3.217
1957	3.283	3.288	3.034	3.054	3.245	3.232	3.158	3.497	3.534	3.622	3.158	3.174
1958	2.202	1.202	1.189	1.055	0.635	1.006	0.984	2.162	2.511	2.647	2.723	2.739
1959	2.975	2.589	2.766	2.831	2.878	3.281	3.047	3.824	3.958	4.022	4.279	4.516
1960	4.116	4.168	2.792	3.317	3.497	2.399	2.404	2.518	2.286	2.129	2.396	2.120
1961	2.230	2.496	2.392	2.186	2.354	2.219	2.244	2.321	2.325	2.606	2.606	2.594
1962	2.688	2.664	2.719	2.740	2.656	2.792	2.892	2.806	2.749	2.742	2.853	2.894
1963	2.917	2.870	2.919	2.884	2.974	2.979	3.206	3.396	3.513	3.542	3.567	3.758
1964	3.501	3.547	3.550	3.446	3.475	3.478	3.803	3.855	3.983	4.040	4.104	4.457
1965	3.848	3.989	3.922	3.916	3.889	3.789	3.803	5.087	5.503	5.246	5.202	4.747
1966	4.596	4.696	4.555	4.630	4.641	4.435	4.818	5.087	5.503	5.246	5.202	4.747
1967	4.486	4.538	4.150	3.715	3.477	3.462	4.423	4.490	4.629	4.542	4.957	4.989
1968	4.846	5.063	5.186	5.499	5.696	5.238	5.190	5.194	5.182	5.471	5.488	6.199
1969	6.167	6.080	6.065	6.053	6.124	6.456	7.172	7.098	7.106	7.030	7.476	8.096
1970	7.888	6.812	6.330	6.876	7.133	6.421	6.345	6.342	5.807	5.831	5.084	4.803
1971	4.201	3.497	3.521	3.865	4.344	5.080	5.554	4.549	4.676	4.443	4.324	3.731
1972	3.367	3.446	3.849	3.513	3.762	4.023	3.794	4.332	4.644	4.767	4.886	5.111
1973	5.689	5.811	6.251	6.278	6.694	7.228	8.320	8.778	7.331	7.163	7.695	7.406
1974	7.778	7.188	8.300	8.909	7.983	7.841	7.698	9.908	7.002	7.892	7.328	7.113
1975	5.606	5.455	5.562	5.716	5.206	5.665	6.318	6.593	6.547	5.685	5.520	5.200
1976	4.763	4.870	4.929	4.909	5.495	5.368	5.194	5.091	5.574	4.979	4.466	4.296
1977	4.720	4.708	4.600	4.518	4.993	4.965	5.163	5.574	5.982	6.278	6.057	6.144
1978	6.440	6.429	6.310	6.294	6.658	6.967	6.895	7.323	8.106	8.454	9.166	9.388
1979	9.324	9.451	9.498	9.498	9.526	8.802	9.154	9.855	9.855	12.256	11.018	12.105
1980	12.038	13.700	15.037	10.788	7.675	8.149	8.221	10.124	11.524	12.331	14.384	13.908
1981	15.199	14.103	12.501	14.190	16.750	13.909	15.065	15.583	14.669	13.352	10.400	11.490
1982	13.364	12.430	13.399	12.469	11.520	13.269	10.550	8.604	7.801	8.031	8.280	7.975
1983	8.122	7.944	8.680	8.150	8.650	9.090	9.130	9.280	8.730	8.410	8.900	8.940
1984	8.870	9.200	9.760	9.680	9.830	9.770	10.400	10.600	10.270	9.380	8.430	7.840
1985	7.760	8.360	8.410	7.870	7.220	7.060	7.230	7.070	7.070	7.240	7.150	7.040
1986	6.92	6.96	6.35	6.08	6.17	5.99	5.86	5.32	5.20	5.18	5.53	5.68
1987	5.44	5.40	5.72	5.79	5.70	5.82	5.55	6.19	6.59	5.12	5.49	5.73

Source: *Moody's Municipal & Government Manual*, vol. 2 (New York: Moody's Investor's Service, Inc., 1988).

MOODY'S BOND YIELDS BY RATING GROUPS

MOODY'S AVERAGE OF YIELDS ON Aaa CORPORATE BONDS (IN PERCENT)

Year	Aver.	Jan.	Feb.	Mar.	Apr.	May	Jun.	Jul.	Aug.	Sep.	Oct.	Nov.	Dec.
1988	.....	9.88	9.40	9.39	9.67	9.90	9.86	9.96	.....	.....	.....	.....	.....
1987	9.38	8.36	8.38	8.36	8.85	9.33	9.32	9.42	9.67	10.18	10.52	10.01	10.11
1986	9.02	10.05	9.67	9.00	8.79	9.09	9.13	8.88	8.72	8.89	8.86	8.68	8.49
1985	11.37	12.08	12.13	12.56	12.23	11.72	10.94	10.97	11.05	11.07	11.02	10.55	10.16
1984	12.71	12.20	12.08	12.57	12.81	13.28	13.55	13.44	12.87	12.66	12.63	12.29	12.13
1983	12.04	11.79	12.01	11.73	11.51	11.46	11.74	12.15	12.51	12.37	12.25	12.41	12.57
1982	13.79	15.18	15.27	14.58	14.46	14.26	14.81	14.61	13.71	12.94	12.12	11.68	11.83
1981	14.17	12.81	13.35	13.33	13.88	14.32	13.75	14.38	14.89	15.49	15.40	14.22	14.23
1980	11.94	11.09	12.38	12.96	12.04	10.99	10.58	11.07	11.64	12.02	12.31	12.97	13.21
1979	9.63	9.25	9.26	9.37	9.38	9.50	9.29	9.20	9.23	9.44	10.13	10.76	10.74
1978	8.73	8.41	8.47	8.47	8.56	8.69	8.76	8.88	8.69	8.69	8.89	9.03	9.16
1977	8.02	7.96	8.04	8.10	8.04	8.05	7.95	7.94	7.98	7.92	8.04	8.08	8.19
1976	8.43	8.60	8.55	8.52	8.40	8.58	8.62	8.56	8.45	8.38	8.32	8.25	7.98
1975	8.83	8.83	8.62	8.67	8.95	8.90	8.77	8.84	8.95	8.95	8.86	8.78	8.79
1974	8.57	7.83	7.85	8.01	8.25	8.37	8.47	8.72	9.00	9.24	9.27	8.89	8.89
1973	7.44	7.15	7.22	7.29	7.26	7.29	7.37	7.45	7.68	7.63	7.60	7.67	7.68
1972	7.21	7.19	7.27	7.24	7.30	7.30	7.23	7.21	7.19	7.22	7.21	7.12	7.08
1971	7.39	7.36	7.08	7.21	7.25	7.53	7.64	7.64	7.59	7.44	7.39	7.26	7.25
1970	8.04	7.91	7.93	7.84	7.83	8.11	8.48	8.44	8.13	8.09	8.03	8.05	7.64
1969	7.03	6.59	6.66	6.85	6.89	6.79	6.98	7.08	6.97	7.14	7.33	7.35	7.72
1968	6.18	6.17	6.10	6.11	6.21	6.27	6.28	6.24	6.02	5.97	6.09	6.19	6.45
1967	5.51	5.20	5.03	5.13	5.11	5.24	5.44	5.58	5.62	5.65	5.82	6.07	6.19
1966	5.13	4.74	4.78	4.92	4.96	4.98	5.07	5.16	5.31	5.49	5.41	5.35	5.39
1965	4.49	4.43	4.41	4.42	4.43	4.44	4.46	4.48	4.49	4.52	4.56	4.60	4.68
1964	4.40	4.37	4.36	4.38	4.40	4.41	4.41	4.40	4.41	4.42	4.42	4.43	4.44
1963	4.26	4.21	4.19	4.19	4.21	4.22	4.23	4.26	4.29	4.31	4.32	4.33	4.35
1962	4.33	4.42	4.42	4.39	4.33	4.28	4.28	4.34	4.35	4.32	4.28	4.25	4.24
1961	4.35	4.32	4.27	4.22	4.25	4.27	4.33	4.41	4.45	4.45	4.42	4.39	4.42
1960	4.41	4.61	4.56	4.49	4.45	4.46	4.45	4.41	4.28	4.25	4.30	4.31	4.35
1959	4.38	4.12	4.14	4.13	4.23	4.37	4.46	4.47	4.43	4.52	4.57	4.56	4.58
1958	3.79	3.60	3.59	3.63	3.60	3.57	3.57	3.67	3.85	4.09	4.11	4.09	4.08
1957	3.89	3.77	3.67	3.66	3.67	3.74	3.91	3.99	4.10	4.12	4.10	4.08	3.81
1956	3.36	3.11	3.08	3.10	3.24	3.28	3.26	3.28	3.43	3.56	3.59	3.69	3.75
1955	3.06	2.93	2.93	3.02	3.01	3.04	3.05	3.06	3.11	3.13	3.10	3.10	3.15
1954	2.90	3.06	2.95	2.86	2.85	2.88	2.90	2.89	2.87	2.89	2.87	2.89	2.90
1953	3.20	3.02	3.07	3.12	3.23	3.34	3.40	3.28	3.24	3.29	3.16	3.11	3.13
1952	2.96	2.98	2.93	2.96	2.93	2.93	2.94	2.95	2.94	2.95	3.01	2.98	2.97
1951	2.86	2.66	2.66	2.78	2.87	2.89	2.94	2.94	2.88	2.84	2.89	2.96	3.01
1950	2.62	2.57	2.58	2.58	2.60	2.61	2.62	2.65	2.61	2.64	2.67	2.67	2.67
1949	2.66	2.71	2.71	2.70	2.70	2.71	2.71	2.67	2.62	2.60	2.61	2.60	2.58
1948	2.82	2.86	2.85	2.83	2.78	2.76	2.76	2.81	2.84	2.84	2.84	2.84	2.79
1947	2.61	2.57	2.55	2.55	2.53	2.53	2.55	2.55	2.56	2.61	2.70	2.77	2.86
1946	2.53	2.54	2.48	2.47	2.46	2.51	2.49	2.48	2.51	2.58	2.60	2.59	2.61
1945	2.62	2.69	2.65	2.62	2.61	2.62	2.61	2.60	2.61	2.62	2.62	2.62	2.61
1944	2.72	2.72	2.74	2.74	2.74	2.73	2.73	2.72	2.71	2.72	2.72	2.72	2.70
1943	2.73	2.79	2.77	2.76	2.76	2.74	2.72	2.69	2.69	2.72	2.70	2.71	2.74
1942	2.83	2.83	2.85	2.86	2.83	2.85	2.85	2.83	2.81	2.80	2.80	2.79	2.81
1941	2.77	2.75	2.78	2.80	2.82	2.81	2.77	2.74	2.74	2.75	2.73	2.72	2.80
1940	2.84	2.88	2.86	2.84	2.82	2.93	2.96	2.88	2.85	2.82	2.79	2.75	2.71
1939	3.01	3.01	3.00	2.99	3.02	2.97	2.92	2.89	2.93	3.25	3.15	3.00	2.94
1938	3.19	3.17	3.20	3.22	3.30	3.22	3.26	3.22	3.18	3.21	3.15	3.10	3.08
1937	3.26	3.10	3.22	3.32	3.42	3.33	3.25	3.24	3.27	3.27	3.24	3.21	3.10
1936	3.24	3.37	3.32	3.29	3.29	3.27	3.24	3.23	3.21	3.18	3.18	3.15	3.10
1935	3.60	3.77	3.69	3.67	3.66	3.65	3.61	3.56	3.60	3.59	3.52	3.47	3.44
1934	4.00	4.35	4.20	4.13	4.07	4.01	3.93	3.89	3.93	3.96	3.90	3.86	3.81
1933	4.49	4.44	4.48	4.68	4.78	4.63	4.46	4.36	4.30	4.36	4.34	4.54	4.50
1932	5.01	5.20	5.23	4.98	5.17	5.36	5.41	5.26	4.91	4.70	4.64	4.63	4.59
1931	4.58	4.42	4.43	4.39	4.40	4.37	4.36	4.36	4.40	4.55	4.99	4.94	5.32
1930	4.55	4.66	4.69	4.62	4.60	4.60	4.57	4.52	4.47	4.42	4.42	4.47	4.52
1929	4.83	4.62	4.66	4.70	4.69	4.70	4.77	4.77	4.79	4.80	4.77	4.76	4.67
1928	4.55	4.46	4.46	4.46	4.46	4.49	4.57	4.61	4.64	4.61	4.61	4.58	4.61
1927	4.57	4.66	4.67	4.62	4.58	4.57	4.58	4.60	4.56	4.54	4.51	4.49	4.46
1926	4.73	4.82	4.77	4.79	4.74	4.71	4.72	4.71	4.72	4.72	4.71	4.68	4.68
1925	4.88	4.95	4.95	4.91	4.87	4.83	4.83	4.87	4.90	4.87	4.85	4.84	4.85
1924	5.00	5.09	5.09	5.10	5.08	5.04	4.99	4.95	4.95	4.95	4.92	4.94	4.95
1923	5.12	5.04	5.07	5.18	5.22	5.16	5.15	5.14	5.08	5.12	5.11	5.09	5.09
1922	5.10	5.34	5.29	5.23	5.13	5.13	5.08	5.00	4.96	4.93	4.97	5.09	5.08
1921	5.97	6.14	6.08	6.08	6.06	6.11	6.18	6.12	5.99	5.93	5.84	5.60	5.50
1920	6.12	5.75	5.86	5.92	6.04	6.25	6.38	6.34	6.30	6.22	6.05	6.08	6.26
1919	5.49	5.35	5.35	5.39	5.44	5.39	5.40	5.44	5.56	5.60	5.54	5.66	5.73

Source: *Moody's Municipal & Government Manual,* vol. 2 (New York: Moody's Investor's Service, Inc., 1988).

MOODY'S AVERAGE OF YIELDS ON Aa CORPORATE BONDS (IN PERCENT)

Year	Aver.	Jan.	Feb.	Mar.	Apr.	May	Jun.	Jul.	Aug.	Sep.	Oct.	Nov.	Dec.
1988		10.09	9.60	9.59	9.86	10.10	10.13	10.26					
1987	9.68	8.86	8.88	8.84	9.15	9.59	9.65	9.64	9.86	10.35	10.74	10.27	10.33
1986	9.47	10.46	10.13	9.49	9.21	9.43	9.49	9.28	9.22	9.36	9.33	9.20	9.02
1985	11.82	12.43	12.49	12.91	12.69	12.30	11.46	11.42	11.47	11.46	11.45	11.07	10.63
1984	13.31	12.71	12.70	13.22	13.48	14.10	14.33	14.12	13.47	13.27	13.11	12.66	12.50
1983	12.42	12.35	12.58	12.32	12.06	11.95	12.15	12.39	12.72	12.62	12.49	12.61	12.76
1982	14.41	15.75	15.72	15.21	14.90	14.77	15.26	15.21	14.48	13.72	12.97	12.51	12.44
1981	14.75	13.52	13.89	13.90	14.39	14.88	14.41	14.79	15.42	15.95	15.82	14.97	15.00
1980	12.50	11.56	12.73	13.51	13.06	11.91	11.39	11.43	12.09	12.52	12.68	13.34	13.78
1979	9.94	9.48	9.50	9.61	9.65	9.86	9.66	9.49	9.53	9.70	10.46	11.22	11.15
1978	8.92	8.59	8.65	8.66	8.73	8.84	8.95	9.07	8.96	8.92	9.07	9.24	9.33
1977	8.24	8.16	8.26	8.28	8.28	8.28	8.19	8.12	8.17	8.15	8.26	8.34	8.405
1976	8.75	9.13	9.02	9.01	8.89	8.92	8.89	8.81	8.66	8.54	8.48	8.46	8.245
1975	9.17	9.13	8.91	8.92	9.19	9.24	9.13	9.13	9.23	9.35	9.32	9.23	9.255
1974	8.84	8.00	8.05	8.18	8.43	8.58	8.75	9.01	9.28	9.66	9.64	9.34	9.20
1973	7.66	7.37	7.47	7.49	7.49	7.49	7.55	7.64	7.84	7.86	7.84	7.90	7.92
1972	7.48	7.52	7.52	7.53	7.57	7.56	7.51	7.50	7.43	7.41	7.45	7.39	7.36
1971	7.78	7.90	7.67	7.73	7.74	7.84	7.96	7.96	7.93	7.81	7.69	7.56	7.57
1970	8.32	8.15	8.13	8.06	8.03	8.24	8.58	8.64	8.49	8.47	8.44	8.42	8.13
1969	7.20	6.73	6.77	6.95	7.02	6.96	7.12	7.24	7.23	7.36	7.53	7.58	7.93
1968	6.38	6.29	6.27	6.28	6.38	6.48	6.50	6.45	6.25	6.23	6.32	6.45	6.66
1967	5.66	5.30	5.18	5.23	5.26	5.42	5.63	5.72	5.76	5.87	6.01	6.23	6.35
1966	5.23	4.83	4.90	5.05	5.10	5.10	5.16	5.25	5.38	5.58	5.50	5.46	5.48
1965	4.57	4.48	4.46	4.48	4.48	4.49	4.52	4.56	4.59	4.63	4.66	4.69	4.80
1964	4.49	4.49	4.46	4.47	4.49	4.50	4.51	4.50	4.49	4.48	4.49	4.49	4.50
1963	4.39	4.37	4.36	4.34	4.35	4.36	4.36	4.39	4.40	4.41	4.43	4.44	4.46
1962	4.47	4.55	4.56	4.53	4.49	4.43	4.44	4.49	4.49	4.46	4.41	4.40	4.38
1961	4.48	4.48	4.40	4.33	4.37	4.41	4.45	4.53	4.57	4.59	4.56	4.54	4.56
1960	4.56	4.77	4.71	4.62	4.58	4.61	4.60	4.56	4.44	4.41	4.44	4.47	4.50
1959	4.51	4.22	4.24	4.23	4.32	4.46	4.56	4.58	4.58	4.69	4.76	4.70	4.74
1958	3.94	3.81	3.77	3.78	3.78	3.78	3.78	3.83	3.98	4.20	4.21	4.21	4.18
1957	4.03	3.89	3.83	3.80	3.79	3.83	3.98	4.10	4.21	4.26	4.28	4.29	4.08
1956	3.45	3.19	3.16	3.18	3.30	3.34	3.35	3.39	3.50	3.63	3.69	3.76	3.85
1955	3.16	3.06	3.10	3.13	3.13	3.15	3.14	3.14	3.20	3.22	3.19	3.18	3.22
1954	3.06	3.22	3.12	3.03	3.00	3.03	3.06	3.04	3.03	3.04	3.04	3.04	3.04
1953	3.31	3.09	3.14	3.18	3.29	3.41	3.50	3.42	3.39	3.43	3.33	3.27	3.28
1952	3.04	3.05	3.01	3.03	3.01	3.00	3.03	3.03	3.06	3.07	3.08	3.06	3.05
1951	2.91	2.71	2.71	2.82	2.93	2.93	2.99	2.99	2.92	2.88	2.93	3.02	3.06
1950	2.69	2.65	2.65	2.66	2.66	2.69	2.69	2.72	2.67	2.71	2.72	2.72	2.72
1949	2.75	2.81	2.80	2.79	2.79	2.78	2.78	2.75	2.71	2.69	2.70	2.68	2.67
1948	2.90	2.94	2.93	2.90	2.87	2.86	2.85	2.89	2.94	2.93	2.94	2.92	2.88
1947	2.70	2.65	2.64	2.64	2.63	2.63	2.64	2.64	2.64	2.69	2.79	2.85	2.94
1946	2.62	2.62	2.56	2.54	2.56	2.58	2.59	2.59	2.62	2.68	2.70	2.69	2.69
1945	2.71	2.76	2.73	2.72	2.73	2.72	2.69	2.68	2.70	2.70	2.70	2.68	2.68
1944	2.81	2.83	2.83	2.82	2.82	2.81	2.81	2.80	2.79	2.79	2.81	2.80	2.76
1943	2.86	2.93	2.89	2.88	2.88	2.87	2.85	2.82	2.81	2.82	2.83	2.84	2.87
1942	2.98	2.96	2.98	3.00	2.98	3.00	3.01	2.99	2.99	2.98	2.95	2.94	2.96
1941	2.94	2.95	3.00	3.01	3.04	3.04	2.99	2.95	2.90	2.90	2.91	2.87	2.86
1940	3.02	3.08	3.05	3.04	3.04	2.99	3.08	3.10	3.01	3.03	3.01	2.96	2.92
1939	3.22	3.32	3.26	3.22	3.22	3.16	3.13	3.08	3.11	3.49	3.35	3.16	3.14
1938	3.56	3.50	3.51	3.56	3.73	3.56	3.68	3.62	3.57	3.60	3.53	3.46	3.42
1937	3.46	3.30	3.40	3.57	3.57	3.53	3.43	3.41	3.41	3.46	3.53	3.54	3.50
1936	3.46	3.57	3.55	3.55	3.57	3.53	3.51	3.48	3.44	3.41	3.37	3.31	3.28
1935	3.95	4.21	4.13	4.11	4.08	4.03	3.99	3.89	3.87	3.85	3.82	3.73	3.65
1934	4.44	5.00	4.70	4.55	4.43	4.37	4.30	4.28	4.34	4.42	4.36	4.28	4.27
1933	5.23	5.30	5.35	5.61	5.81	5.40	5.09	4.83	4.77	4.96	4.97	5.35	5.27
1932	5.98	6.08	6.13	5.85	6.11	6.38	6.60	6.51	5.83	5.54	5.51	5.57	5.60
1931	5.05	4.70	4.70	4.67	4.76	4.76	4.81	4.81	4.85	5.08	5.57	5.61	6.26
1930	4.77	4.86	4.89	4.80	4.78	4.77	4.76	4.74	4.68	4.65	4.67	4.75	4.85
1929	4.93	4.79	4.86	4.92	4.91	4.91	4.98	4.97	4.99	5.01	5.01	4.94	4.84
1928	4.71	4.61	4.61	4.59	4.60	4.64	4.75	4.79	4.82	4.79	4.78	4.75	4.77
1927	4.77	4.87	4.87	4.83	4.80	4.79	4.80	4.80	4.73	4.73	4.69	4.65	4.62
1926	4.97	5.07	5.04	5.05	4.99	4.94	4.92	4.95	4.95	4.97	4.95	4.93	4.89
1925	5.20	5.30	5.25	5.24	5.24	5.19	5.15	5.17	5.21	5.18	4.17	5.14	5.14
1924	5.44	5.55	5.52	5.57	5.56	5.49	5.43	5.38	5.38	5.38	5.35	5.32	5.31
1923	5.62	5.42	5.49	5.61	5.73	5.66	5.66	5.69	5.63	5.65	5.65	5.63	5.63
1922	5.59	5.94	5.80	5.79	5.71	5.62	5.64	5.57	5.44	5.35	5.36	5.45	5.41
1921	6.55	6.64	6.60	6.59	6.68	6.69	6.76	6.78	6.64	6.56	6.47	6.18	5.95
1920	6.59	6.19	6.28	6.42	6.54	6.78	6.79	6.69	6.76	6.65	6.56	6.63	6.84
1919	5.86	5.75	5.79	5.76	5.80	5.75	5.71	5.76	5.85	5.96	5.96	6.02	6.21

Source: *Moody's Municipal & Government Manual*, vol. 2 (New York: Moody's Investor's Service, Inc., 1988).

MOODY'S AVERAGE OF YIELDS ON A CORPORATE BONDS (IN PERCENT)

Year	Aver.	Jan.	Feb.	Mar.	Apr.	May	Jun.	Jul.	Aug.	Sep.	Oct.	Nov.	Dec.
1988	.....	10.43	9.94	9.89	10.17	10.41	10.42	10.55	.....	.....	.....	.....	.....
1987	9.99	9.23	9.20	9.13	9.36	9.83	9.98	10.00	10.20	10.72	10.98	10.63	10.62
1986	9.95	11.04	10.67	10.15	9.83	9.94	9.96	9.76	9.64	9.73	9.72	9.51	9.41
1985	12.28	12.80	12.80	13.36	13.14	12.70	11.98	11.92	12.00	11.99	11.94	11.54	11.19
1984	13.74	13.13	13.11	13.54	13.77	14.37	14.66	14.57	14.13	13.94	13.61	13.09	12.92
1983	13.10	13.53	13.52	13.15	12.86	12.70	12.68	12.88	12.99	13.17	13.11	12.97	13.21
1982	15.43	16.19	16.35	16.12	15.95	15.70	16.07	16.20	15.70	15.07	14.34	13.81	13.66
1981	15.29	13.83	14.27	14.47	14.82	15.43	15.08	15.36	15.76	16.36	16.47	15.82	15.75
1980	12.89	11.88	12.99	13.97	13.55	12.35	11.89	11.95	12.44	12.97	13.05	13.59	14.03
1979	10.20	9.72	9.68	9.81	9.88	10.00	9.89	9.75	9.85	10.03	10.83	11.50	11.46
1978	9.12	8.76	8.79	8.83	8.93	9.05	9.18	9.33	9.18	9.11	9.26	9.48	9.53
1977	8.49	8.45	8.49	8.55	8.55	8.55	8.46	8.40	8.40	8.37	8.48	8.56	8.57
⊡1976	9.09	9.54	9.43	9.40	9.26	9.28	9.24	9.14	8.98	8.81	8.73	8.69	8.53
⊡1975	9.65	9.81	9.51	9.37	9.62	9.79	9.67	9.61	9.68	9.74	9.72	9.64	9.67
⊡1974	9.20	8.17	8.25	8.32	8.61	8.83	9.07	9.40	9.67	10.04	10.29	9.96	9.80
1973	7.84	7.53	7.60	7.66	7.64	7.64	7.71	7.86	8.11	8.11	7.98	8.07	8.11
1972	7.66	7.70	7.70	7.66	7.74	7.75	7.69	7.71	7.64	7.64	7.64	7.58	7.50
1971	8.03	8.15	7.85	7.96	7.99	8.14	8.20	8.21	8.20	8.04	7.97	7.88	7.81
1970	8.57	8.35	8.31	8.17	8.22	8.49	8.76	8.92	8.85	8.78	8.71	8.74	8.48
1969	7.40	6.93	6.97	7.13	7.21	7.12	7.28	7.40	7.41	7.56	7.79	7.84	8.21
1968	6.54	6.48	6.41	6.43	6.57	6.62	6.60	6.60	6.38	6.39	6.47	6.43	6.85
1967	5.86	5.53	5.38	5.49	5.46	5.60	5.77	5.88	5.94	6.06	6.19	6.43	6.58
1966	5.35	4.91	4.96	5.12	5.18	5.17	5.29	5.36	5.48	5.69	5.67	5.65	5.69
1965	4.63	4.57	4.54	4.54	4.54	4.55	4.58	4.62	4.65	4.69	4.71	4.75	4.85
1964	4.57	4.56	4.56	4.56	4.56	4.59	4.60	4.60	4.58	4.57	4.55	4.57	4.58
1963	4.48	4.48	4.46	4.45	4.46	4.46	4.45	4.47	4.48	4.50	4.51	4.54	4.54
1962	4.65	4.74	4.74	4.71	4.66	4.62	4.62	4.65	4.66	4.62	4.61	4.59	4.54
1961	4.70	4.69	4.63	4.57	4.59	4.63	4.69	4.75	4.80	4.81	4.79	4.75	4.74
1960	4.77	4.93	4.92	4.86	4.79	4.84	4.81	4.77	4.65	4.63	4.67	4.69	4.71
1959	4.67	4.43	4.43	4.40	4.45	4.61	4.71	4.75	4.74	4.87	4.87	4.86	4.89
1958	4.17	4.01	4.00	4.06	4.01	4.02	4.00	4.04	4.19	4.40	4.45	4.43	4.42
1957	4.19	4.01	3.99	3.97	3.95	3.99	4.09	4.20	4.35	4.43	4.46	4.50	4.31
1956	3.57	3.30	3.28	3.30	3.41	3.47	3.48	3.52	3.63	3.73	3.81	3.90	3.98
1955	3.24	3.15	3.17	3.18	3.19	3.21	3.22	3.24	3.28	3.31	3.30	3.29	3.33
1954	3.18	3.35	3.25	3.16	3.15	3.15	3.18	3.17	3.15	3.13	3.14	3.13	3.14
1953	3.47	3.25	3.30	3.36	3.44	3.58	3.67	3.62	3.56	3.22	3.47	3.40	3.40
1952	3.23	3.32	3.25	3.24	3.20	3.20	3.20	3.19	3.21	3.21	3.24	3.24	3.22
1951	3.13	2.89	2.88	3.00	3.11	3.15	3.21	3.23	3.17	3.15	3.18	3.26	3.31
1950	2.89	2.85	2.86	2.86	2.86	2.88	2.90	2.92	2.87	2.88	2.91	2.92	2.91
1949	3.00	3.08	3.05	3.05	3.05	3.04	3.04	3.03	2.96	2.95	2.94	2.93	2.89
1948	3.12	3.17	3.17	3.13	3.08	3.06	3.03	3.07	3.13	3.13	3.15	3.18	3.16
1947	2.87	2.79	2.79	2.80	2.81	2.82	2.83	2.82	2.81	2.86	2.95	3.01	3.16
1946	2.75	2.73	2.70	2.69	2.69	2.73	2.73	2.72	2.74	2.80	2.84	2.84	2.83
1945	2.87	2.98	2.94	2.92	2.90	2.88	2.86	2.85	2.85	2.85	2.84	2.81	2.79
1944	3.06	3.11	3.10	3.10	3.09	3.07	3.07	3.05	3.04	3.05	3.01	3.01	2.98
1943	3.13	3.20	3.17	3.14	3.14	3.13	3.11	3.09	3.08	3.10	3.10	3.11	3.13
1942	3.28	3.30	3.29	3.32	3.30	3.31	3.31	3.28	3.27	3.24	3.24	3.19	3.23
1941	3.30	3.36	3.38	3.37	3.38	3.34	3.31	3.26	3.24	3.24	3.21	3.19	3.27
1940	3.57	3.69	3.68	3.65	3.59	3.65	3.70	3.57	3.55	3.52	3.48	3.40	3.36
1939	3.89	3.97	3.94	3.87	3.97	3.92	3.86	3.83	3.80	4.05	4.08	4.02	4.02
1938	4.22	4.20	4.24	4.34	4.49	4.28	3.98	3.96	3.94	4.02	4.16	4.24	4.20
1937	4.01	3.77	3.85	3.97	4.04	4.12	4.11	4.09	4.05	3.99	3.90	3.85	3.78
1936	4.02	4.21	4.12	4.10	4.12	4.12	4.59	4.52	4.46	4.49	4.49	4.45	4.35
1935	4.55	4.74	4.63	4.67	5.12	4.69	4.96	4.96	4.93	5.09	5.17	5.00	4.93
1934	5.08	5.72	5.24	5.12	4.97	4.97	6.29	5.88	5.58	5.51	5.76	6.22	6.21
1933	6.09	6.16	6.30	6.64	6.85	6.85	8.40	8.50	8.19	6.84	6.45	6.44	6.53
1932	7.20	7.06	7.06	6.80	7.48	5.52	5.75	5.64	5.88	6.29	6.88	6.90	7.70
1931	6.01	5.26	5.29	5.30	5.52	5.07	5.08	5.06	5.00	4.94	5.06	5.21	5.43
1930	5.13	5.23	5.25	5.15	5.12	5.23	5.31	5.32	5.39	5.43	5.38	5.33	5.21
1929	5.28	5.10	5.14	5.24	5.23	4.96	5.07	5.09	5.10	5.07	5.04	4.99	5.08
1928	5.01	4.91	4.92	4.92	4.91	5.06	5.05	5.04	5.01	5.01	4.97	4.94	4.92
1927	5.04	5.11	5.13	5.12	5.06	5.06	5.18	5.18	5.21	5.23	5.23	5.17	5.16
1926	5.24	5.38	5.33	5.34	5.27	5.18	5.18	5.44	5.51	5.56	5.53	5.54	5.46
1925	5.55	5.70	5.61	5.66	5.63	5.46	5.46	5.90	5.79	5.84	5.83	5.78	5.72
1924	5.93	6.16	6.18	6.10	6.09	6.00	6.17	6.19	6.21	6.06	6.15	6.23	6.20
1923	6.17	6.04	6.07	6.24	6.05	6.25	5.93	5.97	5.88	5.85	5.79	5.91	5.99	6.04
1922	6.03	6.41	6.33	6.22	6.05	7.53	7.50	7.58	7.53	7.43	7.23	7.03	6.62	6.39
1921	7.28	7.52	7.50	7.53	7.53	7.34	7.60	7.58	7.62	7.69	7.48	7.34	7.45	7.71
1920	7.41	6.88	7.15	7.11	7.34	6.40	7.60	7.58	7.62	7.69	7.48	7.34	7.45	7.71
1919	6.48	6.42	6.45	6.48	6.40	6.35	6.26	6.26	6.44	6.56	6.52	6.70	6.91

Source: *Moody's Municipal & Government Manual*, vol. 2 (New York: Moody's Investor's Service, Inc., 1988).

MOODY'S AVERAGE OF YIELDS ON Baa CORPORATE BONDS (IN PERCENT)

Year	Aver.	Jan.	Feb.	Mar.	Apr.	May	Jun.	Jul.	Aug.	Sep.	Oct.	Nov.	Dec.
1988	......	11.07	10.62	10.57	10.90	11.04	11.00	11.11	......	......	......	......	......
1987	10.58	9.72	9.65	9.61	10.04	10.51	10.52	10.61	10.80	11.31	11.62	11.23	11.29
1986	10.39	11.44	11.11	10.49	10.19	10.29	10.34	10.16	10.18	10.21	10.24	10.07	9.97
1985	12.72	13.26	13.23	13.69	13.51	13.15	12.40	12.43	12.50	12.48	12.36	11.99	11.58
1984	14.19	13.65	13.59	13.99	14.31	14.74	15.05	15.15	14.63	14.35	13.94	13.48	13.40
1983	13.55	13.94	13.95	13.61	13.29	13.09	13.37	13.39	13.64	13.55	13.46	13.61	13.75
1982	16.11	17.10	17.18	16.82	16.78	16.64	16.92	16.80	16.32	15.63	14.73	14.30	14.14
1981	16.04	15.03	15.37	15.34	15.56	15.95	15.80	16.17	16.34	16.92	17.11	16.39	16.55
1980	13.67	12.42	13.57	14.45	14.19	13.17	12.71	12.65	13.15	13.70	14.23	14.64	15.14
1979	10.69	10.13	10.08	10.26	10.33	10.47	10.38	10.29	10.35	10.54	11.40	11.99	12.06
1978	9.49	9.17	9.20	9.22	9.32	9.49	9.60	9.60	9.48	9.42	9.59	9.83	9.94
1977	8.97	9.08	9.12	9.12	9.07	9.01	8.91	8.87	8.82	8.80	8.89	8.95	8.99
[1]1976...	9.75	10.41	10.24	10.12	9.94	9.86	9.89	9.82	9.64	9.40	9.29	9.23	9.12
[1]1975...	10.61	10.81	10.65	10.48	10.58	10.69	10.62	10.55	10.59	10.61	10.62	10.56	10.56
[1]1974...	9.50	8.48	8.53	8.62	8.87	9.05	9.27	9.48	9.77	10.18	10.48	10.60	10.63
1973	8.24	7.90	7.97	8.03	8.09	8.06	8.13	8.24	8.53	8.63	8.41	8.42	8.48
1972	8.16	8.23	8.23	8.24	8.24	8.23	8.20	8.23	8.19	8.09	8.06	7.99	7.93
1971	8.56	8.74	8.39	8.46	8.45	8.62	8.75	8.76	8.76	8.59	8.48	8.38	8.38
1970	9.11	8.86	8.78	8.63	8.70	8.98	9.25	9.40	9.44	9.39	9.33	9.38	9.12
1969	7.81	7.32	7.30	7.51	7.54	7.52	7.70	7.84	7.86	8.05	8.22	8.25	8.65
1968	6.94	6.84	6.80	6.85	6.97	7.03	7.07	6.98	6.82	6.79	6.84	7.01	7.23
1967	6.23	5.97	5.82	5.85	5.83	5.96	6.15	6.26	6.33	6.40	6.52	6.72	6.93
1966	5.67	5.06	5.12	5.32	5.41	5.48	5.58	5.68	5.83	6.09	6.10	6.13	6.18
1965	4.87	4.80	4.78	4.78	4.78	4.81	4.85	4.85	4.68	4.91	4.93	4.95	5.02
1964	4.83	4.83	4.83	4.83	4.85	4.85	4.85	4.83	4.82	4.82	4.81	4.81	4.81
1963	4.86	4.91	4.89	4.88	4.87	4.85	4.84	4.84	4.83	4.84	4.83	4.84	4.85
1962	5.02	5.08	5.07	5.04	5.02	5.00	5.02	5.05	5.06	5.03	4.99	4.96	4.92
1961	5.08	5.10	5.07	5.02	5.01	5.01	5.03	5.09	5.11	5.12	5.11	5.08	5.10
1960	5.19	5.34	5.34	5.25	5.20	5.28	5.26	5.22	5.08	5.01	5.11	5.08	5.10
1959	5.05	4.87	4.89	4.85	4.86	4.96	5.04	5.08	5.09	5.18	5.28	5.26	5.28
1958	4.73	4.83	4.66	4.68	4.67	4.62	4.55	4.53	4.67	4.87	4.92	4.87	4.85
1957	4.71	4.49	4.47	4.43	4.44	4.52	4.63	4.73	4.82	4.93	4.99	5.09	5.03
1956	3.88	3.60	3.58	3.60	3.68	3.73	3.76	3.80	3.93	4.07	4.17	4.24	4.37
1955	3.53	3.45	3.47	3.48	3.49	3.50	3.51	3.52	3.56	3.59	3.59	3.58	3.62
1954	3.51	3.71	3.61	3.51	3.47	3.47	3.49	3.50	3.49	3.47	3.46	3.45	3.45
1953	3.74	3.51	3.53	3.57	3.65	3.78	3.86	3.86	3.85	3.88	3.82	3.75	3.74
1952	3.52	3.59	3.53	3.51	3.50	3.49	3.50	3.50	3.51	3.52	3.54	3.53	3.51
1951	3.41	3.17	3.16	3.23	3.35	3.40	3.49	3.53	3.50	3.46	3.50	3.56	3.61
1950	3.24	3.24	3.24	3.24	3.23	3.25	3.28	3.32	3.23	3.21	3.22	3.22	3.20
1949	3.42	3.46	3.45	3.47	3.45	3.45	3.47	3.46	3.40	3.37	3.36	3.35	3.31
1948	3.47	3.52	3.53	3.53	3.47	3.48	3.34	3.37	3.44	3.45	3.50	3.53	3.53
1947	3.24	3.13	3.12	3.15	3.16	3.17	3.21	3.18	3.17	3.23	3.35	3.44	3.52
1946	3.05	3.01	2.95	2.94	2.96	3.02	3.03	3.08	3.03	3.10	3.15	3.17	3.17
1945	3.29	3.46	3.41	3.38	3.36	3.32	3.29	3.26	3.26	3.24	3.20	3.15	3.10
1944	3.61	3.76	3.72	3.70	3.68	3.63	3.59	3.57	3.55	3.56	3.55	3.53	3.49
1943	3.91	4.16	4.08	4.01	3.96	3.91	3.88	3.81	3.81	3.83	3.82	3.83	3.82
1942	4.28	4.29	4.29	4.30	4.26	4.27	4.33	4.30	4.28	4.26	4.24	4.25	4.28
1941	4.33	4.38	4.42	4.38	4.33	4.32	4.31	4.28	4.27	4.30	4.28	4.28	4.38
1940	4.75	4.86	4.83	4.80	4.74	4.94	5.11	4.80	4.76	4.66	4.56	4.48	4.45
1939	4.96	5.12	5.05	4.89	5.15	5.07	4.91	4.84	4.85	5.00	4.88	4.85	4.92
1938	5.80	5.89	5.97	6.30	6.47	6.06	6.25	5.63	5.49	5.65	5.36	5.23	5.27
1937	5.03	4.49	4.53	4.68	4.84	4.84	4.93	4.91	4.92	5.16	5.52	5.82	5.73
1936	4.77	5.00	4.80	4.86	4.91	4.94	4.90	4.84	4.74	4.62	4.54	4.52	4.53
1935	5.75	5.98	5.95	6.20	6.13	5.94	5.77	5.67	5.58	5.53	5.54	5.43	5.30
1934	6.32	7.01	6.27	6.26	6.01	6.05	6.06	6.13	6.49	6.57	6.40	6.37	6.23
1933	7.76	8.01	8.37	8.91	9.12	7.74	7.07	6.62	6.77	7.27	7.49	7.98	7.75
1932	9.30	9.13	8.87	8.83	10.46	11.63	11.52	10.79	8.22	7.61	7.87	8.24	8.42
1931	7.62	6.41	6.38	6.44	6.72	7.15	7.36	7.08	7.47	8.07	9.04	8.93	10.42
1930	5.90	5.92	5.89	5.73	5.70	5.72	5.78	5.77	5.73	5.65	5.94	6.25	6.71
1929	5.90	5.63	5.66	5.79	5.80	5.80	5.80	5.94	5.95	6.04	6.12	6.11	5.95
1928	5.48	5.35	5.33	5.32	5.33	5.42	5.55	5.58	5.61	5.59	5.58	5.55	5.60
1927	5.48	5.61	5.59	5.54	5.48	5.50	5.55	5.55	5.48	5.42	5.38	5.35	5.32
1926	5.87	6.09	6.02	6.05	5.98	5.86	5.80	5.79	5.81	5.79	5.81	5.77	5.68
1925	6.27	6.44	6.36	6.36	6.41	6.30	6.18	6.20	6.24	6.20	6.17	6.17	6.15
1924	6.83	7.24	7.14	7.08	7.03	6.97	6.82	6.67	6.69	6.73	6.62	6.54	6.46
1923	7.24	6.98	6.97	7.09	7.17	7.17	7.21	7.34	7.38	7.38	7.46	7.40	7.38
1922	7.08	7.70	7.55	7.45	7.14	6.89	6.97	6.89	6.85	6.75	6.78	6.98	7.02
1921	8.35	8.50	8.42	8.55	8.53	8.52	8.56	8.48	8.51	8.34	8.34	7.88	7.61
1920	8.20	7.78	7.94	7.97	8.17	8.39	8.39	8.52	8.39	8.14	7.99	8.21	8.56
1919	7.25	7.12	7.20	7.15	7.23	7.09	7.04	7.06	7.13	7.27	7.34	7.54	7.77

[1]As of December 20, 1976, railroad bonds were removed from the combined Corporate Averages, retroactive to January 1974. This adjustment was necessary because of a lack of comparability to the Industrial and Public Utility averages, reflecting the limited availability of reasonably-current-coupon railroad bonds.

Source: *Moody's Municipal & Government Manual*, vol. 2 (New York: Moody's Investor's Service, Inc., 1988).

MOODY'S AVERAGE OF YIELDS ON Aaa INDUSTRIAL BONDS (IN PERCENT)

Year	Aver.	Jan.	Feb.	Mar.	Apr.	May	Jun.	Jul.	Aug.	Sep.	Oct.	Nov.	Dec.
1988	......	9.37	9.02	9.05	9.27	9.51	9.43	9.42	......	......	......	......	......
1987	9.22	8.48	8.47	8.51	8.87	9.31	9.26	9.26	9.42	9.83	10.11	9.59	9.58
1986	9.11	9.95	9.68	9.23	9.13	9.11	9.24	9.09	8.85	8.87	8.88	8.77	8.57
1985	11.06	11.67	11.64	12.04	11.67	11.26	10.71	10.74	10.87	10.86	10.80	10.38	10.08
1984	12.61	12.01	12.08	12.57	12.81	13.28	13.55	13.44	12.87	12.66	12.42	11.92	11.76
1983	11.56	11.28	11.54	11.27	11.03	10.91	11.25	11.61	11.99	11.87	11.83	12.00	12.14
1982	13.35	14.57	14.66	14.09	14.07	13.83	14.30	14.24	13.43	12.64	11.81	11.24	11.34
1981	13.70	12.31	12.75	12.81	13.33	13.81	13.35	13.87	14.36	14.92	14.97	13.99	13.93
1980	11.57	10.85	12.01	12.59	11.81	10.74	10.27	10.65	11.17	11.58	11.83	12.53	12.79
1979	9.39	9.01	9.01	9.11	9.15	9.30	9.08	8.98	8.99	9.18	9.87	10.52	10.51
1978	8.58	8.31	8.37	8.36	8.43	8.54	8.60	8.73	8.52	8.54	8.72	8.87	8.98
1977	7.86	7.77	7.86	7.92	7.86	7.87	7.77	7.78	7.82	7.76	7.88	7.93	8.04
1976	8.23	8.33	8.29	8.30	8.20	8.43	8.40	8.33	8.26	8.18	8.14	8.13	7.81
1975	8.61	8.65	8.44	8.52	8.78	8.75	8.61	8.62	8.69	8.68	8.57	8.52	8.51
1974	8.42	7.65	7.70	7.87	8.13	8.26	8.34	8.60	8.89	9.12	9.03	8.69	8.74
1973	7.28	6.96	7.04	7.12	7.08	7.13	7.23	7.28	7.56	7.48	7.43	7.50	7.50
1972	6.97	6.90	7.00	6.93	7.01	7.00	6.93	6.98	6.96	7.03	7.01	6.94	6.90
1971	7.05	7.01	6.68	6.80	6.91	7.21	7.28	7.32	7.28	7.14	7.08	6.97	6.95
1970	7.77	7.76	7.73	7.61	7.58	7.58	7.76	8.16	8.19	7.83	7.79	7.75	7.31
1969	6.93	6.47	6.53	6.73	6.81	6.69	6.88	7.03	6.95	7.04	7.21	7.21	7.58
1968	6.12	6.09	6.05	6.08	6.16	6.22	6.24	6.20	5.97	5.91	6.04	6.12	6.38
1967	5.49	5.13	5.04	5.14	5.13	5.21	5.41	5.58	5.62	5.66	5.77	6.06	6.14
1966	5.12	4.72	4.81	4.95	4.97	4.98	5.05	5.11	5.29	5.49	5.37	5.32	5.36
1965	4.45	4.36	4.35	4.35	4.36	4.39	4.44	4.46	4.47	4.50	4.52	4.58	4.67
1964	4.32	4.28	4.24	4.27	4.31	4.32	4.31	4.32	4.35	4.36	4.38	4.37	4.37
1963	4.14	4.06	4.04	4.04	4.07	4.08	4.09	4.15	4.19	4.21	4.22	4.23	4.26
1962	4.18	4.30	4.31	4.28	4.19	4.11	4.14	4.22	4.22	4.16	4.09	4.07	4.08
1961	4.21	4.16	4.09	4.04	4.09	4.11	4.20	4.28	4.29	4.32	4.29	4.27	4.33
1960	4.28	4.49	4.44	4.37	4.33	4.34	4.34	4.29	4.13	4.12	4.15	4.16	4.21
1959	4.27	4.00	4.03	4.01	4.15	4.28	4.38	4.35	4.30	4.43	4.44	4.43	4.45
1958	3.61	3.42	3.43	3.46	3.39	3.33	3.32	3.46	3.68	4.03	3.98	3.93	3.93
1957	3.76	3.68	3.53	3.54	3.52	3.63	3.89	3.91	4.01	3.97	3.93	3.94	3.58
1956	3.30	3.05	3.01	3.08	3.22	3.22	3.17	3.21	3.36	3.51	3.55	3.59	3.70
1955	3.00	2.86	2.93	2.97	2.95	2.99	3.00	3.06	3.07	3.05	3.07	3.03	3.10
1954	2.82	3.00	2.85	2.78	2.78	2.81	2.84	2.81	2.79	2.80	2.77	2.80	2.84
1953	3.12	2.97	3.01	3.05	3.16	3.29	3.37	3.19	3.12	3.17	3.06	2.91	2.88
1952	2.88	2.87	2.82	2.87	2.85	2.86	2.87	2.87	2.80	2.74	2.81	2.86	2.88
1951	2.78	2.59	2.60	2.74	2.82	2.81	2.87	2.87	2.89	2.84	2.87	2.90	2.88
1950	2.55	2.50	2.51	2.52	2.53	2.53	2.54	2.58	2.54	2.57	2.60	2.60	2.60
1949	2.58	2.60	2.61	2.61	2.61	2.63	2.64	2.59	2.59	2.53	2.52	2.53	2.51
1948	2.71	2.76	2.74	2.71	2.67	2.65	2.65	2.70	2.74	2.73	2.73	2.73	2.67
1947	2.53	2.49	2.47	2.46	2.45	2.46	2.47	2.46	2.47	2.53	2.60	2.68	2.76
1946	2.44	2.42	2.38	2.39	2.43	2.47	2.42	2.40	2.42	2.51	2.50	2.48	2.51
1945	2.49	2.54	2.50	2.47	2.50	2.52	2.51	2.49	2.47	2.48	2.46	2.48	2.48
1944	2.57	2.49	2.53	2.57	2.59	2.58	2.59	2.59	2.58	2.58	2.58	2.59	2.56
1943	2.49	2.54	2.52	2.51	2.51	2.49	2.48	2.46	2.46	2.47	2.48	2.50	2.50
1942	2.57	2.59	2.59	2.61	2.56	2.57	2.60	2.60	2.57	2.56	2.54	2.54	2.56
1941	2.50	2.36	2.44	2.51	2.57	2.57	2.57	2.52	2.49	2.51	2.48	2.48	2.56
1940	2.44	2.47	2.44	2.41	2.38	2.60	2.57	2.57	2.52	2.45	2.40	2.34	2.28
1939	2.67	2.62	2.61	2.63	2.69	2.65	2.65	2.57	2.59	2.90	2.82	2.74	2.72
1938	2.85	2.87	2.93	2.92	2.96	2.85	2.85	2.86	2.82	2.87	2.82	2.74	2.72
1937	3.06	2.90	3.05	3.05	3.10	3.07	3.08	3.07	3.06	3.01	2.99	2.94	2.91
1936	3.03	3.13	3.12	3.05	3.05	3.07	3.08	3.04	3.04	3.06	3.01	2.95	2.99
1935	3.53	3.82	3.72	3.69	3.65	3.62	3.57	3.50	3.53	3.48	3.31	3.24	3.25
1934	4.02	4.37	4.23	4.19	4.13	4.04	3.93	3.87	3.91	3.93	3.89	3.85	3.84
1933	4.53	4.50	4.56	4.74	4.88	4.74	4.50	4.42	4.35	4.39	4.36	4.46	4.46
1932	5.09	5.45	5.37	5.18	5.26	5.35	5.47	5.30	4.96	4.75	4.67	4.68	4.64
1931	4.71	4.59	4.57	4.51	4.54	4.54	4.49	4.47	4.47	4.65	5.12	5.07	5.50
1930	4.69	4.80	4.84	4.76	4.71	4.72	4.69	4.64	4.60	4.57	4.57	4.64	4.68
1929	4.86	4.77	4.81	4.83	4.82	4.85	4.90	4.91	4.90	4.92	4.91	4.91	4.80
1928	4.73	4.66	4.66	4.68	4.66	4.69	4.73	4.79	4.82	4.79	4.77	4.76	4.77
1927	4.76	4.85	4.84	4.81	4.80	4.77	4.76	4.78	4.77	4.75	4.68	4.68	4.64
1926	4.93	5.03	5.01	5.04	5.00	4.95	4.93	4.89	4.88	4.88	4.83	4.85	4.86
1925	5.11	5.19	5.19	5.18	5.10	5.10	5.11	5.09	5.12	5.10	5.03	5.04	5.05
1924	5.28	5.33	5.34	5.35	5.34	5.33	5.29	5.26	5.24	5.25	5.23	5.21	5.21
1923	5.37	5.33	5.33	5.38	5.42	5.42	5.41	5.40	5.38	5.36	5.33	5.31	5.31
1922	5.35	5.60	5.52	5.45	5.38	5.38	5.37	5.27	5.23	5.19	5.21	5.26	5.37
1921	6.15	6.34	6.25	6.23	6.21	6.22	6.28	6.26	6.16	6.16	6.15	5.87	5.65
1920	6.19	5.74	5.83	5.91	6.01	6.21	6.47	6.44	6.41	6.42	6.26	6.26	6.35
1919	5.55	5.53	5.51	5.53	5.58	5.53	5.44	5.45	5.50	5.57	5.60	5.65	5.69

Source: *Moody's Municipal & Government Manual*, vol. 2 (New York: Moody's Investor's Service, Inc., 1988).

MOODY'S AVERAGE OF YIELDS ON Aa INDUSTRIAL BONDS (IN PERCENT)

Year	Aver.	Jan.	Feb.	Mar.	Apr.	May	Jun.	Jul.	Aug.	Sep.	Oct.	Nov.	Dec.
1988	.....	9.65	9.29	9.26	9.41	9.66	9.75	9.76	.....	.....	.....	.....	.....
1987	9.59	9.09	9.04	9.04	9.15	9.56	9.69	9.58	9.68	10.03	10.36	9.91	9.87
1986	9.63	10.47	10.27	9.82	9.55	9.47	9.61	9.51	9.41	9.45	9.42	9.38	9.23
1985	11.57	12.18	12.10	12.32	12.22	11.95	11.24	11.29	11.29	11.24	11.29	11.03	10.69
1984	12.95	12.39	12.37	12.78	13.02	13.54	13.76	13.80	13.26	13.12	12.85	12.32	12.23
1983	12.00	11.94	12.14	11.97	11.69	11.46	11.66	11.93	12.26	12.19	12.09	12.25	12.36
1982	14.03	15.01	15.09	14.85	14.68	14.53	14.73	14.74	14.25	13.51	12.73	12.10	12.12
1981	14.19	13.01	13.13	13.19	13.55	14.14	13.92	14.16	14.69	15.32	15.35	15.04	14.77
1980	11.99	11.16	12.26	12.93	12.63	11.82	11.03	10.89	11.45	11.85	12.02	12.71	13.18
1979	9.65	9.24	9.25	9.33	9.37	9.52	9.36	9.26	9.31	9.46	10.07	10.85	10.82
1978	8.74	8.42	8.50	8.53	8.59	8.66	8.71	8.87	8.80	8.75	8.87	9.02	9.10
1977	8.04	7.90	8.06	8.07	8.05	8.06	8.00	7.92	7.97	7.97	8.08	8.20	8.25
1976	8.59	8.87	8.87	8.88	8.78	8.78	8.71	8.59	8.48	8.39	8.36	8.30	8.04
1975	8.90	8.81	8.60	8.67	8.89	8.96	8.91	8.88	8.94	9.06	9.08	9.00	8.99
1974	8.64	7.85	7.90	8.00	8.29	8.44	8.57	8.85	9.03	9.26	9.35	9.13	9.03
1973	7.40	7.04	7.12	7.20	7.19	7.19	7.26	7.36	7.72	7.73	7.67	7.67	7.69
1972	7.11	7.08	7.13	7.09	7.19	7.18	7.11	7.17	7.10	7.10	7.12	7.02	6.97
1971	7.23	7.18	6.91	7.00	7.08	7.33	7.44	7.49	7.50	7.32	7.27	7.16	7.13
1970	7.94	7.85	7.84	7.79	7.76	7.92	8.35	8.32	8.03	7.97	7.92	7.96	7.51
1969	7.05	6.60	6.67	6.85	6.93	6.83	7.02	7.11	7.06	7.18	7.34	7.37	7.69
1968	6.24	6.17	6.13	6.17	6.24	6.32	6.37	6.33	6.08	6.07	6.18	6.28	6.52
1967	5.55	5.20	5.12	5.17	5.17	5.27	5.49	5.60	5.63	5.73	5.85	6.12	6.24
1966	5.15	4.73	4.82	4.96	4.99	5.01	5.09	5.16	5.32	5.52	5.45	5.38	5.39
1965	4.50	4.42	4.41	4.43	4.43	4.45	4.48	4.51	4.52	4.55	4.56	4.60	4.69
1964	4.41	4.39	4.35	4.37	4.43	4.44	4.43	4.40	4.40	4.41	4.42	4.42	4.44
1963	4.29	4.23	4.23	4.24	4.27	4.27	4.28	4.30	4.31	4.32	4.34	4.35	4.36
1962	4.30	4.38	4.38	4.34	4.28	4.24	4.25	4.32	4.33	4.29	4.26	4.24	4.25
1961	4.33	4.29	4.22	4.18	4.26	4.30	4.35	4.38	4.41	4.40	4.37	4.37	4.40
1960	4.39	4.59	4.54	4.46	4.43	4.44	4.43	4.41	4.28	4.24	4.28	4.30	4.33
1959	4.36	4.10	4.13	4.10	4.18	4.33	4.45	4.45	4.41	4.57	4.58	4.53	4.54
1958	3.78	3.67	3.64	3.64	3.61	3.60	3.57	3.62	3.75	4.09	4.09	4.05	4.06
1957	3.89	3.84	3.74	3.66	3.63	3.70	3.92	3.96	4.04	4.07	4.09	4.12	3.85
1956	3.39	3.12	3.10	3.13	3.27	3.30	3.29	3.32	3.45	3.58	3.63	3.68	3.78
1955	3.11	3.01	3.06	3.08	3.08	3.10	3.09	3.10	3.17	3.16	3.14	3.12	3.15
1954	3.02	3.13	3.06	3.00	3.00	3.01	3.04	3.02	3.01	3.01	3.00	2.99	2.99
1953	3.23	3.00	3.05	3.10	3.21	3.33	3.42	3.37	3.32	3.33	3.27	3.19	3.17
1952	2.93	2.92	2.89	2.91	2.89	2.87	2.90	2.92	2.96	2.97	2.98	2.97	2.94
1951	2.82	2.64	2.64	2.76	2.85	2.84	2.84	2.89	2.83	2.81	2.85	2.88	2.91
1950	2.59	2.54	2.54	2.55	2.56	2.56	2.58	2.61	2.58	2.61	2.63	2.63	2.64
1949	2.64	2.70	2.69	2.68	2.68	2.68	2.69	2.64	2.59	2.57	2.58	2.57	2.56
1948	2.78	2.78	2.80	2.78	2.74	2.72	2.73	2.77	2.81	2.81	2.83	2.79	2.75
1947	2.58	2.53	2.52	2.52	2.51	2.51	2.51	2.53	2.53	2.57	2.66	2.75	2.82
1946	2.52	2.48	2.46	2.46	2.50	2.51	2.49	2.49	2.50	2.56	2.58	2.58	2.57
1945	2.56	2.60	2.56	2.56	2.57	2.56	2.56	2.57	2.59	2.57	2.55	2.55	2.54
1944	2.66	2.67	2.68	2.69	2.69	2.69	2.68	2.66	2.64	2.65	2.66	2.63	2.61
1943	2.68	2.71	2.68	2.68	2.69	2.68	2.68	2.64	2.63	2.66	2.67	2.69	2.71
1942	2.73	2.67	2.69	2.72	2.69	2.73	2.76	2.76	2.77	2.77	2.73	2.71	2.73
1941	2.67	2.63	2.73	2.75	2.83	2.77	2.68	2.62	2.62	2.62	2.58	2.57	2.67
1940	2.67	2.72	2.67	2.66	2.62	2.72	2.76	2.69	2.69	2.70	2.70	2.62	2.53
1939	2.86	2.87	2.83	2.83	2.81	2.77	2.74	2.68	2.73	3.26	3.07	2.86	2.83
1938	3.05	3.13	3.11	3.02	3.11	3.02	3.09	3.04	2.99	3.04	3.02	3.00	2.99
1937	3.20	3.08	3.19	3.25	3.36	3.25	3.18	3.19	3.18	3.21	3.23	3.14	3.19
1936	3.18	3.20	3.24	3.27	3.27	3.22	3.24	3.20	3.17	3.15	3.10	3.07	3.07
1935	3.78	4.15	4.12	4.05	3.96	3.94	3.90	3.71	3.63	3.61	3.57	3.39	3.29
1934	4.20	4.47	4.45	4.33	4.18	4.07	4.05	4.12	4.14	4.18	4.15	4.09	4.165
1933	4.89	5.26	5.26	5.45	5.59	5.19	4.74	4.53	4.46	4.53	4.47	4.59	4.60
1932	6.06	6.08	6.16	6.03	6.27	6.55	6.77	6.61	6.09	5.72	5.51	5.44	5.43
1931	5.07	4.85	4.81	4.80	4.86	4.91	4.97	4.88	4.88	5.06	5.40	5.41	6.06
1930	4.86	4.92	4.92	4.89	4.84	4.85	4.84	4.82	4.79	4.79	4.80	4.88	4.96
1929	4.96	4.82	4.91	4.94	4.94	4.95	5.01	5.01	5.00	5.01	5.02	4.98	4.91
1928	4.82	4.73	4.74	4.71	4.72	4.77	4.83	4.91	4.89	4.81	4.79	4.76	4.74
1927	4.86	4.94	4.97	4.93	4.87	4.85	4.88	4.90	4.83	4.90	4.89	4.90	4.84
1926	5.06	5.16	5.12	5.15	5.09	5.03	5.01	5.04	5.04	5.05	5.05	5.04	4.97
1925	5.33	5.45	5.34	5.37	5.36	5.32	5.30	5.30	5.36	5.33	5.31	5.27	5.29
1924	5.57	5.64	5.60	5.60	5.63	5.61	5.56	5.56	5.56	5.55	5.53	5.51	5.52
1923	5.73	5.55	5.65	5.81	5.83	5.77	5.76	5.78	5.75	5.73	5.74	5.70	5.71
1922	5.66	5.96	5.89	5.86	5.70	5.64	5.68	5.63	5.50	5.41	5.50	5.59	5.57
1921	6.69	6.86	6.76	6.84	6.87	6.84	6.92	6.90	6.85	6.73	6.51	6.20	5.97
1920	6.69	6.05	6.22	6.30	6.57	6.87	6.90	6.86	6.90	6.84	6.78	6.84	7.13
1919	5.97	6.01	6.04	5.98	5.94	5.89	5.84	5.84	5.96	5.99	5.94	6.00	6.15

Source: *Moody's Municipal & Government Manual*, vol. 2 (New York: Moody's Investor's Service, Inc., 1988).

MOODY'S AVERAGE OF YIELDS ON A INDUSTRIAL BONDS (IN PERCENT)

Year	Aver.	Jan.	Feb.	Mar.	Apr.	May	Jun.	Jul.	Aug.	Sep.	Oct.	Nov.	Dec.
1988	.....	10.09	9.79	9.68	9.81	10.00	10.05	10.05	.....	.....	.....	.....	.....
1987	9.88	9.51	9.39	9.33	9.34	9.73	9.93	9.86	9.95	10.22	10.62	10.43	10.25
1986	10.30	11.27	11.07	10.81	10.51	10.28	10.29	10.14	9.97	9.95	9.91	9.73	9.70
1985	12.09	12.61	12.51	12.84	12.71	12.28	11.83	11.77	11.87	11.85	11.85	11.58	11.39
1984	13.43	12.85	12.81	13.21	13.38	13.84	14.22	14.30	13.82	13.70	13.42	12.94	12.72
1983	12.53	12.81	12.77	12.36	12.11	11.86	12.12	12.41	12.77	12.80	12.68	12.79	12.88
1982	15.00	15.54	15.86	15.73	15.58	15.35	15.72	15.98	15.56	14.73	13.88	13.15	12.88
1981	14.62	13.39	13.64	13.80	14.15	14.60	14.43	14.52	14.94	15.55	15.73	15.43	15.21
1980	12.44	11.48	12.42	13.29	13.23	12.18	11.57	11.63	11.93	12.49	12.51	13.06	13.43
1979	9.91	9.54	9.51	9.59	9.65	9.70	9.64	9.52	9.56	9.69	10.26	11.11	11.12
1978	8.94	8.60	8.62	8.69	8.76	8.87	8.96	9.14	9.04	8.94	9.06	9.27	9.35
1977	8.36	8.28	8.33	8.40	8.39	8.39	8.33	8.28	8.30	8.27	8.35	8.46	8.49
1976	8.88	9.18	9.15	9.12	9.00	9.00	8.97	8.91	8.82	8.72	8.66	8.63	8.43
1975	9.21	9.25	9.03	9.01	9.22	9.34	9.23	9.22	9.24	9.28	9.28	9.24	9.23
1974	8.90	7.98	8.07	8.19	8.45	8.66	8.82	9.13	9.31	9.62	9.80	9.44	9.31
1973	7.63	7.26	7.35	7.44	7.44	7.41	7.46	7.64	8.02	7.99	7.80	7.88	7.89
1972	7.36	7.38	7.39	7.31	7.43	7.43	7.37	7.39	7.35	7.35	7.34	7.29	7.23
1971	7.61	7.64	7.31	7.44	7.54	7.67	7.76	7.81	7.84	7.66	7.62	7.53	7.48
1970	8.33	8.14	8.12	7.95	8.01	8.25	8.64	8.69	8.56	8.55	8.50	8.47	8.06
1969	7.26	6.74	6.83	7.04	7.13	6.98	7.10	7.24	7.27	7.42	7.65	7.72	7.95
1968	6.39	6.30	6.25	6.27	6.40	6.46	6.50	6.49	6.24	6.23	6.33	6.45	6.71
1967	5.72	5.43	5.27	5.36	5.35	5.49	5.61	5.75	5.81	5.91	6.03	6.27	6.37
1966	5.26	4.80	4.87	5.03	5.08	5.06	5.23	5.31	5.41	5.63	5.56	5.53	5.57
1965	4.55	4.48	4.47	4.47	4.48	4.49	4.52	4.56	4.57	4.59	4.61	4.65	4.73
1964	4.47	4.43	4.43	4.43	4.49	4.49	4.49	4.48	4.47	4.46	4.47	4.47	4.49
1963	4.37	4.33	4.32	4.32	4.34	4.34	4.35	4.37	4.38	4.41	4.42	4.42	4.41
1962	4.43	4.52	4.53	4.49	4.44	4.40	4.40	4.47	4.45	4.39	4.35	4.35	4.35
1961	4.50	4.49	4.40	4.35	4.41	4.45	4.54	4.58	4.59	4.59	4.56	4.53	4.63
1960	4.58	4.71	4.69	4.64	4.60	4.63	4.60	4.58	4.49	4.49	4.51	4.53	4.54
1959	4.49	4.23	4.28	4.26	4.31	4.42	4.51	4.59	4.55	4.69	4.70	4.70	4.69
1958	3.91	3.78	3.72	3.75	3.76	3.76	3.73	3.76	3.87	4.18	4.21	4.23	4.21
1957	4.03	3.95	3.86	3.83	3.84	3.89	4.00	4.08	4.19	4.19	4.23	4.25	4.03
1956	3.47	3.19	3.16	3.21	3.35	3.37	3.39	3.39	3.51	3.62	3.71	3.79	3.90
1955	3.16	3.07	3.09	3.11	3.12	3.13	3.16	3.18	3.22	3.24	3.21	3.18	3.21
1954	3.09	3.20	3.12	3.05	3.07	3.07	3.11	3.13	3.09	3.07	3.08	3.07	3.07
1953	3.27	3.04	3.09	3.15	3.25	3.38	3.47	3.41	3.34	3.35	3.29	3.23	3.24
1952	3.01	3.03	3.01	3.00	2.98	3.00	3.00	2.99	3.01	3.01	3.03	3.03	3.01
1951	2.90	2.68	2.69	2.81	2.90	2.92	2.98	2.98	2.92	2.90	2.95	2.99	3.02
1950	2.66	2.62	2.63	2.63	2.63	2.64	2.64	2.66	2.69	2.66	2.68	2.70	2.69
1949	2.71	2.78	2.76	2.75	2.75	2.75	2.74	2.73	2.67	2.65	2.65	2.64	2.64
1948	2.86	2.90	2.89	2.87	2.82	2.81	2.79	2.83	2.88	2.87	2.89	2.83	2.84
1947	2.66	2.61	2.60	2.58	2.59	2.60	2.59	2.60	2.61	2.67	2.76	2.83	2.92
1946	2.60	2.56	2.52	2.51	2.54	2.59	2.60	2.59	2.60	2.67	2.68	2.68	2.66
1945	2.69	2.73	2.71	2.69	2.70	2.69	2.68	2.69	2.69	2.68	2.67	2.65	2.64
1944	2.81	2.86	2.85	2.83	2.81	2.81	2.79	2.79	2.82	2.85	2.81	2.79	2.74
1943	2.83	2.87	2.84	2.81	2.82	2.83	2.81	2.79	2.78	2.82	2.83	2.86	2.89
1942	2.98	3.01	3.00	3.04	3.03	3.05	3.05	3.03	2.97	2.94	2.91	2.91	2.90
1941	2.96	3.07	3.05	3.05	3.08	3.03	2.97	2.89	2.87	2.86	2.84	2.83	2.94
1940	3.19	3.24	3.24	3.22	3.19	3.25	3.27	3.20	3.18	3.17	3.16	3.09	3.07
1939	3.41	3.46	3.44	3.46	3.51	3.44	3.37	3.32	3.32	3.61	3.46	3.30	3.26
1938	3.61	3.67	3.72	3.71	3.76	3.63	3.63	3.56	3.51	3.58	3.49	3.48	3.52
1937	3.68	3.53	3.61	3.73	3.76	3.68	3.65	3.65	3.57	3.64	3.75	3.78	3.79
1936	3.71	3.88	3.81	3.77	3.78	3.75	3.74	3.72	3.68	3.65	3.61	3.55	3.53
1935	4.23	4.51	4.40	4.39	4.42	4.32	4.25	4.17	4.13	4.10	4.06	4.00	4.01
1934	4.72	5.08	4.91	4.79	4.70	4.69	4.64	4.59	4.67	4.72	4.67	4.62	4.61
1933	5.56	5.85	5.96	6.24	6.21	5.83	5.55	5.27	5.08	5.06	5.12	5.22	5.36
1932	6.94	7.48	7.38	7.10	7.21	8.00	7.84	7.40	6.49	6.14	6.14	6.08	6.01
1931	6.51	5.62	5.68	5.73	6.00	6.15	6.35	6.10	6.49	6.98	7.48	7.47	7.96
1930	5.35	5.42	5.42	5.34	5.26	5.26	5.30	5.26	5.19	5.14	5.36	5.52	5.77
1929	5.38	5.16	5.19	5.31	5.33	5.36	5.41	5.40	5.45	5.55	5.49	5.53	5.41
1928	5.12	5.08	5.09	5.12	5.08	5.13	5.19	5.18	5.18	5.14	5.12	5.04	5.14
1927	5.17	5.26	5.25	5.23	5.19	5.19	5.18	5.17	5.17	5.15	5.12	5.10	5.08
1926	5.40	5.49	5.48	5.50	5.42	5.31	5.37	5.37	5.38	5.38	5.39	5.33	5.32
1925	5.63	5.71	5.65	5.71	5.70	5.64	5.59	5.59	5.62	5.62	5.62	5.60	5.54
1924	5.85	5.99	5.99	5.96	5.99	5.87	5.83	5.80	5.78	5.79	5.76	5.72	5.70
1923	5.98	5.90	5.92	6.01	6.00	5.93	5.96	6.00	5.97	5.95	6.00	6.02	6.01
1922	6.01	6.41	6.32	6.23	6.08	5.90	5.93	5.83	5.88	5.76	5.85	5.91	5.94
1921	7.21	7.38	7.30	7.40	7.42	7.41	7.41	7.44	7.38	7.22	6.99	6.68	6.45
1920	6.94	6.30	6.59	6.62	6.73	6.92	6.96	6.95	7.17	7.11	7.18	7.28	7.52
1919	6.20	6.27	6.30	6.29	6.26	6.19	6.09	5.99	6.13	6.11	6.09	6.17	6.475

Source: *Moody's Municipal & Government Manual,* vol. 2 (New York: Moody's Investor's Service, Inc., 1988).

MOODY'S AVERAGE OF YIELDS ON Baa INDUSTRIAL BONDS (IN PERCENT)

Year	Aver.	Jan.	Feb.	Mar.	Apr.	May	Jun.	Jul.	Aug.	Sep.	Oct.	Nov.	Dec.
1988	.....	10.79	10.59	10.45	10.56	10.71	10.74	10.70	.....	.....	.....	.....	.....
1987	10.62	10.17	10.06	10.02	10.24	10.62	10.58	.10.59	10.70	11.04	11.33	11.05	11.02
1986	10.77	11.63	11.48	11.07	10.74	10.55	10.65	10.64	10.66	10.46	10.51	10.44	10.45
1985	12.46	13.15	13.00	13.18	12.90	12.68	12.14	12.17	12.27	12.24	12.20	11.93	11.67
1984	13.84	13.24	13.13	13.42	13.78	14.21	14.60	14.79	14.48	14.19	13.71	13.24	13.34
1983	12.90	13.33	13.27	12.89	12.52	12.12	12.57	12.76	13.07	12.99	12.95	13.10	13.27
1982	15.77	16.36	16.51	16.47	16.55	16.60	16.63	16.50	16.28	15.57	14.35	13.79	13.58
1981	15.48	14.76	14.87	14.84	14.98	15.24	15.29	15.35	15.48	16.08	16.50	16.28	16.07
1980	13.39	11.92	12.73	13.64	14.03	13.41	12.78	12.54	12.79	13.33	14.03	14.48	14.98
1979	10.42	9.96	9.89	9.98	10.11	10.24	10.19	10.11	10.20	10.29	10.91	11.50	11.61
1978	9.35	9.07	9.11	9.07	9.10	9.27	9.40	9.45	9.43	9.36	9.49	9.66	9.79
1977	8.87	8.99	9.04	9.04	8.97	8.88	8.80	8.75	8.72	8.74	8.77	8.84	8.90
1976	9.67	10.26	10.17	10.07	9.92	9.81	9.76	9.75	9.61	9.33	9.17	9.12	9.03
1975	10.26	10.02	9.98	10.01	10.30	10.42	10.39	10.30	10.31	10.35	10.34	10.33	10.33
1974	9.14	8.38	8.37	8.42	8.69	8.85	9.03	9.23	9.39	9.78	9.92	9.81	9.85
1973	8.07	7.80	7.85	7.94	8.00	7.89	7.99	8.10	8.34	8.35	8.12	8.17	8.29
1972	7.99	8.01	8.02	8.07	8.07	8.10	8.01	8.01	8.00	7.95	7.96	7.86	7.80
1971	8.37	8.46	8.04	8.18	8.19	8.51	8.71	8.74	8.60	8.43	8.34	8.16	8.13
1970	9.00	8.84	8.76	8.57	8.65	8.82	9.05	9.22	9.32	9.29	9.22	9.28	8.92
1969	7.76	7.29	7.26	7.44	7.41	7.47	7.65	7.76	7.87	8.02	8.17	8.15	8.58
1968	6.90	6.79	6.79	6.81	6.86	6.95	7.05	6.98	6.75	6.76	6.82	7.01	7.25
1967	6.21	6.02	5.90	5.90	5.81	5.87	6.06	6.24	6.31	6.43	6.53	6.67	6.82
1966	5.68	5.09	5.14	5.29	5.32	5.44	5.61	5.74	5.92	6.18	6.14	6.13	6.18
1965	4.92	4.85	4.84	4.83	4.88	4.88	4.91	4.93	4.95	4.96	4.98	5.00	5.05
1964	4.87	4.90	4.88	4.88	4.89	4.91	4.91	4.88	4.85	4.84	4.84	4.84	4.85
1963	4.90	4.90	4.89	4.90	4.91	4.91	4.89	4.90	4.90	4.89	4.89	4.89	4.90
1962	4.98	5.07	5.05	4.96	4.93	4.93	5.00	5.06	5.04	4.96	4.91	4.91	4.90
1961	5.10	5.13	5.08	5.02	5.05	5.05	5.06	5.12	5.13	5.14	5.16	5.13	5.10
1960	5.11	5.17	5.17	5.08	5.06	5.20	5.20	5.17	5.05	4.99	5.05	5.05	5.11
1959	4.91	4.77	4.80	4.76	4.77	4.80	4.87	4.92	4.96	5.02	5.07	5.09	5.12
1958	4.59	4.75	4.63	4.60	4.56	4.50	4.44	4.39	4.44	4.64	4.71	4.72	4.74
1957	4.79	4.62	4.64	4.57	4.55	4.60	4.73	4.81	4.90	5.00	5.03	5.04	4.97
1956	3.84	3.55	3.52	3.55	3.65	3.69	3.71	3.75	3.89	4.02	4.13	4.22	4.42
1955	3.47	3.38	3.40	3.41	3.42	3.44	3.45	3.47	3.53	3.54	3.53	3.53	3.56
1954	3.40	3.59	3.46	3.35	3.31	3.34	3.39	3.43	3.40	3.38	3.37	3.36	3.36
1953	3.55	3.27	3.29	3.34	3.44	3.54	3.65	3.69	3.70	3.72	3.68	3.63	3.64
1952	3.20	3.18	3.15	3.16	3.17	3.16	3.16	3.17	3.18	3.21	3.25	3.29	3.28
1951	3.04	2.84	2.84	2.91	2.98	3.02	3.10	3.13	3.11	3.09	3.12	3.15	3.18
1950	2.86	2.86	2.85	2.83	2.85	2.85	2.86	2.88	2.86	2.85	2.86	2.86	2.85
1949	3.02	3.10	3.09	3.07	3.06	3.05	3.06	3.03	2.99	2.96	2.96	2.93	2.90
1948	3.13	3.18	3.18	3.19	3.16	3.10	3.04	3.04	3.11	3.12	3.16	3.16	3.15
1947	2.92	2.87	2.85	2.86	2.85	2.83	2.86	2.88	2.90	2.92	3.01	3.08	3.16
1946	2.84	2.83	2.80	2.80	2.81	2.84	2.83	2.83	2.80	2.83	2.86	2.88	2.91
1945	2.96	3.02	2.99	2.99	2.98	2.96	2.97	2.97	2.98	2.95	2.93	2.89	2.88
1944	3.15	3.30	3.25	3.24	3.24	3.17	3.09	3.10	3.11	3.10	3.10	3.08	3.05
1943	3.38	3.49	3.47	3.48	3.44	3.42	3.38	3.30	3.29	3.31	3.31	3.33	3.33
1942	3.55	3.62	3.63	3.62	3.54	3.50	3.49	3.47	3.49	3.54	3.56	3.54	3.56
1941	3.65	3.78	3.78	3.76	3.74	3.70	3.67	3.61	3.58	3.54	3.48	3.50	3.60
1940	4.08	4.13	4.11	4.07	4.02	4.22	4.38	4.20	4.15	4.06	3.96	3.88	3.82
1939	4.25	4.27	4.27	4.25	4.39	4.33	4.22	4.20	4.19	4.37	4.27	4.14	4.15
1938	4.49	4.48	4.53	4.67	4.73	4.54	4.60	4.44	4.39	4.49	4.37	4.32	4.365
1937	4.25	3.94	3.99	4.13	4.21	4.16	4.16	4.16	4.12	4.22	4.49	4.69	4.70
1936	4.07	4.16	4.13	4.13	4.15	4.13	4.12	4.11	4.06	4.02	3.99	.3.93	3.96
1935	4.51	4.74	4.70	4.67	4.68	4.57	4.54	4.43	4.45	4.44	4.36	4.30	4.28
1934	5.15	5.54	5.31	5.28	5.09	5.06	5.03	4.98	5.13	5.22	5.17	5.05	4.88
1933	6.36	7.04	7.54	7.99	7.71	6.64	6.03	5.59	5.44	5.49	5.52	5.68	5.70
1932	8.76	9.78	9.16	8.53	9.35	10.30	10.64	10.29	7.93	7.21	7.25	7.39	7.32
1931	8.03	6.59	6.55	6.72	7.17	7.93	8.08	7.65	7.88	8.61	9.46	9.22	10.50
1930	6.09	6.21	6.11	5.91	5.82	5.84	5.99	5.95	5.88	5.81	6.21	6.43	6.90
1929	6.02	5.82	5.79	5.88	5.84	5.89	6.05	5.98	6.01	6.13	6.19	6.35	6.25
1928	5.71	5.54	5.49	5.51	5.55	5.68	5.80	5.86	5.84	5.80	5.79	5.84	5.85
1927	5.61	5.80	5.75	5.63	5.54	5.60	5.63	5.63	5.64	5.56	5.49	5.50	5.52
1926	6.11	6.29	6.23	6.22	6.21	6.12	6.06	6.09	6.04	6.05	6.06	6.06	5.89
1925	6.37	6.54	6.46	6.45	6.47	6.48	6.34	6.35	6.32	6.29	6.21	6.25	6.23
1924	6.87	7.16	7.11	7.08	7.02	6.96	6.87	6.80	6.84	6.75	6.71	6.60	6.55
1923	7.06	7.02	6.99	6.97	6.93	6.84	6.90	7.10	7.17	7.15	7.21	7.24	7.21
1922	7.12	7.50	7.51	7.45	7.15	6.92	6.97	6.92	6.91	6.81	6.86	7.16	7.22
1921	8.10	8.50	8.23	8.42	8.33	8.16	8.14	8.07	8.11	8.14	8.07	7.68	7.36
1920	7.94	7.48	7.63	7.82	7.81	8.04	8.12	8.23	8.12	7.83	7.64	8.06	8.54
1919	6.99	6.96	7.04	7.00	7.07	6.97	6.97	6.78	6.78	6.83	6.90	6.97	7.35

The tables above give the monthly average yields of 37 long-term industrial bonds (7 **Aaa**, 10 **Aa**, 10 **A** and 10 **Baa**). Prior to 1928, 20 bonds were used. All yields are calculated to maturity dates and the list of bonds used is adjusted when required to reflect rating changes or other reasons so that each of the series is comparable throughout the entire period. Average yields for the periods presented are not intended to be indicative of yields which may prevail in the future.

Source: *Moody's Municipal & Government Manual*, vol. 2 (New York: Moody's Investor's Service, Inc., 1988).

Part III: Economic Data
_____

Summary of National Income and Product Series, Annually and Quarterly
1929–87   Annual Gross National Product in Current Dollars
                       Personal consumption expenditure, gross private domestic investment, net exports, government
                       purchase of goods and service, final sales, percent change in GNP, p. 675.
1960–87   Quarterly Gross National Product in Current Dollars
                       Personal consumption expenditure, gross private domestic investment, net exports, government
                       purchase of goods and service, final sales, percent change in GNP, p. 675.
1929–87   Annual Gross National Product in Constant (1982) Dollars
                       Personal consumption expenditure, gross private domestic investment, net exports, government
                       purchase of goods and service, final sales, percent change in GNP, p. 677.
1960–87   Quarterly Gross National Product in Constant (1982) Dollars
                       Personal consumption expenditure, gross private domestic investment, net exports, government
                       purchase of goods and service, final sales, percent change in GNP, p. 677.

Price Indexes
1959–87   Annual Price Indexes and GNP Implicit Price Deflator
                       GNP, personal consumption expenditures, fixed investment, exports, imports, government purchases
                       of goods and services, final sales, percent change in GNP, p. 679.
1959–87   Quarterly Price Indexes and GNP Implicit Price Deflator
                       GNP, personal consumption expenditures, fixed investment, exports, imports, government purchases
                       of goods and services, final sales, percent change in GNP, p. 679.
1961–84   Annual Data for Consumer Prices, p. 681.
1981–84   Quarterly Data for Consumer Prices, p. 681.

National Income and Disposition of Personal Income
1929–87   Annual Data for National Income and Disposition of Personal Income
                       National income, compensation of employees, proprietors' income, rental income, corporate profits,
                       net interest, DPI, savings as percentage of DPI, DPI in constant (1982) dollars, p. 682.
1960–87   Quarterly Data for National Income and Disposition of Personal Income
                       National income, compensation of employees, proprietors' income, rental income, corporate profits,
                       net interest, DPI, savings as percentage of DPI, DPI in constant (1982) dollars, p. 682.
_____

Summary National Income and Product Series: Annually, 1929–87, and Quarterly, 1960–87

Table 1.—Gross National Product

[Billions of dollars; quarterly data are seasonally adjusted at annual rates]

Year and quarter	GNP	Personal consumption expenditures				Gross private domestic investment				Net exports			Government purchases of goods and services			Final sales	Gross domestic purchases	Percent change from preceding period		
		Total	Durable goods	Nondurable goods	Services	Total	Nonresidential	Residential	CBI	Net	Exports	Imports	Total	Federal	State and local			GNP	Final sales	Gross domestic purchases
1929	103.9	77.3	9.2	37.7	30.4	16.7	11.0	4.0	1.7	1.1	7.1	5.9	8.9	1.5	7.4	102.2	102.8	...	...	...
1930	91.1	69.9	7.2	34.0	28.8	10.6	8.6	2.4	−.4	1.0	5.5	4.5	9.5	1.6	7.9	91.5	90.1	−12.3	−10.5	−12.3
1931	76.4	60.5	5.5	29.0	26.1	5.9	5.3	1.8	−1.1	.5	3.7	3.2	9.5	1.7	7.8	77.5	75.9	−16.2	−15.2	−15.8
1932	58.5	48.6	3.6	22.7	22.2	1.1	2.9	.8	−2.5	.4	2.5	2.1	8.4	1.6	6.7	61.0	58.1	−23.4	−21.4	−23.4
1933	56.0	45.8	3.5	22.3	20.1	1.6	2.5	.6	−1.6	.4	2.4	2.1	8.3	2.2	6.1	57.6	55.7	−4.2	−5.5	−4.2
1934	65.6	51.4	4.2	26.7	20.4	3.5	3.3	.9	−.7	.6	3.0	2.4	10.1	3.2	6.9	66.3	65.0	17.0	15.1	16.7
1935	72.8	55.8	5.1	29.3	21.3	6.6	4.3	1.3	1.1	.1	3.3	3.2	10.2	3.1	7.2	71.7	72.7	11.0	8.2	11.9
1936	83.1	62.0	6.3	32.9	22.8	8.7	5.8	1.7	1.3	.1	3.6	3.5	12.2	5.1	7.1	81.8	83.0	14.1	14.1	14.2
1937	91.3	66.7	6.9	35.2	24.5	12.1	7.5	2.1	2.5	.4	4.7	4.3	12.1	4.8	7.3	88.7	90.8	9.8	8.4	9.5
1938	85.4	64.1	5.7	34.0	24.4	6.7	5.5	2.1	−.9	1.3	4.4	3.1	13.2	5.5	7.7	86.3	84.0	−6.5	−2.7	−7.5
1939	91.3	67.0	6.7	35.1	25.2	9.5	6.1	3.0	.4	1.2	4.6	3.4	13.6	5.2	8.3	90.9	90.1	7.0	5.4	7.3
1940	100.4	71.0	7.8	37.0	26.2	13.4	7.7	3.5	2.2	1.8	5.4	3.7	14.2	6.1	8.1	98.3	98.7	10.0	8.1	9.5
1941	125.5	80.8	9.7	42.9	28.3	18.3	9.7	4.1	4.5	1.5	6.1	4.7	25.0	17.0	8.0	121.0	124.1	25.0	23.2	25.7
1942	159.0	88.6	6.9	50.8	31.0	10.3	6.3	2.2	1.8	.2	5.0	4.8	59.9	52.0	7.8	157.2	158.8	26.6	29.9	28.0
1943	192.7	99.5	6.5	58.6	34.3	6.2	5.4	1.4	−.6	−1.9	4.6	6.5	88.9	81.4	7.5	193.4	194.6	21.2	23.0	22.6
1944	211.4	108.2	6.7	64.3	37.2	7.7	7.4	1.4	−1.0	−1.7	5.5	7.2	97.1	89.4	7.6	212.3	213.0	9.7	9.8	9.5
1945	213.4	119.6	8.0	71.9	39.7	11.3	10.6	1.7	−1.0	−.5	7.4	7.9	83.0	74.8	8.2	214.4	213.9	.9	1.0	.4
1946	212.4	143.9	15.8	82.7	45.4	31.5	17.3	7.8	6.4	7.8	15.2	7.3	29.1	19.2	9.9	206.0	204.5	−.5	−3.9	−4.4
1947	235.2	161.9	20.4	90.9	50.6	35.0	23.5	12.1	−.5	11.9	20.3	8.3	26.4	13.6	12.8	235.7	223.3	10.8	14.4	9.2
1948	261.6	174.9	22.9	96.6	55.5	47.1	26.8	15.6	4.7	7.0	17.5	10.6	32.6	17.3	15.3	256.9	254.7	11.2	9.0	14.0
1949	260.4	178.3	25.0	94.9	58.4	36.5	24.9	14.6	−3.1	6.5	16.4	9.8	39.0	21.1	18.0	263.4	253.8	−.5	2.5	−.3
1950	288.3	192.1	30.8	98.2	63.2	55.1	27.8	20.5	6.8	2.2	14.5	12.3	38.8	19.1	19.8	281.4	286.0	10.7	6.8	12.7
1951	333.4	208.1	29.9	109.2	69.0	60.5	31.8	18.4	10.2	4.5	19.8	15.3	60.4	38.6	21.8	323.2	329.0	15.7	14.8	15.0
1952	351.6	219.1	29.3	114.7	75.1	53.5	31.9	18.6	3.1	3.2	19.2	16.0	75.8	52.7	23.1	348.6	348.4	5.5	7.9	5.9
1953	371.6	232.6	32.7	117.8	82.1	54.9	35.1	19.4	.4	1.3	18.1	16.8	82.8	57.9	24.8	371.1	370.3	5.7	6.5	6.3
1954	372.5	239.8	32.1	119.7	88.0	54.1	34.7	21.1	−1.6	2.6	18.8	16.3	76.0	48.4	27.7	374.1	370.0	.2	.8	−.1
1955	405.9	257.9	38.9	124.7	94.3	69.7	39.0	25.0	5.7	3.0	21.1	18.1	75.3	44.9	30.3	400.2	402.9	9.0	7.0	8.9
1956	428.2	270.6	38.2	130.8	101.6	72.7	44.5	23.5	4.6	5.3	25.2	19.9	79.7	46.4	33.3	423.6	422.9	5.5	5.8	5.0
1957	451.0	285.3	39.7	137.1	108.5	71.1	47.5	22.2	1.4	7.3	28.2	20.9	87.3	50.5	36.9	449.6	443.7	5.3	6.1	4.9
1958	456.8	294.6	37.2	141.7	115.7	63.6	42.4	22.7	−1.5	3.3	24.4	21.1	95.4	54.5	40.8	458.3	453.5	1.3	1.9	2.2
1959	495.8	316.3	42.8	148.5	125.0	80.2	46.3	28.1	5.8	1.5	25.0	23.5	97.9	54.6	43.3	490.0	494.3	8.5	6.9	9.0
1960	515.3	330.7	43.5	153.2	134.0	78.2	48.8	26.3	3.1	5.9	29.9	24.0	100.6	54.4	46.1	512.3	509.4	3.9	4.6	3.1
1961	533.8	341.1	41.9	157.4	141.8	77.1	48.3	26.4	2.4	7.2	31.1	23.9	108.4	58.2	50.2	531.4	526.6	3.6	3.7	3.4
1962	574.6	361.9	47.0	163.8	151.1	87.6	52.5	29.0	6.1	6.9	33.1	26.2	118.2	64.6	53.5	568.5	567.7	7.6	7.0	7.8
1963	606.9	381.7	51.8	169.4	160.6	93.1	55.2	32.1	5.8	8.2	35.7	27.5	123.8	65.7	58.1	601.1	598.7	5.6	5.7	5.5
1964	649.8	409.3	56.8	179.7	172.8	99.6	61.4	32.8	5.4	10.9	40.5	29.6	130.0	66.4	63.5	644.4	638.9	7.1	7.2	6.7
1965	705.1	440.7	63.5	191.9	185.4	116.2	73.1	33.1	9.9	9.7	42.9	33.2	138.6	68.7	69.9	695.2	695.4	8.5	7.9	8.8
1966	772.0	477.3	68.5	208.5	200.3	128.6	83.5	30.9	14.2	7.5	46.6	39.1	158.6	80.4	78.2	757.8	764.5	9.5	9.0	9.9
1967	816.4	503.6	70.6	216.9	216.0	125.7	84.4	31.1	10.3	7.4	49.5	42.1	179.7	92.7	87.0	806.1	809.0	5.8	6.4	5.8
1968	892.7	552.5	81.0	235.0	236.4	137.0	91.4	37.7	7.9	5.5	54.8	49.3	197.7	100.1	97.6	884.8	887.2	9.3	9.8	9.7
1969	963.9	597.9	86.2	252.2	259.4	153.2	102.3	41.2	9.8	5.6	60.4	54.7	207.3	100.0	107.2	954.1	958.3	8.0	7.8	8.0
1970	1,015.5	640.0	85.7	270.3	284.0	148.8	105.2	40.5	3.1	8.5	68.9	60.5	218.2	98.8	119.4	1,012.3	1,007.0	5.4	6.1	5.1
1971	1,102.7	691.6	97.6	283.3	310.7	172.5	109.6	55.1	7.8	6.3	72.4	66.1	232.4	99.8	132.5	1,094.9	1,096.4	8.6	8.2	8.9
1972	1,212.8	757.6	111.2	305.1	341.3	202.0	123.0	68.6	10.5	3.2	81.4	78.2	250.0	105.8	144.2	1,202.3	1,209.6	10.0	9.8	10.3
1973	1,359.3	837.2	124.7	339.6	373.0	238.8	145.9	73.3	19.6	16.8	114.1	97.3	266.5	106.4	160.1	1,339.7	1,342.5	12.1	11.4	11.0
1974	1,472.8	916.5	123.8	380.9	411.9	240.8	160.6	64.8	15.4	16.3	151.5	135.2	299.1	116.2	182.9	1,457.4	1,456.5	8.3	8.8	8.5
1975	1,598.4	1,012.8	135.4	416.2	461.2	219.6	162.9	62.3	−5.6	31.1	161.3	130.3	335.0	129.2	205.9	1,604.1	1,567.4	8.5	10.1	7.6
1976	1,782.8	1,129.3	161.5	452.0	515.9	277.7	180.0	81.7	16.0	18.8	177.7	158.9	356.9	136.3	220.6	1,766.8	1,764.0	11.5	10.1	12.5
1977	1,990.5	1,257.2	184.5	490.4	582.3	344.1	214.2	108.6	21.3	1.9	191.6	189.7	387.3	151.1	236.2	1,969.2	1,988.6	11.7	11.5	12.7
1978	2,249.7	1,403.5	205.6	541.8	656.1	416.8	259.0	129.2	28.6	4.1	227.5	223.4	425.2	161.8	263.4	2,221.0	2,245.6	13.0	12.8	12.9
1979	2,508.2	1,566.8	219.0	613.2	734.6	454.8	302.8	139.1	13.0	18.8	291.2	272.5	467.8	178.0	289.9	2,495.2	2,489.4	11.5	12.3	10.9
1980	2,732.0	1,732.6	219.3	681.4	831.9	437.0	322.8	122.5	−8.3	32.1	351.0	318.9	530.3	208.1	322.2	2,740.3	2,699.8	8.9	9.8	8.5
1981	3,052.6	1,915.1	239.9	740.6	934.7	515.5	369.2	122.3	24.0	33.9	382.8	348.9	588.1	242.2	345.9	3,028.6	3,018.7	11.7	10.5	11.8
1982	3,166.0	2,050.7	252.7	771.0	1,027.0	447.3	366.7	105.1	−24.5	26.3	361.9	335.6	641.7	272.7	369.0	3,190.5	3,139.7	3.7	5.3	4.0
1983	3,405.7	2,234.5	289.1	816.7	1,128.7	502.3	356.9	152.5	−7.1	−6.1	352.5	358.7	675.0	283.5	391.5	3,412.8	3,411.8	7.6	7.0	8.7
1984	3,772.2	2,430.5	335.5	867.3	1,227.6	664.8	416.0	181.1	67.7	−58.9	383.5	442.4	735.9	310.5	425.3	3,704.5	3,831.1	10.8	8.5	12.3
1985	4,014.9	2,629.0	372.2	911.2	1,345.6	643.1	442.9	188.8	11.3	−78.0	370.9	448.9	820.8	355.2	465.6	4,003.6	4,092.8	6.4	8.1	6.8
1986	4,240.3	2,807.5	406.5	943.6	1,457.3	665.9	433.9	216.6	15.5	−104.4	378.4	482.8	871.2	366.2	505.0	4,224.7	4,344.7	5.6	5.5	6.2
1987	4,526.7	3,012.1	421.9	997.9	1,592.3	712.9	446.8	226.9	39.2	−123.0	428.0	551.1	924.7	382.0	542.8	4,487.5	4,649.7	6.8	6.2	7.0
1960: I	516.1	325.5	43.3	150.9	131.3	88.7	49.4	28.4	11.0	4.3	28.7	24.4	97.6	53.0	44.5	505.0	511.8	11.4	7.4	9.6
II	514.5	331.6	44.2	153.8	133.5	78.1	49.6	26.1	2.5	5.1	29.7	24.6	99.6	53.8	45.8	512.0	509.4	−1.2	5.7	−1.9
III	517.7	331.7	43.7	153.5	134.5	77.4	48.4	25.3	3.7	6.5	30.6	24.0	102.1	55.3	46.8	514.0	511.2	2.5	1.6	1.4
IV	513.0	333.8	42.5	154.6	136.7	68.5	48.1	25.3	−4.9	7.7	30.6	22.9	103.0	55.6	47.4	517.9	505.3	−3.6	3.1	−4.5
1961: I	517.4	334.4	40.0	156.0	138.4	69.5	47.1	25.3	−2.9	8.3	31.1	22.8	105.3	56.0	49.2	520.4	509.1	3.5	1.9	3.0
II	527.9	339.1	41.0	156.8	141.2	74.7	48.0	25.5	1.1	7.0	30.0	23.1	107.1	57.7	49.4	526.7	520.9	8.4	4.9	9.6
III	538.5	341.9	42.3	157.3	142.3	81.2	48.3	26.9	6.0	6.6	31.2	24.5	108.7	58.5	50.2	532.5	531.8	8.3	4.5	8.6
IV	551.5	349.1	44.3	159.5	145.3	83.0	49.9	27.8	5.4	6.9	32.0	25.1	112.5	60.4	52.1	546.2	544.7	10.0	10.7	10.1
1962: I	564.4	354.0	45.3	161.5	147.2	87.9	51.0	28.4	8.6	6.3	31.7	25.5	116.2	63.8	52.4	555.9	558.2	9.7	7.3	10.3
II	572.2	359.7	46.6	162.9	150.2	88.0	52.6	29.2	6.1	7.6	33.6	26.1	116.9	63.9	53.0	566.1	564.6	5.6	7.5	4.7
III	579.2	363.7	47.1	164.5	152.1	89.3	53.5	29.2	6.6	7.3	33.6	26.3	118.9	65.0	53.8	572.6	571.9	5.0	4.7	5.3
IV	582.8	370.2	49.1	166.4	154.7	85.4	53.0	29.1	3.3	6.6	33.4	26.8	120.6	65.8	54.8	579.5	576.2	2.5	4.9	3.0
1963: I	592.1	374.0	50.2	167.5	156.4	88.9	52.8	30.2	5.9	6.9	33.3	26.4	122.3	66.0	56.3	586.2	585.2	6.5	4.7	6.4
II	600.3	378.2	51.5	168.2	158.6	92.2	54.3	32.2	5.6	8.5	35.7	27.2	121.4	64.3	57.1	594.7	591.9	5.7	5.9	4.7
III	613.1	385.1	52.2	170.6	162.3	95.7	55.9	32.5	7.3	8.0	36.0	28.1	124.4	65.5	58.8	605.8	605.2	8.8	7.7	9.3
IV	622.1	389.6	53.3	171.1	165.2	95.8	57.7	33.7	4.4	9.5	37.6	28.2	127.2	67.0	60.2	617.7	612.6	6.0	8.1	5.0
1964: I	636.9	398.8	55.4	175.2	168.2	98.2	58.8	34.0	5.5	11.5	39.9	28.4	128.5	67.0	61.4	631.5	625.5	9.9	9.2	8.7
II	645.6	406.4	56.8	178.4	171.2	98.7	60.5	32.8	5.4	10.2	39.5	29.2	130.2	67.0	63.2	640.2	635.3	5.6	5.6	6.4
III	656.0	414.9	58.6	182.0	174.3	100.0	62.5	32.4	5.2	10.9	40.9	29.9	130.1	65.9	64.2	650.8	645.1	6.6	6.8	6.3
IV	660.6	417.1	56.6	183.1	177.4	101.6	63.9	32.1	5.6	10.9	41.8	30.9	131.0	65.7	65.3	655.0	649.7	2.8	2.6	2.9
1965: I	682.7	427.6	62.1	185.6	179.9	114.4	68.6	33.3	12.5	9.0	39.1	30.1	131.8	65.2	66.6	670.2	673.8	14.1	9.6	15.7
II	695.0	434.4	61.9	189.1	183.4	114.0	71.5	33.4	9.1	10.8	44.2	33.4	135.8	67.1	68.7	685.9	684.2	7.4	9.7	6.3
III	710.7	443.4	63.8	192.8	186.9	117.4	74.4	33.0	10.0	9.5	43.3	33.8	140.3	69.0	71.4	700.7	701.2	9.3	8.9	10.3
IV	732.0	457.4	66.1	199.9	191.4	118.8	78.0	32.7	8.0	9.5	45.2	35.7	146.3	73.3	73.0	723.9	722.5	12.5	13.9	12.7

Source: *Survey of Current Business* (Washington, D.C.: Department of Commerce, September 1988).

Table 1.—Gross National Product—Continued

[Billions of dollars; quarterly data are seasonally adjusted at annual rates]

Year and quarter	GNP	Personal consumption expenditures				Gross private domestic investment				Net exports			Government purchases of goods and services			Final sales	Gross domestic purchases	Percent change from preceding period		
		Total	Durable goods	Nondurable goods	Services	Total	Nonresidential	Residential	CBI	Net	Exports	Imports	Total	Federal	State and local			GNP	Final sales	Gross domestic purchases
1966: I	754.8	467.7	69.2	204.1	194.5	128.2	81.2	33.2	13.8	8.7	45.6	36.9	150.2	75.1	75.1	741.0	746.1	13.1	9.8	13.7
II	764.6	472.7	66.5	207.6	198.5	129.1	83.4	31.9	13.9	7.6	45.8	38.2	155.2	78.3	76.9	750.7	757.0	5.3	5.3	6.0
III	777.7	481.7	69.1	210.7	202.0	127.6	84.5	30.7	12.4	6.4	46.6	40.2	162.0	83.1	78.9	765.2	771.3	7.0	8.0	7.8
IV	790.9	486.9	69.3	211.4	206.2	129.6	85.0	27.9	16.7	7.3	48.4	41.0	167.1	85.1	82.0	774.2	783.6	7.0	4.8	6.5
1967: I	799.7	491.4	67.8	213.7	209.9	125.5	83.5	27.0	15.0	8.0	49.7	41.6	174.8	90.3	84.4	784.7	791.7	4.5	5.5	4.2
II	805.9	500.5	71.2	215.5	213.8	120.6	83.9	30.5	6.2	7.8	48.9	41.2	177.0	91.1	85.9	799.6	798.1	3.1	7.8	3.3
III	822.9	507.5	71.3	217.8	218.4	126.5	84.0	32.2	10.4	7.4	49.1	41.7	181.4	93.9	87.5	812.5	815.5	8.7	6.6	9.0
IV	837.1	514.7	72.2	220.6	221.9	130.1	86.2	34.6	9.4	6.4	50.4	43.9	185.8	95.5	90.2	827.6	830.6	7.1	7.6	7.6
1968: I	862.9	532.4	77.3	227.6	227.5	133.8	90.1	36.1	7.6	5.2	52.1	46.9	191.4	98.0	93.4	855.3	857.6	12.9	14.1	13.7
II	886.7	545.8	79.3	232.6	233.8	137.4	89.2	37.1	11.1	6.1	54.2	48.1	197.4	100.9	96.5	875.6	880.7	11.5	9.8	11.2
III	903.6	561.6	83.6	238.6	239.3	136.8	91.0	37.8	8.0	5.6	56.8	51.1	199.6	100.8	98.8	895.6	898.0	7.8	9.5	8.1
IV	917.4	570.1	83.8	241.2	245.1	139.9	95.2	39.8	4.9	5.0	56.1	51.1	202.4	100.8	101.6	912.5	912.4	6.3	7.8	6.6
1969: I	941.3	581.7	85.8	245.6	250.3	151.3	98.8	41.7	10.8	5.2	52.4	47.2	203.0	99.4	103.7	930.5	936.1	10.8	8.1	10.8
II	955.6	592.7	86.2	250.2	256.3	151.8	100.9	41.8	9.0	5.1	61.8	56.6	206.0	99.6	106.4	946.6	950.5	6.2	7.1	6.3
III	975.4	602.7	86.4	254.2	262.1	158.1	104.5	41.8	11.9	5.3	62.4	57.0	209.2	100.8	108.5	963.5	970.0	8.5	7.3	8.5
IV	983.5	614.3	86.5	258.7	269.0	151.6	104.9	39.3	7.5	6.8	64.9	58.1	210.8	100.4	110.3	976.0	976.7	3.4	5.3	2.8
1970: I	994.2	625.1	85.4	264.7	275.1	146.2	104.5	39.5	2.2	8.1	66.7	58.6	214.7	100.8	113.9	992.0	986.0	4.4	6.7	3.9
II	1,008.9	635.1	86.7	268.2	280.2	148.2	105.6	38.4	4.2	9.8	69.9	60.1	215.7	98.6	117.1	1,004.6	999.0	6.0	5.2	5.4
III	1,027.9	646.8	87.7	271.9	287.2	153.5	106.7	39.6	7.2	8.4	69.4	61.0	219.1	97.3	121.8	1,020.7	1,019.5	7.7	6.6	8.5
IV	1,030.9	653.0	82.9	276.5	293.6	147.3	104.2	44.3	−1.2	7.5	69.6	62.2	223.1	98.3	124.8	1,032.1	1,023.5	1.2	4.5	1.6
1971: I	1,075.2	671.7	93.4	278.3	300.0	166.6	106.4	47.9	12.3	9.4	71.8	62.4	227.5	99.2	128.3	1,062.9	1,065.8	18.3	12.5	17.6
II	1,094.3	685.2	96.2	282.0	307.0	173.4	109.1	54.0	10.3	5.7	72.6	67.0	230.0	98.5	131.5	1,084.0	1,088.6	7.3	8.2	8.8
III	1,113.9	696.8	98.5	284.4	313.9	177.0	110.2	58.0	8.8	6.1	75.3	69.3	234.0	100.4	133.6	1,105.1	1,107.8	7.4	8.0	7.2
IV	1,127.3	712.4	102.2	288.4	321.7	172.9	112.5	60.7	−.3	4.0	69.7	65.7	238.0	101.3	136.7	1,127.6	1,123.3	4.9	8.4	5.7
1972: I	1,166.5	729.3	105.7	293.1	330.5	188.3	117.7	65.8	4.8	2.1	77.8	75.6	246.8	106.8	140.0	1,161.7	1,164.4	14.7	12.7	15.5
II	1,197.2	747.0	108.9	301.5	336.7	199.1	120.5	66.7	11.9	2.2	77.6	75.4	248.9	107.3	141.6	1,185.3	1,195.0	11.0	8.4	10.9
III	1,223.9	764.8	112.3	308.4	344.0	205.7	123.0	68.3	14.4	3.8	81.9	78.1	249.6	104.4	145.2	1,209.5	1,220.0	9.2	8.4	8.6
IV	1,263.5	789.2	118.0	317.4	353.9	214.9	130.7	73.4	10.8	4.5	88.2	83.7	254.8	104.9	149.9	1,252.7	1,259.0	13.6	15.1	13.4
1973: I	1,311.6	813.2	126.3	327.0	359.9	228.0	137.2	75.9	14.8	9.5	100.1	90.6	261.0	106.8	154.2	1,296.8	1,302.1	16.1	14.8	14.4
II	1,342.9	827.9	125.3	333.5	369.1	237.8	144.9	73.5	19.3	13.9	109.4	95.5	263.3	105.6	157.7	1,323.6	1,329.0	9.9	8.5	8.5
III	1,369.4	846.2	125.0	344.0	377.2	237.2	149.4	72.8	15.0	21.1	118.7	97.6	265.0	103.1	161.9	1,354.4	1,348.3	8.1	9.6	5.9
IV	1,413.3	861.6	122.3	353.7	385.7	252.3	152.2	70.9	29.2	22.5	128.3	105.7	276.8	110.0	166.8	1,384.1	1,390.7	13.5	9.1	13.2
1974: I	1,426.2	880.0	120.2	365.6	394.2	238.1	154.4	67.6	16.1	25.0	141.7	116.8	283.1	109.8	173.3	1,410.1	1,401.2	3.7	7.7	3.1
II	1,459.1	907.8	124.3	376.8	406.7	241.3	159.2	66.1	16.0	14.6	151.5	136.9	295.5	114.6	180.9	1,443.2	1,444.6	9.6	9.7	13.0
III	1,489.1	935.3	130.2	388.1	417.0	238.9	163.4	66.2	9.3	10.7	152.9	142.2	304.1	117.8	186.4	1,479.8	1,478.4	8.5	10.5	9.7
IV	1,516.8	943.0	120.3	393.1	429.7	245.1	165.5	59.2	20.4	14.9	159.9	145.1	313.8	122.6	191.2	1,496.5	1,502.0	7.7	4.6	6.5
1975: I	1,524.6	967.4	124.8	400.5	442.1	204.9	160.5	56.9	−12.5	29.3	162.0	132.8	323.1	125.5	197.6	1,537.1	1,495.3	2.1	11.3	−1.8
II	1,563.5	996.6	130.1	411.2	455.3	204.6	160.0	59.8	−15.2	32.7	155.4	122.7	329.7	127.3	202.4	1,578.7	1,530.8	10.6	11.3	9.8
III	1,627.4	1,029.6	140.0	423.2	466.4	229.5	163.4	64.3	1.8	29.4	159.0	129.7	338.9	129.6	209.2	1,625.5	1,598.0	17.4	12.4	18.7
IV	1,678.2	1,057.5	146.5	429.9	481.1	239.3	167.5	68.4	3.4	32.9	168.9	136.0	348.5	134.3	214.2	1,674.8	1,645.3	13.1	12.7	12.4
1976: I	1,730.9	1,091.8	156.4	439.4	495.9	264.6	171.8	75.9	16.8	23.6	170.6	147.0	350.9	132.3	218.6	1,714.1	1,707.3	13.2	9.7	15.9
II	1,761.8	1,111.2	158.9	446.4	505.8	275.8	176.3	79.9	19.6	20.0	175.1	155.1	354.9	134.9	220.0	1,742.2	1,741.9	7.3	6.7	8.4
III	1,794.7	1,139.8	162.4	456.0	521.4	279.6	182.7	79.5	17.4	17.0	180.5	163.4	358.2	137.5	220.8	1,777.2	1,777.6	7.7	8.3	8.5
IV	1,843.7	1,174.6	168.1	466.0	540.6	290.6	189.2	91.3	10.2	14.7	184.8	170.1	363.8	140.7	223.0	1,833.6	1,829.0	11.4	13.3	12.1
1977: I	1,899.1	1,211.8	177.0	477.5	557.4	311.5	200.1	96.3	15.1	4.0	186.3	182.3	371.8	142.7	229.2	1,884.1	1,895.1	12.6	11.5	15.3
II	1,968.9	1,239.2	181.9	485.6	571.7	341.4	209.5	110.2	21.7	4.2	194.0	189.8	384.1	149.9	234.2	1,947.2	1,964.7	15.5	14.1	15.5
III	2,031.6	1,270.2	186.5	491.9	591.7	363.7	218.0	113.0	32.7	5.3	195.9	190.6	392.3	154.3	238.0	1,998.9	2,026.3	13.4	11.1	13.1
IV	2,062.4	1,307.6	192.6	506.8	608.2	359.6	229.0	115.0	15.6	−5.9	190.3	196.2	401.1	157.6	243.4	2,046.8	2,068.3	6.2	9.9	8.6
1978: I	2,111.4	1,332.6	188.9	516.4	627.3	379.7	235.0	118.4	26.3	−6.6	203.8	210.4	405.6	154.9	250.7	2,085.1	2,117.9	9.8	7.7	9.9
II	2,230.3	1,391.1	207.6	534.4	649.0	420.2	257.3	128.5	34.4	1.3	222.1	220.7	417.6	157.1	260.6	2,195.9	2,228.9	24.5	23.0	22.7
III	2,289.5	1,424.6	210.0	548.5	666.1	424.7	266.8	133.4	24.5	6.8	233.2	226.4	433.4	165.4	268.1	2,265.0	2,282.7	11.0	13.2	10.0
IV	2,367.6	1,465.7	215.8	567.9	682.0	442.7	276.9	136.4	29.4	15.0	250.9	236.0	444.2	169.9	274.3	2,338.2	2,352.6	14.4	13.6	12.8
1979: I	2,420.5	1,501.8	215.6	583.4	702.8	446.9	289.0	136.0	21.9	22.7	265.2	242.6	449.2	172.1	277.1	2,398.7	2,397.9	9.2	10.8	7.9
II	2,474.5	1,537.6	214.4	600.9	722.4	463.2	296.3	138.7	28.1	15.2	278.1	262.9	458.6	173.1	285.4	2,446.4	2,459.3	9.2	8.2	10.6
III	2,546.1	1,590.0	223.9	623.6	742.5	461.5	310.1	141.7	9.7	21.8	301.0	279.2	472.8	178.6	294.2	2,536.4	2,524.3	12.1	15.5	11.0
IV	2,591.5	1,637.5	221.9	645.1	770.5	447.8	315.9	139.8	−7.8	15.4	320.6	305.2	490.7	188.0	302.7	2,599.3	2,576.1	7.3	10.3	8.5
1980: I	2,673.0	1,682.2	225.0	662.0	795.1	461.0	326.7	133.9	.4	20.7	346.5	325.8	509.1	197.0	312.2	2,672.5	2,652.3	13.2	11.7	12.4
II	2,672.2	1,688.9	204.9	671.8	812.2	425.0	314.1	110.5	.5	30.1	348.4	318.3	528.2	208.9	319.2	2,671.7	2,642.1	−.1	−.1	−1.5
III	2,734.0	1,749.3	218.7	686.4	844.2	405.4	319.7	115.3	−29.6	46.8	350.1	303.3	532.6	207.2	325.4	2,763.6	2,687.2	9.6	14.5	7.0
IV	2,848.6	1,810.0	228.5	705.2	876.3	456.4	330.5	130.5	−4.6	30.8	358.9	328.1	551.4	219.3	332.1	2,853.3	2,817.8	17.9	13.6	20.9
1981: I	2,978.8	1,862.9	241.1	726.6	895.2	506.9	347.8	131.1	28.0	38.9	380.7	341.9	570.1	229.3	340.8	2,950.8	2,939.9	19.6	14.4	18.5
II	3,017.7	1,896.4	236.0	737.3	923.2	515.3	364.5	128.1	22.7	29.0	383.4	354.4	577.0	233.9	343.2	2,995.0	2,988.7	5.3	6.1	6.8
III	3,099.6	1,940.9	246.9	745.7	948.4	535.9	380.2	120.1	35.7	30.9	382.3	351.4	591.9	245.4	346.5	3,064.0	3,068.8	11.3	9.5	11.2
IV	3,114.4	1,960.2	235.5	752.7	972.0	504.0	384.5	109.8	9.7	36.9	384.8	347.9	613.3	260.2	353.1	3,104.7	3,077.5	1.9	5.4	1.1
1982: I	3,112.6	1,996.3	245.1	758.1	993.1	459.5	382.0	101.7	−24.1	34.7	373.0	338.4	622.1	262.9	359.2	3,136.7	3,077.9	−.2	4.2	.1
II	3,159.5	2,023.8	248.9	762.6	1,012.2	467.8	369.2	103.6	−5.0	42.1	378.9	336.8	625.7	259.3	366.4	3,164.5	3,117.3	6.2	3.6	5.2
III	3,179.4	2,065.6	252.8	776.7	1,036.1	452.2	360.7	100.5	−9.0	14.5	359.9	345.4	647.1	275.3	371.8	3,188.4	3,164.9	2.5	3.1	6.2
IV	3,212.5	2,117.0	263.8	786.6	1,066.5	409.6	354.9	114.7	−59.9	14.1	335.9	321.9	671.8	293.2	378.7	3,272.4	3,198.5	4.2	11.0	4.3
1983: I	3,265.8	2,146.6	266.7	791.0	1,088.9	428.3	340.8	130.2	−42.6	22.7	343.6	320.9	668.1	285.5	382.7	3,308.4	3,243.1	6.8	4.5	5.7
II	3,367.4	2,213.0	284.5	810.9	1,117.6	481.3	344.7	147.8	−11.2	−2.1	344.1	346.2	675.2	287.7	387.5	3,378.6	3,369.5	13.0	8.8	16.5
III	3,443.9	2,262.8	295.2	827.0	1,140.6	519.7	358.1	167.1	−5.5	−19.3	357.7	376.9	680.7	284.9	395.8	3,449.4	3,463.1	9.4	8.6	11.6
IV	3,545.8	2,315.8	310.0	837.9	1,167.9	579.8	383.9	164.9	31.0	−25.8	364.7	390.5	676.1	276.1	400.0	3,514.8	3,571.6	12.4	7.8	13.1
1984: I	3,674.9	2,361.1	322.7	849.9	1,188.6	663.0	392.7	176.2	94.1	−45.7	374.3	420.0	696.5	284.0	412.5	3,580.8	3,720.6	15.4	7.7	17.8
II	3,754.2	2,417.0	335.1	866.9	1,215.1	664.2	413.2	184.3	66.7	−62.8	383.2	446.1	735.8	315.0	420.8	3,687.4	3,817.0	8.9	12.5	10.8
III	3,807.9	2,450.3	337.7	872.8	1,239.7	670.3	423.3	182.1	65.0	−59.3	390.8	450.1	746.6	317.0	429.6	3,742.9	3,867.2	5.8	6.2	5.4
IV	3,851.8	2,493.4	346.7	879.6	1,267.1	661.8	435.0	181.8	45.0	−67.9	385.7	453.6	764.5	326.0	438.5	3,806.8	3,919.7	4.7	7.0	5.5
1985: I	3,925.6	2,554.9	361.4	890.9	1,302.7	639.3	437.7	183.8	17.8	−53.1	376.8	429.9	784.4	336.1	448.3	3,907.7	3,978.7	7.9	11.0	6.2
II	3,979.0	2,599.3	367.1	905.6	1,326.6	652.3	446.1	186.7	19.5	−74.3	372.6	446.9	801.7	339.6	462.1	3,959.5	4,053.3	5.6	5.4	7.7
III	4,047.0	2,661.4	387.2	915.7	1,358.5	626.7	436.6	189.4	.7	−81.2	365.1	446.2	840.2	368.4	471.8	4,046.3	4,128.2	7.0	9.1	7.6
IV	4,107.9	2,700.4	373.2	932.7	1,394.5	654.1	451.3	195.5	7.2	−103.2	369.2	472.4	856.7	376.6	480.1	4,100.7	4,211.2	6.2	5.5	8.3
1986: I	4,180.4	2,739.0	381.4	938.4	1,419.2	686.6	438.9	203.6	44.0	−93.0	376.9	469.9	847.8	356.6	491.2	4,136.5	4,273.4	7.2	3.5	6.0
II	4,207.6	2,772.1	393.0	937.2	1,441.9	667.8	431.9	216.4	19.5	−101.2	373.9	475.1	868.8	368.7	500.2	4,188.1	4,308.7	2.6	5.1	3.3
III	4,268.4	2,842.8	429.9	944.7	1,468.2	653.0	430.6	221.8	.7	−109.1	377.8	486.9	881.8	372.7	509.1	4,267.7	4,377.6	5.9	7.8	6.6
IV	4,304.6	2,876.0	421.8	954.1	1,500.1	656.4	434.1	224.4	−2.0	−114.3	385.2	499.4	886.5	366.7	519.7	4,306.6	4,418.9	3.4	3.7	3.8
1987: I	4,391.8	2,921.7	403.5	977.5	1,540.7	685.5	422.8	225.0	37.7	−119.1	395.3	514.4	903.8	372.7	531.1	4,354.1	4,510.9	8.4	4.5	8.6
II	4,484.2	2,992.2	420.5	995.3	1,576.4	698.5	438.2	227.6	32.7	−122.2	416.8	539.0	915.7	377.5	538.2	4,451.5	4,606.3	8.7	9.3	8.7
III	4,568.0	3,058.2	441.4	1,006.6	1,610.2	702.8	462.1	226.2	14.5	−125.2	440.4	565.6	932.2	386.3	546.0	4,553.5	4,693.2	7.7	9.5	7.8
IV	4,662.8	3,076.3	422.0	1,012.4	1,641.9	764.9	464.1	228.8	72.0	−125.7	459.7	585.4	947.3	391.4	555.9	4,590.7	4,788.4	8.6	3.3	8.4

NOTE.—GNP = Gross national product; CBI = Change in business inventories.

Source: *Survey of Current Business* (Washington, D.C.: Department of Commerce, September 1988).

Table 2.—Gross National Product in Constant Dollars

[Billions of 1982 dollars; quarterly data are seasonally adjusted at annual rates]

Year and quarter	GNP	Personal consumption expenditures				Gross private domestic investment				Net exports			Government purchases of goods and services			Final sales	Gross domestic purchases	Percent change from preceding period		
		Total	Durable goods	Nondurable goods	Services	Total	Nonresidential	Residential	CBI	Net	Exports	Imports	Total	Federal	State and local			GNP	Final sales	Gross domestic purchases
1929	709.6	471.4	40.3	211.4	219.7	139.2	93.0	35.4	10.8	4.7	42.1	37.4	94.2	18.3	75.9	698.7	704.9	....	....	....
1930	642.8	439.7	31.9	203.1	204.8	97.5	76.9	21.5	-.9	2.3	35.6	33.3	103.3	20.6	82.7	643.6	640.5	-9.4	-7.9	-9.1
1931	588.1	422.1	27.5	201.7	193.0	60.2	49.4	17.9	-7.1	-1.0	29.3	30.4	106.8	21.2	85.6	595.2	589.1	-8.5	-7.5	-8.0
1932	509.2	384.9	21.0	187.0	176.9	22.6	29.6	9.4	-16.4	-.5	23.2	23.7	102.2	21.9	80.3	525.6	509.7	-13.4	-11.7	-13.5
1933	498.5	378.7	20.7	181.8	176.2	22.7	25.8	7.7	-10.7	-1.4	22.7	24.2	98.5	27.0	71.5	509.2	499.9	-2.1	-3.1	-1.9
1934	536.7	390.5	23.4	192.4	174.7	35.3	32.4	10.5	-7.6	.1	24.7	24.6	110.7	34.7	76.1	544.3	536.5	7.7	6.9	7.3
1935	580.2	412.1	28.9	201.5	181.7	60.9	40.0	14.7	6.2	-5.9	26.6	32.5	113.0	34.1	79.0	574.0	586.1	8.1	5.5	9.2
1936	662.2	451.6	35.9	224.3	191.4	82.1	54.4	18.7	9.0	-4.2	28.4	32.5	132.5	53.6	78.9	653.1	666.3	14.1	13.8	13.7
1937	695.3	467.9	37.7	232.8	197.4	99.9	65.5	20.2	14.1	-.3	35.7	35.9	127.8	48.9	79.0	681.2	695.6	5.0	4.3	4.4
1938	664.2	457.1	30.4	235.4	191.3	63.1	48.8	20.4	-6.0	6.0	34.1	28.1	137.9	55.0	82.9	670.2	658.2	-4.5	-1.6	-5.4
1939	716.6	480.5	35.7	248.0	196.7	86.0	53.2	28.9	3.9	6.1	36.2	30.1	144.1	53.8	90.3	712.7	710.5	7.9	6.3	7.9
1940	772.9	502.6	40.6	259.4	202.7	111.8	65.0	32.5	14.4	8.2	40.0	31.7	150.2	63.6	86.6	758.5	764.6	7.8	6.4	7.6
1941	909.4	531.1	46.2	275.6	209.3	138.8	76.6	34.4	27.8	3.9	42.0	38.2	235.6	153.0	82.6	881.6	905.5	17.7	16.2	18.4
1942	1,080.3	527.6	31.3	279.1	217.2	76.7	47.4	17.3	12.0	-7.7	29.1	36.9	483.7	407.1	76.7	1,068.3	1,088.0	18.8	21.2	20.1
1943	1,276.2	539.9	28.1	284.7	227.2	50.4	39.4	10.4	.7	-23.0	25.1	48.0	708.9	638.1	70.8	1,275.5	1,299.2	18.1	19.4	19.4
1944	1,380.6	557.1	26.3	297.9	232.9	56.4	52.6	9.0	-5.2	-23.8	27.3	51.1	790.8	722.5	68.3	1,385.7	1,404.3	8.2	8.6	8.1
1945	1,354.8	592.7	28.7	323.5	240.5	76.5	74.2	10.7	-8.4	-18.9	35.2	54.1	704.5	634.0	70.5	1,363.3	1,373.7	-1.9	-1.6	-2.2
1946	1,096.9	655.0	47.8	344.2	262.9	178.1	105.5	44.7	27.9	27.0	69.0	42.0	236.9	159.3	77.6	1,069.0	1,069.9	-19.0	-21.6	-22.1
1947	1,066.7	666.6	56.5	337.4	272.6	177.9	121.7	57.2	-1.0	42.4	82.3	39.9	179.8	91.9	87.9	1,067.7	1,024.3	-2.8	-.1	-4.3
1948	1,108.7	681.8	61.7	338.7	281.4	208.2	127.4	68.6	12.3	19.2	66.2	47.1	199.5	106.1	93.4	1,096.4	1,089.5	3.9	2.7	6.4
1949	1,109.0	695.4	67.8	342.3	285.3	168.8	114.8	63.6	-9.7	18.8	65.0	46.2	226.0	119.5	106.5	1,118.7	1,090.2	0	2.0	.1
1950	1,203.7	733.2	80.7	352.8	299.8	234.9	124.0	86.7	24.2	4.7	59.2	54.6	230.8	116.7	114.2	1,179.5	1,199.0	8.5	5.4	10.0
1951	1,328.2	748.7	74.7	362.9	311.1	235.2	131.7	72.6	30.8	14.6	72.0	57.4	329.7	214.4	115.4	1,297.4	1,313.6	10.3	10.0	9.6
1952	1,380.0	771.4	73.0	376.6	321.9	211.8	130.6	71.2	10.0	6.9	70.1	63.3	389.9	272.7	117.3	1,370.0	1,373.1	3.9	5.6	4.5
1953	1,435.3	802.5	80.2	388.2	334.1	216.6	140.1	73.8	2.8	-2.7	66.9	69.7	419.0	295.9	123.1	1,432.5	1,438.0	4.0	4.6	4.7
1954	1,416.2	822.7	81.5	393.8	347.4	212.6	137.5	79.8	-4.8	2.5	70.0	67.5	378.4	245.0	133.4	1,421.0	1,413.7	-1.3	-.8	-1.7
1955	1,494.9	873.8	96.9	413.2	363.6	259.8	151.0	92.4	16.3	0	76.9	76.9	361.3	217.9	143.4	1,478.6	1,494.9	5.6	4.1	5.7
1956	1,525.6	899.8	92.8	426.9	380.1	257.8	160.4	84.4	12.9	4.3	87.9	83.6	363.7	215.4	148.3	1,512.7	1,521.3	2.1	2.3	1.8
1957	1,551.1	919.7	92.4	434.7	392.6	243.4	161.1	79.3	3.0	7.0	94.9	87.9	381.1	224.1	157.0	1,548.1	1,544.2	1.7	2.3	1.5
1958	1,539.2	932.9	86.9	439.9	406.1	221.4	143.9	81.0	-3.4	-10.3	82.4	92.8	395.3	224.9	170.4	1,542.6	1,549.6	-.8	-.4	.4
1959	1,629.1	979.4	96.9	455.8	426.7	270.3	153.6	100.2	16.5	-18.2	83.7	101.9	397.7	221.5	176.2	1,612.6	1,647.3	5.8	4.5	6.3
1960	1,665.3	1,005.1	98.0	463.3	443.9	260.5	159.4	93.3	7.7	-4.0	98.4	102.4	403.7	220.6	183.1	1,657.5	1,669.3	2.2	2.8	1.3
1961	1,708.7	1,025.2	93.6	470.1	461.4	259.1	158.2	93.6	7.3	-2.7	100.7	103.3	427.1	232.9	194.2	1,701.4	1,711.3	2.6	2.6	2.5
1962	1,799.4	1,069.0	103.0	484.2	481.8	288.6	170.2	102.2	16.2	-7.5	106.9	114.4	449.4	249.3	200.1	1,783.3	1,807.0	5.3	4.8	5.6
1963	1,873.3	1,108.4	111.8	494.3	502.3	307.1	176.6	113.9	16.6	-1.9	114.7	116.6	459.8	247.8	212.0	1,856.7	1,875.3	4.1	4.1	3.8
1964	1,973.3	1,170.6	120.8	517.5	532.3	325.9	194.9	115.3	15.7	5.9	128.8	122.8	470.8	244.2	226.6	1,957.6	1,967.3	5.3	5.4	4.9
1965	2,087.6	1,236.4	134.6	543.2	558.5	367.0	227.6	114.2	25.2	-2.7	132.0	134.7	487.0	244.4	242.5	2,062.4	2,090.3	5.8	5.4	6.3
1966	2,208.3	1,298.9	144.4	569.3	585.3	390.5	250.4	103.2	36.9	-13.7	138.4	152.1	532.6	273.8	258.8	2,171.5	2,222.1	5.8	5.3	6.3
1967	2,271.4	1,337.7	146.2	579.2	612.3	374.4	245.0	100.6	28.8	-16.9	143.6	160.5	576.2	304.4	271.8	2,242.6	2,288.3	2.9	3.3	3.0
1968	2,365.6	1,405.9	161.6	602.4	641.8	391.8	254.5	116.2	21.0	-29.7	155.7	185.3	597.6	309.6	288.0	2,344.6	2,395.3	4.1	4.5	4.7
1969	2,423.3	1,456.7	167.8	617.2	671.7	410.3	269.7	115.4	25.1	-34.9	165.0	199.9	591.2	295.6	295.6	2,398.1	2,458.1	2.4	2.3	2.6
1970	2,416.2	1,492.0	162.5	632.5	697.0	381.5	264.0	109.3	8.2	-30.0	178.3	208.3	572.6	268.3	304.3	2,407.9	2,446.2	-.3	.4	-.5
1971	2,484.8	1,538.8	178.3	640.3	720.2	419.3	258.4	141.3	19.6	-39.8	179.2	218.9	566.5	250.6	315.9	2,465.2	2,524.6	2.8	2.4	3.2
1972	2,608.5	1,621.9	200.4	665.5	756.0	465.4	277.0	166.6	21.8	-49.4	195.2	244.6	570.7	246.0	324.7	2,586.8	2,658.0	5.0	4.9	5.3
1973	2,744.1	1,689.6	220.3	683.2	786.1	520.8	317.3	163.4	40.0	-31.5	242.3	273.8	565.3	230.0	335.3	2,704.1	2,775.7	5.2	4.5	4.4
1974	2,729.3	1,674.0	204.9	666.1	803.1	481.3	317.8	130.2	33.3	.8	269.1	268.4	573.2	226.4	346.8	2,696.0	2,728.5	-.5	-.3	-1.7
1975	2,695.0	1,711.9	205.6	676.5	829.8	383.3	281.2	114.9	-12.8	18.9	259.7	240.8	580.9	226.3	354.6	2,707.8	2,676.1	-1.3	.4	-1.9
1976	2,826.7	1,803.9	232.3	708.8	862.8	453.5	290.6	140.8	22.1	-11.0	274.4	285.4	580.3	224.2	356.0	2,804.6	2,837.7	4.9	3.6	6.0
1977	2,958.6	1,883.8	253.9	731.4	898.5	521.3	324.0	168.1	29.1	-35.5	281.6	317.1	589.1	231.8	357.2	2,929.5	2,994.1	4.7	4.5	5.5
1978	3,115.2	1,961.0	267.4	753.7	939.8	576.9	362.1	178.0	36.8	-26.8	312.6	339.4	604.1	233.7	370.4	3,078.4	3,142.0	5.3	5.1	4.9
1979	3,192.4	2,004.4	266.5	766.6	971.2	575.2	389.4	170.8	15.0	3.6	356.8	353.2	609.1	236.2	373.0	3,177.4	3,188.8	2.5	3.2	1.5
1980	3,187.1	2,000.4	245.9	762.6	991.9	509.3	379.2	137.0	-6.9	57.0	388.9	332.0	620.5	246.9	373.6	3,194.0	3,130.1	-.2	.5	-1.8
1981	3,248.8	2,024.2	250.8	764.4	1,009.0	545.5	395.2	126.5	23.9	49.4	392.7	343.4	629.7	259.6	370.1	3,225.0	3,199.4	1.9	1.0	2.2
1982	3,166.0	2,050.7	252.7	771.0	1,027.0	447.3	366.7	105.1	-24.5	26.3	361.9	335.6	641.7	272.7	369.0	3,190.5	3,139.7	-2.5	-1.1	-1.9
1983	3,279.1	2,146.0	283.1	800.2	1,062.7	504.0	361.2	149.3	-6.4	-19.9	348.1	368.1	649.0	275.1	373.9	3,285.5	3,299.1	3.6	3.0	5.1
1984	3,501.4	2,249.3	323.1	825.9	1,100.3	658.4	425.2	170.9	62.3	-84.0	371.8	455.8	677.7	290.8	387.0	3,439.1	3,585.4	6.8	4.7	8.7
1985	3,618.7	2,354.8	355.1	847.4	1,152.3	637.0	453.5	174.4	9.1	-104.3	367.2	471.4	731.2	326.0	405.2	3,609.6	3,723.0	3.4	5.0	3.8
1986	3,721.7	2,455.2	385.0	879.5	1,190.7	643.5	433.1	195.0	15.4	-137.5	378.4	515.9	760.5	333.4	427.1	3,706.3	3,859.3	2.8	2.7	3.7
1987	3,847.0	2,521.0	390.9	890.5	1,239.5	674.8	445.1	195.2	34.4	-128.9	427.8	556.7	780.2	339.0	441.2	3,812.6	3,975.9	3.4	2.9	3.0
1960: I	1,671.6	997.1	96.9	460.7	439.6	288.7	161.1	100.9	26.7	-9.4	95.0	104.3	395.2	217.0	178.2	1,644.9	1,681.0	7.0	5.2	5.4
II	1,666.8	1,009.8	99.9	465.9	444.1	261.4	161.4	92.7	7.3	-6.9	98.0	104.9	402.6	220.4	182.2	1,659.5	1,673.8	-1.1	3.6	-1.7
III	1,668.4	1,005.7	98.7	463.1	443.9	258.3	157.7	89.8	10.8	-2.4	99.9	102.3	406.8	221.8	185.0	1,657.6	1,670.8	.4	-.5	-.7
IV	1,654.1	1,007.8	96.4	463.6	447.9	233.6	157.6	89.9	-13.9	2.6	100.5	97.9	410.1	223.2	186.9	1,668.0	1,651.5	-3.4	2.5	-4.5
1961: I	1,671.3	1,009.5	91.2	465.3	453.0	238.3	155.3	90.2	-7.1	3.8	102.1	98.3	419.7	226.9	192.8	1,678.5	1,667.6	4.2	2.5	4.0
II	1,692.1	1,023.5	91.8	470.4	461.3	249.1	157.0	90.5	1.7	-3.0	96.9	99.9	422.4	230.8	191.6	1,690.4	1,695.1	5.1	2.9	6.8
III	1,716.3	1,024.6	93.7	469.2	461.7	270.5	158.0	95.4	17.1	-5.4	100.8	106.2	426.7	233.1	193.5	1,699.2	1,721.7	5.8	2.1	6.4
IV	1,754.9	1,042.9	97.8	475.5	469.7	278.4	162.6	98.4	17.4	-6.0	102.9	109.0	439.6	240.7	198.9	1,737.5	1,761.0	9.3	9.3	9.4
1962: I	1,777.9	1,053.6	99.9	480.2	473.6	287.7	165.5	100.2	22.0	-9.4	102.3	111.7	446.0	248.7	197.3	1,755.9	1,787.3	5.3	4.3	6.1
II	1,796.4	1,063.6	102.0	481.3	480.3	291.2	171.3	103.1	16.7	-5.2	108.9	114.1	446.9	248.1	198.8	1,779.7	1,801.6	4.2	5.5	3.2
III	1,813.1	1,072.8	103.1	485.7	484.0	294.7	173.4	102.9	18.4	-6.5	108.8	115.3	452.1	250.9	201.2	1,794.7	1,819.6	3.8	3.4	4.1
IV	1,810.1	1,085.8	106.8	489.7	489.3	280.7	170.5	102.7	7.5	-9.0	107.5	116.5	452.6	249.4	203.2	1,802.6	1,819.1	-.7	1.8	-.1
1963: I	1,834.6	1,094.1	109.2	492.4	492.6	291.9	168.9	106.1	17.0	-6.6	107.3	113.9	455.2	248.2	207.0	1,817.7	1,841.2	5.5	3.4	4.9
II	1,860.0	1,100.2	111.2	492.2	496.7	306.9	174.3	114.0	18.6	-1.4	114.7	116.1	454.4	245.5	208.9	1,841.4	1,861.5	5.7	5.3	4.5
III	1,892.5	1,115.5	112.9	495.9	506.7	315.6	179.4	116.0	20.2	-2.6	115.8	118.5	464.1	249.5	214.6	1,872.3	1,895.1	7.2	6.9	7.4
IV	1,906.1	1,123.6	113.9	496.5	513.1	314.0	183.9	119.4	10.7	3.0	120.9	117.9	465.5	248.0	217.5	1,895.4	1,903.1	2.9	5.0	1.7
1964: I	1,948.7	1,145.2	118.1	505.1	522.0	324.7	186.5	121.3	16.9	9.7	128.0	118.3	469.2	248.3	220.9	1,931.8	1,939.0	9.2	7.9	7.8
II	1,965.4	1,164.4	120.7	514.6	529.1	323.6	192.3	116.0	15.3	4.8	126.0	121.3	472.7	246.8	225.9	1,950.1	1,960.7	3.5	3.8	4.6
III	1,985.2	1,184.8	124.2	524.4	536.1	324.5	197.9	112.9	13.8	5.6	129.6	124.0	470.3	241.8	228.5	1,971.4	1,979.6	4.1	4.4	3.9
IV	1,993.7	1,188.0	120.3	526.0	541.8	330.8	202.9	111.0	16.9	3.7	131.5	127.8	471.1	239.9	231.2	1,976.8	1,989.9	1.7	1.1	2.1
1965: I	2,036.9	1,208.2	130.7	531.2	546.3	362.1	214.7	115.0	32.3	-3.0	120.1	123.1	469.6	236.3	233.4	2,004.6	2,039.9	9.0	5.7	10.4
II	2,066.4	1,221.7	131.2	536.1	554.4	364.3	224.1	116.4	23.9	-.4	135.8	136.3	480.8	241.3	239.6	2,042.5	2,066.8	5.9	7.8	5.4
III	2,099.3	1,242.3	135.9	544.7	561.7	369.9	231.1	113.3	25.4	-4.3	132.7	137.0	491.5	244.9	246.6	2,073.9	2,103.6	6.5	6.3	7.3
IV	2,147.6	1,273.2	140.8	560.8	571.7	371.8	240.6	111.9	19.2	-3.2	139.3	142.5	505.8	255.2	250.6	2,128.3	2,150.8	9.5	10.9	9.3
1966: I	2,190.1	1,287.6	147.3	563.4	576.9	396.9	247.9	113.3	35.7	-7.9	138.4	146.3	513.5	259.4	254.1	2,154.3	2,198.0	8.2	5.0	9.1
II	2,195.8	1,293.1	140.9	568.6	583.6	390.9	251.2	105.8	33.8	-11.6	136.9	148.5	523.4	267.1	256.2	2,162.0	2,207.4	1.0	1.4	1.7
III	2,218.3	1,305.5	144.8	573.6	587.1	389.1	252.9	102.3	33.9	-18.2	137.8	155.9	541.9	282.9	259.0	2,184.4	2,236.5	4.2	4.2	5.4
IV	2,229.2	1,309.5	144.5	571.5	593.4	385.2	249.7	91.4	44.0	-17.2	140.5	157.8	551.7	285.9	265.8	2,185.1	2,246.4	2.0	.1	1.8
1967: I	2,241.8	1,319.4	142.1	576.3	601.0	368.7	244.5	87.6	36.6	-15.5	144.0	159.5	569.2	300.4	268.8	2,205.2	2,257.3	2.3	3.7	2.0
II	2,255.2	1,336.5	148.4	579.1	609.1	361.7	244.3	99.3	18.1	-16.1	142.3	158.5	573.1	302.8	270.3	2,237.1	2,271.4	2.4	5.9	2.5
III	2,287.7	1,343.3	147.1	578.7	617.5	378.8	243.4	104.3	31.1	-13.5	142.7	156.2	579.1	307.6	271.5	2,256.6	2,301.2	5.9	3.5	5.4
IV	2,300.6	1,351.5	147.2	582.7	621.6	388.4	247.8	111.3	29.3	-22.5	145.2	167.7	583.2	306.6	276.5	2,271.3	2,323.1	2.3	2.6	3.9

Source: *Survey of Current Business* (Washington, D.C.: Department of Commerce, September 1988).

Table 2.—Gross National Product in Constant Dollars—Continued

[Billions of 1982 dollars; quarterly data are seasonally adjusted at annual rates]

Year and quarter	GNP	Personal consumption expenditures				Gross private domestic investment				Net exports			Government purchases of goods and services			Final sales	Gross domestic purchases	Percent change from preceding period		
		Total	Durable goods	Nondurable goods	Services	Total	Nonresidential	Residential	CBI	Net	Exports	Imports	Total	Federal	State and local			GNP	Final sales	Gross domestic purchases
1968: I	2,327.3	1,378.1	155.8	594.2	628.2	387.7	255.7	112.9	19.1	−28.7	149.3	178.0	590.1	309.0	281.1	2,308.1	2,356.0	4.7	6.6	5.8
II	2,366.9	1,396.7	159.1	599.2	638.3	397.2	250.0	115.8	31.4	−27.5	153.1	180.6	600.5	313.4	287.1	2,335.5	2,394.4	7.0	4.8	6.7
III	2,385.3	1,421.5	166.4	608.6	646.5	392.0	252.1	116.8	23.2	−29.2	161.8	191.0	601.0	310.4	290.7	2,362.1	2,414.5	3.1	4.6	3.4
IV	2,383.0	1,427.1	165.3	607.6	654.2	390.2	260.4	119.3	10.5	−33.2	158.5	191.8	599.0	305.7	293.2	2,372.5	2,416.2	−.4	1.8	.3
1969: I	2,416.5	1,442.9	168.8	613.4	660.7	412.0	266.0	119.4	26.6	−31.6	144.9	176.5	593.2	299.0	294.2	2,389.9	2,448.1	5.7	3.0	5.4
II	2,419.8	1,451.7	168.2	616.2	667.3	409.1	267.9	118.3	22.9	−36.9	171.3	208.2	596.0	299.8	296.2	2,397.0	2,456.7	.5	1.2	1.4
III	2,433.2	1,459.9	167.6	617.6	674.7	419.5	273.8	116.5	29.2	−36.6	170.3	206.9	590.4	294.2	296.2	2,403.9	2,469.8	2.2	1.2	2.2
IV	2,423.5	1,472.0	166.7	621.4	683.9	400.5	271.1	107.5	21.9	−34.3	173.3	207.7	585.3	289.5	295.8	2,401.6	2,457.8	−1.6	−.4	−1.9
1970: I	2,408.6	1,481.5	163.5	628.4	689.7	379.9	265.9	108.2	5.8	−31.4	175.8	207.2	578.6	279.8	298.8	2,402.8	2,440.0	−2.4	.2	−2.9
II	2,406.5	1,488.1	165.6	629.6	692.8	376.4	264.3	102.1	10.0	−27.7	181.2	208.9	569.7	268.9	300.8	2,396.5	2,434.1	−.3	−1.0	−1.0
III	2,435.8	1,501.3	166.2	634.3	700.8	390.6	266.9	107.6	16.1	−27.7	178.4	206.1	571.6	264.0	307.7	2,419.7	2,463.5	5.0	3.9	4.9
IV	2,413.8	1,497.2	154.8	637.7	704.6	379.3	259.0	119.2	1.0	−33.3	177.8	211.1	570.6	260.4	310.2	2,412.7	2,447.1	−3.6	−1.2	−2.6
1971: I	2,478.6	1,520.9	170.7	639.4	710.8	415.5	257.7	126.1	31.7	−25.3	178.7	204.0	567.6	255.5	312.1	2,447.0	2,503.9	11.2	5.8	9.6
II	2,478.4	1,533.0	175.1	640.9	717.0	423.1	258.6	139.3	25.2	−41.7	180.2	221.8	564.0	249.1	314.9	2,453.2	2,520.1	0	1.0	2.6
III	2,491.1	1,541.0	180.0	639.0	722.0	425.9	257.6	147.7	20.6	−42.7	187.5	230.2	566.9	251.1	315.8	2,470.5	2,533.8	2.1	2.9	2.2
IV	2,491.0	1,560.1	187.4	641.8	731.0	412.8	259.6	152.2	1.0	−49.3	170.4	219.7	567.4	246.6	320.8	2,489.9	2,540.3	0	3.2	1.0
1972: I	2,545.6	1,581.8	191.7	647.5	742.7	439.5	267.9	163.6	8.1	−52.2	189.5	241.7	576.4	253.6	322.8	2,537.5	2,597.8	9.1	7.9	9.4
II	2,595.1	1,607.9	196.1	661.8	750.0	462.3	272.2	164.5	25.6	−49.2	186.9	236.1	574.1	252.2	321.9	2,569.6	2,644.3	8.0	5.2	7.4
III	2,622.1	1,629.9	201.4	670.4	758.1	473.8	275.9	165.6	32.4	−47.7	196.6	244.3	566.1	241.7	324.4	2,589.7	2,669.8	4.2	3.2	3.9
IV	2,671.3	1,667.8	212.4	682.2	773.2	486.0	292.2	172.8	21.0	−48.6	207.8	256.4	566.1	236.4	329.7	2,650.3	2,719.9	7.7	9.7	7.7
1973: I	2,734.0	1,689.9	225.7	687.8	776.3	515.7	304.5	177.1	34.1	−44.1	227.7	271.8	572.5	240.4	332.2	2,700.0	2,778.1	9.7	7.7	8.8
II	2,741.0	1,687.2	221.8	680.8	784.6	521.7	316.7	165.3	39.6	−36.6	239.2	275.7	568.6	235.8	332.8	2,701.4	2,777.6	1.0	.2	−.1
III	2,738.3	1,694.5	220.0	684.5	790.0	511.4	322.6	158.7	30.1	−23.4	247.8	271.2	555.8	220.0	335.8	2,708.2	2,761.7	−.4	1.0	−2.3
IV	2,762.8	1,686.8	213.8	679.4	793.5	534.2	325.5	152.5	56.3	−22.4	254.1	276.5	564.2	223.9	340.3	2,706.5	2,785.1	3.6	−.3	3.4
1974: I	2,747.4	1,667.5	208.2	664.9	794.4	501.1	324.4	141.4	35.3	11.0	266.8	255.8	567.8	223.9	343.9	2,712.1	2,736.4	−2.2	.8	−6.8
II	2,755.2	1,677.2	209.9	665.4	801.9	496.5	324.7	134.4	37.5	1.4	276.6	275.2	580.2	232.0	348.2	2,717.8	2,753.8	1.1	.8	2.6
III	2,719.3	1,686.7	211.6	670.2	804.9	465.5	316.0	130.6	18.8	−5.5	266.7	272.3	572.6	225.2	347.4	2,700.4	2,724.8	−5.1	−2.5	−4.1
IV	2,695.4	1,664.7	189.7	663.9	811.0	462.2	306.2	114.4	41.5	−3.5	266.7	270.2	572.1	224.4	347.7	2,653.9	2,699.0	−3.5	−6.7	−3.7
1975: I	2,642.7	1,677.1	193.5	666.9	816.7	370.6	285.5	106.9	−21.8	17.4	260.0	242.6	577.5	226.3	351.1	2,664.4	2,625.2	−7.6	1.6	−10.5
II	2,669.6	1,706.0	198.7	677.8	829.6	358.1	277.6	110.8	−30.3	28.2	252.5	224.3	577.2	225.5	351.7	2,699.9	2,641.4	4.1	5.4	2.5
III	2,714.9	1,723.9	211.7	679.8	832.4	394.4	279.6	118.2	−3.4	14.4	256.9	242.5	582.1	225.7	356.5	2,718.3	2,700.5	7.0	2.8	9.3
IV	2,752.7	1,740.4	218.3	681.5	840.5	410.1	282.1	123.6	4.4	15.5	269.3	253.9	586.8	227.8	359.0	2,748.3	2,737.2	5.7	4.5	5.5
1976: I	2,804.4	1,777.5	229.7	696.2	851.7	444.7	284.9	135.4	24.4	−.2	268.5	268.7	582.4	222.1	360.3	2,780.0	2,804.6	7.7	4.7	10.2
II	2,816.9	1,790.4	230.6	705.0	854.8	454.9	286.8	139.1	29.0	−8.7	272.0	280.7	580.3	223.4	357.0	2,787.9	2,825.6	1.8	1.1	3.0
III	2,828.6	1,809.9	232.4	712.1	865.4	452.8	292.8	136.3	23.7	−13.4	277.9	291.3	579.4	225.4	354.0	2,805.0	2,842.1	1.7	2.5	2.4
IV	2,856.8	1,837.8	236.7	721.8	879.4	461.8	297.9	152.4	11.6	−21.8	279.1	300.9	579.0	226.1	352.8	2,845.2	2,878.6	4.0	5.9	5.2
1977: I	2,896.0	1,863.7	246.7	728.8	888.2	492.0	311.5	156.3	24.2	−39.9	277.8	317.7	580.2	223.8	356.3	2,871.8	2,935.9	5.6	3.8	8.2
II	2,942.7	1,869.0	251.8	727.3	889.9	519.0	320.4	172.7	25.9	−32.8	284.8	317.7	587.5	230.8	356.7	2,916.8	2,975.5	6.6	6.4	5.5
III	3,001.8	1,888.0	256.2	728.3	903.5	546.9	327.8	174.4	44.7	−28.1	287.0	315.1	594.9	238.0	357.0	2,957.1	3,029.9	8.3	5.6	7.5
IV	2,994.1	1,914.2	261.1	740.9	912.2	527.2	336.4	169.1	21.7	−41.0	276.9	317.9	593.6	234.8	358.9	2,972.4	3,035.0	−1.0	2.1	.7
1978: I	3,020.5	1,923.0	252.6	745.8	924.6	544.0	339.5	172.9	31.6	−39.0	290.8	329.8	592.5	228.4	364.1	2,988.9	3,059.5	3.6	2.2	3.3
II	3,115.9	1,960.8	272.4	749.1	939.2	584.6	363.6	179.8	41.1	−30.7	307.6	338.3	601.3	230.3	371.0	3,074.8	3,146.6	13.2	12.0	11.9
III	3,142.6	1,970.3	270.9	753.5	945.9	583.3	369.4	180.8	33.1	−22.4	318.5	341.0	611.5	238.3	373.2	3,109.5	3,165.0	3.5	4.6	2.4
IV	3,181.6	1,989.7	273.9	766.3	949.6	595.8	376.0	178.6	41.3	−15.1	333.1	348.2	611.1	237.9	373.2	3,140.3	3,196.7	5.1	4.0	4.1
1979: I	3,181.7	1,997.5	268.9	766.2	962.4	582.2	383.7	174.6	23.9	−4.8	340.4	345.2	606.7	236.4	370.3	3,157.7	3,186.5	0	2.2	−1.3
II	3,178.7	1,994.1	262.9	762.1	969.1	590.1	384.9	172.4	32.8	−12.4	343.6	356.1	606.9	233.9	373.0	3,145.8	3,191.1	−.4	−1.5	.6
III	3,207.4	2,007.9	270.9	766.0	971.0	575.7	394.2	170.6	10.9	12.5	363.5	351.0	611.3	237.3	374.0	3,196.5	3,194.9	3.7	6.6	.5
IV	3,201.3	2,018.0	263.4	772.2	982.4	552.9	394.8	165.7	−7.6	18.7	378.8	360.1	611.7	237.1	374.6	3,208.9	3,182.6	−.8	1.6	−1.5
1980: I	3,233.4	2,015.4	260.6	767.9	986.9	556.7	397.7	154.9	4.1	43.5	398.9	355.4	617.8	243.8	374.5	3,229.3	3,189.9	4.1	2.6	.9
II	3,157.0	1,974.1	231.9	760.9	981.3	499.2	372.9	124.1	2.3	58.6	393.1	334.5	625.1	251.6	373.5	3,154.8	3,098.4	−9.1	−8.9	−11.0
III	3,159.1	1,996.3	242.7	759.9	993.6	467.7	370.4	126.8	−29.5	74.1	383.6	309.6	621.1	248.2	372.9	3,188.6	3,085.1	.3	4.4	−1.7
IV	3,199.2	2,015.6	248.6	761.5	1,005.6	513.5	375.8	142.2	−4.5	52.2	380.6	328.4	617.9	244.4	373.4	3,203.8	3,147.0	5.2	1.9	8.3
1981: I	3,261.1	2,022.9	258.7	763.3	1,000.9	552.3	385.7	139.3	27.3	59.7	394.5	334.8	626.3	252.0	374.2	3,233.8	3,201.4	8.0	3.8	7.1
II	3,250.2	2,022.4	248.4	764.5	1,009.5	551.2	395.3	134.1	21.8	50.2	395.3	345.1	626.4	256.0	370.4	3,228.4	3,200.0	−1.3	−.7	−.2
III	3,264.6	2,031.5	255.5	764.7	1,011.4	560.7	402.7	122.3	35.7	42.1	391.1	349.0	630.2	262.7	367.5	3,228.9	3,222.5	1.8	.1	2.8
IV	3,219.0	2,020.0	240.4	765.2	1,014.3	517.9	397.0	110.4	10.6	45.3	389.8	344.5	635.9	267.5	368.4	3,208.5	3,173.8	−5.5	−2.5	−5.9
1982: I	3,170.4	2,031.2	247.7	764.2	1,019.2	464.2	387.0	101.2	−24.0	40.4	374.1	333.7	634.6	267.0	367.7	3,194.4	3,130.0	−5.9	−1.7	−5.4
II	3,179.9	2,041.0	249.1	768.3	1,023.5	467.5	369.5	103.4	−5.4	41.7	378.5	336.8	629.7	260.5	369.2	3,185.3	3,138.2	1.2	−1.1	1.1
III	3,154.5	2,051.8	251.8	772.8	1,027.2	448.6	358.0	100.1	−9.4	11.7	359.5	347.8	642.5	273.8	368.6	3,164.0	3,142.9	−3.2	−2.6	.6
IV	3,159.3	2,078.7	262.0	778.6	1,038.1	408.8	352.3	115.8	−59.3	11.7	336.0	324.3	660.1	289.5	370.6	3,218.6	3,147.6	.6	7.1	.6
1983: I	3,186.6	2,094.2	263.3	786.3	1,044.6	427.1	341.6	127.8	−42.3	16.1	342.5	326.4	649.2	278.2	371.0	3,228.9	3,170.5	3.5	1.3	2.9
II	3,258.3	2,135.1	280.0	795.7	1,059.4	486.9	348.8	147.4	−9.3	−14.6	341.7	356.3	650.9	278.5	372.4	3,267.6	3,273.0	9.3	4.9	13.6
III	3,306.4	2,163.0	288.5	806.2	1,068.3	524.8	363.9	161.9	−1.0	−35.0	352.8	387.8	653.6	277.6	376.0	3,307.4	3,341.4	6.0	5.0	8.6
IV	3,365.1	2,191.9	300.5	812.7	1,078.6	577.2	390.4	159.9	27.0	−46.2	355.5	401.6	642.2	266.0	376.2	3,338.1	3,411.3	7.3	3.8	8.6
1984: I	3,451.7	2,212.1	312.6	814.5	1,085.0	655.2	401.3	170.5	83.4	−68.6	362.7	431.3	653.0	271.5	381.6	3,368.3	3,520.3	10.7	3.7	13.4
II	3,498.0	2,246.7	322.5	828.2	1,096.1	658.4	422.0	173.1	63.2	−87.3	369.1	456.5	680.2	295.6	384.7	3,434.8	3,585.4	5.5	8.1	7.6
III	3,520.6	2,257.3	324.3	829.6	1,103.5	664.2	433.0	170.3	60.9	−85.5	378.7	464.1	684.5	295.5	388.9	3,459.6	3,606.0	2.6	2.9	2.3
IV	3,535.2	2,281.1	333.1	831.2	1,116.8	655.7	444.4	169.6	41.7	−94.8	376.6	471.4	693.2	300.5	392.7	3,493.5	3,630.0	1.7	4.0	2.7
1985: I	3,577.5	2,319.1	344.8	838.2	1,136.2	634.3	448.2	170.3	15.8	−81.4	371.2	452.6	705.5	309.0	396.4	3,561.7	3,658.9	4.9	8.0	3.2
II	3,599.2	2,337.4	350.3	843.0	1,144.1	647.5	457.8	172.9	16.9	−102.4	367.6	470.0	716.7	313.3	403.4	3,582.3	3,701.6	2.4	2.3	4.8
III	3,635.8	2,375.9	369.1	850.0	1,156.8	618.1	447.1	175.0	−4.0	−107.9	362.6	470.5	749.8	340.9	408.9	3,639.8	3,743.8	4.1	6.6	4.6
IV	3,662.4	2,386.9	356.4	858.3	1,172.2	648.0	460.9	179.4	7.7	−125.3	367.4	492.6	752.7	340.6	412.1	3,654.7	3,787.6	3.0	1.6	4.8
1986: I	3,719.3	2,415.1	363.3	870.4	1,181.4	678.0	446.8	185.5	45.7	−115.7	374.5	490.2	741.8	322.7	419.1	3,673.6	3,834.9	6.4	2.1	5.1
II	3,711.6	2,440.9	374.2	880.9	1,185.8	652.1	432.8	195.7	23.6	−140.2	372.1	512.4	758.8	333.6	425.2	3,688.0	3,851.8	−.8	1.6	1.8
III	3,721.3	2,478.6	405.1	881.4	1,192.0	627.6	425.6	199.0	3.0	−151.8	379.1	530.9	766.9	336.7	430.2	3,718.3	3,873.0	1.0	3.3	2.2
IV	3,734.7	2,486.2	397.3	885.3	1,203.6	616.5	427.3	199.7	−10.5	−142.4	387.8	530.2	774.5	340.5	434.0	3,745.2	3,877.2	1.4	2.9	.4
1987: I	3,776.7	2,490.2	378.3	889.9	1,222.0	646.4	418.2	198.4	29.8	−132.8	394.9	527.7	772.9	334.0	438.9	3,746.9	3,909.5	4.6	.2	3.4
II	3,823.0	2,516.6	391.3	889.8	1,235.5	660.1	434.8	197.6	27.8	−126.0	416.4	542.3	772.2	332.1	440.1	3,795.2	3,949.0	5.0	5.3	4.1
III	3,865.3	2,545.2	406.5	891.9	1,246.8	667.9	462.8	192.1	13.0	−130.7	440.9	571.6	782.9	342.1	440.8	3,852.2	3,996.0	4.5	6.1	4.8
IV	3,923.0	2,531.7	387.6	890.5	1,253.6	724.7	464.8	192.7	67.1	−126.0	459.2	585.2	792.6	347.7	444.9	3,855.9	4,049.0	6.1	.4	5.4

NOTE.—GNP=Gross national product; CBI=Change in business inventories.

Source: *Survey of Current Business* (Washington, D.C.: Department of Commerce, September 1988).

Table 3.—Price Indexes and the Gross National Product Implicit Price Deflator

[Index numbers, 1982=100; quarterly data are seasonally adjusted at annual rates]

Year and quarter	Fixed-weighted price indexes														GNP IPD	Percent change from preceding period			
	GNP	Personal consumption expenditures				Fixed investment			Exports	Imports	Government purchases of goods and services			Final sales		FWPI		GNP IPD	GNP Chain price index
		Total	Durable goods	Nondurable goods	Services	Total	Nonresidential	Residential			Total	Federal	State and local			GNP	PCE		
1959	37.6	35.2	52.3	35.0	31.2	58.0	65.9	30.2	32.8	27.0	25.8	26.9	24.9	37.6	30.4	....	....	2.4	....
1960	38.1	35.7	52.1	35.5	31.9	58.1	66.1	30.3	33.5	27.3	26.4	27.3	25.7	38.1	30.9	1.4	1.5	1.6	1.5
1961	38.4	36.1	51.9	35.8	32.4	58.0	66.0	30.2	34.0	27.0	27.0	27.8	26.4	38.3	31.2	.7	.9	1.0	1.0
1962	38.7	36.4	51.7	36.0	32.9	58.0	66.1	29.9	34.1	26.7	27.8	28.4	27.3	38.7	31.9	.8	.9	2.2	1.2
1963	39.1	36.8	51.6	36.4	33.4	58.0	66.2	29.5	34.4	27.1	28.5	29.3	27.9	39.1	32.4	1.0	1.1	1.6	1.3
1964	39.6	37.2	51.9	36.8	33.9	58.2	66.4	29.6	34.8	27.7	29.3	30.1	28.5	39.5	32.9	1.2	1.2	1.5	1.5
1965	40.1	37.7	51.2	37.5	34.5	58.5	66.7	30.0	35.9	28.1	30.0	30.8	29.3	40.0	33.8	1.4	1.2	2.7	1.8
1966	41.1	38.5	50.6	38.7	35.4	59.3	67.4	30.8	37.1	29.1	31.3	32.0	30.6	41.0	35.0	2.5	2.2	3.6	3.0
1967	42.1	39.5	51.2	39.6	36.5	60.2	68.4	31.6	38.2	29.5	32.7	32.8	32.5	42.0	35.9	2.6	2.5	2.6	2.8
1968	43.7	41.0	52.6	41.2	38.0	61.4	69.5	33.1	39.3	30.1	34.5	34.5	34.4	43.6	37.7	3.7	3.8	5.0	4.3
1969	45.6	42.8	53.8	43.2	39.7	63.2	71.0	36.0	40.9	31.2	36.6	36.4	36.7	45.5	39.8	4.4	4.3	5.6	5.0
1970	47.2	44.7	55.0	45.2	41.9	61.5	68.4	37.4	43.3	33.4	39.6	39.5	39.6	47.2	42.0	3.6	4.6	5.5	5.2
1971	48.8	46.6	56.7	46.6	44.2	60.6	66.6	39.5	45.3	35.6	42.3	42.4	42.2	48.8	44.4	3.5	4.2	5.7	4.8
1972	50.3	48.3	57.1	48.2	46.1	59.8	65.0	41.6	46.5	37.8	45.2	46.0	44.6	50.2	46.5	2.9	3.5	4.7	4.2
1973	53.1	51.0	58.1	52.3	48.3	61.8	66.6	45.1	50.8	42.4	48.8	50.1	47.8	53.0	49.5	5.5	5.7	6.5	5.9
1974	57.2	55.8	61.6	59.0	52.0	64.4	68.5	50.1	59.8	54.5	53.5	54.8	52.6	57.2	54.0	7.8	9.4	9.1	8.9
1975	61.8	60.1	66.7	63.2	56.2	69.0	73.1	54.6	65.4	59.7	58.6	59.4	57.9	61.8	59.3	8.0	7.7	9.8	9.2
1976	65.1	63.5	70.4	65.4	60.4	71.4	75.2	58.4	67.4	61.3	62.2	62.4	62.0	65.1	63.1	5.3	5.6	6.4	5.9
1977	68.4	67.5	73.3	68.5	65.3	72.6	74.9	64.8	70.3	66.1	66.0	65.8	66.2	68.4	67.3	5.1	6.3	6.7	6.1
1978	72.7	72.2	77.3	73.1	70.2	74.5	75.0	72.5	74.5	71.3	70.9	70.6	71.2	72.6	72.2	6.2	7.0	7.3	7.2
1979	78.8	78.6	82.5	80.8	76.0	80.3	80.1	81.2	82.9	80.9	77.3	76.8	77.7	78.8	78.6	8.5	8.8	8.9	8.7
1980	86.1	86.8	89.6	89.6	84.0	86.9	86.1	89.4	90.5	96.3	86.3	86.4	86.2	86.1	85.7	9.3	10.5	9.0	9.0
1981	94.1	94.6	95.8	97.0	92.6	94.5	93.9	96.6	97.7	101.5	94.1	94.9	93.5	94.1	94.0	9.3	9.0	9.7	9.4
1982	100.0	100.0	100.0	100.0	100.0	100.0	100.0	100.0	100.0	100.0	100.0	100.0	100.0	100.0	100.0	6.2	5.6	6.4	6.3
1983	104.1	104.2	102.3	102.1	106.3	100.4	99.9	102.2	101.6	97.7	104.5	104.1	104.8	104.1	103.9	4.1	4.2	3.9	4.1
1984	108.3	108.4	104.1	105.2	111.8	101.5	100.2	106.0	104.3	97.5	109.2	108.0	110.1	108.2	107.7	4.0	4.0	3.7	3.9
1985	111.9	112.2	105.2	107.9	117.2	103.3	101.9	108.3	103.7	95.7	113.2	110.4	115.3	111.8	110.9	3.4	3.5	3.0	3.3
1986	115.0	115.3	106.5	107.8	123.0	105.8	104.3	110.9	103.9	93.6	115.6	110.8	119.1	114.9	113.9	2.8	2.7	2.7	2.5
1987	119.1	120.4	109.7	112.6	129.0	108.8	106.8	115.9	106.0	100.8	119.6	113.5	124.1	119.0	117.7	3.6	4.5	3.3	3.4
1959: I	37.4	35.0	52.1	34.8	30.9	57.9	65.7	30.2	32.7	26.9	25.5	26.9	24.7	37.4	30.2	0	0	4.1	0
II	37.5	35.1	52.3	34.9	31.0	58.0	65.9	30.2	32.8	27.0	25.6	27.0	24.9	37.5	30.4	1.3	1.1	2.7	1.2
III	37.6	35.3	52.3	35.1	31.3	58.0	66.0	30.2	32.9	27.1	25.7	27.1	25.0	37.5	30.6	1.7	2.1	2.7	1.9
IV	37.8	35.5	52.3	35.3	31.5	58.1	66.1	30.2	33.0	27.1	25.9	27.2	25.1	37.7	30.6	1.4	1.9	0	1.6
1960: I	37.8	35.5	52.2	35.2	31.6	58.1	66.1	30.2	33.4	27.2	26.1	27.2	25.5	37.8	30.9	.9	.4	4.0	1.0
II	38.0	35.7	52.2	35.5	31.8	58.2	66.2	30.3	33.5	27.4	26.1	27.1	25.6	37.9	30.9	1.8	2.3	0	2.0
III	38.1	35.8	52.0	35.6	32.0	58.2	66.2	30.3	33.7	27.4	26.4	27.7	25.8	38.1	31.0	1.5	1.4	1.3	1.8
IV	38.2	36.0	51.8	35.8	32.2	58.1	66.1	30.3	33.6	27.2	26.6	27.7	25.9	38.1	31.0	.6	1.4	0	1.2
1961: I	38.2	36.0	51.8	35.8	32.3	58.1	66.1	30.2	33.6	27.2	26.7	27.7	26.1	38.2	31.0	.5	.8	0	.7
II	38.3	36.0	51.9	35.7	32.4	58.0	66.0	30.3	34.1	27.0	26.8	27.9	26.3	38.2	31.2	.5	−.1	2.6	.6
III	38.4	36.1	52.0	35.8	32.5	58.0	66.0	30.2	34.0	27.0	27.0	27.9	26.5	38.3	31.4	.8	1.2	2.6	1.1
IV	38.4	36.1	51.8	35.7	32.6	58.0	66.0	30.1	34.1	26.8	27.2	28.1	26.7	38.3	31.4	.5	.2	0	.7
1962: I	38.5	36.2	51.8	35.9	32.7	58.0	66.1	30.1	34.2	26.6	27.5	28.3	27.2	38.4	31.7	1.1	1.2	3.9	1.7
II	38.6	36.4	51.7	36.0	32.9	58.1	66.1	30.0	34.1	26.6	27.6	28.4	27.3	38.6	31.8	.9	1.4	1.3	1.3
III	38.7	36.4	51.7	36.0	33.0	58.1	66.1	29.9	34.1	26.6	27.7	28.5	27.4	38.6	31.9	.5	.7	1.3	.8
IV	38.8	36.5	51.5	36.2	33.1	58.0	66.1	29.7	34.2	26.6	28.0	29.0	27.4	38.7	32.2	1.1	1.1	3.8	1.8
1963: I	38.9	36.6	51.5	36.3	33.2	58.1	66.2	29.8	34.2	26.7	28.2	29.1	27.7	38.8	32.3	1.1	1.0	1.2	1.4
II	38.9	36.7	51.5	36.3	33.3	58.0	66.2	29.6	34.3	27.0	28.3	29.2	27.8	38.9	32.3	.9	.9	0	.9
III	39.0	36.9	51.6	36.5	33.5	58.0	66.2	29.3	34.3	27.2	28.4	29.2	27.9	39.0	32.4	1.1	1.6	1.2	1.1
IV	39.2	37.0	51.8	36.6	33.6	58.0	66.2	29.5	34.5	27.5	28.7	29.7	28.2	39.2	32.6	1.7	1.4	2.5	2.4
1964: I	39.3	37.1	52.1	36.8	33.7	58.0	66.3	29.3	34.5	27.6	28.8	29.9	28.3	39.3	32.7	1.3	1.5	1.2	1.3
II	39.4	37.2	51.9	36.8	33.8	58.1	66.3	29.5	34.6	27.7	29.0	30.1	28.4	39.4	32.8	.9	.5	1.2	1.1
III	39.6	37.3	51.8	36.9	34.0	58.3	66.4	29.8	34.9	27.7	29.2	30.2	28.6	39.5	33.0	1.2	1.0	2.5	1.7
IV	39.7	37.3	51.7	36.9	34.1	58.3	66.4	30.0	35.1	27.7	29.3	30.4	28.7	39.6	33.1	1.0	.8	1.2	1.3
1965: I	39.9	37.5	51.8	37.0	34.3	58.4	66.5	30.0	35.8	27.7	29.5	30.6	29.0	39.8	33.5	1.8	1.6	4.9	1.8
II	40.0	37.7	51.5	37.4	34.5	58.4	66.6	29.8	35.9	27.9	29.7	30.7	29.1	39.9	33.6	1.6	1.9	1.2	2.0
III	40.1	37.7	51.0	37.6	34.6	58.6	66.7	30.1	35.9	28.1	29.9	31.0	29.4	40.1	33.9	1.3	.8	3.6	2.2
IV	40.2	37.8	50.5	37.8	34.7	58.7	66.9	30.1	35.9	28.6	30.2	31.4	29.6	40.1	34.1	1.3	.8	2.4	2.2
1966: I	40.5	38.1	50.4	38.3	34.9	58.8	67.0	30.2	36.4	28.6	30.5	31.6	30.0	40.4	34.5	2.6	2.8	4.8	3.3
II	40.9	38.4	50.5	38.6	35.2	59.2	67.3	30.9	36.9	29.1	30.9	31.8	30.5	40.8	34.8	3.8	3.1	3.5	4.2
III	41.2	38.7	50.7	38.8	35.6	59.4	67.6	30.8	37.3	29.2	31.4	32.2	30.9	41.1	35.1	3.1	3.0	3.5	3.3
IV	41.5	39.0	50.9	39.1	35.9	59.7	67.9	31.3	37.8	29.3	31.6	32.3	31.3	41.4	35.5	3.3	3.3	4.6	3.3
1967: I	41.7	39.1	50.8	39.2	36.1	60.0	68.2	31.5	38.1	29.4	32.0	32.3	31.9	41.6	35.7	1.9	1.1	2.3	2.1
II	41.9	39.3	50.9	39.3	36.3	60.1	68.3	31.4	38.1	29.4	32.4	32.6	32.3	41.8	35.7	2.0	1.9	0	2.2
III	42.2	39.6	51.3	39.7	36.6	60.3	68.5	31.6	38.2	29.5	32.7	32.9	32.7	42.2	36.0	3.1	3.6	3.4	3.6
IV	42.6	40.0	51.8	40.1	37.0	60.5	68.7	31.8	38.4	29.6	33.2	33.6	33.1	42.5	36.4	3.8	3.6	4.5	4.3
1968: I	43.0	40.4	52.1	40.5	37.4	60.9	69.0	32.6	38.8	29.8	33.8	33.9	33.7	43.0	37.1	3.9	4.0	7.9	4.9
II	43.5	40.8	52.3	41.0	37.8	61.2	69.3	32.7	39.4	30.1	34.2	34.2	34.2	43.4	37.5	4.3	4.3	4.4	4.5
III	43.8	41.2	52.7	41.4	38.2	61.5	69.6	33.0	39.3	30.2	34.7	34.9	34.6	43.8	37.9	3.5	3.9	4.3	4.1
IV	44.4	41.6	53.1	41.9	38.6	62.1	70.2	33.9	39.6	30.4	35.3	35.3	35.2	44.3	38.5	4.8	4.5	6.5	5.5
1969: I	44.8	42.0	53.3	42.3	39.0	62.7	70.6	35.3	40.2	30.7	35.6	35.5	35.7	44.7	39.0	4.1	3.6	5.3	4.7
II	45.3	42.5	53.7	42.9	39.5	63.1	70.9	35.8	40.4	30.9	36.1	35.8	36.3	45.2	39.5	4.3	4.9	5.2	4.9
III	45.8	43.0	53.9	43.5	39.9	63.4	71.2	36.3	41.0	31.3	37.0	36.9	37.0	45.8	40.1	5.2	4.6	6.2	6.2
IV	46.4	43.5	54.3	44.1	40.5	63.7	71.4	36.8	42.0	32.0	37.5	37.3	37.6	46.3	40.6	4.6	5.2	5.1	5.1
1970: I	46.8	44.0	54.4	44.7	41.0	62.7	70.0	37.0	42.5	32.4	38.5	38.6	38.5	46.7	41.3	3.4	4.7	7.1	6.0
II	47.1	44.5	54.7	45.1	41.6	61.6	68.4	37.9	43.3	32.9	39.2	39.2	39.2	47.0	41.9	2.6	4.1	5.9	5.0
III	47.3	44.9	55.0	45.4	42.1	60.9	67.7	37.2	43.5	34.0	39.9	39.8	39.9	47.2	42.2	1.9	3.9	2.9	3.3
IV	47.8	45.5	55.9	45.8	42.8	60.7	67.4	37.6	43.9	34.5	40.5	40.4	40.5	47.7	42.7	4.1	5.4	4.8	5.2
1971: I	48.3	45.9	56.6	45.9	43.3	60.8	67.1	38.5	44.9	35.3	41.5	41.7	41.3	48.2	43.4	4.3	3.8	6.7	5.9
II	48.7	46.4	56.9	46.4	43.9	60.7	66.9	39.3	45.2	35.3	42.1	42.4	42.0	48.7	44.2	4.0	4.4	7.6	5.2
III	49.0	46.9	56.7	46.8	44.5	60.5	66.5	39.7	45.3	35.8	42.6	42.7	42.5	49.0	44.7	2.5	3.9	4.6	3.7
IV	49.3	47.2	56.4	47.1	45.0	60.4	66.1	40.4	45.7	36.1	43.1	43.4	42.8	49.3	45.3	2.3	2.8	5.5	3.4
1972: I	49.9	47.7	56.8	47.6	45.5	60.3	65.9	40.7	46.2	37.0	44.4	45.4	43.6	49.8	45.8	4.4	4.2	4.5	5.8
II	50.1	48.0	57.1	47.9	45.9	59.7	65.0	41.1	46.4	37.6	44.9	45.8	44.2	50.0	46.1	1.5	2.8	2.6	2.8
III	50.4	48.4	57.3	48.3	46.4	59.5	64.6	41.7	46.4	38.1	45.5	46.2	44.9	50.3	46.7	2.4	3.4	5.3	3.8
IV	50.9	48.9	57.2	48.9	46.8	59.7	64.5	42.8	47.1	38.7	46.2	47.0	45.6	50.8	47.3	3.9	3.7	5.2	4.8
1973: I	51.7	49.5	57.5	50.0	47.2	60.5	65.5	43.2	48.1	39.6	47.3	48.3	46.5	51.6	48.0	6.3	5.5	6.1	5.8
II	52.6	50.5	58.0	51.5	47.9	61.8	66.6	44.7	49.6	41.8	48.3	49.3	47.5	52.5	49.0	7.4	8.2	8.6	7.4
III	53.7	51.5	58.3	53.1	48.6	62.5	67.2	46.1	51.6	43.0	49.4	51.0	48.3	53.6	50.0	8.3	7.8	8.4	8.3
IV	54.4	52.4	58.5	54.5	49.4	62.5	67.0	46.7	53.8	45.5	50.2	51.9	49.0	54.4	51.2	5.9	7.7	10.0	6.8
1974: I	55.5	53.8	59.0	56.8	50.3	62.8	67.1	48.0	56.5	49.5	51.5	53.1	50.3	55.5	51.9	8.2	11.2	5.6	8.5
II	56.4	55.2	60.5	58.4	51.4	63.7	67.8	49.4	58.2	53.7	52.5	53.4	51.8	56.4	53.0	6.7	10.1	8.8	8.8
III	57.8	56.4	62.6	59.6	52.5	64.9	68.9	51.0	60.9	56.4	54.2	55.4	53.4	57.7	54.8	9.9	9.4	14.3	12.5
IV	59.3	57.8	64.4	61.1	53.6	66.3	70.4	52.2	63.8	58.3	55.9	57.4	54.8	59.3	56.3	11.2	10.0	11.4	12.3

Source: *Survey of Current Business* (Washington, D.C.: Department of Commerce, September 1988).

Table 3.—Price Indexes and the Gross National Product Implicit Price Deflator—Continued

[Index numbers, 1982=100; quarterly data are seasonally adjusted at annual rates]

Year and quarter	GNP	Fixed-weighted price indexes							Exports	Imports				Final sales	GNP IPD	Percent change from preceding period			
		Personal consumption expenditures				Fixed investment					Government purchases of goods and services					FWPI		GNP IPD	GNP Chain price index
		Total	Durable goods	Nondurable goods	Services	Total	Nonresidential	Residential			Total	Federal	State and local			GNP	PCE		
1975: I	60.4	58.7	65.4	61.8	54.8	68.0	72.1	53.6	65.5	59.6	57.0	58.1	56.1	60.4	57.7	7.8	6.7	10.3	9.3
II	61.1	59.4	66.4	62.3	55.6	68.9	73.1	54.2	65.2	60.3	57.9	58.6	57.4	61.1	58.6	4.6	4.9	6.4	6.0
III	62.3	60.6	67.1	63.8	56.6	69.2	73.4	54.6	65.2	59.5	59.0	59.7	58.6	62.2	59.9	7.7	8.4	9.2	8.3
IV	63.3	61.7	68.1	64.7	57.8	69.8	73.8	55.7	65.7	59.6	60.3	61.1	59.6	63.3	61.0	6.7	6.9	7.6	7.2
1976: I	64.0	62.3	69.1	64.7	58.8	70.7	74.7	56.5	66.4	60.1	61.0	61.6	60.7	64.0	61.7	4.6	4.2	4.7	4.8
II	64.7	62.9	69.9	65.0	59.7	71.4	75.3	57.8	67.0	61.0	61.8	62.0	61.7	64.6	62.5	4.2	4.2	5.3	4.6
III	65.4	63.9	70.7	65.6	60.8	71.7	75.4	58.8	67.5	61.9	62.4	62.2	62.5	65.3	63.4	4.4	6.0	5.4	5.4
IV	66.3	64.8	71.8	66.2	62.1	71.8	75.2	60.3	68.6	62.2	63.4	63.6	63.3	66.3	64.5	5.9	6.2	7.1	6.8
1977: I	67.2	65.9	72.5	67.1	63.5	72.2	75.1	62.0	69.5	64.1	64.6	64.8	64.4	67.2	65.6	5.5	7.0	7.0	6.2
II	68.1	67.0	72.9	68.1	64.7	72.6	75.1	64.1	70.6	65.8	65.6	65.4	65.8	68.1	66.9	5.6	6.8	8.2	6.7
III	68.7	68.0	73.5	69.0	66.0	72.5	74.6	65.0	70.3	67.0	66.2	65.3	66.8	68.7	67.7	3.4	6.2	4.9	4.7
IV	69.7	69.0	74.4	69.7	67.1	73.1	74.6	68.0	70.7	67.6	67.8	67.6	68.0	69.7	68.9	6.0	5.6	7.3	7.5
1978: I	70.7	70.0	75.3	70.6	68.3	73.1	74.4	68.6	72.1	69.0	69.0	69.1	69.0	70.6	69.9	5.4	6.3	5.9	5.8
II	72.0	71.6	76.6	72.7	69.6	73.9	74.7	71.5	73.8	70.9	70.1	69.7	70.3	71.9	71.6	7.7	9.3	10.1	9.1
III	73.2	72.9	78.0	74.0	70.9	74.7	75.0	73.7	74.8	72.0	71.4	70.6	71.9	73.2	72.9	7.0	7.5	7.5	7.8
IV	74.7	74.2	79.2	75.3	72.2	75.9	75.9	76.2	76.9	73.3	73.3	73.0	73.5	74.7	74.4	8.7	7.6	8.5	9.1
1979: I	76.3	75.8	80.5	77.4	73.4	77.6	77.6	77.8	79.5	75.8	74.5	74.1	74.9	76.2	76.1	8.3	8.7	9.5	8.4
II	78.0	77.6	81.9	79.8	74.9	79.6	79.5	80.2	82.3	78.6	76.0	75.2	76.5	77.8	77.8	9.6	10.0	9.2	9.6
III	79.7	79.5	83.0	81.9	76.8	81.3	80.9	82.7	84.0	82.3	77.9	77.0	78.6	79.7	79.4	8.7	9.9	8.5	8.1
IV	81.3	81.4	84.6	83.9	78.7	82.6	82.1	84.2	85.6	86.8	80.8	80.9	80.7	81.3	81.0	8.7	9.9	8.3	8.2
1980: I	83.2	83.7	86.9	86.6	80.8	84.3	83.7	86.3	87.6	92.4	83.0	82.7	83.3	83.2	82.7	9.4	12.1	8.7	9.0
II	85.1	85.8	88.8	88.6	82.9	86.2	85.4	89.1	88.9	95.3	85.4	85.3	85.4	85.1	84.6	9.5	10.1	9.5	9.4
III	86.9	87.8	90.5	90.6	85.1	87.9	87.0	90.9	91.4	98.1	86.8	86.2	87.2	86.9	86.5	9.0	9.9	9.3	9.4
IV	89.3	90.0	92.2	92.8	87.3	89.2	88.5	91.7	94.4	100.0	90.0	90.1	88.9	89.3	89.0	11.3	10.2	12.1	11.3
1981: I	91.5	92.2	93.4	95.4	89.5	91.4	90.7	94.0	96.6	101.9	91.7	92.6	91.0	91.4	91.3	10.0	10.2	10.7	9.8
II	93.1	93.8	95.2	96.5	91.4	93.4	92.8	95.4	97.4	102.5	93.1	93.7	92.7	93.1	92.8	7.5	7.4	6.7	7.5
III	95.1	95.5	96.7	97.6	93.8	95.6	94.8	98.1	98.0	100.7	94.6	95.0	94.3	95.1	94.9	8.8	7.6	9.4	9.0
IV	96.9	97.1	98.0	98.4	95.8	97.7	97.1	99.6	98.7	101.0	96.8	98.1	95.9	96.9	96.7	7.7	6.4	7.8	7.9
1982: I	98.2	98.3	98.9	99.2	97.4	99.2	98.8	100.5	99.7	101.4	98.1	98.7	97.7	98.2	98.2	5.7	5.2	6.4	5.9
II	99.4	99.1	99.9	99.2	98.9	100.0	100.0	100.2	100.1	100.0	99.4	99.6	99.2	99.4	99.4	4.7	3.5	5.0	4.8
III	100.7	100.7	100.4	100.5	100.8	100.6	100.7	100.4	100.1	99.3	100.5	100.0	100.9	100.7	100.8	5.5	6.3	5.8	5.6
IV	101.7	101.8	100.7	101.0	102.7	100.2	100.5	99.1	100.0	99.3	102.0	101.7	102.2	101.7	101.7	4.0	4.8	3.6	4.1
1983: I	102.6	102.6	101.4	100.7	104.3	100.7	100.3	101.9	100.4	98.3	103.0	102.8	103.2	102.6	102.5	3.6	2.8	3.2	3.7
II	103.6	103.7	101.7	102.0	105.5	99.9	99.7	100.4	101.0	97.4	103.9	103.7	104.1	103.5	103.3	3.8	4.6	3.2	3.6
III	104.6	104.8	102.5	102.7	106.9	100.6	99.9	103.2	101.7	97.7	105.0	104.5	105.3	104.6	104.2	4.2	4.1	3.5	4.1
IV	105.7	105.8	103.4	103.3	108.4	100.5	99.6	103.3	103.2	97.6	106.0	105.4	106.4	105.6	105.4	4.0	4.1	4.7	3.9
1984: I	106.8	107.0	103.5	104.6	109.7	100.4	99.5	103.5	103.9	97.7	107.7	106.9	108.2	106.8	106.5	4.5	4.5	4.2	4.5
II	107.8	107.9	104.1	104.9	111.1	101.4	99.9	106.4	104.9	98.1	108.8	107.8	109.6	107.8	107.3	3.8	3.2	3.0	3.8
III	108.7	108.9	104.3	105.4	112.6	101.8	100.4	106.9	104.5	97.4	109.6	108.1	110.7	108.7	108.2	3.4	3.8	3.4	3.4
IV	109.6	109.7	104.5	106.0	113.8	102.3	100.9	107.2	104.0	96.8	110.7	109.0	111.9	109.5	109.0	3.2	3.2	3.0	3.1
1985: I	110.6	110.6	105.0	106.6	115.0	102.6	101.1	107.9	103.8	95.2	112.1	110.4	113.4	110.5	109.7	3.8	3.2	2.6	3.7
II	111.5	111.7	105.1	107.7	116.4	102.9	101.5	107.9	103.9	95.6	112.8	110.9	114.9	111.4	110.6	3.3	4.2	3.3	3.2
III	112.3	112.6	105.1	108.1	117.9	103.5	102.2	108.2	103.5	95.3	113.4	110.0	115.8	112.2	111.3	2.8	3.3	2.6	2.6
IV	113.2	113.8	105.4	109.1	119.5	104.2	102.8	109.0	103.4	96.8	114.4	111.0	117.0	113.1	112.2	3.3	4.3	3.3	3.2
1986: I	113.8	114.3	105.8	108.3	120.8	104.7	103.3	109.7	104.0	95.8	114.9	110.9	117.8	113.7	112.4	2.2	1.5	.7	1.7
II	114.5	114.5	106.0	106.8	122.3	105.5	104.1	110.3	103.9	92.4	115.2	110.8	118.4	114.4	113.4	2.4	.7	3.6	2.0
III	115.4	115.7	106.9	107.7	123.8	106.1	104.6	111.2	103.7	92.8	115.5	110.5	119.3	115.2	114.7	3.0	4.2	4.7	3.1
IV	116.2	116.6	107.4	108.3	125.2	106.8	105.3	112.2	103.9	94.7	116.6	110.8	120.8	116.0	115.3	2.8	3.5	2.1	2.4
1987: I	117.4	118.2	108.5	110.3	126.6	107.6	106.1	113.2	104.7	97.8	118.0	112.5	122.0	117.2	116.3	4.2	5.6	3.5	4.0
II	118.6	119.9	109.2	112.4	128.1	108.4	106.5	114.9	105.5	100.3	119.1	113.3	123.3	118.4	117.3	4.2	5.7	3.5	3.7
III	119.7	121.1	110.2	113.4	129.9	107.0	107.0	117.4	106.4	101.9	120.1	113.7	124.9	119.5	118.2	3.7	4.2	3.1	3.6
IV	120.8	122.5	111.0	114.3	131.5	109.9	107.5	118.3	107.0	103.0	121.2	114.4	126.1	120.6	118.9	3.8	4.6	2.4	3.4

NOTE.—GNP=Gross national product; PCE=Personal consumption expenditures; IPD=Implicit price deflator; FWPI=Fixed-weighted price index.

Source: *Survey of Current Business* (Washington, D.C.: Department of Commerce, September 1988).

COMMODITY PRICES—CONSUMER PRICES

YEAR AND MONTH	All items, wage earners and clerical workers, revised (CPI-W)	All items, all urban consumers (CPI-U) ★	All items less shelter	All items less food	All items less medical care ★	Commodities Total ★	Nondurables Total	Nondurables less food	Durables	Commodities less food	Services ★	Food Total ★	Food at home
						1967 = 100							
1961	89.6	89.6	89.9	89.7	90.3	92.0	90.2	91.2	96.6	93.4	85.2	89.1	90.4
1962	90.6	90.6	90.9	90.8	91.2	92.8	90.9	91.8	97.6	94.1	86.8	89.9	91.0
1963	91.7	91.7	92.1	92.0	92.3	93.6	92.0	92.7	97.9	94.8	88.5	91.2	92.2
1964	92.9	92.9	93.2	93.2	93.5	94.6	93.0	93.5	98.8	95.6	90.2	92.4	93.2
1965	94.5	94.5	94.6	94.5	94.9	95.7	94.6	94.8	98.4	96.2	92.2	94.4	95.5
1966	97.2	97.2	97.4	96.7	97.7	98.2	98.1	97.0	98.5	97.5	95.8	99.1	100.3
1967	100.0	100.0	100.0	100.0	100.0	100.0	100.0	100.0	100.0	100.0	100.0	100.0	100.0
1968	104.2	104.2	104.1	104.4	104.1	103.7	103.9	104.1	103.1	103.7	105.2	103.6	103.2
1969	109.8	109.8	109.0	110.1	109.7	108.4	108.9	108.8	107.0	108.1	112.5	108.9	108.2
1970	116.3	116.3	114.4	116.7	116.1	113.5	114.0	113.1	111.8	112.5	121.6	114.9	113.7
1971	121.3	121.3	119.3	122.1	120.9	117.4	117.7	117.0	116.5	116.8	128.4	118.4	116.4
1972	125.3	125.3	122.9	125.8	124.9	120.9	121.7	119.8	118.9	119.4	133.3	123.5	121.6
1973	133.1	133.1	131.1	130.7	132.9	129.9	132.8	124.8	121.9	123.5	139.1	141.4	141.4
1974	147.7	147.7	146.1	143.7	147.7	145.5	151.0	140.9	130.6	136.6	152.1	161.7	162.4
1975	161.2	161.2	159.1	157.1	160.9	158.4	163.2	151.7	145.5	149.1	166.6	175.4	175.8
1976	170.5	170.5	168.3	167.5	169.7	165.2	169.2	158.3	154.3	156.6	180.4	180.8	179.5
1977	181.5	181.5	179.1	178.4	180.3	174.7	178.9	166.5	163.2	165.1	194.3	192.2	190.2
1978	195.3	195.4	191.3	191.2	194.0	187.1	192.0	174.3	173.9	174.7	210.9	211.4	210.2
1979	217.7	217.4	210.8	213.0	216.1	208.4	215.9	198.7	191.1	195.1	234.2	234.5	232.9
1980	247.0	246.8	235.5	244.0	245.5	233.9	245.0	235.2	221.4	222.0	270.3	254.6	251.5
1981	272.3	272.4	258.5	270.6	270.9	253.6	266.3	257.5	227.1	241.2	305.7	274.6	269.9
1982	288.6	289.1	273.3	288.4	286.8	263.8	273.6	261.6	241.1	250.9	333.3	285.7	279.2
1983	297.4	298.4	283.5	298.3	295.1	271.5	279.0	266.3	253.0	259.0	344.9	291.7	282.2
1984	307.6	311.1	295.1	311.3	307.3	280.7	286.6	270.8	266.5	267.0	363.0	302.9	292.6
1981:													
January	260.7	260.5	247.6	257.6	259.2	245.4	256.9	245.3	221.0	232.4	287.7	268.6	265.6
February	263.5	263.2	251.2	260.4	261.9	248.3	262.3	253.2	220.3	235.4	290.1	270.8	267.3
March	265.2	265.1	253.3	262.3	263.7	249.8	265.2	257.5	219.8	237.0	292.5	272.2	268.6
April	266.8	266.8	254.9	264.2	265.4	250.8	265.9	258.1	221.1	238.0	295.4	272.9	268.7
May	269.1	269.0	256.2	267.0	267.6	251.9	265.8	258.2	223.9	239.6	299.6	272.5	267.7
June	271.4	271.3	257.8	269.5	269.9	253.2	266.2	258.0	226.6	241.1	303.5	273.6	268.7
July	274.6	274.4	259.9	272.7	273.0	255.0	267.1	257.5	229.6	242.6	308.8	276.2	271.6
August	276.5	276.5	261.4	274.9	274.9	256.2	268.1	258.4	230.9	243.8	312.2	277.4	272.8
September	279.1	279.3	263.5	278.2	277.8	257.7	269.5	260.3	232.6	245.5	317.3	278.0	273.2
October	279.7	279.9	264.5	279.0	278.3	257.9	269.5	260.7	232.9	245.9	318.6	277.6	272.1
November	280.4	280.7	265.4	280.1	279.0	258.0	269.5	261.1	233.2	246.2	320.6	277.1	271.0
December	281.1	281.5	266.0	280.8	279.6	258.4	269.8	261.1	233.7	246.5	321.8	277.8	271.7
1982:													
January	282.1	282.5	267.4	281.4	280.6	258.8	270.8	260.2	233.4	245.9	323.9	281.0	275.3
February	282.9	283.4	268.3	282.1	281.5	259.5	271.7	260.1	233.7	246.0	325.3	283.3	278.0
March	282.5	283.1	268.5	281.7	280.9	258.8	270.7	258.4	233.5	245.2	325.5	283.0	277.1
April	283.7	284.3	268.7	282.9	282.1	258.9	269.3	255.0	235.8	245.0	328.4	283.9	277.9
May	286.5	287.1	270.6	286.0	284.9	261.5	270.7	256.2	239.8	247.8	331.8	285.5	279.8
June	290.1	290.6	273.8	289.7	288.4	265.1	274.4	261.2	243.2	251.9	334.9	287.8	282.6
July	291.8	292.2	275.3	291.5	289.9	266.5	275.7	263.0	244.7	253.5	337.0	288.5	282.8
August	292.4	292.8	275.7	292.5	290.5	266.4	275.5	263.6	244.6	253.8	338.9	287.4	280.8
September	292.8	293.3	276.9	292.9	290.8	266.6	276.2	264.6	244.1	253.9	339.7	287.6	280.6
October	293.6	294.1	277.9	294.0	291.5	267.5	276.5	265.7	246.0	255.4	340.3	287.0	279.4
November	293.2	293.6	278.1	293.6	290.8	267.8	276.4	266.1	246.6	256.0	338.6	286.4	278.3
December	292.0	292.4	278.2	292.1	289.5	267.7	275.8	264.7	247.3	255.8	335.6	286.5	277.8
1983:													
January	292.1	3 293.1	278.5	3 292.6	3 290.0	3 267.2	275.2	262.4	3 247.3	3 254.4	3 337.9	288.1	279.3
February	292.3	293.2	278.5	292.6	290.0	266.7	274.6	260.5	247.1	253.2	338.9	289.0	280.3
March	293.0	293.4	278.7	292.4	290.1	266.7	274.4	258.9	247.4	252.4	339.4	290.5	281.9
April	294.9	295.5	280.8	294.7	292.3	269.2	277.3	263.0	248.7	255.4	341.2	291.9	283.4
May	296.3	297.1	282.4	296.5	293.9	270.9	279.3	266.3	249.5	257.6	342.6	292.4	283.8
June	297.2	298.1	283.4	297.8	294.9	271.6	279.7	267.3	251.2	258.9	344.0	292.0	283.0
July	298.2	299.3	284.5	299.3	296.0	272.5	280.3	268.4	252.9	260.2	345.6	292.0	282.8
August	299.5	300.3	285.4	300.5	297.0	273.4	281.0	269.6	254.3	261.4	346.8	292.5	282.5
September	300.8	301.8	286.8	302.3	298.5	274.5	281.8	270.6	256.4	262.9	349.0	292.6	282.3
October	301.3	302.6	287.5	303.2	299.3	275.0	281.7	270.2	258.7	263.6	350.2	292.9	282.3
November	301.4	303.1	287.8	303.9	299.7	275.2	281.1	269.5	261.0	264.1	351.0	292.5	281.4
December	301.5	303.5	288.1	304.0	300.0	275.5	281.2	268.5	261.8	263.8	351.6	293.9	283.0
1984:													
January	302.7	305.2	289.8	304.8	301.6	276.8	283.2	267.4	261.4	263.0	353.9	299.4	290.2
February	303.3	306.6	291.4	305.9	302.9	278.3	285.3	269.1	260.9	263.8	355.3	302.1	293.6
March	303.3	307.3	291.9	306.8	303.6	278.7	285.5	269.3	262.2	264.4	356.5	302.2	293.1
April	304.1,	308.8	293.2	308.6	305.1	280.1	286.3	270.7	265.2	266.5	358.1	302.3	292.8
May	305.4	309.7	294.0	310.0	306.0	280.4	286.1	271.1	267.0	267.4	359.9	301.4	290.7
June	306.2	311.0	294.9	311.0	306.9	280.6	286.0	270.5	267.8	267.4	361.9	302.0	291.4
July	307.5	311.7	295.6	312.0	307.9	280.6	286.0	269.5	267.8	266.8	364.5	303.2	292.5
August	310.3	313.0	296.7	313.2	309.2	281.4	287.1	270.0	267.8	267.1	366.5	304.8	294.4
September	312.1	314.5	298.1	315.2	310.7	282.3	288.0	272.3	268.7	268.8	368.9	304.2	293.4
October	312.2	315.3	298.7	316.1	311.4	283.1	288.8	273.6	269.3	269.8	369.7	304.3	293.4
November	311.9	315.3	298.6	316.2	311.3	283.0	288.5	273.3	270.0	269.9	369.9	304.1	292.4
December	312.2	315.5	298.6	316.2	311.5	282.8	288.3	272.2	269.8	269.2	370.6	305.1	293.2

Footnotes giving source of data and description of series appear in the section immediately following these tables.

★Monthly data prior to 1981 are shown on p. 169.

Source: *Business Statistics, a Supplement to the Survey of Current Business* (Washington, D.C.: U.S. Department of Commerce, Bureau of Economic Analysis, 1984).

Table 4.—National Income and Disposition of Personal Income

[Billions of dollars; quarterly data are seasonally adjusted at annual rates]

Year and quarter	National income	Compensation of employees: Total	Compensation of employees: Wages and salaries	Compensation of employees: Supplements to wages and salaries	Proprietors' income with IVA and CCAdj: Farm	Proprietors' income with IVA and CCAdj: Nonfarm	Rental income of persons with CCAdj	Corporate profits with IVA and CCAdj: Total	Corporate profits: IVA	Corporate profits: CCAdj	Corporate profits: Profits before tax	Corporate profits: Profits after tax	Net interest	Personal income	Less: Personal tax and nontax payments	Equals: DPI	Less: Personal outlays	Equals: Personal saving	Saving as percentage of DPI	DPI in constant (1982) dollars
1929	84.7	51.1	50.5	.7	6.1	8.3	4.9	9.6	.5	−.9	10.0	8.6	4.7	84.3	2.6	81.7	79.2	2.6	3.2	498.6
1930	73.5	46.9	46.2	.7	4.3	6.9	4.2	6.3	3.3	−.7	3.7	2.9	4.9	75.5	2.5	73.0	71.1	1.9	2.6	459.2
1931	58.3	39.8	39.2	.6	3.4	5.2	3.4	1.6	2.4	−.4	−.4	−.9	4.9	64.7	1.8	62.9	61.4	1.4	2.3	438.7
1932	42.0	31.1	30.5	.6	2.1	3.1	2.7	−1.6	1.0	−.3	−2.3	−2.7	4.6	49.4	1.4	48.0	49.3	−1.3	−2.8	380.2
1933	39.4	29.6	29.0	.6	2.5	2.9	2.0	−1.5	−2.1	−.3	1.0	.4	4.1	46.3	1.4	44.9	46.5	−1.6	−3.6	370.8
1934	48.3	34.3	33.7	.6	2.9	4.3	1.6	1.1	−.6	−.6	2.3	1.6	4.1	53.1	1.6	51.6	52.0	−.4	−.9	392.1
1935	56.1	37.4	36.7	.7	5.2	5.1	1.6	2.7	−.2	−.6	3.6	2.6	4.1	59.8	1.9	57.9	56.4	1.5	2.5	427.8
1936	64.0	43.0	42.0	1.0	4.3	6.3	1.7	5.0	−.7	−.6	6.3	4.9	3.8	68.0	2.2	65.8	62.8	3.0	4.5	479.1
1937	72.2	48.0	46.1	1.8	6.0	6.8	1.9	5.8	0	−1.1	6.9	5.4	3.7	73.4	2.9	70.5	67.5	2.9	4.2	494.7
1938	65.8	45.0	43.0	2.0	4.4	6.5	2.4	3.9	1.0	−1.1	4.0	3.0	3.6	67.6	2.8	64.8	64.9	−.1	−.1	462.3
1939	71.2	48.2	46.0	2.2	4.4	7.1	2.6	5.5	−.7	−1.0	7.2	5.7	3.6	72.1	2.4	69.7	67.9	1.8	2.6	499.5
1940	79.6	52.2	49.9	2.3	4.4	8.2	2.7	8.8	−.2	−1.1	10.0	7.2	3.3	77.6	2.6	75.0	72.0	3.0	4.0	530.7
1941	102.8	64.8	62.1	2.8	6.4	10.8	3.2	14.3	−2.5	−1.1	17.9	10.3	3.3	95.2	3.3	91.9	81.9	10.0	10.9	604.1
1942	136.2	85.3	82.1	3.2	10.1	13.8	4.1	19.7	−1.2	−.8	21.7	10.3	3.1	122.4	5.9	116.4	89.5	27.0	23.2	693.0
1943	169.7	109.6	105.8	3.8	12.0	16.8	4.6	24.0	−.8	−.5	25.3	11.2	2.7	150.7	17.8	132.9	100.2	32.7	24.6	721.4
1944	182.6	121.3	116.7	4.5	11.9	18.1	4.8	24.2	−.3	.2	24.2	11.3	2.3	164.5	18.9	145.6	109.0	36.5	25.1	749.3
1945	181.6	123.3	117.5	5.8	12.4	19.1	5.0	19.7	−.6	.4	19.8	9.1	2.2	170.0	20.8	149.2	120.5	28.7	19.2	739.5
1946	180.7	119.6	112.0	7.6	14.8	21.5	5.8	17.2	−5.3	−2.4	24.8	15.7	1.8	177.6	18.7	158.9	145.3	13.6	8.6	723.3
1947	196.6	130.1	123.1	7.0	15.1	20.4	5.8	22.9	−5.9	−2.9	31.8	20.5	2.3	190.2	21.4	168.8	163.6	5.2	3.1	694.8
1948	221.5	142.1	135.5	6.5	17.5	22.9	6.4	30.3	−2.2	−3.2	35.6	23.2	2.4	209.2	21.0	188.1	177.0	11.1	5.9	733.1
1949	215.2	142.0	134.7	7.3	12.8	23.1	6.7	28.0	1.9	−3.0	29.2	19.0	2.6	206.4	18.5	187.9	180.6	7.4	3.9	733.2
1950	239.8	155.4	147.2	8.2	13.6	25.2	7.7	34.9	−5.0	−3.0	42.9	25.0	3.0	228.1	20.6	207.5	194.8	12.6	6.1	791.8
1951	277.3	181.6	171.6	10.0	16.0	28.0	8.3	39.9	−1.2	−3.4	44.5	21.9	3.5	256.5	28.9	227.6	211.0	16.6	7.3	819.0
1952	291.6	196.3	185.6	10.7	15.0	29.4	9.4	37.5	1.0	−3.2	39.6	20.2	3.9	273.8	34.0	239.8	222.4	17.4	7.3	844.3
1953	306.6	210.4	199.0	11.5	13.0	30.4	10.7	37.7	−1.0	−2.5	41.2	20.9	4.4	290.5	35.5	255.1	236.7	18.4	7.2	880.0
1954	306.3	209.4	197.2	12.1	12.4	31.1	11.6	36.6	−.3	−1.8	38.7	21.1	5.2	293.0	32.5	260.5	244.1	16.4	6.3	894.0
1955	336.3	225.9	212.1	13.8	11.3	34.0	12.0	47.1	−1.7	−.4	49.2	27.2	5.8	314.2	35.4	278.8	262.8	16.0	5.8	944.5
1956	356.3	244.7	229.0	15.7	11.1	35.8	12.4	45.7	−2.7	−1.2	49.6	27.6	6.5	337.2	39.7	297.5	276.2	21.3	7.2	989.4
1957	372.8	257.8	239.9	17.8	11.0	37.8	13.1	45.3	−1.5	−1.3	48.1	26.7	7.8	356.3	42.4	313.9	291.2	22.7	7.2	1,012.1
1958	375.0	259.8	241.3	18.5	13.1	38.5	13.9	40.3	−.3	−1.3	41.9	22.9	9.5	367.1	42.2	324.9	300.6	24.3	7.5	1,028.8
1959	409.2	281.2	259.8	21.4	10.8	40.9	14.6	51.4	−.3	−.8	52.6	28.9	10.2	390.7	46.1	344.6	322.8	21.8	6.3	1,067.2
1960	424.9	296.7	272.8	23.8	11.6	40.5	15.3	49.5	−.2	−.3	49.9	27.2	11.3	409.4	50.5	358.9	338.1	20.8	5.8	1,091.1
1961	439.0	305.6	280.5	25.1	12.0	42.3	15.8	50.3	.3	.2	49.8	27.1	12.9	426.0	52.2	373.8	348.9	24.9	6.6	1,123.2
1962	473.3	327.4	299.3	28.1	12.1	44.4	16.5	58.3	0	3.1	55.1	31.2	14.6	453.2	57.0	396.2	370.2	25.9	6.5	1,170.2
1963	500.3	345.5	314.8	30.7	11.9	45.7	17.1	63.6	.1	3.8	59.8	33.5	16.3	476.3	60.5	415.8	391.2	24.6	5.9	1,207.3
1964	537.6	371.0	337.7	33.2	10.7	49.8	17.3	70.7	−.5	4.5	66.7	38.7	18.2	510.2	58.8	451.4	419.9	31.5	7.0	1,291.0
1965	585.2	399.8	363.7	36.1	13.0	52.1	18.1	81.3	−1.2	5.2	77.4	46.5	20.9	552.0	65.2	486.8	452.5	34.3	7.0	1,365.7
1966	642.0	443.0	400.3	42.7	14.0	55.5	18.6	86.6	−2.1	5.4	83.3	49.6	24.3	600.8	74.9	525.9	489.9	36.0	6.8	1,431.3
1967	677.7	475.5	428.9	46.6	12.7	58.4	19.6	84.1	−1.6	5.5	80.1	47.5	27.4	644.5	82.4	562.1	516.9	45.1	8.0	1,493.2
1968	739.1	524.7	471.9	52.8	12.8	62.6	18.4	90.7	−3.7	5.3	89.1	49.7	29.8	707.2	97.7	609.6	567.1	42.5	7.0	1,551.3
1969	798.1	578.4	518.3	60.1	14.6	64.7	18.4	87.4	−5.9	6.1	87.2	47.5	34.6	772.9	116.3	656.7	614.5	42.2	6.4	1,599.8
1970	832.6	618.3	551.5	66.8	14.7	65.4	18.2	74.7	−6.6	5.2	76.0	41.7	41.2	831.8	116.2	715.6	657.9	57.7	8.1	1,668.1
1971	898.1	659.4	584.5	74.9	15.5	71.4	18.6	87.1	−4.6	4.3	87.3	49.6	46.3	894.0	117.3	776.8	710.5	66.3	8.5	1,728.4
1972	994.1	726.2	638.7	87.6	19.4	79.0	17.9	100.7	−6.6	5.8	101.5	59.6	51.0	981.6	142.0	839.6	778.2	61.4	7.3	1,797.4
1973	1,122.7	812.8	708.6	104.2	33.7	85.3	18.0	113.3	−20.0	6.2	127.2	77.9	59.6	1,101.7	152.0	949.8	860.8	89.0	9.4	1,916.3
1974	1,203.5	891.3	772.2	119.1	27.5	91.3	16.1	101.7	−39.5	2.3	138.9	87.1	75.5	1,210.1	171.8	1,038.4	941.7	96.7	9.3	1,896.6
1975	1,289.1	948.7	814.7	134.0	25.4	100.0	13.5	117.6	−11.0	−6.2	134.8	83.9	83.8	1,313.4	170.6	1,142.8	1,038.2	104.6	9.2	1,931.7
1976	1,441.4	1,057.9	899.6	158.3	20.6	117.1	11.9	145.2	−14.9	−10.1	170.3	106.0	88.8	1,451.4	198.7	1,252.6	1,156.9	95.8	7.6	2,001.0
1977	1,617.8	1,176.6	994.0	182.6	20.5	132.4	8.2	174.8	−16.6	−9.0	200.4	127.4	105.3	1,607.5	228.1	1,379.3	1,288.6	90.7	6.6	2,066.6
1978	1,838.2	1,329.2	1,119.6	209.7	27.0	149.2	9.3	197.2	−25.3	−10.9	233.5	150.0	126.3	1,812.4	261.1	1,551.2	1,441.1	110.2	7.1	2,167.4
1979	2,047.3	1,491.4	1,251.9	239.5	31.7	160.1	5.6	200.1	−43.2	−14.0	257.2	169.2	158.3	2,034.0	304.7	1,729.3	1,611.3	118.1	6.8	2,212.6
1980	2,203.5	1,638.2	1,372.0	266.3	20.5	160.1	6.6	177.2	−43.1	−16.8	237.1	152.3	200.9	2,258.5	340.5	1,918.0	1,781.1	136.9	7.1	2,214.3
1981	2,443.5	1,807.4	1,510.4	297.1	30.7	156.1	13.3	188.0	−24.2	−14.4	226.5	145.4	248.1	2,520.9	393.3	2,127.6	1,968.1	159.4	7.5	2,248.6
1982	2,518.4	1,907.0	1,586.1	320.9	24.6	150.9	13.6	150.0	−10.4	−9.2	169.6	106.5	272.3	2,670.8	409.3	2,261.4	2,107.5	153.9	6.8	2,261.5
1983	2,719.5	2,020.7	1,676.2	344.5	12.4	178.4	13.2	213.7	−10.9	17.0	207.6	130.4	281.0	2,838.6	410.5	2,428.1	2,297.4	130.6	5.4	2,331.9
1984	3,028.6	2,213.9	1,838.8	375.1	30.5	204.0	8.5	266.9	−5.8	32.7	240.0	146.1	304.8	3,108.7	440.2	2,668.6	2,504.5	164.1	6.1	2,469.8
1985	3,234.0	2,367.5	1,975.2	392.4	30.2	225.6	9.2	282.3	−1.7	59.7	224.3	127.8	319.0	3,325.3	486.6	2,838.7	2,713.3	125.4	4.4	2,542.8
1986	3,437.1	2,507.1	2,094.0	413.1	36.4	250.3	12.4	298.9	8.3	54.2	236.4	129.8	331.9	3,531.1	511.4	3,019.6	2,898.0	121.7	4.0	2,640.9
1987	3,678.7	2,683.4	2,248.4	435.0	43.0	270.0	18.4	310.4	−18.0	51.7	276.7	142.9	353.6	3,780.0	570.3	3,209.7	3,105.5	104.2	3.2	2,686.3
1960: I	425.3	294.2	270.7	23.5	10.3	40.8	15.2	53.8	−.9	−.4	55.0	29.6	11.0	404.3	49.4	354.9	332.6	22.3	6.3	1,087.3
II	425.3	297.1	273.4	23.8	11.8	40.7	15.3	49.5	−.6	−.4	50.5	27.5	10.9	409.5	50.4	359.1	339.0	20.1	5.6	1,093.6
III	425.7	297.9	273.9	24.0	12.0	40.3	15.4	48.6	.5	−.2	48.3	26.5	11.5	411.4	50.9	360.5	339.3	21.3	5.9	1,093.0
IV	423.1	297.4	273.3	24.1	12.1	40.2	15.5	46.0	.3	−.2	45.9	25.3	11.9	412.4	51.2	361.1	341.5	19.7	5.4	1,090.5
1961: I	424.3	298.3	273.8	24.5	12.1	41.3	15.6	45.0	−.1	0	45.0	24.8	12.1	416.0	51.4	364.6	342.1	22.5	6.2	1,100.8
II	434.1	302.4	277.6	24.8	11.8	42.1	15.7	49.4	1.0	.3	48.0	26.1	12.6	422.1	51.7	370.3	346.8	23.5	6.3	1,117.7
III	442.5	307.4	282.2	25.2	11.9	42.6	15.9	51.6	.3	.3	51.0	27.6	13.1	428.7	52.4	376.2	349.7	26.5	7.0	1,127.4
IV	454.9	314.1	288.4	25.7	12.2	43.3	16.1	55.4	−.2	.3	55.3	29.7	13.8	437.2	53.2	383.9	357.0	26.9	7.0	1,146.8
1962: I	464.4	320.6	293.2	27.4	12.4	43.8	16.2	57.7	.4	3.0	54.3	30.5	13.8	443.7	54.5	389.2	362.0	27.2	7.0	1,158.4
II	470.9	326.6	298.7	27.9	12.2	44.4	16.3	57.0	−.1	3.0	54.0	30.5	14.4	451.4	56.4	394.9	367.9	27.0	6.8	1,167.8
III	475.8	329.5	301.1	28.3	12.0	44.8	16.6	58.1	−.8	3.2	55.7	31.4	14.8	456.1	57.8	398.3	372.2	26.1	6.6	1,174.7
IV	482.2	333.0	304.2	28.8	12.0	44.8	16.9	60.3	.5	3.2	56.6	32.3	15.3	461.5	59.3	402.2	378.9	23.4	5.8	1,179.8
1963: I	487.9	337.9	307.9	30.0	12.1	44.9	17.0	60.3	1.0	3.3	56.1	31.7	15.7	467.0	59.9	407.1	383.0	24.1	5.9	1,190.9
II	496.8	342.7	312.3	30.3	12.1	45.3	17.2	63.5	.2	3.9	59.5	33.3	16.0	472.2	60.3	411.9	387.5	24.5	5.9	1,198.2
III	503.8	347.7	316.8	30.9	11.9	45.9	17.0	64.7	−.2	3.9	61.0	34.1	16.5	478.8	60.7	418.1	394.8	23.3	5.6	1,210.9
IV	512.6	353.9	322.2	31.7	11.6	46.8	17.2	66.0	−.8	4.3	62.5	35.0	17.0	487.4	61.1	426.2	399.5	26.8	6.3	1,229.4
1964: I	524.3	360.3	328.2	32.1	10.6	48.3	17.4	70.3	−.2	4.5	66.0	38.3	17.4	496.5	59.9	436.6	408.9	27.7	6.4	1,253.7
II	533.4	367.7	334.8	32.9	10.5	49.7	17.3	70.3	−.1	4.3	66.1	38.3	17.9	505.9	56.4	449.5	416.8	32.6	7.3	1,287.7
III	543.3	375.0	341.4	33.6	10.5	50.5	17.3	71.5	−.9	4.6	67.8	39.3	18.6	515.2	58.5	456.7	425.7	31.0	6.8	1,304.1
IV	549.4	381.0	346.6	34.3	11.1	50.6	17.3	70.6	−.7	4.4	66.8	38.9	18.8	523.4	60.4	462.9	428.1	34.8	7.5	1,318.6
1965: I	566.4	387.6	352.8	34.9	11.9	50.9	17.7	78.2	−.4	4.8	73.8	44.3	20.1	534.0	64.4	469.6	438.8	30.8	6.6	1,327.1
II	578.6	394.4	358.8	35.6	13.3	51.7	18.1	80.4	−1.1	5.1	76.4	46.0	20.7	544.6	65.7	478.9	446.1	32.7	6.8	1,346.8
III	589.3	402.6	366.2	36.5	13.5	52.2	18.2	81.4	−1.5	5.5	77.5	46.6	21.4	558.3	64.6	493.7	455.4	38.3	7.8	1,383.2
IV	606.7	414.6	377.1	37.5	13.3	53.6	18.3	85.3	−1.9	5.2	82.0	49.1	21.5	571.1	66.1	505.0	469.6	35.5	7.0	1,405.8
1966: I	627.1	426.9	385.7	41.2	15.7	54.8	18.5	88.4	−1.2	5.5	84.1	50.0	22.8	583.4	69.7	513.7	480.1	33.7	6.6	1,414.3
II	636.4	438.1	395.9	42.2	14.1	55.2	18.4	86.8	−2.7	5.3	84.1	50.1	23.8	593.9	74.0	519.9	485.3	34.6	6.7	1,422.3
III	647.0	449.2	406.1	43.1	13.7	55.7	18.7	85.0	−3.6	5.4	83.2	49.7	24.7	606.9	76.5	530.4	494.5	35.9	6.8	1,437.4
IV	657.4	457.6	413.4	44.2	12.7	56.4	18.7	86.2	−1.0	5.5	81.6	48.7	25.8	619.1	79.5	539.6	499.9	39.7	7.4	1,451.1
1967: I	662.7	463.9	418.8	45.1	12.5	57.3	19.2	83.5	−.4	5.3	78.6	46.3	26.2	629.5	80.4	549.0	504.5	44.5	8.1	1,474.0
II	669.3	469.4	423.5	45.8	12.7	58.0	19.8	82.4	−1.3	5.4	78.3	46.4	27.0	637.5	80.2	557.2	514.1	43.1	7.7	1,487.9
III	682.6	479.0	431.9	47.0	13.2	59.2	19.8	83.7	−1.7	5.7	79.7	47.5	27.8	650.3	83.6	566.7	520.9	45.8	8.1	1,500.1
IV	696.3	489.8	441.5	48.3	12.6	59.1	19.5	86.7	−2.8	5.6	83.9	49.7	28.6	660.9	85.5	575.4	528.2	47.2	8.2	1,510.7

Source: *Survey of Current Business* (Washington, D.C.: Department of Commerce, September 1988).

Table 4.—National Income and Disposition of Personal Income—Continued

[Billions of dollars; quarterly data are seasonally adjusted at annual rates]

Year and quarter	National income	Compensation of employees			Proprietors' income with IVA and CCAdj		Rental income of persons with CCAdj	Corporate profits with IVA and CCAdj					Net interest	Personal income	Less: Personal tax and nontax payments	Equals: DPI	Less: Personal outlays	Equals: Personal saving	Saving as percentage of DPI	DPI in constant (1982) dollars
		Total	Wages and salaries	Supplements to wages and salaries	Farm	Nonfarm		Total	IVA	CCAdj	Profits before tax	Profits after tax								
1968: I	713.0	504.5	454.1	50.4	12.6	60.6	18.7	87.5	−4.7	5.5	86.7	48.4	29.1	679.6	88.4	591.3	546.3	45.0	7.6	1,530.5
II	732.4	518.0	465.9	52.1	12.7	62.3	18.5	91.3	−2.9	5.4	88.8	49.6	29.7	699.7	92.2	607.5	560.2	47.3	7.8	1,554.7
III	748.0	531.9	478.3	53.6	12.9	63.6	18.3	91.5	−3.0	5.2	89.2	49.8	29.9	717.2	102.8	614.3	576.5	37.8	6.2	1,555.1
IV	762.9	544.5	489.4	55.1	13.1	64.0	18.1	92.8	−4.1	5.2	91.6	51.0	30.5	732.5	107.3	625.2	585.5	39.8	6.4	1,565.1
1969: I	777.1	556.6	499.0	57.6	12.8	64.6	18.2	92.3	−4.9	5.8	91.4	49.9	32.5	745.5	114.0	631.5	597.6	33.9	5.4	1,566.4
II	792.0	570.4	511.3	59.1	14.5	65.0	18.7	89.4	−5.2	6.1	88.6	48.3	34.0	764.5	117.5	647.0	609.2	37.8	5.8	1,584.7
III	808.1	587.4	526.4	61.0	14.9	65.1	18.5	86.7	−4.9	6.2	85.4	46.6	35.5	783.7	115.9	667.7	619.5	48.2	7.2	1,617.5
IV	815.2	599.1	536.4	62.7	16.3	64.0	18.2	81.2	−8.4	6.1	83.5	45.4	36.4	798.2	117.7	680.5	631.5	48.9	7.2	1,630.6
1970: I	818.8	609.5	545.0	64.5	15.6	64.1	18.0	73.5	−8.8	5.8	76.5	42.2	38.0	808.4	117.3	691.1	642.7	48.5	7.0	1,638.0
II	829.5	615.0	549.0	66.0	14.4	64.7	18.1	76.9	−4.6	5.3	76.2	42.0	40.4	829.6	118.5	711.1	652.9	58.2	8.2	1,666.2
III	841.0	623.4	555.6	67.8	14.9	65.9	17.8	76.6	−6.2	5.0	77.8	42.5	42.5	840.3	113.9	726.5	664.7	61.7	8.5	1,686.2
IV	840.9	625.2	556.3	69.0	14.1	67.1	18.7	71.8	−6.6	4.7	73.6	40.1	44.0	848.9	115.2	733.7	671.1	62.5	8.5	1,682.1
1971: I	872.7	642.2	570.1	72.2	14.7	68.2	18.3	84.1	−3.6	4.2	83.5	46.2	45.1	866.9	112.4	754.5	690.0	64.4	8.5	1,708.1
II	890.6	654.1	580.2	73.9	15.5	70.5	18.8	85.8	−4.7	4.3	86.1	47.8	46.0	889.4	115.3	774.1	703.9	70.3	9.1	1,731.9
III	905.2	664.5	588.6	75.9	15.0	72.3	18.7	87.8	−5.6	4.5	88.9	51.3	46.8	901.9	117.7	784.2	715.9	68.3	8.7	1,734.2
IV	923.9	676.7	598.9	77.7	16.5	74.4	18.5	90.6	−4.5	4.4	90.7	52.8	47.3	918.0	123.6	794.4	732.0	62.4	7.9	1,739.6
1972: I	956.3	701.4	617.8	83.6	15.2	75.8	19.4	96.5	−5.8	5.3	97.0	56.8	47.9	945.6	138.4	807.2	749.1	58.1	7.2	1,750.9
II	973.4	716.9	630.4	86.5	18.1	76.8	15.4	96.8	−5.8	5.1	97.6	57.3	49.5	961.9	140.7	821.2	767.4	53.8	6.5	1,767.6
III	1,002.5	731.2	642.3	88.9	19.5	80.3	18.1	101.4	−5.8	6.1	101.1	59.7	52.0	987.8	142.5	845.3	785.7	59.6	7.1	1,801.5
IV	1,044.3	755.4	664.2	91.3	24.8	82.9	18.5	108.0	−9.0	6.8	110.2	64.7	54.6	1,031.0	146.3	884.6	810.7	73.9	8.4	1,869.4
1973: I	1,084.3	783.5	683.2	100.3	24.7	86.2	18.4	114.7	−16.1	6.5	124.3	75.2	56.7	1,057.1	146.1	911.0	835.3	75.7	8.3	1,893.2
II	1,104.6	802.4	700.0	102.4	32.4	83.9	17.3	111.5	−21.7	5.9	127.3	77.5	57.1	1,084.1	148.1	936.1	850.9	85.2	9.1	1,907.6
III	1,132.3	821.4	716.1	105.3	35.2	85.2	17.8	112.4	−19.0	5.6	125.8	77.8	60.3	1,113.4	153.5	959.9	869.8	90.1	9.4	1,922.2
IV	1,169.6	844.0	735.3	108.7	42.5	86.0	18.4	114.7	−23.4	6.8	131.3	80.9	64.1	1,152.2	160.2	992.1	887.1	105.0	10.6	1,942.1
1974: I	1,178.5	861.7	748.1	113.6	34.7	87.6	18.7	106.3	−33.0	5.6	133.7	85.0	69.4	1,169.9	163.3	1,006.5	904.7	101.8	10.1	1,907.2
II	1,190.6	882.1	765.2	117.0	23.2	90.2	16.6	104.2	−38.3	3.8	138.7	87.4	74.2	1,191.6	169.5	1,022.1	932.8	89.2	8.7	1,888.3
III	1,216.5	904.4	783.0	121.4	25.0	93.4	15.6	100.7	−51.5	1.7	150.6	93.5	77.5	1,228.5	175.7	1,052.8	960.7	92.1	8.8	1,898.6
IV	1,228.2	917.0	792.4	124.6	27.2	94.0	13.6	95.5	−35.0	−2.0	132.5	82.4	81.0	1,250.6	178.5	1,072.0	968.4	103.6	9.7	1,892.4
1975: I	1,228.6	919.4	791.8	127.7	21.9	95.4	13.1	96.6	−12.7	−4.3	113.5	71.1	82.3	1,260.0	179.6	1,080.4	992.7	87.7	8.1	1,873.1
II	1,256.5	931.0	800.2	130.7	23.0	97.4	13.9	108.2	−7.3	−5.7	121.1	75.6	83.0	1,292.0	143.7	1,148.3	1,021.6	126.7	11.0	1,965.7
III	1,315.5	957.2	821.2	136.1	28.6	101.6	13.5	129.7	−12.2	−6.9	148.7	91.7	84.9	1,332.1	176.4	1,155.7	1,055.0	100.7	8.7	1,935.0
IV	1,355.6	987.1	845.6	141.5	28.2	105.4	13.6	136.1	−11.7	−8.1	156.0	97.3	85.2	1,369.4	182.7	1,186.7	1,083.3	103.4	8.7	1,953.1
1976: I	1,403.4	1,021.7	871.1	150.6	23.3	111.4	13.4	148.3	−11.6	−9.4	169.4	104.3	85.2	1,405.2	187.2	1,218.0	1,118.3	99.7	8.2	1,983.1
II	1,425.6	1,045.1	889.2	155.9	20.9	115.2	12.2	144.3	−15.5	−10.6	170.5	106.0	88.0	1,431.8	195.0	1,236.8	1,138.2	98.6	8.0	1,992.8
III	1,452.7	1,069.1	908.3	160.8	20.0	117.7	11.2	145.0	−15.9	−10.5	171.4	107.1	89.7	1,465.7	202.5	1,263.2	1,167.6	95.6	7.6	2,005.9
IV	1,483.9	1,095.6	929.8	165.8	18.1	124.0	10.7	143.2	−16.6	−9.9	169.8	106.7	92.3	1,502.8	210.3	1,292.5	1,203.3	89.2	6.9	2,022.2
1977: I	1,533.5	1,124.0	949.9	174.1	20.3	127.3	10.0	153.5	−22.3	−9.6	185.4	118.4	98.5	1,541.0	223.1	1,317.9	1,241.5	76.4	5.8	2,026.9
II	1,596.9	1,160.5	980.8	179.8	19.4	131.2	8.6	175.0	−16.0	−9.3	200.3	127.1	102.3	1,583.2	224.2	1,359.0	1,270.0	88.9	6.5	2,049.6
III	1,654.8	1,192.7	1,007.3	185.3	21.9	134.1	8.3	189.7	−10.6	−8.1	208.4	132.5	108.1	1,631.4	227.4	1,404.0	1,302.1	101.9	7.3	2,086.9
IV	1,685.9	1,229.3	1,038.0	191.3	20.3	137.2	5.9	181.1	−17.7	−8.9	207.7	131.7	112.1	1,674.3	237.8	1,436.4	1,340.9	95.6	6.7	2,102.8
1978: I	1,724.4	1,263.8	1,063.0	200.8	22.0	139.8	7.5	174.0	−21.2	−9.7	204.9	133.9	117.3	1,716.5	241.6	1,474.9	1,367.3	107.6	7.3	2,128.2
II	1,821.4	1,311.5	1,104.6	206.9	30.0	148.9	8.2	199.1	−24.5	−10.6	234.2	149.0	123.7	1,788.2	253.8	1,534.3	1,427.7	106.6	6.9	2,162.7
III	1,870.3	1,348.8	1,136.6	212.2	26.6	152.3	10.8	203.5	−25.1	−11.7	240.3	153.8	128.2	1,842.2	268.5	1,573.6	1,463.1	110.5	7.0	2,176.4
IV	1,936.9	1,392.8	1,174.0	218.7	29.6	155.7	10.6	212.2	−30.4	−11.8	254.4	163.1	136.1	1,902.7	280.6	1,622.1	1,506.1	116.0	7.1	2,202.0
1979: I	1,986.7	1,438.1	1,208.1	230.0	34.2	157.1	8.3	204.8	−35.3	−12.9	253.0	164.0	144.2	1,954.6	288.0	1,666.6	1,543.7	122.8	7.4	2,216.6
II	2,023.2	1,469.6	1,233.7	235.9	35.2	159.6	4.0	204.1	−40.8	−14.0	258.9	169.7	150.8	1,998.6	297.1	1,701.5	1,581.2	120.3	7.1	2,206.6
III	2,072.1	1,508.4	1,266.0	242.4	31.9	162.3	3.6	201.9	−46.2	−14.1	262.3	173.8	164.1	2,063.7	310.8	1,752.9	1,635.3	117.6	6.7	2,213.7
IV	2,107.1	1,549.5	1,300.0	249.5	25.8	161.6	6.8	189.5	−50.4	−14.9	254.7	169.5	174.0	2,119.0	322.7	1,796.3	1,684.8	111.5	6.2	2,213.7
1980: I	2,161.9	1,590.4	1,332.9	257.5	18.0	162.8	6.4	193.1	−58.7	−15.1	267.0	170.4	191.1	2,181.0	323.4	1,857.6	1,730.4	127.3	6.9	2,225.6
II	2,150.5	1,611.8	1,349.2	262.5	12.1	155.3	4.3	169.2	−29.1	−16.4	214.8	140.7	197.8	2,202.3	332.5	1,869.8	1,736.9	132.9	7.1	2,185.7
III	2,201.0	1,643.5	1,375.4	268.1	22.5	159.5	6.3	169.8	−41.1	−17.6	228.5	147.8	199.5	2,278.5	344.4	1,934.1	1,797.6	136.5	7.1	2,207.2
IV	2,300.8	1,707.2	1,430.3	276.9	29.5	163.0	9.4	176.6	−43.5	−17.9	238.1	150.2	215.0	2,372.3	361.9	2,010.3	1,859.4	150.9	7.5	2,238.8
1981: I	2,388.4	1,759.1	1,468.7	290.3	33.4	161.9	10.6	194.7	−34.8	−13.5	243.0	154.3	228.8	2,440.8	375.2	2,065.6	1,913.4	152.2	7.4	2,242.9
II	2,415.2	1,789.7	1,495.5	294.2	32.1	156.7	12.3	184.3	−23.4	−14.2	222.0	141.8	240.1	2,484.5	388.7	2,095.8	1,948.8	147.0	7.0	2,235.0
III	2,483.1	1,827.3	1,528.1	299.1	33.7	155.5	14.3	192.1	−20.5	−14.5	227.1	144.4	260.3	2,567.5	405.6	2,162.0	1,994.9	167.0	7.7	2,262.9
IV	2,487.2	1,853.6	1,549.0	304.5	23.5	150.3	15.9	180.7	−18.0	−15.3	214.0	141.0	263.2	2,590.9	403.9	2,187.0	2,015.5	171.6	7.8	2,253.7
1982: I	2,483.1	1,879.2	1,566.1	313.1	23.3	143.0	14.8	149.9	−7.7	−14.1	171.7	107.5	273.0	2,614.3	407.1	2,207.2	2,052.2	155.0	7.0	2,245.7
II	2,514.0	1,899.3	1,580.1	319.2	23.6	149.4	11.9	149.6	−10.3	−11.1	171.0	107.0	280.2	2,655.9	414.1	2,241.8	2,080.1	161.7	7.2	2,260.9
III	2,528.4	1,918.4	1,594.6	323.8	22.9	151.7	12.0	154.3	−10.0	−7.3	171.6	107.3	269.1	2,683.6	405.0	2,278.6	2,122.6	156.0	6.8	2,263.4
IV	2,548.2	1,931.1	1,603.7	327.4	28.5	159.8	15.8	146.1	−13.4	−4.5	164.1	104.3	266.9	2,729.2	411.1	2,318.1	2,174.9	143.1	6.2	2,276.1
1983: I	2,599.1	1,958.8	1,622.2	336.6	18.1	165.9	13.8	170.6	−5.9	6.7	169.7	110.6	272.1	2,753.1	407.4	2,345.7	2,206.2	139.5	5.9	2,288.4
II	2,685.5	1,995.0	1,653.3	341.7	15.9	176.4	15.4	207.0	−10.6	15.8	201.8	126.6	275.8	2,812.6	417.1	2,395.4	2,274.4	121.1	5.1	2,311.1
III	2,741.8	2,036.3	1,689.9	346.4	−3.5	183.0	11.2	228.9	−19.0	20.5	227.5	141.0	285.9	2,846.8	403.6	2,443.2	2,326.7	116.4	4.8	2,335.4
IV	2,851.5	2,092.7	1,739.4	353.4	19.3	188.6	12.4	248.5	−8.1	25.1	231.5	143.4	290.2	2,941.8	413.9	2,527.9	2,382.5	145.4	5.8	2,392.7
1984: I	2,962.1	2,152.9	1,784.2	368.7	44.3	197.1	12.3	262.7	−15.5	24.5	253.7	152.5	292.8	3,034.1	422.3	2,611.8	2,430.7	181.1	6.9	2,446.9
II	3,009.0	2,195.2	1,822.0	373.2	26.1	202.0	9.3	275.5	−5.0	29.0	251.4	151.2	301.0	3,074.8	432.1	2,642.8	2,490.0	152.8	5.8	2,456.6
III	3,047.3	2,234.9	1,858.1	376.8	23.3	207.5	6.9	262.6	−1.1	35.2	228.5	141.4	312.2	3,137.8	446.7	2,691.1	2,525.9	165.2	6.1	2,479.2
IV	3,096.1	2,272.7	1,891.1	381.7	28.1	209.7	5.6	266.9	−1.6	42.3	226.1	139.2	313.1	3,188.3	459.7	2,728.6	2,571.3	157.3	5.8	2,496.3
1985: I	3,161.5	2,314.8	1,928.6	386.2	34.6	218.6	9.0	266.0	−2.6	52.4	216.3	122.8	318.4	3,263.0	498.4	2,764.6	2,635.8	128.7	4.7	2,509.4
II	3,209.2	2,347.5	1,957.4	390.1	35.3	222.0	11.2	275.8	−1.2	60.0	217.0	124.2	317.4	3,307.6	456.8	2,850.7	2,682.9	167.8	5.9	2,563.5
III	3,252.4	2,381.2	1,987.3	393.8	21.8	227.0	8.9	296.1	3.7	63.6	228.7	129.2	317.4	3,331.7	491.7	2,840.0	2,746.8	93.3	3.3	2,535.4
IV	3,312.8	2,426.7	2,027.4	399.3	29.2	235.0	7.8	291.4	−6.6	63.0	235.0	135.2	322.7	3,399.1	499.6	2,899.5	2,787.7	111.7	3.9	2,562.8
1986: I	3,378.9	2,461.0	2,055.8	405.2	27.6	245.5	10.6	303.2	21.0	59.8	222.5	123.2	331.1	3,460.7	495.6	2,965.1	2,828.2	136.9	4.6	2,614.5
II	3,421.8	2,483.4	2,074.0	409.5	46.4	248.3	12.5	297.1	11.8	55.0	230.3	125.4	334.1	3,517.3	501.0	3,016.3	2,862.1	154.1	5.1	2,655.9
III	3,450.9	2,518.2	2,103.3	414.8	33.3	251.7	13.1	301.2	8.7	52.0	240.5	132.6	333.3	3,546.7	514.2	3,032.4	2,933.6	98.8	3.3	2,643.9
IV	3,496.6	2,565.8	2,142.8	423.0	38.4	255.8	13.4	293.9	−8.1	49.8	252.1	137.9	329.3	3,599.6	534.9	3,064.7	2,967.9	96.8	3.2	2,649.4
1987: I	3,573.0	2,608.9	2,182.9	426.0	46.7	263.5	17.4	298.3	−14.4	50.8	261.8	135.5	338.3	3,676.1	532.2	3,143.9	3,013.1	130.8	4.2	2,679.6
II	3,631.8	2,652.0	2,220.6	431.3	43.0	265.9	17.8	305.2	−20.0	51.5	273.7	141.1	348.1	3,736.1	582.0	3,154.1	3,084.7	69.5	2.2	2,652.8
III	3,708.0	2,702.8	2,265.3	437.5	35.2	271.5	18.1	322.0	−19.5	52.1	289.4	149.5	358.3	3,801.0	576.2	3,224.9	3,152.3	72.6	2.3	2,683.9
IV	3,802.0	2,769.9	2,324.8	445.1	47.0	279.0	20.5	316.1	−18.2	52.4	281.9	145.7	369.5	3,906.8	591.0	3,315.8	3,171.8	144.0	4.3	2,728.9

NOTE.—IVA = Inventory valuation adjustment; CCAdj = Capital consumption adjustment; DPI = Disposable personal income.

Source: *Survey of Current Business* (Washington, D.C.: Department of Commerce, September 1988).

INDEX